Marketing text in the world?

Answer:
Experience. Leadership. Innovation.

MARKETING

Marketing

10/e

Roger A. Kerin
Southern Methodist University

Steven W. Hartley
University of Denver

William Rudelius
University of Minnesota

McGraw-Hill Irwin

MARKETING

Published by McGraw-Hill/Irwin, a business unit of The McGraw-Hill Companies, Inc., 1221 Avenue of the Americas, New York, NY, 10020. Copyright © 2011, 2009, 2006, 2003, 2000, 1997, 1994, 1992, 1989, 1986 by The McGraw-Hill Companies, Inc. All rights reserved. No part of this publication may be reproduced or distributed in any form or by any means, or stored in a database or retrieval system, without the prior written consent of The McGraw-Hill Companies, Inc., including, but not limited to, in any network or other electronic storage or transmission, or broadcast for distance learning.

Some ancillaries, including electronic and print components, may not be available to customers outside the United States.

This book is printed on acid-free paper.

2 3 4 5 6 7 8 9 0 WVR/WVR 1 0 9 8 7 6 5 4 3 2 1 0

ISBN 978-0-07-352993-6
MHID 0-07-352993-1

Vice president and editor-in-chief: *Brent Gordon*
Publisher: *Paul Ducham*
Executive editor: *Doug Hughes*
Director of development: *Ann Torbert*
Developmental editor: *Gina Huck Siegert*
Editorial coordinator: *Sean M. Pankuch*
Vice president and director of marketing: *Robin J. Zwettler*
Marketing manager: *Katie Mergen*
Vice president of editing, design and production: *Sesha Bolisetty*
Lead project manager: *Christine A. Vaughan*
Lead production supervisor: *Carol A. Bielski*
Lead designer: *Matthew Baldwin*
Senior photo research coordinator: *Jeremy Cheshareck*
Photo researcher: *Mike Hruby*
Senior media project manager: *Susan Lombardi*
Cover image: © *Getty Images*
Typeface: *10.5/12 Times Roman*
Compositor: *Lachina Publishing Services*
Printer: *Quebecor World Versailles Inc.*

Library of Congress Cataloging-in-Publication Data

Kerin, Roger A.
Marketing / Roger A. Kerin, Steven W. Hartley, William Rudelius.—10th ed.
p. cm.
Includes index.
ISBN-13: 978-0-07-352993-6 (alk. paper)
ISBN-10: 0-07-352993-1 (alk. paper)
1. Marketing. I. Hartley, Steven William. II. Rudelius, William. III. Title.
HF5415.M29474 2011
658.8--dc22

2009043835

www.mhhe.com

A MESSAGE FROM THE AUTHORS

Who could have anticipated the incredible changes the past several years have brought to business and marketing? Every aspect of our business lives—from the economy, to government's role, to consumers' attitudes and lifestyles—have changed recently. While many of the changes have been disruptive, they create a unique challenge and opportunity for our discipline.

Marketing, more than any other discipline, is a field that embraces the changes and facilitates the development of new products, services, and ideas to respond to the new environment and improve our marketplace. You've certainly noticed the new focus on issues such as global economic growth, regulation, consumer spending, and employment. The future promises to bring many additional issues to our attention and to be an extraordinarily exciting time for marketing students. Welcome to what will surely be viewed as one of our most dramatic periods of business history. We are excited to be part of the educational journey you are undertaking!

You'll soon discover that your past experiences as a consumer provide you with a rich source of important information that will become part of your business perspective. As a student of marketing you will learn how the dynamic changes taking place change business practices. In the future, as a marketing manager, you will use your experiences and knowledge to become a true business professional. This text is our effort to help you begin the transition. We appreciate the opportunity to share our own managerial and educational expertise with you. From our perspective, your career starts here.

This edition of *Marketing* represents a milestone for us for several reasons. First, it is the 10th edition—a symbolic achievement, but more importantly it is an indication of the need for keeping up with the changes in business and marketing. Second, it is the result of more than 25 years of writing—we began writing in 1983! Finally, this edition represents our most advanced offering as an educational resource. We are committed to (1) building on our past experiences as authors, (2) continuing our leadership role in bringing new topics and perspectives to the classroom, and (3) focusing on pedagogical innovation that truly responds to new teaching and learning styles. We believe our efforts have created the most comprehensive, up-to-date, engaging, and technically advanced textbook available today. We hope you'll agree.

As you begin reading *Marketing* you will find that it uses an active-learning approach to bring marketing theories and concepts to life. Each chapter offers a balance of traditional and contemporary perspectives presented in an easy-to-read style using familiar examples of companies, products and services, and business strategies. This approach has been a "perfect match" for today's practical, visual, connected learners. The response from students and instructors has been extraordinary. *Marketing*, and its translations into 11 other languages, is now the No. 1 marketing text in the world! Our 10th edition strives to continue the tradition of past success.

Thank you for the opportunity to share our passion for marketing with you. We hope we succeed in making your studies fun and interesting and that they will become the foundation of an enlightened and productive career!

Roger A. Kerin
Steven W. Hartley
William Rudelius

Preface

Marketing utilizes a unique, innovative, and effective pedagogical approach developed by the authors through the integration of their combined classroom, college, and university experiences. The elements of this approach have been the foundation for each edition of *Marketing* and serve as the core of the text and its supplements as they evolve and adapt to changes in student learning styles, the growth of the marketing discipline, and the development of new instructional technologies. The distinctive features of the approach are illustrated below:

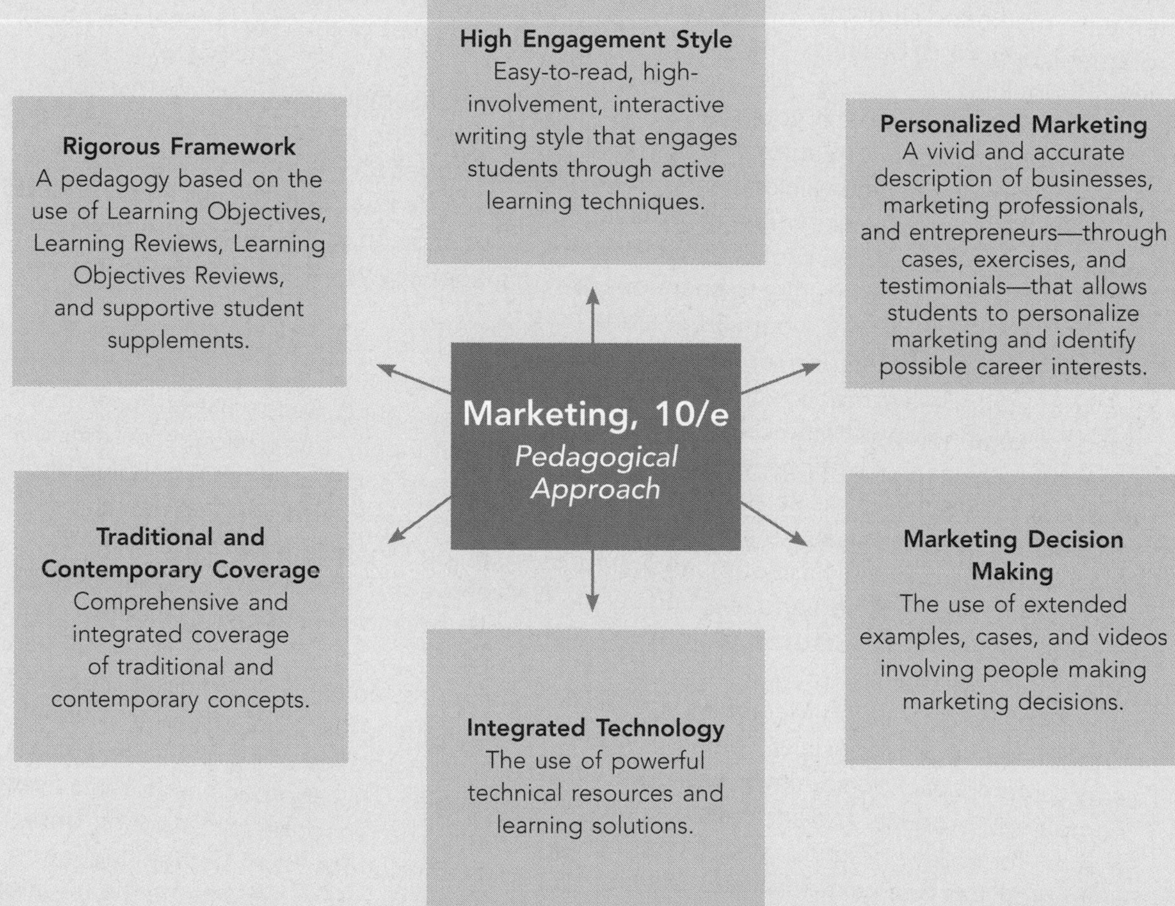

Marketing, 10/e
Pedagogical Approach
High Engagement Style
Easy-to-read, high-involvement, interactive writing style that engages students through active learning techniques.
Personalized Marketing
A vivid and accurate description of businesses, marketing professionals, and entrepreneurs—through cases, exercises, and testimonials—that allows students to personalize marketing and identify possible career interests.
Marketing Decision Making
The use of extended examples, cases, and videos involving people making marketing decisions.
Integrated Technology
The use of powerful technical resources and learning solutions.
Traditional and Contemporary Coverage
Comprehensive and integrated coverage of traditional and contemporary concepts.
Rigorous Framework
A pedagogy based on the use of Learning Objectives, Learning Reviews, Learning Objectives Reviews, and supportive student supplements.

The goal of the 10th edition of *Marketing* is to create an exceptional experience for today's students and instructors of marketing. The development of *Marketing* was based on a rigorous process of assessment, and the outcome of the process is a text and package of learning tools that are based on *experience*, *leadership*, and *innovation* in marketing education.

EXPERIENCE

The Kerin author team brings extraordinary experience to the development of their text. For example, they have benefited from the feedback of many users of previous editions of *Marketing*—a group that now exceeds more than 1 million students! In addition, the authors are experienced instructors who, in their combined careers, have taught more than 50,000 students, using many teaching styles, tools, and technologies. Finally, as researchers and consultants, the authors have worked with many of the world's leading marketing companies.

How has their experience shaped the 10th edition?

- With the development of **Connect Marketing:**

  Connect Marketing is a comprehensive online resource to enable students to learn faster, study more efficiently, and increase knowledge retention. It contains powerful features that allow assignment management and includes a library and a study center.

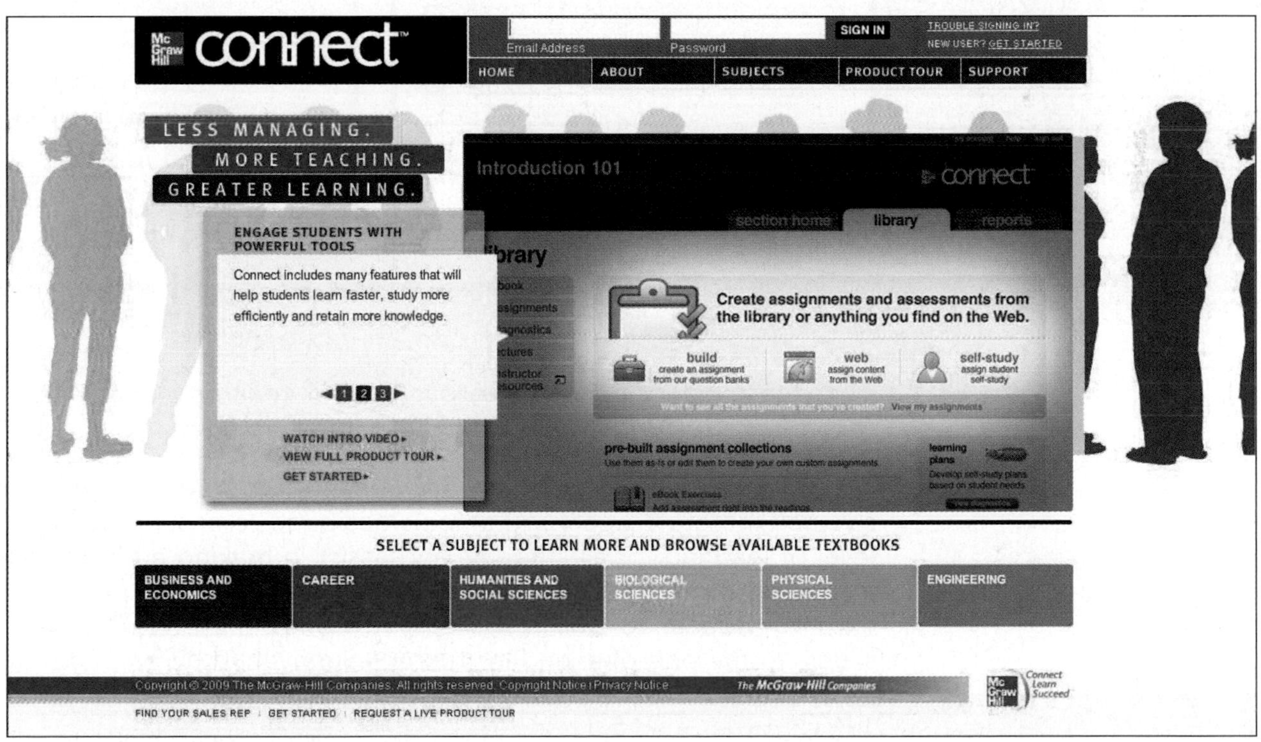

- By integrating assessment tools that allow instructors to meet ***AACSB assurance-of-learning requirements:***

  Each chapter begins with learning objectives, includes in-chapter learning reviews, and ends with learning objective summaries. In addition, the *Marketing*, 10/e, Test Bank includes learning objective, AACSB learning outcome, and Bloom's Taxonomy designations for each question. The combination of the objectives, outcomes, and taxonomy designation with the specific questions provides an important tool for meeting AACSB assurance of learning requirements.

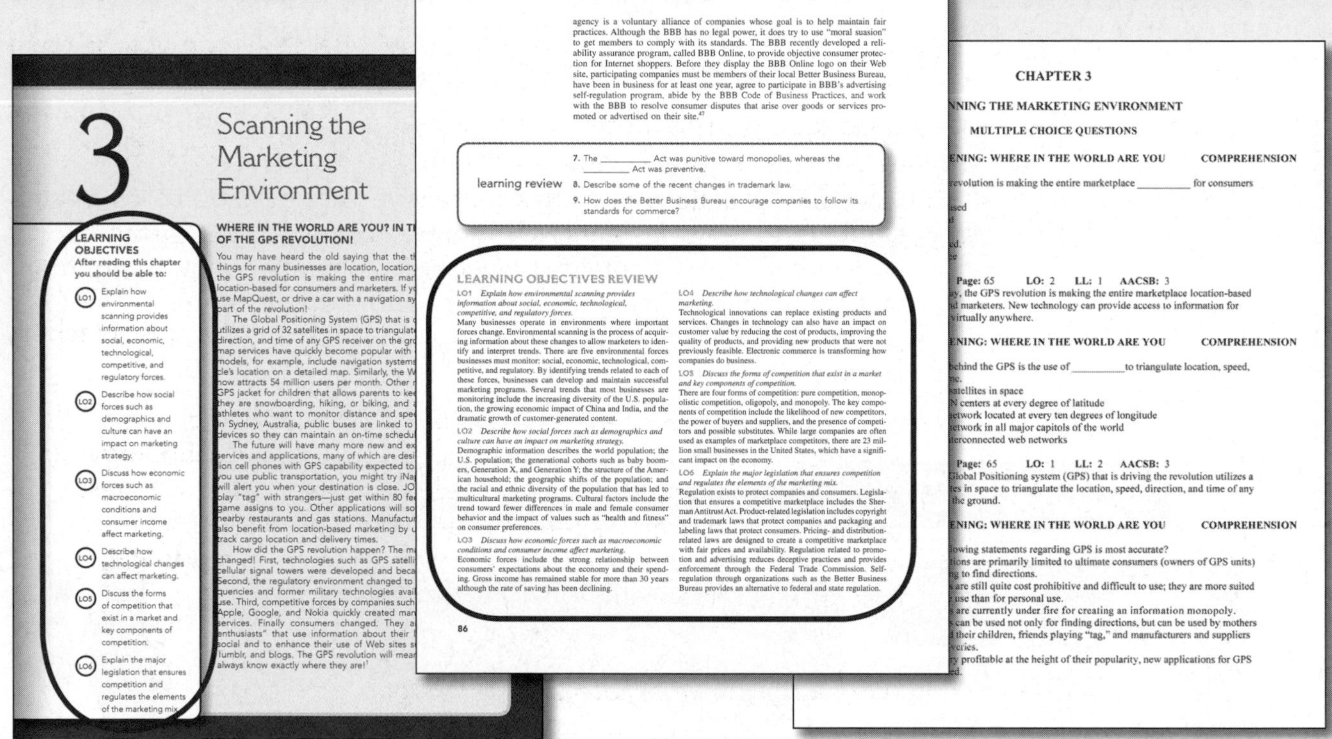

- With the most comprehensive package of ***teaching and learning resources:***

  The resources that accompany *Marketing*, 10/e, are a comprehensive and integrated package of tools designed to ensure the highest level of learning for all students and assist in making an instructor's life easier in the process. The resources range from a package of exciting videos, to online quizzes, to comprehensive PowerPoint slides, to the one-of-a-kind Instructor's Survival Kit, to an integrated Instructor's Manual, to a world-class visually enhanced test bank.

LEADERSHIP

The first text to integrate new content areas such as ethics, technology, interactive marketing, and marketing dashboards and metrics.

The first custom-made videos to accompany a marketing text.

The first teaching package to utilize active learning approaches in the text and the instructor resources.

These are just a few examples that illustrate how the Kerin author team has played a leadership role in the development and delivery of marketing pedagogy. This book is recognized as the market leader in the United States and Canada, and continues to introduce new, leading-edge principles and practices to students and instructors around the world. How does *Marketing*, 10/e, continue this tradition of leadership?

- By integrating **adaptive self-study technology** into the teaching package.

  To help students make the best use of their study time, *Marketing*, 10/e, utilizes a new adaptive self-study technology called **LearnSmart**. This tool provides students with a seamless combination of practice, assessment, and remediation for every concept in the book. The software adapts to every student's response automatically.

- By focusing on ***marketplace diversity:***

  A diverse mix of buyers and sellers populates today's dynamic marketplace. Students will find that successful marketers are not limited to any particular culture, nationality, race, ethnic group, or gender. Rather, like consumers they serve, marketers mirror society, both domestically and globally. This diversity in today's marketplace is reflected in examples throughout the text.

- By emphasizing the feature ***Using Marketing Dashboards:***

The use of marketing dashboards among marketing professionals is popular today. Marketing dashboards graphically portray the measures that marketers use to track and analyze marketing phenomena and performance. Students will find commonly used measures applied by successful marketers throughout the text and be exposed to their calculation, interpretation, and application.

Using Marketing Dashboards
Knowing Your CDI and BDI

Where are sales for my product category and brand strongest and weakest? Data related to this question are displayed in a marketing dashboard using two indexes: (1) category development index and (2) brand development index.

Your Challenge You have joined the marketing team for Hawaiian Punch, the top fruit punch drink sold in the United States. The brand has been marketed to mothers with children under 12 years old. The majority of Hawaiian Punch sales are in gallon and 2-liter bottles. Your assignment is to examine the brand's performance and identify growth opportunities for the Hawaiian Punch brand among households that consume prepared fruit drinks (the product category).

Your marketing dashboard displays a category development index and a brand development index provided by a syndicated marketing research firm. Each index is based on the calculations below:

$$\text{Category Development Index (CDI)} = \frac{\text{Percent of a product category's total U.S. sales in a market segment}}{\text{Percent of the total U.S. population in a market segment}} \times 100$$

$$\text{Brand Development Index (BDI)} = \frac{\text{Percent of a brand's total U.S. sales in a market segment}}{\text{Percent of the total U.S. population in a market segment}} \times 100$$

A CDI over 100 indicates above-average product category purchases by a market segment. A number under 100 indicates below-average purchases. A BDI over 100 indicates a strong brand position in a segment; a number under 100 indicates a weak brand position.

You are interested in CDI and BDI displays for four household segments that consume prepared fruit drinks: (1) households without children; (2) households with children 6 years old or under; (3) households with children aged 7 to 12; and (4) households with children aged 13 to 18.

Your Findings The BDI and CDI measures displayed below show that Hawaiian Punch is consumed by households with children, and particularly households with children under age 12. The Hawaiian Punch BDI is over 100 for both segments—not surprising since the brand is marketed to these segments. Households with children 13 to 18 years old evidence high fruit drink consumption with a CDI over 100. But Hawaiian Punch is relatively weak in this segment with a BDI under 100.

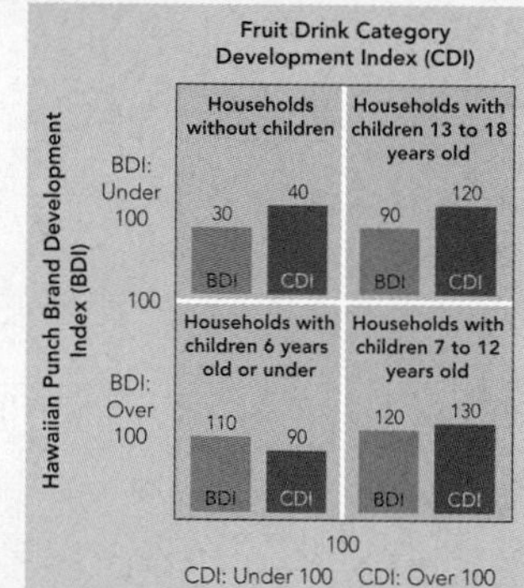

Your Action An opportunity for Hawaiian Punch exists among households with children 13 to 18 years old—teenagers. You might propose that Hawaiian Punch be repositioned for teens. In addition, you might recommend that Hawaiian Punch be packaged in single-serve cans or bottles to attract this segment, much like soft drinks. Teens might also be targeted for advertising and promotions.

Finding New Customers Produce companies have begun marketing and packaging prunes as dried plums to attract younger buyers. Harley-Davidson has tailored a marketing program to encourage women to take up biking, thus doubling the number of potential customers for its motorcycles.[15]

Increasing a Product's Use Promoting more frequent usage has been a strategy of Campbell Soup Company. Because soup consumption rises in the winter and declines during the summer, the company now advertises more heavily in warm months to encourage consumers to think of soup as more than a cold-weather food.

CHAPTER 11 MANAGING SUCCESSFUL PRODUCTS AND BRANDS 279

INNOVATION

What if your research showed that many students in your introductory marketing course don't attempt to read and understand the tables and charts in the textbook? What could you do to increase their interest and involvement? Read on for the answer.

To secure their position in the marketplace, the Kerin author team consistently create innovative pedagogical tools that encourage interaction and match students' learning styles. How did they accomplish this in the 10th edition?

- With the creation of **Lecture Capture** and **eBook**.

  Instructors can now help students focus on in-class discussions rather than note-taking by using **Connect Marketing**'s Lecture Capture to record and distribute lectures and PowerPoint presentations. In addition, the use of eBook provides students with access to the text anytime and anywhere!

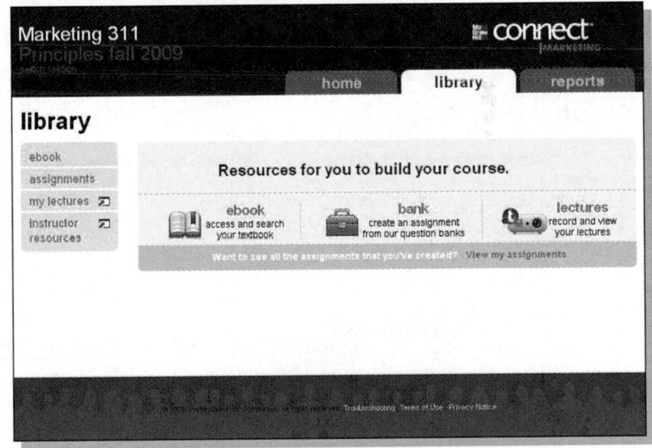

- With the increased emphasis on **visually enhanced test questions.**

The *Marketing*, 10/e, Test Bank has been updated to include the latest concepts and ideas from the textbook. When research by the Kerin author team revealed many students were skipping the tables and charts in the chapter, they decided to do something about it: the visually enhanced test bank! This moves key tables, charts, ads, and photos from the textbook into the test bank to emphasize their importance and reward students who study these key elements.

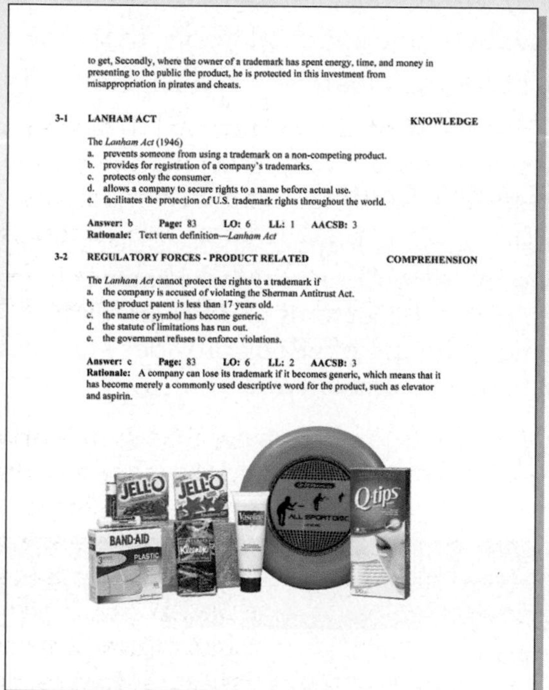
to get, Secondly, where the owner of a trademark has spent energy, time, and money in presenting to the public the product, he is protected in this investment from misappropriation in pirates and cheats.

3-1 LANHAM ACT **KNOWLEDGE**

The *Lanham Act* (1946)
a. prevents someone from using a trademark on a non-competing product.
b. provides for registration of a company's trademarks.
c. protects only the consumer.
d. allows a company to secure rights to a name before actual use.
e. facilitates the protection of U.S. trademark rights throughout the world.

Answer: b **Page:** 83 **LO:** 6 **LL:** 1 **AACSB:** 3
Rationale: Text term definition—*Lanham Act*

3-2 REGULATORY FORCES - PRODUCT RELATED **COMPREHENSION**

The *Lanham Act* cannot protect the rights to a trademark if
a. the company is accused of violating the Sherman Antitrust Act.
b. the product patent is less than 17 years old.
c. the name or symbol has become generic.
d. the statute of limitations has run out.
e. the government refuses to enforce violations.

Answer: c **Page:** 83 **LO:** 6 **LL:** 2 **AACSB:** 3
Rationale: A company can lose its trademark if it becomes generic, which means that it has become merely a commonly used descriptive word for the product, such as elevator and aspirin.

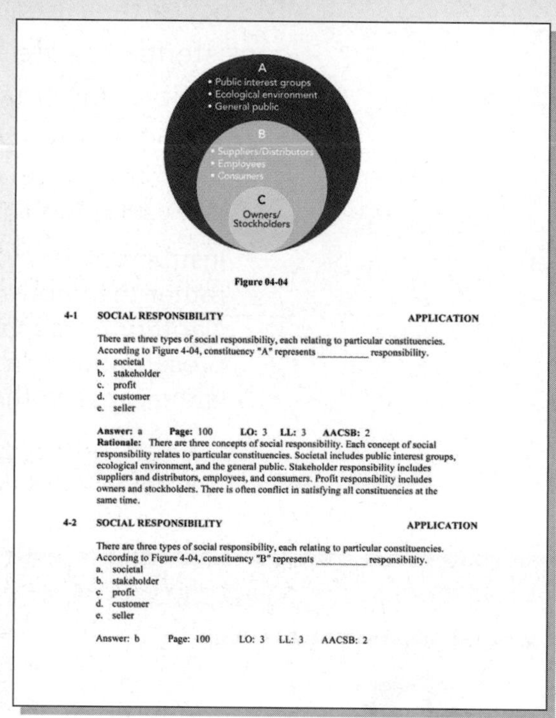

Figure 04-04

4-1 SOCIAL RESPONSIBILITY **APPLICATION**

There are three types of social responsibility, each relating to particular constituencies. According to Figure 4-04, constituency "A" represents __________ responsibility.
a. societal
b. stakeholder
c. profit
d. customer
e. seller

Answer: a **Page:** 100 **LO:** 3 **LL:** 3 **AACSB:** 2
Rationale: There are three concepts of social responsibility. Each concept of social responsibility relates to particular constituencies. Societal includes public interest groups, ecological environment, and the general public. Stakeholder responsibility includes suppliers and distributors, employees, and consumers. Profit responsibility includes owners and stockholders. There is often conflict in satisfying all constituencies at the same time.

4-2 SOCIAL RESPONSIBILITY **APPLICATION**

There are three types of social responsibility, each relating to particular constituencies. According to Figure 4-04, constituency "B" represents __________ responsibility.
a. societal
b. stakeholder
c. profit
d. customer
e. seller

Answer: b Page: 100 LO: 3 LL: 3 AACSB: 2

- Through the ***Instructor's Survival Kit:***

This supplement is exactly what it says it is: an instructor's guide to surviving in today's classroom. Instructors create interaction by breaking the classroom into teams that analyze marketing problems presented through in-class activities. Students who are kinesthetic (tactile) learners especially appreciate the hands-on product samples, brochures, and props that are tied to the activities and are intended to build on the idea of "cooperative learning."

New and Revised Content

New Coverage of Customer Relationships, Customer Value, and Social Entrepreneurship. The efforts of 3M inventor David Windorski to create customer value with the new 3M Post-it® Flag Highlighter are described in the opening example of Chapter 1 and in the end-of-chapter video case. New examples such as Hot Pockets and AT&T's CruiseCast have been added, and a description of a new social entrepreneurship organization called Bridging, Inc., is included in the section on social responsibility.

New Coverage and Examples of Organizational Strategies. Netflix's changing business models are now presented in a Marketing Matters box in Chapter 2. In addition, updated examples of the application of the Boston Consulting Group model to four strategic business units at Kodak are included in the section on business portfolio analysis. Chapter 2 also has an updated introduction to the Using Marketing Dashboards box.

Introduction of the GPS Revolution and New Trends in Marketing. The many new location-aware services and applications that are part of the GPS revolution are described in the opening example of Chapter 3. Recent trends related to authenticity, sustainability, shift to a service economy, mobile marketing, customer-generated content, and regulation related to privacy and customer engagement have been added. Discussions of multicultural advertising, cloud computing, wireless power transmission, software pricing, and the *Internet Tax Freedom Act* are also included.

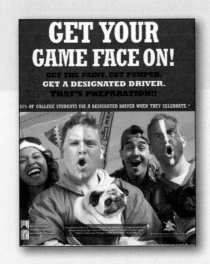

Integration of "Triple Bottom Line," "Greenwashing," and New Examples of Ethics and Social Responsibility in Marketing. The three concepts of social responsibility presented in Chapter 4 now include a discussion of the balance between people, planet, and profits—the triple bottom line. In addition, the discussion of consumer ethics includes "greenwashing," or the confusion caused by some environmental claims. New examples such as the global ethics program at UPS are also included.

New Examples of Consumer Behavior Concepts. The Chapter 5 discussion of alternative evaluation is now based on information about smart phones such as Apple, BlackBerry, and Palm. Other new examples include Hershey's Extra Dark Chocolate advertising, which links the product to improved blood pressure; Unilever's advertising, which features an endorsement from cardiologists to reduce perceived risk; and Oscar Mayer's efforts to change attitudes toward its beef bologna product.

Updated Coverage of Sustainable Procurement. The description of JCPenney's paper procurement process has been expanded to include the growing importance of environmental programs in addition to price, quality, capacity, and other traditional factors. Chapter 6 also includes new coverage of Starbucks' sustainable procurement program, which rewards its coffee bean suppliers for ecologically sound growing practices and invests in the farming communities where the coffee is produced.

New Emphasis on Growth in Emerging Economies. Chapter 7 includes a new chapter opening example featuring Dell's global initiative to begin sales and distribution of low-cost personal computers in Asia, Africa, and Latin America. The section on customs now includes a description of how Siemens AG paid an $800 million fine for alleged bribes of government officials.

New Coverage of Neuromarketing, Buy*ology, and Measuring Social Networks. A new section on neuromarketing, which uses brain scans to record responses to marketing actions, has been added to Chapter 8. A new Marketing Matters box discusses Martin Lindstrom's book, *Buy*ology*, and its conclusions about logos, product placement, advertising with sex appeals, and warning labels on cigarettes. Chapter 8 also now includes a new section on data mining on social networks such as Facebook, LinkedIn, and Twitter.

Updated Coverage of Zappos and Wendy's Segmentation Examples, and Expanded Discussion of Perceptual Maps. The Chapter 9 opening example about Zappos.com has been updated to include the addition of clothes, accessories, and electronics to its original segmentation strategy. The chapter also includes coverage of Wendy's new segmentation strategy to include 25- to 49-year-old customers. Finally, the discussion of perceptual maps and the repositioning of chocolate milk has been expanded.

Introduction of the Stage-Gate® Process, Open Innovation, and Industrial Design. A new Marketing Matters box in Chapter 10 discusses the Stage-Gate® process used by many companies to move a new product idea through all the business steps needed to reach commercialization. The idea generation section of the chapter now covers a method of using outside sources of new-product ideas—called open innovation. In addition, new coverage of industrial design at IDEO, Apple, and Google has been added.

Updated Product Management and Branding Examples. Gatorade's new labels, such as "Bring It" on Gatorade Fierce and "Be Tough" on Gatorade X-Factor, are discussed in the updated opening example for Chapter 11. Ralph Lauren's sunglasses licensing agreement with Luxottica is now included in the Brand Equity section. Finally, Ford's launch of the Fusion and Hyundai's commitment to the best automobile warranty are discussed.

Introduction of the Importance of Authenticity in Services and the Eight Ps of Services Marketing. Chapter 12 now opens with a discussion of the importance of authenticity in service offerings. Strategies for creating authenticity, such as customization, personal interaction, and social networking, are included with examples of companies that are making the change. The section titled "Managing the Marketing of Services" has been updated to utilize the "Eight Ps of Services Marketing" framework. The framework includes product (service), price, place, promotion, people, physical environment, process, and productivity.

New Pricing Examples. The factors that increase or decrease the final price of an offering are illustrated in Chapter 13 with a new example—the 2010 Tesla Roadster Sport. The example includes incentives, allowances, and extra fees in the price equation. A new Making Responsible Decisions box describes the mathematics of credit card debt. In addition, a new Marketing Matters box describing the efforts of an entrepreneur to achieve competitive prices and margins for barbecue sauces has been added. Chapter 14 now opens with a description of Vizio's use of pricing to help it become the fastest growing HDTV company in the United States.

Channel Management and Supply Chain Update. The opening example for Chapter 15 describes how Callaway Golf added an online channel and still maintains its traditional retail partnerships with Golf Galaxy, Dick's Sporting Goods, and PGA Tour Superstores. The use of channels to reach different segments is illustrated with a new example of Fila distributing apparel through Kohl's department stores to reach 25- to 40-year-old consumers. Chapter 15 also describes the trend toward selective distribution for products such as Dell computers. Chapter 16 describes how Apple used its global supply chain to deliver 10 million iPhones to more than 70 countries!

Introduction of Cyber Monday and Other Retailing Trends. The growing importance of online retailing and the recognition of the Monday after Thanksgiving as "Cyber Monday" are now presented in Chapter 17. New discussions of environmentally friendly retailing, the use of self-service kiosks as a method of making customers co-creators of value, electronic payment options, and "green" mailing and digital catalogs have also been added. The new Going Online box describes how some consumers are making shopping a game by subscribing to services that send text messages announcing limited time "flash sales!"

Introduction of the "Age of Engage" in Integrated Marketing Communications. Chapter 18 discusses how consumers increasingly use interactive technologies to stay connected and be engaged with a shopping experience. New forms of integrated marketing communications, including online social viewing rooms for television programs, "fan pages" on Facebook and MySpace, and product integration with video games, have been added to the chapter discussion. New company examples include Gap's iPhone applications, Columbia Pictures' integrated campaign for the movie *Angels and Demons*, and JCPenney's interactive "virtual runway" fashion show. A new Making Responsible Decisions box discusses efforts by direct marketers to "go green" by using recycled paper, removing unresponsive people from mailing lists, and installing "green" printers.

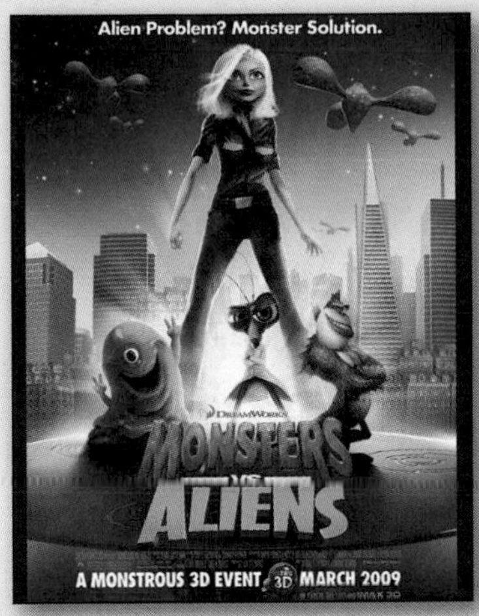

New Advertising and Sales Promotion Examples and Content. Discussion of the trend toward three-dimensional advertising has been added to Chapter 19. Examples of the first 3-D advertisements on the Super Bowl and future applications on digital billboards, video games, and outdoor laser productions are also discussed. Other examples of new forms of advertising include Porsche's "Can You Afford a Porsche?" mobile campaign, Honda's $50 million "From Honda. For Everyone" integrated campaign, Geico's viral video campaign featuring the Geico gecko, Microsoft's "I'm a PC" campaign, and Barack Obama's use of infomercials. Media changes such as the growth of satellite radio, magazines based on user-generated content, the decline of newspaper circulation, the migration of yellow pages users to the Web, the incredible growth of search advertising, and the conversion of outdoor advertising to digital billboards have been added. New examples of sales promotions include Cream of Wheat's online advertising to identify consumers for a coupon offer, Doritos "Crash the Super Bowl" contest asking people to create their own 30-second ad, and *American Idol*'s sweepstakes to win a trip to the season finale.

Updated Description of Salesperson Qualifications. An updated description of salesperson qualifications has been added to the section on salesforce recruitment and selection in Chapter 20. In addition, the methods of evaluating prospective salespeople are discussed.

New and Updated Examples of Interactive Marketing. Chapter 21 includes an updated description of Seven Cycles' use of its interactive, multilanguage Web site to become the world's largest custom bicycle frame builder. Trends in online shopping, total online retail sales, and sales by product category through 2012 are also presented. New examples such as customized M&Ms and online shoe sales at Zappos.com have been added to the chapter.

Increased Emphasis on Marketing Metrics and Marketing Dashboards. New coverage in Chapter 22 provides a numerical example of resource allocation for General Mills products such as Banana Nut Cheerios and Progresso Light Soup. The chapter also includes a new section describing the importance of metrics in marketing planning, an updated Figure 22–9, which reflects the use of marketing dashboards, and an actual dashboard for General Mills' Warm Delights. A new Marketing Matters box describing implementation issues at IBM and a new discussion of the role of a chief marketing officer have also been added.

New and Updated Career Information and Alternate Cases. Appendix C, "Planning a Career in Marketing," has been updated to include new salary information, job descriptions, résumé preparation, job search techniques, and interview skills. Appendix D, Alternate Cases, contains cases for instructors who elect to assign additional cases to students.

Organization

The 10th edition of ***Marketing*** is divided into five parts. Part 1, ***"Initiating the Marketing Process,"*** looks first at what marketing is and how it creates customer value and customer relationships (Chapter 1). Then Chapter 2 provides an overview of the strategic marketing process that occurs in an organization—which provides a framework for the text. Appendix A provides a sample marketing plan as a reference for students. Chapter 3 analyzes the five major environmental factors in our changing marketing environment, while Chapter 4 provides a framework for including ethical and social responsibility considerations in marketing decisions.

Part 2, ***"Understanding Buyers and Markets,"*** first describes, in Chapter 5, how individual consumers reach buying decisions. Next, Chapter 6 looks at organizational buyers and markets and how they make purchase decisions. And finally, in Chapter 7, the dynamics of world trade and the influence of cultural diversity on global marketing practices are explored.

In Part 3, ***"Targeting Marketing Opportunities,"*** the marketing research function and how information about prospective consumers is linked to marketing strategy and decisions is discussed in Chapter 8. The process of segmenting and targeting markets and positioning products appears in Chapter 9.

Part 4, ***"Satisfying Marketing Opportunities,"*** covers the marketing mix elements. The product element is divided into the natural chronological sequence of first developing new products and services (Chapter 10) and then managing the existing products (Chapter 11) and services (Chapter 12). Pricing is covered in terms of underlying pricing analysis (Chapter 13), followed by actual price setting (Chapter 14), and Appendix B, "Financial Aspects of Marketing." Three chapters address the place (distribution) aspects of marketing: "Managing Marketing Channels and Wholesaling" (Chapter 15), "Customer-Driven Supply Chain and Logistics Management" (Chapter 16), and "Retailing" (Chapter 17). Retailing is a separate chapter because of its importance and interest as a career for many of today's students. Promotion is also covered in three chapters. Chapter 18 discusses integrated marketing communications and direct marketing, topics that have grown in importance in the marketing discipline recently. The primary forms of mass market communication—advertising, sales promotion, and public relations—are covered in Chapter 19. Personal selling and sales management are covered in Chapter 20.

Part 5, ***"Managing the Marketing Process,"*** discusses issues and techniques related to interactive marketing technologies and the strategic marketing process. Chapter 21 describes how interactive and multichannel marketing influences customer value and the customer experience through context, content, community, customization, connectivity, and commerce. Chapter 22 expands on Chapter 2 to describe specific techniques and issues related to blending the four marketing mix elements to plan, implement, and evaluate marketing programs.

The book closes with several useful supplemental sections. Appendix C, "Planning a Career in Marketing," discusses marketing jobs and how to get them, and Appendix D provides 22 alternate cases. In addition, a detailed Glossary, Learning Review Answers, and three indexes (name, company/product, and subject) complete the book.

Engaging Features

Chapter-opening vignettes introduce students to chapter concepts by using an exciting company as an example. Students are immediately engaged while learning about real-world companies. Chapter 10 discusses *BusinessWeek*'s most innovative company in 2008, Apple.

nano shoots video.
Introducing the new iPod nano.
Now with video recording,
a larger screen, and FM radio.

10 Developing New Products and Services

LEARNING OBJECTIVES
After reading this chapter you should be able to:

- LO1 Recognize the various terms that pertain to products and services.
- LO2 Identify the ways in which consumer and business products and services can be classified.
- LO3 Explain the significance of "newness" in new products and services as it relates to the degree of consumer learning involved.
- LO4 Describe the factors contributing to a new product's or service's success or failure.
- LO5 Explain the purposes of each step of the new-product process.

APPLE'S NEW-PRODUCT INNOVATION MACHINE

The stage in front of an auditorium is empty except for a desk with an iMac and a huge screen with a large white logo. Then in walks a legend ready for his magic shows in his black turtleneck, jeans, and gray New Balance sneakers.

Apple's Innovation Machine

The legend, of course, is Steve Jobs (opposite page), co-founder and CEO of Apple, Inc. *Fortune* rated Apple as the world's most admired company in 2009 and *BusinessWeek* has perennially rated it as the world's most innovative.[1] The magic shows Jobs has put on over the years have introduced many of Apple's market-changing innovations, such as the:

- Apple II—the first commercial personal computer.
- Macintosh—the first personal computer with a mouse and a graphical user interface.
- iPod—the first commercially successful MP3 digital music player.
- MacBook Air—the world's thinnest notebook that uses a solid state drive instead of a hard disk.
- iPhone 3GS—the revolutionary multi-touch mobile phone and media player.
- iPod nano with Built-in Video Camera—the digital media player that includes a video camera to shoot and play video or enables the user to upload it to a computer and view it on YouTube. The 2009 iPod nano comes in nine different colors and has a FM radio as well as a pedometer. And the larger color display makes it even easier to view images and video. The price? Only $149 for the 8Gb model, similar to what other pocket video cameras cost![2]

The Evolutionary iPod nano and Revolutionary iPod touch

The evolutionary iPod nano, first introduced in 2005 and now in its fifth generation, has sold over 100 million units as of September 2009, making it the most popular media player in the world. Moreover, the iPod family (iPod shuffle, iPod nano, iPod classic, and iPod touch) has sold over 220 million units since the iPod's launch in October 2001. "With iPod, Apple has invented a whole new category of digital music

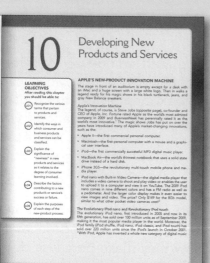

Marketing Matters > > > > > > > > technology

Buy•ology: How "Neuromarketing" Is Trying to Understand Consumers

Is much of the more than $12 *billion* spent on traditional market research (focus groups, surveys, and so on) wasted? Brand guru Martin Lindstrom believes so. Why? Because 85 percent of consumers' thoughts, feelings, or preferences toward products, brands, and advertisements resides deep within the subconscious part of the brain and can't be understood using traditional techniques.

Lindstrom is a believer in the relatively new field of "neuromarketing," which uses high-tech brain scanning instruments to record the brain's responses to various marketing stimuli (package designs, brand logos, fragrances, TV ads, and so on) via the five senses (sight, sound, smell, touch, and taste). Two instruments are typically used when stimuli are presented: (1) An expensive, doughnut-shaped functional magnetic resonance imaging (fMRI) scanner, where different areas of the brain "light up" and can be mapped and (2) a less costly cap with dozens of sensors plugged into an electroencephalograph (EEG), where the real-time changes in brain wave patterns can be seen (see photo).

So why is neuromarketing important to marketers? Lindstrom draws these fascinating conclusions that could have a significant impact on current marketing actions:

- **Brand logos don't work.** Instead, brands should focus on indirect logo signals, such as shapes, sound, smell, color, and so on.
- **Ads with sex appeal don't sell.** Men in particular don't recall these types of ads nearly as much as nonsexually oriented ads.
- **Successful brands function like religion.** Participants' brains respond similarly to brand messages and religious icons.
- **Warning labels on cigarettes don't work.** Interestingly, the labels late the area of the brain resp for cravings.

So, what do you think about neuromarketing? A concerned that marketers will invade your privacy b encing what you buy? Stay tuned!

Marketing Matters boxes highlight real-world examples of customer value creation and delivery, and entrepreneurship that give students further insight into the practical world of marketing.

Making Responsible Decisions > > > > sustainability

Millennials Are Going to Change the World—Through Environmental Sustainability!

Millenials, or Generation Y, are determined to make a difference in the world, and by doing so, make the world a better place. They are idealistic and eager to get started, particularly when it comes to environmental sustainability, which millennials believe is part of what it means to be socially responsible. The group includes students in college and graduate school, and many early career employees. In different ways each group is making its voice heard.

There are approximately 17 million undergraduate millennials who expect sustainable campus communities that include LEED (Leadership in Energy and Environmental Design)-certified housing, campus transit systems, and recycling programs. Graduate students are ... programs with sustainability tainability database specialist at companies that are eco-conscious and advocate good citizenry.

Sara Hochman is a typical example. She was interested in environmental issues in college, and her first job was an environmental consultant. To make a bigger impact on her clients, she decided she "needed to beef up my business skills," so she enrolled in graduate school at the University of Chicago where she could take an elective on renewable energy and join the Energy Club. Similarly, Alix Pryde left a job as head of a wireless telephone group to become the director of environmental strategy at the British Broadcasting Corporation.

Have you made similar choices or decisions bas... your int...

NET IMPACT

Making Responsible Decisions boxes focus on social responsibility, sustainability, and ethics. These boxes provide exciting, current examples of how companies approach these subjects in their marketing strategy.

Going Online

Visit an Apple Store to See What All the Excitement Is About

Interested in visiting an Apple store to see what all the excitement is about? Is one of Apple's 250-plus stores in the world situated near you? If you answered "yes" to the first question and "no" to the second, then log on to www.ifoapplestore.com/db. Here you will find exterior and interior photographs and video tours of various Apple stores. To learn whether an Apple store is planned for your area, visit this Web site to find announcements of grand openings.

Going Online exercises are integrated in the text and ask students to go online and think critically about a specific company's use of the Internet, helping students apply knowledge of key chapter concepts, terms, and topics, as well as evaluate the success or failure of the company's efforts.

building your marketing plan

To do a consumer analysis for the product—the good, service, or idea—in your marketing plan:

1 Identify the consumers who are most likely to buy your product—the primary target market—in terms of (*a*) their demographic characteristics and (*b*) any other kind of characteristics you believe are important.

2 Describe (*a*) the main points of difference of your product for this group and (*b*) what problem they help solve for the consumer, in terms of the first stage in the consumer purchase decision process in Figure 5–1.

3 Identify the one or two key influences for each of the four outside boxes in Figure 5–4: (*a*) marketing mix, (*b*) psychological, (*c*) sociocultural, and (*d*) situational influences.

This consumer analysis will provide the foundation for the marketing mix actions you develop later in your plan.

Building Your Marketing Plan is an end-of-chapter feature that requires students to go through the practical application of creating their own marketing plan.

INSTRUCTOR RESOURCES

Element*	Online Learning Center www.mhhe.com/kerin	Instructor's Resource CD (IRCD)	Other
Using Marketing Dashboards Video	X	X	
Instructor's Manual (IM)	X	X	
Visually Enhanced Test Bank	X	X	
PowerPoint Presentations	X (basic)	X (enhanced)	
Video Cases			Video DVD
Instructor's Survival Kit (ISK)			Stand-alone kit
Instructor Newsletter			e-mail
Connect Marketing			online

*All instructor resources are compatible with any online platform—including Blackboard, WebCT, eCollege, and TopClass.

- Using Marketing Dashboards Video:

  Marketing dashboards are being used among marketing professionals to graphically portray the measures used to track and analyze marketing performance. The key feature in *Marketing*, 10/e, Using Marketing Dashboards, is a way to bring this concept home to your students. Watch this video and even share it with your class for more information on how dashboards are being used today.

- Instructor's Manual:

  The Instructor's Manual (IM) to accompany *Marketing*, 10/e is an all-inclusive resource designed to make an instructor's preparation for teaching much easier. The *Instructor's Manual* includes detailed lectures notes, discussions, and a description of all of the individual multimedia assets from which an instructor can construct a custom presentation. The IM also includes In-Class Activities (ICAs) that link to sample products in the Instructor's Survival Kit to make marketing come to life in the classroom.

- Visually Enhanced Test Bank:

  We offer more than 5,000 test questions categorized by topic and level of learning (knowledge, comprehension, or application) and correlated to both the Learning Objectives and Bloom's Level of Learning to assist instructors in developing their exams. There are also a number of visually enhanced questions in the test bank that include images and figures from the book itself to ensure student learning and preparation.

- Test Bank Online:

A comprehensive bank of test questions is provided within a computerized test bank powered by McGraw-Hill's flexible electronic testing software program EZ Test Online (www.eztestonline.com). EZ Test Online allows you to create paper and online tests or quizzes in this easy-to-use program!

Imagine being able to create and access your test or quiz anywhere, at any time without installing the testing software. Now, with EZ Test Online, instructors can select questions from multiple McGraw-Hill test banks or author their own, and then either print the test for paper distribution or give it online.

Test Creation

- Author/edit questions online using the 14 different question type templates.
- Create printed tests or deliver online to get instant scoring and feedback.
- Create questions pools to offer multiple versions online—great for practice.
- Export your tests for use in WebCT, Blackboard, PageOut and Apple's iQuiz.
- Compatible with EZ Test Desktop tests you've already created.
- Sharing tests with colleagues, adjuncts, TAs is easy

Online Test Management

- Set availability dates and time limits for your quiz or test.
- Control how your test will be presented.
- Assign points by question or question type with drop-down menu.
- Provide immediate feedback to students or delay until all finish the test.
- Create practice tests online to enable student mastery.
- Your roster can be uploaded to enable student self-registration.

Online Scoring and Reporting

- Automated scoring for most of EZ Test's numerous question types.
- Allows manual scoring for essay and other open response questions.
- Manual re-scoring and feedback is also available.
- EZ Test's grade book is designed to easily export to your grade book.
- View basic statistical reports.

Support and Help

- User's Guide and built-in page specific help.
- Flash tutorials for getting started on the support site.
- Support Web site: www.mhhe.com/eztest.
- Product specialist available at 1-800-331-5094.
- Online Training: http://auth.mhhe.com/mpss/workshops/.

- **PowerPoint Presentations:**

  The PowerPoint Presentations feature slides that can be used and personalized by instructors to help present concepts to students efficiently. The Online Learning Center contains a basic version of the media-enhanced PowerPoint Presentations that are found on the IRCD. The media-enhanced version has video and commercials embedded in the presentations and makes for an engaging and interesting classroom lecture.

- **New and Revised Video Cases:**

  A unique series of 22 contemporary marketing video cases is available on DVD. Each video case corresponds with chapter-specific topics and the end-of-chapter case in the text. The video cases feature a variety of organizations and provide balanced coverage of services, consumer products, small businesses, *Fortune* 500 firms, and business-to-business examples. The 10th edition package includes new videos about Google, Under Armour, Pizza Hut, Activeion, and Prince tennis rackets.

- **Instructor's Survival Kit (ISK):**

  The Instructor's Survival Kit contains product samples for use in the classroom to illustrate marketing concepts and encourage student involvement and learning, often with teams working on a task for 5 to 15 minutes in class. Today's students are more likely to learn and be motivated by active participative experiences than by classic classroom lecture and discussion. *Marketing* utilizes product samples from both large and small firms that will interest today's students. When appropriate, sample print and TV ads are included among our PowerPoint Presentations.

- **Instructor Newsletter:**

  The Instructor Newsletter has been developed for adopters of *Marketing*. This newsletter is devoted to providing innovative resources to help improve student learning, offer timely marketing examples, and make class preparation easier. The newsletter includes: links to video clips from *BusinessWeek* and other sources, synopses of articles with in-class discussion questions, teaching tips, and discussion of pedagogical features of *Marketing*. The newsletter will be offered eight times during the academic year and is available through e-mail and on our Web site, www.mhhe.com/kerin.

Less Managing. More Teaching. Greater Learning.

McGraw-Hill *Connect Marketing* is an online assignment and assessment solution that connects students with the tools and resources they'll need to achieve success.

McGraw-Hill *Connect Marketing* helps prepare students for their future by enabling faster learning, more efficient studying, and higher retention of knowledge.

McGraw-Hill *Connect Marketing* Features

Connect Marketing offers a number of powerful tools and features to make managing assignments easier, so faculty can spend more time teaching. With *Connect Marketing,* students can engage with their coursework anytime and anywhere, making the learning process more accessible and efficient. *Connect Marketing* offers you the features described below.

Simple Assignment Management

With *Connect Marketing,* creating assignments is easier than ever, so you can spend more time teaching and less time managing. The assignment management function enables you to:

- Create and deliver assignments easily with selectable end-of-chapter questions and test bank items.
- Streamline lesson planning, student progress reporting, and assignment grading to make classroom management more efficient than ever.
- Go paperless with the eBook and online submission and grading of student assignments.

Smart Grading

When it comes to studying, time is precious. *Connect Marketing* helps students learn more efficiently by providing feedback and practice material when they need it, where they need it. When it comes to teaching, your time also is precious. The grading function enables you to:

- Have assignments scored automatically, giving students immediate feedback on their work and side-by-side comparisons with correct answers.
- Access and review each response; manually change grades or leave comments for students to review.
- Reinforce classroom concepts with practice tests and instant quizzes.

Instructor Library

The *Connect Marketing* Instructor Library is your repository for additional resources to improve student engagement in and out of class. You can select and use any asset that enhances your lecture. The *Connect Marketing* Instructor Library includes:

- *eBook*
- *PowerPoint Presentations*
- *Video Cases*
- *Instructor's Manual*
- *Instructor's Survival Kit and In-Class Activities CD*

Student Study Center

The *Connect Marketing* Student Study Center is the place for students to access additional resources. The Student Study Center:

- Offers students quick access to lectures, practice materials, eBooks, and more.
- Provides instant practice material and study questions, easily accessible on the go.
- Gives students access to the Personalized Learning Plan described below.

Student Progress Tracking

Connect Marketing keeps instructors informed about how each student, section, and class is performing, allowing for more productive use of lecture and office hours. The progress-tracking function enables you to:

- View scored work immediately and track individual or group performance with assignment and grade reports.
- Access an instant view of student or class performance relative to learning objectives.
- Collect data and generate reports required by many accreditation organizations, such as AACSB.

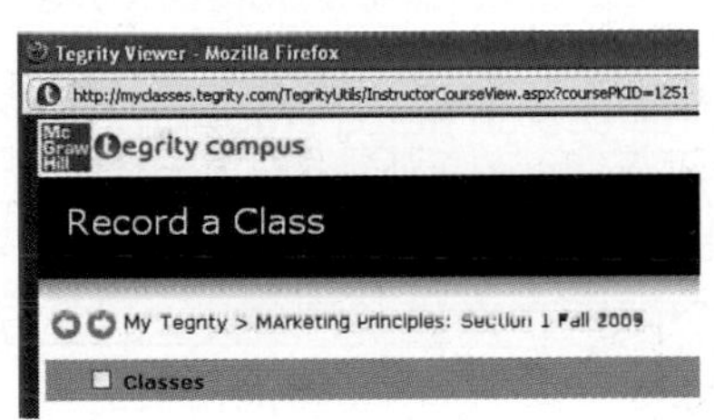

Lecture Capture

Increase the attention paid to lecture discussion by decreasing the attention paid to note taking. For an additional charge Lecture Capture offers new ways for students to focus on the in-class discussion, knowing they can revisit important topics later. Lecture Capture enables you to:

- Record and distribute your lecture with the click of a button.
- Record and index PowerPoint Presentations and anything shown on your computer so it is easily searchable, frame by frame.
- Offer access to lectures anytime and anywhere by computer, iPod, or mobile device.
- Increase intent listening and class participation by easing students' concerns about note-taking. Lecture Capture will make it more likely you will see students' faces, not the tops of their heads.

McGraw-Hill *Connect Plus Marketing*

McGraw-Hill reinvents the textbook learning experience for the modern student with *Connect Plus Marketing*. A seamless integration of an eBook and *Connect Marketing*, *Connect Plus Marketing* provides all of the *Connect Marketing* features plus the following:

- An integrated eBook, allowing for anytime, anywhere access to the textbook.

- Dynamic links between the problems or questions you assign to your students and the location in the eBook where that problem or question is covered.
- A powerful search function to pinpoint and connect key concepts in a snap.

In short, *Connect Marketing* offers you and your students powerful tools and features that optimize your time and energies, enabling you to focus on course content, teaching, and student learning. *Connect Marketing* also offers a wealth of content resources for both instructors and students. This state-of-the-art, thoroughly tested system supports you in preparing students for the world that awaits.

For more information about Connect, go to **www.mcgrawhillconnect.com**, or contact your local McGraw-Hill sales representative.

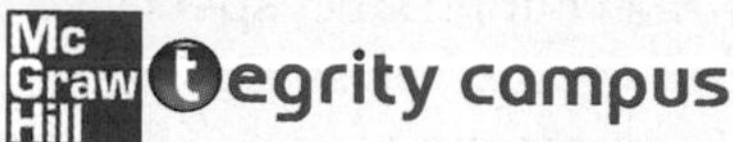

Tegrity Campus: Lectures 24/7

Tegrity Campus is a service that makes class time available 24/7 by automatically capturing every lecture in a searchable format for students to review when they study and complete assignments. With a simple one-click start-and-stop process, you capture all computer screens and corresponding audio. Students can replay any part of any class with easy-to-use browser-based viewing on a PC or Mac.

Educators know that the more students can see, hear, and experience class resources, the better they learn. In fact, studies prove it. With Tegrity Campus, students quickly recall key moments by using Tegrity Campus's unique search feature. This search helps students efficiently find what they need, when they need it, across an entire semester of class recordings. Help turn all your students' study time into learning moments immediately supported by your lecture.

To learn more about Tegrity watch a 2-minute Flash demo at **http://tegritycampus.mhhe.com**.

Assurance of Learning Ready

Many educational institutions today are focused on the notion of *assurance of learning*, an important element of some accreditation standards. *Marketing* is designed specifically to support your assurance of learning initiatives with a simple, yet powerful solution.

Each test bank question for *Marketing* maps to a specific chapter learning outcome/objective listed in the text. You can use our test bank software, EZ Test and EZ Test Online, or in *Connect Marketing* to easily query for learning outcomes/objectives that directly relate to the learning objectives for your course. You can then use the reporting features of EZ Test to aggregate student results in similar fashion, making the collection and presentation of assurance of learning data simple and easy.

AACSB Statement

The McGraw-Hill Companies is a proud corporate member of AACSB International. Understanding the importance and value of AACSB accreditation, *Marketing*, 10e, recognizes the curricula guidelines detailed in the AACSB standards for business accreditation by connecting selected questions in the test bank to the six general knowledge and skill guidelines in the AACSB standards.

The statements contained in *Marketing*, 10e, are provided only as a guide for the users of this textbook. The AACSB leaves content coverage and assessment within the purview of individual schools, the mission of the school, and the faculty. While *Marketing*, 10e, and the teaching package make no claim of any specific AACSB qualification or evaluation, we have within *Marketing*, 10e, labeled selected questions according to the six general knowledge and skills areas.

McGraw-Hill Customer Care Contact Information

At McGraw-Hill, we understand that getting the most from new technology can be challenging. That's why our services don't stop after you purchase our products. You can e-mail our product specialists 24 hours a day to get product-training online. Or you can search our knowledge bank of Frequently Asked Questions on our support Web site. For Customer Support, call **800-331-5094,** e-mail **hmsupport@mcgraw-hill.com,** or visit **www.mhhe.com/support.** One of our technical support analysts will be able to assist you in a timely fashion.

Acknowledgments

To ensure continuous improvement of our textbook and supplements we have utilized an extensive review and development process for each of our past editions. Building on that history, the *Marketing,* 10th edition development process included several phases of evaluation and a variety of stakeholder audiences (e.g., students, instructors, etc.).

Reviewers who were vital in the changes that were made to this edition include:

Wendi Achey
Northampton University

Chris Anicich
California State University—Fullerton

Corinne Asher
Henry Ford Community College

Tim Aurand
Northern Illinois University

Christopher Blocker
Baylor University

Koren Borges
University of North Florida

Glen Brodowsky
California State University—San Marcos

Carmina Cavazos
University of St. Thomas

Debbie Coleman
Miami University—Ohio

Mary Conran
Temple University

Lawrence Duke
Drexel University

Karen Flaherty
Oklahoma State University

Darrell Goudge
University of Central Oklahoma

Santhi Harvey
Central State University

Ron Hasty
University of North Texas

Nathan Himelstein
Essex County College

Donald Hoffer
Miami University—Ohio

Fred Honerkamp
Northwood University

Keith Jones
North Carolina A&T State University

Philip Kearney
Niagara County Community College—SUNY

Kathleen Krentler
San Diego State University

Michelle Kunz
Morehead State University

Christine Lai
Buffalo State University

Donald Larson
Ohio State University

Harold Lucius
Rowan University

Theodore Mitchell
University of Nevada, Reno

Rex Moody
University of Colorado

James Munch
Wright State University

Brian Murray
Jefferson Community College—SUNY

Eric Newman
Cal State San Bernardino

Carmen Powers
Monroe Community College

Philip Shum
William Patterson University

David Smith
Bemidji State University

Cheryl Stansfield
North Hennepin Community College

Gary Tucker
Oklahoma City Community College

Kim Wong
Central New Mexico Community College

Jim Zemanek
East Carolina University

The preceding section demonstrates the amount of feedback and developmental input that went into this project, and we are deeply grateful to the numerous people who have shared their ideas with us. Reviewing a book or supplement takes an incredible amount of energy and attention. We are glad so many of our colleagues took the time to do it. Their comments have inspired us to do our best.

Reviewers who contributed to the first nine editions of this book include:

Nadia J. Abgrab
Kerri Acheson
Roy Adler
Christie Amato
Linda Anglin
Ismet Anitsal
William D. Ash
Gerard Athaide
Andy Aylesworth
Patricia Baconride
Siva Balasubramanian
A. Diane Barlar
James H. Barnes
Karen Becker-Olsen
Frederick J. Beier
Thom J. Belich
Joseph Belonax
Thomas M. Bertsch
Parimal Bhagat
Carol Bienstock
Kevin W. Bittle
Jeff Blodgett
Nancy Bloom
Charles Bodkin

Larry Borgen
Nancy Boykin
Thomas Brashear
Martin Bressler
Bruce Brown
William Brown
William G. Browne
Judy Bulin
David J. Burns
Alan Bush
Stephen Calcich
William J. Carner
Larry Carter
Gerald O. Cavallo
S. Tamer Cavusgil
Bruce Chadbourne
S. Choi Chan
Sang Choe
Kay Chomic
Melissa Clark
Mark Collins
Howard Combs
Clare Comm
Clark Compton
Cristanna Cook
Sherry Cook
John Coppett
John Cox
Scott Cragin
Ken Crocker
Joe Cronin
James Cross
Lowell E. Crow
Brent Cunningham
John H. Cunningham
Bill Curtis
Bob Dahlstrom
Dan Darrow
Neel Das
Hugh Daubek
Martin Decatur
Francis DeFea
Joseph Defilippe
Linda M. Delene
Tino DeMarco
Jobie Devinney-Walsh
Irene Dickey
Paul Dion
William B. Dodds
James H. Donnelly
Michael Drafke
Bob Dwyer
Eddie V. Easley
Eric Ecklund
Roger W. Egerton
Steven Engel
Barbara Evans
Ken Fairweather
Larry Feick
Lori Feldman
Kevin Feldt
Theresa Flaherty
Elizabeth R. Flynn
Charles Ford
Renee Foster
Judy Foxman
Donald Fuller
Stan Garfunkel
Stephen Garrott
Glen Gelderloos
David Gerth
James Ginther
Susan Godar
Dan Goebel
Marc Goldberg
Leslie A. Goldgehn
Kenneth Goodenday
Darrell Goudge
James Gould
Kimberly Grantham
Nancy Grassilli
Barnett Greenberg
James L. Grimm
Pamela Grimm
Pola B. Gupta
Richard Hansen
Donald V. Harper
Dotty Harpool
Lynn Harris
Robert C. Harris
Ernan Haruvy
James A. Henley, Jr.
Ken Herbst
Jonathan Hibbard
Richard M. Hill
Al Holden
Kristine Hovsepian
Jarrett Hudnal
Mike Hyman
Rajesh Iyer
Donald R. Jackson
Kenneth Jameson
David Jamison
Deb Jansky
James C. Johnson
Wesley Johnston
Robert Jones
Mary Joyce
Jacqueline Karen
Janice Karlen
Sudhir Karunakaran
Rajiv Kashyap
Herbert Katzenstein
George Kelley
Katie Kemp
Ram Kesaran
Roy Klages
Douglas Kornemann
Terry Kroeten
Anand Kumar
Nanda Kumar
Ann Kuzma
John Kuzma
Priscilla LaBarbera
Duncan G. LaBay
Jay Lambe
Tim Landry
Jane Lang
Irene Lange
Richard Lapidus
Ron Larson
Ed Laube
J. Ford Laumer
Debra Laverie
Marilyn Lavin
Gary Law
Robert Lawson
Wilton Lelund
Karen LeMasters
Richard C. Leventhal
Leonard Lindenmuth
Ann Little
Eldon L. Little
Yunchuan Liu
James Lollar
Paul Londrigan
Lynn Loudenback
Ann Lucht
Mike Luckett
Robert Luke
Michael R. Luthy
Richard J. Lutz
Marton L. Macchiete
Rhonda Mack
Patricia Manninen
Kenneth Maricle
Tom Marshall
Elena Martinez
Carolyn Massiah
Tamara Masters
Charla Mathwick
Michael Mayo
James McAlexander
Peter J. McClure
Phyllis McGinnis

Jim McHugh
Gary F. McKinnon
Ed McLaughlin
Jo Ann McManamy
Kristy McManus
Bob McMillen
Samuel E. McNeely
Lee Meadow
James Meszaros
George Miaoulis
Soon Hong Min
Ronald Michaels
Herbert A. Miller
Stephen W. Miller
William G. Mitchell
Steven Moff
Kim Montney
Melissa Moore
Linda Morable
Fred Morgan
Gordon Mosley
William Motz
Donald F. Mulvihill
James A. Muncy
Jeanne Munger
Linda Munilla
Bill Murphy
Janet Murray
Keith Murray
Joseph Myslivec
Sunder Narayanan
Bob Newberry
Donald G. Norris
Carl Obermiller
Dave Olson
James Olver
Ben Oumlil
Notis Pagiavlas
Allan Palmer
Dennis Pappas
June E. Parr
Philip Parron
David Terry Paul
Richard Penn
John Penrose
William Pertula
Michael Peters
Susan Peterson
Renee Pfeifer-Luckett
William S. Piper
Stephen Pirog
Gary Poorman
Vonda Powell
Joe Puzi
Edna Ragins
Priyali Rajagopal
Daniel Rajaratnam
James P. Rakowski
Rosemary Ramsey
Barbara Ribbens
Cathie Rich-Duval
Joe Ricks
Heikki Rinne
Linda Rochford
William Rodgers
Jean Romeo
Teri Root
Tom Rossi
Vicki Rostedt
Heidi Rottier
Larry Rottmeyer
Robert W. Ruekert
Maria Sanella
Charles Schewe
Starr F. Schlobohm
Roberta Schultz
Lisa M. Sciulli
Stan Scott
Eberhard Seheuling
Harold S. Sekiguchi
Doris M. Shaw
Eric Shaw
Ken Shaw
Dan Sherrel
Susan Sieloff
Bob E. Smiley
Allen Smith
Kimberly D. Smith
Ruth Ann Smith
Sandra Smith
Norman Smothers
James V. Spiers
Craig Stacey
Miriam B. Stamps
Joe Stasio
Tom Stevenson
Kathleen Stuenkel
Scott Swan
Rick Sweeney
Michael Swenson
Robert Swerdlow
Vincent P. Taiani
Clint Tankersley
Ruth Taylor
Andrew Thacker
Tom Thompson
Dan Toy
Fred Trawick
Thomas L. Trittipo
Sue Umashankar
Bronis J. Verhage
Ottilia Voegtli
Jeff von Freymann
Gerald Waddle
Randall E. Wade
Blaise Waguespack, Jr.
Harlan Wallingford
Mark Weber
Don Weinrauch
Robert S. Welsh
Ron Weston
Michelle Wetherbee
Sheila Wexler
Max White
James Wilkins
Erin Wilkinson
Janice Williams
Kaylene Williams
Robert Williams
Jerry W. Wilson
Joseph Wisenblit
Robert Witherspoon
Van R. Wood
Wendy Wood
Lauren Wright
William R. Wynd
Poh-Lin Yeoh
Mark Young
Sandra Young
Gail M. Zank
Leon Zurawicki

Thanks are also due to many faculty members who contributed to the text chapters and cases. They include: Linda Rochford of the University of Minnesota-Duluth; Kevin Upton of the University of Minnesota-Twin Cities; Nancy Nentl of Metropolitan State University; David Brennan of the University of St. Thomas; and Leigh McAlister of the University of Texas at Austin. Michael Vessey provided cases, research assistance, many special images, and led our efforts on the Instructor's Manual, In-Class Activities, and Instructor's Survival Kit. Kathryn Schifferle of California State University, Steven Rudelius, and Thomas Rudelius assisted with the Instructor

Newsletter. Rick Armstrong of Armstrong Photography, Nick Kaufman and Michelle Morgan of NKP Media, Bruce McLean of World Class Communication Technologies, Paul Fagan of Fagan Productions, Dan Hundley and George Heck of Token Media, Martin Walter of White Room Digital, Scott Bolin of Bolin Marketing, and Dan Stephenson of the Philadelphia Phillies produced the videos. Erica Michaels was responsible for the revision of the test bank.

Many businesspeople also provided substantial assistance by making available information that appears in the text, videos, and supplements—much of it for the first time in college materials. Thanks are due to David Ford and Don Rylander of Ford Consulting Group; Mark Rehborg of Tony's Pizza; Ann Hand and Kathy Seegebrecht of BP; Kimberly Mosford and Ryan Schroeder of Business Incentives; Vivian Callaway, Sandy Proctor, and Anna Stoesz of General Mills; David Windorski of 3M; Nicholas Skally, Linda Glassel, and Tyler Herring of Prince Sports; David Montgomery, David Buck, and Bonnie Clark of the Philadelphia Phillies; Todd Schaeffer, Amber Arnseth, and Chris Deets of Activeion Cleaning Solutions; Ian Wolfman of imc^2; Brian Niccol of Pizza Hut; Stan Jacot of ConAgra Snack Foods; Sandra Smith of Smith Communications; Erin Patton of the MasterMind Group, LLC; Kim Nagele of JCPenney, Inc.; Charles Besio of the Sewell Automotive Group, Inc.; Kate Hodebeck of Cadbury Schweppes America's Beverages, Inc.; Beverly Roberts of U.S. Census Bureau; Jennifer Gebert of Ghirardelli Chocolate Company; Michael Kuhl of 3M Sports and Leisure; Barbara Davis of Ken Davis Products, Inc.; Kerry Barnett of Valassis Communications; and Leslie Herman and Jeff Gerst of Bolin Marketing working with Carma Laboratories (Carmex). We also acknowledge the special help of a team that worked with us on the Fallon Worldwide video case: Fred Senn, Bruce Blister, Kevin Flat, Ginny Grossman, Kim Knutson, Julie Smith, Erin Taut, and Rob White.

Staff support from the Southern Methodist University, the University of Denver, and the University of Minnesota was essential. We gratefully acknowledge the help of Wanda Hanson, Jeanne Milazzo, and Gloria Valdez for their many contributions.

Checking countless details related to layout, graphics, clear writing, and last-minute changes to ensure timely examples is essential for a sound and accurate textbook. This also involves coordinating activities of authors, designers, editors, compositors, and production specialists. Christine Vaughan of McGraw-Hill/Irwin's production staff and editorial consultant, Gina Huck Siegert of Imaginative Solutions, Inc., provided the necessary oversight and hand-holding for us, while retaining a refreshing sense of humor, often under tight deadlines. Thank you again.

Finally, we acknowledge the professional efforts of the McGraw-Hill/Irwin staff. Completion of our book and its many supplements required the attention and commitment of many editorial, production, marketing, and research personnel. Our Burr Ridge-based team included Paul Ducham, Doug Hughes, Sean Pankuch, Melissa Hernandez, Carol Bielski, Matthew Baldwin, Jeremy Cheshareck, Sue Lombardi, Katie Mergen, and many others. In addition we relied on Michael Hruby for constant attention regarding photo elements of the text. Handling the countless details of our text, supplement, and support technologies has become an incredibly complex challenge. We thank all these people for their efforts!

Roger A. Kerin
Steven W. Hartley
William Rudelius

BRIEF CONTENTS

Part 1 Initiating the Marketing Process

1 Creating Customer Relationships and Value through Marketing *2*
2 Developing Successful Marketing and Organizational Strategies *24*
APPENDIX A Building an Effective Marketing Plan 50
3 Scanning the Marketing Environment *64*
4 Ethical and Social Responsibility in Marketing *90*

Part 2 Understanding Buyers and Markets

5 Understanding Consumer Behavior *110*
6 Understanding Organizations as Customers *138*
7 Understanding and Reaching Global Consumers and Markets *160*

Part 3 Targeting Marketing Opportunities

8 Marketing Research: From Customer Insights to Actions *192*
9 Market Segmentation, Targeting, and Positioning *220*

Part 4 Satisfying Marketing Opportunities

10 Developing New Products and Services *244*
11 Managing Successful Products and Brands *268*
12 Services Marketing *296*
13 Building the Price Foundation *318*
14 Arriving at the Final Price *344*
APPENDIX B Financial Aspects of Marketing 370
15 Managing Marketing Channels and Wholesaling *378*
16 Customer-Driven Supply Chain and Logistics Management *404*
17 Retailing *428*
18 Integrated Marketing Communications and Direct Marketing *456*
19 Advertising, Sales Promotion, and Public Relations *484*
20 Personal Selling and Sales Management *518*

Part 5 Managing the Marketing Process

21 Implementing Interactive and Multichannel Marketing *546*
22 Pulling It All Together: The Strategic Marketing Process *570*
APPENDIX C Planning a Career in Marketing 598
APPENDIX D Alternate Cases 616

Glossary 649
Learning Review Answers 660
Chapter Notes 669
Credits 701
Name Index 705
Company/Product Index 713
Subject Index 721

DETAILED CONTENTS

Part 1 Initiating the Marketing Process

1 CREATING CUSTOMER RELATIONSHIPS AND VALUE THROUGH MARKETING 2

Innovation and Marketing at 3M: How Discovering Student Study Habits Launched a New Product 3
What Is Marketing? 4
Marketing and Your Career 4

Marketing Matters: Payoff for the Joys (!) and Sleepless Nights (?) of Starting Your Own Small Business: YouTube!!!! 5

Marketing: Delivering Benefits to the Organization, Its Stakeholders, and Society 6
The Diverse Factors Influencing Marketing Activities 6
What Is Needed for Marketing to Occur 7
How Marketing Discovers and Satisfies Consumer Needs 8
Discovering Consumer Needs 9
The Challenge: Meeting Consumer Needs with New Products 9
Satisfying Consumer Needs 11
The Marketing Program: How Customer Relationships Are Built 12
Customer Value and Customer Relationships 12
Relationship Marketing 13
The Marketing Program 13
3M's Strategy and Marketing Program to Help Students Study 14
How Marketing Became So Important 16
Evolution of the Market Orientation 16
Ethics and Social Responsibility: Balancing the Interests of Different Groups 17

Making Responsible Decisions: Social Entrepreneurship Using Marketing to Help People 18

The Breadth and Depth of Marketing 18

Learning Objectives Review 20
Focusing on Key Terms 20
Applying Marketing Knowledge 21
Building Your Marketing Plan 21

Video Case 1: 3M's Post-it® Flag Highlighter: Extending the Concept! 21

2 DEVELOPING SUCCESSFUL MARKETING AND ORGANIZATIONAL STRATEGIES 24

Where an "A" in a Correspondence Course in Ice Cream Making Can Lead! 25

Today's Organizations 26
Kinds of Organizations 26

Making Responsible Decisions: The Global Dilemma: How to Achieve Sustainable Development 27

What Is Strategy? 27
Structure of Today's Organizations 27
Strategy in Visionary Organizations 28
Organizational Foundation: Why Does It Exist? 29
Organizational Direction: What Will It Do? 30

Marketing Matters: The Netflix Launch and Its Continually . . . Continually . . . Continually . . . Changing Business Model! 31

Organizational Strategies: How Will It Do It? 32
Tracking Strategic Performance with Marketing Dashboards 32

Using Marketing Dashboards: How Well Is Ben & Jerry's Doing? 34

Setting Strategic Directions 34
A Look Around: Where Are We Now? 34
Growth Strategies: Where Do We Want to Go? 35
The Strategic Marketing Process 39
The Planning Phase of the Strategic Marketing Process 40
The Implementation Phase of the Strategic Marketing Process 43
The Evaluation Phase of the Strategic Marketing Process 44

Learning Objectives Review 45
Focusing on Key Terms 46
Applying Marketing Knowledge 47
Building Your Marketing Plan 47

Video Case 2: BP: Transforming Its Strategy "Beyond Petroleum" 47

APPENDIX A Building an Effective Marketing Plan 50

3 SCANNING THE MARKETING ENVIRONMENT 64

Where In the World Are You? In the Middle of the GPS Revolution! 65
Environmental Scanning 66
Tracking Environmental Trends 66
An Environmental Scan of Today's Marketplace 67
Social Forces 68
Demographics 68

Making Responsible Decisions: Millennials Are Going to Change the World—Through Environmental Sustainability! 71

Culture 73
Economic Forces 75
Macroeconomic Conditions 75
Consumer Income 75

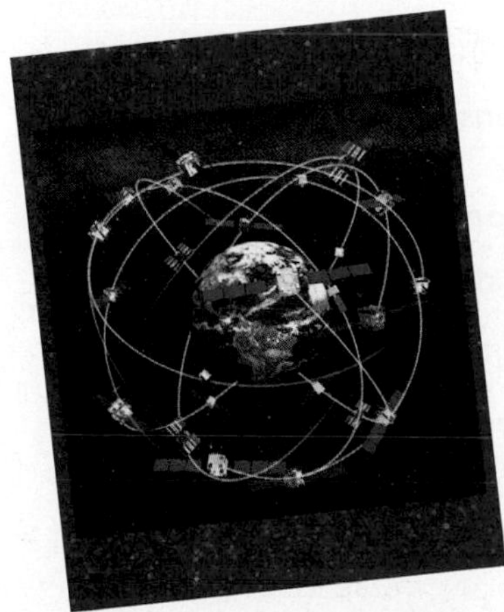

***Going Online: There Are 65 Types of Neighborhoods—Which Type Is Yours?* 77**

Technological Forces 78
- Technology of Tomorrow 78
- Technology's Impact on Customer Value 79
- Electronic Business Technologies 80

Competitive Forces 80
- Alternative Forms of Competition 80
- Components of Competition 81
- Small Businesses as Competitors 81

Regulatory Forces 82
- Protecting Competition 82
- Product-Related Legislation 82

***Marketing Matters: The Web Allows New Uses and Misuses of Trademarks* 84**

- Pricing-Related Legislation 84
- Distribution-Related Legislation 84
- Advertising- and Promotion-Related Legislation 85
- Control through Self-Regulation 85

Learning Objectives Review 86
Focusing on Key Terms 87
Applying Marketing Knowledge 87
Building Your Marketing Plan 87

Video Case 3: Geek Squad: A New Business for a New Environment 87

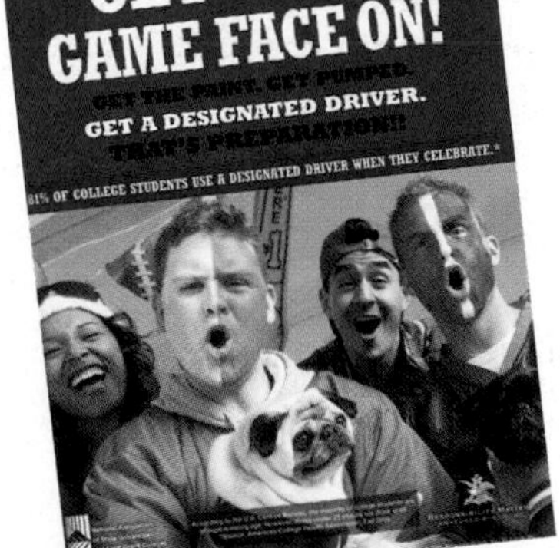

4 ETHICAL AND SOCIAL RESPONSIBILITY IN MARKETING 90

Responsibility Matters at Anheuser-Busch 91

Nature and Significance of Marketing Ethics 92
- Ethical/Legal Framework in Marketing 92
- Current Perceptions of Ethical Behavior 93

Understanding Ethical Marketing Behavior 93
- Societal Culture and Norms 93
- Business Culture and Industry Practices 94

***Making Responsible Decisions: Corporate Conscience in the Cola War* 96**

***Going Online: The Corruption Perceptions Index* 97**

- Corporate Culture and Expectations 97
- Your Personal Moral Philosophy and Ethical Behavior 98

Understanding Social Responsibility in Marketing 100
- Three Concepts of Social Responsibility 100

***Marketing Matters: Will Consumers Switch Brands for a Cause? Yes, If . . .* 103**

The Social Audit and Sustainable Development: Doing Well by Doing Good 103
Turning the Table: Consumer Ethics and Social Responsibility 104

Learning Objectives Review 105
Focusing on Key Terms 106
Applying Marketing Knowledge 106
Building Your Marketing Plan 106

Video Case 4: Starbucks Corporation: Serving More than Coffee 107

Part 2 Understanding Buyers and Markets

5 UNDERSTANDING CONSUMER BEHAVIOR 110

Enlightened Carmakers Know What Custom(h)ers Value 111
Consumer Purchase Decision Process and Experience 112
Problem Recognition: Perceiving a Need 112
Information Search: Seeking Value 112
Alternative Evaluation: Assessing Value 113
Purchase Decision: Buying Value 114
Postpurchase Behavior: Value in Consumption or Use 114

Marketing Matters: The Value of a Satisfied Customer to the Company 115

Consumer Involvement and Problem-Solving Variations 115
Situational Influences 117
Psychological Influences on Consumer Behavior 118
Motivation and Personality 118

Making Responsible Decisions: The Ethics of Subliminal Messages 120

Perception 120
Learning 122
Values, Beliefs, and Attitudes 123

Going Online: Are You an Experiencer? An Achiever?: Identifying Your VALS Profile 124

Consumer Lifestyle 124
Sociocultural Influences on Consumer Behavior 126
Personal Influence 126

Marketing Matters: BzzAgent—The Buzz Experience 127

Reference Groups 128
Family Influence 128
Social Class 130
Culture and Subculture 131

Learning Objectives Review 133
Focusing on Key Terms 134
Applying Marketing Knowledge 134
Building Your Marketing Plan 135

Video Case 5: Best Buy: Using Customer Centricity to Connect with Consumers 135

6 UNDERSTANDING ORGANIZATIONS AS CUSTOMERS 138

Buying Is Marketing, Too! Purchasing Publication Paper at JCPenney 139
The Nature and Size of Organizational Markets 140
Industrial Markets 140
Reseller Markets 140
Government Markets 141
Global Organizational Markets 141
Measuring Domestic and Global Industrial, Reseller, and Government Markets 141
Characteristics of Organizational Buying 143
Demand Characteristics 143
Size of the Order or Purchase 144
Number of Potential Buyers 144
Organizational Buying Objectives 144

Going Online: Supplier Diversity Is a Fundamental Business Strategy at Procter & Gamble 145

Organizational Buying Criteria 145

Marketing Matters: Harley-Davidson's Supplier Collaboration Creates Customer Value . . . and a Great Ride 146

Buyer–Seller Relationships and Supply Partnerships 146

Making Responsible Decisions: Sustainable Procurement for Sustainable Growth 147

The Buying Center: A Cross-Functional Group 147
Charting the Organizational Buying Process 150
Stages in the Organizational Buying Process 150
Buying a Machine Vision System 150
Online Buying in Organizational Markets 153
Prominence of Online Buying in Organizational Markets 153
E-Marketplaces: Virtual Organizational Markets 153

Marketing Matters: eBay Means Business for Entrepreneurs 154

Online Auctions in Organizational Markets 155

Learning Objectives Review 156

Focusing on Key Terms 156
Applying Marketing Knowledge 157
Building Your Marketing Plan 157

Video Case 6: Lands' End: Where Buyers Rule 157

7 UNDERSTANDING AND REACHING GLOBAL CONSUMERS AND MARKETS 160

Dell's Quest for Growth in Emerging Economies 161
Dynamics of World Trade 162
World Trade Flows 162
Competitive Advantage of Nations 164
Marketing in a Borderless Economic World 166
Decline of Economic Protectionism 166

Making Responsible Decisions: Global Ethics and Global Economics—The Case of Protectionism 167

Rise of Economic Integration 168
A New Reality: Global Competition among Global Companies for Global Consumers 169
Emergence of a Networked Global Marketspace 171

Marketing Matters: The Global Teenager—A Market of 2 Billion Voracious Consumers with $200 Billion to Spend 172

A Global Environmental Scan 173
Cultural Diversity 173
Economic Considerations 177
Political-Regulatory Climate 180

Going Online: Checking a Country's Political Risk Rating 181

Comparing Global Market-Entry Strategies 181
Exporting 182
Licensing 182

Marketing Matters: Creative Cosmetics and Creative Export Marketing in Japan 183

Joint Venture 184
Direct Investment 185
Crafting a Worldwide Marketing Program 185
Product and Promotion Strategies 185
Distribution Strategy 187
Pricing Strategy 188

Learning Objectives Review 188
Focusing on Key Terms 189
Applying Marketing Knowledge 189
Building Your Marketing Plan 189

Video Case 7: CNS Breathe Right Strips: Going Global 190

Part 3 Targeting Marketing Opportunities

8 MARKETING RESEARCH: FROM CUSTOMER INSIGHTS TO ACTIONS 192

Test Screenings and Tracking Studies: How Listening to Consumers Reduces Movie Risks 193
The Role of Marketing Research 195
- What Is Marketing Research? 195
- The Challenges in Doing Good Marketing Research 195
- Five-Step Marketing Research Approach 195

Step 1: Define the Problem 195
- Set the Research Objectives 196
- Identify Possible Marketing Actions 196

Step 2: Develop the Research Plan 197
- Specify Constraints 197
- Identify Data Needed for Marketing Actions 197
- Determine How to Collect Data 198

Step 3: Collect Relevant Information 199
- Secondary Data: Internal 199
- Secondary Data: External 199
- Advantages and Disadvantages of Secondary Data 200

Going Online: Online Databases and Internet Resources Useful to Marketers 201

- Primary Data: Watching People 201
- Primary Data: Asking People 203

Marketing Matters: Buy•ology: How "Neuromarketing" Is Trying to Understand Consumers 204

- Primary Data: Other Sources 208
- Advantages and Disadvantages of Primary Data 211

Step 4: Develop Findings 211
- Analyze the Data 211
- Present the Findings 212

Step 5: Take Marketing Actions 213
- Make Action Recommendations 213
- Implement the Action Recommendations 213
- Evaluate the Results 214

Sales Forecasting Techniques 214
- Judgments of the Decision Maker 214
- Surveys of Knowledgeable Groups 215
- Statistical Methods 215

Learning Objectives Review 216
Focusing on Key Terms 216
Applying Marketing Knowledge 217
Building Your Marketing Plan 217

Video Case 8: Ford Consulting Group, Inc.: From Data to Actions 217

9 MARKET SEGMENTATION, TARGETING, AND POSITIONING 220

Zappos.com: Delivering "Wow" through Market Segmentation and Service 221
Why Segment Markets? 222
What Market Segmentation Means 222
When and How to Segment Markets 223
Steps In Segmenting and Targeting Markets 225
Step 1: Group Potential Buyers into Segments 226
Going Online: What "Flock" Do You Belong to? 228
Step 2: Group Products to Be Sold into Categories 231
Step 3: Develop a Market-Product Grid and Estimate the Size of Markets 233
Step 4: Select Target Markets 233
Step 5: Take Marketing Actions to Reach Target Markets 234
Market-Product Synergies: A Balancing Act 236
Marketing Matters: Apple's Segmentation Strategy—Camp Runamok No Longer 237
Positioning the Product 238
Two Approaches to Product Positioning 238
Product Positioning Using Perceptual Maps 238
A Perceptual Map to Reposition Chocolate Milk for Adults 239

Learning Objectives Review 240
Focusing on Key Terms 241
Applying Marketing Knowledge 241
Building Your Marketing Plan 241

Video Case 9: Prince Sports, Inc.: Tennis Racquets for Every Segment 241

Part 4 Satisfying Marketing Opportunities

10 DEVELOPING NEW PRODUCTS AND SERVICES 244

Apple's New-Product Innovation Machine 245
What Are Products and Services? 246
A Look at Goods, Services, and Ideas 246
Classifying Products 246
Product Items, Product Lines, and Product Mixes 248
Using Marketing Dashboards: Which States Are Underperforming? 249
How Marketing Dashboards Can Improve New-Product Performance 249
New Products and Why They Succeed or Fail 250
What Is a New Product? 250

Marketing Matters: Feature Bloat: Geek Squad to the Rescue! 252

Why Products Succeed or Fail 252

Marketing Matters: From Idea to Launch: Stage-Gate® Processes in New-Product Development 255

The New-Product Process 256

Stage 1: New-Product Strategy Development 256

Stage 2: Idea Generation 257

Going Online: IDEO—the Innovation Lab Superstar in Designing New Products 258

Stage 3: Screening and Evaluation 259

Stage 4: Business Analysis 260

Stage 5: Development 260

Marketing Matters: Marissa Mayer: The Talent Behind Google's Familiar White Home Page 261

Stage 6: Market Testing 261

Stage 7: Commercialization 262

Learning Objectives Review 264

Focusing on Key Terms 264

Applying Marketing Knowledge 265

Building Your Marketing Plan 265

Video Case 10: Activeion Cleaning Solutions: Marketing a High-Tech Cleaning Gadget 265

11 MANAGING SUCCESSFUL PRODUCTS AND BRANDS 268

Gatorade: Quenching the Active Thirst within You 269

Charting the Product Life Cycle 270

Introduction Stage 270

Growth Stage 272

Maturity Stage 273

Marketing Matters: Will E-mail Spell Extinction for Fax Machines? 274

Decline Stage 274

Four Aspects of the Product Life Cycle 275

Managing the Product Life Cycle 278

Role of a Product Manager 278

Modifying the Product 278

Modifying the Market 278

Using Marketing Dashboards: Knowing Your CDI and BDI 279

Repositioning the Product 280

Making Responsible Decisions: Consumer Economics of Downsizing—Get Less, Pay More 281

Branding and Brand Management 282
Brand Personality and Brand Equity 283

Going Online: Have an Idea for a Brand or Trade Name? Check It Out 285

Picking a Good Brand Name 285
Branding Strategies 286
Packaging and Labeling Products 288
Creating Customer Value and Competitive Advantage through Packaging and Labeling 288

Marketing Matters: Creating Customer Value through Packaging—Pez Heads Dispense More Than Candy 289

Packaging and Labeling Challenges and Responses 291
Product Warranty 292

Learning Objectives Review 292
Focusing on Key Terms 293
Applying Marketing Knowledge 293
Building Your Marketing Plan 293

Video Case 11: BMW: "Newness" and the Product Life Cycle 294

12 SERVICES MARKETING 296

Services Get Real! 297
The Uniqueness of Services 298
The Four I's of Services 299
The Service Continuum 301
Classifying Services 302

Marketing Matters: Marketing Is a Must for 1.5 Million Nonprofits! 304

How Consumers Purchase Services 305
The Purchase Process 305
Assessing Service Quality 306
Customer Contact and Relationship Marketing 306

Going Online: How Can You Monitor Service Failure? Blog Watching! 307

Managing the Marketing of Services 308
Product (Service) 308
Price 309
Place (Distribution) 309
Promotion 310
People 311
Physical Environment 311
Process 311
Productivity 312

Services in the Future 312

Using Marketing Dashboards: Are JetBlue's Flights Profitably Loaded? 313

Learning Objectives Review 314
Focusing on Key Terms 314
Applying Marketing Knowledge 315
Building Your Marketing Plan 315

Video Case 12: Philadelphia Phillies, Inc.: Sports Marketing 101 315

13 BUILDING THE PRICE FOUNDATION 318

"My Mother Was Not Thrilled . . . ": The Launch of Stubhub.com! 319
Nature and Importance of Price 320
What Is a Price? 320

Marketing Matters: How Flattening the World Affects Prices, Revenues, and Costs: Infosys Technologies, Ltd., IKEA . . . and You! 322

Price and the Global Marketplace 322
Price as an Indicator of Value 322
Price in the Marketing Mix 323
Step 1: Identify Pricing Objectives and Constraints 324
Identifying Pricing Objectives 324
Identifying Pricing Constraints 325

Making Responsible Decisions: Student Credit Cards—What Is the Real Price? 326

Marketing Matters: Small Business Challenge: Finding the Right Prices for Regional Barbecue Sauces 329

Step 2: Estimate Demand and Revenue 329
Fundamentals of Estimating Demand 329
Fundamentals of Estimating Revenue 331
Step 3: Determine Cost, Volume, and Profit Relationships 334

Marketing Matters: Pricing Lessons from Failed Dot-Com Start-ups—Understand Revenues and Expenses 335

The Importance of Controlling Costs 335
Marginal Analysis and Profit Maximization 335
Break-Even Analysis 336

Learning Objectives Review 340
Focusing on Key Terms 340
Applying Marketing Knowledge 341
Building Your Marketing Plan 341

Video Case 13: Washburn Guitars: Using Break-Even Points to Make Pricing Decisions 341

14 ARRIVING AT THE FINAL PRICE 344

Vizio, Inc.—Where Vision Meets Value™ in HDTV 345
Step 4: Select an Approximate Price Level 346
Demand-Oriented Pricing Approaches 346

Marketing Matters: Energizer's Lesson in Price Perception—Value Lies in the Eye of the Beholder 348

Cost-Oriented Pricing Approaches 349
Profit-Oriented Pricing Approaches 351
Competition-Oriented Pricing Approaches 353
Step 5: Set the List or Quoted Price 354

Using Marketing Dashboards: Are Cracker Jack Prices Above, At, or Below the Market? 355

Choosing a Price Policy 355
Company, Customer, and Competitive Effects on Pricing 356

Making Responsible Decisions: Flexible Pricing—Is There Discrimination in Bargaining for a New Car? 357

Balancing Incremental Costs and Revenues 358
Step 6: Make Special Adjustments to the List or Quoted Price 359
Discounts 360
Allowances 361
Geographical Adjustments 362

Marketing Matters: Everyday Low Prices at the Supermarket = Everyday Low Profits—Creating Customer Value at a Cost 363

Legal and Regulatory Aspects of Pricing 363

Going Online: And You Thought That "Free" Is Simply Defined 366

Learning Objectives Review 366
Focusing on Key Terms 367
Applying Marketing Knowledge 367
Building Your Marketing Plan 367

Video Case 14: 3M Greptile™ Grip Golf Glove: Pricing an Innovative Product 368

APPENDIX B Financial Aspects of Marketing 370

15 MANAGING MARKETING CHANNELS AND WHOLESALING 378

Callaway Golf: Designing and Delivering the Goods for Great Golf 379
Nature and Importance of Marketing Channels 380
What Is a Marketing Channel of Distribution? 380
Value Is Created by Intermediaries 380
Channel Structure and Organization 382
Marketing Channels for Consumer Goods and Services 382
Marketing Channels for Business Goods and Services 383

Electronic Marketing Channels 384
Direct and Multichannel Marketing 385
Dual Distribution and Strategic Channel Alliances 386
A Closer Look at Channel Intermediaries 386

Marketing Matters: Nestlé and General Mills—Cereal Partners Worldwide 387

Vertical Marketing Systems and Channel Partnerships 389

Channel Choice and Management 392

Factors Affecting Channel Choice and Management 392

Marketing Matters: Avon Is Calling Again in China 393

Channel Choice Considerations 393

Going Online: Visit an Apple Store to See What All the Excitement Is About 395

Global Dimensions of Marketing Channels 395

Using Marketing Dashboards: Channel Sales and Profit at Charlesburg Furniture 396

Channel Relationships: Conflict, Cooperation, and Law 397

Making Responsible Decisions: Pay to Play: The Ethics of Slotting Allowances 399

Learning Objectives Review 400
Focusing on Key Terms 401
Applying Marketing Knowledge 401
Building Your Marketing Plan 401

Video Case 15: Act II Microwave Popcorn: The Surprising Channel 401

16 CUSTOMER-DRIVEN SUPPLY CHAIN AND LOGISTICS MANAGEMENT 404

Apple Inc.: Supplying the iPhone 3G to the World 405

Significance of Supply Chain and Logistics Management 406

Relating Marketing Channels, Logistics, and Supply Chain Management 406
Supply Chains versus Marketing Channels 406
Global Suppliers and Supply Chains 407
Sourcing, Assembling, and Delivering a New Car: The Automotive Supply Chain 408

Supply Chain Management and Marketing Strategy 408

Going Online: Build Your Own Jetta with a Mouse 409

Aligning a Supply Chain with Marketing Strategy 409
Dell: A Responsive Supply Chain 409

Marketing Matters: IBM's Integrated Supply Chain—Delivering a Total Solution for Its Customers 410

Walmart: An Efficient Supply Chain 410

Objective of Information and Logistics Management in a Customer-Driven Supply Chain 411
Information's Role in Supply Chain Responsiveness and Efficiency 411
Total Logistics Cost Concept 412
Customer Service Concept 413
Marketing Matters: For Fashion and Food Merchandising, Haste Is as Important as Taste 415
Customer Service Standards 415
Using Marketing Dashboards: Diagnosing Out-of-Stocks and On-Time Delivery for Organic Produce 416
Key Logistics Functions in a Supply Chain 417
Transportation 418
Warehousing and Materials Handling 419
Order Processing 420
Inventory Management 421
Making Responsible Decisions: Reverse Logistics and Green Marketing Go Together at Hewlett-Packard: Recycling e-Waste 423
Closing the Loop: Reverse Logistics 423
Learning Objectives Review 424
Focusing on Key Terms 425
Applying Marketing Knowledge 425
Building Your Marketing Plan 425
Video Case 16: Amazon: Delivering the Goods . . . Millions of Times a Day 425

17 RETAILING 428

84 Million Consumers Were Shopping Online on Cyber Monday. Were You One of Them? 429
The Value of Retailing 430
Consumer Utilities Offered by Retailing 430
The Global Economic Impact of Retailing 431
Classifying Retail Outlets 432
Form of Ownership 432
Making Responsible Decisions: Environmentally Friendly Retailing Takes Off! 433
Level of Service 434
Type of Merchandise Line 435
Nonstore Retailing 437
Automatic Vending 437
Direct Mail and Catalogs 438
Television Home Shopping 439
Online Retailing 439
Going Online: For Some Consumers, Shopping Is a Game! 440

Telemarketing 441
Direct Selling 441
Retailing Strategy 442
Positioning a Retail Store 442
Retailing Mix 443

Using Marketing Dashboards: Why Apple Stores May Be the Best in the United States! 447

The Changing Nature of Retailing 448
The Wheel of Retailing 448
The Retail Life Cycle 449
Future Changes in Retailing 450
Multichannel Retailing 450

Marketing Matters: The Multichannel Marketing Multiplier 451

Managing the Customer Experience 451

Learning Objectives Review 452
Focusing on Key Terms 452
Applying Marketing Knowledge 452
Building Your Marketing Plan 453

Video Case 17: Mall of America: Shopping and a Whole Lot More 453

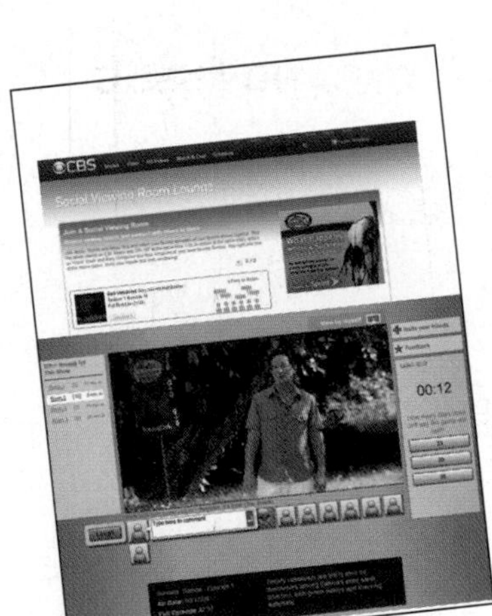

18 INTEGRATED MARKETING COMMUNICATIONS AND DIRECT MARKETING 456

Integrated Marketing Communications Ushers in the 'Age of Engage' 457
The Communication Process 458
Encoding and Decoding 459
Feedback 460
Noise 460
The Promotional Elements 460
Advertising 460
Personal Selling 461
Public Relations 462
Sales Promotion 463
Direct Marketing 463
Integrated Marketing Communications—Developing the Promotional Mix 464
The Target Audience 464

Marketing Matters: Mobile Marketing Reaches Generation Y, 32/7! 465

The Product Life Cycle 465
Product Characteristics 466
Stages of the Buying Decision 467
Channel Strategies 468
Developing an IMC Program 469

Identifying the Target Audience 470
Specifying Promotion Objectives 470
Setting the Promotion Budget 471

Using Marketing Dashboards: How Much Should You Spend on IMC? 472

Selecting the Right Promotional Tools 473
Designing the Promotion 473
Scheduling the Promotion 473

Executing and Assessing the Promotion Program 474

Direct Marketing 475

The Growth of Direct Marketing 475
The Value of Direct Marketing 476
Technological, Global, and Ethical Issues in Direct Marketing 477

Making Responsible Decisions: Can Direct Marketing "Go Green"? 478

Learning Objectives Review 478
Focusing on Key Terms 479
Applying Marketing Knowledge 479
Building Your Marketing Plan 480

Video Case 18: Under Armour: Using IMC to Create a Brand for this Generation's Athletes 480

19 ADVERTISING, SALES PROMOTION, AND PUBLIC RELATIONS 484

Advertising Moves to a New Dimension: The Third Dimension 485

Types of Advertisements 486

Product Advertisements 486
Institutional Advertisements 487

Developing the Advertising Program 488

Identifying the Target Audience 488
Specifying Advertising Objectives 489
Setting the Advertising Budget 489

Going Online: See Your Favorite Super Bowl Ads Again, and Again! 490

Designing the Advertisement 490
Selecting the Right Media 493

Using Marketing Dashboards: What Is the Best Way to Reach 1,000 Customers? 495

Different Media Alternatives 495

Making Responsible Decisions: Who Is Responsible for Click Fraud? 501

Scheduling the Advertising 502

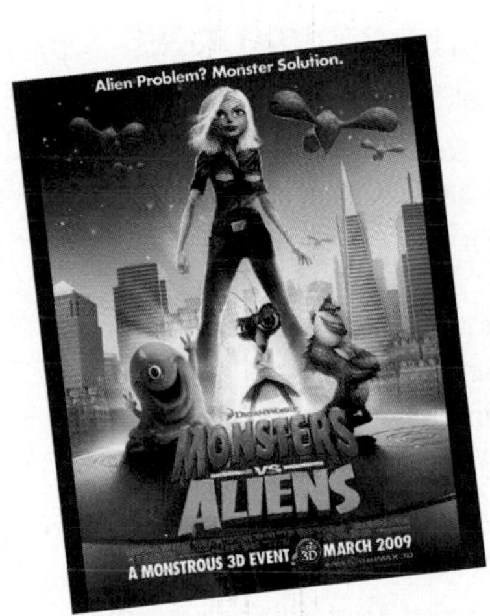

Executing the Advertising Program 503
Pretesting the Advertising 503
Carrying Out the Advertising Program 503
Assessing the Advertising Program 504
Posttesting the Advertising 504
Making Needed Changes 505
Sales Promotion 505
Consumer-Oriented Sales Promotions 505
Trade-Oriented Sales Promotions 510
Public Relations 512
Publicity Tools 512
Increasing the Value of Promotion 512
Building Long-Term Relationships with Promotion 513
Self-Regulation 513

Learning Objectives Review 514
Focusing on Key Terms 514
Applying Marketing Knowledge 514
Building Your Marketing Plan 515

Video Case 19: Google, Inc.: The Right Ads at the Right Time 515

20 PERSONAL SELLING AND SALES MANAGEMENT 518

Xerox Succeeds by Doing What's Right for the Customer 519
Scope and Significance of Personal Selling and Sales Management 520
Nature of Personal Selling and Sales Management 520
Selling Happens Almost Everywhere 520
Personal Selling in Marketing 521
Creating Customer Solutions and Value through Salespeople: Relationship and Partnership Selling 521
The Many Forms of Personal Selling 522
Order-Taking Salespeople 522
Order-Getting Salespeople 523
Customer Sales Support Personnel 524

Marketing Matters: Creating and Sustaining Customer Value through Cross-Functional Team Selling 525

The Personal Selling Process: Building Relationships 526
Prospecting: Identifying and Qualifying Prospective Customers 526
Preapproach: Preparing for the Sales Call 527
Approach: Making the First Impression 528
Presentation: Tailoring a Solution for a Customer's Needs 528

Marketing Matters: Imagine This . . . Putting the Customer into Customer Solutions! 530

Close: Asking for the Customer's Order or Business 531
Follow-Up: Solidifying the Relationship 531

The Sales Management Process 532

Sales Plan Formulation: Setting Direction 532

***Making Responsible Decisions: The Ethics of Asking Customers about Competitors* 533**

Sales Plan Implementation: Putting the Plan into Action 536

***Going Online: What Is Your Emotional Intelligence or EQ?* 538**

Salesforce Evaluation: Measuring Results 539

***Using Marketing Dashboards: Tracking Salesperson Performance at Moore Chemical & Sanitation Supply, Inc.* 540**

Salesforce Automation and Customer Relationship Management 540

Learning Objectives Review 542

Focusing on Key Terms 543

Applying Marketing Knowledge 543

Building Your Marketing Plan 543

Video Case 20: Xerox: Building Customer Relationships through Personal Selling 544

Part 5 Managing the Marketing Process

21 IMPLEMENTING INTERACTIVE AND MULTICHANNEL MARKETING 547

Seven Cycles. One Bike. Yours. 547

Creating Customer Value, Relationships, and Experiences in Marketspace 548

Customer Value Creation in Marketspace 548

Interactivity, Individuality, and Customer Relationships in Marketspace 549

Creating an Online Customer Experience 551

Online Consumer Behavior and Marketing Practice in Marketspace 553

Who Is the Online Consumer? 553

***Using Marketing Dashboards: Sizing Up Site Stickiness at Sewell Automotive Companies* 554**

***Going Online: Are You a Digital Collaborator or a Drifting Surfer?* 555**

***Marketing Matters: Meet Today's Internet Mom—All 38 Million!* 556**

What Online Consumers Buy 556

Why Consumers Shop and Buy Online 557

***Making Responsible Decisions: Let the E-Buyer Beware* 561**

When and Where Online Consumers Shop and Buy 561

Cross-Channel Shoppers and Multichannel Marketing 562
Who Is the Cross-Channel Shopper? 562
Implementing Multichannel Marketing 562

Learning Objectives Review 564
Focusing on Key Terms 565
Applying Marketing Knowledge 565
Building Your Marketing Plan 566

Video Case 21: Pizza Hut and imc²: Becoming a Multichannel Marketer 566

22 PULLING IT ALL TOGETHER: THE STRATEGIC MARKETING PROCESS 570

"Breaking the Rules" at General Mills to Reach Today's On-the-Go Consumer 571
Marketing Basics: Doing What Works and Allocating Resources 572
Finding and Using What Really Works 573
Allocating Marketing Resources Using Sales Response Functions 574
The Planning Phase of the Strategic Marketing Process 577
The Vital Importance of Metrics in Marketing Planning 577
The Variety of Marketing Plans 578
Marketing Planning Frameworks: The Search for Growth 578

Marketing Matters: A Test of Your Skills: Where Are the Synergies? 581

Some Marketing Planning and Strategy Lessons 582
The Implementation Phase of the Strategic Marketing Process 584
Is Planning or Implementation the Problem? 584
Increasing Emphasis on Marketing Implementation 585
Improving Implementation of Marketing Programs 585

Marketing Matters: Implementation Lessons from IBM: Converting Tough Global Problems into Results 587

Organizing for Marketing 589
The Evaluation Phase of the Strategic Marketing Process 590
The Marketing Evaluation Process 590
Evaluation Involves Marketing ROI, Metrics, and Dashboards 591
Evaluation Using Marketing Metrics and Marketing Dashboards at General Mills 592

Learning Objectives Review 594
Focusing on Key Terms 595
Applying Marketing Knowledge 595
Building Your Marketing Plan 595

Video Case 22: General Mills Warm Delights™: Indulgent, Delicious, and Gooey! 596

APPENDIX C Planning a Career in Marketing 598
APPENDIX D Alternate Cases 616
Case D–1 Nike MaxSight Contact Lenses: Seeing a Need 616
Case D–2 Daktronics, Inc.: Global Displays in 68 Billion Colors 617
Case D–3 Jamba Juice: Scanning the Marketing Environment 619
Case D–4 Ford and Firestone: Who's to Blame? 621
Case D–5 The Jamisons Buy an Espresso Machine 623
Case D–6 Motetronix Technology: Marketing Smart Dust 624
Case D–7 Callaway Golf: The Global Challenge 625
Case D–8 HOM Furniture: Where Keen Observation Pays 628
Case D–9 Lawn Mowers: Segmentation Challenges 629
Case D–10 Medtronic in China: Where "Simpler" Serves Patients Better 630
Case D–11 Pampered Pooches Travel in Style 632
Case D–12 DigitalThink: Marketing E-Learning Services 633
Case D–13 Health Cruises, Inc.: Estimating Cost, Volume, and Profit Relationships 635
Case D–14 Bagel Bakes: Pricing a New Breakfast Product 636
Case D–15 Ken Davis Products, Inc.: Finding Success in Retail Channels 638
Case D–16 Dell Inc.: A Foundation Built on Supply Chain Management 640
Case D–17 Trader Joe's: Upscale Value 641
Case D–18 McDonald's Restaurants: An IMC Program to Reach Different Segments 642
Case D–19 Target Corporation: Award-Winning Advertising 644
Case D–20 Morgantown Furniture: Making Promotion Trade-Offs 645
Case D–21 Crate and Barrel: Multichannel Marketing 647
Case D–22 Naked® Juice: Strategy for Growth 647

Glossary 649
Learning Review Answers 660
Chapter Notes 669
Credits 701
Name Index 705
Company/Product Index 713
Subject Index 721

MARKETING

Post-it
3M
Post-it
Post-it
3M
EXAM ON WEDNESDAY - CH. 3,4,5
I. Selecting a speech topic & purpose
°Choosing a topic
- I know a lot about
- I want to know more about it
- Searching for topics
°Personal experience, interests, skills,
Choosing a Topic
87
When you look for a speech topic, keep in mind special expertise you may have or sports, hobbies, travel, and other personal experiences that would make for an interesting presentation.
Topics You

1 Creating Customer Relationships and Value through Marketing

LEARNING OBJECTIVES

After reading this chapter you should be able to:

LO1 Define marketing and identify the diverse factors influencing marketing activities.

LO2 Explain how marketing discovers and satisfies consumer needs.

LO3 Distinguish between marketing mix factors and environmental forces.

LO4 Explain how organizations build strong customer relationships and customer value through marketing.

LO5 Describe how today's customer relationship era differs from prior eras.

INNOVATION AND MARKETING AT 3M: HOW DISCOVERING STUDENT STUDY HABITS LAUNCHED A NEW PRODUCT

David Windorski, a 3M inventor, faced a curious challenge—understanding how college students study!

Specifically, how do they read their textbooks, take class notes, and prepare for exams? After finding the answers, he needed to convert this knowledge into a product that actually helps students improve their studying. Finally, Windorski and 3M had to manufacture and market this product using 3M's world-class adhesive technology.

Sound simple? Perhaps. But David Windorski invested several years of his life conducting marketing research on students' study behavior, developing product ideas, and then creating an actual product students could use.[1] This process of discovering and satisfying consumer needs is the essence of how organizations such as 3M create genuine customer value through effective marketing. In designing a product that satisfies consumer needs, David Windorski's invention got a personal testimonial from host Oprah Winfrey on her 2008 TV show. More on this later.[2]

Discovering Student Study Needs

As an inventor of Post-it® brand products, David Windorski's main job is to design new products. He gets creative "thinking time" under 3M's "15% Rule," in which inventors can use up to 15 percent of their time to do initially unfunded research that might lead to marketable 3M products. Working with a team of four college students, Windorski and the team observed and questioned dozens of students about how they used their textbooks, took notes, wrote term papers, and reviewed for exams.

Windorski describes what college students told him: "It's natural behavior to highlight a passage and then mark the page with a Post-it® Note or Post-it® Flag of some kind. So it's reasonable to put Post-it® products together with a highlighter to have two functions in one."

Satisfying Student Study Needs

Designing a marketable product for students was not done overnight. It took Windorski a few years of creativity, hard work, and attention to countless details. Windorski went back to his drawing board—or more literally to wood blocks and modeling clay—to mock up a number of nonworking models. These nonworking models showed Windorski how the product would feel.

3M's Post-it® Notes or Post-it® Flags

\+

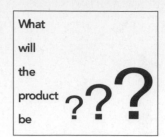

Felt Tip Highlighters

=

What will the product be ???

3M product that will combine Post-it® Notes or Post-it® Flags and Highlighters

For the creative way a student project helped lead to a new product for college students using 3M's technology, see the text.

His search for the 2-in-1 highlighter plus Post-it® Flags produced working models that students could actually use to give him feedback. Windorski had taken some giant steps in trying not only to discover students' needs for his product but also to satisfy those needs with a practical, useful product. Later in the chapter we'll see what products resulted from his innovative thinking and 3M's initial marketing plan that launched his products.

WHAT IS MARKETING?

To see how three 20-somethings launched YouTube, see the text and Marketing Matters box.

The good news is that you are already a marketing expert! You perform many marketing activities and make marketing-related decisions every day. For example, would you sell more Panasonic Viera 50-inch plasma high-definition TVs at $2,499 or $999 each? You answered $999, right? So your experience in shopping gives you some expertise in marketing. As a consumer, you've been involved in thousands of marketing decisions, but mostly on the buying and not the selling side. But to test your expertise, answer the "marketing expert" questions posed in Figure 1–1. You'll find the answers within the next several pages.

The bad news is, good marketing isn't always easy. That's why every year thousands of new products fail in the marketplace and then quietly slide into oblivion. Examples of new products that vary from spectacular successes to dismal failures appear in the next few pages.

Marketing and Your Career

Marketing affects all individuals, all organizations, all industries, and all countries. This book seeks to teach you marketing concepts, often by having you actually

FIGURE 1–1
The see-if-you're-really-a-marketing-expert test

Answer the questions below. The correct answers are given later in the chapter.

1. True or false. You can now buy a satellite TV receiver for your minivan or sport utility vehicle (SUV) so that backseat passengers can watch high-definition television (HDTV) programs.
2. True or false. The 60-year lifetime value of a loyal Kleenex customer is $994.
3. To be socially responsible, 3M puts what recycled material into its very successful ScotchBrite® Never Rust™ soap pads? (*a*) aluminum cans, (*b*) steel-belted tires, (*c*) plastic bottles, (*d*) computer screens.

Marketing Matters > > > > > entrepreneurship

Payoff for the Joys (!) and Sleepless Nights (?) of Starting Your Own Small Business: YouTube!!!!

What happens when you drop Mentos into a bottle of Diet Coke?

Don't know the answer?

Then you're not a serious YouTube viewer! If you need an answer, ask the student sitting next to you in class. But don't try it in your room.

In one 12-month period, a single Web site—YouTube.com—revolutionized the Internet's world of videos and was named *Time* magazine's Invention of the Year for 2006. YouTube's numbers are astounding: In January 2008, 79 million viewers watched more than 3 billion user-posted videos, according to comScore.

The minds behind YouTube are three 20-somethings: Steve Chen, Chad Hurley, and Jawed Karim. Even the three entrepreneurs are astounded at their success. *Time* says the reason for YouTube's success is its rare combination of being both "edgy and easy" for users.

The three men met at PayPal, now the Internet's leading online payment service. Then they left PayPal and worked together on a new concept—a Web site where anyone could upload content that others could view. That was radical because until then only those who owned the Web site would provide the content.

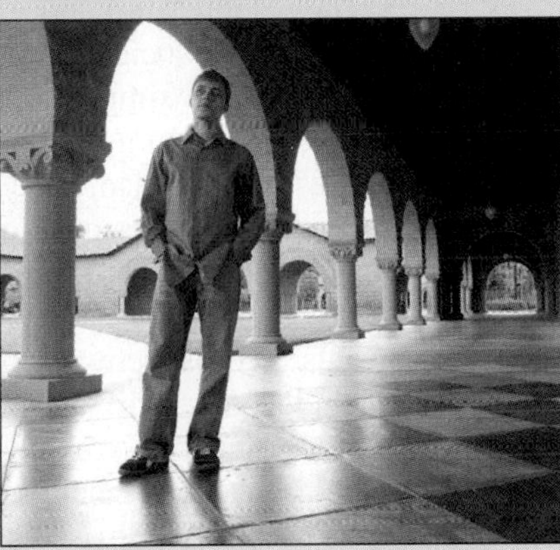

Google bought YouTube in October 2006 for $1.65 billion, only 21 months after its founding. Hurley (standing) and Chen (sitting) in the left photo are now Google employees. They now face issues such as making YouTube.com profitable through its advertising and avoiding potential lawsuits resulting from uploaded content that is copyrighted. Karim (in the right photo) left the company and is doing graduate work in computer science at Stanford University.

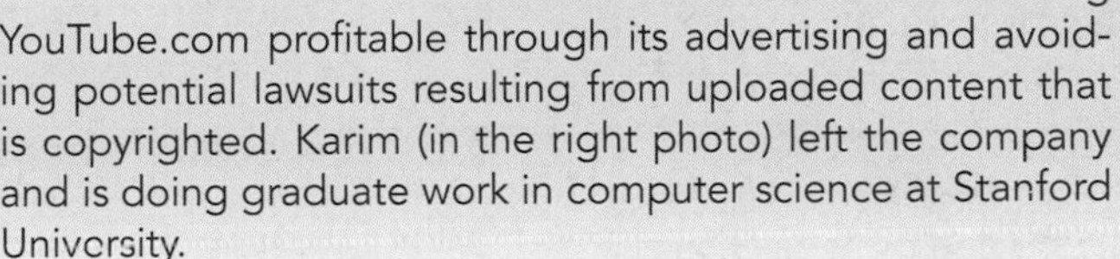

Where will this end? Go to YouTube.com and see for yourself!

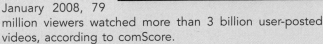

"do marketing"—by putting you in the shoes of a marketing manager facing actual marketing opportunities and problems. The book also shows marketing's many applications and how it affects our lives. This knowledge should make you a better consumer, enable you to be a more informed citizen, and help you in your career planning—as discussed in Appendix C.

Perhaps your future may involve doing sales and marketing for a large organization. Working for a well-known company—Apple, General Electric, Target, or eBay—can be personally satisfying and financially rewarding, and you may gain special respect from your friends.

Small businesses also offer marketing careers. Small businesses are the source of the majority of new U.S. jobs. So you might become your own boss by being an entrepreneur and starting your own business. The Marketing Matters box describes the revolutionary impact three entrepreneurs in their 20s have had on the Internet—and perhaps on how you spend some of your free time.[3] The three entrepreneurs—Steve Chen, Chad Hurley, and Jawed Karim—founded YouTube, which has achieved tremendous Internet success and is now part of Google. Not every Internet start-up reaches the 100 million viewers per month YouTube achieved in late 2008.[4] In fact, more than half of new businesses fail within five years of their launch.

Do you or your friends have a great idea for a start-up business? But you've got no financing? Maybe Jawed Karim can help. He believes that college students have many innovative ideas but don't have the money or know how to get started. In 2008

Karim and two friends launched Youniversity Ventures, which provides venture financing to Internet software start-ups of *college students* and first-time entrepreneurs! To help the start-up team get off the ground Youniversity Ventures will invest $50,000 to $300,000 per company. If you're serious about your idea, e-mail Karim at jawed@youniversityventures.com.[5]

Marketing: Delivering Benefits to the Organization, Its Stakeholders, and Society

The American Marketing Association represents marketing professionals. Combining its 2004 and 2007 definitions, "**marketing** is the activity for creating, communicating, delivering, and exchanging offerings that benefit the organization, its stakeholders and society at large."[6] This definition shows marketing to be a far broader activity than simply advertising or personal selling. It stresses the importance of delivering genuine benefits in the offerings of goods, services, and ideas marketed to customers. Also, note that the organization doing the marketing, the stakeholders affected (such as customers, employees, suppliers, and shareholders), and society should all benefit.

To serve both buyers and sellers, marketing seeks (1) to discover the needs and wants of prospective customers and (2) to satisfy them. These prospective customers include both individuals, buying for themselves and their households, and organizations that buy for their own use (such as manufacturers) or for resale (such as wholesalers and retailers). The key to achieving these two objectives is the idea of **exchange**, which is the trade of things of value between buyer and seller so that each is better off after the trade.[7]

The Diverse Factors Influencing Marketing Activities

Although an organization's marketing activity focuses on assessing and satisfying consumer needs, countless other people, groups, and forces interact to shape the nature of its activities (see Figure 1–2). Foremost is the organization itself, whose

FIGURE 1–2
A marketing department relates to many people, organizations, and forces. Note that the marketing department both *shapes* and *is shaped by* its relationship with these internal and external groups.

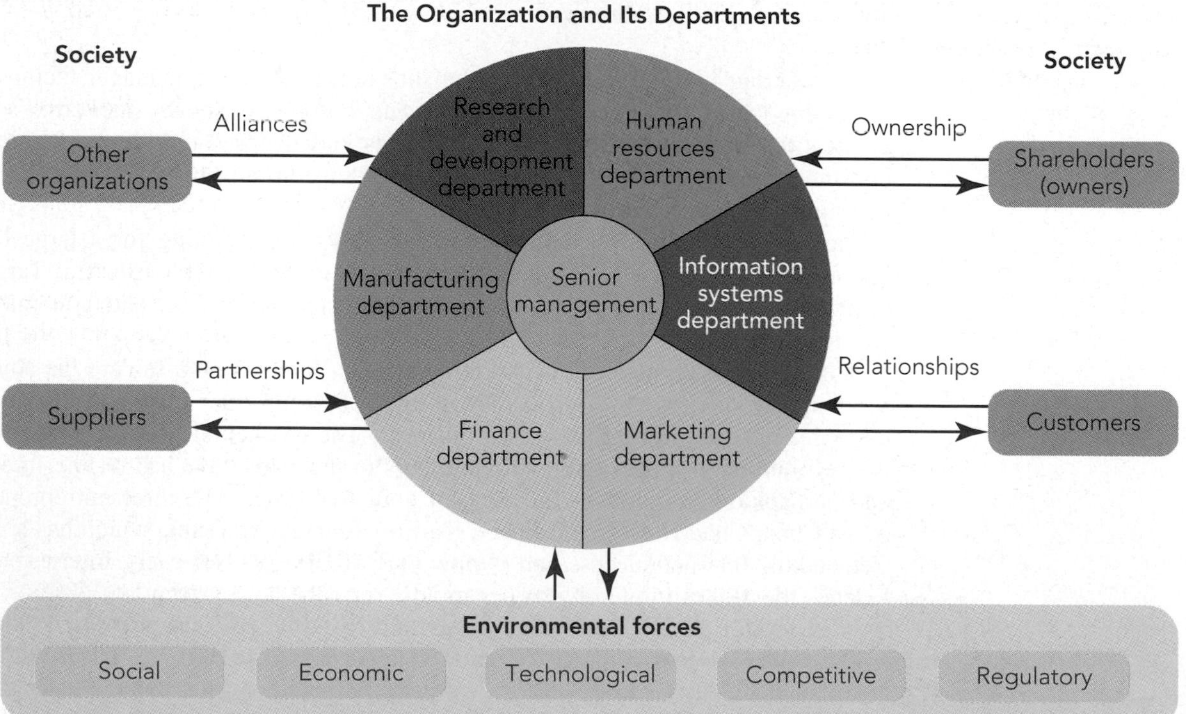

mission and objectives determine what business it is in and what goals it seeks. Within the organization, management is responsible for establishing these goals. The marketing department works closely with a network of other departments and employees to help provide the customer-satisfying products required for the organization to survive and prosper.

Figure 1–2 also shows the key people, groups, and forces outside the organization that influence its marketing activities. The marketing department is responsible for facilitating relationships, partnerships, and alliances with the organization's customers, its shareholders (or often representatives of groups served by a nonprofit organization), its suppliers, and other organizations. Environmental forces involving social, economic, technological, competitive, and regulatory considerations also shape an organization's marketing activities. Finally, an organization's marketing decisions are affected by and, in turn, often have an important impact on society as a whole.

The organization must strike a balance among the sometimes differing interests of these individuals and groups. For example, it is not possible to simultaneously provide the lowest-priced and highest-quality products to customers and pay the highest prices to suppliers, highest wages to employees, and maximum dividends to shareholders.

What Is Needed for Marketing to Occur

For marketing to occur, at least four factors are required: (1) two or more parties (individuals or organizations) with unsatisfied needs, (2) a desire and ability on their part to be satisfied, (3) a way for the parties to communicate, and (4) something to exchange.

Two or More Parties with Unsatisfied Needs Suppose you've developed an unmet need—a desire for information about how computer and telecommunications are interacting to reshape the workplace—but you didn't yet know that *Wired* magazine existed. Also unknown to you was that several copies of *Wired* were sitting on the magazine rack at your nearest bookstore, waiting to be purchased. This is an example of two parties with unmet needs: you, desiring technology-related information, and your bookstore owner, needing someone to buy a copy of *Wired* magazine.

Marketing doesn't happen in a vacuum. The text describes the four factors needed, say, to buy a *Wired* magazine.

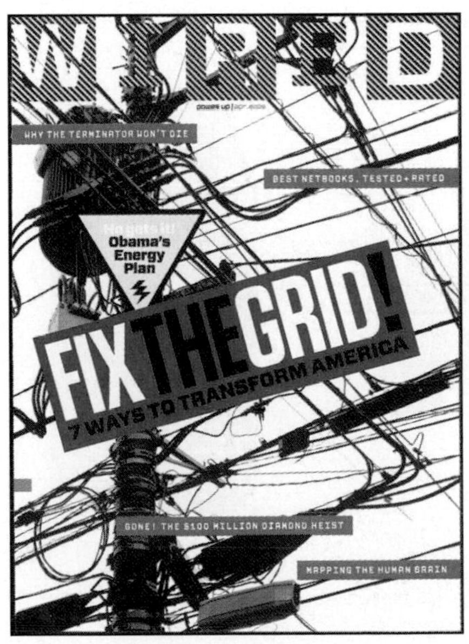

Desire and Ability to Satisfy These Needs Both you and the bookstore owner want to satisfy these unmet needs. Furthermore, you have the money to buy the item and the time to get to the bookstore. The store's owner has not only the desire to sell *Wired* but also the ability to do so since it's stocked on the shelves.

A Way for the Parties to Communicate The marketing transaction of buying a copy of *Wired* will never occur unless you know the product exists and its location. Similarly, the store owner won't stock the magazine unless there's a market of potential buyers nearby. When you receive a free sample in the mail or see the magazine on display in the bookstore, this communications barrier between you (the buyer) and your bookstore (the seller) is overcome.

Something to Exchange Marketing occurs when the transaction takes place and both the buyer and seller exchange something of value. In this case, you exchange your money for the bookstore's magazine. Both you and the bookstore have gained something and also given up something, but you are both better off because you have each satisfied your unmet needs. You have the opportunity to read *Wired*, but you gave up some money; the store gave up the magazine but received money, which enables it to remain in business. This exchange process and, of course, the ethical and legal foundations of exchange are central to marketing.

learning review

1. What is marketing?
2. Marketing focuses on __________ and __________ consumer needs.
3. What four factors are needed for marketing to occur?

HOW MARKETING DISCOVERS AND SATISFIES CONSUMER NEEDS

LO2

The importance of discovering and satisfying consumer needs is so critical to understanding marketing that we look at each of these two steps in detail next.

For these four products, identify (1) what benefits the product provides buyers and (2) what "showstoppers" might kill the product in the marketplace. Answers are discussed in the text.

Vanilla-mint-flavored toothpaste in an aerosol container

Meat and cheese microwavable sandwiches

TV service in backseats of cars, minivans, and SUVs

A diet cola with ginseng and extra caffeine

Discovering Consumer Needs

The first objective in marketing is discovering the needs of prospective customers. But these prospective customers may not always know or be able to describe what they need and want. When Apple built its first Apple II personal computer and started a new industry, consumers didn't really know what the benefits would be. So they had to be educated about how to use personal computers. Also, Bell, a U.S. bicycle helmet maker, listened to its customers, collected hundreds of their ideas, and put several into its new products.[8] This is where effective marketing research, the topic of Chapter 8, can help.

The Challenge: Meeting Consumer Needs with New Products

New-product experts generally estimate that up to 94 percent of the more than 33,000 new consumable products (food, beverage, health, beauty, and other household and pet products) introduced in the United States annually "don't succeed in the long run."[9] Robert M. McMath, who has studied more than 100,000 of these new-product launches, has two key suggestions: (1) focus on what the customer benefit is, and (2) learn from the past.[10]

The solution to preventing such product failures seems embarrassingly obvious. First, find out what consumers need and want. Second, produce what they need and want, and don't produce what they don't need and want. The four products shown on the next page illustrate just how difficult it is to achieve new-product success, a topic covered in more detail in Chapter 10.

Without reading further, think about the potential benefits to customers and possible "showstoppers"—factors that might doom the product—for each of the four products pictured. Some of the products may come out of your past, and others may be on your horizon. Here's a quick analysis of the four products, some with comments adapted from McMath:

- *Dr. Care Toothpaste.* After extensive research, Dr. Care family toothpaste in its aerosol container was introduced more than two decades ago. The vanilla-mint-flavored product's benefits were advertised as being easy to use and sanitary. Pretend for a minute that you are five years old and left alone in the bathroom to brush your teeth using your Dr. Care toothpaste. Hmm! Apparently, surprised parents were not enthusiastic about the bathroom wall paintings sprayed by their future Rembrandts—a showstopper that doomed this creative product.[11]
- *Hot Pockets.* Introduced in 1983, these convenient meat and cheese microwavable sandwiches are a favorite brand among students. More than 80 varieties have been introduced, from Hot Pockets Pizza Snacks to Hot Pockets Subs and now Hot Pockets Paninis. A none-too-serious potential showstopper: Excessive ice crystals can form on the product due to variations in freezer temperatures; if this happens and the sandwich is thawed and refrozen before being microwaved, it may not taste as good.[12]
- *AT&T CruiseCast.* In early 2009, AT&T and RaySat Broadcasting launched the AT&T CruiseCast service that enables families and commuters in the backseat of cars, minivans, and SUVs to watch over 20 channels (Disney Channel, CNBC, Nickelodeon, etc.) of satellite high-definition TV anywhere in the United States (question 1, Figure 1–1). The antenna/receiver is mounted on the roof of the vehicle and incorporates technology that overcomes line-of-sight obstacles, such as overpasses, tunnels, and so on. Potential showstopper: The initial cost of $1,299 for the antenna and $28 per month for the somewhat limited programming.[13]
- *Pepsi Max.* In early 2009, Pepsi launched Pepsi Max. "This is the first diet cola for men" 25 and older who haven't liked the taste of other diet colas, according to the humorous "I'm Good" ad that ran during Super Bowl XLIII (2009).

Pepsi Max is rebranded Diet Pepsi Max, a reformulated soft drink from Britain that was introduced to the U.S. in 2007 as the "Invigorating Zero-Calorie Cola." Pepsi Max has ginseng and extra caffeine to differentiate it from Diet Pepsi. One potential showstopper: women may not consume a soft drink specifically targeted at men.[14]

Firms spend billions of dollars annually on marketing and technical research that significantly reduces, but doesn't eliminate, new-product failure. So meeting the changing needs of consumers is a continuing challenge for firms around the world.

Consumer Needs and Consumer Wants Should marketing try to satisfy consumer needs or consumer wants? Marketing tries to do both. Heated debates rage over this question, fueled by the definitions of needs and wants and the amount of freedom given to prospective customers to make their own buying decisions.

A *need* occurs when a person feels deprived of basic necessities such as food, clothing, and shelter. A *want* is a need that is shaped by a person's knowledge, culture, and personality. So if you feel hungry, you have developed a basic need and desire to eat something. Let's say you then want to eat an apple or a candy bar because, based on your past experience, you know these will satisfy your hunger need. Effective marketing, in the form of creating an awareness of good products at convenient locations, can clearly shape a person's wants.

Certainly, marketing tries to influence what we buy. A question then arises: At what point do we want government and society to step in to protect consumers? Most consumers would say they want government to protect us from harmful drugs and unsafe cars but not from candy bars and soft drinks. To protect college students, should government restrict their use of credit cards?[15] Such questions have no clear-cut answers, which is why legal and social issues are central to marketing. Because even psychologists and economists still debate the exact meanings of *need* and *want*, we shall use the terms interchangeably throughout the book.

As shown in the left side of Figure 1–3, discovering needs involves looking carefully at prospective customers, whether they are children buying M&Ms candy, college students buying highlighters, or firms buying Xerox photocopying machines. A principal activity of a firm's marketing department is to scrutinize its consumers to understand what they need and want and the forces that shape them.

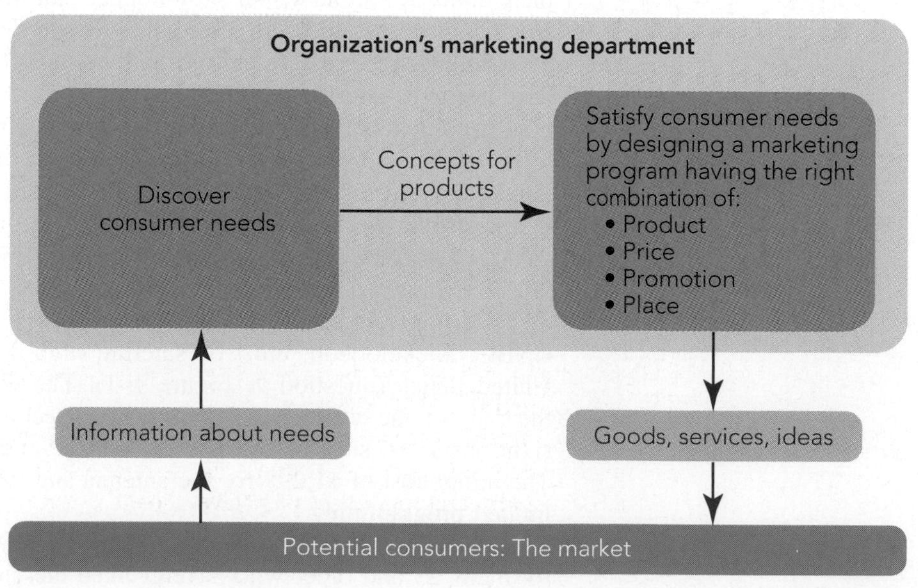

FIGURE 1–3
Marketing seeks first to discover consumer needs through extensive research. It then seeks to satisfy those needs by successfully implementing a marketing program possessing the right combination of the marketing mix—the four Ps.

What a Market Is Potential consumers make up a **market**, which is people with both the desire and the ability to buy a specific offering. All markets ultimately are people. Even when we say a firm bought a Xerox copier, we mean one or several people in the firm decided to buy it. People who are aware of their unmet needs may have the desire to buy the product, but that alone isn't sufficient. People must also have the ability to buy, such as the authority, time, and money. People may even "buy" an idea that results in an action, such as having their blood pressure checked annually or turning down their thermostat to save energy.

Satisfying Consumer Needs

Marketing doesn't stop with the discovery of consumer needs. Because the organization obviously can't satisfy all consumer needs, it must concentrate its efforts on certain needs of a specific group of potential consumers. This is the **target market**—one or more specific groups of potential consumers toward which an organization directs its marketing program.

LO3

The Four Ps: Controllable Marketing Mix Factors Having selected its target market consumers, the firm must take steps to satisfy their needs, as shown in the right side of Figure 1–3. Someone in the organization's marketing department, often the marketing manager, must develop a complete marketing program to reach consumers by using a combination of four tools, often called "the four Ps"—a useful shorthand reference to them first published by Professor E. Jerome McCarthy:[16]

- *Product.* A good, service, or idea to satisfy the consumer's needs.
- *Price.* What is exchanged for the product.
- *Promotion.* A means of communication between the seller and buyer.
- *Place.* A means of getting the product to the consumer.

We'll define each of the four Ps more carefully later in the book, but for now it's important to remember that they are the elements of the **marketing mix**, the marketing manager's controllable factors—product, price, promotion, and place—that can be used to solve a marketing problem. For example, when a company puts a product on sale, it is changing one element of the marketing mix—namely, the price. The marketing mix elements are called controllable factors because they are under the control of the marketing department in an organization.

The Uncontrollable, Environmental Forces While marketers can control their marketing mix factors, there are forces that are mostly beyond their control (see Figure 1–2). These are the **environmental forces** in a marketing decision, those involving social, economic, technological, competitive, and regulatory forces. Examples are what consumers themselves want and need, changing technology, the state of the economy in terms of whether it is expanding or contracting, actions that competitors take, and government restrictions. These five forces may serve as accelerators or brakes on marketing, sometimes expanding an organization's marketing opportunities while at other times restricting them. These five environmental forces are covered in detail in Chapter 3.

Traditionally, many marketing executives have treated these environmental forces as rigid, absolute constraints that are entirely outside their influence. However, recent studies and marketing successes have shown that a forward-looking, action-oriented firm can often affect some environmental forces, for example, by achieving technological or competitive breakthroughs.

THE MARKETING PROGRAM: HOW CUSTOMER RELATIONSHIPS ARE BUILT

An organization's marketing program connects it with its customers. To clarify this link, we shall first discuss the critically important concepts of customer value, customer relationships, and relationship marketing, and then illustrate these concepts with 3M's marketing program for its new Post-it® products for students.

Customer Value and Customer Relationships

Intense competition in today's fast-paced domestic and global markets has caused massive restructuring of many American industries and businesses. American managers are seeking ways to achieve success in this new, more intense level of global competition.

This has prompted many successful U.S. firms to focus on "customer value." That firms gain loyal customers by providing unique value is the essence of successful marketing. What is new, however, is a more careful attempt at understanding how a firm's customers perceive value and then actually creating and delivering that value.[17] For our purposes, **customer value** is the unique combination of benefits received by targeted buyers that includes quality, convenience, on-time delivery, and both before-sale and after-sale service at a specific price. Loyal, satisfied customers are likely to repurchase more over time.[18] Firms now actually try to place a dollar value on the purchases of loyal, satisfied customers during their lifetimes. For example, loyal Kleenex customers average 6.7 boxes a year, about $994 over 60 years in today's dollars (question 2, Figure 1–1).[19]

Research suggests that firms cannot succeed by being all things to all people. Instead, firms must find ways to build long-term customer relationships to provide unique value that they alone can deliver to targeted markets. Many successful firms have chosen to deliver outstanding customer value with one of three value strategies: best price, best product, or best service.[20]

Companies such as Wal-Mart, Southwest Airlines, and Costco have all been successful offering consumers the best price. Other companies such as Starbucks, Nike, and Johnson & Johnson claim to provide the best products on the market. Finally, companies such as Marriott, Lands' End, and Home Depot deliver value by providing exceptional service.

Southwest Airlines, Starbucks, and Home Depot provide customer value using three very different approaches. For their strategies, see the text.

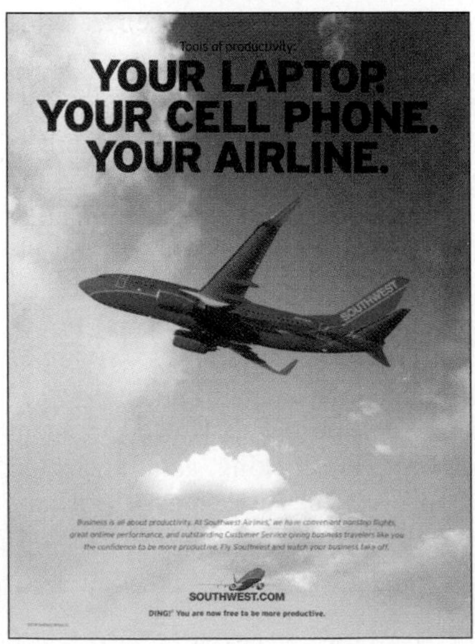

But changing tastes can devastate once-successful marketing strategies. Lands' End, now part of Sears, must focus on strategies to defeat new groups of competitors: boutique specialty stores, catalog retailers, and Internet sellers (see Chapter 2).

Relationship Marketing

Meaningful customer relationships are achieved by a firm identifying creative ways to connect closely to its customers through specific marketing mix actions implemented in its marketing program.

Relationship Marketing: Easy to Understand The hallmark of developing and maintaining effective customer relationships is today called **relationship marketing**, linking the organization to its individual customers, employees, suppliers, and other partners for their mutual long-term benefits. Note that these mutual long-term benefits between the organization and its customers require links to other vital stakeholders, including suppliers, employees, and "partners" such as wholesalers or retailers in a manufacturer's channel of distribution. In many settings, relationship marketing is more effective when there is personal ongoing communication between individuals—both in the selling and buying organizations.[21]

Relationship Marketing: Hard to Do Huge manufacturers find the rigorous standards of relationship marketing difficult to achieve. But today's information technology, along with cutting-edge manufacturing and marketing processes, have led to tailoring goods or services to the tastes of individual customers in high volumes at a relatively low cost. Thus, you can place an Internet order for all the components of an Apple computer and have it delivered in four or five days—in a configuration tailored to your unique wants.

But other forces are working against these kinds of personal relationships between company and customer. Researchers Fournier, Dobscha, and Mick observe that "the number of one-on-one relationships that companies ask consumers to maintain is untenable,"[22] as evidenced by the dozens of credit card and financing offers a typical consumer gets in a year. A decade ago you might have gone to a small store to buy a book or music record, being helped in your buying decision by a salesclerk or the store owner. With today's Internet purchases, you will probably have difficulty achieving the same personal, tender-loving-care connection that you once had with your own favorite book or music store.

The Marketing Program

Effective relationship marketing strategies help marketing managers discover what prospective customers need. They must translate this information into some concepts for products the firm might develop (see Figure 1–3). These concepts must then be converted into a tangible **marketing program**—a plan that integrates the marketing mix to provide a good, service, or idea to prospective buyers. These prospects then react to the offering favorably (by buying) or unfavorably (by not buying), and the process is repeated. As shown in Figure 1–3, in an effective organization this process is continuous: Consumer needs trigger product concepts that are translated into actual products that stimulate further discovery of consumer needs.

learning review

4. An organization can't satisfy the needs of all consumers, so it must focus on one or more subgroups, which are its ________________.

5. What are the four marketing mix elements that make up the organization's marketing program?

6. What are environmental forces?

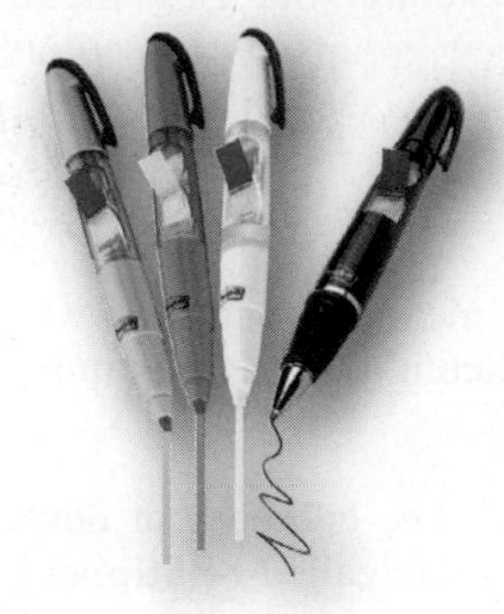

3M's product line of Post-it® Flag Highlighters and Post-it® Flag pens includes variations in color and line widths.

3M's Strategy and Marketing Program to Help Students Study

To see some specifics of an actual marketing program, let's return to our earlier example of 3M inventor David Windorski and his search for a way to combine felt-tip highlighters and 3M's Post-it® Notes or Post-it® Flags to help college students in their studying. We will look at how Windorski worked with 3M: (1) to move his invention from ideas and mock-ups to a commercial highlighter product, (2) to add a new product that extends the product line, and (3) to undertake an actual marketing program to introduce the resulting products.

Moving from Ideas to a Marketable Highlighter Product After working on 15 or 20 wood and clay models, Windorski concluded he had to build a highlighter product that would dispense Post-it® Flags because the Post-it® Notes were simply too large to put inside the barrel of a highlighter.

Hundreds of the initial highlighter prototypes with Post-it® Flags inside were produced and given to students—and also office workers—to get their reactions. Two suggestions from users quickly emerged:

- Because of the abuse the product will take in students' pockets and backpacks, the product must protect the Post-it® Flags so they release easily when needed.
- Package the highlighter two ways—as a single yellow highlighter and as a three-pack in the favorite student colors of yellow, pink, and blue.

This customer feedback, while very useful, also caused special technical challenges for Windorski. For example, he soon discovered that to make the highlighter rugged enough for students, he had to design a rotating cover that would enclose the Post-it® Flags but not pinch them when rotated. Also, Windorski's design required that each injection-molded component of the highlighter meet tolerances less than the thickness of a piece of paper. And he worked closely with the final assembly team to ensure the highlighter achieved 3M's tight quality standards.

Adding the Post-it® Flag Pen Most of David Windorski's initial design energies under 3M's 15% Rule had gone into his Post-it® Flag Highlighter research and development. But Windorski also considered other related products. Many people in offices need immediate access to Post-it® Flags while writing with pens. Students are a potential market for this product, too, but probably a smaller market segment than office workers.

Marketing research among North American office workers refined the design and showed the existence of a sizable market for a Post-it® Flag Pen. Even here, however, Windorski encountered surprises: Consumers in one country may prefer blue ink while those in the country next door prefer black ink. The same is true of the width of line the pen produces.

A Marketing Program for the Post-it® Flag Highlighter and Pen After several years of research, development, and production engineering, 3M introduced its new products. Figure 1–4 outlines the strategies for each of the four marketing mix elements in 3M's program to market its Post-it® Flag Highlighters and Post-it® Flag Pens. We can compare the marketing program for each of the two products:

- *Post-it® Flag Highlighter.* The target market is mainly college students, so 3M's initial challenge was to build student awareness of a product that they didn't know existed. The company used a mix of print ads in college newspapers and a TV ad, and then relied on word-of-mouth advertising—students telling their friends how great the product is. Gaining distribution in college bookstores and having attractive packaging was also critical. Plus, 3M charged a price to

MARKETING MIX ELEMENT	MARKETING PROGRAM ACTIVITY TO REACH: COLLEGE STUDENT SEGMENT	MARKETING PROGRAM ACTIVITY TO REACH: OFFICE WORKER SEGMENT	RATIONALE FOR MARKETING PROGRAM ACTIVITY
Product strategy	Offer Post-it® Flag Highlighter to help college students in their studying	Offer Post-it® Flag Pen to help office workers in their day-to-day work activities	Listen carefully to the needs and wants of potential customer segments to use 3M technology to introduce a useful, innovative product
Price strategy	Seek retail price of about \$3.99 to \$4.99 for a single Post-it® Flag Highlighter or \$5.99 to \$7.99 for a three-pack	Seek retail price of about \$3.99 to \$4.99 for a single Post-it® Flag Pen; wholesale prices are less	Set prices that provide genuine value to the customer segment that is targeted
Promotion strategy	Run limited promotion with a TV ad and some ads in college newspapers and then rely on student word-of-mouth messages	Run limited promotion among distributors to get them to stock the product	Increase awareness of potential users who have never heard of this new, innovative 3M product
Place strategy	Distribute Post-it® Flag Highlighters through college bookstores, office supply stores, and mass merchandisers	Distribute Post-it® Flag Pens through office wholesalers and retailers and mass merchandisers	Make it easy for prospective buyers to buy at convenient retail outlets (both products) or to get at work (Post-it® Flag Pens only)

FIGURE 1–4
Marketing programs for the launch of two Post-it® brand products targeted at two customer market segments.

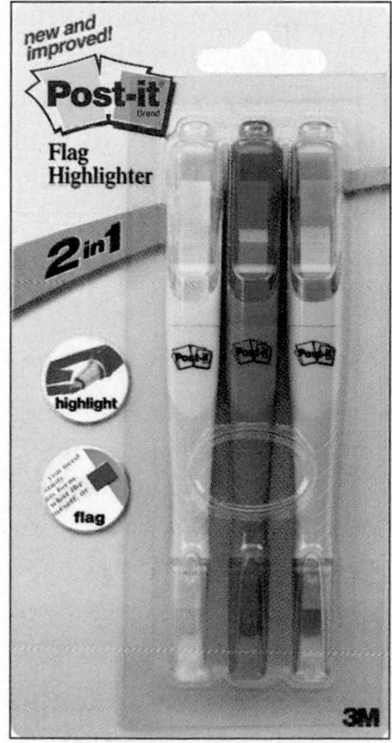

The second generation of Post-it® Flag Highlighters

distributors that it hoped would give a reasonable bookstore price to students and an acceptable profit to distributors and 3M.

- *Post-it® Flag Pen.* The primary target market is people working in offices. But some students are potential customers, so 3M gained distribution in some college bookstores of Post-it® Flag Pens, too. But the Post-it® Flag Pens are mainly business products—bought by the purchasing department in an organization and stocked as office supplies for employees to use. So the marketing program in Figure 1–4 reflects the different distribution or "place" strategies for the two products.

How did these new products do for 3M in the marketplace? They have done so well that 3M bestowed a prestigious award on David Windorski and his team. Their success has also led Windorski to design a second generation of Post-it® Flag Highlighters and Pens *without* the rotating cover that makes it easier to insert replacement flags.

The new tapered design is also easier for students to hold and use. The packaging of the new, second-generation Post-it® Flag Highlighters prominently displays the "2-in-1" benefit.

In what must be the answer to almost every inventor's dream, Oprah Winfrey flew David Windorski to Chicago to appear on her TV show and thank him in person. She told Windorski and her audience that the Post-it® Flag Highlighter is changing the way she does things at home and at work—especially in going through potential books she might recommend for her book club. "David, I know you never thought this would happen when you were in your 3M lab . . . but I want you to take a bow before America for the invention of this . . . (highlighter). It's the most incredible invention," she said.[23]

HOW MARKETING BECAME SO IMPORTANT

To understand why marketing is a driving force in the modern global economy, let us look at the (1) evolution of the market orientation, (2) ethics and social responsibility in marketing, and (3) breadth and depth of marketing activities.

Evolution of the Market Orientation

Many American manufacturers have experienced four distinct stages in the lives of their firms.[24] The first stage, the *production era*, covers the early years of the United States up until the 1920s. Goods were scarce and buyers were willing to accept virtually any goods that were available and make do with them.[25] In the *sales era* from the 1920s to the 1960s, manufacturers found they could produce more goods than buyers could consume. Competition grew. Firms hired more salespeople to find new buyers. This sales era continued into the 1960s for many American firms.

Toyota's world-class reputation among car manufacturers stems from its market orientation and understanding customer needs.

Starting in the late 1950s, marketing became the motivating force among many American firms and the *marketing concept era* dawned. The **marketing concept** is the idea that an organization should (1) strive to satisfy the needs of consumers (2) while also trying to achieve the organization's goals. General Electric probably launched the marketing concept and its focus on consumers when its 1952 annual report stated: "The concept introduces . . . marketing . . . at the beginning rather than the end of the production cycle and integrates marketing into each phase of the business."[26]

Firms such as General Electric, Marriott, and Toyota have achieved great success by putting huge effort into implementing the marketing concept, giving their firms what has been called a *market orientation*. An organization that has a **market orientation** focuses its efforts on (1) continuously collecting information about customers' needs, (2) sharing this information across departments, and (3) using it to create customer value.[27] The result shown in Figure 1–5 is today's *customer relationship era* that started in the 1980s, in which firms seek continuously to satisfy the high expectations of customers.

An important outgrowth of this focus on the customer is the recent attention placed on **customer relationship management (CRM)**, the process of identifying prospective buyers, understanding them intimately, and developing favorable long-term perceptions of the organization and its offerings so that buyers will choose them in the marketplace.[28] This process requires the involvement and commitment of managers and employees throughout the organization[29] and a growing application of information, communication, and Internet technology, as will be described

FIGURE 1–5
Four different orientations in the history of American business. Today's customer relationship era focuses on satisfying the high expectations of customers.

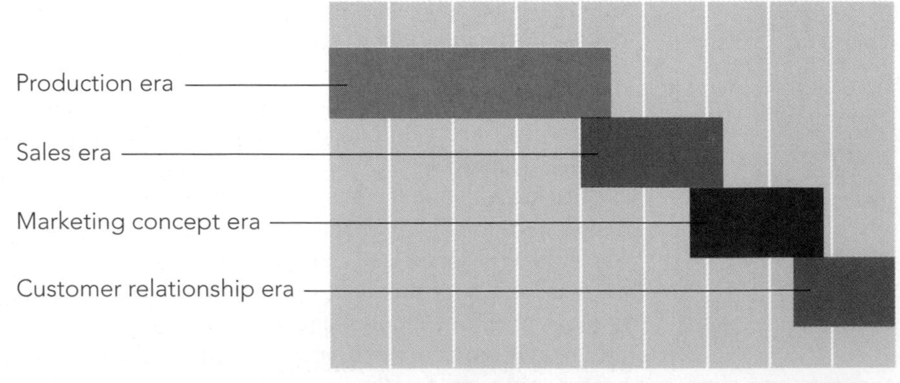

throughout this book. Unfortunately, many expensive CRM computer systems have not provided the expected benefits because they failed to identify exactly which customer segments the company wanted to reach.

The foundation of customer relationship management is really **customer experience**, which is the internal response that customers have to all aspects of an organization and its offering. This internal response includes both the direct and indirect contacts of the customer with the company. Direct contacts include the customer's contacts with the seller through buying, using, and obtaining service. Indirect contacts most often involve unplanned "touches" with the company through word-of-mouth comments from other customers, reviewers, and news reports.

The disconnect between what companies *think they are providing* versus what customers *say they are receiving* shows how important customer experience is. A recent survey of 362 companies showed only 8 percent of them described the experience they received as customers as "superior," but 80 percent actually believed their own companies were supplying "superior" customer experience.[30]

Ethics and Social Responsibility: Balancing the Interests of Different Groups

As organizations have changed their orientation, society's expectations of marketers have also changed. Today, the standards of marketing practice have shifted from an emphasis on producers' interests to consumers' interests. In addition, organizations are increasingly encouraged to consider the social and environmental consequences of their actions for all parties. Guidelines for ethical and socially responsible behavior can help managers balance consumer, organizational, and societal interests.

Ethics Many marketing issues are not specifically addressed by existing laws and regulations. Should information about a firm's customers be sold to other organizations? Should advertising by professional service providers, such as accountants and attorneys, be restricted? Should consumers be on their own to assess the safety of a product? These questions raise difficult ethical issues. Many companies, industries, and professional associations have developed codes of ethics to assist managers.

Social Responsibility While many ethical issues involve only the buyer and seller, others involve society as a whole. For example, suppose you change the oil in your old Chevy yourself and dump the used oil in a corner of your backyard. Is this just a transaction between you and the oil manufacturer? Not quite! The used oil will contaminate the soil, so society will bear a portion of the cost of your behavior. This example illustrates the issue of social responsibility, the idea that organizations are accountable to a larger society.

The well-being of society at large should also be recognized in an organization's marketing decisions. In fact, some marketing experts stress the **societal marketing concept**, the view that organizations should satisfy the needs of consumers in a way that provides for society's well-being.[31] For example, ScotchBrite® Never Rust™ soap pads from 3M—which are made from recycled plastic bottles—are more expensive than competitors' (SOS and Brillo) but superior because they don't rust or scratch (question 3, Figure 1–1). The Making Responsible Decisions box on the next page describes how social entrepreneurship innovates to help solve the practical needs of society.[32]

The societal marketing concept is directly related to *macromarketing*, which is the study of the aggregate flow of a nation's goods and services to benefit society.[33] Macromarketing addresses broad issues such as whether marketing costs too much, whether advertising is wasteful, and what resource scarcities and pollution side effects result from the marketing system. While macromarketing issues are addressed briefly in this book, the book's main focus is on how an individual organization

Making Responsible Decisions > > social responsibility

Social Entrepreneurship Using Marketing to Help People

Fran Heitzman, founder of Bridging, Inc., loves to tell "The Story." It goes something like this: One day, Heitzman was helping a single mom stock her kitchen. When he handed her daughter some silverware, she said, "Just think Mom, now we won't have to share spoons when we eat!" Heitzman then went home and "stole five sets of silverware from our kitchen drawer" to give to those in need. "My wife didn't realize they were missing for a year and a half!"

The moral to Heitzman's story: Everyone's got too much stuff so they should give it away. That's where Bridging comes in. The not-for-profit organization matches people's surpluses of things such as dishes and furniture with other people's needs, an example of what is now called "social entrepreneurship." For example, the men in the photo are retired school teachers whose volunteer work as Bridging truck drivers gives them the personal satisfaction of helping others.

In a nutshell, social entrepreneurship applies innovative approaches to solve the practical needs of society, particularly of those members who lack the financial or political means to solve their own problems. A social entrepreneur is someone who uses inspiration, passion, creativity, and in many cases, capitalistic methods (marketing strategy and tactics, money, technology, etc.) to generate customer value for a significant segment of society through transformational change—much like a business entrepreneur. Social entrepreneurs can organize as either a for- or not-for-profit entity.

Social entrepreneurship occurs globally. For example, Hand in Hand International uses a technique called microfinance to provide small loans (about $125) to women in India who want to start and operate a small business. A Hand in Hand self-help group reaches out to the poorest, least educated, would-be businesswomen and teaches them first the basics (reading, writing, and arithmetic) and then the skills needed to operate a business. Percy Barnevik, the founder of Hand in Hand, says he wanted to "gift" his knowledge, abilities, and passion as a retired CEO to improve society's quality of life.

---

directs its marketing activities and allocates its resources to benefit its customers, or *micromarketing*. Because of the importance of ethical and social responsibility issues in marketing today, Chapter 4 focuses on them, but they are touched on throughout the book.

The Breadth and Depth of Marketing

Marketing today affects every person and organization. To understand this, let's analyze (1) who markets, (2) what is marketed, (3) who buys and uses what is marketed, (4) who benefits from these marketing activities, and (5) how they benefit.

Who Markets? Every organization markets. It's obvious that business firms involved in manufacturing (Heinz), retailing (Target), and providing services (Marriott) market their offerings. And nonprofit organizations such as your local hospital, your college, places (cities, states, countries), and even special causes (Race for the Cure) also engage in marketing. Finally, individuals such as political candidates often use marketing to gain voter attention and preference.[34]

What Is Marketed? Goods, services, and ideas are marketed. *Goods* are physical objects, such as toothpaste, cameras, or computers, that satisfy consumer needs. *Services* are intangible items such as airline trips, financial advice, or art museums. *Ideas* are thoughts about concepts, actions, or causes.

Financial pressures have caused art museums to innovate to market their unique services—the viewing of artworks by visitors—to increase revenues. This often involves levels of rare creativity unthinkable several decades ago. For example, the search for new revenues spurred the Dallas Museum of Art to stay open for 100 consecutive hours to celebrate its centennial.[35]

France's Louvre, home to the Mona Lisa painting and Winged Victory of Samothrace statue, has now launched exotic fund-raising dinners and partnerships with museums around the world.[36] To reach potential future visitors Russia's 1,000-room State Hermitage Museum partnered with IBM to let you take a "virtual tour" of its exhibits. To be a "virtual tourist," go to www.hermitagemuseum.org, and click on the "Virtual Visit" link.

Ideas are most often marketed by nonprofit organizations or the government. For example, your local library may market the idea of developing improved reading skills, and the Nature Conservancy markets the cause of protecting the environment. Charities market the idea that it's worthwhile for you to donate your time or money, and orchestras market fine music. States such as Arizona market themselves as attractive places for tourists to visit.

Who Buys and Uses What Is Marketed? Both individuals and organizations buy and use goods and services that are marketed. **Ultimate consumers** are the people—whether 80 years or eight months old—who use the goods and services purchased for a household. In contrast, **organizational buyers** are those manufacturers, wholesalers, retailers, and government agencies that buy goods and services for their own use or for resale. Although the terms *consumers, buyers,* and *customers* are sometimes used for both ultimate consumers and organizations, there is no consistency on this. In this book you will be able to tell from the example whether the buyers are ultimate consumers, organizations, or both.

France's Louvre and Russia's State Hermitage Museum use creative marketing efforts to generate new revenues and attract first-time visitors.

Who Benefits? In our free-enterprise society there are three specific groups that benefit from effective marketing: consumers who buy, organizations that sell, and society as a whole. True competition between products and services in the marketplace ensures that consumers can find value from the best products, the lowest prices, or exceptional service. Providing choices leads to the consumer satisfaction and quality of life that we have come to expect from our economic system.

Organizations that provide need-satisfying products with effective marketing programs—for example, Target, IBM, and Avon—have blossomed. But competition creates problems for ineffective competitors, such as eToys and hundreds of other dot-com businesses that failed a decade ago.

Finally, effective marketing benefits society.[37] It enhances competition, which both improves the quality of products and services and lowers their prices. This makes countries more competitive in world markets and provides jobs and a higher standard of living for their citizens.

How Do Consumers Benefit? Marketing creates **utility**, the benefits or customer value received by users of the product. This utility is the result of the marketing exchange process and the way society benefits from marketing. There are four different utilities: form, place, time, and possession. The production of the good or service constitutes *form utility. Place utility* means having the offering available where consumers need it, whereas *time utility* means having it available when needed. *Possession utility* is the value of making an item easy to purchase through the provision of credit cards or financial arrangements. Marketing creates its utilities by bridging space (place utility) and hours (time utility) to provide products (form utility) for consumers to own and use (possession utility).

learning review

7. What are the two key characteristics of the marketing concept?
8. What is the difference between ultimate consumers and organizational buyers?

LEARNING OBJECTIVES REVIEW

LO1 *Define marketing and identify the diverse factors influencing marketing activities.*
Marketing is an organizational function and a set of processes for creating, communicating, and delivering value to customers and for managing customer relationships in ways that benefit the organization and its stakeholders. This definition relates to two primary goals of marketing: (*a*) discovering the needs of prospective customers and (*b*) satisfying them. Achieving these two goals also involves the four marketing mix factors largely controlled by the organization and the five environmental forces that are generally outside its control.

LO2 *Explain how marketing discovers and satisfies consumer needs.*
The first objective in marketing is discovering the needs and wants of consumers who are prospective buyers and customers. This is not easy because consumers may not always know or be able to describe what they need and want. A need occurs when a person feels deprived of basic necessities such as food, clothing, and shelter. A want is a need that is shaped by a person's knowledge, culture, and personality. Effective marketing can clearly shape a person's wants and tries to influence what we buy. The second objective in marketing is satisfying the needs of targeted consumers. Because an organization obviously can't satisfy all consumer needs, it must concentrate its efforts on certain needs of a specific group of potential consumers or target market—one or more specific groups of potential consumers toward which an organization directs its marketing program. Having selected its target market consumers, the organization then takes action to satisfy their needs by developing a unique marketing program to reach them.

LO3 *Distinguish between marketing mix factors and environmental forces.*
Four elements in a marketing program designed to satisfy customer needs are product, price, promotion, and place. These elements are called the marketing mix, the four Ps, or the controllable variables because they are under the general control of the marketing department. Environmental forces, also called uncontrollable variables, are largely beyond the organization's control. These include social, economic, technological, competitive, and regulatory forces.

LO4 *Explain how organizations build strong customer relationships and customer value through marketing.*
The essence of successful marketing is to provide sufficient value to gain loyal, long-term customers. Customer value is the unique combination of benefits received by targeted buyers that usually includes quality, price, convenience, on-time delivery, and both before-sale and after-sale service. Marketers do this by using one of three value strategies: best price, best product, or best service.

LO5 *Describe how today's customer relationship era differs from prior eras.*
U.S. business history is divided into four overlapping periods: the production era, the sales era, the marketing concept era, and the current customer relationship era. The production era covers the period to the 1920s when buyers were willing to accept virtually any goods that were available. The central notion was that products would sell themselves. The sales era lasted from the 1920s to the 1960s. Manufacturers found they could produce more goods than buyers could consume, and competition grew, so the solution was to hire more salespeople to find new buyers. In the late 1950s, the marketing concept era dawned when organizations adopted a strong market orientation and integrated marketing into each phase of their business. In today's customer relationship era that started in the 1980s, organizations seek continuously to satisfy the high expectations of customers—an aggressive extension of the marketing concept era.

FOCUSING ON KEY TERMS

customer experience p. 17
customer relationship management (CRM) p. 16
customer value p. 12
environmental forces p. 11
exchange p. 6
market p. 11
market orientation p. 16
marketing p. 6
marketing concept p. 16
marketing mix p. 11
marketing program p. 13
organizational buyers p. 19
relationship marketing p. 13
societal marketing concept p. 17
target market p. 11
ultimate consumers p. 19
utility p. 19

APPLYING MARKETING KNOWLEDGE

1 What consumer wants (or benefits) are met by the following products or services? (*a*) Carnation Instant Breakfast, (*b*) Adidas running shoes, (*c*) Hertz Rent-A-Car, and (*d*) television home shopping programs.

2 Each of the four products, services, or programs in question 1 has substitutes. Respective examples are (*a*) a ham and egg breakfast, (*b*) regular tennis shoes, (*c*) taking a bus, and (*d*) a department store. What consumer benefits might these substitutes have in each case that some consumers might value more highly than those mentioned in question 1?

3 What are the characteristics (e.g., age, income, education) of the target market customers for the following products or services? (*a*) *National Geographic* magazine, (*b*) *Wired* magazine, (*c*) New York Giants football team, and (*d*) the U.S. Open tennis tournament.

4 A college in a metropolitan area wishes to increase its evening-school offerings of business-related courses such as marketing, accounting, finance, and management. Who are the target market customers (students) for these courses?

5 What actions involving the four marketing mix elements might be used to reach the target market in question 4?

6 What environmental forces (uncontrollable variables) must the college in question 4 consider in designing its marketing program?

7 Does a firm have the right to "create" wants and try to persuade consumers to buy goods and services they didn't know about earlier? What are examples of "good" and "bad" want creation? Who should decide what is good and bad?

building your marketing plan

If your instructor assigns a marketing plan for your class, don't make a face and complain about the work—for two special reasons. First, you will get insights into trying to actually "do marketing" that often go beyond what you can get by simply reading the textbook. Second, thousands of graduating students every year get their first job by showing prospective employers a "portfolio" of samples of their written work from college—often a marketing plan if they have one. This can work for you.

This "Building Your Marketing Plan" section at the end of each chapter suggests ways to improve and focus your marketing plan. You will use the sample marketing plan in Appendix A (following Chapter 2) as a guide, and this section after each chapter will help you apply those Appendix A ideas to your own marketing plan.

The first step in writing a good marketing plan is to have a business or product that enthuses you and for which you can get detailed information, so you can avoid glittering generalities. We offer these additional bits of advice in selecting a topic:

- *Do* pick a topic that has personal interest for you—a family business, a business or product you or a friend might want to launch, or a student organization needing marketing help.
- *Do not* pick a topic that is so large it can't be covered adequately or so abstract it will lack specifics.

1 To get started on your marketing plan, list four or five possible topics and compare these with the criteria your instructor suggests and those shown above. Think hard, because your decision will be with you all term and may influence the quality of the resulting marketing plan you show to a prospective employer.

2 When you have selected your marketing plan topic, whether the plan is for an actual business, a possible business, or a student organization, write the "company description" in your plan, as shown in Appendix A.

video case 1 3M's Post-it® Flag Highlighter: Extending the Concept!

"I didn't go out to students and ask, 'What are your needs, or what are your wants?'" 3M inventor David Windorski explains to a class of college students. "And even if I did ask, they probably wouldn't say, 'Put flags inside a highlighter.'"

So Windorski turned the classic textbook approach to marketing on its head.

That classic approach—as you saw earlier in Chapter 1—says to start with needs and wants of potential customers and then develop the product. But sometimes new-product development runs in the opposite direction: Start with a new product idea—such as personal computers—and then see if there is a market. This is really what Windorski did, using a lot of marketing research along the way after he developed the concept of the Post-it® Flag Highlighter.

EARLY MARKETING RESEARCH

During this new-product development process, Windorski and 3M did a lot of marketing research on students. Some was unconventional, while other research was quite traditional. For example, students were asked to dump the contents of their backpacks on the table and to explain what they carried around and then to react to some early highlighter models. Also, several times six or seven students were interviewed together and observed by 3M researchers from behind a one-way mirror—the focus group technique discussed in Chapter 8. Other students were interviewed individually. Windorski's first models were nonworking clay ones like he is holding in the photo below. These nonworking models told him how the innovative highlighters would feel to students eventually using the real ones. When early working models of the Post-it® Flag Highlighter finally existed, several hundred were produced and given to students to use for a month. Their reactions were captured on a questionnaire.

THE NEW-PRODUCT LAUNCH

After the initial marketing research and dozens of technical tests in 3M laboratories, David Windorski's new 3M highlighter product was ready to be manufactured and marketed.

Here's a snapshot of the prelaunch issues that were solved before the product could be introduced:

- *Technical issues.* Can we generate a computer-aided database for injection molded parts? What tolerances do we need? The 3M highlighter is really a technological marvel. For the parts on the highlighter to work, tolerances must be several thousandths of an inch—less than the thickness of a piece of paper.
- *Manufacturing issues.* Where should the product be manufactured? Because 3M chose a company outside the United States, precise translations of critical technical specifications were needed. Windorski spent time in the factory working with engineers and manufacturing specialists there to ensure that 3M's precise production standards would be achieved.
- *Product issues.* What should the brand name be for the new highlighter product? Marketing research and many meetings gave the answer: "The Post-it® Flag Highlighter." How many to a package? What color(s)? What should the packaging look like that can (1) display the product well at retail and (2) communicate its points of difference effectively?
- *Price issues.* With many competing highlighters, what should the price be for 3M's premium highlighter that will provide 3M adequate profit? Should the suggested retail price be the same in college bookstores, mass merchandisers (Wal-Mart, Target), and office supply stores (Office Max, Office Depot)?
- *Promotion issues.* How can 3M tell students the product exists? Might office workers want it and use it? Should there be print ads, TV ads, and point-of-sale displays explaining the product?
- *Place (distribution) issues.* With the limited shelf space in college bookstores and other outlets, how can 3M persuade retailers to stock its new product?

The original designs and packaging of the Post-it® Flag Highlighters and Pens at their new-product launch appear in the photo of the Post-it® product line on the opposite page.

THE MARKETING PROGRAM TODAY AND TOMORROW

The highlighter turned out to be more popular than 3M expected. The company often hears from end users how much they like the product.

So what can 3M do for an encore to build on the initial success? This involves taking great care to introduce product extensions to attract new customers while still retaining its solid foundation of loyal existing customers. Also, 3M's products have to appeal not only to the ultimate consumers but also to retailers who want new items to display in high-traffic areas.

Product and packaging decisions for the Post-it® Flag Highlighter reflect this innovative focus. In terms of product extensions, David Windorski designed new Post-it® Flag Highlighters and Pens that are easier to hold and that have the flags permanently accessible without twisting (see photo on page 15). As to packaging, it's critical that it (1) communicate the 2-products-in-1 idea, (2) be attractive, and (3) achieve both goals with the fewest words.

At 3M, promotion budgets are limited because it relies heavily on its technology for a competitive advantage. This also applies to the Post-it® Flag Highlighter. So you probably have never seen a print or TV ad for it. Yet potential student buyers, the product's main target market, must be made aware that it exists. So 3M searches continually for simple, effective promotions to alert students about this product.

Great technology is meaningless unless the product is available where potential buyers can purchase it. Unlike college bookstores that exist largely to serve students, mass merchandisers and office supply stores track, measure, and seek to maximize the profit of every square foot of selling space. So 3M must convince these retail chains that selling space devoted to its highlighter line will be more profitable than for stocking competing products. The challenge for 3M: Finding ways to make the Post-it® Flag Highlighter prominent on shelves of college bookstores and retail chains.

If the Post-it® Flag Highlighter is doing well in the United States, why not try to sell it around the world? But even here 3M faces critical questions: Which countries will be the best markets? What highlighter colors and packaging works best in each country? How do we physically get the product to these markets in a timely and cost-efficient basis?

Questions

1 *(a)* How did 3M's David Windorski get ideas from college students to help him in designing the final commercial version of the Post-it® Flag Highlighter? *(b)* How were these ideas important to the success of the product?

2 What *(a)* special advantages and *(b)* potential problems did 3M have in introducing a new highlighter-with-flags product for college students?

3 Visit your college bookstore before you answer. *(a)* Where would you display the Post-it® Flag Highlighter in a college bookstore, and *(b)* how can the display increase student awareness of the product?

4 In what ways might 3M try to promote its Post-it® Flag Highlighter and make students more aware of the product?

5 What are *(a)* the special opportunities and *(b)* potential challenges for 3M in taking its Post-it® Flag Highlighter into international markets? *(c)* On which countries should 3M focus its marketing efforts?

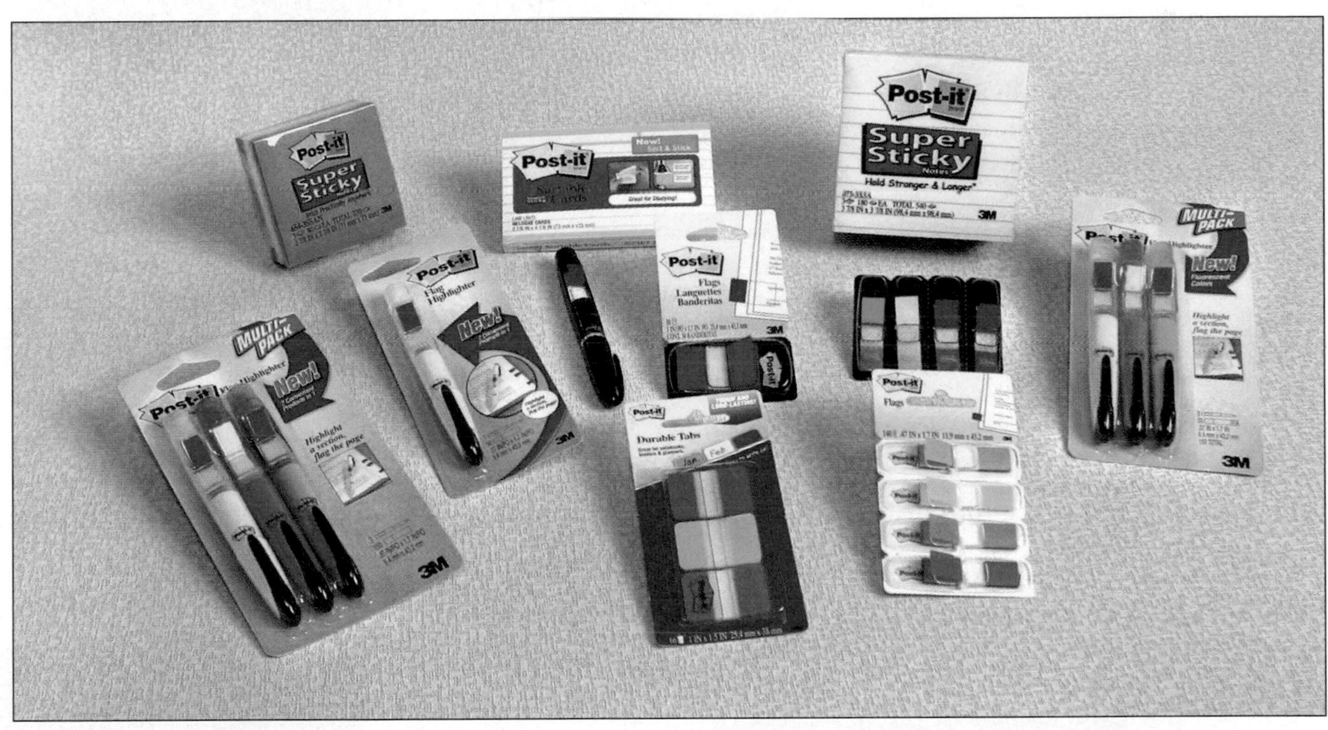

Ben & Jerry's Mission

Ben & Jerry's is founded on & dedicated to a sustainable corporate concept of linked prosperity. Our mission consists of 3 interrelated parts:

SOCIAL mission

To operate the Company in a way that actively recognizes the central role that business plays in society by initiating innovative ways to improve the quality of life locally, nationally and internationally.

PRODUCT mission

To make, distribute and sell the finest quality all natural ice cream and euphoric concoctions with a continued commitment to incorporating wholesome, natural ingredients and promoting business practices that respect the Earth and the Environment.

ECONOMIC mission

To operate the Company on a sustainable financial basis of profitable growth, increasing value for our stakeholders and expanding opportunities for development and career growth for our employees.

Underlying the Mission is the determination to seek new & creative ways of addressing all 3 parts, while holding a deep respect for individuals inside & outside the company, & for the communities of which they are a part.

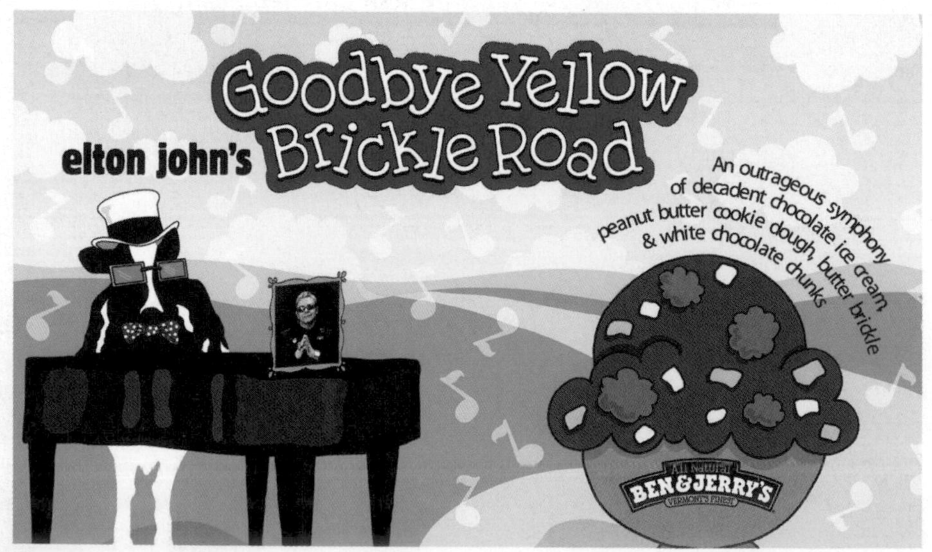

2 Developing Successful Marketing and Organizational Strategies

LEARNING OBJECTIVES
After reading this chapter you should be able to:

LO1 Describe two kinds of organizations and the three levels of strategy in them.

LO2 Describe how core values, mission, organizational culture, business, and goals are important to organizations.

LO3 Explain why managers use marketing dashboards and metrics.

LO4 Discuss how an organization assesses where it is now and seeks to be.

LO5 Explain the three steps of the planning phase of the strategic marketing process.

LO6 Describe the elements of the implementation and evaluation phases of the strategic marketing process.

WHERE AN "A" IN A CORRESPONDENCE COURSE IN ICE CREAM MAKING CAN LEAD!

Here's what the two founding entrepreneurs who aced their $5 college correspondence course in ice cream making are doing in their organization today:

- They buy their milk and cream from one dairy cooperative whose members guarantee the supplies are bovine growth-hormone free.
- Their PartnerShop, Scoopers Making Change, and Cones 2 Career programs help nonprofit organizations give jobs to at-risk youth.
- The summer 2009 limited edition "Goodbye Yellow Brickle Road" (opposite page) ice cream is a partnership with Sir Elton John to help his worldwide AIDS Foundation. The name is a play on one of his most popular song titles. The flavor is "an outrageous symphony of decadent chocolate ice cream, peanut butter cookie dough, butterbrickle and white chocolate chunks." Will it reappear in 2010?
- They are developing a "Cleaner Greener Freezer" for Ben & Jerry's U.S. retail locations, an innovative freezer that uses an eco-friendly refrigerant to save the ozone layer and reduce greenhouse gases.

This creative, funky business is Ben & Jerry's Homemade Holdings, Inc., which links its mission statement to social causes designed to improve humanity, as shown on the opposite page.

Their business started in 1978 when longtime friends Ben Cohen and Jerry Greenfield headed north to Vermont to start an ice cream parlor in a renovated gas station. Buoyed with enthusiasm, $12,000 in borrowed and saved money, and ideas from a $5 Penn State correspondence course in ice cream making, Ben and Jerry were off and scooping.[1] Today, Ben & Jerry's is owned by Unilever, which is the market leader in the global ice cream industry—one that is expected to reach $43 billion by 2013.[2] While customers love Cherry Garcia and the company's other rich premium ice cream flavors, many buy its products to support Ben & Jerry's social mission (opposite page).

Chapter 2 describes how organizations such as Ben & Jerry's, Medtronic, and Kodak set goals to give an overall direction that is linked to their organizational and marketing strategies. The marketing department of an organization converts these strategies into plans that must be implemented. The results are then evaluated to assess the degree to which they accomplish the organization's goals, consistent with its core values and mission.

TODAY'S ORGANIZATIONS

In studying today's visionary organizations, it is important to recognize (1) the kinds of organizations that exist, (2) what strategy is, and (3) how this strategy relates to the three levels found in many large organizations.

Kinds of Organizations

LO1

An *organization* is a legal entity of people who share a common mission. This motivates them to develop *offerings* (products, services, or ideas) that create value for both the organization and its customers by satisfying customer needs and wants.[3] Today's organizations can be divided into business firms and nonprofit organizations.

A *business firm* is a privately owned organization such as Amazon or Nike that serves its customers to earn a profit so that it can survive.[4] **Profit** is the money left after a business firm's total expenses are subtracted from its total revenues and is the reward for the risk it undertakes in marketing its offerings.

In contrast, a *nonprofit organization* is a nongovernmental organization that serves its customers but does not have profit as an organizational goal. Instead, its goals may be operational efficiency or client satisfaction. Regardless, it also must receive sufficient funds above its expenses to continue operations. Charities and farm cooperatives affiliated with Ben & Jerry's are examples of this kind of organization. Both business firms and nonprofit organizations increasingly seek to achieve sustainable development, as described in the Making Responsible Decisions box.[5] For simplicity in the rest of the book, the terms *firm, company, corporation,* and *organization* are used interchangeably to cover both business and nonprofit operations.

Organizations that develop similar offerings create an *industry*, such as the computer industry or the automobile industry.[6] As a result, organizations make strategic decisions that reflect the dynamics of the industry to create a compelling and sustainable advantage for their offerings relative to those of competitors to achieve a superior level of performance.[7] The foundation of much of an organization's marketing strategy is having a clear understanding of the industry within which it competes.

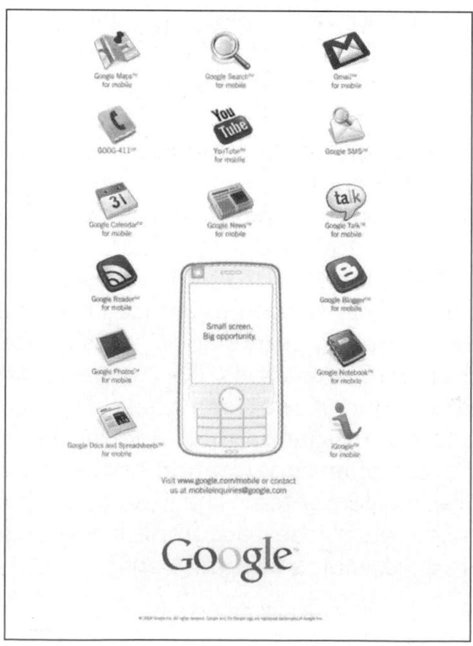

Both business firms such as Google and nonprofit organizations like Nature Conservancy use strategies and organizational structures to achieve their goals.

Making Responsible Decisions > > > > sustainability

The Global Dilemma: How to Achieve Sustainable Development

Corporate executives and world leaders are increasingly asked to address the issue of "sustainable development." This term was formally defined in a 1987 United Nations report as meeting present needs "without compromising the ability of future generations to meet their own needs."

With more than half of the households in many developing nations below the poverty level, should the immediate goal be a cleaner environment or more food, clothing, housing, and consumer goods for its citizens? What should the heads of these governments do? What should business firms and nonprofit organizations trying to enter these developing nations do? What will be the impact on future generations?

The 3M Company developed an innovative program called Pollution Prevention Pays (3P) to reduce harmful environmental impacts, while making a profit doing so. The company estimates that the 3P program in the last quarter century has cut its pollution by 1.6 billion pounds while saving almost $900 million in raw materials and avoiding fines. The company's 2010 environmental goal is to improve energy efficiency per pound of product by 20 percent while reducing waste generated from its operations by 20 percent.

Should the environment or economic growth come first? What are the societal trade-offs?

What Is Strategy?

An organization has limited human, financial, technological, and other resources available to produce and market its offerings—it can't be all things to all people! Every organization must develop strategies to help focus and direct its efforts to accomplish its goals. However, the definition of strategy has been the subject of debate among management and marketing theorists.[8] For our purpose, **strategy** is an organization's long-term course of action designed to deliver a unique customer experience while achieving its goals.[9] Whether explicit or implicit, all organizations set a strategic direction. And marketing helps not only to set this direction but also to move the organization there.

Structure of Today's Organizations

Large organizations such as Medtronic and Kodak are extremely complex. They usually consist of three organizational levels whose strategies are linked to marketing, as shown in Figure 2–1.

FIGURE 2–1
The board of directors oversees the three levels of strategy in organizations: corporate, business unit, and functional.

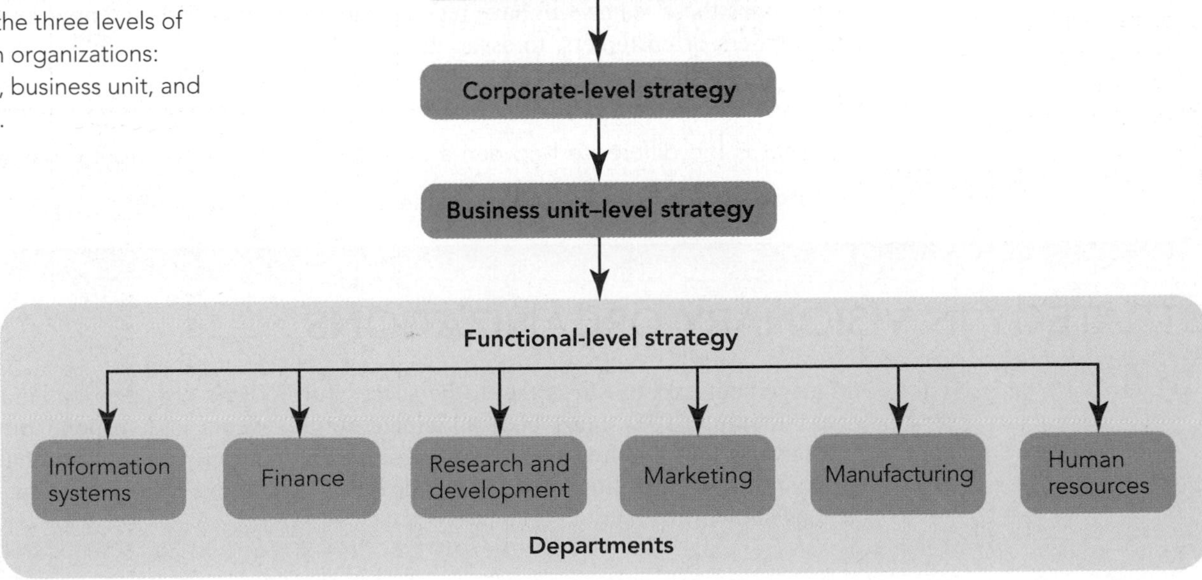

Corporate Level The **corporate level** is where top management directs overall strategy for the entire organization. "Top management" usually means the board of directors and senior management officers with a variety of skills and experiences that are invaluable in establishing overall strategy.

The president or chief executive officer (CEO) is the highest ranking officer in the organization and is usually a member of its board of directors. This person must possess leadership skills and expertise ranging from overseeing the organization's daily operations to spearheading strategy planning efforts that may determine its very survival.

In recent years many large firms have changed the title of the head of marketing from vice president of marketing to chief marketing officer (CMO). These CMOs have an increasingly important role in top management because of their ability to think strategically. Most bring multi-industry backgrounds, cross-functional management expertise, analytical skills, and intuitive marketing insights to their job, which enables them to create and deliver value to the organization and its customers.[10]

Strategic Business Unit Level Some multimarket, multiproduct firms, such as General Electric or Johnson & Johnson, manage a portfolio or group of businesses.[11] Each group is a **strategic business unit (SBU),** which is a subsidiary, division, or unit of an organization that markets a set of related offerings to a clearly defined group of customers. At the *strategic business unit level*, managers set a more specific strategic direction for their businesses to exploit value-creating opportunities. For less complex firms with a single business focus, such as Ben & Jerry's, the corporate and business unit levels may merge.

Functional Level Each strategic business unit has a **functional level**, where groups of specialists actually create value for the organization. The term *department* generally refers to these specialized functions such as marketing and finance (see Figure 2–1). At the functional level, the organization's strategic direction becomes its most specific and focused. Just as there is a hierarchy of levels within an organization, there is a hierarchy of strategic directions set by managers at each level.

A key role of the marketing department is to look outward, keeping the organization focused on creating value both for it and for customers. This is accomplished by listening to customers, developing and producing offerings, and implementing marketing program activities.

When developing marketing programs for new offerings or for improving existing ones, an organization's senior management may form **cross-functional teams**. These consist of a small number of people from different departments who are mutually accountable to accomplish a task or a common set of performance goals. Sometimes these teams will have representatives from outside the organization, such as suppliers or customers, to assist them.

learning review

1. What is the difference between a business firm and a nonprofit organization?
2. What are examples of a functional level in an organization?

STRATEGY IN VISIONARY ORGANIZATIONS

LO2

Management experts stress that to be successful, today's organizations must be forward looking. They must both anticipate future events and respond quickly and effectively. This requires a visionary organization to specify its foundation (why does it exist?), set a direction (what will it do?), and formulate strategies (how will it do it?) as shown in Figure 2–2.[12]

Organizational foundation (why)
- Core values
- Mission (vision)
- Organizational culture

+

Organizational direction (what)
- Business
- Goals (objectives)
  - Long-term
  - Short-term

=

Organizational strategies (how)
- By level
  - Corporate
  - SBU
  - Functional
- By offering
  - Product
  - Service
  - Idea

FIGURE 2–2
Today's visionary organization uses key elements to (1) establish a foundation and (2) set a direction using (3) its strategies that enable it to develop and market its offerings successfully.

Organizational Foundation: Why Does It Exist?

An organization's foundation is its philosophical reason for being—why it exists—and rarely changes. Successful visionary organizations use this foundation to guide and inspire their employees through three elements: core values, mission, and organizational culture.

Core Values An organization's **core values** are the fundamental, passionate, and enduring principles that guide its conduct over time.[13] A firm's founders or senior management develop these core values, which are consistent with their essential beliefs and character.[14] They capture the firm's heart and soul and serve to inspire and motivate its *stakeholders*—employees, shareholders, board of directors, suppliers, distributors, creditors, unions, government, local communities, and customers. Core values also are timeless and should not change due to short-term financial, operational, or marketing concerns. Finally, core values guide the organization's conduct. To be effective, an organization's core values must be communicated to and supported by its top management and employees; if not, they are just hollow words.[15]

Mission By understanding its core values, an organization can take steps to define its **mission**, a statement of the organization's function in society, often identifying its customers, markets, products, and technologies. Often used interchangeably with *vision*, a *mission statement* should be clear, concise, meaningful, inspirational, and long-term.[16]

Medtronic is the world leader in producing heart pacemakers and other medical devices. Earl Bakken, its founder, wrote this mission statement for Medtronic when it was launched a half century ago, which has remained virtually unchanged:

> "To contribute to human welfare by application of biomedical engineering in the research, design, manufacture, and sale of instruments or appliances that alleviate pain, restore health, and extend life."

People see this "rising figure" mural in the headquarters of a world-class corporation. What does it signify? What does it say to employees? To others? For some insights and why it is important, see the text.

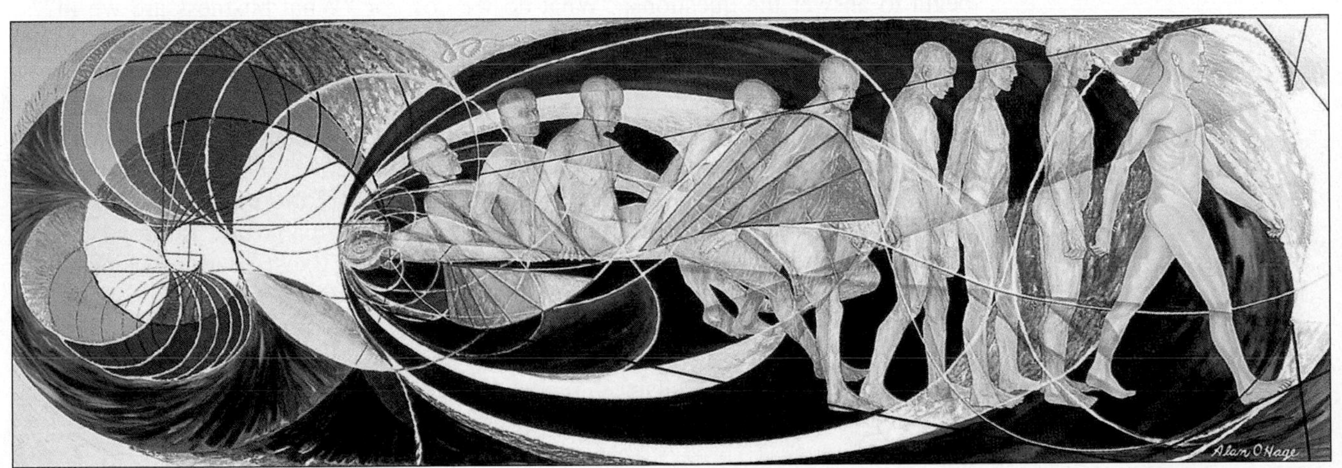

This inspiration and focus appear in the mission statements of both business firms and nonprofit organizations:

- Southwest Airlines: To be dedicated "to the highest quality of Customer Service delivered with a sense of warmth, friendliness, individual pride, and Company Spirit."
- American Red Cross: "To provide relief to victims of disaster and help prevent, prepare for, and respond to emergencies."

In the first half of the 20th century, what "business" did railroads believe they were in? The text reveals their disastrous error.

Each statement exhibits the qualities of a good mission: a clear, challenging, and compelling picture of an envisioned future.

Recently, many organizations have added a social element to their mission statements to reflect an ideal that is morally right and worthwhile.[17] This is what Ben & Jerry's social mission statement is all about, as shown in the chapter opening. Stakeholders, particularly customers, employees, and now society, are asking organizations to be exceptional citizens by providing long-term value while solving society's problems.[18]

Organizational Culture An organization must connect with all of its stakeholders. Thus, an important corporate-level marketing function is communicating its core values and mission to them. Medtronic has a "rising figure" wall mural at its headquarters. The firm also presents every new employee with a medallion depicting this "rising figure" on one side and the company's mission statement on the other. And each December, several patients describe to a large employee holiday celebration how Medtronic devices have changed their lives.[19] These activities send clear messages to employees and other stakeholders about Medtronic's **organizational culture**, the set of values, ideas, attitudes, and norms of behavior that is learned and shared among the members of an organization.

Organizational Direction: What Will It Do?

As shown in Figure 2–1, the organization's foundation enables it to set a direction in terms of (1) the "business" it is in and (2) its specific goals.

For the reasons Netflix is altering its "business model" to respond to changing consumer demand and technologies, see the text and Marketing Matters box.

Business A **business** describes the clear, broad, underlying industry or market sector of an organization's offering. To help define its business, an organization looks at the set of organizations that sell similar offerings—those that are in direct competition with each other—such as "the ice cream business." The organization can then begin to answer the questions, "What do we do?" or "What business are we in?"

In his famous "Marketing Myopia" article, Theodore Levitt argues that senior managers of 20th century American railroads defined their business too narrowly, proclaiming, "We are in the railroad business!" This myopic focus caused these firms to lose sight of who their customers were and what they needed. Thus, railroads only saw other railroads as direct competitors and failed to develop strategies to compete with airlines, barges, pipelines, and trucks—firms whose offerings carry both goods and people. As a result, many railroads merged or went bankrupt. Railroads would have fared better if they had realized they were in "the transportation business."[20]

With today's increased global competition and worldwide financial crises, many organizations are rethinking their *business model*, the strategies an organization develops to provide value to the customers it serves. Technological innovation is often the trigger for this business model change. American newspapers are looking for a new business model as former subscribers get their news online and buy cars

Marketing Matters > > > > > entrepreneurship

The Netflix Launch and Its Continually . . . Continually . . . Continually . . . Changing Business Model!

If in 1997 a customer had been charged a late fee of $40 for a VHS tape of *Apollo 13*, what might she or he have done? Maybe just grumble and pay it?

In the case of Reed Hastings, he was embarrassed, apparently paid the $40 late fee, and—this is where he's different—got to thinking that there's a big market out there. "So I started to investigate the idea of how to create a movie-rental business by mail," he told a *Fortune* magazine interviewer.

The Original Business Model

"Early on, the first concept we launched was rental by mail, but it wasn't subscription based so it worked more like Blockbuster," says Hastings, the founder and chief executive officer of Netflix. It wasn't very popular. So in 1999, he relaunched his idea with a new business model—as a subscription service, pretty much the mail business you see today with 8 million subscribers. "We named the company Netflix, not DVDs by Mail because we knew that eventually we would deliver movies directly over the Internet," Hastings says.

Netflix's Changing Business Model

The Netflix DVDs-by-mail model can deliver any one of 100,000 movies on DVD to you for a fixed monthly fee—$9 for one movie, $14 for two. But look where its business model changed over eight months in 2008: from "Watch Now," enabling regular subscribers to watch any of 1,000 streaming movies on a PC, to using a tiny $100 TV-connect box to let viewers rather awkwardly watch a streaming movie on their TV rather than a PC, to partnering with TiVo, Xbox, and others to enable their systems to let you see one of about 12,000 movies on your TV.

With Netflix breaking a series of technology barriers, its "any movie, any time" business model is literally just around the corner.

---

from Craigslist Inc. rather than using newspaper want ads.[21] Microsoft is rethinking its business model in the new era of $200 laptops.[22] The Marketing Matters box describes how Netflix founder and Chief Executive Officer Reed Hastings got the idea for his start-up and how his business model is changing continuously to reflect the way Internet breakthoughs are able to deliver movies more conveniently to a consumer's TV set.[23]

Goals **Goals** or **objectives** (terms used interchangeably in the textbook) are statements of an accomplishment of a task to be achieved, often by a specific time. For example, Netflix may have the goal of being the top provider of online movies by 2011. Goals convert an organization's mission and business into long- and short-term performance targets to measure how well it is doing (see Figure 2–2).

Business firms can pursue several different types of goals:

- *Profit.* Most firms seek to maximize profits—to get as high a financial return on their investments (ROI) as possible.
- *Sales* (dollars or units). If profits are acceptable, a firm may elect to maintain or increase its sales even though profits may not be maximized.
- *Market share.* **Market share** is the ratio of sales revenue of the firm to the total sales revenue of all firms in the industry, including the firm itself. A firm may choose to maintain or increase its market share, sometimes at the expense of greater profits if industry status or prestige is at stake.
- *Quality.* A firm may offer the highest quality, as Medtronic does with its implantable medical devices.

- *Customer satisfaction.* Customers are the reason the organization exists, so their perceptions and actions are of vital importance. Satisfaction can be measured with surveys or by the number of customer complaints it receives.
- *Employee welfare.* A firm may recognize the critical importance of its employees by stating its goal of providing them with good employment opportunities and working conditions.
- *Social responsibility.* Firms may seek to balance the conflicting goals of stakeholders to promote their overall welfare, even at the expense of profits.

Nonprofit organizations (such as museums and hospitals) also have goals, such as to serve consumers as efficiently as possible. Similarly, government agencies set goals that seek to serve the public good.

Organizational Strategies: How Will It Do It?

As shown in Figure 2–2, the organizational foundation sets the "why" of organizations and organizational direction sets the "what." To convert these into actual results, the organizational strategies are concerned with the "how." These organizational strategies vary in at least two ways, partly depending on the level in the organization and the offerings it provides customers:

Variation by Level Moving from the corporate to the strategic business unit to the functional level involves creating increasingly detailed strategies and plans. For example, at the corporate level, top managers may struggle with writing a meaningful mission statement, while at the functional level the issue may involve whether Joan or Adam makes the sales call tomorrow.

Variation by Offering Organizational strategies also vary by the organization's offering. The strategy will be far different when marketing a very tangible physical product (a Medtronic heart pacemaker), a service (Southwest Airlines flight), or an idea (donate to the American Red Cross).

The remainder of Chapter 2 covers many aspects of developing these organizational strategies.

learning review

3. What is the meaning of an organization's mission?
4. What is the difference between an organization's business and its goals?

LO3

Tracking Strategic Performance with Marketing Dashboards

Although marketing managers can set strategic directions for their organizations, how do they know if they are making progress in getting there? One answer is to measure performance by using marketing dashboards.

Car Dashboards and Marketing Dashboards A **marketing dashboard** is the visual computer display of the essential information related to achieving a marketing objective.[24] Often, it is an Internet-based display with real-time information and active hyperlinks to provide further detail. An example is when a chief marketing officer (CMO) wants to see daily what the effect of a new TV advertising campaign is on a product's sales. This also increases the CMO's accountability in using marketing resources effectively.[25]

The idea of a marketing dashboard really comes from that of a car's dashboard. On a car's dashboard we glance at the fuel gauge and take action when our gas is getting low. With a marketing dashboard, a marketing manager glances at a

FIGURE 2–3
An effective marketing dashboard, like this one from Oracle, helps managers assess a business situation at a glance.

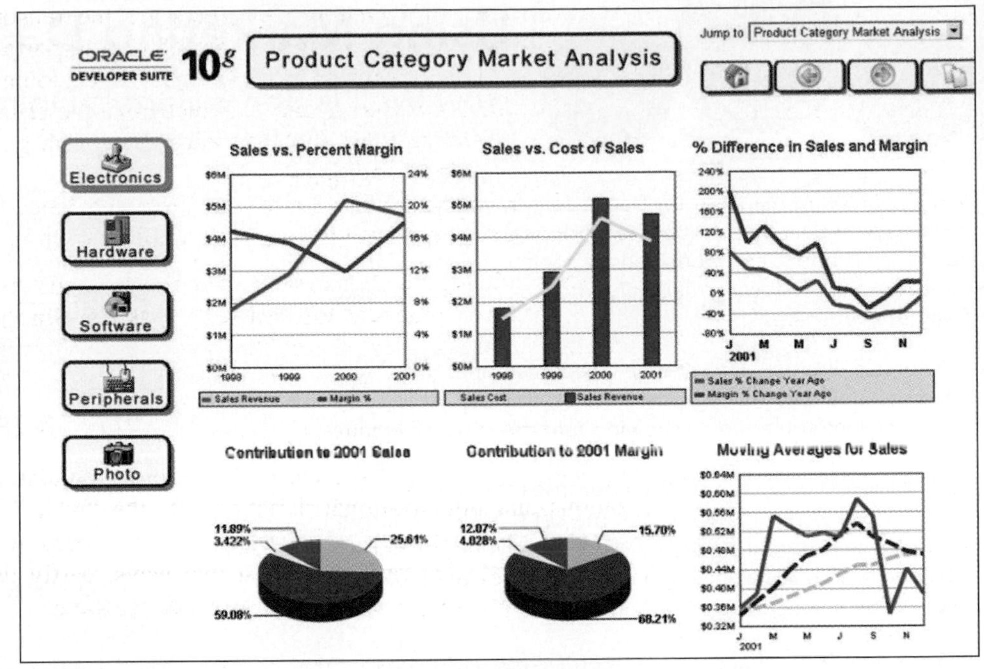

graph or table and makes a decision whether to take action or to analyze the problem further.[26]

Dashboards, Metrics, and Plans The marketing dashboard of Oracle, a large software firm, appears in Figure 2–3. It shows graphic displays of key performance measures of a product category such as sales versus cost of sales.[27] Each variable in a marketing dashboard is a **marketing metric**, which is a measure of the quantitative value or trend of a marketing activity or result.[28] The choice of which marketing metrics to display is critical for a busy marketing manager, who can be overwhelmed with too much or with inappropriate information.[29]

Dashboard designers take great care to show graphs and tables in easy-to-understand formats to enable clear interpretation at a glance.[30] The Oracle marketing dashboard, in Figure 2–3 presents several marketing metrics on the computer screen. The three-step "challenge-findings-action" format in the Using Marketing Dashboards box for Ben & Jerry's on the next page is the one used throughout the textbook. This format stresses the importance of using marketing dashboards and the metrics contained within them to produce effective marketing strategy and program actions. The Ben & Jerry's dashboard shows that both its dollar sales and dollar market share grew from 2008 to 2009.

Most organizations tie the marketing metrics they track in their marketing dashboards to the quantitative objectives established in their **marketing plan**, which is a road map for the marketing activities of an organization for a specified future time period, such as one year or five years. The planning phase of the strategic marketing process (discussed later in this chapter) usually results in a marketing plan that sets the direction for the marketing activities of an organization.

Appendix A at the end of this chapter provides guidelines for writing a marketing plan and also presents a sample marketing plan for Paradise Kitchens® Inc., a firm that produces and distributes a line of spicy chili under the Howlin' Coyote® brand name. Appendix A also links each section of the marketing plan to the relevant textbook chapter to assist students who are writing marketing plans.

Using Marketing Dashboards

How Well Is Ben & Jerry's Doing?

As the marketing manager for Ben & Jerry's, you have been asked to provide a snapshot of the firm's total super-premium ice cream product line performance for the United States. You choose the following marketing metrics: dollar sales and dollar market share.

Your Challenge Information Resources, Inc. (IRI), provides scanner data from grocery stores and other retailers. It has just sent you a report showing that the total ice cream sales for 2009 were $25 billion. Of that total, 5 percent or $1.25 billion (0.05 × $25 billion) comprises the super-premium category—the segment of the market that Ben & Jerry's competes in. Internal company data show you that Ben & Jerry's sold 50 million units at an average price of $5.00 per unit in 2009.

Your Findings Each of the metrics you chose (dollar sales and dollar market share) are goals that firms such as Ben & Jerry's use to measure performance. They can be calculated for 2009 using simple formulas and displayed on the Ben & Jerry's marketing dashboard as follows:

$$\text{Dollar sales (\$)} = \text{Average price} \times \text{Quantity sold} = \$5.00 \times 50 \text{ million units} = \$250 \text{ million}$$

$$\text{Dollar market share (\%)} = \frac{\text{Ben \& Jerry's sales (\$)}}{\text{Total industry sales (\$)}} = \frac{\$250 \text{ million}}{\$1.25 \text{ billion}} = 0.20 \text{ or } 20\%$$

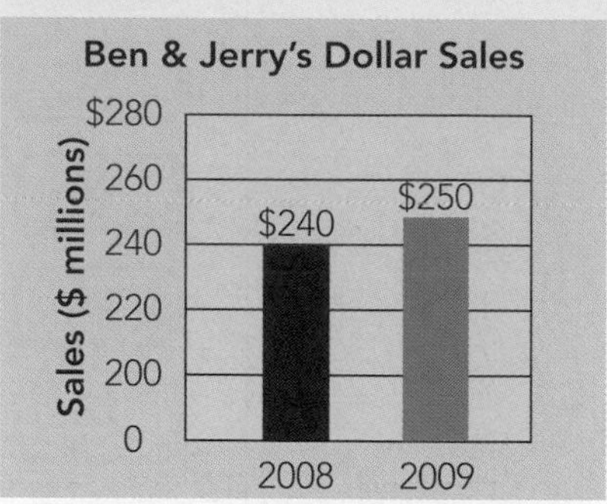

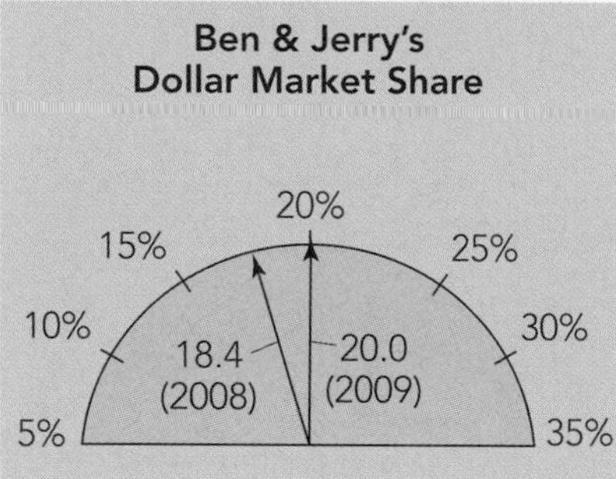

Your dashboard displays show that from 2008 to 2009 dollar sales increased from $240 million to $250 million and that dollar market share grew from 18.4 to 20.0 percent.

Your Action The results need to be compared with the goals established for these metrics. In addition, they should be compared with previous years' results to see if the trends are increasing, flat, or decreasing. NOTE: Marketers also find it useful to calculate market share based on the number of units sold, if data are available.

SETTING STRATEGIC DIRECTIONS

To set a strategic direction, an organization needs to answer two difficult questions: (1) Where are we now? (2) Where do we want to go?

A Look Around: Where Are We Now?

Asking an organization where it is at the present time involves identifying its competencies, customers, and competitors.

Competencies Senior managers must ask the question: What do we do best? The answer involves an assessment of the organization's core *competencies*, which are its special capabilities—the skills, technologies, and resources—that distinguish

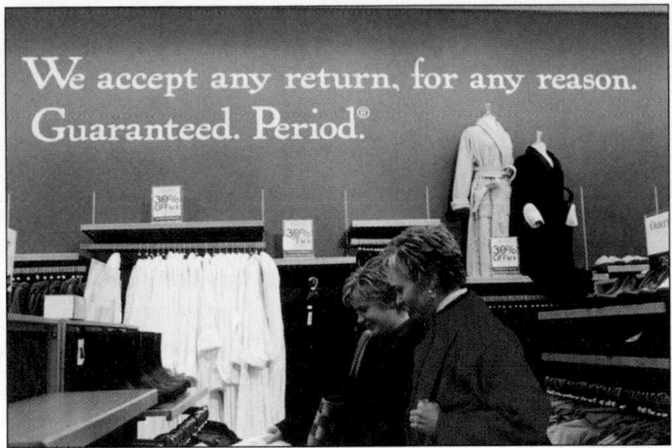

Lands' End's unconditional guarantee for its products highlights its focus on customers.

it from other organizations and provide customer value. Exploiting these competencies can lead to success.[31] Medtronic's competencies include world-class technology, training, and service that respond to life-threatening medical needs. *BusinessWeek* magazine calls Medtronic "the standard setter for quality."[32] Competencies should be distinctive enough to provide a **competitive advantage**, a unique strength relative to competitors that provides superior returns, often based on quality, time, cost, or innovation.[33]

Customers Ben & Jerry's customers are ice cream and frozen yogurt eaters who have different preferences (form, flavor, health, and convenience). Medtronic's customers are cardiologists and heart surgeons who serve patients. Lands' End communicates a remarkable commitment about its customer experience and product quality with these unconditional words:

Guaranteed. Period.®

The Lands' End Web site points out that this guarantee has always been an unconditional one. It reads: "If you're not satisfied with any item, simply return it to us at any time for an exchange or refund of its purchase price." But to get the message across more clearly to its customers, it created the two-word guarantee. The point is that Lands' End's strategy must provide genuine value to customers to ensure that they have a satisfying experience.[34]

Competitors In today's global competition, the distinctions among competitors are increasingly blurred. Lands' End started as a catalog retailer. But today, Lands' End competes with not only other clothing catalog retailers but also traditional department stores, mass merchandisers, and specialty shops. Even well-known clothing brands such as Liz Claiborne now have their own chain stores. Although only some of the clothing in any of these stores directly competes with Lands' End offerings, all these retailers have Web sites to sell their offerings over the Internet. This means there's a lot of competition out there.

Growth Strategies: Where Do We Want to Go?

Knowing where the organization is at the present time enables managers to set a direction for the firm and allocate resources to move in that direction. Two techniques

Kodak today must make a series of difficult marketing decisions. From what you know about cameras and photos, assess Kodak's sales opportunities for the four products shown here. For some possible answers and a way to show these opportunities graphically, see the text and Figure 2–4.

Kodak digital cameras

Kodak digital picture frames

Kodak ink-jet printers and cartridges to print photos at home

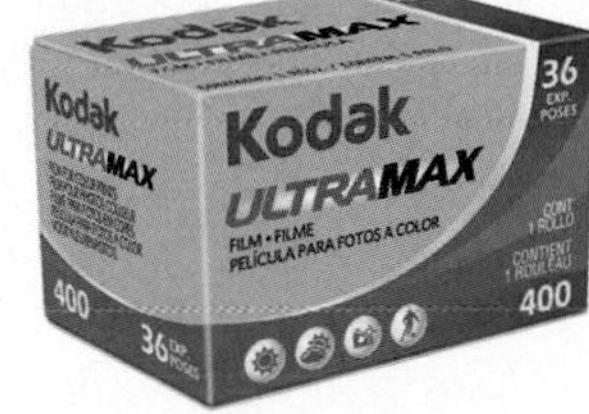

Kodak film

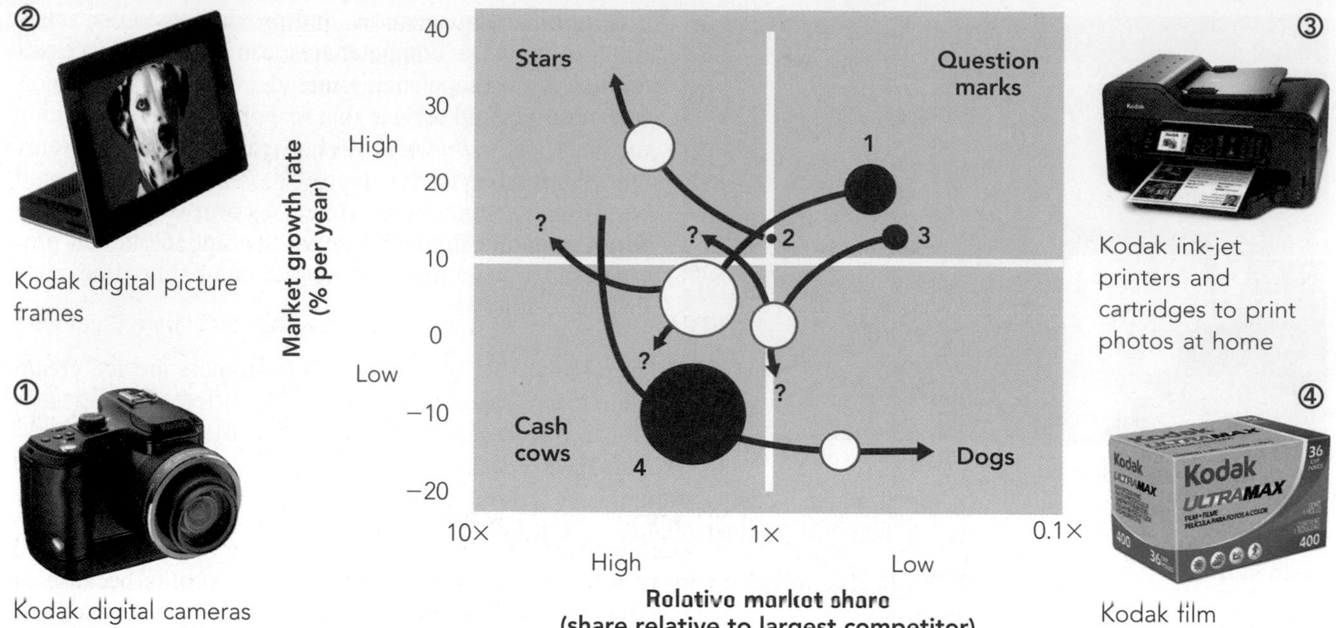

FIGURE 2–4
Boston Consulting Group business portfolio analysis for Kodak's consumer-related SBUs as they appeared in 2003 (solid red circle) and might appear in 2010 (white circle).

to aid managers with these decisions are (1) business portfolio analysis and (2) diversification analysis strategies.

Business Portfolio Analysis The Boston Consulting Group (BCG), a nationally known management consulting firm, uses **business portfolio analysis** to quantify performance measures and growth targets to analyze its clients' strategic business units (SBUs) as though they were a collection of separate investments.[35] The purpose of the tool is to determine the appeal of each SBU or offering and then determine the amount of cash, if any, each should receive. The BCG analysis can also be applied at the offering, product, or brand level. More than 75 percent of the largest U.S. firms have used this analytical tool.

The BCG business portfolio analysis requires an organization to locate the position of each of its SBUs on a growth-share matrix (see Figure 2–4). The vertical axis is the *market growth rate*, which is the annual rate of growth of the SBU's industry. The horizontal axis is the *relative market share*, defined as the sales of the SBU divided by the sales of the largest firm in the industry. A relative market share of 10× (at the left end of the scale) means that the SBU has 10 times the share of its largest competitor, whereas a share of 0.1× (at the right end of the scale) means it has only 10 percent of the share of its largest competitor.

The BCG has given specific names and descriptions to the four resulting quadrants in its growth-share matrix based on the amount of cash they generate for or require from the organization:

- *Cash cows* are SBUs that generate large amounts of cash, far more than they can invest profitably in themselves. They have dominant shares of slow-growth markets and provide cash to cover the organization's overhead and to invest in other SBUs.
- *Stars* are SBUs with a high share of high-growth markets that may need extra cash to finance their own rapid future growth. When their growth slows, they are likely to become cash cows.

- *Question marks* are SBUs with a low share of high-growth markets. They require large injections of cash just to maintain their market share, much less increase it. The name implies management's dilemma for these SBUs: choosing the right ones to invest in and phasing out the rest.
- *Dogs* are SBUs with low shares of slow-growth markets. Although they may generate enough cash to sustain themselves, they do not hold the promise of ever becoming real winners for the organization. Dropping SBUs that are dogs may be required, except when relationships with other SBUs, competitive considerations, or potential strategic alliances exist.[36]

An organization's SBUs often start as question marks and go counterclockwise around Figure 2–4 to become stars, then cash cows, and finally dogs. Because an organization has limited influence on the market growth rate, its main alternative is to try to change its relative market share. To accomplish this, management decides what role each SBU should have in the future and either injects or removes cash from it.

Kodak provides an example of how new technology and changing consumer tastes force a company to convert a crisis into potential long-run opportunities.[37] Until 2000, Kodak relied on its film for the bulk of its revenues and profits because of the billions of photos taken every year. The company made money on repeat business from traditional film sales and *not* on camera purchases. The appearance of digital cameras radically changed Kodak's business forever as film sales began to evaporate.

Four Kodak SBUs (see the solid red circles in Figure 2–4) are shown as they may have appeared in 2003 and can serve as an example of BCG analysis. The area of each solid red circle in Figure 2–4 is roughly proportional to the SBU's 2003 sales revenue. In a more complete analysis, Kodak's other SBUs would be included. This example also shows the agonizing strategic decisions that executives must make in an industry facing profound change—the situation Kodak confronted due to the arrival of digital technology.

The success of Kodak's new digital strategy and its product lines shown in Figure 2–4 depends on how millions of consumers (1) take photos and convert them into printed or online images in the coming years and (2) continue to be affected by the global economic recession. Here is a snapshot of where sales revenues were for four Kodak consumer product lines in 2003 (the solid red circles) and where they now appear headed in 2010 (the white circles).

1. *Kodak digital cameras.* In 2008, about 80 percent of U.S. consumers owned a digital camera because it is now easier to use than a film camera, is cheaper, and allows images to be uploaded and shared online. But Kodak's digital camera sales may flatten due to high household penetration, the economic downturn, and increased competition. Kodak remains No. 3 in market share behind Canon and Sony. Today more women are buying digital cameras because they are small and light. Bottom line: Kodak expects this SBU to continue to be a *cash cow*, with its new digital camera models generating mainly replacement sales.[38]
2. *Kodak digital picture frames.* In 2007, Kodak introduced a line of digital picture frames that allowed consumers to upload, store, and view digital images. In 2008, Kodak expanded its line with more than 10 items ranging in price from $60 to $230. And in 2009, it introduced the $999 OLED (organic light-emitting diode) digital picture frame that features a high-resolution flat-panel display to present extremely sharp photo images. Global demand has exploded, and today Kodak is the market leader—clearly a *star*. By 2012, sales could approach 50 million units.[39]
3. *Kodak ink-jet printers and cartridges to print digital photos at home.* In 2008, the ink-jet printer market dramatically changed as consumers shifted from single-purpose to multi-function machines designed to print photos, make

copies, scan images, and send faxes. Today Kodak now offers only multifunction models. Moreover, Kodak's high-quality ink cartridges make photos at half the cost of Hewlett-Packard's (HP) printers. The result: In two short years, Kodak has sold over 1 million printers. Consumers buy an average of eight ink cartridges a year. Because HP is the entrenched 300-pound gorilla in this market, the future of this *question mark* could evolve into a *star* if Kodak is able to double or triple unit sales. Or this SBU may turn into a *dog* because online printing and sharing have taken off and may soon reach $1 billion.[40]

4. *Kodak film.* An $8 billion *cash cow* in 2003, Kodak film sales were the company's biggest single source of revenue. Now in a free fall because of digital cameras, Kodak film sales dropped to $3 billion in 2008, moving it from being a *cash cow* to a potential *dog*. Kodak stopped producing its Kodachrome slides in late 2009. Experts believe film sales will evaporate by 2012.[41]

How can Ben & Jerry's develop new products and social responsibility programs that contribute to its mission? The text describes how the strategic marketing process and its SWOT analysis can help.

The primary strength of business portfolio analysis lies in forcing a firm to place each of its SBUs in the growth-share matrix, which in turn suggests which SBUs will be cash producers and cash users in the future. Weaknesses of this analysis arise from the difficulty in (1) getting the needed information and (2) incorporating competitive data into business portfolio analysis.[42]

Diversification Analysis **Diversification analysis** is a tool that helps a firm search for growth opportunities from among current and new markets as well as current and new products.[43] For any market, there is both a current product (what the firm now sells) and a new product (what the firm might sell in the future). And for any product there is both a current market (the firm's existing customers) and a new market (the firm's potential customers). As Ben & Jerry's attempts to increase sales revenues, it must consider all four of the market-product strategies shown in Figure 2–5:

- *Market penetration* is a marketing strategy to increase sales of current products in current markets, such as Ben & Jerry's current ice cream products to U.S. consumers. There is no change in either the basic product line or the markets served. Increased sales are generated by selling either more ice cream (through better promotion or distribution) *or* the same amount of ice cream at a higher price to its current customers.
- *Market development* is a marketing strategy to sell current products to new markets. For Ben & Jerry's, Brazil is an attractive new market. There is good news and bad news for this strategy: As household incomes of Brazilians increase, consumers can buy more ice cream; however, the Ben & Jerry's brand may be unknown to Brazilian consumers.

FIGURE 2–5
Four market-product strategies: alternative ways to expand sales revenues for Ben & Jerry's using diversification analysis.

Markets	PRODUCTS: Current	PRODUCTS: New
Current	**Market penetration** Selling more Ben & Jerry's super-premium ice cream to Americans	**Product development** Selling a new product such as children's clothing under the Ben & Jerry's brand to Americans
New	**Market development** Selling Ben & Jerry's super-premium ice cream to Brazilians for the first time	**Diversification** Selling a new product such as children's clothing under the Ben & Jerry's brand to Brazilians for the first time

- *Product development* is a marketing strategy of selling new products to current markets. Ben & Jerry's could leverage its brand by selling children's clothing in the United States. This strategy is risky because Americans may not see a clear connection between the company's expertise in ice cream and children's clothing.
- *Diversification* is a marketing strategy of developing new products and selling them in new markets. This is a potentially high-risk strategy for Ben & Jerry's because the firm has neither previous production nor marketing experience on which to draw to market the offerings to Brazilian consumers.

learning review

5. What is the difference between a marketing dashboard and a marketing metric?
6. What is business portfolio analysis?
7. Explain the four market-product strategies in diversification analysis.

THE STRATEGIC MARKETING PROCESS

After an organization assesses where it is and where it wants to go, other questions emerge, such as:

1. How do we allocate our resources to get where we want to go?
2. How do we convert our plans into actions?
3. How do results compare with our plans, and do deviations require new plans?

To answer these questions, an organization uses the **strategic marketing process**, whereby an organization allocates its marketing mix resources to reach its target markets. This process is divided into three phases: planning, implementation, and evaluation, as shown in Figure 2–6.

FIGURE 2–6
The strategic marketing process has three vital phases: planning, implementation, and evaluation. The figure also shows where these phases are discussed in the text.

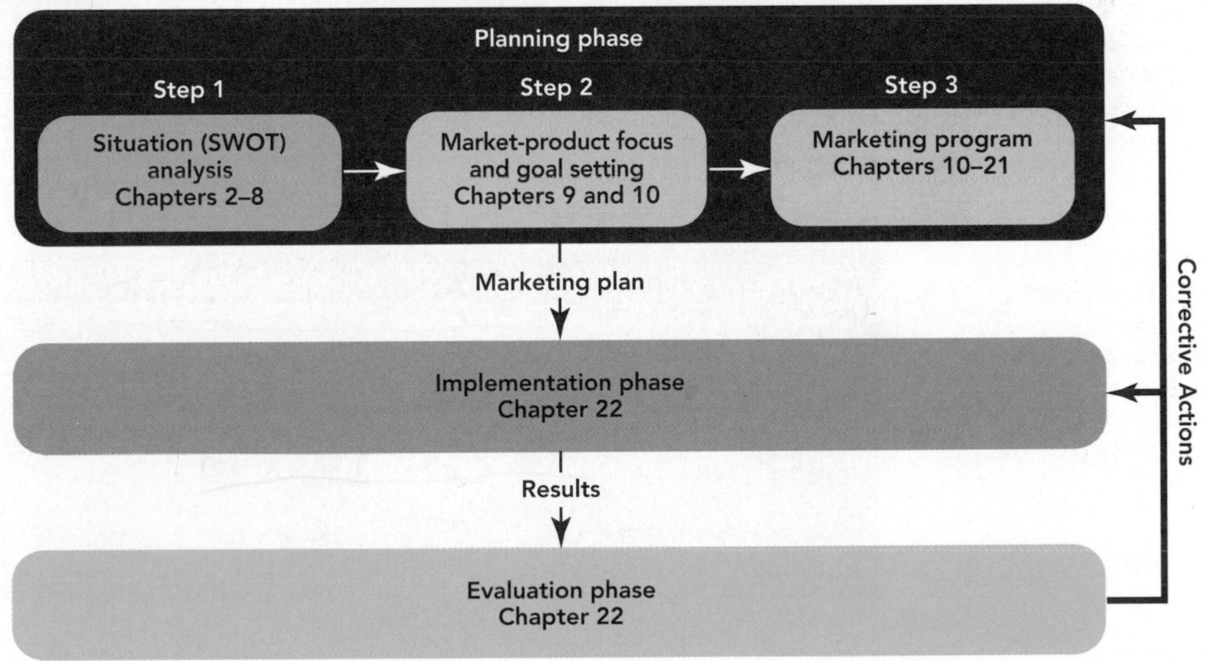

The Planning Phase of the Strategic Marketing Process

LO5

Figure 2–6 shows the three steps in the planning phase of the strategic marketing process: (1) situation (SWOT) analysis, (2) market-product focus and goal setting, and (3) the marketing program.

Step 1: Situation (SWOT) Analysis The essence of **situation analysis** is taking stock of where the firm or product has been recently, where it is now, and where it is headed in terms of the organization's marketing plans and the external forces and trends affecting it. The situation (SWOT) analysis box in Figure 2–6 is the first of the three steps in the planning phase. An effective summary of a situation analysis is a **SWOT analysis**, an acronym describing an organization's appraisal of its internal **S**trengths and **W**eaknesses and its external **O**pportunities and **T**hreats.

The SWOT analysis is based on an exhaustive study of four areas that form the foundation upon which the firm builds its marketing program:

- Identify trends in the organization's industry.
- Analyze the organization's competitors.
- Assess the organization itself.
- Research the organization's present and prospective customers.

Assume you are responsible for doing the SWOT analysis for Unilever, Ben & Jerry's parent company shown in Figure 2–7. Note that the SWOT table has four cells formed by the combination of internal versus external factors (the rows) and favorable versus unfavorable factors (the columns) that identify Ben & Jerry's strengths, weaknesses, opportunities, and threats.

The task is not simply to conduct a SWOT analysis but to translate its results into specific actions to help the firm grow and succeed. The ultimate goal is to identify the *critical* strategy-related factors that impact the firm and then build on vital strengths, correct glaring weaknesses, exploit significant opportunities, and avoid disaster-laden threats.

The Ben and Jerry's SWOT analysis in Figure 2–7 can be the basis for these kinds of specific actions. An action in each of the four cells might be:

FIGURE 2–7
Ben & Jerry's: a SWOT analysis to keep it growing. The picture painted in this SWOT analysis is the basis for management actions.

Location of Factor	TYPE OF FACTOR	
	Favorable	Unfavorable
Internal	**Strengths** • Prestigious, well-known brand name among U.S. consumers • Complements Unilever's other ice cream brands • Recognized for its social mission, values, and actions	**Weaknesses** • B&J's social responsibility actions could reduce focus • Experienced managers needed to help growth • Modest sales growth and profits in recent years
External	**Opportunities** • Growing demand for quality ice cream in overseas markets • Increasing U.S. demand for 100-calorie novelties such as cones and bars • Many U.S. firms successfully use product and brand extensions	**Threats** • B&J customers read nutritional labels and are concerned with sugary and fatty desserts • Competes with General Mills and Nestlé brands • Increasing competition in international markets

- *Build on a strength.* Find specific efficiencies in distribution with Unilever's existing ice cream brands.
- *Correct a weakness.* Recruit experienced managers from other consumer product firms to help stimulate growth.
- *Exploit an opportunity.* Develop new product lines of low-fat, low-carb frozen yogurts and sorbets as well as 100-calorie novelty items to respond to consumer health concerns.[44]
- *Avoid a disaster-laden threat.* Focus on less risky international markets, such as Canada and Mexico.

Step 2: Market-Product Focus and Goal Setting Determining which products will be directed toward which customers (step 2 of the planning phase in Figure 2–6) is essential for developing an effective marketing program (step 3). This decision is often based on **market segmentation**, which involves aggregating prospective buyers into groups, or segments, that (1) have common needs and (2) will respond similarly to a marketing action. This enables an organization to identify the segments on which it will focus its efforts—its target market segments—and develop specific marketing programs to reach them.

As always, understanding the customer is essential. In the case of Medtronic, executives researched a potential new market in Asia by talking extensively with doctors in India and China. They learned that these doctors saw some of the current state-of-the-art features of heart pacemakers as less essential and too expensive. Instead, they wanted an affordable pacemaker that was reliable and easy to implant. This information led Medtronic to develop and market a new product, the Champion heart pacemaker, directed at the needs of these Asian market segments.

Goal setting involves setting measurable marketing objectives to be achieved. For a specific market, the goal may be to introduce a new product, such as Medtronic's Champion pacemaker in Asia or Toyota's launch of its Prius hybrid car in the United States. For a specific brand or product, the goal may be to create a promotional campaign or pricing strategy to get more consumers to purchase.

Let's examine Medtronic's five-year plan to reach the "affordable and reliable" segment of the pacemaker market:[45]

- *Set marketing and product goals.* The chances of new-product success are increased by specifying both market and product goals. Based on their market research showing the need for a reliable yet affordable pacemaker, Medtronic executives set the following as their goal: Design and market such a pacemaker in the next three years that could be manufactured in China for the Asian market.
- *Select target markets.* The Champion pacemaker will be targeted at cardiologists and medical clinics performing heart surgery in India, China, and other Asian countries.
  - *Find points of difference.* **Points of difference** are those characteristics of a product that make it superior to competitive substitutes. Just as a competitive advantage is a unique strength of an entire organization compared to its competitors, points of difference are unique characteristics of one of its products that make it superior to competitive products it faces in the marketplace. For the Champion pacemaker, the key points of difference are *not* the state-of-the-art features that drive up production costs and are important to only a minority of patients. Instead, they are high quality, long life, reliability, ease of use, and low cost.
  - *Position the product.* The pacemaker will be "positioned" in cardiologists' and patients' minds as a medical device that is high

The Champion: Medtronic's high-quality, long-life, low-cost heart pacemaker for Asian market segments.

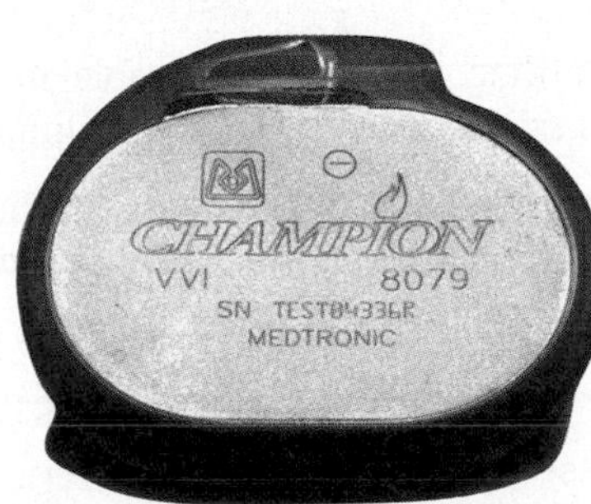

FIGURE 2–8
The 4 Ps elements of the marketing mix must be blended to produce a cohesive marketing program.

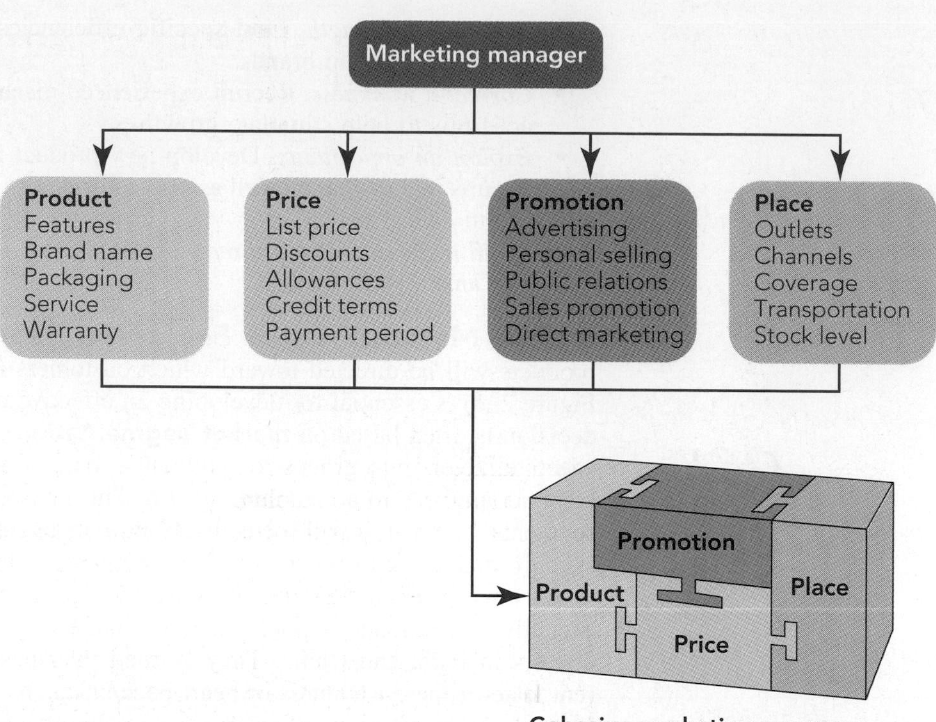

quality and reliable with a long, nine-year life. The name Champion was selected after testing acceptable names among doctors in India, China, Pakistan, Singapore, and Malaysia. So step 2 provides a solid foundation to use in developing the marketing program, step 3 in the planning phase of the strategic marketing process.

Step 3: Marketing Program Activities in step 2 tell the marketing manager which customers to target and which customer needs the firm's product offerings can satisfy—the *who* and *what* aspects of the strategic marketing process. The *how* aspect—step 3 in the planning phase—involves developing the program's marketing mix (the 4 Ps) and its budget. Figure 2–8 shows that each marketing mix element is combined to provide a cohesive marketing program. The five-year marketing plan of Medtronic's Champion pacemaker includes these marketing mix activities:

- *Product strategy.* Offer a Champion brand heart pacemaker with features needed by Asian patients.
- *Price strategy.* Manufacture the Champion to control costs so that it can be priced below $1,000 (in U.S. dollars)—an affordable price for Asian markets.
- *Promotion strategy.* Feature demonstrations at cardiologist and medical conventions across Asia to introduce the Champion and highlight the device's features and application.
- *Place (distribution) strategy.* Search out, utilize, and train reputable medical device distributors across Asia to call on cardiologists and medical clinics.

Putting this marketing program into effect requires that the firm commit time and money to it in the form of a sales forecast (see Chapter 8) and budget that must be approved by top management.

learning review

8. What are the three steps of the planning phase of the strategic marketing process?
9. What are points of difference and why are they important?

The Implementation Phase of the Strategic Marketing Process

LO6

As shown in Figure 2–6, the result of the tens or hundreds of hours spent in the planning phase of the strategic marketing process is the firm's marketing plan. Implementation, the second phase of the strategic marketing process, involves carrying out the marketing plan that emerges from the planning phase. If the firm cannot put the marketing plan into effect—in the implementation phase—the planning phase was a waste of time.

There are four components of the implementation phase: (1) obtaining resources, (2) designing the marketing organization, (3) developing planning schedules, and (4) actually executing the marketing program designed in the planning phase. Kodak provides a case example.

Kodak's new Zi6 pocket video camera can upload its videos to YouTube.

Obtaining Resources In 2003, Kodak announced a bold plan to reenergize the film marketer for the new age of digital cameras and prints. Kodak needed huge sums of cash to implement the plan. So by early 2009, it had sold or transformed several of its SBUs that provided over $300 billion to develop and market new products, such as the exciting Zi6 pocket video camera, which takes HD quality videos that can be uploaded to YouTube.[46]

Designing the Marketing Organization A marketing program needs a marketing organization to implement it. Figure 2–9 shows the organization chart of a typical manufacturing firm, giving some details of the marketing department's structure. Four managers of marketing activities are shown to report to the vice president of marketing. Several regional sales managers and an international sales manager may report to the manager of sales. The product or brand managers and their subordinates help plan, implement, and evaluate the marketing plans for their offerings. However, the entire marketing organization is responsible for converting these marketing plans to reality as part of the corporate marketing team.

Developing Planning Schedules To implement marketing plans, members of the marketing department hold meetings to identify the tasks that need to be done, the

FIGURE 2–9
Organization of a typical manufacturing firm, showing a breakdown of the marketing department.

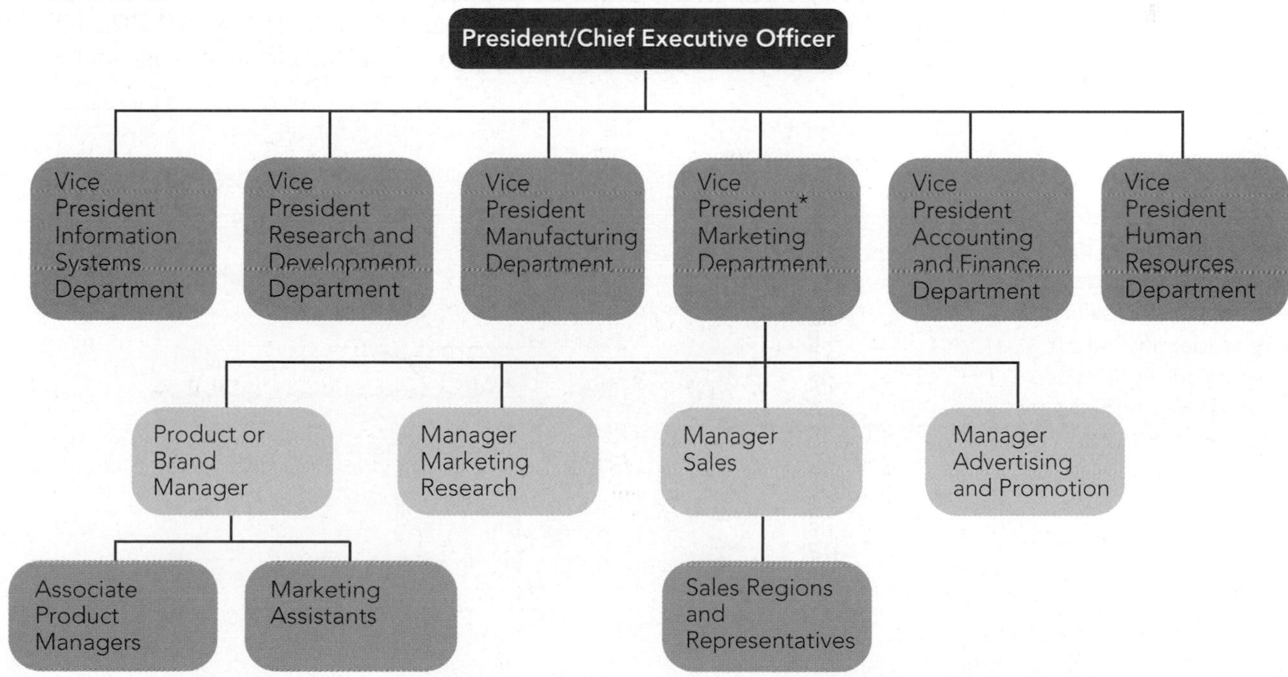

time to allocate to each one, the people responsible, and the deadlines for their accomplishment. In most cases, each team member works on different parts of the plan.

Executing the Marketing Program Marketing plans are meaningless pieces of paper without effective execution of those plans. This effective execution requires attention to detail for both marketing strategies and marketing tactics. A **marketing strategy** is the means by which a marketing goal is to be achieved, usually characterized by a specified target market and a marketing program to reach it. The term implies both the end sought (target market) and the means to achieve it (marketing program). At this marketing strategy level, Kodak will seek to increase sales of digital cameras, ink-jet printers, and digital picture frames.

To implement a marketing program successfully, hundreds of detailed decisions are often required. These decisions, called **marketing tactics**, are detailed day-to-day operational decisions essential to the overall success of marketing strategies. At Kodak, writing ads and setting prices for its new lines of digital cameras are examples of marketing tactics.

The Evaluation Phase of the Strategic Marketing Process

The evaluation phase of the strategic marketing process seeks to keep the marketing program moving in the direction set for it (see Figure 2–6). Accomplishing this requires the marketing manager to (1) compare the results of the marketing program with the goals in the written plans to identify deviations and (2) act on these deviations—correcting negative deviations and exploiting positive ones.

Comparing Results with Plans to Identify Deviations Suppose you are on a Kodak task force in 2003 responsible for making plans through 2010. You observe that Kodak's sales revenues from 1998 through 2003, or AB in Figure 2–10, exhibit a very flat trend. Extending the 1998–2003 trend to 2010 along BC shows very flat sales revenues, a totally unacceptable, no-growth strategy.

Kodak's growth target of 5 to 6 percent annually, the line BD in Figure 2–10, would give sales revenues of $16 billion in 2006 and $20 billion in 2010. This reveals a wedge-shaped shaded gap in the figure. Planners call this the *planning gap*, the difference between the projection of the path to reach a new goal (line BD) and the projection of the path of the results of a plan already in place (line BC). The ultimate purpose of the firm's marketing program is to "fill in" this planning gap—in the case

FIGURE 2–10
The evaluation phase of the strategic marketing process requires that the organization compare actual results with goals to identify and act on deviations to fill in its "planning gap." The text describes how Kodak hopes to fill in its planning gap by 2010.

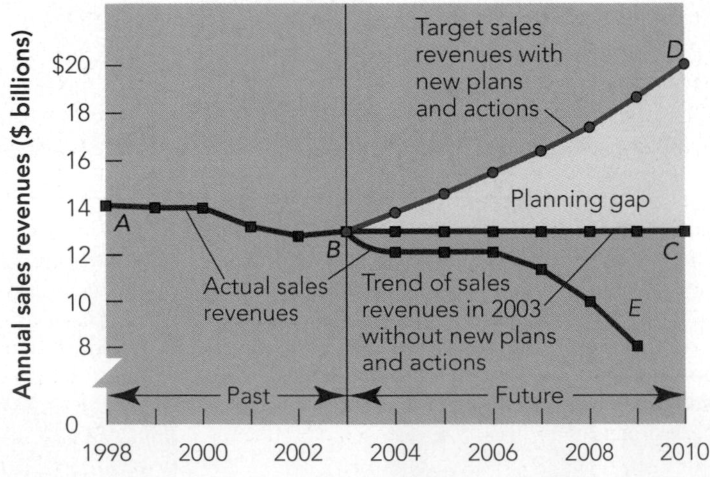

To help fill in its planning gap, Kodak is pursuing opportunities for sales of digital cameras in France.

of your Kodak task force, to move its future sales revenue line from the no-growth line BC up to the challenging target of line BD. But poor performance can result in actual sales revenues being far less than the targeted levels, the actual situation faced by Kodak in 2009 (line BE), where sales were expected to be about $8 billion. This is the essence of evaluation: comparing actual results with goals set.

In this example, the Kodak task force in 2003 used trend extrapolation to project the historic trend through 2010. But as shown by the discrepancy between line BC (the trend extrapolation) and BE (Kodak's actual annual sales revenues), serious forecasting problems can occur. In this case, Kodak failed to anticipate the drastic decline in sales of its film and film cameras.

Acting on Deviations When evaluation shows that actual performance failed to meet expectations, managers need to take corrective actions. Two possible Kodak midcourse corrections for both positive and negative deviations from targets illustrate these management actions your Kodak task force might take in 2009:[47]

- *Exploiting a positive deviation.* If Kodak's innovative digital cameras sell better than expected, Kodak might try to move quickly to offer these to international customers—such as those in France.
- *Correcting a negative deviation.* However, if Panasonic is able to surpass Kodak in global market share of digital cameras, Kodak may need to reduce prices.

Kodak also might (1) develop more feature-laden digital cameras that use its proprietary sensor technologies that improve image (picture) quality to (2) launch a new aggressive global marketing program that integrates its digital camera images into its Kodak digital picture frame.

learning review

10. What is the implementation phase of the strategic marketing process?
11. How do the goals set for a marketing program in the planning phase relate to the evaluation phase of the strategic marketing process?

LEARNING OBJECTIVES REVIEW

LO1 *Describe two kinds of organizations and the three levels of strategy in them.*
An organization is a legal entity of people who share a common mission. There are two kinds. One is a business firm that is a privately owned organization that serves its customers to earn a profit so that it can survive. The other is a nonprofit, nongovernmental organization that serves its customers but does not have profit as a goal. Most large business firms and nonprofit organizations are divided into three levels of strategy: (*a*) the corporate level, where top management directs overall strategy for the entire organization; (*b*) the strategic business unit level, where managers set a more specific strategic direction for their businesses to set value-creating opportunities; and (*c*) the functional level, where groups of specialists actually create value for the organization.

LO2 *Describe how core values, mission, organizational culture, business, and goals are important to organizations.*
Organizations exist to accomplish something for someone. To give organizations direction and focus, they continuously assess their core values, mission, organizational culture, business, and goals. Today's organizations specify their foundation, set a direction, and formulate strategies—"why," "what," and "how" factors, respectively. Core values are the organization's fundamental, passionate, and enduring principles that guide its conduct over time—what Enron forgot when it lost sight of its responsibilities to its stakeholders. The organization's mission is a statement of its function in society, often identifying its customers, markets, products, and technologies. Organizational culture is a set of values, ideas, attitudes, and norms of behavior that is learned and shared among the members of an

organization. To answer the question, "What business are we in?" an organization defines its "business"—the clear, broad, underlying industry category or market sector of its offering. Finally, the organization's goals (or objectives) are statements of an accomplishment of a task to be achieved, often by a specific time.

LO3 *Explain why managers use marketing dashboards and metrics.*
Marketing managers use marketing dashboards to visually display on a single computer screen the essential information to make a decision to take an action or further analyze a problem. This information consists of key performance measures of a product category, such as sales or market share, and is known as a marketing metric, which is a measure of the quantitative value or trend of a marketing activity or result. Most organizations tie their marketing metrics to the quantitative objectives established in their marketing plan, which is a road map for the marketing activities of an organization for a specified future time period, such as one year or five years.

LO4 *Discuss how an organization assesses where it is now and seeks to be.*
Managers of an organization ask two key questions to set a strategic direction. The first question, "Where are we now?" requires an organization to (*a*) reevaluate its competencies to ensure that its special capabilities still provide a competitive advantage; (*b*) assess its present and prospective customers to ensure they have a satisfying customer experience—the central goal of marketing today; and (*c*) analyze its current and potential competitors from a global perspective to determine whether it needs to redefine its business.

The second question, "Where do we want to go?" requires an organization to set a specific direction and allocate resources to move it in that direction. Business portfolio and diversification analyses help an organization do this. Managers use business portfolio analysis to assess its strategic business units (SBUs), product lines, or individual products as though they were a collection of separate investments (cash cows, stars, question marks, and dogs) to determine the amount of cash each should receive. Diversification analysis is a tool that helps managers use one or a combination of four strategies to increase revenues: market penetration (selling more of an existing product to existing markets); market development (selling an existing product to new markets); product development (selling a new product to existing markets); and diversification (selling new products to new markets).

LO5 *Explain the three steps of the planning phase of the strategic marketing process.*
An organization uses the strategic marketing process to allocate its marketing mix resources to reach its target markets. This process is divided into three phases: planning, implementation, and evaluation. The planning phase consists of: (*a*) a situation (SWOT) analysis, which involves taking stock of where the firm or product has been recently, where it is now, and where it is headed. This assessment focuses on the organization's internal factors (strengths and weaknesses) and the external forces and trends affecting it (opportunities and threats); (*b*) a market-product focus through market segmentation—grouping buyers into segments with common needs and similar responses to marketing programs—and goal setting, which in part requires creating points of difference—those characteristics of a product that make it superior to competitive substitutes; and (*c*) a marketing program that specifies the budget and activities (marketing strategies and tactics) for each marketing mix element.

LO6 *Describe the elements of the implementation and evaluation phases of the strategic marketing process.*
The implementation phase of the strategic marketing process carries out the marketing plan that emerges from the planning phase. It has four key elements: (*a*) obtaining resources; (*b*) designing the marketing organization to perform product management, marketing research, sales, and advertising and promotion activities; (*c*) developing schedules to identify the tasks that need to be done, the time that is allocated to each one, the people responsible for each task, and the deadlines for each task's accomplishment; and (*d*) executing the marketing strategies, which are the means by which marketing goals are to be achieved, and their associated marketing tactics, which are the detailed day-to-day operational decisions of a firm's marketing strategies. These are the marketing program actions a firm takes to achieve the goals set forth in its marketing plan.

The evaluation phase of the strategic marketing process seeks to keep the marketing program moving in the direction that was established in the marketing plan. This requires the marketing manager to compare the results from the marketing program with the marketing plan's goals to (*a*) identify deviations or "planning gaps" and (*b*) take corrective actions to exploit positive deviations or correct negative ones.

FOCUSING ON KEY TERMS

business p. 30
business portfolio analysis p. 36
competitive advantage p. 35
core values p. 29
corporate level p. 28
cross-functional teams p. 28
diversification analysis p. 38
functional level p. 28
goals p. 31
market segmentation p. 41
market share p. 31
marketing dashboard p. 32
marketing metric p. 33
marketing plan p. 33
marketing strategy p. 44
marketing tactics p. 44
mission p. 29
objectives p. 31
organizational culture p. 30
points of difference p. 41
profit p. 26
situation analysis p. 40
strategic business unit (SBU) p. 28
strategic marketing process p. 39
strategy p. 27
SWOT analysis p. 40

APPLYING MARKETING KNOWLEDGE

1 (*a*) Using Medtronic as an example, explain how a mission statement gives it a strategic direction. (*b*) Create a mission statement for your own career.
2 What competencies best describe (*a*) your college or university and (*b*) your favorite restaurant?
3 Why does a product often start as a question mark and then move counterclockwise around the BCG's growth-share matrix shown in Figure 2–4?
4 Select one strength, one weakness, one opportunity, and one threat from the Ben & Jerry's SWOT analysis shown in Figure 2–7. Suggest an action that a marketing manager there might take to address each factor.
5 What is the main result of each of the three phases of the strategic marketing process? (*a*) planning, (*b*) implementation, and (*c*) evaluation.
6 The goal-setting step in the planning phase of the strategic marketing process sets quantified objectives for use in the evaluation phase. What does a manager do if measured results are below objectives? Above objectives?

building your marketing plan

1 Read Appendix A, "Building an Effective Marketing Plan." Then write a 600-word executive summary for the Paradise Kitchens marketing plan using the numbered headings shown in the plan. When you have completed the draft of your own marketing plan, use what you learned in writing an executive summary for Paradise Kitchens to write a 600-word executive summary to go in the front of your own marketing plan.
2 Using Chapter 2 and Appendix A as guides, give focus to your marketing plan by (*a*) writing your mission statement in 25 words or less, (*b*) listing three nonfinancial goals and three financial goals, (*c*) writing your competitive advantage in 35 words or less, and (*d*) doing a SWOT analysis table.
3 Draw a simple organization chart for your organization.

video case 2 BP: Transforming Its Strategy "Beyond Petroleum"

"We want to get people to drive an extra block or cut across an extra lane of traffic to choose BP over its competitors," claims Ann Hand, senior vice president—Global Brand Marketing and Innovation (photo below).

BP, formerly known as British Petroleum, is one of the world's largest producers and marketers of petroleum products. Through innovative marketing and with a focus on the environment, BP has been transforming itself into a consumer-centric provider of energy products and services that are broader than just oil and gas.

KEY ELEMENTS IN BP'S "BEYOND PETROLEUM" TRANSFORMATION

Increased energy demand due to the growing economies of both the developed and developing countries as well as supply constraints have caused oil

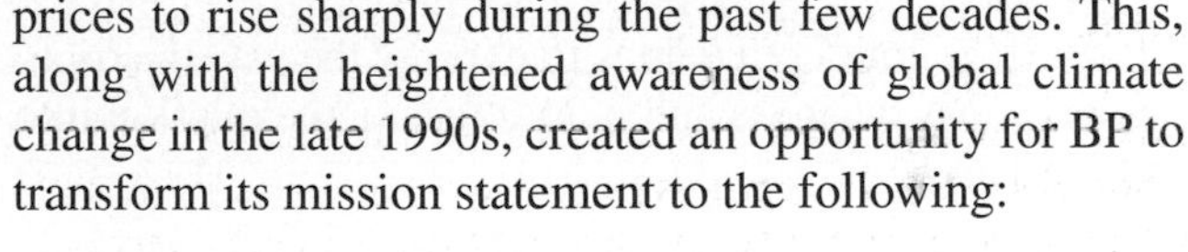

prices to rise sharply during the past few decades. This, along with the heightened awareness of global climate change in the late 1990s, created an opportunity for BP to transform its mission statement to the following:

> Our business is about finding, producing, and marketing the natural energy resources on which the modern world depends.

BP then reorganized itself primarily into two strategic performance (i.e., business) units to support its mission. These "SPUs" consist of activities related to the (1) discovery and production of oil and natural gas and (2) refining and marketing of petroleum products.

BP also identified and evaluated many opportunities to increase its sales and profits. One strategy was through acquisitions. During the late 1990s, BP invested $120 billion to add competitors Amoco, ARCO, and

Castrol to its business portfolio. BP now produces about 3 percent of the planet's oil and gas, operates in over 100 countries around the world, and serves 13 million customers per day at 24,600 retail sites, including 12,300 stations in the United States. The benefits to its stakeholders: BP global sales now exceed $360 billion.

In 2000, BP introduced a new brand identity to reflect the integrated company it had become. The BP shield and Amoco torch were replaced by a new Helios logo that more appropriately reflects BP's corporate and retail brand image as a green, environmentally friendly company. Because a brand image communicates the brand's essence—an emotional tie between the company and its customers—it provides confidence to customers: They know they can get high-quality gas, conveniently purchase food and beverages, and travel onwards refreshed. Thus, BP is not just about gasoline—it goes "beyond petroleum."

Within its refining and marketing SPU, BP sells gasoline at its branded retail gas stations, which include the BP, Amoco Ultimate, Wild Bean Café, BP Connect, and BP Express brands (eastern United States) and the ARCO and *am/pm* brands (western United States). In the near term, BP's retail strategy will focus on high-growth metropolitan areas in the United States through new and franchised service stations. In the long term, BP plans to transform the retail gasoline landscape with its new Helios House and Helios Power strategies.

BP'S FOUR CORE VALUES

BP specifies four core values to express the way the organization does business and help translate the mission into practical action:

- *Progressive:* BP is always looking for new and better ways to conduct business. It has developed a relationship with Ford to build hydrogen vehicles and fueling stations in California, Michigan, and elsewhere. BP also has reformulated its BP Amoco Ultimate fuel to reduce air pollutants.
- *Innovative:* Through the creative approaches of employees, and the development and application of cutting-edge drilling technology, BP seeks breakthrough solutions for its customers.
- *Green:* BP is committed to environmental leadership—the proactive and responsible treatment of the planet's natural resources and developing lower carbon emission energy sources. As a result, BP now stores its gasoline in double-skinned tanks to prevent spills and leaks.
- *Performance-driven:* BP sets the global standards of performance on financial and environmental dimensions, as well as safety, growth, and customer and employee satisfaction.

HELIOS HOUSE: TRANSFORMING BP'S GASOLINE RETAILING

Since 1977, the percentage of gasoline stations in the United States that also contain a convenience store has gone from 5 percent to more than 50 percent. To support the demand for convenience store offerings, BP developed a very successful convenience store concept called *am/pm*. This branded offering was created and tested on ARCO sites in the western United States; in the future, *am/pm* will partner with the BP retail brand and penetrate the eastern United States.

Currently, the *am/pm* stores sell both fuel and more than 2,000 convenience items (snacks, beverages, necessities, etc.). Sales from the more than 1,000 *am/pm* stores now exceed $6 billion; both the number and sales revenues are expected to grow significantly during the next several years as BP transforms many of its existing gas stations into *am/pm* stores.

In early 2007, BP launched a two-part strategy to change the way consumers think about its gas stations. One part was Helios House, a new-look gasoline station located in Los Angeles that will serve as a living laboratory to test ideas in a real environment (photo below). Ann Hand, who manages BP's $280 million global marketing programs, was instrumental in the planning and implementation of Helios House. Becoming operational during April 2007, Helios House was designed to be eco-friendly from the top down. The building itself was constructed from recycled, sustainable, and nontoxic materials. Moreover, its canopy has 90 solar panels to generate its own electricity. The roof is covered with grass to reduce the building's heating and cooling needs and has rain collectors to irrigate the surrounding drought-tolerant landscape. The facility also has energy-efficient lighting, using one-fifth less energy than a traditional gas station. As a result of these and other design features, Helios House became the first gas station to be certified as green by the U.S. Green Building Council.

Helios House also offers customers (1) clean, well-maintained restrooms, (2) friendly "green team" employees who will not only greet customers with a smile but also check their cars' tire pressure to ensure proper inflation—which boosts gas mileage, and (3) tips on creating a green lifestyle through its www.thegreencurve.com Web site. According to Kathy Seegebrecht, BP's U.S. advertising manager, "Helios House will serve as a place where BP can have a conversation with its customers about green ideas and how its gas station can play a part in creating a better environment. It was designed to serve as a beacon to inspire the employees and franchisees through the U.S."

Helios House is *not* a prototype of BP's station of the future. However, it will be an incubator of green ideas that can be implemented among its existing and new stations. It is just too costly to replace 25,000 existing stations throughout the world. Seegebrecht concludes, "Helios House is showing us that in a more brand-conscious world, where we all want the best of everything, people might actually want a better gas station." How successful has the Helios House been? "The site has nearly doubled its fuel volumes."

HELIOS POWER: BP'S PROMOTION OF ITS GASOLINE RETAILING

The second part of BP's strategy was a promotional campaign to transform BP's retail brand image at its locations in the United States. Buying gasoline is a low involvement purchase and consumers have low expectations regarding their purchase experiences. Armed with that consumer insight, BP created and executed the $45 million Helios Power advertising and brand-building campaign, which is an extension of BP's "Beyond Petroleum" corporate campaign that began in the early 2000s. The Helios Power campaign consisted of the following marketing tactics:

- *"A little better" tagline.* BP customers can expect to receive "a little better" experience at its service stations and other retail outlets compared to those of its competitors. Hand elaborates, "In this market, a little better means a lot. People see refueling as a necessary and unpleasant chore. However, BP can be cleaner and friendlier, and that's why people will choose us rather than our competitors." And this choice will be made on an emotional basis because customers "like what we stand for."
- *Animated TV ads.* These feature a family of characters (the Lighthouse family, the Babies, and the Beeps) and a catchy tune designed to reinforce the emotional appeal of the BP brand. The TV ads aired during some of the top U.S. TV shows (*American Idol, Ugly Betty*) and also had exposure on YouTube. The purposes of the ads were to generate awareness of and an emotional connection to the BP brand and its offerings.
- *In-store give-aways.* At the launch in April 2007, environmentally friendly paper bags, T-shirts with a fun new look from the campaign, kids activity books and trading cards featuring the campaign characters, and sunflower seed packets were handed out to customers throughout the entire network of BP stations.
- *Unique Web site.* The www.alittlebettergasstation.com Web site features the "Gas Mania" interactive game, selected animations, ringtones, screensavers, a sweepstakes, and the TV ads.
- *Street teams.* BP and Ford teamed up to promote the use of BP's Ultimate gasoline in Ford's new Edge automobile. Videos featuring groups of college-aged students were created to showcase the BP brand in Florida and the ARCO brand in California.

Questions

1 *(a)* What is BP's "Helios" strategy? *(b)* How does this strategy relate to BP's mission and core values?

2 Conduct a SWOT (strengths, weaknesses, opportunities, and threats) analysis for BP's "Helios" initiative—looking forward globally to the next three years.

3 What are some ways BP could use to effectively communicate its "Helios" strategy to consumers?

4 What are the long-term benefits to (*a*) society and (*b*) BP of its "Helios" initiative?

5 Looking at BP's Helios Power marketing strategy and its "street team" marketing tactic: (*a*) What objectives would you set for this tactic? (*b*) How would you propose BP measure the results?

APPENDIX

A BUILDING AN EFFECTIVE MARKETING PLAN

"New ideas are a dime a dozen," observes Arthur R. Kydd, "and so are new products and new technologies." Kydd should know. As chief executive officer of St. Croix Venture Partners, he and his firm have provided the seed money and venture capital to launch more than 60 start-up firms in the last 25 years. Today, those firms have more than 5,000 employees. Kydd explains:

> I get 200 to 300 marketing and business plans a year to look at, and St. Croix provides start-up financing for only two or three. What sets a potentially successful idea, product, or technology apart from all the rest is markets and marketing. If you have a real product with a distinctive point of difference that satisfies the needs of customers, you may have a winner. And you get a real feel for this in a well-written marketing or business plan.[1]

This appendix (1) describes what marketing and business plans are, including the purposes and guidelines in writing effective plans, and (2) provides a sample marketing plan.

MARKETING PLANS AND BUSINESS PLANS

After explaining the meanings, purposes, and audiences of marketing plans and business plans, this section describes some writing guidelines for them and what external funders often look for in successful plans.

Meanings, Purposes, and Audiences

A marketing plan is a road map for the marketing activities of an organization for a specified future time period, such as one year or five years.[2] No single "generic" marketing plan applies to all organizations and all situations. Rather, the specific format for a marketing plan for an organization depends on the following:

- *The target audience and purpose*. Elements included in a particular marketing plan depend heavily on (1) who the audience is and (2) what its purpose is. A marketing plan for an internal audience seeks to point the direction for future marketing activities and is sent to all individuals in the organization who must implement the plan or who will be affected by it. If the plan is directed to an external audience, such as friends, banks, venture capitalists, or potential investors for the purpose of raising capital, it has the additional function of being an important sales document. In this case, it contains elements such as the strategic plan/focus, organization, structure, and biographies of key personnel that would rarely appear in an internal marketing plan. Also, the financial information is far more detailed when the plan is used to raise outside capital. The elements of a marketing plan for each of these two audiences are compared in Figure A–1.
- *The kind and complexity of the organization*. A small neighborhood restaurant has a somewhat different marketing plan than Medtronic, which serves international markets. The restaurant's plan would be relatively simple and directed at serving customers in a local market. In Medtronic's case, because there is a hierarchy of marketing plans, various levels of detail would be used—such as the entire organization, the strategic business unit, or the product/product line.
- *The industry*. Both the restaurant serving a local market and Medtronic, selling heart pacemakers globally, analyze competition. Not only are their geographic thrusts far different, but also the complexities of their offerings and, hence, the time periods likely to be covered by their plans differ. A one-year marketing plan may be adequate for the restaurant, but Medtronic may need a five-year planning horizon because product-development cycles for complex, new medical devices may be three or four years.

In contrast to a marketing plan, a **business plan** is a road map for the entire organization for a specified future period of time, such as one year or five years.[3] A key difference between a marketing plan and a business plan is that the business plan contains details on the research and development (R&D)/operations/manufacturing activities of the organization. Even for a manufacturing business, the marketing plan is probably 60 or 70 percent of the entire business plan. For firms like a small restaurant or an auto repair shop, their marketing and business plans

Element of the plan	Marketing plan		Business plan	
	For internal audience (to direct the firm)	For external audience (to raise capital)	For internal audience (to direct the firm)	For external audience (to raise capital)
1. Executive summary	✓	✓	✓	✓
2. Description of company		✓		✓
3. Strategic plan/focus		✓		✓
4. Situation analysis	✓	✓	✓	✓
5. Market-product focus	✓	✓	✓	✓
6. Marketing program strategy and tactics	✓	✓	✓	✓
7. R&D and operations program			✓	✓
8. Financial projections	✓	✓	✓	✓
9. Organization structure		✓		✓
10. Implementation plan	✓	✓	✓	✓
11. Evaluation and control	✓		✓	
Appendix A: Biographies of key personnel		✓		✓
Appendix B, etc.: Details on other topics	✓	✓	✓	✓

FIGURE A–1
Elements in typical marketing and business plans targeted at different audiences

are virtually identical. The elements of a business plan typically targeted at internal and external audiences appear in the two right-hand columns in Figure A–1.

The Most-Asked Questions by Outside Audiences

Lenders and prospective investors reading a business or marketing plan that is used to seek new capital are probably the toughest audiences to satisfy. Their most-asked questions include the following:

1. Is the business or marketing idea valid?
2. Is there something unique or distinctive about the product or service that separates it from substitutes and competitors?
3. Is there a clear market for the product or service?
4. Are the financial projections realistic and healthy?
5. Are the key management and technical personnel capable, and do they have a track record in the industry in which they must compete?
6. Does the plan clearly describe how those providing capital will get their money back and make a profit?

Rhonda Abrams, author of *The Successful Business Plan*, observes, "Although you may spend five months preparing your plan, the cold, hard fact is that an investor or lender can dismiss it in less than five minutes."[4] While her comments apply to plans seeking to raise capital, the first five questions just listed apply equally well to plans for internal audiences.

Writing and Style Suggestions

There are no magic one-size-fits-all guidelines for writing successful marketing and business plans. Still, the following writing and style guidelines generally apply:[5]

- Use a direct, professional writing style. Use appropriate business terms without jargon. Present and future tenses with active voice ("I will write an effective marketing plan.") are generally better than past tense and passive voice ("An effective marketing plan was written by me.").
- Be positive and specific to convey potential success. At the same time, avoid superlatives ("terrific," "wonderful"). Specifics are better than glittering generalities.

Use numbers for impact, justifying projections with reasonable quantitative assumptions, where possible.

- Use bullet points for succinctness and emphasis. As with the list you are reading, bullets enable key points to be highlighted effectively.
- Use A-level (the first level) and B-level (the second level) headings under the numbered section headings to help readers make easy transitions from one topic to another. This also forces the writer to organize the plan more carefully. Use these headings liberally, at least one every 200 to 300 words.
- Use visuals where appropriate. Photos, illustrations, graphs, and charts enable massive amounts of information to be presented succinctly.
- Shoot for a plan 15 to 35 pages in length, not including financial projections and appendixes. An uncomplicated small business may require only 15 pages, while a high-technology start-up may require more than 35 pages.
- Use care in layout, design, and presentation. Laser printers give a more professional look than ink-jet printers do. Use 11- or 12-point type (you are now reading 10.5-point type) in the text. Use a serif type (with "feet," like that you are reading now) in the text because it is easier to read, and sans serif (without "feet") in graphs and charts like Figure A–1. A bound report with a nice cover and clear title page adds professionalism.

These guidelines are used, where possible, in the sample marketing plan that follows.

SAMPLE FIVE-YEAR MARKETING PLAN FOR PARADISE KITCHENS,® INC.

To help interpret the marketing plan for Paradise Kitchens, Inc., that follows, we will describe the company and suggest some guidelines in interpreting the plan.

Background on Paradise Kitchens, Inc.

With a degree in chemical engineering, Randall F. Peters spent 15 years working for General Foods and Pillsbury with a number of diverse responsibilities: plant operations, R&D, restaurant operations, and new business development. His wife, Leah, with degrees in both molecular cellular biology and food science, held various Pillsbury executive positions in new category development, packaged goods, and restaurant R&D. In the company's start-up years, Paradise Kitchens survived on the savings of Randy and Leah, the cofounders. With their backgrounds, they decided Randy should serve as president and CEO of Paradise Kitchens, and Leah should focus on R&D and corporate strategy.

Interpreting the Marketing Plan

The marketing plan on the next pages, based on an actual Paradise Kitchens plan, is directed at an external audience (see Figure A–1). To protect proprietary information about the company, some details and dates have been altered, but the basic logic of the plan has been kept.

Notes in the margins next to the Paradise Kitchens plan fall into two categories:

1. *Substantive notes* are in blue boxes. These notes elaborate on the significance of an element in the marketing plan and are keyed to chapter references in this textbook.
2. *Writing style, format, and layout notes* are in red boxes and explain the editorial or visual rationale for the element.

A word of encouragement: Writing an effective marketing plan is hard, but challenging and satisfying, work. Dozens of the authors' students have used effective marketing plans they wrote for class in their interviewing portfolio to show prospective employers what they could do and to help them get their first job.

Color-coding Legend

Blue boxes explain significance of marketing plan elements.

Red boxes give writing style, format, and layout guidelines.

The Table of Contents provides quick access to the topics in the plan, usually organized by section and subsection headings.

Seen by many experts as the single most important element in the plan, the two-page Executive Summary "sells" the plan to readers through its clarity and brevity. For space reasons, it is not shown here, but the Building Your Marketing Plan exercise at the end of Chapter 2 asks the reader to write an Executive Summary for this plan.

The Company Description highlights the recent history and recent successes of the organization.

The Strategic Focus and Plan sets the strategic direction for the entire organization, a direction with which proposed actions of the marketing plan must be consistent. This section is not included in all marketing plans. See Chapter 2.

The qualitative Mission statement focuses the activities of Paradise Kitchens for the stakeholder groups to be served. See Chapter 2.

FIVE-YEAR MARKETING PLAN

Paradise Kitchens,® Inc.

Table of Contents

1. Executive Summary

2. Company Description

Paradise Kitchens®, Inc., was started by cofounders Randall F. Peters and Leah E. Peters to develop and market Howlin' Coyote® Chili, a unique line of single serve and microwavable Southwestern/Mexican style frozen chili products. The Howlin' Coyote line of chili was first introduced into the Minneapolis–St. Paul market and expanded to Denver two years later and Phoenix two years after that.

To the Company's knowledge, Howlin' Coyote is the only premium-quality, authentic Southwestern/Mexican style, frozen chili sold in U.S. grocery stores. Its high quality has gained fast, widespread acceptance in these markets. In fact, same-store sales doubled in the last year for which data are available. The Company believes the Howlin' Coyote brand can be extended to other categories of Southwestern/Mexican food products, such as tacos, enchiladas, and burritos.

Paradise Kitchens believes its high-quality, high-price strategy has proven successful. This marketing plan outlines how the Company will extend its geographic coverage from 3 markets to 20 markets by the year 2014.

3. Strategic Focus and Plan

This section covers three aspects of corporate strategy that influence the marketing plan: (1) the mission, (2) goals, and (3) core competence/sustainable competitive advantage of Paradise Kitchens.

Mission

The mission of Paradise Kitchens is to market lines of high-quality Southwestern/Mexican food products at premium prices that satisfy consumers in this fast-growing food segment while providing challenging career opportunities for employees and above-average returns to stockholders.

The Goals section sets both the nonfinancial and financial targets—where possible in quantitative terms—against which the company's performance will be measured. See Chapter 2.

Lists use parallel construction to improve readability—in this case a series of infinitives starting with "To . . ."

Photos or sample ads can illustrate key points effectively, even if they are not in color as they appear here.

A brief caption on photos and sample ads ties them to the text and highlights the reason for being included.

Goals

For the coming five years Paradise Kitchens seeks to achieve the following goals:

- Nonfinancial goals
  1. To retain its present image as the highest-quality line of Southwestern/Mexican products in the food categories in which it competes.
  2. To enter 17 new metropolitan markets.
  3. To achieve national distribution in two convenience store or supermarket chains by 2010 and five by 2011.
  4. To add a new product line every third year.
  5. To be among the top five chili lines—regardless of packaging (frozen or canned)—in one-third of the metro markets in which it competes by 2011 and two-thirds by 2013.
- Financial goals
  1. To obtain a real (inflation-adjusted) growth in earnings per share of 8 percent per year over time.
  2. To obtain a return on equity of at least 20 percent.
  3. To have a public stock offering by the year 2011.

Core Competency and Sustainable Competitive Advantage

In terms of core competency, Paradise Kitchens seeks to achieve a unique ability to (1) provide distinctive, high-quality chilies and related products using Southwestern/Mexican recipes that appeal to and excite contemporary tastes for these products and (2) deliver these products to the customer's table using effective manufacturing and distribution systems that maintain the Company's quality standards.

To help achieve national distribution through chains, Paradise Kitchens introduced this point-of-purchase ad that adheres statically to the glass door of the freezer case.

To translate these core competencies into a sustainable competitive advantage, the Company will work closely with key suppliers and distributors to build the relationships and alliances necessary to satisfy the high taste standards of our customers.

To improve readability, each numbered section usually starts on a new page. (This is not done in this plan to save space.)

The Situation Analysis is a snapshot to answer the question, "Where are we now?" See Chapter 2.

The SWOT analysis identifies strengths, weaknesses, opportunities, and threats to provide a solid foundation as a springboard to identify subsequent actions in the marketing plan. See Chapter 2.

Each long table, graph, or photo is given a figure number and title. It then appears as soon as possible after the first reference in the text, accommodating necessary page breaks. This also avoids breaking long tables like this one in the middle. Short tables or graphs are often inserted in the text without figure numbers because they don't cause serious problems with page breaks.

Effective tables seek to summarize a large amount of information in a short amount of space.

4. Situation Analysis

This situation analysis starts with a snapshot of the current environment in which Paradise Kitchens finds itself by providing a brief SWOT (strengths, weaknesses, opportunities, threats) analysis. After this overview, the analysis probes ever-finer levels of detail: industry, competitors, company, and consumers.

SWOT Analysis

Figure 1 shows the internal and external factors affecting the market opportunities for Paradise Kitchens. Stated briefly, this SWOT analysis highlights the great strides taken by the company since its products first appeared on grocers' shelves.

Figure 1. SWOT Analysis for Paradise Kitchens

Internal Factors	Strengths	Weaknesses
Management	Experienced and entrepreneurial management and board	Small size can restrict options
Offerings	Unique, high-quality, high-price products	Many lower-quality, lower-price competitors
Marketing	Distribution in three markets with excellent acceptance	No national awareness or distribution; restricted shelf space in the freezer section
Personnel	Good workforce, though small; little turnover	Big gap if key employee leaves
Finance	Excellent growth in sales revenues	Limited resources may restrict growth opportunities when compared to giant competitors
Manufacturing	Sole supplier ensures high quality	Lack economies of scale of huge competitors
R&D	Continuing efforts to ensure quality in delivered products	Lack of canning and microwavable food processing expertise
External Factors	**Opportunities**	**Threats**
Consumer/Social	Upscale market, likely to be stable; Southwestern/Mexican food category is fast-growing segment due to growth in Hispanic American population and desire for spicier foods	Premium price may limit access to mass markets; consumers value a strong brand name
Competitive	Distinctive name and packaging in its markets	Not patentable; competitors can attempt to duplicate product; others better able to pay slotting fees
Technological	Technical breakthroughs enable smaller food producers to achieve many economies available to large competitors	Competitors have gained economies in canning and microwavable food processing
Economic	Consumer income is high; convenience important to U.S. households	More households "eating out," and bringing prepared take-out into home
Legal/Regulatory	High U.S. Food & Drug Administration standards eliminate fly-by-night competitors	Mergers among large competitors being approved by government

The text discussion of Figure 1 (the SWOT Analysis table) elaborates on its more important elements. This "walks" the reader through the information from the vantage of the plan's writer.

The Industry Analysis section provides the backdrop for the subsequent, more detailed analysis of competition, the company, and the company's customers. Without an in-depth understanding of the industry, the remaining analysis may be misdirected. See Chapter 2.

Sales of Mexican entrees are significant and provide a variety of future opportunities for Paradise Kitchens.

Even though relatively brief, this in-depth treatment of sales of Mexican foods in the United States demonstrates to the plan's readers the company's understanding of the industry in which it competes.

As with the Industry Analysis, the Competitors Analysis demonstrates that the company has a realistic understanding of its major chili competitors and their marketing strategies. Again, a realistic assessment gives confidence that subsequent marketing actions in the plan rest on a solid foundation. See Chapters 2, 3, 8, 9, and 22.

In the Company's favor internally are its strengths of an experienced management team and board of directors, excellent acceptance of its lines in the three metropolitan markets in which it competes, and a strong manufacturing and distribution system to serve these limited markets. Favorable external factors (opportunities) include the increasing appeal of Southwestern/Mexican foods, the strength of the upscale market for the Company's products, and food-processing technological breakthroughs that make it easier for smaller food producers to compete.

Among unfavorable factors, the main weakness is the limited size of Paradise Kitchens relative to its competitors in terms of the depth of the management team, available financial resources, and national awareness and distribution of product lines. Threats include the danger that the Company's premium prices may limit access to mass markets and competition from the "eating-out" and "take-out" markets.

Industry Analysis: Trends in Frozen and Mexican Foods

Frozen Foods. According to Grocery Headquarters, consumers are flocking to the frozen food section of grocery retailers. The reasons: hectic lifestyles demanding increased convenience and an abundance of new, tastier, and nutritious products.[6] By 2007, the latest year for which data are available, total sales of frozen food in supermarkets, drugstores, and mass merchandisers, such as Target and Costco (excluding Wal-Mart) reached $29 billion. Prepared frozen meals, which are defined as meals or entrees that are frozen and require minimal preparation, accounted for $8.1 billion, or 26 percent of the total frozen food market.

Sales of Mexican entrees totaled $506 million in 2007.[7] Heavy consumers of frozen meals, those who eat five or more meals every two weeks, tend to be kids, teens, and adults 35–44 years old.[8]

Mexican Foods. Currently, Mexican foods such as burritos, enchiladas, and tacos are used in two-thirds of American households. These trends reflect a generally more favorable attitude on the part of all Americans toward spicy foods that include red chili peppers. The growing Hispanic population in the U.S., about 44 million and almost $798 billion in purchasing power in 2007, partly explains the increasing demand for Mexican food. This Hispanic purchasing power is projected to be $1.2 trillion in 2011.[9]

Competitors in the Chili Market

The chili market represents over $500 million in annual sales. On average, consumers buy five to six servings annually, according to the NPD Group. The products fall primarily into two groups: canned chili (75 percent of sales) and dry chili (25 percent of sales).

This page uses a "block" style and does *not* indent each paragraph, although an extra space separates each paragraph. Compare this page with page 56, which has indented paragraphs. Most readers find indented paragraphs in marketing plans and long reports are easier to follow.

The Company Analysis provides details of the company's strengths and marketing strategies that will enable it to achieve the mission and goals identified earlier. See Chapters 2, 8, and 22.

The higher-level "A heading" of Customer Analysis has a more dominant typeface and position than the lower-level "B heading" of Customer Characteristics. These headings introduce the reader to the sequence and level of topics covered. The organization of this textbook uses this kind of structure and headings.

Satisfying customers and providing genuine value to them is why organizations exist in a market economy. This section addresses the question of "Who are the customers for Paradise Kitchens' products?" See Chapters 5, 6, 7, 8, and 9.

Bluntly put, the major disadvantage of the segment's dominant product, canned chili, is that it does not taste very good. A taste test described in an issue of *Consumer Reports* magazine ranked 26 canned chili products "poor" to "fair" in overall sensory quality. The study concluded, "Chili doesn't have to be hot to be good. But really good chili, hot or mild, doesn't come out of a can."

Company Analysis

The husband-and-wife team that cofounded Paradise Kitchens, Inc., has 44 years of experience between them in the food-processing business. Both have played key roles in the management of the Pillsbury Company. They are being advised by a highly seasoned group of business professionals, who have extensive understanding of the requirements for new-product development.

The Company now uses a single outside producer with which it works closely to maintain the consistently high quality required in its products. The greater volume has increased production efficiencies, resulting in a steady decrease in the cost of goods sold.

Customer Analysis

In terms of customer analysis, this section describes (1) the characteristics of customers expected to buy Howlin' Coyote products and (2) health and nutrition concerns of Americans today.

Customer Characteristics. Demographically, chili products in general are purchased by consumers representing a broad range of socioeconomic backgrounds. Howlin' Coyote chili is purchased chiefly by consumers who have achieved higher levels of education and whose income is $50,000 and higher. These consumers represent 50 percent of canned and dry mix chili users.

The household buying Howlin' Coyote has one to three people in it. Among married couples, Howlin' Coyote is predominantly bought by households in which both spouses work. While women are a majority of the buyers, single men represent a significant segment.

Because the chili offers a quick way to make a tasty meal, the product's biggest users tend to be those most pressed for time. Howlin' Coyote's premium pricing also means that its purchasers are skewed toward the higher end of the income range. Buyers range in age from 25 to 54 and often live in the western United States, where spicy foods are more readily eaten.

The five Howlin' Coyote entrees offer a quick, tasty meal with high-quality ingredients.

This section demonstrates the company's insights into a major trend that has a potentially large impact.

Health and Nutrition Concerns. Coverage of food issues in the U.S. media is often erratic and occasionally alarmist. Because Americans are concerned about their diets, studies from organizations of widely varying credibility frequently receive significant attention from the major news organizations. For instance, a study of fat levels of movie popcorn was reported in all the major media. Similarly, studies on the healthfulness of Mexican food have received prominent play in print and broadcast reports. The high caloric levels of much Mexican and Southwestern-style food have been widely reported and often exaggerated. Some Mexican frozen-food competitors, such as Don Miguel, Mission Foods, Ruiz Foods, and Jose Ole, plan to offer or have recently offered more "carb-friendly" and "fat-friendly" products in response to this concern.

Howlin' Coyote is already lower in calories, fat, and sodium than its competitors, and those qualities are not currently being stressed in its promotions. Instead, in the space and time available for promotions, Howlin' Coyote's taste, convenience, and flexibility are stressed.

Size of headings should give a professional look to the report and not overwhelm the reader. These two headings are too large.

5. Market-Product Focus

This section describes the five-year marketing and product objectives for Paradise Kitchens and the target markets, points of difference, and positioning of its lines of Howlin' Coyote chilies.

Marketing and Product Objectives

Howlin' Coyote's marketing intent is to take full advantage of its brand potential while building a base from which other revenue sources can be mined—both in and out of the retail grocery business. These are detailed in four areas below:

As noted in Chapters 9 and 10, the chances of success for a new product significantly increase if objectives are set for the product itself and if target market segments are identified for it. This section makes these explicit for Paradise Kitchens. The objectives also serve as the planned targets against which marketing activities are measured in program implementation and evaluation.

- Current markets. Current markets will be grown by expanding brand and flavor distribution at the retail level. In addition, same-store sales will be grown by increasing consumer awareness and repeat purchases, thereby leading to the more efficient broker/warehouse distribution channel.
- New markets. By the end of Year 5, the chili, salsa, burrito, and enchilada business will be expanded to a total of 20 metropolitan areas, which represent 53 percent of the 38 major U.S. metropolitan markets. This will represent 70 percent of U.S. food store sales.
- Food service. Food service sales will include chili products and smothering sauces. Sales are expected to reach $693,000 by the end of Year 3 and $1.5 million by the end of Year 5.
- New products. Howlin' Coyote's brand presence will be expanded at the retail

A heading should be spaced closer to the text that follows (and that it describes) than the preceding section to avoid confusion for the reader. This rule is not followed for the Target Markets heading, which now unfortunately appears to "float" between the preceding and following paragraphs.

This section identifies the specific niches or target markets toward which the company's products are directed. When appropriate and when space permits, this section often includes a market-product grid. See Chapter 9.

An organization cannot grow by offering only "me-too products." The greatest single factor in a new product's failure is the lack of significant "points of difference" that set it apart from competitors' substitutes. This section makes these points of difference explicit. See Chapter 10.

A positioning strategy helps communicate the company's unique points of difference of its products to prospective customers in a simple, clear way. This section describes this positioning. See Chapters 9 and 10.

level through the addition of new products in the frozen-foods section. This will be accomplished through new-product concept screening in Year 1 to identify new potential products. These products will be brought to market in Years 2 and 3.

Target Markets

The primary target market for Howlin' Coyote products is households with one to three people, where often both adults work, with individual income typically above $50,000 per year. These households contain more experienced, adventurous consumers of Southwestern/Mexican food and want premium quality products.

To help buyers see the many different uses for Howlin' Coyote chili, recipes are even printed on the *inside* of the packages.

Points of Difference

The "points of difference"—characteristics that make Howlin' Coyote chilies unique relative to competitors—fall into three important areas:

- Unique taste and convenience. No known competitor offers a high-quality, "authentic" frozen chili in a range of flavors. And no existing chili has the same combination of quick preparation and home-style taste that Howlin' Coyote does.
- Taste trends. The American palate is increasingly intrigued by hot spices. In response to this trend, Howlin' Coyote brands offer more "kick" than most other prepared chilies.
- Premium packaging. Howlin' Coyote's packaging graphics convey the unique, high-quality product contained inside and the product's nontraditional positioning.

Positioning

In the past chili products have been either convenient or tasty, but not both. Howlin' Coyote pairs these two desirable characteristics to obtain a positioning in consumers' minds as very high-quality "authentic Southwestern/Mexican tasting" chilies that can be prepared easily and quickly.

Everything that has gone before in the marketing plan sets the stage for the marketing mix actions—the four Ps—covered in the marketing program. See Chapters 10 through 20.

The section describes in detail three key elements of the company's product strategy: the product line, its quality and how this is achieved, and its "cutting edge" packaging. See Chapters 10, 11, and 12.

This Price Strategy section makes the company's price point very clear, along with its price position relative to potential substitutes. When appropriate and when space permits, this section might contain a break-even analysis. See Chapters 13 and 14.

This "introductory overview" sentence tells the reader the topics covered in the section—in this case in-store demonstrations, recipes, and cents-off coupons. While this sentence may be omitted in short memos or plans, it helps readers see where the text is leading. These sentences are used throughout this plan. This textbook also generally utilizes these introductory overview sentences to aid your comprehension.

6. Marketing Program

The four marketing mix elements of the Howlin' Coyote chili marketing program are detailed below. Note that "chile" is the vegetable and "chili" is the dish.

Product Strategy

After first summarizing the product line, the approach to product quality and packaging are covered.

Product Line. Howlin' Coyote chili, retailing for $3.99 for an 11-ounce serving, is available in five flavors. The five are Green Chile Chili, Red Chile Chili, Beef and Black Bean Chili, Chicken Chunk Chili, and Mean Bean Chili.

Unique Product Quality. The flavoring systems of the Howlin' Coyote chilies are proprietary. The products' tastiness is due to extra care lavished upon the ingredients during production. The ingredients used are of unusually high quality. Meats are low-fat cuts and are fresh, not frozen, to preserve cell structure and moistness. Chilies are fire-roasted for fresher taste. Tomatoes and vegetables are select quality. No preservatives or artificial flavors are used.

Packaging. Reflecting the "cutting edge" marketing strategy of its producers, Howlin' Coyote bucks conventional wisdom in packaging. It avoids placing predictable photographs of the product on its containers. Instead, Howlin' Coyote's package shows a Southwestern motif that communicates the product's out-of-the-ordinary positioning.

The Southwestern motif makes Howlin' Coyote's packages stand out in a supermarket's freezer case.

Price Strategy

Howlin' Coyote Chili is, at $3.99 for an 11-ounce package, priced comparably to the other frozen offerings and higher than the canned and dried chili varieties. However, the significant taste advantages it has over canned chilies and the convenience advantages over dried chilies justify this pricing strategy.

Promotion Strategy

Key promotion programs feature in-store demonstrations, recipes, and cents-off coupons.

Elements of the Promotion Strategy are highlighted in terms of the three key promotional activities the company is emphasizing: in-store demonstrations, recipes, and cents-off coupons. For space reasons the company's online strategies are not shown in the plan. See Chapters 18, 19, 20, and 21.

Another bulleted list adds many details for the reader, including methods of gaining customer awareness, trial, and repeat purchases as Howlin' Coyote enters new metropolitan areas.

The Place Strategy is described here in terms of both (1) the present method and (2) the new one to be used when the increased sales volume makes it feasible. See Chapters 15, 16, and 17.

All the marketing mix decisions covered in the just-described marketing program have both revenue and expense effects. These are summarized in this section of the marketing plan.

Note that this section contains no introductory overview sentence. While the sentence is not essential, many readers prefer to see it to avoid the abrupt start with Past Sales Revenues.

In-Store Demonstrations. In-store demonstrations enable consumers to try Howlin' Coyote products and discover their unique qualities. Demos will be conducted regularly in all markets to increase awareness and trial purchases.

Recipes. Because the products' flexibility of use is a key selling point, recipes are offered to consumers to stimulate use. The recipes are given at all in-store demonstrations, on the back of packages, through a mail-in recipe book offer, and in coupons sent by direct-mail or freestanding inserts.

Cents-Off Coupons. To generate trial and repeat-purchase of Howlin' Coyote products, coupons are distributed in four ways:

- In Sunday newspaper inserts. These inserts are widely read and help generate awareness.
- In-pack coupons. Each box of Howlin' Coyote chili will contain coupons for $1 off two more packages of the chili. These coupons will be included for the first three months the product is shipped to a new market. Doing so encourages repeat purchases by new users.
- Direct-mail chili coupons. Those households that fit the Howlin' Coyote demographics described previously will be mailed coupons.
- In-store demonstrations. Coupons will be passed out at in-store demonstrations to give an additional incentive to purchase.

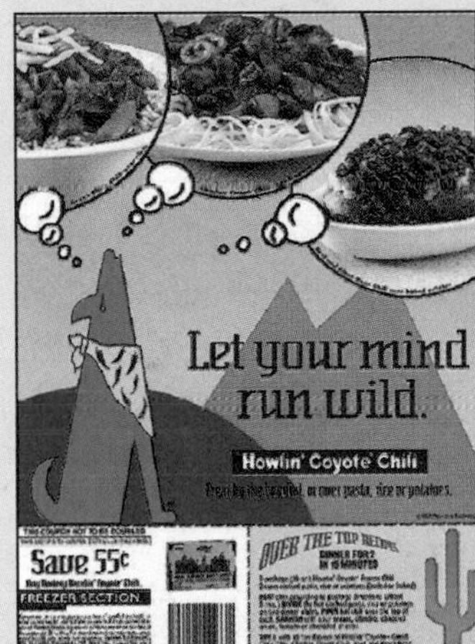

Sunday newspaper inserts encourage consumer trial and provide recipes to show how Howlin' Coyote chili can be used in summer meals.

Place (Distribution) Strategy

Howlin' Coyote is distributed in its present markets through a food distributor. The distributor buys the product, warehouses it, and then resells and delivers it to grocery retailers on a store-by-store basis. As sales grow, we will shift to a more efficient system using a broker who sells the products to retail chains and grocery wholesalers.

7. Financial Data and Projections

Past Sales Revenues

Historically, Howlin' Coyote has had a steady increase in sales revenues since its introduction in 2001. In 2005, sales jumped spectacularly, due largely to new

The graph shows more clearly the dramatic growth of sales revenue than data in a table would do.

The Five-Year Projections section starts with the judgment forecast of cases sold and the resulting net sales. Gross profit and then operating profit—critical for the company's survival—are projected. An actual plan often contains many pages of computer-generated spreadsheet projections, usually shown in an appendix to the plan.

Because this table is very short, it is woven into the text, rather than given a figure number and title.

Because the plan proposes to enter 17 new metropolitan markets in the coming five years (for a total of 20), it is not possible to simply extrapolate the trend in Figure 2. Instead, management's judgment must be used. Methods of making sales forecasts—including the "lost horse" technique used here—are discussed in Chapter 8.

The Organization of Paradise Kitchens appears here. It reflects the bare-bones organizational structure of successful small businesses. Often a more elaborate marketing plan will show the new positions expected to be added as the firm grows.

promotion strategies. Sales have continued to rise, but at a less dramatic rate. Sales revenues appear in Figure 2.

Figure 2. Sales Revenues for Paradise Kitchens, Inc.

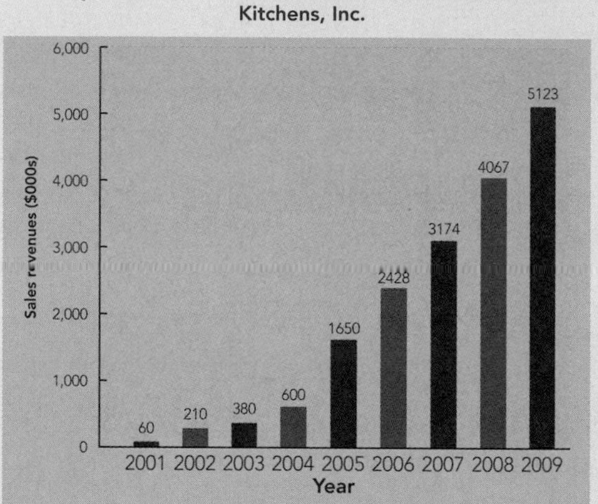

Five-Year Projections

Five-year financial projections for Paradise Kitchens appear below. These projections reflect the continuing growth in number of cases sold (with eight packages of Howlin' Coyote chili per case).

			Projections				
Financial Element	Units	Actual 2009	Year 1 2010	Year 2 2011	Year 3 2012	Year 4 2013	Year 5 2014
Cases sold	1,000	353	684	889	1,249	1,499	1,799
Net sales	$1,000	5,123	9,913	12,884	18,111	21,733	26,080
Gross profit	$1,000	2,545	4,820	6,527	8,831	10,597	12,717
Operating profit (loss)	$1,000	339	985	2,906	2,805	3,366	4,039

8. Organization

Paradise Kitchens' present organization appears in Figure 3. It shows the four people reporting to the President. Below this level are both the full-time and part-time employees of the Company.

Figure 3. The Paradise Kitchens Organization

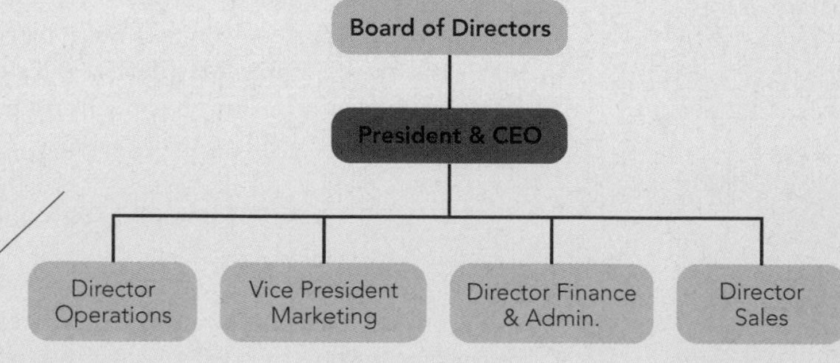

The Implementation Plan shows how the company will turn plans into results. Gantt charts are often used to set deadlines and assign responsibilities for the many tactical marketing decisions needed to enter a new market.

The essence of Evaluation and Control is comparing actual sales with the targeted values set in the plan and taking appropriate actions. Note that the section briefly describes a contingency plan for alternative actions, depending on how successful the entry into a new market turns out to be.

Various appendixes may appear at the end of the plan, depending on the purpose and audience for them. For example, resumes of key personnel or detailed financial spreadsheets often appear in appendixes. For space reasons these are not shown here.

At present Paradise Kitchens operates with full-time employees in only essential positions. It now augments its full-time staff with key advisors, consultants, and subcontractors. As the firm grows, people with special expertise will be added to the staff.

9. Implementation Plan

Introducing Howlin' Coyote chilies to 17 new metropolitan markets is a complex task and requires that creative promotional activities gain consumer awareness and initial trial. Counting the three existing metropolitan markets in which Paradise Kitchens competes, by 2014 it will be in 20 metropolitan markets or 53 percent of the top 38 U.S. metropolitan markets. The anticipated rollout schedule to enter these metropolitan markets appears in Figure 4.

Figure 4. Rollout Schedule to Enter New U.S. Markets

Year	New Markets Added Each Year	Cumulative Markets	Cumulative Percentage of 38 Major U.S. Markets
Today (2009)	2	5	16
Year 1 (2010)	3	8	21
Year 2 (2011)	4	12	29
Year 3 (2012)	2	14	37
Year 4 (2013)	3	17	45
Year 5 (2014)	3	20	53

The diverse regional tastes in chili will be monitored carefully to assess whether minor modifications may be required in the chili recipes. As the rollout to new metropolitan areas continues, Paradise Kitchens will assess manufacturing and distribution trade-offs. This is important in determining whether to start new production with selected high-quality regional contract packers.

10. Evaluation and Control

Monthly sales targets in cases have been set for Howlin' Coyote chili for each metropolitan area. Actual case sales will be compared with these targets and tactical marketing programs modified to reflect the unique sets of factors in each metropolitan area.

Appendix A. Biographical Sketches of Key Personnel

Appendix B. Detailed Financial Projections

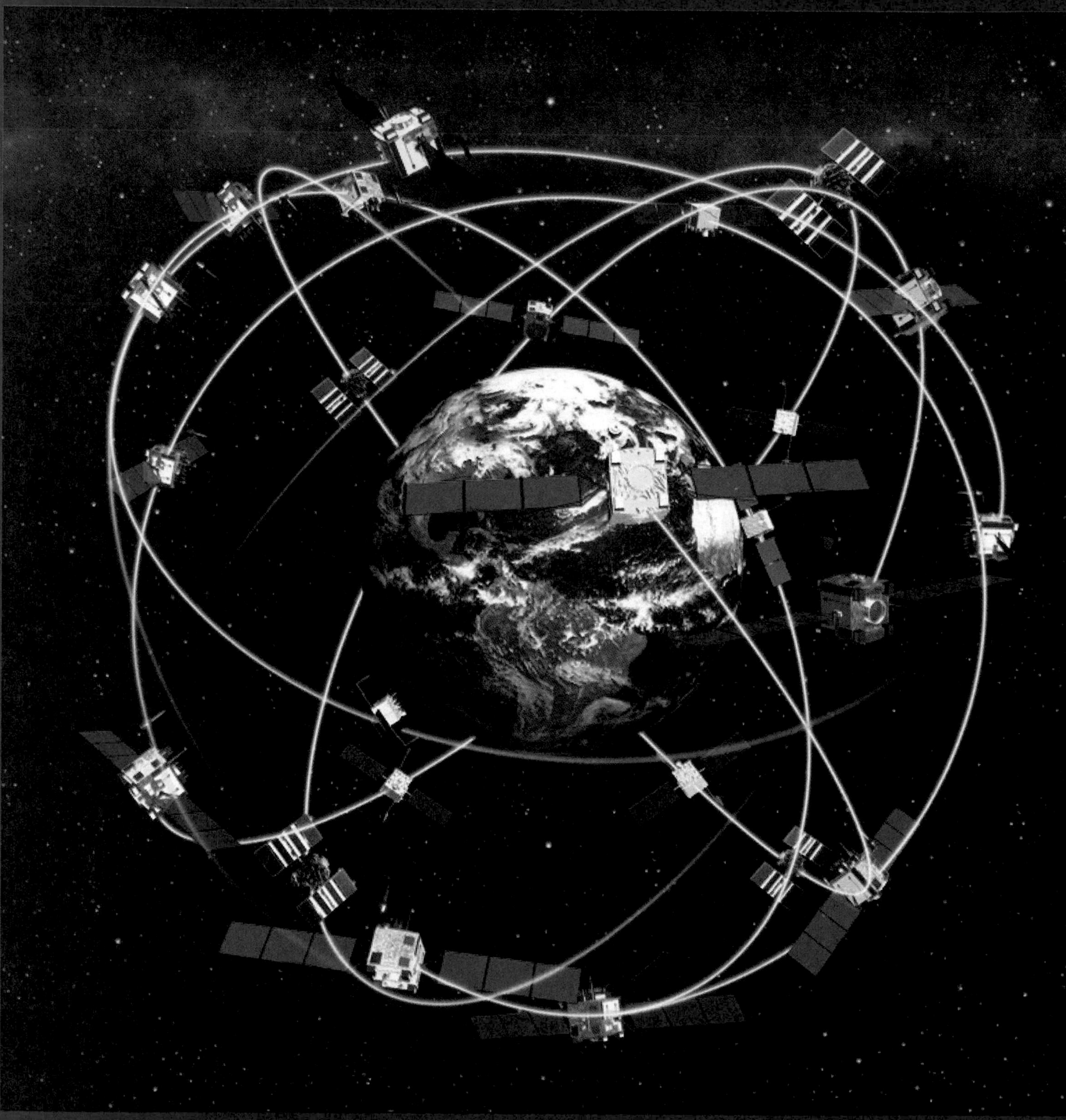

3 Scanning the Marketing Environment

LEARNING OBJECTIVES

After reading this chapter you should be able to:

LO1 Explain how environmental scanning provides information about social, economic, technological, competitive, and regulatory forces.

LO2 Describe how social forces such as demographics and culture can have an impact on marketing strategy.

LO3 Discuss how economic forces such as macroeconomic conditions and consumer income affect marketing.

LO4 Describe how technological changes can affect marketing.

LO5 Discuss the forms of competition that exist in a market and key components of competition.

LO6 Explain the major legislation that ensures competition and regulates the elements of the marketing mix.

WHERE IN THE WORLD ARE YOU? IN THE MIDDLE OF THE GPS REVOLUTION!

You may have heard the old saying that the three most important things for many businesses are location, location, and location. Today, the GPS revolution is making the entire marketplace completely location-based for consumers and marketers. If you have a cell phone, use MapQuest, or drive a car with a navigation system you are already part of the revolution!

The Global Positioning System (GPS) that is driving the revolution utilizes a grid of 32 satellites in space to triangulate the location, speed, direction, and time of any GPS receiver on the ground. Navigation and map services have quickly become popular with consumers. Many car models, for example, include navigation systems that show the vehicle's location on a detailed map. Similarly, the Web-based MapQuest now attracts 54 million users per month. Other recent uses include a GPS jacket for children that allows parents to keep track of kids while they are snowboarding, hiking, or biking, and a tracking device for athletes who want to monitor distance and speed of their workouts. In Sydney, Australia, public buses are linked to traffic lights by GPS devices so they can maintain an on-time schedule.

The future will have many more new and exciting location-aware services and applications, many of which are designed for the 444 million cell phones with GPS capability expected to be in use by 2011. If you use public transportation, you might try iNap, a travel alarm that will alert you when your destination is close. JOYity will allow you to play "tag" with strangers—just get within 80 feet of the subject the game assigns to you. Other applications will soon allow you to find nearby restaurants and gas stations. Manufacturers and retailers will also benefit from location-based marketing by using GPS devices to track cargo location and delivery times.

How did the GPS revolution happen? The marketing environment changed! First, technologies such as GPS satellites, WiFi nodes, and cellular signal towers were developed and became readily available. Second, the regulatory environment changed to make cell phone frequencies and former military technologies available for commercial use. Third, competitive forces by companies such as Garmin, TomTom, Apple, Google, and Nokia quickly created many new products and services. Finally consumers changed. They are becoming "geo-enthusiasts" that use information about their location to be more social and to enhance their use of Web sites such as Flickr, Twitter, Tumblr, and blogs. The GPS revolution will mean that consumers will always know exactly where they are![1]

Many businesses operate in environments where important forces change. Anticipating and responding to changes often means the difference between marketing success and failure. This chapter describes how the marketing environment has changed in the past and how it is likely to change in the future.

ENVIRONMENTAL SCANNING

Changes in the marketing environment are a source of opportunities and threats to be managed. The process of continually acquiring information on events occurring outside the organization to identify and interpret potential trends is called **environmental scanning**.

Tracking Environmental Trends

Environmental trends typically arise from five sources: social, economic, technological, competitive, and regulatory forces. As shown in Figure 3–1 and described later in this chapter, these forces affect the marketing activities of a firm in numerous ways. To illustrate how environmental scanning is used, consider the following trend:[2]

> Coffee industry marketers have observed that the percentage of adults who drink coffee declined from 75 percent in 1962 to 49 percent in 2004, increased to 57 percent in 2007 and declined to 55 percent in 2008. Age-specific analysis indicates that the percentage of 18- to 24-year-olds who drink coffee rose from 16 percent in 2003 to 37 percent in 2007, and then declined to 26 percent in 2008.

What types of businesses are likely to be influenced by these trends? What future would you predict for coffee?

You may have concluded that these changes in coffee consumption are likely to influence coffee manufacturers, coffee shops, and supermarkets. If so, you are correct—the general growth trend has manufacturers offering new flavors and seasonal blends, coffee shops automating to prepare drinks faster, and supermarkets adding boutiques and gourmet brands. The recent decline in consumption has also led to changes. Starbucks, for example, has closed some of its stores and is experimenting

FIGURE 3–1
Environmental forces affect the organization, as well as its suppliers and customers.

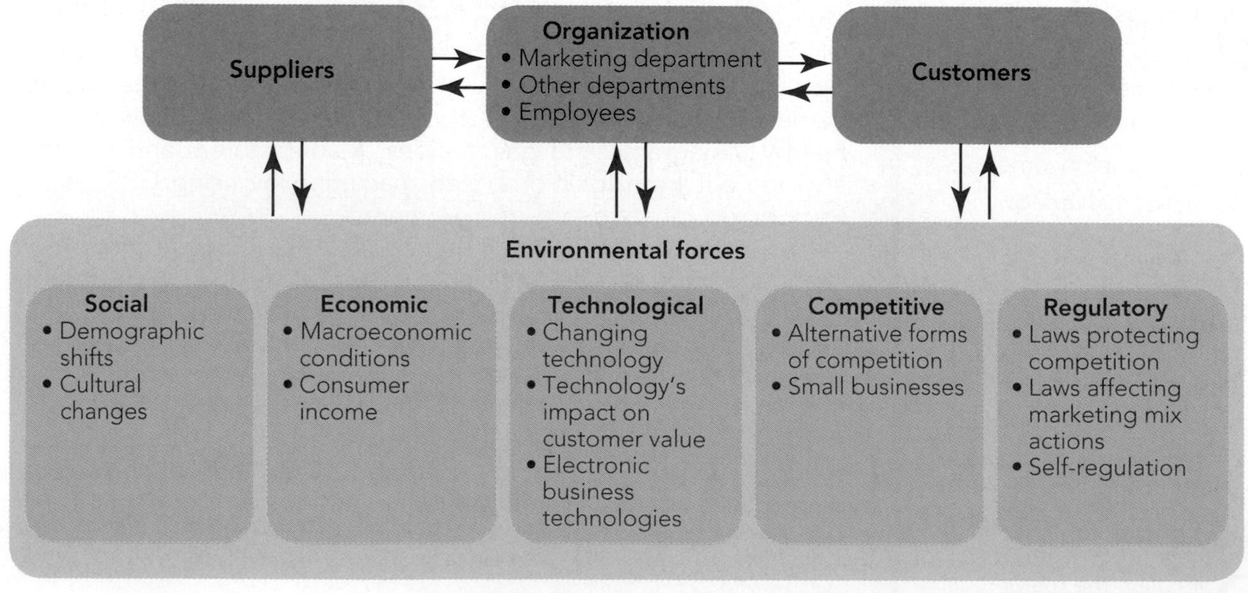

with "short" size cups that sell for $1. Predicting the future requires assumptions about the number of years the trends will continue and the rate of increase or decline in the various age groups. Because experts make different assumptions, their forecasts often cover a large range.

Environmental scanning also involves explaining trends. Why did coffee consumption decline for many years, begin to increase, and then decline again recently? One explanation for the general decline is that consumers switched from coffee to other beverages such as soft drinks, juices, and bottled water. The increase may be the result of new coffee products distributed in coffee shops, supermarkets and vending machines, and gourmet single-serving products for homes and offices. The recent decline may be the result of economic forces that cause consumers to reduce discretionary expenditures. Identifying and interpreting trends such as the changes in coffee consumption, and developing explanations such as those offered in this paragraph, are essential to successful environmental scanning.[3]

An Environmental Scan of Today's Marketplace

What other trends might affect marketing in the future? A firm conducting an environmental scan of the marketplace might uncover key trends such as those listed in Figure 3–2 for each of the five environmental forces.[4] Although the list of trends is far from complete, it reveals the breadth of an environmental scan—from the growing concern for environmental impact and sustainability, to the increasing government ownership of large businesses, to the greater concern for privacy and personal information collection. These trends affect consumers and the businesses and organizations that serve them. Trends such as these are described in the following discussions of the five environmental forces.

FIGURE 3–2
An environmental scan of today's marketplace shows the many important trends that influence marketing.

ENVIRONMENTAL FORCE	TREND IDENTIFIED BY AN ENVIRONMENTAL SCAN
Social	• Shifting of social networks and social media to mainstream forms of communication for consumers • Increasing expectation for authentic and experiential relationships with companies and brands • Growing concern for environmental impact and sustainability
Economic	• Continued shift to a service economy including service components of goods • Growing importance of China, India, and Africa in the world economy • Increasing government ownership and management of large businesses and key industries
Technological	• Greater interest in mobile marketing • Shift from analog to digital technologies in telephone, cable, and Internet industries • Biomimicry, or the emulation of nature, is growing in its impact on innovation
Competitive	• Continued outsoucing of routine business processes and decision-making functions • Growing difficulty recruiting talent from abroad due to increasingly restrictive immigration rules • Dramatic increase in customer-generated content about competitive options
Regulatory	• Growing interest in revising federal and state consumer credit regulations • Greater concern for privacy and personal information collection • New regulations related to customer engagement methods such as e-mail solicitation, promotions, and contests

SOCIAL FORCES

LO2

The **social forces** of the environment include the demographic characteristics of the population and its values. Changes in these forces can have a dramatic impact on marketing strategy.

Demographics

Describing a population according to selected characteristics such as age, gender, ethnicity, income, and occupation is referred to as **demographics**. Several organizations such as the Population Reference Bureau and the United Nations monitor the world population profile, while many other organizations such as the U.S. Census Bureau provide information about the American population.

The World Population at a Glance The most recent estimates indicate there are 6.7 billion people in the world today, and the population is likely to grow to 9.35 billion by 2050. While this growth has led to the term *population explosion*, the increases have not occurred worldwide; they are primarily in the developing countries of Africa, Asia, and Latin America. In fact, India is predicted to have the world's largest population in 2050 with 1.76 billion people, and China will be a close second with 1.44 billion people. Figure 3–3a shows the declining proportion of the world's population in more developed countries such as the United States, Japan, Australia, and those in Europe.[5]

Another important global trend is the shifting age structure of the world population. Figure 3–3b shows the number of people 60 and older is expected to more than triple in the coming decades and reach 2 billion by 2050. Again, the magnitude of this trend varies by region, and developed countries such as the United States are expected to face the highest growth rates of the elderly age group. Global income levels and living standards have also been increasing, although the averages across countries are very different. Per capita income, for example, ranges from \$64,320 in Luxembourg, to \$36,220 in Canada, to \$870 in Ethiopia.

For marketers, global trends such as these have many implications. Obviously, the relative size of countries such as India and China will mean they represent huge markets for many product categories. Elderly populations in developed countries are

FIGURE 3–3
The distribution of the world population is changing. Africa is growing and the population is getting older.

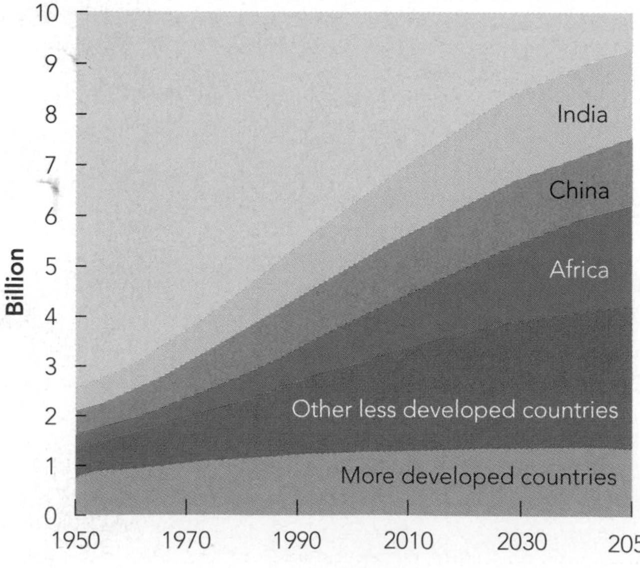

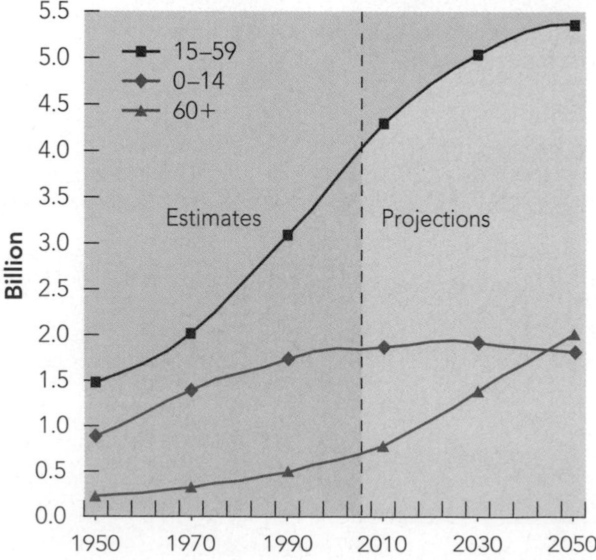

likely to save less and begin spending their funds on health care, travel, and other retirement-related products and services. Economic progress in developing countries will lead to growth in entrepreneurship, new markets for infrastructure related to manufacturing, communication, and distribution, and the growth of exports.[6]

The U.S. Population Studies of the demographic characteristics of the U.S. population suggest several important trends. Generally, the population is becoming larger, older, and more diverse. In 2010, the U.S. population is estimated to be 310 million people. If current trends in life expectancy, birthrates, and immigration continue, by 2030 the U.S. population will exceed 373 million people. This growth suggests that niche markets based on age, life stage, family structure, geographic location, and ethnicity will become increasingly important. The global trend toward an older population is particularly true in the United States. Today, there are approximately 40 million people 65 and older. By 2030, this age group will include more than 72 million people, or almost 20 percent of the population. You may have noticed companies trying to attract older consumers. Mobile phone manufacturer Samsung, for example, recently introduced the Jitterbug with large easy-to-read buttons for seniors. Finally, the term *minority* as it is currently used is likely to become obsolete as the size of most ethnic groups will double during the next two decades.[7]

Generational Cohorts A major reason for the graying of America is that the 76 million **baby boomers**—the generation of children born between 1946 and 1964—are growing older. Baby boomers are retiring at a rate of 10,000 every 24 hours, and they will all be 65 or older by 2030. Their participation in the work force has made them the wealthiest generation in U.S. history, with an estimated $1 trillion in annual buying power. While boomers represent a diverse group in terms of their age and life stages, one commonality is their interest in health, wellness, and appearance. Companies that target boomers will need to respond to their interests in fitness, retirement housing, financial planning, and their appearance. Ameriprise Financial, for example, uses Dennis Hopper as a spokesperson in an ad campaign that claims, "Your generation is definitely not headed for Bingo night."[8] Similarly, Olay offers anti-aging and restoration products for this age group.

The baby boom cohort is followed by **Generation X**, which includes the 15 percent of the population born between 1965 and 1976. This period is also known as the *baby bust*, because the number of children born each year was declining.

Which generational cohorts are these three advertisers trying to reach?

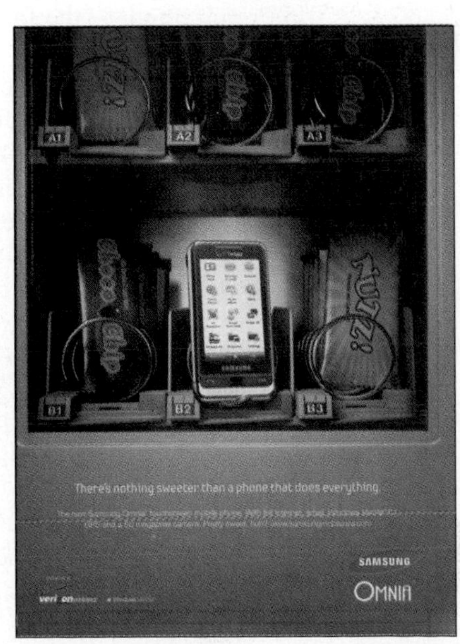

This is a generation of consumers who are self-reliant, supportive of racial and ethnic diversity, and better educated than any previous generation. They are not prone to extravagance and are likely to pursue lifestyles that are a blend of caution, pragmatism, and traditionalism. In terms of net worth, Generation X is the first generation to have less than the previous generation. As baby boomers move toward retirement, however, Generation X is becoming a dominant force in many markets. Generation X, for example, is replacing baby boomers as the largest segment of business travelers. In response, hotel companies are creating new concepts that appeal to the younger market. Surveys of Generation X travelers indicate they want casual, tech-friendly lodging with 24-hour access to food and drinks, so Hyatt Corporation is building 400 new Hyatt Place all-suite hotels featuring free wireless Internet, flat-panel high-definition televisions, a 24-hour guest kitchen, a fitness center, and remote printing.[9]

The generational cohort labeled **Generation Y** includes the 72 million Americans born between 1977 and 1994. This was a period of increasing births, which resulted from baby boomers having children, and it is often referred to as the *echo-boom* or *baby boomlet*. Generation Y exerts influence on music, sports, computers, video games, and especially cell phones. Generation Y views wireless communication as a lifeline to friends and family and was the first to use Web-enabled mobile phones to stream video, send and receive text messages, play games, and access e-mail. They are strong-willed, passionate about the environment, and optimistic. This is also a group that is attracted to purposeful work where they have control. The accompanying Making Responsible Decisions box describes how millennial's interest in sustainability is influencing colleges, graduate schools, and employers. The term *millennials* is also used, with inconsistent definitions, to refer to younger members of Generation Y and sometimes to Americans born since 1994.[10]

Because the members of each generation are distinctive in their attitudes and consumer behavior, marketers have been studying the many groups or cohorts that make up the marketplace and have developed *generational marketing* programs for them.

The American Household As the population age profile has changed, so has the structure of the American household. In 1960, 75 percent of all households consisted of married couples. Today, that type of household is just 50 percent of the population. Only 25 percent of households are married couples with children, and 10 percent are households with working fathers and stay-at-home moms. Some of the fastest-growing types of households are those with a single person, those with a single parent, and those with unmarried partners. Businesses are trying to develop products and services that reflect the changing structure of households. Ocean Village, for example, noticed a 26 percent increase in the number of single parents traveling with children, so it added three-berth cabins on its cruise ships to cater to the trend.[11]

The increase in cohabitation (households with unmarried partners) may be one reason the divorce rate has declined slightly in recent years. Even so, the likelihood that a couple will divorce exceeds 40 percent and the total number of divorced people is 21.6 million. The majority of divorced people eventually remarry, which has given rise to the **blended family**, one formed by merging two previously separated units into a single household. Today, one of every three Americans is a stepparent, stepchild, stepsibling, or some other member of a blended family. Hallmark Cards, Inc., now has specially designed cards and verses for blended families.[12]

Population Shifts A major regional shift in the U.S. population toward Southern and Western states is under way. From 2007 to 2008, the populations of Utah, Arizona, Texas, North Carolina, and Colorado grew at the fastest rates in the nation. Nearly a century ago each of the top 10 most populous cities in the United States was within 500 miles of the Canadian border. Today, seven of the top 10 are in states

Making Responsible Decisions > > > > sustainability

Millennials Are Going to Change the World—Through Environmental Sustainability!

Millenials, or Generation Y, are determined to make a difference in the world, and by doing so, make the world a better place. They are idealistic and eager to get started, particularly when it comes to environmental sustainability, which millennials believe is part of what it means to be socially responsible. The group includes students in college and graduate school, and many early career employees. In different ways each group is making its voice heard.

There are approximately 17 million undergraduate millennials who expect sustainable campus communities that include LEED (Leadership in Energy and Environmental Design)-certified housing, campus transit systems, and recycling programs. Graduate students are looking for programs with sustainability electives, case studies, and potential for involvement with organizations such as Net Impact, a nonprofit for students who want to "use business to improve the world." Early career employees want "green" jobs such as social responsibility officer, environmental consultant, a sustainability database specialist at companies that are eco-conscious and advocate good citizenry.

Sara Hochman is a typical example. She was interested in environmental issues in college, and her first job was an environmental consultant. To make a bigger impact on her clients, she decided she "needed to beef up my business skills," so she enrolled in graduate school at the University of Chicago where she could take an elective on renewable energy and join the Energy Club. Similarly, Alix Pryde left a job as head of a wireless telephone group to become the director of environmental strategy at the British Broadcasting Corporation.

Have you made similar choices or decisions based on your interest and concern about sustainability? What will the world look like after the millennials have made their changes? It is difficult to predict. As experts Peter Leyden and Ruy Teixeira advise, however, we should, "Hang on for the ride!"

that border Mexico. Last year, Texas gained more people than any other state—its population increased by almost 500,000![13]

Populations are also shifting within states. In the early 1900s, the population shifted from rural areas to cities. From the 1930s through the 1980s, the population shifted from the cities to suburbs. More recently, the population began to shift again, from suburbs to more remote suburbs called *exurbs*. Today, 30 percent of all Americans live in central cities, 50 percent live in suburbs, and 20 percent live in rural locations.[14]

To assist marketers in gathering data on the population, the Census Bureau has developed a classification system to describe the varying locations of the population. The system consists of two types of *statistical areas*:

- A *metropolitan statistical area* has at least one urbanized area of 50,000 or more people and adjacent territory that has a high degree of social and economic integration.
- A *micropolitan statistical area* has at least one urban cluster of at least 10,000 but less than 50,000 people and adjacent territory that has a high degree of social and economic integration.

If a metropolitan statistical area contains a population of 2.5 million or more, it may be subdivided into smaller areas called *metropolitan divisions*. In addition, adjacent metropolitan statistical areas and micropolitan statistical areas may be grouped into *combined statistical areas*.[15]

There are currently 363 metropolitan statistical areas, which include 83 percent of the population, and 577 micropolitan areas, which include 10 percent of the population.

Racial and Ethnic Diversity A notable trend is the changing racial and ethnic composition of the U.S. population. Approximately one in four U.S. residents is African American, American Indian, Asian, Pacific Islander, or a representative of another racial or ethnic group. Diversity is further evident in the variety of peoples that make up these groups. For example, Asians consist of Asian Indians, Chinese, Filipinos, Japanese, Koreans, and Vietnamese. For the first time, the 2000 Census allowed respondents to choose more than one of the six race options, and more than 4 million reported more than one race. Hispanics, who may be from any race, currently make up 15 percent of the U.S. population and are represented by Mexicans, Puerto Ricans, Cubans, and others of Central and South American ancestry. While the United States is becoming more diverse, Figure 3–4 suggests that the minority racial and ethnic groups tend to be concentrated in geographic regions.[16]

The racial and ethnic composition of the United States is expected to change even more by 2025. Between 2008 and 2025, the Hispanic population will grow from 44 million to more than 68 million, or almost 20 percent of the total population. The number of Asians in the United States will also double to 24 million, or 7 percent of the population, and the African American population will be approximately 45 million, or 13 percent of the population. The new Census category, *multiracials*, currently makes up 2.4 percent of the population, but because of the limited information about this group, growth forecasts are difficult to make. Overall, the trends in the composition of the population suggest that the U.S. market will no longer be dominated by one group and that non-Hispanic Caucasians will be a declining majority over the next two decades.

While the growing size of these groups has been identified through new Census data, their economic impact on the marketplace is also very noticeable. By 2012, Hispanics, African Americans, and Asians will spend $1.20 trillion, $1.13 trillion, and $670 billion each year, respectively. To adapt to this new marketplace, many companies are developing **multicultural marketing** programs, which are combinations of the marketing mix that reflect the unique attitudes, ancestry, communication preferences, and lifestyles of different races. Because businesses must now market their products to a consumer base with many racial and ethnic identities, in-depth marketing research that allows an accurate understanding of each culture is essential.[17]

FIGURE 3–4
Racial and ethnic groups (excluding Caucasians) are concentrated in geographic regions of the United States.

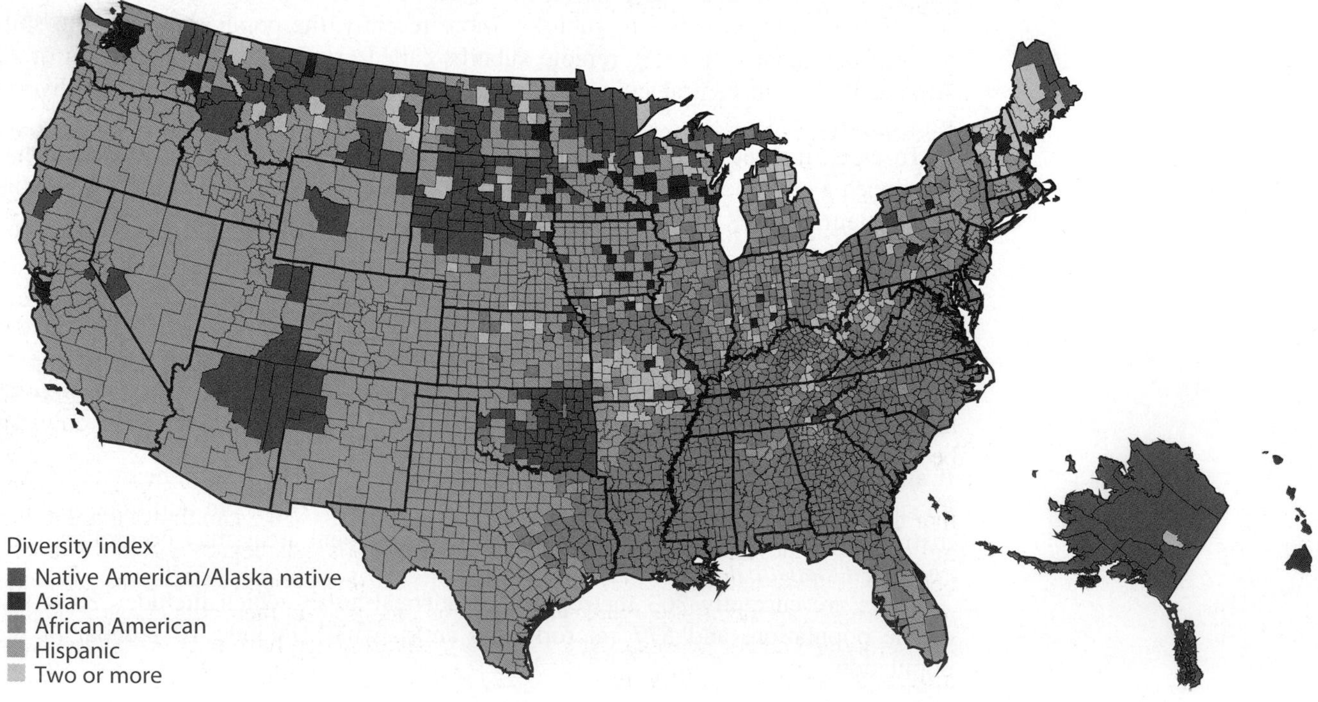

Chevy combined ethnic and regional marketing by using Spanish-language promotions like this one in some states.

Additional analysis of population demographic data, such as the information shown in Figure 3–4, suggests that racial and ethnic groups tend to be concentrated in geographic regions. This information allows companies to combine their multicultural marketing efforts with regional marketing activities. Consider, for example, that 48 percent of Asian Americans live in Los Angeles, New York City, and San Francisco, and that two-thirds of Hispanics live in Florida, Texas, and California. The Texas-based Multi-Cultural Agency of the Year, Dieste, for example, uses its expertise to create regional Hispanic campaigns for Nationwide, Hershey, Pizza Hut, Pepsi, and Nissan. Similarly, companies such as General Mills, Sears, and Tag Heuer are using mobile marketing to reach geographic concentrations of ethnic groups on their cell phones. Occasionally, these campaigns transcend race and ethnicity. The McDonald's "I'm Lovin It" campaign, for example, was a message rooted in hip-hop culture and intended for African American consumers and eventually gained popularity with all audiences around the world.[18]

Culture

A second social force, **culture**, incorporates the set of values, ideas, and attitudes that are learned and shared among the members of a group. Because many of the elements of culture influence consumer buying patterns, monitoring national and global cultural trends is important for marketing. Cross-cultural analysis needed for global marketing is discussed in Chapter 7.

The Changing Attitudes and Roles of Men and Women One of the most notable cultural changes in the United States in the past 30 years has been in the attitudes and roles of men and women in the marketplace. Some experts predict that as this trend continues, the buying patterns of men and women will eventually be very similar.

Your mothers and grandmothers probably remember advertising targeted at them that focused on the characteristics of household products—like laundry detergent that got clothes "whiter than white." In the 1970s and 1980s, ads began to create a bridge between genders with messages such as Secret's "strong enough for a man, but made for a woman." In the 1990s, marketing to women focused on their challenge of balancing family and career interests. Since then, women and men have encouraged the slow movement toward equality in the marketplace. As a result, today's Generation Y represents the first generation of women who have no collective memory of the dramatic changes we have undergone. As one expert explains, "Feminism today is like fluoride; we scarcely notice that we have it."

The video gaming industry is making changes to appeal to women as well as men.

Several factors have contributed to the shift in attitudes. First, many young women had career mothers who provided a reference point for lifestyle choices. Second, increased participation in organized sports eliminated one of the most visible inequalities in opportunities for women. And finally, the Internet has provided exposure to the marketplace through a mechanism that makes gender, race, and ethnicity invisible. Recent surveys, however, suggest that many of the 35 million Generation Y women believe that there is still a need for equal opportunities and treatment in the workplace and in politics.[19]

Many companies that had a consumer base that was primarily men or primarily women in the past are preparing for growth from the other gender. Grocery stores, car dealers, investment services, and many others hope to appeal to both groups in the future. Ugg Australia, for example, built a strong reputation among women with its distinctive boots and is now trying to attract men with new products and advertising. Similarly, Liz Claiborne developed Claiborne for Men, and Cole Haan expanded its line of shoes to include products for women. Some industries have been slower to eliminate stereotypes and gender roles in their business and marketing approaches. The video-gaming industry, for example, has focused on men in the past, offering primarily sports and fighting games. To attract the 50 percent of the population that has been missing, gaming companies are hiring women to help add female characters to games such as Rock Band 2, and to design new games such as Iron Chef America Supreme Cuisine and Imagine Babyz. Another company making the shift to attract both men and women is Harley-Davidson. The motorcycle company now hosts women-only "garage parties," offers motorcycles with smaller frames for women, and creates contests for women to submit essays on motorcycling and why they ride.[20]

Changing Values Culture also includes values, which vary with age but tend to be very similar for men and women. All age groups, for example, rank "protecting the family" and "honesty" as the most important values. Consumers under 20 years old rank "friendship" third, while the 20-to-29 and 30-to-39 age groups rank "self-esteem" and "health and fitness" as their third most important values, respectively.

An increasingly important value for consumers is sustainability and preserving the environment. Concern for the environment is one reason consumers are buying hybrid gas-electric automobiles such as the Toyota Prius and energy-efficient lightbulbs such as General Electric's Energy Smart™ fluorescent bulbs. Companies are also changing their business practices to respond to trends in consumer values. Wal-Mart has set ambitious goals to cut energy use, switch to renewable power, and reduce packaging on the products it carries. Recent research also indicates that consumers around the world are committed to brands with a strong link to social action. For example, Brita's "Filter for Good" campaign asks consumers to take a pledge to reduce their plastic bottle waste.[21]

A change in consumption orientation is also apparent. Today, and for the foreseeable future, **value consciousness**—or the concern for obtaining the best quality, features, and performance of a product or service for a given price—will drive consumption behavior. For many consumers this means bargaining for better price, not just when they are buying a car or a house, but in almost any purchasing situation. Innovative marketers have responded to this new orientation in numerous ways. Some retailers are now authorizing employees to respond to consumers who bargain by giving discounts off of advertised rates. Some companies have created new outlets for value-conscious consumers. Holiday Inn Worldwide, for example, has opened Holiday Inn Express hotels, designed to offer comfortable accommodations with room rates lower than Holiday Inns. Similarly, Nordstrom offers 50 to 75 percent discounts through its Nordstrom Rack Stores.[22]

learning review

1. Describe three generational cohorts.
2. Why are many companies developing multicultural marketing programs?
3. How are important values such as sustainability reflected in the marketplace today?

ECONOMIC FORCES

LO3

The second component of the environmental scan, the **economy**, pertains to the income, expenditures, and resources that affect the cost of running a business and household. We'll consider two aspects of these economic forces: a macroeconomic view of the marketplace and a microeconomic perspective of consumer income.

Macroeconomic Conditions

Of particular concern at the macroeconomic level is the inflationary or recessionary state of the economy, whether actual or perceived by consumers or businesses. In an inflationary economy, the cost to produce and buy products and services escalates as prices increase. From a marketing standpoint, if prices rise faster than consumer incomes, the number of items consumers can buy decreases. This relationship is evident in the cost of a college education. The National Center for Public Policy and Higher Education reports that since 1980 college tuition and fees have increased 440 percent while family income rose less than 150 percent. The share of family income required to pay for tuition at public four-year colleges rose from 12 percent in 1980 to 24 percent today.[23]

Whereas inflation is a period of price increases, recession is a time of slow economic activity. Businesses decrease production, unemployment rises, and many consumers have less money to spend. The U.S. economy experienced recessions from 1973–75, 1981–82, 1990–91, and in 2001. Most recently, a recessionary period began in 2008 and may become the longest in recent history.[24]

Consumer expectations of an inflationary and recessionary U.S. economy are an important element of environmental scanning. Consumer spending, which accounts for two-thirds of U.S. economic activity, is affected by expectations of the future. The two most popular surveys of consumer expectations are the Consumer Confidence Index, conducted by a nonprofit business research organization called the Conference Board, and the Index of Consumer Sentiment, conducted by the Survey Research Center at the University of Michigan. The surveys track the responses of consumers to specific questions about their expectations, and the results are reported once each month. For example, the Index of Consumer Sentiment asks, "Looking ahead, do you think that a year from now you will be better off financially, worse off or just about the same as now?" The answers to the questions are used to construct an index. The higher the index, the more favorable are consumer expectations. Figure 3–5 on the next page shows the fluctuation in the Index of Consumer Sentiment and its close relationship to economic conditions (blue areas represent recessionary periods). The consumer expectations surveys are closely monitored by many companies, particularly manufacturers and retailers of cars, furniture, and major appliances.[25]

Consumer Income

The microeconomic trends in terms of consumer income are also important issues for marketers. Having a product that meets the needs of consumers may be of little value if they are unable to purchase it. A consumer's ability to buy is related to income, which consists of gross, disposable, and discretionary components.

FIGURE 3–5
The Index of Consumer Sentiment (ICS) is closely related to economic conditions.

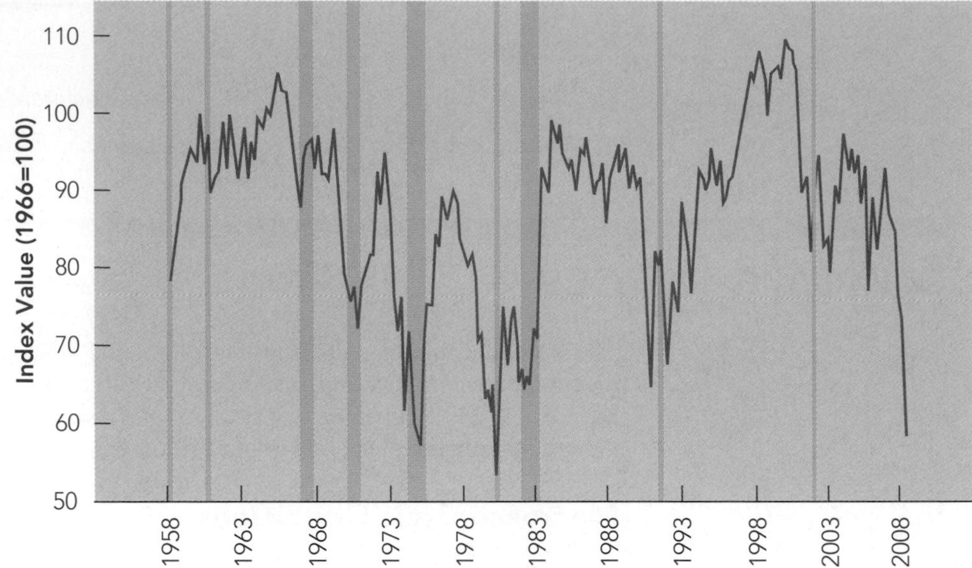

Gross Income The total amount of money made in one year by a person, household, or family unit is referred to as **gross income** (or "money income" at the Census Bureau). While the typical U.S. household earned only about $8,700 of income in 1970, it earned about $50,233 in 2007. When gross income is adjusted for inflation, however, income of that typical U.S. household was relatively stable. In fact, inflation-adjusted income has only varied between $40,442 and $50,641 since 1968. Figure 3–6 shows the distribution of annual income among U.S. households.[26] Are you from a typical household? Read the accompanying Going Online box to learn how you can determine the median household income in your hometown.

Disposable Income The second income component, **disposable income**, is the money a consumer has left after paying taxes to use for necessities such as food, housing, clothing, and transportation. Thus, if taxes rise or fall faster than income, consumers are likely to have more or less disposable income. Similarly, dramatic changes in prices of products can require spending adjustments. In recent years, for example, as the price of gasoline increased and declined dramatically, consumers found themselves adjusting their spending in other categories. In addition, the decline in home prices has had a psychological impact on consumer who tend to spend more when they feel their net worth is rising and postpone purchases when it declines. During a recessionary period, spending, debt, and use of credit are all expected to decline.[27]

FIGURE 3–6
U.S. households have a large range of gross incomes. See the text for descriptions of gross, disposable, and discretionary incomes.

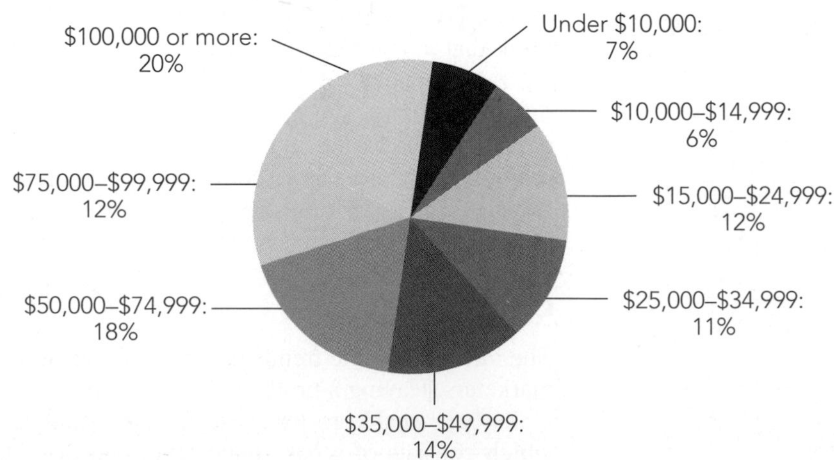

Going Online

There Are 65 Types of Neighborhoods—Which Type Is Yours?

Marketers collect and use environmental information to better understand consumers. One way to begin an environmental scan is to compare economic data about a particular segment of the population to what is "typical" or "average" for the entire population. Do you think your hometown is typical? To find out, visit ESRI's Web site at www.esri.com/data/esri_data/tapestry.html and use the Tapestry Segmentation tool to obtain a profile of your hometown. Just type in the ZIP code of your hometown. ESRI provides a comparison of your ZIP code's population with the averages for the nation. The system also classifies all neighborhoods into 65 segments based on their socioeconomic and demographic composition.

Discretionary Income The third component of income is **discretionary income**, the money that remains after paying for taxes and necessities. Discretionary income is used for luxury items such as a Regent cruise. An obvious problem in defining discretionary versus disposable income is determining what is a luxury and what is a necessity.

The Department of Labor monitors consumer expenditures through its annual Consumer Expenditure Survey. In 2007, consumers spent about 12 percent of their income on food, 34 percent on housing, and 4 percent on clothes. While an additional 24 percent is often spent on transportation, health care, and insurance, the remainder is generally viewed as discretionary. The percentage of income spent on food and housing typically declines as income increases, which can provide an increase in discretionary income. Discretionary expenditures can also be increased by reducing savings. The Bureau of Labor Statistics has observed that since the 1990s the savings rate has been declining and recently reached zero. That trend was reversed in 2008

As consumers' discretionary income increases, so does the opportunity to indulge in the luxurious leisure travel marketed by Regent.

Regent Seven Seas Cruises
www.rssc.com

when the government issued stimulus checks designed to improve the economy, and consumers saved the money rather than spend it. Economists predict that the savings rate will now increase to approximately 5 percent.[28]

TECHNOLOGICAL FORCES

Our society is in a period of dramatic technological change. **Technology**, the third environmental force, refers to inventions or innovations from applied science or engineering research. Each new wave of technological innovation can replace existing products and companies. Do you recognize the items pictured here and what they may replace?

Technology of Tomorrow

Technological change is the result of research, so it is difficult to predict. Some of the most dramatic technological changes occurring now, however, include the following:

- Cloud computing will allow businesses and consumers to access software applications directly from third parties over the Internet and "pay as they go."
- Researchers are developing a wireless power process to transmit power to electrical products without interconnecting wires.
- Advances in nanotechnology, the science of unimaginably small electronics, will lead to smaller microprocessors, efficient fuel cells, and cancer-detection sensors.
- Biotechnology and agricultural genome research is being used to develop genetically modified crops to create enough food for a growing world population.

Some of these trends in technology are already seen in today's marketplace. Google, for example, has developed a cloud computing collection of software including e-mail and word processing called Google Apps. A new company called Powercast is manufacturing holiday lights that run on wireless power, and MIT has developed "WiTricity," which can power a TV from across a room. Nanotechnology is used in the Samsung flash memory chips that are part of the iPod nano. Other technologies such as organic LED televisions, online meeting services, and customized music

Technological change leads to new products. What products might be replaced by these innovations?

services are likely to replace or substitute for existing products and services such as plasma screen televisions, business travel, and radio.[29]

Technology's Impact on Customer Value

Advances in technology have important effects on marketing. First, the cost of technology is plummeting, causing the customer value assessment of technology-based products to focus on other dimensions such as quality, service, and relationships. *PC Magazine* publishes an article titled, "The Best Free Software," each year to tell readers about companies that give their software away, with the expectation that advertising or upgrade purchases will generate revenue. A similar approach is used by many U.S. cellular telephone vendors, who charge little for the telephone if the purchase leads to a long-term telephone service contract.[30]

Technology also provides value through the development of new products. Recent examples that generated extraordinary consumer interest include Nintendo's Wii, Activision's *Guitar Hero* series, and Apple's iPhone. A new version of Amazon's electronic book reader, Kindle, also received attention from many consumers. The new product provides a high-resolution display, holds as many as 1,500 books, and offers a "text-to-speech" feature that allows readers to listen to books. Other new products likely to be available soon include injectable health monitors that will send glucose, oxygen, and other clinical information to a wristwatch-like monitor, LED lights that look like traditional fluorescent light bulbs, and Bluetooth-enabled speakers and video cameras.[31]

Technology can also change existing products and the ways they are produced. Many companies are using technological developments to recycle products through the manufacturing cycle several times. The National Association for PET Container Resources, for example, estimates that 24 percent of all plastic bottles are now recycled, usually to make polyester fibers that are spun into everything from sweaters to upholstery. Tomra Systems has more than 250 rePlanet recycling centers in California and 15,000 reverse vending machines throughout the United States. Another approach is *precycling*, or efforts by manufacturers and consumers to avoid creating waste. For manufacturers this includes decreasing the amount of packaging they use, and for consumers it means buying products that last longer, avoiding products with excess packaging, and reusing as much as possible. According to marketing expert Melissa Lavigne, "It's about being conscious about products you buy in the first place. That's the idea behind precycling."[32]

rePlanet offers recycling through its kiosks and centers. Precycling can also reduce waste.

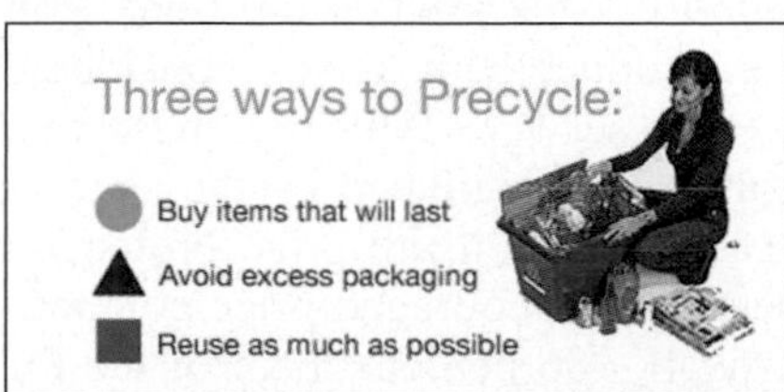

Three ways to Precycle:
Buy items that will last
Avoid excess packaging
Reuse as much as possible

CHAPTER 3 SCANNING THE MARKETING ENVIRONMENT

Electronic Business Technologies

The transformative power of technology may be best illustrated by the rapid growth of the **marketspace**, an information- and communication-based electronic exchange environment mostly occupied by sophisticated computer and telecommunication technologies and digitized offerings. Any activity that uses some form of electronic communication in the inventory, exchange, advertisement, distribution, and payment of goods and services is often called **electronic commerce**. Network technologies are now used for everything from filing expense reports, to monitoring daily sales, to sharing information with employees, to communicating instantly with suppliers.

Many companies have adapted Internet-based technology internally to support their electronic business strategies. An *intranet*, for example, is an Internet-based network used within the boundaries of an organization. It is a private network that may or may not be connected to the public Internet. *Extranets*, which use Internet-based technologies, permit communication between a company and its supplier, distributors, and other partners (such as advertising agencies).

COMPETITIVE FORCES

The fourth component of the environmental scan, **competition**, refers to the alternative firms that could provide a product to satisfy a specific market's needs. There are various forms of competition, and each company must consider its present and potential competitors in designing its marketing strategy.

Alternative Forms of Competition

LO5

Four basic forms of competition form a continuum from pure competition to monopolistic competition to oligopoly to pure monopoly. Chapter 13 contains further discussions on pricing practices under these four forms of competition.

At one end of the continuum is *pure competition*, in which there are many sellers and they each have a similar product. Companies that deal in commodities common to agribusiness (for example, wheat, rice, and grain) often are in a pure competition position in which distribution (in the sense of shipping products) is important but other elements of marketing have little impact.

In the second point on the continuum, *monopolistic competition*, many sellers compete with substitutable products within a price range. For example, if the price of coffee rises too much, consumers may switch to tea. Coupons or sales are frequently used marketing tactics.

Oligopoly, a common industry structure, occurs when a few companies control the majority of industry sales. The wireless telephone industry, for example, is dominated by Verizon, AT&T, Sprint, and T-Mobile, which have 81, 75, 50, and 32 million subscribers, respectively. Similarly, the entertainment industry in the United States is dominated by Viacom, Disney, and Time Warner, and the major firms in the U.S. defense contractor industry are Boeing, Northrup Grumman, and Lockheed Martin. Critics of oligopolies suggest that because there are few sellers, price competition among firms is not desirable because it leads to reduced profits for all producers.[33]

The final point on the continuum, *pure monopoly*, occurs when only one firm sells the product. Monopolies are common for producers of goods considered essential to a community: water, electricity, and cable service. Typically, marketing plays a small role in a monopolistic setting because it is regulated by the state or federal government. Government control usually seeks to ensure price protection for the buyer, although deregulation in recent years has encouraged price competition in the electricity market. Concern that Microsoft's 86 percent share of the PC operating system market is a monopoly has led to lawsuits and consent decrees from the U.S. Justice Department and fines and ongoing investigations from the European Union.[34]

Components of Competition

In developing a marketing program, companies must consider the factors that drive competition: entry, bargaining power of buyers and suppliers, existing rivalries, and substitution possibilities.[35] Scanning the environment requires a look at all of them. These factors relate to a firm's marketing mix decisions and may be used to create a barrier to entry, increase brand awareness, or intensify a fight for market share.

Entry In considering the competition, a firm must assess the likelihood of new entrants. Additional producers increase industry capacity and tend to lower prices. A company scanning its environment must consider the possible **barriers to entry** for other firms, which are business practices or conditions that make it difficult for new firms to enter the market. Barriers to entry can be in the form of capital requirements, advertising expenditures, product identity, distribution access, or the cost to customers of switching suppliers. The higher the expense of the barrier, the more likely it will deter new entrants. For example, Western Union and Moneygram dominate the $7 billion money transfer market because of their huge distribution networks of branch offices and global pickup locations. Potential competitors find it difficult to enter the market because lack of distribution limits consumer access.[36]

Power of Buyers and Suppliers A competitive analysis must consider the power of buyers and suppliers. Powerful buyers exist when they are few in number, there are low switching costs, or the product represents a significant share of the buyer's total costs. This last factor leads the buyer to exert significant pressure for price competition. A supplier gains power when the product is critical to the buyer and when it has built up the switching costs.

Existing Competitors and Substitutes Competitive pressures among existing firms depend on the rate of industry growth. In slow-growth settings, competition is more heated for any possible gains in market share. High fixed costs also create competitive pressures for firms to fill production capacity. For example, airlines offer discounts for making early reservations and charge penalties for changes or cancellations in an effort to fill seats, which represent a high fixed cost.

Small Businesses as Competitors

While large companies provide familiar examples of the forms and components of competition, small businesses make up the majority of the competitive landscape for most businesses. Consider that there are approximately 27 million small businesses in the United States, which employ half of all private sector employees. In addition, small businesses generate 60 to 80 percent of all new jobs annually and 50 percent of the gross domestic product (GDP). Research has shown a strong correlation between national economic growth and the level of new small business activity in the previous years.[37]

learning review

4. What is the difference between a consumer's disposable and discretionary income?
5. How does technology impact customer value?
6. In pure competition there are a ______________ number of sellers.

REGULATORY FORCES

For any organization, the marketing and broader business decisions are constrained, directed, and influenced by regulatory forces. **Regulation** consists of restrictions state and federal laws place on business with regard to the conduct of its activities. Regulation exists to protect companies as well as consumers. Much of the regulation from the federal and state levels is the result of an active political process and has been passed to ensure competition and fair business practices. For consumers, the focus of legislation is to protect them from unfair trade practices and ensure their safety.

Protecting Competition

Major federal legislation has been passed to encourage competition, which is deemed desirable because it permits the consumer to determine which competitor will succeed and which will fail. The first such law was the *Sherman Antitrust Act* (1890). Lobbying by farmers in the Midwest against fixed railroad shipping prices led to the passage of this act, which forbids (1) contracts, combinations, or conspiracies in restraint of trade and (2) actual monopolies or attempts to monopolize any part of trade or commerce. Because of vague wording and government inactivity, however, there was only one successful case against a company in the nine years after the act became law, and the Sherman Act was supplemented with the *Clayton Act* (1914). This act forbids certain actions that are likely to lessen competition, although no actual harm has yet occurred.

In the 1930s, the federal government had to act again to ensure fair competition. During that time, large chain stores appeared, such as the Great Atlantic & Pacific Tea Company (A&P). Small businesses were threatened, and they lobbied for the *Robinson-Patman Act* (1936). This act makes it unlawful to discriminate in prices charged to different purchasers of the same product, where the effect may substantially lessen competition or help to create a monopoly.

Product-Related Legislation

Various federal laws in existence specifically address the product component of the marketing mix. Some are aimed at protecting the company, some at protecting the consumer, and at least one at protecting both.

A company can protect its competitive position in new and novel products under the patent law, which gives inventors the right to exclude others from making, using, or selling products that infringe the patented invention. The federal copyright law is another way for a company to protect its competitive position in a product. The copyright law gives the author of a literary, dramatic, musical, or artistic work the exclusive right to print, perform, or otherwise copy that work. Copyright is secured automatically when the work is created. However, the published work should bear an appropriate copyright notice, including the copyright symbol, the first year of publication, and the name of the copyright owner, and it must be registered under the federal copyright law. Digital technology has necessitated additional copyright legislation, called the *Digital Millenium Copyright Act* (1998), to improve protection of copyrighted digital products. In addition, producers of DVD movies, music recordings, and software want protection from devices designed to circumvent antipiracy elements of their products.[38]

There are many consumer-oriented federal laws regarding products. The various laws include more than 30 amendments and separate laws relating to food, drugs, and cosmetics, such as the *Infant Formula Act* (1980), the *Nutritional Labeling and Education Act* (1990), new labeling requirements for dietary supplements (1997), and proposed labeling guidelines for trans fats (2006).[39] Various other consumer protec-

These products are identified by protected trademarks. Are any of these trademarks in danger of becoming generic?

tion laws have a broader scope, such as the *Fair Packaging and Labeling Act* (1966), the *Child Protection Act* (1966), and the *Consumer Product Safety Act* (1972), which established the Consumer Product Safety Commission to monitor product safety and establish uniform product safety standards. Many of these laws came about because of **consumerism**, a grassroots movement started in the 1960s to increase the influence, power, and rights of consumers in dealing with institutions. This movement continues and is reflected in growing consumer demands for ecologically safe products and ethical and socially responsible business practices. One hotly debated issue concerns liability for environmental abuse.

Trademarks are intended to protect both the firm selling a trademarked product and the consumer buying it. A Senate report states:

> The purposes underlying any trademark statute [are] twofold. One is to protect the public so that it may be confident that, in purchasing a product bearing a particular trademark which it favorably knows, it will get the product which it asks for and wants to get. Secondly, where the owner of a trademark has spent energy, time, and money in presenting to the public the product, he is protected in this investment from misappropriation in pirates and cheats.

This statement was made in connection with another product-related law, the *Lanham Act* (1946), which provides for registration of a company's trademarks. Historically, the first user of a trademark in commerce had the exclusive right to use that particular word, name, or symbol in its business. Registration under the Lanham Act provides important advantages to a trademark owner that has used the trademark in interstate or foreign commerce, but it does not confer ownership. A company can lose its trademark if it becomes generic, which means that it has primarily come to be merely a common descriptive word for the product. Coca-Cola, Whopper, and Xerox are registered trademarks, and competitors cannot use these names. Aspirin and escalator are former trademarks that are now generic terms in the United States and can be used by anyone.

In 1988, the *Trademark Law Revision Act* resulted in a major change to the Lanham Act, allowing a company to secure rights to a name before actual use by declaring an intent to use the name.[40] In 2003, the United States agreed to participate in the *Madrid Protocol,* which is a treaty that facilitates the protection of U.S. trademark rights throughout the world.[41] See the Marketing Matters box on the next page to learn how the Internet and technology have led to a use (or misuse) of trademarks called doppelgangers.[42]

Marketing Matters > > > > > > > > > technology

The Web Allows New Uses and Misuses of Trademarks

Have you see an ad or a logo that looked like a familiar brand but was slightly different? Some examples you might be familiar with include a commercial for Chevy Tahoe saying "global warming is here," and Starbucks logos that read "Evil Empire" or "Frankenbucks Coffee." These parodies—sometimes called doppelgangers—are a growing form of citizen protest called culture jamming. The purpose of culture jamming ranges from offering an alternative, often creative, perspective to undermining the integrity of existing brand marketing. Digital technologies make this possible. Image and video editing software makes changes easy, and Web sites such as YouTube and Adbusters offer outlets for these activities.

Companies currently have different responses to doppelgangers. Some companies ignore them, others try to monitor the parodies for insight about consumer perceptions of the company, and others fight back. Starbucks, for example, has used cease and desist letters, injunctions, and trademark infringement litigation to try to stop the creation and distribution of doppelgangers. Jeben Berg, YouTube's creative strategist, however, argues that culture jamming is important because it is "so disruptive that it forces you to look." Obviously culture jamming and doppelgangers are just two of many possible uses of new technologies. What will be next?

One of the most recent changes in trademark law is the U.S. Supreme Court's ruling that companies may obtain trademarks for colors associated with their products. Over time, consumers may begin to associate a particular color with a specific brand. Examples of products that may benefit from the new law include NutraSweet's sugar substitute in pastel blue packages and Owens-Corning Fiberglas Corporation's pink insulation.[43] Another recent addition to trademark law is the *Federal Dilution Act* (1995), which is used to prevent someone from using a trademark on a noncompeting product (e.g., "Cadillac" brushes).[44]

Pricing-Related Legislation

The pricing component of the marketing mix is the focus of regulation from two perspectives: price fixing and price discounting. Although the Sherman Act did not outlaw price fixing, the courts view this behavior as *per se illegal* (*per se* means "through or of itself"), which means the courts see price fixing itself as illegal.

Certain forms of price discounting are allowed. Quantity discounts are acceptable; that is, buyers can be charged different prices for a product provided there are differences in manufacturing or delivery costs. Promotional allowances or services may be given to buyers on an equal basis proportionate to volume purchased. Also, a firm can meet a competitor's price "in good faith." Legal and regulatory aspects of pricing are covered in more detail in Chapter 14.

Distribution-Related Legislation

The government has four concerns with regard to distribution—earlier referred to as "place" actions in the marketing mix—and the maintenance of competition. The first, *exclusive dealing,* is an arrangement a manufacturer makes with a reseller to handle only its products and not those of competitors. This practice is illegal under the Clayton Act only when it substantially lessens competition.

Requirement contracts require a buyer to purchase all or part of its needs for a product from one seller for a time period. These contracts are not always illegal but depend on the court's interpretation of their impact on distribution.

Exclusive territorial distributorships are a third distribution issue often under regulatory scrutiny. In this situation, a manufacturer grants a distributor the sole rights to sell a product in a specific geographical area. The courts have found few violations with these arrangements.

The fourth distribution strategy is a *tying arrangement,* whereby a seller requires the purchaser of one product to also buy another item in the line. These contracts may be illegal when the seller has such economic power in the tying product that the seller can restrain trade in the tied product. Legal aspects of distribution are reviewed in greater detail in Chapter 15.

Advertising- and Promotion-Related Legislation

Promotion and advertising are aspects of marketing closely monitored by the Federal Trade Commission (FTC), which was established by the *FTC Act of 1914*. The FTC has been concerned with deceptive or misleading advertising and unfair business practices and has the power to (1) issue cease and desist orders and (2) order corrective advertising. In issuing a *cease and desist order*, the FTC orders a company to stop practices the commission considers unfair. With *corrective advertising*, the FTC can require a company to spend money on advertising to correct previous misleading ads. The enforcement powers of the FTC are so significant that often just an indication of concern from the commission can cause companies to revise their promotion.

A landmark legal battle regarding deceptive advertising involved the Federal Trade Commission and Campbell Soup Co. It had been Campbell's practice to insert clear glass marbles into the bottom of soup containers used in print advertisements to bring the soup ingredients (e.g., noodles or chicken) to the surface. The FTC ruled that the advertising was deceptive because it misrepresented the amount of solid ingredients in the soup, and it issued a cease and desist order. Campbell and its advertising agency agreed to discontinue the practice. Future ads used a ladle to show the ingredients.[45]

Companies must meet certain requirements before they can display this logo on their Web sites.

Better Business Bureau
www.bbbonline.com

Other laws have been introduced to regulate promotion practices. The *Deceptive Mail Prevention and Enforcement Act* (1999), for example, provides specifications for direct-mail sweepstakes, such as the requirement that the statement "No purchase is necessary to enter" is displayed in the mailing, in the rules, and on the entry form. Similarly, the *Telephone Consumer Protection Act* (1991) provides requirements for telemarketing promotions, including fax promotions. Telemarketing is also subject to a law that created the *National Do Not Call Registry*, which is a list of consumer phone numbers of people who do not want to receive unsolicited telemarketing calls. Finally, new laws such as the *Children's Online Privacy Protection Act* (1998), the *European Union Data Protection Act* (1998), and the *Controlling the Assault of Non-Solicited Pornography and Marketing (CAN-SPAM) Act* (2004) are designed to restrict information collection and unsolicited e-mail promotions, and specify simple opt-out procedures on the Internet. A related Internet issue, taxation, has generated an ongoing debate and temporary laws such as the *Internet Tax Freedom Act* (2007).[46]

Control through Self-Regulation

The government has provided much legislation to create a competitive business climate and protect the consumer. An alternative to government control is **self-regulation**, where an industry attempts to police itself. The major television networks, for example, have used self-regulation to set their own guidelines for TV ads for children's toys. These guidelines have generally worked well. There are two problems with self-regulation, however: noncompliance by members and enforcement. In addition, if attempts at self-regulation are too strong, they may violate the Robinson-Patman Act. The best-known self-regulatory group is the Better Business Bureau (BBB). This agency is a voluntary alliance of companies whose goal is to help maintain fair practices. Although the BBB has no legal power, it does try to use "moral suasion" to get members to comply with its standards. The BBB recently developed a reliability assurance program, called BBB Online, to provide objective consumer protection for Internet shoppers. Before they display the BBB Online logo on their Web site, participating companies must be members of their local Better Business Bureau, have been in business for at least one year, agree to participate in BBB's advertising self-regulation program, abide by the BBB Code of Business Practices, and work with the BBB to resolve consumer disputes that arise over goods or services promoted or advertised on their site.[47]

learning review

7. The __________ Act was punitive toward monopolies, whereas the __________ Act was preventive.
8. Describe some of the recent changes in trademark law.
9. How does the Better Business Bureau encourage companies to follow its standards for commerce?

LEARNING OBJECTIVES REVIEW

LO1 *Explain how environmental scanning provides information about social, economic, technological, competitive, and regulatory forces.*
Many businesses operate in environments where important forces change. Environmental scanning is the process of acquiring information about these changes to allow marketers to identify and interpret trends. There are five environmental forces businesses must monitor: social, economic, technological, competitive, and regulatory. By identifying trends related to each of these forces, businesses can develop and maintain successful marketing programs. Several trends that most businesses are monitoring include the increasing diversity of the U.S. population, the growing economic impact of China and India, and the dramatic growth of customer-generated content.

LO2 *Describe how social forces such as demographics and culture can have an impact on marketing strategy.*
Demographic information describes the world population; the U.S. population; the generational cohorts such as baby boomers, Generation X, and Generation Y; the structure of the American household; the geographic shifts of the population; and the racial and ethnic diversity of the population that has led to multicultural marketing programs. Cultural factors include the trend toward fewer differences in male and female consumer behavior and the impact of values such as "health and fitness" on consumer preferences.

LO3 *Discuss how economic forces such as macroeconomic conditions and consumer income affect marketing.*
Economic forces include the strong relationship between consumers' expectations about the economy and their spending. Gross income has remained stable for more than 30 years although the rate of saving has been declining.

LO4 *Describe how technological changes can affect marketing.*
Technological innovations can replace existing products and services. Changes in technology can also have an impact on customer value by reducing the cost of products, improving the quality of products, and providing new products that were not previously feasible. Electronic commerce is transforming how companies do business.

LO5 *Discuss the forms of competition that exist in a market and key components of competition.*
There are four forms of competition: pure competition, monopolistic competition, oligopoly, and monopoly. The key components of competition include the likelihood of new competitors, the power of buyers and suppliers, and the presence of competitors and possible substitutes. While large companies are often used as examples of marketplace competitors, there are 23 million small businesses in the United States, which have a significant impact on the economy.

LO6 *Explain the major legislation that ensures competition and regulates the elements of the marketing mix.*
Regulation exists to protect companies and consumers. Legislation that ensures a competitive marketplace includes the Sherman Antitrust Act. Product-related legislation includes copyright and trademark laws that protect companies and packaging and labeling laws that protect consumers. Pricing- and distribution-related laws are designed to create a competitive marketplace with fair prices and availability. Regulation related to promotion and advertising reduces deceptive practices and provides enforcement through the Federal Trade Commission. Self-regulation through organizations such as the Better Business Bureau provides an alternative to federal and state regulation.

FOCUSING ON KEY TERMS

baby boomers p. 69
barriers to entry p. 81
blended family p. 70
competition p. 80
consumerism p. 83
culture p. 73
demographics p. 68
discretionary income p. 77
disposable income p. 76
economy p. 75
electronic commerce p. 80
environmental scanning p. 66
Generation X p. 69
Generation Y p. 70
gross income p. 76
marketspace p. 80
multicultural marketing p. 72
regulation p. 82
self-regulation p. 85
social forces p. 68
technology p. 78
value consciousness p. 74

APPLYING MARKETING KNOWLEDGE

1 For many years Gerber has manufactured baby food in small, single-sized containers. In conducting an environmental scan, identify three trends or factors that might significantly affect this company's future business, and then propose how Gerber might respond to these changes.

2 Describe the new features you would add to an automobile designed for consumers in the 55+ age group. In what magazines would you advertise to appeal to this target market?

3 The population shift from suburbs to exurbs and small towns was discussed in this chapter. What businesses and industries are likely to benefit from this trend? How will retailers need to change to accommodate these consumers?

4 New technologies are continuously improving and replacing existing products. Although technological change is often difficult to predict, suggest how the following companies and products might be affected by the Internet and digital technologies: (*a*) Kodak cameras and film, (*b*) American Airlines, and (*c*) the Metropolitan Museum of Art.

5 In recent years in the brewing industry, a couple of large firms that have historically had most of the beer sales (Anheuser-Busch and Miller) have faced competition from many small "micro" brands. In terms of the continuum of competition, how would you explain this change?

6 The Johnson Company manufactures buttons and pins with slogans and designs. These pins are inexpensive to produce and are sold in retail outlets such as discount stores, hobby shops, and bookstores. Little equipment is needed for a new competitor to enter the market. What strategies should Johnson consider to create effective barriers to entry?

7 Why would Xerox be concerned about its name becoming generic?

8 Develop a "Code of Business Practices" for a new online vitamin store. Does your code address advertising? Privacy? Use by children? Why is self-regulation important?

building your marketing plan

Your marketing plan will include a situation analysis based on internal and external factors that are likely to affect your marketing program.

1 To summarize information about external factors, create a table similar to Figure 3–2 and identify three trends related to each of the five forces (social, economic, technological, competitive, and regulatory) that relate to your product or service.

2 When your table is completed, describe how each of the trends represents an opportunity or a threat for your business.

video case 3 Geek Squad: A New Business for a New Environment

"As long as there's innovation there is going to be new kinds of chaos," explains Robert Stephens, founder of the technology support company Geek Squad. The chaos Stephens is referring to is the difficulty we have all experienced trying to keep up with the many changes in our environment, particularly those related to computers, technology, software, communication, and entertainment. Generally, consumers have found it difficult to install, operate, and use many of the electronic products available today. "It takes time to read the manuals," Stephens says. "I'm going to save you that time because I stay home on Saturday nights and read them for you!"

THE COMPANY

The Geek Squad story begins when Stephens, a native of Chicago, passed up an Art Institute scholarship to pursue a degree in computer science. While Stephens was a computer science student he took a job fixing computers for a research laboratory, and he also started consulting. He could repair televisions, computers, and a variety of other items, although he decided to focus on computers. His experiences as a consultant led him to realize that most people needed help with technology and that they saw value in a service whose employees would show up at a specified time, be friendly, use understandable language, and solve the problem. So, with just $200, Stephens formed Geek Squad in 1994.

Geek Squad set out to provide timely and effective help with all computing needs regardless of the make, model, or place of purchase. Geek Squad employees were called "agents" and wore uniforms consisting of black pants or skirts, black shoes, white shirts, black clip-on ties, a badge, and a black jacket with a Geek Squad logo to create a "humble" attitude that was not threatening to customers. Agents drove black-and-white Volkswagen Beetles, or Geekmobiles, with a logo on the door, and charged fixed prices for services, regardless of how much time was required to provide the service. The "house call" services ranged from installing networks, to debugging a computer, to setting up an entertainment system, and cost from $100 to $300. "We're like 'Dragnet;' we show up at people's homes and help," Stephens says. "We're also like *Ghostbusters*' and there's a pseudogovernment feel to it like *Men in Black*."

In 2002, Geek Squad was purchased by leading consumer electronics retailer Best Buy for about $3 million. Best Buy had observed very high return rates for most of its complex products. Shoppers would be excited about new products, purchase them and take them home, get frustrated trying to make them actually work, and then return them to the store demanding a refund. In fact, Best Buy research revealed that consumers were beginning to see service as a critical element of the purchase. The partnership was an excellent match. Best Buy consumers welcomed the help. Stephens became Geek Squad's chief inspector and a Best Buy vice president and began putting a Geek Squad "precinct" in every Best Buy store, creating some stand-alone Geek Squad Stores, and providing 24-hour telephone support. There are now more than 18,000 agents in the United States, Canada, the United Kingdom, and China, and return rates have declined by 25 to 35 percent. Geek Squad customer materials now suggest that the service is "Saving the World One Computer at a Time. 24 Hours a Day. Your Place or Ours!"

THE CHANGING ENVIRONMENT

Many changes in the environment occurred to create the need for Geek Squad's services. Future changes are also likely to change the way Geek Squad operates. An environmental scan helps understand the changes.

The most obvious changes may be related to technology. Wireless broadband technology, high-definition televisions, products with Internet interfaces, and a general trend toward computers, phones, entertainment systems, and even appliances being interconnected are just a few examples of new products and applications for consumers to learn about. There are also technology-related problems such as viruses, spyware, lost data, and "crashed" or inoperable computers. New technologies have also created a demand for new types of maintenance such as password management, operating system updates, disk cleanup, and "defragging."

Another environmental change that contributes to the popularity of Geek Squad is the change in social factors such as demographics and culture. In the past many electronics manufacturers and retailers focused primarily on men. Women, however, are becoming increasingly interested in personal computing and home entertainment, and, according to the Consumer Electronics Association, are likely to outspend men in the near future. Best Buy's consumer research indicates that women expect personal service during the purchase and installation after the purchase—exactly the service Geek Squad is designed to provide. Our culture is also embracing the Geek Squad concept. If you follow television programming you may have noticed the series *Chuck* where one of the characters works for the "Nerd Herd" at "Buy More" and drives a car like a Geekmobile on service calls!

Competition, economics, and the regulatory environment have also had a big influence on Geek Squad. As discount stores such as Wal-Mart and PC makers such as Dell began to compete with Best Buy and Circuit City new services such as in-home installation were needed to create value for customers. Now, just as changes in competition created an opportunity for Geek Squad, it is also leading to another level of competition as Dell has introduced its own computer support service, Dell-On-Call, and cable companies are offering their own services. The economic situation for electronics continues to improve as prices decline and median income in the United States, particularly for women, is increasing. In 2009, consumers purchased 30 million high-definition televisions, but household penetration is still below 40 percent. Finally, the regulatory environment continues to change with respect to electronic transfer of copyrighted materials such as music and movies and software. Geek Squad must monitor the changes to ensure that its services comply with relevant laws.

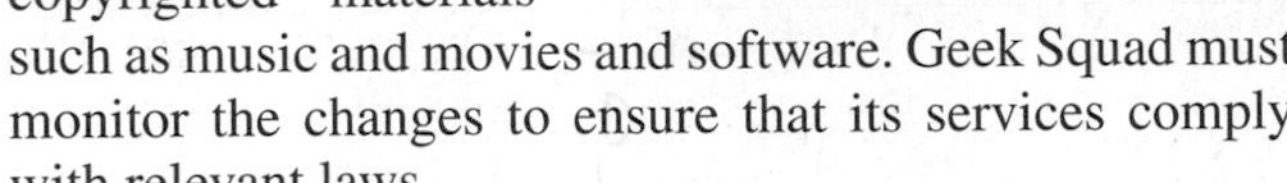

THE FUTURE FOR GEEK SQUAD

The combination of many positive environmental factors helps explain the extraordinary success of Geek Squad. Today, it repairs more than 3,000 PCs a day and generates more than $1 billion in revenue. Because Geek Squad services have a high-profit margin they contribute to the overall performance of Best Buy, and they help generate traffic in the store and create store loyalty. To continue to grow, however, Geek Squad will need to continue to scan the environment and try new approaches to creating customer value.

One possible new approach is to find additional locations that are convenient to consumers. For example, Geek Squad locations are being tested in some FedEx stores and in some Office Depot stores. Another possible approach is to create new houses that are designed for the newest consumer electronics products. To test this idea Best Buy has created partnerships with home builders to wire new houses with high-speed cables and networking equipment that Geek Squad agents can use to create ideal computer and entertainment systems. Geek Squad is also using new technology to improve. Agents now use a smart phone to access updated schedules, log in their hours, and run diagnostics tests on clients' equipment. Finally, to attract the best possible employees, Geek Squad and Best Buy are trying a "results-only work environment" that has no fixed schedules and no mandatory meetings. By encouraging employees to make their own work-life decisions the Geek Squad hopes to keep morale and productivity high.

Other changes and opportunities are certain to appear soon. Despite the success of the Geek Squad, and the potential for additional growth, however, Robert Stephens is modest and claims, "Geeks may inherit the Earth, but they have no desire to rule it!"

Questions

1 What are the key environmental factors that created an opportunity for Robert Stephens to start the Geek Squad?

2 What changes in the purchasing patterns of (*a*) all consumers, and (*b*) women made the acquisition of Geek Squad particularly important for Best Buy?

3 Based on the case information and what you know about consumer electronics, conduct an environmental scan for Geek Squad to identify key trends. For each of the five environmental forces (social, economic, technological, competitive, and regulatory), identify trends likely to influence Geek Squad in the near future.

4 What promotional activities would you recommend to encourage consumers who use independent installers to switch to Geek Squad?

GET YOUR GAME FACE ON!

GET THE PAINT. GET PUMPED.
GET A DESIGNATED DRIVER.
THAT'S PREPARATION!!

81% OF COLLEGE STUDENTS USE A DESIGNATED DRIVER WHEN THEY CELEBRATE.*

4 Ethical and Social Responsibility in Marketing

LEARNING OBJECTIVES
After reading this chapter you should be able to:

- LO1 Explain the differences between legal and ethical behavior in marketing.
- LO2 Identify factors that influence ethical and unethical marketing decisions.
- LO3 Describe the different concepts of social responsibility.
- LO4 Recognize unethical and socially irresponsible consumer behavior.

RESPONSIBILITY MATTERS AT ANHEUSER-BUSCH

Why would a company spend more than $750 million since 1982 trying to persuade people not to abuse its products and millions of dollars more to decrease litter and solid waste? Ask Anheuser-Busch, the leading American brewer.

Anheuser-Busch has been an advocate for responsible drinking for nearly three decades. The company began an aggressive campaign to fight alcohol abuse and underage drinking with its landmark "Know When to Say When" campaign in 1982. In 1989, a Consumer Awareness and Education Department was established within the company. This department, now called the Corporate Social Responsibility (CSR) Department, is charged with developing and implementing programs, advertising, and partnerships that promote responsible drinking; helping prevent alcohol abuse; and helping curb underage drinking before it starts. For example, nearly 7 million copies of the company's *Family Talk about Drinking* guidebook have been distributed free to parents and educators.

In 2004, the brewer began a new chapter in its awareness and education efforts with the launch of its "Responsibility Matters" campaign. This effort emphasizes and implements effective education and awareness programs that promote responsibility and responsible behaviors, such as parents talking with their children about underage drinking, adults being designated drivers, retailers checking IDs to prevent sales to minors, and more. Anheuser-Busch believes these efforts are partly responsible for the sizable decline in drunk-driving accidents, underage drinking, and other forms of alcohol abuse since 1982.

Responsibility at Anheuser-Busch is broader than its successful alcohol awareness and education initiatives. The company is an advocate and sponsor of numerous efforts to preserve the natural environment. A notable example is its massive recycling effort through Anheuser-Busch Recycling Corporation (A-BRC). A-BRC is the world's largest recycler of aluminum cans. A-BRC recycles over 27 billion cans annually, the equivalent of five cans for every four the company packages worldwide. The rationale for founding A-BRC was simple: Voluntary recycling reduces litter and solid waste while conserving natural resources.

Anheuser-Busch acts on what it views as an ethical obligation to its customers and the general public with its alcohol awareness and education programs. At the same time, the company's efforts to protect the environment reflect its broader social responsibility. Not surprisingly, in 2009, the company ranked first among all companies for social responsibility in *Fortune* magazine's "World's Most-Admired Companies" list.[1]

NATURE AND SIGNIFICANCE OF MARKETING ETHICS

Ethics are the moral principles and values that govern the actions and decisions of an individual or group.[2] They serve as guidelines on how to act rightly and justly when faced with moral dilemmas.

Ethical/Legal Framework in Marketing

LO1

A good starting point for understanding the nature and significance of ethics is the distinction between legality and ethicality of marketing decisions. Figure 4–1 helps visualize the relationship between laws and ethics.[3] Whereas ethics deal with personal moral principles and values, **laws** are society's values and standards that are enforceable in the courts. This distinction can sometimes lead to the rationalization that if a behavior is within reasonable ethical and legal limits, then it is not really illegal or unethical. When a recent survey asked the question, "Is it OK to get around the law if you don't actually break it?" about 61 percent of businesspeople who took part responded "yes."[4] How would you answer this question?

Judgment plays a large role in numerous situations in defining ethical and legal boundaries. Consider the following situations. After reading each, assign it to the cell in Figure 4–1 that you think best fits the situation along the ethical–legal continuum.[5]

1. More than 70 percent of the physicians in the Maricopa County (Arizona) Medical Society agreed to establish a maximum fee schedule for health services to curb rising medical costs. All physicians were required to adhere to this schedule as a condition for membership in the society. The U.S. Supreme Court ruled that this agreement to set prices violated the Sherman Act and represented price fixing, which is illegal. Was the society's action ethical?
2. A company in California sells a computer program to auto dealers showing that car buyers should finance their purchase rather than paying cash. The program omits the effect of income taxes and misstates the interest earned on savings over the loan period. The finance option always provides a net benefit over the cash option. Company employees agree that the program does mislead buyers, but say the company will "provide what [car dealers] want as long as it is not against the law." Is this practice ethical?

FIGURE 4–1
Four ways to classify marketing decisions according to ethical and legal relationships

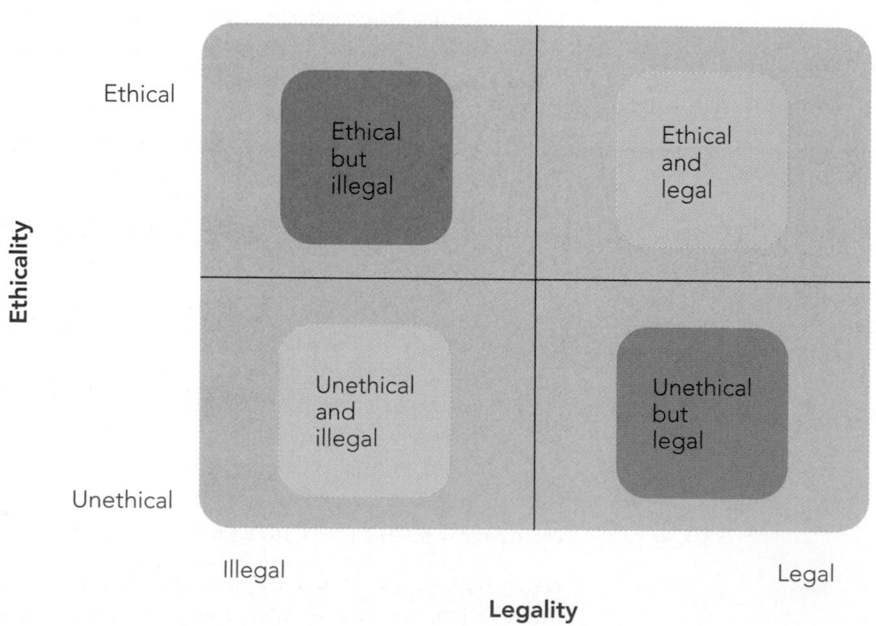

3. China is the world's largest tobacco-producing country and has 300 million smokers. Approximately 700,000 Chinese die annually from smoking-related illnesses. This figure is expected to rise to more than 2 million by 2025. China legally restricts tobacco imports. U.S. trade negotiators advocate free trade, thus allowing U.S. tobacco companies to market their products in China. Is the Chinese trade position ethical?
4. A group of college students recorded movies at a local theater and then uploaded the movies to the Internet. Federal statutes state that the unauthorized reproduction, distribution, or exhibition of copyrighted motion pictures is illegal. The students then directed friends and family to a peer-to-peer Internet network that allowed them to download the movies for free which they did. Are the students ethical? Are the students' friends and family ethical?

Did these situations fit neatly into Figure 4–1 as clearly ethical and legal or unethical and illegal? Probably not. As you read further in this chapter, you will be asked to consider other ethical dilemmas.

Current Perceptions of Ethical Behavior

There has been a public outcry about the ethical practices of businesspeople.[6] Public opinion surveys show that 58 percent of U.S. adults rate the ethical standards of business executives as only "fair" or "poor"; 90 percent think white-collar crime is "very common" or "somewhat common"; 76 percent say the lack of ethics in businesspeople contributes to tumbling societal moral standards; only the U.S. government is viewed as less trustworthy than corporations among institutions in the United States; and advertising practitioners, telemarketers, and car salespeople are thought to be among the least ethical occupations. Surveys of corporate employees generally confirm this public perception. When asked if they were aware of ethical problems in their companies, 56 percent say, "yes."

There are at least four possible reasons the state of perceived ethical business conduct is at its present level. First, there is increased pressure on businesspeople to make decisions in a society characterized by diverse value systems. Second, there is a growing tendency for business decisions to be judged publicly by groups with different values and interests. Third, the public's expectations of ethical business behavior has increased. Finally, and most disturbing, ethical business conduct may have declined.

learning review

1. What are ethics?
2. What are four possible reasons for the present state of ethical conduct in the United States?

UNDERSTANDING ETHICAL MARKETING BEHAVIOR

LO2

Researchers have identified numerous factors that influence ethical marketing behavior.[7] Figure 4–2 on the next page presents a framework that shows these factors and their relationships.

Societal Culture and Norms

As described in Chapter 3, *culture* refers to the set of values, ideas, and attitudes that are learned and shared among the members of a group. Culture also serves as a

FIGURE 4–2
A framework for understanding ethical behavior. Each of these influences will have an effect on ethical marketing behavior.

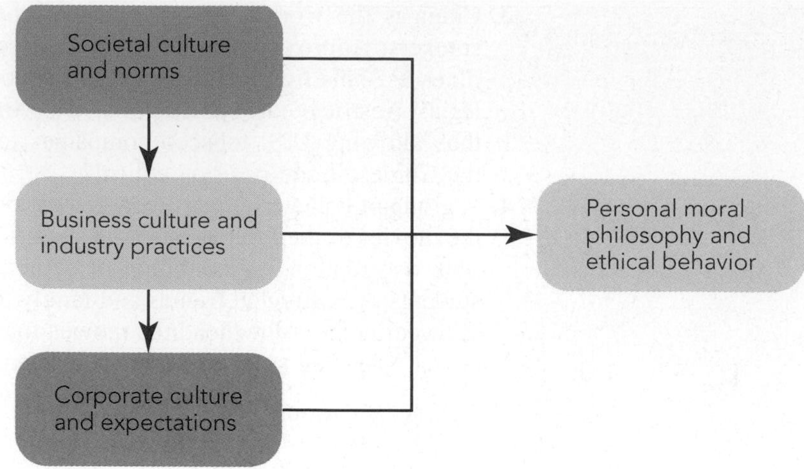

socializing force that dictates what is morally right and just. This means that moral standards are relative to particular societies.[8] These standards often reflect the laws and regulations that affect social and economic behavior, which can create ethical dilemmas. Companies that compete in the global marketplace recognize this fact. Consider UPS, the world's largest package delivery company operating in more than 200 countries and territories worldwide.[9] According to the company's global compliance and ethics coordinator, "Although languages and cultures around the world may be different, we do not change our ethical standards at UPS. Our ethics program is global in nature." Not surprisingly, UPS is consistently ranked among the world's most ethical companies.

Societal values and attitudes also affect ethical and legal relationships among individuals, groups, and business institutions and organizations. Consider the copying of another's copyright, trademark, or patent. These are viewed as intellectual property. Unauthorized use, reproduction, or distribution of intellectual property is illegal in the United States and most countries, which can result in fines and prison terms for perpetrators. The owners of intellectual property also lose. For example, annual worldwide lost sales from the theft of intellectual property amount to $12.5 billion in the music industry, $18.2 billion in the movie industry, and $53.0 billion in the software industry.[10] Lost sales, in turn, result in lost jobs, royalties, wages, and tax revenue. But what about a person downloading copyrighted music, movies, and software over the Internet or from peer-to-peer file-sharing programs, without paying the owner of this property? Is this an ethical or unethical act? It depends on who you ask. Surveys of the U.S. public indicate that the majority consider these acts unethical. However, only a third of U.S. college students say such practices are unethical.[11]

Business Culture and Industry Practices

Societal culture provides a foundation for understanding moral behavior in business activities. *Business cultures* "comprise the effective rules of the game, the boundaries between competitive and unethical behavior, [and] the codes of conduct in business dealings."[12] Consumers have witnessed numerous instances where business cultures in the brokerage (inside trading), insurance (deceptive sales practices), and defense (bribery) industries went awry. Business culture affects ethical conduct both in the exchange relationship between sellers and buyers and in the competitive behavior among sellers.

Ethics of Exchange The exchange process is central to the marketing concept. Ethical exchanges between sellers and buyers should result in both parties being better off after a transaction.

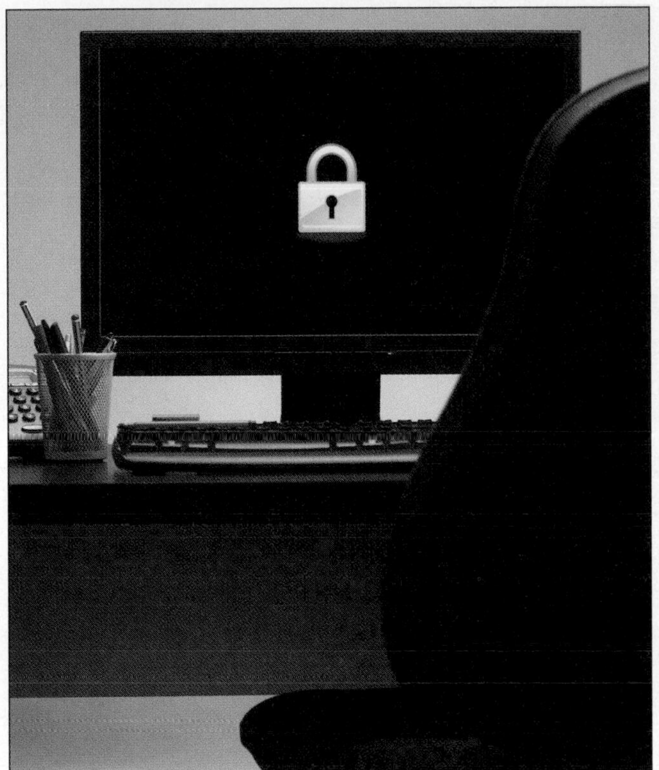

The Federal Trade Commission plays an active role in educating consumers and businesses about the importance of personal information privacy on the Internet. FTC initiatives are detailed on its Web site.

Federal Trade Commission
www.ftc.gov

Before the 1960s, the legal concept of **caveat emptor**—let the buyer beware—was pervasive in the American business culture. In 1962, President John F. Kennedy outlined a **Consumer Bill of Rights** that codified the ethics of exchange between buyers and sellers. These were the right (1) to safety, (2) to be informed, (3) to choose, and (4) to be heard. Consumers expect and often demand that these rights be protected, as have American businesses.

The right to safety manifests itself in industry and federal safety standards for most products sold in the United States. In fact, the U.S. Consumer Product Safety Commission routinely monitors the safety of 15,000 consumer products. However, even the most vigilant efforts to ensure safe products cannot foresee every possibility. Personal claims and property damage from consumer product safety incidents cost companies more than $700 billion annually. Consider the case of batteries used in laptop and notebook computers. Dell Inc. learned that the lithium-ion batteries in its notebook computers, made by Sony Energy Devices Corporation of Japan, posed a fire hazard to consumers. The company recalled 2.7 million batteries and gave consumers a replacement before any personal injuries resulted.[13]

The right to be informed means that marketers have an obligation to give consumers complete and accurate information about products and services. This right also applies to the solicitation of personal information over the Internet and its subsequent use by marketers.[14] A FTC survey of Web sites indicated that 92 percent collect personal information such as consumer e-mail addresses, telephone numbers, shopping habits, and financial data. Yet, only two-thirds of Web sites inform consumers of what is done with this information once obtained. The FTC wants more than posted privacy notices that merely inform consumers of a company's data-use policy, which critics say are often vague, confusing, or too legalistic to be understood. This view is shared by two-thirds of consumers who worry about protecting their personal information online. The consumer right to be informed has spawned much federal legislation, such as the *Children's Online Privacy Protection Act* (1998), and self-regulation initiatives restricting disclosure of personal information.

Relating to the right to choose, today many supermarket chains demand "slotting allowances" from manufacturers, in the form of cash or free goods, to stock new products.[15] This practice could limit the number of new products available to consumers and interfere with their right to choose. One critic of this practice remarked, "If we had had slotting allowances a few years ago, we might not have had granola, herbal tea, or yogurt."

Finally, the right to be heard means that consumers should have access to public-policy makers regarding complaints about products and services. This right is illustrated in limitations put on telemarketing practices. The FTC established the Do Not Call Registry in 2003 for consumers who do not want to receive unsolicited telemarketing calls. Today, almost 167 million U.S. telephone numbers are listed in the registry, which is managed by the FTC. A telemarketer can be fined up to $16,000 for each call made to a telephone number posted on the registry.

Ethics of Competition Business culture also affects ethical behavior in competition. Two kinds of unethical behavior are most common: (1) economic espionage and (2) bribery.

Economic espionage is the clandestine collection of trade secrets or proprietary information about a company's competitors. This practice is illegal and unethical and

Making Responsible Decisions > > > > > > > ethics

Corporate Conscience in the Cola War

Suppose you are a senior executive at Pepsi-Cola and that a Coca-Cola employee offers to sell you the marketing plan and sample for a new Coke product at a modest price? Would you buy it knowing Pepsi-Cola could gain a significant competitive edge in the cola war?

When this question was posed in an online survey of marketing and advertising executives, 67 percent said they would buy the plan and product sample if there were no repercussions. What did Pepsi-Cola do when this offer actually occurred? The company immediately contacted Coca-Cola, which contacted the FBI. An undercover FBI agent paid the employee $30,000 in cash stuffed in a Girl Scout cookie box as a down payment and later arrested the employee and accomplices. When asked about the incident, a Pepsi-Cola spokesperson said: "We only did what any responsible company would do. Competition must be tough, but must always be fair and legal."

Why did the 33 percent of respondents in the online survey say they would decline the offer? Most said they would prefer competing ethically so they could sleep at night. According to a senior advertising agency executive who would decline the offer: "Repercussions go beyond potential espionage charges. As long as we have a conscience, there are repercussions."

So what happened to the Coca-Cola employee and her accomplices? She was sentenced to eight years in prison and ordered to pay $40,000 in restitution. Her accomplices were each sentenced to five years in prison.

carries serious criminal penalties for the offending individual or business. Espionage activities include illegal trespassing, theft, fraud, misrepresentation, wiretapping, the search of a competitor's trash, and violations of written and implicit employment agreements with noncompete clauses. More than half of the largest firms in the United States have uncovered espionage in some form, costing them $300 billion annually in lost sales.[16]

Economic espionage is most prevalent in high-technology industries, such as electronics, specialty chemicals, industrial equipment, aerospace, and pharmaceuticals, where technical know-how and trade secrets separate industry leaders from followers. But espionage can occur anywhere—even in the soft drink industry! Read the accompanying Making Responsible Decisions box to learn how Pepsi-Cola responded to an offer to obtain confidential information about its archrival's marketing plans.[17]

The second form of unethical competitive behavior is giving and receiving bribes and kickbacks. Bribes and kickbacks are often disguised as gifts, consultant fees, and favors. This practice is more common in business-to-business and government marketing than in consumer marketing.

In general, bribery is most evident in industries experiencing intense competition and in countries in the earlier stages of economic development. According to a United Nations study, 15 percent of all companies in industrialized countries have to pay bribes to win or retain business. In Asia, this figure is 40 percent. In Eastern Europe, 60 percent of all companies must pay bribes to do business. A recent poll of senior executives engaged in global marketing revealed that Iraq and Somalia were the most likely countries to evidence bribery to win or retain business. Denmark and New Zealand were the least likely.[18] Bribery on a worldwide scale is monitored by Transparency International. Visit its Web site described in the accompanying Going Online box, and view the most recent country rankings on this practice.

Going Online

The Corruption Perceptions Index

Bribery as a means to win and retain business varies widely by country. Transparency International periodically polls employees of multinational firms and institutions and political analysts and ranks countries on the basis of their perceived level of bribery to win or retain business. To obtain the most recent ranking, visit the Transparency International Web site at www.transparency.org and click Corruption Perceptions Index.

Scroll the Corruption Perceptions Index to see where the United States stands in the worldwide rankings as well as its neighbors, Canada and Mexico. Any surprises? Which country listed in the most recent ranking has the highest ranking and which has the lowest ranking?

The prevalence of economic espionage and bribery in international marketing has prompted laws to curb these practices. Two significant laws, the *Economic Espionage Act* (1996) and the *Foreign Corrupt Practices Act* (1977), address these practices in the United States. Both are detailed in Chapter 7.

Corporate Culture and Expectations

A third influence on ethical practices is corporate culture. *Corporate culture* is the set of values, ideas, and attitudes that is learned and shared among the members of an organization. The culture of a company demonstrates itself in the dress ("We don't wear ties"), sayings ("The IBM Way"), and manner of work (team efforts) of employees. Culture is also apparent in the expectations for ethical behavior present in formal codes of ethics and the ethical actions of top management and co-workers.

Codes of Ethics A **code of ethics** is a formal statement of ethical principles and rules of conduct. It is estimated that 86 percent of U.S. companies have some sort of ethics code and one of every four large companies has corporate ethics officers. At United Technologies, for example, 160 corporate ethics officers distribute the company's ethics code, translated into 24 languages, to employees who work for this defense and engineering giant around the world.[19] Ethics codes and committees typically address contributions to government officials and political parties, relations with customers and suppliers, conflicts of interest, and accurate recordkeeping. For example, General Mills provides guidelines for dealing with suppliers, competitors, and customers, and recruits new employees who share these views.

However, an ethics code is rarely enough to ensure ethical behavior. Coca-Cola has an ethics code and emphasizes that its employees be ethical in their behavior. But that did not stop some Coca-Cola employees from rigging the results of a test market for a frozen soft drink to win Burger King's business. Coca-Cola subsequently agreed to pay Burger King and its operators more than $20 million to settle the matter.[20]

Lack of specificity is a major reason for the violation of ethics codes. Employees must often judge whether a specific behavior is unethical. The American Marketing Association has addressed this issue by providing a detailed statement of ethics, which all members agree to follow. This statement is shown in Figure 4–3 on the next page.

Ethical Behavior of Top Management and Co-Workers A second reason for violating ethics codes rests in the perceived behavior of top management

AMERICAN MARKETING ASSOCIATION STATEMENT OF ETHICS

Preamble

The American Marketing Association commits itself to promoting the highest standard of professional ethical norms and values for its members. Norms are established standards of conduct that are expected and maintained by society and/or professional organizations. Values represent the collective conception of what people find desirable, important and morally proper. Values serve as the criteria for evaluating the actions of others. Marketing practitioners must recognize that they not only serve their enterprises but also act as stewards of society in creating, facilitating and executing the efficient and effective transactions that are part of the greater economy. In this role, marketers should embrace the highest ethical *norms* of practicing professionals and the ethical *values* implied by their responsibility toward stakeholders (e.g., customers, employees, investors, channel members, regulators and the host community).

General Norms

1. Marketers must do no harm. This means doing work for which they are appropriately trained or experienced so that they can actively add value to their organizations and customers. It also means adhering to all applicable laws and regulations and embodying high ethical standards in the choices they make.
2. Marketers must foster trust in the marketing system. This means that products are appropriate for their intended and promoted uses. It requires that marketing communications about goods and services are not intentionally deceptive or misleading. It suggests building relationships that provide for the equitable adjustment and/or redress of customer grievances. It implies striving for good faith and fair dealing so as to contribute toward the efficacy of the exchange process.
3. Marketers must embrace, communicate and practice the fundamental ethical values that will improve consumer confidence in the integrity of the marketing exchange system. These basic *values* are intentionally aspirational and include honesty, responsibility, fairness, respect, openness and citizenship.

Ethical Values

Honesty—to be truthful and forthright in our dealings with customers and stakeholders.

- We will tell the truth in all situations and at all times.
- We will offer products of value that do what we claim in our communications.
- We will stand behind our products if they fail to deliver their claimed benefits.
- We will honor our explicit and implicit commitments and promises.

Responsibility—to accept the consequences of our marketing decisions and strategies.

- We will make strenuous efforts to serve the needs of our customers.
- We will avoid using coercion with all stakeholders.
- We will acknowledge the social obligations to stakeholders that come with increased marketing and economic power.
- We will recognize our special commitments to economically vulnerable segments of the market such as children, the elderly and

FIGURE 4–3
American Marketing Association Statement of Ethics

American Marketing Association
www.marketingpower.com

and co-workers.[21] Observing peers and top management and gauging responses to unethical behavior play an important role in individual actions. A study of business executives reported that 40 percent had been implicitly or explicitly rewarded for engaging in ethically troubling behavior. Moreover, 31 percent of those who refused to engage in unethical behavior were penalized, either through outright punishment or a diminished status in the company.[22] Clearly, ethical dilemmas often bring personal and professional conflict. For this reason, numerous states have laws protecting **whistle-blowers**, employees who report unethical or illegal actions of their employers.

Your Personal Moral Philosophy and Ethical Behavior

Ultimately, ethical choices are based on the personal moral philosophy of the decision maker. Moral philosophy is learned through the process of socialization with friends and family and by formal education. It is also influenced by the societal, busi-

FIGURE 4-3
(Continued)

others who may be substantially disadvantaged.

Fairness—to try to balance justly the needs of the buyer with the interests of the seller.

- We will represent our products in a clear way in selling, advertising and other forms of communication; this includes the avoidance of false, misleading and deceptive promotion.
- We will reject manipulations and sales tactics that harm customer trust.
- We will not engage in price fixing, predatory pricing, price gouging or "bait-and-switch" tactics.
- We will not knowingly participate in material conflicts of interest.

Respect—to acknowledge the basic human dignity of all stakeholders.

- We will value individual differences even as we avoid stereotyping customers or depicting demographic groups (e.g., gender, race, sexual orientation) in a negative or dehumanizing way in our promotions.
- We will listen to the needs of our customers and make all reasonable efforts to monitor and improve their satisfaction on an ongoing basis.
- We will make a special effort to understand suppliers, intermediaries and distributors from other cultures.
- We will appropriately acknowledge the contributions of others, such as consultants, employees and coworkers, to our marketing endeavors.

Openness—to create transparency in our marketing operations.

- We will strive to communicate clearly with all our constituencies.
- We will accept constructive criticism from our customers and other stakeholders.
- We will explain significant product or service risks, component substitutions or other foreseeable eventualities that could affect customers or their perception of the purchase decision.
- We will fully disclose list prices and terms of financing as well as available price deals and adjustments.

Citizenship—to fulfill the economic, legal, philanthropic and societal responsibilities that serve stakeholders in a strategic manner.

- We will strive to protect the natural environment in the execution of marketing campaigns.
- We will give back to the community through volunteerism and charitable donations.
- We will work to contribute to the overall betterment of marketing and its reputation.
- We will encourage supply chain members to ensure that trade is fair for all participants, including producers in developing countries.

Implementation

Finally, we recognize that every industry sector and marketing subdiscipline (e.g., marketing research, e-commerce, direct selling, direct marketing, advertising) has its own specific ethical issues that require policies and commentary. An array of such codes can be accessed through links on the AMA Web site. We encourage all such groups to develop and/or refine their industry and discipline-specific codes of ethics to supplement these general norms and values.

ness, and corporate culture in which a person finds him- or herself. Two prominent personal moral philosophies have direct bearing on marketing practice: (1) moral idealism and (2) utilitarianism.

Moral Idealism

Moral idealism is a personal moral philosophy that considers certain individual rights or duties as universal, regardless of the outcome. This philosophy exists in the Consumer Bill of Rights and is favored by moral philosophers and consumer interest groups. For example, the right to know applies to probable defects in an automobile that relate to safety.

This philosophy also applies to ethical duties. A fundamental ethical duty is to do no harm. Adherence to this duty prompted the recent decision by 3M executives to phase out production of a chemical 3M had manufactured for nearly 40 years. The substance, used in far-ranging products from pet food bags, candy wrappers, carpeting, and 3M's popular Scotchgard fabric protector, had no known harmful health or environmental effect. However, the company discovered that the chemical appeared

What does 3M's Scotchgard have to do with ethics, social responsibility, and a $200 million loss in annual sales? Read the text to find out.

in minuscule amounts in humans and animals around the world and accumulated in tissue. Believing that the substance could be possibly harmful in large doses, 3M voluntarily stopped its production, resulting in a $200 million loss in annual sales.[23]

Utilitarianism An alternative perspective on moral philosophy is **utilitarianism**, which is a personal moral philosophy that focuses on "the greatest good for the greatest number" by assessing the costs and benefits of the consequences of ethical behavior. If the benefits exceed the costs, then the behavior is ethical. If not, then the behavior is unethical. This philosophy underlies the economic tenets of capitalism and, not surprisingly, is embraced by many business executives and students.[24]

Utilitarian reasoning was apparent in Nestlé Food Corporation's marketing of Good Start infant formula, sold by Nestlé's Carnation Company. The formula, promoted as hypoallergenic, was designed to prevent or reduce colic caused by an infant's allergic reaction to cow's milk, a condition suffered by 2 percent of babies. However, some severely milk-allergic infants experienced serious side effects after using Good Start, including convulsive vomiting. Physicians and parents charged that the hypoallergenic claim was misleading, and the Food and Drug Administration investigated the matter. A Nestlé vice president defended the claim and product, saying, "I don't understand why our product should work in 100 percent of cases. If we wanted to say it was foolproof, we would have called it allergy-free. We call it hypo-, or less, allergenic."[25] Nestlé officials seemingly believed that most allergic infants would benefit from Good Start—"the greatest good for the greatest number." However, other views prevailed, and the claim was dropped from the product label.

An appreciation for the nature of ethics, coupled with a basic understanding of why unethical behavior arises, alerts a person to when and how ethical issues exist in marketing decisions. Ultimately, ethical behavior rests with the individual, but the consequences affect many.

learning review

3. What rights are included in the Consumer Bill of Rights?
4. Economic espionage includes what kinds of activities?
5. What is meant by moral idealism?

UNDERSTANDING SOCIAL RESPONSIBILITY IN MARKETING

LO3

As we saw in Chapter 1, the societal marketing concept stresses marketing's social responsibility by not only satisfying the needs of consumers but also providing for society's welfare. **Social responsibility** means that organizations are part of a larger society and are accountable to that society for their actions. Like ethics, agreement on the nature and scope of social responsibility is often difficult to come by, given the diversity of values present in different societal, business, and corporate cultures.

Three Concepts of Social Responsibility

Figure 4–4 shows three concepts of social responsibility: (1) profit responsibility, (2) stakeholder responsibility, and (3) societal responsibility.

Profit Responsibility *Profit responsibility* holds that companies have a simple duty: to maximize profits for their owners or stockholders. This view is expressed by Nobel Laureate Milton Friedman, who said, "There is one and only one social

FIGURE 4–4
Three concepts of social responsibility. Each concept of social responsibility relates to particular constituencies. There is often conflict in satisfying all constituencies at the same time.

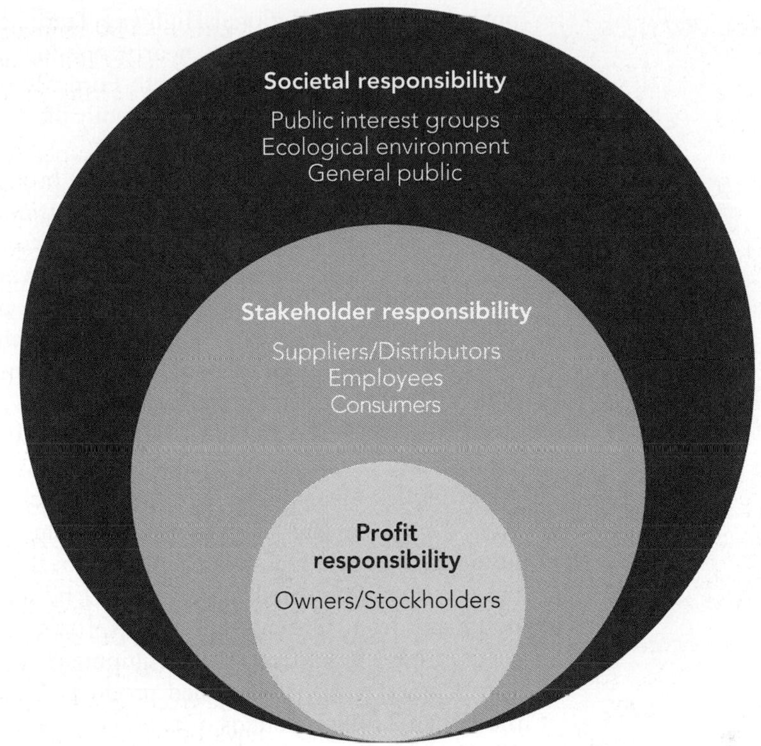

responsibility of business—to use its resources and engage in activities designed to increase its profits so long as it stays within the rules of the game, which is to say, engages in open and free competition without deception or fraud."[26] Genzyme, the maker of Cerezyme, a drug that treats a genetic illness called Gaucher's disease that affects 20,000 people worldwide, has been criticized for apparently adopting this view in its pricing practices. Genzyme charges up to $170,000 for a year's worth of Cerezyme. A Genzyme spokesperson responded saying the company spends about $150 million annually to manufacture Cerezyme and freely gives the drug to patients without insurance. Also, the company invested considerable dollars in research over several years to develop Cerezyme, and the drug's profits are reinvested in ongoing R&D programs.[27]

Stakeholder Responsibility Criticism of the profit view has led to a broader concept of social responsibility. *Stakeholder responsibility* focuses on the obligations an organization has to those who can affect achievement of its objectives. These constituencies include consumers, employees, suppliers, and distributors. Source Perrier S.A., the supplier of Perrier bottled water, exercised this responsibility when it recalled 160 million bottles of water in 120 countries after traces of a toxic chemical were found in 13 bottles. The recall cost the company $35 million, and $40 million more in lost sales. Even though the chemical level was not harmful to humans, Source Perrier's president believed he acted in the best interests of the firm's consumers, distributors, and employees by removing "the least doubt, as minimal as it might be, to weigh on the image of the quality and purity of our product"—which it did.[28]

Failure to consider a company's broader constituencies can have negative consequences. For example, Bridgestone/Firestone, Inc., executives were widely criticized for how they responded to complaints about the safety of selected Firestone-brand tires. These tires had been linked to crashes that killed at least 174 people and injured more than 700 in the United States. The company recalled 6.5 million tires under pressure from the National Highway Traffic Safety Administration. After the recall, Firestone tire sales fell by nearly one-half, which affected Firestone employees, suppliers, and distributors as well. Ford Motor Company, a large buyer of Firestone tires, ended its exclusive contract with the tire producer.[29]

Societal Responsibility An even broader concept of social responsibility has emerged in recent years. *Societal responsibility* refers to obligations that organizations have (1) to the preservation of the ecological environment and (2) to the general public. Today, emphasis is placed on what is termed the **triple-bottom line**—recognition of the need for organizations to improve the state of people, the planet, and profit simultaneously if they are to achieve sustainable, long-term growth.[30] Growing interest in green marketing, cause marketing, social audits, and sustainable development reflect this recognition.

Green marketing—marketing efforts to produce, promote, and reclaim environmentally sensitive products—takes many forms.[31] At 3M, product development opportunities emanate both from consumer research and its "Pollution Prevention Pays" program. This program solicits employee suggestions on how to reduce pollution and recycle materials. Since 1975, this program has generated over 7,400 3P projects that eliminated more than 2.9 billion pounds of air, water, and solid waste pollutants from the environment. Xerox's "Design for the Environment" program focuses on ways to make its equipment recyclable and remanufacturable. Today, 100 percent of Xerox-designed products are remanufacturable. This effort has kept more than 2 billion pounds of equipment from being discarded in U.S. landfills since 1991. Boise Cascade, a leading North American timber manufacturer, and Lowe's and Home Depot, two home-and-garden center retail chains, have discontinued the sale of wood products from the world's endangered forests. Wal-Mart has instituted buying practices that encourage its suppliers to use containers and packaging made from corn, not oil-based resins. The company expects this initiative will save 800,000 barrels of oil annually. These voluntary responses to environmental issues have been implemented with little or no additional cost to consumers and resulted in cost savings to companies.

A global undertaking to further green marketing efforts is the ISO 14000 initiative developed by the International Standards Organization (ISO) in Geneva, Switzerland. *ISO 14000* consists of worldwide standards for environmental quality and green marketing practices. These standards are embraced by 148 countries, including the United States. More than 155,000 companies have met ISO 14000 standards for environmental quality and green marketing.[32]

Socially responsible efforts on behalf of the general public are becoming more common. A formal practice is **cause marketing**, which occurs when the charitable contributions of a firm are tied directly to the customer revenues produced through the promotion of one of its products.[33] This definition distinguishes cause marketing from a firm's standard charitable contributions, which are outright donations. For example, Procter & Gamble raises funds for the Special Olympics when consumers purchase selected company products, and MasterCard International links usage of its card with fund-raising for institutions that combat cancer, heart disease, child abuse, drug abuse, and muscular dystrophy. Barnes & Noble promotes literacy, and Coca-Cola sponsors local Boys and Girls Clubs. Avon Products, Inc., focuses on different issues in different countries. These include breast cancer, domestic violence, disaster relief among many others.

Cause marketing programs incorporate all three concepts of social responsibility by addressing public concerns and satisfying customer needs. They can also enhance corporate sales and profits as described in the Marketing Matters box.[34]

Avon Products, Inc., successfully employs cause marketing programs in the fight against breast cancer.

Avon Products, Inc.
www.avon.com

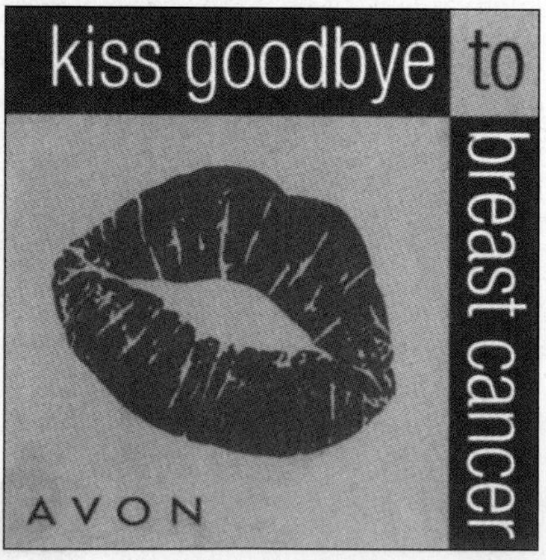

Marketing Matters > > > > > > customer value

Will Consumers Switch Brands for a Cause? Yes, If . . .

American Express Company pioneered cause marketing when it sponsored the renovation of the Statue of Liberty. This effort raised $1.7 million for the renovation, increased card usage among cardholders, and attracted new cardholders. In 2001, U.S. companies raised more than $5 billion for causes they champion. It is estimated that cause marketing will raise over $10 billion in 2010.

Cause marketing benefits companies as well as causes. Research indicates that 85 percent of U.S. consumers say they have a more favorable opinion of companies that support causes they care about. Also, 89 percent of consumers under 25 years old say they will switch to a brand or retailer that supports a good cause if the price and quality of brands or retailers are equal. In short, cause marketing may be a valued point of difference for brands and companies, all other things being equal.

For more information, including news, links, and case studies, visit the Cause Marketing Forum Web site at www.causemarketingforum.com.

The Social Audit and Sustainable Development: Doing Well by Doing Good

Converting socially responsible ideas into actions involves careful planning and monitoring of programs. Many companies develop, implement, and evaluate their social responsibility efforts by means of a **social audit**, which is a systematic assessment of a firm's objectives, strategies, and performance in terms of social responsibility. Frequently, marketing and social responsibility programs are often integrated. Consider McDonald's. The company's concern for the needs of families with children who are chronically or terminally ill was converted into over 286 Ronald McDonald Houses around the world. These facilities, located near treatment centers, enable families to stay together during the child's care. In this case, McDonald's is contributing to the welfare of a portion of its target market.

A social audit consists of five steps:[35]

1. Recognition of a firm's social expectations and the rationale for engaging in social responsibility endeavors.
2. Identification of social responsibility causes or programs consistent with the company's mission.
3. Determination of organizational objectives and priorities for programs and activities it will undertake.
4. Specification of the type and amount of resources necessary to achieve social responsibility objectives.
5. Evaluation of social responsibility programs and activities undertaken and assessment of future involvement.

Corporate attention to social audits will increase as companies seek to achieve sustainable development and improve the quality of life in a global economy.

Marketing and social responsibility programs are often integrated, as is the case with McDonald's. Its concern for ill children worldwide is apparent in the opening of another Ronald McDonald House for children and their families. This time in China.

McDonald's
www.mcdonalds.com

Sustainable development involves conducting business in a way that protects the natural environment while making economic progress. Ecologically responsible initiatives such as green marketing represent one such initiative. Recent initiatives related to working conditions at offshore manufacturing sites that produce goods for U.S. companies focus on quality-of-life issues. Public opinion surveys show that 90 percent of U.S. citizens are concerned about working conditions under which products are made in Asia and Latin America. Companies such as Reebok, Nike, Liz Claiborne, Levi Strauss, and Mattel have responded by imposing codes of conduct to reduce harsh or abusive working conditions at offshore manufacturing facilities.[36] Reebok, for example, now monitors production of its sporting apparel and equipment to ensure that no child labor is used in making its products.

Companies that evidence societal responsibility have been rewarded for their efforts. Research has shown that these companies (1) benefit from favorable word of mouth among consumers and (2) typically outperform less responsible companies on financial performance.[37]

Turning the Table: Consumer Ethics and Social Responsibility

LO4

Consumers also have an obligation to act ethically and responsibly in the exchange process and in the use and disposition of products. Unfortunately, consumer behavior is spotty on both counts.

Unethical practices of consumers are a serious concern to marketers.[38] These practices include: filing warranty claims after the claim period; misredeeming coupons; making fraudulent returns of merchandise; providing inaccurate information on credit applications; tampering with utility meters; tapping cable TV lines; pirating music, movies, and software from the Internet; and submitting phony insurance claims.

The cost to marketers of such behavior in lost sales and prevention expenses is huge. For example, consumers who redeem coupons for unpurchased products or use coupons for other products cost manufacturers $1 billion each year. Fraudulent automobile insurance claims cost insurance companies more than $10 billion annually. In addition, retailers lose about $30 billion yearly from shoplifting and $9.6 billion annually from fraudulent returns of merchandise. Consumers also act unethically toward each other. According to the FBI, consumer complaints about online auction fraud, in which consumers misrepresent their goods to others, outnumber all reports of online crime.

Nike has been a leader in improving workplace conditions in Asian factories that produce its sporting apparel and equipment.

Nike
www.nike.com

Research on unethical consumer behavior indicates that these acts are rarely motivated by economic need. This behavior appears to be influenced by (1) a belief that a consumer can get away with the act and it is worth doing and (2) the rationalization that the act is justified or driven by forces outside the individual—"everybody does it." These reasons were vividly expressed by a 24-year-old who pirated a movie, was sentenced to six months of house arrest, three years of probation, and a $7,000 fine. He said, "I didn't like paying for movies," and added, "so many people do it, you never think you're going to get caught."[39]

Consumer purchase, use, and disposition of environmentally sensitive products relate to consumer social responsibility. Research indicates that consumers are sensitive to ecological issues.[40] For example, a recent survey of U.S. consumers indicated that 50 percent were personally willing to change their lifestyle to improve the environment. However, only 28 percent could identify their own shopping or living habits over the past five years that help protect the environment. Related research shows that consumers (1) may be unwilling to sacrifice convenience and pay higher prices to protect the environment and (2) lack the knowledge to make informed decisions dealing with the purchase, use, and disposition of products.

Consumer confusion over which products are environmentally safe is also apparent, given marketers' rush to produce "green products." For example, few consumers realize that nonaerosol "pump" hair sprays are the second-largest cause of air pollution, after drying paint. In California alone, 27 tons of noxious hair spray fumes are expelled every day. And some environmentally safe claims made by marketers have been labeled *greenwashing*—the practice of making an unsubstantiated or misleading claim about the environmental benefits of a product, service, technology, or company practice.[41]

To address such claims the FTC has drafted guidelines that describe the circumstances when environmental claims can be made and would not constitute misleading information. For example, an advertisement or product label touting a package as "50 percent more recycled content than before" could be misleading if the recycled content has increased from 2 percent to 3 percent.

Ultimately, marketers and consumers are accountable for ethical and socially responsible behavior. The twenty-first century will prove to be a testing period for both.

learning review

6. What is meant by social responsibility?
7. Marketing efforts to produce, promote, and reclaim environmentally sensitive products are called ____________________.
8. What is a social audit?

LEARNING OBJECTIVES REVIEW

LO1 *Explain the differences between legal and ethical behavior in marketing.*
A good starting point for understanding the nature and significance of ethics is the distinction between legality and ethicality of marketing decisions. Whereas ethics deal with personal moral principles and values, laws are society's values and standards that are enforceable in the courts. This distinction can lead to the rationalization that if a behavior is within reasonable ethical and legal limits, then it is not really illegal or unethical. Judgment plays a large role in defining ethical and legal boundaries in marketing. Ethical dilemmas arise when acts or situations are not clearly ethical and legal or unethical and illegal.

LO2 *Identify factors that influence ethical and unethical marketing decisions.*
Four factors influence ethical marketing behavior. First, societal culture and norms serve as socializing forces that dictate what is morally right and just. Second, business culture and industry practices affect ethical conduct both in the exchange relationships between buyers and sellers and the competitive behavior among sellers. Third, corporate culture and expectations are often defined by corporate ethics codes and the ethical behavior of top management and co-workers. Finally, an individual's personal moral philosophy, such as moral idealism or utilitarianism, will dictate ethical choices. Ultimately, ethical behavior rests with the individual, but the consequences affect many.

LO3 *Describe the different concepts of social responsibility.*
Social responsibility means that organizations are part of a larger society and are accountable to that society for their actions. There are three concepts of social responsibility. First, profit responsibility holds that companies have a simple duty: to maximize profits for their owners or stockholders. Second, stakeholder responsibility focuses on the obligations an organization has to those who can affect achievement of its objectives. Those constituencies include consumers, employees, suppliers, and distributors. Finally, societal responsibility focuses on obligations that organizations have to the preservation of the ecological environment and the general public. Companies are placing greater emphasis on societal responsibility today and are reaping the rewards of positive word of mouth from their consumers and favorable financial performance.

LO4 *Recognize unethical and socially irresponsible consumer behavior.*
Consumers, like marketers, have an obligation to act ethically and responsibly in the exchange process and in the use and disposition of products. Unfortunately, consumer behavior is spotty on both counts. Unethical consumer behavior includes filing warranty claims after the claim period, misredeeming coupons, pirating music, movies, and software from the Internet, and submitting phony insurance claims, among other behaviors. Unethical behavior is rarely motivated by economic need. Rather, research indicates that this behavior is influenced by (*a*) a belief that a consumer can get away with the act and it is worth doing and (*b*) the rationalization that such acts are justified or driven by forces outside the individual—"everybody does it." Consumer purchase, use, and disposition of environmentally sensitive products relate to consumer social responsibility. Even though consumers are sensitive to ecological issues they (*a*) may be unwilling to sacrifice convenience and pay potentially higher prices to protect the environment and (*b*) lack the knowledge to make informed decisions dealing with the purchase, use, and disposition of products.

FOCUSING ON KEY TERMS

cause marketing p. 102
caveat emptor p. 95
code of ethics p. 97
Consumer Bill of Rights p. 95
economic espionage p. 95
ethics p. 92
green marketing p. 102
laws p. 92
moral idealism p. 99
social audit p. 103
social responsibility p. 100
sustainable development p. 104
triple-bottom line p. 102
utilitarianism p. 100
whistle-blowers p. 98

APPLYING MARKETING KNOWLEDGE

1 What concepts of moral philosophy and social responsibility are applicable to the practices of Anheuser-Busch described in the introduction to this chapter? Why?
2 Five ethical situations were presented in this chapter: (*a*) a medical society's decision to set fee schedules, (*b*) the use of a computer program by auto dealers to arrange financing, (*c*) smoking in China, (*d*) downloading movies, and (*e*) the pricing of Cerezyme for the treatment of a rare genetic illness. Where would each of these situations fit in Figure 4–1?
3 The American Marketing Association Statement of Ethics shown in Figure 4–3 details the rights and duties of parties in the marketing exchange process. How do these rights and duties compare with the Consumer Bill of Rights?
4 Compare and contrast moral idealism and utilitarianism as alternative personal moral philosophies.
5 How would you evaluate Milton Friedman's view of the social responsibility of a firm?
6 The text lists several unethical practices of consumers. Can you name others? Why do you think consumers engage in unethical conduct?
7 Cause marketing programs have become popular. Describe two such programs with which you are familiar.

building your marketing plan

Consider these potential stakeholders that may be affected in some way by the marketing plan on which you are working: shareholders (if any), suppliers, employees, customers, and society in general. For each group of stakeholders,

1 Identify what, if any, ethical and social responsibility issues might arise.
2 Describe, in one or two sentences, how your marketing plan addresses each potential issue.

video case 4 Starbucks Corporation: Serving More than Coffee

Wake up and smell the coffee—Starbucks is everywhere! As the world's No. 1 specialty coffee retailer, Starbucks serves more than 25 million customers in its stores every week. The concept of Starbucks goes far beyond being a coffeehouse or coffee brand. It represents the dream of its founder, Howard Schultz, who wanted to take the experience of an Italian—specifically, Milan—espresso bar to every corner of every city block in the world. So what is the *Starbucks experience*? According to the company,

> You get more than the finest coffee when you visit Starbucks. You get great people, first-rate music, a comfortable and upbeat meeting place, and sound advice on brewing excellent coffee at home. At home you're part of a family. At work you're part of a company. And somewhere in between there's a place where you can sit back and be yourself. That's what a Starbucks store is to many of its customers—a kind of "third place" where they can escape, reflect, read, chat, or listen.

But there is more. Starbucks has embraced corporate social responsibility like few other companies. A recent Starbucks Corporate Social Responsibility Annual Report described the company's views on social responsibility:

> Starbucks defines corporate social responsibility as conducting our business in ways that produce social, environmental, and economic benefits to the communities in which we operate. In the end, it means being responsible to our stakeholders.
>
> There is a growing recognition of the need for corporate accountability. Consumers are demanding more than "product" from their favorite brands. Employees are choosing to work for companies with strong values. Shareholders are more inclined to invest in business with outstanding corporate reputations. Quite simply, being socially responsible is not only the right thing to do; it can distinguish a company from its industry peers.

Starbucks not only recognizes the central role that social responsibility plays in its business. It also takes constructive action to be socially responsible.

THE COMPANY

Starbucks is the leading retailer, roaster, and brand of specialty coffee in the world with more than 7,500 retail locations in North America, Latin America, Europe, the Middle East, and the Pacific Rim. Beginning in 1971 with a single retail location in Seattle, Washington, Starbucks became a Fortune 500 company in 2003 with annual sales exceeding $4 billion. In addition, Starbucks is ranked as one of the "Ten Most Admired Companies in America" and one of the "100 Best Companies to Work For" by *Fortune* magazine. It has been recognized as one of the "Most Trusted Brands" by *Ad Week* magazine. *Business Ethics* magazine placed Starbucks 21st in its list of the "100 Best Citizens" in 2003. Starbucks' performance can be attributed to a passionate pursuit of its mission and adherence to six guiding principles. Both appear in Figure 1.

COMMITMENT TO CORPORATE SOCIAL RESPONSIBILITY

Starbucks continually emphasizes its commitment to corporate social responsibility. Speaking at the annual shareholders meeting in March 2004, Howard Schultz said,

> From the beginning, Starbucks has built a company that balances profitability with a social conscience. Starbucks business practices are even more relevant today as consumers take a cultural audit of the goods and services they use. Starbucks is known not only for serving the highest quality coffee, but for enriching the daily lives of its people, customers, and coffee farmers. This is the key to Starbucks' ongoing success and we are pleased to report our positive results to shareholders and partners (employees).

FIGURE 1
Starbucks Mission Statement and Guiding Principles

Establish Starbucks as the premier purveyor of the finest coffee in the world while maintaining our uncompromising principles as we grow.

The following six principles will help us measure the appropriateness of our decisions:

1. Provide a great work environment and treat each other with respect and dignity.
2. Embrace diversity as an essential component in the way we do business.
3. Apply the highest standards of excellence to the purchasing, roasting, and fresh delivery of our coffee.
4. Develop enthusiastically satisfied customers all the time.
5. Contribute positively to our communities and our environment.
6. Recognize that profitability is essential to our future success.

Each year, Starbucks makes public a comprehensive report on its corporate social responsibility initiatives. A central feature of this annual report is the alignment of the company's social responsibility decisions and actions with Starbucks Mission Statement and Guiding Principles. The Starbucks 2003 Corporate Social Responsibility Report, titled "Living Our Values," focused on six topical areas: (*a*) partners, (*b*) diversity, (*c*) coffee, (*d*) customers, (*e*) community and environment, and (*f*) profitability.

Partners

Starbucks employs some 74,000 people around the world. The company considers its employees as partners following the creation of Starbucks' stock option plan in 1991, called "Bean Stock." The company believes that giving eligible full- and part-time employees an ownership in the company and sharing the rewards of Starbucks' financial success has made the sense of partnership real. In addition, the company has one of the most competitive employee benefits and compensation packages in the retail industry. Ongoing training, career advancement opportunities, partner recognition programs, and diligent efforts to ensure a healthy and safe work environment have all contributed to the fact that Starbucks has one of the lowest employee turnover rates within the restaurant and fast-food industry.

Diversity

Starbucks strives to mirror the customers and communities it serves. On a quarterly basis, the company monitors the demographics of its workforce to determine whether they reflect the communities in which Starbucks operates. In 2003, Starbucks' U.S. workforce was comprised of 63 percent women and 24 percent people of color. The company also is engaged in a joint venture called Urban Coffee Opportunities (UCO) created to bring Starbucks stores to diverse neighborhoods. There were 52 UCO locations employing almost 1,000 Starbucks partners at the end of 2003.

Supplier diversity is also emphasized. To do business with Starbucks as a diverse supplier, that company must be 51 percent owned, operated, and managed by women, minorities, or socially disadvantaged individuals and meet Starbucks requirements of quality, service, value, stability, and sound business practice. The company spent $80 million with diverse suppliers in 2003 and $95 million with diverse suppliers in 2004.

Coffee

Starbucks' attention to quality coffee extends to its coffee growers located in more than 20 countries. Sustainable development is emphasized. This means that Starbucks pays coffee farmers a fair price for the beans; that the coffee is grown in an ecologically sound manner; and that Starbucks invests in the farming communities where its coffees are produced.

One long-standing initiative is Starbucks' partnership with Conservation International, a nonprofit organization dedicated to protecting soil, water, energy, and biological diversity worldwide. Starbucks is particularly focused on environmental protection and helping local farmers earn more for their crops. In 2003, Starbucks invested more than $1 million in social programs, notably health and education projects, that benefited farming communities in nine countries, from Colombia to Indonesia.

Customers

Starbucks serves customers in 32 countries. The company and its partners are committed to providing each customer the optimal Starbucks experience every time they visit a store. For very loyal Starbucks customers, that translates into 18 visits per month on average.

Making a connection with customers at each store and building the relationship a customer has with Starbucks *baristas*, or coffee brewers, is important in creating the Starbucks experience. Each barista receives 24 hours of training in customer service and basic retail skills, as well as "Coffee Knowledge" and "Brewing the Perfect Cup" classes. Baristas are taught to anticipate the customers' needs and to make eye contact while carefully explaining the various coffee flavors and blends. Starbucks also enhances the customer relationship by soliciting feedback and responding to patrons' experiences and concerns. Starbucks Customer Relations reviews and responds to every inquiry or comment, often within 24 hours for telephone calls and e-mails.

Community and Environment

Efforts to contribute positively to the communities it serves and the environments in which it operates are emphasized in Starbucks' guiding principles. "We aren't in the coffee business, serving people. We are in the people business, serving coffee," says Howard Schultz. Starbucks and its partners have been recognized for volunteer support and

financial contributions to a wide variety of local, national, and international social, economic, and environmental initiatives. For example, the "Make Your Mark" program rewards partners' gifts of time for volunteer work with charitable donations from Starbucks. In addition, Starbucks is a supporter of CARE International, a nonprofit organization dedicated to fighting global poverty.

Starbucks is also committed to environmental responsibility. Starbucks has a longtime involvement with Earth Day activities. It has instituted companywide energy and water conservation programs and waste reduction, recycling, and reuse initiatives proposed by partner *Green Teams*.

Profitability

At Starbucks, profitability is viewed as essential to its future success. When Starbucks' guiding principles were conceived, profitability was included but intentionally placed last on the list. This was done not because profitability was the least important. Instead, it was believed that adherence to the five other principles would ultimately lead to good financial performance. In fact, it has.

Questions

1 How does Starbucks' approach to social responsibility relate to the three concepts of social responsibility described in the text?

2 What role does sustainable development play in Starbucks' approach to social responsibility?

Individuality is Beautiful

AutoPacific VSA

Winner of the Best in Class Vehicle Satisfaction Award for Premium Mid-Size Car* with available touch-screen navigation with XM real time NavTraffic®** reporting, Intelligent Key with Push Button Ignition and an award-winning 270-hp V6 with CVT†–all wrapped in style. It's the sedan for anyone who doesn't want to be like everyone else. **NissanUSA.com**

The New Nissan Altima

SHIFT_individuality

*© 2007 AutoPacific, Inc. Vehicle Satisfaction Award. **XM NavTraffic® functionality not available in all markets. †WardsAuto.com. 2007 Nissan, the Nissan Brand Symbol, "SHIFT_" tagline and Nissan model names are Nissan trademarks. Always wear your seat belt, and please don't drink and drive. © 2007 Nissan North America, Inc.

5 Understanding Consumer Behavior

LEARNING OBJECTIVES

After reading this chapter you should be able to:

LO1 Describe the stages in the consumer purchase decision process.

LO2 Distinguish among three variations of the consumer purchase decision process: routine, limited, and extended problem solving.

LO3 Identify major psychological influences on consumer behavior.

LO4 Identify the major sociocultural influences on consumer behavior.

ENLIGHTENED CARMAKERS KNOW WHAT CUSTOM(H)ERS VALUE

Who buys 68 percent of new cars? Who influences 83 percent of new-car-buying decisions? Women. Yes, women.

Women are a driving force in the U.S. automobile industry. Enlightened carmakers have hired women designers, engineers, and marketing executives to better understand and satisfy this valuable car buyer and influencer. What have they learned? Women and men think and feel differently about key elements of the new-car-buying decision process and experience.

- *The sense of styling.* Women and men care about styling. For men, styling is more about a car's exterior lines and accents. Women are more interested in interior design and finishes. Designs that fit their proportions, provide good visibility, offer ample storage space, and make for effortless parking are particularly important.
- *The need for speed.* Both sexes want speed, but for different reasons. Men think about how many seconds it takes to get from zero to 60 miles per hour. Women want to feel secure that the car has enough acceleration to outrun an 18-wheeler trying to pass them on a freeway entrance ramp.
- *The substance of safety.* Safety for men is about features that help avoid an accident, such as antilock brakes and responsive steering. For women, safety is about features that help to survive an accident, including passenger airbags and reinforced side panels.
- *The shopping experience.* The new-car-buying experience differs between men and women. Generally, men decide upfront what car they want and set out alone to find it. By contrast, women approach it as an intelligence-gathering expedition. They actively seek information and postpone a purchase decision until all options have been evaluated. Women frequently visit auto-buying Web sites, read car-comparison articles, and scan car advertisements. Still, recommendations of friends and relatives matter most. Women typically shop three dealerships before making a purchase decision—one more than men. While only a third of women say that price is the most influential when they shop for a new car, 71 percent say price determines the final decision.

Carmakers have learned that women, more than men, dislike the car-buying experience. In particular, women dread the price negotiations that are often involved in buying a new car. Not surprisingly, 76 percent of women car buyers take a man with them to finalize the terms of sale.[1]

This chapter examines **consumer behavior**, the actions a person takes in purchasing and using products and services, including the mental and social processes that come before and after these actions. This chapter shows how the behavioral sciences help answer questions such as why people choose one product or brand over another, how they make these choices, and how companies use this knowledge to provide value to consumers.

CONSUMER PURCHASE DECISION PROCESS AND EXPERIENCE

LO1

Behind the visible act of making a purchase lies an important decision process and consumer experience that must be investigated. The stages a buyer passes through in making choices about which products and services to buy is the **purchase decision process**. This process has the five stages shown in Figure 5–1: (1) problem recognition, (2) information search, (3) alternative evaluation, (4) purchase decision, and (5) postpurchase behavior.

Problem Recognition: Perceiving a Need

Problem recognition, the initial step in the purchase decision, is perceiving a difference between a person's ideal and actual situations big enough to trigger a decision.[2] This can be as simple as finding an empty milk carton in the refrigerator; noting, as a first-year college student, that your high school clothes are not in the style that other students are wearing; or realizing that your notebook computer may not be working properly.

In marketing, advertisements or salespeople can activate a consumer's decision process by showing the shortcomings of competing (or currently owned) products. For instance, an advertisement for a new generation smart phone could stimulate problem recognition because it emphasizes "maximum use from one device."

Information Search: Seeking Value

After recognizing a problem, a consumer begins to search for information, the next stage in the purchase decision process. First, you may scan your memory for previous experiences with products or brands.[3] This action is called *internal search*. For frequently purchased products such as shampoo and conditioner, this may be enough.

Or a consumer may undertake an *external search* for information.[4] This is needed when past experience or knowledge is insufficient, the risk of making a wrong purchase decision is high, and the cost of gathering information is low. The primary sources of external information are: (1) *personal sources*, such as relatives and friends whom the consumer trusts; (2) *public sources*, including various product-rating organizations such as *Consumer Reports*, government agencies, and TV "consumer programs"; and (3) *marketer-dominated sources*, such as information from sellers including advertising, company Web sites, salespeople, and point-of-purchase displays in stores.

FIGURE 5–1
The purchase decision process consists of five stages.

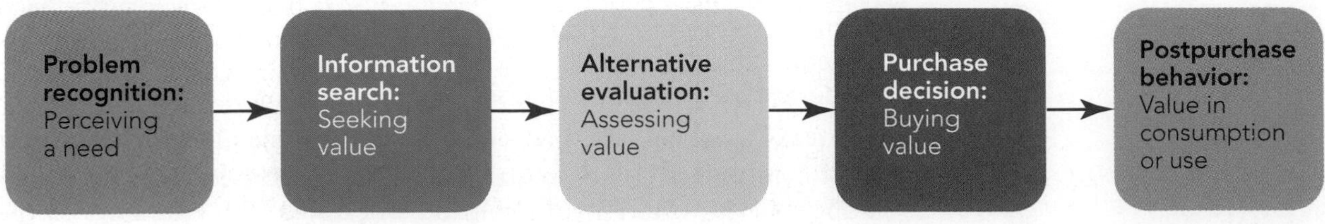

BRAND	MODEL	RETAIL PRICE	DISPLAY	NAVIG-ATION	VOICE QUALITY	BATTERY LIFE	CAMERA RESOLUTION (in megapixels)
Apple	iPhone 3GS	$200	Excellent	Excellent	Fair	Excellent	3.1
BlackBerry	Storm 9530	150	Very Good	Very Good	Fair	Very Good	3.1
HTC	Touch Diamond	200	Very Good	Very Good	Fair	Good	3.1
Palm	Pre	200	Very Good	Excellent	Fair	Good	3.1
LG	Incite	80	Good	Good	Fair	Very Good	3.1
T-Mobile	G1	150	Very Good	Excellent	Fair	Very Good	3.1
Samsung	Blackjack II	50	Good	Good	Good	Excellent	1.9

Rating: Excellent Very Good Good Fair Poor

FIGURE 5–2
Consumer Reports' evaluation of smart phones

Consumer Reports
www.consumerreports.org

Suppose you consider buying a new smart phone. You will probably tap several of these information sources: friends and relatives, advertisements, brand and company Web sites, and stores carrying these phones (for demonstrations). You might study the comparative evaluation of selected smart phones appearing in *Consumer Reports*, a portion of which appears in Figure 5–2.[5]

Alternative Evaluation: Assessing Value

The information search stage clarifies the problem for the consumer by (1) suggesting criteria to use for the purchase, (2) yielding brand names that might meet the criteria, and (3) developing consumer value perceptions. Given only the information shown in Figure 5–2, which selection criteria would you use in buying a smart phone? Would you use price, display quality, navigation or ease of use, battery life, camera resolution, or some other combination of these or other criteria?

For some of you, the information provided may be inadequate because it does not contain all the factors you might consider when evaluating smart phones. These factors are a consumer's **evaluative criteria**, which represent both the objective attributes of a brand (such as display) and the subjective ones (such as prestige) you use to compare different products and brands.[6] Firms try to identify and capitalize on both types of criteria to create the best value for the money paid by you and other consumers. These criteria are often displayed in advertisements.

Consumers often have several criteria for evaluating brands. Knowing this, companies seek to identify the most important evaluative criteria that consumers use when judging brands. For example, among the evaluative criteria shown in the columns of Figure 5–2, suppose you use three in considering smart phones: (1) a retail price of $200 or less, (2) very good or excellent display quality, and (3) excellent navigation. These criteria establish the brands in your **consideration set**—the group of brands that a consumer would consider acceptable from among all the brands of which he or she is aware in the product class.[7] Your evaluative criteria result in three brands and their respective models (Apple iPhone 3GS, Palm Pre, and T-Mobile G1) in your consideration set. If these alternatives are unsatisfactory, you can change your evaluative criteria to create a different consideration set of models and brands. For example, the availability of a memory card or USB slot to download pictures might join the list of evaluative criteria if you take a lot of pictures and want to email them from your PC.

Purchase Decision: Buying Value

Having examined the alternatives in the consideration set, you are almost ready to make a purchase decision. Two choices remain: (1) from whom to buy and (2) when to buy. For a product like a smart phone, the information search process probably involved visiting retail stores, seeing different brands in catalogs, and viewing a smart phone on a seller's Web site. The choice of which seller to buy from will depend on such considerations as the terms of sale, your past experience buying from the seller, and the return policy. Often a purchase decision involves a simultaneous evaluation of both product attributes and seller characteristics. For example, you might choose the second-most preferred smart phone brand at a store or Web site with a liberal refund and return policy versus the most preferred brand with more conservative policies.

Deciding when to buy is determined by a number of factors. For instance, you might buy sooner if one of your preferred brands is on sale or its manufacturer offers a rebate. Other factors such as the store atmosphere, pleasantness or ease of the shopping experience, salesperson assistance, time pressure, and financial circumstances could also affect whether a purchase decision is made or postponed.[8]

Use of the Internet to gather information, evaluate alternatives, and make buying decisions adds a technological dimension to the consumer purchase decision process and buying experience. Consumer benefits and costs associated with this technology and its marketing implications are detailed in Chapter 21.

Postpurchase Behavior: Value in Consumption or Use

After buying a product, the consumer compares it with his or her expectations and is either satisfied or dissatisfied. If the consumer is dissatisfied, marketers must determine whether the product was deficient or consumer expectations were too high. Product deficiency may require a design change. If expectations are too high, perhaps the company's advertising or the salesperson oversold the product's features and benefits.

Sensitivity to a customer's consumption or use experience is extremely important in a consumer's value perception. For example, research on telephone services provided by Sprint and AT&T indicates that satisfaction or dissatisfaction affects consumer value perceptions.[9] Studies show that satisfaction or dissatisfaction affects consumer communications and repeat-purchase behavior. Satisfied buyers tell three other people about their experience. Dissatisfied buyers complain to nine people.[10] Satisfied buyers also tend to buy from the same seller each time a purchase occasion arises. The financial impact of repeat-purchase behavior is signficant, as described in the accompanying Marketing Matters box.[11]

A satisfactory or unsatisfactory consumption or use experience is an important factor in postpurchase behavior. Marketer attention to this stage can pay huge dividends as described in the text.

Firms such as General Electric (GE), Johnson & Johnson, Coca-Cola, and British Airways focus attention on postpurchase behavior to maximize customer satisfaction and retention. These firms, among many others, now provide toll-free telephone numbers, offer liberalized return and refund policies, and engage in extensive staff training to handle complaints, answer questions, record suggestions, and solve consumer problems. For example, GE has a database that stores 750,000 answers about 8,500 of its models in

Marketing Matters > > > > > customer value

The Value of a Satisfied Customer to the Company

Customer satisfaction and experience underlie the marketing concept. But how much is a satisfied customer worth?

This question has prompted firms to calculate the financial value of a satisfied customer over time. Frito-Lay, for example, estimates that the average loyal consumer in the Southwestern United States eats 21 pounds of snack chips a year. At a price of $2.50 a pound, this customer spends $52.50 annually on the company's snacks such as Lays and Ruffles potato chips, Doritos and Tostitos tortilla chips, and Fritos corn chips. Exxon estimates that a loyal customer will spend $500 annually for its branded gasoline, not including candy, snacks, oil, or repair services purchased at its gasoline stations. Kimberly-Clark reports that a loyal customer will buy 6.7 boxes of its Kleenex tissues each year and will spend $994 on facial tissues over 60 years, in today's dollars.

These calculations have focused marketer attention on the buying experience, customer satisfaction, and retention. Ford Motor Company set a target of increasing customer retention—the percentage of Ford owners whose next car is also a Ford—from 60 percent to 80 percent. Why? Ford executives say that each additional percentage point is worth a staggering $100 million in profits.

This calculation is not unique to Ford. Research shows that a 5 percent improvement in customer retention can increase a company's profits by 70 to 80 percent.

It takes 12 muscles to smile
or 3 simple ingredients.
Just potatoes, all natural oil & a dash of salt.
Lay's
Classic
Happiness is simple

120 product lines to handle 3 million calls annually. Such efforts produce positive post-purchase communications among consumers and foster relationship building between sellers and buyers.

Often a consumer is faced with two or more highly attractive alternatives, such as a BlackBerry or Samsung smart phone. If you choose a BlackBerry, you might think, "Should I have purchased the Samsung?" This feeling of postpurchase psychological tension or anxiety is called **cognitive dissonance**. To alleviate it, consumers often attempt to applaud themselves for making the right choice. So after your purchase, you may seek information to confirm your choice by asking friends questions like, "Don't you like my new phone?" or by reading ads of the brand you chose. You might even look for negative features about the brand you didn't buy and decide that the Samsung headset didn't feel right. Firms often use ads or follow-up calls from salespeople in this postpurchase behavior stage to comfort buyers that they made the right decision. For many years, Buick ran an advertising campaign with the message, "Aren't you really glad you bought a Buick?"

Consumer Involvement and Problem-Solving Variations

LO2

Sometimes consumers don't engage in the five-stage purchase decision process. Instead, they skip or minimize one or more stages depending on the level of **involvement**, the personal, social, and economic significance of the purchase to the consumer.[12] High-involvement purchase occasions typically have at least one of three characteristics: The item to be purchased (1) is expensive, (2) can have serious personal consequences, or (3) could reflect on one's social image. For these occasions,

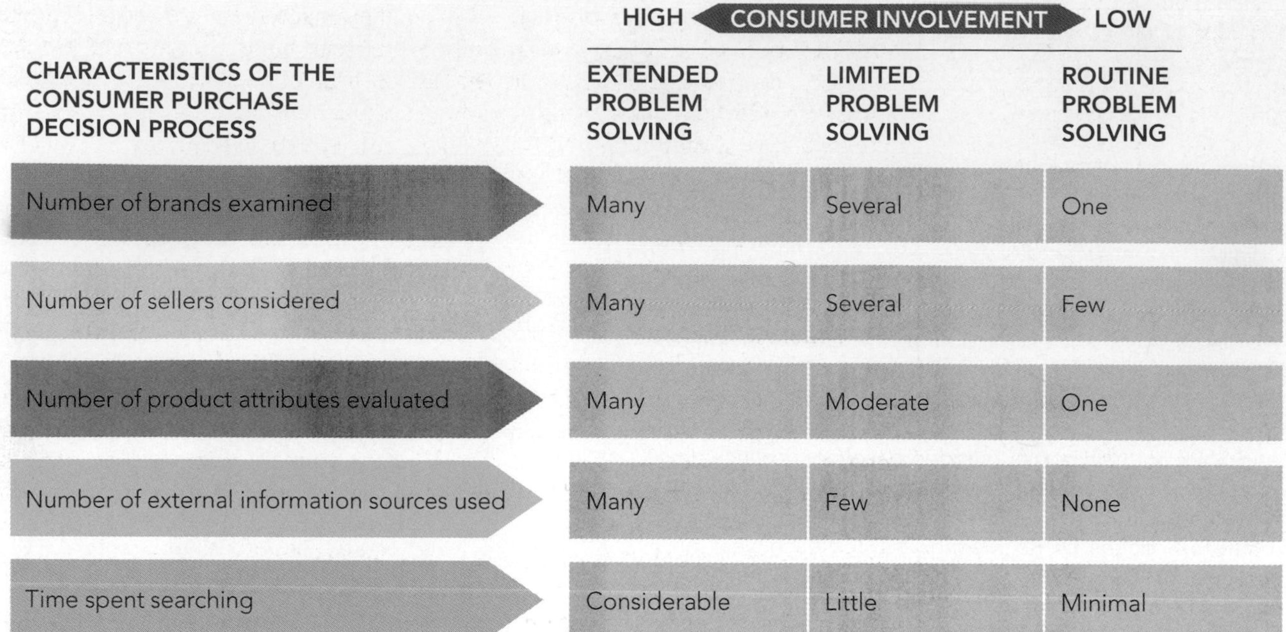

	HIGH ◀ CONSUMER INVOLVEMENT ▶ LOW		
CHARACTERISTICS OF THE CONSUMER PURCHASE DECISION PROCESS	EXTENDED PROBLEM SOLVING	LIMITED PROBLEM SOLVING	ROUTINE PROBLEM SOLVING
Number of brands examined	Many	Several	One
Number of sellers considered	Many	Several	Few
Number of product attributes evaluated	Many	Moderate	One
Number of external information sources used	Many	Few	None
Time spent searching	Considerable	Little	Minimal

FIGURE 5–3
Comparison of problem-solving variations: extended problem solving, limited problem solving, and routine problem solving.

consumers engage in extensive information search, consider many product attributes and brands, form attitudes, and participate in word-of-mouth communication. Low-involvement purchases, such as toothpaste and soap, barely involve most of us, but audio and video systems and automobiles are very involving.

There are three general variations in the consumer purchase decision process based on consumer involvement and product knowledge. Figure 5–3 shows some of the important differences between the three problem-solving variations.

Extended Problem Solving In extended problem solving, each of the five stages of the consumer purchase decision process is used, including considerable time and effort on external information search and in identifying and evaluating alternatives. Several brands are in the consideration set, and these are evaluated on many attributes. Extended problem solving exists in high-involvement purchase situations for items such as automobiles and audio systems.

Limited Problem Solving In limited problem solving, consumers typically seek some information or rely on a friend to help them evaluate alternatives. Several brands might be evaluated using a moderate number of attributes. Limited problem solving might be used in choosing a toaster, a restaurant for lunch, and other purchase situations in which the consumer has little time or effort to spend.

Routine Problem Solving For products such as table salt and milk, consumers recognize a problem, make a decision, and spend little effort seeking external information and evaluating alternatives. The purchase process for such items is virtually a habit and typifies low-involvement decision making. Routine problem solving is typically the case for low-priced, frequently purchased products.

Involvement and Marketing Strategy Low and high consumer involvement has important implications for marketing strategy. If a company markets a low-involvement product and its brand is a market leader, attention is placed on (1) maintaining product quality, (2) avoiding stockout situations so that buyers don't substitute a competing brand, and (3) repetitive advertising messages that reinforce

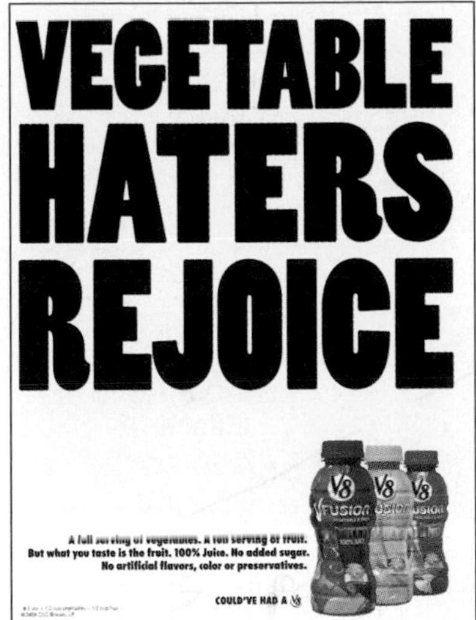

What does this ad for Campbell's V8 vegetable juice have to do with getting it into a consumer's consideration set? Read the text to find out.

a consumer's knowledge or assures buyers they made the right choice. Market challengers have a different task. They must break buying habits and use free samples, coupons, and rebates to encourage trial of their brand. Advertising messages will focus on getting their brand into a consumer's consideration set. For example, Campbell's V8 vegetable juice advertising message—"I could have had a V8!"—is targeted at consumers who routinely purchase fruit juices and soft drinks. Marketers can also link their brand attributes with high-involvement issues. Hershey's does this by linking consumption of Hershey's Extra Dark™ Chocolate with improved blood pressure and blood vessel function in addition to a great taste.

Marketers of high-involvement products know that their consumers constantly seek and process information about objective and subjective brand attributes, form evaluative criteria, rate product attributes in various brands, and combine these ratings for an overall brand evaluation—like that described in the smart phone purchase decision. Market leaders ply consumers with product information through advertising and personal selling and create chat rooms and communities on their company or brand Web sites. Market challengers capitalize on this behavior through comparative advertising that focuses on existing product attributes and often introduce novel evaluative criteria for judging competing brands. Challengers also benefit from Internet search engines such as Microsoft Bing and Google that assist buyers of high-involvement products.

Situational Influences

Often the purchase situation will affect the purchase decision process. Five **situational influences** have an impact on the purchase decision process: (1) the purchase task, (2) social surroundings, (3) physical surroundings, (4) temporal effects, and (5) antecedent states.[13] The purchase task is the reason for engaging in the decision. Information searching and evaluating alternatives may differ depending on whether the purchase is a gift, which often involves social visibility, or for the buyer's own use. Social surroundings, including the other people present when a purchase decision is made, may also affect what is purchased. Consumers accompanied by children buy about 40 percent more items than consumers shopping by themselves. Physical surroundings such as decor, music, and crowding in retail stores may alter how purchase decisions are made. Temporal effects such as time of day or the amount of time available will influence where consumers have breakfast and lunch and what is ordered. Finally, antecedent states, which include the consumer's mood or the amount of cash on hand, can influence purchase behavior and choice. For example, consumers with credit cards purchase more than those with cash or debit cards.

Figure 5–4 on the next page shows the many influences that affect the consumer purchase decision process. The decision to buy a product also involves important psychological and sociocultural influences. These two influences are covered in the remainder of this chapter. Marketing mix influences are described in Chapters 10 through 20.

learning review

1. What is the first stage in the consumer purchase decision process?
2. The brands a consumer considers buying out of the set of brands in a product class of which the consumer is aware is called the ____________.
3. What is the term for postpurchase anxiety?

FIGURE 5–4
Influences on the consumer purchase decision process come from both internal and external sources.

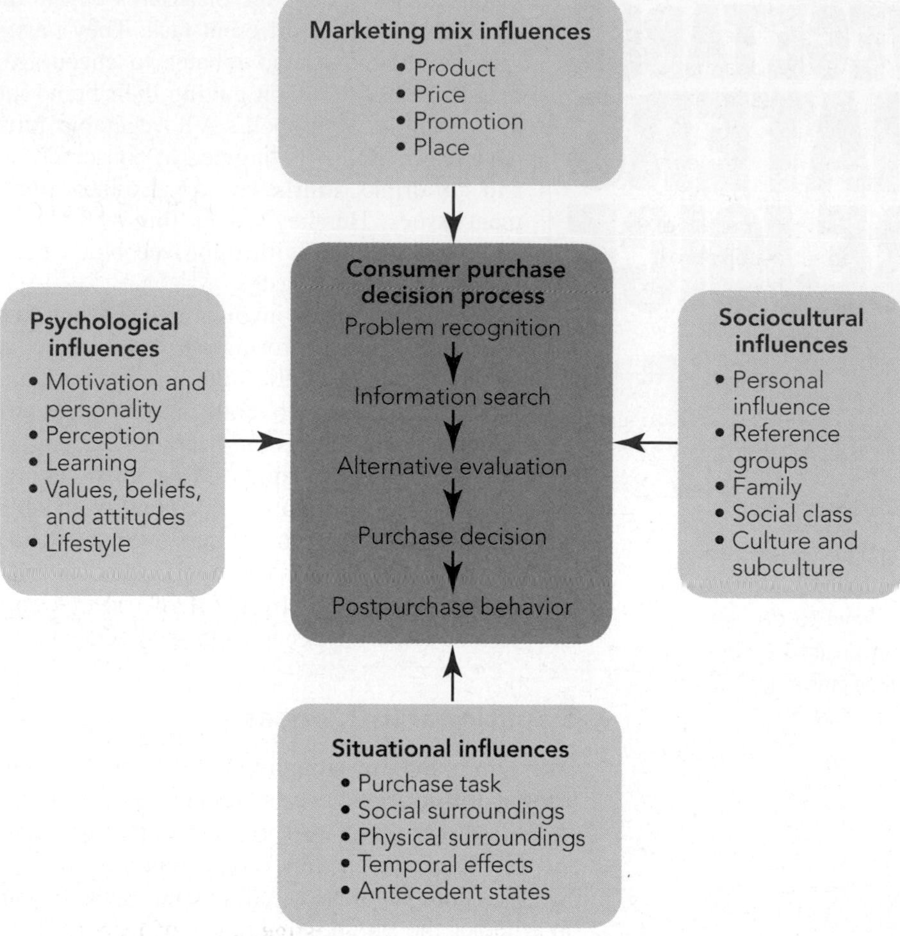

PSYCHOLOGICAL INFLUENCES ON CONSUMER BEHAVIOR

LO3

Psychology helps marketers understand why and how consumers behave as they do. In particular, psychological concepts such as motivation and personality; perception; learning; values, beliefs, and attitudes; and lifestyle are useful for interpreting buying processes and directing marketing efforts.

Motivation and Personality

Motivation and personality are two familiar psychological concepts that have specific meanings and marketing implications. These concepts are closely related and are used to explain why people do some things and not others.

Motivation **Motivation** is the energizing force that stimulates behavior to satisfy a need. Because consumer needs are the focus of the marketing concept, marketers try to arouse these needs.

An individual's needs are boundless. People possess physiological needs for basics such as water, shelter, and food. They also have learned needs, including self-esteem, achievement, and affection. Psychologists point out that these needs may be hierarchical; that is, once physiological needs are met, people seek to satisfy their learned needs.

Figure 5–5 shows one need hierarchy and classification scheme that contains five need classes.[14] *Physiological needs* are basic to survival and must be satisfied first.

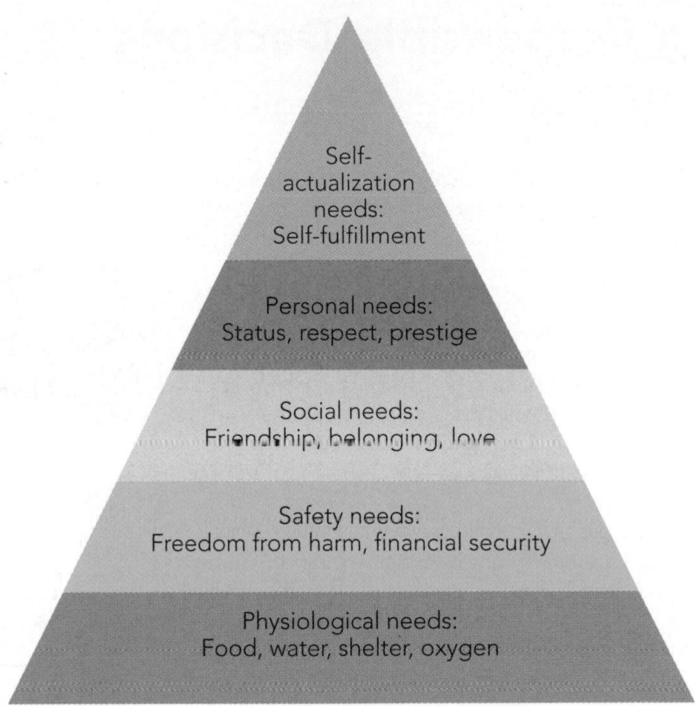

FIGURE 5–5
The hierarchy of needs is based on the idea that motivation comes from a need. If a need is met, it's no longer a motivator, so a higher-level need becomes the motivator. Higher-level needs demand support of lower-level needs.

A Red Lobster advertisement featuring a seafood salad attempts to activate the need for food. *Safety needs* involve self-preservation as well as physical and financial well-being. Smoke detector and burglar alarm manufacturers focus on these needs, as do insurance companies and retirement plan advisors. *Social needs* are concerned with love and friendship. Dating services, such as Match.com and eHarmony, and fragrance companies try to arouse these needs. *Personal needs* include the need for achievement, status, prestige, and self-respect. The American Express Platinum Card and Brooks Brothers Clothiers appeal to these needs. Sometimes firms try to arouse multiple needs to stimulate problem recognition. Michelin has combined safety with parental love to promote tire replacement for automobiles. *Self-actualization needs* involve personal fulfillment. For example, a long-running U.S. Army recruiting program invited enlistees to "Be all you can be."

Personality While motivation is the energizing force that makes consumer behavior purposeful, a consumer's personality guides and directs behavior. **Personality** refers to a person's consistent behaviors or responses to recurring situations.

Although many personality theories exist, most identify *key traits*—enduring characteristics within a person or in his or her relationship with others. Such traits include assertiveness, extroversion, compliance, dominance, and aggression, among others. These traits are inherited or formed at an early age and change little over the years. Research suggests that compliant people prefer known brand names and use more mouthwash and toilet soaps. Aggressive types use razors, not electric shavers, apply more cologne and aftershave lotions, and purchase signature goods such as Gucci, Yves St. Laurent, and Donna Karan as an indicator of status.[15]

These personality characteristics are often revealed in a person's **self-concept**, which is the way people see themselves and the way they believe others see them. Marketers recognize that people have an actual self-concept and an ideal self-concept. The actual self refers to how people actually see themselves. The ideal self describes how people would like to see themselves. These two self-images are reflected in the products and brands a person buys, including automobiles, home appliances and furnishings, magazines, consumer electronics, clothing, grooming and leisure products, and frequently, the stores a person shops. The importance of self-concept is summed

Making Responsible Decisions > > > > > > > ethics

The Ethics of Subliminal Messages

For about 50 years, the topic of subliminal perception and the presence of subliminal messages and images embedded in commercial communications have sparked heated debate.

The Federal Communications Commission has denounced subliminal messages as deceptive. Still, consumers spend $50 million a year for subliminal messages designed to help them raise their self-esteem, quit smoking, or lose weight. Almost two-thirds of U.S. consumers think subliminal messages are present in commercial communications; about half are firmly convinced that this practice can cause them to buy things they don't want.

Subliminal messages are not illegal in the United States, however, and marketers are often criticized for pursuing opportunities to create these messages in both electronic and print media. A book by August Bullock, *The Secret Sales Pitch: An Overview of Subliminal Advertising,* is devoted to this topic. Bullock identifies images and advertisements that he claims contain subliminal messages and describes techniques that can be used for conveying these messages.

Do you believe that a marketer's attempts to implant subliminal messages in electronic and print media are a deceptive practice and unethical, regardless of their intent?

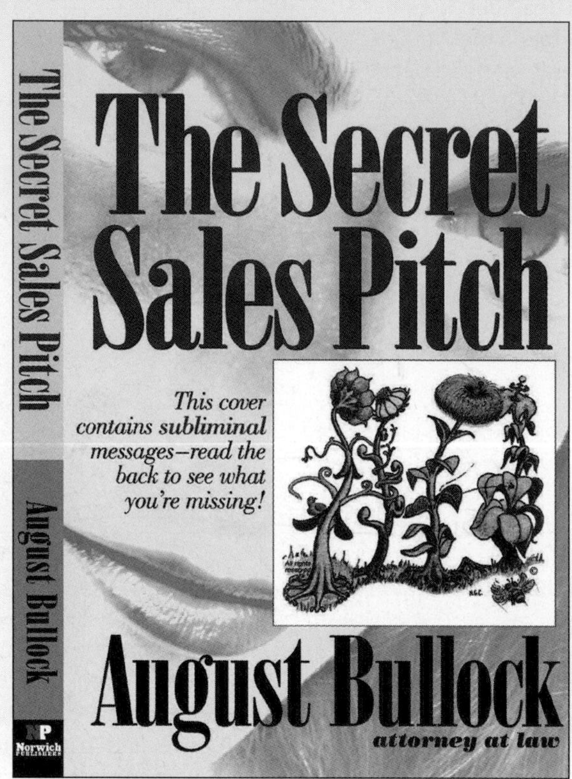

up by a senior marketing executive at Lenovo, a global supplier of notebook computers: "The notebook market is getting more like cars. The car you drive reflects you, and notebooks are becoming a form of self-expression as well."[16]

Perception

One person sees a Cadillac as a mark of achievement; another sees it as ostentatious. This is the result of **perception**—the process by which an individual selects, organizes, and interprets information to create a meaningful picture of the world.

Selective Perception Because the average consumer operates in a complex environment, the human brain attempts to organize and interpret information with a process called *selective perception*, a filtering of exposure, comprehension, and retention. *Selective exposure* occurs when people pay attention to messages that are consistent with their attitudes and beliefs and ignore messages that are inconsistent. Selective exposure often occurs in the postpurchase stage of the consumer decision process, when consumers read advertisements for the brand they just bought. It also occurs when a need exists—you are more likely to "see" a McDonald's advertisement when you are hungry rather than after you have eaten a pizza.

Selective comprehension involves interpreting information so that it is consistent with your attitudes and beliefs. A marketer's failure to understand this can have disastrous results. For example, Toro introduced a small, lightweight snowblower called the Snow Pup. Even though the product worked, sales failed to meet expecta-

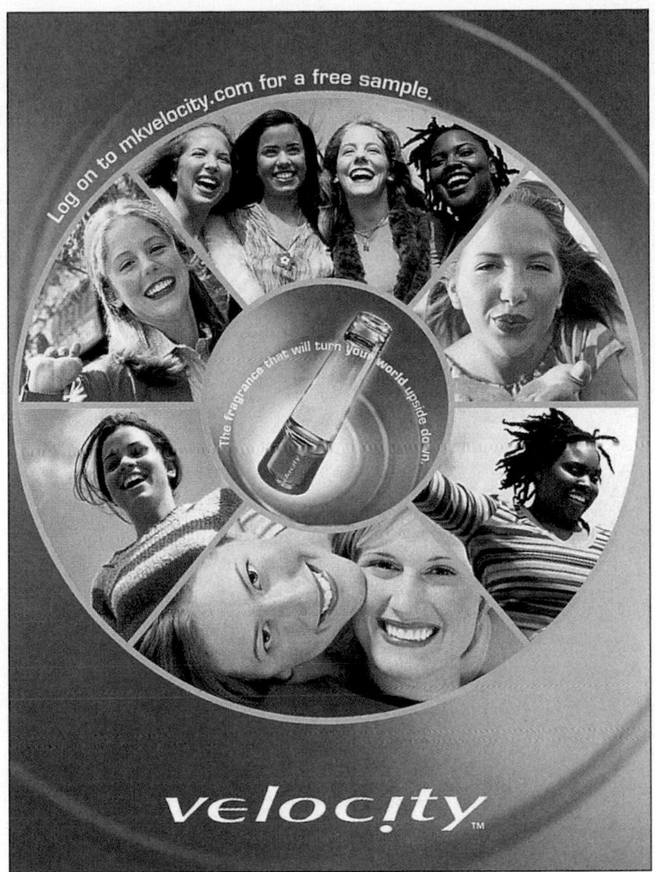

Why does Clorox tout the Good Housekeeping seal for its Fresh Step cat litter? Why does Mary Kay, Inc. offer a free sample of its Velocity brand fragrance through its Web site? The answers appear in the text.

The Clorox Company
www.freshstep.com

Mary Kay, Inc.
www.marykay.com

tions. Why? Toro later found out that consumers perceived the name to mean that Snow Pup was a toy or too light to do any serious snow removal. When the product was renamed Snow Master, sales increased sharply.[17]

Selective retention means that consumers do not remember all the information they see, read, or hear, even minutes after exposure to it. This affects the internal and external information search stage of the purchase decision process. This is why furniture and automobile retailers often give consumers product brochures to take home when they leave the showroom.

Because perception plays an important role in consumer behavior, it is not surprising that the topic of subliminal perception is a popular item for discussion. **Subliminal perception** means that you see or hear messages without being aware of them. The presence and effect of subliminal perception on behavior is a hotly debated issue, with more popular appeal than scientific support. Indeed, evidence suggests that such messages have limited effects on behavior.[18] If these messages did influence behavior, would their use be an ethical practice? (See the accompanying Making Responsible Decisions box.)[19]

Perceived Risk Perception plays a major role in the perceived risk in purchasing a product or service. **Perceived risk** represents the anxiety felt because the consumer cannot anticipate the outcomes of a purchase but believes there may be negative consequences. Examples of possible negative consequences are the size of the financial outlay required to buy the product (Can I afford $500 for those skis?), the risk of physical harm (Is bungee jumping safe?), and the performance of the product (Will the whitening toothpaste work?). A more abstract form is psychosocial (What will my friends say if I get a tattoo?). Perceived risk affects information search, because the greater the perceived risk, the more extensive the external search stage is likely to be.

Recognizing the importance of perceived risk, companies develop strategies to reduce the consumer's risk and encourage purchases. These strategies and examples of firms using them include the following:

- *Obtaining seals of approval:* The Good Housekeeping seal for Fresh Step cat litter.
- *Securing endorsements from influential people:* Endorsements for Promise soft spread from 9 out of 10 cardiologists.
- *Providing free trials of the product:* Samples of Mary Kay's Velocity fragrance.
- *Giving extensive usage instructions:* Clairol hair coloring.
- *Providing warranties and guarantees:* Kia Motors' 10-year, 100,000-mile warranty.

Learning

Much consumer behavior is learned. Consumers learn which information sources to consult for information about products and services, which evaluative criteria to use when assessing alternatives, and, more generally, how to make purchase decisions. **Learning** refers to those behaviors that result from (1) repeated experience and (2) reasoning.

Behavioral Learning *Behavioral learning* is the process of developing automatic responses to a situation built up through repeated exposure to it. Four variables are central to how consumers learn from repeated experience: drive, cue, response, and reinforcement. A *drive* is a need that moves an individual to action. Drives, such as hunger, might be represented by motives. A *cue* is a stimulus or symbol perceived by consumers. A *response* is the action taken by a consumer to satisfy the drive, whereas a *reinforcement* is the reward. Being hungry (drive), a consumer sees a cue (a billboard), takes action (buys a sandwich), and receives a reward (it tastes great!).

Marketers use two concepts from behavioral learning theory. *Stimulus generalization* occurs when a response elicited by one stimulus (cue) is generalized to another stimulus. Using the same brand name for different products is an application of this concept, such as Tylenol Cold & Flu and Tylenol P.M. *Stimulus discrimination* refers to a person's ability to perceive differences in stimuli. Consumers' tendency to perceive all light beers as being alike led to Budweiser Light commercials that distinguished between many types of "light beers" and Bud Light.

Cognitive Learning Consumers also learn through thinking, reasoning, and mental problem solving without direct experience. This type of learning, called *cognitive learning*, involves making connections between two or more ideas or simply observing the outcomes of others' behaviors and adjusting your own accordingly. Firms also influence this type of learning. Through repetition in advertising, messages such as "Advil is a headache remedy" attempt to link a brand (Advil) and an idea (headache remedy) by showing someone using the brand and finding relief.

Brand Loyalty Learning is also important to marketers because it relates to habit formation—the basis of routine problem solving. Furthermore, there is a close link between habits and **brand loyalty**, which is a favorable attitude toward and consistent purchase of a single brand over time. Brand loyalty results from the positive reinforcement of previous actions. A consumer reduces risk and saves time by consistently purchasing the same brand of shampoo and has favorable results—healthy,

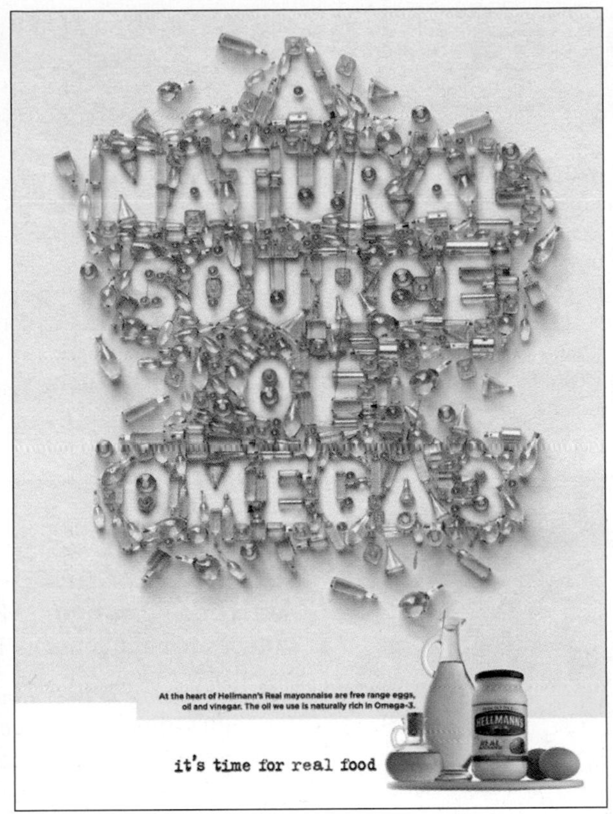

Attitudes toward Colgate Total toothpaste and Hellmann's Real Mayonnaise were successfully changed by these ads. How? Read the text to find out how marketers can change consumer attitudes toward products and brands.

Colgate-Palmolive
www.colgate.com

Hellmann's
www.hellmanns.com

shining hair. There is evidence of brand loyalty in many commonly purchased products in the United States and the global marketplace. However, the incidence of brand loyalty appears to be declining in North America, Western Europe, and Japan.[20]

Values, Beliefs, and Attitudes

Values, beliefs, and attitudes play a central role in consumer decision making and related marketing actions.

Attitude Formation An **attitude** is a "learned predisposition to respond to an object or class of objects in a consistently favorable or unfavorable way."[21] Attitudes are shaped by our values and beliefs, which are learned. Values vary by level of specificity. We speak of American core values, including material well-being and humanitarianism. We also have personal values, such as thriftiness and ambition. Marketers are concerned with both but focus mostly on personal values. Personal values affect attitudes by influencing the importance assigned to specific product attributes. Suppose thriftiness is one of your personal values. When you evaluate cars, fuel economy (a product attribute) becomes important. If you believe a specific car brand has this attribute, you are likely to have a favorable attitude toward it.

Beliefs also play a part in attitude formation. **Beliefs** are a consumer's subjective perception of how a product or brand performs on different attributes. Beliefs are based on personal experience, advertising, and discussions with other people. Beliefs about product attributes are important because, along with personal values, they create the favorable or unfavorable attitude the consumer has toward certain products, services, and brands.

Going Online

Are You an Experiencer? An Achiever?: Identifying Your VALS Profile

The VALS™ system run by SRI Consulting Business Intelligence has identified eight unique consumer segments based on a person's primary motivation and resources. The text provides a brief description of each segment.

Do you wish to know your VALS profile? If you do, respond to the questions on the VALS survey at www.sric-bi.com. Simply click "VALS Survey." In addition to obtaining your profile in real time, you can examine the characteristics of your and other profiles in greater detail.

Attitude Change Marketers use three approaches to try to change consumer attitudes toward products and brands, as shown in the following examples.[22]

1. *Changing beliefs about the extent to which a brand has certain attributes.* To allay mothers' concerns about ingredients in its mayonnaise, Hellmann's successfully communicated the product's high Omega 3 content which is essential to human health.
2. *Changing the perceived importance of attributes.* Pepsi-Cola made freshness an important product attribute when it stamped freshness dates on its cans. Before doing so, few consumers considered cola freshness an issue. After Pepsi spent about $25 million on advertising and promotion, a consumer survey found that 61 percent of cola drinkers believed freshness dating was an important attribute.
3. *Adding new attributes to the product.* Colgate-Palmolive included a new antibacterial ingredient, tricloson, in its Colgate Total toothpaste and spent $100 million marketing the brand. The result? Colgate replaced Crest as the market leader for the first time in 25 years.

Consumer Lifestyle

Lifestyle is a mode of living that is identified by how people spend their time and resources, what they consider important in their environment, and what they think of themselves and the world around them. The analysis of consumer lifestyles, called *psychographics*, provides insights into consumer needs and wants. Lifestyle analysis has proven useful in segmenting and targeting consumers for new and existing products and services (see Chapter 9).

Psychographics, the practice of combining psychology, lifestyle, and demographics, is often used to uncover consumer motivations for buying and using products and services. A prominent psychographic system is VALS from SRI Consulting Business Intelligence (SRIC-BI).[23] The VALS system identifies eight consumer segments based on (1) their primary motivation for buying and having certain products and services and (2) their resources.

According to SRIC-BI researchers, consumers are motivated to buy products and services and seek experiences that give shape, substance, and satisfaction to their lives. But not all consumers are alike. Consumers are inspired by one of three primary motivations—ideals, achievement, and self-expression—that give meaning to their self or the world and govern their activities. The different levels of resources enhance or constrain a person's expression of his or her primary motivation. A person's resources include psychological, physical, demographic, and material capacities such as income, self-confidence, and risk-taking. Before reading further, visit the VALS Web site shown in the accompanying Going Online box. Complete the short survey to learn which segment best describes you.

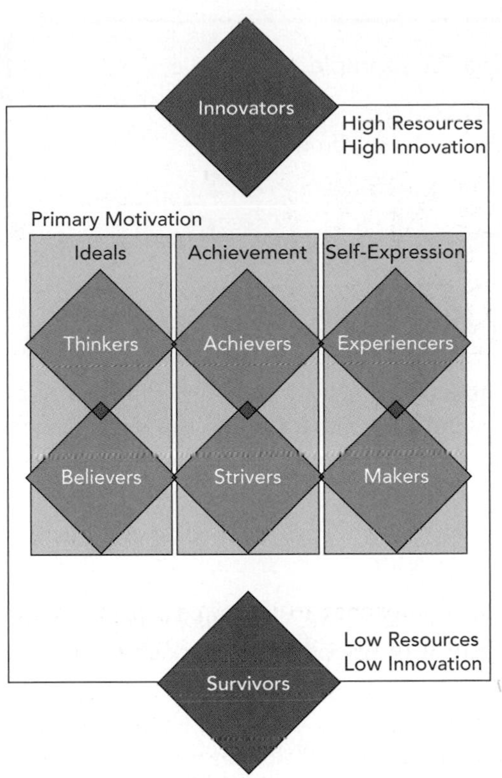

The VALS classification system places consumers with abundant resources—psychological, physical, and material means and capacities—near the top of the chart and those with minimal resources near the bottom. The chart segments consumers by their basis for decision making: ideals, achievement, or self-expression. The boxes intersect to indicate that some categories may be considered together. For instance, a marketer may categorize Thinkers and Believers together.

The VALS system seeks to explain why and how consumers make purchase decisions.

- *Ideals-motivated groups.* Consumers motivated by ideals are guided by knowledge and principle. *Thinkers* are mature, reflective, and well-educated people who value order, knowledge, and responsibility. They are practical consumers, deliberate information-seekers, who value durability and functionality in products over styling and newness. *Believers*, with fewer resources, are conservative, conventional people with concrete beliefs based on traditional, established codes: family, religion, community, and the nation. They choose familiar products and brands, favor American-made products, and are generally brand loyal.
- *Achievement-motivated groups.* Consumers motivated by achievement look for products and services that demonstrate success to their peers or to a peer group they aspire to. These consumers include *Achievers*, who have a busy, goal-directed lifestyle and a deep commitment to career and family. Image is important to them. They favor established, prestige products and services and are interested in time-saving devices given their hectic schedules. *Strivers* are trendy, fun-loving, and less self-confident than Achievers. They also have lower levels of education and household income. Money defines success for them. They favor stylish products and are as impulsive as their financial circumstances permit.
- *Self-expression-motivated groups.* Consumers motivated by self-expression desire social or physical activity, variety, and risk. *Experiencers* are young, enthusiastic, and impulsive consumers who become excited about new possibilities but are equally quick to cool. They savor the new, the offbeat, and the risky. Their energy finds an outlet in exercise, sports, outdoor recreation, and social activities. Much of their income is spent on fashion items, entertainment, and socializing and particularly on looking good and having the latest things. *Makers*, with fewer resources, express themselves and experience the world by working on it—raising children or fixing a car. They are practical people who have constructive skills, value self-sufficiency, and are unimpressed by material possessions except those with a practical or functional purpose.
- *High- and low-resource groups.* Two segments stand apart. *Innovators* are successful, sophisticated, take-charge people with high self-esteem and abundant resources of all kinds. Image is important to them, not as evidence of power or status, but as an expression of cultivated tastes, independence, and character. They are receptive to new ideas and technologies. Their lives are characterized by variety. *Survivors*, with the least resources of any segment, focus on meeting basic needs (safety and security) rather than fulfilling desires. They represent a modest market for most products and services and are loyal to favorite brands, especially if they can be purchased at a discount.

Each of these segments exhibits unique media preferences. Experiencers and Strivers are the most likely to visit Internet chat rooms. Innovators, Thinkers, and Achievers tend to read business and news magazines such as *Fortune and Time*. Makers read automotive magazines. Believers are the heaviest readers of *Reader's Digest*. GeoVALS™ estimates the percentage of each VALS group by zip code.

learning review

4. The problem with the Toro Snow Pup was an example of selective ____________.
5. What three attitude-change approaches are most common?
6. What does *lifestyle* mean?

SOCIOCULTURAL INFLUENCES ON CONSUMER BEHAVIOR

LO4

Sociocultural influences, which evolve from a consumer's formal and informal relationships with other people, also exert a significant impact on consumer behavior. These involve personal influence, reference groups, family influence, social class, culture, and subculture.

Personal Influence

A consumer's purchases are often influenced by the views, opinions, or behaviors of others. Two aspects of personal influence are very important to marketing: opinion leadership and word-of-mouth activity.

Opinion Leadership Individuals who exert direct or indirect social influence over others are called **opinion leaders**. Opinion leaders are considered to be knowledgeable about or users of particular products and services, so their opinions influences others' choices. Opinion leadership is widespread in the purchase of cars and trucks, entertainment, clothing and accessories, club membership, consumer electronics, vacation locations, food, and financial investments. A study by *Popular Mechanics* magazine identified 18 million opinion leaders who influence the purchases of some 85 million consumers for do-it-yourself products.

About 10 percent of U.S. adults are opinion leaders.[24] Identifying, reaching, and influencing opinion leaders is a major challenge for companies. Some firms use

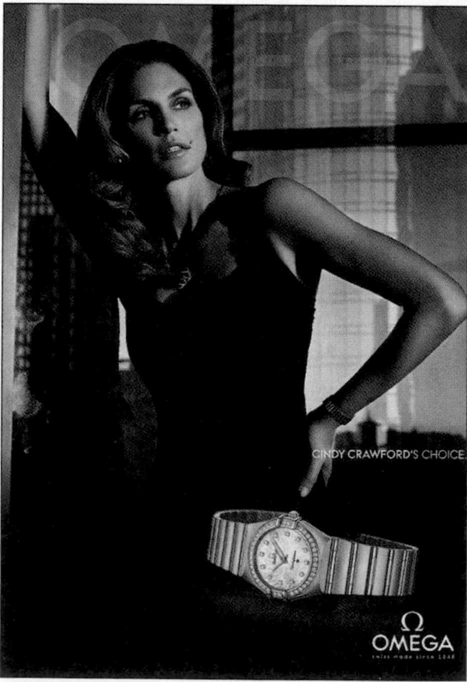

Firms use actors or athletes as spokespersons to represent their products, such as Cindy Crawford and Michael Phelps for OMEGA watches.

OMEGA
www.omegawatches.com

Marketing Matters > > > > > > customer value

BzzAgent—The Buzz Experience

Have you recently heard about a new product, movie, Web site, book, or restaurant from someone you know . . . or a complete stranger? If so, you may have had a word-of-mouth experience.

Marketers recognize the power of word of mouth. The challenge has been to harness that power. BzzAgent Inc. does just that. Its worldwide volunteer army of over 600,000 natural-born talkers channel their chatter toward products and services they deem authentically worth talking about. "Our goal is to capture honest word of mouth," says David Balter, BzzAgent's founder, "and to build a network that turns passionate customers into brand evangelists."

BzzAgent's method is simple. Once a client signs on with Bzz-Agent, the company searches its "agent" database for those who match the demographic and psychographic profile of the target market for a client's offering. Agents then can sign up for a buzz campaign and receive a sample product and a training manual for buzz-creating strategies. Each time an agent completes an activity, he or she is expected to file an online report describing the nature of the buzz and its effectiveness. BzzAgent coaches respond with encouragement and feedback on additional techniques.

Agents keep the products they promote. They also earn points redeemable for books, CDs, and other items by filing detailed reports. Who are the agents? About 65 percent are older than 25, 70 percent are women, and two are Fortune 500 CEOs. All are gregarious and genuinely like the product or service, otherwise they wouldn't participate in the buzz campaign.

Estée Lauder, Monster.com, Anheuser-Busch, Penguin Books, Lee jeans, Arby's, Nestlé, Hershey Foods, and Volkswagen have used BzzAgent. But BzzAgent's buzz isn't cheap, and not everything is buzz worthy. Deploying 1,000 agents on a 12-week campaign can cost a company $95,000, exclusive of product samples. BzzAgent researches a product or service before committing to a campaign and rejects about 80 percent of the companies that seek its service. It also refuses campaigns for politicians, religious groups, and certain products, such as firearms. Interested in BzzAgent? Visit its Web site at www.bzzagent.com.

sports figures or celebrities as spokespersons to represent their products, such as actor Cindy Crawford and swimmer Michael Phelps for OMEGA watches. Others promote their products in media believed to reach opinion leaders. Still others use more direct approaches. For example, a carmaker recently invited influential community leaders and business executives to test-drive its new models. Some 6,000 accepted the offer, and 98 percent said they would recommend their tested car. The company estimated that the number of favorable recommendations totaled 32,000.

Word of Mouth The influencing of people during conversations is called **word of mouth**. Word of mouth is the most powerful and authentic information source for consumers because it typically involves friends viewed as trustworthy. According to a recent study, 67 percent of U.S. consumer product sales are directly based on word-of-mouth activity among friends, family, and colleagues.[25]

The power of personal influence has prompted firms to promote positive and retard negative word of mouth. For instance, "teaser" advertising campaigns are run in advance of new-product introductions to stimulate conversations. Other techniques such as advertising slogans, music, and humor also heighten positive word of mouth. Many commercials shown during the Super Bowl are created expressly to initiate conversations about the advertisements and featured product or service the next day. Increasingly, companies recruit and deploy people to produce *buzz*—popularity created by consumer word of mouth. Read the accompanying Marketing Matters box to learn how this is done by BzzAgent.[26]

On the other hand, rumors about Kmart (snake eggs in clothing), McDonald's (worms in hamburgers), Corona Extra beer (contaminated beer), and Snickers candy bars in Russia (a cause of diabetes) have resulted in negative word of mouth, none of which was based on fact. Overcoming or neutralizing negative word of mouth is difficult and costly. Marketers have found that supplying factual information, providing toll-free numbers for consumers to call the company, and giving appropriate product demonstrations have proven helpful.

The power of word of mouth has been magnified by the Internet through online forums, chat rooms, blogs, bulletin boards, and Web sites. In fact, Ford uses special software to monitor online messages and find out what consumers are saying about its vehicles. Chapter 21 describes how marketers track, initiate, and manage word of mouth in an online environment.

Reference Groups

Reference groups are people to whom an individual looks as a basis for self-appraisal or as a source of personal standards. Reference groups affect consumer purchases because they influence the information, attitudes, and aspiration levels that help set a consumer's standards. For example, one of the first questions one asks others when planning to attend a social occasion is, "What are you going to wear?" Reference groups influence the purchase of luxury products but not necessities—reference groups exert a strong influence on the brand chosen when its use or consumption is highly visible to others.

Consumers have many reference groups, but three groups have clear marketing implications. A *membership group* is one to which a person actually belongs, including fraternities and sororities, social clubs, and the family. Such groups are easily identifiable and are targeted by firms selling insurance, insignia products, and charter vacations. An *aspiration group* is one that a person wishes to be a member of or wishes to be identified with, such as a professional society. Firms frequently rely on spokespeople or settings associated with their target market's aspiration group in their advertising. A *dissociative group* is one that a person wishes to maintain a distance from because of differences in values or behaviors.

Family Influence

Family influences on consumer behavior result from three sources: consumer socialization, passage through the family life cycle, and decision making within the family or household.

Consumer Socialization The process by which people acquire the skills, knowledge, and attitudes necessary to function as consumers is **consumer socialization.**[27] Children learn how to purchase (1) by interacting with adults in purchase situations and (2) through their own purchasing and product usage experiences. Research shows that children evidence brand preferences at age two, and these preferences often last a lifetime. This knowledge prompted the licensing of the well-known Craftsman brand name to MGA Entertainment for its children's line of My First Craftsman power tools; Time, Inc., to launch *Sports Illustrated for Kids*; and Yahoo! and America Online to offer special areas where young audiences can view their children's menu—Yahoo! Kids and Kids Only, respectively.

Family Life Cycle Consumers act and purchase differently as they go through life. The **family life cycle** concept describes the distinct phases that a family progresses through from formation to retirement, each phase bringing with it identifiable purchasing behaviors.[28] Figure 5–6 illustrates the traditional progression as well as contemporary variations of the family life cycle. Today, the *traditional family*—

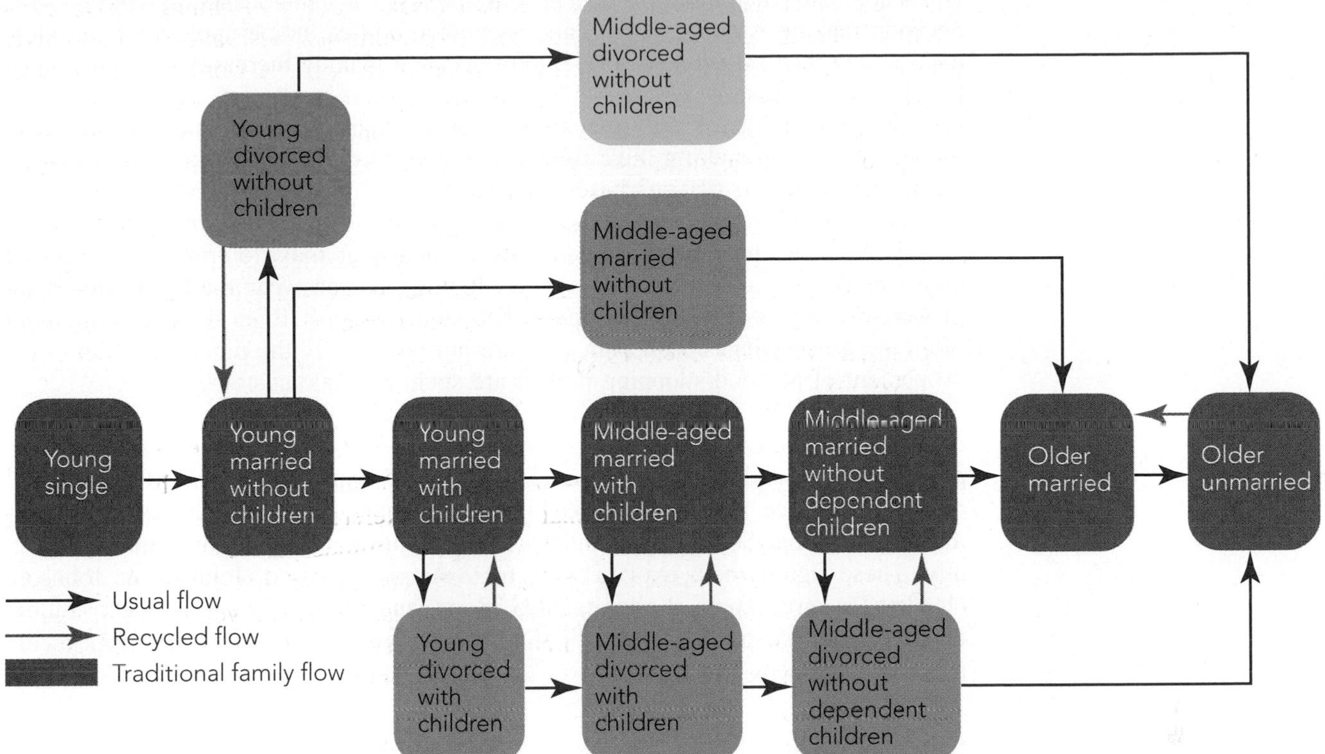

FIGURE 5–6
Modern family life cycle stages and flows. Can you identify people you know in different stages? Do they follow the purchase patterns described in the text?

married couple with children younger than 18 years—constitutes just 22 percent of all U.S. households. The remaining 78 percent of U.S. households include single parents, unmarried couples, divorced, never-married, or widowed individuals, and older married couples whose children no longer live at home.

Young singles' buying preferences are for nondurable items, including prepared foods, clothing, personal care products, and entertainment. They represent a target market for recreational travel, automobile, and consumer electronics firms. Young married couples without children are typically more affluent than young singles because usually both spouses are employed. These couples exhibit preferences for furniture, housewares, and gift items for each other. Young marrieds with children are driven by the needs of their children. They make up a sizable market for life insurance, various children's products, and home furnishings. Single parents with children are the least financially secure of households with children. Their buying preferences are often affected by a limited economic status and tend toward convenience foods, child care services, and personal care items.

Middle-aged married couples with children are typically better off financially than their younger counterparts. They are a significant market for leisure products and home improvement items. Middle-aged couples without children typically have a large amount of discretionary income. These couples buy better home furnishings, status automobiles, and financial services. Persons in the last two phases—older married and older unmarried—make up a sizable market for prescription drugs, medical services, vacation trips, and gifts for younger relatives.

Family Decision Making A third influence in the decision-making process occurs within the family.[29] Two decision-making styles exist: spouse-dominant and joint decision making. With a joint decision-making style, most decisions are made by both husband and wife. Spouse-dominant decisions are those for which either the husband or the wife is mostly responsible. Research indicates that wives tend to have more say when purchasing groceries, children's toys, clothing, and medicines.

Husbands tend to be more influential in home and car maintenance purchases. Joint decision making is common for cars, vacations, houses, home appliances and electronics, and medical care. As a rule, joint decision making increases with the education of the spouses.

Roles of individual family members in the purchase process are another element of family decision making. Five roles exist: (1) information gatherer, (2) influencer, (3) decision maker, (4) purchaser, and (5) user. Family members assume different roles for different products and services. This knowledge is important to firms. For example, 89 percent of wives either influence or make outright purchases of men's clothing. Knowing this, Haggar Clothing, a menswear marketer, advertises in women's magazines such as *Vanity Fair* and *Redbook*. Even though women are often the grocery decision maker, they are not necessarily the purchaser. More than 40 percent of all food-shopping dollars are spent by male customers.

Increasingly, preteens and teenagers are the information gatherers, influencers, decision makers, and purchasers of products and services for the family, given the prevalence of working parents and single-parent households. Children under 12 directly influence more than $365 billion in annual family purchases. Teenagers influence another $650 billion and spend $200 million of their own money annually. These figures help explain why, for example, Nabisco, Johnson & Johnson, Hewlett-Packard, Apple, Kellogg, P&G, Sony, and Oscar Mayer, among countless other companies, spend more than $55 billion annually in electronic and print media that reach preteens and teens.

Social Class

A more subtle influence on consumer behavior than direct contact with others is the social class to which people belong. **Social class** may be defined as the relatively permanent, homogeneous divisions in a society into which people sharing similar values, interests, and behavior can be grouped. A person's occupation, source of income (not level of income), and education determine his or her social class. Generally speaking, three major social class categories exist—upper, middle, and lower—with subcategories within each. This structure has been observed in the United States, Great Britain, Western Europe, and Latin America.[30]

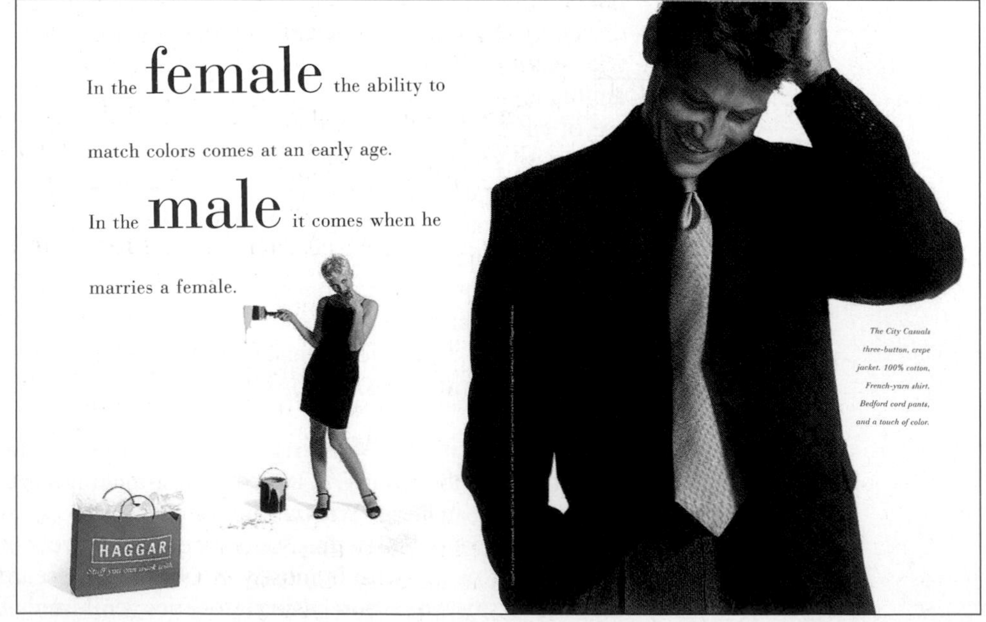

The Haggar Clothing Co. recognizes the important role women play in the choice of men's clothing. The company directs a large portion of its advertising toward women because they influence and purchase men's clothing.

Haggar Clothing Co.
www.haggar.com

To some degree, persons within social classes exhibit common values, attitudes, beliefs, lifestyles, and buying behaviors. Compared with the middle classes, people in the lower classes have a more short-term time orientation, think in concrete rather than abstract terms, and see fewer personal opportunities. Members of the upper classes focus on achievements and the future and think in abstract or symbolic terms.

Companies use social class as a basis for identifying and reaching particularly good prospects for their products and services. For instance, JCPenney has historically appealed to the middle classes. *New Yorker* magazine reaches the upper classes. In general, people in the upper classes are targeted by companies for items such as financial investments, expensive cars, and formal evening wear. The middle classes represent a target market for home improvement centers, automobile parts stores, and personal hygiene products. Firms also recognize differences in media preferences among classes: lower and working classes prefer tabloid magazines; middle classes read fashion, romance, and celebrity (*People*) magazines; and upper classes tend to subscribe to literary, travel, and news magazines.

Culture and Subculture

As described in Chapter 3, *culture* refers to the set of values, ideas, and attitudes that are learned and shared among the members of a group. Thus, we often refer to the American culture, the Latin American culture, or the Japanese culture. Cultural underpinnings of American buying patterns were described in Chapter 3; Chapter 7 will explore the role of culture in global marketing.

Subgroups within the larger, or national, culture with unique values, ideas, and attitudes are referred to as **subcultures**. Various subcultures exist within the American culture. The three largest racial/ethnic subcultures in the United States are Hispanics, African Americans, and Asian Americans. Collectively, they are expected to account for one in four U.S. consumers and spend about $3.4 trillion for goods and services in 2013.[31] Each group exhibits sophisticated social and cultural behaviors that affect buying patterns, which provides the basis for multicultural marketing programs described in Chapter 3.

Why does Best Foods advertise its Mazola Corn Oil in Spanish? Read the text for the answer.

Mazola Corn Oil
www.mazola.com

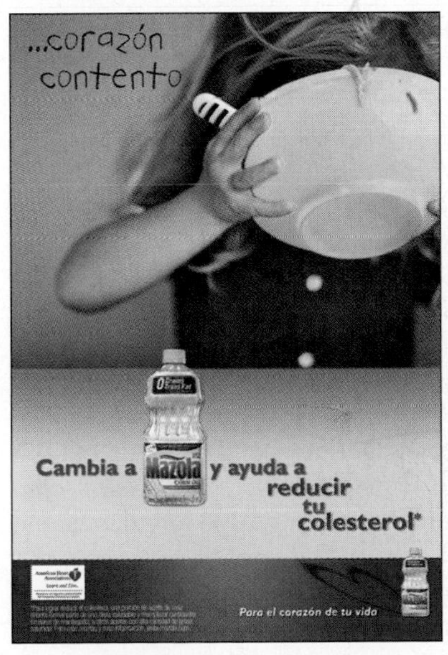

Hispanic Buying Patterns Hispanics represent the largest racial/ethnic subculture in the United States in terms of population and spending power. About 50 percent of Hispanics in the United States are immigrants, and the majority are under the age of 25. One-third of Hispanics are younger than 18.

Research on Hispanic buying practices has uncovered several consistent patterns:[32]

1. Hispanics are quality and brand conscious. They are willing to pay a premium price for premium quality and are often brand loyal.
2. Hispanics prefer buying American-made products, especially those offered by firms that cater to Hispanic needs.
3. Hispanic buying preferences are strongly influenced by family and peers.
4. Hispanics consider advertising a credible product information source, and U.S. firms spend more than $4 billion annually on advertising to Hispanics.
5. Convenience is not an important product attribute to Hispanic homemakers with respect to food preparation or consumption, nor is low caffeine in coffee and soft drinks, low fat in dairy products, and low cholesterol in packaged foods.

Despite some consistent buying patterns, marketing to Hispanics has proven to be a challenge for two reasons. First, the Hispanic subculture is diverse and composed of Mexicans, Puerto Ricans, Cubans, and others of Central and South American ancestry. Cultural differences among these nationalities often affect product preferences. For example, Campbell Soup Company sells its Casera

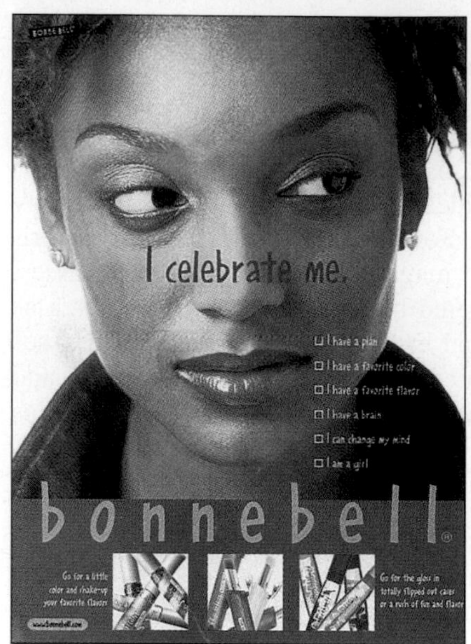

African American women represent a large market for health and beauty products. Cosmetic companies such as Bonne Bell Cosmetics, Inc., actively seek to serve this market.

Bonne Bell Cosmetics, Inc.
www.bonnebell.com

line of soups, beans, and sauces using different recipes to appeal to Puerto Ricans on the East Coast and Mexicans in the Southwest. Second, a language barrier exists, and commercial messages are frequently misinterpreted when translated into Spanish. Volkswagen learned this lesson when the Spanish translation of its "Drivers Wanted" slogan suggested "chauffeurs wanted." The Spanish slogan was changed to "*Agarra calle*," a slang expression that can be loosely translated as "let's hit the road."

Sensitivity to the unique needs of Hispanics by firms has paid huge dividends. For example, Metropolitan Life Insurance is the largest insurer of Hispanics. Goya Foods dominates the market for ethnic food products sold to Hispanics. Best Foods' Mazola Corn Oil captures two-thirds of the Hispanic market for this product category. Time, Inc., has more than 750,000 subscribers to its *People en Español*.

African American Buying Patterns African Americans have the second-largest spending power of the three racial/ethnic subcultures in the United States. Consumer research on African American buying patterns has focused on similarities and differences with Caucasians. When socioeconomic status differences between African Americans and Caucasians are removed, there are more similarities than points of difference. Differences in buying patterns are greater within the African American subculture, due to levels of socioeconomic status, than between African Americans and Caucasians of similar status.

Even though similarities outweigh differences, there are consumption patterns that do differ between African Americans and Caucasians.[33] For example, African Americans spend far more than Caucasians on boy's clothing, rental goods, and audio equipment. Adult African Americans are twice as likely to own a pager and spend twice as much for online services, on a per capita basis, than Caucasians. African American women spend three times more on health and beauty products than Caucasian women. Furthermore, the typical African American family is five years younger than the typical Caucasian family. This factor alone accounts for some of the observed differences in preferences for clothing, music, shelter, cars, and many other products, services, and activities. Finally, it must be emphasized that, historically, African Americans have been deprived of employment and educational opportunities in the United States. Both factors have resulted in income disparities between African Americans and Caucasians, which influence purchase behavior.

Recent research indicates that while African Americans are price conscious, they are strongly motivated by quality and choice. They respond more to products such as apparel and cosmetics and advertising that appeal to their African American pride and heritage as well as address their ethnic features and needs regardless of socioeconomic status.

Asian American Buying Patterns About 70 percent of Asian Americans are immigrants. Most are under the age of 30.

The Asian subculture is composed of Chinese, Japanese, Filipinos, Koreans, Asian Indians, people from Southeast Asia, and Pacific Islanders. The diversity of the Asian subculture is so great that generalizations about buying patterns of this group are difficult to make.[34] Consumer research on Asian Americans suggests that individuals and families divide into two groups. *Assimilated* Asian Americans are conversant in English, highly educated, hold professional and managerial positions, and exhibit buying patterns very much like the typical American consumer. *Nonassimilated* Asian Americans are recent immigrants who still cling to their native languages and customs.

The diversity of Asian Americans evident in language, customs, and tastes requires marketers to be sensitive to different Asian nationalities. For example, Anheuser-

This advertisement featured NBA basketball star Yao Ming and ran in Asian-language print publications nationwide, focusing on Asian Americans.

McDonald's Corporation
www.mcdonalds.com

Busch's agricultural products division sells eight varieties of California-grown rice, each with a different Asian label to cover a range of nationalities and tastes. The company's advertising also addresses the preferences of Chinese, Japanese, and Koreans for different kinds of rice bowls. McDonald's actively markets to Asian Americans. According to a company executive, "We recognize diversity in this market. We try to make our messages in the language they prefer to see them." Recently, McDonald's launched an advertising campaign that emphasized the company's Chicken Select product for Chinese, Vietnamese, and Korean consumers.

Studies show that the Asian American subculture as a whole is characterized by hard work, strong family ties, appreciation for education, and median family incomes exceeding those of any other ethnic group. This subculture is also the most entrepreneurial in the United States, as evidenced by the number of Asian-owned businesses. These qualities led Metropolitan Life Insurance to identify Asian Americans as a target for insurance following the company's success in marketing to Hispanics.

learning review

7. What are the two primary forms of personal influence?
8. Marketers are concerned with which types of reference groups?
9. What two challenges must marketers overcome when marketing to Hispanics?

LEARNING OBJECTIVES REVIEW

LO1 *Describe the stages in the consumer purchase decision process.*
The consumer purchase decision process consists of five stages. They are problem recognition, information search, alternative evaluation, purchase decision, and postpurchase behavior. Problem recognition is perceiving a difference between a person's ideal and actual situation big enough to trigger a decision. Information search involves remembering previous purchase experiences (internal search) and external search behavior such as seeking information from other sources. Alternative evaluation clarifies the problem for the consumer by (*a*) suggesting the evaluative criteria to use for the purchase, (*b*) yielding brand

names that might meet the criteria, and (*c*) developing consumer value perceptions. The purchase decision involves the choice of an alternative, including from whom to buy and when to buy. Postpurchase behavior involves the comparison of the chosen alternative with a consumer's expectations, which leads to satisfaction or dissatisfaction and subsequent purchase behavior.

LO2 *Distinguish among three variations of the consumer purchase decision process: routine, limited, and extended problem solving.*
Consumers don't always engage in the five-stage purchase decision process. Instead, they skip or minimize one or more stages depending on the level of involvement—the personal, social, and economic significance of the purchase. For low-involvement purchase occasions, consumers engage in routine problem solving. They recognize a problem, make a decision, and spend little effort seeking external information and evaluating alternatives. For high-involvement purchase occasions, each of the five stages of the consumer purchase decision process is used, including considerable time and effort on external information search and in identifying and evaluating alternatives. With limited problem solving, consumers typically seek some information or rely on a friend to help them evaluate alternatives.

LO3 *Identify major psychological influences on consumer behavior.*
Psychology helps marketers understand why and how consumers behave as they do. In particular, psychological concepts such as motivation and personality; perception; learning; values, beliefs, and attitudes; and lifestyle are useful for interpreting buying processes. Motivation is the energizing force that stimulates behavior to satisfy a need. Personality refers to a person's consistent behaviors or responses to recurring situations. Perception is the process by which an individual selects, organizes, and interprets information to create a meaningful picture of the world. Consumers filter information through selective exposure, comprehension, and retention.

Much consumer behavior is learned. Learning refers to those behaviors that result from (*a*) repeated experience and (*b*) reasoning. Brand loyalty results from learning. Values, beliefs, and attitudes are also learned and influence how consumers evaluate products, services, and brands. A more general concept is lifestyle. Lifestyle, also called psychographics, combines psychology and demographics and focuses on how people spend their time and resources, what they consider important in their environment, and what they think of themselves and the world around them.

LO4 *Identify the major sociocultural influences on consumer behavior.*
Sociocultural influences, which evolve from a consumer's formal and informal relationships with other people, also affect consumer behavior. These involve personal influence, reference groups, the family, social class, culture, and subculture. Opinion leadership and word-of-mouth behavior are two major sources of personal influence on consumer behavior. Reference groups are people to whom an individual looks as a basis for self-approval or as a source of personal standards. Family influences on consumer behavior result from three sources: consumer socialization, passage through the family life cycle, and decision making within the family or household. A more subtle influence on consumer behavior than direct contact with others is the social class to which people belong. Persons within social classes tend to exhibit common values, attitudes, beliefs, lifestyles, and buying behaviors. Finally, a person's culture and subculture have been shown to influence product preferences and buying patterns.

FOCUSING ON KEY TERMS

attitude p. 123
beliefs p. 123
brand loyalty p. 122
cognitive dissonance p. 115
consideration set p. 113
consumer behavior p. 112
consumer socialization p. 128
evaluative criteria p. 113
family life cycle p. 128
involvement p. 115
learning p. 122
lifestyle p. 124
motivation p. 118
opinion leaders p. 126
perceived risk p. 121
perception p. 120
personality p. 119
purchase decision process p. 112
reference groups p. 128
self-concept p. 119
situational influences p. 117
social class p. 130
subcultures p. 131
subliminal perception p. 121
word of mouth p. 127

APPLYING MARKETING KNOWLEDGE

1 Review Figure 5–2, which shows the smart phone attributes identified by *Consumer Reports*. Which attributes are important to you? What other attributes might you consider? Which brand would you prefer?

2 Suppose research at Panasonic reveals that prospective buyers are anxious about buying high-definition television sets. What strategies might you recommend to the company to reduce consumer anxiety?

3 A Porsche salesperson was taking orders on new cars because he was unable to satisfy the demand with the limited number of cars in the showroom and lot. Several persons had backed out of the contract within two weeks of signing the order. What explanation can you give for this behavior, and what remedies would you recommend?

4 Which social class would you associate with each of the following items or actions: (*a*) tennis club membership, (*b*) an arrangement of plastic flowers in the kitchen, (*c*) *True Romance* magazine, (*d*) *Smithsonian* magazine, (*e*) formally dressing for dinner frequently, and (*f*) being a member of a bowling team.

5 Assign one or more levels of the hierarchy of needs and the motives described in Figure 5–5 to the following products: (*a*) life insurance, (*b*) cosmetics, (*c*) *The Wall Street Journal*, and (*d*) hamburgers.

6 With which stage in the family life cycle would the purchase of the following products and services be most closely identified: (*a*) bedroom furniture, (*b*) life insurance, (*c*) a Caribbean cruise, (*d*) a house mortgage, and (*e*) children's toys?

7 "The greater the perceived risk in a purchase situation, the more likely that cognitive dissonance will result." Does this statement have any basis given the discussion in the text? Why?

building your marketing plan

To do a consumer analysis for the product—the good, service, or idea—in your marketing plan:

1 Identify the consumers who are most likely to buy your product—the primary target market—in terms of (*a*) their demographic characteristics and (*b*) any other kind of characteristics you believe are important.

2 Describe (*a*) the main points of difference of your product for this group and (*b*) what problem they help solve for the consumer, in terms of the first stage in the consumer purchase decision process in Figure 5–1.

3 Identify the one or two key influences for each of the four outside boxes in Figure 5–4: (*a*) marketing mix, (*b*) psychological, (*c*) sociocultural, and (*d*) situational influences.

This consumer analysis will provide the foundation for the marketing mix actions you develop later in your plan.

video case 5 Best Buy: Using Customer Centricity to Connect with Consumers

"So much of our business success comes down to understanding consumer behavior," explains Joe Brandt, a store service manager at one of Best Buy's newest stores. "What we do is we try to keep our ear to the railroad tracks. In essence, we listen to the customer to be able to change on a dime when a customer wants us to tailor that experience a certain way and provide certain shopping experiences and certain services.

"Consumers look at a lot of different things," Joe added. "They look at brands, shopability of the store, how easy it is to navigate the store, how pleasant the employees are, price, and how we take care of the customer." Overall there are many factors that "customers look at when they're making a purchase decision."

THE COMPANY

Best Buy is the world's largest consumer electronics retailer with 1,172 stores, 140,000 employees, and $35.9 billion in revenue. Its U.S. and Canadian market share is almost 20 percent, far ahead of rivals Circuit City, Wal-Mart, and Costco.

Best Buy operates superstores that provide a limited number of product categories with great depth within the categories. The retailer sells consumer electronics, home office products, appliances, entertainment software, and related services. In addition to its U.S. and Canadian stores, Best Buy has recently opened stores in China and has announced plans to open stores in Puerto Rico, Mexico, and Turkey. Best Buy also offers its products online through bestbuy.com, and design and installation services through Geek Squad and Magnolia Audio and Video.

Best Buy began as The Sound of Music, a small specialty audio retailer, in 1966. A tornado severely damaged one of its stores in 1981. Instead of closing the store for repairs, Dick Schulze, the owner, had a tornado sale in which more goods were brought in from its other stores and prices were slashed. The sale was so successful that it was repeated the following two years. "When the tornado hit, we decided to market to the community as a whole, and get electronics out there to everybody. We geared ourselves up to win by understanding what consumers want in technology," said Joe Brandt. In 1983, The Sound of Music changed its name to Best Buy and opened its first superstore.

The company continued to grow as the consumer electronics category exploded in the 1980s and 1990s. Based on consumer feedback, Best Buy moved away from the traditional sales approach in 1989 by eliminating commissioned sales representatives. This move was embraced by customers, but questioned by some suppliers and Wall Street analysts who thought it would reduce sales and profits. Best Buy's approach was successful at generating growth in stores and revenues. However, company expenses increased and profits declined. When growth of the consumer electronics market slowed and mass marketers such as Wal-Mart, Target, Costco, and Sam's Club became competitors, Best Buy considered changes to its approach.

Best Buy began to differentiate itself from the mass marketers by offering more services, delivery, and installation. Instead of selling individual products, it concentrated on selling entire systems. The acquisition of Geek Squad to provide in-store, home, and office computer services and Magnolia Home Theater to provide complete audio and home theater systems reflect these changes. These additions significantly increased profit and insulated the company from discount store competition. Responding to customer needs and competitive changes was an important part of Best Buy's strategy.

ADOPTING "CUSTOMER CENTRICITY" AT BEST BUY

When Dick Schulze stepped down as CEO, his successor, Brad Anderson, began looking for new ideas to continue the company's growth. He invited Larry Seldon of Columbia University to present his theory of "customer centricity." Seldon's theory suggested that some customers account for a disproportionate amount of a firm's sales and profits. Anderson adapted the theory to try to understand the needs and behaviors of specific types of customers, or segments. Initial research identified five segments:

- **Barry:** The affluent professional who wants the best technology and entertainment, and who demands excellent service.
- **Jill:** The prototypical "soccer mom" who is a busy suburban mom who wants to enrich her children's lives with technology and entertainment.
- **Carrie and Buzz:** The "early adopter," active, younger customer who wants the latest technology and entertainment.
- **Ray:** The "practical adopter" who is a family man who wants technology that improves his life through technology and entertainment.
- **Small business:** The customer who runs his or her own business and has specific needs relating to growing sales and increasing the profitability of the business.

Best Buy used "lab" stores to test product offerings, store designs, and service offerings targeted at each segment. Successful offerings and designs were then expanded to a larger number of pilot stores that would undergo significant physical changes and require substantial new training of sales associates. The cost of applying customer centricity to a store was often as much as $600,000. Early results were impressive as customer centricity stores reported sales much higher than the chain average. As Best Buy began rapid conversion of hundreds of Best Buy stores to the centricity formats, however, expenses increased and profits declined.

THE ISSUES

The impact of Best Buy's new approach on profitability led the company to continue to adapt its ideas about customers. One consideration, for example, was that the "Jill" segment should be broadened to include all females. Research showed that women spend $68 billion on consumer electronics each year and influence 89 percent of all purchases. Unfortunately, females did not embrace the Best Buy experience, largely because its stores were male-oriented in merchandise, appearance, and staffing. "Men and women shop very differently," observes Brandt. Men "typically love the technology" and they like to "play with it" while women are "looking for a knowledgeable person who can answer their questions in a simple manner." To address this problem Best Buy began to implement many changes that would make Best Buy *the* place for women to shop (and work!).

Today, Best Buy is trying a variety of new approaches. Its stores, for example, are being changed to be more appealing to women. Store layout has been changed to include larger aisles, softer colors, less noise, and reduced visibility of boxes and extra stock. In addition, Best Buy now offers women, and all customers, a personal shopping assistant who will walk a customer through the store, demonstrate how the products function, and arrange for delivery and installation after the sale. Best Buy has also created rooms that resemble a home in the store to show customers exactly how the products will look when they are installed. According to Brandt, "We try to personalize the experience as much as possible, and we really try to build a relationship. Once we do that we have the opportunity to really listen and answer questions that customers have." Best Buy is undertaking other initiatives as well. It created the Women's Leadership Forum (WOLF) to develop female leaders within the company. Early results have yielded an increase in applications and a decline in turnover. Overall, these changes appear to be working. Best Buy has observed an increase in its female market share in consumer electronics!

In the future Best Buy's customer centricity efforts will continue to focus on understanding consumer behavior and improving the customer experience. Brandt explains: "Customer centricity, in simple terms, is listening to the customer, putting the customer at the forefront of everything we do. That is, whatever shopping experience that they are looking for, we gear our company and our structure to satisfy that need as much as possible."

Questions

1 How has an understanding of consumer behavior helped Best Buy grow from a small specialty audio retailer to the world's largest consumer electronics retailer?

2 What were the advantages and disadvantages of using "customer centricity" to create five segments of Best Buy customers?

3 How are men and women different in their consumer behavior when they are shopping in a Best Buy store?

4 What are two or three (*a*) objective evaluative criteria and (*b*) subjective evaluative criteria female consumers use when shopping for electronics at Best Buy?

5 What challenges does Best Buy face in the future?

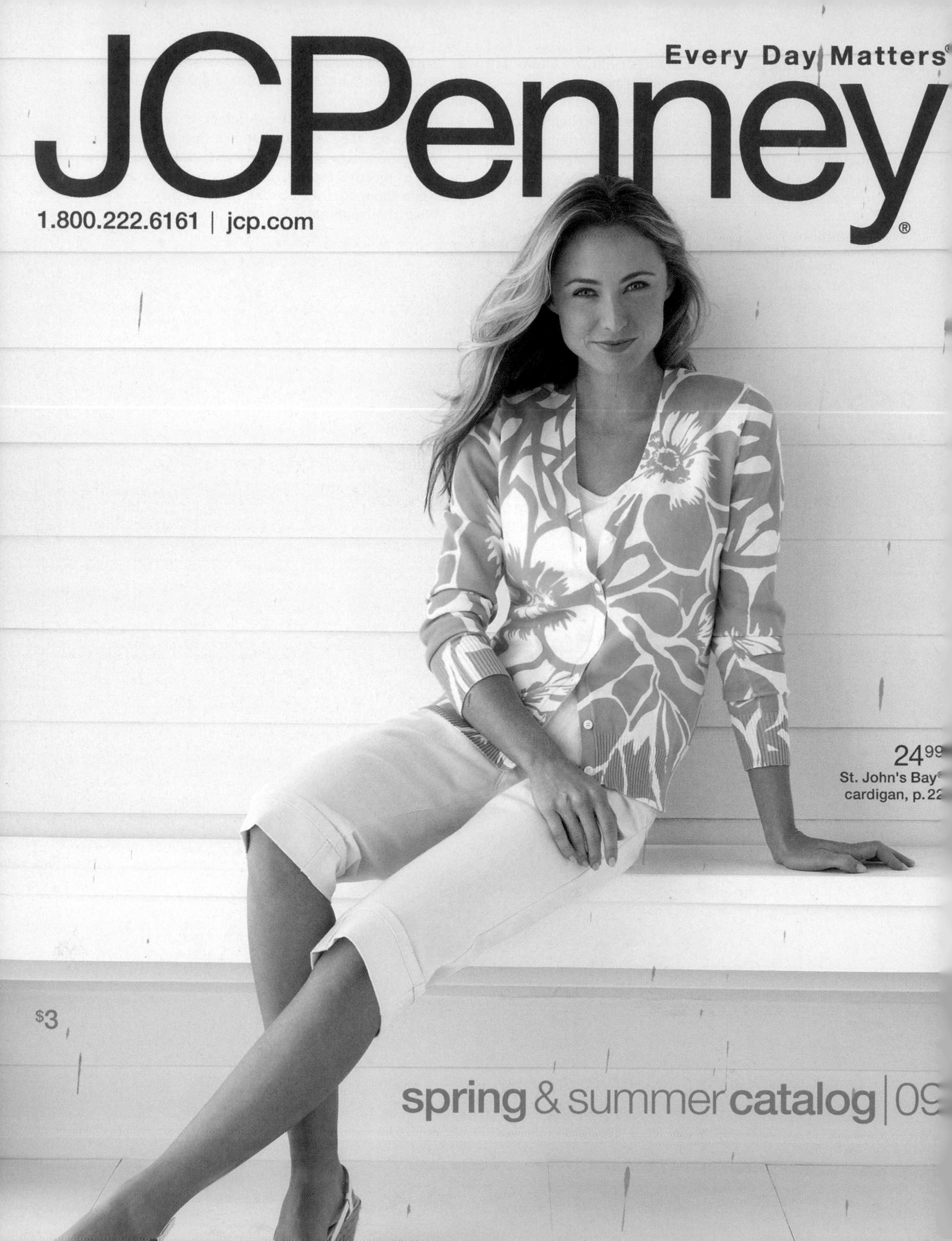
JCPenney
Every Day Matters®
1.800.222.6161 | jcp.com
24.99
St. John's Bay®
cardigan, p. 22
$3
spring & summer catalog | 09

6 Understanding Organizations as Customers

LEARNING OBJECTIVES

After reading this chapter you should be able to:

LO1 Distinguish among industrial, reseller, and government organizational markets.

LO2 Describe the key characteristics of organizational buying that make it different from consumer buying.

LO3 Explain how buying centers and buying situations influence organizational purchasing.

LO4 Recognize the importance and nature of online buying in industrial, reseller, and government organizational markets.

BUYING IS MARKETING, TOO! PURCHASING PUBLICATION PAPER AT JCPENNEY

Kim Nagele views paper differently than most people do. As the senior procurement agent at JCPMedia, he and a team of purchasing professionals buy more than 260,000 tons of publication paper annually at a cost of hundreds of millions of dollars.

JCPMedia is the print and paper purchasing arm for JCPenney, the fifth-largest retailer in the United States and the largest catalog merchant of general merchandise in the Western Hemisphere. Paper is serious business at JCPMedia, which buys publication paper for JCPenney catalogs, newspaper inserts, and direct-mail pieces. Some 10 companies from around the world including Verso Paper in the United States, Catalyst Paper Inc. in Canada, Norski Skog in Norway, and UPM-Kymmene Inc. in Finland, supply paper to JCPMedia.

The choice of paper and suppliers is also a significant business decision given the sizable revenue and expense consequences. Therefore, JCPMedia paper buyers work closely with JCPenney marketing personnel and within budget constraints to assure that the right quality and quantity of publication paper is purchased at the right price point for the millions of catalogs, newspaper inserts, and direct-mail pieces distributed every year.

In addition to paper quality and price, buyers formally evaluate supplier capabilities, often by extended visits to supplier facilities. These include a supplier's capacity to deliver on time selected grades of paper from specialty items to magazine papers, the availability of specific types of paper to meet printing deadlines, and ongoing environmental programs. For example, a supplier's forestry management and sustainability practices are considered in the JCPMedia buying process.

The next time you thumb through a JCPenney catalog, newspaper insert, or direct-mail piece, notice the paper. Considerable effort and attention was given to its selection and purchase by Kim Nagele and JCPMedia paper buyers.[1]

Purchasing paper for JCPMedia is one example of organizational buying. This chapter examines types of organizational buyers; key characteristics of organizational buying, including online buying; different buying situations; unique aspects of the organizational buying process; and typical buying procedures and decisions in today's organizational markets.

THE NATURE AND SIZE OF ORGANIZATIONAL MARKETS

LO1

Understanding organizational markets and buying behavior is a necessary prerequisite for effective business marketing. **Business marketing** is the marketing of goods and services to companies, governments, or not-for-profit organizations for use in the creation of goods and services that they can produce and market to others. Because over half of all U.S. business school graduates take jobs in firms that engage in business marketing, it is important to understand the characteristics of organizational buyers and their buying behavior.

Organizational buyers are those manufacturers, wholesalers, retailers, and government agencies that buy goods and services for their own use or for resale. For example, these organizations buy computers and telephone services for their own use. However, manufacturers buy raw materials and parts that they reprocess into the finished goods they sell. Wholesalers and retailers resell the goods they buy without reprocessing them. Organizational buyers include all buyers in a nation except ultimate consumers. These organizational buyers purchase and lease large volumes of capital equipment, raw materials, manufactured parts, supplies, and business services. In fact, because they often buy raw materials and parts, process them, and sell the upgraded product several times before it is purchased by the final organizational buyer or ultimate consumer, the total annual purchases of organizational buyers are far greater than those of ultimate consumers. IBM alone buys nearly $40 billion in goods and services each year for its own use or resale.[2]

Organizational buyers are divided into three markets: (1) industrial, (2) reseller, and (3) government.[3] Each market is described next.

Industrial Markets

There are about 7.2 million firms in the industrial, or business, market. These *industrial firms* in some way reprocess a product or service they buy before selling it again to the next buyer. This is certainly true of Corning, Inc., which transforms an exotic blend of materials to create optical fiber capable of carrying much of the telephone traffic in the United States on a single strand. It is also true (if you stretch your imagination) of a firm selling services, such as a bank that takes money from its depositors, reprocesses it, and "sells" it as loans to borrowers.

The importance of services in the United States today is emphasized by the composition of industrial markets. Companies that primarily sell physical goods (manufacturers; mining; construction; and farms, timber, and fisheries) represent 25 percent of all the industrial firms. The services market sells diverse services such as legal advice, auto repair, and dry cleaning. Along with finance, insurance, and real estate businesses, and transportation, communication, public utility firms, and not-for-profit organizations, service companies represent 75 percent of all industrial firms. Because of the size and importance of service companies and not-for-profit organizations (such as the American Red Cross), services marketing is discussed in detail in Chapter 12.

Reseller Markets

Wholesalers and retailers that buy physical products and resell them again without any reprocessing are *resellers*. In the United States there are almost 2 million retailers and 430,000 wholesalers. In Chapters 15 through 17 we shall see how manufacturers use wholesalers and retailers in their distribution ("place") strategies as channels through which their products reach ultimate consumers. In this chapter, we look at these resellers mainly as organizational buyers in terms of (1) how they make their own buying decisions and (2) which products they choose to carry.

The Orion lunar spacecraft to be designed, developed, tested, and evaluated by Lockheed Martin Corp. is an example of a purchase by a government unit, namely the National Aeronautics and Space Administration (NASA). Read the text to find out how much NASA will pay for the Orion lunar spacecraft.

Lockheed Martin Corporation
www.lockheedmartin.com

Government Markets

Government units are the federal, state, and local agencies that buy goods and services for the constituents they serve. There are about 89,500 of these government units in the United States. These purchases include the $3.9 billion the National Aeronautics and Space Administration (NASA) intends to pay to Lockheed Martin to develop and produce the Orion lunar spacecraft scheduled for launch in 2014 as well as lesser amounts spent by local school and sanitation districts.[4]

Global Organizational Markets

Industrial, reseller, and government markets also exist on a global scale. International trade statistics indicate that the largest exporting industries in the United States focus on organizational buyers, not ultimate consumers. Capital equipment (such as construction equipment, computers, and telecommunications) and industrial supplies (such as machine parts) account for about 46 percent of all U.S. product exports.

The majority of world trade involves exchange relationships that span the globe. Consider the ingredients found in Kellogg's popular Nutri-Grain cereal bar. Kellogg buyers purchase ingredients from farmers, food processors, and wholesalers in eight countries on three continents.[5] Additional examples of business marketing in the global arena appear in Chapter 7.

MEASURING DOMESTIC AND GLOBAL INDUSTRIAL, RESELLER, AND GOVERNMENT MARKETS

The measurement of industrial, reseller, and government markets is an important first step for a firm interested in gauging the size of one, two, or all three of these markets in the United States and around the world. This task has been made easier with the **North American Industry Classification System (NAICS)**.[6] The NAICS provides common industry definitions for Canada, Mexico, and the United States, which

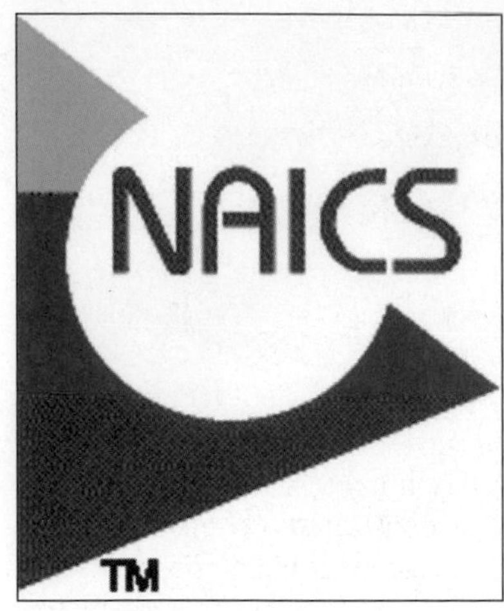

makes it easier to measure economic activity in the three member countries of the North American Free Trade Agreement (NAFTA). The NAICS replaced the Standard Industrial Classification (SIC) system, a version of which has been in place for more than 50 years in the three NAFTA member countries. The SIC neither permitted comparability across countries nor accurately measured new or emerging industries. Furthermore, the NAICS is consistent with the International Standard Industrial Classification of All Economic Activities, published by the United Nations, to facilitate measurement of global economic activity.

The NAICS groups economic activity to permit studies of market share, demand for goods and services, import competition in domestic markets, and similar studies. It designates industries with a numerical code in a defined structure. A six-digit coding system is used. The first two digits designate a sector of the economy, the third digit designates a subsector, and the fourth digit represents an industry group. The fifth digit designates a specific industry and it is the most detailed level at which comparable data is available for Canada, Mexico, and the United States. The sixth digit designates individual country-level national industries. Figure 6–1 shows a breakdown within the information industries sector (code 51) to illustrate the classification scheme.

The NAICS permits a firm to find the NAICS codes of its present customers and then obtain NAICS-coded lists for similar firms. Also, it is possible to monitor NAICS categories to determine the growth in various sectors and industries to identify promising marketing opportunities. However, the NAICS has an important limitation. Five-digit national industry codes are not available for all three countries because the respective governments will not reveal data when too few organizations exist in a category.

A further refinement in the measurement of organizational markets is the *North American Product Classification System* (NAPCS).[7] The NAPCS provides a classification system for products and services that is consistent across Canada, Mexico, and the United States and international classification systems, such as the Central Product Classification System of the United Nations. The NAICS and NAPCS represent the continued effort toward economic integration in North America and the world.

FIGURE 6–1
NAICS breakdown for information industries sector: NAICS code 51 (abbreviated)

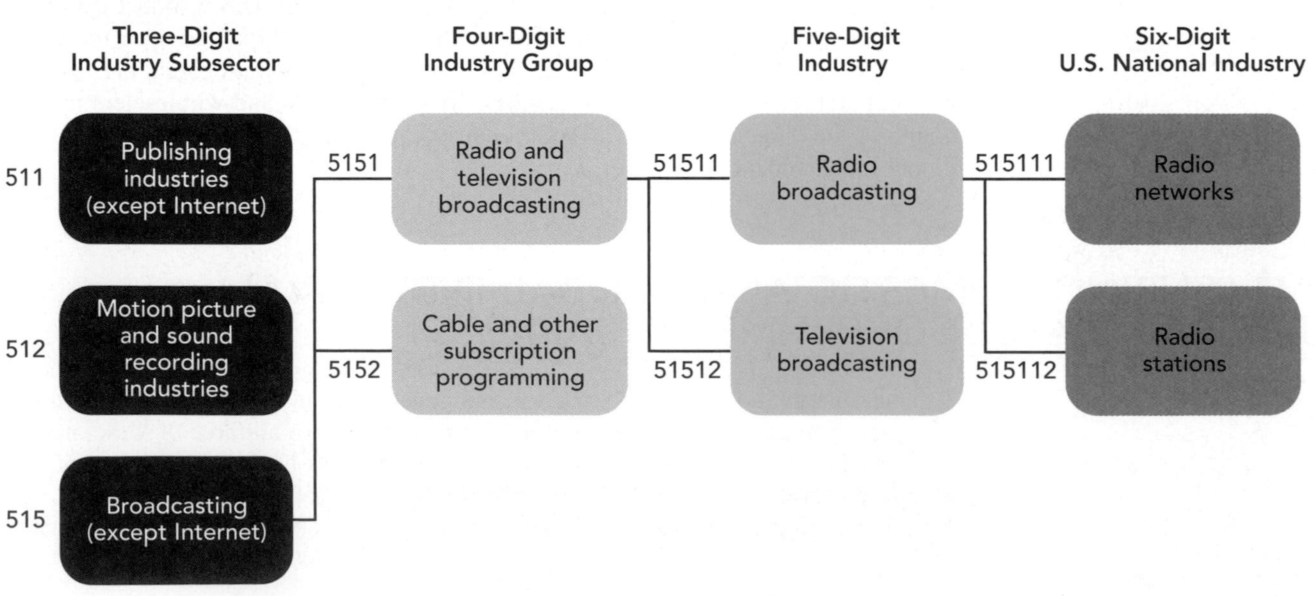

learning review	1. What are the three main types of organizational buyers? 2. What is the North American Industry Classification System (NAICS)?

CHARACTERISTICS OF ORGANIZATIONAL BUYING

LO2

Organizations are different from individuals, so buying for an organization is different from buying for yourself or your family. In both cases the objective in making the purchase is to solve the buyer's problem—to satisfy a need or want. But unique objectives and policies of an organization put special constraints on how it makes buying decisions. Understanding the characteristics of organizational buying is essential in designing effective marketing programs to reach these buyers. Key characteristics of organizational buying are listed in Figure 6–2 and discussed next.[8]

Demand Characteristics

Consumer demand for products and services is affected by their price and availability and by consumers' personal tastes and discretionary income. By comparison, industrial demand is derived. **Derived demand** means that the demand for industrial products and services is driven by, or derived from, demand for consumer products and services. For example, the demand for Weyerhaeuser's pulp and paper products is based on consumer demand for newspapers, FedEx packages, and disposable diapers. Derived demand is based on expectations of future consumer demand. For

FIGURE 6–2
Key characteristics and dimensions of organizational buying behavior

CHARACTERISTICS	DIMENSIONS
Market characteristics	• Demand for industrial products and services is derived. • Few customers typically exist, and their purchase orders are large.
Product or service characteristics	• Products or services are technical in nature and purchased on the basis of specifications. • Many of goods purchased are raw and semifinished. • Heavy emphasis is placed on delivery time, technical assistance, and postsale service.
Buying process characteristics	• Technically qualified and professional buyers follow established purchasing policies and procedures. • Buying objectives and criteria are typically spelled out, as are procedures for evaluating sellers and their products or services. • There are multiple buying influences, and multiple parties participate in purchase decisions. • There are reciprocal arrangements, and negotiation between buyers and sellers is commonplace. • Online buying over the Internet is widespread.
Marketing mix characteristics	• Direct selling to organizational buyers is the rule, and distribution is very important. • Advertising and other forms of promotion are technical in nature. • Price is often negotiated, evaluated as part of broader seller and product or service qualities, and frequently affected by quantity discounts.

instance, Whirlpool buys parts for its washers and dryers in anticipation of consumer demand, which is affected by the replacement cycle for these products and by consumer income.

Size of the Order or Purchase

The size of the purchase involved in organizational buying is typically much larger than that in consumer buying. The dollar value of a single purchase made by an organization often runs into thousands or millions of dollars. For example, Siemens Energy & Automation's Airport Logistics Division was awarded a $28 million contract to build a baggage handling and security system for JetBlue Airways' terminal at John F. Kennedy International Airport.[9] With so much money at stake, most organizations place constraints on their buyers in the form of purchasing policies or procedures. Buyers must often get competitive bids from at least three prospective suppliers when the order is above a specific amount, such as $5,000. When the order is above an even higher amount, such as $50,000, it may require the review and approval of a vice president or even the president of the company. Knowing how order size affects buying practices is important in determining who participates in the purchase decision and makes the final decision, and the length of time required to arrive at a purchase agreement.

Number of Potential Buyers

Firms selling consumer products or services often try to reach thousands or millions of individuals or households. For example, your local supermarket or bank probably serves thousands of people. Kellogg tries to reach 80 million North American households with its breakfast cereals and probably succeeds in selling to a third or half of these in any given year. Firms selling to organizations are often restricted to far fewer buyers. Gulfstream Aerospace Corporation can sell its business jets to a few thousand organizations throughout the world, and Goodyear sells its original equipment tires to fewer than 10 car manufacturers.

Organizational Buying Objectives

Organizations buy products and services for one main reason: to help them achieve their objectives. For business firms the buying objective is usually to increase profits through reducing costs or increasing revenues. For example, 7-Eleven buys automated inventory systems to increase the number of products that can be sold through its convenience stores and to keep them fresh. Nissan Motor Company switched its advertising agency because it expects the new agency to devise a more effective ad campaign to help it sell more cars and increase revenues. To improve executive decision making, many firms buy advanced computer systems to process data. The objectives of nonprofit firms and government agencies are usually to meet the needs of the groups they serve. Recognizing the high costs of energy, Sylvania promotes to prospective buyers cost savings and increased profits made possible by its fluorescent and halogen lights.

Many companies today have broadened their buying objectives to include an emphasis on buying from minority- and women-owned suppliers and vendors. Companies such as Pitney Bowes, PepsiCo, Coors, and JCPenney report that sales, profits, and customer satisfaction have increased because of their minority- and women-owned supplier and vendor initiatives.[10] Learn about Procter & Gamble's commitment to and success of its supplier diversity efforts in the accompanying Going Online box.[11] Other companies include environmental initiatives. For example, Lowe's and Home Depot no longer purchase lumber from companies that harvest timber from the world's endangered forests.[12] Successful business market-

Going Online

Supplier Diversity Is a Fundamental Business Strategy at Procter & Gamble

"Supplier diversity is no longer an issue of social conscience," says A. G. Lafley, chairman of the board, president, and chief executive officer at Procter & Gamble, Inc. "It is a fundamental business strategy." At P&G, purchases from minority- and women-owned suppliers are targeted to reach $2.5 billion by 2010 . . . and for good reason.

Minority- and women-owned suppliers deliver a competitive advantage to P&G. They (1) provide innovative and new ways to help P&G deliver greater value to its consumers; (2) help P&G achieve greater cost efficiencies; and (3) assist P&G in finding new ways to market its brands to consumers.

To learn more about P&G's supplier diversity initiatives and hear from many of its minority- and women-owned suppliers, visit the P&G Web site at www.pg.com/supplier_diversity and watch the video titled, "Economic Inclusion: A Corporate Commitment."

ers recognize that understanding buying objectives is a necessary first step in marketing to organizations.

Organizational Buying Criteria

In making a purchase, the buying organization must weigh key buying criteria that apply to the potential supplier and what it wants to sell. **Organizational buying criteria** are the objective attributes of the supplier's products and services and the capabilities of the supplier itself. These criteria serve the same purpose as the evaluative criteria used by consumers and described in Chapter 5. The most commonly used criteria are: (1) price, (2) ability to meet the quality specifications required for the item, (3) ability to meet required delivery schedules, (4) technical capability, (5) warranties and claim policies in the event of poor performance, (6) past performance on previous contracts, and (7) production facilities and capacity.[13] Suppliers that meet or exceed these criteria create customer value.

Organizational buyers who purchase products and services in the global marketplace often supplement their buying criteria with supplier ISO 9000 standards certification. **ISO 9000** standards, developed by the International Standards Organization (ISO) in Geneva, Switzerland, refer to standards for registration and certification of a manufacturer's quality management and assurance system based on an on-site audit of practices and procedure. The 3M Co., which buys and markets its products globally, has over 80 percent of its manufacturing and service facilities ISO 9000 certified. This certification also gives 3M confidence in the consistent quality of its suppliers' manufacturing systems and products.[14]

Many organizational buyers today are transforming their buying criteria into specific requirements that are communicated to prospective suppliers. This practice, called **supplier development**, involves the deliberate effort by organizational buyers to build relationships that shape suppliers' products, services, and capabilities to fit a buyer's needs and those of its customers. Consider Deere & Company, the maker of John Deere farm, construction, and lawn-care equipment. Deere employs supplier-development engineers who work full-time with the company's suppliers to improve their efficiency and quality and reduce their costs. According to a Deere senior executive, "Their quality, delivery, and costs are, after all, our quality, delivery, and costs."[15] Read the Marketing Matters box on the next page to learn how Harley-Davidson emphasizes supplier collaboration in its product design.[16]

With many U.S. manufacturers using a *just-in-time* (JIT) inventory system that reduces the inventory of production parts to those to be used within hours or days, on-time delivery is becoming an even more important buying criterion and, in some instances, a requirement. Caterpillar trains its key suppliers in JIT inventory system

Marketing Matters > > > > > > customer value

Harley-Davidson's Supplier Collaboration Creates Customer Value . . . and a Great Ride

It's nice to be admired. Harley-Davidson's well-deserved reputation for innovation, product quality, and talented management and employees has made it a perennial member of *Fortune* magazine's list of "America's Most Admired Companies."

Harley-Davidson is also respected by suppliers for the way it collaborates with them in product design. According to Jeff Bluestein, the company's chairman: "We involve our suppliers as much as possible in future products, new-product development, and get them working with us." Emphasis is placed on quality benchmarks, cost control, delivery schedules, and technological innovation as well as building mutually beneficial, long-term relationships. Face-to-face communication is encouraged, and many suppliers have personnel stationed at Harley-Davidson's Product Development Center.

The relationship between Harley-Davidson and Milsco Manufacturing is a case in point. Milsco has been the sole source of original equipment motorcycle seats and a major supplier of aftermarket parts and accessories, such as saddlebags, for Harley-Davidson since 1934. Milsco engineers and designers work closely with their Harley counterparts in the design of each year's new products.

The notion of a mutually beneficial relationship is expressed by Milsco's manager of industrial design: "Harley-Davidson refers to us as stakeholders, someone who can win or lose from a successful or failed program. We all share responsibility toward one another." He also notes that Harley-Davidson is not Milsco's only customer. It is simply the customer that he most respects.

and conducts supplier seminars on how to diagnose, correct, and implement continuous quality improvement programs. The just-in-time inventory system is discussed further in Chapter 16.

Buyer–Seller Relationships and Supply Partnerships

Another distinction between organizational and consumer buying behavior lies in the nature of the relationship between organizational buyers and suppliers. Specifically, organizational buying is more likely to involve complex negotiations concerning delivery schedules, price, technical specifications, warranties, and claim policies. These negotiations also can last for an extended period. This was the case when the Lawrence Livermore National Laboratory acquired two IBM supercomputers—each with capacity to perform 360 trillion mathematical operations per second—at a cost of $290 million.[17]

Reciprocal arrangements also exist in organizational buying. **Reciprocity** is an industrial buying practice in which two organizations agree to purchase each other's products and services. The U.S. Justice Department disapproves of reciprocal buying because it restricts the normal operation of the free market. However, the practice exists and can limit the flexibility of organizational buyers in choosing alternative suppliers.

Long-term contracts are also prevalent.[18] For instance, Kraft Foods, Inc. is spending $1.7 billion over seven years for global information technology services provided by Electronic Data Systems. Hewlett-Packard has a 10-year, $3 billion contract to manage Procter & Gamble's information technology in 160 countries.

In some cases, buyer–seller relationships evolve into supply partnerships.[19] A **supply partnership** exists when a buyer and its supplier adopt mutually beneficial

Making Responsible Decisions > > > > sustainability

Sustainable Procurement for Sustainable Growth

Manufacturers, retailers, wholesalers, and governmental agencies are increasingly sensitive to how their buying decisions affect the environment. Concerns about the depletion of natural resources; air, water, and soil pollution; and the social consequences of economic activity have given rise to the concept of sustainable procurement. Sustainable procurement aims to integrate environmental considerations into all stages of an organization's buying process with the goal of reducing the impact on human health and the physical environment.

Starbucks is a pioneer and worldwide leader in sustainable procurement. The company's attention to quality coffee extends to its coffee growers located in more than 20 countries. This means that Starbucks pays coffee farmers a fair price for the beans; that the coffee is grown in an ecologically sound manner; and that Starbucks invests in the farming communities where its coffees are produced. In this way, Starbucks focuses on the sustainable growth of its suppliers.

objectives, policies, and procedures for the purpose of lowering the cost or increasing the value of products and services delivered to the ultimate consumer. Intel, a manufacturer of microprocessors and the "computer inside" of most personal computers, is an example. Intel supports its suppliers by offering them quality management programs and by investing in supplier equipment that produces fewer product defects and boosts supplier productivity. Suppliers, in turn, provide Intel with consistent high-quality products at a lower cost for its customers, the makers of personal computers, and finally you, the ultimate customer. Retailers, too, have forged partnerships with their suppliers. Wal-Mart has such a relationship with Procter & Gamble for ordering and replenishing P&G's products in its stores. By using computerized cash register scanning equipment and direct electronic linkages to P&G, Wal-Mart can tell P&G what merchandise is needed, along with how much, when, and to which store to deliver it on a daily basis.

Supply partnerships often include provisions for what is called *sustainable procurement*. This buying practice is described in the accompanying Making Responsible Decisions box.[20] Because supply partnerships also involve the physical distribution of goods, they are again discussed in Chapter 16 in the context of supply chain management.

The Buying Center: A Cross-Functional Group

LO3

For routine purchases with a small dollar value, a single buyer or purchasing manager often makes the purchase decision alone. In many instances, however, several people in the organization participate in the buying process. The individuals in this group, called a **buying center**, share common goals, risks, and knowledge important to a purchase decision. For most large multistore chain resellers, such as Sears, 7-Eleven convenience stores, Target, or Safeway, the buying center is highly formalized and is called a *buying committee*. However, most industrial firms or government units use informal groups of people or call meetings to arrive at buying decisions.

The importance of the buying center requires that a firm marketing to many industrial firms and government units understand the structure, technical and business functions represented, and behavior of these groups.[21] Four questions provide guidance in understanding the buying center in these organizations: Which individuals are in the buying center for the product or service? What is the relative influence of each member of the group? What are the buying criteria of each member? How does each member of the group perceive our firm, our products and services, and our salespeople?

Answers to these questions are difficult to come by. This is particularly true when dealing with industrial firms, resellers, and governments outside the United States. For example, U.S. firms are often frustrated by the fact that Japanese buyers "ask a thousand questions" but give few answers, sometimes rely on third-party individuals to convey views on proposals, are prone to not "talk business," and often say "yes" to be courteous when they mean "no."

People in the Buying Center The composition of the buying center in a given organization depends on the specific item being bought. Although a buyer or purchasing manager is almost always a member of the buying center, individuals from other functional areas are included, depending on what is to be purchased. In buying a million-dollar machine tool, the president (because of the size of the purchase) and the production vice president or manager would probably be members. For key components to be included in a final manufactured product, a cross-functional group of individuals from research and development (R&D), engineering, and quality control are likely to be added. For new word-processing equipment, experienced secretaries who will use the equipment would be members. Still, a major question in penetrating the buying center is finding and reaching the people who will initiate, influence, and actually make the buying decision.

Roles in the Buying Center Researchers have identified five specific roles that an individual in a buying center can play.[22] In some purchases the same person may perform two or more of these roles.

- *Users* are the people in the organization who actually use the product or service, such as a secretary who will use a new word processor.
- *Influencers* affect the buying decision, usually by helping define the specifications for what is bought. The information systems manager would be a key influencer in the purchase of a new mainframe computer.
- *Buyers* have formal authority and responsibility to select the supplier and negotiate the terms of the contract. Kim Nagele performs this role as senior procurement agent at JCPMedia as described in the chapter opening example.
- *Deciders* have the formal or informal power to select or approve the supplier that receives the contract. In routine orders the decider is usually the buyer or purchasing manager; in important technical purchases it is more likely to be someone from R&D, engineering, or quality control. The decider for a key component being incorporated in a final manufactured product might be any of these three people.
- *Gatekeepers* control the flow of information in the buying center. Purchasing personnel, technical experts, and secretaries can all keep salespeople or information from reaching people performing the other four roles.

Effective marketing to organizations requires an understanding of buying centers and their role in purchase decisions.

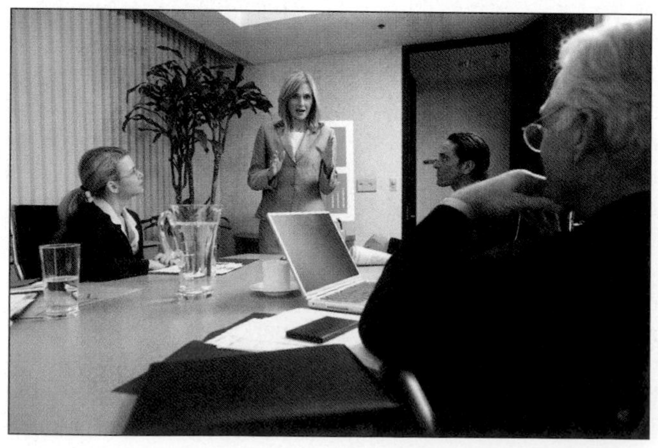

Buying Situations and the Buying Center The number of people in the buying center largely depends on the specific buying situation. Researchers who have studied organizational buying identify three types of buying situations, called **buy classes**. These buy classes vary from the routine reorder, or *straight rebuy*, to the completely new purchase, termed *new buy*.

In between these extremes is the *modified rebuy*. Some examples will clarify the differences.[23]

- *New buy*. Here the organization is a first-time buyer of the product or service. This involves greater potential risks in the purchase, so the buying center is enlarged to include all those who have a stake in the new buy. Procter & Gamble's purchase of a multimillion-dollar fiber-optic network from Corning, Inc., for its corporate offices in Cincinnati, represented a new buy.[24]
- *Straight rebuy*. Here the buyer or purchasing manager reorders an existing product or service from the list of acceptable suppliers, probably without even checking with users or influencers from the engineering, production, or quality control departments. Office supplies and maintenance services are usually obtained as straight rebuys.
- *Modified rebuy*. In this buying situation the users, influencers, or deciders in the buying center want to change the product specifications, price, delivery schedule, or supplier. Although the item purchased is largely the same as with the straight rebuy, the changes usually necessitate enlarging the buying center to include people outside the purchasing department.

Figure 6–3 summarizes how buy classes affect buying center tendencies.[25]

The marketing and sales strategies of the sellers facing each of these three buying situations can vary greatly because the importance of personnel from functional areas such as purchasing, engineering, production, and R&D often varies with (1) the type of buying situation and (2) the stage of the purchasing process. If it is a new buy for the manufacturer, you should be prepared to act as a consultant to the buyer, work with technical personnel, and expect a long time for a buying decision to be reached. However, if the manufacturer has bought the item from you before (a straight or modified rebuy), you might emphasize a competitive price and a reliable supply in meetings with the purchasing agent.

FIGURE 6–3
The buying situation affects buying center behavior in different ways. Understanding these differences can pay huge dividends.

	BUY-CLASS SITUATION		
BUYING CENTER DIMENSION	NEW BUY	STRAIGHT REBUY	MODIFIED REBUY
People involved	Many	One	Two to three
Decision time	Long	Short	Moderate
Problem definition	Uncertain	Well-defined	Minor modifications
Buying objective	Good solution	Low-priced supplier	Low-priced supplier
Suppliers considered	New/present	Present	Present
Buying influence	Technical/operating personnel	Purchasing agent	Purchasing agent and others

learning review

3. What one department is almost always represented by a person in the buying center?
4. What are the three types of buying situations or buy classes?

CHARTING THE ORGANIZATIONAL BUYING PROCESS

Organizational buyers, like consumers, engage in a decision process when selecting products and services. **Organizational buying behavior** is the decision-making process that organizations use to establish the need for products and services and identify, evaluate, and choose among alternative brands and suppliers. There are important similarities and differences between the two decision-making processes. To better understand the nature of organizational buying behavior, we first compare it with consumer buying behavior and then describe an actual organizational purchase in detail.

Stages in the Organizational Buying Process

As shown in Figure 6–4 (and covered in Chapter 5), the five stages a student might use in buying a smart phone also apply to organizational purchases. However, comparing the two right-hand columns in Figure 6–4 reveals key differences. For example, when a smart phone manufacturer buys earbud headsets for its units from a supplier, more individuals are involved, supplier capability becomes more important, and the postpurchase evaluation behavior is more formalized.

The headset-buying decision process is typical of the steps made by organizational buyers. Let's now examine in detail the decision-making process for a more complex product—machine vision systems.

Buying a Machine Vision System

Machine vision is widely regarded as one of the keys to the factory of the future. The chief elements of a machine vision system are its optics, light source, camera, video processor, and computer software. Vision systems are mainly used for product inspection. They are also becoming important as one of the chief elements in the information feedback loop of systems that control manufacturing processes. Vision systems, selling for $25,000 to $250,000, are mostly sold to original equipment manufacturers (OEMs) who incorporate them in still larger industrial automation systems, which sell for millions of dollars. Companies worldwide are expected to spend more than $10 billion for machine vision systems in 2010.[26]

Finding productive applications for machine vision involves the constant search for technology and designs that satisfy user needs. The buying process for machine vision components and assemblies is frequently a new buy because many machine vision systems contain elements that require some custom design. Let's track five purchasing stages that a company such as the Industrial Automation Division of Siemens, a large German industrial firm, would follow when purchasing components and assemblies for the machine vision systems it produces and installs.

Problem Recognition Sales engineers constantly canvass industrial automation equipment users such as American National Can, Ford Motor Company, Grumman Aircraft, and many Asian and European firms for leads on upcoming industrial automation projects. They also keep these firms current on Siemens' technology, products, and services. When a firm needing a machine vision capability identifies a project

STAGE IN THE BUYING DECISION PROCESS	CONSUMER PURCHASE: SMART PHONE FOR A STUDENT	ORGANIZATIONAL PURCHASE: EARBUD HEADSET FOR A SMART PHONE
Problem recognition	Student doesn't like the features of the smart phone now owned and desires a new one.	Marketing research and sales departments observe that competitors are improving the earbud headsets for their smart phones. The firm decides to improve the earbud headsets on its own new models, which will be purchased from an outside supplier.
Information search	Student uses past experience, that of friends, ads, the Internet, and *Consumer Reports* to collect information and uncover alternatives.	Design and production engineers draft specifications for earbud headsets. The purchasing department identifies suppliers of earbud headsets.
Alternative evaluation	Alternative smart phones are evaluated on the basis of important attributes desired in a phone, and several stores are visited.	Purchasing and engineering personnel visit with suppliers and assess (1) facilities, (2) capacity, (3) quality control, and (4) financial status. They drop any suppliers not satisfactory on these factors.
Purchase decision	A specific brand of smart phone is selected, the price is paid, and the student leaves the store.	They use (1) quality, (2) price, (3) delivery, and (4) technical capability as key buying criteria to select a supplier. Then they negotiate terms and award a contract.
Postpurchase behavior	Student reevaluates the purchase decision, may return the phone to the store if it is unsatisfactory.	They evaluate suppliers using a formal vendor rating system and notify a supplier if the earbud headsets do not meet their quality standard. If the problem is not corrected, they drop the firm as a future supplier.

FIGURE 6–4
Comparing the stages in a consumer and organizational purchase decision process

that would benefit from Siemens' expertise, company engineers typically work with the firm to determine the kind of system required to meet the customer's need.

After a contract is won, project personnel must often make a **make-buy decision**—an evaluation of whether components and assemblies will be purchased from outside suppliers or built by the company itself. (Siemens produces many components and assemblies.) When these items are to be purchased from outside suppliers, the company engages in a thorough supplier search and evaluation process.

Information Search Companies such as Siemens employ a sophisticated process for identifying outside suppliers of components and assemblies. For standard items such as connectors, printed circuit boards, and components such as resistors and capacitors, the purchasing agent consults the company's purchasing databank, which contains information on hundreds of suppliers and thousands of products. All products in the databank have been prenegotiated as to price, quality, and delivery time, and many have been assessed using **value analysis**—a systematic appraisal of the design, quality, and performance of a product to reduce purchasing costs.

For one-of-a-kind components or assemblies such as new optics, cameras, and light sources, the company relies on its engineers to keep current on new developments in product technology. This information is often found in technical journals and industry magazines or at international trade shows where suppliers display their most recent innovations. In some instances, supplier representatives might be asked to make presentations to the buying center at Siemens. Such a group often consists of a project engineer; several design, system, and manufacturing engineers; and a purchasing agent.

Alternative Evaluation The main buying criteria used to select machine vision suppliers and products are displayed in Figure 6–5.[27] Product performance, a supplier's technical support, and ease of use are the three most frequently mentioned buying criteria for machine vision suppliers and products. Interestingly, price is among the least frequently mentioned. Typically, two or three suppliers for each standard component and assembly are identified from a **bidder's list**—a list of firms believed to be qualified to supply a given item. This list is generated from the company's purchasing databank as well as from engineering inputs. Specific items that are unique may be obtained from a single supplier after careful evaluation by the buying center.

Firms selected from the bidder's list are sent a quotation request from the purchasing agent, describing the desired quantity, delivery date(s), and specifications of the components or assemblies. Suppliers are expected to respond within 30 days.

Purchase Decision Unlike the short purchase stage in a consumer purchase, the period from supplier selection to order placement to product delivery can take several weeks or even months. Even after bids for components and assemblies are submitted, further negotiation concerning price, performance, and delivery terms is likely. Sometimes conditions related to warranties, indemnities, and payment schedules have to be agreed on. The purchase decision is further complicated by the fact that two or more suppliers of the same item might be awarded contracts. This practice can occur when large orders are requested. Suppliers who are not chosen are informed why their bids were not selected.

Postpurchase Behavior As in the consumer purchase decision process, postpurchase evaluation occurs in the industrial purchase decision process, but it is formalized and often more sophisticated. All items purchased are examined in a formal product acceptance process. The performance of the supplier is also monitored and recorded. Performance on past contracts determines a supplier's chances of being asked to bid on future purchases, and poor performance may result in a supplier's name being dropped from the bidder's list.

This example of an organizational purchase suggests four lessons for marketers who want to increase their chances of selling products and services to organiza-

FIGURE 6–5
Product and supplier selection criteria for buying machine vision equipment emphasize factors other than price.

An optic component in a larger machine vision system for soft drink cans.

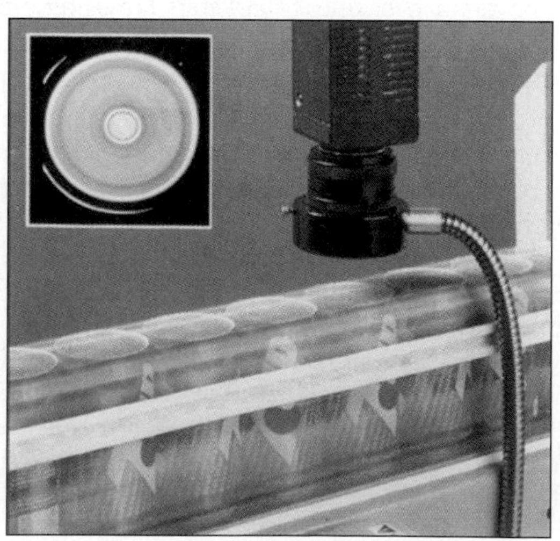

Percentage of machine vision buyers citing individual selection criteria.

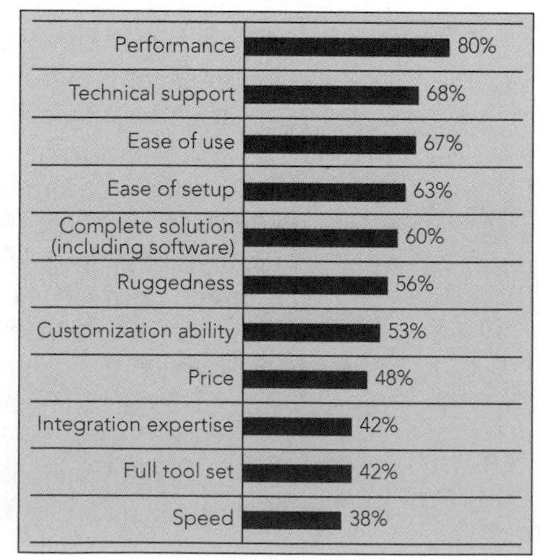

Performance	80%
Technical support	68%
Ease of use	67%
Ease of setup	63%
Complete solution (including software)	60%
Ruggedness	56%
Customization ability	53%
Price	48%
Integration expertise	42%
Full tool set	42%
Speed	38%

tions. Firms selling to organizations must: (1) understand the organization's needs, (2) get on the right bidder's list, (3) find the right people in the buying center, and (4) provide value to organizational buyers.

learning review

5. What is a make-buy decision?

6. What is a bidder's list?

ONLINE BUYING IN ORGANIZATIONAL MARKETS

LO4

Organizational buying behavior and business marketing continues to evolve with the application of Internet technology. Organizations dwarf consumers in terms of online transactions made, average transaction size, and overall purchase volume. In fact, organizational buyers account for about 80 percent of the global dollar value of all online transactions.

Prominence of Online Buying in Organizational Markets

Online buying in organizational markets is prominent for three major reasons.[28] First, organizational buyers depend heavily on timely supplier information that describes product availability, technical specifications, application uses, price, and delivery schedules. This information can be conveyed quickly via Internet technology. Second, this technology has been shown to substantially reduce buyer order processing costs. At General Electric, online buying has cut the cost of a transaction from $50 to $100 per purchase to about $5. Third, business marketers have found that Internet technology can reduce marketing costs, particularly sales and advertising expense, and broaden their potential customer base for many types of products and services.

For these reasons, online buying is popular in all three kinds of organizational markets. For example, airlines electronically order over $400 million in spare parts from the Boeing Company each year. Customers of W. W. Grainger, a large U.S. wholesaler of maintenance, repair, and operating supplies, buy more than $425 million worth of these products annually online. Supply and service purchases totaling $650 million each year are made online by the Los Angeles County government.

Online buying can assume many forms. Organizational buyers can purchase directly from suppliers. For instance, a buyer might acquire a dozen desktop photocopiers from Xerox at www.xerox.com. This same buyer might purchase office furniture and supplies through a reseller such as Office Depot at www.officedepot.com. Increasingly, organizational buyers and business marketers are using e-marketplaces and online auctions to purchase and sell products and services.

E-Marketplaces: Virtual Organizational Markets

A significant development in organizational buying has been the creation of online trading communities, called **e-marketplaces**, that bring together buyers and supplier organizations. These online communities go by a variety of names, including B2B exchanges and e-hubs, and make possible the real-time exchange of information, money, products, and services.

E-marketplaces can be independent trading communities or private exchanges. Independent e-marketplaces act as a neutral third party and provide an Internet technology trading platform and a centralized market that enable exchanges between buyers and sellers. They charge a fee for their service and exist in settings that have one or more of the following features: (1) thousands of geographically dispersed buyers and sellers, (2) volatile prices caused by demand and supply fluctuations,

Marketing Matters > > > > > entrepreneurship

eBay Means Business for Entrepreneurs

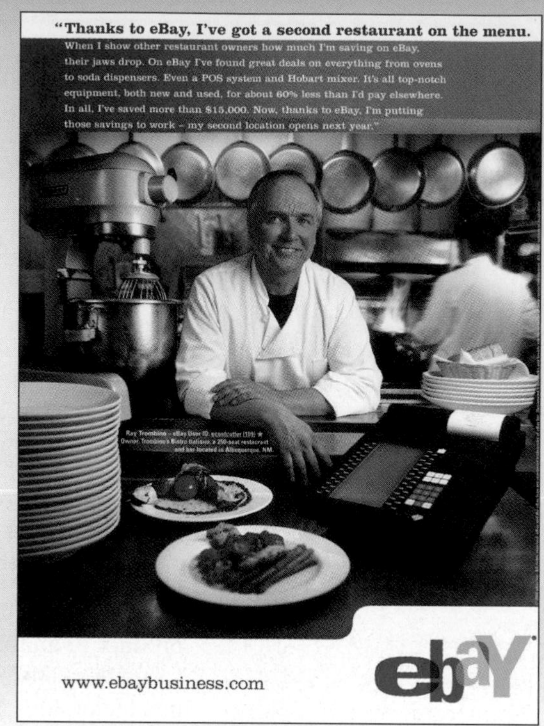

San Jose, California–based eBay Inc. is a true Internet phenomenon. By any measure, it is the predominant person-to-person trading community in the world. But there is more.

Now eBayBusiness offers a trading platform for over 23 million small businesses in the United States and even greater numbers around the world. Transactions on eBayBusiness exceed sales of $20 billion annually.

The eBayBusiness platform has proven to be a boon for small businesses. According to an eBay-commissioned survey conducted by ACNielsen, 82 percent of small businesses using eBayBusiness report that it helped their business grow and expand, 78 percent say it helped to reduce their costs, and 79 percent say their business had become more profitable. Additionally, eBayBusiness promotes entrepreneurship. According to the general manager of eBayBusiness, "Many of our sellers started their businesses specifically as a result of the ability to use eBay as their e-commerce platform."

Today, more than 724,000 Americans report that eBay is their primary or secondary source of income—up 68 percent from 2003 when 430,000 Americans were making some or all of their income selling on eBay. According to a spokesperson from the American Enterprise Institute for Public Policy Research, "The potential for entrepreneurs to realize success through eBay is significant."

(3) time sensitivity due to perishable offerings and changing technologies, and (4) easily comparable offerings between a variety of sellers.

Examples of independent e-marketplaces include PlasticsNet (plastics), Hospital Network.com (healthcare supplies and equipment), and Textile Web (garment and apparel products). Small business buyers and sellers, in particular, benefit from independent e-marketplaces. These e-marketplaces offer them an economical way to expand their customer base and reduce the cost of products and services. To serve entrepreneurs and the small business market in the United States, eBay launched eBayBusiness. Read the accompanying Marketing Matters box to learn more about this independent trading community.[29]

Large companies tend to favor private exchanges that link them with their network of qualified suppliers and customers. Private exchanges focus on streamlining a company's purchase transactions with its suppliers and customers. Like independent e-marketplaces, they provide a technology trading platform and central market for buyer–seller interactions. They are not a neutral third party, however, but represent the interests of their owners. For example, Agentrics is an international business-to-business private exchange. It connects more than 250 retail customers with 80,000 suppliers. Its members include Best Buy, Campbell Soup, Costco, Radio Shack, Safeway, Target, Tesco, and Walgreens.[30] The Global Healthcare Exchange engages in the buying and selling of health care products for over 1,400 hospitals and more than 100 health care suppliers, such as Abbott Laboratories, GE Medical Systems, Johnson & Johnson, Medtronic USA, and McKesson Corporation.[31] Each of these private exchanges has saved their members over $2 billion since 2000 due to efficiencies in purchase transactions.

Online Auctions in Organizational Markets

Online auctions have grown in popularity among organizational buyers and business marketers. Many e-marketplaces offer this service. Two general types of auctions are common: (1) a traditional auction and (2) a reverse auction.[32] Figure 6–6 shows how buyer and seller participants and price behavior differ by type of auction. Let's look at each auction type more closely to understand the implications of each for buyers and sellers.

In a **traditional auction** a seller puts an item up for sale and would-be buyers are invited to bid in competition with each other. As more would-be buyers become involved, there is an upward pressure on bid prices. Why? Bidding is sequential. Prospective buyers observe the bids of others and decide whether or not to increase the bid price. The auction ends when a single bidder remains and "wins" the item with its highest price. Traditional auctions are often used to dispose of excess merchandise. For example, Dell, Inc., sells surplus, refurbished, or closeout computer merchandise at its www.dellauction.com Web site.

A reverse auction works in the opposite direction from a traditional auction. In a **reverse auction**, a buyer communicates a need for a product or service and would-be suppliers are invited to bid in competition with each other. As more would-be suppliers become involved, there is a downward pressure on bid prices for the buyer's business. Why? Like traditional auctions, bidding is sequential and prospective suppliers observe the bids of others and decide whether or not to decrease the bid price. The auction ends when a single bidder remains and "wins" the business with its lowest price. Reverse auctions benefit organizational buyers by reducing the cost of their purchases. As an example, United Technologies Corp., estimates that it has saved $600 million on the purchase of $6 billion in supplies using online reverse auctions.[33]

Clearly, buyers welcome the lower prices generated by reverse auctions. Suppliers often favor reverse auctions because they give them a chance to capture business that they might not have otherwise had because of a long-standing purchase relationship between the buyer and another supplier. On the other hand, suppliers say reverse auctions put too much emphasis on prices, discourage consideration of other important buying criteria, and may threaten supply partnership opportunities.[34]

FIGURE 6–6
Buyer and seller participants and price behavior differ by type of online auction. As an organizational buyer, would you prefer to participate in a traditional auction or a reverse auction?

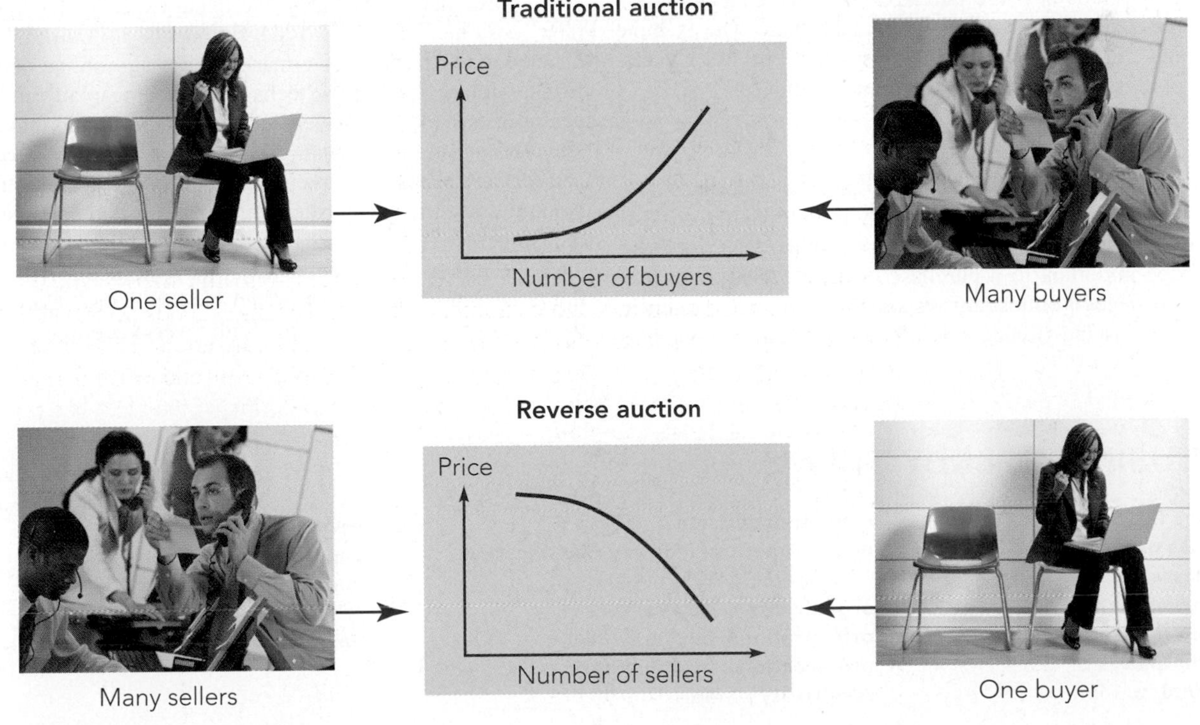

learning review

7. What are e-marketplaces?
8. In general, which type of online auction creates upward pressure on bid prices and which type creates downward pressure on bid prices?

LEARNING OBJECTIVES REVIEW

LO1 *Distinguish among industrial, reseller, and government organizational markets.*
There are three different organizational markets: industrial, reseller, and government. Industrial firms in some way reprocess a product or service they buy before selling it to the next buyer. Resellers—wholesalers and retailers—buy physical products and resell them again without any reprocessing. Government agencies, at the federal, state, and local levels, buy goods and services for the constituents they serve. The North American Industry Classification System (NAICS) provides common industry definitions for Canada, Mexico, and the United States, which facilitates the measurement of economic activity for these three organizational markets.

LO2 *Describe the key characteristics of organizational buying that make it different from consumer buying.*
Seven major characteristics of organizational buying make it different from consumer buying. These include demand characteristics, size of the order or purchase, number of potential buyers, buying objectives, buying criteria, buyer–seller relationships and supply partnerships, and multiple buying influences within organizations. The organizational buying process itself is more formalized, more individuals are involved, supplier capability is more important, and the postpurchase evaluation behavior often includes performance of the supplier and the item purchased. Figure 6–4 details how the purchase of a smart phone differs between a consumer and organizational purchase. The example describing the purchase of machine vision systems by an industrial firm illustrates this process in greater depth.

LO3 *Explain how buying centers and buying situations influence organizational purchasing.*
Buying centers and buying situations have an important influence on organizational purchasing. A buying center consists of a group of individuals who share common goals, risks, and knowledge important to a purchase decision. A buyer or purchasing manager is almost always a member of a buying center. However, other individuals may affect organizational purchasing due to their unique roles in a purchase decision. Five specific roles that a person may play in a buying center include users, influencers, buyers, deciders, and gatekeepers. The specific buying situation will influence the number of people in and the different roles played in a buying center. For a routine reorder of an item—a straight rebuy situation—a purchasing manager or buyer will typically act alone in making a purchasing decision. When an organization is a first-time purchaser of a product or service—a new buy situation—a buying center is enlarged and all five roles in a buying center often emerge. A modified rebuy buying situation lies between these two extremes. Figure 6–3 offers additional insights into how buying centers and buying situations influence organization purchasing.

LO4 *Recognize the importance and nature of online buying in industrial, reseller, and government organizational markets.*
Organizations dwarf consumers in terms of online transactions made and purchase volume. Online buying in organizational markets is popular for three reasons. First, organizational buyers depend on timely supplier information that describes product availability, technical specifications, application uses, price, and delivery schedules. This information can be conveyed quickly via Internet technology. Second, this technology substantially reduces buyer order processing costs. Third, business marketers have found that Internet technology can reduce marketing costs, particularly sales and advertising expense, and broaden their customer base. Two developments in online buying have been the creation of e-marketplaces and online auctions. E-marketplaces provide a technology trading platform and a centralized market for buyer–seller transactions and make possible the real-time exchange of information, money, products, and services. These e-marketplaces can be independent trading communities, such as PlasticsNet, or private exchanges such as the Global Healthcare Exchange. Online traditional and reverse auctions represent a second major development. With traditional auctions, the highest-priced bidder "wins." Conversely, the lowest-priced bidder "wins" with reverse auctions.

FOCUSING ON KEY TERMS

bidder's list p. 152
business marketing p. 140
buy classes p. 148
buying center p. 147
derived demand p. 143
e-marketplaces p. 153
ISO 9000 p. 145
make-buy decision p. 151
North American Industry Classification System (NAICS) p. 141
organizational buyers p. 140
organizational buying behavior p. 150
organizational buying criteria p. 145
reciprocity p. 146
reverse auction p. 155
supplier development p. 145
supply partnership p. 146
traditional auction p. 155
value analysis p. 151

APPLYING MARKETING KNOWLEDGE

1 Describe the major differences among industrial firms, resellers, and government units in the United States.

2 Explain how the North American Industry Classification System (NAICS) might be helpful in understanding industrial, reseller, and government markets, and discuss the limitations inherent in this system.

3 List and discuss the key characteristics of organizational buying that make it different from consumer buying.

4 What is a buying center? Describe the roles assumed by people in a buying center and what useful questions should be raised to guide any analysis of the structure and behavior of a buying center.

5 Effective marketing is of increasing importance in today's competitive environment. How can firms more effectively market to organizations?

6 A firm that is marketing multimillion-dollar wastewater treatment systems to cities has been unable to sell a new type of system. This setback has occurred even though the firm's systems are cheaper than competitive systems and meet U.S. Environmental Protection Agency (EPA) specifications. To date, the firm's marketing efforts have been directed to city purchasing departments and the various state EPAs to get on approved bidder's lists. Talks with city-employed personnel have indicated that the new system is very different from current systems and therefore city sanitary and sewer department engineers, directors of these two departments, and city council members are unfamiliar with the workings of the system. Consulting engineers, hired by cities to work on the engineering and design features of these systems and paid on a percentage of system cost, are also reluctant to favor the new system. (*a*) What roles do the various individuals play in the purchase process for a wastewater treatment system? (*b*) How could the firm improve the marketing effort behind the new system?

building your marketing plan

Your marketing plan may need an estimate of the size of the market potential or industry potential (see Chapter 9) for a particular product market in which you compete. Use these steps:

1 Define the product market precisely, such as ice cream.

2 Visit the NAICS Web site at www.census.gov.

3 Click "NAICS" and enter a keyword that describes your product market (e.g., ice cream).

4 Follow the instructions to the specific NAICS code and economic census data that details the dollar sales and provides the estimate of market or industry potential.

video case 6 Lands' End: Where Buyers Rule

Organizational buying is a part of the marketing effort that influences every aspect of business at Lands' End. As senior vice president of operations Phil Schaecher explains, "When we talk about purchasing at Lands' End, most people think of the purchase of merchandise for resale, but we buy many other things aside from merchandise, everything from the simplest office supply to the most sophisticated piece of material-handling equipment." As a result, Lands' End has developed a sophisticated approach to organizational buying, which is one of the keys to its success.

THE COMPANY

The company started by selling sailboat equipment, duffle bags, rainsuits, and sweaters from a basement location in Chicago's old tannery district. In its first catalog, the company name was printed with a typing error—the apostrophe in the wrong place—but the fledgling company couldn't afford to correct and reprint it. So ever since, the company name has been Lands' End—with the misplaced apostrophe.

When the company outgrew its Chicago location, founder Gary Comer relocated it to Dodgeville, Wisconsin, where he had fallen in love with the rolling hills and changing seasons. The original business ideas were simple: "Sell only things we believe in, ship every order the day it arrives, and unconditionally guarantee everything." Over time, the company developed eight principles of doing business:

- Never reduce the quality of a product to make it cheaper.
- Price products fairly and honestly.
- Accept any return for any reason.

- Ship items in stock the day after the order is received.
- What is best for the customer is best for Lands' End.
- Place contracts with manufacturers who are cost-conscious and efficient.
- Operate efficiently.
- Encourage customers to shop in whatever way they find most convenient.

These principles became the guidelines for the company's dedicated local employees and helped create extraordinary expectations from Lands' End customers.

Today, Lands' End is one of the world's largest direct merchants of traditionally styled clothing for the family, soft luggage, and products for the home. The products are offered through catalogs, on the Internet, and in retail stores. In one year, Lands' End distributes more than 200 million catalogs designed for specific segments, including *The Lands' End Catalog, Lands' End Men, Lands' End Plus Size Collection, Lands' End Kids, Lands' End for School Uniforms, Lands' End Home,* and *Lands' End Business Outfitters*. In a typical day, catalog shoppers place more than 40,000 telephone calls to the company. The Lands' End Web site (www.landsend.com) also offers every Lands' End product and a wide variety of Internet shopping innovations such as a 3-D model customized to each customer (called My Virtual Model™); individually tailored clothes (called Lands' End Custom™); and a feature that allows customers to "chat" online directly with a customer service representative (called Lands' End Live™). Lands' End also operates stores in the United States, the United Kingdom, Germany, and Japan. Selected Lands' End merchandise is also sold in Sears stores, following the purchase of Lands' End by Sears in 2002.

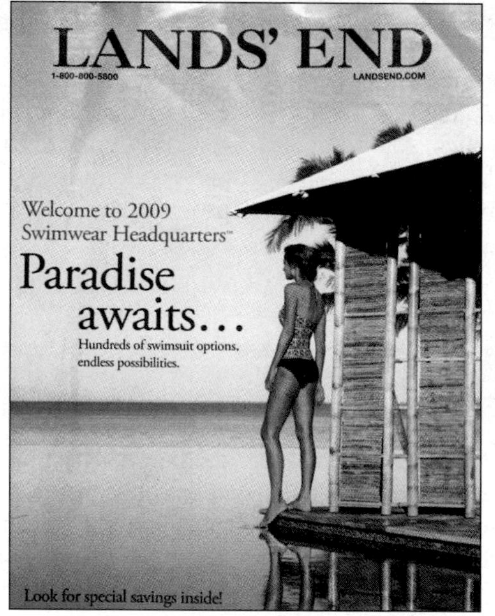

The company's goal is to please customers with the highest levels of quality and service in the industry. Lands' End maintains the high quality of its products through several important activities. For example, the company works directly with mills and manufacturers to retain control of quality and design. "The biggest difference between Lands' End and some other retailers or catalog businesses is that we actually design all the product here and we do all the specifications. Therefore, the manufacturer is building that product directly to our specs, we are not buying off of somebody else's line," explains Joan Mudget, vice president of quality assurance. In addition, Lands' End tests its products for comfort and fit by paying real people (local residents and children) to "wear-test" and "fit-test" all types of garments.

Service has also become an important part of the Lands' End reputation. Customers expect prompt, professional service at every step—initiating the order, making selections, shipping, and follow-up (if necessary). Some of the ways Lands' End meets these expectations include offering the simplest guarantee in the industry—"Guaranteed. Period."—toll-free telephone lines open 24 hours a day, 364 days a year, continuous product training for telephone representatives, and two-day shipping. Lands' End operators even send personal responses to all e-mail messages, approximately 230,000 per year.

ORGANIZATIONAL BUYING AT LANDS' END

The sixth Lands' End business principle (described earlier) is accomplished through the company's organizational buying process. First, its buyers specify fabric quality, construction, and sizing standards, which typically exceed industry standards, for current and potential Lands' End products. Then the buyers literally search around the world for the best possible source of fabrics and products. Once a potential supplier is identified, one of the company's 150 quality assurance personnel makes an information-gathering visit. The purpose of the visit is to understand the supplier's values, to assess four criteria (economic, quality, service, and vendor), and to determine if the Lands' End standards can be achieved.

Lands' End evaluations of potential suppliers lead to the selection of what the company hopes will become long-term partners. As Mudget explains, "When we're looking for new manufacturers we are looking for the long term. I think one of the most interesting things is we're not out there looking for new vendors every year to fill the same products." In fact, Lands' End believes that the term *supplier* does not adequately describe the importance the company places on the relationships. Lands' End suppliers are viewed as allies, supporters, associates, colleagues, and stakeholders in the future of the company. Once an alliance is formed the product specifications and the performance on those specifications are regularly evaluated.

Lands' End buyers face a variety of buying situations. Straight rebuys involve reordering an existing product—such as shipping boxes—without evaluating or changing specifications. Modified rebuys involve changing some aspect of a previously ordered product—such as the collar of a knit shirt—based on input from consumers, retailers, or other people involved in the purchase decision. Finally, new buys involve first-time purchases—such as Lands' End addition of men's suits to its product line. The complexity of the process can vary with the type of purchase. Schaecher explains, "As you get more complicated in the purchase there are more things you look at to decide on a vendor."

FUTURE CHALLENGES FOR LANDS' END

Lands' End faces several challenges as it pursues improvements in its organizational buying process. First, new technologies offer opportunities for fast, efficient, and accurate communication with suppliers. Ed Smidebush, general inventory manager, describes a new system at Lands' End: "Our quick response system is a computerized system where we transmit electronically to our vendors each Sunday night, forecast information as well as stock positions and purchase order information so that on Monday morning this information will be incorporated directly into their manufacturing reports so that they can prioritize their production." Occasionally Lands' End must work with its suppliers to improve their technology and information system capabilities.

Another challenge for Lands' End is to anticipate changes in consumer interests. While it has many years of experience with retail consumers, preferences for colors, fabrics, and styles change frequently, requiring buyers to constantly monitor the marketplace. In addition, Lands' End's more recent offerings to corporate customers require constant attention "because business customers' wants and incentives, and the environment in which they're shopping, are very different from consumers at home," explains marketing manager Hilary Kleese.

Finally, Lands' End must anticipate the quantities of each of its products consumers are likely to order. To do this, historical information is used to develop forecasts. One of the best tests of their forecast accuracy is the holiday season, when Lands' End receives more than 100,000 calls each day. Having the right products available is important because, as every employee knows from Principle 4, every order must be shipped the day after it is received.

Questions

1 *(a)* Who is likely to comprise the buying center in the decision to select a new supplier for Lands' End? *(b)* Which of the buying center members are likely to play the roles of users, influencers, buyers, deciders, and gatekeepers?

2 *(a)* Which stages of the organizational buying decision process does Lands' End follow when it selects a new supplier? *(b)* What selection criteria does the company utilize in the process?

3 Describe purchases Lands' End buyers typically face in each of the three buying situations: straight rebuy, modified rebuy, and new buy.

DELL
I CHOOSE TO
TAKE MY OWN PATH
I CHOOSE DELL
It was an unlikely pairing. By marrying tradition and technology, Anupam gave life to a whole new way for Indians to find love. Shaadi now caters to two million members and is a household name in matrimonial services. Shaadi relies on secure and highly scalable Dell PowerEdge™ 2900 Servers, powered by Intel® Xeon® Processors, to match its ever-growing data management needs.
What's your path?
SMS 'TYOP6' TO 56767
TAKEYOUROWNPATH.COM
Anupam Mittal
Creator of popular marriage website, Shaadi.com and Founder of People Group
intel
Xeon inside
Powerful. Efficient.
Standard messaging rates apply. TRADEMARKS: Celeron, Celeron Inside, Centrino, Centrino Inside, Core Inside, Intel, Intel Logo, Intel Atom, Intel Atom Inside, Intel Core, Intel Inside, Intel Inside Logo, Intel Viiv, Intel vPro, Itanium, Itanium Inside, Pentium, Pentium Inside, Viiv Inside, vPro Inside, Xeon, and Xeon Inside are trademarks of Intel Corporation in the U.S. and other countries. COPYRIGHT: © 2009 Dell Inc. All rights reserved.

DELL
I CHOOSE TO
TAKE MY OWN PATH
I CHOOSE DELL
Giving up a secure job to help others realise their dreams, Satya launched his first program for IIM aspirants. Today Career Launcher has presence in four countries serving over 100,000 learners across K-12 schools, higher education, employability skills and Test preparation. Satya relies on Dell Vostro™ laptops, powered by Intel® Core™2 Duo Processors, for worry-free performance that both he and his students demand.
What's your path?
SMS 'TYOP9' TO 56767
TAKEYOUROWNPATH.COM
Satya Narayanan R
Founder of Asia's Leading education corporate - Career Launcher
intel
Core 2 Duo inside
Do More
Standard messaging rates apply. TRADEMARKS: Celeron, Celeron Inside, Centrino, Centrino Inside, Core Inside, Intel, Intel Logo, Intel Atom, Intel Atom Inside, Intel Core, Intel Inside, Intel Inside Logo, Intel Viiv, Intel vPro, Itanium, Itanium Inside, Pentium, Pentium Inside, Viiv Inside, vPro Inside, Xeon, and Xeon Inside are trademarks of Intel Corporation in the U.S. and other countries. COPYRIGHT: © 2009 Dell Inc. All rights reserved.

DELL
I CHOOSE TO
TAKE MY OWN PATH
I CHOOSE DELL
Believing in empowering kids with computer skills, Kishore turned his vision into one of the largest education systems in the world. Today, he provides virtual and interactive learning classrooms to over 40,000 schools in India. Kishore uses reliable Dell Vostro™ 220 Desktops, powered by Intel® Core™ 2 Duo Processors, to keep his business at the top of its class.
What's your path?
SMS 'TYOP8' TO 56767
TAKEYOUROWNPATH.COM
P. Kishore
Founder of Everonn Systems, Pioneer in computerising school education
intel
Core 2 Duo inside
Do More
Standard messaging rates apply. TRADEMARKS: Celeron, Celeron Inside, Centrino, Centrino Inside, Core Inside, Intel, Intel Logo, Intel Atom, Intel Atom Inside, Intel Core, Intel Inside, Intel Inside Logo, Intel Viiv, Intel vPro, Itanium, Itanium Inside, Pentium, Pentium Inside, Viiv Inside, vPro Inside, Xeon, and Xeon Inside are trademarks of Intel Corporation in the U.S. and other countries. COPYRIGHT © 2009 Dell Inc. All rights reserved.

DELL
I CHOOSE TO
TAKE MY OWN PATH
I CHOOSE DELL
With a relentless passion to bring enjoyment to people, Neeraj created India's most popular music, video, and gaming entertainment portals. Today, Hungama is the leading South Asian mobile and digital content publisher. Neeraj trusts Dell PowerEdge™ 2950 Servers, powered by Intel® Xeon® Processors, for their high-speed performance to keep up with his fast-paced business.
What's your path?
SMS 'TYOP7' TO 56767
TAKEYOUROWNPATH.COM
Neeraj Roy
CEO of Hungama, India's premier digital and mobile entertainment company
intel
Xeon inside
Powerful. Efficient.
Standard messaging rates apply. TRADEMARKS: Celeron, Celeron Inside, Centrino, Centrino Inside, Core Inside, Intel, Intel Logo, Intel Atom, Intel Atom Inside, Intel Core, Intel Inside, Intel Inside Logo, Intel Viiv, Intel vPro, Itanium, Itanium Inside, Pentium, Pentium Inside, Viiv Inside, vPro Inside, Xeon, and Xeon Inside are trademarks of Intel Corporation in the U.S. and other countries. COPYRIGHT: © 2009 Dell Inc. All rights reserved.

7 Understanding and Reaching Global Consumers and Markets

LEARNING OBJECTIVES
After reading this chapter you should be able to:

LO1 Describe the nature and scope of world trade from a global perspective and its implications for the United States.

LO2 Identify the major trends that have influenced the landscape of global marketing in the past decade.

LO3 Identify the environmental forces that shape global marketing efforts.

LO4 Name and describe the alternative approaches companies use to enter global markets.

LO5 Explain the distinction between standardization and customization when companies craft worldwide marketing programs.

DELL'S QUEST FOR GROWTH IN EMERGING ECONOMIES

Why has Dell, Inc., embarked on a bold global growth initiative? Simply put, "Our success is going to be largely dependent on our ability to expand globally," says Steve Felice, president of Dell Asia Pacific and Japan.

Dell's global initiative focuses on emerging economies in Asia, Africa, and Latin America. Compared with mature economies in North America and Western Europe, emerging economies offer significant growth potential, according to Michael Dell, Dell's founder and chief executive officer.

Dell's global initiative is bold in its departure from prior product development practices and in its change to its sales and distribution strategy. The company now designs low-cost notebook and desktop personal computers for customers in China, India, and other emerging economies. "We used to design products for global requirements and distribute the same product globally," says Felice. "In this situation, we started with talking to emerging country customers, designing a product for emerging countries, and initially launching the product in only emerging countries. That's a big departure in our strategy."

Dell's signature direct sales and distribution strategy has broadened as part of its global growth initiative. The company built its U.S. business with telephone- and Internet-based sales without retailers. In emerging economies, however, customers prefer to see, touch, and use a personal computer before they buy. Also, credit cards aren't widespread and customers are often leery of purchasing personal computers online or over the phone. In response, Dell has opened "experience centers" to help customers get comfortable with "buying direct." More boldly, the company decided to distribute its products through electronics retailers to reach more buyers quickly. Commenting on this move, Felice said: "These [emerging] economies are growing so fast that we didn't want to miss out on the opportunity. But if we just use the direct model, it might take us too long to get there." Dell's global growth initiative illustrates the importance of understanding global customers and reaching them by adapting to their needs.[1]

This chapter describes today's complex and dynamic global marketing environment. It begins with an overview of world trade and the emergence of a borderless economic world. Attention is then focused on prominent cultural, economic, and political-regulatory factors that present both an opportunity and a challenge for global marketers. Four major global market entry strategies are then detailed. Finally, the task of designing, implementing, and evaluating worldwide marketing programs for companies such as Dell, Inc., is described.

DYNAMICS OF WORLD TRADE

LO1

The dollar value of world trade has more than doubled in the past decade and will exceed $20 trillion in 2012. Manufactured goods and commodities account for 75 percent of world trade. Service industries, including telecommunications, transportation, insurance, education, banking, and tourism, represent the other 25 percent.

World Trade Flows

All nations and regions of the world do not participate equally in world trade. World trade flows reflect interdependencies among industries, countries, and regions and manifest themselves in country, company, industry, and regional exports and imports.

Global Perspective Figure 7–1 shows the estimated dollar value of exports and imports among North American countries, Europe, Asian/Pacific Rim countries, and the rest of the world, including intraregional trade flows.[2] The United States, Europe, Canada, China, and Japan together account for more than two-thirds of world trade.

Not all trade involves the exchange of money for goods or services. In a world where 70 percent of all countries do not have convertible currencies or where government-owned enterprises lack sufficient cash or credit for imports, other means of payment are used. An estimated 15 to 20 percent of world trade involves **countertrade**, the practice of using barter rather than money for making global sales.[3]

Countertrade is popular with many Eastern European nations, Russia, and Asian countries. For example, the Malaysian government recently exchanged 20,000 tons of rice for an equivalent amount of Philippine corn. Volvo of North America delivered automobiles to the Siberian police force when Siberia had no cash to pay for them. It accepted payment in oil, which it then sold for cash to pay for media advertising in the United States.

A global perspective on world trade views exports and imports as complementary economic flows: A country's imports affect its exports and exports affect its imports. Every nation's imports arise from the exports of other nations. As the exports of one country increase, its national output and income rise, which in turn leads to an increase in the demand for imports. This nation's greater demand for imports stimulates the exports of other countries. Increased demand for exports of other nations energizes their economic activity, resulting in higher national income, which stimulates their demand for imports. In short, imports affect exports and vice versa. This phenomenon is called the *trade feedback effect* and is one argument for free trade among nations.

United States Perspective The United States is the world's perennial leader in terms of **gross domestic product** (GDP), which is the monetary value of all goods and services produced in a country during one year. The United States is also among the world's leaders in exports due in large part to its global prominence in the aerospace, chemical, office equipment, information technology, pharmaceutical, telecommunications, and professional service industries. However, the U.S. percentage share of world exports has shifted downward over the past 30 years, whereas its percentage share of world imports has increased. Therefore, the relative position of the United States as a supplier to the world has diminished despite an absolute growth in exports. At the same time, its relative role as a marketplace for the world has increased, particularly for automobile, oil, textile, apparel, and consumer electronics products.

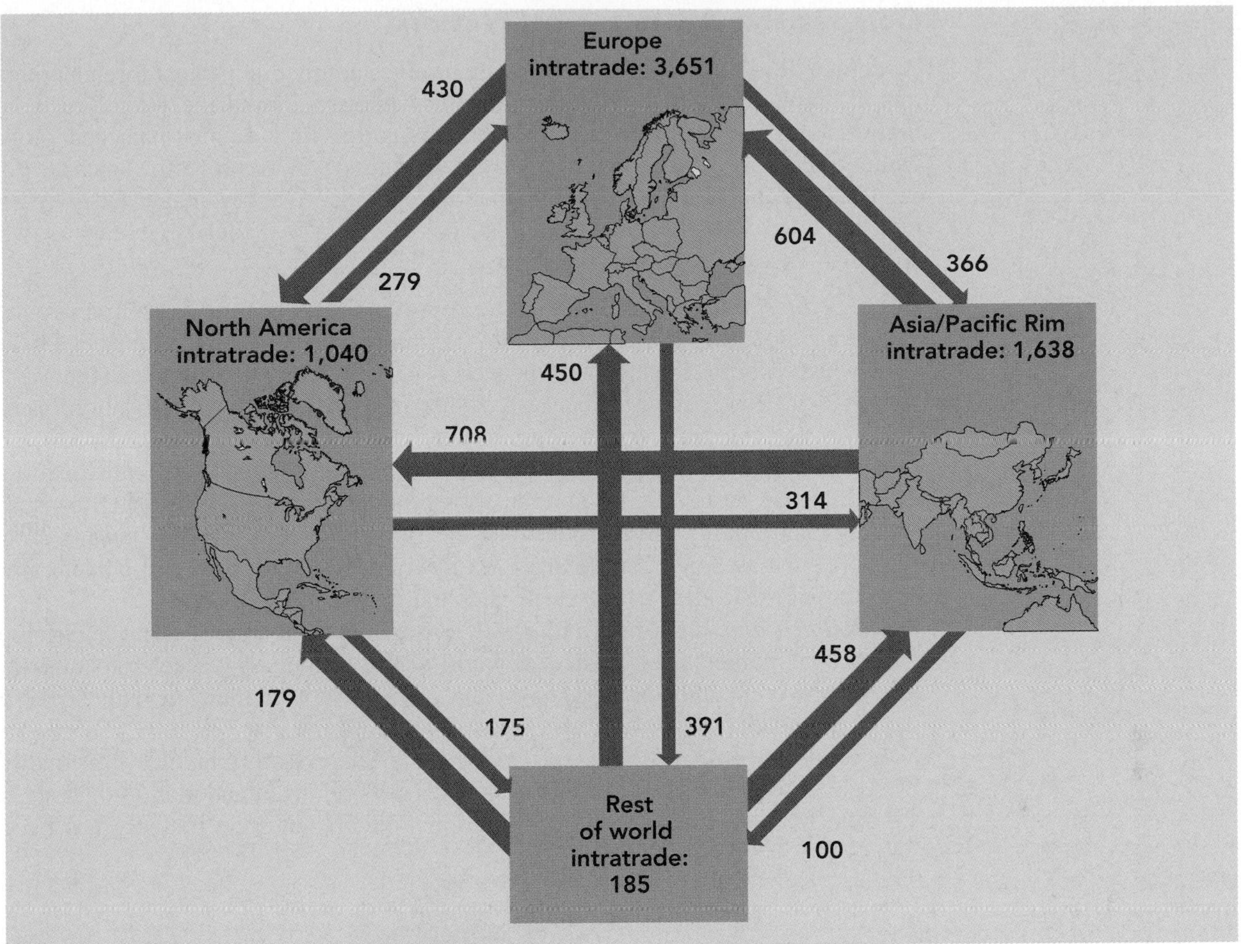

FIGURE 7–1
Illustrative world trade flows for manufactured goods and commodities within and between geographic regions (billions of U.S. dollars)

The difference between the monetary value of a nation's exports and imports is called the **balance of trade**. When a country's exports exceed its imports, it incurs a surplus in its balance of trade. When imports exceed exports, a deficit results. World trade trends in U.S. exports and imports are reflected in the U.S. balance of trade. Two important things have happened in U.S. exports and imports over the past 30 years. First, imports have exceeded exports each year, indicating that the United States has a continuing balance of trade deficit. Second, the volume of both exports and imports has increased dramatically, showing why almost every American is significantly affected. The effect varies from the products they buy (Samsung DVD players from South Korea, Waterford crystal from Ireland, Louis Vuitton luggage from France) to those they sell (Cisco Systems' Internet technology to Europe, DuPont's chemicals to the Far East, Merck pharmaceuticals to Africa) and the jobs and improved standard of living that result.

World trade flows to and from the United States reflect demand and supply interdependencies for goods and services among nations and industries. The four largest importers of U.S. goods and services are Canada, China, Mexico, and Japan. These countries purchase approximately 67 percent of U.S. exports. The four largest exporters to the United States are Canada, China, Mexico, and Japan.

The United States is Asia's largest export market, buying about 40 percent of the exports of Japan, Taiwan, South Korea, and China, a quarter of Hong Kong's exports, and 40 percent of the Philippines's exports. The trade imbalance between the United States and Asia is illustrated by the fact that China, Japan, and South Korea combine for about 80 percent of the total U.S. balance of trade deficit.

Competitive Advantage of Nations

As companies in many industries find themselves competing against foreign competitors at home and abroad, government policy makers around the world are increasingly asking why some companies and industries in a country succeed globally while others lose ground or fail. Harvard Business School professor Michael Porter suggests a "diamond" to explain a nation's competitive advantage and why some industries and firms become world leaders.[4] He identified four key elements, which appear in Figure 7–2:

1. *Factor conditions.* These reflect a nation's ability to turn its natural resources, education, and infrastructure into a competitive advantage. Consider Holland, which exports 58 percent of the world's cut flowers. The Dutch lead the world in the cut-flower industry because of their research in flower cultivation, packaging, and shipping—not because of their weather.
2. *Demand conditions.* These include both the number and sophistication of domestic customers for an industry's product. Japan's sophisticated consumers demand quality in their consumer electronics, thereby making Japan's producers such as Sony, Sanyo, Sharp, Pioneer, JVC, Matsushita, and Hitachi among the world leaders in the electronics industry.
3. *Related and supporting industries.* Firms and industries seeking leadership in global markets need clusters of world-class suppliers that accelerate innovation. Swiss companies are leaders in the global watch market, in part, because of high quality supporting watch-movement makers.
4. *Company strategy, structure, and rivalry.* These factors include the conditions governing the way a nation's businesses are organized and managed, along with the intensity of domestic competition. The Italian shoe industry has become

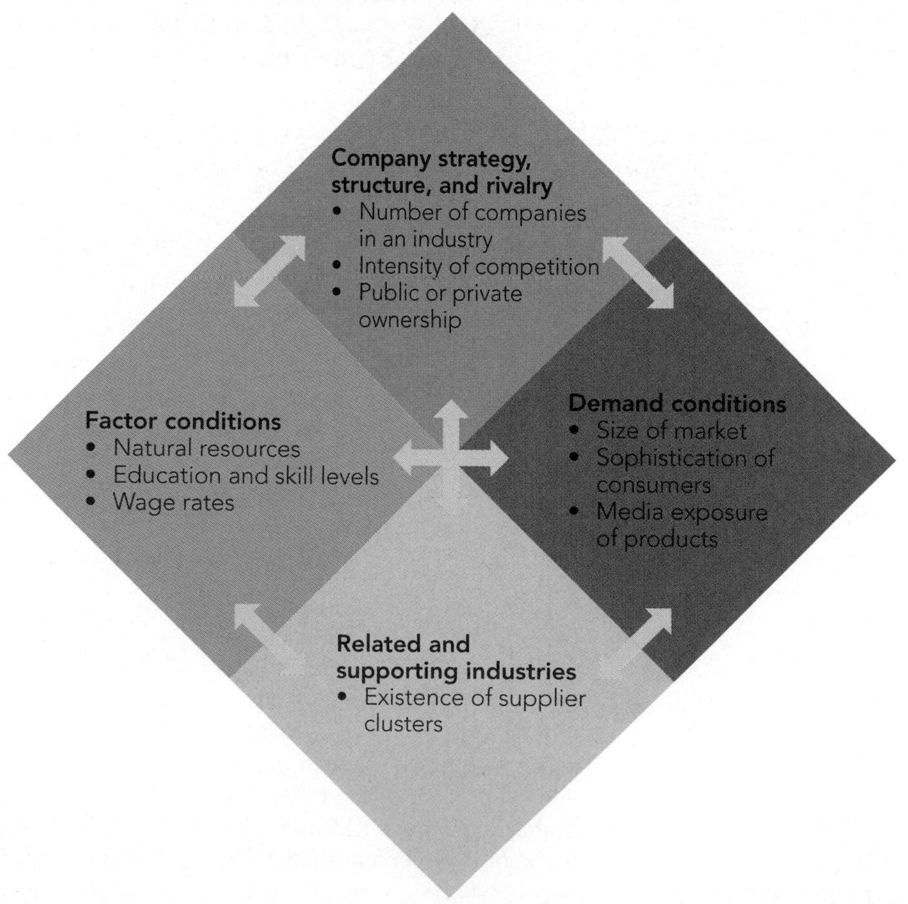

FIGURE 7–2
Porter's diamond of national competitive advantage contains four key elements that explain why some industries and firms in different countries become world leaders.

Sharp and Bruno Magli have succeeded in the global marketplace as well as in their domestic markets.

Sharp Corporation
www.sharpusa.com

Bruno Magli
www.brunomagli.it

a world leader because of intense domestic competition among firms such as MAB, Bruno Magli, and Rossimoda, which has made shoes for Christian Dior and Anne Klein Couture.

Case histories of firms in more than 100 industries were analyzed in Porter's study. While the strategies used by successful global competitors differed in many respects, a common theme emerged: A firm that succeeds in global markets has first succeeded in intense domestic competition. Hence, competitive advantage for global firms grows out of continuous improvement, innovation, and change.

However, pursuit of a country's competitive advantage in global markets has a dark side—economic espionage.[5] *Economic espionage* is the clandestine collection of trade secrets or proprietary information about competitors. This practice is common in high-technology industries such as electronics, specialty chemicals, industrial equipment, aerospace, and pharmaceuticals, where technical know-how and trade secrets separate global industry leaders from followers. It is estimated that economic espionage costs U.S. firms $250 billion a year. The intelligence services of some 23 nations routinely target U.S. firms for information about research and development efforts, manufacturing and marketing plans, and customer lists. To counteract this threat, the **Economic Espionage Act (1996)** makes the theft of trade secrets by foreign entities a federal crime in the United States. This act prescribes prison sentences of up to 15 years and fines up to $500,000 for individuals. Agents of foreign governments found guilty of economic espionage face a 25-year prison sentence and a $10 million fine.

learning review

1. What is the trade feedback effect?
2. What variables influence why some companies and industries in a country succeed globally while others lose ground or fail?

MARKETING IN A BORDERLESS ECONOMIC WORLD

LO2

Global marketing has been and continues to be affected by a growing borderless economic world. Four trends in the past decade have significantly influenced the landscape of global marketing:

Trend 1: Gradual decline of economic protectionism by individual countries.

Trend 2: Formal economic integration and free trade among nations.

Trend 3: Global competition among global companies for global customers.

Trend 4: Emergence of a networked global marketspace.

Decline of Economic Protectionism

Protectionism is the practice of shielding one or more industries within a country's economy from foreign competition through the use of tariffs or quotas. The argument for protectionism is that it limits the outsourcing of jobs, protects a nation's political security, discourages economic dependency on other countries, and promotes development of domestic industries. Read the accompanying Making Responsible Decisions box and ask yourself if protectionism has an ethical dimension.[6]

Tariffs and quotas discourage world trade as depicted in Figure 7–3. **Tariffs**, which are a government tax on goods or services entering a country, primarily serve to raise prices on imports. The average tariff on manufactured goods in industrialized countries is 4 percent. However, wide differences exist across nations. For example, European Union countries have a 10 percent tariff on cars imported from Japan, which is about four times higher than the tariff imposed by the United States on Japanese cars.

The effect of tariffs on consumer prices is substantial. Consider U.S. rice exports to Japan. The U.S. Rice Millers' Association claims that if the Japanese rice market were opened to imports by lowering tariffs, lower prices would save Japanese consumers $6 billion annually, and the United States would gain a large share of the Japanese rice market. Tariffs imposed on bananas by European Union countries cost

FIGURE 7–3
How does protectionism affect world trade? Protectionism hinders world trade through tariff and quota policies of individual countries. Tariffs increase prices and quotas limit supply.

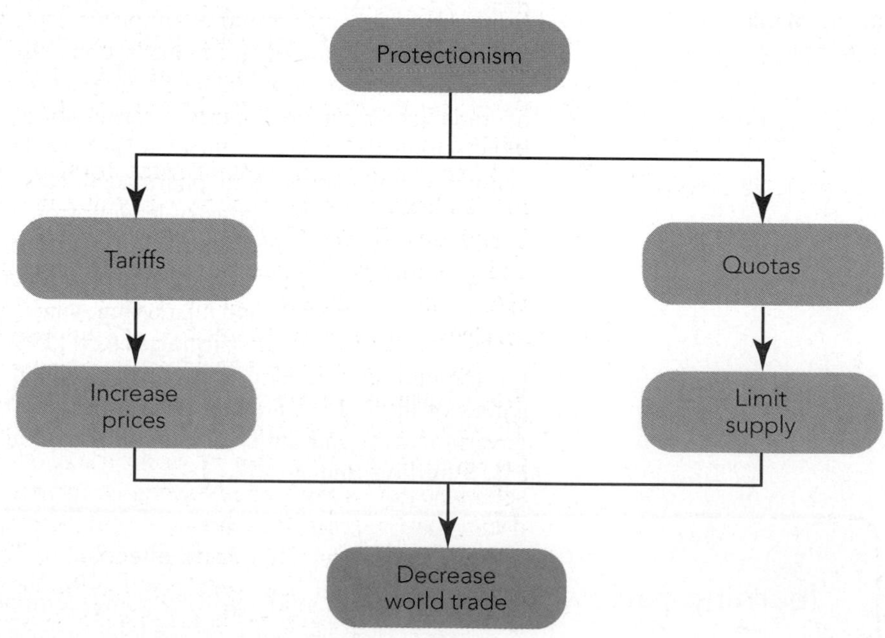

Making Responsible Decisions > > > > > > > ethics

Global Ethics and Global Economics—The Case of Protectionism

World trade benefits from free and fair trade among nations. Nevertheless, governments of many countries continue to use tariffs and quotas to protect their various domestic industries. Why? Protectionism earns profits for domestic producers and tariff revenue for the government. There is a cost, however. Protectionist policies cost Japanese consumers between $75 billion and $110 billion annually. U.S. consumers pay about $70 billion each year in higher prices because of tariffs and other protective restrictions.

Sugar and textile import quotas in the United States, automobile and banana import tariffs in European countries, shoe import tariffs in the United States, beer import tariffs in Canada, and rice import tariffs in Japan protect domestic industries but also interfere with world trade for these products. Regional trade agreements, such as those found in the provisions of the European Union and the North American Free Trade Agreement, may also pose a situation whereby member nations can obtain preferential treatment in quotas and tariffs but nonmember nations cannot.

Protectionism, in its many forms, raises an interesting global ethical question. Is protectionism, no matter how applied, an ethical practice?

consumers $2 billion a year, and U.S. consumers pay $5 billion annually for tariffs on imported shoes.

A **quota** is a restriction placed on the amount of a product allowed to enter or leave a country. Quotas can be mandated or voluntary and may be legislated or negotiated by governments. Import quotas seek to guarantee domestic industries access to a certain percentage of their domestic market. For example, there is a limit on imported television sets to Great Britain and Italian quotas on Japanese motorcycles. China has import quotas on corn, cotton, rice, and wheat. The United States also imposes quotas. For instance, U.S. sugar import quotas have existed for more than 50 years and preserve about half of the U.S. sugar market for domestic producers. American consumers pay $1.5 billion annually in extra food costs because of this quota.

Every country engages in some form of protectionism. However, protectionism has declined over the past 50 years due in large part to the *General Agreement on Tariffs and Trade (GATT)*. This international treaty intended to limit trade barriers and promote world trade through the reduction of tariffs, which it did. However, GATT did not address nontariff trade barriers, such as quotas and world trade in services, which often sparked heated trade disputes between nations.

As a consequence, the major industrialized nations of the world formed the **World Trade Organization** (WTO) in 1995 to address an array of world trade issues.[7] There are 153 WTO member countries, including the United States, which account for more than 90 percent of world trade. The WTO is a permanent institution that sets rules governing trade between its members through panels of trade experts who decide on trade disputes between members and issue binding decisions. The WTO reviews more than 200 disputes annually. For instance, the WTO denied Kodak's multimillion-dollar damage claim that the Japanese government protected Fuji Photo from import competition. In another decision, the WTO allowed Britain, Ireland, and the European Union to reclassify U.S.-produced local area network (LAN) computer equipment as telecommunications gear. The new classification effectively doubled the import tariff on these U.S. goods.

Rise of Economic Integration

In recent years, a number of countries with similar economic goals have formed transnational trade groups or signed trade agreements for the purpose of promoting free trade among member nations and enhancing their individual economies. Three of the best-known examples are the European Union (or simply EU), the North American Free Trade Agreement (NAFTA), and the Asian Free Trade Areas.

European Union The European Union consists of 27 member countries that have eliminated most barriers to the free flow of goods, services, capital, and labor across their borders (see Figure 7–4).[8] This single market houses more than 500 million consumers with a combined gross domestic product larger than that of the United States. In addition, 16 countries have adopted a common currency called the *euro*. Adoption of the euro has been a boon to electronic commerce in the EU by eliminating the need to continually monitor currency exchange rates.

The EU creates abundant marketing opportunities because firms do not need to market their products and services on a nation-by-nation basis. Rather, pan-European

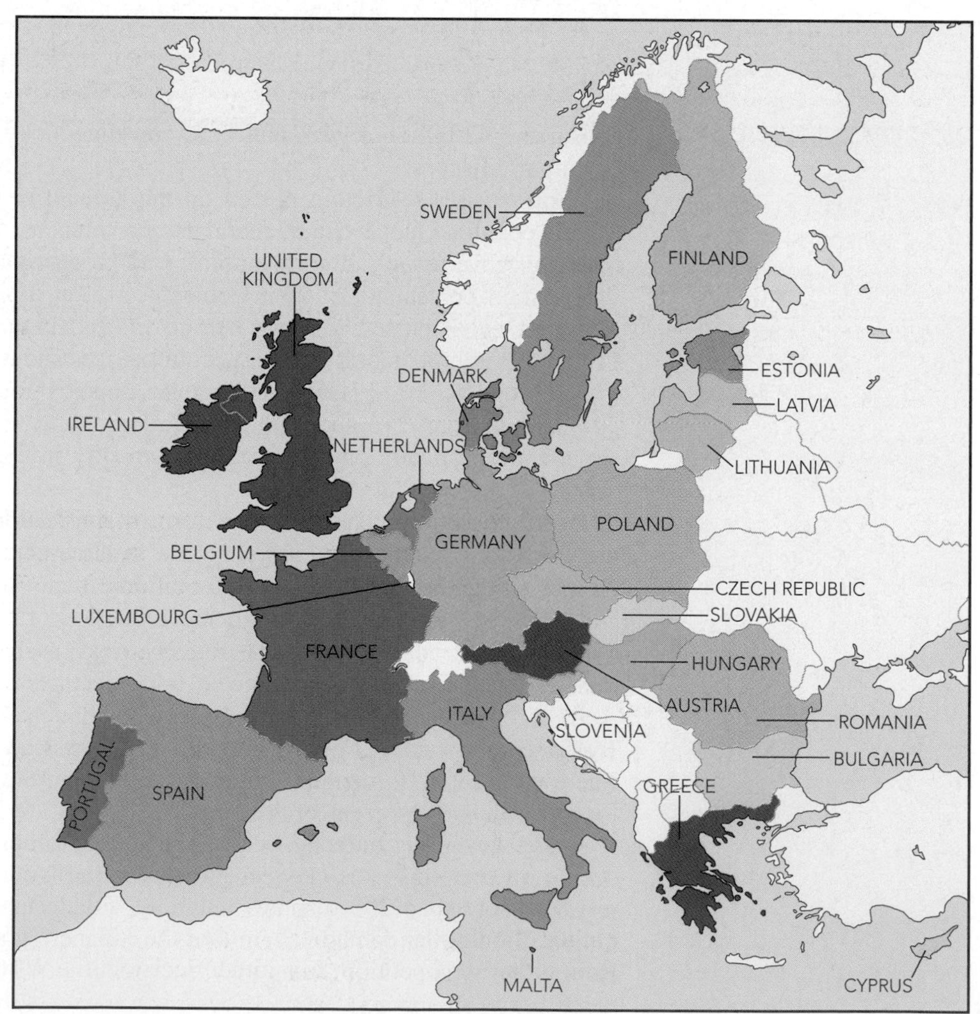

FIGURE 7–4
The European Union in early 2010 consists of 27 countries with more than 500 million consumers.

European Union
www.europa.eu.int

marketing strategies are possible due to greater uniformity in product and packaging standards; fewer regulatory restrictions on transportation, advertising, and promotion imposed by countries; and removal of most tariffs that affect pricing practices. For example, Colgate-Palmolive Company now markets its Colgate toothpaste with one formula and package across EU countries at one price. Black & Decker—the maker of electrical hand tools, appliances, and other consumer products—now produces 8, not 20, motor sizes for the European market, resulting in production and marketing cost savings. These practices were previously impossible because of different government and trade regulations. Europeanwide distribution from fewer locations is also feasible given open borders. French tire maker Michelin closed 180 of its European distribution centers and now uses just 20 to serve all EU countries.

North American Free Trade Agreement The North American Free Trade Agreement lifted many trade barriers between Canada, Mexico, and the United States and created a marketplace with more than 450 million consumers.[9] NAFTA has stimulated trade flows among member nations as well as cross-border retailing, manufacturing, and investment. For example, NAFTA paved the way for Wal-Mart to move to Mexico and Mexican supermarket giant, Gigante, to move into the United States. Whirlpool Corporation's Canadian subsidiary stopped making washing machines in Canada and moved that operation to Ohio. Whirlpool then shifted the production of kitchen ranges and compact dryers to Canada. Ford invested $60 million in its Mexico City manufacturing plant to produce smaller cars and light trucks for global sales.

In 2006, a comprehensive free trade agreement among Costa Rica, the Dominican Republic, El Salvador, Guatemala, Honduras, Nicaragua, and the United States extended many NAFTA benefits to Central American countries and the Dominican Republic. Called CAFTA-DR, this agreement is viewed as a step toward a 34-country Free Trade Area of the Americas for the Western Hemisphere.

Asian Free Trade Agreements Efforts to liberalize trade in East Asia—from Japan and the four "Little Dragons" (Hong Kong, Singapore, South Korea, and Taiwan) through Thailand, Malaysia, and Indonesia—are also growing. Although the trade agreements are less formal than those underlying the EU and NAFTA, they have reduced tariffs among countries and promoted trade.

A New Reality: Global Competition among Global Companies for Global Consumers

The emergence of a largely borderless economic world has created a new reality for marketers of all shapes and sizes. Today, world trade is driven by global competition among global companies for global consumers.

Global Competition **Global competition** exists when firms originate, produce, and market their products and services worldwide. The automobile, pharmaceutical, apparel, electronics, aerospace, and telecommunication fields represent well-known industries with sellers and buyers on every continent. Other industries that are increasingly global in scope include soft drinks, cosmetics, ready-to-eat cereals, snack chips, and retailing.

Global competition broadens the competitive landscape for marketers. The familiar "cola war" waged by Pepsi-Cola and Coca-Cola in the United States has been repeated around the world, including in India, China, and Argentina. Procter & Gamble's Pampers and Kimberly-Clark's Huggies have taken their disposable diaper rivalry from the United States to Western Europe. Boeing and Europe's Airbus vie for lucrative commercial aircraft contracts on virtually every continent.

Pepsi-Cola, now available in more than 190 countries and territories, accounts for a quarter of all soft drinks sold internationally. This Brazilian ad—"How to make jeans last 10 years"—features the popular Diet Pepsi brand targeted at weight-conscious consumers.

PepsiCo, Inc.
www.pepsico.com

Collaborative relationships also are a common way to meet the demands of global competition. Global **strategic alliances** are agreements among two or more independent firms to cooperate for the purpose of achieving common goals such as a competitive advantage or customer value creation. For example, General Mills and Nestlé of Switzerland created Cereal Partners Worldwide to fine-tune Nestlé's European cereal marketing and distribute General Mills cereals worldwide. Today this global alliance produces almost $2 billion in annual sales in more than 130 countries.

Global Companies Three types of companies populate and compete in the global marketplace: (1) international firms, (2) multinational firms, and (3) transnational firms.[10] All three employ people in different countries, and many have administrative, marketing, and manufacturing operations (often called *divisions* or *subsidiaries*) around the world. However, a firm's orientation toward and strategy for global markets and marketing defines the type of company it is or attempts to be.

An *international firm* engages in trade and marketing in different countries as an extension of the marketing strategy in its home country. Generally, these firms market their existing products and services in other countries the same way they do in their home country. Avon, for example, successfully distributes its product line through direct selling in Asia, Europe, and South America, employing virtually the same marketing strategy used in the United States.

A *multinational firm* views the world as consisting of unique parts and markets to each part differently. Multinationals use a **multidomestic marketing strategy**, which means that they have as many different product variations, brand names, and advertising programs as countries in which they do business. For example, Lever Europe, a division of Unilever, markets its fabric softener known as Snuggle in the United States in 10 European countries under seven brand names, including Kuschelweich in Germany, Coccolino in Italy, and Mimosin in France. These products have different packages, different advertising programs, and occasionally different formulas. Procter & Gamble markets Mr. Clean, its popular multipurpose cleaner, in North America and Asia. But you won't necessarily find the Mr. Clean brand in other parts of the world. In many Latin American countries, Mr. Clean is Mastro Limpio. Mr. Clean is Mr. Proper in most parts of Europe, Africa, and the Middle East.

A *transnational firm* views the world as one market and emphasizes cultural similarities across countries or universal consumer needs and wants more than differences. Transnational marketers employ a **global marketing strategy**—the practice of standardizing marketing activities when there are cultural similarities and adapting them when cultures differ. This approach benefits marketers by allowing them to realize economies of scale from their production and marketing activities.

Global marketing strategies are popular among many business-to-business marketers such as Caterpillar and Komatsu (heavy construction equipment) and Texas Instruments, Intel, Hitachi, and Motorola (semiconductors). Consumer goods marketers such as Timex, Seiko, and Swatch (watches), Coca-Cola and Pepsi-Cola (cola soft drinks), Mattel and Lego (children's toys), Nike and Adidas (athletic shoes), Gillette (personal care products), L'Oréal and Shiseido (cosmetics), and McDonald's (quick-service restaurants) successfully execute this strategy.

Each of these companies markets a **global brand**—a brand marketed under the same name in multiple countries with similar and centrally coordinated marketing programs.[11] Global brands have the same product formulation or service concept, deliver the same benefits to consumers, and use consistent advertising across multiple countries and cultures. This isn't to say that global brands are not sometimes tailored to specific cultures or countries. However, adaptation is used only when necessary to better connect the brand to consumers in different markets. Consider McDonald's.[12] This global marketer has adapted its proven formula of "food, fun, and families" across 118 countries on six continents. Although the Golden Arches and Ronald McDonald appear worldwide, McDonald's tailors other aspects of its marketing program. It serves beer in Germany, wine in France, and coconut, mango, and tropical mint shakes in Hong Kong. Hamburgers are made with different meat and spices in Japan, Thailand, India, and the Philippines. But McDonald's world-famous French fry is standardized. Its French fry in Beijing, China, tastes like the one in Paris, France, which tastes like the one in your neighborhood.

Global Consumers Global competition among global companies often focuses on the identification and pursuit of global consumers as described in the Marketing Matters box on the next page.[13] **Global consumers** consist of consumer groups living in many countries or regions of the world who have similar needs or seek similar features and benefits from products or services. Evidence suggests the presence of a global middle-income class, a youth market, and an elite segment, each consuming or using a common assortment of products and services, regardless of geographic location. A variety of companies have capitalized on the global consumer. Whirlpool, Sony, and IKEA have benefited from the growing global middle-income class desire for kitchen appliances, consumer electronics, and home furnishings, respectively. Levi Strauss, Nike, Coca-Cola, and Apple have tapped the global youth market. DeBeers, Chanel, Gucci, Rolls-Royce, and Sotheby's and Christie's, the world's largest fine art and antique auction houses, cater to the elite segment for luxury goods worldwide.

Emergence of a Networked Global Marketspace

The use of Internet technology as a tool for exchanging goods, services, and information on a global scale is the fourth trend affecting world trade. Over 1.7 billion businesses, educational institutions, government agencies, and households worldwide are expected to have Internet access by 2012. The broad reach of this technology suggests that its potential for promoting world trade is huge.

A networked global marketspace enables the exchange of goods, services, and information from sellers *anywhere* to buyers *anywhere* at *any time* and at a lower cost. In particular, companies engaged in business-to-business marketing have spurred the growth of global electronic commerce.[14] Ninety percent of global

Marketing Matters > > > > > > > customer value

The Global Teenager—A Market of 2 Billion Voracious Consumers with $200 Billion to Spend

The "global teenager" market consists of 2 billion 13- to 19-year-olds in Europe, North and South America, and industrialized nations of Asia and the Pacific Rim who have experienced intense exposure to television (MTV broadcasts in 169 countries in 33 languages), movies, travel, the Internet, and global advertising by companies such as Apple, Sony, Nike, and Coca-Cola. The similarities among teens across these countries are greater than their differences. For example, a global study of middle-class teenagers' rooms in 25 industrialized countries indicated it was difficult, if not impossible, to tell whether the rooms were in Los Angeles, Mexico City, Tokyo, Rio de Janeiro, Sydney, or Paris. Why? Teens spend $200 billion annually for a common gallery of products: Nintendo video games, Tommy Hilfiger apparel, Levi's blue jeans, Nike and Adidas athletic shoes, Swatch watches, Apple iPods, Benetton apparel (shown in the photo), and Procter & Gamble Clearasil facial medicine.

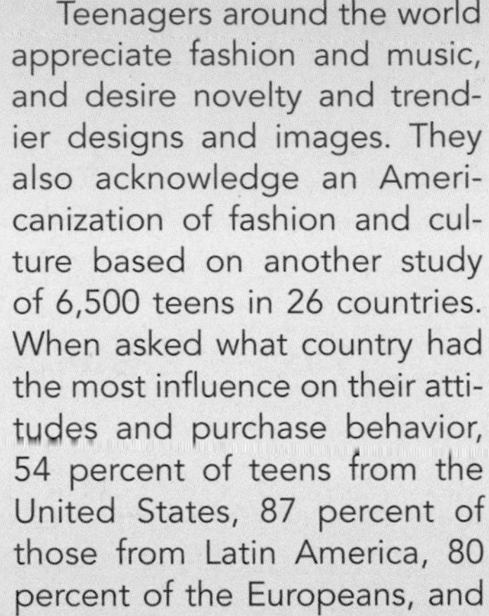

Teenagers around the world appreciate fashion and music, and desire novelty and trendier designs and images. They also acknowledge an Americanization of fashion and culture based on another study of 6,500 teens in 26 countries. When asked what country had the most influence on their attitudes and purchase behavior, 54 percent of teens from the United States, 87 percent of those from Latin America, 80 percent of the Europeans, and 80 percent of those from Asia named the United States. This phenomenon has not gone unnoticed by parents. As one parent in India said, "Now the youngsters dress, talk, and eat like Americans."

electronic commerce revenue arises from business-to-business transactions among a dozen countries in North America, Western Europe, and the Asia/Pacific Rim region. Industries that have benefited from this technology include industrial chemicals and controls; maintenance, repair, and operating supplies; computer and electronic equipment and components; aerospace parts; and agricultural and energy products. The United States, Canada, United Kingdom, Germany, Sweden, Japan, India, China, and Taiwan are among the most active participants in worldwide business-to-business electronic commerce.

Sweden's IKEA is capitalizing on the home-improvement trend sweeping through China. The home-furnishings retailer is courting young Chinese consumers who are eagerly updating their housing with modern, colorful but inexpensive furniture. IKEA entered China in 1998. The company expected to have at least 10 stores open in China by 2010.

IKEA
www.ikea.com

Marketers recognize that the networked global marketspace offers unprecedented access to prospective buyers on every continent. Companies that have successfully capitalized on this access manage multiple country and language Web sites that customize content and communicate with consumers in their native tongue. Nestlé, the world's largest packaged food manufacturer, coffee roaster, and chocolate maker, is a case in point. The company operates 65 individual country Web sites in more than 20 languages that span five continents.

learning review

3. What is protectionism?
4. The North American Free Trade Agreement was designed to promote free trade among which countries?
5. What is the difference between a multidomestic marketing strategy and a global marketing strategy?

A GLOBAL ENVIRONMENTAL SCAN

LO3

Global companies conduct continuing environmental scans of the five sets of environmental factors described earlier in Figure 3–1 (social, economic, technological, competitive, and regulatory forces). This section focuses on three kinds of uncontrollable environmental variables—cultural, economic, and political-regulatory—that affect global marketing practices in strikingly different ways than those in domestic markets.

Cultural Diversity

Marketers must be sensitive to the cultural underpinnings of different societies if they are to initiate and consummate mutually beneficial exchange relationships with global consumers. A necessary step in this process is **cross-cultural analysis**, which involves the study of similarities and differences among consumers in two or more nations or societies.[15] A thorough cross-cultural analysis involves an understanding of and an appreciation for the values, customs, symbols, and language of other societies.

Values A society's **values** represent personally or socially preferable modes of conduct or states of existence that tend to persist over time. Understanding and working with these aspects of a society are important factors in global marketing. For example,

- McDonald's does not sell beef hamburgers in its restaurants in India because the cow is considered sacred by almost 85 percent of the population. Instead, McDonald's sells the Maharaja Mac: two all-chicken patties, special sauce, lettuce, cheese, pickles, onions on a sesame-seed bun.
- Germans have not been overly receptive to the use of credit cards such as Visa or MasterCard and installment debt to purchase goods and services. Indeed, the German word for debt, *Schuld*, is the same as the German word for guilt.

These examples illustrate how cultural values can influence behavior in different societies. Cultural values become apparent in the personal values

McDonald's sells its popular Maharaja Mac in India. Read the text to find the ingredients.

McDonald's
www.mcdonalds.com

Cultural symbols evoke deep feelings. What cultural lesson did Coca-Cola executives learn when they used the Eiffel Tower and the Parthenon in a global advertising campaign? Read the text to find the answer.

of individuals that affect their attitudes and beliefs and the importance assigned to specific behaviors and attributes of goods and services. These personal values affect consumption-specific values, such as the use of installment debt by Germans, and product-specific values, such as the importance assigned to credit card interest rates.

Customs **Customs** are what is considered normal and expected about the way people do things in a specific country. Clearly customs can vary significantly from country to country. For example, 3M Company executives were perplexed when the company's Scotch-Brite floor-cleaning product initially produced lukewarm sales in the Philippines. When a Filipino employee explained that consumers there customarily clean floors by pushing coconut shells around with their feet, 3M changed the shape of the pad to a foot and sales soared. Some other customs may seem unusual to Americans. Consider, for example, that in France, men wear more than twice the number of cosmetics that women do and that Japanese women give Japanese men chocolates on Valentine's Day.

The custom of giving token business gifts is popular in many countries where they are expected and accepted. However, bribes, kickbacks, and payoffs offered to entice someone to commit an illegal or improper act on behalf of the giver for economic gain is considered corrupt in any culture. The prevalence of bribery in global marketing has led to an agreement among the world's major exporting nations to make bribery of foreign government officials a criminal offense. This agreement is patterned after the **Foreign Corrupt Practices Act (1977)**, as amended by the *International Anti-Dumping and Fair Competition Act* (1998). These acts make it a crime for U.S. corporations to bribe an official of a foreign government or political party to obtain or retain business in a foreign country. For example, the German engineering company Siemens AG paid an $800 million fine for $1 billion in alleged bribes of government officials around the globe.[16]

Customs also relate to nonverbal behavior of individuals in different cultural settings. The story is told of U.S. executives negotiating a purchase agreement with their Japanese counterparts. The chief American negotiator made a proposal that was met with silence by the Japanese head negotiator. The American assumed the offer was not acceptable and raised the offer, which again was met with silence. A third offer was made, and an agreement was struck. Unknown to the American, the silence of the Japanese head negotiator meant that the offer was being considered, not rejected. The Japanese negotiator obtained several concessions from the American because of a misreading of silence. Unlike U.S. businesspeople, who tend to express opinions early in meetings and negotiations, Japanese executives prefer to wait and listen. The higher their position, such as chief negotiator, the more they listen.[17]

Cultural Symbols **Cultural symbols** are things that represent ideas and concepts. Symbols and symbolism play an important role in cross-cultural analysis because different cultures attach different meanings to things. So important is the role of symbols that a field of study, called **semiotics**, has emerged that examines the correspondence between symbols and their role in the assignment of meaning for people. By adroitly using cultural symbols, global marketers can tie positive symbolism to their products, services, and brands to enhance their attractiveness to consumers. However, improper use of symbols can spell disaster. A culturally sensitive global marketer will know that:[18]

- North Americans are superstitious about the number 13, and Japanese feel the same way about the number 4. *Shi*, the Japanese word for four, is also the word for death. Knowing this, Tiffany & Company sells its fine glassware and china in sets of five, not four, in Japan.
- "Thumbs-up" is a positive sign in the United States. However, in Russia and Poland, this gesture has an offensive meaning when the palm of the hand is shown, as AT&T learned. The company reversed the gesture depicted in ads, showing the back of the hand, not the palm.

Microsoft operates in over 100 countries and more often than not speaks to its customers in their own language. Read the text to learn how language affects global marketing.

Microsoft Corporation
www.microsoft.com

Cultural symbols evoke deep feelings. Consider how executives at Coca-Cola Company's Italian office learned this lesson. In a series of advertisements directed at Italian vacationers, the Eiffel Tower, the Empire State Building, and the Tower of Pisa were turned into the familiar Coca-Cola bottle. However, when the white marble columns in the Parthenon that crowns the Acropolis in Athens were turned into Coca-Cola bottles, the Greeks were outraged. Greeks refer to the Acropolis as the "holy rock," and a government official said the Parthenon is an "international

What does the Nestlé Kit Kat bar have to do with academic achievement in Japan? Read the text to find out.

Nestlé Company
www.nestle.com

symbol of excellence" and that "whoever insults the Parthenon insults international culture." Coca-Cola apologized for the ad.[19]

Global marketers are also sensitive to the fact that the country of origin or manufacture of products and services can symbolize superior or poor quality in some countries. For example, Russian consumers believe products made in Japan and Germany are superior in quality to products from the United States and the United Kingdom. Japanese consumers believe Japanese products are superior to those made in Europe and the United States. About a third of Americans say the quality of products from other countries are not as good as products made in the United States.[20]

Language Global marketers should not only know the native tongues of countries in which they market their products and services but also the nuances and idioms of a language. Even though about 100 official languages exist in the world, anthropologists estimate that at least 3,000 different languages are spoken. There are 20 official languages spoken in the European Union, and Canada has two official languages (English and French). Seventeen major languages are spoken in India alone.

English, French, and Spanish are the principal languages used in global diplomacy and commerce. However, the best language to communicate with consumers is their own, as any seasoned global marketer will attest to. Unintended meanings of brand names and messages have ranged from the absurd to the obscene:

- When the advertising agency responsible for launching Procter & Gamble's successful Pert shampoo in Canada realized that the name means "lost" in French, it substituted the brand name Pret, which means "ready."
- In Italy, Cadbury Schweppes, the world's third-largest soft-drink manufacturer, realized that its Schweppes Tonic Water brand had to be renamed Schweppes Tonica because "il water" turned out to be the idiom for a bathroom.
- The Vicks brand name common in the United States is German slang for sexual intimacy; therefore, Vicks is called Wicks in Germany.

Experienced global marketers use **back translation**, where a translated word or phrase is retranslated into the original language by a different interpreter to catch errors. For example, IBM's first Japanese translation of its "Solution for a small planet" advertising message yielded "Answers that make people smaller." The error was caught and corrected. Nevertheless, unintended translations can produce favorable results. Consider Kit Kat bars marketed by Nestlé worldwide. Kit Kat is pronounced "kitto katsu" in Japanese, which roughly translates to "I hope you win." Japanese teens eat Kit Kat bars for good luck, particularly when taking crucial school exams.[21]

The importance of language in global marketing is assuming greater importance in an increasingly networked and borderless economic world. For example, Oracle Corporation, a leading worldwide supplier of software, markets its products by language groups instead of through 145 country-specific efforts. The French group markets to France, Belgium, Switzerland, and Canada. A Spanish-language group oversees Spain and Latin America. Eight other language groups—English, Japanese, Korean, Chinese, Portuguese, Italian, Dutch, and German—cover Oracle's top revenue-producing countries.[22]

Cultural Ethnocentricity The tendency for people to view their own values, customs, symbols, and language favorably is well-known. However, the belief that aspects of one's culture are superior to another's is called *cultural ethnocentricity* and is a sure impediment to successful global marketing.

An outgrowth of cultural ethnocentricity exists in the purchase and use of goods and services produced outside of a country. Global marketers are acutely aware that certain groups within countries disfavor imported products, not on the basis of price, features, or performance, but purely because of their foreign origin. **Consumer**

ethnocentrism is the tendency to believe that it is inappropriate, indeed immoral, to purchase foreign-made products.[23] Ethnocentric consumers believe that buying imported products is wrong because such purchases are unpatriotic, harm domestic industries, and cause domestic unemployment. Consumer ethnocentrism has been observed among a segment of the population in the United States, France, Japan, Korea, and Germany as well as other parts of Europe and Asia. The prevalence of consumer ethnocentrism makes the job of global marketers more difficult.[24]

Economic Considerations

Global marketing is also affected by economic considerations. Therefore, a scan of the global marketplace should include: (1) a comparative analysis of the economic development in different countries, (2) an assessment of the economic infrastructure in these countries, (3) measurement of consumer income in different countries, and (4) recognition of a country's currency exchange rates.

Stage of Economic Development There are 195 independent countries in the world today, each of which is at a slightly different point in terms of its stage of economic development. However, they can be classified into two major groupings that will help the global marketer better understand their needs:

- *Developed* countries have somewhat mixed economies. Private enterprise dominates, although they have substantial public sectors as well. The United States, Canada, Japan, and most of Western Europe can be considered developed.
- *Developing* countries are in the process of moving from an agricultural to an industrial economy. There are two subgroups within the developing category: (1) those that have already made the move and (2) those that remain locked in a preindustrial economy. Countries such as Brazil, Poland, Hungary, India, China, Slovenia, Australia, Israel, Venezuela, and South Africa fall into the first group. In the second group are Afghanistan, Sri Lanka, Ethiopia, Tanzania, and Chad, where living standards are low and improvement will be slow.

About 86 percent of the world's population of roughly 6.9 billion people reside in developing countries on one-fifth of total world income. Four billion of these people live on less than $2 per day. In global marketing terms, they are viewed as being at the **bottom of the pyramid**, which is the largest, but poorest socioeconomic group of people in the world.[25]

Today, global companies are choosing to serve people at the bottom of the pyramid by being responsive to their conditions and needs. Motorola is an example. The company developed a low-cost cell phone with battery life as long as 500 hours for rural villagers without regular electricity and an extra-loud volume for use in noisy markets. Motorola's cell phone, a no-frills design priced at $40, has a standby time of two weeks and conforms to local languages and customs. Motorola has been successful selling this cell phone design in rural areas across China, India, and Turkey. Still, the task facing global marketers is not easy. A country's stage of economic development affects and is affected by other economic factors, as described next.

Economic Infrastructure The *economic infrastructure*—a country's communications, transportation, financial, and distribution systems—is a critical consideration in determining whether to try to market to a country's consumers and organizations. Parts of the infrastructure that North Americans or Western Europeans take for granted can be huge problems elsewhere—not only in developing nations but even in Eastern Europe, the Indian subcontinent, and China where such an infrastructure is assumed to be in place.[26] Two-lane roads outside major urban centers that limit average speeds to 35 to 40 miles per hour are common and a nightmare for firms requiring prompt truck delivery in these countries. In China, the bicycle is

The Coca-Cola Company has made a huge financial investment in bottling and distribution facilities in Russia.

The Coca-Cola Company
www.thecoca-colacompany.com

the preferred mode of transportation. This is understandable because China has few navigable roads outside its major cities where 80 percent of the population lives. In India, Coca-Cola uses large tricycles to distribute cases of Coke along narrow streets in many cities. Wholesale and retail institutions tend to be small, and a majority are operated by new owner–managers in many of these countries who are still learning the ways of a free market system.

The communication infrastructures in these countries also differ. This infrastructure includes telecommunication systems and networks in use, such as telephones, cable television, broadcast radio and television, computer, satellite, and wireless telephone. In general, the communication infrastructure in many developing countries is limited or antiquated compared with that of developed countries.

Even the financial and legal system can cause problems. Formal operating procedures among financial institutions and the notion of private property is still limited. As a consequence, it is estimated that two-thirds of the commercial transactions in Russia involve nonmonetary forms of payment. The legal red tape involved in obtaining titles to buildings and land for manufacturing, wholesaling, and retailing operations also has been a huge problem. Still, the Coca-Cola Company invested $750 million from 1991 through 1998 to build bottling and distribution facilities in Russia, and Frito-Lay spent $60 million to build a plant outside Moscow to make Lay's potato chips.

Consumer Income and Purchasing Power A global marketer selling consumer goods must also consider what the average per capita or household income is among a country's consumers and how the income is distributed to determine a nation's purchasing power. Per capita income varies greatly between nations. Average yearly per capita income in EU countries is about $34,000 and is less than $500 in some developing countries such as Liberia. A country's income distribution is important because it gives a more reliable picture of a country's purchasing power. Generally, as the proportion of middle-income households in a country increases, the greater a nation's purchasing power tends to be.

Figure 7–5 shows the worldwide disparity in the percentage distribution of households by level of purchasing power. In established market economies such as those in North America and Western Europe, 65 percent of households have an annual purchasing capability of $20,000 or more. In comparison, 75 percent of households

FIGURE 7–5
Clear differences exist in household purchasing power around the world. This figure shows that 65 percent of households in established market economies, such as those in North America and Western Europe, have an annual purchasing power of $20,000 or more. By comparison, 75 percent of households in South Asia and Sub-Saharan Africa have a purchasing power of less than $5,000.

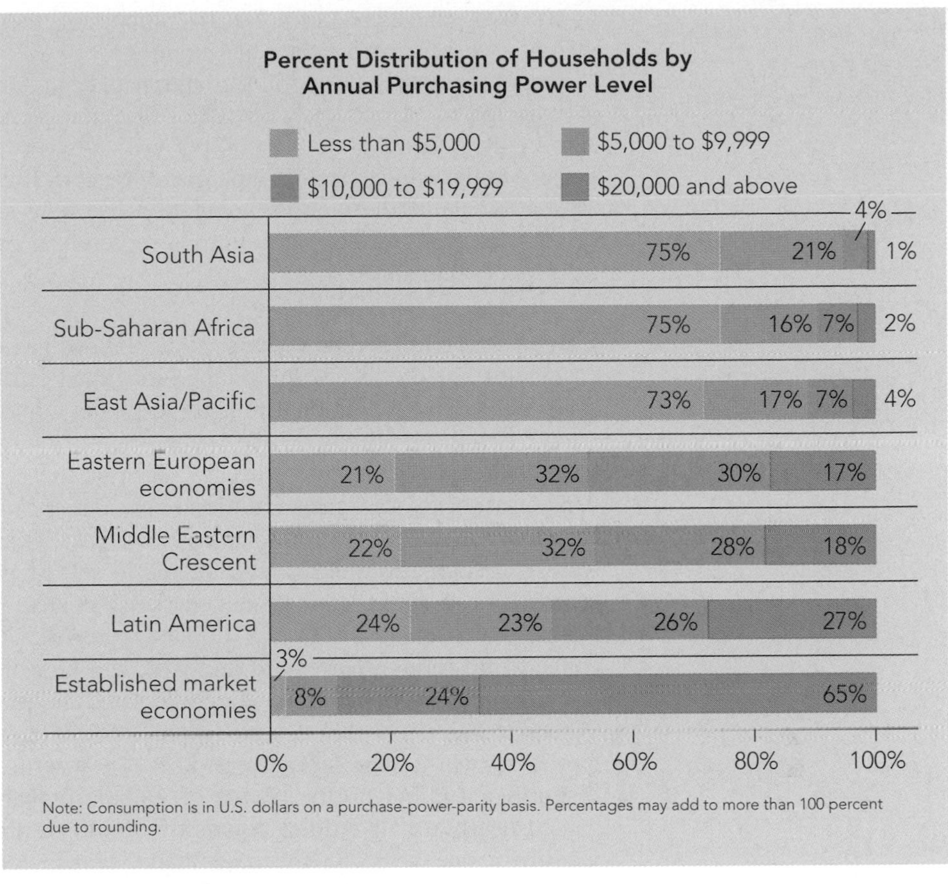

in the developing countries of Sub-Saharan Africa have an annual purchasing power of less than $5,000.[27]

Seasoned global marketers recognize that people in developing countries often have government subsidies for food, housing, and health care that supplement their income. So people with seemingly low incomes are actually promising customers for a variety of products. For instance, a consumer in South Asia earning the equivalent of $250 per year can afford Gillette razors. When that consumer's income rises to $1,000, a Sony television becomes affordable, and a new Volkswagen or Nissan can be bought with an annual income of $10,000. In developing countries of Eastern Europe, a $1,000 annual income makes a refrigerator affordable, and $2,000 brings an automatic washer within reach—good news for Whirlpool, the world's leading manufacturer and marketer of major home appliances.

Hindustan Lever's Project Shakti initiative in India has resulted in 45,000 women entrepreneurs selling Lever products in 100,000 villages—with more to come.

Unilever
www.unilever .com

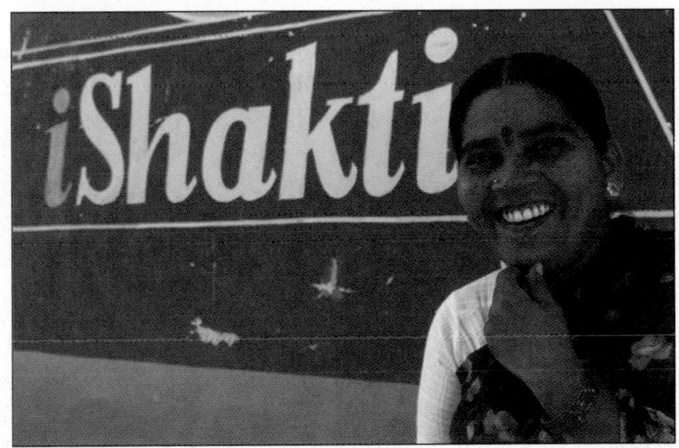

Efforts to raise household incomes in developing countries is evident in the popularity of microfinance. **Microfinance** is the practice of offering small, collateral-free loans to individuals who otherwise would not have access to the capital necessary to begin small businesses or other income-generating activities. An example of microfinance is found in Hindustan Lever's Project Shakti initiative in India. The company realized it could not sell to the rural poor in India unless it found ways to distribute its products such as soap, shampoos, and laundry detergents. Lever provided start-up loans to women to buy stocks of products to sell to local villagers. Today, about 45,000 women entrepreneurs sell Lever products in 100,000 villages in India. Equally important, these women now have a source of income, whereas before they had nothing.[28]

Income growth in developing countries of Asia, Latin America, and Eastern Europe is expected to stimulate world trade. The number of consumers in these countries earning the equivalent of $10,000 per year is expected to surpass the number of consumers in the United States, Japan, and Western Europe combined by 2015. By one estimate, half of the world's population has now achieved "middle-class" status.[29] For this reason, developing countries represent a prominent marketing opportunity for global companies.

Currency Exchange Rates Fluctuations in exchange rates among the world's currencies are of critical importance in global marketing. Such fluctuations affect everyone, from international tourists to global companies.

A **currency exchange rate** is the price of one country's currency expressed in terms of another country's currency, such as the U.S. dollar expressed in Japanese yen, euros, or Swiss francs. Failure to consider exchange rates when pricing products for global markets can have dire consequences. Mattel learned this lesson the hard way. The company was recently unable to sell its popular Holiday Barbie doll and accessories in some international markets because they were too expensive. Why? Barbie prices, expressed in U.S. dollars, were set without regard for how they would convert into foreign currencies and were too high for many buyers.[30]

Exchange rate fluctuations affect the sales and profits made by global companies. When foreign currencies can buy more U.S. dollars, for example, U.S. products are less expensive for the foreign customer. Short-term fluctuations, however, can have a significant effect on the profits of global companies.[31] Hewlett-Packard recently gained nearly a half million dollars of additional profit through exchange rate fluctuation in one year. On the other hand, Honda recently lost $408 million on its European operations alone because of currency swings in the Japanese yen compared with the euro and British pound. Severe and protracted fluctuations in a country's currency can affect trade as well. For example, Procter & Gamble briefly suspended product shipments to Turkey, one of its largest export markets, because of instability of the Turkish currency.

Political-Regulatory Climate

The political and regulatory climate for marketing in a country or region of the world lies not only in identifying the current climate but in determining how long a favorable or unfavorable climate will last. An assessment of a country or regional political-regulatory climate includes an analysis of its political stability and trade regulations.

Political Stability Trade among nations or regions depends on political stability. Billions of dollars have been lost in the Middle East and Africa as a result of internal political strife, terrorism, and war. Losses such as these encourage careful selection of politically stable countries and regions of the world for trade.

Political stability in a country is affected by numerous factors, including a government's orientation toward foreign companies and trade with other countries. These factors combine to create a political climate that is favorable or unfavorable for marketing and financial investment in a country or region of the world. Marketing managers monitor political stability using a variety of measures and often track country risk ratings supplied by agencies such as the PRS Group. Visit the PRS Group Web site shown in the accompanying Going Online box to see political risk ratings for 140 countries. Expect to be surprised by the ranking of countries.

Going Online

Checking a Country's Political Risk Rating

The political climate in every country is regularly changing. Governments can make new laws or enforce existing policies differently. Numerous consulting firms prepare political risk analyses that incorporate a variety of variables such as the risk of internal turmoil, external conflict, government restrictions on company operations, and tariff and nontariff trade barriers.

The PRS Group maintains multiple databases of country-specific information and projections, including country political risk ratings. These ratings can be accessed at www.prsgroup.com. Click "Intl. Country Risk Guide" followed by "Sample Tables." Then click "Table 1: Country Risk, Ranked by Composite Rating" (you will need to give your name and e-mail address to obtain the table). Which three countries have the highest rating (lowest risk), and which three have the lowest rating (highest risk)? Which countries have risk ratings closest to the United States?

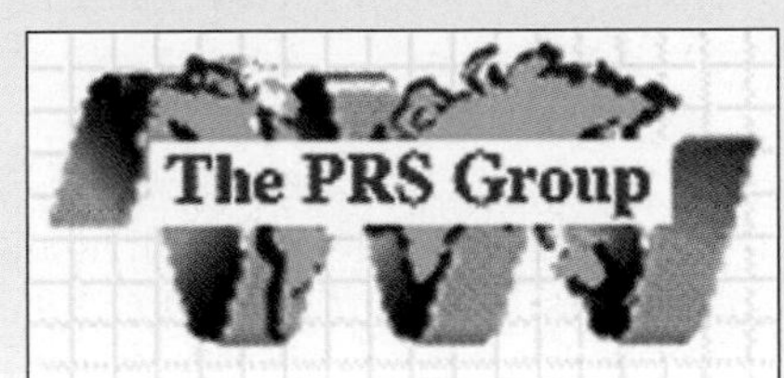

Trade Regulations Countries have a variety of rules that govern business practices within their borders. These rules often serve as trade barriers.[32] For example, Japan has some 11,000 trade regulations. Japanese car safety rules effectively require all automobile replacement parts to be Japanese and not American or European; public health rules make it illegal to sell aspirin or cold medicine without a pharmacist present. The Malaysian government has advertising regulations stating that "advertisements must not project or promote an excessively aspirational lifestyle," Sweden outlaws all advertisements to children, and Saudi Arabia bans Mattel's Barbie dolls because they are a symbol of Western decadence.

Trade regulations also appear in free trade agreements among countries. EU nations abide by some 10,000 rules that specify how goods are to be made and marketed. For instance, the rules for a washing machine's electrical system are detailed on more than 100 typed pages. Regulations related to contacting consumers via telephone, fax, and e-mail without their prior consent also exist. The European Union's ISO 9000 quality standards, though not a trade regulation, have the same effect on business practice. These standards, described in Chapter 6, involve registration and certification of a manufacturer's quality management and quality assurance system. Many European companies require suppliers to be ISO 9000 certified as a condition of doing business with them.

learning review

6. Semiotics involves the study of ______________.
7. When foreign currencies can buy more U.S. dollars, are U.S. products more or less expensive for a foreign consumer?

COMPARING GLOBAL MARKET-ENTRY STRATEGIES

LO4

Once a company has decided to enter the global marketplace, it must select a means of market entry. Four general options exist: (1) exporting, (2) licensing, (3) joint venture, and (4) direct investment.[33] As Figure 7–6 on the next page demonstrates, the amount of financial commitment, risk, marketing control, and profit potential increases as the firm moves from exporting to direct investment.

FIGURE 7–6
A firm's profit potential and control over marketing activities increase as it moves from exporting to direct investment as a global market-entry strategy. But so does a firm's financial commitment and risk. Firms often engage in exporting, licensing, and joint ventures before pursuing a direct investment strategy.

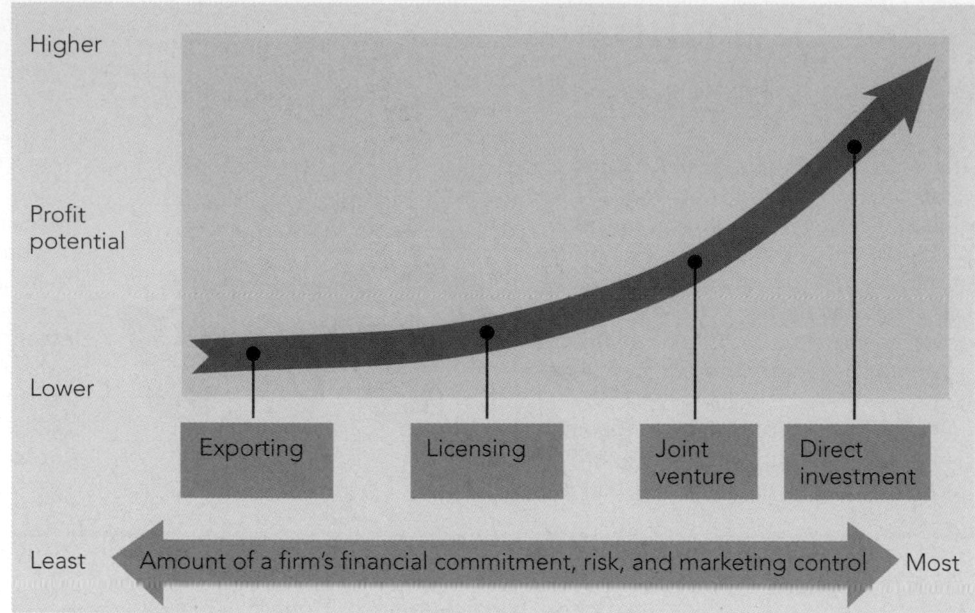

Exporting

Exporting is producing goods in one country and selling them in another country. This entry option allows a company to make the least number of changes in terms of its product, its organization, and even its corporate goals. Host countries usually do not like this practice because it provides less local employment than under alternative means of entry.

Indirect exporting is when a firm sells its domestically produced goods in a foreign country through an intermediary. It has the least amount of commitment and risk but will probably return the least profit. Indirect exporting is ideal for a company that has no overseas contacts but wants to market abroad. The intermediary is often a distributer that has the marketing know-how and resources necessary for the effort to succeed. Fran Wilson Creative Cosmetics uses an indirect exporting approach to sell its products in Japan. Read the accompanying Marketing Matters box to find out how this innovative marketer and its Japanese distributors sell 20 percent of the lipsticks exported to Japan by U.S. cosmetic companies.[34]

Direct exporting is when a firm sells its domestically produced goods in a foreign country without intermediaries. Most companies become involved in direct exporting when they believe their volume of sales will be sufficiently large and easy to obtain so that they do not require intermediaries. For example, the exporter may be approached by foreign buyers that are willing to contract for a large volume of purchases. Direct exporting involves more risk than indirect exporting for the company but also opens the door to increased profits. The Boeing Company applies a direct exporting approach. Boeing is the world's largest aerospace company and the largest U.S. exporter.

Even though exporting is commonly employed by large firms, it is the prominent global market-entry strategy among small- and medium-sized companies. For example, 60 percent of U.S. firms exporting products have fewer than 100 employees. These firms account for about 29 percent of total U.S. merchandise exports.[35]

Licensing

Under licensing, a company offers the right to a trademark, patent, trade secret, or other similarly valued items of intellectual property in return for a royalty or a fee. The advantages to the company granting the license are low risk and a capital-free

Marketing Matters > > > > > entrepreneurship

Creative Cosmetics and Creative Export Marketing in Japan

How does a medium-sized U.S. cosmetics firm sell 1.5 million tubes of lipstick in Japan annually? Fran Wilson Creative Cosmetics can attribute its success to a top-quality product, effective advertising, and a novel export marketing program. The firm's Moodmatcher lip coloring comes in green, orange, silver, black, and six other hues that change to a shade of pink, coral, or red, depending on a woman's chemistry when it's applied.

The company does not sell to department stores. According to a company spokesperson, "Shiseido and Kanebo (two large Japanese cosmetics firms) keep all the other Japanese or import brands out of the major department stores." Rather, the company sells its Moodmatcher lipstick through a network of Japanese distributors that reach Japan's 40,000 beauty salons.

The result? The company, with its savvy Japanese distributors, accounts for 20 percent of the lipsticks exported annually to Japan by U.S. cosmetic companies.

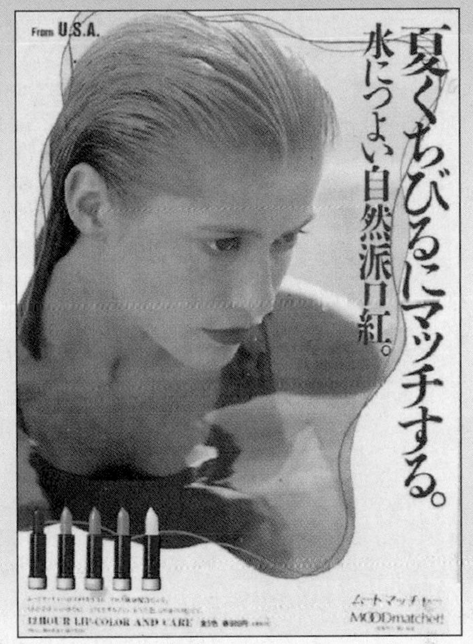

entry into a foreign country. The licensee gains information that allows it to start with a competitive advantage, and the foreign country gains employment by having the product manufactured locally. For instance, Yoplait yogurt is licensed from Sodima, a French cooperative, by General Mills for sales in the United States.

There are some serious drawbacks to this mode of entry, however. The licensor forgoes control of its product and reduces the potential profits gained from it. In addition, while the relationship lasts, the licensor may be creating its own competition. Some licensees are able to modify the product somehow and enter the market with product and marketing knowledge gained at the expense of the company that got them started. To offset this disadvantage, many companies strive to stay innovative so that the licensee remains dependent on them for improvements and successful operation. Finally, should the licensee prove to be a poor choice, the name or reputation of the company may be harmed.

McDonald's uses franchising as a market-entry strategy, and about 66 percent of the company's sales come from non-U.S. operations. Note that the golden arches appear prominently—one aspect of its global brand promise.

McDonald's
www.mcdonalds.com

Two variations of licensing, *contract manufacturing* and *contract assembly*, represent alternative ways to produce a product within the foreign country. With contract manufacturing, a U.S. company may contract with a foreign firm to manufacture products according to stated specifications. The product is then sold in the foreign country or exported back to the United States. With contract assembly, the U.S. company may contract with a foreign firm to assemble (not manufacture) parts and components that have been shipped to that country. In both cases, the advantage to the foreign country is the employment of its people, and the U.S. firm benefits from the lower wage rates in the foreign country.

Contract manufacturing and assembly in developing countries has sparked controversy in the toy, textile, and apparel industries where poor working conditions, low pay, and child labor practices have been documented. However, this practice has been an economic boon to Taiwan where 55 percent of the world's notebook computers are made. In a typical year, U.S. companies such as Dell will have Taiwanese firms supply over half of their notebook computer needs.[36]

A third variation of licensing is *franchising*. Franchising is one of the fastest-growing market-entry strategies. More than 75,000 franchises of U.S. firms are located in countries throughout the world. Franchises include soft-drink, motel, retailing, fast-food, and car rental operations and a variety of business services. McDonald's is a premier global franchiser. With some 18,000 units outside the United States, about 66 percent of McDonald's sales come from non-U.S. operations.[37]

Strauss Group's joint venture with PepsiCo. markets Frito-Lay's Cheetos, Ruffles, Doritos and other snacks in Israel.

Strauss Group
www.strauss-group.com

Joint Venture

When a foreign company and a local firm invest together to create a local business, it is called a **joint venture**. These two companies share ownership, control, and profits of the new company. For example, the Strauss Group has a joint venture with PepsiCo to market Frito-Lay's Cheetos, Ruffles, and Doritos and other snacks in Israel.[38]

The advantages of this option are twofold. First, one company may not have the necessary financial, physical, or managerial resources to enter a foreign market alone. The joint venture between Ericsson, a Swedish telecommunications firm, and CGCT, a French switch maker, enabled them together to beat out AT&T for a $100 million French contract. Ericsson's money and technology combined with CGCT's knowledge of the French market helped them to win the contract that neither of them could have won alone. Second, a government may require or strongly encourage a joint venture before it allows a foreign company to enter its market. This was the case in China. More than 50,000 Chinese-foreign joint ventures now operate in China.

The disadvantages arise when the two companies disagree about policies or courses of action for their joint venture or when governmental bureaucracy bogs down the effort. For example, U.S. firms often prefer to reinvest earnings gained, whereas some foreign companies may want to spend those earnings. Or a U.S. firm may want to return profits earned to the United States, while the local firm or its government may oppose this—the problem faced by many potential joint ventures in Eastern Europe, Russia, Latin America, and South Asia.

Nestlé has made a sizable direct investment in ice cream manufacturing in China to produce its global brands such as Drumstick. Nestlé operates 26 factories in China.

Direct Investment

The biggest commitment a company can make when entering the global market is **direct investment**, which entails a domestic firm actually investing in and owning a foreign subsidiary or division. Examples of direct investment are Nissan's Smyrna, Tennessee, plant that produces pickup trucks and the Mercedes-Benz factory in Vance, Alabama, that makes the M-class sports utility vehicle. Many U.S.-based global companies also use this mode of entry. Reebok entered Russia by creating a subsidiary known as Reebok Russia.

For many companies, direct investment often follows one of the other three market-entry strategies.[39] For example, both FedEx and UPS entered China through joint ventures with Chinese companies. Each subsequently purchased the interests of its partner and converted the Chinese operations into a division. Following on the success of its European and Asian exporting strategy, Harley-Davidson now operates wholly owned marketing and sales subsidiaries in Germany, Italy, the United Kingdom, and Japan, among other countries.

The advantages to direct investment include cost savings, better understanding of local market conditions, and fewer local restrictions. Firms entering foreign markets using direct investment believe that these advantages outweigh the financial commitments and risks involved.

learning review

8. What mode of entry could a company follow if it has no previous experience in global marketing?
9. How does licensing differ from a joint venture?

CRAFTING A WORLDWIDE MARKETING PROGRAM

LO5

The choice of a market-entry strategy is a necessary first step for a marketer when joining the community of global companies. The next step involves the challenging task of planning, implementing, and evaluating marketing programs worldwide.

Successful global marketers standardize global marketing programs whenever possible and customize them wherever necessary. The extent of standardization and customization is often rooted in a careful global environment scan supplemented with judgment based on experience and marketing research.

Product and Promotion Strategies

Global companies have five strategies for matching products and their promotion efforts to global markets. As Figure 7–7 on the next page shows, the strategies focus on whether a company extends or adapts its product and promotion message for consumers in different countries and cultures.

A product may be sold globally in one of three ways: (1) in the same form as in its home market, (2) with some adaptations, or (3) as a totally new product:[40]

1. *Product extension.* Selling virtually the same product in other countries is a product extension strategy. It works well for products such as Coca-Cola, Gillette razors, Wrigley's gum, Levi's jeans, Sony consumer electronics, Harley-Davidson motorcycles, Nike apparel and shoes, and Nokia cell phones. As a general rule, product extension seems to work best when the consumer market target for the product is alike across countries and cultures—that is, consumers share the same desires, needs, and uses for the product.

FIGURE 7–7
Five product and promotion strategies for global marketing exist based on whether a company extends or adapts its product and promotion message for consumers in different countries and cultures.

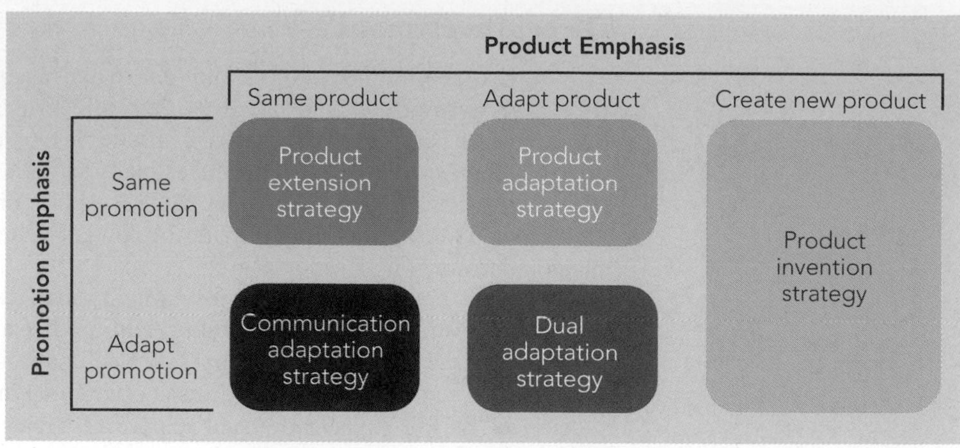

2. *Product adaptation.* Changing a product in some way to make it more appropriate for a country's climate or consumer preferences is a product adaptation strategy. Exxon sells different gasoline blends based on each country's climate. Frito-Lay produces and markets its potato chips in Russia, but don't expect them to taste like the chips eaten in North America. Russians prefer dairy, meat, and seafood-flavored potato chips. Likewise, Gerber baby food comes in different varieties in different countries. Vegetable and rabbit meat is a favorite food in Poland. Freeze-dried sardines and rice is popular in Japan. Maybelline's makeup is formulaically adapted to local skin types and weather across the globe, including an Asia-specific mascara that doesn't run during the rainy season.
3. *Product invention.* Alternatively, companies can invent totally new products designed to satisfy common needs across countries. Black & Decker did this with its Snake Light flexible flashlight. Created to address a global need for portable lighting, the product became a best seller in North America, Europe, Latin America, and Australia and is the most successful new product developed by Black & Decker. Similarly, Whirlpool developed a compact, automatic clothes washer specifically for households in developing countries with annual household incomes of $2,000. Called Ideale, the washer features bright colors because washers are often placed in home living areas, not hid in laundry rooms (which don't exist in many homes in developing countries).

An identical promotion message is used for the product extension and product adaptation strategies around the world. Gillette uses the same global message for its men's toiletries: "Gillette, the Best a Man Can Get." Even though Exxon adapts its gasoline blends for different countries based on climate, the promotion message is unchanged: "Put a Tiger in Your Tank."

Global companies may also adapt their promotion message. For instance, the same product may be sold in many countries but advertised differently. As an example, L'Oréal, a French health and beauty products marketer, introduced its Golden Beauty brand of sun care products through its Helena Rubenstein subsidiary in Western Europe with a communication adaptation strategy. Recognizing that cultural and buying motive differences related to skin care and tanning exist, Golden Beauty advertising features dark tanning for northern Europeans, skin protection to avoid wrinkles among Latin Europeans, and beautiful skin for Europeans living along the Mediterranean Sea, even though the products are the same.

Other companies use a dual adaptation strategy by modifying both their products and promotion messages. Nestlé does this with Nescafé coffee. Nescafé is marketed using different coffee blends and promotional campaigns to match consumer preferences in different countries. For example, Nescafé, the world's largest brand of

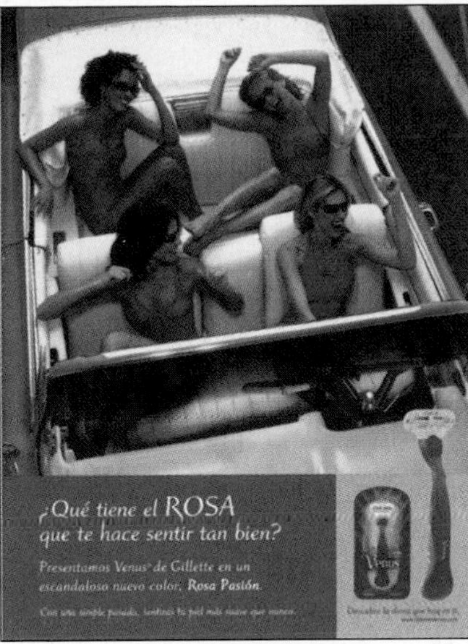

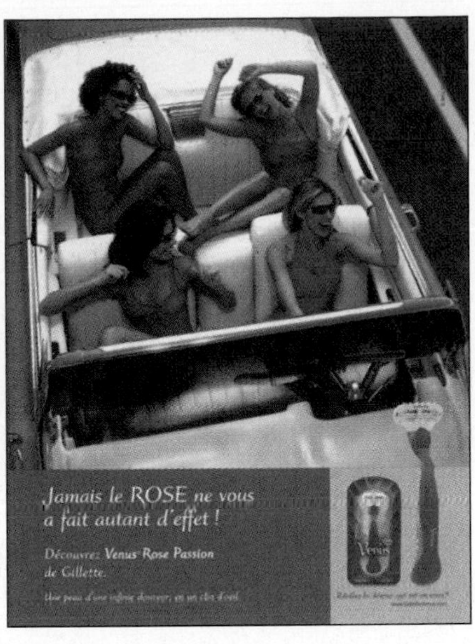

Gillette delivers the same global message whenever possible as shown in the Gillette for Women Venus ads from the United States, Mexico, and France.

The Gillette Company
www.gillette.com

coffee, generally emphasizes the taste, aroma, and warmth of shared moments in its advertising around the world. However, Nescafé is advertised in Thailand as a way to relax from the pressures of daily life.

These examples illustrate the simple rule applied by global companies: Standardize product and promotion strategies whenever possible and customize them wherever necessary. This is the art of global marketing.[41]

Distribution Strategy

Distribution is of critical importance in global marketing. The availability and quality of retailers and wholesalers as well as transportation, communication, and warehousing facilities are often determined by a country's stage of economic development. Figure 7–8 outlines the channel through which a product manufactured in one country must travel to reach its destination in another country. The first step involves the seller; its headquarters is the starting point and is responsible for the successful distribution to the ultimate consumer.

The next step is the channel between two nations, moving the product from one country to another. Intermediaries that can handle this responsibility include resident buyers in a foreign country, independent merchant wholesalers who buy and sell the product, or agents who bring buyers and sellers together.

Once the product is in the foreign nation, that country's distribution channels take over. These channels can be very long or surprisingly short, depending on the product line. In Japan, fresh fish go through three intermediaries before getting to a retail outlet. Conversely, shoes only go through one intermediary. In other cases, the channel does not even involve the host country. Procter & Gamble sells its soap door-to-door in the Philippines because there are no other alternatives in many parts of that country. Dell has had to revise its direct-marketing channel that originally featured online and phone buying in China. Today, Dell markets its home computers and accessories through Gome, China's largest electronics retailer.[42]

FIGURE 7–8
Channels of distribution in global marketing are often long and complex.

Pricing Strategy

Global companies also face many challenges in determining a pricing strategy as part of their worldwide marketing effort. Individual countries, even those with free trade agreements, may impose considerable competitive, political, and legal constraints on the pricing latitude of global companies. For example, antitrust authorities in Germany limited Wal-Mart from selling some items below cost to lure shoppers. Without the practice, Wal-Mart was unable to compete against German discount stores. This, and other factors, led Wal-Mart to leave Germany in 2006 following eight years without a profit.[43] Of course, economic factors such as the costs of production, selling, and tariffs, plus transportation and storage costs, also affect global pricing decisions.

Pricing too low or too high can have dire consequences. When prices appear too low in one country, companies can be charged with dumping, a practice subject to severe penalties and fines. **Dumping** is when a firm sells a product in a foreign country below its domestic price or below its actual cost. This is often done to build a company's share of the market by pricing at a competitive level. Another reason is that the products being sold may be surplus or cannot be sold domestically and, therefore, are already a burden to the company. The firm may be glad to sell them at almost any price. A recent trade dispute involving U.S. apple growers and Mexico is a case in point. Mexican trade officials claimed that U.S. growers were selling their red and golden delicious apples in Mexico below the actual cost of production. They imposed a 101 percent tariff on U.S. apples, and a severe drop in U.S. apple exports to Mexico resulted. Subsequent negotiations set a floor on the price of U.S. apples sold to Mexico.[44]

When companies price their products very high in some countries but competitively in others, they face a gray market problem. A **gray market**, also called *parallel importing*, is a situation where products are sold through unauthorized channels of distribution.[45] A gray market comes about when individuals buy products in a lower-priced country from a manufacturer's authorized retailer, ship them to higher-priced countries, and then sell them below the manufacturer's suggested retail price through unauthorized retailers. Many well-known products have been sold through gray markets, including Seiko watches, Chanel perfume, and Mercedes-Benz cars. Parallel importing is legal in the United States. It is illegal in the European Union.

learning review

10. Products may be sold globally in three ways. What are they?

11. What is dumping?

LEARNING OBJECTIVES REVIEW

LO1 *Describe the nature and scope of world trade from a global perspective and its implications for the United States.*
A global perspective on world trade views exports and imports as complementary economic flows: A country's imports affect its exports and exports affect its imports. World trade flows to and from the United States reflect demand and supply interdependencies for goods among nations and industries. The four largest importers of U.S. goods and services are Canada, China, Mexico, and Japan. The four largest exporters to the United States are Canada, China, Mexico, and Japan. The United States imports more goods than it exports.

LO2 *Identify the major trends that have influenced the landscape of global marketing in the past decade.*
Four major trends have influenced the landscape of global marketing in the past decade. First, there has been a gradual decline of economic protectionism by individual countries, leading to a reduction in tariffs and quotas. Second, there is growing economic integration and free trade among nations, reflected in the creation of the European Union and the North American Free Trade Agreement. Third, there exists global competition among global companies for global consumers, resulting in firms adopting global marketing strategies and promoting global brands. And finally, a networked global marketspace has emerged using Internet technology as a tool for exchanging goods, services, and information on a global scale.

LO3 *Identify the environmental forces that shape global marketing efforts.*
Three major environmental forces shape global marketing efforts. First, there are cultural forces, including values, customs, cultural symbols, and language. Economic forces also

shape global marketing efforts. These include a country's stage of economic development and economic infrastructure, consumer income and purchasing power, and currency exchange rates. Finally, political-regulatory forces in a country or region of the world create a favorable or unfavorable climate for global marketing efforts.

LO4 *Name and describe the alternative approaches companies use to enter global markets.*
Companies have four alternative approaches for entering global markets. These are exporting, licensing, joint venture, and direct investment. Exporting involves producing goods in one country and selling them in another country. Under licensing, a company offers the right to a trademark, patent, trade secret, or similarly valued items of intellectual property in return for a royalty or fee. In a joint venture, a foreign company and a local firm invest together to create a local business. Direct investment entails a domestic firm actually investing in and owning a foreign subsidiary or division.

LO5 *Explain the distinction between standardization and customization when companies craft worldwide marketing programs.*
Companies distinguish between standardization and customization when crafting worldwide marketing programs. Standardization means that all elements of the marketing program are the same across countries and cultures. Customization means that one or more elements of the marketing program are adapted to meet the needs or preferences of consumers in a particular country or culture. Global marketers apply a simple rule when crafting worldwide marketing programs: Standardize marketing programs whenever possible and customize them wherever necessary.

FOCUSING ON KEY TERMS

back translation p. 176
balance of trade p. 163
bottom of the pyramid p. 177
consumer ethnocentrism p. 176
countertrade p. 162
cross-cultural analysis p. 173
cultural symbols p. 175
currency exchange rate p. 180
customs p. 174
direct investment p. 185
dumping p. 188
Economic Espionage Act (1996) p. 165
exporting p. 182
Foreign Corrupt Practices Act (1977) p. 174
global brand p. 171
global competition p. 169
global consumers p. 171
global marketing strategy p. 171
gray market p. 188
gross domestic product (GDP) p. 162
joint venture p. 184
microfinance p. 179
multidomestic marketing strategy p. 170
protectionism p. 166
quota p. 167
semiotics p. 175
strategic alliances p. 170
tariffs p. 166
values p. 173
World Trade Organization p. 167

APPLYING MARKETING KNOWLEDGE

1 What is meant by this statement: "Quotas are a hidden tax on consumers, whereas tariffs are a more obvious one."?

2 Is the trade feedback effect described in the text a long-run or short-run view on world trade flows? Explain your answer.

3 The United States is considered to be a global leader in the development and marketing of pharmaceutical products, and Merck & Co. of New Jersey is a world leader in prescription drug sales. What explanation can you give for this situation based on the text discussion concerning the competitive advantage of nations?

4 How successful would a television commercial in Japan be if it featured a husband surprising his wife in her dressing area on Valentine's Day with a small box of chocolates containing four candies? Why?

5 As a novice in global marketing, which alternative for global market-entry strategy would you be likely to start with? Why? What other alternatives do you have for a global market entry?

6 Coca-Cola is sold worldwide. In some countries, Coca-Cola owns the bottling facilities; in others, it has signed contracts with licensees or relies on joint ventures. When selecting a licensee in each country, what factors should Coca-Cola consider?

building your marketing plan

Does your marketing plan involve reaching global customers outside the United States? If the answer is no, read no further and do not include a global element in your plan. If the answer is yes, try to identify:

1 What features of your product are especially important to potential customers.

2 In which countries these potential customers live.

3 Special marketing issues that are involved in trying to reach them.

Answers to these questions will help in developing more detailed marketing mix strategies described in later chapters.

video case 7 CNS Breathe Right Strips: Going Global

"It's naive to treat 'international' as one big market—particularly within OTC," explains Marti Morfitt, president and CEO of CNS, the company that manufactures Breathe Right® nasal strips. "There are many discrete, unique markets, and local expertise is needed to understand the dynamics within each and address them effectively."

"OTC" refers to over-the-counter medical products such as aspirin or cough syrup that customers can buy without a doctor's prescription. Breathe Right nasal strips qualify as an OTC product. But that doesn't mean there isn't a lot of technology and medical science behind it.

Breathe Right nasal strips are innovative adhesive strips with patented dual flex bars inside. When attached to the nose, they gently lift and hold open nasal passages, making it easier to breathe. Breathe Right strips are used for a variety of reasons, all to help breathe better through the nose: athletes hoping to play their best (particularly when wearing mouth guards); snorers (and their spouses) hoping for a quiet night's sleep; and allergy, sinusitis, and cold sufferers looking for drug-free relief from nasal congestion.

HOW IT ALL BEGAN

Breathe Right strips were invented by Bruce Johnson, a chronic nasal congestion sufferer. At times Johnson put straws or paper clips in his nose at night to keep his nasal passages open. He eventually came up with a prototype for Breathe Right strips. He brought his invention to CNS, Inc., which recognized its market potential. CNS took the strips to the Food and Drug Administration for approval of claims for relief of snoring and nasal congestion.

CNS, a small company, had a limited marketing budget. However, it got a big public relations break when Jerry Rice, the wide receiver for the San Francisco 49ers, wore a Breathe Right strip on national TV and scored two touchdowns during the 49ers' 1995 Super Bowl victory. Demand for the strips soared.

"What really helped sales of Breathe Right strips was that CNS had done a very effective job of getting press kits in the hands of news and sports media," says Morfitt. "When people on television asked, 'What is that funny looking thing on his nose?' the reporters could talk about how the strip was an effective consumer product for everyone. And a $1.4 million business turned into a $45 million business in just one year."

THE DECISION TO GO GLOBAL

As awareness and trial in the United States was building, CNS began to get inquiries from people in other countries

asking where they could buy strips. In 1995 CNS decided to take advantage of global interest and introduce Breathe Right strips internationally.

What countries did CNS choose to enter with its Breathe Right strips? "Countries we focus on are those with a large OTC market, high per-capita spending in the OTC market, and future prospects for growth," says Kevin McKenna, vice president for international at CNS. All these factors relate to market size. "But the real key to success in a market is a local partner that is entrepreneurial and has an ability to execute in terms of achieving distribution and sales."

IMPORTANCE OF LOCAL PARTNERS

Dynamic world market changes in the past 30 years have influenced opportunities for global sales of Breathe Right strips. Key trends include increased availability of OTC products formerly available only by prescription; and a global push toward self-care, spurred by the increasing cost of health and medical care. Additionally, OTC products have extended beyond the traditional boundary of the pharmacy and into grocery and other channels; and the role of the pharmacist has expanded from that of medical professional to one that includes selling and marketing OTC products to consumers.

At the same time, changes were taking place within CNS. When Morfitt joined CNS in 1998, she began pulling together a new management group with extensive experience in marketing consumer packaged goods, both in the United States and abroad. CNS began seeking "hungry" international partners who would bring greater localized market expertise and direct-selling capabilities than past partners. Morfitt also wanted partners with demonstrated entrepreneurial spirit to match that of the new management team.

The company's partner in Italy, BluFarm Group, uses its local knowledge and direct-selling skills to partner with pharmacists to teach them how to increase sales of Breathe Right strips in their stores. In Italy, as throughout much of Europe, OTC products such as antacids, aspirin, and nasal strips are typically placed behind pharmacy counters and therefore not visible to customers. The only way to sell a product is for a customer to ask for it by name. BluFarm Group recognized the importance of in-store advertising and sales execution to build awareness and created point-of-sale materials such as window and counter displays to let customers know that Breathe Right strips were available in the store. "BluFarm's ability to capture consumers' awareness of Breathe Right strips as they walk in the retailer's door has beneficial results for CNS, BluFarm, pharmacists, and consumers," says McKenna.

"Working with an experienced local partner helps overcome surprises in global markets," says Nick Naumann, senior marketing communications manager at CNS. One surprise: universal product codes (UPC) on packaging aren't "universal"—they are used only in the United States and Canada. "Different forms of those codes in other countries can take a few weeks to six months or more of government review to obtain," he says.

Even the same packaging colors don't work around the globe. Research with U.S. consumers revealed they wanted darker packaging to suggest the strips' use at night by snorers and those with stuffed noses. "'Too grim and negative' Asian and European consumers told us," says Naumann. Breathe Right strips in those countries have a lighter, airier look than in the United States to convey the open feeling one gets from the nasal strips.

MANAGING GLOBAL GROWTH

Today, Breathe Right strips are sold in more than 25 countries. To ensure the Breathe Right brand continues to meet growth expectations, CNS now uses a three-stage approach to penetrate and develop new markets:

- Stage 1: Explore/test the concept.
  —Use screening criteria to identify high-potential markets.
  —Identify potential partners.
  —Validate concept with research.
  —Develop strategy and launch test market.
- Stage 2: Establish the product.
  —Penetrate the marketplace.
  —Refine messages for local market.
  —Evaluate partnership and marketing strategies.
- Stage 3: Manage the product.
  —Achieve sustainability/profitability.
  —Exploit new product and new use opportunities.

Overall, this approach starts with what works in the United States and extends it into new markets, paying close attention to local needs and customs. Throughout the three stages CNS conducts market research and makes financial projections.

As shown in the figure, at each stage of the market development process, performance must be met for the product to enter the next stage. Once success with Breathe Right nasal strips is established in a country, the groundwork is laid and international partners have the ability to introduce other Breathe Right products.

Stage 1: Explore/Test

↓

Stage 1 to Stage 2 Criteria Screen

- Relevant market: Cough/cold category size, GDP and GDP growth
- Quality of partners
- Product acceptance
- Cost to launch/support
- Political stability

↓

Stage 2: Establish the Product

↓

Stage 2 to Stage 3 Criteria Screen

- Proven partner and distribution strength
- Effective consumer ad and education programs
- Met initial trial and repeat targets
- Clear path to profits

↓

Stage 3: Manage the Product

LOOKING FORWARD

"We believe the Breathe Right brand has great potential, both domestically and around the world," says Morfitt. "Growth will come both from further expansion of Breathe Right nasal strips and from other drug-free, better-breathing line extensions."

Questions

1 What are the advantages and disadvantages for CNS taking Breathe Right strips into international markets?

2 What are the advantages to CNS of (*a*) using its three-stage process to enter new global markets and (*b*) having specific criteria to move through the stages?

3 Using the CNS criteria, with what you know, which countries should have highest priority for CNS?

4 Which single segment of potential Breathe Right strip users would you target to enter new markets?

5 Which marketing mix variables should CNS emphasize the most to succeed in a global arena? Why?

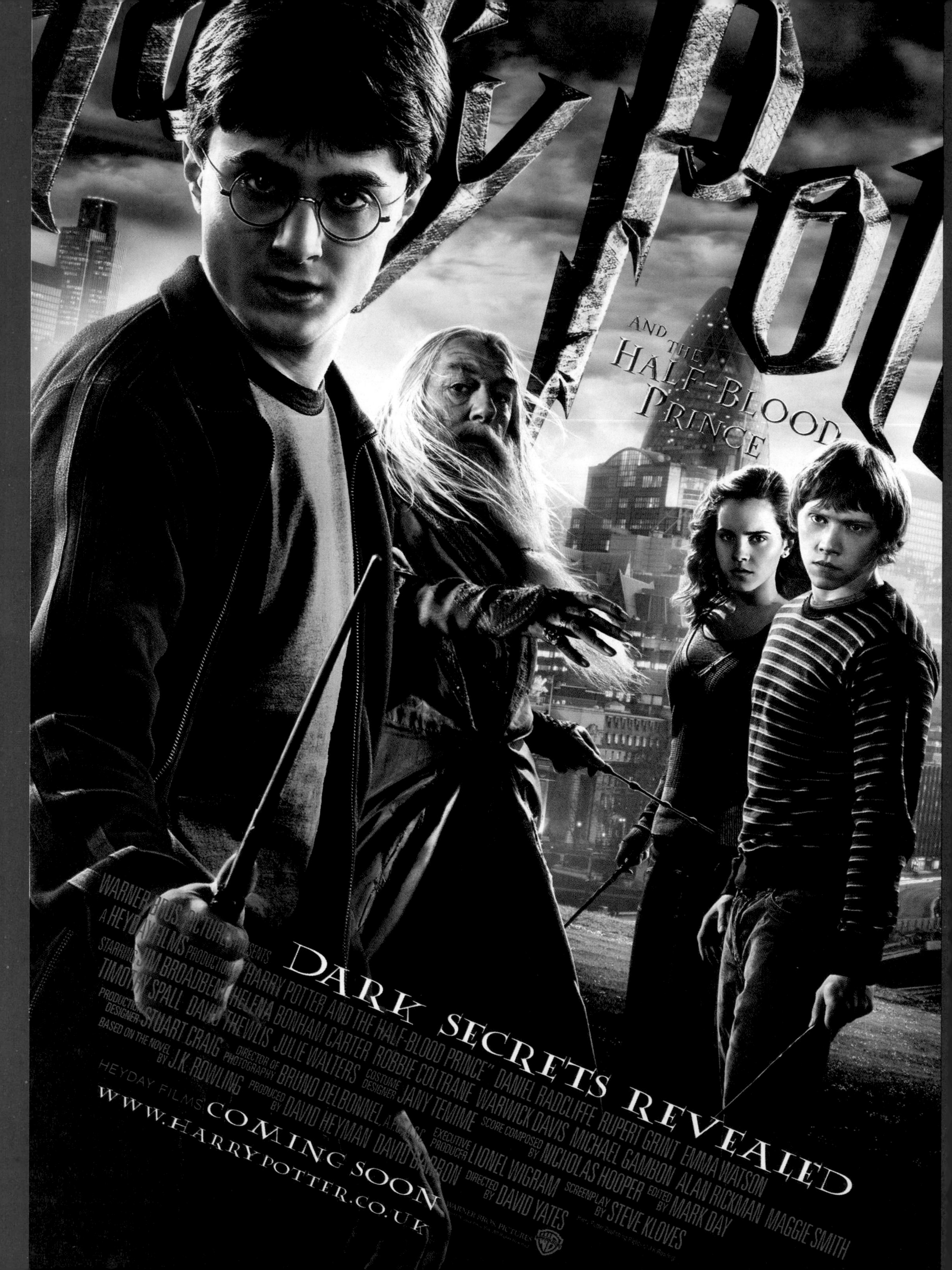
AND THE HALF-BLOOD PRINCE
DARK SECRETS REVEALED
"HARRY POTTER AND THE HALF-BLOOD PRINCE" DANIEL RADCLIFFE RUPERT GRINT EMMA WATSON
HELENA BONHAM CARTER ROBBIE COLTRANE WARWICK DAVIS MICHAEL GAMBON ALAN RICKMAN MAGGIE SMITH
JULIE WALTERS
PRODUCTION DESIGNER STUART CRAIG
COSTUME DESIGNER JANY TEMIME
SCORE COMPOSED BY NICHOLAS HOOPER
EDITED BY MARK DAY
DIRECTOR OF PHOTOGRAPHY BRUNO DELBONNEL
EXECUTIVE PRODUCER LIONEL WIGRAM
SCREENPLAY BY STEVE KLOVES
BASED ON THE NOVEL BY J.K. ROWLING
PRODUCED BY DAVID HEYMAN
DIRECTED BY DAVID YATES
HEYDAY FILMS
COMING SOON
WWW.HARRYPOTTER.CO.UK

8 Marketing Research: From Customer Insights to Actions

LEARNING OBJECTIVES
After reading this chapter you should be able to:

LO1 Identify the reason for conducting marketing research.

LO2 Describe the five-step marketing research approach that leads to marketing actions.

LO3 Explain how marketing uses secondary and primary data.

LO4 Discuss the uses of observations, questionnaires, panels, experiments, and newer data collection methods.

LO5 Explain how information technology and data mining lead to marketing actions.

LO6 Describe three approaches to developing a company's sales forecast.

TEST SCREENINGS AND TRACKING STUDIES: HOW LISTENING TO CONSUMERS REDUCES MOVIE RISKS

Harry Potter and the Half Blood Prince, *Star Trek*, and *Transformers: Revenge of the Fallen* are movies that their studios count on for huge profits. But what can these studios do to try to reduce the costly risks of a movie's box-office failure?[1]

What's in a Movie Name?

Fixing bad names for movies—such as *Shoeless Joe* and *Rope Burns*—can turn potential disasters into hugely successful blockbusters. Don't remember seeing these movies? Well, test screenings, a form of marketing research, found that moviegoers like you had problems with these titles. Here's what happened:

- Shown frequently on television now, *Shoeless Joe* became *Field of Dreams* because audiences thought Kevin Costner might be playing a homeless person.
- *Rope Burns* became *Million Dollar Baby* because audiences didn't like the original name. The movie won the 2005 Academy Award™ for Best Picture and starred Hilary Swank as a woman boxer and Clint Eastwood as her trainer.

Filmmakers want movie titles that are concise, grab attention, capture the essence of the film, and have no legal restrictions to reduce risk to both the studio and audiences—the same factors that make a good brand name.[2]

Using Marketing Research to Reduce Movie Risks

Bad titles, poor scripts, temperamental stars, costly special effects, and several blockbuster movies released at the same time are just a few of the nightmares studios face. According to the latest data, today's films now average $107 million to produce and market.[3] So studios try to reduce their risks by doing marketing research that includes conducting test screenings and using tracking studies.

Without reading ahead, think about the answers to these questions:

- Whom would you recruit for movie test screenings?
- What questions would you ask to help you edit or modify the title or other aspects of a film?

Test screenings and tracking studies can help avoid potential dangers, such as improving movie titles, endings, and characters.

Virtually every major U.S. movie produced today uses test screenings to obtain the key reactions of consumers likely to be in the target audience. In test screenings, 300 to 400 prospective moviegoers are recruited to attend a "sneak preview" of a film before its release. After viewing the movie, the audience fills out an exhaustive survey to critique its title, plot, characters, music, and ending as well as the marketing program (posters, trailers, and so on) to identify improvements to make in the final edit.[4]

Test screenings resulted in *Fatal Attraction* having one of the most commercially successful "ending-switches" of all time. In sneak previews, audiences liked everything but the ending, which had Alex (Glenn Close) committing suicide and framing Dan (Michael Douglas) as her murderer by leaving his fingerprints on the knife she used. The studio shot $1.3 million of new scenes for the ending that audiences eventually saw. The new ending for *Fatal Attraction* undoubtedly contributed to the movie's box-office success.[5]

Figure 8–1 summarizes some key questions used in these test screenings both to select the people for the screenings and to obtain key reactions of those sitting in the screenings. Note how specific the studio's action is for each question asked. This is an example of effective, action-oriented marketing research.

Marketing researchers use tracking studies immediately before an upcoming film's release to forecast its opening week's box-office revenues. The tracking studies ask prospective target audience moviegoers who have seen at least six movies in the last year three key questions: (1) Are you aware of the film? (2) Are you interested in seeing the film? and (3) Will you see the film this week?[6] Depending on the research results, the movie studio may run last-minute ads to increase awareness, interest, and attendance at the film. Industry "wisdom" says that the total U.S. box-office revenues will be two and one-half times the opening week's box office revenues.[7]

This example shows how marketing research, the main topic of this chapter, links marketing strategy and decisive marketing actions. Also, marketing research is often used to help a firm develop its sales forecasts, the final topic of this chapter.

FIGURE 8–1
Marketing research questions asked in test screenings of movies. Note each kind of question leads to a specific action—a characteristic of effective marketing research.

POINT WHEN ASKED	KEY QUESTIONS	ACTION AND USE OF QUESTION
Before the test screening	• How old are you? • How frequently do you pay to see movies?	• Find people who fit the target audience profile for movie. • Find people who frequently attend movies.
After the test screening	• What do you think of the title? What title would you suggest? • Were any characters too distasteful? Who? How? • Did you like the ending? If not, how would you change it?	• Change movie title. • Change aspects of some characters in the movie. • Change or clarify ending of the movie.

THE ROLE OF MARKETING RESEARCH

LO1

Let's look at (1) what marketing research is, (2) identify some difficulties with it, and (3) describe the five steps marketers use to conduct it.

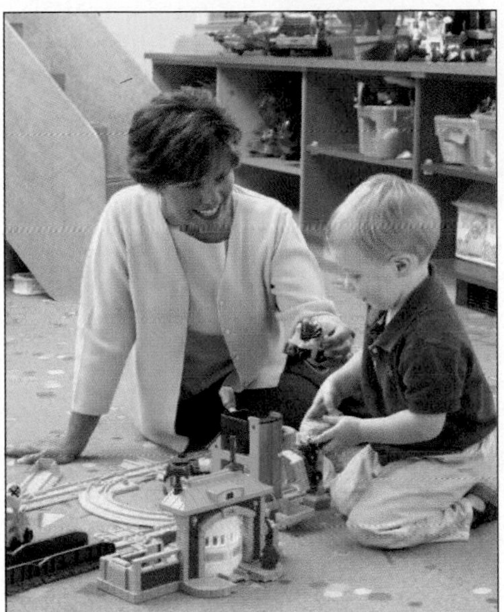

For how Fisher-Price does marketing research on young children who can't read, see the text.

What Is Marketing Research?

Marketing research is the process of defining a marketing problem and opportunity, systematically collecting and analyzing information, and recommending actions.[8] Although imperfect, marketers conduct marketing research to reduce risk of and thereby improve marketing decisions.

The Challenges in Doing Good Marketing Research

Whatever the marketing issue involved—whether discovering consumer tastes or setting the right price—good marketing research is challenging. For example:

- Suppose your firm is developing a new product never before seen by consumers. Would consumers really know whether they are likely to buy a product that they have never thought about before?
- Imagine if you, as a consumer, were asked about your personal hygiene habits. Even though you know the answers, would you reveal them? When personal or status questions are involved, will people give honest answers?
- Will consumers' actual purchase behavior match their stated interest or intentions? Will they buy the same brand they say they will?

Marketing research must overcome these difficulties and obtain the information needed so that marketers can make reasonable estimates about what consumers want and will buy.

Five-Step Marketing Research Approach

A **decision** is a conscious choice from among two or more alternatives. All of us make many such decisions daily. At work we choose from alternative ways to accomplish an assigned task. At college we choose from alternative courses. As consumers we choose from alternative brands. No magic formula guarantees correct decisions.

Managers and researchers have tried to improve the outcomes of decisions by using more formal, structured approaches to *decision making,* the act of consciously choosing from alternatives. The systematic marketing research approach used to collect information to improve marketing decisions and actions described in this chapter uses five steps and is shown in Figure 8–2 on the next page. Although the five-step approach described here focuses on marketing decisions, it provides a systematic checklist for making both business and personal decisions.

STEP 1: DEFINE THE PROBLEM

Every marketing problem faces its own research challenges. For example, toy designers at Fisher-Price conduct marketing research to discover how children play, how

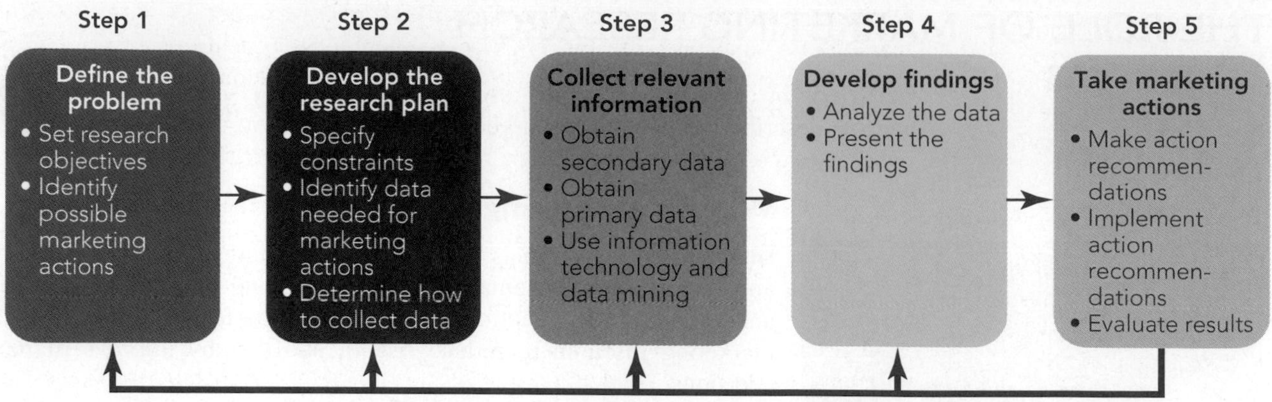

FIGURE 8–2
Five-step marketing research approach leading to marketing actions. Lessons learned from past research mistakes are fed back to improve each of the steps.

they learn, and what they like to play with.[9] As part of its marketing research, Fisher-Price invites children to play at its state-licensed nursery school in East Aurora, New York. From behind one-way mirrors, toy designers and marketing researchers watch the children use—and abuse—toys, which helps the firm develop better products.

The original model of a classic Fisher-Price toy, the Chatter Telephone™, was simply a wooden phone with a dial that rang a bell. However, observers noted that the children kept grabbing the receiver like a handle to pull the phone along behind them, so a designer added wheels, a noisemaker, and eyes that bobbed up and down.

A careful look at Fisher-Price's toy marketing research shows the two key elements of defining a problem: setting the research objectives and identifying possible marketing actions.

Set the Research Objectives

Research objectives are specific, measurable goals the decision maker—in this case, an executive at Fisher-Price—seeks to achieve in conducting the marketing research. For Fisher-Price, the immediate research objective was to decide whether to market the old or new telephone design.

In setting these research objectives, marketers have to be clear on the purpose of the research that leads to marketing actions. The three main types of marketing research, with examples explained in more detail later in the chapter, are:

1. *Exploratory research* provides ideas about a relatively vague problem. General Mills discovered that the initial version of its Hamburger Helper wasn't satisfactory for many consumers, so it interviewed them to get ideas to improve the product.
2. *Descriptive research* generally involves trying to find the frequency that something occurs or the extent of a relationship between two factors. So when General Mills wants to study how loyal consumers are to its Wheaties, it can obtain data on the number of households buying Wheaties and competitive products.
3. *Causal research*, the most sophisticated, tries to determine the extent to which the change in one factor changes another one. In the Fisher-Price example discussed next, changing the toy designs is related to changes in the amount of time children play with the toy. Experiments and test markets, discussed later, are examples of causal research.

The wheels, noisemaker, and bobbing eyes on Fisher-Price's hugely successful Chatter Telephone resulted from careful marketing research on children.

Identify Possible Marketing Actions

Effective decision makers develop specific **measures of success**, which are criteria or standards used in evaluating proposed solutions to the problem.

Marketing research isn't perfect. Recently it correctly identified Cybertron Transformers as a "hot toy" . . .

. . . but missed on Hasbro's FurReal Friends Butterscotch Pony.

Different research outcomes—based on the measure of success—lead to different marketing actions. For the Fisher-Price problem, if a measure of success were the total time children spent playing with each of the two telephone designs, the results of observing them would lead to clear-cut actions as follows:

Measure of Success: Playtime	Possible Marketing Action
• Children spent more time playing with old design.	• Continue with old design; don't introduce new design.
• Children spent more time playing with new design.	• Introduce new design; drop old design.

One test of whether marketing research should be done is if different outcomes will lead to different marketing actions. If all the research outcomes lead to the same action—such as top management sticking with the older design regardless of what the observed children liked—the research is useless and a waste of money. In this case, research results showed that kids liked the new design, so Fisher-Price introduced its noisemaking pull-toy Chatter Telephone, which became a toy classic and has sold millions.

Each year, *FamilyFun* magazine has dozens of children—and their parents—evaluate hundreds of new toys from over 100 toy manufactures to select its Toy of the Year awards. Over the years, the magazine has been right on the money in selecting Barney the TV dinosaur, Tickle Me Elmo, and Fisher-Price's Love to Dance Bear™ as hot toys—ones that jumped off retailers' shelves. But as shown with the toys in the margin, even careful marketing research can sometimes overlook hot toys. Forecasting which toys are hot and will sell well is critical for retailers, which must place orders to manufacturers 8 to 10 months before holiday shoppers walk into their stores. Bad forecasts can lead to lost sales for understocks and severe losses for overstocks.

Marketing researchers know that defining a problem is an incredibly difficult task. For example, if the objectives are too broad, the problem may not be researchable. If they are too narrow, the value of the research results may be seriously lessened. This is why marketing researchers spend so much time defining a marketing problem precisely and writing a formal proposal that describes the research to be done.[10]

STEP 2: DEVELOP THE RESEARCH PLAN

The second step in the marketing research process requires that the researcher (1) specify the constraints on the marketing research activity, (2) identify the data needed for marketing decisions, and (3) determine how to collect the data.

Specify Constraints

The **constraints** in a decision are the restrictions placed on potential solutions to a problem. Examples include the limitations on the time and money available to solve the problem. Thus, Fisher-Price might set two constraints on its decision to select either the old or new version of the Chatter Telephone: The decision must be made in 10 weeks and no research budget is available beyond that needed for collecting data in its nursery school.

Identify Data Needed for Marketing Actions

Often marketing research studies wind up collecting a lot of data that are interesting but irrelevant for marketing decisions that result in marketing actions. In the

Fisher-Price Chatter Telephone case, it might be nice to know the children's favorite colors, whether they like wood or plastic toys better, and so on. In fact, knowing answers to these questions might result in later modifications of the toy, but right now the problem is to select one of two toy designs. So this study must focus on collecting data that help managers make a clear choice between the two telephone designs.

Determine How to Collect Data

Determining how to collect useful marketing research data is often as important as actually collecting the data—step 3 in the process, which is discussed later. Two key elements in deciding how to collect the data are (1) concepts and (2) methods.

Concepts In the world of marketing, *concepts* are ideas about products or services. To find out about consumer reaction to a potential new product, marketing researchers frequently develop a *new-product concept*, that is, a picture or verbal description of a product or service the firm might offer for sale. For example, Fisher-Price's addition of a noisemaker, wheels, and eyes to the basic design of its Chatter Telephone made the toy more fun for children and increased sales.

Methods *Methods* are the approaches that can be used to collect data to solve all or part of a problem. For example, if you are the marketing researcher at Fisher-Price responsible for the Chatter Telephone, you face a number of methods issues in developing your research plan, including the following:

- Can we actually ask three- or four-year-olds meaningful questions they can answer about their liking or disliking of the two designs?
- Are we better off not asking them questions but simply observing their behavior?
- If we simply observe the children's behavior, how can we do this in a way to get the best information without biasing the results?

Millions of other people have asked similar questions about millions of other products and services. How can you find and use the methods that other marketing researchers have found successful? Information on useful methods is available in tradebooks, textbooks, and handbooks that relate to marketing and marketing research. Some periodicals and technical journals, such as the *Journal of Marketing* and the *Journal of Marketing Research* both published by the American Marketing Association, summarize methods and techniques valuable in addressing marketing problems.

Special methods vital to marketing are (1) sampling and (2) statistical inference. For example, marketing researchers often use *sampling*, which is a technique to select a group of distributors, customers, or prospects and treating the information they provide as typical of all those in whom they are interested. They may then use *statistical inference* to generalize the results from the sample to much larger groups of distributors, customers, or prospects to help decide on marketing actions.

learning review

1. What is marketing research?
2. What is the five-step marketing research approach?
3. What are constraints, as they apply to developing a research plan?

STEP 3: COLLECT RELEVANT INFORMATION

LO3

Collecting enough relevant information to make a rational, informed marketing decision sometimes simply means using your knowledge to decide immediately. At other times it entails collecting an enormous amount of information at great expense.

Figure 8–3 shows how the different kinds of marketing information fit together. **Data**, the facts and figures related to the problem, are divided into two main parts: secondary data and primary data. **Secondary data** are facts and figures that have already been recorded before the project at hand. As shown in Figure 8–3, secondary data divide into two parts—internal and external secondary data—depending on whether the data come from inside or outside the organization needing the research. **Primary data** are facts and figures that are newly collected for the project. Figure 8–3 shows that primary data can be divided into observational data, questionnaire data, and other sources of data.

Secondary Data: Internal

Examples of internal secondary data include detailed sales breakdowns by product line, by region, by customer, and by sales representative, as well as customer inquiries and complaints. So internal secondary data are often the starting point for a new marketing research study because using this information can result in huge time and cost savings.

Secondary Data: External

Published data from outside the organization are external secondary data. The U.S. Census Bureau publishes a variety of useful reports. Best known is the Census 2000, which is the most recent count of the U.S. population that occurs every 10 years. Recently, the Census Bureau began collecting data annually from a smaller number

FIGURE 8–3
Types of marketing information. Researchers must choose carefully among these to get the best results, considering time and cost constraints.

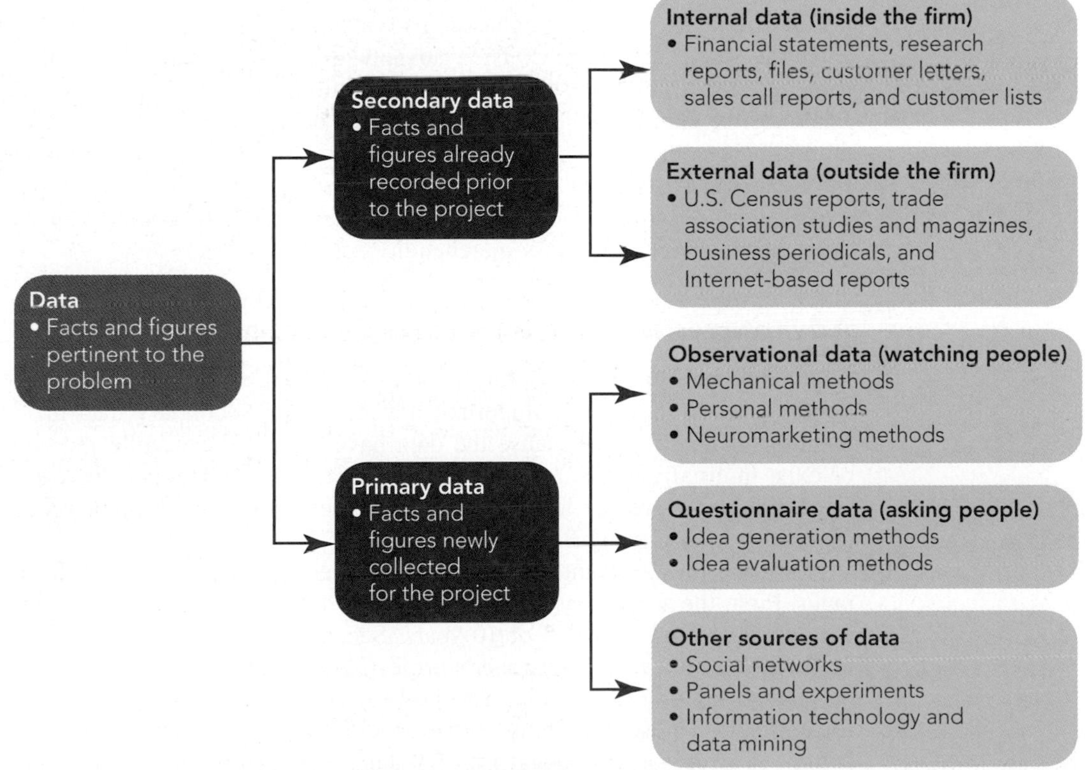

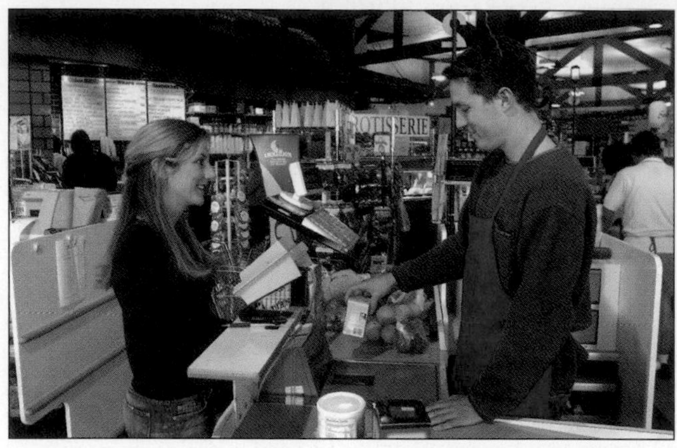

Scanner data at supermarket checkout counters provide valuable information for marketing decisions.

of people through the American Community Survey. Both surveys contain detailed information on American households, such as the number of people per household and their age, sex, race/ethnic background, income, occupation, and education. Marketers use these data to identify characteristics and trends of ultimate consumers.

The Census Bureau also publishes the Economic Census, which is conducted every five years. These reports are vital to business firms selling products and services to organizations. The 2007 Economic Census contains data on the number and sales of establishments in the United States that produce a good or service based on its geography (states, counties, ZIP codes, etc.), industry sector (Manufacturing, Retail Trade, etc.), and North American Industry Classification System (NAICS) code. The Current Industrial Reports are periodic studies that provide data on the production quantity and shipment value of selected products. Finally, trade associations, universities, and business periodicals provide detailed data of value to market researchers and planners. These data are now available online via the Internet and can be identified and located using a search engine such as Google. The accompanying Going Online box provides examples.

Several market research companies pay households and businesses to record all their purchases using a paper or electronic diary. Such *syndicated panel* data economically answer questions that require consistent data collection over time, such as how many times did our customers buy our products this year compared to last year? One syndicated panel sample with almost 100,000 households gives each household an electronic wand to scan the bar codes on purchases it makes. Other examples of specialized syndicated services that provide a standard set of data on a regular basis are the Nielsen Media Research's TV ratings and the J. D. Power's automotive quality and customer satisfaction surveys.

Some data services provide comprehensive information on household demographics and lifestyle, product purchases, TV viewing behavior, and responses to coupon and free-sample promotions. Their advantage is that a single firm can collect, analyze, interrelate, and present all this information. For consumer product firms such as Procter & Gamble, sales data from various channels are critical to allocate scarce marketing resources. As a result, they use services such as Information Resources' InfoScan and ACNielsen's ScanTrack to collect product sales and coupon/free-sample redemptions that have been scanned at the checkout counters of supermarket, drug, convenience, and mass merchandise retailers.

Advantages and Disadvantages of Secondary Data

A general rule among marketing people is to obtain secondary data first and then collect primary data. Two important advantages of secondary data are (1) the tremendous time savings because the data have already been collected and published or exist internally and (2) the low cost, such as free or inexpensive Census reports. Furthermore, a greater level of detail is often available through secondary data, especially U.S. Census Bureau data.

However, these advantages must be weighed against some significant disadvantages. First, the secondary data may be out of date, especially if they are U.S. Census data collected only every 5 or 10 years. Second, the definitions or categories might not be quite right for a researcher's project. For example, the age groupings or product categories might be wrong for the project. Also, because the data are collected for another purpose, they may not be specific enough for the project. In such cases it may be necessary to collect primary data.

Going Online

Online Databases and Internet Resources Useful to Marketers

Information contained in online databases available via the Internet consists of indexes to articles in periodicals and statistical or financial data on markets, products, and organizations that are accessed either directly or via Internet search engines or portals through keyword searches.

Statistical and financial data on markets, products, and organizations include:

- *The Wall Street Journal* (www.wsj.com), CNBC (www.cnbc.com), and *Fox Business News* (www.foxbusiness.com) provide up-to-the-minute business news and security prices plus research reports on companies, industries, and countries.
- STAT-USA (www.stat-usa.gov) and the Census Bureau (www.census.gov) of the U.S. Department of Commerce provide information on U.S. business, economic, and trade activity collected by the federal government.

Portals and search engines include:

- USA.gov (www.usa.gov) is the portal to all U.S. government Web sites. Users click on links to browse by topic or enter keywords for specific searches.
- Google (www.google.com) is the most popular portal to the entire Internet. Users click on links to browse by topic or enter keywords for specific searches.

Some of these Web sites are accessible only if your educational institution has paid a subscription fee. Check with your institution's Web site.

learning review

4. What is the difference between secondary and primary data?

5. What are some advantages and disadvantages of secondary data?

Primary Data: Watching People

LO4

Observing people and asking them questions are the two principal ways to collect new or primary data for a marketing study. Facts and figures obtained by watching, either mechanically or in person, how people actually behave is the way marketing researchers collect **observational data**. Observational data can be collected by mechanical (including electronic), personal, or neuromarketing methods.

Mechanical Methods National TV ratings, such as those of Nielsen Media Research shown in Figure 8–4 on the next page are an example of mechanical observational data collected by a "people meter." The people meter is a box that (1) is attached to TV sets, VCRs, cable boxes, and satellite dishes in more than 25,000 homes across the country; (2) has a remote that operates the meter when a viewer begins and finishes watching a TV program; and (3) stores and then transmits the viewing information each night to Nielsen Media Research. Data are also collected using less sophisticated meters or TV diaries (a paper-pencil measurement system).[11]

By 2011, Nielsen will implement a new measurement program dubbed the *Anytime Anywhere Media Measurement (A2/M2) Initiative*. The purpose of A2/M2 is to "follow the video" of 21st century viewers. New "active/passive" people meter technology will measure all types of TV viewing behavior from a variety of devices and sources: DVR (digital video recorders), VOD (video on demand), Internet-delivered TV shows on computers via iTunes, streaming media, mobile media devices (cell phones, iPods, etc.), as well as outside the home in bars, fitness clubs, airports, and so on.

On the basis of all these observational data, Nielsen Media Research then calculates the rating and share of each TV program. With 114.5 million TV households

FIGURE 8–4
Nielsen Television Index Ranking Report for network TV prime-time households, week of May 18–24, 2009. The difference of a few share points in Nielsen TV ratings affects the cost of a TV ad on a show and even whether the show remains on the air.

Rank	Program	Network	Rating	Share
1	*American Idol—Wednesday*	FOX	16.1	27
2	*American Idol—Tuesday*	FOX	13.5	22
3	*Dancing with the Stars—Results*	ABC	12.6	20
4	*Dancing with the Stars*	ABC	12.2	20
5	*The Mentalist*	CBS	10.4	16
6	*NCIS*	CBS	10.3	17
7	*Two and a Half Men*	CBS	9.9	15
8	*CSI: Miami*	CBS	8.9	15
9	*Criminal Minds*	CBS	8.7	14
10	*Rules of Engagement*	CBS	7.9	12

Source: Copyright 2009, The Nielsen Company. All times Eastern. Viewing estimates include live viewing and DVR playback on the same day, defined as 3 A.M. to 3 A.M. Rank is based on U.S. Household Rating % from Nielsen Media Research's National People Meter Sample.

in the United States, based on the 2000 U.S. Census, a single ratings point equals 1 percent, or 1,145,000 TV households.[12] For TV viewing, a share point is the percentage of TV sets in use tuned to a particular program. Because TV and cable networks sell almost $65 billion annually in advertising and set advertising rates to advertisers on the basis of those data, precision in the Nielsen data is critical.[13] Thus, a change of one percentage point in a rating can mean gaining or losing millions of dollars in advertising revenues because advertisers pay rates on the basis of the size of the audience for a TV program. So as Figure 8–4 shows, we might expect to pay more for a 30-second TV ad on *The Mentalist* than one on *CSI: Miami*. Broadcast and cable networks may change the time slot or even cancel a TV program if its ratings are consistently poor and advertisers are unwilling to pay a rate based on a higher guaranteed rating.

But TV advertisers today have a special problem: With about three out of four TV viewers skipping ads with TiVo or channel surfing during commercials, how many people are actually seeing their TV ad? Now services such as Nielsen Media Research and Media Check offer advertisers minute-by-minute measurement of how many viewers stay tuned during commercials. The viewership data in Figure 8–4 includes not only live TV but also programs taped on digital video recorders (DVRs). With these more precise measures of who is likely to see a TV ad, buying TV ads is becoming a lot more scientific.[14]

Nielsen Online Ratings also uses an electronic meter to record Internet user behavior. These data are collected via a meter installed on computers by tracking the actual mouse clicks made by a large sample of 230,000 panelists in the U.S. as they surf the Internet. Nielsen Online Ratings identifies the top Web sites—or "brands"—that have the largest unique audiences and "active reach," which is the percent of total home and office users that visited the Web site. In 2009, the five most popular U.S. Web site brands were Google, Microsoft, Yahoo!, Facebook, and AOL.

What determines if *American Idol* stays on the air? For the importance of the TV "ratings game," see the text.

Personal Methods Observational data can take some strange twists. Jennifer Voitle, a laid-off investment bank employee with four advanced degrees, responded to an Internet ad and found a new career: *mystery shopper*. Companies pay mystery shoppers to check on the quality and pricing of their products and the integrity of and customer service provided by their employees. Jennifer

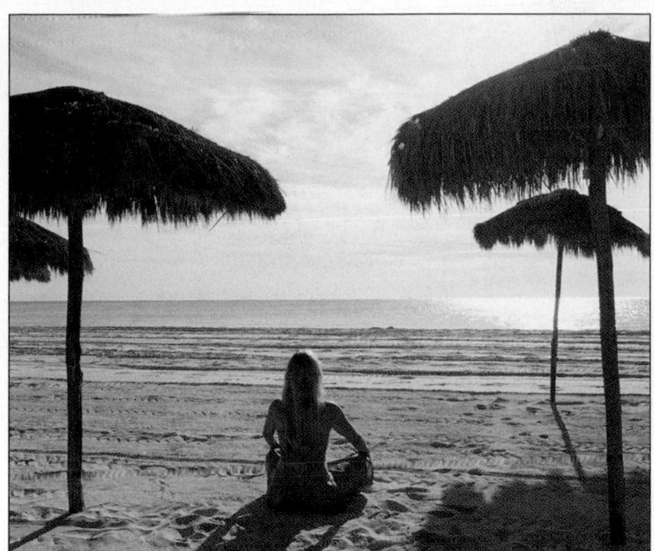

Is this *really* marketing research? A *mystery shopper* at work.

gets paid to travel to exotic hotels, eat at restaurants, play golf, test-drive new cars, shop for clothes, and play arcade games. But her role posing as a customer gives her client unique marketing research information that can be obtained in no other way. Says Jennifer, "Can you believe they call this work?"[15]

Watching consumers in person or videotaping them are two other observational approaches. For example, Procter & Gamble watched women do their laundry, clean the floor, put on makeup, and so on because they comprise 80 percent of its customers! And Gillette videotaped consumers brushing their teeth in their own bathrooms to see how they really brush—not just how they say they brush. The new-product result: Gillette's Oral-B CrossAction toothbrush.[16]

Ethnographic research is a specialized observational approach in which trained observers seek to discover subtle behavioral and emotional reactions as consumers encounter products in their "natural use environment," such as in their home or car.[17] Recently, Kraft launched Deli Creations, which are sandwiches made with its Oscar Mayer meats, Kraft cheeses, and Grey Poupon mustard, after spending several months with consumers in their kitchens. Kraft discovered that consumers wanted complete, ready-to-serve meals that are easy to prepare—and it had the products to create them.[18]

Personal observation is both useful and flexible, but it can be costly and unreliable when different observers report different conclusions when watching the same event. And while observation can reveal *what* people do, it cannot easily determine *why* they do it. This is the principal reason for using neuromarketing and questionnaires, our next topics.

Neuromarketing Methods As a global brand expert, Martin Lindstrom has consulted for clients that market everything from chocolate and TV remote controls to toothpaste and iPod speakers. Not being satisfied with the results obtained from traditional marketing research, Lindstrom undertook a three-year, $7 million study that used brain scanning to analyze the buying processes of more than 2,000 participants. And how was his study different from traditional marketing research? Lindstrom merged neuroscience—the study of the brain—with marketing! His controversial findings using "neuromarketing" are summarized in his 2008 breakthrough book *Buy•ology*. Several of his findings appear in the Marketing Matters box on the next page.[19]

Primary Data: Asking People

How many dozens of times have you filled out some kind of a questionnaire? Maybe a short survey at school or a telephone or e-mail survey to see if you are pleased with the service you received. Asking consumers questions and recording their answers is the second principal way of gathering information.

We can divide this primary data collection task into (1) idea generation methods and (2) idea evaluation methods, although they sometimes overlap and each has a number of special techniques.[20] Each survey method results in valuable **questionnaire data**, which are facts and figures obtained by asking people about their attitudes, awareness, intentions, and behaviors.

Idea Generation Methods—Coming Up with Ideas In the past the most common way of collecting questionnaire data to generate ideas was through

Marketing Matters > > > > > > > > technology

Buy•ology: How "Neuromarketing" Is Trying to Understand Consumers

Is much of the more than $12 *billion* spent on traditional market research (focus groups, surveys, and so on) wasted? Brand guru Martin Lindstrom believes so. Why? Because 85 percent of consumers' thoughts, feelings, or preferences toward products, brands, and advertisements resides deep within the subconscious part of the brain and can't be understood using traditional techniques.

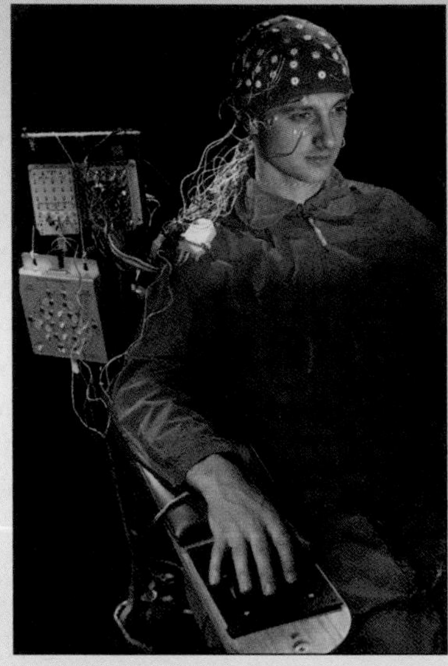

Lindstrom is a believer in the relatively new field of "neuromarketing," which uses high-tech brain scanning instruments to record the brain's responses to various marketing stimuli (package designs, brand logos, fragrances, TV ads, and so on) via the five senses (sight, sound, smell, touch, and taste). Two instruments are typically used when stimuli are presented: (1) An expensive, doughnut-shaped functional magnetic resonance imaging (fMRI) scanner, where different areas of the brain "light up" and can be mapped and (2) a less costly cap with dozens of sensors plugged into an electroencephalograph (EEG), where the real-time changes in brain wave patterns can be seen (see photo).

So why is neuromarketing important to marketers? Lindstrom draws these fascinating conclusions that could have a significant impact on current marketing actions:

- **Brand logos don't work.** Instead, brands should focus on indirect logo signals, such as shapes, sound, smell, color, and so on.
- **Ads with sex appeal don't sell.** Men in particular don't recall these types of ads nearly as much as nonsexually oriented ads.
- **Successful brands function like religion.** Participants' brains respond similarly to brand messages and religious icons.
- **Warning labels on cigarettes don't work.** Interestingly, the labels stimulate the area of the brain responsible for cravings.

So, what do you think about neuromarketing? Are you concerned that marketers will invade your privacy by influencing what you buy? Stay tuned!

---

an *individual interview*, which involves a single researcher asking questions of one respondent. This approach has many advantages, such as being able to probe for additional ideas using follow-up questions to a respondent's initial answers, but it is very expensive. Later in the chapter we'll discuss some alternatives.

Individual interviews have the advantage of enabling interviewers to ask probing follow-up questions about a respondent's answers.

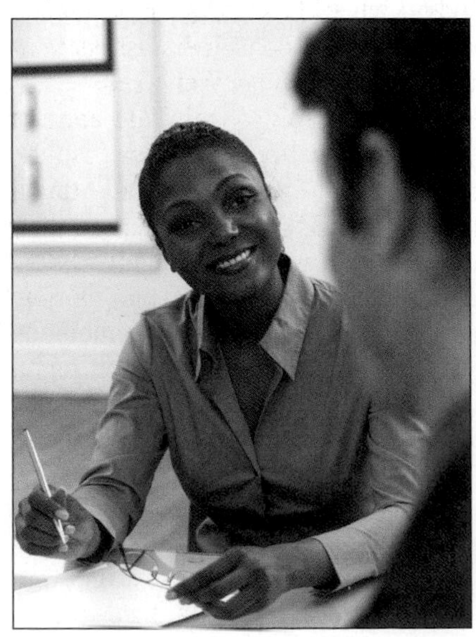

General Mills sought ideas about why Hamburger Helper didn't fare well when introduced. Initial instructions called for cooking a half-pound of hamburger separately from the noodles or potatoes, which were later mixed with the hamburger. So General Mills researchers used a special kind of individual interview called *depth interviews* in which researchers ask lengthy, free-flowing kinds of questions to probe for underlying ideas and feelings. These depth interviews showed that consumers (1) didn't think it contained enough meat and (2) didn't want the hassle of cooking in two different pots. So the Hamburger Helper product manager changed the recipe to call for a full pound of meat and to allow users to prepare it in one dish. This marketing action converted a potential failure into a success.[21]

Focus groups are informal sessions of 6 to 10 past, present, or prospective customers in which a discussion leader, or moderator, asks their opinions about the firm's and its competitors' products, how they use these products, and special needs they have that these products don't address. Often recorded and conducted in special interviewing rooms with a one-way mirror, these groups enable marketing researchers and managers to hear and watch consumer reactions. The informality and peer support in an effective focus group help uncover ideas that are often difficult to obtain with individual interviews. For example, 3M ran eight focus groups around the United States and heard consumers complain that standard steel wool pads scratched their

Listening carefully in focus groups to student and instructor suggestions benefits this text, such as providing answers to the Learning Review questions.

expensive cookware. These interviews led to 3M's internationally successful Scotch-Brite® Never Scratch soap pad.[22]

Finding "the next big thing" for consumers has become the obsession not only for consumer product firms but also for firms in many other industries. The result is that marketing researchers have come to rely on other—many would say bizarre—techniques than more traditional individual or focus group interviews. These "fuzzy front end" methods attempt early identification of elusive consumer tastes or trends. For example, Trend Hunter is a firm that seeks to anticipate and track "the evolution of cool." Trend hunting (or watching) is the practice of identifying "emerging shifts in social behavior," which are driven by changes in pop culture that can lead to new products. Trend Hunter has identified over 47,000 "micro trends" through its global network of 27,000 spotters and features several of these trends on its daily Trend Hunter TV broadcast via its Web site (see www.trendhunter.com/tv).[23]

Idea Evaluation Methods—Testing an Idea In idea evaluation, the marketing researcher tries to test ideas discovered earlier to help the marketing manager recommend marketing actions. Idea evaluation methods often involve conventional questionnaires using personal, mail, telephone, fax, and online (e-mail or Internet) surveys of a large sample of past, present, or prospective consumers. In choosing among them, the marketing researcher balances the cost of the particular method against the expected quality of and speed with which the information is obtained. Personal interview surveys enable the interviewer to be flexible in asking probing questions or getting reactions to visual materials but are very costly. Mail surveys are usually biased because those most likely to respond have had especially positive or negative experiences with the product or brand. While telephone interviews allow flexibility, unhappy respondents may hang up on the interviewer, even with the efficiency of computer-assisted telephone interviewing (CATI). Fax surveys, a method in decline, are restricted to respondents having the technology.

Increasingly, marketing researchers have begun to use online (e-mail and Internet) surveys to collect primary data. The reason: Most consumers have an Internet connection and an e-mail account. Marketers can embed a survey in an e-mail sent to targeted respondents. When they open the e-mail, consumers can either see the survey or click on a link to access it from a Web site. Marketers can also ask consumers to complete a "pop up" survey in a separate window when they access an organization's Web site. Many organizations use this method to have consumers assess their products and services or evaluate the design and usability of their Web sites.

The advantages of online surveys are that the cost is relatively minimal and the turnaround time from data collection to report presentation is much quicker than the traditional methods discussed earlier. However, online surveys have serious drawbacks: Some consumers may view e-mail surveys as "junk" or "spam" and either do not receive them if they have a "spam blocker" or purposely or inadvertently delete them without opening. For Internet surveys, some consumers have a "pop-up blocker" that prohibits a browser from opening a separate window that contains the survey; thus, they may not be able to participate in the research. For both e-mail and Internet surveys, consumers can complete the survey multiple times, creating a significant bias in the results. This is especially true for online panels. Research firms, such as MarketTools that markets Zoomerang, have developed sampling technology to prohibit this practice.[24]

The high cost of reaching respondents in their homes using personal interviews has led to a dramatic increase in the use of *mall intercept interviews*, which are personal interviews of consumers visiting shopping centers. These face-to-face

1. What things are most important to you when you decide to eat out and go to a fast-food restaurant?

____

____

____

2. Have you eaten at a fast-food restaurant in the past month?

☐ Yes ☐ No

3. If you answered yes to question 2, how often do you eat fast food?

☐ Once a week ☐ 2 to 3 times a month ☐ Once a month or less

4. How important is it to you that a fast-food restaurant satisfies you on the following characteristics? [Check the box that describes your feelings for each item listed]

CHARACTERISTIC	VERY IMPORTANT	SOMEWHAT IMPORTANT	IMPORTANT	UNIMPORTANT	SOMEWHAT UNIMPORTANT	VERY UNIMPORTANT
• Taste of food	☐	☐	☐	☐	☐	☐
• Cleanliness	☐	☐	☐	☐	☐	☐
• Price	☐	☐	☐	☐	☐	☐
• Variety of menu	☐	☐	☐	☐	☐	☐

5. For each of the characteristics listed below, check the space on the scale that describes how you feel about Wendy's. Mark an X on only **one** of the five spaces listed for each item listed.

CHARACTERISTIC	CHECK THE SPACE THAT DESCRIBES THE DEGREE TO WHICH WENDY'S IS . . .						
• Taste of food	Tasty	____	____	____	____	____	Not tasty
• Cleanliness	Clean	____	____	____	____	____	Dirty
• Price	Inexpensive	____	____	____	____	____	Expensive
• Variety of menu	Broad	____	____	____	____	____	Narrow

FIGURE 8–5

To obtain the most valuable information from consumers, the Wendy's survey utilizes five different kinds of questions discussed in the text.

interviews reduce the cost of personal visits to consumers in their homes while providing the flexibility to show respondents visual cues such as ads or actual product samples. However, a critical disadvantage of mall intercept interviews is that the people selected for the interviews may not be representative of the consumers targeted, giving a biased result.

The foundation of all research using questionnaires is designing precise questions that get clear, unambiguous answers very efficiently. Figure 8–5 shows a number of formats for questions taken from a Wendy's survey that assessed fast-food restaurant preferences among present and prospective consumers. Question 1 is an example of an *open-ended question*, which allows respondents to express opinions, ideas, or behaviors in their own words without being forced to choose among alternatives that have been predetermined by a marketing researcher. This information is invaluable to marketers because it captures the "voice" of respondents, which is useful in understanding consumer behavior, identifying product benefits, or developing advertising messages. In contrast, *closed-end* or *fixed alternative questions* require respondents to select one or more response options from a set of predetermined choices. Question

6. Check one box that describes your agreement or disagreement with each statement listed below:

STATEMENT	STRONGLY AGREE	AGREE	DON'T KNOW	DISAGREE	STRONGLY DISAGREE
• Adults like to take their families to fast-food restaurants	☐	☐	☐	☐	☐
• Our children have a say in where the family chooses to eat	☐	☐	☐	☐	☐

7. How important are each of the following sources of information to you when selecting a fast-food restaurant to eat at? [Check one box for each source listed]

SOURCE OF INFORMATION	VERY IMPORTANT	SOMEWHAT IMPORTANT	NOT AT ALL IMPORTANT
• Television	☐	☐	☐
• Newspapers	☐	☐	☐
• Radio	☐	☐	☐
• Billboards	☐	☐	☐
• Flyers	☐	☐	☐

8. How often do you eat out at each of the following fast-food restaurants? [Check one box for each source listed]

RESTAURANT	ONCE A WEEK OR MORE	2 TO 3 TIMES A MONTH	ONCE A MONTH OR LESS
• Burger King	☐	☐	☐
• McDonald's	☐	☐	☐
• Wendy's	☐	☐	☐

9. Please answer the following questions about you and your household. [Check only one for each item]

a. What is your gender? ☐ Male ☐ Female

b. What is your marital status? ☐ Single ☐ Married ☐ Other (widowed, divorced, etc.)

c. How many children under age 18 live in your home? ☐ 0 ☐ 1 ☐ 2 ☐ 3 or more

d. What is your age? ☐ Under 25 ☐ 25–44 ☐ 45 or older

e. What is your total annual individual or household income?

☐ <$15,000 ☐ $15,000–49,000 ☐ $50,000 or more

FIGURE 8–5
(continued)

2 is an example of a *dichotomous question*, the simplest form of a fixed alternative question that allows only a "yes" or "no" response.

A fixed alternative question with three or more choices uses a *scale*. Question 5 is an example of a question that uses a *semantic differential scale*, a five-point scale in which the opposite ends have one- or two-word adjectives that have opposite meanings. For example, depending on how clean the respondent feels that Wendy's is, he or she would check the left-hand space on the scale, the right-hand space, or one of the five intervening points. Question 6 uses a *Likert scale*, in which the respondent indicates the extent to which he or she agrees or disagrees with a statement.

The questionnaire in Figure 8–5 provides valuable information to the marketing researcher at Wendy's. Questions 1 to 8 inform him or her about the likes and dislikes in eating out, frequency of eating out at fast-food restaurants generally and at Wendy's specifically, and sources of information used in making decisions about fast-food restaurants. Question 9 gives details about the personal or household characteristics, which can be used in trying to segment the fast-food market, a topic discussed in Chapter 9.

Wendy's does marketing research continuously to discover changing customer wants.

Wendy's Restaurant
www.wendys.com

Figure 8–6 shows typical problems to guard against when wording questions to obtain meaningful answers from respondents. For example, in a question of whether you eat at fast-food restaurants regularly, the word *regularly* is ambiguous. Two people might answer "yes" to the question, but one might mean "once a day" while the other means "once or twice a month." Both answers appear as "yes" to the researcher who tabulates them, but they suggest that dramatically different marketing actions be directed to each of these two prospective consumers. Therefore, it is essential that marketing research questions be worded precisely so that all respondents interpret the same question similarly.

Electronic technology has revolutionized traditional concepts of interviews or surveys. Today, respondents can walk up to a kiosk in a shopping center, read questions off a screen, and key their answers into a computer on a touch screen. Even fully automated telephone interviews exist: An automated voice questions respondents over the telephone, who then key their replies on a touch-tone telephone.

Primary Data: Other Sources

Three other methods of collecting primary data exist that overlap somewhat with the observational or questionnaire methods just discussed. These involve using (1) social networks, (2) panels and experiments, and (3) information technology and data mining.

Social Networks At this moment, someone—maybe even you!—is communicating with someone else online using a social network. Many consumers use social networking Web sites such as Facebook, LinkedIn, and Twitter to communicate with and share opinions among friends, family, and other like-minded individuals around the world. Social networks allow for more intimate and frequent contact among people who share common interests—at a lower cost than other media.

Why is this important to marketers? Because consumers often share their opinions about the offerings they use or want on these social networking Web sites or in

FIGURE 8–6
Typical problems when wording questions

PROBLEM	SAMPLE QUESTION	EXPLANATION OF PROBLEM
Leading question	Why do you like Wendy's fresh meat hamburgers better than those of competitors?	Consumer is led to make statement favoring Wendy's hamburgers.
Ambiguous question	Do you eat at fast-food restaurants regularly? ☐ Yes ☐ No	What is meant by word *regularly*—once a day, once a month, or what?
Unanswerable question	What was the occasion for eating your first hamburger?	Who can remember the answer? Does it matter?
Two questions in one	Do you eat Wendy's hamburgers and chili? ☐ Yes ☐ No	How do you answer if you eat Wendy's hamburgers but not chili?
Nonmutually exclusive answers	What is your age? ☐ Under 20 ☐ 20–40 ☐ 40 and over	What answer does a 40-year-old check?

How do marketers track information on social networks such as Facebook or Twitter? Why do they care? For the answers, see the text.

online blogs (a personal diary or commentary) and forums (a place to hold discussions that allows participants to post comments)—it's like an online version of word of mouth! As a result, marketing researchers increasingly want to glean information from these sites to "mine" their raw consumer-generated content in real time. When collected, transcribed, tabulated, and analyzed, this content may signal a trend in the marketplace that can lead to marketing actions. While most social networks are consumer-driven, not marketer-driven, some organizations have established their own brand-related social networks to obtain consumer insights about both the organization and its offerings, which can increase brand loyalty.

What's likely to happen in the future? For marketers such as Procter & Gamble (P&G) and Unilever, a much larger portion of their market research budgets will be allocated to online research such as social network data mining. They believe that social networks are more in touch with today's consumer lifestyles. Moreover, many consumers are frustrated with research methods such as focus groups, mail surveys, and telephone surveys. However, when relying on consumer-generated content, the sample of individuals from whom this content was gleaned may not be statistically representative of the marketplace.[25]

Panels and Experiments Two special ways that observations and questionnaires are sometimes used are panels and experiments.

Marketing researchers often want to know if consumers change their behavior over time, so they take successive measurements of the same people. A *panel* is a sample of consumers or stores from which researchers take a series of measurements. For example, the NPD Group collects data about consumer purchases such as apparel, food, and electronics from its Online Panel, which consists of more than 3 million individuals worldwide. So a firm like General Mills can use descriptive research—counting the frequency of consumer purchases—to measure switching behavior from one brand of its breakfast cereal (Wheaties) to another (Cheerios) or to a competitor's brand (Kellogg's Special K). A disadvantage of panels is that the marketing research firm needs to recruit new members continually to replace those who drop out. These new recruits must match the characteristics of those they replace to keep the panel representative of the marketplace.

How might Wal-Mart have done early marketing research to help develop its supercenters, which have achieved international success? For its unusual research, see the text.

An *experiment* involves obtaining data by manipulating factors under tightly controlled conditions to test cause and effect, an example of causal research. The interest is in whether changing one of the independent variables (a cause) will change the behavior of the dependent variable that is studied (the result). In marketing experiments, the independent variables of interest—sometimes called the marketing *drivers*—are often one or more of the marketing mix elements, such as a product's features, price, or promotion (like advertising messages or coupons). The ideal dependent variable usually is a change in purchases (incremental unit or dollar sales) of individuals, households, or organizations. For example, food companies often use *test markets*, which offer a product for sale in a small geographic area to help evaluate potential marketing actions. So a test market is really a kind of marketing experiment to reduce risks. In 1988, Wal-Mart opened three experimental stand-alone supercenters to gauge consumer acceptance before deciding to open others. Today, Wal-Mart operates 2,500 supercenters around the world.

A potential difficulty with experiments is that outside factors (such as actions of competitors) can distort the results of an experiment and affect the dependent variable (such as sales). A researcher's task is to identify the effect of the marketing variable of interest on the dependent variable when the effects of outside factors in an experiment might hide it.

learning review

6. What is the difference between observational and questionnaire data?
7. Which survey provides the greatest flexibility for asking probing questions: mail, telephone, or personal interview?
8. What is the difference between a panel and an experiment?

LO5

Information Technology and Data Mining Today's marketing managers can be drowned in an ocean of data; they need to adopt strategies for dealing with complex, changing views of the competition, the market, and the consumer. The Internet and PC power help make sense out of this data ocean. The marketer's task is to convert this data ocean into useful information that leads to marketing actions.

Information technology involves operating computer networks that can store and process data. Today information technology can extract hidden information from large databases such as households' product purchases, TV viewing behavior, and responses to coupon or free-sample promotions. As noted earlier, firms such as Information Resources' InfoScan and AC Nielsen's ScanTrack collect this information through bar-code scanners at the checkout counters in supermarket, drug, convenience, and mass merchandise retailers in the United States.[26]

Figure 8–7 shows how marketing researchers and managers use information technology to frame questions that provide answers leading to marketing actions. At the bottom of Figure 8–7 the marketer queries the databases in the information system with marketing questions needing answers. These questions go through statistical models that analyze the relationships that exist among the data. The databases form the core, or *data warehouse,* where the ocean of data is collected and stored. After the search of this data warehouse, the models select and link the pertinent data, often presenting them in tables and graphics for easy interpretation. Marketers can also use *sensitivity analysis* to query the database with "what if" questions to determine how a hypothetical change in a driver such as advertising can affect sales.

Traditional marketing research typically involves identifying possible drivers and then collecting data. For example, we might collect data to test the hypothesis that increasing couponing (the driver) during spring will increase trials by first-time buyers (the result).

In contrast, **data mining** is the extraction of hidden predictive information from large databases to find statistical links between consumer purchasing patterns and marketing actions. Some of these are common sense: Since many consumers buy peanut butter and grape jelly together, it may be a good idea to run a joint promotion between Skippy peanut butter and Welch's grape jelly. But would you have expected that men buying diapers in the evening sometimes buy a six-pack of beer as well? This is exactly what supermarkets discovered when they mined checkout data from scanners. So they placed diapers and beer near each other, then placed potato chips between them—and increased sales on all three items!

On the near horizon: RFID technology using a "smart tag" microchip on the diapers and beer to tell whether they wind up in the same shopping bag—at 10 in the evening.[27] Still, the success in data mining depends on

At 10 P.M. what is this man likely to buy besides these diapers? For the curious answer data mining gives, see the text.

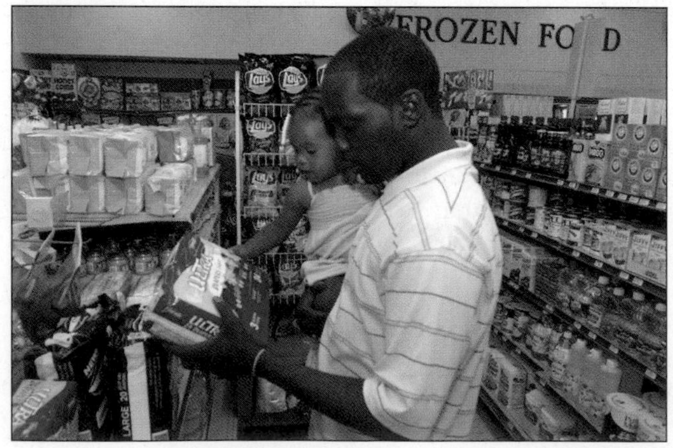

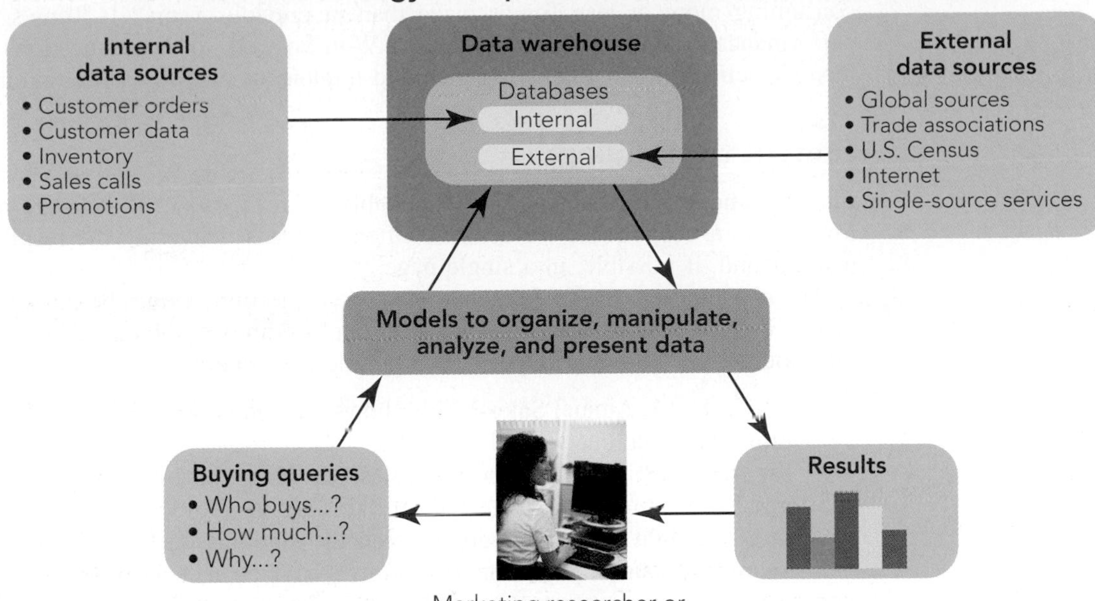

FIGURE 8–7
How marketing researchers and managers use information technology to turn information into action

the judgments of the marketing managers and researchers in how to select, analyze, and interpret the information.

Advantages and Disadvantages of Primary Data

Compared with secondary data, primary data have the advantage of being more specific to the problem being studied. The main disadvantages are that primary data are usually far more costly and time consuming to collect than secondary data.

STEP 4: DEVELOP FINDINGS

How are sales doing? To see how marketers at Tony's Pizza assessed this question and the results, read the text.

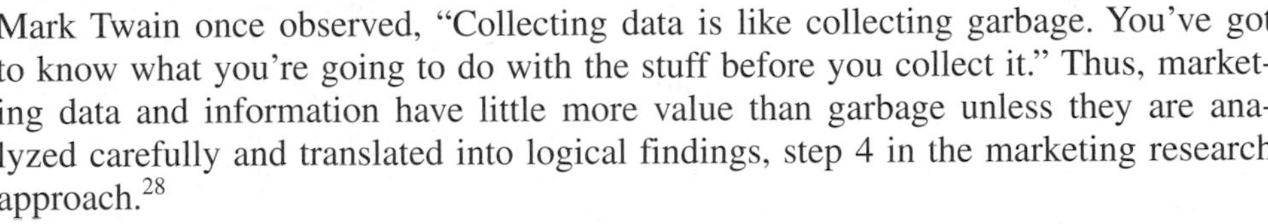

Mark Twain once observed, "Collecting data is like collecting garbage. You've got to know what you're going to do with the stuff before you collect it." Thus, marketing data and information have little more value than garbage unless they are analyzed carefully and translated into logical findings, step 4 in the marketing research approach.[28]

Analyze the Data

Let's consider the case in early 2010 of Tony's Pizza and Teré Carral, the marketing manager responsible for the Tony's brand. We will use hypothetical data to protect Tony's proprietary information.

Teré is concerned about the limited growth in the Tony's brand over the past four years. She hires a consultant to collect and analyze data to explain what's going on with her brand and to recommend ways to improve its growth. Teré asks the consultant to put together a proposal that includes the answers to two key questions:

1. How are Tony's sales doing on a household basis? For example, are fewer households buying Tony's pizzas, or is each household buying fewer Tony's? Or both?
2. What factors might be contributing to Tony's very flat sales over the past four years?

Facts uncovered by the consultant are vital. For example, is the average household consuming more or less Tony's pizza than in previous years? Is Tony's flat sales performance related to a specific factor? With answers to these questions Teré can identify actions in her marketing plan and implement them over the coming year.

Present the Findings

Findings should be clear and understandable from the way the data are presented. Managers are responsible for *actions*. Often it means delivering the results in clear pictures and, if possible, in a single page.

The consultant gives Teré the answers to her questions using the marketing dashboards in Figure 8–8, a creative way to present findings graphically. Let's look over the shoulders of Teré and the consultant while they interpret these findings:

FIGURE 8–8
These marketing dashboards present findings to Tony's marketing manager that lead to recommendations and actions.
Source: Teré Carral, Tony's Pizza.

- Figure 8–8A, Annual Sales—This shows the annual growth of the Tony's Pizza brand is stable but virtually flat from 2006 through 2009.
- Figure 8–8B, Average Annual Sales per Household—Look closely at this graph. At first glance, it may seem like sales in 2009 are *half* what they were in 2006, right? But be careful to read the numbers on the vertical axis. They show that household purchases of Tony's have been steadily declining over the

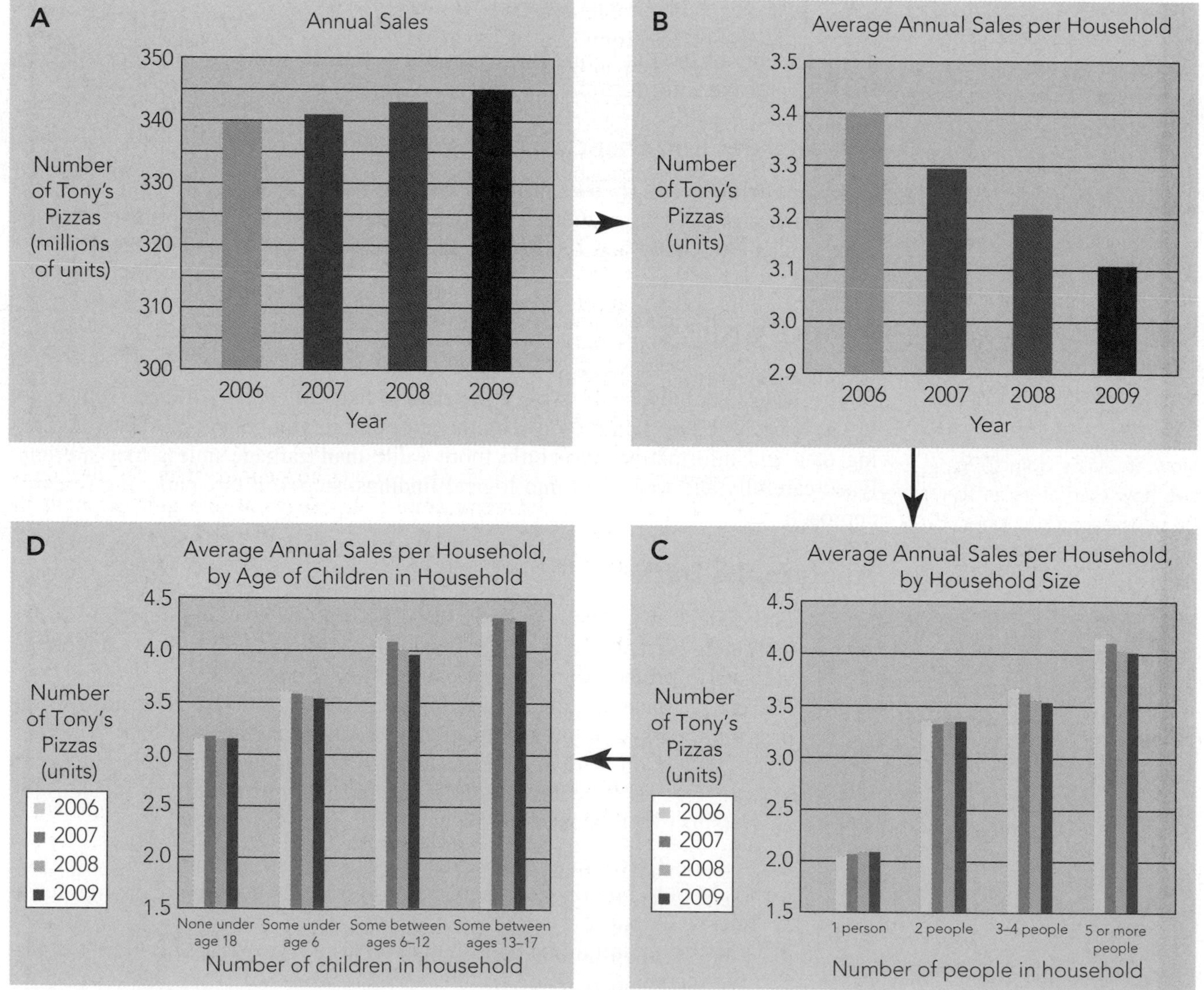

past four years, from an average of 3.4 pizzas per household in 2006 to 3.1 pizzas per household in 2009. (Significant, but hardly a 50 percent drop.) Now the question is, if Tony's annual sales are stable, yet the average individual household is buying fewer Tony's pizzas, what's going on? The answer is, more households are buying pizzas—it's just that each household is buying fewer Tony's pizzas. That households aren't choosing Tony's is a genuine source of concern. But again, here's a classic example of a marketing problem representing a marketing opportunity. The number of households buying pizza is *growing*, and that's good news for Tony's.

- Figure 8–8C, Average Annual Sales per Household, by Household Size—This chart starts to show a source of the problem: Even though average sales of pizza to households with only one or two people is stable, households with three or four people and those with five or more are declining in average annual pizza consumption. Which households tend to have more than two people? Answer: Households *with children*. Therefore, we should look more closely at the pizza-buying behavior of households with children.
- Figure 8–8D, Average Annual Sales per Household, by Age of Children in the Household—The picture is becoming very clear now: The real problem is in the serious decline in average consumption in the households with younger children, especially in households with children in the 6- to 12-year-old age group.

Identifying a sales problem in households with children 6 to 12 years old is an important discovery, as Tony's sales are declining in a market segment that is known to be one of the heaviest in buying pizzas.

STEP 5: TAKE MARKETING ACTIONS

Effective marketing research doesn't stop with findings and recommendations—someone has to identify the marketing actions, put them into effect, and monitor how the decisions turn out, which is the essence of step 5.

Marketing research at Tony's Pizza helped develop this colorful, friendly ad targeted at families with 6 to 12 year olds.

Make Action Recommendations

Teré Carral, the marketing manager for Tony's Pizza, met with her team to convert the market research findings into specific marketing recommendations with a clear objective: Target households with children ages 6 to 12 to reverse the trend among this segment and gain strength in one of the most important segments in the frozen pizza category. Her recommendation is to develop:

- An advertising campaign that will target children 6 to 12.
- A monthly promotion calendar with this age group target in mind.
- A special event program reaching children 6 to 12.

Implement the Action Recommendations

As her first marketing action, Teré undertakes advertising research to develop ads that appeal to children in the 6-to-12 age group and their families. The research shows that children like colorful ads with funny, friendly characters. She gives these research results to her advertising agency, which develops several sample ads for her review. Teré selects three that are tested on children to identify the most appealing one, which is then used in her next advertising campaign for Tony's Pizza. This is the ad at left.

Evaluate the Results

Evaluating results is a continuing way of life for effective marketing managers. There are really two aspects of this evaluation process:

- *Evaluating the decision itself.* This involves monitoring the marketplace to determine if action is necessary in the future. For Teré, is her new ad successful in appealing to 6-to-12-year-olds and their families? Are sales increasing to this target segment? The success of this strategy suggests Teré add more follow-up ads with colorful, funny, friendly characters.
- *Evaluating the decision process used.* Was the marketing research and analysis used to develop the recommendations effective? Was it flawed? Could it be improved for similar situations in the future? Teré and her marketing team must be vigilant for ways to improve the analysis and results—to learn lessons that might apply to future marketing research efforts at Tony's.

Again, systematic analysis does not guarantee success. But, as in the case of Tony's Pizza, it can improve a firm's success rate for its marketing decisions.

learning review

9. How does data mining differ from traditional marketing research?
10. In the marketing research for Tony's Pizza, what is an example of (*a*) a finding and (*b*) a marketing action?

SALES FORECASTING TECHNIQUES

Forecasting or estimating potential sales is often a key goal in a marketing research study. Good sales forecasts are important for a firm as it schedules production. The term **sales forecast** refers to the total sales of a product that a firm expects to sell during a specified time period under specified environmental conditions and its own marketing efforts. For example, Betty Crocker might develop a sales forecast of 4 million cases of cake mix for U.S. consumers in 2011, assuming consumers' dessert preferences remain constant and competitors don't change prices.

Three main sales forecasting techniques are often used: (1) judgments of the decision maker, (2) surveys of knowledgeable groups, and (3) statistical methods.

Judgments of the Decision Maker

Probably 99 percent of all sales forecasts are simply the judgment of the person who must act on the results of the forecast—the individual decision maker. *A direct forecast* involves estimating the value to be forecast without any intervening steps. Examples appear daily: How many quarts of milk should I buy? How much money should I get out of the ATM?

A *lost-horse forecast* involves starting with the last known value of the item being forecast, listing the factors that could affect the forecast, assessing whether they have a positive or negative impact, and making the final forecast. The technique gets its name from how you'd find a lost horse: go to where it was last seen, put yourself in its shoes, consider those factors that could affect where you might go (to the pond if you're thirsty, the hayfield if you're hungry, and so on), and go there.

How might a marketing manager at Under Armour forecast running shoe sales through 2012? Use a lost-horse forecast, as described in the text.

For example, in early 2009 Under Armour introduced its first line of running shoes. This required it to broaden its appeal from boys and young men who often used its knee pads and cleats in team sports to women, older consumers, and casual athletes. Suppose an Under Armour marketing manager in early 2010 needs to make a sales forecast through 2012. She would take the known value of 2009 sales and list positive factors (good acceptance of its high-tech designs, great publicity) and the negative factors (the economic recession, competition from established name brands) to arrive at the final series of sales forecasts.[29]

Surveys of Knowledgeable Groups

If you wonder what your firm's sales will be next year, ask people who are likely to know something about future sales. Two common groups that are surveyed to develop sales forecasts are prospective buyers and the firm's salesforce.

A *survey of buyers' intentions forecast* involves asking prospective customers if they are likely to buy the product during some future time period. For industrial products with few prospective buyers, this can be effective. There are only a few hundred customers in the entire world for Boeing's large airplanes, so Boeing surveys them to develop its sales forecasts and production schedules.

A *salesforce survey forecast* involves asking the firm's salespeople to estimate sales during a coming period. Because these people are in contact with customers and are likely to know what customers like and dislike, there is logic to this approach. However, salespeople can be unreliable forecasters—painting too rosy a picture if they are enthusiastic about a new product and too grim a forecast if their sales quota and future compensation are based on it.

Statistical Methods

The best-known statistical method of forecasting is *trend extrapolation*, which involves extending a pattern observed in past data into the future. When the pattern is described with a straight line, it is *linear trend extrapolation*. Suppose that in early 2000 you were a sales forecaster for the Xerox Corporation and had actual sales data running from 1988 to 1999 (see Figure 8–9). Using linear trend extrapolation, you draw a line to fit the past sales data and project it into the future to give the forecast values shown for 2000 to 2012.

If in 2008 you want to compare your forecasts with actual results, you are in for a surprise—illustrating the strength and weakness of trend extrapolation. Trend extrapolation assumes that the underlying relationships in the past will continue into the future, which is the basis of the method's key strength: simplicity. If this assumption

FIGURE 8–9
Linear trend extrapolation of sales revenues at Xerox, made at the start of 2000

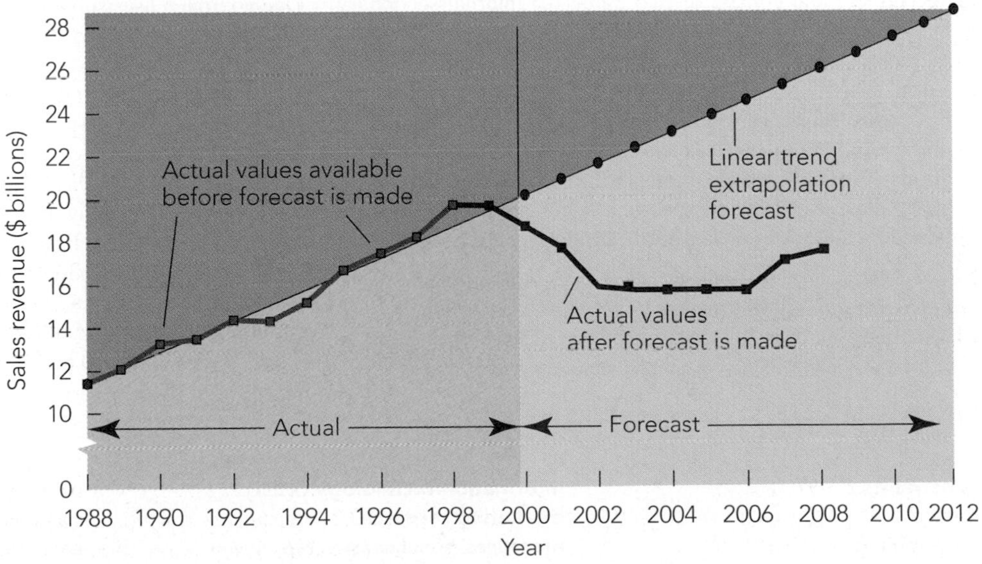

proves correct, you have an accurate forecast. However, if this proves wrong, the forecast is likely to be wrong. In this case your forecasts from 2001 through 2007 were too high, as shown in Figure 8–9, largely because of fierce competition in the photocopying industry.

learning review

11. What are the three kinds of sales forecasting techniques?
12. How do you make a lost-horse forecast?

LEARNING OBJECTIVES REVIEW

LO1 *Identify the reason for conducting marketing research.*
To be successful, products and marketing programs must meet the wants and needs of potential customers. So marketing research reduces risk by providing the vital information to help marketing managers understand those wants and needs and translate them into marketing actions.

LO2 *Describe the five-step marketing research approach that leads to marketing actions.*
Marketing researchers engage in a five-step decision-making process to collect information that improves marketing decisions. The first step is to define the problem, which requires setting the research objectives and identifying possible marketing actions. The second step is to develop the research plan, which involves specifying the constraints, identifying data needed for marketing decisions, and determining how to collect the data. The third step is to collect the relevant information, which includes considering pertinent secondary data (both internal and external) and primary data (by observing and questioning consumers) as well as using information technology and data mining to trigger marketing actions. The fourth step is to develop findings from the marketing research data collected. This involves analyzing the data and presenting the findings of the research. The fifth and last step is to take marketing actions, which involves making and implementing the action recommendations.

LO3 *Explain how marketing uses secondary and primary data.*
Secondary data have already been recorded before the start of the project and consist of two parts: (*a*) internal secondary data, which originate from within the organization, such as sales reports and customer comments, and (*b*) external secondary data, which are created by other organizations, such as the U.S. Census Bureau (provides data on the country's population, manufacturers, retailers, and so on) or business and trade publications (provide data on industry trends, market size, etc.). Primary data are collected specifically for the project and are obtained by either observing or questioning people.

LO4 *Discuss the uses of observations, questionnaires, panels, experiments, and newer data collection methods.*
Marketing researchers observe people in various ways, such as electronically using Nielsen people meters to measure TV viewing behavior or personally using mystery shoppers or ethnographic techniques. A recent electronic innovation is neuromarketing—using high-tech brain scanning to record the responses of a consumer's brain to marketing stimuli like packages or TV ads. Questionnaires involve asking people questions (*a*) in person using interviews or focus groups or (*b*) via a questionnaire using a telephone, fax, print, e-mail, or an Internet survey. Panels involve a sample of consumers or stores that are repeatedly measured through time to see if their behaviors change. Experiments, such as test markets, involve measuring the effect of marketing variables such as price or advertising on sales. Collecting data from social networks like Facebook or Twitter is increasingly important because users can share their opinions about products and services with countless "friends" around the globe.

LO5 *Explain how information technology and data mining lead to marketing actions.*
Today's marketing managers are often overloaded with data—from internal sales and customer data to external data on TV viewing habits or grocery purchases from the scanner data at checkout counters. Information technology enables this massive amount of marketing data to be stored, accessed, and processed. The resulting databases can be queried using data mining to find statistical relationships useful for marketing decisions and actions.

LO6 *Describe three approaches to developing a company's sales forecast.*
One approach uses subjective judgments of the decision maker, such as direct or lost-horse forecasts. A direct forecast involves estimating the value to be forecast without any intervening steps. A lost horse forecast starts with the last known value of the item being forecast, listing the factors that could affect the forecast, assessing whether they have a positive or negative impact, and making the final forecast. Surveys of knowledgeable groups is a second method. It involves obtaining information such as the intentions of potential buyers or estimates of the salesforce. Statistical methods involving extending a pattern observed in past data into the future is a third example. The best-known statistical method is linear trend extrapolation.

FOCUSING ON KEY TERMS

constraints p. 197
data p. 199
data mining p. 210
decision p. 195
information technology p. 210
marketing research p. 195
measures of success p. 196
observational data p. 201
primary data p. 199
questionnaire data p. 203
sales forecast p. 214
secondary data p. 199

APPLYING MARKETING KNOWLEDGE

1 Suppose your dean of admissions is considering surveying high school seniors about their perceptions of your school to design better informational brochures for them. What are the advantages and disadvantages of doing (*a*) telephone interviews and (*b*) an Internet survey of seniors requesting information about the school?

2 Nielsen Media Research obtains ratings of local TV stations in small markets by having households fill out diary questionnaires. These give information on (*a*) who is watching TV and (*b*) what program. What are the limitations of this questionnaire method?

3 The format in which information is presented is often vital. (*a*) If you were a harried marketing manager and queried your information system, would you rather see the results in tables or charts and graphs? (*b*) What are one or two strengths and weaknesses of each format?

4 Wisk detergent decides to run a test market to see the effect of coupons and in-store advertising on sales. The index of sales is as follows:

Element in Test Market	Weeks Before Coupon	Week of Coupon	Week after Coupon
Without in-store ads	100	144	108
With in-store ads	100	268	203

What are your conclusions and recommendations?

5 Suppose Fisher-Price wants to run a simple experiment to evaluate a proposed chatter telephone design. It has two different groups of children on which to run its experiment for one week each. The first group has the old toy telephone, whereas the second group is exposed to the newly designed pull toy with wheels, a noisemaker, and bobbing eyes. The dependent variable is the average number of minutes during the two-hour play period that one of the children is playing with the toy, and the results are as follows:

Element in Experiment	First Group	Second Group
Independent variable	Old design	New design
Dependent variable	13 minutes	62 minutes

Should Fisher-Price introduce the new design? Why?

6 (*a*) Why might a marketing researcher prefer to use secondary data rather than primary data in a study? (*b*) Why might the reverse be true?

7 Which of the following variables would linear trend extrapolation be more accurate for? (*a*) Annual population of the United States or (*b*) annual sales of cars produced in the United States by Ford. Why?

building your marketing plan

To help you collect the most useful data for your marketing plan, develop a three-column table:

1 In column 1, list the information you would ideally like to have to fill holes in your marketing plan.

2 In column 2, identify the source for each bit of information in column 1, such as an Internet search, talking to prospective customers, looking at internal data, and so forth.

3 In column 3, set a priority on information you will have time to spend collecting by ranking them: 1 = most important; 2 = next most important, and so forth.

video case 8 Ford Consulting Group, Inc.: From Data to Actions

"The fast pace of working as a marketing professional isn't getting any easier," agrees David Ford, as he talks with Mark Rehborg, Tony's Pizza brand manager. "The speed of communication, the availability of real-time market information, and the responsibility for a brand's profit make marketing one of the most challenging professional jobs today."

Mark responds, "Ten years ago, we could reach 80 percent of our target market with 3 television spots—but today, to reach the same 80 percent, we would have to buy 97 spots. We haven't the luxury to be complacent—our core consumer, the 6- to 12-year-old 'big kid,' is part of a savvy, wired culture that is changing rapidly."

DASHBOARDS: DATA INTO ACTIONS

David Ford, president of Ford Consulting Group (FCG), prepares business analysis, often in the form of a dashboard, to assist clients such as Tony's in translating the market and sales information into marketing actions. David works with Mark to grow Tony's sales and profit performance. Mark uses information to choose where to spend his funds to promote his products. Many times, the sales force requests additional promotion funds to help them hit their sales targets.

The information used most often for sales and promotion analysis comes from places like ACNielsen's ScanTrack and Information Resources' InfoScan (IRI) that summarize sales data from grocery stores and other outlets that scan purchases at the checkout.

FCG helps clients make sense of their existing information, *not* collect more information. The project that follows is typical of the work Ford Consulting Group (www.fordconsultinggroup.com) undertakes for a client. The data are hypothetical, but the situation is a very typical one in the grocery products industry. Here's a snapshot of some of the terms in the case:

- "You" have just come on the job, as the new marketing person.
- "NE" is the Northeastern sales region of Tony's.
- "SW, NW, SW" are the other sales regions.

PART 1: A TYPICAL QUESTION, ON A TYPICAL DAY

Let's dive into the background of a typical question you might face on a typical day. You are given two memos (one from Mark to you) as background.

You dig into data files and develop Table 1 that shows how Tony's is doing in the company's four sales regions and the entire United States on key marketing dimensions. Without reading further, take a deep breath and try to answer question 1.

PART 2: UNCOVERING THE TRUTH

Let's assume your analysis (question 1) shows the NE is a problem, so we need to understand what's going on in the NE. Further effort enables you to develop Table 2. It shows the situation for the four largest supermarket chains in the Northeast sales region that carry Tony's. Now answer question 2.

Questions

1 Study Table 1. (*a*) How does the situation in the Northeast compare with the other regions in the United States? (*b*) What are reasons that sales are soft? (*c*) Write a 150-word e-mail with attachments to Mark Rehborg, your boss, giving your answers to *b*.

2 Study Table 2. (*a*) What do you conclude from this information? (*b*) Summarize your conclusions in a 150-word e-mail with attachments to Mark, who needs them for a meeting tomorrow with Margaret, the Northeast sales region manager. (*c*) What marketing actions might your memo suggest?

TO: Mark Rehborg, Tony's Brand Manager
FROM: Steve Quam, Tony's Field Sales
CC: Margaret Loiaza, NE Sales Region Manager

RE: Feedback on Sales Call at Food-Fast

Hi Mark—

Our sales call at Food-Fast wasn't so great. They don't see how our Tony's is going to sell well enough to justify the additional shelf-space. I also talked to Margaret and she said that second quarter may be weaker than planned across all the NE, and I should give you a heads-up. She's on vacation this week. She's planning to schedule some time with you to talk about additional promotion money to do catch-up in the third quarter. She'll be there next week.

Steve

TO: You, the New Marketing Person
FROM: Mark Rehborg, Tony's Brand Manager (Your Boss)

RE: Small Project due Friday

Hi You,

Can you help out here? I've got a meeting with Margaret on Friday afternoon, and she's concerned that Food-Fast and the whole NE is going to need some additional promotion dollars.

Lauretta started the analysis and was hurt in a kickboxing accident yesterday and won't be back to work for a week. Her files are attached. Can you look through her files and summarize what's going on in the NE and the rest of the U.S.? Does Margaret need more promotion money?

Let's discuss Friday A.M.

Mark

TABLE 1. COMPARISON OF TONY'S PERFORMANCE, BY REGION						
					Promotion	
Region	Quarterly Change in Volume (%)	Distribution[a] (%)	Price ($)	Price Gap[b] ($)	Support[c] (%)	Volume[d] (%)
NE	3%	93%	$1.29	+8	7%	14%
SE	5	95	1.11	−1	9	16
NW	8	98	1.19	+1	8	15
SW	6	96	1.25	0	8	15
U.S.	6	97	1.19	0	8	15

[a] % of outlets carrying Tony's.
[b] Price gap = (Our price) − (Competitor's price).
[c] Promotion support = % of the time brand was promoted.
[d] Promotion volume = % of the volume sold on promotion.

TABLE 2. COMPARISON OF MAJOR SUPERMARKET CHAINS IN THE NORTHEAST						
					Promotion	
Super-Market Chain	Quarterly Change in Volume (%)	Distribution[a] (%)	Price ($)	Price Gap[b] ($)	Support[c] (%)	Volume[d] (%)
Save-a-lot	5%	95%	$1.39	+10	10%	19%
Food-Fast	0	90	1.28	−1	3	4
Get-Fresh	0	90	1.30	+1	3	4
Dollars-Off	7	97	1.34	+5	7	14

24/7 Customer Service 1.800.927.7671 • Español 1.888.927.4104 Cart My Account • My Favorites | Help

Zappos.com ZETA POWERED by SERVICE™

Free Shipping Both Ways!* 365-Day Return Policy

--Search-- Search

Search by: Size • Narrow Shoes • Wide Shoes • Popular Searches

Go to Zappos.com Classic

--Visit Our Other Sites--

View All Departments | Shoes | Clothing | Bags & Handbags | Watches | Sunglasses | New Arrivals | Brands | Women's | Men's | Kids'

Alphabetical Brand Index # A B C D E F G H I J K L M N O P Q R S T U V W X Y Z

Women's Shoes

What's New
Sandals
Heels
Boots
Sneakers
Slippers
Flats
Clogs & Mules
More Women's Shoes

Men's Shoes

What's New
Boots
Sneakers
Oxfords
Sandals
Loafers
Boat Shoes
Slippers
More Men's Shoes

Kids' Shoes

What's New
Sneakers
Flats
Sandals
Boots
First Walkers
More Kids' Shoes

Women's Clothing

What's New
Tops
Shorts
Skirts
Pants
Jackets & Coats
Swimsuits
Sleepwear
More Women's Clothing

Men's Clothing

What's New
Shirts
Shorts
Pants
Jackets & Coats
Suits
Swimsuits
Sleepwear
More Men's Clothing

Kids' Clothing

What's New
Clothing Sets
Shirts
Shorts
Pants
Jackets & Coats
Swimwear
Baby One-Pieces
More Kids' Clothing

Bags and Handbags

Backpacks
Messenger Bags
Diaper Bags
Laptop Bags
Tote Bags
Hobo Bags
Shoulder Bags
Clutch Bags
More Bags

More Departments

What's New
Accessories
Housewares
Beauty
Jewelry
Watches
Sporting Goods
More Departments

FREE RETURNS · 365-DAY RETURN POLICY · 24/7 CUSTOMER SERVICE · 1.800.927.7671

Shopping Recommendations For You

Onitsuka Tiger by Asics
Ultimate 81
$66.95

Converse
All Star Core OX
$45.00

Converse
Chuck Taylor All Star Ox
$45.00

Sperry Top-Sider
Authentic Original
$64.95

Vans
Classic Slip-On Core Classics
$42.00

What's New At Zappos!

Women's

Zappos Top Sellers!

Women's

Find What You Need Quickly

By Gender

Special Interest

Specialty Site

The Zappos Culture

Learn about what inspires Zappos to provide the best service!

Zappos Core Values:
10 Values We Live By

Customer Testimonials:
Our Customers Connect

Enjoy Fun and A Little Weirdness:
Check out Zappos Blogs

The Zappos Experience:
Share Your Zappos Videos

Unique Customers:
Zappos Furry Customers
Zappos Customers In Training

Become a Part of Our Culture:
Careers at Zappos

Get Inspired:

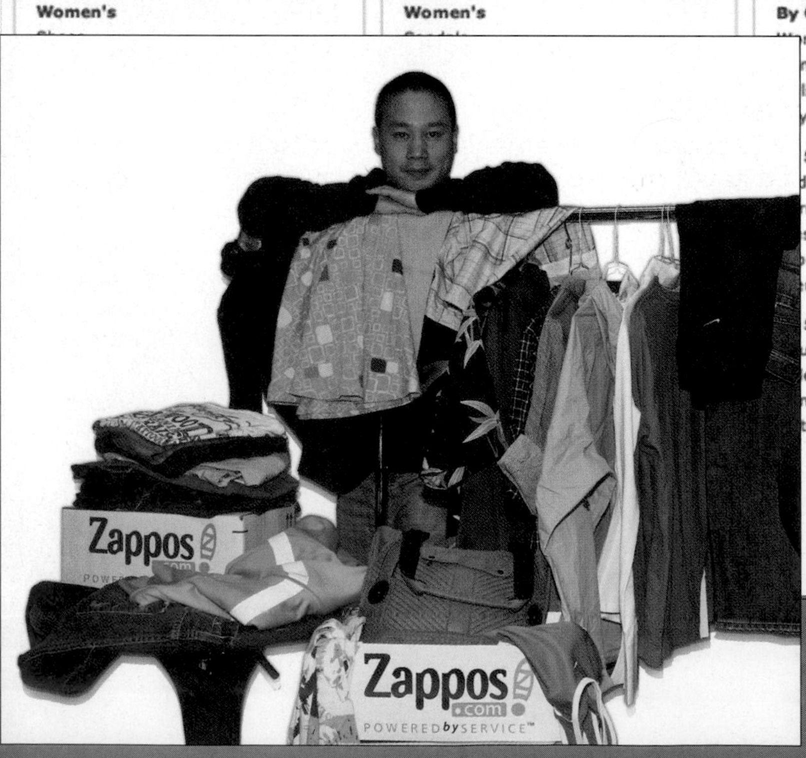

9 Market Segmentation, Targeting, and Positioning

LEARNING OBJECTIVES
After reading this chapter you should be able to:

LO1 Explain what market segmentation is and when to use it.

LO2 Identify the five steps involved in segmenting and targeting markets.

LO3 Recognize the bases used to segment consumer and organizational markets.

LO4 Develop a market-product grid to identify a target market and recommend resulting actions.

LO5 Explain how marketing managers position products in the marketplace.

ZAPPOS.COM: DELIVERING "WOW" THROUGH MARKET SEGMENTATION AND SERVICE

Tony Hsieh (opposite page) showed signs of being an entrepreneur early in life. He's now chief executive officer (CEO) of online retailer Zappos.com. The company name is derived from the Spanish word *zapatos,* which means shoes.

At age 12, Hsieh brought in several hundred dollars a month with his button-making business. In college, Hsieh sold pizzas out of his dorm room. Fellow entrepreneur Alfred Lin bought pizzas from Hsieh and then sold them by the slice to other students. And where is pizza-slice marketer Alfred Lin today? He's the chief operating officer at Zappos.com.[1]

A Clear Market Segmentation Strategy

Hsieh, Lin, and founder Nick Swinmurn have given Zappos.com a clear, specific market segmentation strategy: Offer a huge selection of shoes to people who will buy them online. Recently Zappos.com has added lines of clothes, accessories, beauty, and housewares. This focus on the segment of online buyers generated over $1 billion in sales in 2008.[2]

"With Zappos, the shoe store comes to you," says Pamela Leo, a New Jersey customer. "I can try the shoes in the comfort of my own home. . . . It's fabulous."[3] Besides the in-home convenience, Zappos .com offers free shipping both ways.[4] The choices for its online customers are staggering. A recent Zappos.com home page described "Today at Zappos" as 1,136 brands, with over 3 million products.

Delivering WOW Customer Service

Asked about Zappos.com, Hsieh says, "We try to spend most of our time on stuff that will improve customer-service levels."[5] This customer-service obsession for its market segment of online customers means that all new Zappos.com employees—whether the chief financial officer or children's footwear buyer—go through four weeks of customer-loyalty training. Hsieh offers $2,000 to anyone completing the training who wants to leave Zappos.com. The theory: If you take the money and run, you're not right for Zappos.com. Few take the money!

Ten "core values" are the foundation for the Zappos.com culture, brand, and business strategies. Some examples:[6]

#1. Deliver WOW through service. This focus on exemplary customer service encompasses all 10 core values.

#3. Create fun and a little weirdness. In a Zappos.com day, cowbells ring, parades appear, and modified-blaster gunfights arise.

#6. Build open and honest relationships with communications. Employees are told to say what they think.

The other Zappos.com core values appear on its Web site: www.Zappos.com.

The Zappos.com strategy illustrates successful market segmentation and targeting, the first topics in Chapter 9. The chapter ends with the topic of positioning the organization, product, or brand.

WHY SEGMENT MARKETS?

LO1

A business firm segments its markets so it can respond more effectively to the wants of groups of potential buyers and thus increase its sales and profits. Not-for-profit organizations also segment the clients they serve to satisfy client needs more effectively while achieving the organization's goals. Let's describe (1) what market segmentation is and (2) when to segment markets, sometimes using the Zappos.com segmentation strategy as an example.

What Market Segmentation Means

People have different needs and wants, even though it would be easier for marketers if they didn't. **Market segmentation** involves aggregating prospective buyers into groups that (1) have common needs and (2) will respond similarly to a marketing action. **Market segments** are the relatively homogeneous groups of prospective buyers that result from the market segmentation process. Each market segment consists of people who are relatively similar to each other in terms of their consumption behavior.

The existence of different market segments has caused firms to use a marketing strategy of **product differentiation**. This strategy involves a firm using different marketing mix activities, such as product features and advertising, to help consumers perceive the product as being different and better than competing products. The perceived differences may involve physical features, such as size or color, or nonphysical ones, such as image or price.

Segmentation: Linking Needs to Actions The process of segmenting a market and selecting specific segments as targets is the link between the various buyers' needs and the organization's marketing program, as shown in Figure 9–1. Market segmentation is only a means to an end: to lead to tangible marketing actions that can increase sales and profitability.

Effective market segmentation does two key things: (1) forms meaningful groupings and (2) develops specific marketing mix actions. People or organizations should be grouped into a market segment according to the similarity of their needs and the benefits they look for in making a purchase. The market segments must relate to specific marketing actions that the organization can take. These actions may involve separate offerings or other aspects of the marketing mix, such as price, promotion, or distribution strategies.

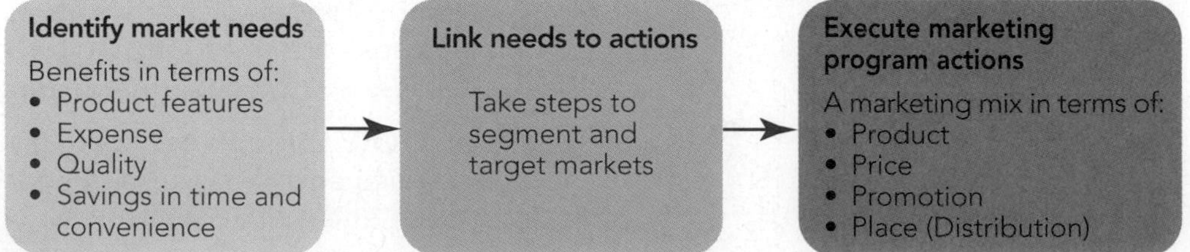

FIGURE 9–1
Market segmentation links market needs to an organization's marketing program—specific marketing mix actions to satisfy those needs.

Core value #3—"create fun and a little weirdness"—helped in naming Zappos .com one of the 2008 "Marketers of the Year" by *Advertising Age* magazine.

The Successful Zappos.com Footwear Segmentation Strategy The Zappos.com target customer segment consists of people who want (1) a wide selection of shoes, (2) to shop online in the convenience of their own home, and (3) to receive the guarantee of quick delivery and free returns. Zappos' actions include offering a huge inventory of shoes and other products, using an online selling strategy, and providing overnight delivery. This enables Zappos .com to create a positive customer experience and generate repeat purchases. On any given day, about 75 percent of Zappos.com shoppers are repeat customers.

With over 8 million customers and 5,000 calls daily to Zappos' service center, Zappos.com executives believe that the speed with which a customer receives an online purchase plays a big role in gaining repeat customers.[7] The company will continue to stress this point of difference, made possible by stocking in its warehouse every item it sells. And if customers continue to associate Zappos.com with the absolute best service among online sellers with its footwear, clothing, and other offerings, both Zappos.com weirdness (its fifth core value) and its sales are on solid footing!

When and How to Segment Markets

The one-size-fits all mass markets—like that for Tide laundry detergent of 40 years ago—no longer exist. The global marketing officer at Procter & Gamble, which markets Tide, says, "Every one of our brands is targeted." Welcome to today's customer relationship era that consists of market segmentation and target marketing.[8]

A business goes to the trouble and expense of segmenting its markets when it expects that this will increase its sales, profit, and return on investment. When expenses are greater than the potentially increased sales from segmentation, a firm should not attempt to segment its market. Three specific segmentation strategies that illustrate this point are: (1) one product and multiple market segments, (2) multiple products and multiple market segments, and (3) "segments of one," or mass customization.

One Product and Multiple Market Segments When an organization produces only a single product or service and attempts to sell it to two or more market segments, it avoids the extra costs of developing and producing additional versions of the product. In this case, the incremental costs of taking the product into new market segments are typically those of a separate promotional campaign or a new channel of distribution.

These *different* covers for the *same* magazine issue show a very effective market segmentation strategy. For which specific one it is and why it works, see the text.

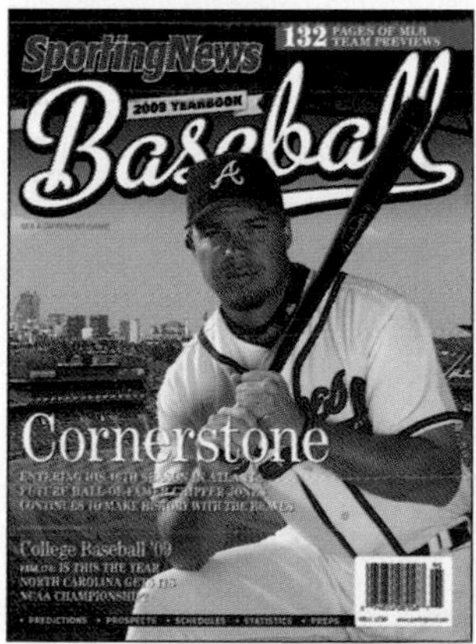

Does Harry Potter appeal only to the English-speaking kids' segment? See the text about this amazing publishing success story.

Magazines and books are single products frequently directed to two or more distinct market segments. The *Sporting News Baseball Yearbook* uses 16 different covers featuring a baseball star from each of its regions in the United States. Harry Potter's phenomenal seven-book success is based both on author J. K. Rowling's fiction-writing wizardry and her publisher's creativity in marketing to preteen, teen, and adult segments of readers around the world. By 2008, more than 400 million Harry Potter books had been sold in 64 languages.[9] In the United States, the books were often at the top of *The New York Times* fiction best-seller list—for adults. Although separate covers for magazines or separate advertisements for books are expensive, these expenses are minor compared with the costs of producing multiple versions of magazines or books for multiple age or geographic market segments.

Multiple Products and Multiple Market Segments Ford's different lines of cars, SUVs, and pickup trucks are each targeted at a different type of customer—examples of multiple products aimed at multiple market segments. Producing these different vehicles is clearly more expensive than producing only a single vehicle. But this strategy is very effective if it meets customers' needs better, doesn't reduce quality or increase price, and adds to Ford's sales revenues and profits.

Marketers increasingly emphasize a two-tier marketing strategy—what some call "Tiffany/Wal-Mart strategies." Many firms now offer different variations of the same basic offering to high-end and low-end segments. Gap's Banana Republic chain sells blue jeans for $58, whereas its Old Navy stores sell a slightly different version for $22.

Segments of One: Mass Customization American marketers are rediscovering today what their ancestors running the corner general store knew a century ago: Each customer has unique needs and wants, and desires special tender loving care. Economies of scale in manufacturing and marketing during the past century made mass-produced goods so affordable that most customers were willing to compromise their individual tastes and settle for standardized products. Today's Internet ordering and flexible manufacturing and marketing processes have made *mass customization* possible, which means tailoring goods or services to the tastes of individual customers on a high-volume scale.

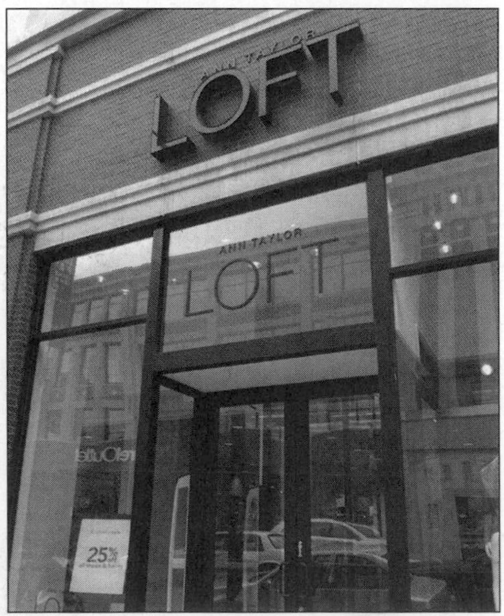

Ann Taylor Stores Corporation's LOFT chain tries to reach value-conscious women with a casual lifestyle while its flagship Ann Taylor chain targets more sophisticated women. Do these store fronts convey this difference? For the potential dangers of this two-segment strategy, see the text.

Mass customization is the next step beyond *build-to-order* (BTO), manufacturing a product only when there is an order from a customer. Dell uses BTO systems that trim work-in-progress inventories and shorten delivery times to customers. To do this, Dell restricts its computer manufacturing line to only a few basic models that can be assembled in four minutes. This gives customers a good choice with quick delivery. But even this system falls a bit short of total mass customization because customers do not have an unlimited number of features they can choose from.[10]

The Segmentation Trade-Off: Synergies versus Cannibalization

The key to successful product differentiation and market segmentation strategies is finding the ideal balance between satisfying a customer's individual wants and achieving *organizational synergy*, the increased customer value achieved through performing organizational functions such as marketing or manufacturing more efficiently. The "increased customer value" can take many forms: more products, improved quality on existing products, lower prices, easier access to products through improved distribution, and so on. So the ultimate criterion for an organization's marketing success is that customers should be better off as a result of the increased synergies.

The organization should also achieve increased revenues and profits from the product differentiation and market segmentation strategies it uses. When the increased customer value involves adding new products or a new chain of stores, the product differentiation–market segmentation trade-off raises a critical issue: Are the new products or new chain simply stealing customers and sales from the older, existing ones? This is known as *cannibalization*.

However, the lines between customer segments can often blur, which can lead to problems, such as the Ann Taylor flagship store competing with its LOFT outlets. The flagship Ann Taylor chain targets polished, sophisticated women while its sister Ann Taylor LOFT chain targets women wanting moderately priced, trendy, casual clothes they can wear to the office. The nightmare: Annual sales of the LOFT stores recently passed those of the Ann Taylor chain, which has struggled to reach its target customers. The result: More than 100 stores from both chains were to be closed by 2010.[11]

learning review

1. Market segmentation involves aggregating prospective buyers into groups that have two key characteristics. What are they?
2. In terms of market segments and products, what are the three market segmentation strategies?

STEPS IN SEGMENTING AND TARGETING MARKETS

LO2

Figure 9–2 identifies the five-step process used to segment a market and select the target segments on which it wants to focus. Segmenting a market requires both detailed analysis and large doses of common sense and managerial judgment. So market segmentation is both science and art!

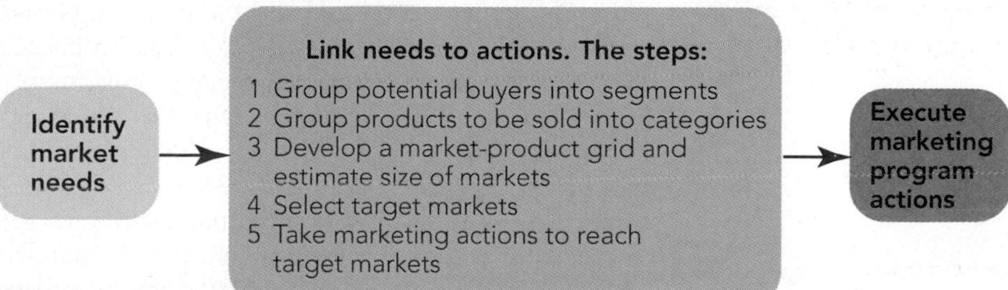

Identify market needs
Link needs to actions. The steps:
1 Group potential buyers into segments
2 Group products to be sold into categories
3 Develop a market-product grid and estimate size of markets
4 Select target markets
5 Take marketing actions to reach target markets
Execute marketing program actions

FIGURE 9–2
The five key steps in segmenting and targeting markets link market needs of customers to the organization's marketing program.

MICROFRIDGE REVOLUTIONIZES
THE REFRIGERATOR.
AGAIN.
The leader in combination appliances brings you a newly engineered design to deliver the ultimate in convenience for any small space environment.
The most popular combination appliance in America now offers new features. A fully integrated Dual Charging Station allows you to charge laptops, cell
conservation benefits of Safe Plug® technology.
This is no ordinary refrigerator. So if you haven't seen the new MicroFridge®, now's the time to see how the best just got better.
Dual Charging Station - A brand new feature that makes it easy and convenient to charge personal electronic devices.
Safe Plug® Technology - A patent-pending power management system that conserves energy and prevents circuit overloads.
10-Year Warranty - Our on-site service only adds to what is by far an industry best warranty.
To get the world's most revolutionary refrigerator, call 1-800-994-0165 or visit microfridge.com
MICRO FRIDGE.
SAFE PLUG

This appliance includes everything from a small refrigerator, freezer, and microwave oven to a charging station for laptops and cell phones. To which market segment might this appeal? The answer appears in the text.

Mac-Gray Corporation
www.microfridge.com

Use market segmentation to choose target markets and take useful marketing actions for the Wendy's restaurant we assume you just bought. Your Wendy's is located next to a large urban university, one that offers both day and evening classes. Your restaurant offers the basic Wendy's fare: hamburgers, chicken and deli sandwiches, salads, French fries, and Frosty desserts. Even though you are part of a chain that has some restrictions on menu and décor, you are free to set your hours of business and to develop local advertising. How can market segmentation help?

Step 1: Group Potential Buyers into Segments

It's not always a good idea to segment a market. Grouping potential buyers into meaningful segments involves meeting some specific criteria that answer the questions, "Would segmentation be worth doing?" and "Is it possible?" If so, a marketer must find specific variables that can be used to create these various segments.

Criteria to Use in Forming the Segments A marketing manager should develop segments for a market that meet five essential criteria:[12]

- *Simplicity and cost-effectiveness of assigning potential buyers to segments.* A marketing manager must be able to put a market segmentation plan into effect. This means identifying the characteristics of potential buyers in a market and then cost-effectively assigning them to a segment.
- *Potential for increased profit.* The best segmentation approach is the one that maximizes the opportunity for future profit and return on investment (ROI). If this potential is maximized without segmentation, don't segment. For nonprofit organizations, the criterion is the potential for serving clients more effectively.
- *Similarity of needs of potential buyers within a segment.* Potential buyers within a segment should be similar in terms of common needs that, in turn, leads to a common marketing action, such as product features sought or advertising media used.
- *Difference of needs of buyers among segments.* If the needs of the various segments aren't very different, combine them into fewer segments. A different segment usually requires a different marketing action that, in turn, means greater costs. If increased sales don't offset extra costs, combine segments and reduce the number of marketing actions.
- *Potential of a marketing action to reach a segment.* Reaching a segment requires a simple but effective marketing action. If no such action exists, don't segment.

LO3

Ways to Segment Consumer Markets Figure 9–3 shows four general bases of segmentation and the typical variables that can be used to segment U.S. consumer markets. These four segmentation bases are: (1) *geographic segmentation*, which is based on where prospective customers live or work (region, city size); (2) *demographic segmentation*, which is based on some *objective* physical (gender, race), measurable (age, income), or other classification attribute (birth era, occupation) of prospective customers; (3) *psychographic segmentation*, which is based on some subjective mental or emotional attributes (personality), aspirations (lifestyle), or needs of prospective customers; and (4) *behavioral segmentation*, which is based on some observable actions or attitudes by prospective customers—such as where they buy, what benefits they seek, how frequently they buy, and why they buy. Some examples are:

- *Geographic segmentation: Region.* Campbell's found that its canned nacho cheese sauce, which could be heated and poured directly onto nacho chips, was too spicy for Americans in the East and not spicy enough for those in the West and Southwest. The result: Today, Campbell's plants in Texas and California produce a hotter nacho cheese sauce than that produced in the other plants to serve their regions better.
- *Demographic segmentation: Household size.* More than half of all U.S. households are made up of only one or two persons, so Campbell's packages meals with only one or two servings—from Great Starts breakfasts to L'Orient dinners.
- *Psychographic segmentation: Lifestyle.* Nielsen Claritas' lifestyle segmentation is based on the belief that "birds of a feather flock together." Thus, people of similar lifestyles tend to live near one another, have similar interests, and buy similar offerings. This is of great value to marketers. Claritas' PRIZM classifies every household in the United States into one of 66 unique market segments. See the Going Online box on the next page for a profile of where you live.
- *Behavioral segmentation: Product features.* Understanding what features are important to different customers is a useful way to segment markets because it can lead directly to specific marketing actions, such as a new product, an ad campaign, or a distribution system. For example, college dorm residents frequently want to keep and prepare their own food to save money or have a

FIGURE 9–3
Segmentation bases, variables, and breakdowns for U.S. consumer markets. In selecting a segmentation variable, a marketing manager needs it to lead to a marketing action.

Basis of Segmentation	Segmentation Variables	Typical Breakdowns
Geographic	Region	Northeast; Midwest; South; West; etc.
	City size	Under 10,000; 10,000–24,999; 25,000–49,999; 50,000–99,999; etc.
	Statistical area	Metropolitan and micropolitan statistical areas; Census tract; etc.
	Media-television	210 designated market areas (DMA) in the U.S. (Nielsen)
	Density	Urban; suburban; small town; rural
Demographic	Gender	Male; female
	Age	Under 6 yrs; 6–11 yrs; 12–17 yrs; 18–24 yrs; 25–34 yrs; etc.
	Race/ethnicity	African American; Asian; Hispanic; White/Caucasian; etc.
	Life stage	Infant; preschool; child; youth; collegiate; adult; senior
	Birth era	Baby boomer (1946–1964); Generation X (1965–1976); etc.
	Household size	1; 2; 3–4; 5 or more
	Marital status	Never married; married; separated; divorced; widowed; domestic partner
	Income	Under $15,000; $15,000–$24,999; $25,000–$34,999; etc.
	Education	Some high school or less; high school graduate (or GED); etc.
	Occupation	Managerial & professional; technical, sales; farming; etc.
Psychographic	Personality	Gregarious; compulsive; extroverted; aggressive; ambitious; etc.
	Values (VALS2)	Innovators; Thinkers; Achievers; Experiencers; Believers; Strivers; etc.
	Lifestyle (Claritas PRIZM)	Blue Blood Estates; Single City Blues; etc. 66 total neighborhood clusters
	Needs	Quality; service; price/value; health; convenience; etc.
Behavioral	Retail store type	Department; specialty; outlet; convenience; mass merchandiser; etc.
	Direct marketing	Mail order/catalog; door-to-door; direct response; Internet
	Product features	Situation-specific; general
	Usage rate	Light user; medium user; heavy user
	User status	Nonuser; ex-user; prospect; first-time user; regular user
	Awareness/intentions	Unaware; aware; interested; intending to buy; purchaser; rejection

Going Online

What "Flock" Do You Belong to?

Who are your target customers? What are they like? Where do they live? How can you reach them? These questions are answered by Nielsen Claritas, whose PRIZM classifies every household into one of 66 demographically and behaviorally distinct neighborhood segments to identify lifestyles and purchase behavior within a defined geographic market area, such as zip code.

Want to know what your neighborhood is like? Go to claritas.com/MyBestSegments/Default.jsp and click the "You Are Where You Live" image. Then, type in your zip code (and security code) to find out what the most common segments are in your neighborhood. For a description of these segments, click the "Segment Look-Up" tab. Is this your "flock"?

late-night snack. However, their dorm rooms are often woefully short of space. MicroFridge understands this and markets a combination microwave, refrigerator, freezer, and charging station targeted to these students.

- *Behavioral segmentation: Usage rate.* **Usage rate** is the quantity consumed or patronage—store visits—during a specific period. It varies significantly among different customer groups. Airlines have developed frequent-flier programs to encourage passengers to use the same airline repeatedly to create loyal customers. This technique, sometimes called *frequency marketing*, focuses on usage rate. One key conclusion emerges about usage: In market segmentation studies, some measure of usage by, or sales obtained from, various segments is central to the analysis.

The Aberdeen Group recently analyzed which segmentation bases were used by the 20 percent most profitable organizations of the 220 surveyed. From highest to lowest, these were the segmentation bases they used:

- Geographic bases—88 percent.
- Behavioral bases—65 percent.
- Demographic bases—53 percent.
- Psychographic bases—43 percent.

The top 20 percent often use more than one of these bases in their market segmentation studies, plus measures such as purchase histories and usage rates of customers.[13]

To obtain quarterly, projectable usage rate data to the U.S. national population for more than 450 consumer product categories, and 8,000+ brands, Experian Simmons continuously surveys over 25,000 adults each year. The purpose is to discover how the products and services they buy and the media they use relate to their behavioral, psychographic, and demographic characteristics. Figure 9–4 shows the results of a question Simmons asked about adult respondents' frequency of use (or patronage) of fast-food restaurants.[14]

As shown by the arrow in the far right column of Figure 9–4, the importance of the segment increases as we move up the table. Among nonusers of these restaurants, prospects (who might become users) are more important than nonprospects (who are never likely to become users). Moving up the rows to users, it seems logical that light users of these restaurants (0 to 5 times per month) are important but less so than medium users (6 to 13 times per month), who, in turn, are a less important segment than the critical group: heavy users (14 or more times per month). The Actual

Consumption column in Figure 9–4 shows how much of the total monthly usage of these restaurants is accounted for by heavy, medium, and light users.

Usage rate is sometimes referred to in terms of the **80/20 rule**, a concept that suggests 80 percent of a firm's sales are obtained from 20 percent of its customers. The percentages in the 80/20 rule are not really fixed at exactly 80 percent and 20 percent but suggest that a small fraction of customers provides a large fraction of a firm's sales. For example, Figure 9–4 shows that the 45.4 percent of the U.S. population who are heavy users of fast-food restaurants provide 70.6 percent of the consumption volume. These high percentages are most likely due to the recession that began in late 2008 as consumers increasingly patronized fast food restaurants due to their inexpensive "value meal" offerings.

The Usage Index per Person column in Figure 9–4 emphasizes the importance of the heavy-user segment even more. Giving the light users (0 to 5 restaurant visits per month) an index of 100, the heavy users have an index of 640. In other words, for every $1.00 spent by a light user in one of these restaurants in a month, each heavy user spends $6.40. This is the reason that as a Wendy's restaurant owner, you want to focus most of your marketing efforts on reaching the highly attractive heavy-user market segment.

As part of its survey, Experian Simmons asked adults which fast-food restaurant(s) were (1) the sole or only restaurant, (2) the primary one, or (3) one of several secondary ones they patronized. As a Wendy's restaurant owner, the information depicted in Figure 9–5 on the next page should give you some ideas in developing a marketing program for your local market. For example, the Wendy's bar graph in Figure 9–5 shows that your sole (0.6 percent) and primary (17.2 percent) user segments are somewhat behind Burger King and far behind McDonald's. Thus, your challenge is to look at these two competitors and devise a marketing program to win customers from them.

The nonusers part of the Wendy's bar graph in Figure 9–5 also provides ideas. It shows that 13.8 percent of adult Americans don't go to fast-food restaurants in a typical month and are really nonprospects—unlikely to ever patronize your restaurant. However, 56.6 percent of nonusers are prospects who may be worth a targeted marketing program. These adults use the product category (fast food) but do not yet

FIGURE 9–4
Patronage of fast-food restaurants by adults 18 years and older. The table shows the critical importance of attracting heavy users and medium users to a fast-food restaurant.

User or Nonuser	Specific Segment	Number (1,000s)	Percentage	Actual Consumption (%)	Usage Index per Person	Importance of Segment
Users	Heavy users (14 + per month)	100,739	45.4%	70.6%	640	High
	Medium users (6–13 per month)	64,724	29.2	26.9	380	↑
	Light users (0–5 or per month)	22,051	9.9	2.4	100	
Total users		187,514	84.5	100.0	—	
Nonusers	Prospects	3,758	1.7	—	—	
	Nonprospects	30,569	13.8	—	—	
Total nonusers		34,327	15.5	—	—	Low
Total	Users + nonusers	221,841	100.0	—	—	

Source: Experian Simmons Spring 2009 Full-Year NCS/NHCS Choices 3 System Crosstabulation Report based on visits within the past 30 days.

FIGURE 9–5 Comparison of various kinds of users and nonusers for Wendy's, Burger King, and McDonald's fast-food restaurants. This table gives a Wendy's restaurant a snapshot of its customers compared to those of its major competitors.

Percentage of respondents (adults, 18 and over)

		Wendy's	Burger King	McDonald's
Users	Sole restaurant	0.6%	0.8%	3.7%
	Primary restaurant	17.2%	23.5%	46.0%
	Secondary restaurant	11.8%	13.9%	11.4%
Nonusers	Prospects	56.6%	48.0%	25.1%
	Nonprospects	13.8%	13.8%	13.8%

Source: Experian Simmons Spring 2009 Full-Year NCS/NHCS Choices 3 System Crosstabulation Report based on visits within the past 30 days.

patronize Wendy's. New menu items, such as the Coffee Toffee Twisted Frosty, or promotional strategies, such as the "Lessons in 3conomics" TV ad that introduces three sandwiches for 99¢ to beat the recession, may succeed in converting these prospects into users that patronize Wendy's.

Variables to Use in Forming Segments To analyze your Wendy's customers, you need to identify which variables to use to segment them. Because the restaurant is located near a large urban university, the most logical starting point for segmentation is really behavioral: Are the prospective customers students or nonstudents?

To segment the students, you could try a variety of (1) geographic variables, such as city or zip code, (2) demographic variables, such as gender, age, year in school, or college major, or (3) psychographic variables, such as personality or needs. But none of these variables really meets the five criteria listed previously—particularly, the fifth criterion about leading to a doable marketing action to reach the various segments. The bases of segmentation for the "students" segment really combines two variables: (1) where students live and (2) when they are on campus. This results in four "student" segments:

- Students living in dormitories (university residence halls, sororities, fraternities).
- Students living near the university in apartments.
- Day commuter students living outside the area.
- Night commuter students living outside the area.

The three main segments of "nonstudents" include:

- Faculty and staff members who work at the university.
- People who live in the area but aren't connected with the university.
- People who work in the area but aren't connected with the university.

People in each of these nonstudent segments aren't quite as similar as those in the student segments, which makes them harder to reach with a marketing program or action. Think about (1) whether the needs of all these segments are different and (2) how various advertising media can be used to reach these groups effectively.

What variables might Xerox use to segment organizational markets to respond to a firm's color copying problems? For the possible answer and related marketing actions, see the text.

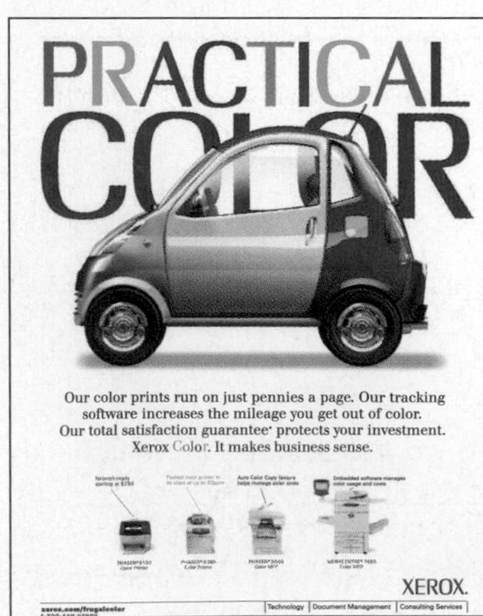

Ways to Segment Organizational Markets A number of variables can be used to segment organizational markets (see Figure 9–6). For

Basis of Segmentation	Segmentation Variables	Typical Breakdowns
Geographic	Global region or country Statistical area Density	European Union, South America, etc.; U.S., Japan, India, etc. Metropolitan and micropolitan statistical areas; Census tract; etc. Urban; suburban; small town; rural
Demographic	NAICS code NAICS sector Number of employees Annual sales	2 digit: Sector; 3 digit: subsector; 4 digit: industry group; etc. Agriculture, forestry (11); mining (21); utilities (22); etc. 1–99; 100–499; 500–999; 1,000–4,999; 5,000 + Under $1 million; $1 million–$9.9 million; $10 million–$49.9 million; etc.
	Number of locations	1–9; 10–49; 50–99; 100–499; 500–999; 1,000+
Behavioral	Kind Where used Application Purchase location Who buys Type of buy	Product; service Installation, component; supplies; etc. Office; production; etc. Centralized; decentralized Individual buyer; industrial buying group New buy; modified rebuy; straight rebuy

FIGURE 9–6
Segmentation bases, variables, and breakdowns for U.S. organizational markets. These variables are used in business-to-business marketing.

example, a product manager at Xerox responsible for its new line of color printers might use these segmentation bases and corresponding variables:

- *Geographic segmentation: Statistical area.* Firms located in a metropolitan statistical area might receive a personal sales call, whereas those in a micropolitan statistical area might be contacted by telephone.
- *Demographic segmentation: NAICS code.* Firms categorized by the North American Industry Classification System code as manufacturers that deal with customers throughout the world might have different document printing needs than do retailers or lawyers serving local customers.
- *Demographic segmentation: Number of employees.* The size of the firm is related to the volume of digital documents produced, so firms with varying numbers of employees might be specific target markets for different Xerox copier systems.
- *Behavioral segmentation: Usage rate.* Similar to this segmentation variable for consumer markets, features are often of major importance in organizational markets. So Xerox can target organizations needing fast printing, copying, and scanning in color—the benefits and features emphasized in the ad for its Xerox WorkCentre 7655 Color MFP system.

learning review

3. The process of segmenting and targeting markets is a bridge between which two marketing activities?
4. What is the difference between the demographic and behavioral bases of market segmentation?

Step 2: Group Products to Be Sold into Categories

What does your Wendy's restaurant sell? Of course you are selling individual products such as Frostys, hamburgers, and fries. But for marketing purposes you're really selling combinations of individual products that become a "meal." This distinction is critical, so let's discuss both (1) individual Wendy's products and (2) groupings of Wendy's products.

MARKET SEGMENT		PRODUCT OR INNOVATION								
GENERAL	GROUP WITH NEED	HOT 'N JUICY HAMBURGER (1969)	DRIVE-THRU (1970)	99¢ SUPER VALUE MEALS (1989)	SALAD SENSATIONS (2002)	E-PAY (2003)	ADULT COMBO MEALS (2004)	LOW TRANS FAT CHICKEN SANDWICHES (2006)	FRESCATA DELI SANDWICHES (2006)	BREAKFAST SANDWICHES (2007)
GENDER	Male	P	P	P	S	P	P	S	P	P
	Female				P	P	S	P	P	
NEEDS	Price/Value			P	S		P			
	Health-Conscious				P			P	P	
	Convenience	S	P		S	P	S			P
	Meat Lovers	P		S			P	S	S	S
UNIVERSITY AFFILIATION	Affiliated (Students, Faculty, Staff)	P	S	P	P	P	S	P	P	S
	Nonaffiliated (Residents, Workers)	S	P	S	S	S	P	S	S	P

Key: P = Primary market S = Secondary market

FIGURE 9–7
Wendy's new products and other innovations target specific market segments based on a customer's gender, needs, or university affiliation.

Individual Wendy's Products When Dave Thomas founded Wendy's in 1969, he offered only four basic items: "hot 'n juicy" hamburgers, Frosty Dairy Desserts (Frostys), French fries, and soft drinks. Since then, Wendy's has introduced many new products and innovations to compete for customers' fast-food dollars. Some of these are shown in Figure 9–7. New products include salads, low trans fat chicken sandwiches, and Frescata deli sandwiches. But there are also nonproduct innovations to increase consumer convenience like drive-thru services and E-Pay to enable credit card purchases.

Figure 9–7 also shows that each product or innovation is not targeted equally to all market segments based on gender, needs, or university affiliation. The cells in Figure 9–7 labeled "P" represent Wendy's primary target market segments when it introduced each product or innovation. The boxes labeled "S" represent the secondary target market segments that also bought these products or used these innovations. In some cases, Wendy's discovered that large numbers of people in a segment not originally targeted for a particular product or innovation bought it anyway.

Groupings of Wendy's Products: Meals Finding a means of grouping the products a firm sells into meaningful categories is as important as grouping customers into segments. If the firm has only one product or service, this isn't a problem. But when it has dozens or hundreds, these must be grouped in some way so buyers can relate to them. This is why department stores and supermarkets are organized into product groups, with the departments or aisles containing related merchandise. Likewise, manufacturers have product lines that are the groupings they use in the catalogs sent to customers.

What are the product groupings for your Wendy's restaurant? It could be the item purchased, such as, hamburgers, salads, a Frosty, and French fries. This is where judgment—the qualitative aspect of marketing—comes in. Customers really buy an eating experience—a meal occasion that satisfies a need at a particular time of day. So the product grouping that makes the most marketing sense is the five "meals" based on the time of day consumers buy them: breakfast, lunch, between-meal snack, dinner, and after-dinner snack. These groupings are more closely related to the way purchases are actually made and permit you to market the entire meal, not just your French fries or hamburgers.

LO4

Step 3: Develop a Market-Product Grid and Estimate the Size of Markets

A **market-product grid** is a framework to relate the market segments of potential buyers to products offered or potential marketing actions by an organization. In a complete market-product grid analysis, each cell in the grid can show the estimated market size of a given product sold to a specific market segment. Let's first look at forming a market-product grid for your Wendy's restaurant and then at estimating market sizes.

Forming a Market-Product Grid Developing a market-product grid means identifying and labeling the markets (or horizontal rows) and product groupings (or vertical columns), as shown in Figure 9–8. From our earlier discussion we've chosen to divide the market segments as students versus nonstudents, with subdivisions of each. The columns—or "products"—are really the meals (or eating occasions) customers enjoy at the restaurant.

Estimating Market Sizes Now the size of the market in each cell (the unique market-product combination) of the market-product grid must be estimated. For your Wendy's restaurant, this involves estimating the sales of each kind of meal expected to be sold to each student and nonstudent market segment.

The market size estimates in Figure 9–8 vary from a large market ("3") to no market at all ("0") for each cell in the market-product grid. These may be simple guesstimates if you don't have the time or money to conduct formal marketing research (as discussed in Chapter 8). But even such crude estimates of the size of specific markets using a market-product grid are helpful in determining which target market segments to select and which product groupings to offer.

Step 4: Select Target Markets

A firm must take care to choose its target market segments carefully. If it picks too narrow a set of segments, it may fail to reach the volume of sales and profits it needs.

FIGURE 9–8
Selecting a target market for your Wendy's fast-food restaurant next to an urban university. The numbers show the estimated size of market in that cell, which leads to selecting the shaded target market.

MARKET SEGMENTS	PRODUCTS: MEALS				
	Break-fast	Lunch	Between-Meal Snack	Dinner	After-Dinner Snack
Student					
Dormitory	0	1	3	0	3
Apartment	1	3	3	1	1
Day commuter	0	3	2	1	0
Night commuter	0	0	1	3	2
Nonstudent					
Faculty or staff	0	3	1	1	0
Live in area	0	1	2	2	1
Work in area	1	3	0	1	0

Key: 3 = Large market; 2 = Medium market; 1 = Small market; 0 = No market.

If it selects too broad a set of segments, it may spread its marketing efforts so thin that the extra expense exceeds the increased sales and profits.

Criteria to Use in Selecting the Target Segments Two kinds of criteria in the market segmentation process are those used to (1) divide the market into segments (discussed earlier) and (2) actually pick the target segments. Even experienced marketing executives often confuse these two different sets of criteria. Five criteria can be used to select the target segments for your Wendy's restaurant:

- *Market size.* The estimated size of the market in the segment is an important factor in deciding whether it's worth going after. There is really no market for breakfasts among dormitory students (Figure 9–8), so you should not devote any marketing effort toward reaching this tiny segment.
- *Expected growth.* Although the size of the market in the segment may be small now, perhaps it is growing significantly or is expected to grow in the future. Sales of fast-food meals eaten outside the restaurants are projected to exceed those eaten inside. And Wendy's is the fast-food leader in average time to serve a drive-thru order—it is 16.7 seconds faster than McDonald's. This speed and convenience is potentially very important to night commuters in adult education programs.[15]
- *Competitive position.* Is there a lot of competition in the segment now or is there likely to be in the future? The less the competition, the more attractive the segment is. For example, if the college dormitories announce a new policy of "no meals on weekends," this segment is suddenly more promising for your restaurant. Wendy's recently introduced E-Pay pay-by-credit-card service at its restaurants to keep up with this new service at McDonald's.
- *Cost of reaching the segment.* A segment that is inaccessible to a firm's marketing actions should not be pursued. For example, the few nonstudents who live in the area may not be reachable with ads in newspapers or other media. As a result, do not waste money trying to advertise to them.
- *Compatibility with the organization's objectives and resources.* If your Wendy's restaurant doesn't yet have the cooking equipment to make breakfasts and has a policy against spending more money on restaurant equipment, then don't try to reach the breakfast segment. As is often the case in marketing decisions, a particular segment may appear attractive according to some criteria and very unattractive according to others.

How can Wendy's target different market segments like late-night customers or commuting college students? For the answer, see the text and Figure 9–9.

Choose the Segments Ultimately, a marketing executive has to use these criteria to choose the segments for special marketing efforts. As shown in Figure 9–8, let's assume you've written off the breakfast product grouping for two reasons: It's too small a market and it's incompatible with your objectives and resources. In terms of competitive position and cost of reaching the segment, you choose to focus on the four student segments and *not* the three nonstudent segments (although you're certainly not going to turn away business from the nonstudent segments!). This combination of market-product segments—your target market—is shaded in Figure 9–8.

Step 5: Take Marketing Actions to Reach Target Markets

The purpose of developing a market-product grid is to trigger marketing actions to increase sales and profits. This means that someone must develop and execute an action plan in the form of a marketing program.

Your Immediate Wendy's Segmentation Strategy With your Wendy's restaurant you've already reached one significant decision: There is a limited market for breakfast, so you won't open for business until 10:30 A.M. In fact, Wendy's first attempt at a breakfast menu was a disaster and was discontinued in 1986. Wendy's evaluates possible new menu items continuously to compete not only with McDonald's and Burger King but also with a complex array of convenience stores and gas stations that sell reheatable packaged foods as well as new "easy-lunch" products.

Another essential decision is where and what meals to advertise to reach specific market segments. An ad in the student newspaper could reach all the student segments, but you might consider this approach too expensive and want a more focused effort to reach smaller segments. If you choose three segments for special actions (Figure 9–9), advertising actions to reach them might include:

- *Day commuters* (an entire market segment). Run ads inside commuter buses and put flyers under the windshield wipers of cars in parking lots used by day commuters. These ads and flyers promote all the meals at your restaurant to a single segment of students, a horizontal cut through the market-product grid.
- *Between-meal snacks* (directed to all four student markets). To promote eating during this downtime for your restaurant, offer "Ten percent off all purchases between 2:00 and 4:30 P.M. during winter quarter." This ad promotes a single meal to all four student segments, a vertical cut through the market-product grid.
- *Dinners to night commuters.* The most focused of all three campaigns, this ad promotes a single meal to the single segment of night commuter students. The campaign might consist of a windshield flyer offering a free Frosty with the coupon when the person buys a drive-thru meal between 5 P.M. and 8 P.M.

Depending on how your advertising actions work, you can repeat, modify, or drop them and design new campaigns for other segments you deem are worth the effort. This advertising example is just a small piece of a complete marketing program for your Wendy's restaurant. And Wendy's focus on the late-night customers shown in its

FIGURE 9–9
Advertising actions to market various meals to a range of possible market segments of students

MARKET SEGMENTS	PRODUCTS: MEALS			
	Lunch	Between-Meal Snack	Dinner	After-Dinner Snack
Dormitory students	1	3	0	3
Apartment students	3	3	1	1
Day commuter students	3	2	1	0
Night commuter students	0	1	3	2

Ads in buses; flyers under windshield wipers of cars in parking lots

Ad campaign: "Ten percent off all purchases between 2:00 and 4:30 P.M. during winter quarter"

Ad on flyer under windshield wipers of cars in night parking lots: "Free Frosty with this coupon when you buy a drive-thru meal between 5:00 P.M. and 8:00 P.M."

Key: 3 = Large market; 2 = Medium market; 1 = Small market; 0 = No market.

ad on page 234 has been successful because customers like that the late-night pickup window is open until midnight or later.

Future Strategies for Your Wendy's Restaurant Changing customer tastes and competition mean you must alter your strategies when necessary. This involves looking at (1) what Wendy's headquarters is doing, (2) what competitors are doing, and (3) what might be changing in the area served by your restaurant.

Wendy's headquarters recently announced an aggressive new marketing program that includes:[16]

- Targeting 25-to-49-year-old customers, not just 18-to-24-year-old ones.
- Positioning Wendy's as a lower-cost fast-food chain.
- Responding to the 2009 recession by aggressively marketing three 99-cent sandwiches.
- Introducing new menu items as the chain breaks into the breakfast market again.

The Wendy's strategy has been remarkably successful.

But other competitors such as McDonald's and Burger King are not sitting still, and you must be aware of their strategies. For example, in 2009 McDonald's actively promoted its lower-priced items that customers perceive as having good value, such as its Dollar Menu loaded with "choice choices." Also, individual McDonald's restaurants were given the flexibility to change prices in light of local demand.[17] And Burger King rolled out its $1.39 BK Burger Shots™—"tiny flame-broiled burgers."

With these corporate Wendy's plans and new actions from competitors, maybe you'd better rethink your market segmentation decisions on hours of operation and breakfasts. Also, if new businesses have moved into your area, what about a new strategy to reach people that work in the area? Or a new promotion for the night owls and early birds—the 12 A.M. to 5 A.M. customers—that now generate one-sixth of revenues at some McDonald's restaurants?[18]

How has Apple moved from its 1977 Apple II to today's Mac Pro? The Marketing Matters box and text discussion provide insights into Apple's current market segmentation strategy.

Apple's Ever-Changing Segmentation Strategy Steve Jobs and Steve Wozniak didn't realize they were developing today's multibillion-dollar PC industry when they invented the Apple I in a garage on April Fool's Day in 1976. Hobbyists, the initial target market, were not interested in the product. However, when the Apple II was displayed at a computer trade show in 1977, consumers loved it and Apple Computer was born. Typical of young companies, Apple focused on its products and had little concern for its markets. Its creative, young engineers were often likened to "Boy Scouts without adult supervision."[19]

Steve Jobs left Apple in 1985, the company languished, and it constantly altered its market-product strategies. When Steve Jobs returned in 1997, he detailed his vision for a reincarnated Apple by describing a new market segmentation strategy that he called the "Apple Product Matrix." This strategy consisted of developing two general types of computers (desktops and portables) targeted at two general kinds of market segments—the consumer and professional sectors.

In most segmentation situations, a single product does not fit into an exclusive market niche. Rather, product lines and market segments overlap. So Apple's market segmentation strategy enables it to offer different products to meet the needs of different market segments, as shown in the Marketing Matters box.

Market-Product Synergies: A Balancing Act

Recognizing opportunities for key synergies—that is, efficiencies—is vital to success in selecting target market segments and making marketing decisions. Market-product grids illustrate where such synergies can be found. How? Let's consider Apple's

Marketing Matters > > > > > > > > > technology

Apple's Segmentation Strategy—Camp Runamok No Longer

Camp Runamok was the nickname given to Apple in the early 1980s because the innovative company had no coherent series of product lines directed at identifiable market segments. Today, Apple has targeted its various lines of Macintosh computers at specific market segments, as shown in the accompanying market-product grid. Because the market-product grid shifts as a firm's strategy changes, the one here is based on Apple's product lines in late-2009. The grid suggests the market segmentation strategy Steve Jobs is using to compete in the digital age.

MARKETS		COMPUTER PRODUCTS					
Sector	Segment	Mac Pro	MacBook Pro	iMac	MacBook	MacBook Air	Mac Mini
Consumer	Individuals	✓	✓	✓	✓	✓	✓
	Small/home office	✓	✓	✓	✓	✓	
	Students			✓	✓		✓
	Teachers		✓	✓			
Professional	Medium/large business	✓	✓	✓		✓	
	Creative	✓	✓	✓			
	College faculty	✓	✓	✓		✓	
	College staff			✓	✓		✓

market-product grid in the accompanying Marketing Matters box and examine the difference between marketing synergies and product synergies shown there.

- *Marketing synergies.* Running horizontally across the grid, each row represents an opportunity for efficiency in terms of a market segment. Were Apple to focus on just one group of consumers, such as the medium/large business segment, its marketing efforts could be streamlined. Apple would not have to spend time learning about the buying habits of students or college faculty. So it could probably create a single ad to reach the medium/large business target segment (the yellow row), highlighting the only products they'd need to worry about developing: the Mac Pro, the MacBook Pro, the iMac, and the MacBook Air. Although clearly not Apple's strategy today, new firms often focus only on a single customer segment.
- *Product synergies.* Running vertically down the market-product grid, each column represents an opportunity for efficiency in research and development (R&D) and production. If Apple wanted to simplify its product line, reduce R&D and production expenses, and manufacture only one computer, which might it choose? Based on the market-product grid, Apple might do well to focus on the iMac (the orange column), because every segment purchases it.

Marketing synergies often come at the expense of product synergies because a single customer segment will likely require a variety of products, each of which will have to be designed and manufactured. The company saves money on marketing but spends more in production. Conversely, if product synergies are emphasized, marketing will have to address the concerns of a wide variety of consumers, which costs more time and money. Marketing managers responsible for developing a company's product line must balance both product and marketing synergies as they try to increase the company's profits.

learning review

5. What factor is estimated or measured for each of the cells in a market-product grid?
6. What are some criteria used to decide which segments to choose for targets?
7. How are marketing and product synergies different in a market-product grid?

POSITIONING THE PRODUCT

LO5

When a company introduces a new product, a decision critical to its long-term success is how prospective buyers view it in relation to those products offered by its competitors. **Product positioning** refers to the place a product occupies in consumers' minds on important attributes relative to competitive products. By understanding where consumers see a company's product or brand today, a marketing manager can seek to change its future position in their minds. This requires **product repositioning**, *changing* the place a product occupies in a consumer's mind relative to competitive products.

Two Approaches to Product Positioning

Marketers follow two main approaches to positioning a new product in the market. *Head-to-head positioning* involves competing directly with competitors on similar product attributes in the same target market. Using this strategy, Dollar rental car competes directly with Avis and Hertz.

Differentiation positioning involves seeking a less-competitive, smaller market niche in which to locate a brand. McDonald's tried to appeal to the health-conscious segment when it introduced the low-fat McLean Deluxe hamburger to avoid competing directly with Wendy's and Burger King. However, it was eventually dropped from the menu. Companies also follow a differentiation positioning strategy among brands within their own product line to minimize the cannibalization of a brand's sales or market shares.

Marketing managers often convert their positioning ideas for the product or brand into a succinct written positioning statement. The positioning statement not only is used internally within the marketing department but also for others, outside it, such as research and development engineers or advertising agencies.[20]

Product Positioning Using Perceptual Maps

A key to positioning a product or brand effectively is discovering the perceptions of its potential customers. In determining its positioning in the minds of customers, companies take four steps:

1. Identify the important attributes for a product or brand class.
2. Discover how target customers rate competing products or brands with respect to these attributes.

More "zip" for chocolate milk? The text and Figure 9–11 describe how American dairies have successfully repositioned chocolate milk to appeal to American adults.

3. Discover where the company's product or brand is on these attributes in the minds of potential customers.
4. Reposition the company's product or brand in the minds of potential customers.

From these data, it is possible to develop a **perceptual map**, a means of displaying or graphing in two dimensions the location of products or brands in the minds of consumers to enable a manager to see how consumers perceive competing products or brands, as well as its own product or brand. The firm can then develop marketing actions to move its product or brand to an ideal position.

A Perceptual Map to Reposition Chocolate Milk for Adults

Recently U.S. dairies were struggling to increase milk sales. So they hit on a wild idea. Try to reposition chocolate milk in the minds of American adults to increase their sales revenues. Let's use the four steps above to show how dairies repositioned chocolate milk for American adults:

1. *Identify the important attributes (or scales) for adult drinks.* Research reveals the key attributes adults use to judge various drinks are (*a*) low versus high nutrition and (*b*) children's drinks versus adult drinks, as shown by the two axes in Figure 9–10.
2. *Discover how adults see various competing drinks.* Locate various adult drinks on these axes, as shown in Figure 9–10.
3. *Discover how potential customers see chocolate milk.* Figure 9–10 shows adults see chocolate milk as moderately nutritious (on the vertical axis) but as mainly a child's drink (on the horizontal axis).
4. *Reposition chocolate milk to make it more appealing to adults.* Looking at the circled letters in Figure 9–10, to which one should the dairies try to move chocolate milk to increase sales?

What actions did dairies take? They repositioned chocolate milk to the location of the star shown in the perceptual map in Figure 9–11 on the next page, the position of letter "B" in Figure 9–10. Their arguments are nutritionally powerful. For women,

FIGURE 9–10
A perceptual map of the location of beverages in the minds of American adults. Toward which letter would you try to move the perception of chocolate milk to make it more appealing to these adults?

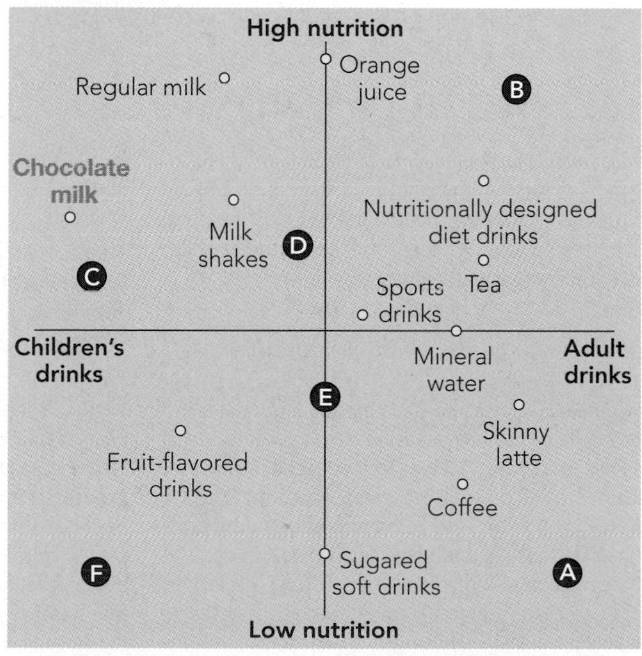

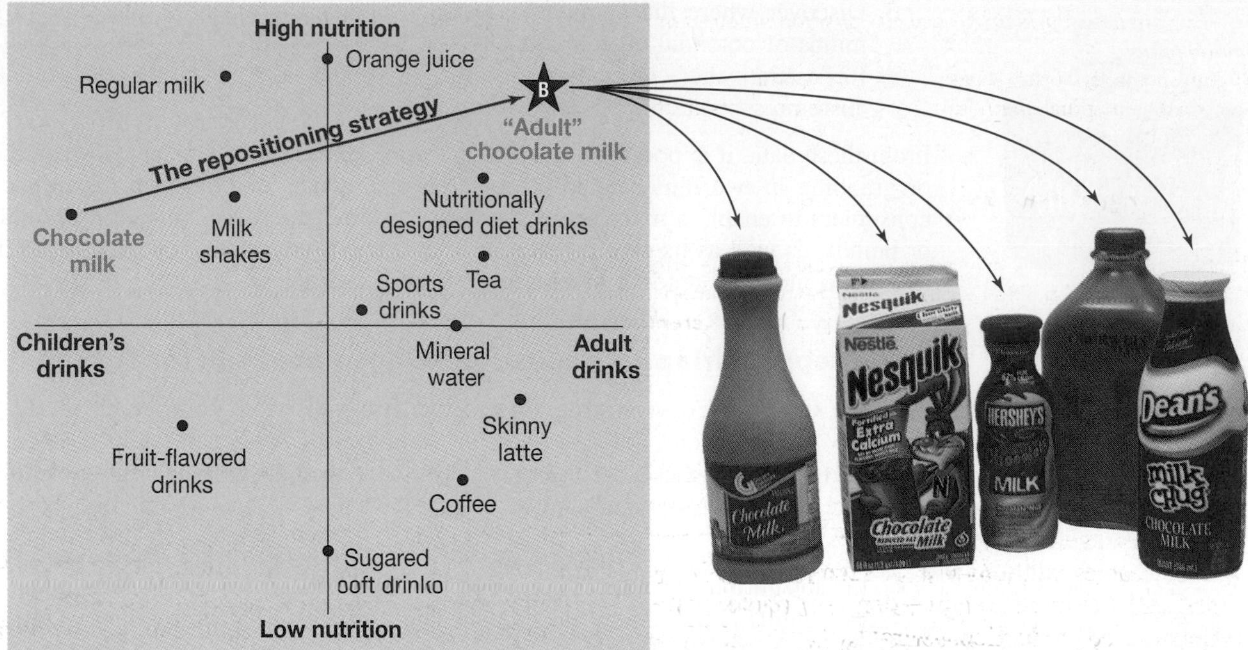

FIGURE 9–11
The strategy American dairies are using to reposition chocolate milk to reach adults: Have adults view chocolate milk both as more nutritional and "more adult."

chocolate milk provides calcium, critically important in female diets. And dieters get a more filling, nutritious beverage than with a soft drink for about the same calories.[21] The result: Chocolate milk sales increased dramatically, much of it because of adult consumption.[22] Part of this is due to giving chocolate milk "nutritional respectability" for adults, but another part is due to the innovative packaging that enables many new chocolate milk containers to fit in a car's cup holders.

learning review

8. What is the difference between product positioning and product repositioning?
9. Why do marketers use perceptual maps in product positioning decisions?

LEARNING OBJECTIVES REVIEW

LO1 *Explain what market segmentation is and when to use it.*
Market segmentation involves aggregating prospective buyers into groups that (*a*) have common needs and (*b*) will respond similarly to a marketing action. Organizations go to the expense of segmenting their markets when it increases their sales, profits, and ability to serve customers better.

LO2 *Identify the five steps involved in segmenting and targeting markets.*
Step 1 is to group potential buyers into segments. Buyers within a segment should have similar characteristics to each other and respond similarly to marketing actions like a new product or a lower price. Step 2 involves putting related products to be sold into meaningful groups. In step 3, organizations develop a market-product grid with estimated sizes of markets in each of the market-product cells of the resulting table. Step 4 involves selecting the target market segments on which the organization should focus. Step 5 involves taking marketing mix actions—often in the form of a marketing program—to reach the target market segments.

LO3 *Recognize the bases used to segment consumer and organizational markets.*
Bases used to segment consumer markets include geographic, demographic, psychographic, and behavioral ones. Organizational markets use the same bases except for psychographic ones.

LO4 *Develop a market-product grid to identify a target market and recommend resulting actions.*
Organizations use five key criteria to segment markets, whose groupings appear in the rows of the market-product grid. Groups of related products appear in the columns. After estimating the size of market in each cell in the grid, they select the target market segments on which to focus. They then identify marketing mix actions—often in a marketing program—to reach the target market most efficiently.

LO5 *Explain how marketing managers position products in the marketplace.*
Marketing managers often locate competing products on two-dimensional perceptual maps to visualize the products in the minds of consumers. They then try to position new products or reposition existing products in this space to attain the maximum sales and profits.

FOCUSING ON KEY TERMS

80/20 rule p. 229
market-product grid p. 233
market segmentation p. 222
market segments p. 222
perceptual map p. 239
product differentiation p. 222
product positioning p. 238
product repositioning p. 238
usage rate p. 228

APPLYING MARKETING KNOWLEDGE

1 What variables might be used to segment these consumer markets? (*a*) lawn mowers, (*b*) frozen dinners, (*c*) dry breakfast cereals, and (*d*) soft drinks.
2 What variables might be used to segment these industrial markets? (*a*) industrial sweepers, (*b*) photocopiers, (*c*) computerized production control systems, and (*d*) car rental agencies.
3 In Figure 9–8, the dormitory market segment includes students living in college-owned residence halls, sororities, and fraternities. What market needs are common to these students that justify combining them into a single segment in studying the market for your Wendy's restaurant?
4 You may disagree with the estimates of market size given for the rows in the market-product grid in Figure 9–8. Estimate the market size, and give a brief justification for these market segments: (*a*) dormitory students, (*b*) day commuters, and (*c*) people who work in the area.
5 Suppose you want to increase revenues for your fast-food restaurant even further. Referring to Figure 9–9, what advertising actions might you take to increase revenues from (*a*) dormitory students, (*b*) dinners, and (*c*) after-dinner snacks from night commuters?
6 Locate these drinks on the perceptual map in Figure 9–10: (*a*) cappuccino, (*b*) beer, and (*c*) soy milk?

building your marketing plan

Your marketing plan (*a*) needs a market-product grid to focus your marketing efforts and also (*b*) leads to a forecast of sales for the company. Use these steps:
1 Define the market segments (the rows in your grid) using the bases of segmentation used to segment consumer and organizational markets.
2 Define the groupings of related products (the columns in your grid).
3 Form your grid and estimate the size of market in each market-product cell.
4 Select the target market segments on which to focus your efforts with your marketing program.
5 Use the information and the lost-horse forecasting technique to make a sales forecast (company forecast).

video case 9 Prince Sports, Inc.: Tennis Racquets for Every Segment

"Over the last decade we've seen a dramatic change in the media to reach consumers," says Linda Glassel, vice president of sports marketing and brand image of Prince Sports, Inc.

PRINCE SPORTS IN TODAY'S CHANGING WORLD

"Today—particularly in reaching younger consumers—we're now focusing so much more on social marketing and social networks, be it Facebook, Twitter, MySpace, and internationally with Hi5, Bebo, and Orkut," she adds.

Linda Glassel's comments are a snapshot look at what Prince Sports faces in the changing world of tennis in the 2010s.

Prince Sports is a racquet sports company whose portfolio of brands includes Prince (tennis, squash, and badminton), Ektelon (racquetball), and Viking (platform/paddle tennis). Its complete line of tennis products alone is astounding: more than 150 racquet models; more than

50 tennis strings; over 50 footwear models; and countless types of bags, apparel, and other accessories.

Prince prides itself on its history of innovation in tennis—including inventing the first "oversize" and "long-body" racquets, the first "synthetic gut" tennis string, and the first "Natural Foot Shape" tennis shoe. Its challenge today is to continue to innovate to meet the needs of all levels of tennis players.

"One favorable thing for Prince these days is the dramatic growth in tennis participation—higher than it's been in many years," says Nick Skally (center in the photo below), senior marketing manager. A recent study by the Sporting Goods Manufacturers confirms this point: Tennis participation in the U.S. was up 43 percent from 2000 to 2008—the fastest growing traditional individual sport in the country.

TAMING TECHNOLOGY TO MEET PLAYERS' NEEDS

Every tennis player wants the same thing: to play better. But they don't all have the same skills, or the same ability to swing a racquet fast. So adult tennis players fall very broadly into three groups, each with special needs:

- *Those with shorter, slower strokes.* They want maximum power in a lightweight frame.
- *Those with moderate to full strokes.* They want the perfect blend of power and control.
- *Those with longer, faster strokes.* They want greater control with less power.

To satisfy all these needs in one racquet is a big order.

"When we design tennis racquets, it involves an extensive amount of market research on players at all levels," explains Tyler Herring, Global Business Director for Performance Tennis Racquets. In 2005, Prince's research led it to introduce its breakthrough O^3 technology. "Our O^3 technology solved an inherent contradiction between racquet speed and sweet spot," he says. Never before had a racquet been designed that simultaneously delivers faster racquet speed with a dramatically increased "sweet spot." The "sweet spot" in a racquet is the middle of the frame that gives the most power and consistency when hitting. In 2009 Prince introduced their latest evolution of the O^3 platform called EXO^3. Its newly patented design suspends the string bed from the racquet frame—thereby increasing the sweet spot by up to 83 percent while reducing frame vibration up to 50 percent.

SEGMENTING THE TENNIS MARKET

"The three primary market segments for our tennis racquets are our performance line, our recreational line, and our junior line," says Herring. He explains that within each of these segments Prince makes difficult design trade-offs to balance (1) the price a player is willing to pay, (2) what playing features (speed versus spin, sweet spot versus control, and so on) they want, and (3) what technology can be built into the racquet for the price point.

Within each of these three primary market segments, there are at least two sub-segments—sometimes overlapping! Figure 1 gives an overview of Prince's market segmentation strategy and identifies sample racquet models. The three right-hand columns show the design variations of length, unstrung weight, and head size. The table shows the complexities Prince faces in converting its technology into a racquet with physical features that satisfy players' needs.

DISTRIBUTION AND PROMOTION STRATEGIES

"Prince has a number of different distribution channels—from mass merchants like Wal-Mart and Target, to sporting goods chains, to smaller specialty tennis shops," says Nick Skally. For the large chains Prince contributes co-op advertising for their in-store circulars, point-of-purchase displays, in-store signage, consumer brochures, and even "space planograms" to help the retailer plan the layout of Prince products in their tennis area. Prince aids for small tennis specialty shops include a supply of demo racquets, detailed catalogs, posters, racquet and string guides, merchandising fixtures, and hardware, such as racquet hooks and footwear shelves, in addition to other items. Prince also provides these shops with "player standees," which are corregated life-size cut outs of professional tennis players.

Prince reaches tennis players directly through its Web site (www.princetennis.com), which gives product information, tennis tips, and the latest tennis news. Besides using social networks like Facebook and Twitter, Prince runs ads in regional and national tennis publications, and develops advertising campaigns for online sites and broadcast outlets.

In addition to its in-store activities, advertising, and online marketing, Prince invests heavily in its Teaching

Pro program. These sponsored teaching pros receive all the latest product information, demo racquets, and equipment from Prince, so they can truly be Prince ambassadors in their community. Aside from their regular lessons, instructors and teaching professionals hold local "Prince Demo events" around the country to give potential customers a hands-on opportunity to see and try various Prince racquets, strings, and grips.

Prince also sponsors over 100 professional tennis players who appear in marquee events such as the four Grand Slam tournaments (Wimbledon and the Australian, French, and U.S. Opens). TV viewers can watch Russia's Maria Sharapova walk onto a tennis court carrying a Prince racquet bag or France's Gael Monfils hit a service ace using his Prince racquet.

Where is Prince headed in the 2010s? "As a marketer, one of the biggest challenges is staying ahead of the curve," says Glassel. And she stresses, "It's learning, it's studying, it's talking to people who understand where the market is going."

Questions

1 In the 2010s what trends in the environmental forces (social, economic, technological, competitive, and regulatory) (*a*) work for and (*b*) work against success for Prince Sports in the tennis industry?

2 Because sales of Prince Sports in tennis-related products depends heavily on growth of the tennis industry, what marketing activities might it use in the U.S. to promote tennis playing?

3 What promotional activities might Prince use to reach (*a*) recreational players and (*b*) junior players?

4 What might Prince do to help it gain distribution and sales in (*a*) mass merchandisers like Target and Wal-Mart and (*b*) specialty tennis shops?

5 In reaching global markets outside the U.S. (*a*) what are some criteria that Prince should use to select countries in which to market aggressively, (*b*) what three or four countries meet these criteria best, and (*c*) what are some marketing actions Prince might use to reach these markets?

FIGURE 1
Prince Targets Racquets at Specific Market Segments

Market Segments			Product Features in Racquet			
Main Segments	Sub-Segments	Segment Characteristics (Skill level, age)	Brand Name	Length (Inches)	Unstrung Weight (Ounces)	Head Size (Sq. In.)
Performance	Precision	For touring professional players wanting great feel, control, and spin	EXO³ Ignite 95	27.0	11.8	95
	Thunder	For competitive players wanting a bigger sweet spot and added power	EXO³ Red 95	27.25	9.9	105
Recreational	Small head size	Players looking for a forgiving racquet with added control	AirO Lightning MP	27.0	9.9	100
	Larger head size	Players looking for a larger sweet spot and added power	AirO Maria Lite OS	27.0	9.7	110
Junior	More experienced young players	Ages 8 to 15; somewhat shorter and lighter racquets than high school adult players	AirO Team Maria 23	23.0	8.1	100
	Beginner	Ages 5 to 11; much shorter and lighter racquets; tennis balls with 50% to 75% less speed for young beginners	Air Team Maria 19	19.0	7.1	82

nano shoots video.

Introducing the new iPod nano.
Now with video recording,
a larger screen, and FM radio.

Buy now

Shop online now and get free shipping or pick one up Thursday at the Apple Retail Store.

Video recording with effects

The new video camera in iPod nano lets you shoot video—even with video effects—wherever you are. Yet the new iPod nano is still the same ultraportable size. Learn more ›

Genius Mixes

Genius acts as your personal DJ, searching your iTunes library to find songs that go great together, then organizing them into mixes you'll love. All automatically.
Learn more ›

FM radio with Live Pause

10 Developing New Products and Services

LEARNING OBJECTIVES
After reading this chapter you should be able to:

LO1 Recognize the various terms that pertain to products and services.

LO2 Identify the ways in which consumer and business products and services can be classified.

LO3 Explain the significance of "newness" in new products and services as it relates to the degree of consumer learning involved.

LO4 Describe the factors contributing to a new product's or service's success or failure.

LO5 Explain the purposes of each step of the new-product process.

APPLE'S NEW-PRODUCT INNOVATION MACHINE

The stage in front of an auditorium is empty except for a desk with an iMac and a huge screen with a large white logo. Then in walks a legend ready for his magic shows in his black turtleneck, jeans, and gray New Balance sneakers.

Apple's Innovation Machine

The legend, of course, is Steve Jobs (opposite page), co-founder and CEO of Apple, Inc. *Fortune* rated Apple as the world's most admired company in 2009 and *BusinessWeek* has perennially rated it as the world's most innovative.[1] The magic shows Jobs has put on over the years have introduced many of Apple's market-changing innovations, such as the:

- Apple II—the first commercial personal computer.
- Macintosh—the first personal computer with a mouse and a graphical user interface.
- iPod—the first commercially successful MP3 digital music player.
- MacBook Air—the world's thinnest notebook that uses a solid state drive instead of a hard disk.
- iPhone 3GS—the revolutionary multi-touch mobile phone and media player.
- iPod nano with Built-in Video Camera—the digital media player that includes a video camera to shoot and play video or enables the user to upload it to a computer and view it on YouTube. The 2009 iPod nano comes in nine different colors and has an FM radio as well as a pedometer. And the larger color display makes it even easier to view images and video. The price? Only $149 for the 8Gb model, similar to what other pocket video cameras cost![2]

The Evolutionary iPod nano and Revolutionary iPod touch

The evolutionary iPod nano, first introduced in 2005 and now in its fifth generation, has sold over 100 million units as of September 2009, making it the most popular media player in the world. Moreover, the iPod family (iPod shuffle, iPod nano, iPod classic, and iPod touch) has sold over 220 million units since the iPod's launch in October 2001. "With iPod, Apple has invented a whole new category of digital music player. . . [and] listening to music will never be the same again," said Steve Jobs. This prophetic statement back in 2001 has certainly come true! And what about the revolutionary iPod touch that was launched in 2007? Its multi-touch graphical user interface, which was borrowed from the iPhone, has "buttons" that are transforming the device into an exciting portable game machine![3]

The life of an organization depends on how it conceives, produces, and markets *new* products (goods, services, and ideas), the topic of this chapter. Chapter 11 discusses the process of managing *existing* products, services, and brands.

WHAT ARE PRODUCTS AND SERVICES?

LO1

The essence of marketing is in developing products and services to meet buyer needs. A **product** is a good, service, or idea consisting of a bundle of tangible and intangible attributes that satisfies consumers' needs and is received in exchange for money or something else of value. Let's look more carefully at the meanings of goods, services, and ideas.

A Look at Goods, Services, and Ideas

A *good* has tangible attributes that a consumer's five senses can perceive. For example, Apple's latest iPhone 3GS can be touched and its features can be seen and heard. A good also may have intangible attributes consisting of its delivery or warranties and embody more abstract concepts, such as becoming healthier or wealthier.[4] Goods can also be divided into nondurable goods and durable goods. A *nondurable* good is an item consumed in one or a few uses, such as food products and fuel. A *durable* good is one that usually lasts over many uses, such as appliances, cars, and mobile phones. This classification method also provides direction for marketing actions. For example, nondurable goods such as Wrigley's gum rely heavily on consumer advertising. In contrast, costly durable goods, such as cars, generally emphasize personal selling.

Services are intangible activities or benefits that an organization provides to satisfy consumers' needs in exchange for money or something else of value. Services have become a significant part of the U.S. economy, exceeding 40 percent of its gross domestic product. Hence, a good may be the breakfast cereal you eat, whereas a service may be a tax return an accountant fills out for you.

Finally, in marketing, an *idea* is a thought that leads to an action such as a concept for a new invention, or getting people out to vote.

Throughout this book *product* generally includes not only physical goods but services and ideas as well. When *product* is used in its narrower meaning of "goods," it should be clear from the example or sentence.

LO2

Classifying Products

Two broad categories of products widely used in marketing relate to the type of user. **Consumer products** are products purchased by the ultimate consumer, whereas **business products** (also called *B2B products or industrial products*) are products that organizations buy that assist in providing other products for resale. But some products can be considered both consumer and business items. For example, an Apple iMac computer can be sold to consumers for personal use or to business firms for office use. Each classification results in different marketing actions. Viewed as a consumer product, the iMac would be sold through its retail stores or directly from its Web site. As a business product, an Apple salesperson might contact a firm's purchasing department directly and offer discounts for multiple purchases.

The iPhone's innovative touch screen emerged after Apple engineers studied tablet PCs, portable computers using touch screens.

Consumer Products The four types of consumer products shown in Figure 10–1 on the next page differ in terms of the (1) effort the consumer spends on the decision, (2) attributes used in making the purchase decision, and (3) frequency of purchase. **Convenience products** are items that the consumer purchases frequently, conveniently, and with a minimum of shopping effort. **Shopping products** are items for which the consumer compares several alternatives on criteria such as price, quality, or style. **Specialty products** are items that the consumer makes a special effort to search out and buy. **Unsought products** are items that the consumer does not know about or knows about but does not initially want.

Figure 10–1 shows how each type of consumer product stresses different marketing mix actions, degrees of brand loyalty, and shopping effort. But how a consumer product is classified depends on the individual. One woman may view a camera as a shopping product and visit several stores before deciding on a brand, whereas her friend may view a camera as a specialty product and will make a special effort to buy only a Nikon.

Business Products A major characteristic of business products is that their sales are often the result of *derived demand*; that is, sales of business products frequently result (or are derived) from the sale of consumer products. For example, as consumer demand for Ford cars (a consumer product) increases, the company may increase its demand for paint spraying equipment (a business product).

Business products may be classified as components or support products. *Components* are items that become part of the final product. These include raw materials such as grain or lumber, as well as assemblies or parts, such as a Ford car

BASIS OF COMPARISON	CONVENIENCE PRODUCT	SHOPPING PRODUCT	SPECIALTY PRODUCT	UNSOUGHT PRODUCT
	TYPE OF CONSUMER PRODUCT			
Product	Toothpaste, cake mix, hand soap, ATM cash withdrawal	Cameras, TVs, briefcases, airline tickets	Rolls-Royce cars, Rolex watches, heart surgery	Burial insurance, thesaurus
Price	Relatively inexpensive	Fairly expensive	Usually very expensive	Varies
Place (distribution)	Widespread; many outlets	Large number of selective outlets	Very limited	Often limited
Promotion	Price, availability, and awareness stressed	Differentiation from competitors stressed	Uniqueness of brand and status stressed	Awareness is essential
Brand loyalty of consumers	Aware of brand but will accept substitutes	Prefer specific brands but will accept substitutes	Very brand loyal; will not accept substitutes	Will accept substitutes
Purchase behavior of consumers	Frequent purchases; little time and effort spent shopping	Infrequent purchases; needs much comparison shopping time	Infrequent purchases; needs extensive search and decision time	Very infrequent purchases; some comparison shopping

FIGURE 10–1
How a consumer product is classified significantly affects which products consumers buy and the marketing strategies used.

engine or car door hinges. *Support products* are items used to assist in producing other goods and services. These include:

- *Installations*, such as buildings and fixed equipment.
- *Accessory equipment*, such as tools and office equipment.
- *Supplies*, such as stationery, paper clips, and brooms.
- *Industrial services*, such as maintenance, repair, and legal services.

Strategies to market business products reflect both the complexities of the product involved (paper clips versus computer-machine tools) and the buy-class situations discussed in Chapter 6.

A broad product line can benefit both consumers and retailers. The text shows how Little Remedies' product line does this.

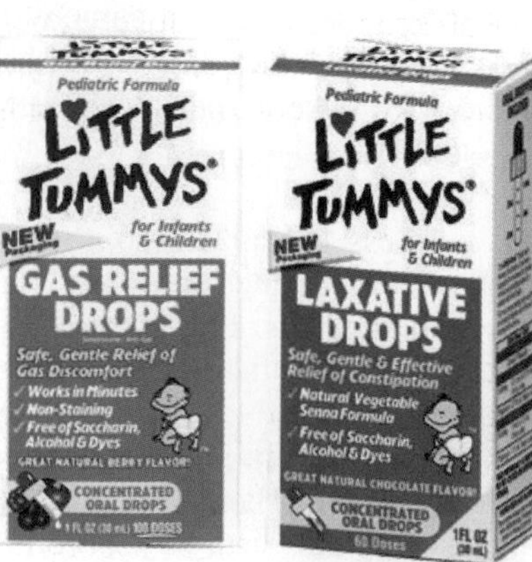

Product Items, Product Lines, and Product Mixes

Most organizations offer a range of products and services to consumers. A **product item** is a specific product that has a unique brand, size, or price. For example, Ultra Downy softener for clothes comes in several different sizes. Each size is a separate *stock keeping unit* (SKU), which is a unique identification number that defines an item for ordering or inventory purposes.

A **product line** is a group of product or service items that are closely related because they satisfy a class of needs, are used together, are sold to the same customer group, are distributed through the same outlets, or fall within a given price range. Nike's product lines include shoes and clothing, whereas the Mayo Clinic's service lines consist of inpatient hospital care and outpatient physician services. Each product line has its own marketing strategy.

Using Marketing Dashboards
Which States Are Underperforming?

In 2008, you started your own company to sell a nutritious, high-energy snack you developed. It is now January 2011. As a marketer, you ask yourself, "How well is my business growing?"

Your Challenge The snack is sold in all 50 states. Your goal is 10 percent annual growth. To begin 2011, you want to quickly solve any sales problems that occurred during 2010. You know that states whose sales are stagnant or in decline are offset by those with greater than 10 percent growth.

Studying a table of the sales and percent change versus a year ago in each of the 50 states would work but be very time consuming. A good graphic is better. You choose the following marketing metric, where "sales" are measured in units:

$$\text{Annual \% sales change} = \frac{(\text{2010 Sales} - \text{2009 Sales}) \times 100}{\text{2009 Sales}}$$

You want to act quickly to improve sales. In your map, growth that is greater than 10 percent is green, 0 to 10 percent growth is orange, and decline is red. Notice that you (1) picked a metric and (2) made your own rules that green is good, orange is bad, and red is very bad.

Your Findings You see that sales growth in the Northeastern states is weaker than the 10 percent target, and sales are actually declining in many of the states.

Annual Percentage Change in Unit Volume, by State

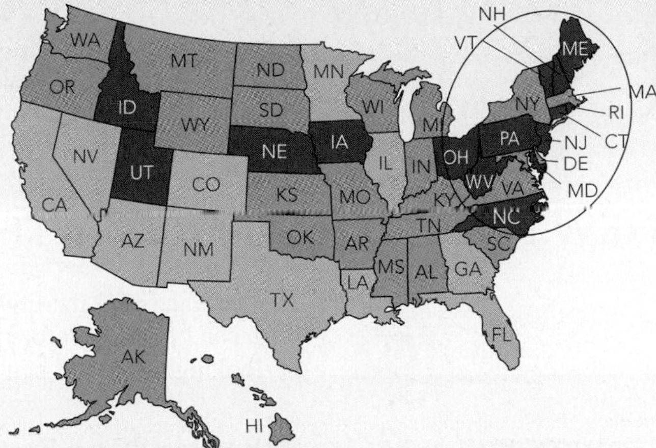

Your Action Marketing is often about grappling with sales shortfalls. You'll need to start by trying to identify and correct the problems in the largest volume states that are underperforming—in this case in the northeastern United States.

You'll want to do marketing research to see if the problem starts with (1) an external factor such as changing consumer tastes or (2) an internal factor such as a breakdown in your distribution system.

The Little Remedies® product line consists of more than a dozen nonprescription medicines for infants and young children sold in a family of creative packages. A broad product line enables both consumers and retailers to simplify their buying decisions. If a family has a good experience with one Little Remedies product, it might buy another one in the line. And an extensive line enables Little Remedies to obtain distribution chains such as Babies "Я" Us and Wal-Mart, avoiding the need for retailers to deal with many different suppliers.

Many firms offer a **product mix** that consists of all of the product lines offered by an organization. For example, Cray Inc. has a small product mix of three supercomputer lines that are sold mostly to governments and large businesses. Fortune Brands, however, has a large product mix that includes product lines such as sporting equipment (Titleist golf balls) and plumbing supplies (Moen faucets).

How Marketing Dashboards Can Improve New-Product Performance

The Using Marketing Dashboards box shows how marketers measure actual market performance versus the goals set in new-product planning. It shows that you have set a goal of 10 percent annual growth for the new snack you developed. You choose a marketing metric of "annual % sales change"—to measure the annual growth rate from 2009 to 2010 for each of the 50 states. Your special concerns in the marketing dashboard are the states shown in red, where sales have actually declined. As shown in the box, having identified the Northeastern United States as a problem region, you conduct in-depth marketing research to lead to corrective actions.

learning review

1. What are the four main types of consumer products?
2. What is the difference between a product line and a product mix?
3. What marketing metric might you use in a marketing dashboard to discover which states have weak sales?

NEW PRODUCTS AND WHY THEY SUCCEED OR FAIL

New products are the lifeblood of a company and keep it growing, but the financial risks can be large. Before discussing how new products reach the market, we'll begin by looking at *what* a new product is.

What Is a New Product?

The term *new* is difficult to define. Is Sony's PlayStation 3 *new* when there was a PlayStation 2? Is Nintendo's Wii *new* when its GameCube launch goes back to 2001? What does *new* mean for new-product marketing? Newness from several points of view are discussed next.

Newness Compared with Existing Products If a product is functionally different from existing products, it can be defined as new. Sometimes this newness is revolutionary and creates a whole new industry, as in the case of the Apple II computer. At other times additional features are added to an existing product to try to make it appeal to more customers. And as microprocessors now appear not only in computers and cell phones but also in countless applications in vehicles and

As you read the discussion about what *new* means in new-product development, think about how it affects the marketing strategies of Sony and Nintendo in their *new* video-game console launches.

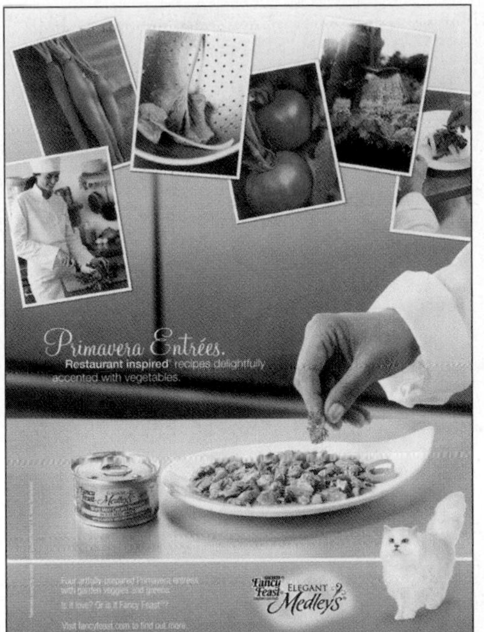

The text describes the potential benefits and dangers of an incremental innovation such as Purina's Elegant Medleys, its restaurant-inspired food for cats.

appliances, consumers' lives get far more complicated. This proliferation of extra features—sometimes called "feature bloat"—overwhelms many consumers. The Marketing Matters box on the next page describes how founder Richard Stephens and his Geek Squad work to address the rise of feature bloat.[5]

Newness in Legal Terms The U.S. Federal Trade Commission (FTC) advises that the term *new* be limited to use with a product up to six months after it enters regular distribution. The difficulty with this suggestion is in the interpretation of the term *regular distribution*.

Newness from the Organization's Perspective Successful organizations view newness and innovation in their products at three levels. At the lowest level, which usually involves the least risk, is a product line extension. This is an incremental improvement of an existing product for the company. For example, Purina added its "new" line of Elegant Medleys®, a "restaurant-inspired food for cats," to its existing line of 50 varieties of its Fancy Feast® gourmet cat food. This has the potential benefit of adding new customers but the twin dangers of increasing expenses and cannibalizing its existing line.

At the next level is a significant jump in the innovation or technology, such as from a regular landline telephone to a cell phone. The third level is true innovation, a truly revolutionary new product, such as the first Apple computer in 1976. Effective new-product programs in large firms deal at all three levels.

Newness from the Consumer's Perspective A fourth way to define new products is in terms of their effects on consumption. This approach classifies new products according to the degree of learning required by the consumer, as shown in Figure 10–2.

With a *continuous innovation*, consumers don't need to learn new behaviors. Toothpaste manufacturers can add new attributes or features like "whitens teeth" or "removes plaque," as when they introduce a new or improved product. But the extra features in the new toothpaste do not require buyers to learn new tooth-brushing behaviors, so it is a continuous innovation. The benefit of this simple innovation is that effective marketing mainly depends on generating awareness and not needing to reeducate customers.

FIGURE 10–2
The degree of "newness" in a new product affects the amount of learning effort consumers must exert to use the product and the resulting marketing strategy.

	LOW	Degree of New Consumer Learning Needed	HIGH
BASIS OF COMPARISON	CONTINUOUS INNOVATION	DYNAMICALLY CONTINUOUS INNOVATION	DISCONTINUOUS INNOVATION
Definition	Requires no new learning by consumers	Disrupts consumer's normal routine but does not require totally new learning	Requires new learning and consumption patterns by consumers
Examples	New improved shaver or detergent	Electric toothbrush, compact disc player, and automatic flash unit for cameras	VCR, digital video recorder, electric car
Marketing strategy	Gain consumer awareness and wide distribution	Advertise points of difference and benefits to consumers	Educate consumers through product trial and personal selling

Marketing Matters > > > > > > > > > technology

Feature Bloat: Geek Squad to the Rescue!

Adding more features to a product to satisfy more consumers seems like a no-brainer strategy.

Feature Bloat

In fact, most marketing research with potential buyers of a product done *before* they buy shows they say they *do want* more features in the product. It's when the new product gets home that the "feature bloat" problems occur—often overwhelming the consumer with mind-boggling complexity.

Computers pose a special problem for homeowners because there's no in-house technical assistance like that existing in large organizations. Also, to drive down prices of home computers, usually little customer support service is available. Ever call the manufacturer's toll-free "help" line? One survey showed that 29 percent of the help-line callers wound up swearing at the customer service representative and 21 percent just screamed.

The Geek Squad to the Rescue

Computer feature bloat has given rise to what TV's *60 Minutes* says is "the multibillion-dollar service industry populated by the very people who used to be shunned in the high-school cafeteria: Geeks like Robert Stephens!"

More than a decade ago he turned his geekiness into the Geek Squad—a group of technically savvy people who can fix almost any computer problem. "There's usually some frantic customer at the door pointing to some device in the corner that will not obey," Stephens explains.

"The biggest complaint about tech support people is rude, egotistical behavior," says Stephens. So he launched the Geek Squad to show some friendly humility by having team members work their wizardry while:

1. Showing genuine concern to customers.
2. Dressing in geeky white shirts, black clip-on ties, and white socks, a "uniform" borrowed from NASA engineers.
3. Driving to customer homes or offices in black-and-white VW "geekmobiles."

Do customers appreciate the 6,000-person Geek Squad, now owned by Best Buy? Robert Stephens answers by explaining, "People will say, 'They saved me . . . they saved my data.'" This includes countless college students working on their papers or theses with data lost somewhere in their computers—"data they promised themselves they'd back up next week."

For how the kind of innovation present in this ketchup bottle affects the marketing strategy, see the text.

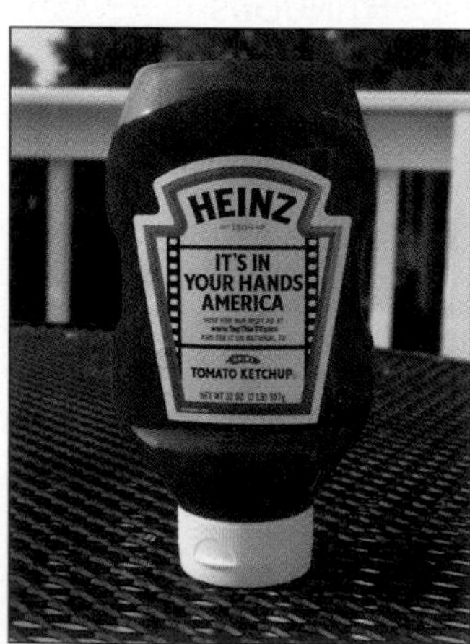

With a *dynamically continuous innovation*, only minor changes in behavior are required. Heinz launched its EZ Squirt Ketchup in an array of unlikely hues—from green and orange to pink and teal—with kid-friendly squeeze bottles and nozzles.[6] Encouraging kids to write their names on hot dogs or draw dinosaurs on burgers as they use this new product requires only minor behavioral changes. So the marketing strategy here is to educate prospective buyers on the product's benefits, advantages, and proper use.

A *discontinuous innovation* involves making the consumer learn entirely new consumption patterns to use the product. Have you bought a wireless router for your computer? Congratulations if you installed it yourself! Recently, one-third of those bought at Best Buy were returned because they were too complicated to set up—the problem with a discontinuous innovation.[7] So marketing efforts for discontinuous innovations usually involve not only gaining initial consumer awareness but also educating consumers on both the benefits and proper use of the innovative product, activities that can cost millions of dollars—and maybe rely on Geek Squad help.

Why Products Succeed or Fail

We all know the giant product successes—such as Apple's iPhone, Google, and CNN. Yet the thousands of product failures every year that slide quietly into oblivion cost American businesses billions of dollars. Ideally, a new product needs a precise

New-product success or failure? For the special problems these two products face, see the text.

protocol, a statement that, before product development begins, identifies: (1) a well-defined target market; (2) specific customers' needs, wants, and preferences; and (3) what the product will be and do.

Research suggests that it takes about 3,000 raw unwritten ideas to produce a single commercially successful new product.[8] To learn marketing lessons and convert potential failures to successes, we can analyze why new products fail and then study several failures in detail. As we go through the new-product process later in the chapter, we can identify ways such failures might have been avoided—admitting that hindsight is clearer than foresight.

LO4

Marketing Reasons for New-Product Failures Both marketing and nonmarketing factors contribute to new-product failures. Using the research results from several studies on new-product success and failure, we can identify critical marketing factors—which sometimes overlap—that often separate new-product winners and losers:[9]

1. *Insignificant point of difference.* Research shows that a distinctive point of difference is the single most important factor for a new product to defeat competitive ones—having superior characteristics that deliver unique benefits to the user. In the mid-1990s, General Mills introduced Fingos, a sweetened cereal flake about the size of a corn chip. Consumers were supposed to snack on them dry, but they didn't.[10] The point of difference was not important enough to get consumers to stop eating competing snacks such as popcorn and potato chips.
2. *Incomplete market and product protocol before product development starts.* Without this protocol, firms try to design a vague product for a phantom market. Developed by Kimberly-Clark, Avert Virucidal tissues contained vitamin C derivatives scientifically designed to kill cold and flu germs when users sneezed, coughed, or blew their noses into them. It failed in test market. People didn't believe the claims and were frightened by the "cidal" in the brand name, which they connected to words like *suicidal*. A big part of Avert's failure was its lack of a product protocol that clearly defined how it would satisfy consumer wants and needs.[11]
3. *Not satisfying customer needs on critical factors.* Overlapping somewhat with point 1, this factor stresses that problems on one or two critical factors can kill the product, even though the general quality is high. For example, the Japanese, like the British, drive on the left side of the road. Until 1996, U.S. carmakers

Lessons from new-product failures: Why might consumers not buy a tissue to kill sneezing germs (below) . . .

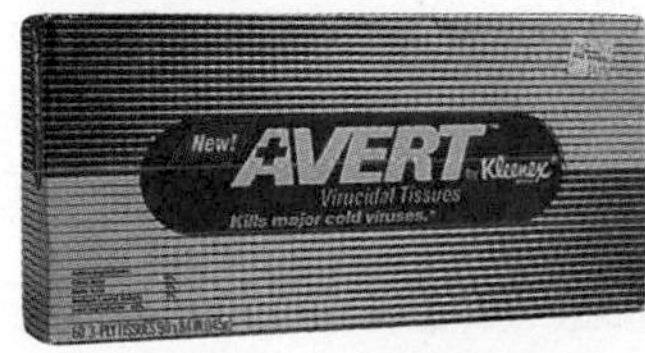

sent Japan few right-hand-drive cars—unlike German carmakers who exported right-hand-drive models in several of their brands.[12]

. . . or a spray to get rid of scary creatures from a child's bedroom (above)? Answers appear in the text.

4. *Bad timing.* This results when a product is introduced too soon, too late, or when consumer tastes are shifting dramatically. Bad timing gives new-product managers nightmares. Microsoft, for example, introduced its Zune player a few years after Apple launched its iPod and other competitors offered new MP3 players.
5. *Too little market attractiveness.* The ideal is a large target market with high growth and real buyer need. But often the target market is too small or competitive to warrant the huge expenses necessary to reach it. OUT! International's Hey! There's A Monster In My Room spray was designed to rid scary creatures from a kid's bedroom and had a bubble-gum fragrance. While a creative and cute product, the brand name probably kept the kids awake at night more than their fear of the monsters because it implied the monster was still hiding in the bedroom. Also, was this a real market?
6. *Poor product quality.* This factor often results when a product is not thoroughly tested. The costs to an organization for poor quality can be staggering and include the labor, materials, and other expenses to fix the problem—not to mention the lost sales, profits, and market share that usually result. For example, after Microsoft launched its Xbox 360 video game console, millions began to experience the "red ring of death." The problem: The consoles' microprocessors ran too hot, causing them to "pop off" their motherboards. Microsoft had to set aside $1.1 billion to extend its warranty and fix any affected console for free—costing it future sales and reducing its market share lead in the multibillion dollar market over rivals Sony and Nintendo.[13]
7. *Poor execution of the marketing mix: brand name, package, price, promotion, distribution.* Somewhere in the marketing mix there can be a showstopper that kills the product. Introduced by Gunderson & Rosario, Inc., Garlic Cake was supposed to be served as an hors d'oeuvre with sweet breads, spreads, and meats, but somehow the company forgot to tell this to potential consumers. Garlic Cake died because consumers were left to wonder just what a Garlic Cake is and when on earth a person would want to eat it.
8. *No economical access to buyers.* Grocery products provide an example. Today's mega-supermarkets carry more than 30,000 different SKUs. With about 20,000 new packaged goods (food, beverage, health and beauty aids, household, and pet items) introduced each year, the cost to gain access to retailer shelf space is huge.[14] Because shelf space is judged in terms of sales per square foot, Thirsty Dog! (a zesty beef-flavored, vitamin-enriched, mineral-loaded, lightly carbonated bottled water for your dog) must displace an existing product on the supermarket shelves, a difficult task with the high sales per square foot demands of these stores. Thirsty Dog! failed to generate enough sales to meet these requirements.

Simple marketing research should have revealed the problems. Developing successful new products may sometimes involve luck, but more often it involves having a product that really meets a need and has significant points of difference over competitive products.

What Were They Thinking? Organizational Problems in New-Product Failure A number of other organizational problems can cause new-product disasters. Key ones—some that overlap—include:

1. *Not really listening to the "voice of the consumer."* Product managers may believe they "know better" than their customers or feel they "can't afford" the valuable marketing research that could uncover problems.
2. *Skipping stages in the new-product process.* Although details may vary, the seven-stage new-product process discussed in the next section is a sequence

Marketing Matters > > > > > > > > technology

From Idea to Launch: Stage-Gate® Processes in New-Product Development

In the 1960s, the National Aeronautics and Space Administration (NASA) developed an engineering phase-review process to keep its missile and satellite programs on schedule. Today's Stage-Gate® process is adapted from NASA's system, but it covers all the business steps in converting a new-product idea to its commercialization launch—the idea-to-launch sequence.

The Stage-Gate process incorporates ideas uncovered by studying best practices of exemplary new-product-development projects and teams as they drive their projects to market quickly and effectively. The system is a series of stages, with each stage consisting of a set of activities whose purpose is to improve the project outcome.

Stage-Gate gets its name because preceding each stage in the new-product development is a "gate." Team members (the gatekeepers) make the key "go/kill" decision at each gate in the sequence to commit the resources required to move the project forward. Two important problems can cause ineffective gates:

- *Gates can lack teeth.* The gate review meetings are held, but bad projects aren't killed, often for the groupthink reason discussed in the text.
- *Gates can be hollow.* Go decisions are made, but inadequate resources are committed to ensure success.

Too often the project emphasis is simply getting through each gate to move into the next stage.

Today firms such as Procter & Gamble and Johnson & Johnson have a clearer innovation goal: To win in the marketplace with a successful new product—not simply go through the Stage-Gate process.

used in some form by most large organizations. Skipping a stage often leads to disaster. This is why many firms have a "gate" to ensure that one step is completed satisfactorily before going on to the next step, as discussed in the Marketing Matters box.[15]

3. *Pushing a poorly conceived product into the market to generate quick revenue.* Today's marketing managers are under incredible pressure from top management to meet quarterly revenue targets. This focus on speed often results in overlooking the network of services needed to support the physical product.[16]
4. *Encountering "groupthink" in task force and committee meetings.* Someone in the new-product planning meeting knows or suspects the product concept is a dumb idea. But that person is afraid to speak up for fear of being cast as a "negative thinker" and "not a team player" and then being ostracized from real participation in the group. And a strong public commitment to a new product by its key advocate may make it difficult to kill the product even when new negative information comes to light.[17]
5. *Not learning critical takeaway lessons from past failures.* The easiest lessons are from "intelligent failures"—ones that happen early in the new-product process. At this point these failures are less expensive and immediately give better understanding of customers' wants and needs.

Many of these organizational problems cause the eight marketing reasons for new-product failure listed above.

learning review

4. What kind of innovation would an improved electric toothbrush be?
5. Why can an "insignificant point of difference" lead to new-product failure?
6. How might using the Stage-Gate process reduce the chances of skipping a stage in new-product development?

THE NEW-PRODUCT PROCESS

LO5

Finding ways to stimulate American innovation and provide jobs is a vital concern to federal and state governments, business firms, and citizens alike.[18] Organizations conduct global searches to find the scientists and engineers that can achieve the creative breakthroughs needed for new high-tech products. For example, Chinese, Indian, Russian, and other immigrant engineers represent half the total number of engineers in California's Silicon Valley.[19]

To develop new products efficiently, companies such as General Electric and 3M use a specific sequence of steps to make their products ready for market. Figure 10–3 shows the **new-product process**, the seven stages an organization goes through to identify business opportunities and convert them to a salable good or service.

Stage 1: New-Product Strategy Development

For companies, **new-product strategy development** is the stage of the new-product process that defines the role for a new product in terms of the firm's overall objectives. During this stage, the firm uses both a SWOT analysis (Chapter 2) and environmental scanning (Chapter 3) to assess its strengths and weaknesses relative to the trends it identifies as opportunities or threats. The outcome not only defines the vital "protocol" for each new-product idea but also identifies the strategic role it might serve in the firm's portfolio.

New-product development in services, such as buying a stock or airline ticket or watching a Major League Baseball game, is often difficult. Why? Because services are intangible and performance-oriented. Nevertheless, service innovations can have a huge impact on our lives. For example, the online brokerage firm E*TRADE has revolutionized the financial services industry through its online trading.

A Major League Baseball park is a study in new-product innovation. If you visit Turner Field, home of the Atlanta Braves, you may be in for a shock about what's going on besides baseball on the field. There's the members-only 755 club—honoring Hank Aaron's home run total—and the Chophouse bar and grill for 20-somethings and a big playground sponsored by Cartoon Network. Each of these attractions become part of the customer experience that the team wants its fans to enjoy—and the attractions are almost as important as fielding a winning team.[20]

A visit to watch an Atlanta Braves baseball game is often a lot more than the game itself. As described in the text, it may involve a meal at the Chophouse or many other services.

FIGURE 10–3
Carefully using the seven stages in the new-product process increases the chances of new-product success.

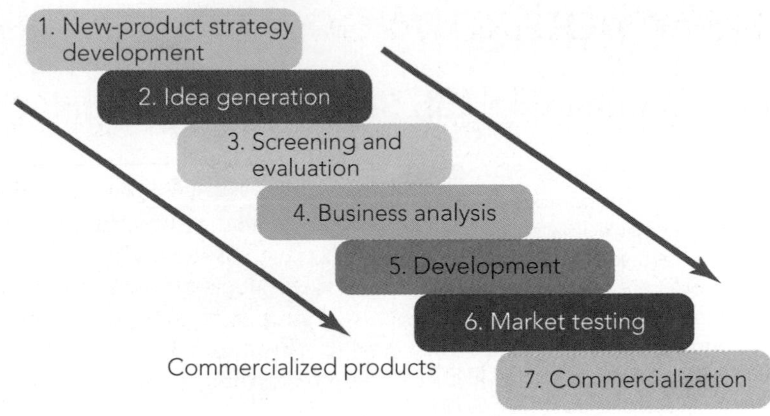

Stage 2: Idea Generation

Idea generation is the stage of the new-product process that develops a pool of concepts as candidates for new products, building upon the previous stage's results. Many forward-looking companies have discovered their own organization is not generating enough useful new-products ideas. This has led to *open innovation*, in which an organization finds and executes creative new-product ideas by developing strategic relationships with outside individuals and organizations. This section contains examples of open innovation relationships.[21]

Customer and Supplier Suggestions Firms ask their salespeople to talk to customers and ask their purchasing personnel to talk to suppliers to discover new-product ideas.[22] Whirlpool gets ideas from customers on ways to standardize components so that it can cut the number of different product platforms to reduce costs.[23] Business researchers emphasize that firms must actively involve customers and suppliers in the new-product development process.[24] This means the focus should be on what the new product will actually *do* for them rather than simply *what they want*.[25]

A. G. Lafley, CEO of Procter & Gamble (P&G), gave his executives a *revolutionary* thought: "Look outside the company for solutions to problems rather than insisting P&G knows best." When he ran P&G's laundry detergent business, he had to redesign the laundry boxes so they were easier to open. Why? While consumers *said* P&G's laundry boxes were "easy to open," cameras they agreed to have installed in their laundry rooms showed they opened the boxes with *screwdrivers*![26]

Employee and Co-Worker Suggestions Employees should be encouraged to suggest new-product ideas through suggestion boxes. The idea for Nature Valley granola bars from General Mills came when one of its marketing managers observed co-workers bringing granola to work in plastic bags.

Would women *really* help design this car? For how Volvo said "yes," see the text.

Auto industry studies show that women buy about two-thirds of all vehicles and influence about 85 percent of all sales. However, many auto-makers do marketing research on car-loving, "gear-head" guys to get ideas on new-car features. To bridge the gender gap, Volvo obtained ideas on new-car features from all-female focus groups from its Swedish workforce. It then named a five-woman team of Volvo managers to design a "concept car"—what the auto industry uses to test new designs, technical innovations, and consumer reactions. One innovative feature: when pressing an ignition key button, the car's gull-wing doors pop open and the steering wheel pulls in so the driver can enter the car more easily.[27]

Research and Development Laboratories Another source of new products is a firm's own research and development laboratories.

Going Online

IDEO—the Innovation Lab Superstar in Designing New Products

The Apple mouse. The Palm V PDA. The Crest Neat Squeeze toothpaste dispenser. The Steelecase Leap adjustable office chair. These are just some of the thousands of new products designed by IDEO, an innovation lab you've probably never heard of but benefit from everyday.

For David Kelley, co-founder of IDEO, product design is really "industrial design" and includes both artistic and functional elements. And to foster this creativity, IDEO allows its designers and engineers much freedom—its offices look like schoolrooms; employees can hang their bicycles from the ceiling; there are rubber-band fights; and on Monday mornings, there are show-and-tell sessions.

Fresh Express asked IDEO to design an innovative single-serve package for salads. IDEO's solution (photo): A five-section package—one large section for the salad greens and four smaller ones for proteins, dressings, and so on—each section sealed in plastic.

Visit IDEO's Web site (www.ideo.com) to view its recent inventions and innovations for clients such as McDonald's self-ordering kiosk, the Zyliss' Mandolin fruit and vegetable slicer, LifePort's kidney transporter, Pepsi's High Visibility vending machine, and Nike's all-terrain sunglasses.

Apple is a world leader in new-product development in computers and electronics. Apple is also world-class in *industrial design*, an applied art that improves the aesthetics and usefulness of mass-produced products for users. Apple's sleek iPhone and iMac models came out of its Apple Industrial Design Group, which is driven by the obsessive concerns of Steve Jobs for cutting-edge industrial design in all the company's products.[28] But even Apple sometimes goes outside its own labs—for example, when it found its original "mouse" at IDEO.

Professional R&D laboratories that are outside the walls of large corporations are sources of open innovation and provide new-product ideas.[29] Labs at Arthur D. Little helped put the "crunch" in the Quaker Oats Company's Cap'n Crunch cereal and the flavor in Carnation's Instant Breakfast. As described in the Going Online box, IDEO is a world-class new-product development firm, having designed more than 4,000 of them.[30]

Brainstorming sessions conducted at IDEO can generate 100 new ideas in an hour. IDEO's "shop-a-long" visits with client firms let their managers experience firsthand what one of its customers does. A sample recommendation from a shop-a-long with managers from a large U.S. health maintenance organization who actually could play the part of a patient: Make examining rooms larger to enable the nervous patient to have a friend or relative in the room while waiting for the doctor.[31]

Competitive Products Analyzing the competition can lead to new-product ideas. For six months, the Marriott Corporation sent a six-person intelligence team to travel and stay at economy hotels around the country. The team assessed the competitions' strengths and weaknesses on everything from the soundproof qualities of the rooms to the softness of the towels. Marriott then budgeted $500 million for a new economy hotel chain—Fairfield Inns.

Universities, Inventors, and Smaller Firms Many firms look for outside visionaries that have inventions or innovative ideas that can become products. Some sources of this open innovation strategy include:

- *Universities.* Many universities have technology transfer centers that often partner with business firms to commercialize faculty inventions. The first-of-its-kind carbonated yogurt Go-Gurt Fizzix was launched in late 2007 as a result

Gary Schwartzberg partnered with Kraft Foods to get his cream cheese-filled bagels in stores across the United States.

of General Mills partnering with Brigham Young University to license the university's patent to put the "fizz" into the yogurt.[32]

- *Inventors.* Many lone inventors and entrepreneurs develop brilliant new-product ideas—like Gary Schwartzberg's tube-shaped bagel filled with cream cheese. A portable breakfast for the on-the-go person, the innovative bagel couldn't get widespread distribution. So Schwartzberg sold his idea to Kraft Foods, Inc., which now markets its Bagel-Fuls filled with Kraft's best-selling Philadelphia cream cheese in supermarkets across the United States.[33]
- *Smaller, nontraditional firms.* Small technology firms and even small, nontraditional firms in adjacent industries provide creative advances. General Mills partnered with Weight Watchers to develop Progresso Light soups, the first consumer packaged product in any grocery category to carry the Weight Watchers endorsement with a 0 points value per serving.[34]

Great ideas can come from almost anywhere—the challenge is recognizing them.

Stage 3: Screening and Evaluation

Screening and evaluation is the stage of the new-product process that internally and externally evaluates new-product ideas to eliminate those that warrant no further effort.

Internal Approach A firm's employees evaluate the technical feasibility of a proposed new-product idea to determine whether it meets the objectives defined in the new-product strategy development step. For example, 3M scientists develop many world-class innovations in the company's labs. A recent innovation was its micro-replication technology—one that has 3,000 tiny gripping "fingers" per square inch. An internal assessment showed 3M that this technology could be used to improve the gripping of golf or work gloves.

Organizations that develop service-dominated offerings need to ensure that employees have the commitment and skills to meet customer expectations and sustain customer loyalty—an important criterion in screening a new-service idea. This is the essence of **customer experience management (CEM)**, which is the process of managing the entire customer experience within the firm. Marketers must consider employees' interactions with customers so that the new services are consistently delivered and experienced, clearly differentiated from other service offerings, and relevant and valuable to the target market.

External Approach Firms use *concept tests*, external evaluations with consumers that consist of preliminary testing of a new-product idea rather than an actual product. Generally, these tests are more useful with minor modifications of existing products than with new, innovative products with which consumers are not familiar.[35] Concept tests rely on written descriptions of the product but may be augmented with sketches, mock-ups, or promotional literature. Key questions for concept testing include: How does the customer perceive the product? Who would use it? and How would it be used?

learning review

7. What is the new-product strategy development stage in the new-product process?
8. What are the main sources of new-product ideas?
9. How do internal and external screening and evaluation approaches differ?

How do you print ink-jet images on Pringles chips safely and inexpensively? The text describes how a global search found the critical technology.

Stage 4: Business Analysis

Business analysis specifies the features of the product and the marketing strategy needed to bring it to market and make financial projections. This is the last checkpoint before significant resources are invested to create a *prototype*—a full-scale operating model of the product. The business analysis stage assesses the total "business fit" of the proposed new product with the company's mission and objectives—from whether the product can be economically developed and manufactured to the marketing strategy needed to have it succeed in the marketplace.

This process requires not only detailed financial projections but also assessments of the marketing and product synergies related to the company's existing operations. Will the new product require a lot of new machinery to produce it or can we use unused capacity of existing machines? Will the new product cannibalize sales of our existing products or increase revenues by reaching new market segments? Can the new product be protected with a patent or copyright? Financial projections of expected profits require estimates of expected prices per unit and units sold, as well as detailed estimates of the costs of R&D, production, and marketing.

For services, business analysis must consider *capacity management*, integrating the service component of the marketing mix with efforts to influence consumer demand. Most services are perishable and have a limited capacity due to the inseparability of the service from its provider. Therefore, a service provider must manage the availability of the offering so that demand matches capacity over the duration of the demand cycle (one day, a week, and so on). For example, airlines and mobile phone service providers use *off-peak pricing* to charge different prices for different times of the day or week to reflect the variations in demand for their services. This enables them to maximize profit.[36]

Stage 5: Development

Development is the stage of the new-product process that turns the idea on paper into a prototype. This results in a demonstrable, producible product that involves not only manufacturing the product but also performing laboratory and consumer tests to ensure it meets the standards established for it in the protocol. Moreover, the new product must be able to be manufactured at reasonable cost with the required quality.

A brainstorming session at Procter & Gamble produced the idea of printing pop culture images on its Pringles chips. But how do you print sharp images—like those for *Spider-Man 3*—using edible dyes on millions of chips? Internal development would be too long and costly, so P&G circulated a description of its unusual printing need globally. A university professor in Bologna, Italy, had invented an ink-jet method for printing edible images on cakes and cookies. In less than a year, P&G adapted the process and launched its new "Pringle Prints"—at a fraction of the time and cost internal development would have taken.[37]

Does this Google home page look like a no-brainer to design? To read how Google designers spend thousands of hours to provide "favorable user experiences," see the text and Marketing Matters box.

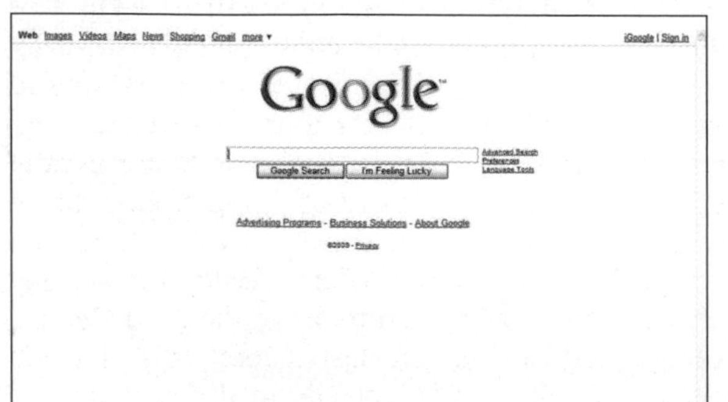

For services, developing customer service delivery expectations is critical. This involves analyzing the entire sequence of steps or "service encounters" that make up the service to study the points of interaction between consumers and the service provider.[38] High-contact services such as hotels, car rental agencies, and Web sites use this approach to enhance customer relationships. That white, plain-vanilla Google home page may look like it was designed by a child. But the Marketing Matters box describes how Google's Marissa Mayer has spent thousands of hours and done countless experiments to get exactly the right "feel" for Google's millions of users.[39]

Safety tests are also critical for when the product isn't used as planned. To make sure seven-year-olds can't bite Barbie's

Marketing Matters > > > > > > customer value

Marissa Mayer: The Talent Behind Google's Familiar *White* Home Page

Unknown to you, Google Employee No. 20, Marissa Mayer, probably impacts your life at least 5 or 10 times a week.

The New York Times calls her the "gatekeeper of Google's home page," the one person who "controls the look, feel, and functionality of the Internet's most heavily trafficked search engine." Virtually every new design or feature—from the color of the Google tool bar to the exact words on a Google page—needs her stamp of approval. The very clear, very plain, very white Google home page reflects Mayer's passion about obtaining a favorable user experience. Her job title: vice president of search products and user experience.

At Google, Mayer has introduced over 100 products and features, such as Google News, Gmail, and Image Search. Sounding like a combination English teacher and art instructor, Mayer sets the design standards for Google. Many of these are based on her internal Google experiments to measure user preferences. Her precise design rules include:

- Avoid first- and second-person pronouns.
- Write "Google" instead of "we."
- Don't switch tenses.
- Avoid italics because they are hard to read on a computer screen.

And beyond the grammar lessons, there are also precise design and graphic arts guidelines: "If you want to make the design on the page simpler, take away one of these: A type of font, a color, or an image."

An engineer, Mayer has a Google life that goes far beyond pronouns and colors of Google's Web pages. As *The New York Times* notes, "She oversees 200 product managers who in turn supervise 3,000 engineers, or more than 10 percent of Google's work force." Comments one colleague, "She functions at the executive level but is just as comfortable at the engineer level."

head off and choke, Mattel clamps her foot in steel jaws in a test stand and then pulls on her head with a wire. Similarly, car manufacturers have done extensive safety tests by crashing their cars into concrete walls.

Stage 6: Market Testing

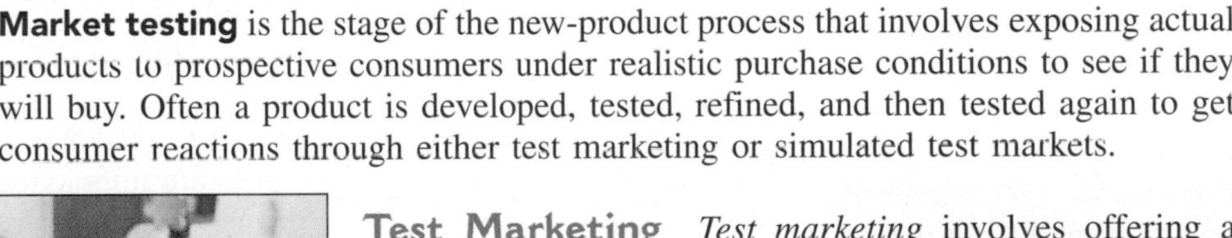

Market testing is the stage of the new-product process that involves exposing actual products to prospective consumers under realistic purchase conditions to see if they will buy. Often a product is developed, tested, refined, and then tested again to get consumer reactions through either test marketing or simulated test markets.

During development, laboratory tests like this one on Barbie result in safer dolls and toys for children.

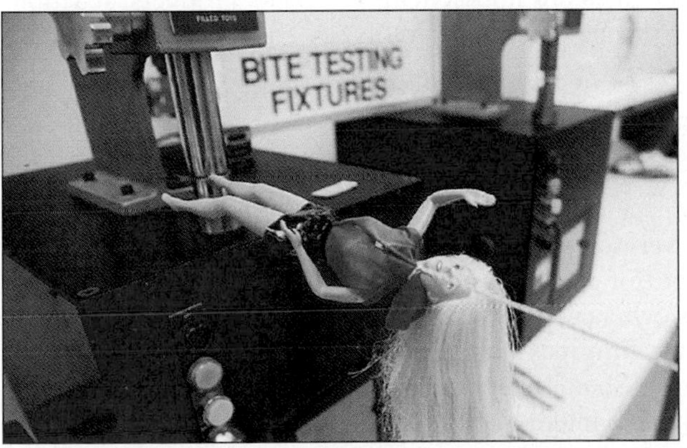

Test Marketing *Test marketing* involves offering a product for sale on a limited basis in a defined area. This test is done to determine whether consumers will actually buy the product and to try different ways of marketing it. Only about a third of the products tested do well enough to go on to the next stage. These market tests are usually conducted in cities that are viewed as being representative of U.S. consumers like the six shown in Figure 10–4 on the next page.[40] Of these cities, Wichita Falls, Texas, most closely matches the U.S. average found in the 2000 Census. Other criteria used in selecting test market cities include cable systems to deliver different ads to different homes,

Demographic Characteristic	USA	Wichita Falls, TX
2000 population	281.4 mil.	140,518
Median age (years)	35.3	33.6
% of family households with children under 18	32.8%	33.8%
% Hispanic or Latino of any race	12.5%	11.8%
% African American	12.3%	9.6%
% Asian American	3.6%	1.7%
% Native American	1.5%	1.7%

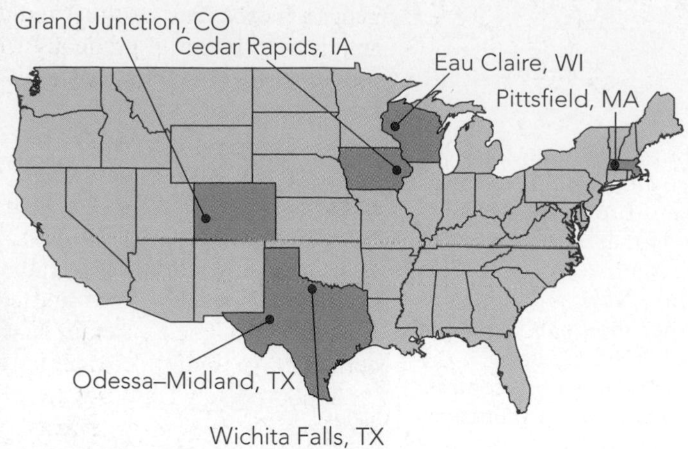

FIGURE 10–4
Six important U.S. test markets and the "demographics winner": the Wichita Falls, Texas, metropolitan statistical area

and tracking systems such as those of ACNielsen to measure sales resulting from different advertising campaigns. The 2010 Census will probably reveal different U.S. cities that better represent the national average demographic characteristics. These cities will become the new preferred test market cities.

This information indicates potential sales volume and market share in the test area. Companies also use market tests to check other elements of the marketing mix, such as price, level of advertising support, and distribution. Because market tests are so time consuming and expensive and can alert competitors to a firm's plans, some firms skip test markets or use simulated test markets.

Simulated Test Markets Because of the time, cost, and confidentiality problems of test markets, consumer packaged goods companies often turn to *simulated* (or *laboratory*) *test markets (STM)*, a technique that simulates a full-scale test market but in a limited fashion. STMs are often run in shopping malls, where consumers are questioned to identify who uses the product class being tested. Next, willing participants are questioned on usage, reasons for purchase, and important product attributes. Qualified persons are then shown TV commercials or print ads for the test product along with competitors' advertising. Finally, they are given money to make a decision to buy or not buy the firm's product—or the competitors' product—from a real or simulated store environment.

Commercializing a new French fry: To learn how Burger King's improved French fries confronted McDonald's fries, see the text.

When Test Markets Don't Work Not all products can use test marketing. Test marketing a service is very difficult because it is intangible and consumers can't see what they are buying. For example, how do you test market a new building for an art museum?

Similarly, test markets for expensive consumer products such as cars or costly industrial products such as jet engines are impractical. For these products, reactions of potential buyers to mockups or one-of-a-kind prototypes are all that is feasible.

Stage 7: Commercialization

Finally, the product is brought to the point of **commercialization**—the stage of the new-product process that positions and launches a new product in full-scale production and sales. Companies proceed very carefully at the commercialization stage because this is the most expensive stage for most new products. If competitors introduce a product that leapfrogs the firm's own new product or if cannibalization of its own existing products looks significant, the firm may halt the new-product launch permanently.

Countless other questions arise. Should we make an advance announcement of the new-product introduction to stimulate interest and potential sales?[41] Do we need to add new salespeople?[42] Do the salespeople need extra training?

Large companies use *regional rollouts*, introducing the product sequentially into geographical areas of the United States, to allow production levels and marketing activities to build up gradually to minimize the risk of new-product failure. Grocery product manufacturers and telephone service providers are examples of firms that use this strategy.

Burger King's French Fries: The Complexities of Commercialization Burger King's "improved French fries" are an example of what can go wrong at the commercialization stage. In the fast-food industry, McDonald's French fries are the gold standard against which all other fries are measured. Burger King decided to take on McDonald's fries and spent millions of R&D dollars developing a starch-coated fry designed to retain heat longer and add crispiness. This crispiness was even defined: "An audible crunch that should be present for seven or more chews!"

A 100-person team set to work and developed the starch-coated fry that beat McDonald's fries in taste tests, 57 percent to 35 percent, with 8 percent having no opinion. After "certifrying" 300,000 managers and employees on the new frying procedures, the fries were launched with a $70 million marketing budget. The launch turned into disaster. The reason: The new fry proved too complicated to get right day after day in Burger King restaurants, except under ideal conditions, and was dropped.[43]

Effective cross-functional teams at Hewlett-Packard have reduced new-product development times significantly—often with the aid of "fences."

The Special Risks in Commercializing Grocery Products New grocery products pose special commercialization problems. Because shelf space is so limited, many supermarkets require a *slotting fee* for new products, a payment a manufacturer makes to place a new item on a retailer's shelf. This can run to several million dollars for a single product. But there's even another potential expense. If a new grocery product does not achieve a predetermined sales target, some retailers require a *failure fee*, a penalty payment a manufacturer makes to compensate a retailer for sales its valuable shelf space failed to make. These costly slotting fees and failure fees are further examples of why large grocery product manufacturers use regional rollouts.

Speed as a Factor in New-Product Success In recent years, companies have discovered that speed or *time to market* (TtM) is often vital in introducing a new product. Recent studies have shown that high-tech products coming to market on time are far more profitable than those arriving late. So some companies—such as Sony, BMW, 3M, and Hewlett-Packard—have overlapped the sequence of stages described in this chapter.

With this approach, termed *parallel development*, cross-functional team members who conduct the simultaneous development of both the product and the production process stay with the product from conception to production. This has enabled Hewlett-Packard to reduce the development time for notebook computers from 12 to 7 months. In software development, *fast prototyping* uses a "do it, try it, fix it" approach—encouraging continuing improvement even after the initial design. To speed up time to market, many large companies are building "fences" around their new product teams to keep them from getting bogged down in red tape.[44]

learning review

10. How does the development stage of the new-product process involve testing the product inside and outside the firm?

11. What is a test market?

12. What is the commercialization of a new product?

LEARNING OBJECTIVES REVIEW

LO1 *Recognize the various terms that pertain to products and services.*
A product is a good, service, or idea consisting of a bundle of tangible and intangible attributes that satisfies consumers and is received in exchange for money or something else of value.

A good has tangible attributes that a consumer's five senses can perceive and intangible ones such as warranties; a laptop computer is an example. Goods can also be divided into nondurable goods, which are consumed in one or a few uses, and durable goods, which usually last over many uses. Services are intangible activities or benefits that an organization provides to satisfy consumer needs in exchange for money or something else of value, such as an airline trip. An idea is a thought that leads to a product or action, such as eating healthier foods.

LO2 *Identify the ways in which consumer and business products and services can be classified.*
By type of user, the major distinctions are consumer products, which are products purchased by the ultimate consumer, and business products, which are products that assist in providing other products for resale.

Consumer products can be broken down based on the effort involved in the purchase decision process, marketing mix attributes used in the purchase, and the frequency of purchase: (*a*) convenience products are items that consumers purchase frequently and with a minimum of shopping effort; (*b*) shopping products are items for which consumers compare several alternatives on selected criteria; (*c*) specialty products are items that consumers make special efforts to seek out and buy; and (*d*) unsought products are items that consumers do not either know about or initially want.

Business products can be broken down into (*a*) components, which are items that become part of the final product, such as raw materials or parts, and (*b*) support products, which are items used to assist in producing other goods and services and include installations, accessory equipment, supplies, and industrial services.

Services can be classified in terms of whether they are delivered by (*a*) people or equipment, (*b*) business firms or nonprofit organizations, or (*c*) government agencies.

Firms can offer a range of products, which involve decisions regarding the product item, product line, and product mix.

LO3 *Explain the significance of "newness" in new products and services as it relates to the degree of consumer learning involved.*
From the important perspective of the consumer, "newness" is often seen as the degree of learning that a consumer must engage in to use the product. With a continuous innovation, no new behaviors must be learned. With a dynamically continuous innovation, only minor behavioral changes are needed. With a discontinuous innovation, consumers must learn entirely new consumption patterns.

LO4 *Describe the factors contributing to a new product's or service's success or failure.*
A new product or service often fails for these marketing reasons: (*a*) insignificant points of difference, (*b*) incomplete market and product protocol before product development starts, (*c*) not satisfying customer needs on critical factors, (*d*) bad timing, (*e*) too little market attractiveness, (*f*) poor product quality, (*g*) poor execution of the marketing mix, and (*h*) no economical access to buyers.

LO5 *Explain the purposes of each step of the new-product process.*
The new-product process consists of seven stages a firm uses to develop a salable good or service: (*a*) New-product strategy development involves defining the role for the new product within the firm's overall objectives. (*b*) Idea generation involves developing a pool of concepts from consumers, employees, basic R&D, and competitors to serve as candidates for new products. (*c*) Screening and evaluation involves evaluating new product ideas to eliminate those that are not feasible from a technical or consumer perspective. (*d*) Business analysis involves defining the features of the new product, developing the marketing strategy and marketing program to introduce it, and making a financial forecast. (*e*) Development involves not only producing a prototype product but also testing it in the lab and on consumers to see that it meets the standards set for it. (*f*) Market testing involves exposing actual products to prospective consumers under realistic purchasing conditions to see if they will buy the product. (*g*) Commercialization involves positioning and launching a product in full-scale production and sales with a specific marketing program.

FOCUSING ON KEY TERMS

business analysis p. 260
business products p. 246
commercialization p. 262
consumer products p. 246
convenience products p. 247
customer experience management (CEM) p. 259
development p. 260
idea generation p. 257
market testing p. 261
new-product process p. 256
new-product strategy development p. 256
product p. 246
product item p. 248
product line p. 248
product mix p. 249
protocol p. 253
screening and evaluation p. 259
services p. 246
shopping products p. 247
specialty products p. 247
unsought products p. 247

APPLYING MARKETING KNOWLEDGE

1 Products can be classified as either consumer or business goods. How would you classify the following products? (*a*) Johnson's baby shampoo, (*b*) a Black & Decker two-speed drill, and (*c*) an arc welder.
2 Are Nature Valley Granola bars and Eddie Bauer hiking boots convenience, shopping, specialty, or unsought products?
3 Based on your answer to question 2, how would the marketing actions differ for each product and the classification to which you assigned it?
4 In terms of the behavioral effect on consumers, how would a computer, such as an Apple iMac, be classified? In light of this classification, what actions would you suggest to the manufacturers of these products to increase their sales in the market?
5 What methods would you suggest to assess the potential commercial success for the following new products? (*a*) a new, improved ketchup; (*b*) a three-dimensional television system that took the company 10 years to develop; and (*c*) a new children's toy on which the company holds a patent.
6 Concept testing is an important step in the new-product process. Outline the concept tests for (*a*) an electrically powered car and (*b*) a new loan payment system for automobiles that is based on a variable interest rate. What are the differences in developing concept tests for products as opposed to services?

building your marketing plan

In fine-tuning the product strategy for your marketing plan, do these two things:
1 Develop a simple three-column table in which (*a*) market segments of potential customers are in the first column and (*b*) the one or two key points of differences of the product to satisfy the segment's needs are in the second column.
2 In the third column of your table, write ideas for specific new products for your business in each of the rows in your table.

video case 10 Activeion Cleaning Solutions: Marketing a High-Tech Cleaning Gadget

If a company told you it was marketing a handheld, on-demand cleaning gadget that also sanitizes, eliminating greater than 99.9 percent of harmful bacteria—and uses simply the tap water from your faucet—what would you think?

You'd probably think it was just another overly hyped gadget involving false, exaggerated claims and featured on late-night infomercials!

That's exactly the problem that Activeion Cleaning Solutions, a small startup company with a revolutionary technology, faced in late 2009. Let's have you give the company some *pro bono* (free!) marketing advice.

THE TECHNOLOGY: SAFE, SMART, SUSTAINABLE CLEANING

Activeion Cleaning Solutions is a privately held technology company created to revolutionize the cleaning industry through the manufacturing, marketing, and distribution of advanced technologies and products that address the ever-growing need for sustainable cleaning.

In 2008, Activeion licensed a new chemical-free cleaning technology from a mid-sized industrial company using the technology on the large scrubbing machines it sells to factories and warehouses. Other forms of the base chemical-free cleaning technology are used in hospitals for wound cleaning, in food-processing plants for sanitizing produce, and in pharmaceutical plants for maximizing cleanliness. Activeion decided to miniaturize these large, expensive versions of the technology, integrate the technology into a portable handheld sprayer, and market it to commercial cleaning professionals, as well as consumers, at a reasonable price.

The technology makes use of the energy stored in water molecules. First, tap water is passed through a membrane to create oxygen-rich micro-bubbles. Next, this water passes through an electrical charge to separate it into acidic and alkaline ionized or "activated" water. Because dirt and grime are naturally charged themselves, they are attracted to the activated water, which then breaks down the dirt and grime, lifts them from the surface, and enables the resulting dirt and grime particles to be wiped away easily.

Effective on a range of surfaces—from glass and stainless steel to wood and carpet—*R&D Magazine* named the technology as one of the most technologically significant developments of 2008. Through the innovation, cleaning professionals can meet the demand for green cleaning without the negative environmental and health concerns associated with producing, packaging, transporting, using, and disposing of traditional cleaning chemicals.

PRODUCTS AND MARKETS

In 2009 Activeion Cleaning Solutions introduced the Ionator for professional commercial cleaners as well as a consumer version for homes.

"The benefits from the Ionator are dramatic," explains Scott Beine, custodial manager for the Target Center Arena in Minneapolis, Minnesota, and a believer in the technology. "With its activated water-cleaning process, we've been able to eliminate most general-purpose cleaning products, thereby providing health and safety benefits to our custodial staff and building occupants."

The most stunning benefit of the Ionator is in the environmental area. It avoids the problems associated with traditional chemical detergents and their related packaging, which must be produced, transported, and then disposed of into the waste stream. The Ionator also can replace the hundreds of millions of chemical-laden cleaning bottles used—and disposed of—everyday, around the world. On April 22, 2009 Ellen DeGeneres featured the product on her "Earth Day" show—calling it one of the best green products available. The Ionator is now priced at $299.

Markets for the Ionator range from schools and hospitals to hotels and restaurants—virtually anywhere traditional, general-purpose cleaning chemicals are in use. There are millions of these locations in the United States that use general purpose cleaning chemicals.

To reach consumers, the company has recently introduced a version for home use, selling at about half the price of the commercial Ionator. This product seeks to reach the 117 million single-family homes, especially those with families interested in creating a safer, healthier, more sustainable living space.

BENEFITS

"We believe we have a fantastic story to tell," says Amber Arnseth, product marketing manager for Activeion. She lists the key benefits Activeion technology offers both professional cleaners and consumers:

- *Safety*. By converting tap water into a powerful cleaner and sanitizer, the Ionator eliminates cleaning chemicals. The technology is one of the only cleaning products in the world without a health-related warning label.
- *Simplicity*. Just fill with tap water and go! This is the ultimate form of "cleaning on the go" that so many households and cleaning professionals want and need. There's nothing to add, mix, or batch (it's portable)—just spray, clean, and wipe dry whenever and wherever there's a spill or a mess (it's on-demand).
- *Sustainability*. In a carbon footprint analysis, the University of Tennessee/Eco-Form compared cleaning with the Ionator to cleaning with traditional general-purpose chemicals. It found significant benefits to using the Ionator. It not only reduces environmental problems but also significantly reduces energy consumption.
- *Savings*. With a technology that works as well as or better than existing general-purpose cleaning chemicals, the Ionator eliminates the purchasing, storing, refilling, and managing of toxic cleaning supplies most organizations face today when they clean. The Grand Haven (Michigan) Area Public School District reports savings of over $20,000 annually by converting to the Ionator. Many other testimonials just like this one exist.
- *Fun*. In a recent blogging event with the Silicon Valley Moms group (www.svmoms.com), virtually all bloggers reported the same: The Ionator is cool, it helps make cleaning fun, and kids love using it because of the futuristic green glow and the buzzing sound.

CHALLENGES

Despite the numerous benefits, introducing a new, disruptive technology comes with challenges. "Almost everyone who hears about our product and technology loves the promise of what it can do," says Arnseth. "Yet we know it won't be easy to get people to convert."

Among the obvious challenges:

- *Defining "clean."* Aside from the removal of visible dirt and grime, how can one tell if a surface is clean? Or if harmful bacteria have been eliminated? Chemical companies mitigate this challenge by adding scents, bubbles, and colors—to "signal" clean.

- *Assessing new technology risk*. It's difficult enough to introduce any new technology to a fast-paced, short-attention-spanned world—much less a technology that is seemingly so unbelievable. Consumers are notoriously finicky in adopting new technologies.
- *Defining a new category*. The category of "high-tech cleaning gadgets for everyday, hard-surface, cleaning on-the-go throughout the home" does not exist today. Activeion is creating a new category in the marketplace—which has historically been one of the most difficult of marketing objectives.

Welcome to the challenges of bringing a new technology into the world!

Questions

1 What are the major points of difference for the Activeion portable handheld cleaning and sanitizing devices for (*a*) business users and (*b*) households?

2 From information in the case and a visit to the Activeion Web site (www.activeion.com), what are the characteristics of the main target markets for the Activeion cleaning tools among (*a*) business users and (*b*) households?

3 Look again at the eight key reasons for new product success and failure in the chapter. Using a five-point scale (5 = very favorable, 3 = neutral, 1 = very unfavorable), evaluate (*a*) the Ionator for business users and (*b*) the consumer version for households on each of the eight reasons and briefly justify your answers.

4 When introducing the consumer version for households, (*a*) identify three key target markets, (*b*) suggest media you might use to reach them, and (*c*) create one or two simple messages to communicate the product's points of difference.

5 What other handheld applications could Activeion pursue for its technology?

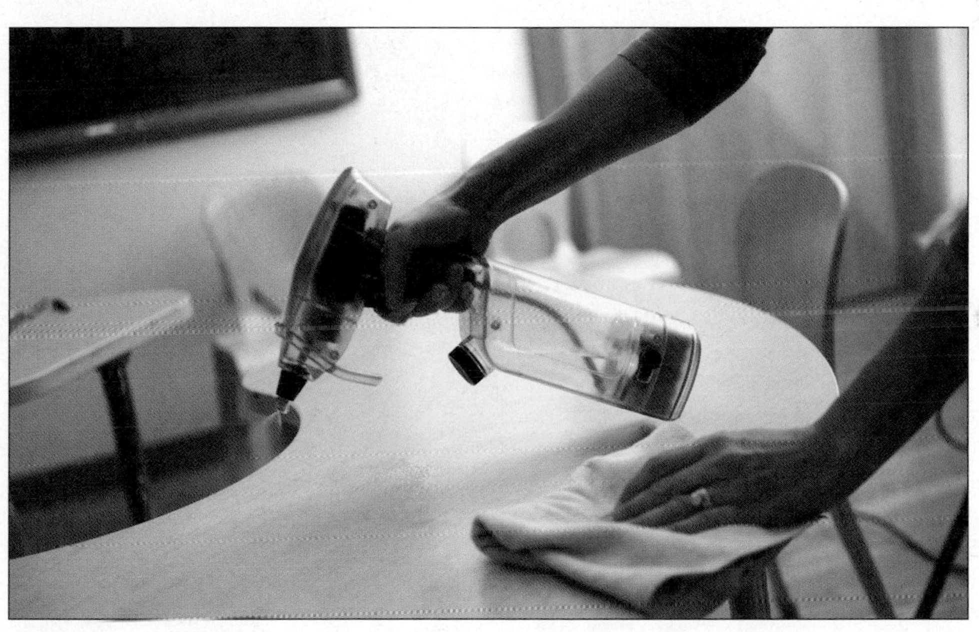

SERENA
SERENA

G2
LESS CALORIES
FOR MORE ATHLETES

11 Managing Successful Products and Brands

LEARNING OBJECTIVES

After reading this chapter you should be able to:

LO1 Explain the product life-cycle concept.

LO2 Identify ways that marketing executives manage a product's life cycle.

LO3 Recognize the importance of branding and alternative branding strategies.

LO4 Describe the role of packaging, labeling, and warranties in the marketing of a product.

GATORADE: QUENCHING THE ACTIVE THIRST WITHIN YOU

Why is the thirst for Gatorade unquenchable? Look no further than constant product improvement and masterful brand development.

Like Kleenex in the tissue market, Jell-O among gelatin desserts, and iPod for digital music players, Gatorade is synonymous with sports drinks. Concocted in 1965 at the University of Florida as a rehydration beverage for the school's football team, the drink was coined "Gatorade" by an opposing team's coach after watching his team lose to the Florida Gators in the Orange Bowl. The name stuck, and a new beverage product class was born. Stokely-Van Camp Inc. bought the Gatorade formula in 1967 and commercialized the product. The original Gatorade had one flavor—lemon-lime.

The Quaker Oats Company acquired Stokely-Van Camp in 1983 and quickly increased Gatorade sales through a variety of means. More flavors were added. Multiple package sizes were offered using different containers. Distribution expanded from convenience stores and supermarkets to mass merchandisers such as Wal-Mart. Consistent advertising and promotion effectively conveyed the product's unique performance benefits and links to athletic competition. International opportunities were vigorously pursued. Today, Gatorade is sold in more than 80 countries in North America, Europe, Latin America, the Middle East, Africa, Asia, and Australia and has become a global brand.

Masterful brand management spurred Gatorade's success. Gatorade Frost® was introduced in 1997 and aimed at expanding the brand's reach beyond organized sports to other usage occasions. Gatorade Fierce® appeared in 1999. In the same year, Gatorade entered the bottled-water category with Propel Fitness Water, a lightly flavored water fortified with vitamins. The Gatorade Performance Series was introduced in 2001, featuring a Gatorade Energy Bar, Gatorade Energy Drink, and Gatorade Nutritional Shake.

Brand development accelerated after PepsiCo Inc. purchased Quaker Oats and the Gatorade brand in 2001. Gatorade All Stars, designed for teens, and Gatorade Xtremo, developed with a bilingual label for Latino consumers, were launched in 2002. Gatorade X-Factor followed in 2003. In 2005, Gatorade Endurance Formula was created for serious runners, construction workers, and other people doing long, sweaty workouts. Gatorade Rain, a lighter tasting version of regular Gatorade, arrived in 2006. In 2007, Gatorade AM, with no caffeine, debuted for the morning workout consumer. Gatorade Tiger, named for Tiger Woods, and a low-calorie Gatorade called G2 were successfully marketed in 2008.

G2's new "Everyday Athletic" campaign has been a resounding success. Gatorade's marketing performance is a direct result of continuous product improvement and masterful brand management.

Gatorade
www.Gatorade.com

In 2009, Gatorade executives unleashed a bevy of enhanced beverages in bold new packaging. "Just like any good athlete, Gatorade is taking it to the next level," said Sarah Rob O'Hagan, Gatorade's chief marketing officer. "Whether you're in it for the win, for the thrill or for better health, if your body is moving, Gatorade sees you as an athlete, and we're inviting you into the brand." According to a company announcement, "The new Gatorade attitude would be most visible through a total packaging redesign." For example, Gatorade Thirst Quencher now displays the letter G front and center along with the brand's iconic bolt. "For Gatorade, G represents the heart, hustle, and soul of athleticism and will become a badge of pride for anyone who sweats, no matter where they're active"

To differentiate the range of Gatorade offerings from the traditional Gatorade Thirst Quencher, newly enhanced beverages conveyed the attitude of a tough-love coach or personal trainer through in-your-face names on the label and nutrition benefits inside. Gatorade Fierce is now Bring It™, Gatorade X-Factor is now Be Tough™, Gatorade AM is now Shine On™, and Gatorade Rain is now No Excuses™. Additionally, Gatorade Tiger was updated to emphasize its new focus benefit derived from the product's reformulation. Some 45 years after its creation, Gatorade remains a vibrant multibillion-dollar growth brand with seemingly unlimited potential.[1]

The marketing of Gatorade illustrates continuous product development and masterful brand management in a dynamic marketplace. This chapter shows how the actions taken by Gatorade executives exemplify those made by successful marketers.

CHARTING THE PRODUCT LIFE CYCLE

Products, like people, are viewed as having a life cycle. The concept of the **product life cycle** describes the stages a new product goes through in the marketplace: introduction, growth, maturity, and decline (Figure 11–1).[2] The two curves shown in this figure, total industry sales revenue and total industry profit, represent the sum of sales revenue and profit of all firms producing the product. The reasons for the changes in each curve and the marketing decisions involved are detailed in the following pages.

Introduction Stage

The introduction stage of the product life cycle occurs when a product is introduced to its intended target market. During this period, sales grow slowly, and profit is minimal. The lack of profit is often the result of large investment costs in product development, such as the millions of dollars spent by Gillette to develop the Gillette Fusion razor shaving system. The marketing objective for the company at this stage is to create consumer awareness and stimulate *trial*—the initial purchase of a product by a consumer.

Companies often spend heavily on advertising and other promotion tools to build awareness and stimulate product trial among consumers in the introduction stage. For example, Gillette budgeted $200 million in advertising to introduce the Fusion

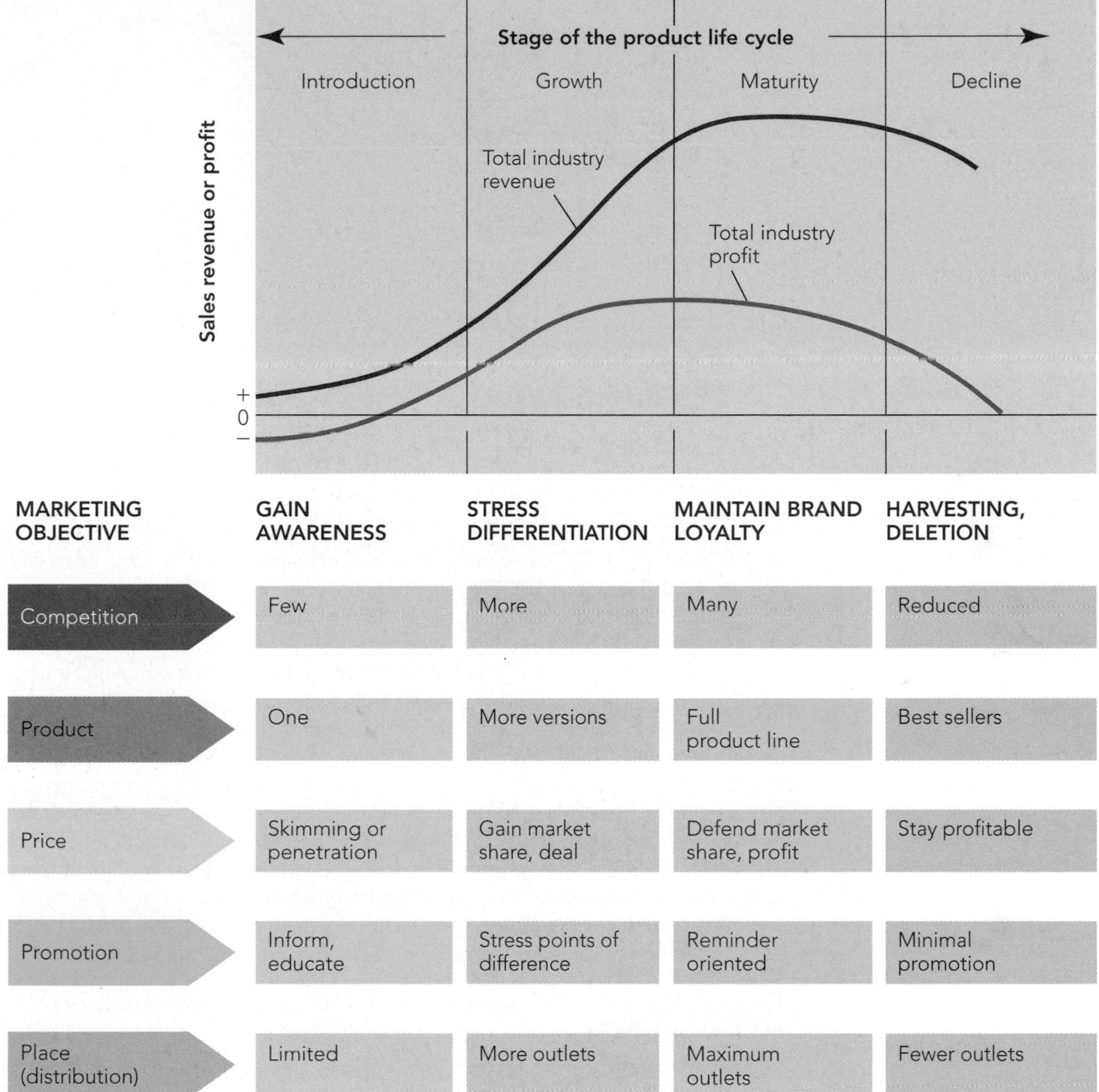

FIGURE 11–1
How stages of the product life cycle relate to a firm's marketing objectives and marketing mix actions

shaving system to male shavers. The result? Over 60 percent of male shavers became aware of the new razor within six months and 26 percent tried the product.[3]

Advertising and promotion expenditures in the introduction stage are often made to stimulate *primary demand*, the desire for the product class rather than for a specific brand, since there are few competitors with the same product. As more competitors launch their own products and the product progresses along its life cycle, company attention is focused on creating *selective demand*, the preference for a specific brand.

Other marketing mix variables also are important at this stage. Gaining distribution can be a challenge because channel intermediaries may be hesitant to carry a new product. Also, a company often restricts the number of variations of the product to ensure control of product quality. Remember that the original Gatorade came in only one flavor.

During introduction, pricing can be either high or low. A high initial price may be used as part of a *skimming* strategy to help the company recover the costs of

FIGURE 11–2
Product life cycle for the stand-alone fax machine for business use: 1970–2012. All four product life-cycle stages appear: introduction, growth, maturity, and decline.

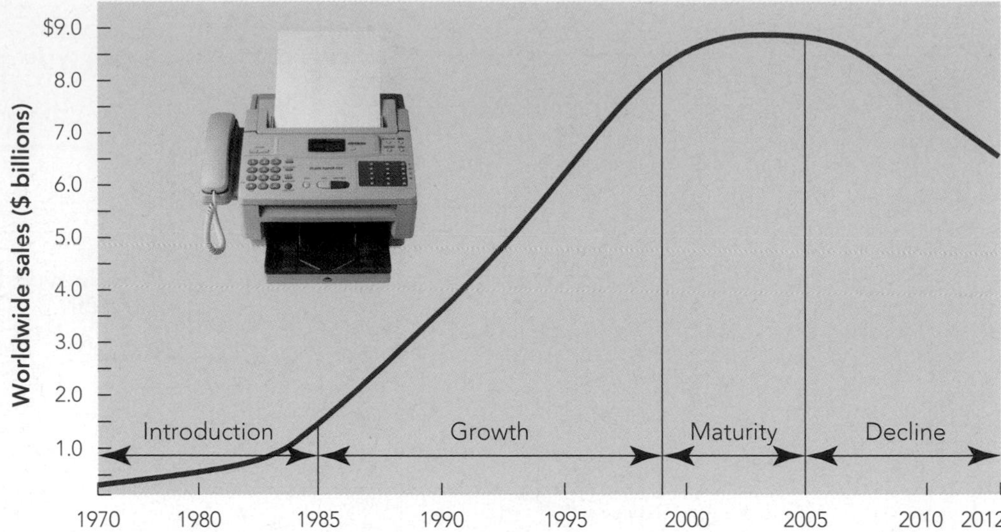

development as well as capitalize on the price insensitivity of early buyers. A master of this strategy is 3M. According to a 3M manager, "We hit fast, price high, and get the heck out when the me-too products pour in."[4] High prices tend to attract competitors eager to enter the market because they see the opportunity for profit. To discourage competitive entry, a company can price low, referred to as *penetration pricing*. This pricing strategy helps build unit volume, but a company must closely monitor costs. These and other pricing techniques are covered in Chapter 14.

Figure 11–2 charts the stand-alone fax machine product life cycle for business use in the United States from the early 1970s to 2012.[5] As shown, sales grew slowly in the 1970s and early 1980s after Xerox pioneered the first portable fax machine. Fax machines were first sold direct to businesses by company salespeople and were premium priced. The average price for a fax machine in 1980 was a hefty $12,700. Those fax machines were primitive by today's standards. They contained mechanical parts, not electronic circuitry, and offered few features seen in today's models.

Several product classes are in the introductory stage of the product life cycle. These include pocket video cameras and electric-powered automobiles.

Growth Stage

The growth stage of the product life cycle is characterized by rapid increases in sales. It is in this stage that competitors appear. For example, Figure 11–2 shows the dramatic increase in sales of fax machines from 1986 to 1998. The number of companies selling fax machines also increased, from one in the early 1970s to four in the late 1970s to seven manufacturers in 1983, which sold nine brands. By 1998 there were some 25 manufacturers and 60 brands from which to choose.

The result of more competitors and more aggressive pricing is that profit usually peaks during the growth stage. For instance, the average price for a fax machine plummeted from $3,300 in 1985 to $500 in 1995. At this stage, advertising shifts emphasis to stimulating selective demand; product benefits are compared with those of competitors' offerings for the purpose of gaining market share.

Product sales in the growth stage grow at an increasing rate because of new people trying or using the product and a growing proportion of *repeat purchasers*—people who tried the product, were satisfied, and bought again. For the Gillette Fusion razor, over 60 percent of men who tried the razor adopted the product permanently. For successful products, the ratio of repeat to trial purchases grows as the product moves through the life cycle. Durable fax machines meant that replacement purchases were

Electric automobiles made by General Motors are in the introductory stage of the product life cycle. Digital cameras produced by OLYMPUS are in the growth stage. Each product and company faces unique challenges based on its product life-cycle stage.

General Motors Company
www.gm.com

OLYMPUS America, Inc.
www.olympusamerica.com

rare. However, it became common for more than one machine to populate a business as the machine's use became more widespread.

Changes appear in the product in the growth stage. To help differentiate a company's brand from competitors, an improved version or new features are added to the original design, and product proliferation occurs. Changes in fax machines included (1) models with built-in telephones; (2) models that used plain, rather than thermal, paper for copies; and (3) models that integrated electronic mail.

In the growth stage, it is important to gain as much distribution for the product as possible. In the retail store, for example, this often means that competing companies fight for display and shelf space. Expanded distribution in the fax industry is an example. Early in the growth stage, just 11 percent of office machine dealers carried this equipment. By the mid-1990s, more than 70 percent of these dealers sold fax equipment, and distribution was expanded to other stores selling electronic equipment.

Numerous product classes or industries are in the growth stage of the product life cycle. Examples include smart phones and digital cameras.

Maturity Stage

The maturity stage is characterized by a slowing of total industry sales or product class revenue. Also, marginal competitors begin to leave the market. Most consumers who would buy the product are either repeat purchasers of the item or have tried and abandoned it. Sales increase at a decreasing rate in the maturity stage as fewer new buyers enter the market. Profit declines due to fierce price competition among many sellers, and the cost of gaining new buyers at this stage rises.

Marketing attention in the maturity stage is often directed toward holding market share through further product differentiation and finding new buyers. Fax machine

Marketing Matters > > > > > > customer value

Will E-mail Spell Extinction for Fax Machines?

Technological substitution that creates value for customers often causes the decline stage in the product life cycle. Will e-mail replace fax machines?

This question has been debated for years. Even though e-mail continues to grow with broadening Internet access, millions of fax machines are still sold each year. Industry analysts estimate that the number of e-mail mailboxes worldwide will grow to 2.5 billion in 2012. However, the phenomenal popularity of e-mail has not brought fax machines to extinction. Why? The two technologies do not directly compete for the same messaging applications.

E-mail is used for text messages, and faxing is predominately used for communicating formatted documents by business users. Fax usage is expected to increase through 2010, even though unit sales of fax machines have declined on a worldwide basis. Internet technology and e-mail may eventually replace facsimile technology and paper and make fax machines extinct, but not in the immediate future.

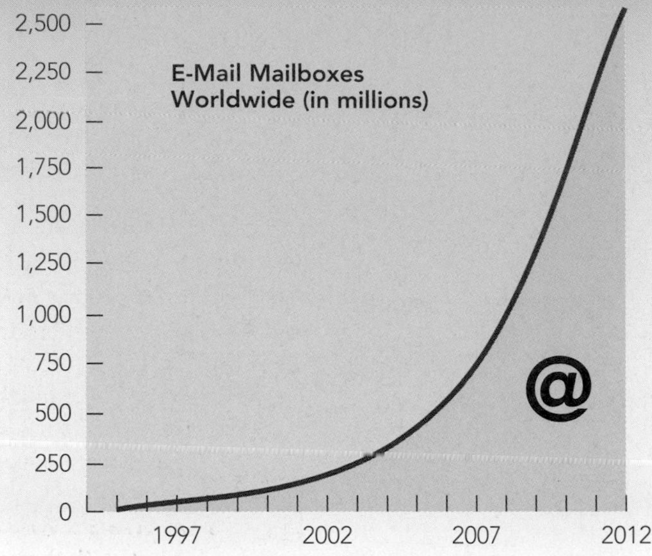

manufacturers developed Internet-enabled multifunctional models with new features such as scanning, copying, and color reproduction. They also designed fax machines suitable for small and home businesses, which today represent a substantial portion of sales. Still, a major consideration in a company's strategy in this stage is to control overall marketing cost by improving promotional and distribution efficiency.

Fax machines entered the maturity stage in the late 1990s. At the time, about 90 percent of industry sales were captured by five producers (Hewlett-Packard, Brother, Sharp, Lexmark, and Samsung), reflecting the departure of marginal competitors. By 2004, 200 million stand-alone fax machines were installed throughout the world, sending more than 120 billion faxes annually.

Numerous product classes and industries are in the maturity stage of their product life cycle. These include soft drinks and DVD players.

Decline Stage

The decline stage occurs when sales drop. Fax machines for business use moved to this stage in early 2005 and the average price for a fax machine had sunk below $100. Frequently, a product enters this stage not because of any wrong strategy on the part of companies, but because of environmental changes. For example, digital music players pushed compact discs into decline in the recorded music industry. Will Internet technology and e-mail make fax machines extinct any time soon? The accompanying Marketing Matters box offers one perspective on this question.[6]

Products in the decline stage tend to consume a disproportionate share of management and financial resources relative to their future worth. A company will follow one of two strategies to handle a declining product: deletion or harvesting.

Deletion Product *deletion*, or dropping the product from the company's product line, is the most drastic strategy. Because a residual core of consumers still consume or use a product even in the decline stage, product elimination decisions are not taken lightly. For example, Sanford Corporation continues to sell its Liquid Paper correction fluid for use with typewriters in the era of word-processing equipment.

Harvesting A second strategy, *harvesting*, is when a company retains the product but reduces marketing costs. The product continues to be offered, but salespeople do not allocate time in selling nor are advertising dollars spent. The purpose of harvesting is to maintain the ability to meet customer requests. Coca-Cola, for instance, still sells Tab, its first diet cola, to a small group of die-hard fans. According to Coke's CEO, "It shows you care. We want to make sure those who want Tab, get Tab."[7]

Four Aspects of the Product Life Cycle

Some important aspects of product life cycles are (1) their length, (2) the shape of their sales curves, (3) how they vary with different levels of products, and (4) the rate at which consumers adopt products.

Length of the Product Life Cycle There is no set time that it takes a product to move through its life cycle. As a rule, consumer products have shorter life cycles than business products. For example, many new consumer food products such as Frito-Lay's Baked Lay's potato chips move from the introduction stage to maturity in 18 months. The availability of mass communication vehicles informs consumers quickly and shortens life cycles. Also, technological change tends to shorten product life cycles as new-product innovation replaces existing products.

Shape of the Product Life Cycle The product life-cycle sales curve shown in Figure 11–1 is the *generalized life cycle*, but not all products have the same shape to their curve. In fact, there are several life-cycle curves, each type suggesting different marketing strategies. Figure 11–3 shows the shape of life-cycle sales curves for four different types of products: high-learning, low-learning, fashion, and fad products.

A *high-learning product* is one for which significant customer education is required and there is an extended introductory period (Figure 11–3A). It may surprise you, but personal computers had this life-cycle curve. Consumers in the 1980s had to learn the benefits of owning the product or be educated in a new way of performing familiar tasks. Convection ovens for home use required consumers to learn a new way of cooking and alter familiar recipes used with conventional ovens. As a result, these ovens spent years in the introductory period.

In contrast, sales for a *low-learning product* begin immediately because little learning is required by the consumer, and the benefits of purchase are readily understood

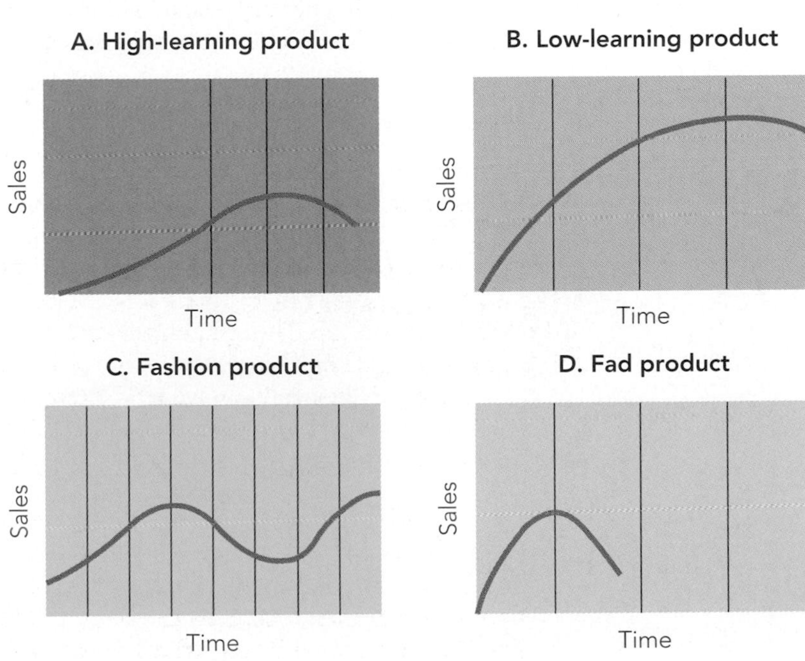

FIGURE 11–3
Alternative product life-cycle curves based on product types. Note the long introduction stage for a high-learning product compared with a low-learning product. Read the text for an explanation of different product life-cycle curves.

(Figure 11–3B). This product often can be easily imitated by competitors, so the marketing strategy is to broaden distribution quickly. In this way, as competitors rapidly enter, most retail outlets already have the innovator's product. It is also important to have the manufacturing capacity to meet demand. A successful low-learning product is Gillette's Fusion razor. This product achieved $1 billion in worldwide sales in less than three years.

A *fashion product* (Figure 11–3C) is a style of the times. Life cycles for fashion products frequently appear in women's and men's apparel. Fashion products are introduced, decline, and then seem to return. The length of the cycles may be months, years, or decades. Consider women's hosiery. Product sales have been declining for years. Women consider it more fashionable to not wear hosiery—bad news for Hanes brands, the leading marketer of women's sheer hosiery. According to an authority on fashion, "Companies might as well let the fashion cycle take its course and wait for the inevitable return of pantyhose."[8]

A *fad* experiences rapid sales on introduction and then an equally rapid decline (Figure 11–3D). These products are typically novelties and have a short life cycle. They include car tattoos sold in Southern California and described as the first removable and reusable graphics for automobiles, and vinyl dresses and fleece bikinis made by a Minnesota clothing company.[9]

The Product Level: Class and Form The product life cycle shown in Figure 11–1 is a total industry or product class sales curve. Yet, in managing a product it is important to often distinguish among the multiple life cycles (class and form) that may exist. **Product class** refers to the entire product category or industry, such as prerecorded music. **Product form** pertains to variations within the product class. For prerecorded music, product form exits in the technology used to provide the music such as cassette types, compact discs, and digital music players. Figure 11–4 shows the life cycles for these three product forms.[10]

The Life Cycle and Consumers The life cycle of a product depends on sales to consumers. Not all consumers rush to buy a product in the introductory stage, and the shapes of the life-cycle curves indicate that most sales occur after the

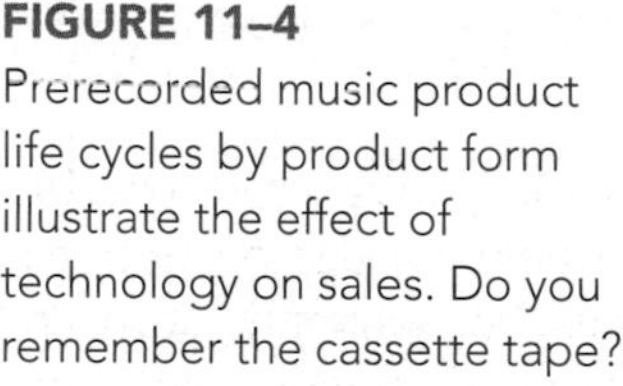
FIGURE 11–4
Prerecorded music product life cycles by product form illustrate the effect of technology on sales. Do you remember the cassette tape?

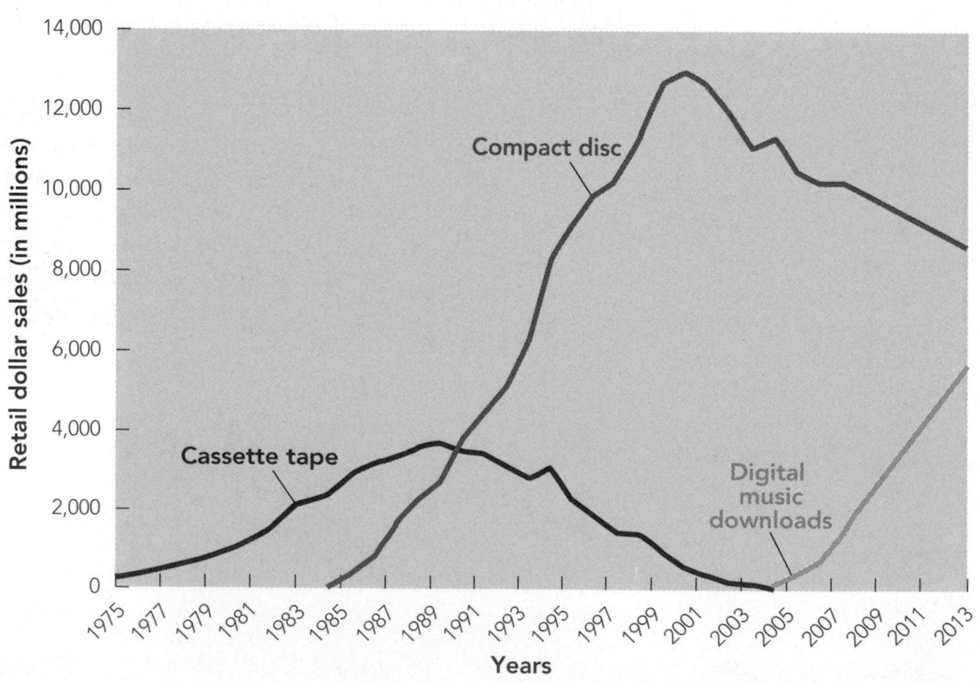

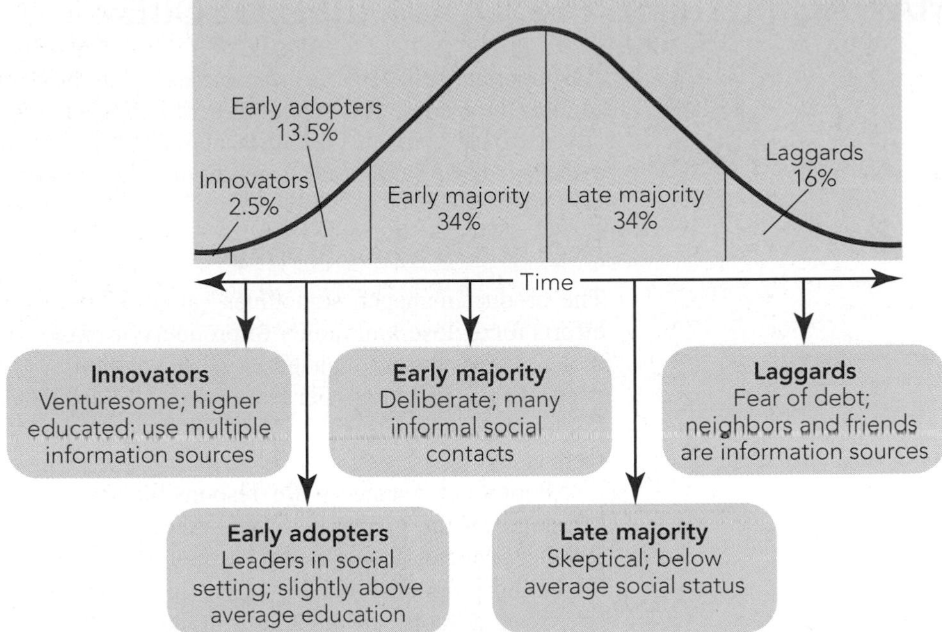

FIGURE 11–5
Five categories and profiles of product adopters. For a product to be successful, it must be purchased by innovators and early adopters.

product has been on the market for some time. In essence, a product diffuses, or spreads, through the population, a concept called the *diffusion of innovation*.[11]

Some people are attracted to a product early. Others buy it only after they see their friends or opinion leaders with the item. Figure 11–5 shows the consumer population divided into five categories of product adopters based on when they adopt a new product. Brief profiles accompany each category. For any product to be successful, it must be purchased by innovators and early adopters. This is why manufacturers of new pharmaceuticals try to gain adoption by respected hospitals, clinics, and physicians. Once accepted by innovators and early adopters, the adoption of new products moves on to the early majority, late majority, and laggard categories.

Several factors affect whether a consumer will adopt a new product or not. Common reasons for resisting a product in the introduction stage are usage barriers (the product is not compatible with existing habits), value barriers (the product provides no incentive to change), risk barriers (physical, economic, or social), and psychological barriers (cultural differences or image).[12]

Companies attempt to overcome these barriers in numerous ways. They provide warranties, money-back guarantees, extensive usage instructions, demonstrations, and free samples to stimulate initial trial of new products. For example, software developers offer demonstrations downloaded from the Internet. Cosmetic consumers can browse through the Cover Girl ColorMatch system on its Web site to find out how certain makeup products will look. Free samples are one of the most popular means to gain consumer trial. In fact, 71 percent of consumers consider a sample to be the best way to evaluate a new product.[13]

learning review

1. Advertising plays a major role in the _______________ stage of the product life cycle, and _______________ plays a major role in maturity.
2. How do high-learning and low-learning products differ?
3. What are the five categories of product adopters?

MANAGING THE PRODUCT LIFE CYCLE

An important task for a firm is to manage its products through the successive stages of their life cycles. This section describes the role of the product manager who is usually responsible for this and presents three ways to manage a product through its life cycle: modifying the product, modifying the market, and repositioning the product.

Role of a Product Manager

The product manager, sometimes called a *brand manager*, manages the marketing efforts for a close-knit family of products or brands. Introduced by Procter & Gamble in 1928, the product manager style of marketing organization is used by consumer goods firms, including General Mills and PepsiCo, and by industrial firms such as Intel and Hewlett-Packard. The U.S. Postal Service employs product managers as well.

All product managers are responsible for managing existing products through the stages of the life cycle. Some are also responsible for developing new products. Product managers' marketing responsibilities include developing and executing a marketing program for the product line described in an annual marketing plan and approving ad copy, media selection, and package design.

Product managers also engage in extensive data analysis related to their products and brands. Sales, market share, and profit trends are closely monitored. Managers often supplement these data with two measures: (1) a category development index (CDI) and (2) a brand development index (BDI). These indexes help to identify strong and weak market segments (usually demographic or geographic segments) for specific consumer products and brands and provide direction for marketing efforts. The calculation, visual display, and interpretation of these two indexes for Hawaiian Punch are described in the Using Marketing Dashboards box.

Harley-Davidson redesigned some of its motorcycle models to feature smaller hand grips, a lower seat, and an easier-to-pull clutch lever to create a more comfortable ride for women. According to Genevieve Schmitt, founding editor of WomenRidersNow.com, "They realize that women are an up-and-coming segment and that they need to accommodate them."

Harley-Davidson, Inc.
www.harley-davidson.com

Modifying the Product

Product modification involves altering a product's characteristic, such as its quality, performance, or appearance, to increase the product's value to customers and increase sales. Wrinkle-free and stain-resistant clothing made possible by nanotechnology revolutionized the men's and women's apparel business and stimulated industry sales of casual pants, shirts, and blouses. Nokia's global leadership position among cell phone handset manufacturers is due to continuous product modification. For example, Nokia offers a cell phone handset that plays music, displays maps, takes pictures, surfs the Internet, and holds a 3.5-inch screen for watching TV and playing video games. Nokia's effort is called *product bundling*—the sale of two or more separate products in one package. In this case, the Nokia handset integrates seven separate products: telephone, camera, computer, video game player, GPS, television, and MP3 player in one handset package.[14]

New features, packages, or scents can be used to change a product's characteristics and give the sense of a revised product. Procter & Gamble revamped Pantene shampoo and conditioner with a new vitamin formula and relaunched the brand with a multimillion-dollar advertising and promotion campaign. The result? Pantene, a brand first introduced in the 1940s, is now the top-selling shampoo and conditioner in the United States in an industry with more than 1,000 competitors.

Modifying the Market

With **market modification** strategies, a company tries to find new customers, increase a product's use among existing customers, or create new use situations.

Using Marketing Dashboards
Knowing Your CDI and BDI

Where are sales for my product category and brand strongest and weakest? Data related to this question are displayed in a marketing dashboard using two indexes: (1) category development index and (2) brand development index.

Your Challenge You have joined the marketing team for Hawaiian Punch, the top fruit punch drink sold in the United States. The brand has been marketed to mothers with children under 12 years old. The majority of Hawaiian Punch sales are in gallon and 2-liter bottles. Your assignment is to examine the brand's performance and identify growth opportunities for the Hawaiian Punch brand among households that consume prepared fruit drinks (the product category).

Your marketing dashboard displays a category development index and a brand development index provided by a syndicated marketing research firm. Each index is based on the calculations below:

$$\text{Category Development Index (CDI)} = \frac{\text{Percent of a product category's total U.S. sales in a market segment}}{\text{Percent of the total U.S. population in a market segment}} \times 100$$

$$\text{Brand Development Index (BDI)} = \frac{\text{Percent of a brand's total U.S. sales in a market segment}}{\text{Percent of the total U.S. population in a market segment}} \times 100$$

A CDI over 100 indicates above-average product category purchases by a market segment. A number under 100 indicates below-average purchases. A BDI over 100 indicates a strong brand position in a segment; a number under 100 indicates a weak brand position.

You are interested in CDI and BDI displays for four household segments that consume prepared fruit drinks: (1) households without children; (2) households with children 6 years old or under; (3) households with children aged 7 to 12; and (4) households with children aged 13 to 18.

Your Findings The BDI and CDI measures displayed below show that Hawaiian Punch is consumed by households with children, and particularly households with children under age 12. The Hawaiian Punch BDI is over 100 for both segments—not surprising since the brand is marketed to these segments. Households with children 13 to 18 years old evidence high fruit drink consumption with a CDI over 100. But Hawaiian Punch is relatively weak in this segment with a BDI under 100.

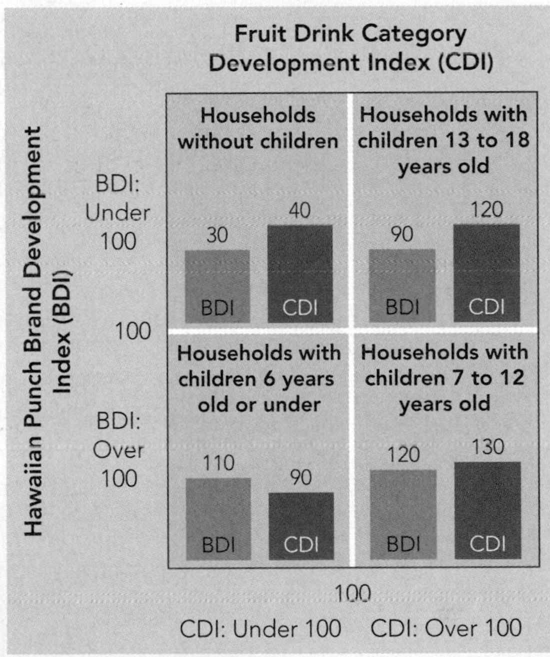

Your Action An opportunity for Hawaiian Punch exists among households with children 13 to 18 years old—teenagers. You might propose that Hawaiian Punch be repositioned for teens. In addition, you might recommend that Hawaiian Punch be packaged in single-serve cans or bottles to attract this segment, much like soft drinks. Teens might also be targeted for advertising and promotions.

Finding New Customers Produce companies have begun marketing and packaging prunes as dried plums to attract younger buyers. Harley-Davidson has tailored a marketing program to encourage women to take up biking, thus doubling the number of potential customers for its motorcycles.[15]

Increasing a Product's Use Promoting more frequent usage has been a strategy of Campbell Soup Company. Because soup consumption rises in the winter and declines during the summer, the company now advertises more heavily in warm months to encourage consumers to think of soup as more than a cold-weather food.

Similarly, the Florida Orange Growers Association advocates drinking orange juice throughout the day rather than for breakfast only.

Creating a New Use Situation Finding new uses for an existing product has been the strategy behind Dockers, the U.S. market leader in casual pants. Originally intended as a single pant for every situation, Dockers now promotes different looks for different usage situations: work, weekend, dress, and golf.[16]

Repositioning the Product

Often a company decides to reposition its product or product line in an attempt to bolster sales. *Product repositioning* changes the place a product occupies in a consumer's mind relative to competitive products. A firm can reposition a product by changing one or more of the four marketing mix elements. Four factors that trigger the need for a repositioning action are discussed next.

Reacting to a Competitor's Position One reason to reposition a product is because a competitor's entrenched position is adversely affecting sales and market share. New Balance, Inc. successfully repositioned its athletic shoes to focus on fit, durability, and comfort rather than competing head-on against Nike and Adidas on fashion and professional sports. The company offers an expansive range of shoes and it networks with podiatrists, not sport celebrities.[17]

Reaching a New Market When Unilever introduced iced tea in Britain, sales were disappointing. British consumers viewed it as leftover hot tea, not suitable for drinking. The company made its tea carbonated and repositioned it as a cold soft drink to compete as a carbonated beverage and sales improved. Johnson & Johnson effectively repositioned St. Joseph aspirin from one for infants to an adult low-strength aspirin to reduce the risk of heart problems or strokes.[18]

Catching a Rising Trend Changing consumer trends also lead to repositioning. Growing consumer interest in foods that offer health and dietary benefits is an example. Many products have been repositioned to capitalize on this trend. Quaker

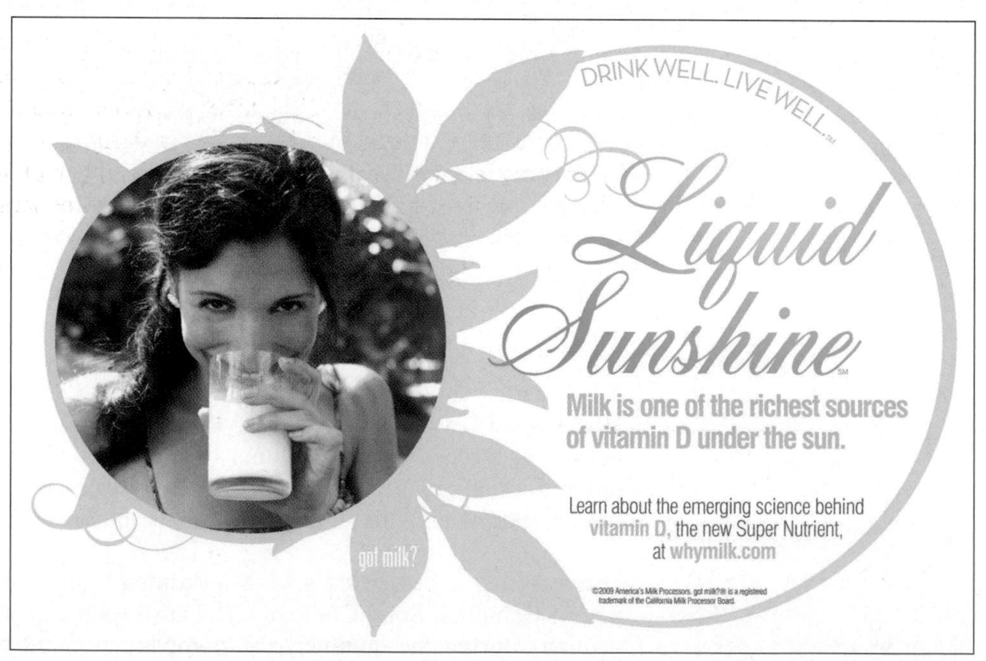

The Milk Processor Education Program (MilkPEP) promotes the nutritional qualities of milk, notably vitamin D, in its advertising.

The Milk Processor Education Program
www.whymilk.com

Making Responsible Decisions > > > > > > > ethics

Consumer Economics of Downsizing—Get Less, Pay More

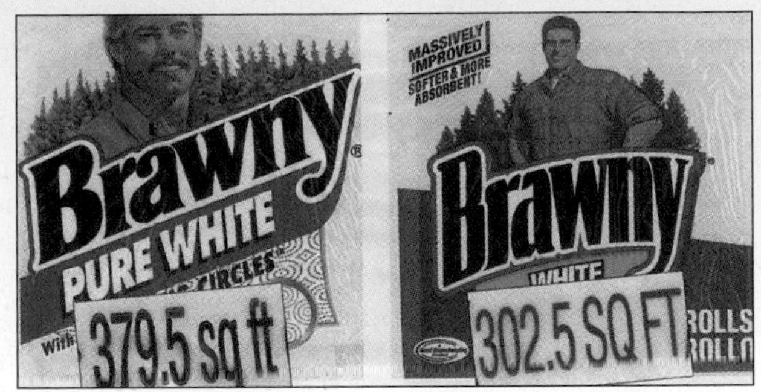

For more than 30 years, Starkist put 6.5 ounces of tuna into its regular-sized can. Today, Starkist puts 6.125 ounces of tuna into its can, but charges the same price. Frito-Lay (Doritos and Lay's snack chips), Procter & Gamble (Pampers and Luvs disposable diapers), Nestlé (Poland Spring and Calistoga bottled waters) have whittled away at package contents 5 to 10 percent while maintaining their products' package size, dimensions, and prices. Kimberly-Clark cut its retail price on its jumbo pack of Huggies diapers from $13.50 to $12.50, but reduced the number of diapers per pack from 48 to 42. Georgia-Pacific reduced the content of its Brawny paper towel six-roll pack by 20 percent without lowering the price.

Consumer advocates charge that downsizing the content of packages while maintaining prices is a subtle and unannounced way of taking advantage of consumer buying habits. They also say downsizing is a price increase in disguise and deceptive, but legal. Manufacturers argue that this practice is a way of keeping prices from rising beyond psychological barriers for their products.

Is downsizing an unethical practice if manufacturers do not inform consumers that the package contents are less than they were previously?

Oats makes the FDA-approved claim that oatmeal, as part of a low-saturated-fat, low-cholesterol diet, may reduce the risk of heart disease. Calcium-enriched products, such as Kraft American cheese and Uncle Ben's Calcium Plus rice, emphasize healthy bone structure for children and adults. Weight-conscious consumers have embraced low-fat and low-calorie diets in growing numbers. Today, most food and beverage companies offer reduced-fat and low-calorie versions of their products.

Changing the Value Offered In repositioning a product, a company can decide to change the value it offers buyers and trade up or down. **Trading up** involves adding value to the product (or line) through additional features or higher-quality materials. Michelin, Bridgestone, and Goodyear have done this with a "run-flat" tire that can travel up to 50 miles at 55 miles per hour after suffering total air loss. Dog food manufacturers, such as Ralston Purina, also have traded up by offering super-premium foods based on "life-stage nutrition." Mass merchandisers, such as Target and JCPenney, can trade up by adding a designer clothes section to their stores.

Trading down involves reducing the number of features, quality, or price. For example, airlines have added more seats, thus reducing legroom, and limited snack service. Trading down exists when companies engage in *downsizing*—reducing the package content without changing package size and maintaining or increasing the package price. Firms are criticized for this practice, as described in the Making Responsible Decisions box.[19]

learning review

4. How does a product manager help manage a product's life cycle?
5. What does "creating a new use situation" mean in managing a product's life cycle?
6. Explain the difference between trading up and trading down in repositioning.

BRANDING AND BRAND MANAGEMENT

LO3

A basic decision in marketing products is **branding**, in which an organization uses a name, phrase, design, symbols, or combination of these to identify its products and distinguish them from those of competitors. A **brand name** is any word, device (design, sound, shape, or color), or combination of these used to distinguish a seller's goods or services. Some brand names can be spoken, such as a Gatorade or Rollerblade. Other brand names cannot be spoken, such as the colored apple (the *logotype* or *logo*) that Apple puts on its machines and in its ads. A **trade name** is a commercial, legal name under which a company does business. The Coca-Cola Company is the trade name of that firm.

A **trademark** identifies that a firm has legally registered its brand name or trade name so the firm has its exclusive use, thereby preventing others from using it. In the United States, trademarks are registered with the U.S. Patent and Trademark Office and protected under the Lanham Act. A well-known trademark can help a company advertise its offerings to customers and develop their brand loyalty.

Because a good trademark can help sell a product, *product counterfeiting*, which involves low-cost copies of popular brands not manufactured by the original producer, is a serious problem. Counterfeit products can steal sales from the original manufacturer or harm the company's reputation. U.S. companies lose between $200 billion and $250 billion each year to counterfeit products.[20] To counteract counterfeiting, the U.S. government passed the *Stop Counterfeiting in Manufactured Goods Act* (2006), which makes counterfeiters subject to 20-year prison sentences and $15 million in fines.

Consumers may benefit most from branding. Recognizing competing products by distinct trademarks allows them to be more efficient shoppers. Consumers can recognize and avoid products with which they are dissatisfied, while becoming loyal

Can you describe the brand personality traits for these two brands?

got2b
www.got2b.com

Degree Fine Fragrance Collection
www.degree.com

to other, more satisfying brands. As discussed in Chapter 5, brand loyalty often eases consumers' decision making by eliminating the need for an external search.

Brand Personality and Brand Equity

Product managers recognize that brands offer more than product identification and a means to distinguish their products from competitors.[21] Successful and established brands take on a **brand personality**, a set of human characteristics associated with a brand name. Research shows that consumers often assign personality traits to products—traditional, romantic, rugged, sophisticated, rebellious—and choose brands that are consistent with their own or desired self-image. Marketers can and do imbue a brand with a personality through advertising that depicts a certain user or usage situation and conveys certain emotions or feelings to be associated with the brand. For example, the personality traits associated with Coca-Cola are all American and real; with Pepsi, young and exciting; and with Dr Pepper, nonconforming and unique. The traits often linked to Harley-Davidson are masculinity, defiance, and rugged individualism.

Brand name importance to a company has led to a concept called **brand equity**, the added value a brand name gives to a product beyond the functional benefits provided. This value has two distinct advantages. First, brand equity provides a competitive advantage. The Sunkist brand implies quality fruit. The Disney name defines children's entertainment. A second advantage is that consumers are often willing to pay a higher price for a product with brand equity. Brand equity, in this instance, is represented by the premium a consumer will pay for one brand over another when the functional benefits provided are identical. Gillette razors and blades, Bose audio systems, Duracell batteries, and Louis Vuitton luggage all enjoy a price premium arising from brand equity.

Creating Brand Equity Brand equity doesn't just happen. It is carefully crafted and nurtured by marketing programs that forge strong, favorable, and unique customer associations and experiences with a brand. Brand equity resides in the minds of consumers and results from what they have learned, felt, seen, and heard about a brand over time. Marketers recognize that brand equity is not easily or quickly achieved. Rather, it arises from a sequential building process consisting of four steps (see Figure 11–6).[22]

- The first step is to develop positive brand awareness and an association of the brand in consumers' minds with a product class or need to give the brand an identity. Gatorade and Kleenex have achieved this in the sports drink and facial tissue product classes, respectively.
- Next, a marketer must establish a brand's meaning in the minds of consumers. Meaning arises from what a brand stands for and has two dimensions—a functional, performance-related dimension and an abstract, imagery-related dimension. Nike has done this through continuous product development and improvement and its links to peak athletic performance in its integrated marketing communications program.
- The third step is to elicit the proper consumer responses to a brand's identity and meaning. Here attention is placed on how consumers think and feel about a brand. Thinking focuses on a brand's perceived quality, credibility, and superiority relative to other brands. Feeling

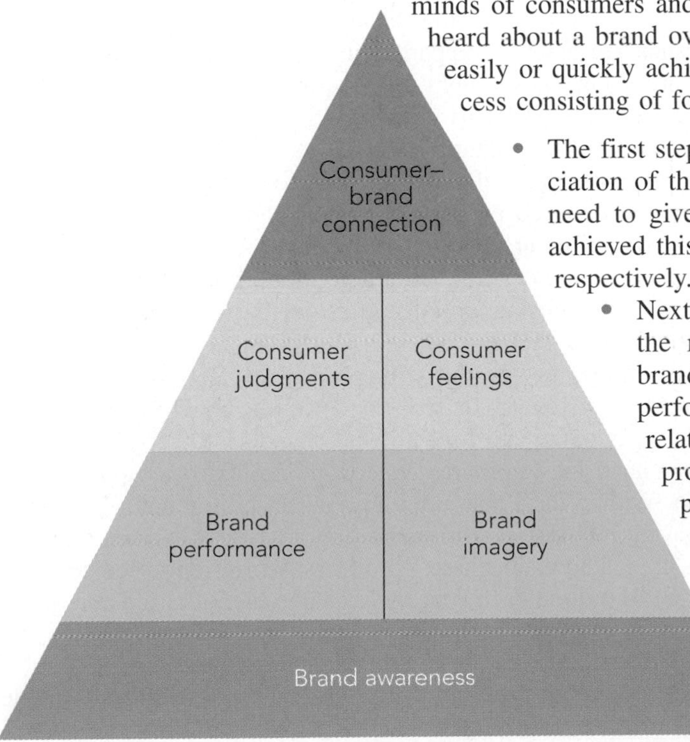

FIGURE 11–6
The customer-based brand equity pyramid shows the four-step building process that forges strong, favorable, and unique customer associations with a brand.

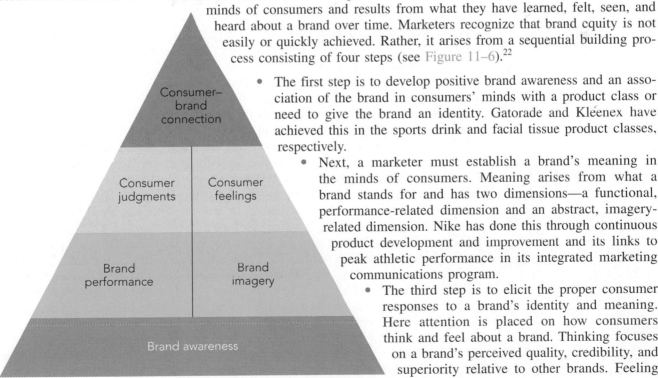

Ralph Lauren has a long-term licensing agreement with Luxottica Group, S.P.A. of Milan for the design, production, and worldwide distribution of prescription frames and sunglasses under the Ralph Lauren brand. The agreement is an ideal fit for both companies. Ralph Lauren is a leader in the design, marketing, and distribution of premium lifestyle products. Luxottica is the global leader in the premium and luxury eyewear sector.

Luxottica Group, S.P.A.
www.luxottica.com

Ralph Lauren Corporation
www.ralphlauren.com

relates to the consumer's emotional reaction to a brand. Michelin elicits both responses for its tires. Not only is Michelin thought of as a credible and superior-quality brand, but consumers also acknowledge a warm and secure feeling of safety, comfort, and self-assurance without worry or concern about the brand.

- The final, and most difficult, step is to create a consumer–brand connection evident in an intense, active loyalty relationship between consumers and the brand. A deep psychological bond characterizes a consumer–brand connection and the personal identification customers have with the brand. Brands that have achieved this status include Harley-Davidson, Apple, and eBay.

Valuing Brand Equity Brand equity also provides a financial advantage for the brand owner.[23] Successful, established brand names, such as Gillette, Nike, Gatorade, and Nokia, have an economic value in the sense that they are intangible assets. The recognition that brands are assets is apparent in the decision to buy and sell brands. For example, Triarc Companies bought the Snapple brand from Quaker Oats for $300 million and sold it three years later to Cadbury Schweppes for $900 million. This example illustrates that brands, unlike physical assets that depreciate with time and use, can appreciate in value when effectively marketed. However, brands can lose value when they are not managed properly. Consider the purchase and sale of Lender's Bagels. Kellogg bought the brand for $466 million only to sell it to Aurora Foods for $275 million three years later following deteriorating sales and profits.

Financially lucrative brand licensing opportunities arise from brand equity.[24] **Brand licensing** is a contractual agreement whereby one company (licensor) allows its brand name(s) or trademark(s) to be used with products or services offered by another company (licensee) for a royalty or fee. For example, Playboy earns more than $260 million licensing its name and logo for merchandise. Disney makes billions of dollars each year licensing its characters for children's toys, apparel, and games. Licensing fees for Winnie the Pooh alone exceed $3 billion annually.

Successful brand licensing requires careful marketing analysis to assure a proper fit between the licensor's brand and the licensee's products. World-renowned designer Ralph Lauren earns over $140 million each year by licensing his Ralph Lauren, Polo, and Chaps brands for dozens of products, including paint by Glidden, furniture by Henredon, footwear by Rockport, eyewear by Luxottica, and fragrances by L'Oreal.[25] Mistakes, such as Kleenex diapers, Bic perfume, and Domino's fruit-favored bubble gum, are a few examples of poor matches and licensing failures.

Going Online

Have an Idea for a Brand or Trade Name? Check It Out

More than a million brand names or trade names are registered with the U.S. Patent and Trademark Office. Thousands more are registered each year.

An important step in choosing a brand or trade name is to determine whether the name has been already registered. The U.S. Patent and Trademark Office (www.uspto.gov) offers a valuable service by allowing individuals and companies to quickly check to see if a name has been registered.

Do you have an idea for a brand or trade name for a new snack, software package, retail outlet, or service? Check to see if the name has been registered by clicking "Trademarks," then "Search." Enter your brand name to find out if someone has registered your chosen name(s).

Picking a Good Brand Name

We take brand names such as Red Bull, iPod, and Axe for granted, but it is often a difficult and expensive process to pick a good name. Companies will spend between $25,000 and $100,000 to identify and test a new brand name. Five criteria are mentioned most often when selecting a good brand name.[26]

- *The name should suggest the product benefits.* For example, Accutron (watches), Easy Off (oven cleaner), Glass Plus (glass cleaner), Cling-Free (antistatic cloth for drying clothes), Chevy Volt (electric car), and Tidy Bowl (toilet bowl cleaner) all clearly describe the benefits of purchasing the product.
- *The name should be memorable, distinctive, and positive.* In the auto industry, when a competitor has a memorable name, others quickly imitate. When Ford named a car the Mustang, Pintos, Colts, and Broncos soon followed. The Thunderbird name led to the Phoenix, Eagle, Sunbird, and Firebird.
- *The name should fit the company or product image.* Sharp is a name that can apply to audio and video equipment. Bufferin, Excedrin, Anacin, and Nuprin are scientific-sounding names, good for analgesics. Eveready, Duracell, and DieHard suggest reliability and longevity—two qualities consumers want in a battery.
- *The name should have no legal or regulatory restrictions.* Legal restrictions produce trademark infringement suits, and regulatory restrictions arise through improper use of words. For example, the U.S. Food and Drug Administration discourages the use of the word *heart* in food brand names. This restriction led to changing the name of Kellogg's Heartwise cereal to Fiberwise, and Clorox's Hidden Valley Ranch Take Heart Salad Dressing had to be modified to Hidden Valley Ranch Low-Fat Salad Dressing. Increasingly, brand names need a corresponding address on the Internet. This further complicates name selection because about 140 million domain names are already registered.
- *The name should be simple* (such as Bold laundry detergent, Axe deodorant and body spray, and Bic pens) *and should be emotional* (such as Joy and Obsession perfumes). In the development of names for international use, having a nonmeaningful brand name has been considered a benefit. A name such as Exxon does not have any prior impressions or undesirable images among a diverse world population of different languages and cultures. The 7Up name is another matter. In Shanghai, China, the phrase means "death through drinking" in the local dialect. Sales have suffered as a result.

Do you have an idea for a brand name? If you do, check to see if the name has been already registered with the U.S. Patent and Trademark Office by visiting its Web site described in the Going Online box.

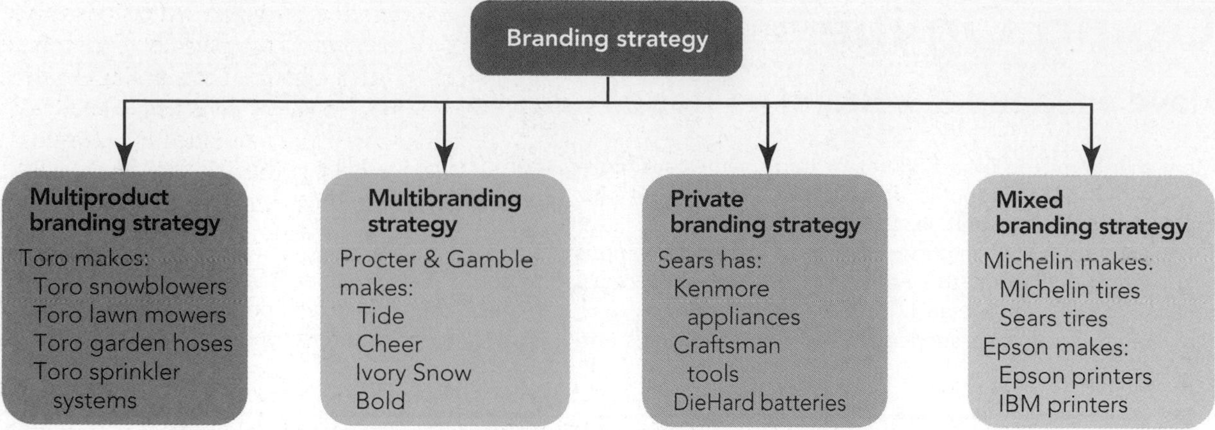

FIGURE 11–7
Alternative branding strategies are available to marketers. Each has advantages and disadvantages described in the text.

Branding Strategies

Companies can employ several different branding strategies, including multiproduct branding, multibranding, private branding, or mixed branding (see Figure 11–7).

Multiproduct Branding Strategy

With **multiproduct branding**, a company uses one name for all its products in a product class. This approach is sometimes called *family branding* or *corporate branding* when the company's trade name is used. For example, Microsoft, General Electric, Samsung, Gerber, and Sony engage in corporate branding—the company's trade name and brand name are identical. Church & Dwight uses the Arm & Hammer family brand name for all its products featuring baking soda as the primary ingredient.

There are several advantages to multiproduct branding. Capitalizing again on brand equity, consumers who have a good experience with the product will transfer this favorable attitude to other items in the product class with the same name. Therefore, this brand strategy makes possible *product line extensions*, the practice of using a current brand name to enter a new market segment in its product class. Campbell Soup Company employs a multiproduct branding strategy with soup line extensions. It offers regular Campbell soup, home-cooking style, and chunky varieties and more than 100 soup flavors. This strategy can result in lower advertising and promotion costs because the same name is used on all products, thus raising the level of brand awareness. A risk with line extension is that sales of an extension may come at the expense of other items in the company's product line. Line extensions work best when they provide incremental company revenue by taking sales away from competing brands or attracting new buyers.[27]

Some multiproduct branding companies employ *subbranding*, which combines a corporate or family brand with a new brand, to distinguish a part of its product line from others. Gatorade successfully used subbranding with the introduction of Gatorade G2. Similarly, Porsche successfully markets its higher-end Porsche Carrera and its lower-end Porsche Boxster.

A strong brand equity also allows for *brand extension*, the practice of using a current brand name to enter a different product class. For instance, equity in the Huggies family brand name has allowed Kimberly-Clark to successfully extend its name to a full line of baby and toddler toiletries. Honda's established name for motor vehicles has extended easily to snowblowers, lawn mowers, marine engines, and snowmobiles.

However, there is a risk with brand extensions. Too many uses for one brand name can dilute the meaning of a brand for consumers. Marketing experts claim this has happened to the Arm & Hammer brand given its use for toothpaste, laundry detergent, gum, cat litter, air freshener, carpet deodorizer, and antiperspirant.[28]

Kimberly-Clark was able to leverage the strong Huggies brand equity among mothers when it introduced a full line of baby and toddler toiletries first in the United States and then globally. The success of this brand extension strategy is evident in the $500 million in annual sales generated globally.

Kimberly-Clark Corporation
www.kimberly-clark.com

A variation on brand extensions is the practice of *co-branding*; the pairing of two brand names of two manufacturers on a single product.[29] For example, Hershey Foods has teamed with General Mills to offer a co-branded breakfast cereal called Reese's Peanut Butter Puffs and with Nabisco to provide Chips Ahoy! cookies using Hershey's chocolate morsels. Co-branding benefits firms by allowing them to enter new product classes and capitalize on an already established brand name in that product class.

Multibranding Strategy Alternately, a company can engage in **multibranding**, which involves giving each product a distinct name. Multibranding is a useful strategy when each brand is intended for a different market segment. P&G makes Camay soap for those concerned with soft skin and Safeguard for those who want deodorant protection. Black & Decker markets its line of tools for the household do-it-yourselfer segment with the Black & Decker name but uses the DeWalt name for its professional tool line. Disney uses the Miramax and Touchstone Pictures names for films directed at adults and its Disney name for children's films.

Multibranding is applied in a variety of ways. Some companies array their brands on the basis of price-quality segments.[30] Marriott International offers 15 hotel and resort brands, each suited for a particular traveler experience and budget. To illustrate, Marriott Marquis hotels and Vacation Clubs offer luxury amenities at a premium price. Marriott and Renaissance hotels offer medium- to high-priced accommodations. Courtyard hotels and TownPlace Suites appeal to economy-minded travelers, whereas the Fairfield Inn is for those on a very low travel budget.

Other multibrand companies introduce new product brands as defensive moves to counteract competition. Called *fighting brands*, their chief purpose is to confront competitor brands. For instance, Frito-Lay introduced Santitas brand tortilla chip to go head-to-head against regional tortilla chip brands that were biting into sales of its flagship Doritos and Tostitos brand tortilla chips. Ford launched its Fusion brand to halt the defection of Ford owners who were buying competitors' midsize cars. According to Ford's car group marketing manager, "Every year we're losing around 50,000 people from our products to competitors' midsize cars. We're losing Mustang, Focus, and Taurus owners. Fusion is our interceptor."[31]

Compared with the multiproduct strategy, advertising and promotion costs tend to be higher with multibranding. The company must generate awareness among consumers and retailers for each new brand name without the benefit of any previous impressions. The advantages of this strategy are that each brand is unique to each market segment and there is no risk that a product failure will affect other products in the line. Still, some large multibrand firms have found that the complexity and expense of implementing this strategy can outweigh the benefits. For example, Unilever recently pruned its brands from some 1,600 to 400 through product deletion and sales to other companies.[32]

Private Branding Strategy A company uses **private branding**, often called *private labeling* or *reseller branding*, when it manufactures products but sells them under the brand name of a wholesaler or retailer. Rayovac, Paragon Trade Brands, and Ralcorp Holdings are major suppliers of private-label alkaline batteries, diapers, and grocery products, respectively. Radio Shack, Costco, Sears, Wal-Mart, and Kroger are large retailers that have their own brand names. Private branding is popular because it typically produces high profits for manufacturers and resellers. Consumers also buy them. It is estimated that one of every five items purchased at U.S. supermarkets, drugstores, and mass merchandisers bears a private brand.[33]

Black & Decker uses a multibranding strategy to reach different market segments. Black & Decker markets its tool line for the do-it-yourselfers with the Black & Decker name, but uses the DeWalt name for professionals.

Black & Decker
www.blackanddecker.com

Mixed Branding Strategy A fourth branding strategy is **mixed branding**, where a firm markets products under its own name(s) and that of a reseller because the segment attracted to the reseller is different from its own market. Beauty and fragrance marketer Elizabeth Arden is an example. The company sells its Elizabeth Arden brand through department stores and a line of skin care products at Wal-Mart with the "skinsimple" brand name. Companies such as Del Monte, Whirlpool, and Dial produce private brands of pet foods, home appliances, and soap, respectively, for resellers.

PACKAGING AND LABELING PRODUCTS

The **packaging** component of a product refers to any container in which it is offered for sale and on which label information is conveyed. A **label** is an integral part of the package and typically identifies the product or brand, who made it, where and when it was made, how it is to be used, and package contents and ingredients. To a great extent, the customer's first exposure to a product is the package and label and both are an expensive and important part of marketing strategy. For Pez Candy, Inc., the character head-on-a-stick plastic container that dispenses a miniature tablet candy is the central element of its marketing strategy as described in the Marketing Matters box.[34]

Creating Customer Value and Competitive Advantage through Packaging and Labeling

Packaging and labeling cost U.S. companies more than $120 billion annually and account for about 15 cents of every dollar spent by consumers for products.[35] Despite

Marketing Matters > > > > > > customer value

Creating Customer Value through Packaging—Pez Heads Dispense More Than Candy

Customer value can assume numerous forms. For Pez Candy, Inc. (www.pez.com), customer value manifests itself in some 450 Pez character candy dispensers. Each refillable dispenser ejects tasty candy tablets in a variety of flavors that delight preteens and teens alike in more than 60 countries.

Pez was formulated in 1927 by Austrian food mogul Edward Haas III and successfully sold in Europe as an adult breath mint. Pez, which comes from the German word for peppermint, *pfefferminz*, was originally packaged in a hygienic, headless plastic dispenser. Pez first appeared in the United States in 1953 with a headless dispenser, marketed to adults. After conducting extensive marketing research, Pez was repositioned with fruit flavors, repackaged with licensed character heads on top of the dispenser, and remarketed as a children's product in the mid-1950s. Since then, most top-level licensed characters and hundreds of other characters have become Pez heads. Consumers eat more than 3 billion Pez tablets annually in the United States alone, and company sales growth exceeds that of the candy industry as a whole.

The unique Pez package dispenses a "use experience" for its customers beyond the candy itself, namely, fun. And fun translates into a 98 percent awareness level for Pez among teenagers and 89 percent among mothers with children. Pez has not advertised its product for years. With that kind of awareness, who needs advertising?

the cost, packaging and labeling are essential because both provide important benefits for the manufacturer, retailer, and ultimate consumer. Packaging and labeling also can provide a competitive advantage.

Communication Benefits A major benefit of packaging is the label information on it conveyed to the consumer, such as directions on how, where, and when to use the product and the source and composition of the product, which is needed to satisfy legal requirements of product disclosure. For example, the labeling system for packaged and processed foods in the United States provides a uniform format for nutritional and dietary information. Many packaged foods contain informative recipes to promote usage of the product. Campbell Soup estimates that the green bean casserole recipe on its cream of mushroom soup can accounts for $20 million in soup sales each year![36] Other information consists of seals and symbols, either government required or commercial seals of approval (such as the Good Housekeeping seal).

Can you name this soft-drink brand? If you can, then the package has fulfilled its purpose.

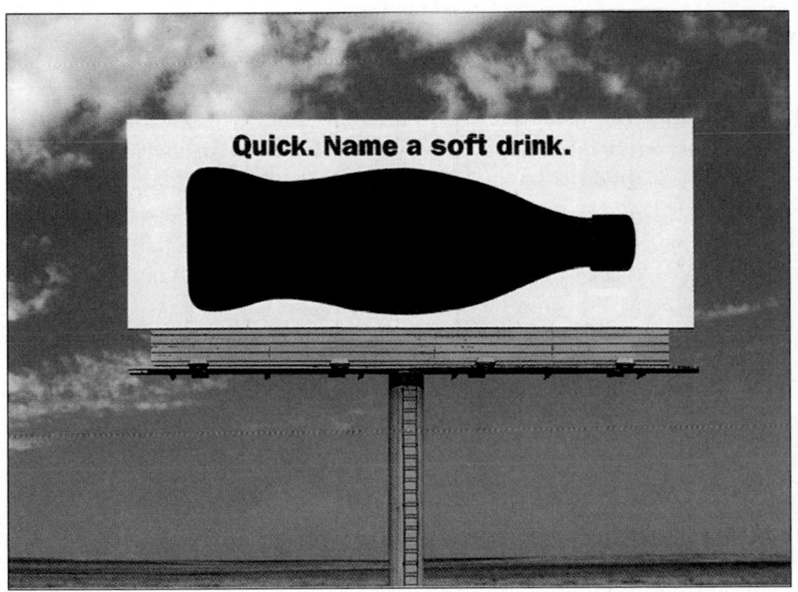

Functional Benefits Packaging often plays a functional role, such as storage, convenience, protection, or product quality. Storing food containers is one example, and beverage companies have developed lighter and easier ways to stack products on shelves and in refrigerators. Examples include Coca-Cola beverage packs designed to fit neatly onto refrigerator shelves and Ocean Spray Cranberries' rectangular juice bottles that allow 10 units per package versus 8 of its former round bottles.

The convenience dimension of packaging is increasingly important. Kraft Miracle Whip salad dressing, Heinz ketchup, and Skippy Squeez'It peanut butter are sold in squeeze bottles; microwave popcorn has been a major market success; and Chicken of the Sea tuna and Folgers coffee are packaged in single-serving portions. Nabisco offers portion-control package sizes for the convenience of weight-conscious consumers. It offers 100-calorie packs of Oreos, Cheese Nips, and other products in individual pouches.

Which chip stacks up better? Frito-Lay's launch of Lay's Stax potato crisps to compete against Procter & Gamble's Pringles illustrates the role of packaging in product and brand management.

Consumer protection is another important function of packaging, including the development of tamper-resistant containers. Today, companies commonly use safety seals or pop-tops that reveal previous opening. But, no package is truly tamper resistant. U.S. law now provides for maximum penalties of life imprisonment and $250,000 fines for package tampering. Consumer protection through labeling exists in "open dating," which states the expected shelf life of the product.

Functional features of packaging also can affect product quality. Procter & Gamble's Pringles, with its cylindrical packaging, offers uniform chips, minimal breakage, and for some consumers, better value for the money than flex-bag packages for chips. Not to be outdone, Frito-Lay, the world's leading producer of snack chips, "stands up" to Pringles with its own line of Lay's Stax potato crisps. Consumers are the final judge of which chip stacks up better.

Perceptual Benefits A third component of packaging and labeling is the perception created in the consumer's mind. Package and label shape, color, and graphics distinguish one brand from another, convey a brand's positioning, and build brand equity. According to the director of marketing for L'eggs hosiery, "Packaging is important to the positioning and equity of the L'eggs brand."[37] Why? Packaging and labeling have been shown to enhance brand recognition and facilitate the formation of strong, favorable, and unique brand associations.[38] This logic applies to Celestial Seasonings' packaging and labeling, which uses delicate illustrations, soft and warm colors, and quotations about life to reinforce the brand's positioning as a New Age, natural herbal tea.

The distinctive design of Celestial Seasonings' tea boxes reinforces the brand's positioning as a New Age, natural herbal tea.

Successful marketers recognize that changes in packages and labels can update and uphold a brand's image in the customer's mind. Just Born, Inc., a candy manufacturer of such brands as Jelly Joes and Mike and Ike Treats, is a case in point. For many years these brands were sold in old-fashioned black-and-white packages. However, when the packaging was updated to four color, with animated grape and cherry characters, sales jumped 25 percent. Pepsi-Cola has embarked on a packaging change to uphold its image among teens and young adults. Beginning in 2007, Pepsi-Cola debuted new graphics on its cans and bottles every three or four weeks to reflect the "fun, optimistic, and youthful spirit" of the brand to its customers.[39]

Because labels list a product's source, brands competing in the global marketplace can benefit from "country of origin or manufacture" perceptions as described in Chapter 7. Consumers tend to have stereotypes about country-product pairings that they judge "best"—English tea, French perfume, Italian leather, and Japanese electronics—which can affect a brand's image. Increasingly, Chinese firms are adopting the English language and Roman letters for their brand labels. This is being done because of a common perception in many Asian countries that "things Western are good."[40]

Packaging and Labeling Challenges and Responses

Package and label designers face four challenges. They are: (1) the continuing need to connect with customers; (2) environmental concerns; (3) health, safety, and security issues; and (4) cost reduction.

Connecting with Customers Packages and labels must be continually updated to connect with customers. The challenge lies in creating aesthetic and functional design features that attract customer attention and deliver customer value in their use. If done right, the rewards can be huge.[41]

For example, the marketing team responsible for Kleenex tissues converted its standard rectangular box into an oval shape with colorful seasonal graphics. Sales soared with this aesthetic change in packaging. After months of in-home research, Kraft product managers discovered that consumers often transferred Chips Ahoy! cookies to jars for easy access and to avoid staleness. The company solved both problems by creating a patented resealable opening on the top of the bag. The result? Sales of the new package doubled that of the old package with the addition of this functional feature.

Environmental Concerns Because of widespread worldwide concern about the growth of solid waste and the shortage of viable landfill sites, the amount, composition, and disposal of packaging material continues to receive much attention. For example, PepsiCo, Coca-Cola, and Nestlé have decreased the amount of plastic in their beverage bottles to reduce solid waste.[42] Recycling packaging material is another major thrust. Procter & Gamble now uses recycled cardboard in over 70 percent of its paper packaging. Its Spic and Span liquid cleaner is packaged in 100 percent recycled material. Other firms, such as Wal-Mart, are emphasizing the use of less packaging material. In 2008, the company began working with its 600,000 global suppliers to reduce overall packaging and shipping material by 5 percent by 2013.[43]

European countries have been trendsetters concerning packaging guidelines and environmental sensitivity. Many of these guidelines now exist in provisions governing trade to and within the European Union. In Germany, 80 percent of packaging material must be collected, and 80 percent of this amount must be recycled or reused to reduce solid waste in landfills. U.S. firms marketing in Europe have responded to these guidelines and ultimately benefited U.S. consumers.

Health, Safety, and Security Issues A third challenge involves the growing health, safety, and security concerns of packaging materials. Today, most U.S. and European consumers believe companies should make sure products and their packages are safe and secure, regardless of the cost, and companies are responding in numerous ways. Most butane lighters sold today, like those made by Scripto, contain a child-resistant safety latch to prevent misuse and accidental fire. Child-proof caps on pharmaceutical products and household cleaners and sealed lids on food packages are now common. New packaging technology and materials that extend a product's *shelf life* (the time a product can be stored) and prevent spoilage continue to be developed with special applications for developing countries.

Cost Reduction About 80 percent of packaging material used in the world consists of paper, plastics, and glass. As the cost of these materials rises, companies are constantly challenged to find innovative ways to cut packaging costs while delivering value to their customers. As an example, Hewlett-Packard reduced the size and weight of its Photosmart product package and shipping container. Through design and material changes, packaging material costs fell by more than 50 percent. Shipping costs per unit dropped 41 percent.[44]

PRODUCT WARRANTY

A final component for product consideration is the **warranty**, which is a statement indicating the liability of the manufacturer for product deficiencies. There are various types of product warranties with different implications for manufacturers and customers.

America's Best Warranty

Hyundai has made a commitment to offer the best automobile warranty for buyers.

Hyundai Motor America
www.hyundaiusa.com

Some companies like Hyundai, offer *express warranties*, which are written statements of liabilities. In recent years, the FTC has required greater disclosure on express warranties to indicate whether the warranty is a limited-coverage or full-coverage alternative. A *limited-coverage warranty* specifically states the bounds of coverage and, more important, areas of noncoverage. A *full warranty* has no limits of noncoverage. The *Magnuson-Moss Warranty/FTC Improvement Act* (1975) regulates the content of consumer warranties and so has strengthened consumer rights with regard to warranties. Increasingly, manufacturers are being held to *implied warranties*, which assign responsibility for product deficiencies to the manufacturer. Studies show that the type of warranty can affect a consumer's product evaluation. Brands with limited warranties tend to receive less positive evaluations compared with full-warranty items.[45]

Warranties are also important in light of product liability claims. In the early part of the 20th century, the courts protected companies. The trend now is toward "strict liability" rulings, where a manufacturer is liable for any product defect, whether it followed reasonable research standards or not. This issue remains hotly contested between companies and consumer advocates.

Warranties represent much more to the buyer than just protection from negative consequences—they offer a significant marketing advantage for the producer. Sears has built a strong reputation for its Craftsman tool line with a simple warranty: If you break a tool, it's replaced with no questions asked. Zippo has an equally simple warranty: "If it ever fails, we'll fix it free."

learning review

7. What are the five criteria mentioned most often when selecting a good brand name?
8. What are the three major benefits of packaging and labeling?
9. What is the difference between an expressed and an implied warranty?

LEARNING OBJECTIVES REVIEW

LO1 *Explain the product life-cycle concept.*
The product life cycle describes the stages a new product goes through in the marketplace: introduction, growth, maturity, and decline. Product sales growth and profitability differ at each stage, and marketing managers have marketing objectives and marketing mix strategies unique to each stage based on consumer behavior and competitive factors. In the introductory stage, the need is to establish primary demand, whereas the growth stage requires selective demand strategies. In the maturity stage, the need is to maintain market share; the decline stage necessitates a deletion or harvesting strategy. Some important aspects of product life cycles are (*a*) their length, (*b*) the shape of the sales curve, (*c*) how they vary by product classes and forms, and (*d*) the rate at which consumers adopt products.

LO2 *Identify ways that marketing executives manage a product's life cycle.*
Marketing executives manage a product's life cycle three ways. First, they can modify the product itself by altering its characteristics, such as product quality, performance, or appearance. Second, they can modify the market by finding new customers for the product, increasing a product's use among existing customers, or creating new use situations for the product. Finally, they can reposition the product using any one or a combination of marketing mix elements. Four factors trigger a repositioning

action. They include reacting to a competitor's position, reaching a new market, catching a rising trend, and changing the value offered to consumers.

LO3 *Recognize the importance of branding and alternative branding strategies.*
A basic decision in marketing products is branding, in which an organization uses a name, phrase, design, symbols, or a combination of these to identify its products and distinguish them from those of its competitors. Product managers recognize that brands offer more than product identification and a means to distinguish their products from competitors. Successful and established brands take on a brand personality and acquire brand equity—the added value a given brand name gives to a product beyond the functional benefits provided—that is crafted and nurtured by marketing programs that forge strong, favorable, and unique consumer associations with a brand. A good brand name should suggest the product benefits, be memorable, fit the company or product image, be free of legal restrictions, and be simple and emotional. Companies can and do employ several different branding strategies. With multiproduct branding, a company uses one name for all its products in a product class. A multibranding strategy involves giving each product a distinct name. A company uses private branding when it manufactures products but sells them under the brand name of a wholesaler or retailer. Finally, a company can employ mixed branding, where it markets products under its own name(s) and that of a reseller.

LO4 *Describe the role of packaging, labeling, and warranties in the marketing of a product.*
Packaging, labeling, and warranties play numerous roles in the marketing of a product. The packaging component of a product refers to any container in which it is offered for sale and on which label information is conveyed. Manufacturers, retailers, and consumers acknowledge that packaging and labeling provide communication, functional, and perceptual benefits. Contemporary packaging and labeling challenges include (*a*) the continuing need to connect with customers, (*b*) environmental concerns, (*c*) health, safety, and security issues, and (*d*) cost reduction. Warranties indicate the liability of the manufacturer for product deficiencies and are an important element of product and brand management.

FOCUSING ON KEY TERMS

brand equity p. 283
brand licensing p. 284
brand name p. 282
brand personality p. 283
branding p. 282
label p. 288
market modification p. 278
mixed branding p. 288
multibranding p. 287
multiproduct branding p. 286
packaging p. 288
private branding p. 287
product class p. 276
product form p. 276
product life cycle p. 270
product modification p. 278
trade name p. 282
trademark p. 282
trading down p. 281
trading up p. 281
warranty p. 292

APPLYING MARKETING KNOWLEDGE

1 Listed here are three different products in various stages of the product life cycle. What marketing strategies would you suggest to these companies? (*a*) Canon digital cameras—growth stage, (*b*) Hewlett Packard tablet computers—introductory stage, and (*c*) handheld manual can openers—decline stage.

2 It has often been suggested that products are intentionally made to break down or wear out. Is this strategy a planned product modification approach?

3 The product manager of GE is reviewing the penetration of trash compactors in American homes. After more than two decades in existence, this product is in relatively few homes. What problems can account for this poor acceptance? What is the shape of the trash compactor life cycle?

4 For years, Ferrari has been known as the manufacturer of expensive luxury automobiles. The company plans to attract the major segment of the car-buying market who purchase medium-priced automobiles. As Ferrari considers this trading-down strategy, what branding strategy would you recommend? What are the trade-offs to consider with your strategy?

5 The nature of product warranties has changed as the federal court system reassesses the meaning of warranties. How does the regulatory trend toward warranties affect product development?

building your marketing plan

For the product offering in your marketing plan,

1 Identify (*a*) its stage in the product life cycle and (*b*) key marketing mix actions that might be appropriate, as shown in Figure 11–1.

2 Develop (*a*) branding and (*b*) packaging strategies, if appropriate for your offering.

video case 11 BMW: "Newness" and the Product Life Cycle

"We're fortunate right now at BMW in that all of our products are new and competitive," says Jim McDowell, vice president of marketing at BMW, as he explains BMW's product life cycle. "Now, how do you do that? You have to introduce new models over time. You have to logically plan out the introductions over time, so you're not changing a whole model range at the same time you're changing another model range."

BMW's strategy is to keep its products in the introduction and growth stages by periodically introducing new models in each of its product lines. In fact, in contrast to many auto manufacturers that launch a new model and then leave it unchanged, BMW works continually to improve its existing products. Explains McDowell, "Anyone can sell a lot of cars the first year, when a car is new. It is our challenge to constantly improve the car and to continuously find new innovative ways to market it."

BMW—THE COMPANY AND ITS PRODUCTS

BMW started in 1916 as a manufacturer of airplane engines. "When you look at our roundel, the BMW symbol, it is a blue-and-white circle," says McDowell, "that is meant to represent the spinning propeller on a plane, to remind us of our heritage." Since then the company has added motorcycle and automobile production. Today, BMW is one of the preeminent luxury car manufacturers in Europe, North America, and the world.

BMW produces several lines of cars including the 1, 3, 5, 6, and 7 series, the Z line of roadsters, the X line of "sport activity vehicles," and the M line of "motor sport" sedans. Currently, the United States, Germany, and the United Kingdom are BMW's largest markets. BMW introduced its 1 series—a compact car designed to compete with the Volkswagen Golf in Europe and the Rabbit in the United States—to attract a new younger audience. In addition BMW owns the MINI and Rolls-Royce brands. Combined sales of BMW, MINI, and Rolls-Royce exceed $59 billion and are expected to increase 40 percent by 2020. Reasons for the growing popularity of BMW include high-performance products, unique advertising, an award-winning Web site, innovations such as "smart" electronics that "learn" what the driver prefers, and new vehicles such as the V-series, which will compete with minivans.

PRODUCT LIFE CYCLE

BMW cars typically have a product life cycle of seven years. To keep products in the introductory and growth stages, BMW regularly introduces new models for each of its series to keep the entire series "new." For instance, with the 3 series, it will introduce the new sedan model one year, the new coupe the next year, then the convertible, then the station wagon, and then the sport hatchback. That's a new product introduction for five of the seven years of the product life cycle. McDowell explains, "So, even though we have seven-year life cycles, we constantly try to make the cars meaningfully different and new about every three years. And that involves adding features and other capabilities to the cars as well." How well does this strategy work? BMW often sees its best sales numbers in either the sixth or seventh year after the product introduction.

As global sales have increased, BMW has become aware of some international product life-cycle differences. For example, it has discovered that some competitive products have life cycles that are shorter or longer than seven years. In Sweden and Britain, automotive product life cycles are eight years, while in Japan they are typically only four years long.

BMW uses a system of "product advocates" to manage the marketing efforts of its product lines. McDowell explains that a series advocate would actually use and drive that series and would constantly be thinking "How can I better serve my customer?" In addition to modifying each model throughout the product life cycle, BMW modifies the markets it serves. For example, during the past 10 years BMW has expanded its market by appealing to a much larger percentage of women, African Americans, Asians, and Hispanics. BMW's positioning strategy is the same worldwide and that is to offer high-performance, luxury vehicles to individuals. "You won't find it as a taxi or a fleet car," says McDowell. Generally, once a model is positioned and introduced, BMW avoids trying to reposition it.

BRANDING

"BMW is fortunate—we don't have too much of a dilemma as to what we're going to call our cars." McDowell is referring to BMW's trademark naming system that consists of the product line number and the motor type. For example, the designation "328" tells you the car is in the 3 series and the engine is 2.8 liters in size. BMW has found this naming system to be clear and logical and can be easily understood around the world.

The Z, X, and M series don't quite fit in with this system. BMW had a tradition of building experimental, open-air cars and calling them Z's, so when one of them was selected for production, BMW decided to continue with the Z name. For the sport activity vehicles BMW also used a letter name—the X series—since the four-wheel-drive vehicle didn't fit with the sedan-oriented 1, 3, 5, 6, and 7 series. The M series has a 20-year history with BMW as the line with the luxury and racing-level performance. The lettered series now includes the Z4, X3, X5, M3, M5, and M6. Compared to the evocative names many car manufacturers choose to garner excitement for their new models, the BMW numbers and letters are viewed as a simple and effective branding strategy.

In the past BMW has built a brand personality for its vehicles with high-visibility product placements. BMW products, for example, have been featured in four James Bond films. Similarly, BMW hired master directors to create a series of Internet-based mini-movies called "The Hire"–which featured "the ultimate driving machine" and edgy actors. The movies were so successful and attracted so much attention from consumers and industry experts that the movies have been placed into the Museum of Modern Art. Other marketing programs that contribute to the BMW brand personality include the BMW Art Car Collection, created by internationally acclaimed artists; sponsorship of America's Cup and Formula 1 Series racing teams; and events such as the BMW Golf Club International tournament.

MANAGING THE PRODUCT THROUGH THE WEB—THE WAVE OF THE FUTURE

One of the ways BMW is improving its product offerings even further is through its innovative Web site (www.bmwusa.com). At the site, customers can learn about the particular models, e-mail questions, and request literature or test-drives from their local BMW dealership. What really sets BMW's Web site apart from other car manufacturers, though, is the ability for customers to configure a car to their own specifications (interior choices, exterior choices, engine, packages, and options) and then transfer that information to their local dealer. As Carol Burrows, product communications manager for BMW, explains, "The BMW Web site is an integrated part of the overall marketing strategy for BMW. The full range of products can be seen and interacted with online. We offer pricing options online. Customers can go to their local dealership via the Web site to further discuss costs for purchase of a car. And it is a distribution channel for information that allows people access to the information 24 hours a day at their convenience." The ultimate extravagance in buying a car is having everything customized to the owner's preferences. Today, 80 percent of European buyers and 30 percent of U.S. buyers use the BMW Web site to choose from 350 model variations, 500 options, 90 exterior colors, and 170 interior trims to create their perfect vehicle!

Questions

1 Compare the product life cycle described by BMW for its cars to the product life cycle shown in Figure 11–1. How are they (*a*) similar and (*b*) dissimilar?

2 Based on BMW's typical product life cycle, what marketing strategies are appropriate for the 3 series? The X5?

3 Which of the three ways to manage the product life cycle does BMW utilize with its products—modifying the product, modifying the market, or repositioning the product?

4 How would you describe BMW's branding strategy (manufacturer branding, private branding, or mixed branding)? Why?

5 Go to the BMW Web site (www.bmwusa.com) and design a car to your own specifications. How does this enable you as a customer to evaluate the product differently than would be otherwise possible?

CIRQUE DU SOLEIL®
KOOZÅ™
CIRQUE DU SOLEIL®

12 Services Marketing

LEARNING OBJECTIVES
After reading this chapter you should be able to:

LO1 Describe four unique elements of services.

LO2 Recognize how services differ and how they can be classified.

LO3 Explain how consumers purchase and evaluate services.

LO4 Develop a customer contact audit to identify service advantages.

LO5 Explain the role of the eight Ps in the services marketing mix.

LO6 Discuss the important roles of internal marketing and customer experience management in service organizations.

SERVICES GET REAL!

Have you recently heard someone use the words *fake* or *phony* or even *counterfeit*? It's a common concern of many consumers today and part of a growing trend that will change most services. As authors James Gilmore and Joseph Pine explain, "The more contrived the world seems, the more we all demand what is real." In their book, *Authenticity,* they suggest that what consumers really want are engaging, personal, memorable, and authentic offerings. Cirque du Soleil, for example, offers a completely new art form, but manages the perception of authenticity by combining the original elements of street performance, the circus, and live theater.[1]

Our economy has shifted from the production of goods, to the delivery of services, and more recently, to the staging of experiences. The "experience economy" focuses on performing services that provide a unique experience. Disneyland, for example, was one of the first service organizations to recognize the importance of sights, sounds, tastes, aromas, and textures in creating experiences for consumers. Hard Rock Café and Planet Hollywood restaurants used a similar approach to sell dining experiences that included food, music, entertainment, and a fun environment. Many other companies such as Starbucks and Apple stores also have strategies designed to provide compelling experiences.

The growth of produced, sometimes contrived experiences, however, has led consumers to search for sincere, or authentic, offerings. Consumers are no longer content with affordable, high-quality purchases; they want offerings that reflect their self-image—who they are or who they aspire to be. How can service providers ensure that they are offering authentic experiences? There are many options!

First, services that facilitate customization increase authenticity. Creating custom playlists for iPods, for example, allows consumers to participate in the production process. Another option is to provide personal interaction rather than automation. ATMs, kiosks, credit card readers, and Web sites are not viewed as authentic. Geico advertisements address this issue by emphasizing that "insurance specialists are available 24/7." Authenticity can also result from a social process that allows consumers to share their interests. YouTube, MySpace, and Facebook are obvious outlets, although companies can create their own social networking opportunities. The advertising agency for Doritos, for example, created a contest to encourage consumers to submit their own TV commercial, and then ran the winning entry during the Super Bowl. Finally, institutions that provide services must manage any dimension of their reputation that might influence perceptions of authenticity.

If you look closely you'll see that many services are adding dimensions of authenticity. Nike's customization service, NIKEiD.com, allows customers to design shoes according to their exact preferences. Progressive Insurance provides personal attention by sending Immediate Response Vehicles to the site of an accident so an adjuster can handle emergencies, arrange for new transportation, and provide the policyholder with a check—in person. Retailers such as Bloomingdale's now facilitate the social aspects of shopping by providing dressing rooms large enough for friends and electronic mirrors that allow texting anyone whose opinion might be needed.

As the actions of Disneyland, Planet Hollywood, NikeiD, Progressive Insurance, Cirque du Soleil, and many others illustrate, the marketing of services is dynamic and exciting. In this chapter, we discuss how services differ from traditional products (goods), how consumers make purchase decisions, and the ways in which the marketing mix is used.

THE UNIQUENESS OF SERVICES

Services are intangible activities or benefits (such as airline trips, financial advice, or automobile repair) that an organization provides to satisfy consumers' needs in exchange for money or something else of value.

Services have become a significant component of the global economy and one of the most important components of the U.S. economy. The World Trade Organization estimates that all countries exported merchandise valued at $13.5 trillion and commercial services valued at $3.2 trillion. In the United States, more than 42 percent of the gross domestic product (GDP) now comes from services. As shown in Figure 12–1, the value of services in the economy has increased more than 70 percent since 1990. Projections indicate that by 2016, goods-producing firms will employ 21.7 million people and service firms will employ more than 130 million. Services also

FIGURE 12–1
Services are now a larger part of the U.S. gross domestic product (GDP) than goods.

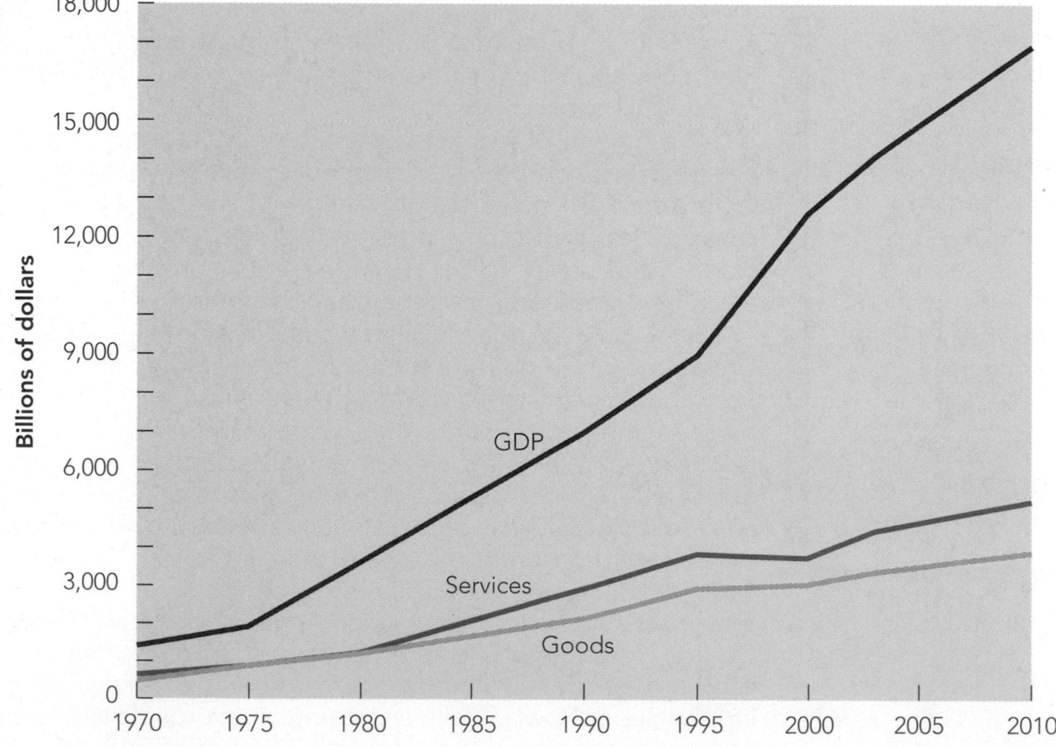

represent a large export business—the $512 billion of services exports in 2009 is one of the few areas in which the United States has a trade surplus.[2]

The growth of this sector is the result of increased demand for services that have been available in the past and the increasing interest in new services. Concierge services, for example, have been popular in hotels such as the Breakers in Palm Beach, Florida, which has a staff of 11 concierges, and the Ritz-Carlton, which offers concierges who specialize in technology support, shopping, and medical issues. Outside the hotel industry, Famous Friends Concierge service offers clients opportunities to fly on private jets with celebrities, private check-in at resorts, hard-to-get restaurant and nightclub reservations, and special event tickets. Concierge services are even available for daily lifestyle needs. Ace Concierge, for example, will schedule car maintenance, pick up and deliver dry cleaning, walk your dog, or even shop for groceries and gifts! Other new services include: The Luggage Club, which offers door-to-door luggage delivery to and from 220 countries; Virgin Galactic, which offers private space travel; and friendorfollow.com, which helps you determine if the people you are following on Twitter are also following you. These firms and many others like them are examples of the imaginative services that will play a role in our economy in the future.[3]

The Four I's of Services

LO1

There are four unique elements to services—*intangibility, inconsistency, inseparability,* and *inventory*—referred to as the **four I's of services**.

Intangibility Services are intangible; that is, they can't be held, touched, or seen before the purchase decision. In contrast, before purchasing a traditional product, a consumer can touch a box of laundry detergent, kick the tire of an automobile, or sample a new breakfast cereal. Because services tend to be a performance rather than an object, they are much more difficult for consumers to evaluate. To help consumers assess and compare services, marketers try to make them tangible or show the benefits of using the service.

The Singapore Airlines ad shows the airline's new seats and emphasizes their size and other tangible benefits. American Express also provides tangible benefits by allowing cardmembers to earn points for redemption of airline tickets, electronics, and gift cards through its Membership Rewards® program.

Why do many services emphasize their tangible benefits? The answer appears in the text.

Singapore Airlines
www.singaporeair.com

American Express Co.
www.americanexpress.com

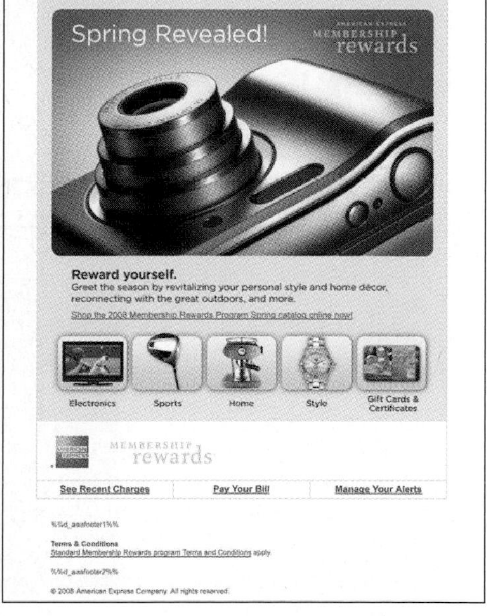

Inconsistency Developing, pricing, promoting, and delivering services is challenging because the quality of a service is often inconsistent. Because services depend on the people who provide them, their quality varies with each person's capabilities and day-to-day job performance. Inconsistency is much more of a problem in services than it is with tangible goods. Tangible products can be good or bad in terms of quality, but with modern production lines the quality will at least be consistent. On the other hand, one day the Philadelphia Phillies baseball team may have great hitting and pitching and look like a pennant winner and the next day lose by 10 runs. Or a soprano at New York's Metropolitan Opera may have a bad cold and give a less-than-perfect performance. Whether the service involves tax assistance at H&R Block or guest relations at the Ritz-Carlton, organizations attempt to reduce inconsistency through standardization and training.[4]

Inseparability A third difference between services and goods, and related to problems of consistency, is inseparability. In most cases, the consumer cannot (and does not) separate the deliverer of the service from the service itself. For example, to receive an education, a person may attend a university. The quality of the education may be high, but if the student has difficulty interacting with instructors, finds counseling services poor, or does not receive adequate library or computer assistance, he or she may not be satisfied with the educational experience. Students' evaluations of their education will be influenced primarily by their perceptions of instructors, counselors, librarians, and other people at the university. Allstate's reminder that "You're in good hands" emphasizes the importance of its agents.

The amount of interaction between the consumer and the service provider depends on the extent to which the consumer must be physically present to receive the service. Some services such as haircuts, golf lessons, medical diagnoses, and food service require the customer to participate in the delivery of the services. Other services such as car repair, dry cleaning, and waste disposal process tangible objects with less involvement from the customer. Finally, services such as banking, consulting, and insurance can now be delivered electronically, often requiring no face-to-face customer interaction.[5] While this approach can create value for consumers, a disadvantage of some *self-service technologies* such as ATMs, grocery store scanning

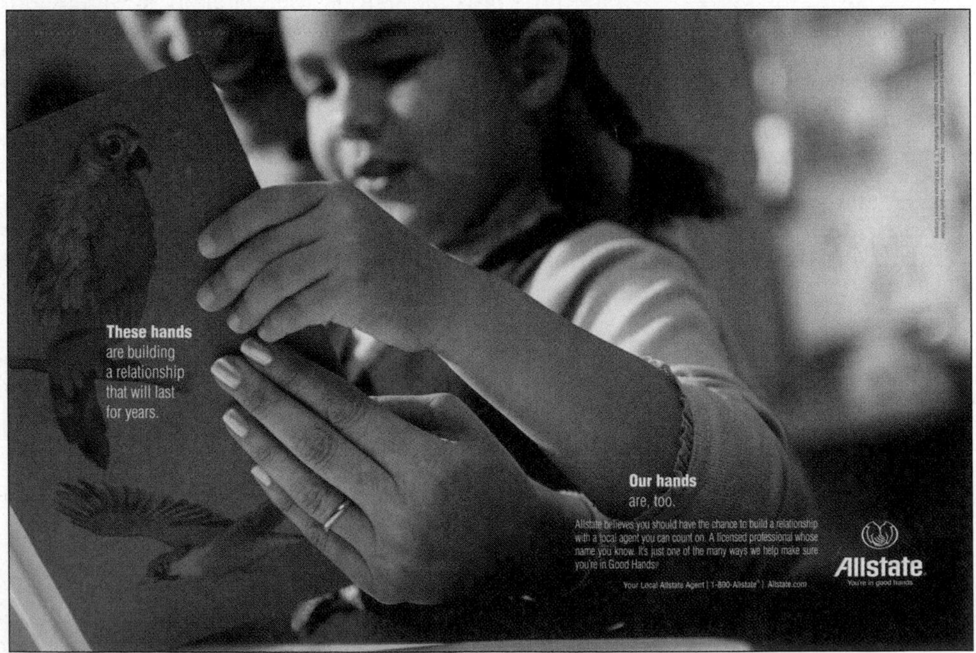

People play an important role in the delivery of many services.

Allstate
www.allstate.com

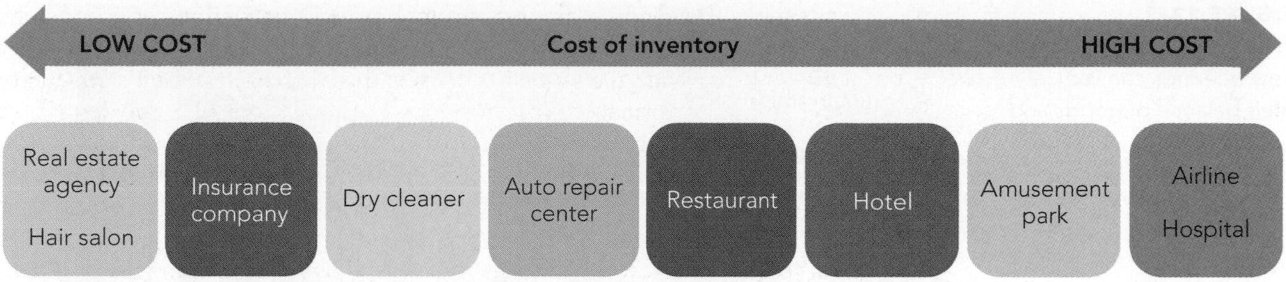

LOW COST — Cost of inventory — HIGH COST

Real estate agency / Hair salon	Insurance company	Dry cleaner	Auto repair center	Restaurant	Hotel	Amusement park	Airline / Hospital

FIGURE 12–2
Inventory carrying costs of services depend on the cost of employees and equipment.

stations, and self-service gas station pumps is that they are perceived as being less personal.[6]

Inventory Inventory of services is different from that of goods. Inventory problems exist with goods because many items are perishable and because there are costs associated with handling inventory. With services, inventory carrying costs are more subjective and are related to **idle production capacity**, which is when the service provider is available but there is no demand. The inventory cost of a service is the cost of paying the person used to provide the service along with any needed equipment. If a physician is paid to see patients but no one schedules an appointment, the fixed cost of the idle physician's salary is a high inventory carrying cost. In some service businesses, however, the provider of the service is on commission (a Merrill Lynch stockbroker) or is a part-time employee (a clerk at Macy's). In these businesses, inventory carrying costs can be significantly lower or nonexistent because the idle production capacity can be cut back by reducing hours or having no salary to pay because of the commission compensation system. Figure 12–2 shows a scale of inventory carrying costs represented on the low end by real estate agencies and hair salons and on the high end by airlines and hospitals. The inventory carrying costs of airlines is high because of high-salaried pilots and very expensive equipment. In contrast, real estate agencies and hair salons have employees who work on commission and need little expensive equipment to conduct business. One reason service providers must maintain production capacity is because of the importance of time to today's customers.

The Service Continuum

LO2

The four I's differentiate services from goods in most cases, but many companies are not clearly service-based or good-based organizations. Is Hewlett-Packard a computer company or service business? Although Hewlett-Packard manufactures computers, printers, and other goods, many of the company's employees work in its services division providing systems integration, networking, consulting, education, and product support.[7] What companies bring to the market ranges from the tangible to the intangible or good-dominant to service-dominant offerings referred to as the **service continuum** (Figure 12–3 on the next page).

Teaching, nursing, and the theater are intangible, service-dominant activities, and intangibility, inconsistency, inseparability, and inventory are major concerns in their marketing. Salt, neckties, and dog food are tangible goods, and the problems represented by the four I's are not relevant in their marketing. However, some businesses are a mix of intangible service and tangible good factors. A clothing tailor provides a service but also a good, the finished suit. How pleasant, courteous, and attentive the tailor is to the customer is an important component of the service, and how well the clothes fit is an important part of the product. As shown in Figure 12–3, a fast-food

FIGURE 12–3
The service continuum shows how offerings can vary in their balance of goods and services.

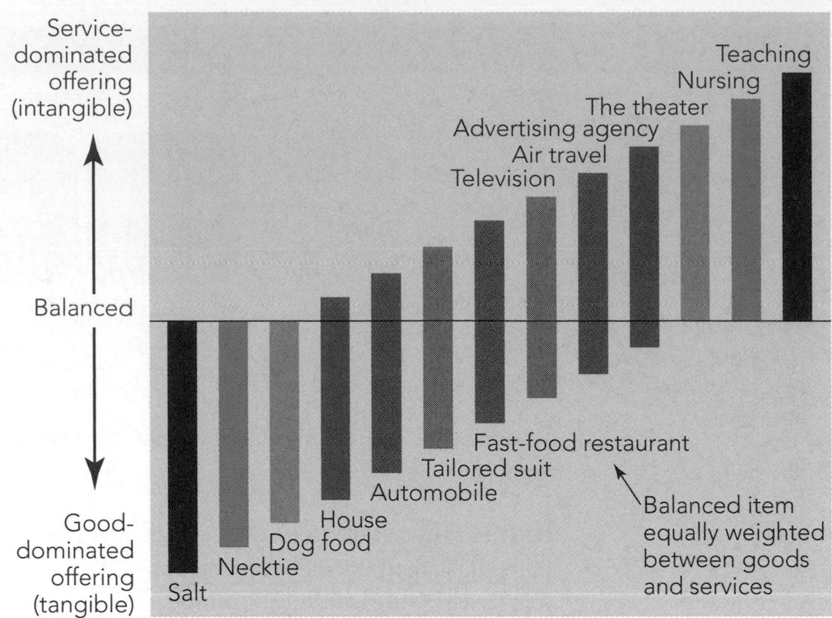

restaurant is about half tangible goods (the food) and half intangible services (courtesy, cleanliness, speed, and convenience).

For many businesses today it is useful to distinguish between their core product—either a good or a service—and supplementary services. A core service offering such as a bank account, for example, also has supplementary services such as deposit assistance, parking or drive-through availability, ATMs, and monthly statements. Supplementary services often allow service providers to differentiate their offering from competitors, and they may add value for consumers. While there are many potential supplementary services, key categories of supplementary services include consultation, finance, order taking, billing, and upgrades.[8]

Classifying Services

Throughout this book, marketing organizations, techniques, and concepts are classified to show the differences and similarities in an organized framework. Services can also be classified in several ways, according to whether (1) they are delivered by people or equipment, (2) they are profit or nonprofit, or (3) they are government sponsored.

Delivery by People or Equipment As seen in Figure 12–4, many companies offer services. Professional services include management consulting firms such as Booz, Allen & Hamilton, or Accenture. Skilled labor is required to offer services such as Sears appliance repair or Sheraton catering service. Unskilled labor such as that used by Brinks store-security forces is also a service provided by people.

Equipment-based services do not have the marketing concerns of inconsistency because people are removed from the provision of the service. Electric utilities, for example, can provide service without frequent personal contact with customers. Motion picture theaters have projector operators that consumers never see. A growing number of customers use self-service technologies such as Home Depot's self checkout, Southwest Airlines' self check-in, and Schwab's online stock trading without interacting with any service employees.[9]

Profit or Nonprofit Organizations Many organizations involved in services also distinguish themselves by their tax status as profit or nonprofit organiza-

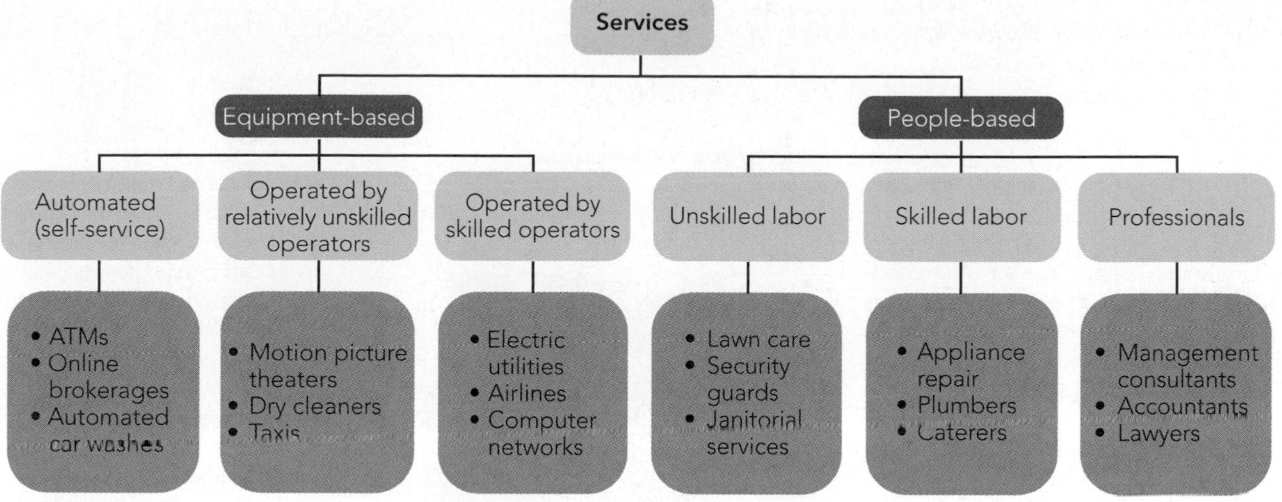

FIGURE 12–4
Services can be classified as equipment-based or people-based.

tions. In contrast to *profit organizations, nonprofit organizations'* excesses in revenue over expenses are not taxed or distributed to shareholders. When excess revenue exists, the money goes back into the organization's treasury to allow continuation of the service. Based on the corporate structure of the nonprofit organization, it may pay tax on revenue-generating holdings not directly related to its core mission. Nonprofit organizations in the United States now have expenditures of $1.9 trillion and employ 10 percent of the work force.[10]

The United Way, Greenpeace, Outward Bound, The Salvation Army, and The Nature Conservancy are examples of nonprofit organizations. Historically, misconceptions have limited the use of marketing practices by such organizations.[11] In recent years, however, nonprofit organizations have turned to marketing to help achieve their goals. The American Red Cross is a good example. To increase the organization's blood donor base, it recently hired an advertising agency to develop a campaign that includes advertising, direct marketing, public relations, and customer relationship management. Another agency was hired to focus on raising awareness in Hispanic communities through outdoor murals. Other promotional activities include

Nonprofit services often advertise.

Red Cross
www.redcross.org

United Nations Children's Fund
www.unicef.org

Marketing Matters > > > > > > > customer value

Marketing Is a Must for 1.5 Million Nonprofits!

For many years "the M-word was not considered a good thing," explains Tom Peterson, the vice president for marketing at anti-poverty nonprofit Heifer International. As the 1.5 million charitable causes, universities, foundations, hospitals, and other nonprofits began to compete for members and donations, however, the need for marketing became apparent. The *Susan G. Komen for the Cure* organization has been one of the most successful to adapt. Its walks and races and partnerships with companies such as Yoplait, American Airlines, and Bank of America now generate more than $180 million annually and have allowed it to invest nearly $1 billion in cancer research and community outreach programs.

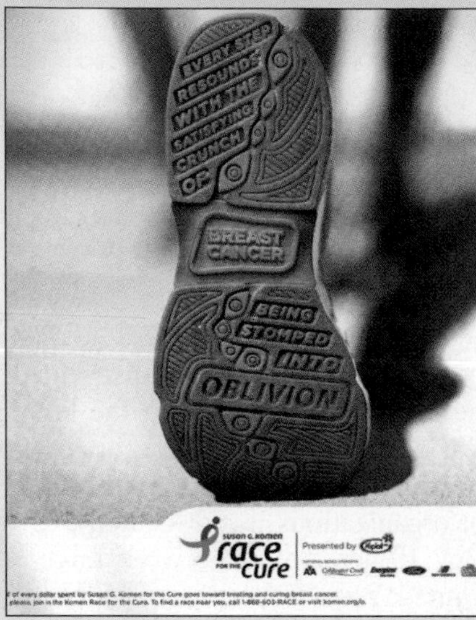

Nonprofit organizations should follow many of the same principles businesses use. First, they should create a specific and realistic mission statement. The Chicago Children's Museum's mission statement, for example, is "to create a community where play and learning connect." Second, the organizations should have a unique selling proposition that will help consumers understand what the organization will do for sponsors, members, or others. St. Jude Children's Research Hospital emphasizes that it is "Finding cures. Saving children." Nonprofits should also use common branding practices to select a name, logo, or tagline. The Museum of Modern Art's acronym "MoMA," the Komen pink ribbon logo, and the American Heart Association's tagline "Learn and Live" are all successful examples.

In the past many nonprofit organizations relied solely on free public service announcements for their communication. Now successful nonprofit budgets include advertising and Web-based tools to facilitate awareness and engagement. For example, the American Heart Association allocated $12 million to its advertising activities, which led to $40 million in contributions. Similarly, the March of Dimes created an online forum where people can share stories, and it now has an average of 8,100 posts each month.

Businesses are responding also. Some become sponsors of events or encourage employees to make donations. They can also become members of nonprofit organizations. The 1% for the Planet organization has 700 member companies that donate 1 percent of their sales to approved nonprofit groups such as the Surfrider Foundation, Amazon Conservation Association, and Rainforest Relief.

---

a campaign called Red Cross Racing, which is targeted at the 75 million NASCAR fans across the country, and the National Celebrity Cabinet, which currently includes Miley Cyrus, Pierce Brosnan, Heidi Klum, Eli Manning, and Patti LaBelle. The American Marketing Association Foundation recently began honoring extraordinary achievement in nonprofit marketing and recognized UNICEF for its "Tap Project" campaign that created 1 billion impressions about clean water.[12] See the accompanying Marketing Matters box to learn about essential marketing activities for nonprofit organizations.[13]

Government Sponsored A third way to classify services is based on whether they are government sponsored. Although there is no direct ownership and they are nonprofit organizations, governments at the federal, state, and local levels provide a broad range of services. The United States Postal Service, for example, has adopted many marketing activities. First-class postage revenue has declined as postal service customers have increased their use of the Internet to send e-mail, pay bills, and file taxes. Rather than fight the trend, however, the Postal Service is embracing the Internet. Its Web site, www.usps.com, allows consumers to buy stamps, arrange deliveries, and manage mailing lists online. In addition, new post office boxes are designed in a shoebox size to better meet the needs of consumers who shop for clothing and shoes online. Businesses can even buy stamps with their company brand and logo on them. The Postal Service's marketing activities are designed to allow it to compete with UPS, FedEx, DHL, and foreign postal services for global package delivery business. Finally, you may have noticed that many post offices are now also retail outlets that sell collector stamps, Pony Express sweatshirts, and even neckties![14]

learning review

1. What are the four I's of services?
2. To eliminate service inconsistencies, companies rely on ________________ and ________________.
3. Would inventory carrying costs for an accounting firm with certified public accountants be (*a*) high, (*b*) low, or (*c*) nonexistent?

HOW CONSUMERS PURCHASE SERVICES

LO3

Colleges, hospitals, hotels, and even charities are facing an increasingly competitive environment. Successful service organizations, like successful product-oriented firms, must understand how the consumer makes a service purchase decision and quality evaluation and in what ways a company can present a differential advantage relative to competing offerings.

The Purchase Process

Many aspects of services affect the consumer's evaluation of the purchase. Because services cannot be displayed, demonstrated, or illustrated, consumers cannot make a prepurchase evaluation of all the characteristics of services.[15] Similarly, because service providers may vary in their delivery of a service, an evaluation of a service may change with each purchase. Figure 12–5 portrays how different types of goods and services are evaluated by consumers. Tangible goods such as clothing, jewelry, and furniture have *search* properties, such as color, size, and style, which can be determined before purchase. Services such as restaurants and child care have *experience* properties, which can be discerned only after purchase or during consumption. Finally, services provided by specialized professionals such as medical diagnoses and legal services have *credence* properties, or characteristics that the consumer may find impossible to evaluate even after purchase and consumption.[16] To reduce the uncertainty created by these properties, service consumers turn to personal sources

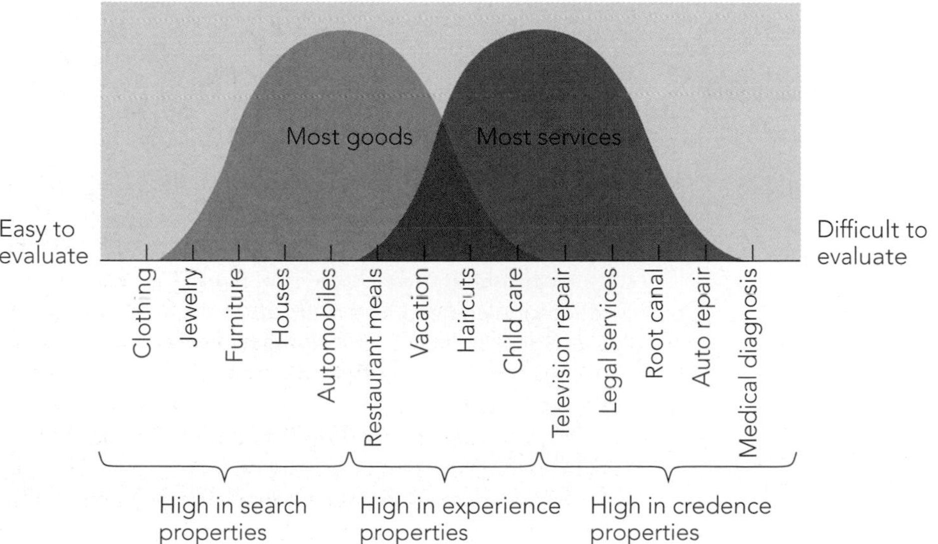

FIGURE 12–5
Consumers use search, experience, and credence properties to evaluate services.

of information such as early adopters, opinion leaders, and reference group members during the purchase decision process.[17] The Mayo Clinic uses an organized, explicit approach called "evidence management" to present customers with concrete and convincing evidence of its strengths.[18]

Assessing Service Quality

Once a consumer tries a service, how is it evaluated? Primarily by comparing expectations about a service offering to the actual experience a consumer has with the service.[19] Differences between the consumer's expectations and experience are identified through **gap analysis**. This type of analysis asks consumers to assess their expectations and experiences on dimensions of service quality such as those described in Figure 12–6.[20] Expectations are influenced by word-of-mouth communications, personal needs, past experiences, and promotional activities, while actual experiences are determined by the way an organization delivers its service.[21] The relative importance of the various dimensions of service quality varies by the type of service.[22] What if someone is dissatisfied and complains? Recent studies suggest that customers who experience a "service failure" will increase their satisfaction if the service makes a satisfactory service recovery effort, although they may not increase their intent to repurchase.[23] See the Going Online box for ideas about monitoring service failures.[24]

Customer Contact and Relationship Marketing

LO4

Consumers judge services on the entire sequence of steps that make up the service process. To focus on these steps, or "service encounters," a firm can develop a **customer contact audit**—a flowchart of the points of interaction between consumer and service provider.[25] This is particularly important in high-contact services such as hotels, educational institutions, and automobile rental agencies. Figure 12–7 is a consumer contact audit for renting a car from Hertz. The interactions identified in a customer contact audit often serve as the basis for developing relationships with

FIGURE 12–6
There are five dimensions of service quality.

DIMENSION	DEFINITION	EXAMPLES OF QUESTIONS AIRLINE CUSTOMERS MIGHT ASK
Reliability	Ability to perform the promised service dependably and accurately	Is my flight on time?
Tangibles	Appearance of physical facilities, equipment, personnel, and communication materials	Are the gate, the plane, and the baggage area clean?
Responsiveness	Willingness to help customers and provide prompt service	Are the flight attendants willing to answer my questions?
Assurance	Knowledge and courtesy of employees and their ability to convey trust and confidence	Are the ticket counter attendants, flight attendants, and pilots knowledgeable about their jobs?
Empathy	Caring, individualized attention provided to customers	Do the employees determine if I have special seating, meal, baggage, transfer or rebooking needs?

Going Online

How Can You Monitor Service Failure? Blog Watching!

Only 5 to 10 percent of dissatisfied customers choose to complain—the rest switch companies or make negative comments to other people. Increasingly, the forum for personal comments is on the Web through blogs or video sites. Domino's Pizza, for example, discovered that a negative video of two Domino's employees was viewed almost 1 million times on YouTube in just two days. Companies can monitor the postings for insights into service failures. Try using www.blogsearch.google.com or www.technorati.com to find blog entries about a service you know. There are also Web services such as www.buzzlogic.com and www.reputationdefender.com available to monitor blogs. Most public relations experts agree that it is best to respond to, rather than ignore, comments on the Web. Domino's posted a response on YouTube and created a Twitter account to try to counter the bad publicity and to answer questions. To find out what consumers are saying about your favorite brands try your own blog search now!

customers. Recent research suggests that authenticity and sincerity of the interactions affect the success of the relationships.[26]

A Customer's Car Rental Activities A customer decides to rent a car and (1) contacts the rental company (see Figure 12–7). A customer service representative receives the information (2) and checks the availability of the car at the desired location. When the customer arrives at the rental site (3), the reservation system is again accessed, and the customer provides information regarding payment, address, and driver's license (4). A car is assigned to the customer (5), who proceeds by bus to the car pickup (6). On return to the rental location (7), the customer checks in (8),

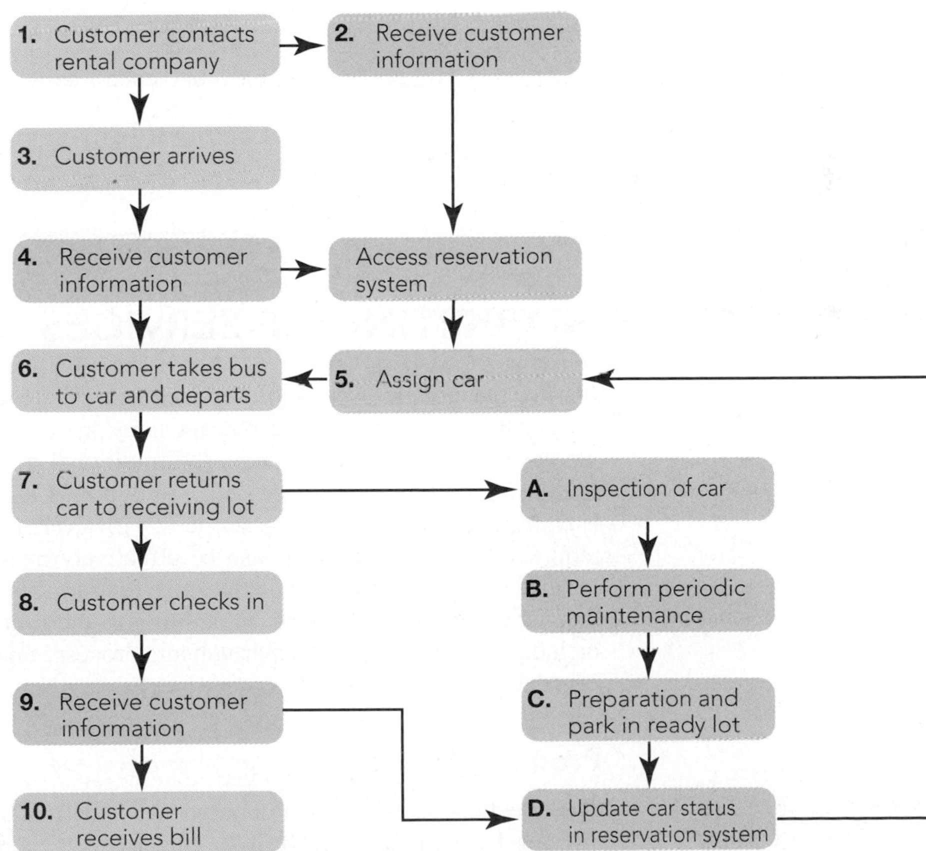

FIGURE 12–7
Customer contact audit for a car rental (green shaded boxes indicate customer activity)

The Hertz Corporation
www.hertz.com

a customer service representative collects information on mileage, gas consumption, and damages (9), and a bill is printed (10).

Each of the steps numbered 1 to 10 is a customer contact point where the tangible aspects of Hertz service are seen by the customer. Figure 12–7, however, also shows a series of steps lettered A to D that involve an inspection, maintenance, preparation for the next customer, and an update of the reservation system. These steps are essential in providing a clean, well-maintained car, but they are not points of customer interaction. To create a service advantage, Hertz must create a competitive advantage in the sequence of interactions with the customer. For example, Hertz has attempted to eliminate step 4 for some customers with its Hertz #1 Club—these customers simply show their drivers license and pick up the car's keys.

Relationship Marketing The contact between a service provider and a customer represents a service encounter that is likely to influence the customer's assessment of the purchase. The number of encounters in a service experience may vary. Disney, for example, estimates that a park visitor will have 74 encounters with Disney employees in a single visit. These encounters represent opportunities to develop social bonds, or relationships, with customers. The relationship may also be developed through loyalty incentives such as airline frequent flyer programs. Relationship marketing provides several benefits for service customers including the continuity of a single provider, customized service delivery, reduced stress due to a repetitive purchase process, and an absence of switching costs. Recent surveys of consumers have indicated that while customers of many services are interested in being "relationship customers," they require that the relationship be balanced in terms of loyalty, benefits, and respect for privacy,[27] and that there is a higher expectation of future use of the service.[28] Understanding the service characteristics that lead to repeat purchases can help services managers allocate their resources to appropriate relationship marketing activities.[29]

learning review

4. What are the differences between search, experience, and credence properties?
5. Hertz created its differential advantage at the points of ________________ in its customer contact audit.

MANAGING THE MARKETING OF SERVICES

LO5

Just as the unique aspects of services necessitate changes in the consumer's purchase process, the marketing management process requires special adaptation.[30] As we have seen in earlier chapters, the traditional marketing mix is composed of the four Ps: product, price, place, and promotion. Careful management of the four Ps is important when marketing services. However, the distinctive nature of services requires that other variables also be effectively managed by service marketers. The concept of an expanded marketing mix for services has been adopted by many service-marketing organizations. In addition to the four Ps, the services marketing mix includes people, physical environment, process, and productivity, or the **eight Ps of services marketing**.[31]

Product (Service)

The concepts of the product component of the marketing mix discussed in Chapters 10 and 11 apply equally well to Cheerios (a good) and to American Express (a

American Red Cross

Logos create service identities.

service). Managers of goods and services must design the product concept with the features and benefits desired by customers. An important aspect of the product concept is branding. Because services are intangible, and more difficult to describe, the brand name or identifying logo of the service organization is particularly important when a consumer makes a purchase decision.[32] Therefore, service organizations, such as banks, hotels, rental car companies, and restaurants, rely on branding strategies to distinguish themselves in the minds of the consumers. Strong brand names and symbols are important for service marketers, not only as a means of differentiation, but also to convey an image of quality. A service firm with a well-established brand reputation will also find it easier to introduce new services than firms without a brand reputation.[33]

Many services have undertaken creative branding activities. Hotels, for example, have begun to extend their branding efforts to consumers' homes through services such as *Hotels at Home*, which offers Westin's "Heavenly Bed," Hilton's bathrobes, and even artwork from Sheraton hotel rooms for consumers to buy and use at home.[34] Look at the logos on this page to determine how successful some companies have been in branding their service with a name and symbol.

Price

In service businesses, price is referred to in many ways. Hospitals refer to *charges*; consultants, lawyers, physicians, and accountants to *fees*; airlines to *fares*; hotels to *rates*; and colleges and universities to *tuition*. Because of the intangible nature of services, price is often perceived by consumers as a possible indicator of the quality of the service. Do you expect higher quality from an expensive restaurant? Would you wonder about the quality of a $100 surgery? In many cases there may be few other available cues for the customer to judge, so price becomes very important as a quality indicator.[35]

Pricing of services also goes beyond the traditional tasks of setting the selling price. When customers buy a service, they also consider nonmonetary costs, such as the mental and physical efforts required to consume the service. Service marketers must also try to minimize the effort required to purchase and use the service. Pricing also plays a role in balancing consumer demand for services. Many service businesses use **off-peak pricing**, which consists of charging different prices during different times of the day or during different days of the week to reflect variations in demand for the service. Airlines, for example, offer discounts for weekend travel, while movie theaters offer matinee prices.

Price influences perceptions of services.

Place (Distribution)

Place or distribution is a major factor in developing a service marketing strategy because of the inseparability of services from the producer. Rarely are intermediaries involved in the distribution of a service; the distribution site and the service deliverer are the tangible components of the service. Until recently customers generally had to go to the service provider's physical location to purchase the service. Increased competition, however, has forced many service firms to consider the value of convenient distribution and to find new ways of distributing services to customers. Hairstyling chains such as Cost Cutters Family Hair Salon, tax preparation offices such as H&R Block, and accounting firms such as Ernst & Young all use multiple locations for the distribution of services. Technology is also being used to deliver services beyond the provider's physical locations. In the banking industry, for example, customers of participating banks using the Cirrus system can access any one of thousands of automatic teller machines throughout the United States. The availability of electronic distribution through the Internet also allows for global reach and coverage for a variety of services, including travel, education, entertainment, and insurance.[36] With speed and convenience becoming increasingly important to customers when they select service providers, service firms can leverage the use of the Internet to deliver services on a 24/7 basis, in real time, on a global scale.

Promotion

The value of promotion, especially advertising, for many services is to show consumers the benefits of purchasing the service. It is valuable to stress availability, location, consistent quality, and efficient, courteous service,[37] and to provide a physical representation of the service or a service encounter.[38] The Accenture ad, for example, describes the benefits available to its customers—"High Performance. Delivered." The Space Adventures ad describes several benefits of spaceflight, such as traveling at 17,500 miles per hour and orbiting the Earth, and it provides a photo of the service encounter—a private astronaut in space! In most cases promotional concerns of services are similar to those of products.

Another form of promotion, *publicity*, has played a major role in the promotional strategy of many service organizations. Nonprofit organizations such public schools, religious organizations, and hospitals, for example, often use publicity to disseminate their messages. For many of these organizations the most common form of publicity is the *public service announcement* (PSA) because it is free.[39] As discussed later in Chapter 19, however, using PSAs as the foundation of a promotion program is unlikely to be effective because the timing and location of the PSA are under the control of the medium, not the organization.

Personal selling, sales promotion, and direct marketing can also play an important role in services marketing. Service firm representatives, such as hotel employees handling check-in, or wait-staff in restaurants, are often responsible for selling their services. Similarly, sales promotions such as coupons, free trials, and contests are often effective tools for service firms. Finally, direct marketing activities are often used to reach specific audiences with interest in specific types of services. Increasingly, service firms are adopting an integrated marketing communications approach, similar to the approach used by many consumer packaged goods firms, to ensure that the

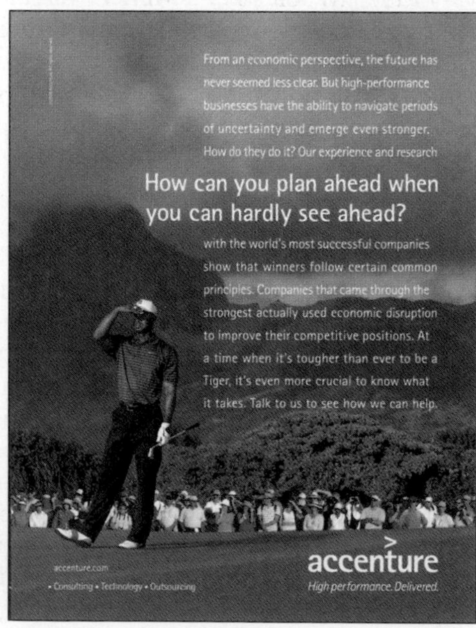

Services use promotional programs to communicate benefits and provide a representation of the service encounter.

Accenture
www.accenture.com

Space Adventures
www.spaceadventures.com

many forms of promotion are providing a consistent message and contributing to a common objective.

People

LO6

Many services depend on people for the creation and delivery of the customer service experience.[40] The nature of the interaction between employees and customers strongly influences the customer's perceptions of the service experience. Customers will often judge the quality of the service experience based on the performance of the people providing the service. This aspect of services marketing has led to a concept called internal marketing.[41]

Internal marketing is based on the notion that a service organization must focus on its employees, or internal market, before successful programs can be directed at customers.[42] Service firms need to ensure that employees have the attitude, skills, and commitment needed to meet customer expectations and to sustain customer loyalty. This idea suggests that employee development through recruitment, training, communication, coaching, management, and leadership are critical to the success of service organizations.[43] Finally, many service organizations, such as educational institutions and athletic teams, must recognize that individual customer behavior may also influence the service outcome for other customers. These interactions suggest that the people element in services includes employees and all customers.

Once internal marketing programs have prepared employees for their interactions with customers, organizations can better manage the services they provide. **Customer experience management (CEM)** is the process of managing the entire customer experience with the company. CEM experts suggest that the process should be intentional and planned, consistent so that every experience is similar, differentiated from other service offerings, and relevant and valuable to the target market. Companies such as Disney, Southwest Airlines, the Ritz-Carlton, and Starbucks all manage the experience they offer customers. They integrate their activities to connect with customers at each contact point to move beyond customer relationships to customer loyalty.[44] Zappos.com, an online shoe retailer, for example, requires that all employees complete a four-week customer loyalty training program to help deliver one of the company's core concepts—"Deliver WOW through service."[45]

Physical Environment

The appearance of the environment in which the service is delivered and where the firm and customer interact can influence the customer's perception of the service. The physical evidence of the service includes all the tangibles surrounding the service: the buildings, landscaping, vehicles, furnishings, signage, brochures, and equipment. Service firms need to manage physical evidence carefully and systematically to convey the proper impression of the service to the customer. This is sometimes referred to as impression, or evidence, management.[46] For many services, the physical environment provides an opportunity for the firm to send consistent and strong messages about the nature of the service to be delivered.

Process

Process refers to the actual procedures, mechanisms, and flow of activities by which the service is created and delivered. The actual creation and delivery steps that the customer experiences provide customers with evidence on which to judge the service. These steps involve not only "what" gets created but also "how" it is created. The customer contact audit discussed earlier in the chapter is relevant to understanding the service process discussed here. The customer contact audit can serve as a basis for ensuring better service creation and delivery processes. Grease Monkey believes that it has the right process in the vehicle oil change and fluid exchange service

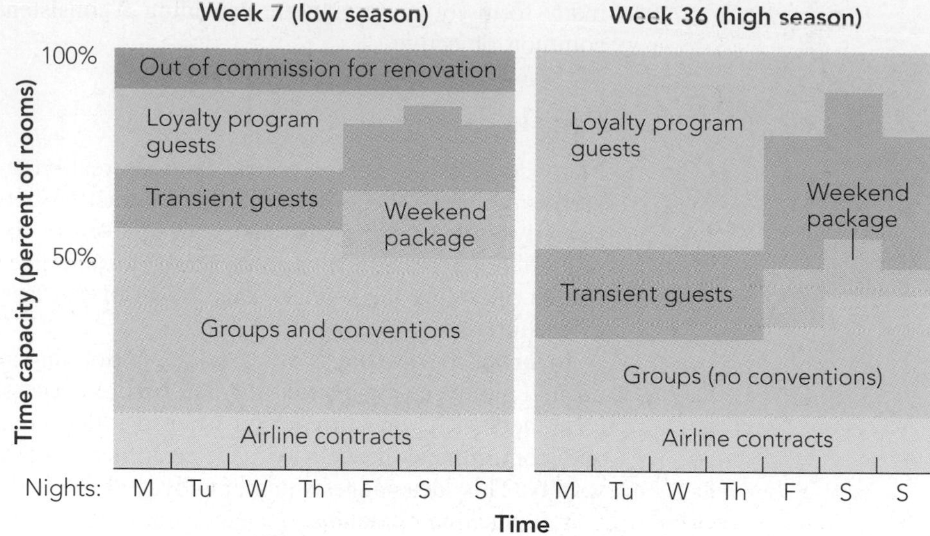

FIGURE 12–8 Different prices and packages help match hotel demand to capacity.

business. Customers do not need appointments, stores are open six days per week, the service is completed in 15–20 minutes, and a waiting room allows customers to read or work while the service is being completed.

Productivity

Most services have a limited capacity due to the inseparability of the service from the service provider and the perishable nature of the service. For example, to "buy" an appendectomy, a patient must be in the hospital at the same time as the surgeon and only one patient can be helped at that time. Similarly, no additional surgery can be conducted tomorrow because of an unused operating room or an available surgeon today—the service capacity is lost if it is not used. So the service component of the marketing mix must be integrated with efforts to influence consumer demand.[47] This is referred to as **capacity management**.

Service organizations must manage the availability of the offering so that (1) demand matches capacity over the duration of the demand cycle (for example, one day, week, month, or year), and (2) the organization's assets are used in ways that will maximize the return on investment (ROI).[48] Figure 12–8 shows how a hotel tries to manage its capacity during the high and low seasons. Differing price structures are assigned to each segment of consumers to help moderate or adjust demand for the service. Airline contracts fill a fixed number of rooms throughout the year. In the low season, when more rooms are available, tour packages at appealing prices are used to attract groups or conventions, such as an offer for seven nights in Orlando at a reduced price. Weekend packages are also offered to vacationers. In the high-demand season, groups are less desirable because guests who will pay high prices travel to Florida on their own. The accompanying Using Marketing Dashboards box demonstrates how JetBlue Airways uses a capacity management measure called *load factor* to assess its profitability.

SERVICES IN THE FUTURE

What can we expect from the services industry in the future? New and better services, of course, and an unprecedented variety of choices. Many of the changes will be the result of two factors: technological development and an expanding scope in the global economy.

Technogical advances are rapidly changing the service industry. In fact, many of the likely changes in the United States are already occurring in Europe and Asia

Using Marketing Dashboards
Are JetBlue's Flights Profitably Loaded?

Capacity management is critical in the marketing of many services. For example, having the right number of airline seats or hotel rooms available at the right time, price, and place can spell the difference between a profitable or unprofitable service operation.

Airlines feature *load factor* as a capacity management measure on their marketing dashboards, along with two other measures; namely the *operating expense* per available seat flown one mile and the revenue generated by each seat flown one mile called *yield*. Load factor is the percentage of available seats flown one mile occupied by a paying customer.

These three measures combine to show airline operating income or loss per available seat flown one mile:

Operating income (loss) per available seat flown one mile
= [Yield × Load factor] − Operating expense

Your Challenge As a marketing analyst for New York City-based JetBlue Airways, you have been asked to determine the operating income or loss per available seat flown one mile for the first six months of 2010. In addition, you have been asked to determine what load factor JetBlue must reach to break even assuming its current yield and operating expense will not change in the immediate future.

Your Findings JetBlue's yield, load factor, and operating expense marketing dashboard displays are shown below.

You can conclude from these measures that JetBlue Airways posted about a 0.21¢ loss per available seat flown one mile in the first six months of 2010:

Operating loss per available seat flown one mile
= [9.83¢ × 82.1%] − 8.28¢ = −.2096¢

Assuming JetBlue's yield and operating expense will not change and using a little algebra, the airline's load factor will have to increase from 82.1 percent to 84.23 percent to break even:

Operating income (loss) per available seat flown one mile
= [9.83¢ × Load factor] − 8.28¢ = 0¢
Load factor = 84.23%

Your Action Assuming yield and operating expenses will not change, you should recommend that JetBlue consider revising its flight schedules to better accommodate traveler needs and advertise these changes. Consideration might be also given to how JetBlue utilizes its existing airplane fleet to serve its customers and produce a profit.

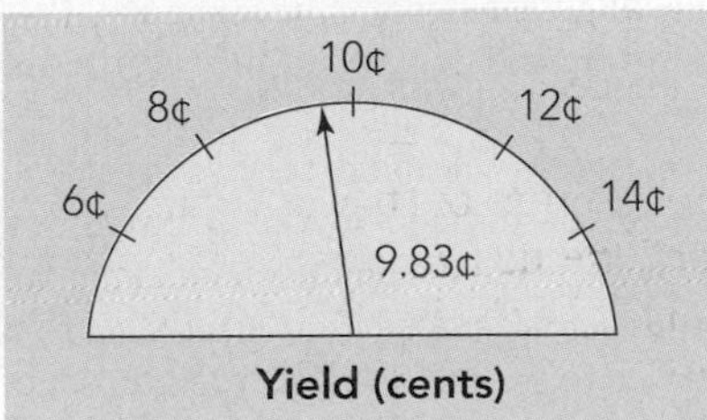

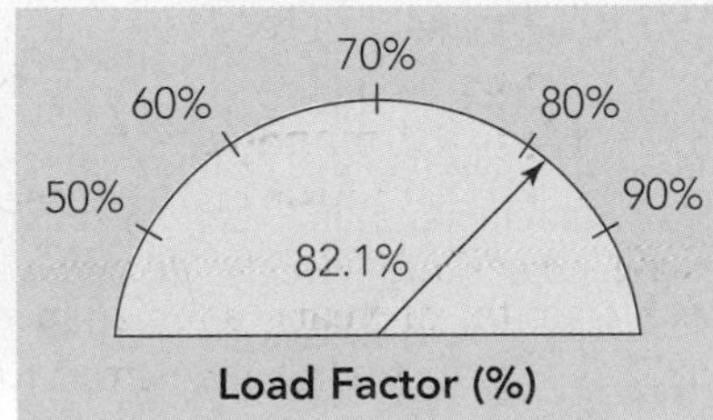

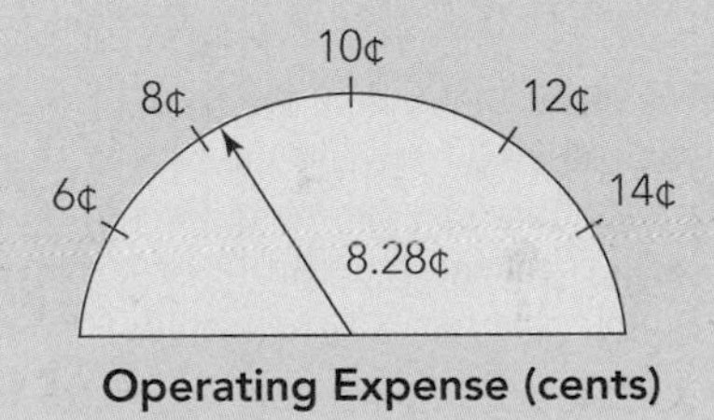

where new generations of technology have leapfrogged North America. The key elements of future services include mobility, convergence, personalization, and collaboration. Mobility will be provided by new generations of networks that will allow TV, GPS, high-speed data transfer, and audio programming on portable digital devices. Products such as the Apple iPhone are indications of the coming convergence of voice, video, and data in a single product. Personalization is also under way at services such as Amazon.com where past transactions are analyzed to customize information seen by customers. Technology-mediated personalization can increase the customers' perceptions of value; however, excessive attempts at personalization can also trigger privacy concerns.[49] Finally, collaboration services that allow Web-conferencing, dating and matchmaking, and even remote involvement of friends when someone is shopping are coming![50]

An expanding scope of influence in the global economy is also changing the service industry. While the past decade has seen services grow to become the dominant part of the economy in the United States, the future is likely to see more emphasis on the global marketing of services and increasing attention to cross-cultural implications for services. Recent studies indicate that consumers in countries such as Australia, China, Germany, India, and the United States place varying emphasis on service quality and underscore the need to "think global and act local." Finally, some experts predict that the dominant view of economic exchange will shift from its current focus on goods and tangible resources to services and intangible attributes.[51] Countries that expect to compete globally will need to invest in service industry growth and service innovation.[52] In fact, recent research suggests that services marketing strategies create a competitive advantage and are very profitable.[53]

learning review

6. How does a movie theater use off-peak pricing?
7. Matching demand with capacity is the focus of _____________ management.
8. What factors will influence future changes in services?

LEARNING OBJECTIVES REVIEW

LO1 *Describe four unique elements of services.*
The four unique elements of services—the four I's—are intangibility, inconsistency, inseparability, and inventory. Intangibility refers to the tendency of services to be a performance that cannot be held or touched, rather than an object. Inconsistency is a characteristic of services because they depend on people to deliver them, and people vary in their capabilities and in their day-to-day performance. Inseparability refers to the difficulty of separating the deliverer of the service (hair stylist) from the service itself (hair salon). Inventory refers to the need to have service production capability when there is service demand.

LO2 *Recognize how services differ and how they can be classified.*
Services differ in terms of the balance of the part of the offering that is based on goods and the part of the offering that is based on service. Services can be delivered by people or equipment, they can be provided by profit or nonprofit organizations, and they can be government sponsored.

LO3 *Explain how consumers purchase and evaluate services.*
Because services are intangible, prepurchase evaluation is difficult for consumers. To choose a service, consumers use search, experience, and credence qualities to evaluate the good and service elements of an offering. Once a consumer tries a service, it is evaluated by comparing expectations with the actual experience on five dimensions of quality—reliability, tangibles, responsiveness, assurance, and empathy. Differences between expectations and experience are identified through gap analysis.

LO4 *Develop a customer contact audit to identify service advantages.*
A customer contact audit is a flowchart of the points of interaction between a consumer and a service provider. The interactions identified in a customer contact audit often serve as the basis for developing relationships with customers.

LO5 *Explain the role of the eight Ps in the services marketing mix.*
The services marketing mix includes eight Ps. An important aspect of the product element is branding—the use of a brand name or logo to help consumers identify a service. Pricing is reflected in charges, fees, fares, and rates and can be used to influence perceptions of the quality of a service and to balance demand for services. Place (or distribution) is used to provide access and convenience. Promotional tools such as advertising and publicity are a means of communicating the benefits of a service. People are responsible for the creation and delivery of the service. Internal marketing and customer experience management are concepts that result from a focus on people within the service organization and their interactions with customers. Physical environment refers to the appearance of the place where the services are delivered. Process refers to the actual procedures, mechanisms, and activities by which a service is created and delivered. Productivity is related to the inseparability of the service from the service provider and is influenced by capacity management.

LO6 *Discuss the important roles of internal marketing and customer experience management in service organizations.*
Because the employee plays a central role in creating the service experience, and in building and maintaining relationships with customers, services have adopted a concept called internal marketing. This concept suggests that services need to ensure that employees (the internal market) have the attitude, skills, and commitment needed to meet customer expectations. Customer experience management is the process of managing the entire customer experience with the company to ensure customer loyalty.

FOCUSING ON KEY TERMS

capacity management p. 312
customer contact audit p. 306
customer experience management p. 311
eight Ps of services marketing p. 308
four I's of services p. 299
gap analysis p. 306
idle production capacity p. 301
internal marketing p. 311
off-peak pricing p. 309
service continuum p. 301
services p. 298

APPLYING MARKETING KNOWLEDGE

1 Explain how the four I's of services would apply to a Marriott Hotel.

2 Idle production capacity may be related to inventory or capacity management. How would the pricing component of the marketing mix reduce idle production capacity for (*a*) a car wash, (*b*) a stage theater group, and (*c*) a university?

3 Look back at the service continuum in Figure 12–3. Explain how the following points in the continuum differ in terms of consistency: (*a*) salt, (*b*) automobile, (*c*) advertising agency, and (*d*) teaching.

4 What are the search, experience, and credence properties of an airline for the business traveler and pleasure traveler? What properties are most important to each group?

5 Outline the customer contact audit for the typical deposit you make at your neighborhood bank.

6 How does off-peak pricing influence demand for services?

7 Draw the channel of distribution for the following services: (*a*) a restaurant, (*b*) a hospital, and (*c*) a hotel.

8 The text suggests that internal marketing is necessary before a successful marketing program can be directed at consumers. Why is this particularly true for service organizations?

9 Outline the capacity management strategies that an airline must consider.

10 In recent years, many service businesses have begun to provide their employees with uniforms. Explain the rationale behind this strategy in terms of the concepts discussed in this chapter.

building your marketing plan

In this section of your marketing plan you should distinguish between your core product—a good or a service—and supplementary services.

1 Develop an internal marketing program that will ensure that employees are prepared to deliver the core and supplementary services.

2 Conduct a customer contact audit and create a flowchart similar to Figure 12–7 to identify specific points of interaction with customers.

3 Describe marketing activities that will (*a*) address each of the four I's as they relate to your service and (*b*) encourage the development of relationships with your customers.

Add this as an appendix to your marketing plan and use the results in developing your marketing mix strategy.

video case 12 Philadelphia Phillies, Inc.: Sports Marketing 101

"Unfortunately we can't promise fans in the stands a win every game," laughs David Montgomery, president and chief executive officer of the Philadelphia Phillies, Inc. But in 2008 his Phillies came close enough to that: They beat the Tampa Bay Rays to win the World Series (photo).

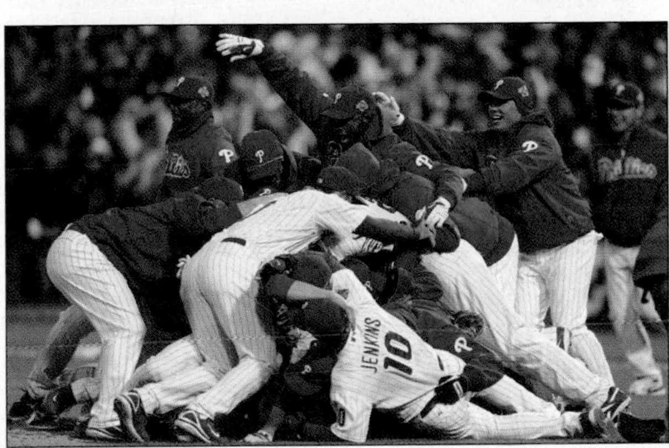

Montgomery goes on to explain key elements of the Phillies' marketing strategy, starting with moving into its new Citizens Bank Park baseball stadium in 2004. "Bring everyone in closer. Have fans feel 'I'm not alone here; lots of others are in the seats. This is a *happening*!'" he says. Our new facility and the fact that it's a game played in summer out in the open air really takes you to a much broader audience," he says. "Our challenge is to appeal to all the segments in that audience." In the new baseball-only ballpark, every seat is angled toward home plate to give fans the best view of the action.

The new fan-friendly Phillies stadium is just one element in today's complex strategy to effectively market the Philadelphia Phillies to several different segments of fans—a far different challenge than in the past. A century ago Major League Baseball was pretty simple. You built a stadium. You hired the ballplayers. You printed tickets—hoping and praying a winning team would bring in fans and sell those tickets. And your advertising consisted of printing the team's home schedule in the local newspaper.

THE PHILLIES TODAY: APPEALS, SEGMENTS, AND ACTIVITIES

Baseball, like other sports, is a service whose primary benefit is entertainment. Marketing a Major League Baseball team is far different today.

"How do you market a product that is all over the board?" asks David Buck, the Phillies' vice president of marketing. He first gives a general answer to his question: "The ballpark experience is the key. As long as you project an image of a fun ballpark experience in everything you do, you're going to be in good shape. Our best advertising is word of mouth from happy fans." Next come the specifics. Marketing the appeal of a fun ballpark experience to all segments of fans is critical because the Phillies can't promise a winning baseball team.

Reaching the different segments of fans is a special challenge because each segment attends a game for different reasons and therefore will respond to different special promotions:

- *The diehards.* Intense baseball fans who are there to watch the strategy and see the Phillies win.
- *Kids 14 years and under.* At the game with their families, to get bat or bobble-head doll premiums, and have a "run-the-bases" day.
- *Women and men 15 years and older.* Special "days out," such as Mother's Day or Father's Day.
- *Seniors, 60 years and over.* A "stroll-the-bases" day.
- *The 20- and 30-somethings.* Meet friends at the ballpark and restaurants for a fun night out.
- *Corporate and community groups.* At the game to have fun but also to get to know members of their respective organizations better.

It's clear that not all fans are there for exactly the same "fun ballpark experience."

The "fun ballpark experience" today also goes beyond simply watching the Phillies play a baseball game. Fans at Citizens Bank Park can:

- Buy souvenirs at the Phanatic Attic, within the Majestic Clubhouse Store.
- Romp in the Phanatic Phun Zone, the largest soft-play area for kids in Major League Baseball.
- Test their skills in a pitching game.
- Stroll through Ashburn Alley (named for a famous Phillie), an outdoor food and entertainment area.
- Eat at McFadden's Restaurant and Saloon year round or Harry the K's Bar & Grill.

PROMOTIONAL ACTIVITIES

The range of the Phillies' promotional activities today is mind numbing. Before and during the season, the Phillies run a series of TV ads to generate and/or maintain fan interest. A recent ad campaign targeted kids by showing that the Phillies' players themselves are just like them. The tagline: "There's a little fan in all of us."

The Phillies also use "special promotion days," which typically increase fan attendance by 30 to 35 percent for a game, according to David Buck. These days often generate first-time visits by people who have never seen a Major League Baseball game. They generally fall into three categories: (1) theme nights, (2) event days, and (3) premium gift days.

Theme nights are devoted to special community groups or other fan segments. Examples include College Nights (fellow classmates, alumni, and faculty), dates for families of the military and law enforcement, Rooftop Thursdays (having a luau with friends on the stadium rooftop), among others. Event days can involve camera days where fans can have their photo taken with a favorite Phillies player. Or they can involve fireworks, an old-timers' game, or running or strolling the bases. Five "Dollar Dog Nights" during the season let fans eat as many hot dogs as they can for $1.

The Phillies premiums or giveaways are also directed at specific market segments. These premiums range from baseball caps, beach towels, and T-shirts to a Phillies team photo or bobble-head dolls. To control expenses, the Phillies try to keep the cost of the premiums in the range of $1 to $3.

Other promotional activities fall in both the traditional and nontraditional categories. Personal appearances at public and charity events by Phillies players and their wives, radio and TV ads, and special events paid for by sponsors have been used by baseball teams for decades. The "Phillies Ballgirls" involve a clearly new, nontraditional promotional activity. These 20 women are all college softball players and are ambassadors for the Phillies. Besides taking on other softball teams on the diamond, they make four or five appearances a week at charity events, schools, or golf outings. They also help promote the Phillies sense of social responsibility and its focus on recycling and the environment.

The Internet and social networks have revolutionized the Phillies media strategies. "I remember the days we used to mail press releases that took four or five days to get to recipients," says the Phillies vice president of communications, Bonnie Clark. Fans not only can order tickets on the team's Web site (www.phillies.com), but also can buy Phillies jerseys and caps and get the inside scoop on players—like who's going on the disabled list and so on. The social networks now have huge importance. "Six months after launching a Phillies Twitter, we have 7,400 followers," she says. "And we now have more than 190,000 Facebook friends."

Probably the best-known mascot in professional sports, the Phillie Phanatic is a Philadelphia legend. This oversized, green furry mascot has been around for over 25 years. It not only appears in the ballpark at all Phillies' home games, but also makes appearances at charity and public events year round. Or rather the *three* Phanatics do so, because the demand is too great for a single Phanatic. "The Phanatic is a great character because he doesn't carry wins or losses," says David Montgomery. "Fans young and old can relate to him . . . he makes you smile, makes you laugh, and adds to the enjoyment of the game."

BOTTOM LINE: REVENUES AND EXPENSES

"We're a private business that serves the public," David Montgomery points out. "And we've got to make sure our revenues more than cover our expenses." He identifies five key sources of revenues and the approximate annual percentages for each:

Sources of Revenue	Approx. %
1. Ticket sales (home and away games)	52%
2. National media (network TV and radio)	13
3. Local media (over-the-air TV, pay TV, radio)	13
4. Advertising (publications, co-sponsorship promotions)	12
5. Concessions (food, souvenirs, restaurants)	10
Total	100

Balanced against these revenues are some major expenses that include players' salaries (about $130 million) and salaries of more than 150 full-time employees. Other expenses are those for scouting and drafting 40 to 60 new players per year, operating six minor-league farm clubs, and managing a labor force of 400 persons for each of the Phillies' 81 regular-season home games at Citizens Bank Park.

David Montgomery never gets bored. "When I finished business school, I had to choose between a marketing research job at a large paper products company or marketing the Philadelphia Phillies," explains Montgomery, who started with the Phillies by selling season and group tickets. "And it was no real decision because there never has been one day on this job that wasn't different and exciting."

Questions

1 (*a*) What is the "product" that the Phillies market? (*b*) What "products" are the Phillies careful not to market?

2 How does the "quality" dimension in marketing the Philadelphia Phillies as an entertainment service differ from that in marketing a consumer product such as a breakfast cereal?

3 In terms of a social network marketing strategy, (*a*) what are the likely characteristics of the Phillies fans and (*b*) what should the Phillies' Facebook fan page contain?

4 Considering all five elements of the promotional mix (advertising, personal selling, public relations, sales promotion, and direct marketing), what specific promotional activities should the Phillies use? Which should be used off-season? During the season?

5 What kind of special promotion gift days (with premiums) and event days (no premiums) can the Phillies use to increase attendance by targeting these fan segments: (*a*) 14 and under, (*b*) 15 and over, (*c*) other special fan segments, and (*d*) all fans?

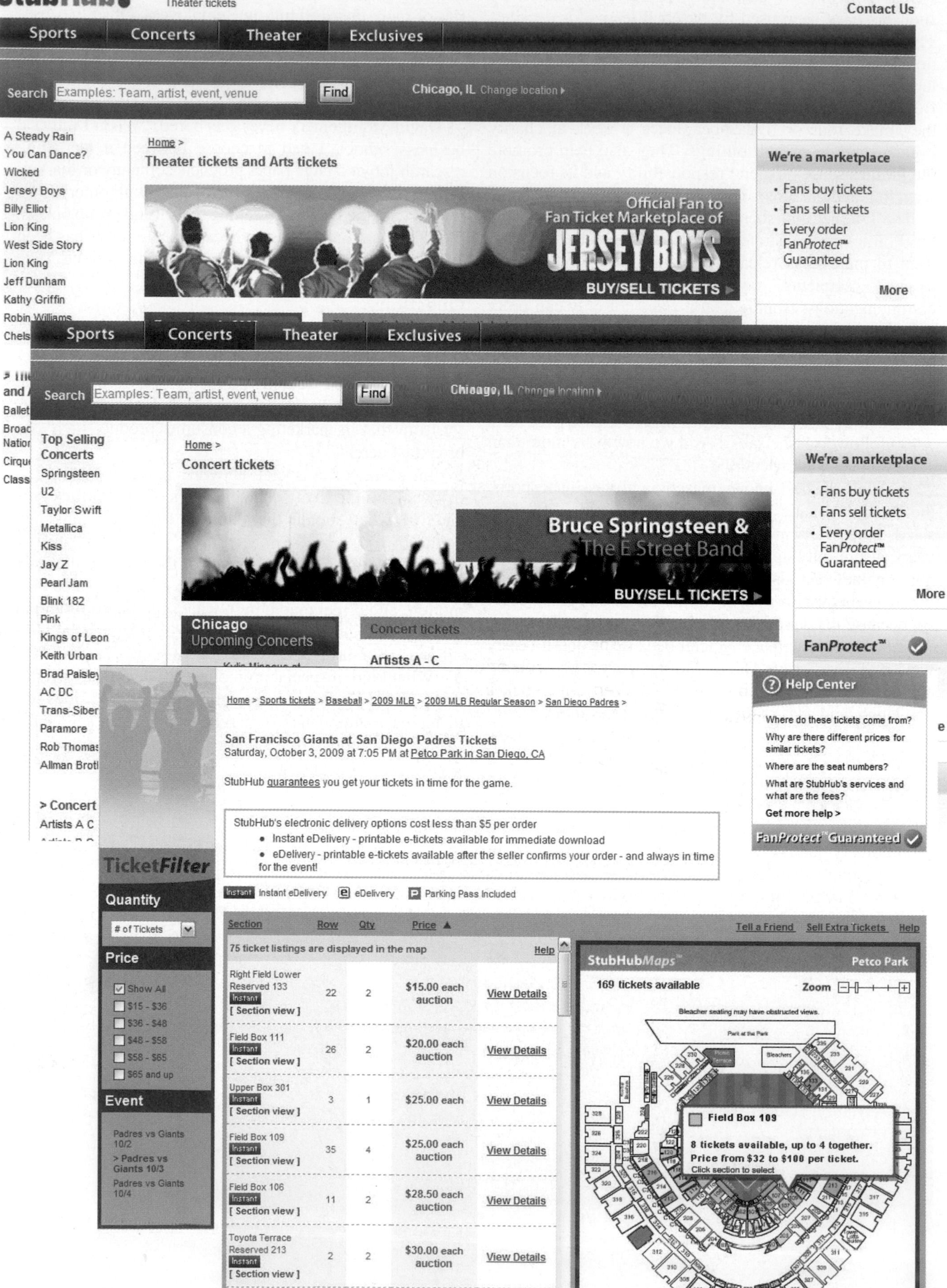

StubHub!
Theater tickets
Tickets Home | Register | Login | My Account | Buy | Sell | Help
Contact Us
Sports
Concerts
Theater
Exclusives
Search
Examples: Team, artist, event, venue
Find
Chicago, IL Change location
A Steady Rain
You Can Dance?
Wicked
Jersey Boys
Billy Elliot
Lion King
West Side Story
Lion King
Jeff Dunham
Kathy Griffin
Robin Williams
Home >
Theater tickets and Arts tickets
Official Fan to Fan Ticket Marketplace of
JERSEY BOYS
BUY/SELL TICKETS
We're a marketplace
Fans buy tickets
Fans sell tickets
Every order FanProtect™ Guaranteed
More
Sports
Concerts
Theater
Exclusives
Search
Examples: Team, artist, event, venue
Find
Chicago, IL Change location
Top Selling Concerts
Springsteen
U2
Taylor Swift
Metallica
Kiss
Jay Z
Pearl Jam
Blink 182
Pink
Kings of Leon
Keith Urban
Home >
Concert tickets
Bruce Springsteen &
The E Street Band
BUY/SELL TICKETS
Chicago
Upcoming Concerts
Concert tickets
Artists A - C
We're a marketplace
Fans buy tickets
Fans sell tickets
Every order FanProtect™ Guaranteed
More
FanProtect™
Home > Sports tickets > Baseball > 2009 MLB > 2009 MLB Regular Season > San Diego Padres >
San Francisco Giants at San Diego Padres Tickets
Saturday, October 3, 2009 at 7:05 PM at Petco Park in San Diego, CA
StubHub guarantees you get your tickets in time for the game.
StubHub's electronic delivery options cost less than $5 per order
Instant eDelivery - printable e-tickets available for immediate download
eDelivery - printable e-tickets available after the seller confirms your order - and always in time for the event!
Instant eDelivery
eDelivery
Parking Pass Included
Help Center
Where do these tickets come from?
Why are there different prices for similar tickets?
Where are the seat numbers?
What are StubHub's services and what are the fees?
Get more help >
FanProtect™ Guaranteed
TicketFilter
Quantity
# of Tickets
Price
Show All
$15 - $36
$36 - $48
$48 - $58
$58 - $65
$65 and up
Event
Padres vs Giants 10/2
> Padres vs Giants 10/3
Padres vs Giants 10/4
Section
Row
Qty
Price
Tell a Friend
Sell Extra Tickets
Help
75 ticket listings are displayed in the map
Right Field Lower Reserved 133 [Section view] 22 2 $15.00 each auction View Details
Field Box 111 [Section view] 26 2 $20.00 each auction View Details
Upper Box 301 [Section view] 3 1 $25.00 each View Details
Field Box 109 [Section view] 35 4 $25.00 each auction View Details
Field Box 106 [Section view] 11 2 $28.50 each auction View Details
Toyota Terrace Reserved 213 [Section view] 2 2 $30.00 each auction View Details
Field 120
StubHubMaps™
Petco Park
169 tickets available
Zoom
Bleacher seating may have obstructed views.
Park at the Park
Bleachers
Field Box 109
8 tickets available, up to 4 together.
Price from $32 to $100 per ticket.
Click section to select

13 Building the Price Foundation

LEARNING OBJECTIVES

After reading this chapter you should be able to:

- LO1 Identify the elements that make up a price.
- LO2 Recognize the objectives a firm has in setting prices and the constraints that restrict the range of prices a firm can charge.
- LO3 Explain what a demand curve is and the role of revenues in pricing decisions.
- LO4 Describe what price elasticity of demand means to a manager facing a pricing decision.
- LO5 Explain the role of costs in pricing decisions.
- LO6 Describe how various combinations of price, fixed cost, and unit variable cost affect a firm's break-even point.

"MY MOTHER WAS NOT THRILLED . . . ": THE LAUNCH OF STUBHUB.COM!

"It was definitely something that my mother was *not* thrilled about," recalls Jeff Fluhr.[1] The "it" Fluhr's mother was concerned about was his dropping out of the Stanford University MBA program his first year there.

Plan for the Start-up

Fluhr and his classmate, Eric Baker, had entered a class competition for the best business plan. Their idea: "Need A Ticket.com," a centralized Web site where people owning tickets to sporting events or concerts could auction them off. The idea seemed so great that Fluhr dropped out of graduate school to start the new business. But, as with most marketing or business plans for start-ups, actually turning the plan into reality wasn't as easy as the two entrepreneurs expected.

Fluhr and Baker launched their ticket-selling business in late 2000, right after the dot-com crash, so they had trouble raising money from investors. The original business plan focused on selling tickets on other Web sites such as Microsoft's MSN and then having StubHub split the revenues from the resold tickets. In 2003, the approach changed to what it is today. The StubHub Web site lets sellers either sell their tickets directly to buyers at a fixed price, a price that declines as the date of the event approaches, or sell them by auction.

How StubHub's Pricing Works Now

The StubHub pricing formula is very straightforward. Suppose you want to sell a ticket for $100. The buyer pays $110 for the ticket, the extra $10 being the 10 percent commission to StubHub. It, in turn, pays you $85 for the ticket you sold, factoring in its $15 or 15 percent commission to you, the seller.[2] So StubHub makes $25 on the sale.

Internet Web sites have revolutionized pricing and efficiently connecting buyers and sellers—from eBay and Amazon.com to travel sites such as Priceline.com and Expedia. In the ticket reselling business, StubHub competes with giants like Ticketmaster, and smaller firms such as Craigslist, TicketsNow, and Razor Gator.[3]

With over half of tickets to major events sold online, StubHub's Web site can help generate *extra ticket sales* for the original sponsors of the events. This is why StubHub now has formal relationships not only with professional sports leagues, but also with many sports programs at

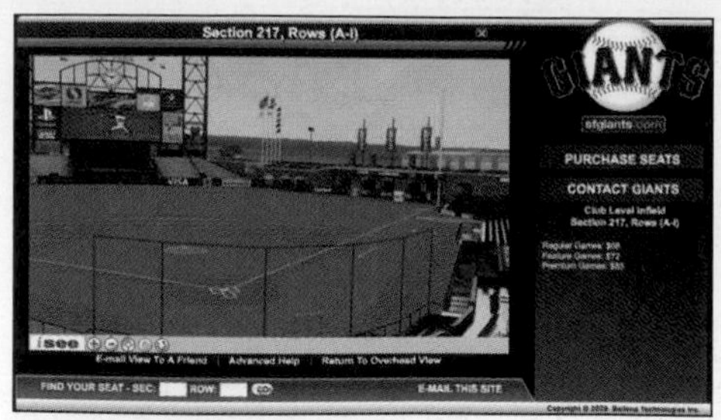

Want to see what the view of the field is for the San Francisco Giants home game tickets you can buy? To find out how the Giants and StubHub can help, read the text.

major universities such as Alabama, Southern California, Stanford, Kansas State, and Purdue. In early 2009 the San Francisco Giants announced a partnership with StubHub (now part of eBay) to enable fans buying resold tickets to have a simulated view of the field from the seats they are thinking about buying.[4]

Pricing decisions involve carefully assessing consumer demand, revenues, fixed costs, and variable costs before setting a final price. If the answers were easy, hundreds of failed dot-com firms with brilliant ideas, technologies, and marketing plans would still be going strong today.

Welcome to the fascinating—and intense—world of pricing, where many forces come together in the price buyers are asked to pay. This chapter covers important factors used in setting prices.

NATURE AND IMPORTANCE OF PRICE

The price paid for goods and services goes by many names. You pay *tuition* for your education, *rent* for an apartment, *interest* on a bank credit card, and a *premium* for car insurance. Your dentist or physician charges you a *fee*, a professional or social organization charges *dues*, and airlines charge a *fare*. In business, an executive is given a *salary*, a salesperson receives a *commission*, and a worker is paid a *wage*. And what you pay for clothes or a haircut is termed a *price*.

Among all marketing and operations factors in a business firm, price has a unique role. It is the place where all other business decisions come together. The price must be "right"—in the sense that customers must be willing to pay it; it must generate enough sales dollars to pay for the cost of developing, producing, and marketing the product; *and* it must earn a profit for the company. Small changes in price can have big effects on both the number of units sold and company profit. Research on 1,000 large U.S. companies shows that a 1 percent price increase translates to a 12 percent increase in profitability, other factors remaining the same.[5]

What Is a Price?

LO1

These examples highlight the many varied ways that price plays a part in our daily lives. From a marketing viewpoint, **price** is the money or other considerations (including other products and services) exchanged for the ownership or use of a product or service. Recently, Wilkinson Sword exchanged some of its knives for advertising used to promote its razor blades. This practice of exchanging products and services for other products and services rather than for money is called **barter**. These transactions account for billions of dollars annually in domestic and international trade.

For most products, money is exchanged. However, the amount paid is not always the same as the list, or quoted, price because of discounts, allowances, and extra fees. While discounts, allowances, and rebates make the effective price lower, other marketing tactics raise the real price. One new 21st century pricing tactic is to use "special fees" and "surcharges." This practice is driven by consumers' zeal for low prices combined with the ease of making price comparisons on the Internet. Buyers are more willing to pay extra fees than a higher list price, so sellers use add-on charges as a way of having the consumer pay more without raising the list price.[6] For airline ticket pricing this changed in late 2009 when new software programs included the extra fees—like that for checking a bag—in the "ticket price" of a flight.[7]

In deciding whether to buy a new Tesla Roadster Sport electric car, consider incentives, allowances, and extra fees—as well as the original list price!

All the factors that increase or decrease the final price of an offering help construct a "price equation," which is shown for a few products in Figure 13–1. They are key considerations when you buy your next car. For example, suppose you want to get "plugged in" and buy a 2010 Tesla Roadster Sport, the world's leading all-electric, zero-emission car that has a 245-mile range and can be recharged in three hours. This exciting "green" vehicle can move you from 0 to 60 mph in 3.7 seconds at a top speed of 125 mph.

The Tesla Roadster Sport has a list price of $128,500, but you want several options (leather interior, carbon fiber hard top, electronics upgrade, metallic paint, performance wheels, and others) that will cost $20,000. An extended warranty will add an additional $5,000. However, if you put $50,000 down now and finance the balance over the next year, you will receive a rebate of $3,500 off the list price.

Using the *Kelley Blue Book* (www.kbb.com) trade-in value for your 2005 Honda Civic DX four-door sedan that has 75,000 miles and is in good condition, the dealer gives you a trade-in allowance of $5,000. In addition, you will have to pay a 7.5 percent sales tax of $10,200, an auto registration fee of $500 to the state, and a $500 destination charge to ship the car. But because the Tesla Roadster Sport is an alternative energy vehicle, you qualify for a $2,500 state rebate and a $7,500 federal tax credit! Finally, your total finance charge is $2,687 based on an annual interest rate of 5 percent.[8]

Applying the price equation shown in Figure 13–1 to your purchase, your final price is:

Final price = [List price] − [(Incentives) + (Allowances)] + [Extra fees]

= [$128,500] − [($3,500 + $2,500 + $7,500) + ($5,000)]

+ [$20,000 + $5,000 + $500 + $500 + $10,200 + $2,687]

= $148,887

Note that your final price is $20,387 more than the list price. Your monthly payment for the one-year loan of $96,200 (including the total finance charge) is $8,241. Are you still interested in the Tesla Roadster Sport? If so, put yourself on the waiting list!

FIGURE 13–1
The "price" a buyer pays can take different names, depending on what is purchased, and can change depending on the price equation.

ITEM PURCHASED	PRICE	= LIST PRICE	INCENTIVES AND − ALLOWANCES	+ EXTRA FEES
New car bought by an individual	Final price	= List price	− Rebate Cash discount Old car trade-in	+ Financing charges Special accessories Destination charges
Term in college bought by a student	Tuition	= Published tuition	− Scholarship Other financial aid Discounts for number of credits taken	+ Special activity fees
Merchandise bought from a wholesaler by a retailer	Invoice price	= List price	− Quantity discount Cash discount Seasonal discount Functional or trade discount	+ Penalty for late payment

Marketing Matters > > > > > > > > technology

How Flattening the World Affects Prices, Revenues, and Costs: Infosys Technologies, Ltd., IKEA . . . and You!

The New York Times writer Tom Friedman says he got the idea for the title of his award-winning book *The World Is Flat* on a trip to Bangalore, India, a place he describes as "India's Silicon Valley."

Columbus sailed *west* from Europe to try to find India and the sources of wealth in his day—precious metals, silks, and spices. Friedman was flying *east* to India from New York to try to learn more about the key sources of wealth of our day—computer software algorithms, information technology, call centers, and efficient manufacturing.

In visiting Infosys Technologies, Ltd., 40 minutes from Bangalore, Friedman found himself on a park-like campus with manicured lawns and many glass-and-steel buildings (photo). Nandan Nilekani, chief executive officer of Infosys, told Friedman that outsourcing was just one dimension of fundamental changes in world business. Nilekani went on to explain that broadband connectivity, the explosion of software and search engines, and lower-priced computers have made it easy for anyone to do remote development. This means today's intellectual work can be delivered from almost anywhere, often with far lower prices to the organizations buying.

Nilekani looked at Friedman and summed up his comments with, "Tom, the playing field is being leveled."

Hundreds of global companies are looking to developing economies not only as sources of trained personnel in information technology and outsourced manufacturing, but also to generate new revenues from sales of their products and services. Some examples:

- Intel has trained more than 600,000 teachers in India and 700,000 in China and placed PCs in 6,000 villages in India.
- China Mobile Ltd. with over 300 million customers is the world's largest cell phone system and is adding 5 million new customers a month.
- Swedish retailer IKEA, which has sold 32 million Billy bookcases since 1978, now carries its contemporary designs in 226 stores in Europe, Asia, the United States, and Australia and uses suppliers from around the world.

Maybe—just maybe—the world *is* flattening! And students reading these words must prepare themselves for future jobs on this leveled playing field.

For what "flattening the world" means to IKEA and other global marketers, see the text and the Marketing Matters box.

Price and the Global Marketplace

To generate profits in today's global marketplace, international firms look around the world to find both new markets to increase revenues and suppliers whose efficiencies and lower hourly wages can reduce the prices the buying firms must pay. The Marketing Matters box describes how the "world is flattening," or how the global "playing field is being leveled," as the chief executive officer of India's Infosys Technologies, Ltd., says.[9]

IKEA, the huge Swedish retailer, understands this. It is *both* opening new stores *and* contracting with furniture manufacturers around the world. To compete in China, IKEA has slashed prices to appeal to consumers in the country's growing middle class. The strategy seems to be working: IKEA's new store in Beijing—opened in 2006—has floor space the size of eight football fields and forecasts 6 million visitors annually.

Price as an Indicator of Value

From a consumer's standpoint, price is often used to indicate value when it is compared with the perceived benefits such as quality, durability, and so

For how a McDonald's "Extra Value Meal" is an example of applying a "value pricing" strategy, see the text.

on of a product or service. Specifically, **value** is the ratio of perceived benefits to price, or[10]

$$\text{Value} = \frac{\text{Perceived benefits}}{\text{Price}}$$

This relationship shows that for a given price, as perceived benefits increase, value increases. For example, if you're used to paying $9.99 for a medium pizza, wouldn't a large pizza at the same price be more valuable? Conversely, for a given price, value decreases when perceived benefits decrease.

Creative marketers engage in **value-pricing**, the practice of simultaneously increasing product and service benefits while maintaining or decreasing price. For some products, price influences consumers' perception of overall quality and ultimately its value to consumers.[11] In a survey of home furnishing buyers, 84 percent agreed with the statement: "The higher the price, the higher the quality."[12] For example, Kohler introduced a walk-in bathtub that is safer for children and the elderly. Although priced higher than conventional step-in bathtubs, it has proven very successful because buyers are willing to pay more for what they perceive as the value of the extra safety.

Here "value" involves the judgment by a consumer of the worth and desirability of a product or service relative to substitutes that satisfy the same need. In this instance a "reference value" emerges, which involves comparing the costs and benefits of substitute items. The value of "supersizing" at fast-food restaurants comes from getting "more bang for your buck"—generally, a larger quantity for the same or a lower price. For example, if you order an "Extra Value Meal" at McDonald's, the price you pay is less than if you bought each item in the meal separately.

Price in the Marketing Mix

Pricing is a critical decision made by a marketing executive because price has a direct effect on a firm's profits. This is apparent from a firm's **profit equation**:

$$\begin{aligned}\text{Profit} &= \text{Total revenue} - \text{Total cost}\\ &= (\text{Unit price} \times \text{Quantity sold}) - (\text{Fixed cost} + \text{Variable cost})\end{aligned}$$

What makes this relationship even more complicated is that price affects the quantity sold, as illustrated with demand curves later in this chapter. Furthermore, since the quantity sold usually affects a firm's costs because of efficiency of production, price also indirectly affects costs. Thus, pricing decisions influence both total revenue (sales) and total cost, which makes pricing one of the most important decisions marketing executives face.

The importance of price in the marketing mix necessitates an understanding of six major steps in the process organizations go through in setting prices (see Figure 13–2 on the next page):

1. Identify pricing objectives and constraints.
2. Estimate demand and revenue.
3. Determine cost, volume, and profit relationships.

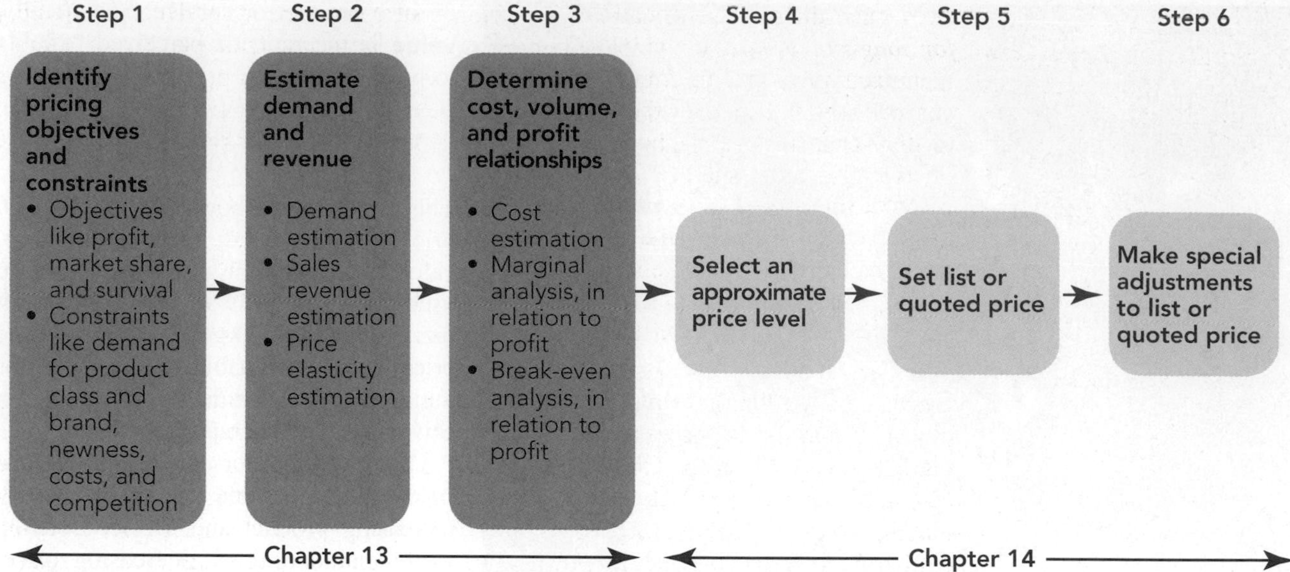

FIGURE 13–2
The six steps in setting price. The first three steps are covered in this chapter and the last three steps in Chapter 14.

4. Select an approximate price level.
5. Set list or quoted price.
6. Make special adjustments to list or quoted price.

The first three steps are covered in this chapter and the last three in Chapter 14.

learning review

1. What is price?
2. What factors impact the list price to determine the final price?

STEP 1: IDENTIFY PRICING OBJECTIVES AND CONSTRAINTS

With such a variety of alternative pricing strategies available, a marketing manager must consider the pricing objectives and constraints that will narrow the range of choices. While pricing objectives frequently reflect corporate goals, pricing constraints often relate to conditions existing in the marketplace.

Identifying Pricing Objectives

LO2

Pricing objectives involve specifying the role of price in an organization's marketing and strategic plans. To the extent possible, these pricing objectives are carried to lower levels in the organization, such as in setting objectives for marketing managers responsible for an individual brand. These objectives may change depending on the financial position of the company as a whole, the success of its products, or the segments in which it is doing business. H. J. Heinz, for example, has specific pricing objectives for its Heinz Ketchup brand that vary by country. Chapter 2 discussed seven broad objectives that an organization may pursue, which tie in directly to the organization's pricing policies.

Profit Three different objectives relate to a firm's profit, which is often measured in terms of return on investment (ROI) or return on assets (ROA). These objec-

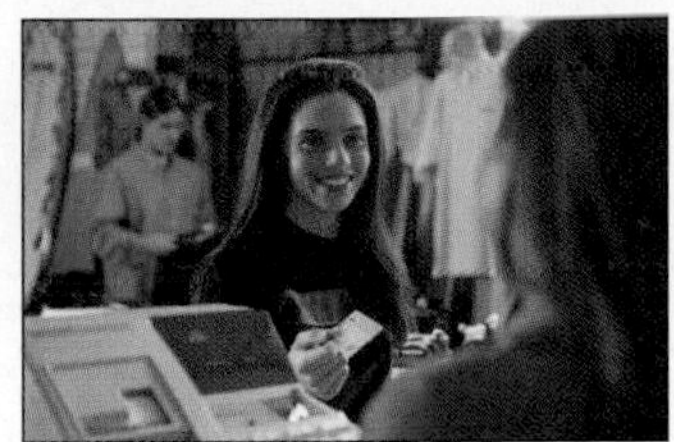

For how credit cards pose issues for both students and social responsibility, see the text and the Making Responsible Decisions box.

tives have different implications for pricing strategy. One objective is *managing for long-run profits*, in which companies—such as many Japanese car or TV set manufacturers—give up immediate profit by developing quality products to penetrate competitive markets over the long term. Products are priced relatively low compared to their cost to develop, but the firm expects to make greater profits later because of its high market share.

A *maximizing current profit* objective, such as for a quarter or year, is common in many firms because the targets can be set and performance measured quickly. American firms are sometimes criticized for this short-run orientation. As noted earlier, a *target return* objective occurs when a firm sets a profit goal (such as 20 percent for pretax ROI), usually determined by its board of directors.

Sales Given that a firm's profit is high enough for it to remain in business, an objective may be to increase sales revenue, which will in turn lead to increases in market share and profit. Objectives related to sales revenue or unit sales have the advantage of being translated more easily into meaningful targets for marketing managers responsible for a product line or brand than profit objectives. However, cutting price on one product in a firm's line may increase its sales revenue but reduce those of related products.

Market Share Market share is the ratio of the firm's sales revenues or unit sales to those of the industry (competitors plus the firm itself). Companies often pursue a market share objective when industry sales are relatively flat or declining. In the late 1990s, Boeing cut prices drastically to try to maintain its 60 percent market share and encountered huge losses. Although increased market share is a primary goal of some firms, others see it as a means to other ends: increasing sales and profits.

Unit Volume Many firms use *unit volume*, the quantity produced or sold, as a pricing objective. These firms often sell multiple products at very different prices and need to match the unit volume demanded by customers with price and production capacity. Using unit volume as an objective can be counterproductive if a volume objective is achieved, say, by drastic price cutting that drives down profit.

Survival In some instances, profits, sales, and market share are less important objectives of the firm than mere survival. Specialty-toy retailers increasingly are facing survival problems because they can't match price cuts by big discount retailers like Wal-Mart and Target, the reason FAO Schwartz recently filed for bankruptcy.

Social Responsibility A firm may forgo higher profit on sales and follow a pricing objective that recognizes its obligations to customers and society in general. Medtronics followed this pricing policy when it introduced the world's first heart pacemaker. That monthly payment on your credit card seem a bit too high? Of course, and it's a painful question for many students using credit cards. So study the Making Responsible Decisions box on the next page to see the potential pitfalls students face using their credit cards—and how to try to avoid them. Also, think about the social responsibility repercussions credit card issuers face today.[13]

Identifying Pricing Constraints

Factors that limit the range of prices a firm may set are **pricing constraints**. Consumer demand for the product clearly affects the price that can be charged. Other constraints on price vary from factors within the organization to competitive factors outside the organization. Legal and regulatory constraints on pricing are discussed in Chapter 14.

Making Responsible Decisions > > social responsibility

Student Credit Cards—What Is the Real Price?

Thousands of American college students are drowning in credit card debt.

The picture is bleak. Only one in five college students pays off the credit card balance each month. In 2008 three-quarters of undergraduates owning credit cards had an average credit card debt of $2,169. And 10 percent of those graduating had more than $10,000 in credit card debt. Even scarier—the interest rate goes up for a missed monthly payment. One credit card holder made his payment one day late and saw his interest rate skyrocket from 9.99 to 29 percent.

The mathematics of credit card debt is frightening. Let's suppose that you've found a good interest rate and that at graduation your credit card company is charging 13 percent annual interest on your $2,000 balance. Paying this balance off at 2 percent a month will require 18 years and seven months of payments with $1,996.75 in interest—about the amount of the original balance!

In early 2009 these credit card problems got the attention of Congress and the President. So the "Credit Card Bill of Rights" was signed into law in May 2009. It introduces many features to protect consumers using credi cards. These include (1) restricting when credit card issuers can raise interest rates; (2) requiring them to give users greater disclosure of rates and also 45 days notice on interest rate, fee, and finance charge increases; and (3) banning interest charges on paid-off balances from previous billing cycles.

Using credit cards still requires a lot of common sense. Financial experts advise students using credit cards to:

- Pay off the balance monthly—and on time. Experts shout: Don't miss a payment!
- Find a card with a low interest rate, especially when *not* paying off the monthly balance. Compare credit card features you want at www.creditcards.com.
- Make purchases with cash whenever possible because that forces serious thinking that is skipped by bringing out that plastic card.

Also, Nellie Mae, the nation's leading educational lender, provides students with debt-management tools and help at www.nelliemae.com.

What should be done to help students address their credit card debt problems? Require them to take personal finance training? Restrict the number of cards they own? Lower the maximum credit line? What do you think?

Demand for the Product Class, Product, and Brand The number of potential buyers for the product class (cars), product (sports cars), and brand (Tesla Roadster Sport) clearly affects the price a seller can charge. So does whether the item is a luxury—like the Tesla—or a necessity—like bread and a roof over your head. Generally, the greater the demand for a product, the higher the price that can be set. For example, the New York Mets set different ticket prices for their games based on the appeal of their opponent—higher prices when they play the New York Yankees and lower ones when they play the Pittsburgh Pirates.[14]

The text describes factors that affect a product's price. And you can check eBay to see if those old Beanie Babies in your attic or a 2001 Ichiro Suzuki bobble-head doll have value.

Newness of the Product: Stage in the Product Life Cycle The newer a product and the earlier it is in its life cycle, the higher is the price that can usually be charged. Willing to spend up to $5,000 for a new high-definition (HD) Panasonic 65-inch plasma TV? The high initial price is possible because of patents and limited competition early in its product life cycle. By the time you read this, the price will probably be much lower.

Sometimes—when nostalgia or fad factors come into play—prices may rise later in the product's life cycle. Collectibles can experience skyrocketing prices, such as $260 for a Zip the Cat Beanie Baby (if it has black paws) or $305 for a 2001 Ichiro Suzuki bobble-head doll. But these prices can nosedive, too, when the fad wears off or a recession appears.[15]

Single Product versus a Product Line When Sony introduced its Walkman CD player, it was not only unique and in the introductory stage of its product life cycle but also the *only* portable CD player Sony sold. As a result, the firm had great latitude in setting a price. Now, with a wide range of Sony CD products and technologies, the price of individual models has to be consistent with the others based on features provided, and meaningful price differentials must communicate value to consumers.

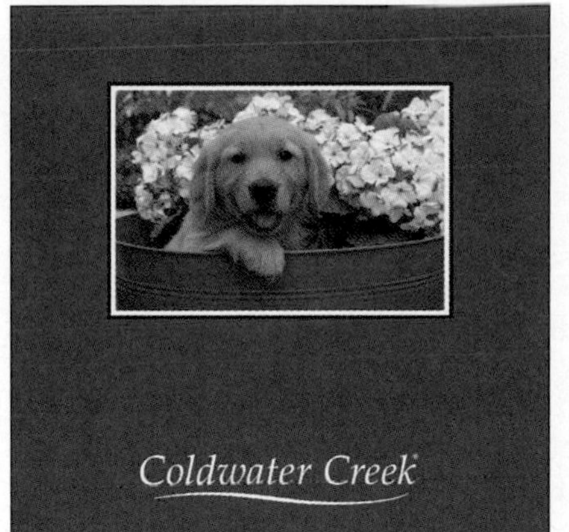

Setting hundreds of prices that will be valid for the life of a catalog involves many risky decisions.

Cost of Producing and Marketing the Product In the long run, a firm's price must cover all the costs of producing and marketing a product. If the price doesn't cover these costs, the firm will fail; so in the long run, a firm's costs set a floor under its price. In the 1990s, no-frills airlines such as Southwest, JetBlue, and AirTran set low airfares, forcing large competing U.S. airlines to cut costs and lower ticket prices. But times change. In 2009, the recession, fluctuating fuel prices, mothballed planes, and layoffs have caused turmoil in airline ticket pricing.[16]

Cost of Changing Prices and Time Period They Apply If Scandinavian Airlines asks General Electric (GE) to provide spare jet engines to power the new Boeing 737 it just bought, GE can easily set a new price for the engines to reflect its latest information since only one buyer has to be informed. But if Coldwater Creek decides that sweater prices are too low in its catalogs after thousands of catalogs have been mailed to customers, it has a big problem. It must consider the cost of changing prices and the time period for which they apply in developing the price list for its catalog items. A study of four supermarket chains found the average annual cost of these price changes was $105,887, which represents 0.70 percent of revenues and an astounding 35.2 percent of net margins.[17] In actual practice, research indicates that most firms change the prices of their major products once a year. But on a Web site, prices can change from minute to minute.[18]

Type of Competitive Market The seller's price is constrained by the type of market in which it competes. Economists generally delineate four types of competitive markets. From most competitive to least competitive, these are pure competition, monopolistic competition, oligopoly, and pure monopoly. Figure 13–3 shows that the type of competition dramatically influences the range of price competition and, in turn, the nature of product differentiation and extent of advertising. A firm must recognize the general type of competitive market it is in to understand the range of

FIGURE 13–3
Pricing, product, and advertising strategies available to firms in four types of competitive markets

TYPE OF COMPETITIVE MARKET

STRATEGIES AVAILABLE	PURE COMPETITION (Many sellers who follow the market price for identical, commodity products)	MONOPOLISTIC COMPETITION (Many sellers who compete on nonprice factors)	OLIGOPOLY (Few sellers who are sensitive to each other's prices)	PURE MONOPOLY (One seller who sets the price for a unique product)
Extent of price competition	Almost none: market sets price	Some: compete over range of prices	Some: price leader or follower of competitors	None: sole seller sets price
Extent of product differentiation	None: products are identical	Some: differentiate products from competitors	Various: depends on industry	None: no other producers
Extent of advertising	Little: purpose is to inform prospects that seller's products are available	Much: purpose is to differentiate firm's products from competitors	Some: purpose is to inform but avoid price competition	Little: purpose is to increase demand for product class

both its price and nonprice strategies. Examples of how prices can be affected by the four competitive situations follow:

- *Pure competition.* Hundreds of local grain elevators sell corn whose price per bushel is set by the marketplace. Within strains, the corn is identical, so advertising only informs buyers that the seller's corn is available.
- *Monopolistic competition.* Dozens of regional, private brands of peanut butter compete with national brands like Skippy and Jif. Both price competition (regional, private brands being lower than national brands) and nonprice competition (product features and advertising) exist.
- *Oligopoly.* The few sellers of aluminum (Reynolds, Alcoa) or large jetliners (Boeing, Airbus) try to avoid price competition because it can lead to disastrous price wars in which all lose money. Yet firms in such industries stay aware of a competitor's price cuts or increases and may follow suit. The products can be undifferentiated (aluminum) or differentiated (large jetliners), and informative advertising that avoids head-to-head price competition is used.[19] In video games the Microsoft Xbox 360's oligopolistic competition with Sony and Nintendo is so severe that it was losing $126 on every unit sold at its $399 introductory price.[20]
- *Pure monopoly.* In 1994, Johnson & Johnson (J&J) revolutionized the treatment of coronary heart diseases by introducing the stent—a tiny mesh tube "spring" that props open clogged arteries. Initially a monopoly, J&J stuck with its early $1,595 price and achieved $1 billion in sales and 91 percent market share by the end of 1996. But its reluctance to give price reductions for large-volume purchases to hospitals antagonized them. When competitors like Medtronic introduced an improved stent at lower prices, J&J's market share plummeted to 8 percent two years later.[21]

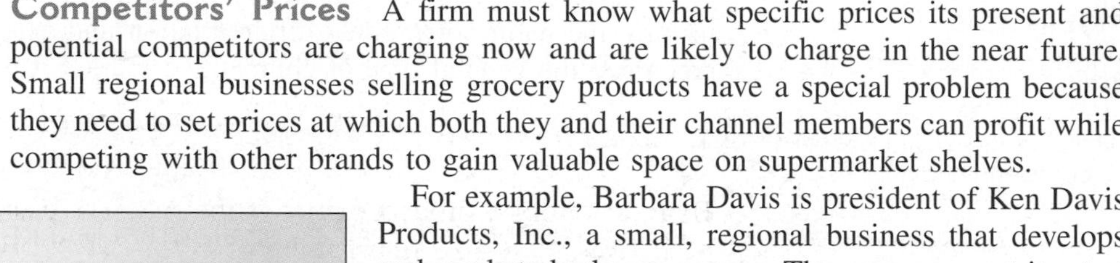

For some of the pricing challenges of a regional small business, see the Marketing Matters box and text.

Competitors' Prices A firm must know what specific prices its present and potential competitors are charging now and are likely to charge in the near future. Small regional businesses selling grocery products have a special problem because they need to set prices at which both they and their channel members can profit while competing with other brands to gain valuable space on supermarket shelves.

For example, Barbara Davis is president of Ken Davis Products, Inc., a small, regional business that develops and markets barbecue sauces. The company got its start when Ken Davis, Barbara's late husband, used his grandmother's recipe for barbecue sauce in his restaurant. Customers loved the sauce, even though it was "a little of this and that" and different every time. So Barbara Davis, a home economist experienced in corporate test kitchens, standardized the original sauce recipe that launched the company. It now competes with national brands like Kraft and Heinz and other regional brands. The Marketing Matters box describes how Barbara Davis keeps an eye on competitors' prices to help set those for her company's barbecue sauces.[22]

learning review

3. What is the difference between pricing objectives and pricing constraints?
4. How does the type of competitive market a firm is in affect its range in setting price?

Marketing Matters > > > > > entrepreneurship

A Small Business Challenge: Finding the Right Prices for Regional Barbecue Sauces

"We position Ken Davis® Bar-B-Q-Sauce not just as something you use for grilling, but as something that adds flavor to ordinary food—a spice kit in a jar," explains Barbara Davis, president of Ken Davis Products, Inc. (shown in photo).

Compared with other condiments, barbecue sauce is a highly regional business due to consumer taste preferences. For example, sweet, smoky, "tomato-y" sauces are preferred in the Midwest, while in other parts of the country people like vinegar-based, mustard-based, or hot and spicy sauces. Each area typically has market leaders that are local or regional brands, not one of the national giants, and they compete directly with each other.

To enable Ken Davis Bar-B-Q-Sauce to remain a regional market leader, Barbara Davis spends time in her test kitchen to develop new recipes that use the sauce as an ingredient. The recipes are published on its Web site: www.kendavis-bbq.com.

A special challenge for Barbara Davis is to achieve retail prices and shelf space that allow the company to compete with other regional favorites and protect her company's profit margins. Barbecue sauces are categorized in the marketplace by price—regular, premium, and super premium. Typical prices consumers see on supermarket shelves, and their retail margins for 18- or 19-ounce bottles include:

- Kraft (regular)—$2.29; 12 to 15 percent margin.
- Ken Davis (premium)—$2.99; 18 to 20 percent margin.
- Daddy Sam's (super premium)—$5.99; over 20 percent margin.

The company has succeeded in this fiercely competitive business first by creating a niche market—premium barbecue sauce—and second by offering high quality at competitive prices within that niche. While it is important to cover all the company's expenses with the pricing, it is just as important to keep on a par with the major competitors' prices.

STEP 2: ESTIMATE DEMAND AND REVENUE

LO3

Basic to setting a product's price is the extent of customer demand for it. Marketing executives must also translate this estimate of customer demand into estimates of revenues the firm expects to receive.

Fundamentals of Estimating Demand

The text describes a creative pricing experiment of *Newsweek* magazine.

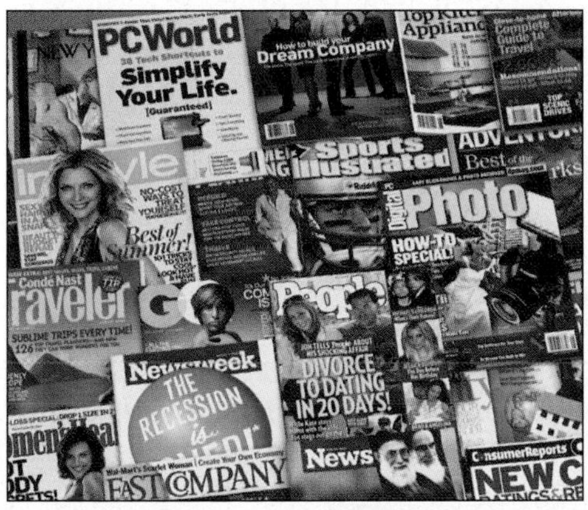

How much money would you pay for your favorite magazine? If the price kept going up, at some point you would probably quit buying it. Conversely, if the price kept going down, you might eventually decide not only to keep buying your magazine but also to get your friend a subscription too. The lower the price, the higher the demand. The publisher wants to sell more magazines, but will it sell enough additional copies to make up for the lower price per copy? Here's how one firm decided to find out.

Newsweek conducted a pricing experiment at newsstands in 11 cities throughout the United States. At that time, Houston newsstand buyers paid $2.25 per copy, while in Fort Worth, New York, Los Angeles, and Atlanta they paid the regular $2.00 price. In San Diego, the price was $1.50, while in Detroit it was only $1.00. By comparison, the regular newsstand price for *Time* and *U.S. News & World Report*, *Newsweek*'s competitors, was $1.95. Why did *Newsweek* conduct the experiment? According to a *Newsweek* executive, "We want to figure out what the demand curve for our magazine at the newsstand is."[23]

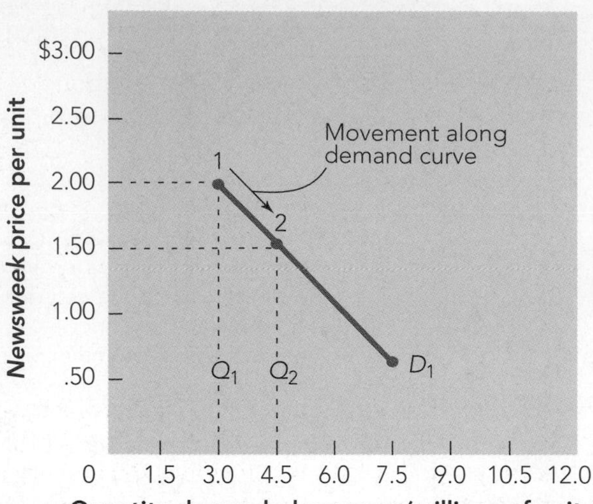

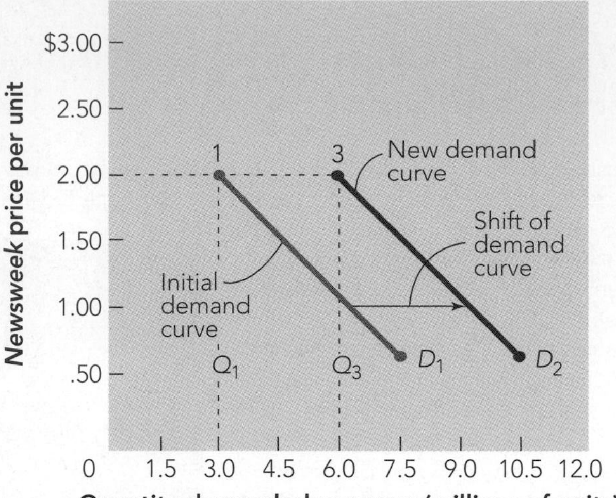

FIGURE 13–4

Demand curves for *Newsweek* showing the effect on annual sales (quantity demanded per year) by a change in price caused by (A) a movement along the demand curve and (B) a shift of the demand curve.

The Demand Curve A **demand curve** is a graph relating the quantity sold and price, which shows the maximum number of units that will be sold at a given price. Demand curve D_1 in Figure 13–4A shows the newsstand demand for *Newsweek* under the existing conditions. Note that as price falls, more people decide to buy and unit sales increase. But price is not the complete story in estimating demand. Economists emphasize three other key factors:

1. *Consumer tastes.* As we saw in Chapter 3, these depend on many factors such as demographics, culture, and technology. Because consumer tastes can change quickly, up-to-date marketing research is essential to estimate demand.
2. *Price and availability of similar products.* The laws of demand work for one's competitors, too. If the price of *Time* magazine falls, more people will buy it. That then means fewer people will buy *Newsweek. Time* is considered by economists to be a substitute for *Newsweek.* Online magazines are also a substitute, one whose availability has increased tremendously in recent years. The point to remember is, as the price of substitutes falls or their availability increases, the demand for a product (*Newsweek*, in this case) will fall.
3. *Consumer income.* In general, as real consumer income (allowing for inflation) increases, demand for a product also increases.

The first two factors influence what consumers *want* to buy, and the third affects what they *can* buy. Along with price, these are often called **demand factors**, or factors that determine consumers' willingness and ability to pay for products and services. As discussed in Chapters 8 and 10, it is often very difficult to estimate demand for new products, especially because consumer likes and dislikes are often so difficult to read clearly. For example, Campbell Soup spent seven years and $55 million on a super secret project to produce a line of Intelligent Quisine (IQ) food products "scientifically proven to lower high levels of cholesterol, blood sugar, and blood pressure." After 15 months in an Ohio test market, Campbell Soup yanked the entire IQ line because customers found the line too pricey and lacking in variety.[24]

Movement Along versus Shift of a Demand Curve Demand curve D_1 in Figure 13–4A shows that as the price of *Newsweek* is lowered from $2.00 (point 1) to $1.50 (point 2) an issue, the quantity demanded increases from 3.0 million (Q_1) to 4.5 million (Q_2) units per year. This is an example of a *movement along a demand curve* and assumes that other factors (consumer tastes, price and availability of substitutes, and consumer income) remain unchanged.

What if some of these factors do change? For example, if advertising causes more people to want *Newsweek*, newsstand demand is increased; or if consumer incomes rise, then the demand for all magazines, including *Newsweek*, increases. Now the initial demand curve, D_1 (the blue line in Figure 13–4B), no longer represents the newsstand demand; instead, a new curve, D_2, must be drawn. D_2 (the red line in Figure 13–4B) represents the new demand for *Newsweek*. Economists call this a *shift in the demand curve*—in this case, a shift to the right from D_1 to D_2. This increased demand means that more *Newsweek* magazines are wanted for a given price: At a price of $2.00 (point 3), the demand is 6 million units per year (Q_3) on D_2 rather than 3 million units per year (Q_1) on D_1.

Fundamentals of Estimating Revenue

While economists may talk about "demand curves," marketing executives are more likely to speak in terms of "revenues generated," which are the monies received by the firm for selling its products. Demand curves lead directly to three related revenue concepts critical to pricing decisions: **total revenue (TR)**, **average revenue (AR)**, and **marginal revenue (MR)** (Figure 13–5).

Demand Curves and Revenue Figure 13–6A on the next page again shows the demand curve for *Newsweek*, but it is now extended to intersect both the price and quantity axes. The demand curve shows that as price is changed, the quantity of *Newsweek* magazines sold throughout the United States changes. This relationship holds whether the price is increased from $2.50 to $3.00 on the demand curve or is reduced from $1 to $0 on the curve. In the former case the market demands no *Newsweek* magazines, whereas in the latter case 9 million could be given away at $0 per unit.

It is likely that if *Newsweek* was given away, more than 9 million would be demanded. This fact illustrates two important points. First, it can be dangerous to extend a demand curve beyond the range of prices for which it really applies. Second, most demand curves are rounded (or convex) to the origin, thereby avoiding an unrealistic picture of what demand looks like when a straight-line curve intersects either the price axis or the quantity axis.

FIGURE 13–5
Fundamental concepts about "revenues," which are the monies received from selling the product: Total revenue, average revenue, and marginal revenue

Total revenue (TR) is the total money received from the sale of a product. If

TR = Total revenue
P = Unit price of the product
Q = Quantity of the product sold

Then:

$$TR = P \times Q$$

Average revenue (AR) is the average amount of money received for selling one unit of a product, or simply the price of that unit. Average revenue is the total revenue divided by the quantity sold:

$$AR = \frac{TR}{Q} = P$$

Marginal revenue (MR) is the change in total revenue that results from producing and marketing one additional unit of a product:

$$MR = \frac{\text{Change in TR}}{\text{1 unit increase in Q}} = \frac{\Delta TR}{\Delta Q} = \text{slope of TR curve}$$

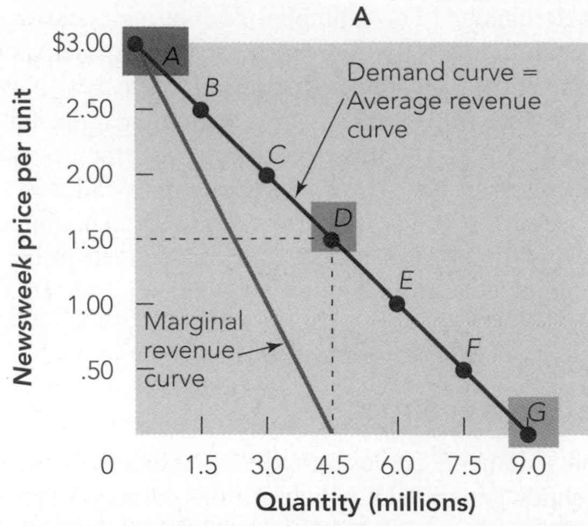

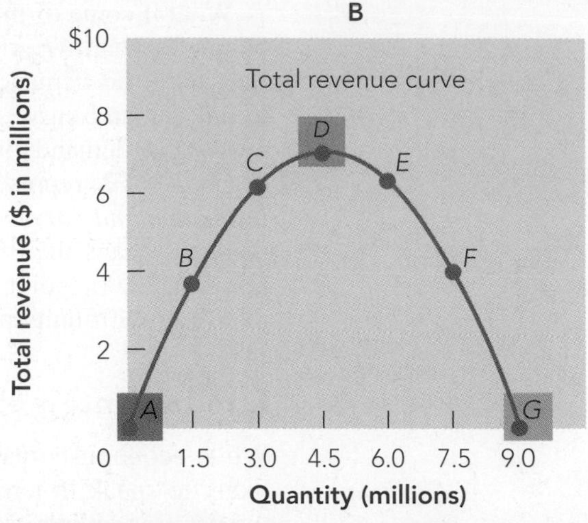

Point on Demand Curve	Price (P)	Quantity Sold (Q)	Total Revenue (P × Q)	Average Revenue (TR/Q = P)	Marginal Revenue (ΔTR/ΔQ)
A	$3.00	0	$0	$3.00	$3.00
B	2.50	1,500,000	3,750,000	2.50	2.00
C	2.00	3,000,000	6,000,000	2.00	1.00
D	1.50	4,500,000	6,750,000	1.50	0
E	1.00	6,000,000	6,000,000	1.00	−1.00*
F	.50	7,500,000	3,750,000	.50	−2.00*
G	0	9,000,000	0	0	−3.00*

*Not shown in Figure 13–6A. (Note that the marginal revenue (MR) curve in Figure 13–6A is the slope of the total revenue curve in Figure 13–6B.)

FIGURE 13–6
How *Newsweek's* downward-sloping demand curve affects its total, average, and marginal revenues

Figure 13–6B shows the total revenue curve for *Newsweek* calculated from the demand curve shown in Figure 13–6A. The total revenue curve is developed by simply multiplying the unit price times the quantity for each of the points on the demand curve. Total revenue starts at $0 (point *A*), reaches a maximum of $6,750,000 at point *D*, and returns to $0 at point *G*. This shows that as price is reduced in the *A*-to-*D* segment of the curve, total revenue is increased. However, cutting price in the *D*-to-*G* segment results in a decline in total revenue.

Marginal revenue, which is the slope of the total revenue curve, is positive but decreasing when the price lies in the range from $3 to above $1.50 per unit. Below $1.50 per unit, though, marginal revenue is actually negative, so the extra quantity of magazines sold is more than offset by the decrease in the price per unit.

For any downward-sloping, straight-line demand curve, the marginal revenue curve always falls at a rate twice as fast as the demand curve. As shown in Figure 13–6A, the marginal revenue becomes $0 per unit at a quantity sold of 4.5 million units—the very point at which total revenue is maximum (see Figure 13–6B). A rational marketing manager would never operate in the region of the demand curve in which marginal revenue is negative. This means that in Figure 13–6A this manager would set prices only in the *A*-to-*D* segment of the demand curve. Also, when market share falls, the easy answer is to cut price, often with devastating results: A 1 percent price cut in the food and drug industry results in a 24 percent decline in profits, other factors being equal.[25]

What price did *Newsweek* select after conducting its experiment? It kept the price at $2.00 per copy. However, through expanded newsstand distribution and more aggressive advertising, *Newsweek* was later able to shift its demand curve to the right and charge a price of $2.50 without affecting its newsstand volume.

LO4

Price Elasticity of Demand With a downward-sloping demand curve, marketing managers are especially interested in how sensitive consumer demand and the firm's revenues are to changes in the product's price. This can be conveniently measured by **price elasticity of demand**, or the percentage change in quantity demanded relative to a percentage change in price. Price elasticity of demand (E) is expressed as follows:

$$\text{Price elasticity of demand} = \text{E} = \frac{\text{Percentage change in quantity demanded}}{\text{Percentage change in price}}$$

Because quantity demanded usually decreases as price increases, price elasticity of demand is usually a negative number. However, for the sake of simplicity and by convention, elasticity figures are shown as positive numbers. Finally, price elasticity of demand assumes three forms: elastic demand, inelastic demand, and unitary demand.

Elastic demand exists when a 1 percent decrease in price produces more than a 1 percent increase in quantity demanded, thereby actually increasing sales revenue. This results in a price elasticity that is greater than 1 with elastic demand. In other words, a product with elastic demand is one in which a slight decrease in price results in a relatively large increase in demand or units sold. The reverse is also true; with elastic demand, a slight increase in price results in a relatively large decrease in demand. So marketers may cut price to increase consumer demand, the units sold, and total revenue for one of these products, depending on what competitors' prices are.

Inelastic demand exists when a 1 percent decrease in price produces less than a 1 percent increase in quantity demanded, thereby actually decreasing sales revenue. This results in a price elasticity that is less than 1 with inelastic demand. So a product with inelastic demand means that slight increases or decreases in price will not significantly affect the demand, or units sold, for the product. The concern for marketers is that while lowering price will increase the quantity sold, revenues will actually fall. *Unitary demand* exists when the percentage change in price is identical to the percentage change in quantity demanded so that sales revenue remains the same. In this instance, price elasticity is equal to 1.

Price elasticity is important to marketing managers because of its relationship to total revenue, so it is important that marketing managers recognize that price elasticity of demand is not the same over all possible prices of a product. Figure 13–6B illustrates this point using the *Newsweek* demand curve shown in Figure 13–6A. As the price decreases from $2.50 to $2.00 per copy, total revenue increases, indicating an elastic demand. However, when the price decreases from $1.00 to 50 cents, total revenue declines, indicating an inelastic demand. Unitary demand elasticity exists at a price of $1.50 per copy.

Decisions Involving Price Elasticity Price elasticity of demand is determined by a number of factors. First, the more substitutes a product or service has, the more likely it is to be price elastic. For example, a new sweater, shirt, or blouse has many possible substitutes and is price elastic, but gasoline has almost no substitutes and is price inelastic. In fact, with the American love affair with cars and driving, we are surprisingly insensitive to a price increase in gasoline: A recent study showed a 10 percent increase in price results in only a 0.6 percent decrease in gasoline consumption.[26]

Fast-forward to today: Price sensitivity is especially critical for *Newsweek* and other consumer magazines because of the recession and fewer pages of ads. Figure 13–7 on the next page shows that in the last half of 2008 subscribers paid an average of 47 cents for an issue of *Newsweek*, far below the newsstand price of $4.95 and barely covering mailing costs. *Newsweek* executives look at the higher subscription and newsstand prices for *The Economist* magazine, a major competitor. Then they ask themselves again about price elasticity and whether raising prices might not make sense. Their decision? Look at your local newsstand![27]

Second, products and services considered to be necessities are price inelastic, so open-heart surgery is price inelastic, whereas airline tickets for a vacation are price

FIGURE 13–7
A continuing question for *Newsweek* executives: Should we raise subscription and newsstand prices? The data here and the earlier text discussion about price elasticity of demand show their pricing dilemma.

elastic. Toothpaste is an example of a consumer product with inelastic demand. So even in the current recession, Procter & Gamble's Crest and Colgate's Total toothpastes often show price *increases* on shelves of retailers.[28]

Third, items that require a large cash outlay compared with a person's disposable income are price elastic. Accordingly, cars and yachts are price elastic; soft drinks tend to be price inelastic.

Because 12- to 17-year-olds often have limited spending money, this group is very price elastic in its demand for cigarettes. As a result, many legislators recommend far higher excise taxes on cigarettes to increase their prices significantly with the goal of reducing teenage smoking. In April 2009, the federal cigarette tax more than doubled to $1.01 per pack. So in New York City, which has the highest combined state and local tax in the United States, a box of Marlboro Light Kings costs over $10 at many stores. The result of high prices for cigarettes in New York: High school smoking hit a new low of 13.8 percent, far below the national average.[29] Price elasticity is not only a relevant concept for marketing managers but is also important for public policy affecting pricing practices.

learning review

5. What is the difference between a movement along and a shift of a demand curve?
6. What is total revenue and how is it calculated?
7. What does it mean if a product has a price elasticity of demand that is greater than 1?

STEP 3: DETERMINE COST, VOLUME, AND PROFIT RELATIONSHIPS

While revenues are the monies received by the firm from selling its products or services to customers, costs or expenses are the monies the firm pays out to its employees and suppliers. Marketing managers often use marginal analysis and break-even analysis to relate revenues and costs, topics covered in this section.

Marketing Matters > > > > > entrepreneurship

Pricing Lessons from Failed Dot-Com Start-ups—Understand Revenues and Expenses

Price, revenue, fixed cost, variable cost. Boring topics from finance or economics? But they are also critical to marketing success.

Everyone Deserves a Second Chance, BarNone

Dot-Com Failures

During the past decade, hundreds of dot-com start-ups have failed, many of them brick-and-mortar businesses like Pets.com (pet products) and Webvan (online groceries). Here are some reasons for these failures:

- Setting prices too low to cover the huge fixed costs of inventory, warehouses, and order fulfillment, especially on low-margin goods like groceries (Webvan).
- Spending too much on promotion, such as Pets.com's $2.2 million on Super Bowl XXXV ads.
- Believing people would forgo shopping at traditional stores, a problem encountered by Pets.com competing with PetSmart and Petco.

As a result, Pets.com was liquidated. However, the Pets.com sock puppet, because of its visibility, was bought by and serves as the "spokespuppet" for BarNone, a firm that helps consumers with poor credit obtain automobiles.

Dot-Com Successes

Besides time and money savings for customers, the travel dot-coms like Orbitz or Travelocity have special strategies for success:

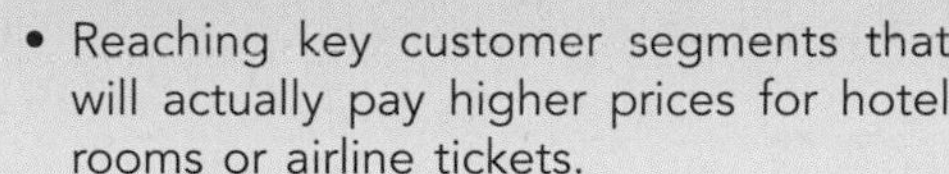

- Reaching key customer segments that will actually pay higher prices for hotel rooms or airline tickets.
- Finding customer segments (students or senior citizens) whose last-minute or last-week flexibility enables them to reserve hotel rooms or airline seats that would otherwise go unsold.
- Being able to conduct almost all operations electronically, without the warehousing and order fulfillment problems of their failed dot-com cousins.

Still, travel dot-coms face major uncertainties, such as higher airline ticket prices and reduced number of flights. Also very significant is the fluctuation in demand for airline tickets due to the state of the U.S. economy and terrorism concerns.

The Importance of Controlling Costs

Understanding the role and behavior of costs is critical for all marketing decisions, particularly pricing decisions. Five cost concepts are important in pricing decisions: **total cost (TC)**, **fixed cost (FC)**, **variable cost (VC)**, **unit variable cost (UVC)**, and **marginal cost (MC)** (see Figure 13–8 on the next page).

Many firms go bankrupt because their costs get out of control, causing their total costs to exceed their total revenues over an extended period. This is why sophisticated marketing managers make pricing decisions that balance both their revenues and costs. Out-of-control manufacturing costs compared to foreign car companies is the exact problem General Motors, Ford, and Chrysler face. This has caused the government to invest billions of dollars in them, hoping that restructuring will make them cost competitive.

As described in the Marketing Matters box, travel dot-com firms have often been more successful than others, at least partly because of far lower fixed costs.[30]

Marginal Analysis and Profit Maximization

LO5

A basic idea in business, economics, and indeed everyday life is **marginal analysis**, which is a continuing, concise trade-off of incremental costs against incremental revenues. In personal terms, marginal analysis means that people will continue to do something as long as the incremental return exceeds the incremental cost. This same idea holds true in marketing and pricing decisions. In this setting, marginal analysis means that as long as revenue received from the sale of an additional product

FIGURE 13–8
Fundamental concepts about "costs," which are the monies the firm pays out to its employees and suppliers: Total cost, fixed cost, variable cost, unit variable cost, and marginal cost

Total cost (TC) is the total expense incurred by a firm in producing and marketing a product. Total cost is the sum of fixed cost and variable cost.

Fixed cost (FC) is the sum of the expenses of the firm that are stable and do not change with the quantity of a product that is produced and sold. Examples of fixed costs are rent on the building, executive salaries, and insurance.

Variable cost (VC) is the sum of the expenses of the firm that vary directly with the quantity of a product that is produced and sold. For example, as the quantity sold doubles, the variable cost doubles. Examples are the direct labor and direct materials used in producing the product and the sales commissions that are tied directly to the quantity sold. As mentioned above:

$$TC = FC + VC$$

Unit variable cost (UVC) is variable cost expressed on a per unit basis for a product:

$$UVC = \frac{VC}{Q}$$

Marginal cost (MC) is the change in total cost that results from producing and marketing one additional unit of a product:

$$MC = \frac{\text{Change in TC}}{\text{1 unit increase in Q}} = \frac{\Delta TC}{\Delta Q} = \text{slope of TC curve}$$

(marginal revenue) is greater than the additional cost of producing and selling it (marginal cost), a firm will expand its output of that product.

Break-Even Analysis

LO6

Marketing managers often employ an approach that considers cost, volume, and profit relationships based on the profit equation. **Break-even analysis** is a technique that analyzes the relationship between total revenue and total cost to determine profitability at various levels of output. The **break-even point (BEP)** is the quantity at which total revenue and total cost are equal. Profit then comes from all units sold beyond the BEP. In terms of the definitions in Figure 13–8,

$$BEP_{\text{Quantity}} = \frac{\text{Fixed cost}}{\text{Unit price} - \text{Unit variable cost}} = \frac{FC}{P - UVC}$$

Calculating a Break-Even Point Consider a picture frame store. Suppose you wish to identify how many pictures you must sell to cover your fixed cost at a given price. Let's assume demand for your framed pictures is strong so the average price customers are willing to pay for each picture is $120. Also, suppose your fixed cost (FC) is $32,000 (for real estate taxes, interest on a bank loan, and other fixed expenses) and unit variable cost (UVC) for a picture is now $40 (for labor, glass, frame, and matting). Your break-even quantity (BEP_{Quantity}) is 400 pictures, as follows:

$$BEP_{\text{Quantity}} = \frac{\text{Fixed cost}}{\text{Unit price} - \text{Unit variable cost}} = \frac{FC}{P - UVC}$$
$$= \frac{\$32{,}000}{\$120 - \$40}$$
$$= 400 \text{ pictures}$$

Marginal analysis is central to the concept of maximizing profits. In Figure 13–9A, marginal revenue and marginal cost are graphed. Marginal cost starts out high at lower quantity levels, decreases to a minimum through production and marketing

FIGURE 13–9
Profit is a maximum at the quantity at which marginal revenue and marginal cost are equal.

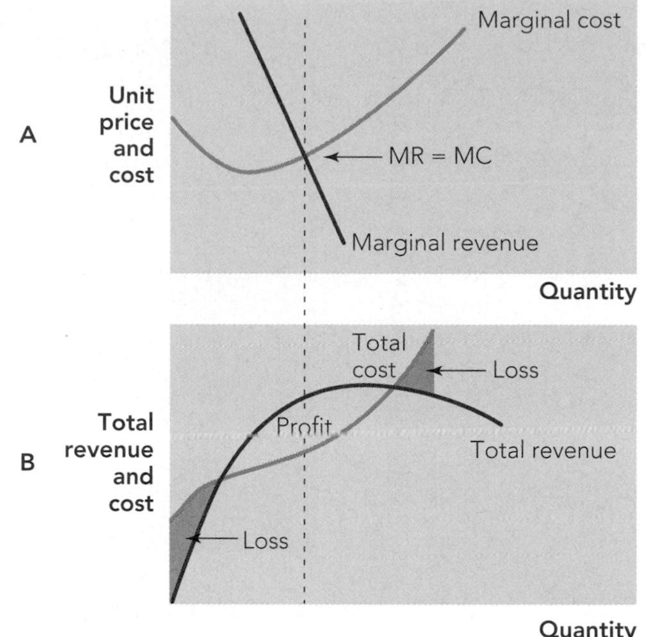

efficiencies, and then rises again due to the inefficiencies of overworked labor and equipment. Marginal revenue follows a downward slope. In Figure 13–9B, total cost and total revenue curves corresponding to the marginal cost and marginal revenue curves are graphed. Total cost initially rises as quantity increases but increases at the slowest rate at the quantity where marginal cost is lowest. The total revenue curve increases to a maximum and then starts to decline, as shown in Figure 13–9B.

The message of marginal analysis, then, is to operate up to the quantity and price level where marginal revenue equals marginal cost (MR = MC). Up to the output quantity at which MR = MC, each increase in total revenue resulting from selling one additional unit exceeds the increase in the total cost of producing and marketing that unit. Beyond the point at which MR = MC, however, the increase in total revenue from selling one more unit is less than the cost of producing and marketing that unit. At the quantity at which MR = MC, the total revenue curve lies farthest above the total cost curve because they are parallel, and profit is a maximum.

The row shaded in orange in Figure 13–10 shows that your break-even quantity at a price of $120 per picture is 400 pictures. At less than 400 pictures, your picture frame store incurs a loss, and at more than 400 pictures it makes a profit. Figure

FIGURE 13–10
Calculating a break-even point for the picture frame store in the text example shows its profit starts at 400 framed pictures per year.

Quantity of Pictures Sold (Q)	Price Per Picture (P)	Total Revenue (TR) = (P × Q)	Unit Variable Cost (UVC)	Total Variable Cost (VC) = (UVC × Q)	Fixed Cost (FC)	Total Cost (TC) = (FC + VC)	Profit = (TR – TC)
0	$120	$0	$40	$0	$32,000	$32,000	–$32,000
200	120	24,000	40	8,000	32,000	40,000	–16,000
400	120	48,000	40	16,000	32,000	48,000	0
600	120	72,000	40	24,000	32,000	56,000	16,000
800	120	96,000	40	32,000	32,000	64,000	32,000
1,000	120	120,000	40	40,000	32,000	72,000	48,000
1,200	120	144,000	40	48,000	32,000	80,000	64,000

FIGURE 13–11
Break-even analysis chart for a picture store shows the break-even point at 400 pictures.

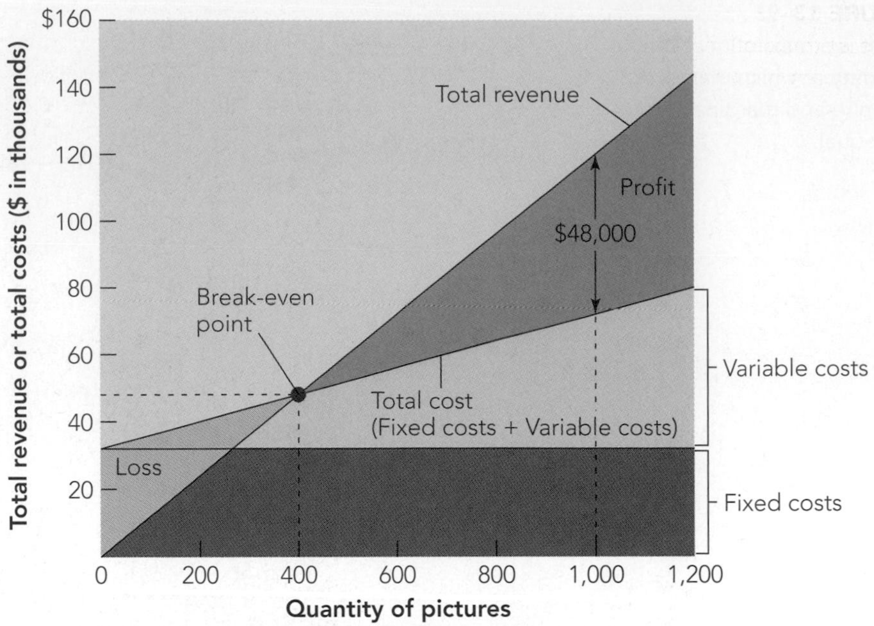

13–10 also shows that if you could increase your annual picture sales to 1,000, your store would make a profit of $48,000—the row shaded in green in the figure.

Figure 13–11 shows a graphic presentation of the break-even analysis, called a **break-even chart**. It shows that total revenue and total cost intersect and are equal at a quantity of 400 pictures sold, which is the break-even point at which profit is exactly $0. You want to do better? If your frame store could increase the quantity sold annually to 1,000 pictures, the graph in Figure 13–11 shows you can earn an annual profit of $48,000, just as shown by the row shaded in green in Figure 13–10. Other financial aspects of a picture frame store appear in Appendix B.

Applications of Break-Even Analysis Because of its simplicity, break-even analysis is used extensively in marketing, most frequently to study the impact on profit of changes in price, fixed cost, and variable cost. The mechanics of break-even analysis are the basis of the widely used electronic spreadsheets offered by computer programs such as Microsoft Excel. These permit managers to answer hypothetical "what if" questions about the effect of changes in prices and costs on their profit.

The power of break-even analysis is shown in Figure 13–12. If an electronic calculator manufacturer automates its production, thereby increasing fixed cost and reducing variable cost by substituting machines for workers, this increases the break-even point from 333,333 to 500,000 units per year. Note in this example that only the fixed costs increase immediately. The manufacturer hopes these fixed costs will be offset in the longer run by reduced unit variable costs.

But what about the impact of the higher level of fixed costs on profit? Remember, profit at any output quantity is given by:

$$\text{Profit} = \text{Total revenue} - \text{Total cost}$$
$$= (P \times Q) - [FC + (UVC \times Q)]$$

Before automation, profit at 1 million units of sales is:

$$\text{Profit} = (P \times Q) - [FC = (UVC \times Q)]$$
$$= (\$10 \times 1{,}000{,}000) - [\$1{,}000{,}000 + (\$7 \times 1{,}000{,}000)]$$
$$= \$10{,}000{,}000 - \$8{,}000{,}000$$
$$= \$2{,}000{,}000$$

FIGURE 13–12
The cost trade-off: fixed versus variable costs

Executives in virtually every mass-production industry—from locomotives and cars to electronic calculators and breakfast cereals—are searching for ways to increase quality and reduce production costs to remain competitive in world markets. Increasingly they are substituting robots, automation, and computer-controlled manufacturing systems for blue- and white-collar workers.

To understand the implications of this on the break-even point (BEP) and profit, consider this example of an electronic calculator manufacturer such as Hewlett-Packard:

Before Automation	After Automation
P = \$10 per unit	P = \$10 per unit
FC = \$1,000,000	FC = \$4,000,000
UVC = \$7 per unit	UVC = \$2 per unit
$BEP_{Quantity} = \frac{FC}{P - UVC}$	$BEP_{Quantity} = \frac{FC}{P - UVC}$
$= \frac{\$1,000,000}{\$10 - \$7}$	$= \frac{\$4,000,000}{\$10 - \$2}$
= 333,333 units	= 500,000 units

The automation increases the fixed cost and increases the break-even quantity from 333,333 to 500,000 units per year. So if annual sales fall within this range, the calculator manufacturer will incur a loss with the automated plant, whereas it would have made a profit if it had not automated.

But what about its potential profit if it sells 1 million units a year? Look carefully at the two break-even charts below, and see the text to check your conclusions.

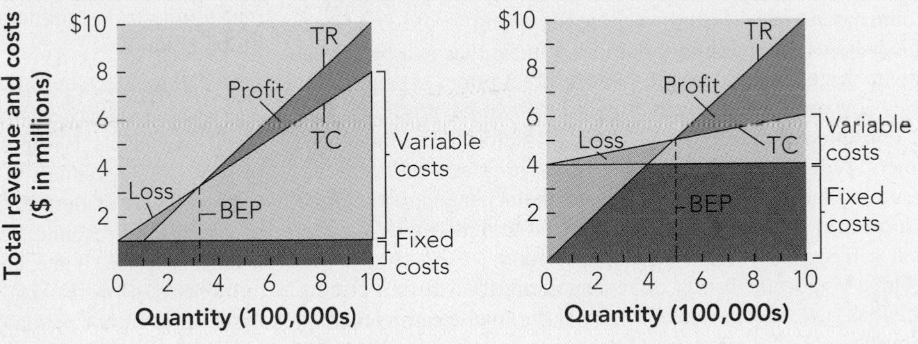

After automation, profit at 1 million units of sales is:

$$\text{Profit} = (P \times Q) - [FC + (UVC \times Q)]$$
$$= (\$10 \times 1,000,000) - [\$4,000,000 + (\$2 \times 1,000,000)]$$
$$= \$10,000,000 - \$6,000,000$$
$$= \$4,000,000$$

Automation, by adding to fixed costs, increases profit by \$2 million at 1 million units of sales. Thus, as the quantity sold increases for the automated plant, the potential increase in profit can be huge. This is shown by comparing the size of the two orange wedges in Figure 13–12 break-even charts before and after automation. So with large production and sales volumes, automated plants for Hewlett-Packard calculators produce large profits. Also, firms in other industries, such as airline, railroad, and hotel and motel industries, that require high fixed costs can reap large profits when they go even slightly beyond the break-even point.

learning review

8. What is the difference between fixed costs and variable costs?
9. What is a break-even point?

LEARNING OBJECTIVES REVIEW

LO1 *Identify the elements that make up a price.*
Price is the money or other considerations (such as barter) exchanged for the ownership or use of a good or service. Although price typically involves money, the amount exchanged is often different from the list or quoted price because of incentives (rebates, discounts, etc.), allowances (trade), and extra fees (finance charges, surcharges, etc.).

LO2 *Recognize the objectives a firm has in setting prices and the constraints that restrict the range of prices a firm can charge.*
Pricing objectives specify the role of price in a firm's marketing strategy and may include profit, sales revenue, market share, unit volume, survival, or some socially responsible price level. Pricing constraints that restrict a firm's pricing flexibility include demand, product newness, other products sold by the firm, production and marketing costs, cost of price changes, type of competitive market, and the prices of competitive substitutes.

LO3 *Explain what a demand curve is and the role of revenues in pricing decisions.*
A demand curve is a graph relating the quantity sold and price, which shows the maximum number of units that will be sold at a given price. Three demand factors affect price: (*a*) consumer tastes, (*b*) price and availability of substitute products, and (*c*) consumer income. These demand factors determine consumers' willingness and ability to pay for goods and services. Assuming these demand factors remain unchanged, if the price of a product is lowered or raised, then the quantity demanded for it will increase or decrease, respectively.

Three important forms of revenues impact a firm's pricing decisions: (*a*) total revenue, which is the total money received from the sale of a product; (*b*) average revenue, which is the average amount of money received for selling one unit of a product (which is simply the price of the unit); and (*c*) marginal revenue, which is the change in total revenue that results from producing and marketing one additional unit.

LO4 *Describe what price elasticity of demand means to a manager facing a pricing decision.*
Price elasticity of demand measures the responsiveness of units of a product sold to a change in price, which is expressed as the percentage change in the quantity of a product demanded divided by the percentage change in price. Price elasticity is important to marketing managers because a change in price usually has an important effect on the number of units of the product sold and on total revenue.

LO5 *Explain the role of costs in pricing decisions.*
Five important costs impact a firm's pricing decisions: (*a*) total cost, or total expenses, the sum of fixed cost and variable cost incurred by a firm in producing and marketing a product; (*b*) fixed cost, the sum of expenses of the firm that are stable and do not change with the quantity of a product that is produced and sold; (*c*) variable cost, the sum of expenses of the firm that vary directly with the quantity of a product that is produced and sold; (*d*) unit variable cost, variable cost expressed on a per unit basis; and (*e*) marginal cost, the change in total cost that results from producing and marketing one additional unit of the product.

LO6 *Describe how various combinations of price, fixed cost, and unit variable cost affect a firm's break-even point.*
Break-even analysis is a technique that analyzes the relationship between total revenue and total cost to determine profitability at various levels of output. The break-even point is the quantity at which total revenue and total cost are equal. Assuming no change in price, if the costs of a firm's product increase due to higher fixed costs (manufacturing or advertising) or variable costs (direct labor or materials), then its break-even point will be higher. And if total cost is unchanged, an increase in price will reduce the break-even point.

FOCUSING ON KEY TERMS

average revenue (AR) p. 331
barter p. 320
break-even analysis p. 336
break-even chart p. 338
break-even point (BEP) p. 336
demand curve p. 330
demand factors p. 330
fixed cost (FC) p. 335
marginal analysis p. 335
marginal cost (MC) p. 335
marginal revenue (MR) p. 331
price p. 320
price elasticity of demand p. 333
pricing constraints p. 325
pricing objectives p. 324
profit equation p. 323
total cost (TC) p. 335
total revenue (TR) p. 331
unit variable cost (UVC) p. 335
value p. 323
value-pricing p. 323
variable cost (VC) p. 335

APPLYING MARKETING KNOWLEDGE

1 How would the price equation apply to the purchase price of (*a*) gasoline, (*b*) an airline ticket, and (*c*) a checking account?

2 What would be your response to the statement, "Profit maximization is the only legitimate pricing objective for the firm"?

3 How is a downward-sloping demand curve related to total revenue and marginal revenue?

4 A marketing executive once said, "If the price elasticity of demand for your product is inelastic, then your price is probably too low." What is this executive saying in terms of the economic principles discussed in this chapter?

5 A marketing manager reduced the price on a brand of cereal by 10 percent and observed a 25 percent increase in quantity sold. The manager then thought that if the price were reduced by another 20 percent, a 50 percent increase in quantity sold would occur. What would be your response to the marketing manager's reasoning?

6 A student theater group at a university has developed a demand schedule that shows the relationship between ticket prices and demand based on a student survey, as follows: (*a*) Graph the demand curve and the total revenue curve based on these data. What ticket price might be set based on this analysis? (*b*) What other factors should be considered before the final price is set?

Ticket Price	Number of Students Who Would Buy
$1	300
2	250
3	200
4	150
5	100

7 Touché Toiletries, Inc., has developed an addition to its Lizardman Cologne line tentatively branded Ode d'Toade Cologne. Unit variable costs are 45 cents for a three-ounce bottle, and heavy advertising expenditures in the first year would result in total fixed costs of $900,000. Ode d'Toade Cologne is priced at $7.50 for a three-ounce bottle. How many bottles of Ode d'Toade must be sold to break even?

8 Suppose that marketing executives for Touché Toiletries reduced the price to $6.50 for a three-ounce bottle of Ode d'Toade and the fixed costs were $1,100,000. Suppose further that the unit variable cost remained at 45 cents for a three-ounce bottle. (*a*) How many bottles must be sold to break even? (*b*) What dollar profit level would Ode d'Toade achieve if 200,000 bottles were sold?

9 Executives of Random Recordings, Inc., produced a CD titled *Sunshine/Moonshine* by the Starshine Sisters Band. (*a*) Using the price and cost information in the table, prepare a chart like that in Figure 13–10 showing total cost, fixed cost, and total revenue for album quantity sold levels starting at 10,000 CDs through 100,000 CDs at 10,000 intervals, that is, 10,000; 20,000; 30,000; and so on. (*b*) What is the break-even point for the CD?

Selling price	$9.00 per CD
CD cover	$1.00 per CD
Songwriter's royalties	$0.30 per CD
Recording artists' royalties	$0.70 per CD
Direct material and labor costs to produce the CD	$1.00 per CD
Fixed cost of producing a CD (advertising, studio fee, etc.)	$100,000

building your marketing plan

In starting to set a final price:

1 List two pricing objectives and three pricing constraints.

2 Think about your customers and competitors and set three possible prices.

3 Assume a fixed cost and unit variable cost and (*a*) calculate the break-even points and (*b*) plot a break-even chart for the three prices specified in step 2.

video case 13 Washburn Guitars: Using Break-Even Points to Make Pricing Decisions

"We offer a guitar at every price point for every skill level," explains Kevin Lello, vice president of marketing at Washburn Guitars. Washburn is one of the most prestigious guitar manufacturers in the world, offering instruments that range from one-of-a-kind, custom-made acoustic and electric guitars and basses to less-expensive, mass-produced guitars. Lello has responsibility for marketing Washburn's products and ensuring that the price of each product matches the company's objectives related to sales, profit, and market share. "We do pay attention to break-even points," adds Lello. "We need to know exactly how much a guitar costs us, and how much the overhead is for each guitar."

THE COMPANY

The modern Washburn Guitars company started in 1977 when a small Chicago firm bought the century-old Washburn brand name and a small inventory of guitars, parts, and promotional supplies. At that time, annual company sales of about 2,500 guitars generated revenues of $300,000. Washburn's first catalog, appearing in 1978, told a frightening truth:

> Our designs are translated by Japan's most experienced craftsmen, assuring the consistent quality and craftsmanship for which they are known.

At that time, the American guitar-making craft was at an all-time low. Guitars made by Japanese firms, such as Ibane and Yamaha, were in use by an increasing number of professionals.

Times have changed for Washburn. Today, the company sells about 50,000 guitars each year and annual revenues exceed $40 million. All this resulted from Washburn's aggressive marketing strategies to develop product lines with different price points targeted at musicians in distinctly different market segments.

THE PRODUCTS AND MARKET SEGMENTS

One of Washburn's early successes was the trendsetting Festival Series of cutaway, thin-bodied flattops, with built-in bridge pickups and controls. This guitar became the standard for live performances as its popularity with rock and country stars increased. Over the years several generations of musicians have used Washburn guitars. Early artists included Bob Dylan, Dolly Parton, Greg Allman, and the late George Harrison of the Beatles. In recent years, Mike Kennerty of the All American Rejects, Rick Savage of Def Leppard, and Hugh McDonald of Bon Jovi have been among the many musicians who use Washburn products.

Until 1991, all Washburn guitars were manufactured in Asia. That year Washburn started building its high-end guitars in the United States. Today, Washburn marketing executives divide its product line into four categories to appeal to different market segments. From high end to low end these are:

- One-of-a-kind, custom instruments.
- Batch-custom instruments.
- Mass-customized instruments.
- Mass-produced instruments.

The one-of-a-kind custom products appeal to the many stars who use Washburn instruments as well as collectors. The batch-custom products appeal to professional musicians. The mass-customized products appeal to musicians with intermediate skill levels who may not yet be professionals. Finally, the mass-produced units are targeted at first-time buyers and are still manufactured in Asian factories.

PRICING ISSUES

Setting prices for its various lines presents a continuing challenge for Washburn. Not only do the prices have to reflect the changing tastes of its various segments of musicians, but the prices must also be competitive with the prices of other guitars manufactured and marketed globally. The price elasticity of demand, or price sensitivity, for Washburn's products varies between its segments. To reduce the price sensitivity for some of its products Washburn uses endorsements by internationally known musicians who play its instruments and lend their names to lines of Washburn signature guitars. Stars playing Washburn guitars such as Nuno Bettencourt of Extreme; Paul

Stanley of KISS; Scott Ian of Anthrax; and Dan Donegan of Disturbed have their own lines of signature guitars—the "batch-custom" units mentioned earlier. These guitars receive excellent reviews. *Total Guitar* magazine, for example, recently said, "If you want a truly original axe that has been built with great attention to detail . . . then the Washburn Maya Pro DD75 could be the one."

Bill Abel, Washburn's vice president of sales, is responsible for reviewing and approving prices for the company's lines of guitars. Setting a sales target of 2,000 units for a new line of guitars, he is considering a suggested retail price of $349 per unit for customers at one of the hundreds of retail outlets carrying the Washburn line. For planning purposes, Abel estimates half of the final retail price will be the price Washburn nets when it sells its guitar to the wholesalers and dealers in its channel of distribution.

Looking at Washburn's financial data for its present plant, Abel estimates that this line of guitars must bear these fixed costs:

Rent and taxes	= $14,000
Depreciation of equipment	= $ 4,000
Management and quality control program	= $20,000

In addition, he estimates the variable costs for each unit to be:

Direct materials = $25/unit

Direct labor = 15 hours/unit @$8/hour

Carefully kept production records at Washburn's plant make Abel believe that these are reasonable estimates. He explains, "Before we begin a production run, we have a good feel for what our costs will be. The U.S.-built N-4, for example, simply costs more than one of our foreign-produced electrics."

Caught in the global competition for guitar sales, Washburn continually searches for ways to reduce and control costs. For example, Washburn recently purchased Parker Guitar, another guitar manufacturer that designed products for professionals and collectors, and will combine the two production facilities in a new location. Washburn expects the acquisition to lower its fixed and variable costs. Specifically, Washburn projects that its new factory location will reduce its rent and taxes expense by 40 percent, and the new skilled employees will reduce the hours of work needed for each unit by 15 percent.

By managing the prices of its products, Washburn also helps its dealers and retailers. In fact, Abel believes it is another reason for Washburn's success: "We have excellent relationships with the independent retailers. They're our lifeblood, and our outlet to sell our product. We sell through chains and online dealers, but it's the independent dealer that sells the guitars. So we take a smaller margin from them because they have to do more work. They appreciate it, and they go the extra mile for us."

Questions

1 What factors are most likely to affect the demand for the lines of Washburn guitars (*a*) bought by a first-time guitar buyer and (*b*) bought by a sophisticated musician who wants a signature model?

2 For Washburn, what are examples of (*a*) shifting the demand curve to the right to get a higher price for a guitar line (movement of the demand curve) and (*b*) pricing decisions involving moving along a demand curve?

3 In Washburn's factory, what is the break-even point for the new line of guitars if the retail price is (*a*) $349, (*b*) $389, and (*c*) $309? Also, (*d*) if Washburn achieves the sales target of 2,000 units at the $349 retail price, what will its profit be?

4 Assume that the merger with Parker leads to the cost reductions projected in the case. What will be the (*a*) new break-even point at a $349 retail price for this line of guitars and (*b*) new profit if it sells 2,000 units?

5 If for competitive reasons, Washburn eventually has to move all its production back to Asia, (*a*) which specific fixed and variable costs might be lowered and (*b*) what additional fixed and variable costs might it expect to incur?

14 Arriving at the Final Price

LEARNING OBJECTIVES

After reading this chapter you should be able to:

LO1 Describe how to establish the "approximate price level" using demand-oriented, cost-oriented, profit-oriented, and competition-oriented approaches.

LO2 Recognize the major factors considered in deriving a final list or quoted price from the approximate price level.

LO3 Identify the adjustments made to the approximate price level on the basis of discounts, allowances, and geography.

LO4 Name the principal laws and regulations affecting specific pricing practices.

VIZIO, INC.—WHERE VISION MEETS VALUE™ IN HDTV

Can you name North America's fastest-growing HDTV and consumer electronics company? It's Vizio, Inc., an entrepreneurial Irvine, California-based company with a bold agenda. "Our goal is to be the next Sony in 20 to 30 years," says William Wang, Vizio's co-founder and chief executive officer, who is shown on the opposite page.

In 2002, Wang was struck by an ad for a $10,000 flat-panel HDTV set and immediately saw an opportunity. Instead of marketing these sets as luxury items, Wang thought he could make and market a flat-panel HDTV that was affordable to the average consumer. Like many entrepreneurs, he borrowed money from friends and family and mortgaged his home. Within a year, he formed a company that is now known as Vizio, Inc., and delivered its first HDTV to Costco for distribution through that company's stores. Vizio HDTVs are now sold through Costco, Wal-Mart, BJ's Wholesale, Sears, Sam's Club, and Target Stores nationwide along with authorized online partners.

Vizio's ability to deliver affordable flat-panel HDTVs to the average consumer is based on a novel strategy. Instead of investing in expensive manufacturing facilities, Vizio relies on contract manufacturers in Taiwan to build its products. Product development and marketing specialists in the United States handle product design and marketing. That's "Where Vision Meets Value," the company's motto, comes into play. "The whole goal is to ensure that we have the right product at the right time and the right price and really drive a seamless end-to-end value chain," says John Morriss, Vizio's partner manager vice president. "Vizio HDTVs are more popular and in greater demand than ever," added Laynie Newsome, Vizio's co-founder and vice president of sales and marketing communications. "Consumers want to save money without sacrificing quality or technology, which is why we continue to be the fastest growing HDTV company in the United States.[1]

Vizio's powerful and profitable price-value position has resonated with consumers and produced annual sales that exceed $2 billion. Remember Sony? Vizio is now challenging Sony to become the second largest seller of HDTVs in North America. Not bad for a company with about 100 employees that is less than 10 years old!

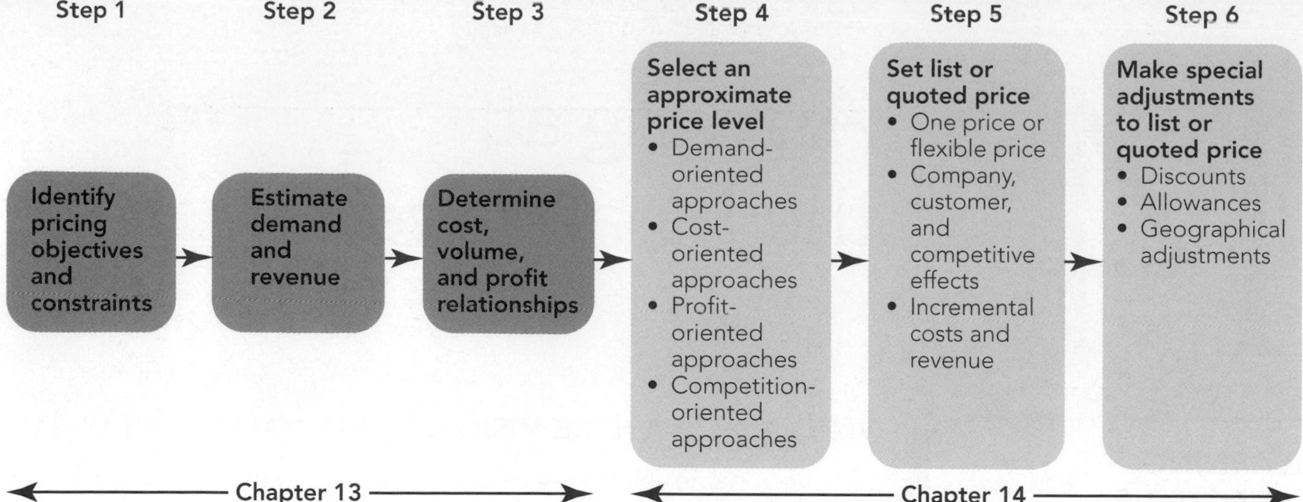

FIGURE 14–1
The six steps in setting price. The first three steps were covered in Chapter 13. The last three steps are covered in this chapter.

This chapter describes how companies like Vizio set an approximate price level for their offerings, highlights important considerations in setting a list or quoted price, and identifies various price adjustments that can be made to prices set by a company—the last three steps involved in setting prices (Figure 14–1). Legal and regulatory aspects of pricing are also described.

STEP 4: SELECT AN APPROXIMATE PRICE LEVEL

LO1

A key for a marketing manager setting a final price for a product is to find an approximate price level to use as a reasonable starting point. Four common approaches to helping find this approximate price level are (1) demand-oriented, (2) cost-oriented, (3) profit-oriented, and (4) competition-oriented approaches (see Figure 14–2). Although these approaches are discussed separately below, some of them overlap, and a seasoned marketing manager will consider several in selecting an approximate price level.

Demand-Oriented Pricing Approaches

Demand-oriented approaches weigh factors underlying expected customer tastes and preferences more heavily than such factors as cost, profit, and competition when selecting a price level.

Skimming Pricing A firm introducing a new or innovative product can use **skimming pricing**, setting the highest initial price that customers really desiring the product are willing to pay. These customers are not very price sensitive because they weigh the new product's price, quality, and ability to satisfy their needs against the same characteristics of substitutes. As the demand of these customers is satisfied, the firm lowers the price to attract another, more price-sensitive segment. Thus, skimming pricing gets its name from skimming successive layers of "cream," or customer segments, as prices are lowered in a series of steps.

Skimming pricing is an effective strategy when: (1) enough prospective customers are willing to buy the product immediately at the high initial price to make these sales profitable, (2) the high initial price will not attract competitors, (3) lowering price has only a minor effect on increasing the sales volume and reducing the unit costs, and (4) customers interpret the high price as signifying high quality. These four conditions are most likely to exist when the new product is protected by patents or copyrights or its uniqueness is understood and valued by consumers. Gillette, for

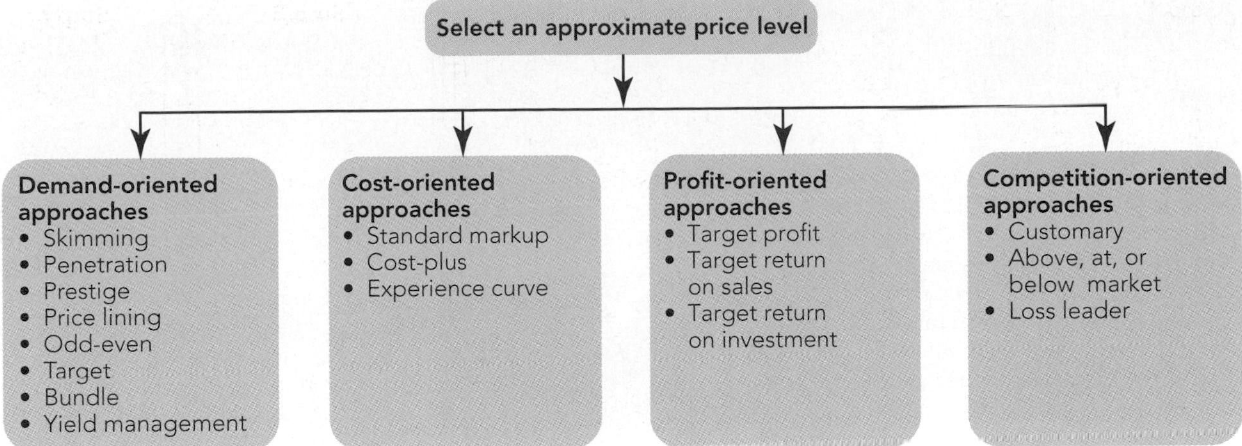

FIGURE 14–2
Four approaches for selecting an approximate price level

example, adopted a skimming strategy for its five-blade Fusion brand shaving system since many of these conditions applied. The Gillette Fusion shaving system has 70 patents that protect its product technology.

Penetration Pricing Setting a low initial price on a new product to appeal immediately to the mass market is **penetration pricing**, the exact opposite of skimming pricing. Nintendo consciously chose a penetration strategy when it introduced the Nintendo Wii, its newest generation video game console.

The conditions favoring penetration pricing are the reverse of those supporting skimming pricing: (1) many segments of the market are price sensitive, (2) a low initial price discourages competitors from entering the market, and (3) unit production and marketing costs fall dramatically as production volumes increase. A firm using penetration pricing may (1) maintain the initial price for a time to gain profit lost from its low introductory level or (2) lower the price further, counting on the new volume to generate the necessary profit.

In some situations, penetration pricing may follow skimming pricing. A company might initially price a product high to attract price-insensitive consumers and recoup initial research and development costs and introductory promotional expenditures. Once this is done, penetration pricing is used to appeal to a broader segment of the population and increase market share.[2]

Prestige Pricing As noted in Chapter 13, consumers may use price as a measure of the quality or prestige of an item so that as price is lowered beyond some point, demand for the item actually falls. **Prestige pricing** involves setting a high price so that quality- or status-conscious consumers will be attracted to the product and buy it (see Figure 14–3A on the next page). The demand curve slopes downward and to the right between points *A* and *B* but turns back to the left between points *B* and *C* because demand is actually reduced between points *B* and *C*. From *A* to *B* buyers see the lowering of price as a bargain and buy more; from *B* to *C* they become dubious about the quality and prestige and buy less. A marketing manager's pricing strategy here is to stay above price P_0 (the initial price).

Rolls-Royce cars, Chanel perfume, Cartier jewelry, Lalique crystal, and Swiss watches have an element of prestige pricing in them and may sell worse at lower prices than at higher ones.[3] The recent success of Swiss watchmaker TAG Heuer is an example. The company raised the average price of its watches from $250 to $1,000, and its sales volume jumped sevenfold.[4] Recently, Energizer learned that buyers of high-performance alkaline batteries tend to link a lower price with lower quality. The Marketing Matters box on the next page describes the pricing lesson learned by Energizer.[5]

Marketing Matters > > > > > > customer value

Energizer's Lesson in Price Perception—Value Lies in the Eye of the Beholder

Battery manufacturers are as tireless as a certain drum-thumping bunny in their efforts to create products that perform better, last longer, and not incidentally, outsell the competition. The commercialization of new alkaline battery technology at a price that creates value for consumers is not always obvious or easy. Just ask the marketing executives at Energizer about their experience with pricing Energizer Advanced Formula and Energizer e^2 AA alkaline batteries.

When Duracell launched its high-performance Ultra brand AA alkaline battery with a 25 percent price premium over standard Duracell batteries, Energizer quickly countered with its own high-performance battery—Energize Advanced Formula. Believing that consumers would not pay the premium price, Energizer priced its Advanced Formula brand at the same price as its standard AA alkaline battery, expecting to gain market share from Duracell. It did not happen. Why? According to industry analysts, consumers associated Energizer's low price with inferior quality in the high-performance segment. Instead of gaining market share, Energizer lost market share to Duracell and Rayovac, the number three battery manufacturer.

Having learned its lesson, Energizer subsequently released its e^2 high-performance battery, this time priced 4 percent higher than Duracell Ultra and about 50 percent higher than Advanced Formula. The result? Energizer recovered lost sales and market share. The lesson learned? Value lies in the eye of the beholder.

Price Lining Often a firm that is selling not just a single product but a line of products may price them at a number of different specific pricing points, which is called **price lining**. For example, a department store manager may price a line of women's casual slacks at $59, $79, and $99. As shown in Figure 14–3B, this assumes that demand is elastic at each of these price points but inelastic between these price points. In some instances, all the items might be purchased for the same cost and then marked up at different percentages to achieve these price points based on color, style, and expected demand. In other instances, manufacturers design products for different price points, and retailers apply approximately the same markup percentages to achieve the three or four different price points offered to consumers. Sellers often feel that a limited number (such as three or four) of price points is preferable to 8 or 10, which may only confuse prospective buyers.[6]

FIGURE 14–3
Demand curves for two types of demand-oriented pricing approaches—prestige pricing and price lining—apply to different kinds of products.

A. Prestige pricing

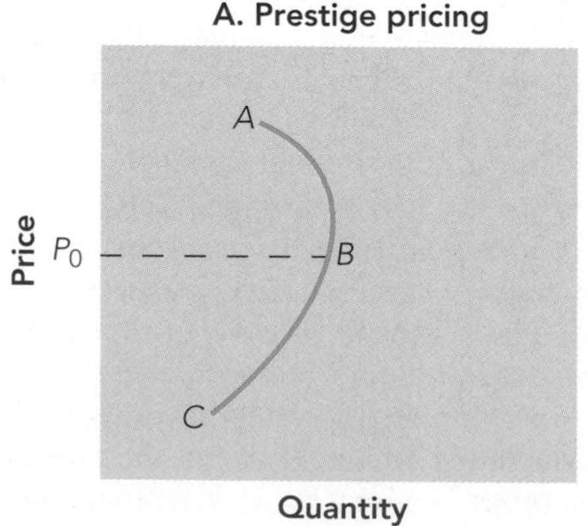

B. Price lining

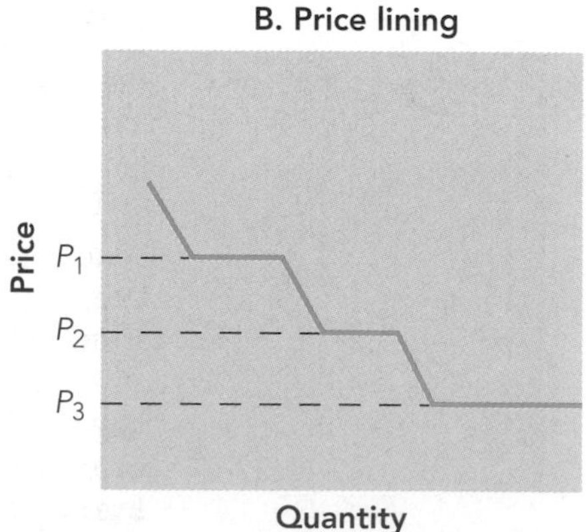

Odd-Even Pricing Sears offers a Craftsman radial saw for $499.99, the suggested retail price for the Gillette Fusion shaving system is $11.99, and Amazon sold a recent U2 CD for $3.99. Why not simply price these items at $500, $12, and $4, respectively? These firms are using **odd-even pricing**, which involves setting prices a few dollars or cents under an even number. The presumption is that consumers see the Sears radial saw as priced at "something over $400" rather than "about $500." In theory, demand increases if the price drops from $500 to $499.99. There is some evidence to suggest this does happen. However, research suggests that overuse of odd-ending prices tends to mute its effect on demand.[7]

Target Pricing Manufacturers will sometimes estimate the price that the ultimate consumer would be willing to pay for a product. They then work backward through markups taken by retailers and wholesalers to determine what price they can charge wholesalers for the product. This practice, called **target pricing**, results in the manufacturer deliberately adjusting the composition and features of a product to achieve the target price to consumers. Canon uses this practice for pricing its cameras.[8]

Bundle Pricing A frequently used demand-oriented pricing practice is **bundle pricing**—the marketing of two or more products in a single package price. For example, Delta Air Lines offers vacation packages that include airfare, car rental, and lodging. Bundle pricing is based on the idea that consumers value the package more than the individual items. This is due to benefits received from not having to make separate purchases and enhanced satisfaction from one item given the presence of another. Moreover, bundle pricing often provides a lower total cost to buyers and lower marketing costs to sellers.[9]

Yield Management Pricing Have you noticed seats on airline flights are priced differently within coach class? What you observed is **yield management pricing**—the charging of different prices to maximize revenue for a set amount of capacity at any given time. As described in Chapter 12, service businesses engage in capacity management, and an effective way to do this is by varying prices by time, day, week, or season. Yield management pricing is a complex approach that continually matches demand and supply to customize the price for a service. Airlines, hotels, cruise ships, and car rental companies frequently use it. American Airlines estimates that yield management pricing produces an annual revenue that exceeds $500 million.[10]

learning review

1. What are the circumstances in pricing a new product that might support skimming or penetration pricing?
2. What is odd-even pricing?

Cost-Oriented Pricing Approaches

With cost-oriented approaches a price setter stresses the cost side of the pricing problem, not the demand side. Price is set by looking at the production and marketing costs and then adding enough to cover direct expenses, overhead, and profit.

Standard Markup Pricing Managers of supermarkets and other retail stores have such a large number of products that estimating the demand for each product as a means of setting price is impossible. Therefore, they use **standard markup pricing**,

How was the price of the Rock and Roll Hall of Fame determined? Read the text to find out.

Rock and Roll Hall of Fame and Museum
www.rockhall.com

which entails adding a fixed percentage to the cost of all items in a specific product class. This percentage markup varies depending on the type of retail store (such as furniture, clothing, or grocery) and on the product involved. High-volume products usually have smaller markups than do low-volume products. Supermarkets such as Kroger, Safeway, and Jewel have different markups for staple items and discretionary items. The markup on staple items such as sugar, flour, and dairy products varies from 10 percent to 23 percent, whereas markups on discretionary items like snack foods and candy ranges from 27 percent to 47 percent. These markups must cover all expenses of the store, pay for overhead costs, and contribute something to profits. For supermarkets these markups, which may appear very large, result in only a 1 percent profit on sales revenue if the store is operating efficiently.

By comparison, consider the markups on snacks and beverages purchased at your local movie theater. The markup is 87 percent on soft drinks, 65 percent on candy bars, and 90 percent on popcorn. These markups might sound high, but consider the consequences. "If we didn't charge as much for concessions as we did, a movie ticket would cost $20," says the CEO of Regal Entertainment, the largest U.S. theater chain.[11] An explanation of how to compute a markup, along with operating statement data and other ratios, is given in Appendix B to this chapter.

Cost-Plus Pricing Many manufacturing, professional services, and construction firms use a variation of standard markup pricing. **Cost-plus pricing** involves summing the total unit cost of providing a product or service and adding a specific amount to the cost to arrive at a price. Cost-plus pricing generally assumes two forms. With *cost-plus percentage-of-cost pricing*, a fixed percentage is added to the total unit cost. This is often used to price one- or few-of-a-kind items, as when an architectural firm charges a percentage of the construction costs of, say, the $92 million Rock and Roll Hall of Fame and Museum in Cleveland, Ohio.

In buying highly technical, few-of-a-kind products such as hydroelectric power plants or space satellites, governments have found that general contractors are reluctant to specify a formal, fixed price for the procurement. Therefore, they use *cost-plus fixed-fee pricing*, which means that a supplier is reimbursed for all costs, regardless of what they turn out to be, but is allowed only a fixed fee as profit that is independent of the final cost of the project. For example, suppose the National Aeronautics and Space Administration agreed to pay Boeing $1.2 billion as the cost of a space shuttle and agreed to a $100 million fee for providing that space shuttle. Even if Boeing's cost increased to $2 billion for the space shuttle, its fee would remain $100 million.

Cost-plus pricing is the most commonly used method to set prices for business products.[12] Increasingly, however, this method is finding favor among business-to-business marketers in the service sector. For example, the rising cost of legal fees has prompted some law firms to adopt a cost-plus pricing approach. Rather than billing business clients on an hourly basis, lawyers and their clients agree on a fixed fee based on expected costs plus a profit for the law firm. Many advertising agencies now use this approach. Here, the client agrees to pay the agency a fee based on the cost of its work plus some agreed-on profit, which is often a percentage of total cost.[13]

Experience Curve Pricing The method of **experience curve pricing** is based on the learning effect, which holds that the unit cost of many products and services declines by 10 percent to 30 percent each time a firm's experience at producing and selling them doubles. This reduction is regular or predictable enough that

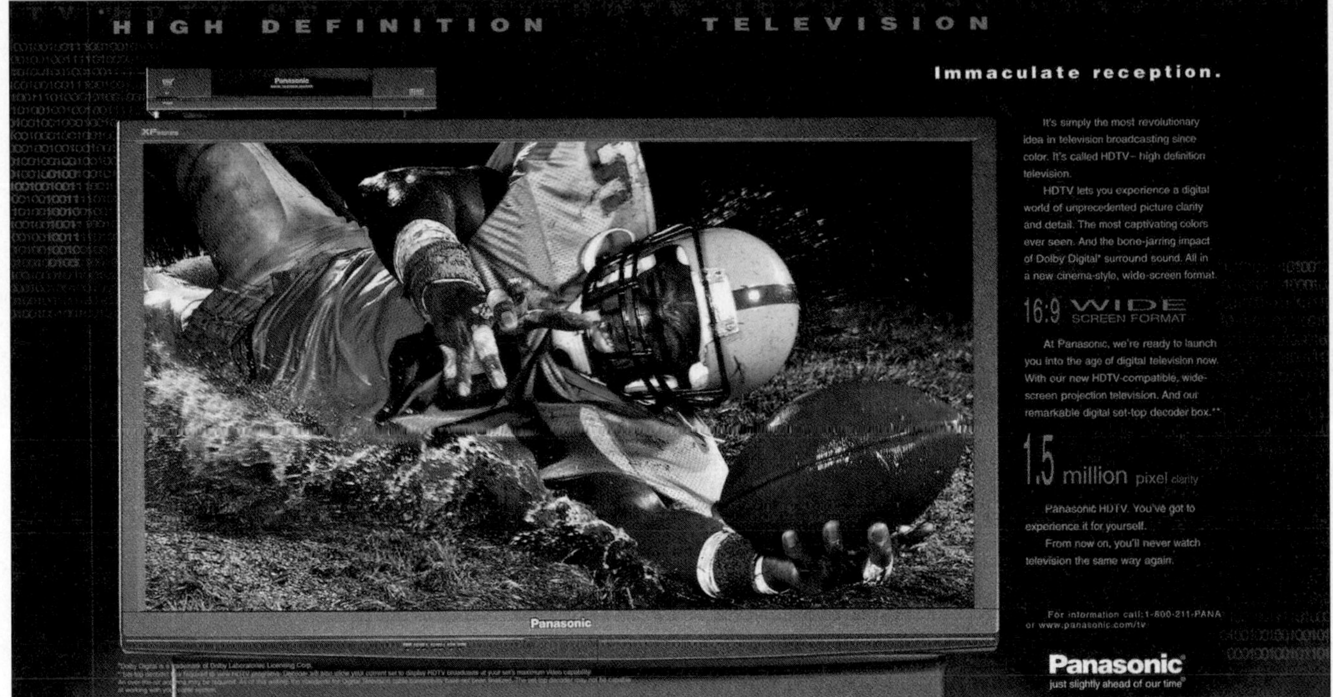

Panasonic is a pioneer in the successful commercialization of flat-panel HDTVs. It, like its competitors, relies on experience curve pricing to drive down prices.

Panasonic
www.panasonic.com

the average cost per unit can be mathematically estimated. For example, if the firm estimates that costs will fall by 15 percent each time volume doubles, then the cost of the 100th unit produced and sold will be about 85 percent of the cost of the 50th unit, and the 200th unit will be 85 percent of the 100th unit. Therefore, if the cost of the 50th unit is $100, the 100th unit would cost $85, the 200th unit would be $72.25, and so on. Because prices often follow costs with experience curve pricing, a rapid decline in price is possible.

Japanese, Korean, and U.S. firms in the electronics industry often adopt this pricing approach. This cost-based pricing approach complements the demand-based pricing strategy of skimming followed by penetration pricing. For example, DVD player prices have decreased from $900 to less than $100, fax machine prices have declined from $1,000 to under $100, and cellular telephones that once sold for $4,000 are now priced below $99. Panasonic, Sony, Samsung, LG, Vizio, and other television manufacturers use experience curve pricing for flat panel, HDTV sets.[14] Consumers benefit because prices will decline as cumulative sales volume grows.

Profit-Oriented Pricing Approaches

A price setter may choose to balance both revenues and costs to set price using profit-oriented approaches. These might either involve a target of a specific dollar volume of profit or express this target profit as a percentage of sales or investment.

Target Profit Pricing

A firm may set an annual target of a specific dollar volume of profit, which is called **target profit pricing**. Suppose a picture framing store owner wishes to use target profit pricing to establish a price for a typical framed picture and assumes the following:

- Variable cost is a constant $22 per unit.
- Fixed cost is a constant $26,000.
- Demand is insensitive to price up to $60 per unit.
- A target profit of $7,000 is sought at an annual volume of 1,000 units (framed pictures).

The price can be calculated as follows:

$$\text{Profit} = \text{Total revenue} - \text{Total cost}$$
$$\text{Profit} = (P \times Q) - [FC + (UVC \times Q)]$$
$$\$7{,}000 = (P \times 1{,}000) - [\$26{,}000 + (\$22 \times 1{,}000)]$$
$$\$7{,}000 = 1{,}000P - (\$26{,}000 + \$22{,}000)$$
$$1{,}000P = \$7{,}000 + \$48{,}000$$
$$P = \$55$$

Note that a critical assumption is that this higher average price of a framed picture will not cause the demand to fall.

Target Return-on-Sales Pricing A shortcoming with target profit pricing is that although it is simple and the target involves only a specific dollar volume, there is no benchmark of sales or investment used to show how much of the firm's effort is needed to achieve the target. Firms such as supermarket chains often use **target return-on-sales pricing** to set typical prices that will give them a profit that is a specified percentage, say, 1 percent, of the sales volume. Suppose the owner decides to use target return-on-sales pricing for the frame shop and makes the same first three assumptions shown previously. The owner now sets a target of 20 percent return on sales at an annual volume of 1,250 units. This results in the following price:

$$\text{Target return on sales} = \frac{\text{Target profit}}{\text{Total revenue}}$$
$$20\% = \frac{TR - TC}{TR}$$
$$0.20 = \frac{P \times Q - [FC + (UVC \times Q)]}{TR}$$
$$0.20 = \frac{P \times 1{,}250 - [\$26{,}000 + (\$22 \times 1{,}250)]}{P \times 1{,}250}$$
$$P = \$53.50$$

So at a price of $53.50 per unit and an annual quantity of 1,250 frames,

$$TR = P \times Q = \$53.50 \times 1{,}250 = \$66{,}875$$
$$TC = FC + (UVC \times Q) = \$26{,}000 + (\$22 \times 1{,}250) = \$53{,}500$$
$$\text{Profit} = TR - TC = \$66{,}875 - \$53{,}500 = \$13{,}375$$

As a check,

$$\text{Target return on sales} = \frac{\text{Target profit}}{\text{Total revenue}} = \frac{\$13{,}375}{\$66{,}875} = 20\%$$

Target Return-on-Investment Pricing Large, publicly owned corporations and many public utilities set annual return-on-investment (ROI) targets such as a ROI of 20 percent. **Target return-on-investment pricing** is a method of setting prices to achieve this target.

Suppose the store owner sets a target ROI of 10 percent, which is twice that achieved the previous year. She considers raising the average price of a framed picture to $54 or $58—up from last year's average of $50. To do this, she might improve product quality by offering better frames and higher-quality matting, which will increase the cost but will probably offset the decreased revenue from the lower number of units that can be sold next year.

Assumptions or Results	Financial Element	Last Year	SPREADSHEET SIMULATION			
			A	B	C	D
ASSUMPTIONS	Price per unit (P)	$50	$54	$54	$58	$58
	Units sold (Q)	1,000	1,200	1,100	1,100	1,000
	Change in unit variable cost (UVC)	0%	+10%	+10%	+20%	+20%
	Unit variable cost	$22.00	$24.20	$24.20	$26.20	$26.40
	Total expenses	$8,000	Same	Same	Same	Same
	Owner's salary	$18,000	Same	Same	Same	Same
	Investment	$20,000	Same	Same	Same	Same
	State and federal taxes	50%	Same	Same	Same	Same
SPREADSHEET RESULTS	Net sales (P × Q)	$50,000	$64,800	$59,400	$63,800	$58,000
	Less: COGS (Q × UVC)	22,000	29,040	26,620	29,040	26,400
	Gross margin	$28,000	$35,760	$32,780	$34,760	$31,600
	Less: total expenses	8,000	8,000	8,000	8,000	8,000
	Less: owner's salary	18,000	18,000	18,000	18,000	18,000
	Net profit before taxes	$2,000	$9,760	$6,780	$8,760	$5,600
	Less: taxes	1,000	4,880	3,390	4,380	2,800
	Net profit after taxes	$1,000	$4,880	$3,390	$4,380	$2,800
	Investment	$20,000	$20,000	$20,000	$20,000	$20,000
	Return on investment	5.0%	24.4%	17.0%	21.9%	14.0%

FIGURE 14–4
Results of a spreadsheet simulation to select a price to achieve a target return on investment

To handle this wide variety of assumptions, managers use spreadsheets to project operating statements based on a set of assumptions. Figure 14–4 shows the results of a spreadsheet simulation, with assumptions shown at the top and the projected results at the bottom. A previous year's operating statement results are shown in the column headed "Last Year." The assumptions and spreadsheet results for four different sets of assumptions are shown in columns A, B, C, and D.

In choosing a price or another action using spreadsheet results, the manager must (1) study the results of the simulation projections and (2) assess the realism of the assumptions underlying each set of projections. For example, the store owner sees from the bottom row of Figure 14–4 that all four spreadsheet simulations exceed the after-tax target ROI of 10 percent. But after more thought, she judges it to be more realistic to set an average price of $58 per unit, allow the unit variable cost to increase by 20 percent to account for more expensive framing and matting, and settle for the same unit sales as the 1,000 units sold last year. She selects simulation D in this spreadsheet approach to target ROI pricing and has a goal of 14 percent after-tax ROI.

Competition-Oriented Pricing Approaches

Rather than emphasize demand, cost, or profit factors, a price setter can stress what competitors or "the market" is doing.

Customary Pricing For some products where tradition, a standardized channel of distribution, or other competitive factors dictate the price, **customary pricing** is used. Tradition prevails in the pricing of Swatch watches. The $40 customary price for the basic model changed little in 10 years. Candy bars offered through standard vending machines have a customary price of 75 cents. A significant departure from this price may result in a loss of sales for the manufacturer. Hershey changes the amount of chocolate in its candy bars depending on the price of raw chocolate rather than vary its customary retail price so that it can continue selling through vending machines.

Above-, At-, or Below-Market Pricing For most products, it is difficult to identify a specific market price for a product or product class. Still, marketing managers often have a subjective feel for the competitors' price or market price. Using this benchmark, they then may deliberately choose a strategy of **above-, at-, or below-market pricing**.

Among watch manufacturers, Rolex takes pride in emphasizing that it makes one of the most expensive watches you can buy, a clear example of above-market pricing. Manufacturers of national brands of clothing such as Hart Schaffner & Marx and Christian Dior and retailers such as Neiman Marcus deliberately set premium prices for their products.

Large department store chains such as JCPenney generally use at-market pricing. These chains often establish the going market price in the minds of their competitors. Similarly, Revlon cosmetics and Arrow brand shirts are generally priced "at market." They also provide a reference price for competitors that use above- and below-market pricing.

A number of firms use below-market pricing. Manufacturers and retailers that offer private brands of products ranging from peanut butter to shampoo deliberately set prices for these products about 8 percent to 10 percent below the prices of nationally branded competitive products such as Skippy peanut butter and Vidal Sassoon shampoo. Below-market pricing also exists in business-to-business marketing. Hewlett-Packard, for instance, initially priced its office personal computers below competitors to promote a value image among corporate buyers.[15]

Companies use a "price premium" to assess whether its products and brands are above, at, or below the market. An illustration of how the price premium measure is calculated, displayed, and interpreted appears in the Using Marketing Dashboards box.

Loss-Leader Pricing For a special promotion retail stores deliberately sell a product below its customary price to attract attention to it. The purpose of this **loss-leader pricing** is not to increase sales but to attract customers in hopes they will buy other products as well, particularly the discretionary items with large markups. For example, Best Buy, Target, and Wal-Mart sell CDs at about half of music companies' suggested retail price to attract customers to their stores.[16]

learning review

3. What is standard markup pricing?
4. What profit-based pricing approach should a manager use if he or she wants to reflect the percentage of the firm's resources used in obtaining the profit?
5. What is the purpose of loss-leader pricing when used by a retail firm?

STEP 5: SET THE LIST OR QUOTED PRICE

LO2

The first four steps in setting price covered in Chapter 13 and this chapter result in an approximate price level for the product that appears reasonable. But it still remains for the manager to set a specific list or quoted price in light of all relevant factors.

Using Marketing Dashboards

Are Cracker Jack Prices Above, At, or Below the Market?

How would you determine whether a firm's retail prices are above, at, or below the market? You might visit retail stores and record what prices retailers are charging for products or brands. This laborious activity can be simplified by combining two consumer market share measures to create a "price premium" display on your marketing dashboard.

Your Challenge Frito-Lay is considering whether to buy the Cracker Jack brand of caramel popcorn from Borden, Inc. Frito-Lay research shows that Cracker Jack has a strong brand equity. But, Cracker Jack's dollar sales market share and pound volume market share declined recently and trailed the Crunch 'n Munch brand as shown in the table.

Borden's management used an above-market, premium pricing strategy for Cracker Jack. Specifically, Cracker Jack's suggested retail price was set to yield an average price premium per pound of 28 percent relative to Crunch 'n Munch. As a Frito-Lay marketer studying Cracker Jack, your challenge is to calculate and display Cracker Jack's actual price premium relative to Crunch 'n Munch. A price premium is the percentage by which the actual price charged for a specific brand exceeds (or falls short of) a benchmark established for a similar product or basket of products. This premium can be calculated as follows:

$$\text{Price Premium (\%)} = \frac{\text{Dollar Sales Market Share for a Brand}}{\text{Unit Volume Market Share for a Brand}} - 1$$

Brand	Dollar Sales Market Share	Pound Volume Market Share
Crunch 'n Munch	32%	32%
Cracker Jack	26	19
Fiddle Faddle	7	8
Private Brands	4	8
Seasonal, Specialty, and Regional (S,S,R) Brands	31	33
	100%	100%

Your Findings Using caramel popcorn brand market share data, the Cracker Jack price premium is 1.368, or 36.8 percent, calculated as follows: (26 percent ÷ 19 percent) − 1 = .368. By comparison, Crunch 'n Munch enjoys no price premium. Its dollar sales market share and unit (pound) volume market share are equal: (32 percent ÷ 32 percent) − 1 = 0, or zero percent. The price premium, or lack thereof, of other brands can be displayed in a marketing dashboard as shown below.

Your Action Cracker Jack's price premium clearly exceeds the 28 percent Borden benchmark relative to Crunch 'n Munch. Cracker Jack's price premium may have overreached its brand equity. Consideration might be given to assessing Cracker Jack's price premium relative to its market position should Frito-Lay purchase the brand.

Price Premium Display

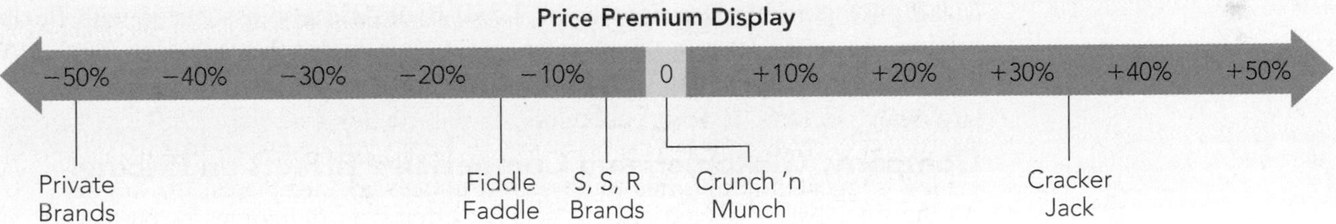

Choosing a Price Policy

Choosing a price policy is important in setting a list or quoted price. Two options are common—a one-price policy or a flexible-price policy.

One-Price Policy A **one-price policy**, also called *fixed pricing*, is setting one price for all buyers of a product or service. For example, when you buy a Wilson (K) factor tennis racket from a sporting goods store, you are offered the product at a single price. You can buy it or not, but there is no variation in the price under the seller's one-price policy. CarMax uses this approach in its stores and features a "no haggle, one price" price for cars. Some retailers have married this policy with

What price policy does Family Dollar Stores use? Read the text to find the answer.

a below-market approach. Dollar Valley Stores and 99¢ Only Stores sell everything in their stores for $1 or less. Family Dollar Stores sell everything for $2.

Flexible-Price Policy In contrast, a **flexible-price policy**, also called *dynamic pricing*, involves setting different prices for products and services depending on individual buyers and purchase situations. A flexible-price policy gives sellers considerable discretion in setting the final price in light of demand, cost, and competitive factors. Yield management pricing is a form of flexible pricing because prices vary by an individual buyer's purchase situation, company cost considerations, and competitive conditions. Dell Inc. uses flexible pricing. It continually adjusts prices in response to changes in its own costs, competitive pressures, and demand from customers, from one segment of the personal computer market to another. "Our flexibility allows us to be [priced] different even within a day," says a Dell spokesperson.[17]

Most companies use a one-price policy. However, flexible pricing has grown in popularity because of increasingly sophisticated information technology. Today, many marketers have the ability to customize a price for an individual on the basis of his or her purchasing patterns, product preferences, and price-sensitivity, all of which are stored in company data warehouses. For example, online marketers routinely adjust prices in response to purchase situations and past purchase behaviors of online buyers. Some online marketers monitor an online shopper's *clickstream*—the way that person navigates through the Web site. If the visitor behaves like a price-sensitive shopper—perhaps by comparing many different products and prices—that person may be offered a lower price.[18]

Flexible pricing means that some customers pay more and others less for the same product or service. And flexible pricing is not without its critics because of this discriminatory potential. For example, car dealers have traditionally used flexible pricing on the basis of buyer–seller negotiations to agree on a final sales price. However, flexible pricing may result in discriminatory practices in car buying as detailed in the Making Responsible Decisions box.[19] Legal issues are also associated with flexible pricing. As noted later in this chapter, constraints under the Robinson-Patman Act prevent carrying a flexible-price policy to the extreme of price discrimination.

Company, Customer, and Competitive Effects on Pricing

As the final list or quoted price is set, the effects on the company, customers, and competitors must be assessed.

Company Effects For a firm with more than one product, a decision on the price of a single product must consider the price of other items in its product line or related product lines in its product mix. Within a product line or mix there are usually some products that are substitutes for one another and some that complement each other.[20] Frito-Lay recognizes that its tortilla chip product line consisting of Baked Tostitos, Tostitos, and Doritos brands are partial substitutes for one another and its bean and cheese chip-dip line and salsa sauces complement the tortilla chip line.

A manager's challenge when marketing multiple products is **product-line pricing**, the setting of prices for all items in a product line. When setting prices, the manager seeks to cover the total cost and produce a profit for the complete line, not necessarily for each item. For example, the penetration price for Nintendo's Wii video game console was likely at or below its cost, but the price of its video games

Making Responsible Decisions > > > > > > > ethics

Flexible Pricing—Is There Discrimination in Bargaining for a New Car?

What do 60 percent of prospective buyers dread when looking for a new car? That's right! They dread negotiating the price. Price bargaining demonstrates shortcomings of flexible pricing when purchasing a new car: the potential for price discrimination.

A National Bureau of Economic Research study of 750,000 car purchases indicated that African Americans, Hispanics, and women, on average, paid roughly $423, $483, and $105 more, respectively, for a new car in the $21,000 range than the typical purchaser. Smaller price premiums remained after adjusting for income, education, and other factors that may affect price negotiations.

Research shows that searching automotive and car dealer Web sites before buying a new car reduces price premiums paid by African Americans, Hispanics, and women.

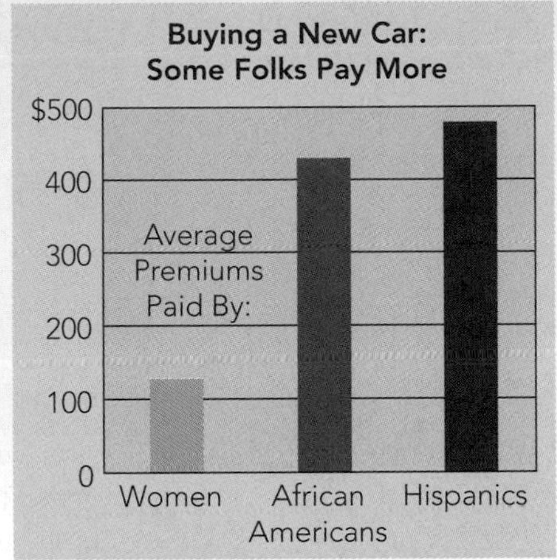

(complementary products) was set high enough to cover the loss and deliver a handsome profit for the Nintendo product line.

Product-line pricing involves determining (1) the lowest-priced product and price, (2) the highest-priced product and price, and (3) price differentials for all other products in the line.[21] The lowest- and highest-priced items in the product line play important roles. The highest-priced item is typically positioned as the premium item in quality and features. The lowest-priced item is the traffic builder designed to capture the attention of the hesitant or first-time buyer. Price differentials between items in the line should make sense to customers and reflect differences in their perceived value of the products offered. Behavioral research also suggests that the price differentials should get larger as one moves up the product line.

Customer Effects In setting price, marketers weigh factors heavily that satisfy the perceptions or expectations of ultimate consumers, such as the customary prices for a variety of consumer products. Retailers have found that they should not price their store brands 20 to 25 percent below manufacturers' brands.[22] When they do, consumers often view the lower price as signaling lower quality and don't buy. Manufacturers and wholesalers must choose prices that result in profit for resellers in the channel to gain their cooperation and support. Toro failed to do this on its lines of lawn mowers and snow throwers. It decided to augment its traditional hardware outlet distribution by also selling through mass merchandisers. To do so, it set mass merchandiser prices far below those for its traditional hardware outlets. Unhappy hardware stores abandoned Toro products in favor of mowers and snow throwers from competitors.

Competitive Effects A manager's pricing decision is immediately apparent to most competitors, who may retaliate with price changes of their own. Therefore, a manager who sets a final list or quoted price must anticipate potential price responses from competitors. Regardless of whether a firm is a price leader or follower, it wants to avoid cutthroat price wars in which no firm in the industry makes a profit.

A **price war** involves successive price cutting by competitors to increase or maintain their unit sales or market share. Price wars erupt in a variety of industries, from consumer electronics to disposable diapers, from soft drinks to airlines, and from

Frito-Lay recognizes that its tortilla chip products are partial substitutes for one another. Its bean and cheese dips and salsa sauces complement tortilla chips. This knowledge is used for Frito-Lay product-line pricing.

Frito-Lay, Inc.
www.frito-lay.com

grocery retailing to telephone services. Managers expecting that a lower price will result in a larger market share, higher unit sales, and greater profit for their company often initiate them. These results may occur. But, if competitors match the lower price, other things being equal, the expected market share, sales, and profit gain are lost. According to an analysis of large U.S. companies, a 1 percent price cut—assuming no change in unit volume or costs—lowers a company's net profit by an average of 8 percent.[23]

Marketers are advised to consider price cutting only when one or more conditions exist: (1) the company has a cost or technological advantage over its competitors, (2) primary demand for a product class will grow if prices are lowered, and (3) the price cut is confined to specific products or customers (as with airline tickets), and not across the board.[24]

Balancing Incremental Costs and Revenues

When a price is changed or new advertising or selling programs are planned, their effect on the quantity sold must be considered. This assessment, called *marginal analysis* (Chapter 13), involves a continuing, concise trade-off of incremental costs against incremental revenues.

Do marketing and business managers really use marginal analysis? Yes, they do, but they often don't use phrases such as *marginal revenue*, *marginal cost*, and *elasticity of demand.*

Think about these managerial questions:

- How many extra units do we have to sell to pay for that $1,000 advertisement?
- Should we hire three more salespeople or not?

These questions are a form of marginal or incremental analysis, even though these exact words are not used.

Figure 14–5 shows the power, and some limitations, of marginal analysis applied to a marketing decision. Note that the frame store owner must either conclude that a simple advertising campaign will more than pay for itself in additional sales or not undertake the campaign. The decision could also have been made to increase the average price of a framed picture to cover the cost of the campaign, but the principle still applies: Expected incremental revenues from pricing and other marketing actions must more than offset incremental costs.

FIGURE 14–5
Expected incremental revenue from pricing and other marketing actions must more than offset incremental costs to achieve an incremental profit.

Suppose the owner of a picture framing store is considering buying a series of magazine ads to reach her upscale target market. The cost of the ads is $1,000, the average price of a framed picture is $50, and the unit variable cost (materials plus labor) is $30.

This is a direct application of marginal analysis that an astute manager uses to estimate the incremental revenue or incremental number of units that must be obtained to at least cover the incremental cost. In this example, the number of extra picture frames that must be sold is obtained as follows:

$$\text{Incremental number of frames} = \frac{\text{Extra fixed cost}}{\text{Price} - \text{Unit variable cost}}$$

$$= \frac{\$1{,}000 \text{ of advertising}}{\$50 - \$30}$$

$$= 50 \text{ frames}$$

So unless there are other benefits of the ads, such as long-term goodwill, she should buy the ads only if she expects they will increase frame sales by at least 50 units.

The example in Figure 14–5 shows both the main advantage and difficulty of marginal analysis. The advantage is its commonsense usefulness, and the difficulty is obtaining the necessary data to make decisions. The owner can measure the cost quite easily, but the incremental revenue generated by the ads is difficult to measure. She could partly solve this problem by offering $2 off the purchase price with use of a coupon printed in the ad to see which sales resulted from the ad.

STEP 6: MAKE SPECIAL ADJUSTMENTS TO THE LIST OR QUOTED PRICE

LO3

When you pay 75 cents for a bag of M&Ms in a vending machine or receive a quoted price of $10,000 from a contractor to renovate a kitchen, the pricing sequence ends with the last step just described: setting the list or quoted price. But when you are a manufacturer of M&M candies or gas grills and sell your product to dozens or hundreds of wholesalers and retailers in your marketing channel, you may need to make special adjustments to the list or quoted price. Wholesalers adjust list or quoted prices they set for retailers. Retailers, in turn, do the same for consumers. Three special adjustments to the list or quoted price are (1) discounts, (2) allowances, and (3) geographical adjustments (see Figure 14–6).

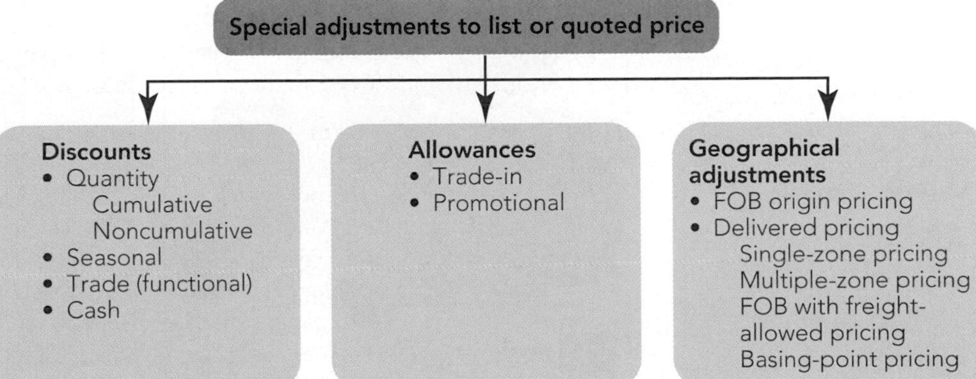

FIGURE 14–6
Three special adjustments to list or quoted price include discounts, allowances, and geographical adjustments. Each can substantially change the final price.

Special adjustments to list or quoted price

Discounts
- Quantity
  - Cumulative
  - Noncumulative
- Seasonal
- Trade (functional)
- Cash

Allowances
- Trade-in
- Promotional

Geographical adjustments
- FOB origin pricing
- Delivered pricing
  - Single-zone pricing
  - Multiple-zone pricing
  - FOB with freight-allowed pricing
  - Basing-point pricing

Discounts

Discounts are reductions from the list price that a seller gives a buyer as a reward for some activity of the buyer that is favorable to the seller. Four kinds of discounts are especially important in marketing strategy: (1) quantity, (2) seasonal, (3) trade (functional), and (4) cash.[25]

Quantity Discounts

To encourage customers to buy larger quantities of a product, firms at all levels in the marketing channel offer **quantity discounts**, which are reductions in unit costs for a larger order. For example, a photocopying service such as AlphaGraphics might set a price of 10 cents a copy for 1 to 25 copies, 9 cents a copy for 26 to 100, and 8 cents a copy for 101 or more. Because the photocopying service gets more of the buyer's business and has longer production runs that reduce its order-handling costs, it is willing to pass on some of the cost savings in the form of quantity discounts to the buyer.

Quantity discounts are of two general kinds: noncumulative and cumulative. *Noncumulative quantity discounts* are based on the size of an individual purchase order. They encourage large individual purchase orders, not a series of orders. This discount is used by FedEx to encourage companies to ship a large number of packages at one time. *Cumulative quantity discounts* apply to the accumulation of purchases of a product over a given time period, typically a year. Cumulative quantity discounts encourage repeat buying by a single customer to a far greater degree than do noncumulative quantity discounts.

Seasonal Discounts

To encourage buyers to stock inventory earlier than their normal demand would require, manufacturers often use seasonal discounts. A firm such as Toro that manufactures lawn mowers and snow throwers offers seasonal discounts to encourage wholesalers and retailers to stock up on lawn mowers in January and February and on snow throwers in July and August—five or six months before the seasonal demand by ultimate consumers. This enables Toro to smooth out seasonal manufacturing peaks and troughs, thereby contributing to more efficient production. It also rewards wholesalers and retailers for the risk they accept

Marketers provide a variety of discounts to marketing channel members who in turn often pass them along to consumers. Toro uses seasonal discounts to stimulate consumer demand and smooth out seasonal manufacturing peaks and troughs. Promotional discounts are used by retailers such as Payless to offer items at sale prices.

The Toro Company
www.toro.com

Payless Shoe Source
www.payless.com

in assuming increased inventory carrying costs and having supplies in stock at the time they are wanted by customers.

Trade (Functional) Discounts To reward wholesalers and retailers for marketing functions they will perform in the future, a manufacturer often gives *trade*, or *functional discounts*. These reductions off the list or base price are offered to resellers in the marketing channel on the basis of (1) where they are in the channel and (2) the marketing activities they are expected to perform in the future.

Suppose a manufacturer quotes price in the following form: list price—$100 less 30/10/5. The first number in the percentage sequence always refers to the retail end of the channel. The last number always refers to the wholesaler or jobber closest to the manufacturer in the channel. The trade discounts are simply subtracted one at a time. This price quote shows $100 is the manufacturer's suggested retail price; 30 percent of the suggested retail price is available to the retailer to cover costs and provide a profit of $30 ($100 × 0.3 = $30); wholesalers closest to the retailer in the channel get 10 percent of their selling price ($70 × 0.1 = $7); and the final group of wholesalers in the channel (probably jobbers) that are closest to the manufacturer get 5 percent of their selling price ($63 × 0.05 = $3.15). Thus, starting with the manufacturer's suggested retail price and subtracting the three trade discounts shows that the manufacturer's selling price to the wholesaler or jobber closest to it is $59.85 (see Figure 14–7).

Traditional trade discounts have been established in various product lines such as hardware, food, and pharmaceutical items. Although the manufacturer may suggest the trade discounts shown in the example just cited, the sellers are free to alter the discount schedule depending on their competitive situation.

Cash Discounts To encourage retailers to pay their bills quickly, manufacturers offer them *cash discounts*. Suppose a retailer receives a bill quoted at $1,000, 2/10 net 30. This means that the bill for the product is $1,000, but the retailer can take a 2 percent discount ($1,000 × 0.02 = $20) if payment is made within 10 days and send a check for $980. If the payment cannot be made within 10 days, the total amount of $1,000 is due within 30 days. It is usually understood by the buyer that an interest charge will be added after the first 30 days of free credit.

Retailers provide cash discounts to consumers as well to eliminate the cost of credit granted to consumers. These discounts take the form of discount-for-cash policies.

Allowances

Allowances, like discounts, are reductions from list or quoted prices to buyers for performing some activity. They include trade-in and promotional allowances.

FIGURE 14–7
The structure of trade discounts affects the manufacturer's selling price and margins made by resellers in a marketing channel.

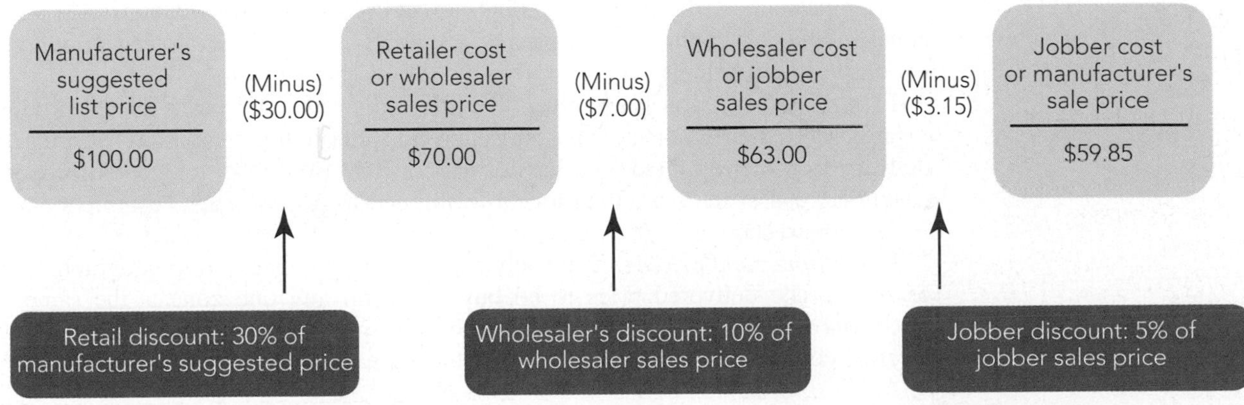

Trade-in Allowances A new-car dealer can offer a substantial reduction in the list price of that new Toyota Camry by offering you a trade-in allowance of $1,000 for your Chevrolet Cavalier. A *trade-in allowance* is a price reduction given when a used product is part of the payment on a new product. Trade-ins are an effective way to lower the price a buyer has to pay without formally reducing the list price.

Promotional Allowances Sellers in the marketing channel can qualify for **promotional allowances** for undertaking certain advertising or selling activities to promote a product. Various types of allowances include an actual cash payment or an extra amount of "free goods" (as with a free case of frozen pizzas to a retailer for every dozen cases purchased). Frequently, a portion of these savings is passed on to the consumer by retailers.

Some companies, such as Procter & Gamble, have chosen to reduce promotional allowances for retailers by using everyday low pricing. **Everyday low pricing** (EDLP) is the practice of replacing promotional allowances with lower manufacturer list prices. EDLP promises to reduce the average price to consumers while minimizing promotional allowances that cost manufacturers billions of dollars every year. However, EDLP does not necessarily benefit supermarkets as described in the Marketing Matters box.[26]

Geographical Adjustments

Geographical adjustments are made by manufacturers or even wholesalers to list or quoted prices to reflect the cost of transportation of the products from seller to buyer. The two general methods for quoting prices related to transportation costs are (1) FOB origin pricing and (2) uniform delivered pricing.

FOB Origin Pricing FOB means "free on board" some vehicle at some location, which means the seller pays the cost of loading the product onto the vehicle that is used (such as a barge, railroad car, or truck). **FOB origin pricing** usually involves the seller's naming the location of this loading as the seller's factory or warehouse (such as "FOB Detroit" or "FOB factory"). The title to the goods passes to the buyer at the point of loading, so the buyer becomes responsible for picking the specific mode of transportation, for all the transportation costs, and for subsequent handling of the product. Buyers farthest from the seller face the big disadvantage of paying the higher transportation costs.

Uniform Delivered Pricing When a **uniform delivered pricing** method is used, the price the seller quotes includes all transportation costs. It is quoted in a contract as "FOB buyer's location," and the seller selects the mode of transportation, pays the freight charges, and is responsible for any damage that may occur because the seller retains title to the goods until delivered to the buyer. Although they go by various names, there are four kinds of delivered pricing methods: (1) single-zone pricing, (2) multiple-zone pricing, (3) FOB with freight-allowed pricing, and (4) basing-point pricing.

In *single-zone pricing*, all buyers pay the same delivered price for the products, regardless of their distance from the seller. So, although a retail store offering free delivery in a metropolitan area has lower transportation costs for goods shipped to customers nearer the store than for those shipped to distant ones, customers pay the same delivered price.

In *multiple-zone pricing*, a firm divides its selling territory into geographic areas or zones. The delivered price to all buyers within any one zone is the same, but prices across zones vary depending on the transportation cost to the zone and the level of competition and demand within the zone.

Marketing Matters > > > > > > customer value

Everyday Low Prices at the Supermarket = Everyday Low Profits—Creating Customer Value at a Cost

Who wouldn't welcome low retail prices every day? The answer is supermarket chains—76 percent of U.S. grocery stores have not adopted this practice. Supermarkets prefer Hi-Lo pricing based on frequent specials where prices are temporarily lowered then raised again. Hi-Lo pricing reflects allowances that manufacturers give supermarkets to push their product. Consider a New York City supermarket whose advertisement is shown here. It regularly pays $1.15 for a can of Bumble Bee white tuna ($55.43 ÷ 48 = $1.15), but the allowances reduce the cost to 96 cents. A price special of 99 cents still provides a 3 cent retail markup ($0.99 retail price in ad − $0.96 cost). When the price on tuna returns to its regular level, the store's gross margin on tuna increases substantially on those cans that were bought with the allowance but not sold during the price special promotion.

BUMBLE BEE white tuna	
List price per 48-can case:	$55.43
Allowance:	$9.50
Net cost per can:	96 cents

RAGÚ spaghetti sauce	
List price per 12-jar case:	$9.50
Allowance:	96 cents
Net cost per jar:	71 cents

MAXWELL HOUSE instant coffee	
List price per 18-jar case:	$83.72
Allowance:	$13.50
Net cost per jar:	$3.90

Everyday low pricing (EDLP) eliminates manufacturer allowances and can reduce average retail prices by up to 10 percent. While EDLP provides lower average prices than Hi-Lo pricing, EDLP does not allow for deeply discounted price specials. EDLP can create everyday customer value and modestly increase supermarket sales—but at a cost. Already slim supermarket chain profits can slip by 18 percent with EDLP without the benefit of allowances as described earlier. Also, some argue that EDLP without price specials is boring for many grocery shoppers who welcome price specials. EDLP has been hailed as "value pricing" by manufacturers, but supermarkets view it differently. For them, EDLP means "Everyday Low Profits!"

With *FOB with freight-allowed pricing*, also called *freight absorption pricing*, the price is quoted by the seller as "FOB plant—freight allowed." The buyer is allowed to deduct freight expenses from the list price of the goods, so the seller agrees to pay, or "absorb," the transportation costs.

Basing-point pricing involves selecting one or more geographical locations (basing point) from which the list price for products plus freight expenses are charged to the buyer. For example, a company might designate St. Louis as the basing point and charge all buyers a list price of $100 plus freight from St. Louis to their location. Basing-point pricing methods have been used in the steel, cement, and lumber industries where freight expenses are a significant part of the total cost to the buyer and products are largely undifferentiated.

Legal and Regulatory Aspects of Pricing

LO4

Arriving at a final price is clearly a complex process. The task is further complicated by legal and regulatory restrictions. Five pricing practices have received the most scrutiny: (1) price fixing, (2) price discrimination, (3) deceptive pricing, (4) geographical pricing, and (5) predatory pricing (see Figure 14–8 on the next page).

Price Fixing A conspiracy among firms to set prices for a product is termed **price fixing**. Price fixing is illegal per se under the Sherman Act (*per se* means in and of itself). When two or more competitors explicitly or implicitly set prices, this practice is called *horizontal price fixing*. For example, six foreign vitamin companies

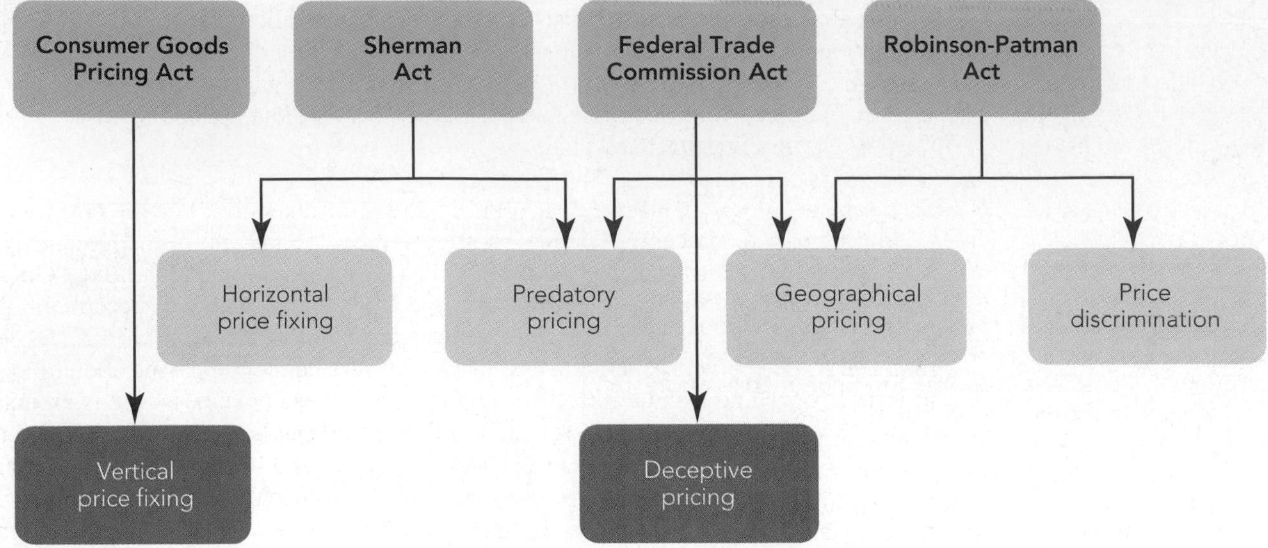

FIGURE 14–8
Several pricing practices are affected by legal and regulatory restrictions. These restrictions seek to benefit both consumers and companies.

pled guilty to price fixing in the human and animal vitamin industry and paid the largest fine in U.S. history, a hefty $335 million.[27]

Vertical price fixing involves controlling agreements between independent buyers and sellers (a manufacturer and a retailer) whereby sellers are required to not sell products below a minimum retail price. This practice, called *resale price maintenance*, was declared illegal per se in 1975 under provisions of the *Consumer Goods Pricing Act*. Nevertheless, this practice is not uncommon. Shoe supplier Nine West recently agreed to settle government charges that the company restricted competition by coercing retailers to adhere to its resale prices. Nine West agreed to pay $34 million in the settlement.[28] However, manufacturers and wholesalers can fix the maximum retail price for their products provided the price agreement does not create an "unreasonable restraint of trade" or is anticompetitive.

It is important to recognize that a "manufacturer's suggested retail price," or MSRP, is not illegal per se. The issue of legality only arises when manufacturers enforce such a practice by coercion. Furthermore, there appears to be a movement toward a "*rule of reason*" in horizontal and vertical price fixing cases.[29] This rule holds that circumstances surrounding a practice must be considered before making a judgment about its legality. The rule of reason perspective is the direct opposite of the per se rule.

Price Discrimination The Clayton Act as amended by the Robinson-Patman Act prohibits **price discrimination**—the practice of charging different prices to different buyers for goods of like grade and quality. However, not all price differences are illegal; only those that substantially lessen competition or create a monopoly are deemed unlawful. Moreover, "goods" is narrowly defined and does not include discrimination in services.

A unique feature of the Robinson-Patman Act is that it allows for price differentials to different customers under the following conditions:

1. When price differences charged to different customers do not exceed the differences in the cost of manufacture, sale, or delivery resulting from differing methods or quantities in which such goods are sold or delivered to buyers. This condition is called the cost justification defense.
2. When price differences result from changing market conditions, avoiding obsolescence of seasonal merchandise, including perishables, or closing out sales.
3. When price differences are quoted to selected buyers in good faith to meet competitors' prices and are not intended to injure competition. This condition is called the meet-the-competition defense.

The Robinson-Patman Act also covers promotional allowances. To legally offer promotional allowances to buyers, the seller must do so on a proportionally equal basis to all buyers distributing the seller's products. In general, the rule of reason applies frequently in price discrimination cases and is often applied to cases involving flexible pricing practices of firms.

Deceptive Pricing Price deals that mislead consumers fall into the category of *deceptive pricing*. Deceptive pricing is outlawed by the Federal Trade Commission Act. The FTC monitors such practices and has published a regulation titled "Guides against Deceptive Pricing" to help businesspeople avoid a charge of deception. The five most common deceptive pricing practices are described in Figure 14–9. As you read about these practices it should be clear that laws cannot be passed and enforced to protect consumers and competitors against all of these practices, so it is essential to rely on the ethical standards of those making and publicizing pricing decisions. An often used pricing practice is to promote products and services for free—a great price! It would seem that the meaning of "free" is obvious. Think again. Visit the FTC Web site described in the Going Online box on the next page to learn what *free* means.

Geographical Pricing FOB origin pricing is legal, as are FOB freight-allowed pricing practices, providing no conspiracy to set prices exists. Basing-point pricing can be viewed as illegal under the Robinson-Patman Act and the Federal Trade Commission Act if there is clear-cut evidence of a conspiracy to set prices. In general, geographical pricing practices have been immune from legal and regulatory restrictions, except in those instances in which a conspiracy to lessen competition exists under the Sherman Act or price discrimination exists under the Robinson-Patman Act.

Predatory Pricing **Predatory pricing** is the practice of charging a very low price for a product with the intent of driving competitors out of business. Once competitors have been driven out, the firm raises its prices. This practice is illegal under the Sherman Act and the Federal Trade Commission Act. Proving the presence

FIGURE 14–9
Five most common deceptive pricing practices

DECEPTIVE PRICING PRACTICE	DESCRIPTION
Bait and switch	A deceptive practice exists when a firm offers a very low price on a product (the bait) to attract customers to a store. Once in the store, the customer is persuaded to purchase a higher priced item (the switch) using a variety of tricks, including (1) downgrading the promoted item, (2) not having the item in stock, or (3) refusing to take orders for the item.
Bargains conditional on other purchases	This practice may exist when a buyer is offered "1-Cent Sales," "Buy 1, Get 1 Free," and "Get 2 for the Price of 1." Such pricing is legal only if the first items are sold at the regular price, not a price inflated for the offer. Substituting lower quality items on either the first or second purchase is also considered deceptive.
Comparable value comparisons	Advertising such as "Retail Value $100.00, Our Price $85.00" is deceptive if a verified and substantial number of stores in the market area did not price the item at $100.
Comparisons with suggested prices	A claim that a price is below a manufacturer's suggested or list price may be deceptive if few or no sales occur at that price in a retailer's market area.
Former price comparisons	When a seller represents a price as reduced, the item must have been offered in good faith at a higher price for a substantial previous period. Setting a high price for the purpose of establishing a reference for a price reduction is deceptive.

Going Online

And You Thought That "Free" Is Simply Defined

The offer of "free" merchandise or service is a promotional device often used to attract customers. The Federal Trade Commission (FTC) acknowledges that such offers are a useful and valuable marketing practice. However, the FTC also recognizes that such offers must be made with extreme care so as to avoid any possibility that consumers will be misled or deceived.

The FTC has issued its "Guide Concerning Use of the Word 'Free' and Similar Representations" at www.ftc.gov/bcp/guides/free.htm. This guide illustrates that the term *free* has multiple dimensions. Suppose a marketer substitutes similar words for *free*, such as *gift*, *given without charge*, or *bonus*. What is the FTC's position on this practice?

BUY THREE, GET ONE FREE

of this practice has been difficult and expensive because it must be shown that the predator explicitly attempted to destroy a competitor and the predatory price was below the defendant's average cost.

learning review

6. Why would a seller choose a flexible-price policy over a one-price policy?
7. If a firm wished to encourage repeat purchases by a buyer throughout a year, would a cumulative or noncumulative quantity discount be a better strategy?
8. Which pricing practices are covered by the Sherman Act?

LEARNING OBJECTIVES REVIEW

LO1 *Describe how to establish the "approximate price level" using demand-oriented, cost-oriented, profit-oriented, and competition-oriented approaches.*

Demand, cost, profit, and competition influence the initial consideration of the approximate price level for a product or service. Demand-oriented pricing approaches stress consumer demand and revenue implications of pricing and include eight types: skimming, penetration, prestige, price lining, odd-even, target, bundle, and yield management. Cost-oriented pricing approaches emphasize the cost aspects of pricing and include three types: standard markup, cost-plus, and experience curve pricing. Profit-oriented pricing approaches focus on a balance between revenues and costs to set a price and include three types: target profit, target return-on-sales, and target return-on-investment pricing. And finally, competition-oriented pricing approaches stress what competitors or the marketplace are doing and include three types: customary; above-, at-, or below-market; and loss-leader pricing. Although these approaches are described separately, some of them overlap, and an effective marketing manager will consider several in searching for an approximate price level.

LO2 *Recognize the major factors considered in deriving a final list or quoted price from the approximate price level.*

Given an approximate price level for a product or service, a manager sets a list or quoted price by considering three additional factors. First, a manager must decide whether to follow a one-price versus a flexible-price policy. Second, the manager should consider the effects of the proposed price on the company, customer, and competitors. Finally, consideration should be given to balancing incremental costs and revenues, particularly when price and cost changes are planned.

LO3 *Identify the adjustments made to the approximate price level on the basis of discounts, allowances, and geography.*

Numerous adjustments can be made to the approximate price level. Discounts are reductions from the list or quoted price that a seller gives a buyer as a reward for some activity of the buyer that is favorable to the seller. These include quantity, seasonal, trade (functional), and cash discounts. Allowances offered to buyers also reduce list or quoted prices. Trade-in allowances and promotional allowances are most common. Finally, geographical adjustments are made to list or quoted prices to reflect transportation costs from sellers to buyers. The two general methods for quoting prices related to transportation costs are FOB origin pricing and uniform delivered pricing.

LO4 *Name the principal laws and regulations affecting specific pricing practices.*

There are four principal laws that affect six major pricing practices. The Sherman Act specifically prohibits horizontal price fixing and predatory pricing. The Consumer Goods Pricing Act makes it illegal for companies to engage in vertical price fixing or resale price maintenance agreements. The Federal Trade Commission Act outlaws deceptive pricing. Provisions in this act also address aspects of predatory pricing and geographical pricing. Finally, the Robinson-Patman Act prohibits price discrimination for goods of like grade and quality, covers the use of promotional allowances, and addresses certain aspects of geographical pricing.

FOCUSING ON KEY TERMS

above-, at-, or below-market pricing p. 354
basing-point pricing p. 363
bundle pricing p. 349
cost-plus pricing p. 350
customary pricing p. 353
everyday low pricing p. 362
experience curve pricing p. 350
flexible-price policy p. 356
FOB origin pricing p. 362
loss-leader pricing p. 354
odd-even pricing p. 349
one-price policy p. 355
penetration pricing p. 347
predatory pricing p. 365
prestige pricing p. 347
price discrimination p. 364
price fixing p. 363
price lining p. 348
price war p. 357
product-line pricing p. 356
promotional allowances p. 362
quantity discounts p. 360
skimming pricing p. 346
standard markup pricing p. 349
target pricing p. 349
target profit pricing p. 351
target return-on-investment pricing p. 352
target return-on-sales pricing p. 352
uniform delivered pricing p. 362
yield management pricing p. 349

APPLYING MARKETING KNOWLEDGE

1 Under what conditions would a digital camera manufacturer adopt a skimming price approach for a new product? A penetration approach?

2 What are some similarities and differences between skimming pricing, prestige pricing, and above-market pricing?

3 A producer of microwave ovens has adopted an experience curve pricing approach for its new model. The firm believes it can reduce the cost of producing the model by 20 percent each time volume doubles. The cost to produce the first unit was $1,000. What would be the approximate cost of the 4,096th unit?

4 The Hesper Corporation is a leading manufacturer of high-quality upholstered sofas. Current plans call for an increase of $600,000 in the advertising budget. If the firm sells its sofas for an average price of $850 and the unit variable costs are $550, then what dollar sales increase will be necessary to cover the additional advertising?

5 Suppose executives estimate that the unit variable cost for their VCR is $100, the fixed cost related to the product is $10 million annually, and the target volume for next year is 100,000 recorders. What sales price will be necessary to achieve a target profit of $1 million?

6 A manufacturer of motor oil has a trade discount policy whereby the manufacturer's suggested retail price is $30 per case with the terms of 40/20/10. The manufacturer sells its products through jobbers, who sell to wholesalers, who sell to gasoline stations. What will the manufacturer's sale price be?

7 Suppose a manufacturer of exercise equipment sets a suggested price to the consumer of $395 for a particular piece of equipment to be competitive with similar equipment. The manufacturer sells its equipment to a sporting goods wholesaler who receives 25 percent of the selling price and a retailer who receives 50 percent of the selling price. What demand-oriented pricing approach is being used, and at what price will the manufacturer sell the equipment to the wholesaler?

8 Is there any truth in the statement, "Geographical pricing schemes will always be unfair to some buyers"? Why or why not?

building your marketing plan

To arrive at the final price(s) for your offering(s):

1 Modify the three prices from your Chapter 13 analysis in light of (*a*) pricing considerations for demand-, cost-, profit-, and competition-oriented Chapter 14 approaches and (*b*) possibilities for discounts, allowances, and geographic adjustments.

2 Do a break-even analysis for each of these three new prices.

3 Choose the final price(s).

video case 14 3M Greptile™ Grip Golf Glove: Pricing an Innovative Product

"Marketing is not brain surgery," says Dr. George Dierberger, Marketing and International Manager of 3M's Sports and Leisure Products Project. "We tend to make it a lot more difficult than it is. 3M wins with its technology. We're not in the 'me-too' business, and in marketing we've got to remember that."

3M'S MICROREPLICATION TECHNOLOGY AND ITS GREPTILE GRIP GOLF GLOVE

The 3M Company is a $25 billion global, diversified technology business. Among its well-known brands are Post-it® Notes™, Scotch® tape, Scotch Brite® scouring pads, and Nexcare™ bandages. The key to 3M's marketing successes is its commitment to innovation. For more than a century, 3M's management has given its employees the freedom to try new ideas. This "culture of creativity" has led to the commercialization of more than 50,000 products.

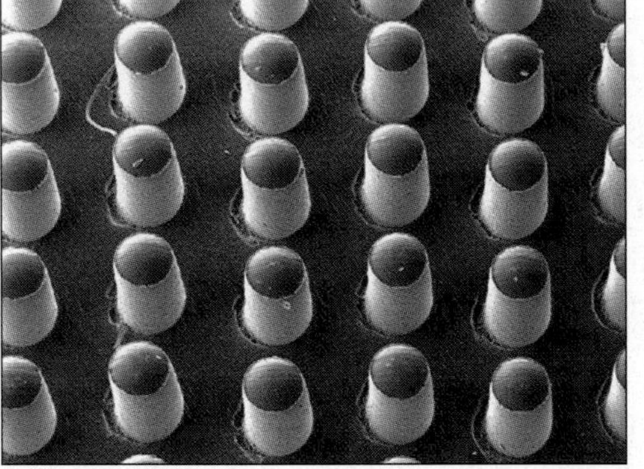

The Sports and Leisure Products Project is a business unit that Dierberger manages with his marketing staff. Recently, Dierberger and his staff tried to change the conventional thinking about golfing. Using 3M's proprietary "microreplication" technology, and applying it to a golf glove, the new Greptile™ gripping material consists of thousands of tiny "gripping fingers" sewn into the upper palm and lower fingers of a golf glove (photo).

The 3M Greptile Grip golf glove is made primarily of high-quality Cabretta sheep leather to give it a soft, comfortable feel. The golf glove is offered in both men's and women's versions and in small, medium, medium/large, large, and extra-large hand sizes. Initially, 3M sold the Greptile Grip golf glove through Walmart and other mass merachandisers. Then golf retailers like Golfsmith, Austad's, and Golf Galaxy began to carry it.

According to Dierberger, "It is the only glove on the market that actively improves a golfer's hold on the club by allowing a more relaxed grip, leading to greater driving distance with less grip pressure, even under wet conditions." Laboratory tests found that the Greptile material offers 610 percent greater gripping power than leather and 340 percent greater than tackified (sticky) grips. The result: On drives, the golf ball travels an average 10.5 feet farther!

3M'S NEW PRODUCT PROCESS

Since about half of 3M's products are less than five years old, the process used by 3M to develop new-product innovations is critical to its success and continued growth. Every innovation must meet 3M's new product criteria: (1) be a patentable or trademarked technology; (2) offer a superior value proposition to consumers; and (3) change the basis of competition by achieving a significant point of difference.

When developing a new product innovation such as the 3M Greptile Grip golf glove, 3M uses a rigorous seven-step process: (1) idea, (2) concept, (3) feasibility, (4) development, (5) scale-up, (6) launch, and (7) post-launch. "But innovation is not a linear path—not just A, then B, then C," says Dierberger. "It's the adjustments you make after you've developed the product that determines your success. And it's learning lessons from testing on real customers to make the final tweaks—changing the price points, improving the benefits statement on the packaging, and sharpening the advertising appeals."

In the case of the 3M Greptile Grip golf glove, countless other examples of these adjustments appeared. Mike Kuhl, marketing coordinator at 3M, points out, "Consumer testing labs said the information on the back of our package was incomplete so we had dozens of golfers hit drives using our glove and competitive gloves to compare driving distance." And says 3M packaging engineer Travis Strom, "Our first glove package 'pillowed'—bulked up—on the shelf, had hard-to-read text, and wasn't appealing to golfers, so we had to redesign it. After all, you only have a few seconds to capture the customer's attention with the package and make a sale."

THE GOLF AND GOLF GLOVE MARKETS

Several socioeconomic and demographic trends impact the golf glove market favorably. First, the huge baby boomer population (those born between 1946 and 1964) has matured, reaching its prime earning potential. This allows for greater discretionary spending on leisure activities, such as golf. According to the National Golf Foundation (NGF), consumers 50 and older—today's baby boomers—spend the most on golf equipment (clubs, bags, balls, shoes, gloves, etc.). Second, according to U.S. Census Bureau data, the U.S. population has shifted regionally from the East and North to the South and West, where golfing is popular year-round due to the temperate weather. On the negative side, the number of U.S. golf courses has been declining slightly due to the recession, totaling about 16,000 at the end of 2008.

Finally, golf is becoming an increasingly popular leisure activity for all age groups and ethnic backgrounds. According to the NGF, golf participants in the United States totaled 28.6 million in 2008. Female golfers now account for about 25 percent of all golfers while minority participation is about 10 percent. For 2009, the National Sporting Goods Association estimated that sales of golf equipment were $3.4 billion, down about 8 percent from its peak in 2007 as a result of the recession.

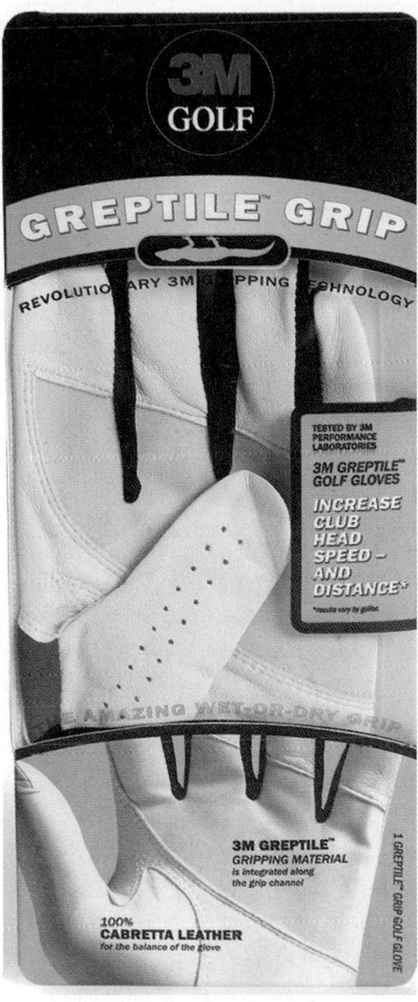

The global market for golf gloves is estimated at $300 million, with the United States at $180 million or 60 percent of worldwide sales. Historically, about 80 percent of golf gloves are sold through public and private on- and off-course golf pro specialty shops, golf superstores, and sporting good superstores. However, mass merchandisers like Wal-Mart and Target have recently increased their shares due to the typically lower prices offered by these retailers. FootJoy and Titleist, both owned by Acushnet, are the top two golf glove market share leaders. Nike, which entered the golf equipment market with Tiger Woods as its spokesperson, along with Calloway and TaylorMade, also have measurable shares of the global golf glove market.

SETTING A PRICE

Golf glove marketers focus on technology, comfort, durability, and price/value to create points of difference from their competition. This is the basis of 3M's stress on the improved gripping with its golf glove. So in 2005, 3M Golf launched its premium Greptile Grip golf glove consisting of the highest quality Cabretta leather and selling for a suggested retail price of $16.95 to $19.95. The next year, 3M introduced versions of its Greptile Grip golf gloves in Japan and Europe, the second and third largest golf markets behind the United States.

Recently, golf glove marketer Bionic introduced the Classic ($24.95) and the Pro ($39.95) gloves designed by an orthopedic hand surgeon. FootJoy also launched the innovative "tailored cut" Pure Touch Limited ($28) for a "precision fit" and the SciFlex ($18), which incorporates new "microfiber" technology for comfort and durability.

Many golf glove marketers now focus on price/value due to the recession. Several, such as FootJoy, Titleist, and Calloway, offer single gloves within three basic price points: $6.00 to $9.99; $10.00 to $16.99; and $17.00 and up. However, these and other firms also offer gloves in 2-packs (Calloway's Warbird—$15.99) and/or 3-packs (FootJoy's StaSof—$26.99).

Questions

1 What are the characteristics of the target market for the 3M Greptile Grip golf glove?

2 (*a*) What are the key points of difference of the 3M Greptile Grip golf glove when compared to competitors' products, such as FootJoy and Bionic? (*b*) Substitute products, such as golf grips?

3 How does the Greptile Grip golf glove meet 3M's three criteria for new products?

4 Since 3M has no prior products for the golf market, what special promotion and distribution problems might 3M have?

5 (*a*) Looking at the competitors' prices today, should 3M use a demand-oriented, cost-oriented, profit-oriented, or competition-oriented pricing strategy for its Greptile Grip golf glove? (*b*) Give your reasons. (*c*) For the strategy you selected, recommend a price point, justifying your answer.

APPENDIX B FINANCIAL ASPECTS OF MARKETING

Basic concepts from accounting and finance provide valuable tools for marketing executives. This appendix describes an actual company's use of accounting and financial concepts and illustrates how they assist the owner in making marketing decisions.

THE CAPLOW COMPANY

An accomplished artist and calligrapher, Jane Westerlund decided to apply some of her experience to the picture framing business in Minneapolis. She bought an existing retail frame store, The Caplow Company, from a friend who owned the business and wanted to retire. She avoided the do-it-yourself end of the framing business and chose three kinds of business activities: (1) cutting the frame, mats, and glass for customers who brought in their own pictures or prints to be framed; (2) selling prints and posters that she had purchased from wholesalers; and (3) restoring high-quality frames and paintings.

To understand how accounting, finance, and marketing relate to each other, let's analyze (1) the operating statement for her frame shop, (2) some general ratios of interest that are derived from the operating statement, and (3) some ratios that pertain specifically to her pricing decisions.

The Operating Statement

The *operating statement* (also called an *income statement* or *profit-and-loss statement*) summarizes the profitability of a business firm for a specific time period, usually a month, quarter, or year. The title of the operating statement for The Caplow Company shows it is for a one-year period (Figure B–1). The purpose of an operating statement is to show the profit of the firm and the revenues and expenses that led to that profit. This information tells the owner or manager what has happened in the past and suggests actions to improve future profitability.

The left side of Figure B–1 shows that there are three key elements to all operating statements: (1) sales of the firm's goods and services, (2) costs incurred in making and selling the goods and services, and (3) profit or loss, which is the difference between sales and costs.

Sales Elements The sales elements of Figure B–1 have four terms that need explanation:

- *Gross sales* are the total amount billed to customers. Dissatisfied customers or errors may reduce the gross sales through returns or allowances.
- *Returns* occur when a customer gives the item purchased back to the seller, who either refunds the purchase price or allows the customer a credit on subsequent purchases. In any event, the seller now owns the item again.
- *Allowances* are given when a customer is dissatisfied with the item purchased and the seller reduces the original purchase price. Unlike returns, in the case of allowances the buyer owns the item.
- *Net sales* are simply gross sales minus returns and allowances.

The operating statement for The Caplow Company shows that:

Gross sales	$80,500
Less: Returns and allowances	500
Net sales	$80,000

The low level of returns and allowances shows the shop generally has done a good job in satisfying customers, which is essential in building the repeat business necessary for success.

Cost Elements The *cost of goods sold* (COGS) is the total cost of the products sold during the period. This

FIGURE B–1
Examples of an operating statement

THE CAPLOW COMPANY
Operating Statement
For the Year Ending December 31, 2009

Sales	Gross sales			$80,500
	Less: Returns and allowances			500
	Net sales			$80,000
Costs	Cost of goods sold:			
	Beginning inventory at cost		$ 6,000	
	Purchases at billed cost	$21,000		
	Less: Purchase discounts	300		
	Purchases at net cost	20,700		
	Plus: freight-in	100		
	Net cost of delivered purchases		20,800	
	Direct labor (framing)		14,200	
	Cost of goods available for sale		41,000	
	Less: Ending inventory at cost		5,000	
	Cost of goods sold			36,000
	Gross margin (gross profit)			$44,000
	Expenses:			
	Selling expenses:			
	Sales salaries	2,000		
	Advertising expense	3,000		
	Total selling expense		5,000	
	Administrative expenses:			
	Owner's salary	18,000		
	Bookkeeper's salary	1,200		
	Office supplies	300		
	Total administrative expense		19,500	
	General expenses:			
	Depreciation expense	1,000		
	Interest expense	500		
	Rent expense	2,100		
	Utility expenses (heat, electricity)	3,000		
	Repairs and maintenance	2,300		
	Insurance	2,000		
	Social security taxes	2,200		
	Total general expense		13,100	
	Total expenses			37,600
Profit or loss	Profit before taxes			$ 6,400

item varies according to the kind of business. A retail store purchases finished goods and resells them to customers without reworking them in any way. In contrast, a manufacturing firm combines raw and semifinished materials and parts, uses labor and overhead to rework these into finished goods, and then sells them to customers. All these activities are reflected in the cost of goods sold item on a manufacturer's operating statement. Note that the frame shop has some features of a pure retailer (prints and posters it buys that are resold without alteration) and a pure manufacturer (assembling the raw materials of molding, matting, and glass to form a completed frame).

Some terms that relate to cost of goods sold need clarification:

- *Inventory* is the physical material that is purchased from suppliers, may or may not be reworked, and is available for sale to customers. In the frame shop, inventory includes molding, matting, glass, prints, and posters.

- *Purchase discounts* are reductions in the original billed price for reasons such as prompt payment of the bill or the quantity bought.
- *Direct labor* is the cost of the labor used in producing the finished product. For the frame shop, this is the cost of producing the completed frames from the molding, matting, and glass.
- *Gross margin (gross profit)* is the money remaining to manage the business, sell the products or services, and give some profit. Gross margin is net sales minus cost of goods sold.

The two right-hand columns in Figure B–1 between "Net sales" and "Gross margin" calculate the cost of goods sold:

Net sales		$80,000
Cost of goods sold		
Beginning inventory at cost	$ 6,000	
Net cost of delivered purchases	20,800	
Direct labor (framing)	14,200	
Cost of goods available for sale	41,000	
Less: ending inventory at cost	5,000	
Cost of goods sold		36,000
Gross margin (gross profit)		$44,000

This section considers the beginning and ending inventories, the net cost of purchases delivered during the year, and the cost of the direct labor going into making the frames. Subtracting the $36,000 cost of goods sold from the $80,000 net sales gives the $44,000 gross margin.

Jane Westerlund (left) and an assistant assess the restoration of a gold frame for regilding.

Three major categories of expenses are shown in Figure B–1 below the gross margin:

- *Selling expenses* are the costs of selling the product or service produced by the firm. For The Caplow Company there are two such selling expenses: sales salaries of part-time employees waiting on customers and the advertising expense of simple newspaper ads and direct-mail ads sent to customers.
- *Administrative expenses* are the costs of managing the business, and for The Caplow Company include three expenses: the owner's salary, a part-time bookkeeper's salary, and office supplies expense.
- *General expenses* are miscellaneous costs not covered elsewhere; for the frame shop these include seven items: depreciation expense (on equipment), interest expense, rent expense, utility expenses, repairs and maintenance expense, insurance expense, and social security taxes.

As shown in Figure B–1, selling, administrative, and general expenses total $37,600 for The Caplow Company.

Profit Element What the company has earned, the *profit before taxes,* is found by subtracting cost of goods sold and expenses from net sales. For The Caplow Company, Figure B–1 shows that profit before taxes is $6,400.

General Operating Ratios to Analyze Operations

Looking only at the elements of Caplow's operating statement that extend to the right-hand column highlights the firm's performance on some important dimensions. Using operating ratios such as *expense-to-sales ratios* for expressing basic expense or profit elements as a percentage of net sales gives further insights:

Element in Operating Statement	Dollar Value	Percentage of Net Sales
Gross sales	$80,500	
Less: Returns and allowances	500	
Net sales	80,000	100%
Less: Cost of goods sold	36,000	45
Gross margin	44,000	55
Less: Total expenses	37,600	47
Profit (or loss) before taxes	$ 6,400	8%

Westerlund can use this information to compare her firm's performance from one time period to the next. To do so, it is especially important that she keep the same definitions for each element of her operating statement, also a significant factor in using the electronic spreadsheets discussed in Chapter 14. Performance comparisons between periods are more difficult if she changes definitions for the accounting elements in the operating statement.

She can use either the dollar values or the operating ratios (the value of the element of the operating statement divided by net sales) to analyze the firm's performance. However, the operating ratios are more valuable than the dollar values for two reasons: (1) the simplicity of working with percentages rather than dollars and (2) the availability of operating ratios of typical firms in the same industry, which are published by Dun & Bradstreet and trade associations. Thus, Westerlund can compare her firm's performance not only with that of *other* frame shops but also with that of *small* frame shops that have annual net sales, for example, under $100,000. In this way, she can identify where her operations are better or worse than other similar firms. For example, if trade association data showed a typical frame shop of her size had a ratio of cost of goods sold to net sales of 37 percent, compared with her 45 percent, she might consider steps to reduce this cost through purchase discounts, reducing inbound freight charges, finding lower-cost suppliers, and so on.

Ratios to Use in Setting and Evaluating Price

Using The Caplow Company as an example, we can study four ratios that relate closely to setting a price: (1) markup, (2) markdown, (3) stockturns, and (4) return on investment. These terms are defined in Figure B–2 and explained below.

Markup Both *markup* and gross margin refer to the amount added to the cost of goods sold to arrive at the selling price, and they may be expressed either in dollar or percentage terms. However, the term *markup* is more commonly used in setting retail prices. Suppose the average price Westerlund charges for a framed picture is $80. Then in terms of the first two definitions in Figure B–2 and the earlier information from the operating statement,

Element of Price	Dollar Value
Cost of goods sold	$36
Markup (or gross margin)	44
Selling price	$80

The third definition in Figure B–2 gives the percentage markup on selling price:

$$\text{Markup on selling price (\%)} = \frac{\text{Markup}}{\text{Selling price}} \times 100$$

$$= \frac{44}{80} \times 100 = 55\%$$

FIGURE B–2
How to calculate selling price, markups, markdown, stockturn rate, and return on investment

Name of Financial Element or Ratio	What It Measures	Equation
Selling price ($)	Price customer sees	Cost of goods sold (COGS) + Markup
Markup ($)	Dollars added to COGS to arrive at selling price	Selling price − COGS
Markup on selling price (%)	Relates markup to selling price	$\frac{\text{Markup}}{\text{Selling price}} \times 100 = \frac{\text{Selling price} - \text{COGS}}{\text{Selling price}} \times 100$
Markup on cost (%)	Relates markup to cost	$\frac{\text{Markup}}{\text{COGS}} \times 100 = \frac{\text{Selling price} - \text{COGS}}{\text{COGS}} \times 100$
Markdown (%)	Ability of firm to sell its products at initial selling price	$\frac{\text{Markdowns}}{\text{Net sales}} \times 100$
Stockturn rate	Ability of firm to move its inventory quickly	$\frac{\text{COGS}}{\text{Average inventory at cost}}$ or $\frac{\text{Net sales}}{\text{Average inventory at selling price}}$
Return on investment (%)	Profit performance of firm compared with money invested in it	$\frac{\text{Net profit after taxes}}{\text{Investment}} \times 100$

And the percentage markup on cost is obtained as follows:

$$\text{Markup on cost (\%)} = \frac{\text{Markup}}{\text{Cost of goods sold}} \times 100$$

$$= \frac{44}{36} \times 100 = 122.2\%$$

Inexperienced retail clerks sometimes fail to distinguish between the two definitions of markup, which (as the preceding calculations show) can represent a tremendous difference, so it is essential to know whether the base is cost or selling price. Marketers generally use selling price as the base for talking about markups unless they specifically state that they are using cost as a base.

Retailers and wholesalers that rely heavily on markup pricing (discussed in Chapter 14) often use standardized tables that convert markup on selling price to markup on cost, and vice versa. The two equations below show how to convert one to the other:

$$\text{Markup on selling price (\%)} = \frac{\text{Markup on cost (\%)}}{100\% + \text{Markup on cost (\%)}} \times 100$$

$$\text{Markup on cost (\%)} = \frac{\text{Markup on selling price (\%)}}{100\% - \text{Markup on selling price (\%)}}$$

Using the data from The Caplow Company gives:

$$\text{Markup on selling price (\%)} = \frac{\text{Markup on cost (\%)}}{100\% + \text{Markup on cost (\%)}} \times 100$$

$$= \frac{122.2}{100 + 122.2} \times 100 = 55\%$$

$$\text{Markup on cost (\%)} = \frac{\text{Markup on selling price (\%)}}{100\% - \text{Markup on selling price (\%)}} \times 100$$

$$= \frac{55}{100 - 55} \times 100 = 122.2\%$$

The use of an incorrect markup base is shown in Westerlund's business. A markup of 122.2 percent on her cost of goods sold for a typical frame she sells gives 122.2% × \$36 = \$44 of markup. Added to the \$36 cost of goods sold, this gives her a selling price of \$80 for the framed picture. However, a new clerk working for her who erroneously priced the framed picture at 55 percent of cost of goods sold set the final price at \$55.80 (\$36 of cost of goods sold plus 55% × \$36 = \$19.80). The error, if repeated, can be disastrous: frames would be accidentally sold at \$55.80, or \$24.20 below the intended selling price of \$80.

Markdown A *markdown* is a reduction in a retail price that is necessary if the item will not sell at the full selling price to which it has been marked up. The item might not sell for a variety of reasons: the selling price was set too high or the item is out of style or has become soiled or damaged. The seller "takes a markdown" by lowering the price to sell it, thereby converting it to cash to buy future inventory that will sell faster.

The markdown percentage cannot be calculated directly from the operating statement. As shown in the fifth item of Figure B–2, the numerator of the markdown percentage is the total dollar markdowns. Markdowns are reductions in the prices of goods that are purchased by customers. The denominator is net sales.

Suppose The Caplow Company had a total of \$700 in markdowns on the prints and posters that are stocked and available for sale. Since the frames are custom made for individual customers, there is little reason for a markdown there. Caplow's markdown percent is then:

A customer discusses choices of framing and matting for her print with Jane Westerlund.

$$\text{Markdown (\%)} = \frac{\text{Markdowns}}{\text{Net sales}} \times 100$$

$$= \frac{\$700}{\$80{,}000} \times 100$$

$$= 0.875\%$$

Other kinds of retailers often have markdown ratios several times this amount. For example, women's dress stores have markdowns of about 25 percent, and menswear stores have markdowns of about 2 percent.

Stockturn Rate A business firm is eager to have its inventory move quickly, or "turn over." *Stockturn rate,* or simply stockturns, measures this inventory movement. For a retailer, a slow stockturn rate may show it is buying merchandise customers don't want, so this is a critical measure of performance. When a firm sells only a single product, one convenient way to measure stockturn rate is simply to divide its cost of goods sold by average inventory at cost. The sixth item in Figure B–2 shows how to calculate stockturn rate using information in the operating statement:

$$\text{Stockturn rate} = \frac{\text{Cost of goods sold}}{\text{Average inventory at cost}}$$

The dollar amount of average inventory at cost is calculated by adding the beginning and ending inventories for the year and dividing by 2 to get the average. From Caplow's operating statement, we have:

$$\text{Stockturn rate} = \frac{\text{Cost of goods sold}}{\text{Average inventory at cost}}$$

$$= \frac{\text{Cost of goods sold}}{\dfrac{\text{Beginning inventory} + \text{Ending inventory}}{2}}$$

$$= \frac{\$36{,}000}{\dfrac{\$6{,}000 + \$5{,}000}{2}}$$

$$= \frac{\$36{,}000}{\$5{,}500}$$

$$= 6.5 \text{ stockturns per year}$$

What is considered a "good stockturn" varies by industry. For example, supermarkets have limited shelf space for thousands of new products from manufacturers each year, so they watch stockturn carefully by product line. The stockturn rate in supermarkets for breakfast foods is about 17 times per year, for pet food about 22 times per year, and for paper products about 25 times per year.

Return on Investment A better measure of the performance of a firm than the amount of profit it makes in a year is its *return on investment* (ROI), which is the ratio of net income to the investment used to earn that net income. To calculate ROI, it is necessary to subtract income taxes from profit before taxes to obtain net income, then divide this figure by the investment that can be found on a firm's balance sheet (which is another accounting statement that shows the firm's assets, liabilities, and net worth). While financial and accounting experts have many definitions for *investment,* an often-used definition is "total assets."

For our purposes, let's assume that Westerlund has total assets (investment) of \$20,000 in The Caplow Company, which covers inventory, store fixtures, and framing equipment. If she pays \$1,000 in income taxes, her store's net income is \$5,400, so her ROI is given by the seventh item in Figure B–2:

$$\begin{aligned}\text{Return on investment} &= \text{Net income/Investment} \times 100\\ &= \$5{,}400/\$20{,}000 \times 100\\ &= 27\%\end{aligned}$$

If Westerlund wants to improve her ROI next year, the strategies she might take are found in this alternative equation for ROI:

$$\begin{aligned}\text{ROI} &= \text{Net sales/Investment} \times \text{Net income/Net sales}\\ &= \text{Investment turnover} \times \text{Profit margin}\end{aligned}$$

This equation suggests that The Caplow Company's ROI can be improved by raising investment turnover or increasing profit margin. Increasing stockturns will accomplish the former, whereas lowering cost of goods sold to net sales will cause the latter.

Callaway
PURE

BOMB IT
OR BEND IT.

The FT-9™ Driver is designed for both.

Golf Digest Hot List

Carbon composite construction, External Web Weighting and explosive titanium Hyperbolic Face Cup Technology™ combine to provide unbelievable distance and shot-shaping control. So go ahead. Hit a draw. Hit a fade. Hit it pure.

callawaygolf.com/pure

Callaway

© 2009 Callaway Golf Company. FT-9, Hyperbolic Face Cup Technology, the Chevron Device and Callaway Golf are trademarks and/or registered trademarks of Callaway Golf Company.

15 Managing Marketing Channels and Wholesaling

LEARNING OBJECTIVES

After reading this chapter you should be able to:

LO1 Explain what is meant by a marketing channel of distribution and why intermediaries are needed.

LO2 Distinguish among traditional marketing channels, electronic marketing channels, and different types of vertical marketing systems.

LO3 Describe the factors and considerations that affect a company's choice and management of a marketing channel.

LO4 Recognize how conflict, cooperation, and legal considerations affect marketing channel relationships.

CALLAWAY GOLF: DESIGNING AND DELIVERING THE GOODS FOR GREAT GOLF

What do Ernie Els, a world-class golf professional, and Justin Timberlake, a pop icon and avid amateur golfer, have in common? Both use Callaway Golf equipment, accessories, and apparel when playing their favorite sport.

With annual sales exceeding $1 billion annually, Callaway Golf is one of the most recognized and highly regarded companies in the golf industry. With its commitment to continuous product innovation and broad distribution in the United States and more than 100 countries worldwide, Callaway Golf has built a strong reputation for designing and delivering the goods for great golf for golfers of all skill levels, both amateur and professional.

Callaway Golf primarily markets its products through more than 15,000 on- and off-course golf retailers and sporting goods retailers, such as Golf Galaxy, Inc.; Dick's Sporting Goods, Inc.; and PGA Tour Superstores, that sell quality golf products and provide a level of customer service appropriate for the sale of such products. The company also has its own online store (Shop.Callawaygolf.com), which makes it a full-fledged multichannel marketer, and a successful one as well. The chief executive of PGA America called Callaway's online store "innovative in that it combines that old legacy relationship with the retail channel with the new innovation of the Web" soon after the online store was launched. Callaway's chief executive officer, George Fellows, says Callaway's online store is useful for consumers who are looking for accessories or apparel, and for those who know their preferred golf club specifications: "There are always going to be certain people that will not feel comfortable buying online. But for those that do feel comfortable, we really represent the most seamless process."

Callaway Golf considers its marketing channel partners a valued marketing asset. For example, when the company opened its online store, careful attention was placed on how Callaway Golf "could satisfy the consumer but do so in a way that didn't violate our relationships with our loyal trade partners," Fellows said. The solution? Callaway Golf has one of its retailers get credit for the sale. This retailer then fulfills a buyer's order within 24 hours. Consumers, retailers, and Callaway Golf all benefit from this arrangement.[1]

This chapter focuses on marketing channels of distribution and why they are an important component in the marketing mix. It then shows how such channels benefit consumers and the sequence of firms that make up a marketing channel. Finally, it describes factors that influence the choice and management of marketing channels, including channel conflict, cooperation, and legal restrictions.

NATURE AND IMPORTANCE OF MARKETING CHANNELS

Reaching prospective buyers, either directly or indirectly, is a prerequisite for successful marketing. At the same time, buyers benefit from distribution systems used by companies.

What Is a Marketing Channel of Distribution?

LO1

You see the results of distribution every day. You may have purchased Lay's Potato Chips at a 7-Eleven convenience store, a book online through Amazon.com, and Levi's jeans at Kohl's department stores. Each of these items was brought to you by a marketing channel of distribution, or simply a **marketing channel**, which consists of individuals and firms involved in the process of making a product or service available for use or consumption by consumers or industrial users.

Marketing channels can be compared with a pipeline through which water flows from a source to terminus. Marketing channels make possible the flow of goods from a producer, through intermediaries, to a buyer. Intermediaries go by various names (see Figure 15–1) and perform various functions. Some intermediaries actually purchase items from the seller, store them, and resell them to buyers. For example, Celestial Seasonings produces specialty teas and sells them to food wholesalers. The wholesalers then sell these teas to supermarkets and grocery stores, which, in turn, sell them to consumers. Other intermediaries such as brokers and agents represent sellers but do not actually take title to products—their role is to bring a seller and buyer together. Century 21 real estate agents are examples of this type of intermediary. The importance of intermediaries is made even clearer when we consider the functions they perform and the value they create for buyers.

Value Is Created by Intermediaries

Few consumers appreciate the value created by intermediaries; however, producers recognize that intermediaries make selling goods and services more efficient because they minimize the number of sales contacts necessary to reach a target market.

FIGURE 15–1
A variety of terms is used for marketing intermediaries. They vary in specificity and use in consumer and business markets.

TERM	DESCRIPTION
Middleman	Any intermediary between manufacturer and end-user markets
Agent or broker	Any intermediary with legal authority to act on behalf of the manufacturer
Wholesaler	An intermediary who sells to other intermediaries, usually to retailers; term usually applies to consumer markets
Retailer	An intermediary who sells to consumers
Distributor	An imprecise term, usually used to describe intermediaries who perform a variety of distribution functions, including selling, maintaining inventories, extending credit, and so on; a more common term in business markets but may also be used to refer to wholesalers
Dealer	A more imprecise term than *distributor* that can mean the same as distributor, retailer, wholesaler, and so forth

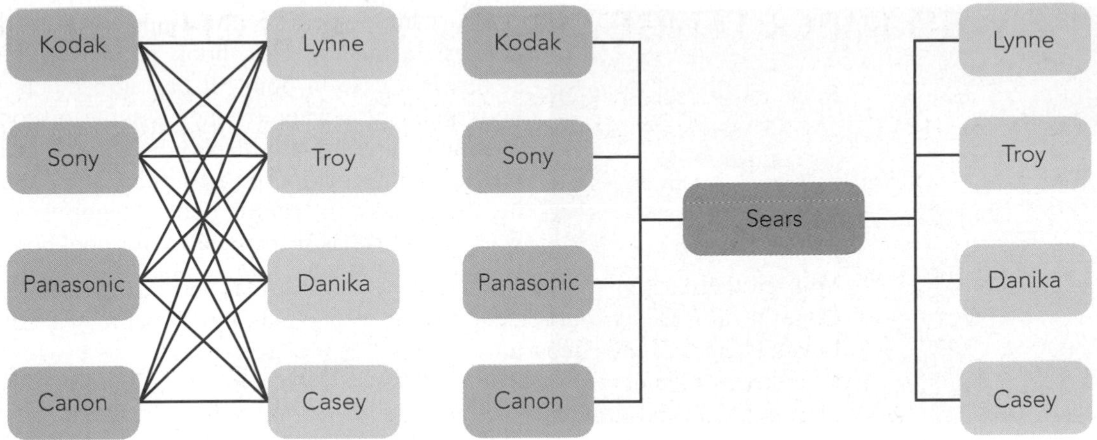

FIGURE 15–2
Intermediaries minimize transactions and the cost of distribution for producers and customers.

Figure 15–2 shows a simple example of how this comes about in the digital camera industry. Without a retail intermediary (such as Sears), Kodak, Sony, Panasonic, and Canon would each have to make four contacts to reach the four buyers shown who are in the target market. However, each producer has to make only one contact when Sears acts as an intermediary. Equally important from a macromarketing perspective, the total number of industry transactions is reduced from 16 to 8, which reduces producer cost and hence benefits the customer.

Important Functions Performed by Intermediaries Intermediaries make possible the flow of products from producers to buyers by performing three basic functions (Figure 15–3). Intermediaries perform a *transactional function* that involves buying, selling, and risk taking because they stock merchandise in anticipation of sales. Intermediaries perform a *logistical function* evident in the gathering, storing, and dispersing of products (see Chapter 16 on supply chain and logistics management). Finally, intermediaries perform *facilitating functions*, which assist producers in making goods and services more attractive to buyers.

All three functions must be performed in a marketing channel, even though each channel member may not participate in all three. Channel members often negotiate

FIGURE 15–3
Marketing channel intermediaries perform three fundamental functions, each of which consists of different activities.

TYPE OF FUNCTION	ACTIVITIES RELATED TO FUNCTION
Transactional function	• *Buying*: Purchasing products for resale or as an agent for supply of a product • *Selling*: Contacting potential customers, promoting products, and seeking orders • *Risk taking*: Assuming business risks in the ownership of inventory that can become obsolete or deteriorate
Logistical function	• *Assorting*: Creating product assortments from several sources to serve customers • *Storing*: Assembling and protecting products at a convenient location to offer better customer service • *Sorting*: Purchasing in large quantities and breaking into smaller amounts desired by customers • *Transporting*: Physically moving a product to customers
Facilitating function	• *Financing*: Extending credit to customers • *Grading*: Inspecting, testing, or judging products, and assigning them quality grades • *Marketing information and research*: Providing information to customers and suppliers, including competitive conditions and trends

Borders, a leading U.S. book retailer, works closely with book publishers. Read the text to learn how this is done.

Borders Group, Inc.
www.borders.com

about which specific functions they will perform. Borders, a leading U.S. book retailer with over 1,000 stores, is a case in point. It has agreements with major book publishers whereby they assume responsibility for recommending how to display books on its shelves, and providing information on new titles and consumer reading preferences in specific book categories. For example, HarperCollins has responsibility for cookbooks, Random House for children's books, and Pearson for computer books.[2]

Consumers Also Benefit from Intermediaries

Consumers also benefit from intermediaries. Having the goods and services you want, when you want them, where you want them, and in the form you want them is the ideal result of marketing channels.

In more specific terms, marketing channels help create value for consumers through the four utilities described in Chapter 1: time, place, form, and possession. Time utility refers to having a product or service when you want it. For example, FedEx provides next-morning delivery. Place utility means having a product or service available where consumers want it, such as having a Texaco gas station located on a long stretch of lonely highway. Form utility involves enhancing a product or service to make it more appealing to buyers. Consider the importance of bottlers in the soft-drink industry. Coca-Cola and Pepsi-Cola manufacture the flavor concentrate (cola, lemon-lime) and sell it to bottlers—intermediaries—which then add sweetener and the concentrate to carbonated water and package the beverage in bottles and cans, which are then sold to retailers. Possession utility entails efforts by intermediaries to help buyers take possession of a product or service, such as having airline tickets delivered by a travel agency.

learning review

1. What is meant by a marketing channel?
2. What are the three basic functions performed by intermediaries?

CHANNEL STRUCTURE AND ORGANIZATION

LO2

A product can take many routes on its journey from a producer to buyers. Marketers continually search for the most efficient route from the many alternatives available. As you'll see, there are some important differences between the marketing channels for consumer goods and those for business goods.

Marketing Channels for Consumer Goods and Services

Figure 15–4 shows the four most common marketing channels for consumer goods and services. It also shows the number of levels in each marketing channel, as evidenced by the number of intermediaries between a producer and ultimate buyers. As the number of intermediaries between a producer and buyer increases, the channel is viewed as increasing in length. Thus, the producer → wholesaler → retailer → consumer channel is longer than the producer → consumer channel.

Direct Channel Channel A represents a *direct channel* because a producer and ultimate consumers deal directly with each other. Many products and services are distributed this way. Many insurance companies sell their financial services using

FIGURE 15–4
Common marketing channels for consumer goods and services differ by the kind and number of intermediaries.

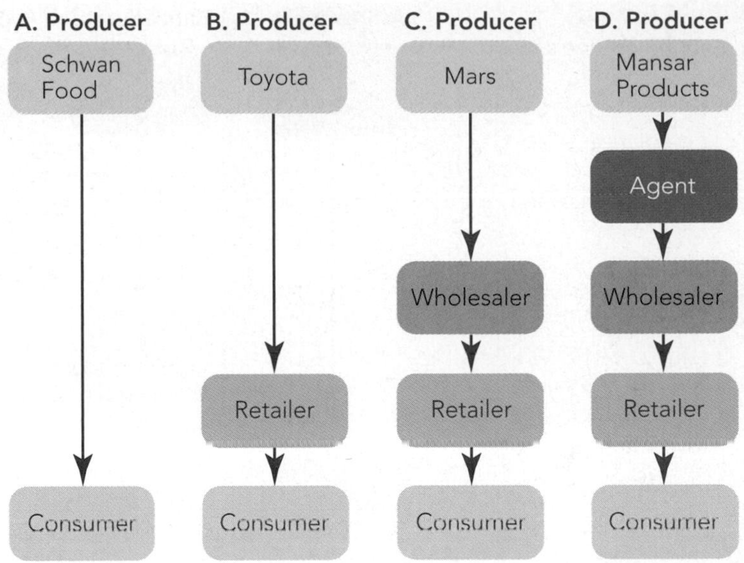

a direct channel and branch sales offices. The Schwan Food Company of Marshall, Minnesota markets a full line of frozen foods in 50 countries, including the United States, using route salespeople who sell from refrigerated trucks. Because there are no intermediaries with a direct channel, the producer must perform all channel functions.

Indirect Channel The remaining three channel forms are *indirect channels* because intermediaries are inserted between the producer and consumers and perform numerous channel functions. Channel B, with a retailer added, is most common when a retailer is large and can buy in large quantities from a producer or when the cost of inventory makes it too expensive to use a wholesaler. Automobile manufacturers such as Toyota use this channel, and a local car dealer acts as a retailer. Why is there no wholesaler? So many variations exist in the product that it would be impossible for a wholesaler to stock all the models required to satisfy buyers; in addition, the cost of maintaining an inventory would be too high. However, large retailers such as Sears, 7-Eleven, Staples, Safeway, and Home Depot buy in sufficient quantities to make it cost effective for a producer to deal with only a retail intermediary.

Adding a wholesaler in Channel C is most common for low-cost, low-unit value items that are frequently purchased by consumers, such as candy, confectionary items, and magazines. For example, Mars sells its line of candies to wholesalers in case quantities, who then break down (sort) the cases so that individual retailers can order in boxes or much smaller quantities.

Channel D, the most indirect channel, is employed when there are many small manufacturers and many small retailers, and an agent is used to help coordinate a large supply of the product. Mansar Products, Ltd., is a Belgian producer of specialty jewelry that uses agents to sell to wholesalers in the United States, which then sell to many small independent jewelry retailers.

Marketing Channels for Business Goods and Services

The four most common channels for business goods and services are shown in Figure 15–5 on the next page. In contrast with channels for consumer products, business channels typically are shorter and rely on one intermediary or none at all because business users are fewer in number, tend to be more concentrated geographically, and buy in larger quantities (see Chapter 6).

FIGURE 15–5
Common marketing channels for business goods and services differ by the kind and number of intermediaries.

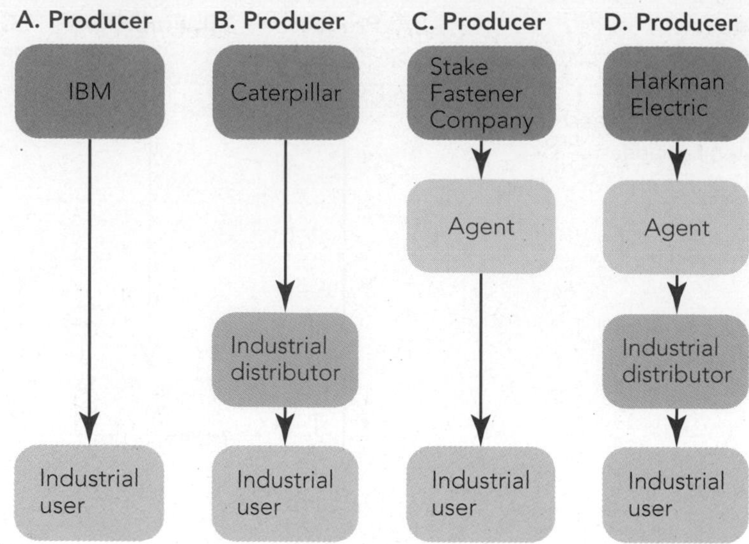

Direct Channel Channel A, represented by IBM's large, mainframe computer business, is a direct channel. Firms using this channel maintain their own salesforce and perform all channel functions. This channel is employed when buyers are large and well defined, the sales effort requires extensive negotiations, and the products are of high unit value and require hands-on expertise in terms of installation or use.

Indirect Channel Channels B, C, and D are indirect channels with one or more intermediaries to reach industrial users. In Channel B, an **industrial distributor** performs a variety of marketing channel functions, including selling, stocking, delivering a full product assortment, and financing. In many ways, industrial distributors are like wholesalers in consumer channels. Caterpillar uses industrial distributors to sell its construction and mining equipment in over 200 countries. In addition to selling, Caterpillar distributors stock 40,000 to 50,000 parts and service equipment using highly trained technicians.

Channel C introduces a second intermediary, an *agent*, who serves primarily as the independent selling arm of producers and represents a producer to industrial users. For example, Stake Fastener Company, a producer of industrial fasteners, has an agent call on industrial users rather than employing its own salesforce.

Channel D is the longest channel and includes both agents and distributors. For instance, Harkman Electric, a producer of electric products, uses agents to call on electrical distributors who sell to industrial users.

Electronic Marketing Channels

These common marketing channels for consumer and business goods and services are not the only routes to the marketplace. Advances in electronic commerce have opened new avenues for reaching buyers and creating customer value.

Interactive electronic technology has made possible **electronic marketing channels**, which employ the Internet to make goods and services available for consumption or use by consumers or business buyers. A unique feature of these channels is that they combine electronic and traditional intermediaries to create time, place, form, and possession utility for buyers.

Figure 15–6 shows the electronic marketing channels for books (Amazon.com), automobiles (Autobytel.com), reservation services (Orbitz.com), and personal computers (Dell.com). Are you surprised that they look a lot like common consumer product marketing channels? An important reason for the similarity resides in channel functions detailed in Figure 15–3. Electronic intermediaries can and do perform

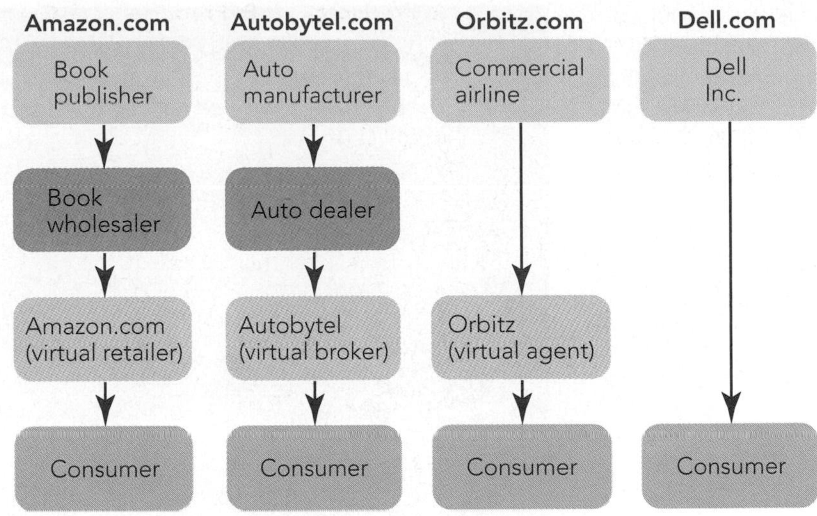

FIGURE 15–6
Consumer electronic marketing channels look much like those for consumer goods and services. Read the text to learn why.

transactional and facilitating functions effectively and at a relatively lower cost than traditional intermediaries because of efficiencies made possible by information technology. However, electronic intermediaries are incapable of performing elements of the logistical function, particularly for products such as books and automobiles. This function remains with traditional intermediaries or with the producer, as evident with Dell, Inc., and its direct channel.

Many services can be distributed through electronic marketing channels, such as car rental reservations marketed by Alamo.com, financial securities by Schwab.com, and insurance by MetLife.com. However, many other services such as health care and auto repair still involve traditional intermediaries.

Direct and Multichannel Marketing

Many firms also use direct and multichannel marketing to reach buyers. **Direct marketing channels** allow consumers to buy products by interacting with various advertising media without a face-to-face meeting with a salesperson. Direct marketing channels include mail-order selling, direct-mail sales, catalog sales, telemarketing, interactive media, and televised home shopping (the Home Shopping Network). Some firms sell products almost entirely through direct marketing. These firms include L.L. Bean (apparel) and Newegg.com (consumer electronics). Marketers such as Nestlé and Sunkist, in addition to using traditional channels composed of wholesalers and retailers, employ direct marketing through catalogs and telemarketing to reach more buyers. Direct marketing is covered in greater depth in Chapter 18.

Multichannel marketing is the *blending* of different communication and delivery channels that are *mutually reinforcing* in attracting, retaining, and building relationships with consumers who shop and buy in traditional intermediaries and online. Multichannel marketing seeks to integrate a firm's electronic and delivery channels. At Eddie Bauer, for example, every effort is made to make the apparel shopping and purchase experience for its customers the same in its retail stores, with its catalog, and at its Web site. According to an Eddie Bauer marketing manager, "We don't distinguish between channels because it's all Eddie Bauer to our customers."[3]

Multichannel marketing also can leverage the value-adding capabilities of different channels. For example, retail stores can leverage their physical presence by allowing customers to pick up their online orders at a nearby store or return or exchange nonstore purchases if they wish. Catalogs can serve as shopping tools for online purchasing, as they do for store purchasing. Web sites can help consumers do their homework before visiting a store. Office Depot has leveraged its store, catalog, and Web site channels with impressive results. The company does more than $5 billion

Eddie Bauer successfully engages in multichannel marketing through its 375 retail and outlet stores in North America, Japan, and Germany, its Web site, and catalog.

Eddie Bauer
www.eddiebauer.com

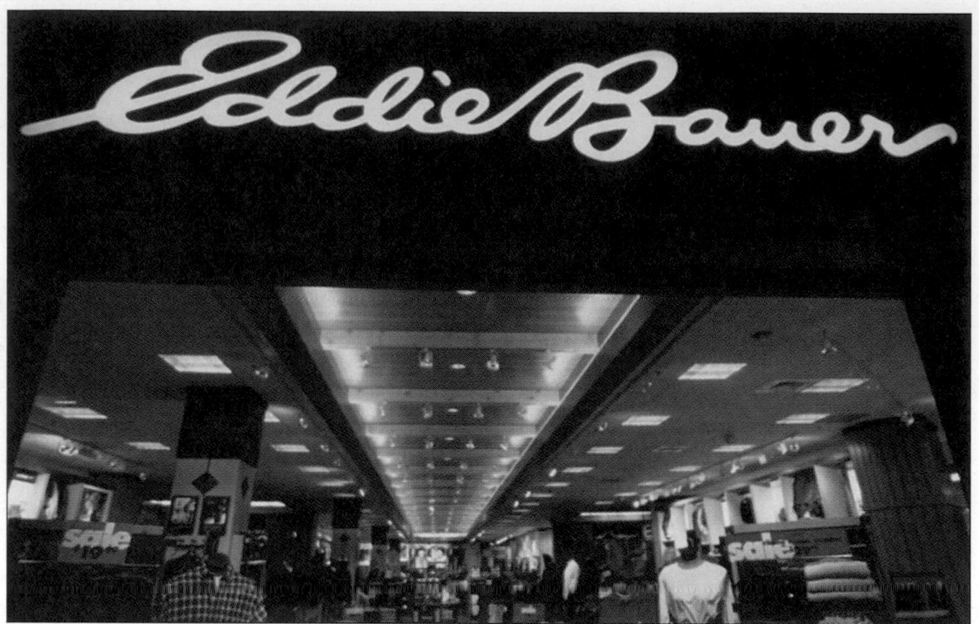

in online retail sales annually. Multichannel marketing is discussed further in Chapter 21 on interactive marketing.

Dual Distribution and Strategic Channel Alliances

In some situations, producers use **dual distribution**, an arrangement whereby a firm reaches different buyers by employing two or more different types of channels for the same basic product. For example, GE sells its large appliances directly to home and apartment builders but uses retail stores, including Lowe's home centers, to sell to consumers. In some instances, firms pair multiple channels with a multibrand strategy (see Chapter 11). This is done to minimize cannibalization of the firm's family brand and differentiate the channels. For example, Hallmark sells its Hallmark greeting cards through Hallmark stores and select department stores, and its Ambassador brand of cards through discount and drugstore chains.

A recent innovation in marketing channels is the use of **strategic channel alliances**, whereby one firm's marketing channel is used to sell another firm's products. An alliance between Kraft Foods and Starbucks is a case in point. Kraft distributes Starbucks coffee in U.S. supermarkets and internationally. Strategic alliances are popular in global marketing, where the creation of marketing channel relationships is expensive and time consuming. For example, General Mills and Nestlé have an extensive alliance that spans 130 international markets from Mexico to China. Read the Marketing Matters box so you won't be surprised when you are served Nestlé (not General Mills) Cheerios when traveling outside North America.[4]

A Closer Look at Channel Intermediaries

Channel structures for consumer and business products assume various forms based on the number and type of intermediaries. Knowledge of the roles played by these intermediaries is important for understanding how channels operate in practice.

The terms *wholesaler*, *agent*, and *retailer* have been used in a general fashion consistent with the meanings given in Figure 15–1. However, on closer inspection, a variety of specific types of intermediaries emerges. These intermediaries engage in wholesaling activities—those activities involved in selling products and services to

Marketing Matters > > > > > > customer value

Nestlé and General Mills—Cereal Partners Worldwide

Can you say Nestlé Cheerios *miel amandes*? Millions of French start their day with this European equivalent of General Mills' Honey Nut Cheerios, made possible by Cereal Partners Worldwide (CPW). CPW is a strategic alliance designed from the start to be a global business. It joined the cereal manufacturing and marketing capability of U.S.-based General Mills with the worldwide distribution clout of Swiss-based Nestlé.

From its headquarters in Switzerland, CPW first launched General Mills cereals under the Nestlé label in France, the United Kingdom, Spain, and Portugal in 1990. Today, CPW competes in 130 countries that span the globe.

The General Mills–Nestlé strategic channel alliance also increased the ready-to-eat cereal worldwide market share of these companies, which are already rated as the two best-managed firms in the world. CPW currently accounts for over 25 percent of global cereal sales with about $2 billion in annual revenue.

those who are buying for the purposes of resale or business use. Intermediaries engaged in retailing activities are discussed in detail in Chapter 17. Figure 15–7 on the next page describes the functions performed by major types of independent wholesalers.[5]

Merchant Wholesalers **Merchant wholesalers** are independently owned firms that take title to the merchandise they handle. They go by various names, including industrial distributor (described earlier). Most firms engaged in wholesaling activities are merchant wholesalers.

Merchant wholesalers are classified as either full-service or limited-service wholesalers, depending on the number of functions performed. Two major types of full-service wholesalers exist. *General merchandise* (or *full-line*) *wholesalers* carry a broad assortment of merchandise and perform all channel functions. This type of wholesaler is most prevalent in the hardware, drug, and clothing industries. However, these wholesalers do not maintain much depth of assortment within specific product lines. *Specialty merchandise* (or *limited-line*) *wholesalers* offer a relatively narrow range of products but have an extensive assortment within the product lines carried. They perform all channel functions and are found in the health foods, automotive parts, and seafood industries.

Four major types of limited-service wholesalers exist. *Rack jobbers* furnish the racks or shelves that display merchandise in retail stores, perform all channel functions, and sell on consignment to retailers, which means they retain the title to the products displayed and bill retailers only for the merchandise sold. Familiar products such as hosiery, toys, housewares, and health and beauty items are sold by rack jobbers. *Cash and carry wholesalers* take title to merchandise but sell only to buyers who call on them, pay cash for merchandise, and furnish their own transportation for merchandise. They carry a limited product assortment and do not make deliveries, extend credit, or supply market information. This wholesaler is common in electric supplies, office supplies, hardware products, and groceries.

FUNCTIONS PERFORMED	MERCHANT WHOLESALERS: FULL SERVICE: GENERAL MERCHANDISE	MERCHANT WHOLESALERS: FULL SERVICE: SPECIALTY MERCHANDISE	MERCHANT WHOLESALERS: LIMITED SERVICE: RACK JOBBERS	MERCHANT WHOLESALERS: LIMITED SERVICE: CASH AND CARRY	MERCHANT WHOLESALERS: LIMITED SERVICE: DROP SHIPPERS	MERCHANT WHOLESALERS: LIMITED SERVICE: TRUCK JOBBERS	AGENTS AND BROKERS: MANUFACTURER'S AGENTS	AGENTS AND BROKERS: SELLING AGENTS	AGENTS AND BROKERS: BROKERS
Transactional functions									
Buying	Yes★	Yes	Yes	Yes	Yes	Yes	No	No	No
Sales calls on customers	Yes	Yes	Yes	No	Yes	Yes	Yes	Yes	Yes
Risk taking (taking title to products)	Yes	Yes	Yes	Yes	Yes	Yes	No	No	No
Logistical functions									
Creates product assortments	Yes	Yes	Yes	Yes	No	Yes	Sometimes	No	Yes
Stores products (maintains inventory)	Yes	Yes	Yes	Yes	No	Yes	No	No	Sometimes
Sorts products	Yes	Yes	Yes	Yes	Yes	Yes	No	No	No
Transports products	Yes	Yes	Yes	No	No	Yes	Sometimes	Sometimes	Sometimes
Facilitating functions									
Provides financing (credit)	Yes	Yes	Yes	No	Yes	No	No	Sometimes	No
Provides market information and research	Yes	Yes	Sometimes	No	Sometimes	No	Sometimes	Sometimes	Yes
Grading	Yes	Yes	Sometimes	No	Sometimes	No	No	Sometimes	Yes

★ Key: Yes Sometimes No

FIGURE 15–7
Functions performed by independent wholesaler types vary. Only full-service wholesalers perform all channel functions.

Drop shippers, or *desk jobbers*, are wholesalers that own the merchandise they sell but do not physically handle, stock, or deliver it. They simply solicit orders from retailers and other wholesalers and have the merchandise shipped directly from a producer to a buyer. Drop shippers are used for bulky products such as coal, lumber, and chemicals, which are sold in extremely large quantities. *Truck jobbers* are small wholesalers that have a small warehouse from which they stock their trucks for distribution to retailers. They usually handle limited assortments of fast-moving or perishable items that are sold for cash directly from trucks in their original packages. Truck jobbers handle products such as bakery items, dairy products, and meat.

Agents and Brokers Unlike merchant wholesalers, agents and brokers do not take title to merchandise and typically perform fewer channel functions. They make their profit from commissions or fees paid for their services, whereas merchant wholesalers make their profit from the sale of the merchandise they own.

Manufacturer's agents and selling agents are the two major types of agents used by producers. **Manufacturer's agents**, or *manufacturer's representatives*, work for several producers and carry noncompetitive, complementary merchandise in an exclusive territory. Manufacturer's agents act as a producer's sales arm in a territory and are principally responsible for the transactional channel functions, primarily sell-

Century 21 has about 7,700 independently owned and operated broker offices in 68 countries and territories worldwide.

Century 21 Real Estate, LLC
www.century21.com

ing. They are used extensively in the automotive supply, footwear, and fabricated steel industries.

By comparison, **selling agents** represent a single producer and are responsible for the entire marketing function of that producer. They design promotional plans, set prices, determine distribution policies, and make recommendations on product strategy. Selling agents are used by small producers in the textile, apparel, food, and home furnishing industries.

Brokers are independent firms or individuals whose principal function is to bring buyers and sellers together to make sales. Brokers, unlike agents, usually have no continuous relationship with the buyer or seller but negotiate a contract between two parties and then move on to another task. Brokers are used extensively by producers of seasonal products (such as fruits and vegetables) and in the real estate industry.

A unique broker that acts in many ways like a manufacturer's agent is a food broker, representing buyers and sellers in the grocery industry. Food brokers differ from conventional brokers because they act on behalf of producers on a permanent basis and receive a commission for their services. For example, Nabisco uses food brokers to sell its candies, margarine, and Planters peanuts, but it sells its line of cookies and crackers directly to retail stores.

Manufacturer's Branches and Offices Unlike merchant wholesalers, agents, and brokers, manufacturer's branches and sales offices are wholly owned extensions of the producer that perform wholesaling activities. Producers assume wholesaling functions when there are no intermediaries to perform these activities, customers are few in number and geographically concentrated, or orders are large or require significant attention. A *manufacturer's branch office* carries a producer's inventory and performs the functions of a full-service wholesaler. A *manufacturer's sales office* does not carry inventory, typically performs only a sales function, and serves as an alternative to agents and brokers.

Vertical Marketing Systems and Channel Partnerships

The traditional marketing channels described so far represent a loosely knit network of independent producers and intermediaries brought together to distribute goods and services. However, other channel arrangements exist for the purpose of

Tiffany & Co. and H&R Block represent two different types of vertical marketing systems. Read the text to find out how they differ.

Tiffany & Co.
www.tiffany.com

H&R Block
www.hrblock.com

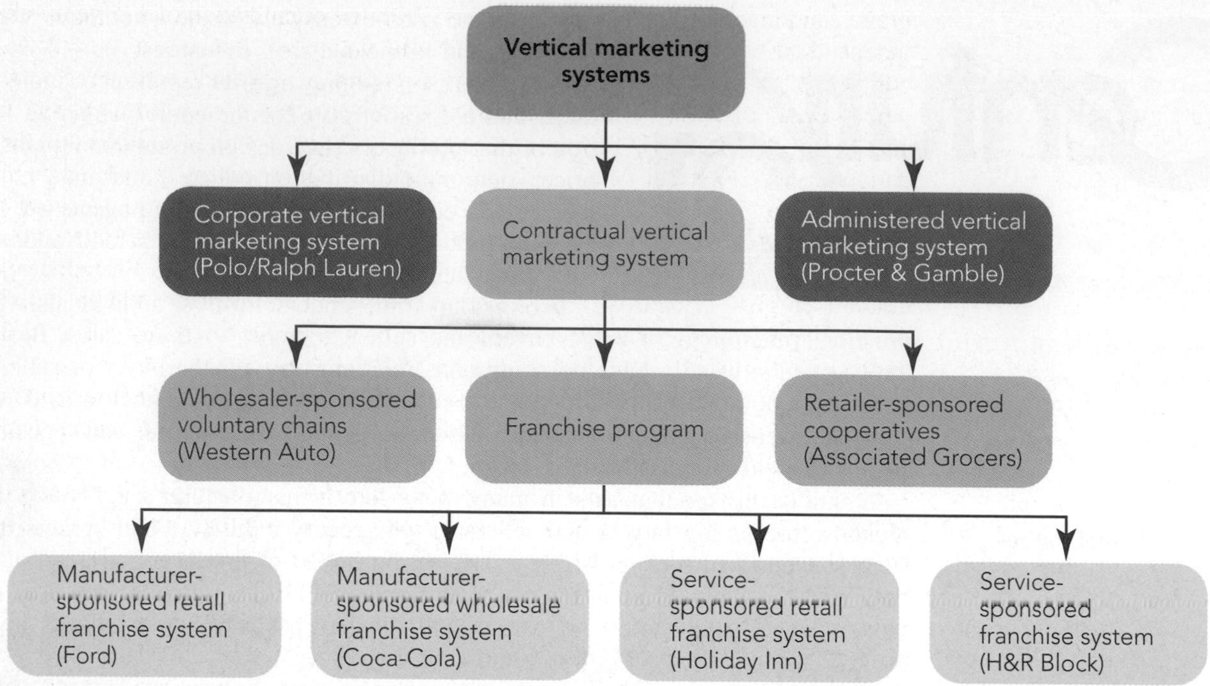

FIGURE 15–8
There are three major types of vertical marketing systems—corporate, contractual, and administered. Contractual systems are the most popular for reasons described in the text.

improving efficiency in performing channel functions and achieving greater marketing effectiveness. These arrangements are called vertical marketing systems and channel partnerships. **Vertical marketing systems** are professionally managed and centrally coordinated marketing channels designed to achieve channel economies and maximum marketing impact.[6] Figure 15–8 depicts the major types of vertical marketing systems: corporate, contractual, and administered.

Corporate Systems The combination of successive stages of production and distribution under a single ownership is a *corporate vertical marketing system*. For example, a producer might own the intermediary at the next level down in the channel. This practice, called *forward integration*, is exemplified by Ralph Lauren, which manufactures clothing and also owns apparel shops. Other examples of forward integration include Goodyear, Apple, and Sherwin-Williams. Alternatively, a retailer might own a manufacturing operation, a practice called *backward integration*. For example, Kroger supermarkets operate manufacturing facilities that produce everything from aspirin to cottage cheese for sale under the Kroger label. Tiffany & Co., the exclusive jewelry retailer, manufactures about half of the fine jewelry items for sale through its 150 stores and boutiques worldwide.

Companies seeking to reduce distribution costs and gain greater control over supply sources or resale of their products pursue forward and backward integration. However, both types of integration increase a company's capital investment and fixed costs. For this reason, many companies favor contractual vertical marketing systems to achieve channel efficiencies and marketing effectiveness.

Contractual Systems Under a *contractual vertical marketing system*, independent production and distribution firms integrate their efforts on a contractual basis to obtain greater functional economies and marketing impact than they could achieve alone. Contractual systems are the most popular among the three types of vertical marketing systems.

Three variations of contractual systems exist. *Wholesaler-sponsored voluntary chains* involve a wholesaler that develops a contractual relationship with small, independent retailers to standardize and coordinate buying practices, merchandising programs, and inventory management efforts. With the organization of a large number of independent retailers, economies of scale and volume discounts can be achieved to compete with chain stores. IGA and Ben Franklin variety and craft stores represent wholesaler-sponsored voluntary chains. *Retailer-sponsored cooperatives* exist when small, independent retailers form an organization that operates a wholesale facility cooperatively. Member retailers then concentrate their buying power through the wholesaler and plan collaborative promotional and pricing activities. Examples of retailer-sponsored cooperatives include Associated Grocers and Ace Hardware.

The most visible variation of contractual systems is franchising. **Franchising** is a contractual arrangement between a parent company (a franchisor) and an individual or firm (a franchisee) that allows the franchisee to operate a certain type of business under an established name and according to specific rules.

Four types of franchise arrangements are most popular. *Manufacturer-sponsored retail franchise systems* are prominent in the automobile industry, where a manufacturer such as Ford licenses dealers to sell its cars subject to various sales and service conditions. *Manufacturer-sponsored wholesale systems* exist in the soft-drink industry, where Pepsi-Cola licenses wholesalers (bottlers) that purchase concentrate from Pepsi-Cola and then carbonate, bottle, promote, and distribute its products to retailers and restaurants. *Service-sponsored retail franchise systems* are provided by firms that have designed a unique approach for performing a service and wish to profit by selling the franchise to others. Holiday Inn, Avis, and McDonald's represent this franchising approach. *Service-sponsored franchise systems* exist when franchisors license individuals or firms to dispense a service under a trade name and specific guidelines. Examples include Snelling and Snelling, Inc., employment services and H&R Block tax services. Franchising is discussed further in Chapter 17.

Administered Systems In comparison, *administered vertical marketing systems* achieve coordination at successive stages of production and distribution by the size and influence of one channel member rather than through ownership. Procter & Gamble, given its broad product assortment ranging from disposable diapers to detergents, is able to obtain cooperation from supermarkets in displaying, promoting, and pricing its products. Wal-Mart can obtain cooperation from manufacturers in terms of product specifications, price levels, and promotional support, given its position as the world's largest retailer.

Channel Partnerships Increasingly, channel members are forging channel partnerships akin to supply partnerships described in Chapter 6. A **channel partnership** consists of agreements and procedures among channel members for ordering and physically distributing a producer's products through the channel to the ultimate consumer.[7] A central feature of channel partnerships is the collaborative use of information and communication technology to better serve customers and reduce the time and cost of performing channel functions. Channel partnerships are elaborated upon in Chapter 16 on supply chain and logistics management.

learning review

3. What is the difference between a direct and an indirect channel?
4. Why are channels for business products typically shorter than channels for consumer products?
5. What is the principal distinction between a corporate vertical marketing system and an administered vertical marketing system?

CHANNEL CHOICE AND MANAGEMENT

LO3

Marketing channels not only link a producer to its buyers but also provide the means through which a firm implements various elements of its marketing strategy. Therefore, choosing a marketing channel is a critical decision.

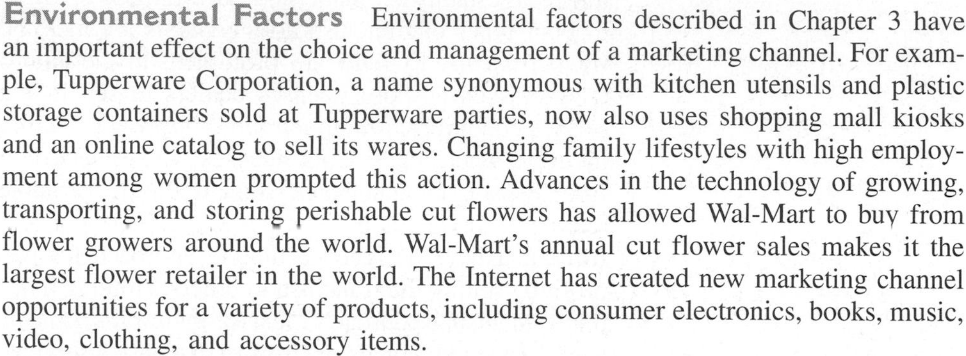

Factors Affecting Channel Choice and Management

Environmental forces have broadened Tupperware Corporation's marketing channel.

Tupperware Corporation
www.tupperware.com

The final choice of a marketing channel by a producer depends on a number of factors that often interact with each other.

Environmental Factors Environmental factors described in Chapter 3 have an important effect on the choice and management of a marketing channel. For example, Tupperware Corporation, a name synonymous with kitchen utensils and plastic storage containers sold at Tupperware parties, now also uses shopping mall kiosks and an online catalog to sell its wares. Changing family lifestyles with high employment among women prompted this action. Advances in the technology of growing, transporting, and storing perishable cut flowers has allowed Wal-Mart to buy from flower growers around the world. Wal-Mart's annual cut flower sales makes it the largest flower retailer in the world. The Internet has created new marketing channel opportunities for a variety of products, including consumer electronics, books, music, video, clothing, and accessory items.

Regulatory factors also influence channel choice, notably in global markets. Read the Marketing Matters box to learn how Avon responded to China's ban on direct selling and subsequent lifting of the ban.[8]

Consumer Factors Consumer characteristics have a direct bearing on the choice and management of a marketing channel. Determining which channel is most appropriate is based on answers to fundamental questions such as: Who are potential customers? Where do they buy? When do they buy? How do they buy? What do they buy? These answers also indicate the type of intermediary best suited to reaching target buyers.

For example, Fila, a higher-end activewear apparel manufacturer that sold its product line through specialty athletic stores and pro shops, realized that it needed to broaden its market coverage. It signed a distribution agreement with Kohl's department stores for a line of moderately priced activewear bearing the Fila brand. According to a company spokesperson, "The (Fila) labels sell mainly to 14- to 24-year olds. (Kohl's) gives a chance to reach women between 25 and later 40s, the family consumer."[9]

Product Factors In general, highly sophisticated products such as large, scientific computers, unstandardized products such as custom-built machinery, and products of high unit value, such as commercial aircraft, are distributed directly to buyers. Unsophisticated, standardized products with low unit value, such as table salt, are typically distributed through indirect channels. A product's stage in the life cycle also affects marketing channels. This was shown in the description of the fax machine product life cycle in Chapter 11.

Company Factors A firm's financial, human, or technological capabilities affect channel choice. For example, firms that are unable to employ a salesforce might use manufacturer's agents or selling agents to reach wholesalers or buyers. If a firm has multiple products for a particular target market, it might use a direct channel. Firms with a limited product line might use intermediaries to reach buyers.

Marketing Matters > > > > > entrepreneurship

Avon Is Calling Again in China

What do you do when your marketing channel is banned by a government? Just ask executives at Avon, Inc., the world's largest cosmetic and beauty products direct selling company.

Avon pioneered direct selling in China in 1990. By 1998, the company had about 75,000 active independent representatives successfully selling its product line in China. The entrepreneurial spirit among Chinese women had proven to fit well with Avon's direct selling channel. Then, in April 1998, the Chinese State Council issued an order banning all forms of direct selling in China.

In response, Avon established a retail distribution network that grew to include some 6,300 independent beauty boutiques and over 1,000 cosmetic parlors in department stores across China by 2005. Then, in December 2005, direct selling was permitted in China provided companies met specific operating and licensing requirements. Avon was the first company to meet these standards and began recruiting representatives. By 2009, Avon had over 230,000 active representatives in China. Avon's retail network has been retained to offer after-sales services—including order pick-ups and product returns—and sell Avon products.

Andrea Jung, Avon's chairwoman and CEO, says the market in China could soon add $1 billion to the company's annual profit.

Company factors also influence a change in marketing strategy. Nike withdrew its Starter line of athletic shoes and apparel from Wal-Mart after the company decided it was "a business that did not play to Nike's strengths" and "did not provide the avenue for growth necessary for Nike to reach its target revenue of $23 billion by 2011."[10]

Channel Choice Considerations

Recognizing that numerous routes to buyers exist and also recognizing the factors just described, marketing executives typically consider three questions when choosing a marketing channel and intermediaries:

1. Which channel and intermediaries will provide the best coverage of the target market?
2. Which channel and intermediaries will best satisfy the buying requirements of the target market?
3. Which channel and intermediaries will be the most profitable?

Target Market Coverage Achieving the best coverage of the target market requires attention to the *density*—that is, the number of stores in a geographical area—and type of intermediaries to be used at the retail level of distribution. Three degrees of distribution density exist: intensive, exclusive, and selective.

Intensive distribution means that a firm tries to place its products and services in as many outlets as possible. Intensive distribution is usually chosen for convenience products or services such as candy, fast food, newspapers, and soft drinks. For example, Coca-Cola's retail distribution objective is to place its products "within an arm's reach of desire." Cash, yes cash, is distributed intensively by Visa. It operates over 1 million automatic teller machines in more than 170 countries.

Exclusive distribution is the extreme opposite of intensive distribution because only one retailer in a specified geographical area carries the firm's products. Exclusive distribution is typically chosen for specialty products or services, such as some women's fragrances, men's and women's apparel and accessories, and yachts. Gucci, one

Read the text to learn which buying requirements are satisfied by Jiffy Lube and PETCO.

Jiffy Lube International
www.jiffylube.com

PETCO
www.petco.com

of the world's leading luxury goods companies, uses exclusive distribution in the marketing of its Yves Saint Laurent, Sergio Rossi, Boucheron, Opium, and Gucci brands.

Selective distribution lies between these two extremes and means that a firm selects a few retailers in a specific geographical area to carry its products. Selective distribution weds some of the market coverage benefits of intensive distribution to the control over resale evident with exclusive distribution. For example, Dell, Inc., chose selective distribution when it decided to sell its products through U.S. retailers along with its direct channel.[11] According to Michael Dell, the company's CEO, "There were plenty of retailers who said, 'sell through us,' but we didn't want to show up everywhere." The company now sells a limited range of its products through Wal-Mart, Best Buy, and Staples, an office-products retailer. Dell's decision was consistent with current trends. Today, selective distribution is the most common form of distribution intensity.

Satisfying Buyer Requirements A second consideration in channel choice is gaining access to channels and intermediaries that satisfy at least some of the interests buyers might want fulfilled when they purchase a firm's products or services. These interests fall into four broad categories: (1) information, (2) convenience, (3) variety, and (4) pre- or postsale services. Each relates to customer experience.

Information is an important requirement when buyers have limited knowledge or desire specific data about a product or service. Properly chosen intermediaries communicate with buyers through in-store displays, demonstrations, and personal selling. Consumer electronics manufacturers such as Apple have opened their own retail outlets staffed with highly trained personnel to inform buyers how their products can better satisfy each customer's needs.

Convenience has multiple meanings for buyers, such as proximity or driving time to a retail outlet. For example, 7-Eleven stores, with more than 36,000 outlets worldwide, many of which are open 24 hours a day, satisfy this interest for buyers. Candy and snack-food firms benefit by gaining display space in these stores. For other consumers, convenience means a minimum of time and hassle. Jiffy Lube, which promises to change engine oil and filters quickly, appeals to this aspect of convenience. For those who shop on the Internet, convenience means that Web sites must be easy to locate and navigate, and image downloads must be fast. A commonly held view among Web site developers is the "eight second rule": Consumers

Going Online

Visit an Apple Store to See What All the Excitement Is About

Interested in visiting an Apple store to see what all the excitement is about? Is one of Apple's 250-plus stores in the world situated near you? If you answered "yes" to the first question and "no" to the second, then log on to www.ifoapplestore.com/db. Here you will find exterior and interior photographs and video tours of various Apple stores. To learn whether an Apple store is planned for your area, visit this Web site to find announcements of grand openings.

will abandon their efforts to enter or navigate a Web site if download time exceeds eight seconds.[12]

Variety reflects buyers' interest in having numerous competing and complementary items from which to choose. Variety is evident in the breadth and depth of products and brands carried by intermediaries, which enhances their attraction to buyers. Thus, manufacturers of pet food and supplies seek distribution through pet superstores such as PETCO and PetSmart, which offer a wide array of pet products.

Pre- or postsale services provided by intermediaries are an important buying requirement for products such as large household appliances that require delivery, installation, and credit. Therefore, Whirlpool seeks dealers that provide such services.

Steven Jobs' decision to distribute Apple products through company-owned stores was motivated by the failure of retailers to deliver on these four consumer interests for Apple. Visit the Web site in the Going Online box to learn more about Apple stores.

For the answer to how Schick became a razor and blade market share leader in Japan, read the text.

Schick
www.schick.com

Profitability The third consideration in choosing a channel is profitability, which is determined by the margins earned (revenue minus cost) for each channel member and for the channel as a whole. Channel cost is the critical dimension of profitability. These costs include distribution, advertising, and selling expenses associated with different types of marketing channels. The extent to which channel members share these costs determines the margins received by each member and by the channel as a whole.

Companies routinely monitor the performance of their marketing channels. Read the Using Marketing Dashboards box on the next page to see how Charlesburg Furniture views the sales and profit performance of its marketing channels.

Global Dimensions of Marketing Channels

Marketing channels around the world reflect traditions, customs, geography, and the economic history of individual countries and societies. Even so, the basic marketing channel functions must be performed. But differences do exist and are illustrated by marketing channels in Japan, one of the world's largest economies and a major U.S. trade partner.

Intermediaries outside Western Europe and North America tend to be small, numerous, and often owner operated as described in Chapter 7. Japan, for example,

Using Marketing Dashboards

Channel Sales and Profit at Charlesburg Furniture

Charlesburg Furniture is one of 1,000 wood furniture manufacturers in the United States. The company sells its furniture through furniture store chains, independent furniture stores, and department store chains in the southern United States. The company has traditionally allocated its marketing funds for cooperative advertising, in-store displays, and retail sales support on the basis of dollar sales by channel.

Your Challenge As the Vice President of Sales & Marketing at Charlesburg Furniture, you have been asked to review the company's sales and profit in its three channels and recommend a course of action. The question: Should Charlesburg Furniture continue to allocate its marketing funds on the basis of channel dollar sales or profit?

Your Findings Charlesburg Furniture tracks the sales and profit from each channel (and individual customer) and the three-year trend of sales by channel on its marketing dashboard. This information is displayed in the marketing dashboard below.

Several findings stand out. Furniture store chains and independent furniture stores account for 85.2 percent of Charlesburg Furniture sales and 93 percent of company profit. These two channels also evidence growth as measured by annual percentage change in sales. By comparison, department store chains annual percentage sales growth has declined and recorded negative growth in 2009. This channel accounts for 14.8 percent of company sales and 7 percent of company profit.

Your Action Charlesburg Furniture should consider abandoning the practice of allocating marketing funds solely on the basis of channel sales volume. The importance of independent furniture stores to Charlesburg's profitability warrants further spending, particularly given this channel's favorable sales trend. Doubling the percentage allocation for marketing funds for this channel may be too extreme, however. Rather, an objective-task promotional budgeting method should be adopted (see Chapter 18). Charlesburg Furniture might also consider the longer term role of department store chains as a marketing channel.

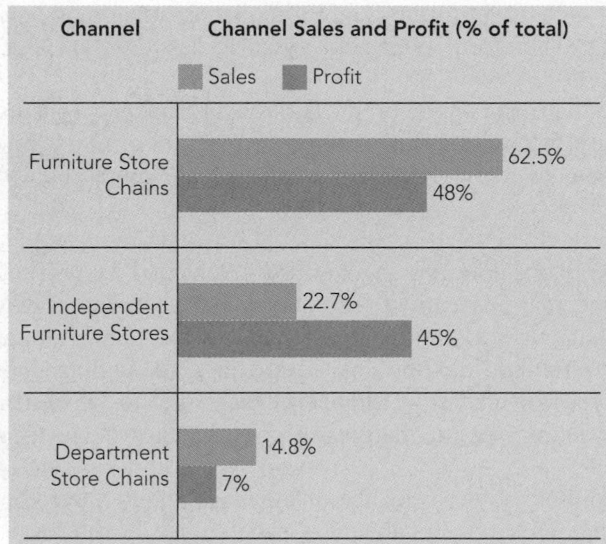

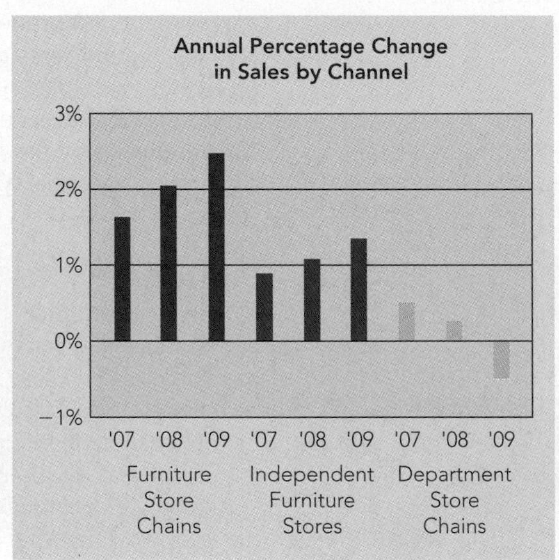

has less than one-half of the population and a land mass less than 5 percent of the United States. However, Japan and the United States have about the same number of wholesalers and retailers. Why? Japanese marketing channels tend to include many intermediaries based on tradition and lack of storage space. As many as five intermediaries are involved in the distribution of soap in Japan compared with one or two in the United States.

Understanding marketing channels in global markets is often a prerequisite to successful marketing. For example, Gillette attempted to sell its razors and blades through company salespeople in Japan as it does in the United States, thus eliminating wholesalers traditionally involved in marketing toiletries. However, Schick sold its razors and blades through the traditional Japanese channel involving wholesalers. The result? Schick achieved a commanding lead over Gillette in the Japanese razor and blade market.[13]

Channel relationships also must be considered. In Japan, the distribution *keiretsu* (translated as "alignments") bonds producers and intermediaries together. The bond, through vertical integration and social and economic ties, ensures that each channel member benefits from the distribution alignment. The dominant member of the distribution *keiretsu*, which is typically a producer, has considerable influence over channel member behavior, including which competing products are sold by other channel members. Well-known Japanese companies such as Matsushita (electronics), Nissan and Toyota (automotive products), and Kirin (and other brewers and distillers) employ the distribution *keiretsu* extensively. Shiseido and Kanebo, for instance, influence the distribution of cosmetics through Japanese department stores.

Channel Relationships: Conflict, Cooperation, and Law

LO4

Unfortunately, because channels consist of independent individuals and firms, there is always potential for disagreements concerning who performs which channel functions, how profits are allocated, which products and services will be provided by whom, and who makes critical channel-related decisions. These channel conflicts necessitate measures for dealing with them. Sometimes they result in legal action.

Channel conflict is sometimes visible to consumers. Read the text to learn what antagonized independent Goodyear tire dealers.

Goodyear Tire and Rubber Company
www.goodyear.com

Sources of Conflict in Marketing Channels

Channel conflict arises when one channel member believes another channel member is engaged in behavior that prevents it from achieving its goals. Two types of conflict occur in marketing channels: vertical conflict and horizontal conflict.

Vertical conflict occurs between different levels in a marketing channel—for example, between a manufacturer and a wholesaler or retailer or between a wholesaler and a retailer. Three sources of vertical conflict are most common.[14] First, conflict arises when a channel member bypasses another member and sells or buys products direct, a practice called **disintermediation**. This conflict emerged when Jenn-Air, a producer of kitchen appliances, decided to terminate its distributors and sell directly to retailers. Second, disagreements over how profit margins are distributed among channel members produce conflict. This happened when the world's biggest music company, Universal Music Group, adopted a pricing policy for CDs that squeezed the profit margins for specialty music retailers. A third conflict situation arises when manufacturers believe wholesalers or retailers are not giving their products adequate attention. For example, Nike stopped shipping popular sneakers such as Nike Shox NZ to Foot Locker in retaliation for the retailer's decision to give more shelf space to shoes costing under $120.

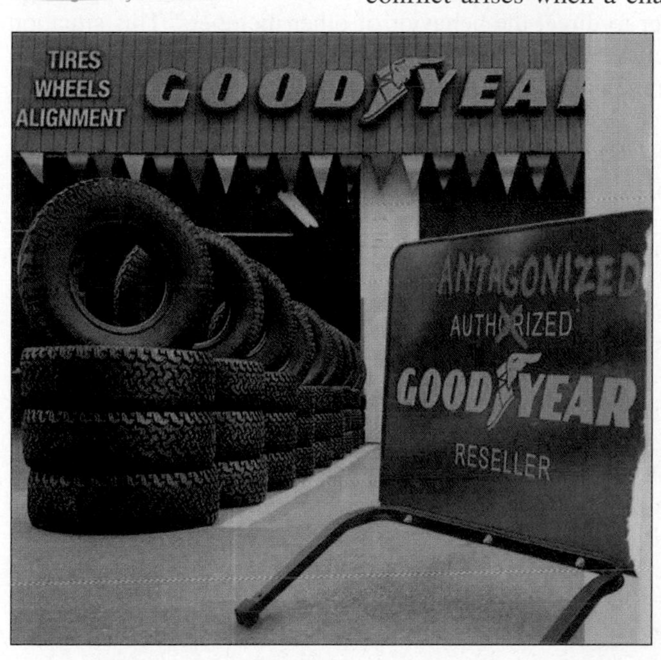

Horizontal conflict occurs between intermediaries at the same level in a marketing channel, such as between two or more retailers (Target and Kmart) or two or more wholesalers that handle the same manufacturer's brands. Two sources of horizontal conflict are common.[15] First, horizontal conflict arises when a manufacturer increases its distribution coverage in a geographical area. For example, a franchised Lexus dealer in Chicago might complain to Toyota that another franchised Lexus dealer has located too close to its dealership. Second, dual distribution causes conflict when different types of retailers carry the same brands. For instance, Goodyear tire dealers became irate when Goodyear Tire Company decided to sell its brands through Sears, Wal-Mart, and Sam's Clubs. Many switched to competing tire makers.

Securing Cooperation in Marketing Channels Conflict can have destructive effects on the workings of a marketing channel, so it is necessary to secure cooperation among channel members.

Channel Captain One means is through a **channel captain**, a channel member that coordinates, directs, and supports other channel members. Channel captains can be producers, wholesalers, or retailers. P&G assumes this role because it has a strong consumer following in brands such as Crest, Tide, and Pampers. Therefore, it can set policies or terms that supermarkets will follow. McKesson, a pharmaceutical drug wholesaler, is a channel captain because it coordinates and supports the product flow from numerous small drug manufacturers to drugstores and hospitals nationwide. Wal-Mart and Office Depot are retail channel captains because of their strong consumer image, number of outlets, and purchasing volume.

Channel Influence A firm becomes a channel captain because it is the channel member with the ability to influence the behavior of other members.[16] Influence can take four forms. First, economic influence arises from the ability of a firm to reward other members given its strong financial position or customer franchise. Microsoft Corporation and Wal-Mart have such influence. Expertise is a second source of influence. For example, American Hospital Supply helps its customers (hospitals) manage inventory and streamline order processing for hundreds of medical supplies. Third, identification with a particular channel member can create influence for that channel member. For instance, retailers may compete to carry the Ralph Lauren line, or clothing manufacturers may compete to be carried by Neiman Marcus, Nordstrom, or Bloomingdale's. In both instances, the desire to be identified with a channel member gives that firm influence over others. Finally, influence can arise from the legitimate right of one channel member to direct the behavior of other members. This situation would occur under contractual vertical marketing systems where a franchisor can legitimately direct how a franchisee behaves. Other means for securing cooperation in marketing channels rest in the different variations of vertical marketing systems.

Channel influence can be used to gain concessions from other channel members. For instance, some large supermarket chains expect manufacturers to pay allowances, in the form of cash or free goods, to stock and display their products. Some manufacturers call these allowances "extortion" as described in the Making Responsible Decisions box.[17]

Legal Considerations Conflict in marketing channels is typically resolved through negotiation or the exercise of influence by channel members. Sometimes conflict produces legal action. Therefore, knowledge of legal restrictions affecting channel strategies and practices is important. Some restrictions were described in Chapter 14, namely vertical price fixing and price discrimination. However, other legal considerations unique to marketing channels warrant attention.[18]

In general, suppliers can select whomever they want as channel intermediaries and may refuse to deal with whomever they choose. However, the Federal Trade Commission and the Justice Department monitor channel practices that restrain competition, create monopolies, or otherwise represent unfair methods of competition

Making Responsible Decisions > > > > > > > ethics

Pay to Play: The Ethics of Slotting Allowances

Have you ever wondered why your favorite cookies are no longer to be found at your local supermarket? Or that delicious tortilla chip you like to serve at parties is missing from the shelf and replaced by another brand?

Blame it on slotting allowances. Some large supermarket chains demand slotting allowances from food manufacturers, paid in the form of money or free goods to stock and display products. These allowances, which can run up to $25,000 per item per store for a supermarket chain, cost U.S. food makers about $1 billion annually. Not surprisingly, slotting allowances have been labeled "ransom," "extortional allowances," and "commercial bribery" by manufacturers because they already pay supermarkets $25 billion a year in "trade dollars" to promote and discount their products. Small food manufacturers, in particular, view slotting allowances as an economic barrier to distribution for their products. Supermarket operators see these allowances as a reasonable cost of handling business for manufacturers. Incidentally, Wal-Mart and Costco do not solicit slotting allowances from manufacturers.

Is the practice of charging slotting allowances unethical behavior?

under the Sherman Act (1890) and the Clayton Act (1914). Six channel practices have received the most attention (see Figure 15–9).

Dual distribution, although not illegal, can be viewed as anticompetitive in some situations. The most common situation arises when a manufacturer distributes through its own vertically integrated channel in competition with independent wholesalers and retailers that also sell its products. If the manufacturer's behavior is viewed as an attempt to lessen competition by eliminating wholesalers or retailers, then such action would violate both the Sherman and Clayton Acts.

Vertical integration is viewed in a similar light. Although not illegal, this practice is sometimes subject to legal action under the Clayton Act if it has the potential to lessen competition or foster monopoly.

The Clayton Act specifically prohibits exclusive dealing and tying arrangements when they lessen competition or create monopolies. *Exclusive dealing* exists when a supplier requires channel members to sell only its products or restricts distributors from selling directly competitive products. *Tying arrangements* occur when a supplier requires a distributor purchasing some products to buy others from the supplier. These arrangements often arise in franchising. They are illegal if the tied products could be purchased at fair market values from other suppliers at desired quality standards of the franchiser. *Full-line forcing* is a special kind of tying arrangement. This practice involves a supplier requiring that a channel member carry its full line of products in order to sell a specific item in the supplier's line.

Even though a supplier has a legal right to choose intermediaries to carry and represent its products, a *refusal to deal* with existing channel members may be illegal

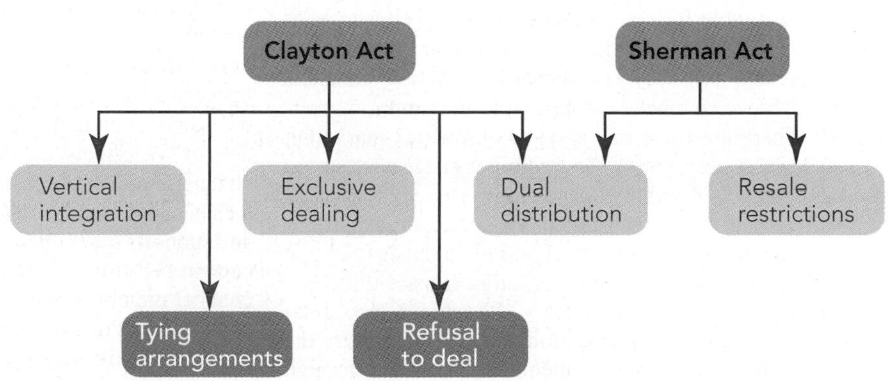

FIGURE 15–9
Channel strategies and practices are affected by legal restrictions. The Clayton Act and the Sherman Act restrict specific strategies and practices.

under the Clayton Act. *Resale restrictions* refer to a supplier's attempt to stipulate to whom distributors may resell the supplier's products and in what specific geographical areas or territories they may be sold. These practices have been prosecuted under the Sherman Act. Today, however, the courts apply the "rule of reason" in such cases and consider whether such restrictions have a "demonstrable economic effect."

learning review

6. What are the three questions marketing executives consider when choosing a marketing channel and intermediaries?
7. What are the three degrees of distribution density?
8. What is meant by exclusive dealing?

LEARNING OBJECTIVES REVIEW

LO1 *Explain what is meant by a marketing channel of distribution and why intermediaries are needed.*
A marketing channel of distribution, or simply a marketing channel, consists of individuals and firms involved in the process of making a product or service available for use or consumption by consumers or industrial users. Intermediaries make possible the flow of products from producers to buyers by performing three basic functions. The transactional function involves buying, selling, and risk taking because intermediaries stock merchandise in anticipation of sales. The logistical function involves the gathering, storing, and dispensing of products. The facilitating function assists producers in making goods and services more attractive to buyers. The performance of these functions by intermediaries creates time, place, form, and possession utility for consumers.

LO2 *Distinguish among traditional marketing channels, electronic marketing channels, and different types of vertical marketing systems.*
Traditional marketing channels describe the route taken by products and services from producers to buyers. This route can range from a direct channel with no intermediaries, because a producer and ultimate consumers deal directly with each other, to indirect channels where intermediaries (agents, wholesalers, distributors, or retailers) are inserted between a producer and consumer and perform numerous channel functions. Electronic marketing channels employ the Internet to make goods and services available for consumption or use by consumer or business buyers. Vertical marketing systems are professionally managed and centrally coordinated marketing channels designed to achieve channel economics and maximum marketing impact. There are three major types of vertical marketing systems (VMS). A corporate VMS combines successive stages of production and distribution under a single ownership. A contractual VMS exists when independent production and distribution firms integrate their efforts on a contractual basis to obtain greater functional economies and marketing impact than they could achieve alone. An administered VMS achieves coordination at successive stages of production and distribution by the size and influence of one channel member rather than through ownership.

LO3 *Describe the factors and considerations that affect a company's choice and management of a marketing channel.*
Four factors affect a company's choice and management of a marketing channel. These are environmental factors, consumer factors, product factors, and company factors, all of which interact with each other. Recognizing that numerous routes to buyers exist and also recognizing the factors just described, marketers consider three questions when choosing and managing a marketing channel and intermediaries. First, which channel and intermediaries will provide the best coverage of the target market? Marketers typically choose one of three levels of market coverage: intensive, selective, or exclusive distribution. Second, which channel and intermediaries will best satisfy the buying requirements of the target market? These buying requirements fall into four categories: information, convenience, variety, and attendant services. Finally, which channel and intermediaries will be the most profitable? Here marketers look at the margins earned (revenues minus cost) for each channel member and for the channel as a whole.

LO4 *Recognize how conflict, cooperation, and legal considerations affect marketing channel relationships.*
Because marketing channels consist of independent individuals and firms, there is always potential for conflict which sometimes results in legal action. So channel members try to find ways to cooperate for their mutual benefit. Two types of conflict occur in marketing channels. Vertical conflict occurs between different levels in a marketing channel, for example, between a manufacturer and a wholesaler or retailer, or between a wholesaler and a retailer. Horizontal conflict occurs between intermediaries at the same level in a marketing channel, such as between two retailers or two or more wholesalers that handle the same manufacturer's brands. Because conflict can have destructive effects on the workings of a marketing channel, channel members seek ways to cooperate. One way is through a channel captain—a channel member that coordinates, directs, and supports other channel members. A firm becomes a channel captain because of its ability to influence the behavior of other channel members. Nevertheless, channel conflict can result in legal action. The most common legal actions arise from channel practices that restrain competition, create monopolies, or represent unfair methods of competition.

FOCUSING ON KEY TERMS

brokers p. 389
channel captain p. 398
channel conflict p. 397
channel partnership p. 391
direct marketing channels p. 385
disintermediation p. 397
dual distribution p. 386
electronic marketing channels p. 384
exclusive distribution p. 393
franchising p. 391
industrial distributor p. 384
intensive distribution p. 393
manufacturer's agents p. 388
marketing channel p. 380
merchant wholesalers p. 387
multichannel marketing p. 385
selective distribution p. 394
selling agents p. 389
strategic channel alliances p. 386
vertical marketing systems p. 390

APPLYING MARKETING KNOWLEDGE

1 A distributor for Celanese Chemical Company stores large quantities of chemicals, blends these chemicals to satisfy requests of customers, and delivers the blends to a customer's warehouse within 24 hours of receiving an order. What utilities does this distributor provide?

2 Suppose the president of a carpet manufacturing firm has asked you to look into the possibility of bypassing the firm's wholesalers (who sell to carpet, department, and furniture stores) and selling direct to these stores. (*a*) What caution would you voice on this matter, and (*b*) what type of information would you gather before making this decision?

3 What type of channel conflict is likely to be caused by dual distribution, and what type of conflict can be reduced by direct distribution? Why?

4 How does the channel captain idea differ among corporate, administered, and contractual vertical marketing systems with particular reference to the use of the different forms of influence available to firms?

5 Comment on this statement: "The only distinction among merchant wholesalers and agents and brokers is that merchant wholesalers take title to the products they sell."

6 (*a*) How do specialty, shopping, and convenience goods generally relate to intensive, selective, and exclusive distribution? (*b*) Give a brand name that is an example of each goods-distribution matchup.

7 How would you respond to the statement: "Marketing channels with the highest sales always produce the highest profit."

building your marketing plan

Does your marketing plan involve selecting channels and intermediaries? If the answer is no, read no further and do not include this element in your plan. If the answer is yes:

1 Identify which channel and intermediaries will provide the best coverage of the target market for your product or service.

2 Specify which channel and intermediaries will best satisfy the important buying requirements of the target market.

3 Determine which channel and intermediaries will be the most profitable.

4 Select your channel(s) and intermediary(ies).

video case 15 Act II Microwave Popcorn: The Surprising Channel

"We developed the technology that launched the microwave popcorn business and helped make ACT II the number one brand in the world," says Jack McKeon, president of Golden Valley Microwave Foods, a division of ConAgra Foods, Inc. "But we were also lucky along the way, as we backed into what has become one of the biggest distribution channels in the industry today, one that no one ever saw coming." Founded in 1978, ACT II is a global leader in producing and marketing microwave popcorn. But it hasn't always been easy.

THE LAUNCH: THE IDEA AND THE TECHNOLOGY

In the mid-1980s, only about 15 percent of U.S. households had microwave ovens, so launching a microwave foods business was risky. ACT II's initial marketing research turned up two key points of difference or benefits that people wanted in their microwave popcorn: (1) fewer unpopped kernels and (2) good popping results in all types of microwave ovens, even low-powered ovens—the kind that many households with microwaves had at the time. ACT II's research and development (R&D) staff successfully addressed these wants by developing a microwave popcorn bag utilizing a thin strip of material laminated between layers of paper, which focused the microwave energy to produce high-quality popped corn, regardless of an oven's power. This breakthrough significantly increased the size of the microwave popcorn market (and is still used in all microwave popcorn bags today). Using its revolutionary package, ACT II was introduced in 1984.

THE LUCKY DAY: BOTH CAPITAL AND MASS MERCHANDISERS

From 1978 until it became public in September 1986, ACT II was privately owned. Like most start-ups, ACT II was severely undercapitalized due to the cost of developing and introducing the brand. As a result, ACT II needed a partner to help develop the business. Its solution was to enter into a licensing agreement to share its technology for packaging microwave popcorn with one of the largest food manufacturers in the industry. The licensing partner would sell the popcorn under its own brand name in grocery stores and supermarkets. In turn, ACT II agreed it would not distribute its ACT II brand in U.S. grocery stores or supermarkets for 10 years. This meant that ACT II had to find other channels of distribution in which to sell its microwave popcorn.

For the next 10 years, the company developed many new channels. ACT II products were sold through vending machines, video stores (Blockbuster), institutions (movie theaters, colleges, military bases), drugstores (Walgreen's, Rite-Aid, CVS/Pharmacy), warehouse club stores (e.g., Sam's Club, Costco, BJ's), and convenience stores (7-Eleven, Circle K). "But the huge opportunity we discovered and developed was the mass merchandiser channel through chains like Wal-Mart and Target," says McKeon. "ACT II microwave popcorn was the first item of any kind to sell a million units in a week for Target, and that happened in 1987. Wal-Mart, too, was on the front end of this market and today is the top seller of microwave popcorn in any channel, selling far more popcorn than the leading grocery chains. Mass merchandisers now account for over a third of all the microwave popcorn sold in the U.S. They created the ACT II business as we know it today, and it was accomplished without a dime of conventional consumer promotions. That's one of the really unique parts of the ACT II story."

THE SITUATION TODAY

In the United States, more than 90 percent of households own microwave ovens. In addition, more than 60 percent of households are microwave popcorn consumers who spent more than $665 million on the product category in 2008. Orville Redenbacher's popcorn, also owned by ConAgra Foods, is now the market share leader with $142 million in sales while ACT II is #5 with $59 million in sales. "Our marketing research shows ACT II is especially strong in young families with kids," says Frank Lynch, vice president of marketing at Golden Valley. This conjures up an image of Mom and Dad watching a movie on TV with the kids and eating ACT II popcorn, a picture

close to reality. "ACT II has good market penetration in almost all age, income, urban versus rural, and ethnic segments," he continues.

"From the beginning, ACT II has been a leader in the microwave popcorn industry," says McKeon, "and we plan to continue that record." As evidence, he cites a number of ACT II "firsts":

- First mass-marketed microwave popcorn.
- First flavored microwave popcorn.
- First microwave popcorn tub.
- First fat-free microwave popcorn.
- First extra-butter microwave popcorn.
- First one-step sweetened microwave popcorn.

This list highlights a curious market segmentation phenomenon that has emerged in the last five years—the no-butter versus plenty-of-butter consumers. Originally, popcorn was seen as junk food. Later studies by nutritionists pointed out its health benefits: low calories and high fiber. This caused ACT II to introduce its low-fat popcorn to appeal to the health-conscious segment of consumers. However, when it comes to eating popcorn while watching a movie at home on TV, the more butter on their popcorn, the better. Recently, much of the growth in popcorn sales has been in the spoil-yourself-with-a lot-of-butter-on-your-popcorn segment.

Because of these diverse consumer tastes in popcorn, ACT II has developed a variety of popcorn products around its brand. Besides the low-fat and extra butter versions, these include the original flavors (natural, butter, and Kettle Corn), sweet glazed products (Caramel Corn and Buttery Cinnamon), and popcorn in tubs, mini-bags, and balls.

ACT II is positioned as unpretentious, fun, and youthful—a great product at a reasonable price. By stressing value, ACT II is responding to today's growing value consciousness of consumers seeking quality products at reasonable prices. These strategies have enabled ACT II to remain a leader in the microwave popcorn market.

OPPORTUNITIES FOR FUTURE GROWTH

For many years, the growth of the microwave popcorn industry closely followed the growth of household ownership of microwave ovens—from under 20 percent to more than 90 percent. But now, with a microwave oven in virtually every U.S. home, ACT II is trying to identify new market segments, new products, and innovative ways to appeal to all the major marketing channels.

In the United States, ACT II's strategy must include finding creative ways to continue to work with existing channels where it has special strength, such as the mass merchandiser channel. It also needs to further develop opportunities in the grocery store and supermarket channel. Now that the 10-year restriction on sales in grocery stores and supermarkets has expired, distribution through wholesalers that reach grocery stores and supermarkets is possible.

Global markets also present opportunities. ACT II has followed the penetration of microwave ovens in countries around the world, and used brokers to help gain distribution in those markets. However, foreign markets represent foreign tastes, something that does not always lend itself to standardized products. United Kingdom consumers, for example, think of popcorn as a candy or child's food rather than the salty snack it is in the United States. Even in DisneylandParis, France, American-style popcorn is absent, as French consumers sprinkle sugar on their popcorn. On the other hand, Swedes like theirs very buttery while many Mexicans like jalapeno-flavored popcorn.

Questions

1 Visit ACT II's Web site at www.ACTII.com and examine the assortment of products offered today. Are the assortment or the packaging related to its distribution channels or the segments they serve?

2 Use Figure 15–4 to create a description of the channels of distribution used for ACT II popcorn today.

3 Compared to selling through the nongrocery channels, what kind of product, price, and promotion strategies might ConAgra Foods use to reach the grocery channel more effectively?

4 What special marketing issues does ConAgra Foods face as it pursues growth in global markets?

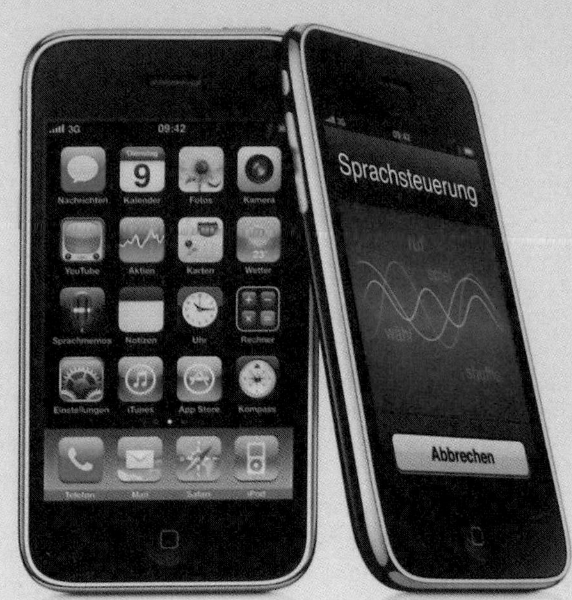

iPhone 3G S
Sprachsteuerung
Abbrechen
Jetzt bei Orange oder Swisscom kaufen.

16 Customer-Driven Supply Chain and Logistics Management

LEARNING OBJECTIVES

After reading this chapter you should be able to:

- LO1 Recognize the relationship between marketing channels, logistics, and supply chain management.
- LO2 Describe how a company's supply chain aligns with its marketing strategy.
- LO3 Identify the major logistics cost and customer service factors that managers consider when making supply chain decisions.
- LO4 Describe the key logistics functions in a supply chain.

APPLE INC.: SUPPLYING THE IPHONE 3G TO THE WORLD

Apple excels in innovation . . . in global supply chain management. Yes, that's right, global supply chain management! Why?

Consider this. On July 11, 2008, the iPhone 3G was simultaneously launched in 21 countries: Australia, Austria, Belgium, Canada, Denmark, Finland, Germany, Hong Kong, Ireland, Italy, Japan, Mexico, the Netherlands, New Zealand, Norway, Portugal, Spain, Sweden, Switzerland, the United Kingdom, and the United States (1 million units were sold during the first weekend). Then, on August 22, 2008, the phone was introduced in 22 more countries: Argentina, Chile, Colombia, Czech Republic, Ecuador, El Salvador, Estonia, Greece, Guatemala, Honduras, Hungary, India, Liechtenstein, Macau, Paraguay, Peru, the Philippines, Poland, Romania, Singapore, Slovakia, and Uruguay. By late 2009, Apple expected to have its iPhone 3GS available in 70 countries with over 30 million units sold.

This feat was made possible by a carefully orchestrated supply chain consisting of no fewer than 10 component suppliers from three countries that produced circuit boards, tough-screen controllers, digital camera modules, video processing chips, and a host of other components. All of these were assembled, stored, and delivered to Apple's Shenzhen, China, facility to Apple Stores and authorized dealers in 70 countries in sufficient quantities to satisfy the enormous demand for the iPhone 3G. Not surprisingly, Apple was recognized by its peers as having the world's top supply chain in 2008.[1]

Welcome to the critical world of customer-driven supply chain and logistics management. The essence of the problem is simple: It makes no sense to have brilliant marketing programs to sell world-class products if the products aren't available at the right time, at the right place, and in the right form and condition that customers want them.

This chapter describes the significance of supply chains and logistics management to the practice of marketing. In particular, attention is placed on the necessary alignment between supply chain management and marketing strategy, the trade-offs managers make between total distribution costs and customer service, and the increased application of information in managing the physical flow of goods to the final customer. Finally, the importance of reclaiming recyclable and reusable materials from customers for repair, remanufacturing, redistribution, and disposal is addressed in the context of reverse logistics.

SIGNIFICANCE OF SUPPLY CHAIN AND LOGISTICS MANAGEMENT

We often hear or use the term *distribution* but seldom appreciate its significance in marketing. U.S. companies spend $560 billion transporting raw materials and finished goods each year, another $332 billion on material handling, warehousing, storage, and holding inventory, and $40 billion managing the distribution process, including the cost of information technology. Worldwide, these activities and investments cost companies about $3.4 trillion each year.[2] In this section, we highlight contemporary perspectives on distribution, including supply chains and logistics, and describe the linkage between supply chain management and marketing strategy.

Relating Marketing Channels, Logistics, and Supply Chain Management

A marketing channel relies on logistics to make products available to consumers and industrial users, a point emphasized in Chapter 15. **Logistics** involves those activities that focus on getting the right amount of the right products to the right place at the right time at the lowest possible cost. The performance of these activities is **logistics management**, the practice of organizing the *cost-effective flow* of raw materials, in-process inventory, finished goods, and related information from point of origin to point of consumption to satisfy *customer requirements*.

Three elements of this definition deserve emphasis. First, logistics deals with decisions needed to move a product from the source of raw materials to consumption, or the *flow* of the product. Second, those decisions have to be made in a *cost-effective* manner. While it is important to drive down logistics costs, there is a limit—the third point of emphasis. A firm needs to drive down logistics costs as long as it can deliver expected *customer service*, which means satisfying customer requirements. The role of management is to see that customer needs are satisfied in the most cost-effective manner. When properly done, the results can be spectacular.

For example, Procter & Gamble set out to meet the needs of consumers more effectively by collaborating and partnering with its suppliers and retailers to ensure that the right products reached store shelves at the right time and at a lower cost. The effort was judged a success when, during an 18-month period, P&G's retail customers recorded a $65 million savings in logistics costs while customer service increased.[3]

The Procter & Gamble experience is not an isolated incident. Today, logistics management is embedded in a broader view of distribution, consistent with the emphasis on supply and channel partnering described in Chapters 6 and 15. Companies now recognize that getting the right items needed for consumption or production to the right place at the right time in the right condition at the right cost is often beyond their individual capabilities and control. Instead, collaboration, coordination, and information sharing among manufacturers, suppliers, and distributors are necessary to create a seamless flow of goods and services to customers. This perspective is represented in the concept of a supply chain and the practice of customer-driven supply chain management.

Supply Chains versus Marketing Channels

A **supply chain** is a sequence of firms that perform activities required to create and deliver a product or service to ultimate consumers or industrial users. It differs from a marketing channel in terms of membership. A supply chain includes suppliers that provide raw material inputs to a manufacturer as well as the wholesalers and retailers that deliver products to you. The management process is also different.

FIGURE 16–1
Relating logistics management and supply chain management to supplier networks and marketing channels

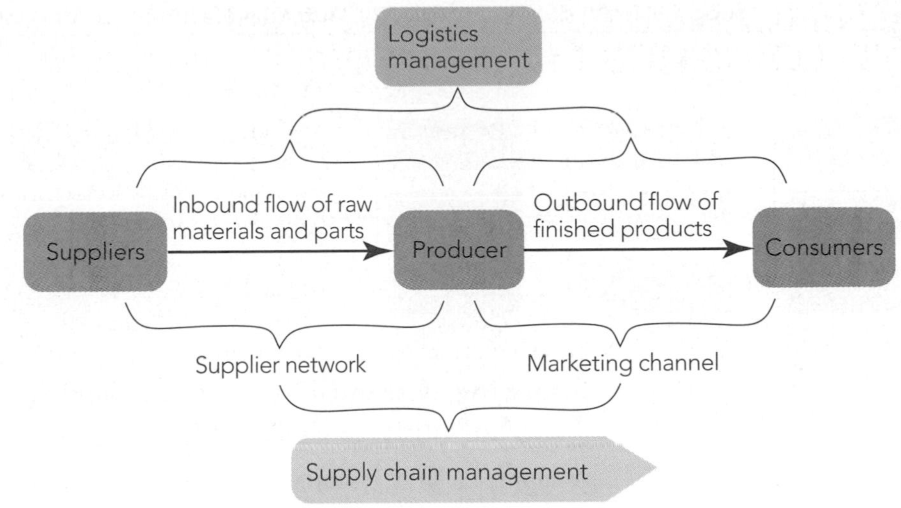

Supply chain management is the integration and organization of information and logistics activities *across firms* in a supply chain for the purpose of creating and delivering products and services that provide value to ultimate consumers. The relation among marketing channels, logistics management, and supply chain management is shown in Figure 16–1. An important feature of customer-driven supply chain management is its application of sophisticated information technology that allows companies to share and operate systems for order processing, transportation scheduling, and inventory and facility management.

Global Suppliers and Supply Chains

All companies are members of one or more supply chains. Supply chains span the globe; few companies rely only on domestic suppliers today.

Global suppliers provide ingredients in processed food, materials and parts in cars and trucks, components in consumer electronics, textiles and dyes in clothing—and the list goes on. For example, more than 80 percent of the active pharmaceutical ingredients in prescription and over-the-counter drugs sold in the United States are produced overseas, with the majority coming from manufacturers in India and China.[4] Even a simple product like a cereal bar contains additives and ingredients from around the world (see Figure 16–2).[5]

FIGURE 16–2
Cereal bars sold in stores and vending machines everywhere seem as American as apple pie—but their ingredients and additives come from all over the world thanks to global suppliers and supply chains. Enjoy your Kellogg's Nutri-Grain cereal bar!

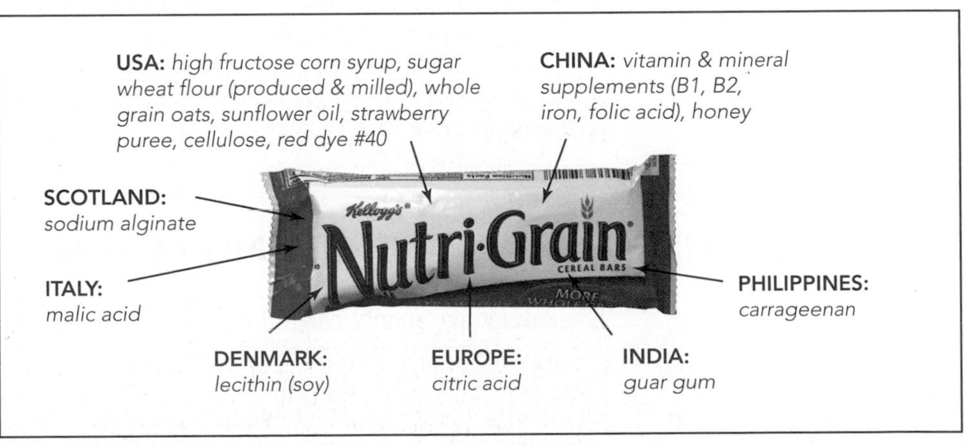

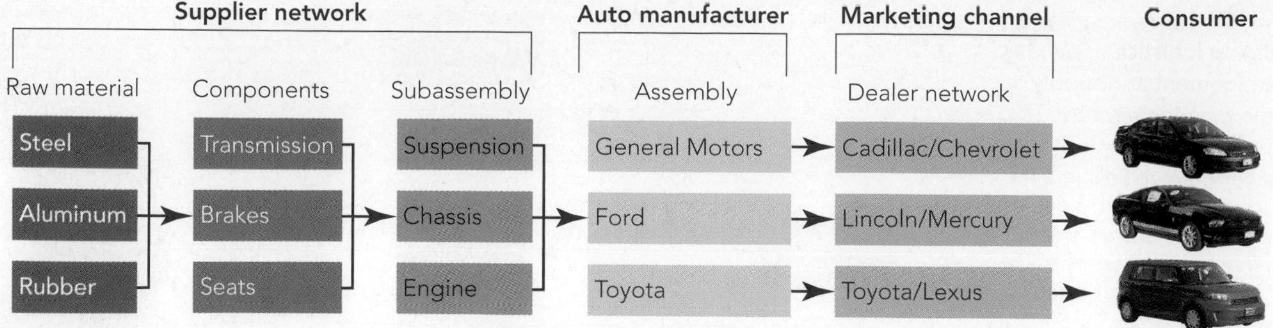

FIGURE 16–3
The automotive supply chain includes thousands of firms that provide the 5,000 or so electronic components and parts in a typical car.

Sourcing, Assembling, and Delivering a New Car: The Automotive Supply Chain

A supply chain is essentially a sequence of linked suppliers and customers in which every customer is, in turn, a supplier to another customer until a finished product reaches the final consumer. Even a simplified supply chain diagram for carmakers shown in Figure 16–3 illustrates how complex a supply chain can be.[6] A carmaker's supplier network includes thousands of firms worldwide that provide the 5,000 or so electronic components and parts in a typical automobile. They provide items ranging from raw materials, such as steel and rubber, to components, including transmissions, tires, brakes, and seats, to complex subassemblies and assemblies evident in chassis and suspension systems that make for a smooth, stable ride. Coordinating and scheduling material and component flows for their assembly into actual automobiles by carmakers is dependent on logistical activities, including transportation, order processing, inventory control, materials handling, and information technology.

A central link is the carmaker supply chain manager, who is responsible for translating customer requirements into actual orders and arranging for delivery dates and financial arrangements for car dealers. This is not an easy task given different consumer preferences and how much consumers are willing to pay. To appreciate the challenge facing supply chain managers, visit the Volkswagen Web site described in the Going Online box, and assemble your own Jetta based on your preferences and price.

Logistical aspects of the automobile marketing channel are also an integral part of the supply chain. Major responsibilities include transportation (which involves the selection and oversight of external carriers—trucking, airline, railroad, and shipping companies—for cars and parts to dealers), the operation of distribution centers, the management of finished goods inventories, and order processing for sales. Supply chain managers also play an important role in the marketing channel. They work with car dealers to ensure that the right automobiles are delivered to different locations. In addition, they make sure that spare and service parts are available so that dealers can meet the car maintenance and repair needs of consumers. All of this is done with the help of information technology that links the entire automotive supply chain. What does all of this cost? Logistics costs represent 25 percent to 30 percent of the retail price of a typical new car.

SUPPLY CHAIN MANAGEMENT AND MARKETING STRATEGY

The automotive supply chain illustration shows how information and logistics activities are integrated and organized across firms to create and deliver a car for you. What's missing from this illustration is the linkage between a specific company's supply chain and its marketing strategy. Just as companies have different marketing strategies, they also design and manage supply chains differently. The goals to be

Going Online

Build Your Own Jetta with a Mouse

Supply chain managers are responsible for having the right products at the right place at the right time at the right price for customers. In the automotive industry, this task is complex given the variety of car options available.

To appreciate the challenge, visit the Volkswagen Web site at www.VW.com. Click the link and choose a model such as a Jetta. Then click the "Start Building" button to select your trim, color, interior, and options. You will immediately obtain the manufacturer's suggested retail price (MSRP).

This easy task for you represents a sizable undertaking for a VW supply manager. You may not realize it, but VW comes in thousands of versions, including dealer-installed options you might want. A supply of these items has to be at the VW dealer for installation when you pick up your new car.

achieved by a firm's marketing strategy determine whether its supply chain needs to be more responsive or efficient in meeting customer requirements.

Aligning a Supply Chain with Marketing Strategy

There are a variety of supply chain configurations, each of which is designated to perform different tasks well. Marketers today recognize that the choice of a supply chain follows from a clearly defined marketing strategy and involves three steps:[7]

1. *Understand the customer.* To understand the customer, a company must identify the needs of the customer segment being served. These needs, such as a desire for a low price or convenience of purchase, help a company define the relative importance of efficiency and responsiveness in meeting customer requirements.
2. *Understand the supply chain.* Second, a company must understand what a supply chain is designed to do well. Supply chains range from those that emphasize being responsive to customer requirements and demand to those that emphasize efficiency with a goal of supplying products at the lowest possible delivered cost.
3. *Harmonize the supply chain with the marketing strategy.* Finally, a company needs to ensure that what the supply chain is capable of doing well is consistent with the targeted customer's needs and its marketing strategy. If a mismatch exists between what the supply chain does particularly well and a company's marketing strategy, the company will either need to redesign the supply chain to support the marketing strategy or change the marketing strategy. Read the Marketing Matters box on the next page to learn how IBM overhauled its complete supply chain to support its marketing strategy.[8]

How are these steps applied and how are efficiency and responsive considerations built into a supply chain? Let's look at how two well-known companies—Dell and Walmart—have harmonized their supply chain and marketing strategy.[9]

Dell: A Responsive Supply Chain

The Dell marketing strategy primarily targets customers who desire having the most up-to-date computer systems customized to their needs. These customers are also

Marketing Matters > > > > > > customer value

IBM's Integrated Supply Chain—Delivering a Total Solution for Its Customers

IBM is one of the world's great business success stories because of its ability to reinvent itself to satisfy shifting customer needs in a dynamic global marketplace. The company's transformation of its supply chain is a case in point.

Beginning in 2001, IBM set about to build a single integrated supply chain that would handle raw material procurement, manufacturing, logistics, customer support, order entry, and customer fulfillment across all of IBM—something that had never been done before. Why would IBM undertake this task? According to IBM's CEO, Samuel J. Palmisano, "You cannot hope to thrive in the IT industry if you are a high-cost, slow-moving company. Supply chain is one of the new competitive battlegrounds. We are committed to being the most efficient and productive player in our industry."

The task wasn't easy. With factories in 10 countries, IBM buys 2 billion parts a year from 33,000 suppliers, offers 78,000 products available in 3 million possible variations, moves over 2 billion pounds of machines and parts annually, processes 1.7 million customer orders annually in North America alone, and operates in 150 countries. Yet with surprising efficiency, IBM overhauled its supply chain from raw material sourcing to postsales support.

Today, IBM is uniquely poised to configure and deliver a tailored mix of hardware, software, and service to provide a total solution for its customers. Not surprisingly, IBM's integrated supply chain is now heralded as one of the best in the world!

---

willing to: (1) wait to have their customized computer system delivered in a few days, rather than picking out a model at a retail store, and (2) pay a reasonable, though not the lowest, price in the marketplace. Given Dell's customer segment, the company has the option of adopting an efficient or responsive supply chain.

An efficient supply chain may use inexpensive, but slower, modes of transportation, emphasize economies of scale in its production process by reducing the variety of system configurations offered, and limit its assembly and inventory storage facilities to a single location, say Austin, Texas, where the company is headquartered. If Dell opted only for efficiency in its supply chain, it would be difficult if not impossible to satisfy its target customer's desire for rapid delivery and a wide variety of customizable products. Dell instead opted for a responsive supply chain. It relies on more expensive express transportation for receipt of components from suppliers and delivery of finished products to customers. The company achieves product variety and manufacturing efficiency by designing common platforms across several products and using common components. Moreover, Dell has invested heavily in information technology to link itself with suppliers and customers.

Walmart: An Efficient Supply Chain

Now let's consider Walmart. Walmart's marketing strategy is to be a reliable, lower-price retailer for a wide variety of mass consumption consumer goods. This strategy favors an efficient supply chain designed to deliver products to consumers at the lowest possible cost. Efficiency is achieved in a variety of ways. For instance, Walmart keeps relatively low inventory levels, and most is stocked in stores available for sale, not in warehouses gathering dust. The low inventory arises from Walmart's innovative use of *cross-docking*—a practice that involves unloading products from suppliers, sorting products for individual stores, and quickly reloading products onto its trucks for a particular store. No warehousing or storing of products occurs, except for a few hours or, at most, a day. Cross-docking allows Walmart to operate only a small number of distribution centers to service its vast network of Walmart Stores, Supercenters, Neighborhood Markets, Marketside, and Sam's Clubs, which contributes to efficiency. On the other hand, the company runs its own fleet of trucks to

Dell and Walmart emphasize responsiveness and efficiency in their supply chains, respectively. The text details how they do this.

Dell, Inc.
www.dell.com

Walmart, Inc.
www.walmartstores.com

service its stores. This does increase cost and investment, but the benefits in terms of responsiveness justify the cost in Walmart's case.

Walmart has invested much more than its competitors in information technology to operate its supply chain. The company feeds information about customer requirements and demand from its stores back to its suppliers, which manufacture only what is being demanded. This large investment has improved the efficiency of Walmart's supply chain and made it responsive to customer needs.

Three lessons can be learned from these two examples. First, there is no one best supply chain for every company. Second, the best supply chain is the one that is consistent with the needs of the customer segment being served and complements a company's marketing strategy. And finally, supply chain managers are often called upon to make trade-offs between efficiency and responsiveness on various elements of a company's supply chain.

learning review

1. What is the principal difference between a marketing channel and a supply chain?
2. The choice of a supply chain involves what three steps?

OBJECTIVE OF INFORMATION AND LOGISTICS MANAGEMENT IN A CUSTOMER-DRIVEN SUPPLY CHAIN

LO3

The objective of information and logistics management in a customer-driven supply chain is to minimize logistics costs while delivering maximum customer service. The Dell and Walmart examples highlighted how two well-known companies have realized this objective by different means. An important similarity between these two companies is that both use information to leverage logistics activities, reduce logistics costs, and improve customer service.

Information's Role in Supply Chain Responsiveness and Efficiency

Information consists of data and analysis regarding inventory, transportation, distribution facilities, and customers throughout the supply chain.[10] Continuing advances in information technology make it possible to track logistics activities and customer service variables and manage them for efficiency and responsiveness. For example, information on customer demand patterns allows pharmaceutical companies such as Eli Lilly and GlaxoSmithKline to produce and stock drugs in anticipation of customer needs. This improves supply chain responsiveness because customers will find the drugs when and where they want them. Demand information improves supply chain efficiency because pharmaceutical firms are better able to meet customer needs and produce, transport, and store the required amount of inventory.

change
hp
How to light up a supply chain.
Advance Transformer, a leading component manufacturer for lighting systems, had legacy IT systems that no longer kept up with production demands. They turned to HP to help them better manage their supply chain. Now, with a unified management of the whole infrastructure, their systems automatically solve problems as they occur. All this has reduced production time from 28 to 5 days, cut inventory levels by 50% and revealed the bright side of change. www.hp.com/adapt
Solutions for the adaptive enterprise.
hp
invent

Hewlett-Packard is a leader in the application of information technology to supply chain management.

Hewlett-Packard
www.hp.com

A variety of technologies are used to transmit and manage information in a supply chain. An **electronic data interchange (EDI)** combines proprietary computer and telecommunication technologies to exchange electronic invoices, payments, and information among suppliers, manufacturers, and retailers. When linked with store scanning equipment and systems, EDI provides a seamless electronic link from a retail checkout counter to suppliers and manufacturers. EDI is commonly used in retail, apparel, transportation, pharmaceutical, grocery, health care, and insurance industries, as well as by local, state, and federal government agencies. About 95 percent of the companies listed in the Fortune 1000 use EDI. At Hewlett-Packard, for example, 1 million EDI transactions are made every month.

Another technology is the *extranet*, which is an Internet-based network that permits secure business-to-business communication between a manufacturer and its suppliers, distributors, and sometimes other partners (such as advertising agencies). Extranets are less expensive and more flexible to operate than EDI because of their connection to the public Internet. This technology is prominent in private electronic exchanges described in Chapter 6. For example, Whirlpool's private exchange allows it to fulfill retailer orders quickly and inexpensively and better match appliance demand and supply.

Whereas EDI and extranets transmit information, other technologies help manage information in a supply chain. Enterprise resource planning (ERP) technology and supply chain management software track logistics cost and customer service variables, both of which are described next.

Total Logistics Cost Concept

For our purposes, **total logistics cost** includes expenses associated with transportation, materials handling and warehousing, inventory, stockouts (being out of inven-

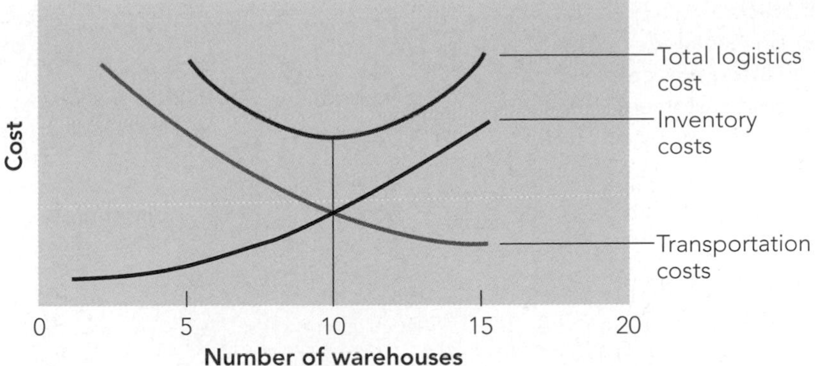

FIGURE 16–4
How total logistics cost varies with the number of warehouses used based on inventory costs and transportation costs. The goal is to minimize total logistics cost.

tory), order processing, and return goods handling. Many of these costs are interrelated so changes in one will impact the others. For example, as the firm attempts to minimize its transportation costs by shipping in larger quantities, it will also experience an increase in inventory levels. Larger inventory levels will not only increase inventory costs but should also reduce stockouts. It is important, therefore, to study the impact on all of the logistics decision areas when considering a change.

Figure 16–4 provides a graphic example. An oft-used supply chain strategy is for a firm to have a number of warehouses, which receive shipments in large quantities and then redistribute smaller shipments to local customers. As the number of warehouses increases, inventory costs rise and transportation costs fall. That is, more inventory is warehoused, but it is transported in volume closer to customers. The net effect is to minimize the total costs of logistics shown in Figure 16–4 by having 10 warehouses. This means the total cost curve is minimized at a point where neither of the two individual cost elements is at a minimum but the overall system is.

Studying its total logistics cost has had revolutionary consequences for National Semiconductor, which produces computer chips. In two years, it cut its standard delivery time 47 percent, reduced distribution costs 2.5 percent, and increased sales 34 percent by shutting down six warehouses around the world and air-freighting its microchips from its huge distribution center in Singapore. It does this even though it has six factories in Israel, Britain, and the United States. National also discovered that a lot of its chips were actually profit-losers, and it cut the number of products it sells by 45 percent, thereby simplifying logistics and increasing profits.[11]

Customer Service Concept

If a supply chain is a *flow*, the end of it—or *output*—is the service delivered to customers. However, service can be expensive. One company found that to increase on-time delivery from a 95 percent rate to a 100 percent rate tripled total logistics costs. Higher levels of service require tactics such as more inventory to reduce stockouts, more expensive transportation to improve speed and lessen damage, and double or triple checking of orders to ensure correctness. A firm's goal should be to provide superior customer service while controlling logistics costs. Customer service is now seen not merely as an expense but as a means to increase customer satisfaction and sales. For example, a 3M survey about customer service among 18,000 European customers in 16 countries revealed surprising agreement in all countries about the importance of customer service. Respondents stressed factors such as condition of product delivered, on-time delivery, quick delivery after order placement, and effective handling of problems.[12]

Within the context of a supply chain, **customer service** is the ability of logistics management to satisfy users in terms of time, dependability, communication, and convenience. As suggested by Figure 16–5 on the next page, a supply chain manager's key task is to balance these four customer service factors against total logistics cost factors.

FIGURE 16–5
Supply chain managers balance total logistics cost factors against customer service factors.

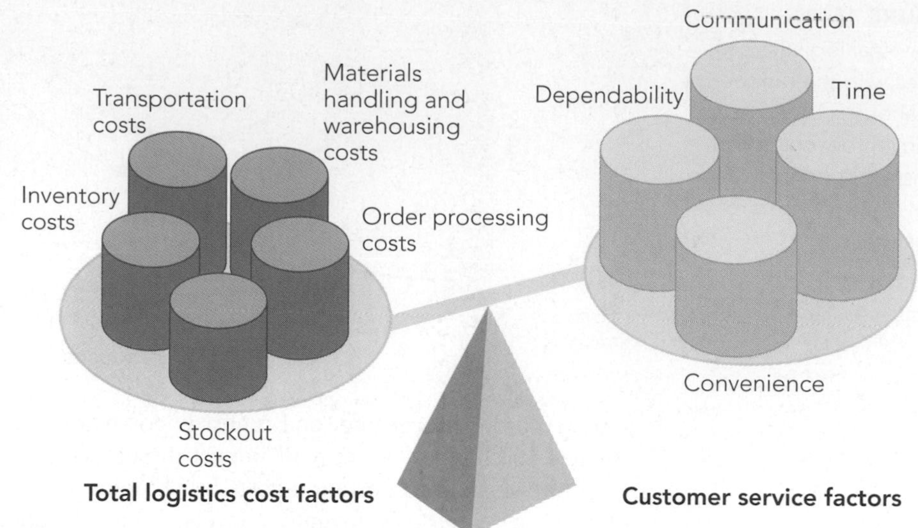

Time In a supply chain setting, time refers to **lead time** for an item, which means the lag from ordering an item until it is received and ready for use or sale. This is also referred to as *order cycle time* or *replenishment time* and may be more important to retailers or wholesalers than consumers. The various elements that make up the typical order cycle include recognition of the need to order, order transmittal, order processing, documentation, and transportation. A current emphasis in supply chain management is to reduce lead time so that customer inventory levels may be minimized. Another emphasis is to make the process of reordering and receiving products as simple as possible, often through electronic data and inventory systems called **quick response** or **efficient consumer response** delivery systems. These inventory management systems reduce the retailer's lead time for receiving merchandise, thereby lowering a retailer's inventory investment, improving customer service levels, and reducing logistics expense (see the Marketing Matters box).[13] The order processing portion of lead time will be discussed later in this chapter.

Dependability Dependability is the consistency of replenishment. This is important to all firms in a supply chain and to consumers. It can be broken into three elements: consistent lead time, safe delivery, and complete delivery. Consistent service allows planning (such as appropriate inventory levels). Inconsistencies create surprises. Intermediaries may be willing to accept longer lead times if they know about them in advance and can thus make plans. While surprise delays may shut down a production line, early deliveries will be almost as troublesome because of the problems of storing the extra inventory. Dependability is essential for the just-in-time inventory strategies discussed at the end of the chapter.

Communication Communication is a two-way link between buyer and seller that helps in monitoring service and anticipating future needs. Status reports on orders are a typical example of improved communication between buyer and seller. The increased communication capability of transportation carriers has enhanced the accuracy of such tracing information and improved the ability of buyers to schedule shipments. Note, however, that such information is still reactive and is not a substitute for consistent on-time deliveries. Therefore, some firms have partnered with firms specializing in logistics in an effort to institutionalize a more proactive flow of useful information. Unisys, a major technology firm, relies on DHL's global service parts logistics system to enable monitoring, management, and inventory level reporting across regions of the world. This system provides timely information about the status of orders throughout the Unisys supply chain from multiple suppliers.[14]

Marketing Matters > > > > > > > > > technology

For Fashion and Food Merchandising, Haste Is as Important as Taste

Fashion and food have a lot in common. Both depend a lot on taste and both require timely merchandising. By its nature, fashion dictates that suppliers and retailers be able to adjust to new styles, colors, and different seasons. Fashion retailers need to identify what's hot, so it can be ordered quickly, and what's not, to avoid markdowns. Saks employs a *quick response* delivery system for fashion merchandise. Saks' point-of-sale scanner system records each day's sales. When stock falls below a minimum level, the system automatically generates a replenishment order. Vendors of fashion merchandise, such as Donna Karan (DKNY), receive an electronic order, which is processed within 48 hours.

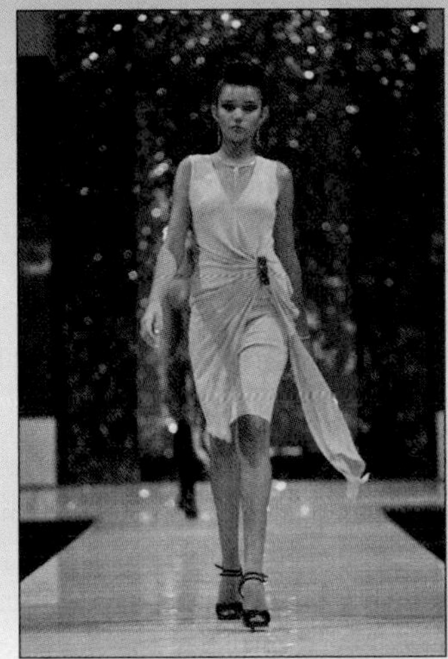

Food marketers and retailers use the term *efficient consumer response* to describe their replenishment systems. All major food companies, including General Mills, Del Monte, Heinz, Nestlé, and Beatrice Foods, and many supermarket chains such as Kroger, Safeway, and A&P rely on electronic replenishment systems to minimize stockouts of popular items and overstocks of slow-moving items. Lowered retailer inventories and efficient logistics practices have been projected to save U.S. grocery shoppers $30 billion a year.

Convenience The concept of convenience means that there should be a minimum of effort on the part of the buyer in doing business with the seller. Is it easy for the customer to order? Are the products available from many outlets? Does the buyer have to buy huge quantities of the product? Will the seller arrange all necessary details, such as transportation? The seller must concentrate on removing unnecessary barriers to customer convenience. This customer service factor has promoted the use of vendor-managed inventory practices discussed later in the chapter.

Customer Service Standards

Firms that operate effective supply chains usually develop a set of written customer service standards. These serve as objectives and provide a benchmark against which results can be measured for control purposes. In developing these standards, information is collected on customers' needs. It is also necessary to know what competitors offer as well as the willingness of customers to pay a bit more for better service. After these and similar questions are answered, realistic standards are set and an ongoing monitoring program is established. The examples below suggest that customer service standards will differ by type of firm.

Type of Firm	Customer Service Standard
Wholesaler	At least 98 percent of orders filled accurately
Manufacturer	Order cycle time of no more than five days
Retailer	Returns accepted within 30 days
Airline	At least 90 percent of arrivals on time
Trucker	A maximum of 5 percent loss and damage per year
Restaurant	Lunch served within five minutes of order

Effective customer service can yield substantial returns. The head of IBM's integrated supply chain group estimates that a 1 percent increase in customer service

Using Marketing Dashboards

Diagnosing Out-of-Stocks and On-Time Delivery for Organic Produce

Supply chain managers recognize that out-of-stocks mean lost sales. And poor on-time delivery is often the culprit. These measures are routinely compared on a weekly or monthly basis against a numerical standard and each other.

Your Challenge You have just joined Superior Supermarkets as a distribution analyst. Superior Supermarkets is a 150-store chain that serves small cities and towns in the south central United States through its own distribution center. During your first meeting with the vice president of distribution, the topic of produce out-of-stocks arose. Specifically, organic produce (fresh fruits and vegetables) out-of-stocks had increased. Out-of-stocks are calculated as follows:

$$\text{Out-of-Stocks (\%)} = \frac{\text{Number of outlets where a brand or product is listed but unavailable}}{\text{Total number of outlets where a brand or product is listed}}$$

Poor on-time delivery of produce was the suspected reason for the rise in out-of-stocks. On-time delivery is calculated as follows:

$$\text{On-Time Delivery (\%)} = \frac{\text{Number of deliveries achieved in the time frame promised}}{\text{Total number of deliveries initiated in a time period}}$$

Your challenge is to examine whether on-time delivery performance might be the reason for the organic produce out-of-stocks situation at Superior Supermarkets.

Your Findings Superior Supermarkets monitors out-of-stocks and on-time delivery on a monthly basis. A 3 percent out-of-stock standard and a 98 percent on-time delivery standard have been set by the company. Monthly results for organic produce are displayed on the company's marketing dashboard shown below.

Clearly, the downward trend in on-time delivery corresponds with the upward trend in out-of-stocks for organic produce.

Your Action As a distribution analyst, you might recommend that the transportation department needs to improve its performance. However, the issue might reach deeper into the order cycle time for organic produce. Recall that order cycle time includes the recognition of the need to place, transmit, process, document, and transport the order. The actual *cause* of out-of-stocks might reside in the four prior elements of order cycle time and not just transportation.

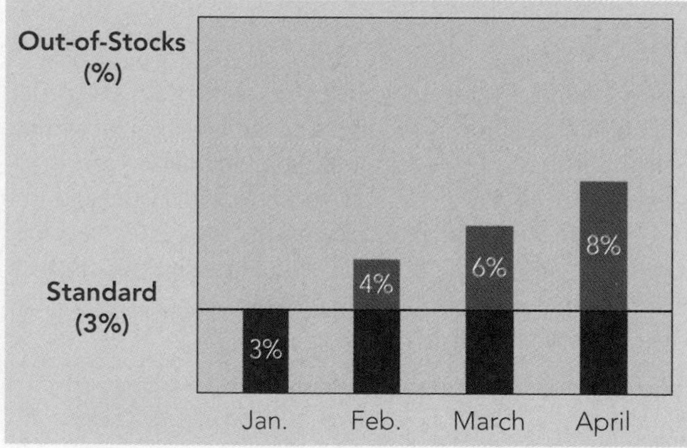

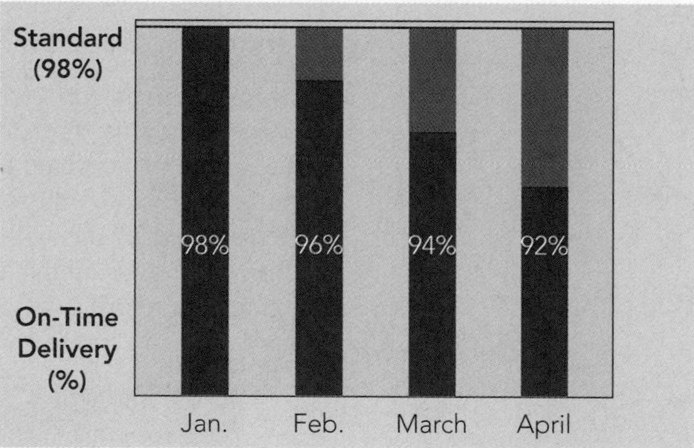

satisfaction translates into $2 billion to $3 billion of additional revenue to his company.[15]

Companies rely on marketing dashboards to monitor customer service standards. Read the Using Marketing Dashboards box to see one application and interpretation of the link between out-of-stocks and on-time delivery.

learning review

3. The objective of information and logistics management in a supply chain is to ______________.
4. How does consumer demand information increase supply chain responsiveness and efficiency?
5. What is the relationship between the number of warehouses a company operates, its inventory costs, and its transportation costs?

KEY LOGISTICS FUNCTIONS IN A SUPPLY CHAIN

FedEx Supply Chain Services and Ryder Systems are two third-party logistics providers that perform most or all of the logistics functions that manufacturers, suppliers, and distributors would normally perform.

FedEx Supply Chain Services
www.fedex.com

Ryder Systems
www.ryder.com

The four key logistic functions in a supply chain include (1) transportation, (2) warehousing and materials handling, (3) order processing, and (4) inventory management. These functions have become so complex and interrelated that many companies have outsourced them to third-party logistics providers.

Third-party logistics providers are firms that perform most or all of the logistics functions that manufacturers, suppliers, and distributors would normally perform themselves. Today, 77 percent of manufacturers listed in the Fortune 500 outsource one or more logistics functions, at least on a limited basis.[16] Ryder Systems, UPS Supply Chain Solutions, FedEx Supply Chain Services, DHL, and Penske Logistics are just a few of the companies that specialize in handling logistics functions for their clients.

The four major logistics functions and the involvement of third-party logistics providers are described next.

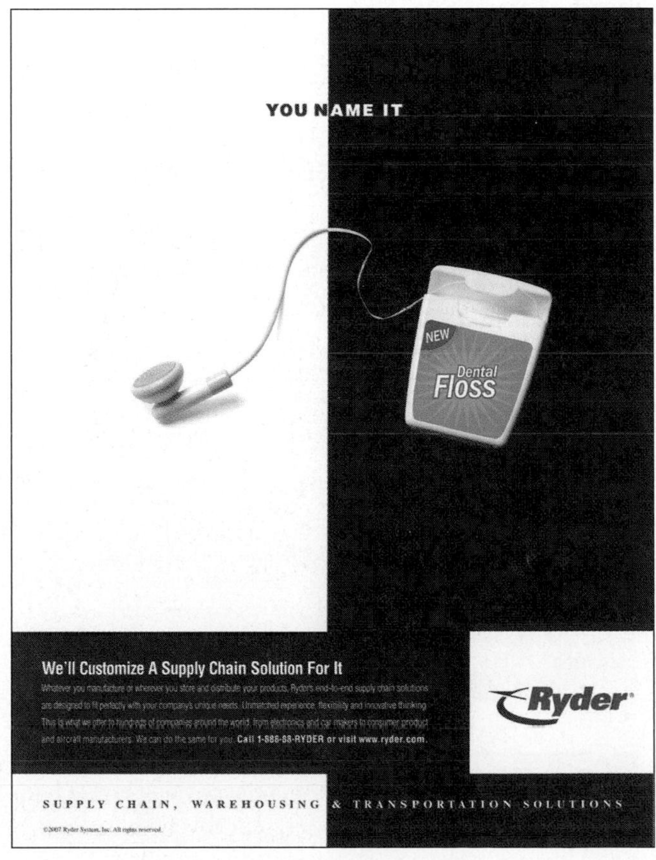

Transportation

LO4

Transportation provides the movement of goods necessary in a supply chain. There are five basic modes of transportation: railroads, motor carriers, air carriers, pipelines, and water carriers, and modal combinations involving two or more modes, such as truck trailers on a rail flatcar.

All transportation modes can be evaluated on six basic service criteria:

- *Cost.* Charges for transportation.
- *Time.* Speed of transit.
- *Capability.* What can be realistically carried with this mode.
- *Dependability.* Reliability of service regarding time, loss, and damage.
- *Accessibility.* Convenience of the mode's routes (such as pipeline availability).
- *Frequency.* Scheduling.

Figure 16–6 summarizes the relative service advantages and disadvantages of five modes of transportation available.[17]

Railroads Railroads typically carry heavy, bulky items over long distances. Railroads can carry larger shipments than trucks (in terms of total weight per vehicle), but their routes are less extensive. Services include unit trains and intermodal service. A *unit train* is dedicated to one commodity (often coal), using permanently coupled cars that run a continuous loop from a single origin to a single destination and back. Even though the train returns empty, the process captures enough operating efficiencies to make it one of the lowest-cost transportation alternatives available. Unit trains keep to a specific schedule so that the customers can plan on reliable delivery, and they usually carry products that can be loaded and unloaded quickly and automatically.

Railroads also apply the unit train concept to *intermodal transportation*, which involves combining different transportation modes to get the best features of each. The result is a service that attracts high-value freight, which would normally go by

FIGURE 16–6
Advantages and disadvantages of five modes of transportation

TRANSPORTATION MODE	RELATIVE ADVANTAGES	RELATIVE DISADVANTAGES
Railroads	• Full capability • Extensive routes • Low cost	• Some reliability, damage problems • Not always complete pickup and delivery • Sometimes slow
Motor carriers	• Complete pickup and delivery • Extensive routes • Fairly fast	• Size and weight restrictions • Higher cost • More weather sensitive
Air carriers	• Fast • Low damage • Frequent departures	• High cost • Limited capabilities
Pipeline	• Low cost • Very reliable • Frequent departures	• Limited routes (accessibility) • Slow
Water carriers	• Low cost • Huge capacities	• Slow • Limited routes and schedules • More weather sensitive

truck. The most popular combination is truck-rail, called *piggyback* or *trailer on flat-car (TOFC)*. The other popular use of an intermodal combination is associated with export/import traffic and uses containers in place of trailers. These containers can be loaded on ships, trains, and truck trailers. So in terms of the on-land segment of international shipments, a container is handled the same way as a trailer. Containers are used in international trade because they use less space on oceangoing vessels.

Motor Carriers In contrast to the railroad industry, the for-hire motor carrier industry is composed of many small firms, including independent truckers and firms that own their own trucks for transporting their own products.

The greatest advantage of motor carriers is the complete door-to-door service. Trucks can go almost anywhere there is a road, and with the design of specialized equipment, they can carry a variety of products. Their physical limitations are size and weight restrictions enforced by the states. Trucks have the reputation for maintaining a better record than rail for loss and damage and providing faster, more reliable service, especially for shorter distances. As a result, trucks carry higher-value goods that are time-sensitive and expensive to carry in inventory. The trade-off is that truck rates are substantially higher than rail rates.

Air Carriers and Express Companies Air freight is costly, but its speed may create savings in lower inventory. The items that can be carried are limited by space constraints and are usually valuable, time-sensitive, and lightweight, such as perishable flowers, clothing, and electronic parts. Specialized firms provide ground support in terms of collecting shipments and delivering them to the air terminal. When air freight is handled by major airlines—such as American, United, or Delta—it is often carried as cargo using the excess luggage space of scheduled passenger flights.

Freight Forwarders *Freight forwarders* are firms that accumulate small shipments into larger lots and then hire a carrier to move them, usually at reduced rates. Recall that transportation companies provide rate incentives for larger quantities. Forwarders collect many small shipments consigned to a common destination and pay the carrier the lower rate based on larger volume, so they often convert shipments that are less-than-truckload (LTL) into full truckloads, thereby receiving better shipping rates. The rates charged by the forwarder to the individual shippers, in turn, are somewhat less than the small quantity rate, and the difference is the forwarder's margin. In general, the shipment receives improved service at lower cost.

Warehousing and Materials Handling

Warehouses may be classified in one of two ways: (1) storage warehouses and (2) distribution centers. In *storage warehouses*, products are intended to come to rest for some period of time, as in the aging of products or in storing household goods. *Distribution centers*, on the other hand, are designed to facilitate the timely movement of goods and represent a very important part of a supply chain. They represent the second most significant cost in a supply chain after transportation.

Distribution centers not only allow firms to hold their stock in decentralized locations but are also used to facilitate sorting and consolidating products from different manufacturing plants or suppliers. For example, a distribution center operated by ODW Logistics, Inc., a third-party logistics provider, provides these services. Pioneer Electronics, Inc., relies on ODW not just for warehousing and distribution, but for basic assembly as well. ODW employees put plasma television sets and stereo speakers delivered separately from China in a single box with receivers from Thailand, other smaller parts from around the world, and installation instructions. The boxes are then shipped to the home-theater sections of Walmart stores and Best

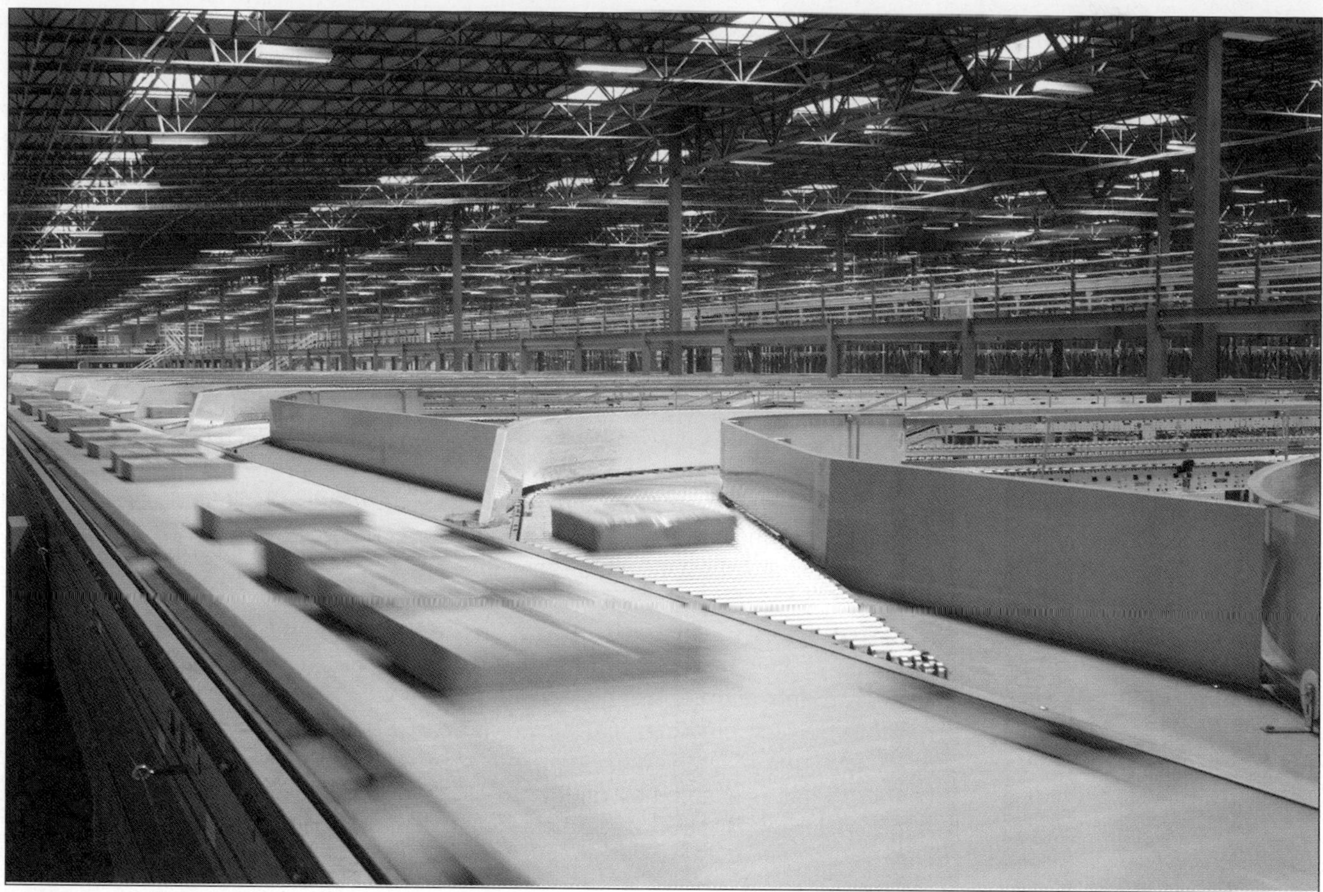

Amazon.com operates 30 highly automated warehouses in the United States, Europe, and Asia.

Amazon.com
www.amazon.com

Buy.[18] Some physical transformation can also take place in distribution centers such as mixing or blending ingredients, labeling, and repackaging. Paint companies such as Sherwin-Williams and Benjamin Moore use distribution centers for this purpose. In addition, distribution centers may serve as manufacturers' sales offices, described in Chapter 15, and order processing centers.

Materials handling, which involves moving goods over short distances into, within, and out of warehouses and manufacturing plants, is a key part of warehouse operations. The two major problems with this activity are high labor costs and high rates of loss and damage. Every time an item is handled, there is a chance for loss or damage. Common materials handling equipment includes forklifts, cranes, and conveyors. Today, materials handling in warehouses is automated by using computers and robots to reduce the cost of holding, moving, and recording inventories.

Order Processing

There are several stages in the processing of an order, and a failure at any one of them can cause a problem with the customer. The process starts with transmitting the order by a variety of means such as the Internet, an extranet, or electronic data interchange. This is followed by entering the order in the appropriate databases and sending the information to those needing it. For example, a regional warehouse is notified to prepare an order. After checking inventory, a new quantity may need to be reordered from the production line, or purchasing may be requested to reorder from a vendor. If the item is currently out of stock, a *back order* is created, and the whole process of keeping track of a small part of the original order must be managed. In addition, credit may have to be checked for some customers, all docu-

United Airlines Cargo provides fast, global delivery, often utilizing containers.

United Airlines
www.unitedcargo.com

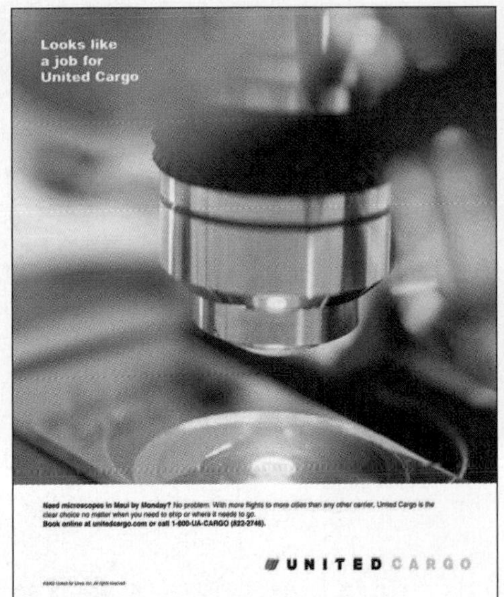

mentation for the order must be prepared, transportation must be arranged, and an order confirmation must be sent. Order processing systems are evaluated in terms of speed and accuracy.

Electronic order processing has replaced manual processing for most large companies. For example, 96 percent of IBM's purchase transactions with suppliers are conducted on the Internet. Kiwi Brands, the Douglassville, Pennsylvania, marketer of Kiwi shoe polish, Endust, and Behold, receives 75 percent of its retailers' purchase orders via EDI. The company has also implemented financial EDI, sending invoices to retailers and receiving payment order/remittance advice documents and electronic funds transfer (EFT) payments. Shippers as well are linked to the system, allowing Kiwi to receive shipment status messages electronically.

Inventory Management

Inventory management is one of the primary responsibilities of the supply chain manager. The major problem is maintaining the delicate balance between too little and too much. Too little inventory may result in poor service, stockouts, brand switching, and loss of market share; too much leads to higher costs because of the money tied up in inventory and the chance that it may become obsolete.

Reasons for Inventory Traditionally, carrying inventory has been justified on several grounds: (1) to offer a buffer against variations in supply and demand, often caused by uncertainty in forecasting demand; (2) to provide better service for those customers who wish to be served on demand; (3) to promote production efficiencies; (4) to provide a hedge against price increases by suppliers; (5) to promote purchasing and transportation discounts; and (6) to protect the firm from contingencies such as strikes and shortages.

However, companies today view inventory as something to be moved, not stored, and more of a liability than an asset. The traditional justification for inventory has resulted in excessive inventories that have proven costly to maintain. Consider the U.S. automobile industry. Despite efforts to streamline its supply chain, industry analysts estimate that $230 billion worth of excess inventory piles up annually in the form of unused raw materials, parts waiting to be delivered, and vehicles sitting on dealers' lots.[19]

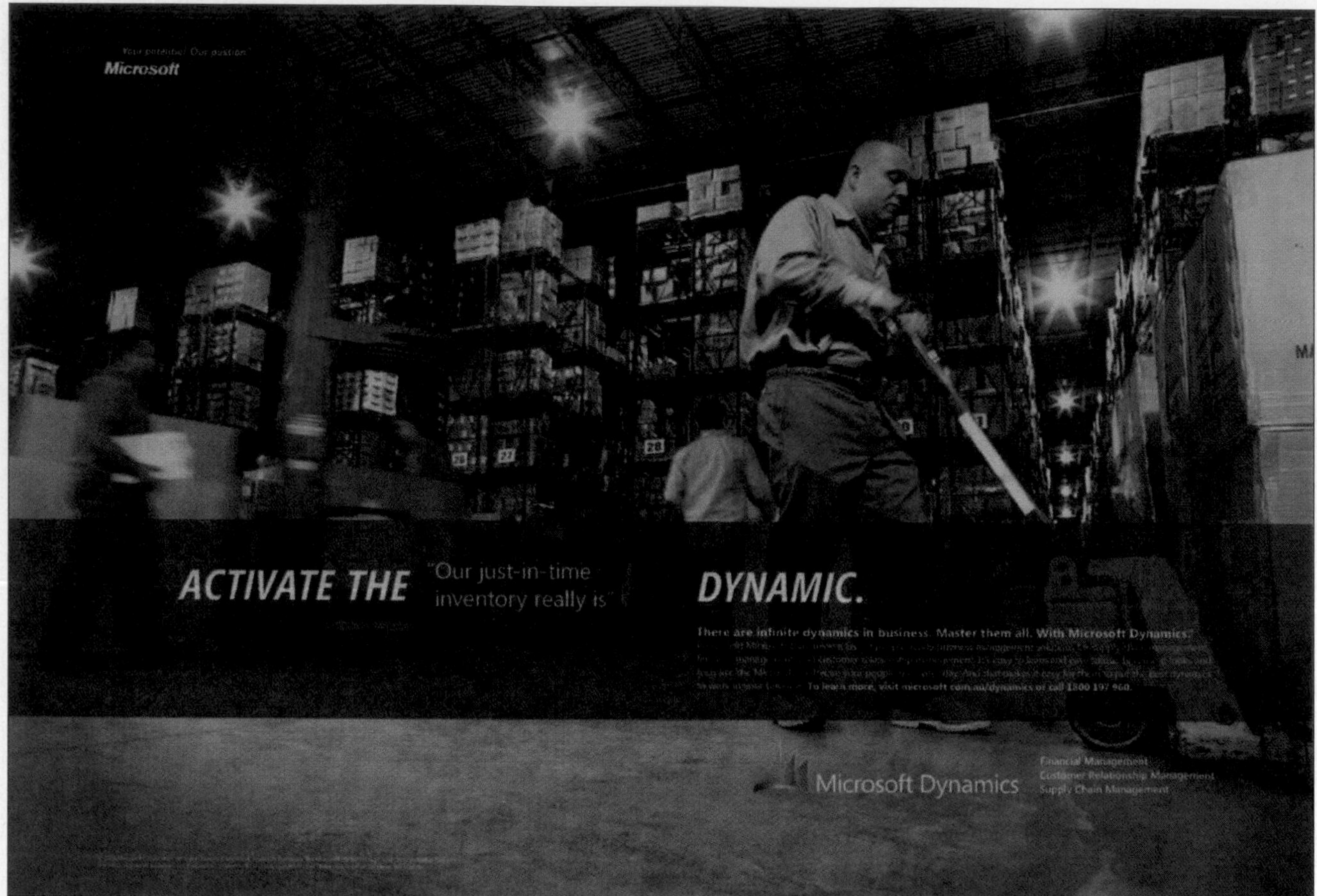

Microsoft
ACTIVATE THE
"Our just-in-time inventory really is"
DYNAMIC.
There are infinite dynamics in business. Master them all. With Microsoft Dynamics.
Microsoft Dynamics
Financial Management
Customer Relationship Management
Supply Chain Management

Did you know Microsoft Corporation is also involved in supply chain management? This advertisement features Microsoft Dynamics and its just-in-time solution for supply chain management.

Microsoft Dynamics
www.microsoft.com/dynamics

Inventory Costs Specific inventory costs are often hard to detect because they are difficult to measure and occur in many different parts of the firm. A classification of inventory costs includes the following:

- *Capital costs.* The opportunity costs resulting from tying up funds in inventory instead of using them in other, more profitable investments; these are related to interest rates.
- *Inventory service costs.* Items such as insurance and taxes that are present in many states.
- *Storage costs.* Warehousing space and materials handling.
- *Risk costs.* Possible loss, damage, pilferage, perishability, and obsolescence.

Storage costs, risk costs, and some inventory service costs vary according to the characteristics of the item inventoried. For example, perishable products or highly seasonal items have higher risk costs than a commodity type product such as lumber. Capital costs are always present and are proportional to the *values* of the item and prevailing interest rates. The costs of carrying inventory vary with the particular circumstances but quite easily could range from 10 to 35 percent for different firms.

Supply Chain Inventory Strategies Conventional wisdom a decade ago was that a firm should protect itself against uncertainty by maintaining a reserve inventory at each of its production and stocking points. This has been described as a "just-in-case" philosophy of inventory management and led to unnecessary high levels of inventory. In contrast is the **just-in-time (JIT) concept**, which is an inventory supply system that operates with very low inventories and requires fast, on-time delivery. When parts are needed for production, they arrive from suppliers "just in

Making Responsible Decisions > > > > sustainability

Reverse Logistics and Green Marketing Go Together at Hewlett-Packard: Recycling e-Waste

Between 20 and 50 million tons of electronic waste find their way to landfills around the world annually. Americans alone are expected to discard 400 million analog TV sets and computer monitors and Japanese consumers will trash 610 million cell phones in 2010. The result? Landfills are seeping lead, chromium, mercury, and other toxins, prevalent in digital debris, into the environment.

Fortunately, Hewlett-Packard has taken it upon itself to act responsibly and address this issue through its highly regarded reverse logistics program. Hewlett-Packard has recycled computer and printer hardware since 1987 and is an industry leader in this practice. The company's recycling service is available today in more than 40 countries, regions, and territories. By 2010, Hewlett-Packard will have recycled over 1 billion pounds of used products to be refurbished for resale or donation or for recovery of materials.

The recycling effort at Hewlett-Packard is also part of the company's Design for Supply Chain program. Among other initiatives in this program, emphasis is placed on product and packaging changes to reduce reverse supply chain and environmental costs. For example, design changes have increased the recycling of its popular ink-jet supplies by 25 percent.

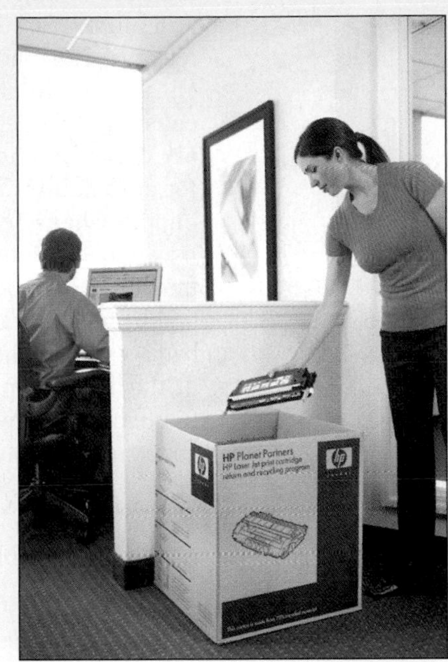

time," which means neither before nor after they are needed. Note that JIT is used in situations where demand forecasting is reliable, such as when supplying an automobile production line, and is not suitable for inventories that are to be stored over significant periods of time.

Electronic data interchange and electronic messaging technology coupled with the constant pressure for faster response time in replenishing inventory have also changed the way suppliers and customers do business in a supply chain. The approach, called **vendor-managed inventory (VMI)**, is an inventory-management system whereby the *supplier* determines the product amount and assortment a customer (such as a retailer) needs and automatically delivers the appropriate items.

Campbell Soup's system illustrates how VMI works.[20] Campbell first establishes EDI links with retailers. Every morning, retailers electronically inform the company of their demand for all Campbell products and the inventory levels in their distribution centers. Campbell uses that information to forecast future demand and determine which products need replenishment based on upper and lower inventory limits established with each retailer. Trucks leave the Campbell shipping plant that afternoon and arrive at the retailer's distribution centers with the required replenishments the same day.

CLOSING THE LOOP: REVERSE LOGISTICS

The flow of products in a supply chain does not end with the ultimate consumer or industrial user. Companies today recognize that a supply chain can work in reverse.

Reverse logistics is a process of reclaiming recyclable and reusable materials, returns, and reworks from the point of consumption or use for repair, remanufacturing, redistribution, or disposal. The effect of reverse logistics can be seen in the reduced waste in landfills and lowered operating costs for companies. The Making Responsible Decisions box on the previous page describes the successful reverse logistics initiative at Hewlett-Packard.[21]

Companies such as Kodak (reusable cameras), Motorola and Nokia (return and reuse of cell phones), and Caterpillar, Xerox, and IBM (remanufacturing and recycling) have implemented acclaimed reverse logistics programs.[22] Other firms have enlisted third-party logistics providers to handle this process along with other supply chain functions. GNB Technologies, Inc., a manufacturer of lead-acid batteries for automobiles and boats, has outsourced much of its supply chain activity to UPS Supply Chain Services.[23] The company contracts with UPS to manage its shipments between plants, distribution centers, recycling centers, and retailers. This includes movement of both new batteries and used products destined for recycling and covers both truck and railroad shipments. This partnership along with the initiatives of other battery makers has paid economic and ecological dividends. By recycling 90 percent of the lead from used batteries, manufacturers have kept the demand for new lead in check, thereby holding down costs to consumers. Also, solid waste management costs and the environmental impact of lead in landfills are reduced.

learning review

6. What are the basic trade-offs between the five modes of transportation?
7. What types of inventory should use storage warehouses and which type should use distribution centers?
8. What are the strengths and weaknesses of a just-in-time system?

LEARNING OBJECTIVES REVIEW

LO1 *Recognize the relationship between marketing channels, logistics, and supply chain management.*
A marketing channel relies on logistics to make products available to consumers and industrial users. Logistics involves those activities that focus on getting the right amount of the right products to the right place at the right time at the lowest possible cost. The performance of these activities is logistics management—the practice of organizing the cost-effective flow of raw materials, in-process inventory, finished goods, and related information from point of origin to point of consumption to satisfy customer requirements.

A supply chain is a sequence of firms that perform activities required to create and deliver a product or service to ultimate consumers or industrial users. It differs from a marketing channel in terms of membership. A supply chain includes suppliers that provide raw material inputs to a manufacturer as well as the wholesalers and retailers that deliver products. The management process is also different. Supply chain management is the integration and organization of information and logistics activities across firms in a supply chain for the purpose of creating and delivering products and services that provide value to consumers.

LO2 *Describe how a company's supply chain aligns with its marketing strategy.*
A company's supply chain follows from a clearly defined marketing strategy. The alignment of a company's supply chain with its marketing strategy involves three steps. First, a supply chain must reflect the needs of the customer segment being served. Second, a company must understand what a supply chain is designed to do well. Supply chains range from those that emphasize being responsive to customer requirements and demands to those that emphasize efficiency with the goal of supplying products at the lowest possible delivered cost. Finally, a supply chain must be consistent with the targeted customer's needs and the company's marketing strategy. The Dell and Wal-Mart examples in the chapter illustrate how this alignment is achieved by two well-known companies.

LO3 *Identify the major logistics cost and customer service factors that managers consider when making supply chain decisions.*
Companies strive to provide superior customer service while controlling logistics cost. The major customer service factors include the length of time between orders and deliveries, dependability in replenishing inventory, communication between buyers and sellers, and convenience in buying from the seller. Logistics cost factors include transportation, materials handling and warehousing, order processing, inventory, and stockouts.

LO4 *Describe the key logistics functions in a supply chain.*
The four key logistics functions in a supply chain include transportation, warehousing and materials handling, order process-

ing, and inventory management. Transportation provides the movement of goods necessary in a supply chain. The five major transportation modes are railroads, motor carriers, air carriers, pipelines, and water carriers. Warehousing and materials handling include the storing, sorting, and handling of products at storage warehouses or distribution centers. Order processing includes order receipt, delivery, invoicing, and collection from customers. Inventory management involves minimizing inventory-carrying costs while maintaining sufficient stocks of products to satisfy anticipated customer needs. Two popular inventory management practices are just-in-time (JIT) and vendor-managed inventory (VMI) systems.

FOCUSING ON KEY TERMS

customer service p. 413
efficient consumer response p. 414
electronic data interchange (EDI) p. 412
just-in-time (JIT) concept p. 422
lead time p. 414
logistics p. 406
logistics management p. 406
quick response p. 414
reverse logistics p. 424
supply chain p. 406
supply chain management p. 407
third-party logistics providers p. 417
total logistics cost p. 412
vendor-managed inventory (VMI) p. 423

APPLYING MARKETING KNOWLEDGE

1 List several companies to which logistical activities might be unimportant. Also list several whose focus is only on the inbound or outbound side.
2 What are some types of businesses in which order processing may be among the paramount success factors?
3 List the customer service factors that would be vital to buyers in the following types of companies: (*a*) manufacturing, (*b*) retailing, (*c*) hospitals, and (*d*) construction.
4 Name some cases when extremely high service levels (e.g., 99 percent) would be warranted.
5 Name the mode of transportation that would be the best for the following products: (*a*) farm machinery, (*b*) cut flowers, (*c*) frozen meat, and (*d*) coal.
6 The auto industry is a heavy user of the just-in-time concept. Why? What other industries would be good candidates for its application? What do they have in common?
7 Look again at Figure 16–4. Explain why as the number of warehouses increases, (*a*) inventory costs rise and (*b*) transportation costs fall.
8 What relationship would you expect to see between a company's on-time delivery percentage and its out-of-stock percentage?

building your marketing plan

Does your marketing plan involve a product? If the answer is no, read no further and do not include this element in your plan. If the answer is yes:

1 If inventory is involved, (*a*) identify the three or four major kinds of inventory needed for your organization (retail stock, finished products, raw materials, supplies, and so on), and (*b*) suggest ways to reduce their costs.

2 (*a*) Rank the four customer service factors (time, dependability, communication, and convenience) from most important to least important from your customers' point of view, and (*b*) identify actions for the one or two most important to serve customers better.

video case 16 Amazon: Delivering the Goods . . . Millions of Times a Day

"The new economy means that the balance of power has shifted toward the consumer," explains Jeff Bezos, CEO of Amazon.com, Inc. The global online retailer is a pioneer of fast, convenient, low-cost virtual shopping that has attracted millions of consumers. Of course, while Amazon has changed the way many people shop, the company still faces the traditional and daunting task of creating a seamless flow of deliveries to its customers—often millions of times each day.

THE COMPANY

Bezos started Amazon.com with a simple idea: to use the Internet to transform book buying into the fastest, easiest, and most enjoyable shopping experience possible.

The company was incorporated in 1994 and opened its virtual doors in July 1995. At the forefront of a huge growth of dot-com businesses, Amazon pursued a get-big-fast business strategy. Sales grew rapidly and Amazon began adding products and services other than books. In fact, Amazon soon set its goal on being the world's most customer-centric company, where customers can find and discover anything they might want to buy online!

Today Amazon claims to have the "Earth's Biggest Selection™" of products and services in the following categories: Books; Movies, Music & Games; Digital Downloads; Kindle; Computers & Office; Electronics; Home & Garden; Grocery, Health & Beauty; Toys, Kids & Baby; Clothing, Shoes & Jewelry; Sports & Outdoors; and Tools, Auto & Industrial. Other services allow customers to:

- Search for a product or brand using all or part of its name.
- Place orders with one click using "Buy Now with 1-Click" button.
- Receive personalized recommendations based on past purchases through opt-in e-mails.

These products and services have attracted millions of people around the globe. This has made Amazon.com, along with its international sites in Canada, the United Kingdom, Germany, Japan, France, and China, the leading online retailer.

Despite its incredible success with consumers and continuing growth in sales, Amazon.com found it difficult to be profitable. Many industry observers questioned the viability of online retailing and Amazon's business model. Then, in 2002, Amazon shocked many people by becoming profitable. The company has remained profitable. There are a variety of explanations for the turnaround. Generally, Bezos suggests that "efficiencies allow for lower prices, spurring sales growth across the board, which can be handled by existing facilities without much additional cost." More specifically, the facilities Bezos is referring to are the elements of its supply chain, which are one of the most complex and expensive aspects of the company's business.

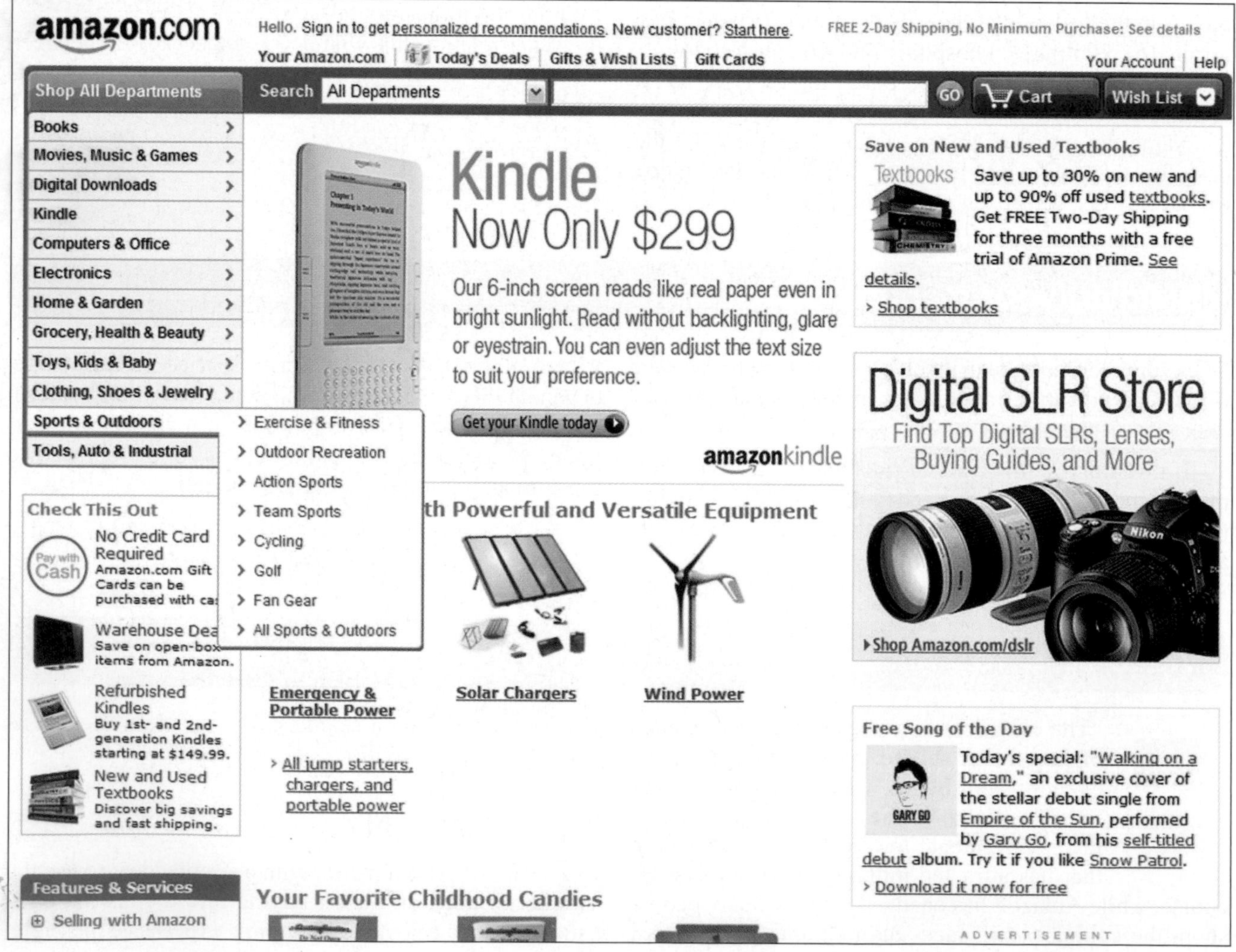

SUPPLY CHAIN AND LOGISTICS MANAGEMENT AT AMAZON.COM

What happens after an order is submitted on Amazon's Web site but before it arrives at the customer's door? A lot. Amazon.com maintains huge distribution, or "fulfillment," centers where it keeps inventory of millions of products. This is one of the key differences between Amazon.com and some of its competitors—it actually stocks products. So Amazon must manage the flow of products from its 15 million suppliers to its distribution and customer service centers with the flow of customer orders from the distribution centers to individuals' homes or offices.

The process begins with the suppliers. "Amazon's goal is to collaborate with our suppliers to increase efficiencies and improve inventory turnover," explains Jim Miller, vice president of supply chain at Amazon.com. "We want to bring to suppliers the kind of interactive relationship that has inspired customers to shop with us." For example, Amazon is using software to more accurately forecast purchasing patterns by region, which allows it to give its suppliers better information about delivery dates and volumes. Before the development of this software, 12 percent of incoming inventory was sent to the wrong location, leading to lost time and delayed orders. Now only 4 percent of the incoming inventory is mishandled.

At the same time, Amazon has been improving the part of the process that sorts the products into the individual orders. Jeffrey Wilke, Amazon's senior vice president of operations, says, "We spent the whole year really focused on increasing productivity." Again, technology has been essential. "The speed at which telecommunications networks allow us to pass information back and forth has enabled us to do the real-time work that we keep talking about. In the past, it would have taken too long to get this many items through a system," explains Wilke. Once the order is in the system, computers ensure that all items are included in the box before it is taped and labeled. A network of trucks and regional postal hubs then conclude the process with delivery of the order.

The success of Amazon's logistics and supply chain management activities may be most evident during the year-end holiday shopping season. Amazon received orders for 37.9 million items between November 9 and December 21 one year, including orders for 450,000 Harry Potter books and products, and orders for 36,000 items placed just before the holiday delivery deadline. Well over 99 percent of the orders were shipped and delivered on time.

AMAZON'S CHALLENGES

Despite all of Amazon's recent improvements, logistics experts estimate that the company's distribution centers are operating at approximately 40 percent of their capacity. This situation suggests that Amazon must reduce its capacity or increase its sales.

Several sales growth options are possible. First, Amazon can continue to pursue growth through sales of hundreds of thousands of electronic books, magazines, and newspapers through its new Kindle devices and store. The 6" Kindle 2 is capable of storing 1,500 publications while the 9.7" Kindle DX can hold over 3,500. Second, Amazon can continue its expansion into new product and service categories. Recently, it launched its Outdoor Recreation store—the latest in over a dozen such categories. This approach would prevent Amazon from becoming a niche merchant and position it as a true online retail department store. Third, Amazon can increase the availability of products from other retailers through its Amazon WebStore. These retailers can create a customized, branded Web site that uses Amazon eCommerce technology. Finally, Amazon can pursue a strategy of providing access to its existing operations for other retailers through its Fulfillment by Amazon (FBA) service. Online retailers store their products at Amazon's distribution centers and when they sell a product—Amazon ships it!

Amazon.com has come a long way toward proving that online retailing can work. Its logistics and supply chain management activities have provided Amazon with a cost-effective and efficient distribution system that combines automation and communication technology with superior customer service. To continue its drive to increase future sales, profits, and customer service, Amazon acquired Zappos.com in mid-2009. According to Bezos, "We see great opportunities for both companies to learn from each other and create even better experiences for our customers."

Questions

1 How do Amazon.com's logistics and supply chain management activities help the company create value for its customers?

2 What systems did Amazon develop to improve the flow of products from suppliers to Amazon distribution centers? What systems improved the flow of orders from the distribution centers to customers?

3 Why will logistics and supply chain management play an important role in the future success of Amazon.com?

GLOBAL
globalcomputer.com

CYBER MONDAY
MADNESS
1 DAY SALE!
CLICK HERE

Search over 100,000 Products in Stock...

Deal Alerts via RSS

We are open 24 hours a day, 7 days a week. **Call us at 888-845-6225**
WHEN CALLING USE **PRIORITY CODE:** GLOEM609

17 Retailing

LEARNING OBJECTIVES

After reading this chapter you should be able to:

LO1 Identify retailers in terms of the utilities they provide.

LO2 Explain the alternative ways to classify retail outlets.

LO3 Describe the many methods of nonstore retailing.

LO4 Classify retailers in terms of the retail positioning matrix, and specify retailing mix actions.

LO5 Explain changes in retailing with the wheel of retailing and the retail life cycle concepts.

84 MILLION CONSUMERS WERE SHOPPING ONLINE ON CYBER MONDAY. WERE YOU ONE OF THEM?

Two of the biggest days of the retailing year are the Friday after Thanksgiving—Black Friday—and the Monday after Thanksgiving—Cyber Monday. The days are so popular for shoppers that retailers report more than $20 billion in sales on Black Friday and almost $1 billion in sales on Cyber Monday. The names have interesting histories. Black Friday was an accounting term used to suggest when retailers finally became profitable, and Cyber Monday was the result of consumers shopping from their broadband connections at work on their first day back after the holiday. The number of Cyber Monday shoppers has been growing dramatically. Are you one of them?

Several factors account for the growth in Cyber Monday shopping and online shopping in general. First, the number of fast Internet connections in homes and businesses has grown to about 100 million. Second, large retailers such as Amazon, Home Depot, and Walmart have given online shopping a lot of visibility. Many retailers now move their Friday in-store sales and promotions to their Web sites on Monday to attract the shoppers who didn't want to park, stand in line, or deal with crowds in the stores.

While retailers may encourage online shopping with promotions as simple as e-mail notifications, cyber shopping is also the result of many new, interesting, and exciting online approaches. OfficeMax, for example, drives traffic to its Web site with an online application called "Elf Yourself" that allows visitors to e-mail an animated elf to friends. New Web sites such as Mpire.com track the price of products like TVs, clothing, and books to let consumers know if prices are increasing or decreasing. Like.com provides a visual search engine that finds products that are similar in appearance—just draw a box around the product or part of the product that you like and the site shows other products that are similar! For many consumers, buying new products leads to selling old products, and sites such as gazelle.com now calculate the value of used products, offer users a price for the product, and even send a box to mail it. There is even an official Cyber Monday Web site where more than 500 retailers have special online offers![1]

Cyber Monday and online shopping are just a few examples of the many exciting changes occurring in retailing today. This chapter examines the critical role of retailing in the marketplace and the challenging decisions retailers face as they strive to create value for customers.

What types of products will consumers buy through catalogs, television, the Internet, or by telephone? In what type of store will consumers look for products they don't buy directly? How important is the location of the store? Will customers expect services such as alterations, delivery, installation, or repair? What price should be charged for each product? These are difficult and important questions that are an integral part of retailing. In the channel of distribution, retailing is where the customer meets the product. It is through retailing that exchange (a central aspect of marketing) occurs. **Retailing** includes all activities involved in selling, renting, and providing products and services to ultimate consumers for personal, family, or household use.

THE VALUE OF RETAILING

LO1

Retailing is an important marketing activity. Not only do producers and consumers meet through retailing actions, but retailing also creates customer value and has a significant impact on the economy. To consumers, the value of retailing is in the form of utilities provided (Figure 17–1). Retailing's economic value is represented by the people employed in retailing as well as by the total amount of money exchanged in retail sales (Figure 17–2).

Consumer Utilities Offered by Retailing

The utilities provided by retailers create value for consumers. Time, place, form, and possession utilities are offered by most retailers in varying degrees, but one utility is often emphasized more than others. Look at Figure 17–1 to see how well you can match the retailer with the utility being emphasized in the description.

FIGURE 17–1
Which retailer best provides which utilities?

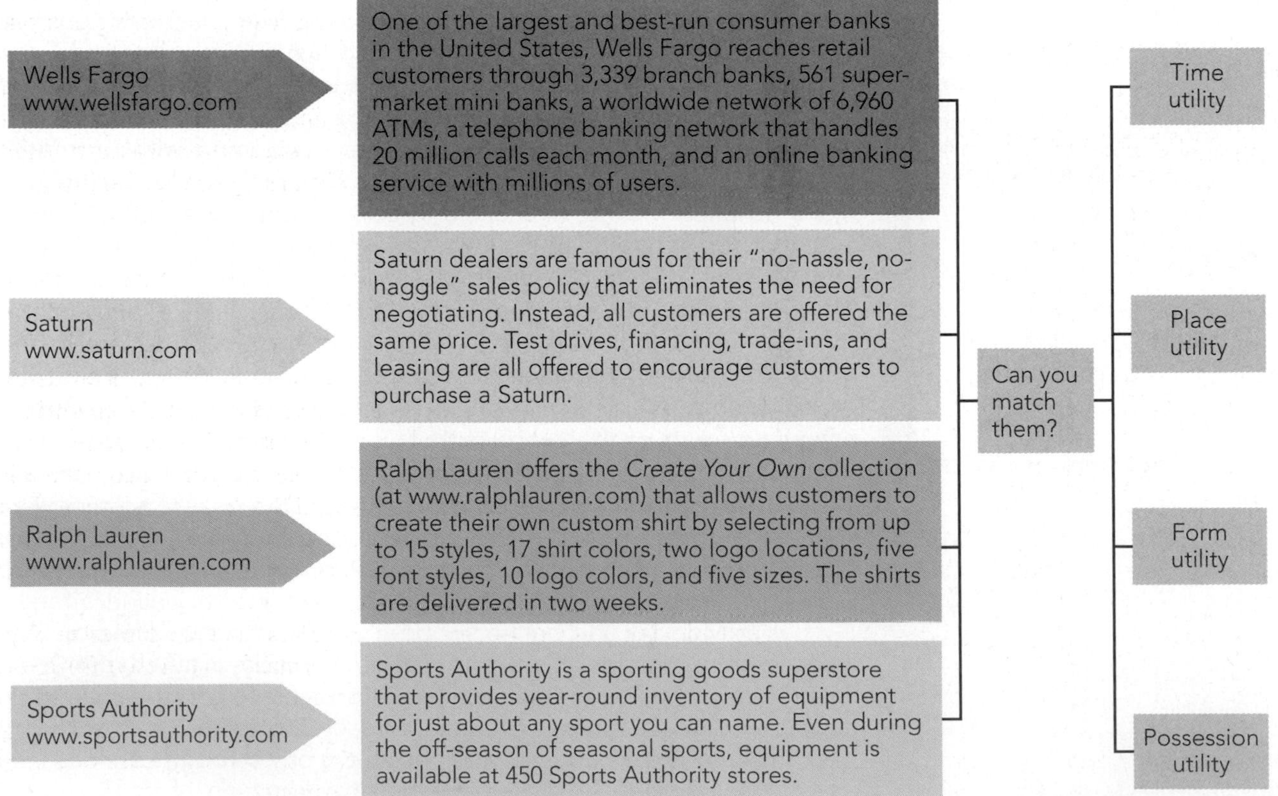

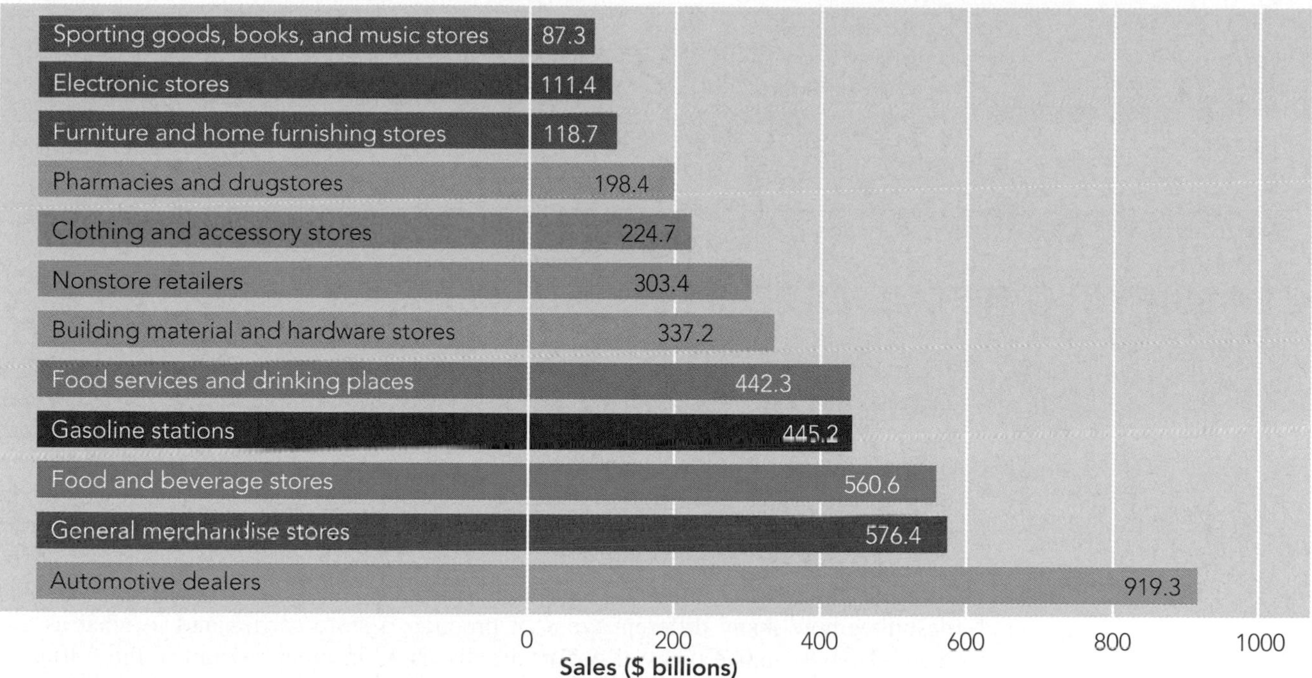

FIGURE 17–2
Are you surprised by the relative size of different types of retailers?

Providing mini banks in supermarkets, as Wells Fargo does, puts the bank's products and services close to the consumer, providing place utility. By providing financing or leasing and taking used cars as trade-ins, Saturn makes the purchase easier and provides possession utility. Form utility—production or alteration of a product—is offered by Ralph Lauren through its online *Create Your Own* program, which offers shirts that meet each customer's specifications. Finding the right sporting equipment during the off-season is the time utility provided by Sports Authority. Many retailers offer a combination of the four basic utilities. Some supermarkets, for example, offer convenient locations (place utility); are open 24 hours a day (time utility); customize purchases in the bakery, deli, and florist (form utility); and allow several payment and credit options (possession utility).

Tesco is one of the largest retailers outside the United States.

The Global Economic Impact of Retailing

Retailing is important to the U.S. and global economies. Four of the 30 largest businesses in the United States are retailers (Walmart, Costco, Home Depot, and Target). Walmart's $405 billion in annual sales in 2008 surpassed the gross domestic product of all but 27 countries for that same year. Walmart, Costco, Home Depot, and Target together have more than 2.8 million employees—more than the combined populations of Jacksonville, Florida; El Paso, Texas; and Stockton, California.[2] Figure 17–2 shows that many other retailers, including food stores, automobile dealers, and general merchandise outlets, are also significant contributors to the U.S. economy.[3]

Outside the United States large retailers include Daiei in Japan, Carrefour in France, Metro Group in Germany, and Tesco in Britain.[4] In emerging economies such as China and Mexico, a combination of local and global retailers is evolving. Walmart, for example, has more than 3,600 stores outside the United States, including stores in Brazil, China, Japan, Mexico, and the United Kingdom.[5]

learning review

1. When Ralph Lauren makes shirts to a customer's exact preferences, what utility is provided?
2. Two measures of the impact of retailing in the global economy are ____________ and ____________.

CLASSIFYING RETAIL OUTLETS

LO2

For manufacturers, consumers, and the economy, retailing is an important component of marketing that has several variations. Because of the large number of alternative forms of retailing, it is easier to understand the differences among retail institutions by recognizing that outlets can be classified in several ways. First, **form of ownership** distinguishes retail outlets based on whether individuals, corporate chains, or contractual systems own the outlet. Second, **level of service** is used to describe the degree of service provided to the customer. Three levels of service are provided by self-, limited-, and full-service retailers. Finally, the type of **merchandise line** describes how many different types of products a store carries and in what assortment. The alternative types of outlets are discussed in greater detail in the following pages. For many consumers today, each of the types of outlets discussed are viewed in terms of their environmentally friendly, or green, activities. The accompanying Making Responsible Decisions box gives examples of the green activities of several retailers.[6]

Form of Ownership

There are three general forms of retail ownership—individual, corporate chain, and contractual system.

Independent Retailer One of the most common forms of retail ownership is the independent business owned by an individual. Independent retailers account for most of the 1.1 million retail establishments in the United States and include hardware stores, convenience stores, clothing stores, and computer and software stores. In addition, there are 29,600 jewelry stores, 21,100 florists, and 43,100 sporting good and hobby stores. The advantage of this form of ownership for the owner is that he or she can be his or her own boss. More than 50 percent of all retail establishments have four or fewer employees.[7] For customers, the independent store can offer convenience, personal service, and lifestyle compatibility.

Corporate Chain A second form of ownership, the corporate chain, involves multiple outlets under common ownership. Many of the department store names you may know—Bon Marche, Lazurus, Burdines, Famous Barr, Filenes, Foleys, and Marshall Field's—are now one of 810 Macy's stores nationwide. Macy's Inc. also owns 40 Bloomingdale's, which compete with other chainstores such as Saks Fifth Avenue and Neiman Marcus.

In a chain operation, centralization in decision making and purchasing is common. Chain stores have advantages in dealing with manufacturers, particularly as the size of the chain grows. A large chain can bargain with a manufacturer to obtain good service or volume discounts on orders. Target's large volume makes it a strong negotiator with manufacturers of most products. The buying power of chains is seen when consumers compare chain store prices with other types of stores. Consumers also benefit in dealing with chains because there are multiple outlets with similar merchandise and consistent management policies.

Making Responsible Decisions > > > > sustainability

Environmentally Friendly Retailing Takes Off!

Sustainability has been a topic of interest for some retailers for many years. Recently, however, it has become a movement for the entire industry. What happened? A combination of factors contributed to the change: environmental consciousness among consumers has reached an all-time high, publicity related to global warming has increased, "green" has become an important element of company image and reputation, and most environmental initiatives save retailers money!

When consumers learned that food packaging creates 50 percent of all household waste, they added packaging to their purchase decision criteria. Walmart responded by requiring its suppliers to trim one square inch of packaging from its toy lines and reduced packaging by 3,500 tons. Electronics retailer Best Buy recently began using solar energy in some of its stores with the goal of reducing CO_2 emissions by 8 percent by 2012. Mountain Equipment company is building on its green image by collecting rainwater to water grass at the store and to use in its toilets. When Home Depot switched its in-store light fixture displays to compact fluorescent light bulbs it saved $16 million per year. Other companies are using motion detectors to turn lights on and off, improving the fuel economy of delivery vehicles, and designing "zero waste" stores.

Are your favorite retailers "green"? Do sustainability efforts influence your purchase decisions?

Retailing has become a high-tech business for many large chains. Walmart, for example, has developed a sophisticated inventory management and cost control system that allows rapid price changes for each product in every store. In addition, stores such as Walmart and Target are implementing pioneering new technologies such as radio frequency identification (RFID) tags to improve the quality of information available about products.

Contractual Systems Contractual systems involve independently owned stores that band together to act like a chain. The three kinds described in Chapter 15 are retailer-sponsored cooperatives, wholesaler-sponsored voluntary chains, and franchises. One retailer-sponsored cooperative is the Associated Grocers, which consists of neighborhood grocers that all agree with several other independent grocers to buy their goods directly from food manufacturers. In this way, members can take advantage of volume discounts commonly available to chains and also give the impression of being a large chain, which may be viewed more favorably by some consumers. Wholesaler-sponsored voluntary chains such as Independent Grocers' Alliance (IGA) try to achieve similar benefits.

Subway is a popular business-format franchisor.

As noted in Chapter 15, in a franchise system an individual or firm (the franchisee) contracts with a parent company (the franchisor) to set up a business or retail outlet. The franchisor usually assists in selecting the location, setting up the store or facility, advertising, and training personnel. The franchisee usually pays a onetime franchise fee and an annual royalty, usually tied to franchise's sales. There are two general types of franchises: *business-format franchises*, such as McDonald's, Radio Shack, and Subway, and *product-distribution franchises*, such as a Ford dealership or a Coca-Cola distributor. In business-format franchising, the franchisor provides step-by-step procedures for most aspects of the business and guidelines for the most likely decisions a franchisee will face.

Franchising is attractive because it offers an opportunity for people to enter a well-known, established business for which managerial advice is provided. Also, the franchise fee may be less than the cost of setting up an independent business. The International Franchise Association recently reported that there are 909,000 franchised businesses in the United States, which generate $880 billion in annual sales and employ more than 11 million people. Franchising is popular in international markets also: more than half of all U.S. franchisors have operations in other countries. What is the fastest growing franchise? Subway now has 29,612 locations, including 7,927 stores outside the United States.[8]

Franchise fees paid to the franchisor can range from $15,000 for a Subway franchise to $45,000 for a McDonald's restaurant franchise. When the fees are combined with other costs such as real estate and equipment, however, the total investment can be much higher. Franchisees also pay an ongoing royalty fee that ranges from 2 percent for a Sonic Drive In to 12.5 percent for a McDonald's. Figure 17–3 shows the top five franchises, as rated by *Entrepreneur* magazine, based on factors such as size, financial strength, stability, years in business, and costs. By selling franchises, an organization reduces the cost of expansion but loses some control. A good franchisor, however, will maintain strong control of the outlets in terms of delivery and presentation of merchandise and try to enhance recognition of the franchise name.[9]

Level of Service

Even though most customers perceive little variation in retail outlets by form of ownership, differences among retailers are more obvious in terms of level of service. In some department stores, such as Loehmann's, very few services are provided. Some grocery stores, such as the Cub Foods chain, encourage customers to bag the food themselves and recycle their plastic bags. Other outlets, such as Neiman Marcus, provide a wide range of customer services from gift wrapping to wardrobe consultation.

Self-Service Self-service requires that the customers perform many functions and little is provided by the outlet. Warehouse clubs such as Costco, for example, are usually self-service, with all nonessential customer services eliminated. Similarly, most gas stations today are self-service. New forms of self-service are being developed at airlines, hotels, and even libraries! Lufthansa airline, for example, is installing 300 self-service check-in terminals that feature an integrated radio frequency identification (RFID) scanner to read passports or ID cards, in addition to allowing passengers to select seats, print boarding passes, and check baggage. Hilton Hotels now includes self-service kiosks in the lobby of each of its hotels. The kiosks allow guests to check in, print keys, check for messages, check out, print hotel receipts, and print airline boarding passes. The Palm Beach County library system is mov-

FIGURE 17–3
The top five franchises in the United States vary from sandwich restaurants to tax preparation services.

Franchise	Type of Business	Total Start-up Cost	Number of Franchises
Subway	Sandwich restaurant	$78,600–$238,300	29,612
McDonald's	Fast-food restaurant	$950,200–$1,800,000	25,465
Liberty Tax Service	Tax preparation service	$53,800–$66,900	2,579
Sonic Drive In Restaurants	Drive-In restaurant	$1,200,000–$3,200,000	2,768
InterContinental Hotels	Hotel	Variable	3,498

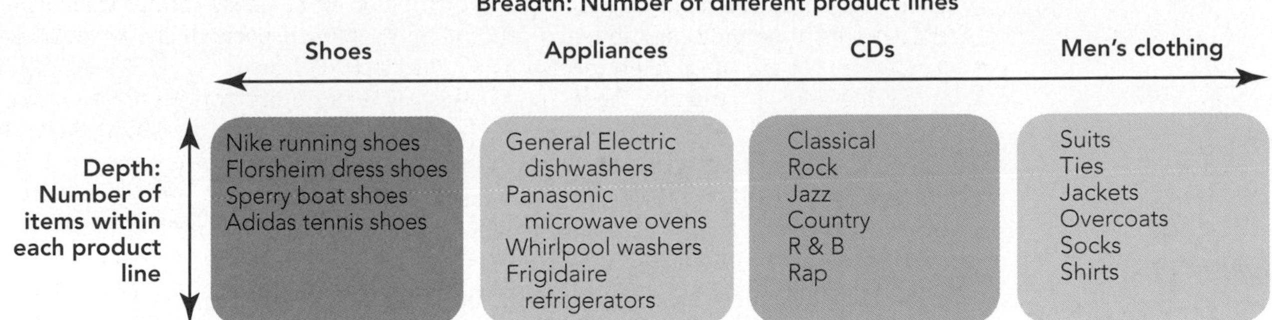

FIGURE 17–4
Stores vary in terms of the breadth and depth of their merchandise lines.

ing in the same direction; it is adding self-service checkout machines to each of its branches. In general, the trend is toward retailing experiences that make customers co-creators of the value they receive.[10]

Limited Service Limited-service outlets provide some services, such as credit and merchandise return, but not others, such as clothing alterations. General merchandise stores such as Walmart, Kmart, and Target are usually considered limited service outlets. Customers are responsible for most shopping activities, although salespeople are available in departments such as consumer electronics, jewelry, and lawn and garden.

Full Service Full-service retailers, which include most specialty stores and department stores, provide many services to their customers. Neiman Marcus, Nordstrom, and Saks Fifth Avenue, for example, all rely on better service to sell more distinctive, higher-margin goods and to retain their customers. Nordstrom offers a wide variety of services, including free exchanges, easy returns, credit cards through Nordstrom bank, a live help line, an online gift finder, catalogs, a four-level loyalty program called Nordstrom Fashion Rewards, and an online beauty specialist. Some Nordstrom stores also offer a "Personal Touch" department, which provides shopping assistants for consumers who need help with style, color, and size selection, and a concierge service for assistance with anything else. Nordstrom stores typically have 50 percent more salespeople on the floor than similarly sized stores, and the salespeople are renowned for their professional and personalized attention to customers. Nordstrom also offers e-mail and RSS feeds to notify customers when new merchandise is available.[11]

Type of Merchandise Line

Retail outlets also vary by their merchandise lines, the key distinction being the breadth and depth of the items offered to customers (see Figure 17–4). **Depth of product line** means the store carries a large assortment of each item, such as a shoe store that offers running shoes, dress shoes, and children's shoes. **Breadth of product line** refers to the variety of different items a store carries, such as appliances and CDs.

Staples is the category killer in office supplies.

Depth of Line Stores that carry a considerable assortment (depth) of a related line of items are limited-line stores. Sports Authority sporting goods stores carry considerable depth in sports equipment ranging from weight-lifting accessories to running shoes. Stores that carry tremendous depth in one primary line of merchandise are single-line stores. Victoria's Secret, a nationwide chain, carries great depth in women's lingerie. Both limited- and single-line stores are often referred to as *specialty outlets*.

Specialty discount outlets focus on one type of product, such as electronics (Best Buy), office supplies (Staples), or books (Barnes and Noble) at very competitive

	Hypermarket	Supercenter
Region of Popularity	Europe	United States
Average size	90,000–300,000 sq. ft.	100,000–215,000 sq. ft.
Number of products	20,000–80,000	35,000
Annual revenue	$100,000,000 per store	$60,000,000 per store

FIGURE 17–5
Hypermarkets are popular in Europe, and supercenters are popular in the U.S.

prices. These outlets are referred to in the trade as *category killers* because they often dominate the market. Best Buy, for example, is the largest consumer electronics retailer with more than 1,000 stores, and Staples is the leader in office supplies.[12]

Breadth of Line Stores that carry a broad product line, with limited depth, are referred to as *general merchandise stores*. For example, large department stores such as Dillard's, Macy's, and Neiman Marcus carry a wide range of different types of products but not unusual sizes. The breadth and depth of merchandise lines are important decisions for a retailer. Traditionally, outlets carried related lines of goods. Today, however, **scrambled merchandising**, offering several unrelated product lines in a single store, is common. The modern drugstore carries food, camera equipment, magazines, paper products, toys, small hardware items, and pharmaceuticals. Supermarkets rent videos, print photos, and sell flowers.

A form of scrambled merchandising, the **hypermarket**, has been successful in Europe. These hypermarkets are large stores (more than 200,000 square feet) based on a simple concept: offer "everything under one roof," eliminating the need to stop at more than one location. The stores provide variety, quality, and low price for groceries and general merchandise. Carrefour, one of the largest hypermarket retailers, has 1,163 hypermarkets, including 218 in France, 160 in Spain, and 71 in Poland. The growth of hypermarkets may be slowing in Europe, however, as the availability of smaller discount stores in more convenient locations has increased. The concept is growing in popularity outside of Europe though; in China, for example, Carrefour, RT-Mart, and Geant are expanding the hypermarket format.[13]

In the United States, retailers discovered that shoppers were uncomfortable with the huge size of hypermarkets. They developed a variation of the hypermarket called the *supercenter*, which combines a typical merchandise store (approximately 70,000 square feet) with a full-size grocery store. Walmart, Kmart, and Target are now using the concept very successfully. Walmart currently operates 2,700 supercenters in the United States and plans to open 100 to 200 new stores each year in the near future. Supercenters have seen an increase in popularity in the United States as the changes in the economy have encouraged shoppers to save money by buying in bulk. Figure 17–5 shows the differences between the supercenter and hypermarket concepts.[14]

Scrambled merchandising is convenient for consumers because it eliminates the number of stops required in a shopping trip. However, for the retailer this merchandising policy means there is competition between very dissimilar types of retail outlets, or **intertype competition**. A local bakery may compete with a department store, discount outlet, or even a local gas station. Scrambled merchandising and intertype competition make it more difficult to be a retailer.

learning review

3. Centralized decision making and purchasing are an advantage of _______________ ownership.

4. What are some examples of new forms of self-service retailers?

5. Would a shop for big men's clothes carrying pants in sizes 40 to 60 have a broad or deep product line?

NONSTORE RETAILING

LO3

Most of the retailing examples discussed earlier in the chapter, such as corporate chains, department stores, and limited- and single-line specialty stores, involve store retailing. Many retailing activities today, however, are not limited to sales in a store. Nonstore retailing occurs outside a retail outlet through activities that involve varying levels of customer and retailer involvement. Figure 17–6 shows six forms of nonstore retailing: automatic vending, direct mail and catalogs, television home shopping, online retailing, telemarketing, and direct selling.

Get a "FREE" YoZone VENDING MACHINE TODAY!

BENEFITS

FREE DELIVERY AND INSTALLATION

PROFESSIONAL OPERATORS

ON-LINE REPORTING

FREE PRODUCT SAMPLING EVENTS

INSURANCE

1000's of GREAT LOCATIONS!

CHOOSE FROM OVER 100 NATURAL AND ORGANIC SNACKS AND DRINKS

Sign up for a YoZone or YoThirsty NOW!

Vending machines offer many products found in convenience stores.

Automatic Vending

Nonstore retailing includes vending machines, which make it possible to serve customers when and where stores cannot. Machine maintenance, operating costs, and location leases can add to the cost of the products, so prices in vending machines tend to be higher than those in stores. About 48 percent of the products sold from vending machines are cold beverages, another 19 percent are candy and snacks, and 10 percent is food. Many new types of products are quickly becoming available in vending machines. Best Buy now uses vending machines to sell cell phone and computer accessories, digital cameras, flash drives, and other consumer electronics products in airports. Similarly, YoNaturals uses vending machines to distribute healthy and organic snacks in schools, health clubs, and hospitals in 135 U.S. cities. The 11.5 million vending machines currently in use in the United States generate more than $46 billion in annual sales.[15]

Improved technology is making vending machines easier to use by reducing the need for cash. In the United States, about 17,500 machines currently accept credit cards or PayPass cards and many more will be equipped with card readers soon. In Japan, Korea, and the Philippines consumers use cell phones that transmit payments to vending machines via an infrared beam or a radio wave. Another improvement in vending machines is the trend toward "green" machines that

FIGURE 17–6
Many types of retailers do not have stores.

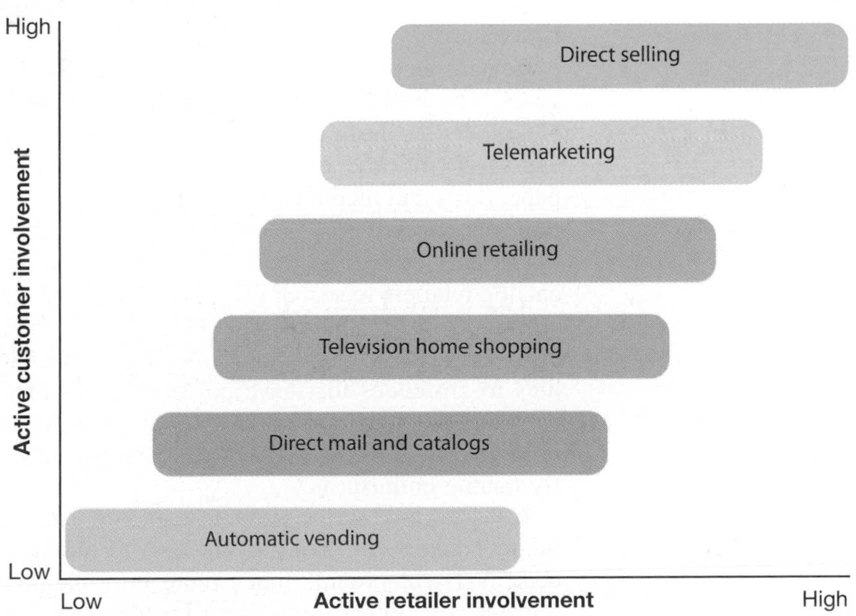

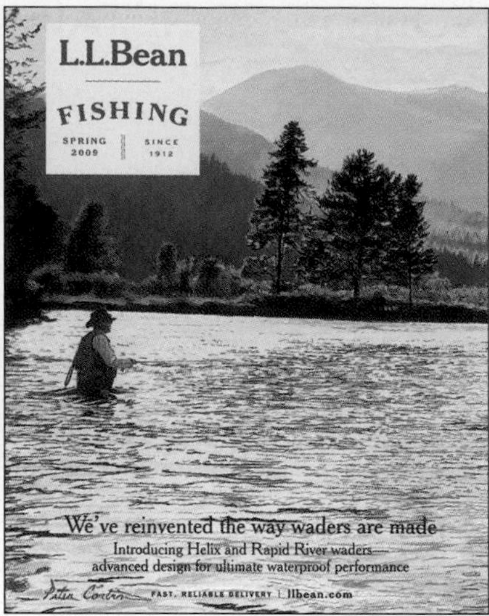

Specialty catalogs appeal to market niches.

consume less energy by using more efficient compressors, more efficient lighting, and better insulation. Vending machines are popular with consumers; recent consumer satisfaction research indicates that 82 percent of consumers believe purchasing from a vending machine is equal to or superior to a store purchase.[16]

Direct Mail and Catalogs

Direct-mail and catalog retailing is attractive because it eliminates the cost of a store and clerks. For example, it costs a traditional retail store $34 to acquire a new customer, whereas catalog customers are acquired for approximately $14. In addition, direct mail and catalogs improve marketing efficiency through segmentation and targeting, and they create customer value by providing a fast and convenient means of making a purchase. The average U.S. household now receives 18 direct-mail items or catalogs each week. The Direct Marketing Association estimates that direct-mail and catalog retailing creates 1.7 million jobs and $1.9 trillion in sales. Direct-mail and catalog retailing is popular outside of the United States also. Furniture retailer IKEA delivered 198 million copies of its catalog in 27 languages to 35 countries last year.[17]

Several factors have had an impact on direct-mail and catalog retailing in recent years. The influence of large retailers such as IKEA, Crate and Barrel, JCPenney, and others has been positive as their marketing activities have increased the number and variety of products consumers purchase through direct mail and catalogs. Higher paper costs and increases in postage rates, the growing interest in do-not-mail legislation, the concern for "green" mailings and catalogs, and the possibility of the U.S. Postal Service reducing delivery to five days, however, have caused direct-mail and catalog retailers to search for ways to improve their efficiency and provide additional customer value. One approach has been to focus on proven customers rather than prospective customers. Some merchants, such as Williams-Sonoma, reduce mailings to zip codes that have not been profitable. Another successful approach used by many catalog retailers is to send specialty catalogs to market niches identified in their databases. L.L. Bean, for example, has developed an individual catalog for fly-fishing enthusiasts.[18]

New, creative forms of direct-mail and catalog retailing are also being developed. Some retailers are investing in new technologies such as the intelligent mail bar code that will provide much more information about mail and catalog delivery at a lower cost. Other innovations include digital catalogs that are searchable, in PDF format, and embedded with links to complementary products. You will also see merchants using direct mail and catalogs to direct customers to personalized URLs (PURLs, such as www.JohnSmith.offer.com), which are Web pages preloaded with information and offerings specific to an individual. To recognize companies that successfully integrate their direct-mail and catalog activities with other marketing activities, *Multichannel Merchant* magazine evaluates hundreds of entries to select the winners of the Multichannel Merchant Awards in 18 categories. Recent winners might be retailers you already know. They include L.L. Bean, The Republic of Tea, Ebags, and Harry and David.[19]

Television Home Shopping

Television home shopping is possible when consumers watch a shopping channel on which products are displayed; orders are then placed over the telephone or the Internet. Currently, the three largest programs are QVC, HSN, and ShopNBC. QVC ("quality, value, convenience") broadcasts live 24 hours each day, 364 days a year and reaches 166 million cable and satellite homes in the United States, United Kingdom, Germany, Japan, and Italy. The company generates sales of $7 billion from its 50 million customers by offering more than 1,150 products each week, answering 181 million telephone calls, and shipping more than 166 million packages each year. The television home shopping channels offer apparel, jewelry, cooking, home improvement products, electronics, toys, and even food. Of all these products, the best-selling item ever was a Dell personal computer.[20]

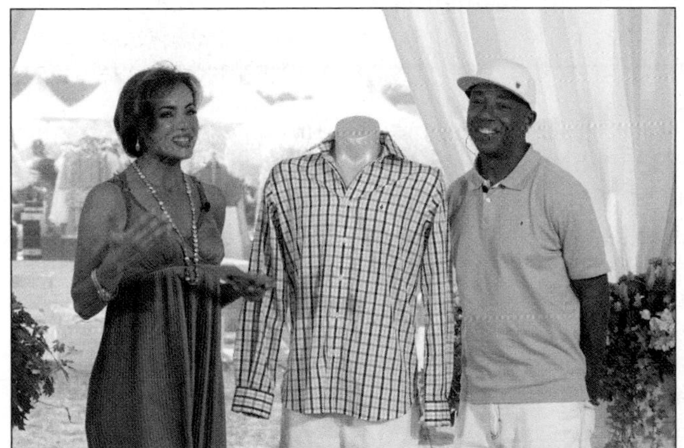

Television home shopping programs serve millions of customers each year.

In the past, television home shopping programs have attracted mostly 40- to 60-year-old women. To begin to attract a younger audience, QVC has invited celebrities onto the show. For example, Ellen DeGeneres has been on the show promoting her collection of holistic pet care products and supermodel Heidi Klum has been a host selling her line of jewelry. Broadcasting from remote locations such as Yankee Stadium and airing live acts such as LeAnn Rimes also help attract new customers. The shopping programs are also using other forms of retailing. QVC now has three types of retail stores: a studio store at its headquarters, QVC@THE MALL in Minnesota's Mall of America, and four outlet stores. Similarly, the Home Shopping Network now offers retail experiences on TV, online, in catalogs, and in stores. Finally, several television shopping programs are developing online video platforms, which may attract as many as 50 percent of all new customers, and interactive technology that allows viewers to place orders with their remote control rather than the telephone.[21]

Online Retailing

Online retailing allows consumers to search for, evaluate, and order products through the Internet. For many consumers the advantages of this form of retailing are the 24-hour access, the ability to comparison shop, in-home privacy, and variety. Studies of online shoppers indicated that men were initially more likely than women to buy something online. As the number of online households increased, however, the profile of online shoppers changed to include all shoppers. In addition, the number of online retailers grew rapidly for several years and then declined as many standalone, Internet-only businesses failed or consolidated. Today, traditional and online retailers—"bricks and clicks"—are melding, using experiences from both approaches to create better value and experiences for customers. Walmart (www.walmart.com) recently introduced "site-to-store" service that allows customers to order online and

Going Online

For Some Consumers, Shopping Is a Game!

If you love shopping, particularly for bargains, there are several new Web sites and shopping services for you. Gilt.com, Ideeli.com, HauteLook.com and RueLaLa.com all send text messages announcing limited-time "flash sales" on luxury goods. Consumers then log on to the Web site to make their purchases. Alexandra Wilson, co-founder of Gilt.com, reports that one of the company's messages sold 600 dresses in six minutes!

A variation of these sites is the Web retailer TextBuyIt, a service that allows shoppers to text a product name, universal product code, or ISBN number from a mobile phone and receive price comparison information without getting on the Web.

For some consumers these new services make shopping fun, engaging, even a game! Quick, check your phone for information about the next flash sale!

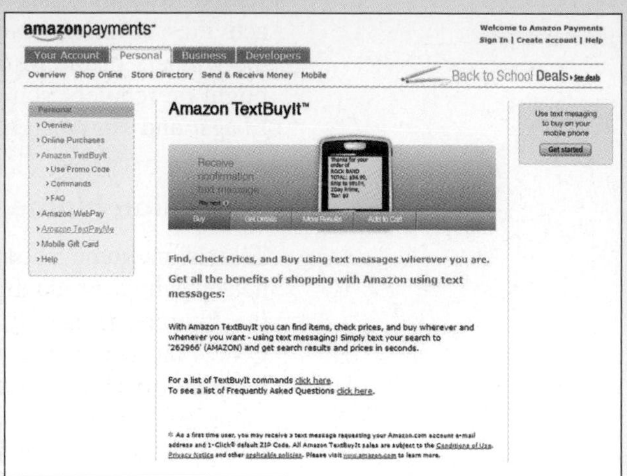

pick up the order without a shipping fee at the store of their choice. Experts predict that online sales will reach $335 billion by 2012.[22]

Online retail purchases can be the result of several very different approaches. First, consumers can pay dues to become a member of an online discount service such as www.netMarket.com. The service offers tens of thousands of products and more than 1,200 brand names at very low prices to its 25 million subscribers. Another approach to online retailing is to use a shopping "bot" such as www.mysimon.com. This site searches the Internet for a product specified by the consumer and provides a report on the locations of the best prices available. Consumers can also use the Internet to go directly to online malls (www.fashionmall.com), apparel retailers (www.gap.com), bookstores (www.amazon.com), computer manufacturers (www.dell.com), grocery stores (www.peapod.com), music and video stores (www.tower.com), and travel agencies (www.travelocity.com). A final approach to online retailing is the online auction, such as www.ebay.com, where consumers bid on more than 50,000 categories of products.[23] See the Going Online box for a description of new forms of online and mobile shopping.[24]

One of the biggest problems online retailers face is that nearly two-thirds of online shoppers make it to "checkout" and then leave the Web site to compare shipping costs and prices on other sites. Of the shoppers who leave, 70 percent do not return. One way online retailers are addressing this issue is to offer consumers a comparison of competitors' offerings. At Allbookstores.com, for example, consumers can use a "comparison engine" to compare prices with Amazon.com, Barnesandnoble.com, and as many as 25 other bookstores. Experts suggest that online retailers should think of their Web sites as dynamic billboards and be visible to search engines if they are to attract and retain customers.[25]

Shopping "bots" like mysimon.com find the best prices for products consumers specify.

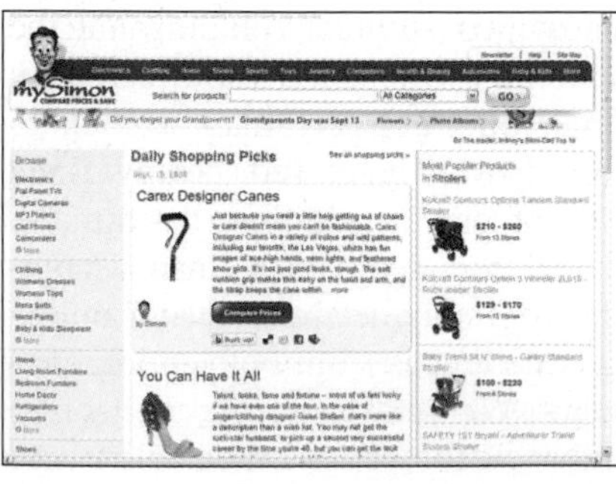

Online retailers are also trying to improve the online retailing experience by adding experiential or interactive activities to their Web sites. Similarly, car manufacturers such as BMW, Mercedes, and Jaguar encourage Web site visitors to "build" a vehicle by selecting interior and exterior colors, packages, and options and then view the customized virtual car. In addition, the merger of television home shopping and online retailing will be possible through TV-based Internet platforms such as Microsoft's MSN TV2, which

Consumers can easily access the Internet in many locations today.

uses an Internet appliance attached to a television to connect to the Internet. Owning a television or a computer isn't a necessity for online retailing, however, as many hotels, bars, libraries, airports, and other public locations offer Internet kiosks. In China, the world's largest population of Internet users (253 million), consumers can shop online in more than 185,000 Internet cafes.[26]

Telemarketing

Another form of nonstore retailing, called **telemarketing**, involves using the telephone to interact with and sell directly to consumers. Compared with direct mail, telemarketing is often viewed as a more efficient means of targeting consumers. Insurance companies, brokerage firms, and newspapers have often used this form of retailing as a way to cut costs but still maintain access to their customers. According to the Direct Marketing Association, annual telemarketing sales exceed $330 billion.[27]

The telemarketing industry has recently gone through dramatic changes as a result of new legislation related to telephone solicitations. Issues such as consumer privacy, industry standards, and ethical guidelines have encouraged discussion among consumers, Congress, the Federal Trade Commission, and businesses. The result was legislation that created the National Do-Not-Call registry (www.donotcall.gov) for consumers who do not want to receive telephone calls related to company sales efforts. Currently, there are more than 157 million phone numbers on the registry. Companies that use telemarketing have already adapted by adding compliance software to ensure that numbers on the list are not called. In addition, some firms are considering shifting their telemarketing budgets to direct-mail and door-to-door techniques.[28]

Direct Selling

Direct selling, sometimes called door-to-door retailing, involves direct sales of goods and services to consumers through personal interactions and demonstrations in their home or office. A variety of companies, including familiar names such as Avon, Fuller Brush, Mary Kay Cosmetics, and World Book, have created an industry with more than $110 billion in worldwide sales by providing consumers with personalized service and convenience. In the United States, there are more than 15 million direct salespeople working full-time and part-time in 70 product categories.[29]

Growth in the direct-selling industry is the result of two trends. First, many direct selling retailers are expanding into markets outside of the United States. Avon, for example, has 5.8 million sales representatives in 100 countries. More than 77 percent of Amway's $10.7 billion in sales now comes from outside the United States.[30] Similarly, other retailers such as Herbalife and Electrolux are rapidly expanding into new markets. Direct selling is likely to continue to grow in markets where the lack of effective distribution channels increases the importance of door-to-door convenience and where the lack of consumer knowledge about products and brands will increase the need for a person-to-person approach.

The second trend is the growing number of companies that are using direct selling to reach consumers who prefer one-on-one customer service and a social shopping experience rather than online shopping or big discount stores. The Direct Selling Association reports that the number of companies using direct selling has increased by 30 percent in the past five years. Pampered Chef, for example, has 60,000 independent sales reps who sell the company's products at in-home kitchen parties. Interest among potential sales representatives has grown during the recent economic downturn as people seek independence and control of their work activities.[31]

learning review

6. Successful catalog retailers often send _____________ catalogs to _____________ markets identified in their databases.
7. How are retailers increasing consumer interest and involvement in online retailing?
8. Where are direct selling retail sales growing? Why?

RETAILING STRATEGY

This section describes how a retailer develops and implements a retailing strategy. Research suggests that factors related to market and competitor characteristics may influence strategic choices and that the combination of choices is an important consideration for retailers.[32] Figure 17–7 identifies the relationship between strategy, positioning, and the retailing mix.

Positioning a Retail Store

LO4

The classification alternatives presented in the previous sections help determine one store's position relative to its competitors. The **retail positioning matrix** is a matrix developed by the MAC Group, Inc., a management consulting firm.[33] This matrix positions retail outlets on two dimensions: breadth of product line and value added. As defined previously, *breadth of product line* is the range of products sold through each outlet. The second dimension, *value added*, includes elements such as location

FIGURE 17–7
Elements of a retailing strategy

FIGURE 17–8
Four positioning strategies for retailers

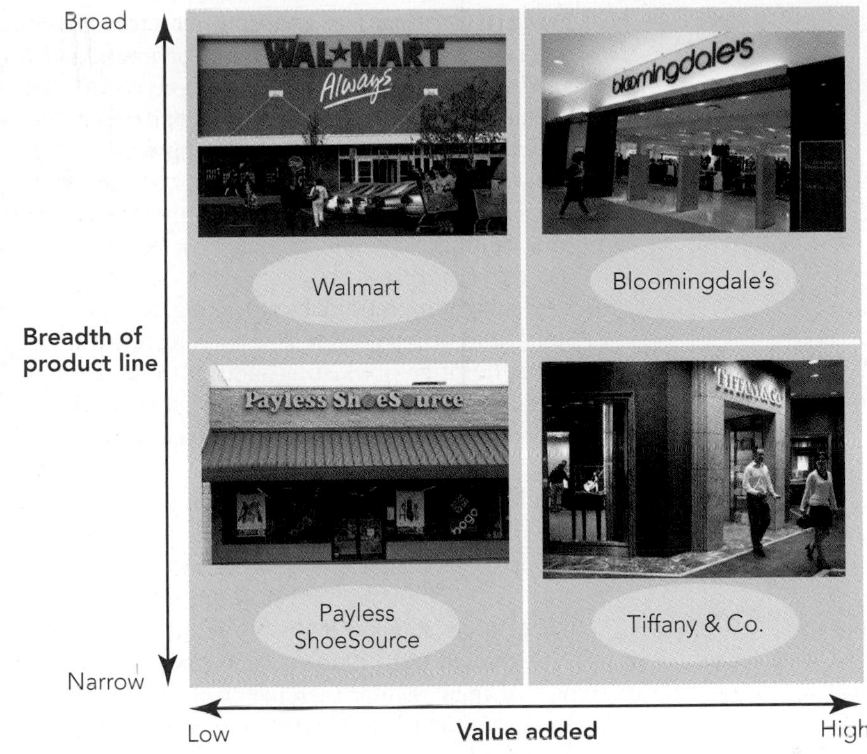

(as with 7-Eleven stores), product reliability (as with Holiday Inn or McDonald's), or prestige (as with Saks Fifth Avenue or Brooks Brothers).

The retail positioning matrix in Figure 17–8 shows four possible positions. An organization can be successful in any position, but unique strategies are required within each quadrant. Consider the four stores shown in the matrix:

1. Bloomingdale's has high value added and a broad product line. Retailers in this quadrant pay great attention to store design and product lines. Merchandise often has a high margin of profit and is of high quality. The stores in this position typically provide high levels of service.
2. Walmart has low value added and a broad line. Walmart and similar firms typically trade a lower price for increased volume in sales. Retailers in this position focus on price with low service levels and an image of being a place for good buys.
3. Tiffany & Co. has high value added and a narrow line. Retailers of this type typically sell a very restricted range of products that are high in status and quality. Customers are also provided with high levels of service.
4. Payless ShoeSource has low value added and a narrow line. Such retailers are specialty mass merchandisers. Payless ShoeSource, for example, carries athletic shoes at a discount. These outlets appeal to value-conscious consumers. Economies of scale are achieved through centralized advertising, merchandising, buying, and distribution. Stores are usually the same in design, layout, and merchandise; hence they are often referred to as "cookie-cutter" stores.

Retailing Mix

In developing retailing strategy, managers work with the **retailing mix**, which includes activities related to managing the store and the merchandise in the store. The retailing mix is similar to the marketing mix and includes retail pricing, store location, retail communication, and merchandise.

Retail Pricing In setting prices for merchandise, retailers must decide on the markup, markdown, and timing for markdowns. As mentioned in Appendix B, the *markup* refers to how much should be added to the cost the retailer paid for a product to reach the final selling price. Retailers decide on the *original markup*, but by the time the product is sold, they end up with a *maintained markup*. The original markup is the difference between retailer cost and initial selling price. When products do not sell as quickly as anticipated, their price is reduced. The difference between the final selling price and retailer cost is the maintained markup, which is also called the *gross margin*.

Discounting a product, or taking a *markdown*, occurs when the product does not sell at the original price and an adjustment is necessary. Often new models or styles force the price of existing models to be marked down. Discounts may also be used to increase demand for complementary products.[34] For example, retailers might take a markdown on CD players to increase sales of CDs or reduce the price of cake mix to generate frosting purchases. The *timing* of a markdown can be important. Many retailers take a markdown as soon as sales fall off to free up valuable selling space and cash. However, other stores delay markdowns to discourage bargain hunters and maintain an image of quality. There is no clear answer, but retailers must consider how the timing might affect future sales. Research indicates that frequent promotions increase consumers' ability to remember regular prices.[35]

Although most retailers plan markdowns, many retailers use price discounts as a part of their regular merchandising policy. Walmart and Home Depot, for example, emphasize consistently low prices and eliminate most markdowns with a strategy often called *everyday low pricing*.[36] Because consumers often use price as an indicator of product quality, however, the brand name of the product and the image of the store become important decision factors in these situations.[37] Another strategy, *everyday fair pricing*, is advocated by retailers that may not offer the lowest price but try to create value for customers through service and the total buying experience.[38] Consumers often use the prices of *benchmark* or *signpost* items, such as a can of Coke, to form an overall impression of the store's prices.[39] In addition, price is the most likely to influence consumers' assessment of merchandise value.[40] When store prices are based on rebates, retailers must be careful to avoid negative consumer perceptions if the rebate processing time is long (e.g., six weeks).[41]

A special issue for retailers trying to keep prices low is shrinkage, or breakage, theft, and fraud by customers and employees. The National Retail Federation estimates that the average retailer loses 1.6 percent of sales to shrinkage each year. Fraudulent returns alone account for $15 billion. About 50 percent of retail shrinkage is due to employee theft. Some retailers have noticed an increase in theft and fraud as economic conditions have declined. In general, the issue has increased retailers' interest in new technical and surveillance techniques to reduce shrinkage.[42]

Off-price retailing is a retail pricing practice that is used by retailers such as T.J. Maxx, Burlington Coat Factory, and Ross Stores. **Off-price retailing** involves selling brand-name merchandise at lower than regular prices. The difference between the off-price retailer and a discount store is that off-price merchandise is bought by the retailer from manufacturers with excess inventory at prices below wholesale prices. The discounter, however, buys at full wholesale price but takes less of a markup than do traditional department stores. Because of this difference in the way merchandise is purchased by the retailer, selection at an off-price retailer is unpredictable, and searching for bargains has become a popular activity for many consumers. "It's more like a sport than it is like ordinary shopping," says Christopher Boring of Columbus, Ohio's Retail Planning Associates.[43] Savings to the consumer at off-price retailers are reported as high as 70 percent off the prices of a traditional department store.

T.J. Maxx is a popular off-price retailer.

Off 5th provides an outlet for excess merchandise from Saks Fifth Avenue.

There are several variations of off-price retailing. One is the *warehouse club*. These large stores (100,000 to 140,000 square feet) are rather stark outlets with no elaborate displays, customer service, or home delivery. They require an annual membership fee (ranging from $30 to $100) for the privilege of shopping there. While a typical Walmart stocks 30,000 to 60,000 items, warehouse clubs carry 4,000 to 8,000 items and usually stock just one brand of appliance or food product. Service is minimal, and customers usually pay by cash or check. Customers are attracted by the ultralow prices and surprise deals on selected merchandise, although several of the clubs have recently started to add ancillary services such as optical shops and pharmacies to differentiate themselves from competitors. The major warehouse clubs in the United States include Walmart's Sam's Club, BJ's Wholesale Club, and Costco's Warehouse Club. Sales of these off-price retailers have grown to approximately $200 billion annually.[44]

A second variation is the *outlet store*. Factory outlets, such as Van Heusen Factory Store, Bass Shoe Outlet, and Gap Factory Store, offer products for 25 to 30 percent off the suggested retail price. Manufacturers use the stores to clear excess merchandise and to reach consumers who focus on value shopping. Retail outlets such as Nordstrom Rack and Off 5th (Saks Fifth Avenue outlet) allow retailers to sell excess merchandise and still maintain an image of offering merchandise at full price in their primary store. The number of factory outlet centers has decreased recently as factory outlet stores are competing with the sales in mall and discount stores. In markets such as China, however, the outlet concept is still growing.[45]

A third variation of off-price retailing is offered by *single-price*, or *extreme value, retailers* such as Family Dollar, Dollar General, and Dollar Tree. These stores average about 6,000 square feet in size and attract customers who want value and a "corner store" environment rather than a large supercenter experience. Some experts predict extraordinary growth of these types of retailers. Dollar General, for example, already has 8,000 stores in 35 states and plans to open more.[46]

Store Location A second aspect of the retailing mix involves deciding where to locate the store and how many stores to have. Department stores, which started downtown in most cities, have followed customers to the suburbs, and in recent years more stores have been opened in large regional malls. Most stores today are near several others in one of five settings: the central business district, the regional center, the community shopping center, the strip mall, or the power center.

The **central business district** is the oldest retail setting, the community's downtown area. Until the regional outflow to suburbs, it was the major shopping area, but the suburban population has grown at the expense of the downtown shopping area. Consumers often view central business district shopping as less convenient because of lack of parking, higher crime rates, and exposure to the weather. Many cities such as Louisville, Denver, and San Antonio have implemented plans to revitalize shopping in central business districts by attracting new offices, entertainment, and residents to downtown locations.

Regional shopping centers consist of 50 to 150 stores that typically attract customers who live or work within a 5- to 10-mile range. These large shopping areas often contain two or three *anchor stores*, which are well-known national or regional stores such as Sears, Saks Fifth Avenue, and Bloomingdale's. The largest variation of a regional center is the West Edmonton Mall in Alberta, Canada. The shopping center is a conglomerate of more than 800 stores, 21 movie theaters, the world's largest indoor amusement park, 110 restaurants, and a 354-room Fantasyland hotel.[47]

A more limited approach to retail location is the **community shopping center**, which typically has one primary store (usually a department store branch) and often about 20 to 40 smaller outlets. Generally, these centers serve a population of consumers who are within a 10- to 20-minute drive.

Not every suburban store is located in a shopping mall. Many neighborhoods have clusters of stores, referred to as a **strip mall**, to serve people who are within a 5- to 10-minute drive. Gas station, hardware, laundry, grocery, and pharmacy outlets are commonly found in a strip mall. Unlike the larger shopping centers, the composition of these stores is usually unplanned. A variation of the strip mall is called the **power center**, which is a huge shopping strip with multiple anchor (or national) stores such as Home Depot, Best Buy, or JCPenney. Power centers are seen as having the convenient location found in many strip malls and the additional power of national stores. These large strip malls often have two to five anchor stores and often contain a supermarket, which brings the shopper to the power center on a weekly basis.[48]

Retail Communication A retailer's communication activities can play an important role in positioning a store and creating its image. While the traditional elements of communication and promotion are discussed in Chapter 19 on advertising and Chapter 20 on personal selling, the message communicated by the many other elements of the retailing mix are also important.

Deciding on the image of a retail outlet is an important retailing mix factor that has been widely recognized and studied since the late 1950s. Pierre Martineau described image as "the way in which the store is defined in the shopper's mind," partly by its functional qualities and partly by an aura of psychological attributes.[49] In this definition, *functional* refers to mix elements such as price ranges, store layouts, and breadth and depth of merchandise lines. The psychological attributes are the intangibles such as a sense of belonging, excitement, style, or warmth. Image has been found to include impressions of the corporation that operates the store, the category or type of store, the product categories in the store, the brands in each category, merchandise and service quality, and the marketing activities of the store.[50]

Closely related to the concept of image is the store's atmosphere or ambience. Many retailers believe that sales are affected by layout, color, lighting, and music in the store as well as by how crowded it is. In addition, the physical surroundings that influence customers may affect the store's employees.[51] In creating the right image and atmosphere, a retail store tries to attract its target audience with what those consumers seek from the buying experience, so the store will fortify the beliefs and the emotional reactions buyers are seeking.[52] While store image perceptions can exist independently of shopping experiences, consumers' shopping experiences can also influence store perceptions.[53]

Merchandise A final element of the retailing mix is the merchandise offering. Managing the breadth and depth of the product line requires retail buyers who are familiar with the needs of the target market and the alternative products available from the many manufacturers that might be interested in having a product available in the store. A popular approach to managing the assortment of merchandise today is called **category management**. This approach assigns a manager the responsibility for selecting all products that consumers in a market segment might view as substitutes for each other, with the objective of maximizing sales and profits in the category. For example, a category manager might be responsible for shoes in a department store or paper products in a grocery store.

Many retailers are developing an advanced form of category management called *consumer marketing at retail* (CMAR). Recent surveys show that, as part of their CMAR programs, retailers are conducting research, analyzing the data to identify shopper problems, translating the data into retailing mix actions, executing shopper-friendly in-store programs, and monitoring the performance of the merchandise. Walmart, for example, has used the approach to test baby-product and dollar-product categories. Grocery stores such as Safeway and Kroger use the approach to deter-

Using Marketing Dashboards

Why Apple Stores May Be the Best in the United States!

How effective is my retail format compared to other stores? How are my stores performing this year compared to last year? Information related to this question is often displayed in a marketing dashboard using two measures: (1) sales per square foot, and (2) same store sales growth.

Your Challenge You have been assigned to evaluate the Apple store retail format. The store's simple, inviting, and open atmosphere has been the topic of discussion among many retailers. Apple, however, is relatively new to the retailing business and many experts have been skeptical of the format. To allow an assessment of Apple stores, use *sales per square foot* as an indicator of how effectively retail space is used to generate revenue and *same store sales growth* to compare the increase in sales of stores that have been open for the same period of time. The calculations for these indicators are:

$$\text{Sales per square foot} = \frac{\text{Total sales}}{\text{Selling area in square feet}}$$

$$\text{Same store sales growth} = \frac{\text{Store sales in year 2} - \text{Store sales in year 1}}{\text{Store sales in year 1}}$$

Your Findings You decide to collect sales information for Saks, Neiman Marcus, Best Buy, Tiffany, and Apple stores to allow comparisons with other successful retailers. The information you collect allows the calculation of *sales per square foot* and *same store growth* for each store. The results are then easy to compare in the graphs below.

Your Action The results of your investigation indicate that Apple stores' sales per square foot are higher than any of the comparison stores at $4,000. In addition, Apple's same store growth rate of 45 percent is higher than all of the other stores. You conclude that the elements of Apple's format are very effective and even indicate that Apple may currently be the best retailer in the United States.

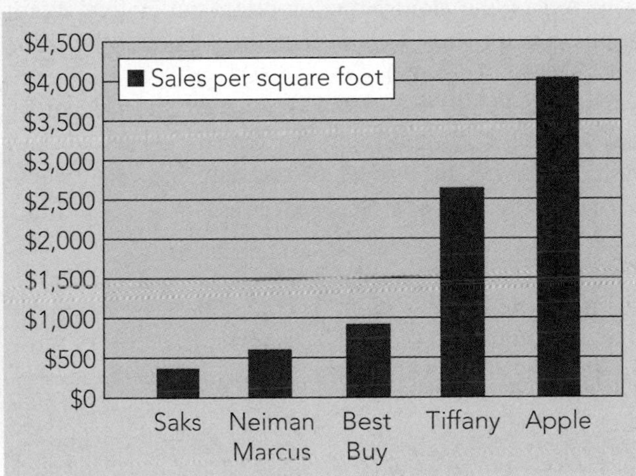

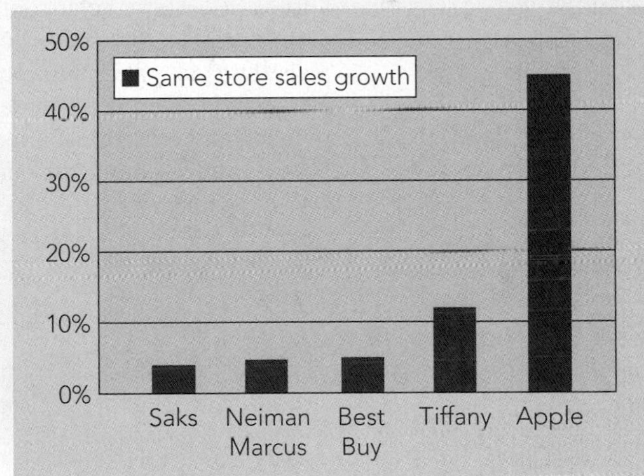

mine the appropriate mix of brand name and private-label products. Specialty retailer Barnes & Noble recently won a best practice award for its application of the approach to the selection, presentation, and promotion of magazines.[54]

Retailers have a variety of marketing metrics that can be used to assess the effectiveness of a store or retail format. First, there are measures related to customers such as the number of transactions per customer, the average transaction size per customer, the number of customers per day or per hour, and the average length of a store visit. Second, there are measures related to products such as number of returns, inventory turnover, inventory carrying cost, and average number of items per transaction. Finally, there are financial measures, such as gross margin, sales per employee, return on sales, and markdown percentage.[55] The two most popular measures for retailers are *sales per square foot* and *same store sales growth*. The Using Marketing Dashboards box describes the calculation of these measures for Apple stores.[56]

learning review

9. What are the two dimensions of the retail positioning matrix?
10. How does original markup differ from maintained markup?
11. A huge shopping strip mall with multiple anchor stores is a ________ center.

THE CHANGING NATURE OF RETAILING

LO5

Retailing is the most dynamic aspect of a channel of distribution. New types of retailers are always entering the market, searching for a new position that will attract customers. The reason for this continual change is explained by two concepts: the wheel of retailing and the retail life cycle.

The Wheel of Retailing

The **wheel of retailing** describes how new forms of retail outlets enter the market.[57] Usually they enter as low-status, low-margin stores such as a drive in hamburger stand with no indoor seating and a limited menu (Figure 17–9, box 1). Gradually these outlets add fixtures and more embellishments to their stores (in-store seating, plants, and chicken sandwiches as well as hamburgers) to increase the attractiveness for customers. With these additions, prices and status rise (box 2). As time passes, these outlets add still more services and their prices and status increase even further (box 3). These retail outlets now face some new form of retail outlet that again appears as a low-status, low-margin operator (box 4), and the wheel of retailing turns as the cycle starts to repeat itself.

When Ray Kroc started the first McDonald's in 1955, it opened shortly before lunch and closed just after dinner, offering a limited menu for the two meals without any inside seating for customers. Over time, the wheel of retailing has led to new

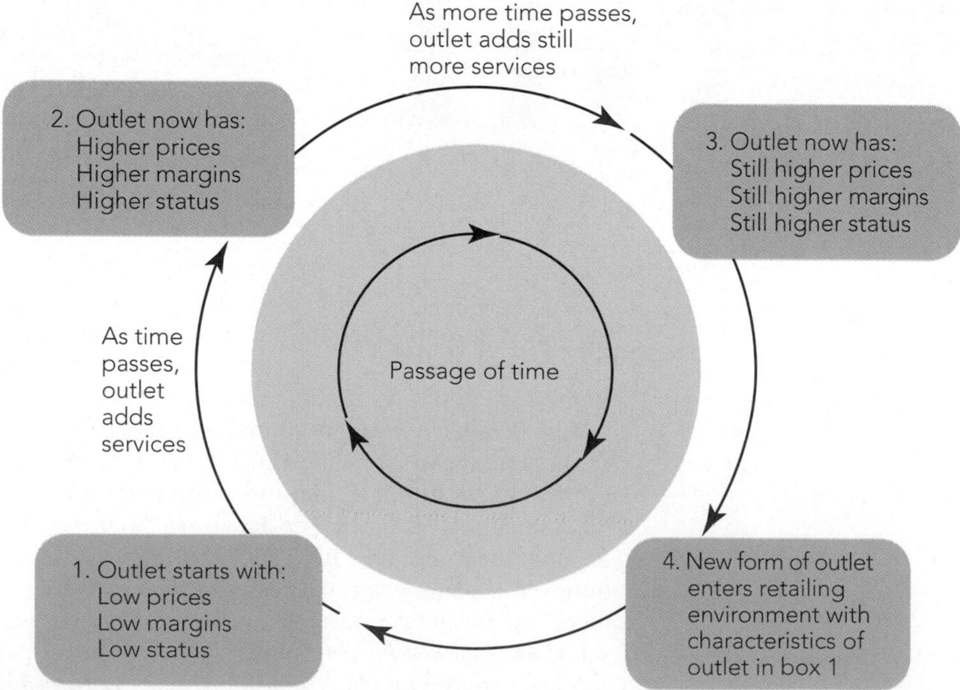

FIGURE 17–9
The wheel of retailing describes how retail outlets change.

Outlets such as Checkers enter the wheel of retailing as low-status, low-margin stores.

products and services. In 1975, McDonald's introduced the Egg McMuffin and turned breakfast into a fast-food meal. Today, McDonald's has an extensive menu, seating, and services such as wireless Internet connections and McCafé premium coffee. For the future, McDonald's is testing new products such as fried chicken biscuits, frying oil without trans fats, and fruit smoothies; new formats such as seating "zones" for different types of customers; and 24/7 "always open" hours.

The changes are leaving room for new forms of outlets such as Checkers Drive-In Restaurants. The chain opened fast-food stores that offered only basics—burgers, fries, and cola, a drive-through window, and no inside seating—and now has more than 800 stores. The wheel is turning for other outlets too—Boston Market has added pick-up, delivery, and full-service catering to its original restaurant format, and it also provides Boston Market meal solutions through supermarket delis and Boston Market frozen meals in the frozen food sections. For still others, the wheel has come full circle. Taco Bell is now opening small, limited-offering outlets in gas stations, discount stores, or "wherever a burrito and a mouth might possibly intersect."[58]

Discount stores were a major new retailing form in the 1960s and priced their products below those of department stores. As prices in discount stores rose in the 1980s, they found themselves overpriced compared with a new form of retail outlet—the warehouse club. Today, off-price retailers and factory outlets are offering prices even lower than warehouse clubs.

The Retail Life Cycle

The process of growth and decline that retail outlets, like products, experience is described by the **retail life cycle**.[59] Figure 17–10 shows the retail life cycle and the position of various current forms of retail outlets on it. Early growth is the stage

FIGURE 17–10
The retail life cycle describes stages of growth and decline for retail outlets.

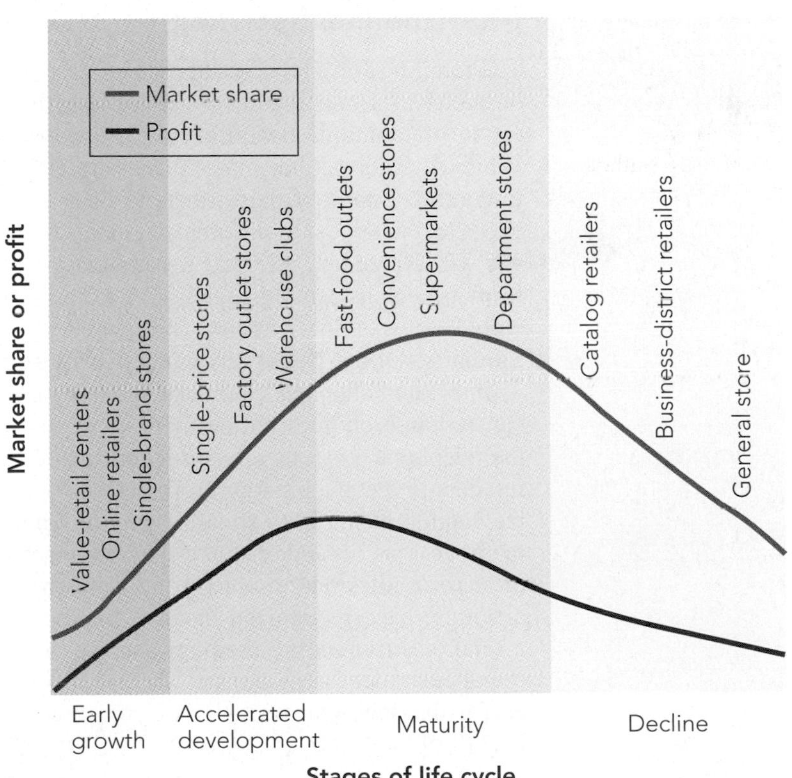

of emergence of a retail outlet, with a sharp departure from existing competition. Market share rises gradually, although profits may be low because of start-up costs. In the next stage, accelerated development, both market share and profit achieve their greatest growth rates. Usually multiple outlets are established as companies focus on the distribution element of the retailing mix. In this stage, some later competitors may enter. Wendy's, for example, appeared on the hamburger chain scene almost 20 years after McDonald's had begun operation. The key goal for the retailer in this stage is to establish a dominant position in the fight for market share.

The battle for market share is usually fought before the maturity stage, and some competitors drop out of the market. In the wars among hamburger chains, Jack in the Box, Gino's Hamburgers, and Burger Chef used to be more dominant outlets. New retail forms such as Fatburger and In-N-Out Burger enter in the maturity stage, stores try to maintain their market share, and price discounting occurs.

The challenge facing retailers is to delay entering the decline stage in which market share and profit fall rapidly. Specialty apparel retailers, such as the Gap, Limited, Benetton, and Ann Taylor, have noticed a decline in market share after years of growth. To prevent further decline, these retailers will need to find ways of discouraging their customers from moving to low-margin, mass-volume outlets or high-price, high-service boutiques.[60]

FUTURE CHANGES IN RETAILING

Two exciting trends in retailing—the growth of multichannel retailing and the increasing focus on customer experience management—are likely to lead to many changes for retailers and consumers in the future.

Multichannel Retailing

The retailing formats described previously in this chapter represent an exciting menu of choices for creating customer value in the marketplace. Each format allows retailers to offer unique benefits and meet particular needs of various customer groups. While each format has many successful applications, retailers in the future are likely to combine many of the formats to offer a broader spectrum of benefits and experiences and to appeal to different segments of consumers.[61] These **multichannel retailers** will utilize and integrate a combination of traditional store formats and nonstore formats such as catalogs, television, home shopping, and online retailing.[62] Barnes & Noble, for example, created Barnesandnoble.com to compete with Amazon.com. Similarly, Office Depot has integrated its store, catalog, and Internet operations.

Integrated channels can make shopping simpler and more convenient. A consumer can research choices online or in a catalog and then make a purchase online, over the telephone, or at the closest store. In addition, the use of multiple channels allows retailers to reach a broader profile of customers. While online retailing may cannibalize catalog business to some degree, an online transaction costs about half as much to process as a catalog order. Multichannel retailers also benefit from the synergy of sharing information among the different channel operations. Online retailers, for example, have recognized that the Internet is more of a transactional medium than a relationship-building medium and are working to find ways to complement traditional customer interactions.[63] The benefits of multichannel marketing are also apparent in the spending behavior of consumers as described in the Marketing Matters box.[64]

Marketing Matters > > > > > > customer value

The Multichannel Marketing Multiplier

Multichannel marketing is the blending of different communication and delivery channels that are mutually reinforcing in attracting, retaining, and building relationships with consumers who shop and buy in the traditional marketplace and marketspace. Industry analysts refer to the complementary role of different communication and delivery channels as an *influence effect.*

Retailers that integrate and leverage their stores, catalogs, and Web sites have seen a sizable lift in yearly sales recorded from individual customers. Eddie Bauer is a good example. Customers who shop only one of its channels spend $100 to $200 per year. Those who shop in two channels spend $300 to $500 annually. Customers who shop all these channels—store, catalog, and Web site—spend $800 to $1,000 per year. Moreover, multichannel customers have been found to be *three times* as profitable as single-channel customers.

JCPenney has seen similar results. The company is a leading multichannel retailer and reports that a JCPenney customer who shops in all three channels—store, catalog, and Web site—spends *four to eight times* as much as a customer who shops in only one channel, as shown in the chart.

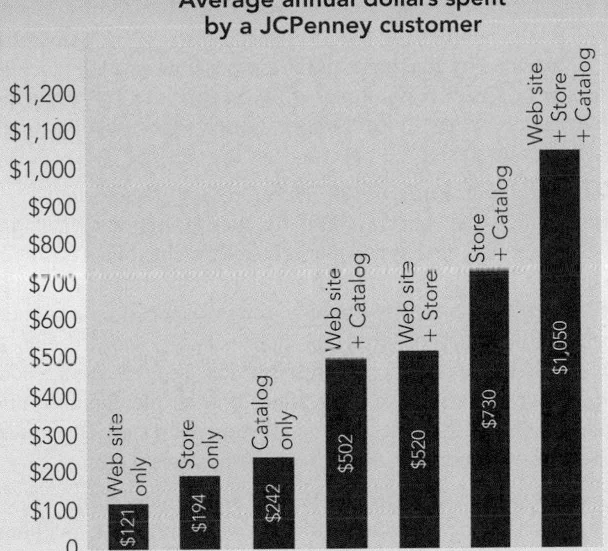

Managing the Customer Experience

Department stores are changing to create social retailing experiences. While many of those changes appeal to women and address the way women like to shop, retailers are also paying more attention to men and their shopping behavior. Men have typically been viewed as infrequent "mission shoppers" who go to a store only as a means of obtaining a product as efficiently as possible. Today's young men, however, are changing their shopping behavior. Recent research found that 84 percent of men said they purchase their own clothes, compared with just 65 percent four years ago. To appeal to men, many stores are creating stand-alone men's sections that combine clothes, accessories, and gadgets in one place. The new sections use "masculine" interior designs with simple colors, stainless-steel fixtures, and dark wood floors. Bloomingdale's in Manhattan has even added seating, sports magazines, and televisions to the men's areas. All of these changes are intended to create a better experience for male shoppers. As Jack Hruska, executive vice president at Bloomingdale's, explains, "We hope to make men feel more comfortable and at home by giving them a place to unwind while they are shopping."[65]

learning review

12. According to the wheel of retailing, when a new retail form appears, how would you characterize its image?

13. Market share is usually fought out before the ______________ stage of the retail life cycle.

14. What is an influence effect?

LEARNING OBJECTIVES REVIEW

LO1 *Identify retailers in terms of the utilities they provide.*
Retailers provide time, place, form, and possession utilities. Time utility is provided by stores with convenient time-of-day (e.g., open 24 hours) or time-of-year (e.g., seasonal sports equipment available all year) availability. Place utility is provided by the number and location of the stores. Possession utility is provided by making a purchase possible (e.g., financing) or easier (e.g., delivery). Form utility is provided by producing or altering a product to meet the customer's specifications (e.g., custom-made shirts).

LO2 *Explain the alternative ways to classify retail outlets.*
Retail outlets can be classified by their form of ownership, level of service, and type of merchandise line. The forms of ownership include independent retailers, corporate chains, and contractual systems that include retailer-sponsored cooperatives, wholesaler-sponsored voluntary chains, and franchises. The levels of service include self-service, limited-service, and full-service outlets. Stores classified by their merchandise line include stores with depth, such as sporting good specialty stores, and stores with breadth, such as large department stores.

LO3 *Describe the many methods of nonstore retailing.*
Nonstore retailing includes automatic vending, direct mail and catalogs, television home shopping, online retailing, telemarketing, and direct selling. The methods of nonstore retailing vary by the level of involvement of the retailer and the level of involvement of the customer. Vending, for example, has low involvement, whereas both the consumer and the retailer have high involvement in direct selling.

LO4 *Classify retailers in terms of the retail positioning matrix, and specify retailing mix actions.*
The retail positioning matrix positions retail outlets on two dimensions: breadth of product line and value added. There are four possible positions in the matrix—broad product line/low value added (Walmart), narrow product line/low value added (Payless Shoe Source), broad product line/high value added (Bloomingdale's), and narrow product line/high value added (Tiffany). Retailing mix actions are used to manage a retail store and the merchandise in a store. The mix variables include pricing, store location, communication activities, and merchandise. Two common forms of assessment for retailers are "sales per square foot" and "same store growth."

LO5 *Explain changes in retailing with the wheel of retailing and the retail life cycle concepts.*
The wheel of retailing concept explains how retail outlets typically enter the market as low-status, low-margin stores. Over time, stores gradually add new products and services, increasing their prices, status, and margins, and leaving an opening for new low-status, low-margin stores. The retail life cycle describes the process of growth and decline for retail outlets through four stages: early growth, accelerated development, maturity, and decline.

FOCUSING ON KEY TERMS

breadth of product line p. 435
category management p. 446
central business district p. 445
community shopping center p. 445
depth of product line p. 435
form of ownership p. 432
hypermarket p. 436
intertype competition p. 436
level of service p. 432
merchandise line p. 432
multichannel retailers p. 450
off-price retailing p. 444
power center p. 446
regional shopping centers p. 445
retail life cycle p. 449
retail positioning matrix p. 442
retailing p. 430
retailing mix p. 443
scrambled merchandising p. 436
strip mall p. 446
telemarketing p. 441
wheel of retailing p. 448

APPLYING MARKETING KNOWLEDGE

1 Discuss the impact of the growing number of dual-income households on (*a*) nonstore retailing and (*b*) the retail mix.
2 How does value added affect a store's competitive position?
3 In retail pricing, retailers often have a maintained markup. Explain how this maintained markup differs from original markup and why it is so important.
4 What are the similarities and differences between the product and retail life cycles?
5 How would you classify Walmart in terms of its position on the wheel of retailing versus that of an off-price retailer?
6 Develop a chart to highlight the role of each of the four main elements of the retailing mix across the four stages of the retail life cycle.
7 In Figure 17–8 Payless ShoeSource was placed on the retail positioning matrix. What strategies should Payless ShoeSource follow to move itself into the same position as Tiffany?
8 Breadth and depth are two important components in distinguishing among types of retailers. Discuss the breadth and depth implications of the following retailers discussed in this chapter: (*a*) Nordstrom, (*b*) Walmart, (*c*) L. L. Bean, and (*d*) Best Buy.
9 According to the wheel of retailing and the retail life cycle, what will happen to factory outlet stores?
10 The text discusses the development of online retailing in the United States. How does the development of this retailing form agree with the implications of the retail life cycle?

building your marketing plan

Does your marketing plan involve using retailers? If the answer is no, read no further and do not include a retailing element in your plan. If the answer is yes:

1 Use Figure 17–8 to develop your retailing strategy by (*a*) selecting a position in the retail positioning matrix and (*b*) specifying the details of the retailing mix.

2 Develop a positioning statement describing the breadth of the product line (broad versus narrow) and value added (low versus high).

3 Describe an appropriate combination of retail pricing, store location, retail communication, and merchandise assortment.

video case 17 Mall of America: Shopping and a Whole Lot More

"If you build it, they will come" not only worked in the movie *Field of Dreams* but also applies—big time—to Mall of America.

Located in a suburb of Minneapolis, Mall of America (www.mallofamerica.com) is the largest completely enclosed retail and family-entertainment complex in the United States. "We're more than a mall, we're a destination," explains Maureen Cahill, an executive at Mall of America. More than 100,000 people each day—40 million visitors each year—visit the one-stop complex offering retail shopping, guest services, convenience, a huge variety of entertainment, and fun for all. "Guest services" include everything from high school and college classrooms to a doctor's office and a wedding chapel.

THE CONCEPT AND CHALLENGE

The idea for the Mall of America came from the West Edmonton Mall in Alberta, Canada. The Ghermezian Brothers, who developed that mall, sought to create a unique mall that would attract not only local families but also tourists from the Upper Midwest, the nation, and even from abroad.

The two challenges for Mall of America: How can it (1) attract and keep the large number of retail establishments needed to (2) continue to attract even more millions of visitors than today? A big part of the answer is in Mall of America's positioning—"There is a place for fun in your life!"

THE STAGGERING SIZE AND OFFERINGS

Opened August 1992 amid tremendous worldwide publicity, Mall of America faced skeptics who had their doubts because of its size, its unique retail-entertainment mix, and the nationwide recession. Despite these concerns, it opened with more than 80 percent of its space leased and attracted more than 1 million visitors its first week.

Mall of America is 4.2 million square feet, the equivalent of 88 football fields. This makes it three to four times

the size of most other regional malls. It includes four anchor department stores: Nordstrom, Macy's, Bloomingdale's, and Sears. It also includes more than 520 specialty stores, from Brooks Brothers to DSW Shoe Warehouse. Approximately 36 percent of Mall of America's space is devoted to anchors and 64 percent to specialty stores. This makes the space allocation the reverse of most regional malls.

The retail-entertainment mix of Mall of America is incredibly diverse. For example, there are more than 100 apparel and accessory stores, 18 jewelry stores, and 33 shoe stores. Two food courts with 27 restaurants plus more than 30 other restaurants scattered throughout the building meet most food preferences of visitors. Another surprise: Mall of America is home to many "concept stores," where retailers introduce a new type of store or design. Because of its incredible size, the mall has 194 stores not found at competing regional malls. In addition, it has an entrepreneurial program for people with an innovative retail idea and limited resources. They can open a kiosk, wall unit, or small store for a specified time period or as a temporary seasonal tenant.

Unique features of Mall of America include:

- A seven-acre theme park with more than 50 attractions and rides, including a roller coaster, Ferris wheel, and games in a glass-enclosed, skylighted area with more than 400 trees.
- Underwater Adventures, where visitors are surrounded by sharks, stingrays, and sea turtles; can adventure among fish native to the north woods; and can discover what lurks at the bottom of the Mississippi River.
- Entertainment choices that include a 14-screen theater, A.C.E.S. Flight Simulation, NASCAR Silicon Motor Speedway, and Dinosaur Walk Museum.
- The LEGO Land Imagination Center, a 6,000-square-foot showplace with more than 30 full-sized models.

As a host to corporate events and private parties, Mall of America has a rotunda that opens to all four floors that facilitates presentations, demonstrations, and exhibits. Organizations such as PepsiCo, Visa-USA, and Chevrolet have used the facilities to gain shopper awareness. Mall of America is a rectangle with the anchor department stores at the corners and amusement park in the skylighted central area, making it easy for shoppers to understand and navigate. It has 12,550 free parking ramp spaces on site and another 7,000 spaces nearby during peak times.

THE MARKET

The Minneapolis–St. Paul metropolitan area is a market with more than 3 million people. A total of 30 million people live within a day's drive of Mall of America. A survey of its shoppers showed that 32 percent of the shoppers travel 150 miles or more and account for more than 50 percent of the sales revenues. Located three miles from the Minneapolis/St. Paul International Airport, Mall of America provides a shuttle bus from the airport every half hour. Light-rail service from the airport and downtown Minneapolis is also available.

Tourism accounts for 4 out of 10 visits to Mall of America. About 6 percent of visitors come from outside the United States. Some come just to see and experience Mall of America, while others take advantage of the cost savings available on goods (Japan) or taxes (Canada and states with sales taxes on clothing).

THE FUTURE: FACING THE CHALLENGES

Where does Mall of America head in the future?

"We just did a brand study and found that Mall of America is one of the most recognized brands in the world," Cahill says. "They might not know where we are sometimes, but they've heard of Mall of America and they know they want to come.

"What we've learned since 1992 is to keep the Mall of America fresh and exciting," she explains. "We're constantly looking at what attracts people and adding to that. We're adding new stores, new attractions, and new events. We hold more than 350 events a year and with everyone from Garth Brooks to Sarah Ferguson to N Sync."

Mall of America announced a plan for a 5.6 million-square-foot expansion, the area of another 117 football fields, connected by pedestrian skyway to the present building. "The second phase will not be a duplicate of what we have," Cahill says. "We have plans for at least three hotels, a performing arts center, a business office complex, an art or history museum, and possibly even a television broadcast facility." The expansion is expected to attract an additional 20 million visitors annually. In addition, the development is designed to exceed environmental certification standards.

One of the first elements of the expansion includes a now open 306,000-square-foot IKEA store. Other new elements will include a 13,000-square-foot restaurant called Cantina Corona, a 6,000-seat performing arts auditorium created by AEG, a 300,000-square-foot Bass Pro store, a 500-room hotel and a Mayo Clinic facility. All of these new additions and the many offerings of the current mall reinforce that Mall of America is a shopping destination and a whole lot more!

Questions

1 Why has Mall of America been such a marketing success so far?

2 What (*a*) retail and (*b*) consumer trends have occurred since Mall of America was opened in 1992 that it should consider when making future plans?

3 (*a*) What criteria should Mall of America use in adding new facilities to its complex? (*b*) Evaluate (*i*) retail stores, (*ii*) entertainment offerings, and (*iii*) hotels on these criteria.

4 What specific marketing actions would you propose that Mall of America managers take to ensure its continuing success in attracting visitors (*a*) from the local metropolitan area and (*b*) from outside of it?

TV Celebrity Food Games News Sports Mobile Shop

Shows Video HD Videos Watch & Chat Schedule

Login Register

Social Viewing Room Lounge

Join A Social Viewing Room

Browse viewing rooms and connect with others to share

Join family, friends and fellow fans and watch your favorite episodes of your favorite shows together. Boo the latest villains on CSI: Miami and CSI: NY at the same time, LOL in unison at the same crazy antics on Worst Week and Gary UnMarried and toss tomatoes at your least favorite Survivor. Hop right into one of the rooms below, invite your friends and start socializing!

2 / 2

Gary Unmarried Gary And His Half Brother
Season 1: Episode 19
Full Episode (21:36)

Join Now

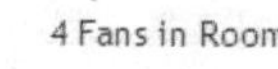

4 Fans in Room

View by myself

Other Rooms for This Show

Room 1	[3]	12 min. in
Room 2	[10]	2 min. in
Room 3	[2]	29 min. in
Room 4	[2]	25 min. in

Invite your friends

Feedback

Quick Quiz

00:12

How many days dc Jeff say the game last?

33

39

55

Want your own avatar picture? Register, it's free! | No, thanks

Laugh

Type here to comment

Survivor: Samoa - Episode 1
Air Date: 09/17/09
Full Episode 42:37

Twenty castaways are left to fend for themselves among Samoa's white sand beaches, lush green valleys and towering waterfalls.

18 Integrated Marketing Communications and Direct Marketing

LEARNING OBJECTIVES
After reading this chapter you should be able to:

LO1 Discuss integrated marketing communication and the communication process.

LO2 Describe the promotional mix and the uniqueness of each component.

LO3 Select the promotional approach appropriate to a product's target audience, life-cycle stage, and characteristics, as well as stages of the buying decision and channel strategies.

LO4 Describe the elements of the promotion decision process.

LO5 Explain the value of direct marketing for consumers and sellers.

INTEGRATED MARKETING COMMUNICATIONS USHERS IN THE 'AGE OF ENGAGE'

How would you characterize today's marketplace? For most consumers the answer is interactive and connected—through cell phones, computers, the Web, and social networks such as Facebook, MySpace, Twitter, LinkedIn, and Flickr. In this marketplace the key to communicating with consumers is to engage them—a perfect job for integrated marketing communications campaigns!

How can media engage consumers? The options are endless for traditional and new forms of media. TV networks, for example, now offer online video streams of many series. CBS recently created social viewing rooms at CBS.com for programs such as *CSI* and *Survivor*. The rooms allow viewers to chat about what they are watching and to offer critical reactions to the program. Senior Vice President Anthony Soohoo explains, "When people are online they want to engage in a different way, they want to share the experience." The audience for online viewing is now 162 million viewers, compared to the 282 million who watch on their television.

New forms of communicating with customers, such as social media, also offer opportunities to engage consumers. Recent research shows that 85 percent of consumers believe that companies should be interacting through social channels. Many companies create a branded presence such as a fan page within virtual communities such as Facebook or MySpace to generate word-of-mouth advertising. Some companies, such as Saturn, have even created their own online communities as showcases for their brands and products. One advantage of this medium is that it is less expensive than other forms of marketing, even though it may require constant monitoring by someone at the company or its advertising agency.

Many other media can also engage consumers today. When Disney created a contest for the chance to play a fantasy role at Disneyland, more than 10,000 people submitted videos! eBay Motors worked with the makers of a car racing game called "Grid" for Xbox 360, Playstation 3, and Nintendo so that the auction platform would be integrated into the game, and seen by a potential audience of 40 million game enthusiasts. Procter & Gamble used product placement to include its Crest Whitestrips in the movie *He's Just Not That into You*, and then passed out free samples at the exits of the movie theaters. E-mail, blogs, gift cards, magazines, and sweepstakes are also potential forms of media that can engage today's consumers.[1]

The many types of promotion in these examples demonstrate the opportunity for engaging potential customers and the importance of integrating the various elements of a communication program.

Promotion represents the fourth element in the marketing mix. The promotional element consists of communication tools, including advertising, personal selling, sales promotion, public relations, and direct marketing. The combination of one or more of these communication tools is called the **promotional mix**. All of these tools can be used to: (1) inform prospective buyers about the benefits of the product, (2) persuade them to try it, and (3) remind them later about the benefits they enjoyed by using the product. In the past, marketers often viewed these communication tools as separate and independent. The advertising department, for example, often designed and managed its activities without consulting departments or agencies that had responsibility for sales promotion or public relations. The result was often an overall communication effort that was uncoordinated and, in some cases, inconsistent. Today, the concept of designing marketing communications programs that coordinate all promotional activities—advertising, personal selling, sales promotion, public relations, and direct marketing—to provide a consistent message across all audiences is referred to as **integrated marketing communications (IMC)**. In addition, by taking consumer expectations into consideration, IMC is a key element in a company's customer experience management strategy.[2]

This chapter provides an overview of the communication process, a description of the promotional mix elements, several tools for integrating the promotional mix, and a process for developing a comprehensive promotion program. One of the promotional mix elements, direct marketing, is also discussed in this chapter. Chapter 19 covers advertising, sales promotion, and public relations, and Chapter 20 discusses personal selling.

THE COMMUNICATION PROCESS

LO1

Communication is the process of conveying a message to others and it requires six elements: a source, a message, a channel of communication, a receiver, and the processes of encoding and decoding[3] (see Figure 18–1). The **source** may be a company or person who has information to convey. The information sent by a source, such as a description of a new cellular telephone, forms the **message**. The message is conveyed by means of a **channel of communication** such as a salesperson, advertising media, or public relations tools. Consumers who read, hear, or see the message are the **receivers**.

FIGURE 18–1

The communication process consists of six key elements.

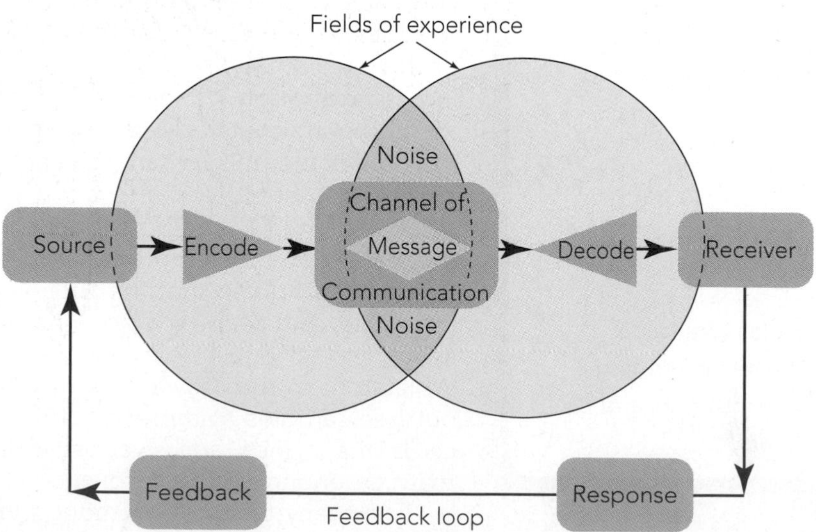

Welcome to the open
PECKINPAH ROAD, CA – 48 miles northeast of Fresno.
To get to some of the most spectacular trails on Earth, you'll need one of the most capable off-road vehicles on Earth. You'll also need available front and rear locking differentials, a 45.0:1 crawl ratio, and full underbody protection. All engineered to take you anywhere in the midsize HUMMER H3. Find out more at HUMMER.com.
HUMMER
LIKE NOTHING ELSE.

How would you decode this ad?

HUMMER
www.HUMMER.com

Encoding and Decoding

Encoding and decoding are essential to communication. **Encoding** is the process of having the sender transform an idea into a set of symbols. **Decoding** is the reverse, or the process of having the receiver take a set of symbols, the message, and transform the symbols back to an idea. Look at the accompanying automobile advertisement: Who is the source, and what is the message?

Decoding is performed by the receivers according to their own frame of reference: their attitudes, values, and beliefs.[4] HUMMER is the source and the advertisement is the message, which appeared in *BusinessWeek* magazine (the channel). How would you interpret (decode) this advertisement? The picture and text in the advertisement show that the source's intention is to generate interest in its product with the headline "Welcome to the open"—a statement the source believes will appeal to the readers of the magazine.

The process of communication is not always a successful one. Errors in communication can happen in several ways. The source may not adequately transform the abstract idea into an effective set of symbols, a properly encoded message may be sent through the wrong channel and never make it to the receiver, the receiver may not properly transform the set of symbols into the correct abstract idea, or finally, feedback may be so delayed or distorted that it is of no use to the sender. Although communication appears easy to perform, truly effective communication can be very difficult.

For the message to be communicated effectively, the sender and receiver must have a mutually shared **field of experience**—a similar understanding and knowledge they apply to the message. Figure 18–1 shows two circles representing the fields of experience of the sender and receiver, which overlap in the message. Some of the better-known message problems have occurred when U.S. companies have taken their messages to cultures with different fields of experience. Many misinterpretations are merely the result of bad translations. For example, KFC made a mistake when its "finger-lickin' good" slogan was translated into Mandarin Chinese as "eat your fingers off!"[5]

Feedback

Figure 18–1 shows a line labeled *feedback loop*, which consists of a response and feedback. A **response** is the impact the message had on the receiver's knowledge, attitudes, or behaviors. **Feedback** is the sender's interpretation of the response and indicates whether the message was decoded and understood as intended. Chapter 19 reviews approaches called *pretesting* which ensure that messages are decoded properly.

Noise

Noise includes extraneous factors that can work against effective communication by distorting a message or the feedback received (Figure 18–1). Noise can be a simple error, such as a printing mistake that affects the meaning of a newspaper advertisement or using words or pictures that fail to communicate the message clearly. Noise can also occur when a salesperson's message is misunderstood by a prospective buyer, such as when a salesperson's accent, use of slang terms, or communication style make hearing and understanding the message difficult.

learning review

1. What are the six elements required for communication to occur?
2. A difficulty for U.S. companies advertising in international markets is that the audience does not share the same ________________.
3. A misprint in a newspaper ad is an example of _______________.

THE PROMOTIONAL ELEMENTS

LO2

To communicate with consumers, a company can use one or more of five promotional alternatives: advertising, personal selling, public relations, sales promotion, and direct marketing. Figure 18–2 summarizes the distinctions among these five elements. Three of these elements—advertising, sales promotion, and public relations—are often said to use *mass selling* because they are used with groups of prospective buyers. In contrast, personal selling uses *customized interaction* between a seller and a prospective buyer. Personal selling activities include face-to-face, telephone, and interactive electronic communication. Direct marketing also uses messages customized for specific customers.

Advertising

Advertising is any paid form of nonpersonal communication about an organization, good, service, or idea by an identified sponsor. The *paid* aspect of this definition is important because the space for the advertising message normally must be bought. An occasional exception is the public service announcement, where the advertising time or space is donated. A full-page, four-color ad in *Time* magazine, for example, costs $273,750. The *nonpersonal* component of advertising is also important. Advertising involves mass media (such as TV, radio, and magazines), which are nonpersonal and do not have an immediate feedback loop as does personal selling.

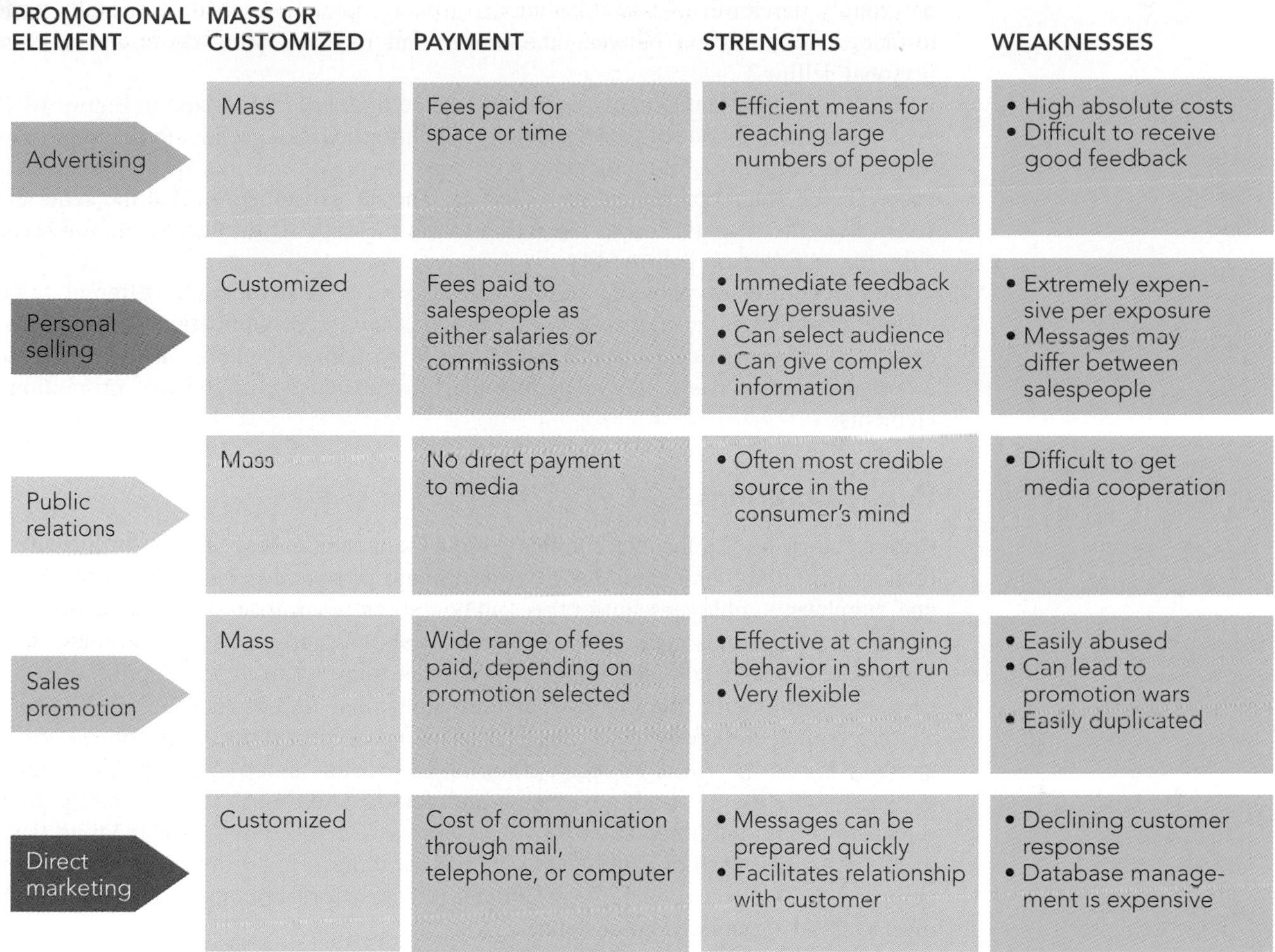

PROMOTIONAL ELEMENT	MASS OR CUSTOMIZED	PAYMENT	STRENGTHS	WEAKNESSES
Advertising	Mass	Fees paid for space or time	• Efficient means for reaching large numbers of people	• High absolute costs • Difficult to receive good feedback
Personal selling	Customized	Fees paid to salespeople as either salaries or commissions	• Immediate feedback • Very persuasive • Can select audience • Can give complex information	• Extremely expensive per exposure • Messages may differ between salespeople
Public relations	Mass	No direct payment to media	• Often most credible source in the consumer's mind	• Difficult to get media cooperation
Sales promotion	Mass	Wide range of fees paid, depending on promotion selected	• Effective at changing behavior in short run • Very flexible	• Easily abused • Can lead to promotion wars • Easily duplicated
Direct marketing	Customized	Cost of communication through mail, telephone, or computer	• Messages can be prepared quickly • Facilitates relationship with customer	• Declining customer response • Database management is expensive

FIGURE 18–2
The five elements of the promotional mix

So before the message is sent, marketing research plays a valuable role; for example, it determines that the target market will actually see the medium chosen and that the message will be understood.

There are several advantages to a firm using advertising in its promotional mix. It can be attention-getting—as with the Havaianas ad shown on the next page—and also can communicate specific product benefits to prospective buyers. By paying for the advertising space, a company can control *what* it wants to say and, to some extent, to *whom* the message is sent. Advertising also allows the company to decide *when* to send its message (which includes how often). The nonpersonal aspect of advertising also has its advantages. Once the message is created, the same message is sent to all receivers in a market segment. If the pictorial, text, and brand elements of an advertisement are properly pretested, an advertiser can ensure the ad's ability to capture consumers' attention and trust that the same message will be decoded by all receivers in the market segment.[6]

Advertising has some disadvantages. As shown in Figure 18–2 and discussed in depth in Chapter 19, the costs to produce and place a message are significant, and the lack of direct feedback makes it difficult to know how well the message was received.

Personal Selling

The second major promotional alternative is **personal selling**, which is the two-way flow of communication between a buyer and seller designed to influence a person's or group's purchase decision. Unlike advertising, personal selling is usually face-to-face communication between the sender and receiver. Why do companies use personal selling?

There are important advantages to personal selling, as summarized in Figure 18–2. A salesperson can control to *whom* the presentation is made, reducing the amount of *wasted coverage*, or communication with consumers who are not in the target audience. The personal component of selling has another advantage in that the seller can see or hear the potential buyer's reaction to the message. If the feedback is unfavorable, the salesperson can modify the message.

The flexibility of personal selling can also be a disadvantage. Different salespeople can change the message so that no consistent communication is given to all customers. The high cost of personal selling is probably its major disadvantage. On a cost-per-contact basis, it is generally the most expensive of the five promotional elements.

Public Relations

Public relations is a form of communication management that seeks to influence the feelings, opinions, or beliefs held by customers, prospective customers, stockholders, suppliers, employees, and other publics about a company and its products or services.[7] Many tools such as special events, lobbying efforts, annual reports, press conferences, RSS feeds, and image management may be used by a public relations department, although publicity often plays the most important role.[8] **Publicity** is a nonpersonal, indirectly paid presentation of an organization, good, or service. It can take the form of a news story, editorial, or product announcement. A difference between publicity and both advertising and personal selling is the "indirectly paid" dimension. With publicity a company does not pay for space in a mass medium (such as television or radio) but attempts to get the medium to run a favorable story on the company. In this sense, there is an indirect payment for publicity in that a company must support a public relations staff.

An advantage of publicity is credibility. When you read a favorable story about a company's product (such as a glowing restaurant review), there is a tendency to

Advertising, public relations, and sales promotion are three elements of the promotional mix.

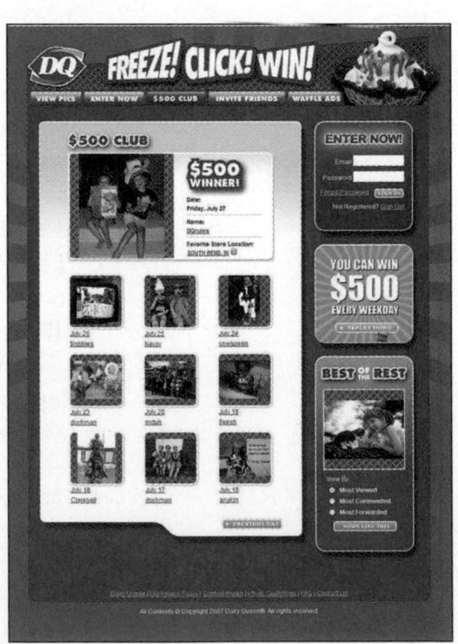

believe it. Travelers throughout the world have relied on Frommer's guides such as *Australia from $60 a Day*. These books outline out-of-the-way, inexpensive restaurants and hotels, giving invaluable publicity to these establishments. Such businesses do not (nor can they) buy a mention in the guide.

The disadvantage of publicity relates to the lack of the user's control over it. A company can invite media to cover an interesting event such as a store opening or a new product release, but there is no guarantee that a story will result, if it will be positive, or who will be in the audience. Social media, such as blogs, have grown dramatically and allow uncontrollable public discussions of almost any company activity. Many public relations departments now focus on facilitating and responding to online discussions. McDonald's, for example, responds to comments about McDonald's products and promotions on its corporate social responsibility blog, *Open for Discussion*.[9] Generally, publicity is an important element of most promotional campaigns, although the lack of control means that it is rarely the primary element. Research related to the sequence of IMC elements, however, indicates that publicity followed by advertising with the same message increases the positive response to the message.[10]

Sales Promotion

A fourth promotional element is **sales promotion**, a short-term inducement of value offered to arouse interest in buying a good or service. Used in conjunction with advertising or personal selling, sales promotions are offered to intermediaries as well as to ultimate consumers. Coupons, rebates, samples, and sweepstakes, such as the "Shop Smart for College" promotion, are just a few examples of sales promotions discussed later in this chapter.

The advantage of sales promotion is that the short-term nature of these programs (such as a coupon or sweepstakes with an expiration date) often stimulates sales for their duration. Offering value to the consumer in terms of a cents-off coupon or rebate may increase store traffic from consumers who are not store-loyal.[11]

Sales promotions cannot be the sole basis for a campaign because gains are often temporary and sales drop off when the deal ends. Advertising support is needed to convert the customer who tried the product because of a sales promotion into a long-term buyer. If sales promotions are conducted continuously, they lose their effectiveness. Customers begin to delay purchase until a coupon is offered, or they question the product's value. Some aspects of sales promotions also are regulated by the federal government.[12] These issues are reviewed in detail in Chapter 19.

Direct Marketing

Another promotional alternative, **direct marketing**, uses direct communication with consumers to generate a response in the form of an order, a request for further information, or a visit to a retail outlet. The communication can take many forms including face-to-face selling, direct mail, catalogs, telephone solicitations, direct response advertising (on television and radio and in print), and online marketing.[13] Like personal selling, direct marketing often consists of interactive communication. It also has the advantage of being customized to match the needs of specific target markets. Messages can be developed and adapted quickly to facilitate one-to-one relationships with customers.

While direct marketing has been one of the fastest-growing forms of promotion, it has several disadvantages. First, most forms of direct marketing require a comprehensive and up-to-date database with information about the target market. Developing and maintaining the database can be expensive and time consuming. In addition, growing concern about privacy has led to a decline in response rates among some customer groups. Companies with successful direct marketing programs are sensitive to these issues and often use a combination of direct marketing alternatives together, or direct marketing combined with other promotional tools, to increase value for customers.

learning review

4. Explain the difference between advertising and publicity when both appear on television.
5. Cost per contact is high with the ______________ element of the promotional mix.
6. Which promotional element should be offered only on a short-term basis?

INTEGRATED MARKETING COMMUNICATIONS—DEVELOPING THE PROMOTIONAL MIX

A firm's promotional mix is the combination of one or more of the promotional tools it chooses to use. In putting together the promotional mix, a marketer must consider two issues. First, the balance of the elements must be determined. Should advertising be emphasized more than personal selling? Should a promotional rebate be offered? Would public relations activities be effective? Several factors affect such decisions: the target audience for the promotion, the stage of the product's life cycle, characteristics of the product, decision stage of the buyer, and even the channel of distribution. Second, because the various promotional elements are often the responsibility of different departments, coordinating a consistent promotional effort is necessary. A promotional planning process designed to ensure integrated marketing communications can facilitate this goal.

The Target Audience

Publications such as *Restaurant News* reach business buyers.

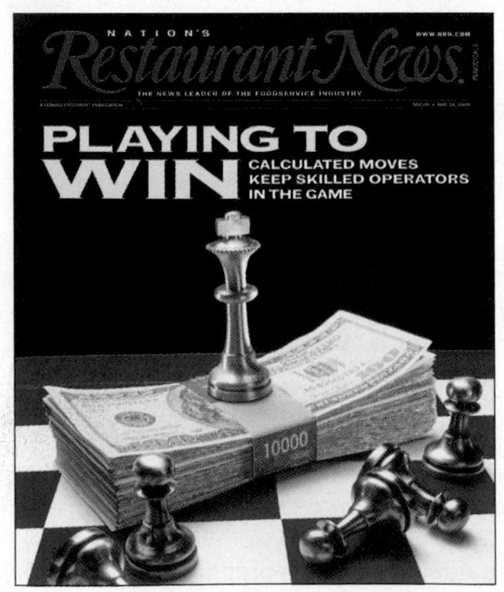

Promotional programs are directed to the ultimate consumer, to an intermediary (retailer, wholesaler, or industrial distributor), or to both. Promotional programs directed to buyers of consumer products often use mass media because the number of potential buyers is large. Personal selling is used at the place of purchase, generally the retail store. Direct marketing may be used to encourage first-time or repeat purchases. Combinations of many media alternatives are a necessity for some target audiences today. The Marketing Matters box describes how Generation Y consumers can be reached through mobile marketing programs.[14]

Advertising directed to business buyers is used selectively in trade publications, such as *Restaurant News* magazine for buyers of restaurant equipment and supplies. Because business buyers often have specialized needs or technical questions, personal selling is particularly important. The salesperson can provide information and the necessary support after sales.

Intermediaries are often the focus of promotional efforts. As with business buyers, personal selling is the major promotional ingredient. The salespeople assist intermediaries in making a profit by coordinating promotional campaigns sponsored by the manufacturer and by providing marketing advice and expertise. Intermediaries' questions often pertain to the allowed markup, merchandising support, and return policies.

Marketing Matters > > > > > > > > technology

Mobile Marketing Reaches Generation Y, 32/7!

The marketplace is flooded with new forms of media. In addition to traditional media such as television, radio, magazines, and newspapers, marketers can now use cell phones, social networks, RSS feeds, blogs, and a variety of other means to deliver messages. To cope with the volume of messages, consumers have applied multitasking to media use. A recent study of television viewers, for example, found that 58 percent were instant messaging, e-mailing, texting, or talking on the phone while they watched TV. This simultaneous media use is so common it has created 32-hour "media days" for consumers.

Generation Y is particularly adept, as up to 72 percent of that group is "connected" while watching television. Since using a single medium alone is a thing of the past for young consumers, advertising agencies, broadcasters, cable and satellite providers, and retailers must change their views of consumers' ability to absorb and remember advertising messages. Marketers can still communicate with Generation Y, however, by integrating new media into their campaigns and facilitating the connected conversations.

With 259 million wireless phones in the United States, many experts believe that marketing through cell phones, or mobile marketing, is a logical addition to integrated campaigns. The Gap, for example, created a free iPhone application that allows consumers to put together an outfit and then generate a list of the items. According to Executive Vice President Ivy Ross, "We want to engage our customers where they're playing and really be where they are." Similarly, Kraft created the iFood Assistant to create recipes made with Kraft products. The application is now one of the iPhone's 100 most popular applications. Phones are also offering access to the Internet and social networks—an essential element as Generation Y members keep in touch with an average of 47 "friends."

Watch for other brands to try similar mobile programs, particularly for consumers who are connected multitaskers.

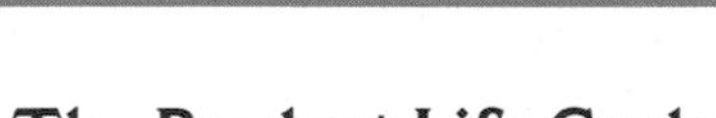

The Product Life Cycle

All products have a product life cycle (see Chapter 11), and the composition of the promotional mix changes over the four life-cycle stages, as shown for Purina Dog Chow in Figure 18–3.

Introduction Stage Informing consumers in an effort to increase their level of awareness is the primary promotional objective in the introduction stage of the

FIGURE 18–3
Promotional tools used over the product life cycle of Purina Dog Chow

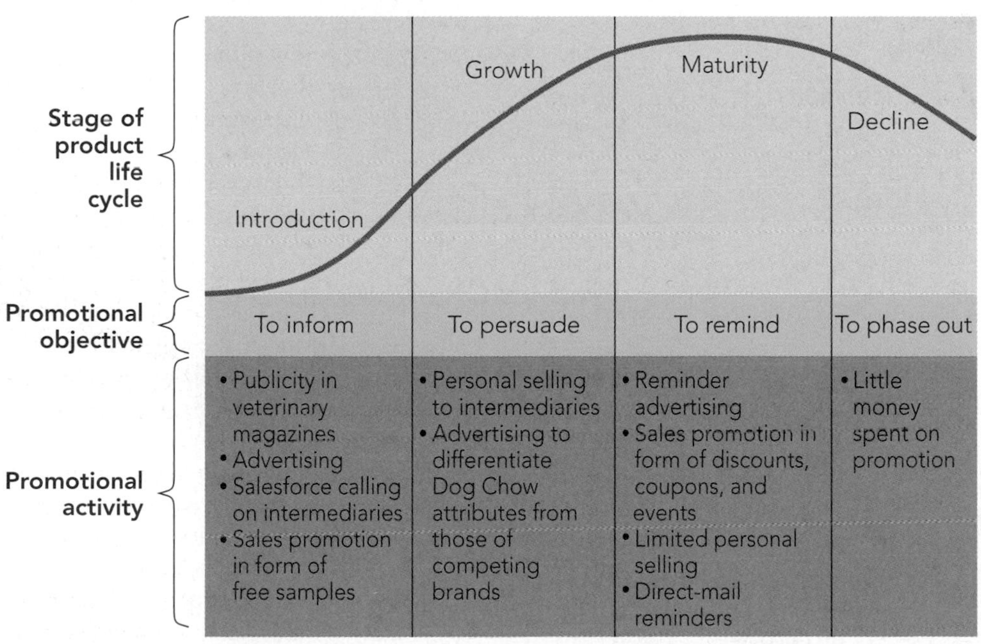

product life cycle. In general, all the promotional mix elements are used at this time, although the use of specific mix elements during any stage depends on the product and situation. News releases about Purina's new nutritional product are sent to veterinary magazines, trial samples are sent to registered dog owners, advertisements are placed in *Dog World* magazine, and the salesforce begins to approach supermarkets to get orders. Advertising is particularly important as a means of reaching as many people as possible to build awareness and interest. Publicity may even begin slightly before the product is commercially available.

Growth Stage The primary promotional objective of the growth stage is to persuade the consumer to buy the product—Purina Dog Chow—rather than substitutes, so the marketing manager seeks to gain brand preference and solidify distribution. Sales promotion assumes less importance in this stage, and publicity is not a factor because it depends on novelty of the product. The primary promotional element is advertising, which stresses brand differences. Personal selling is used to solidify the channel of distribution. For consumer products such as dog food, the salesforce calls on the wholesalers and retailers in hopes of increasing inventory levels and gaining shelf space. For business products, the salesforce often tries to get contractual arrangements to be the sole source of supply for the buyer.

Maturity Stage In the maturity stage, the need is to maintain existing buyers, and advertising's role is to remind buyers of the product's existence. Sales promotion, in the form of discounts and coupons offered to both ultimate consumers and intermediaries, is important in maintaining loyal buyers. In a test of one mature consumer product, it was found that 80 percent of the product's sales at this stage resulted from sales promotions.[15] Sponsoring events can also help maintain loyalty. For the past 12 years, Purina has sponsored the Incredible Dog Challenge, which is now covered by ABC and is available as podcasts from the Purina Web site.[16] Direct marketing actions such as direct mail are used to maintain involvement with existing customers and to encourage repeat purchases. Price cuts and discounts can also significantly increase a mature brand's sales. The salesforce at this stage seeks to satisfy intermediaries. An unsatisfied customer who switches brands is hard to replace.

Purina sponsors the Incredible Dog Challenge to maintain existing buyers.

Decline Stage The decline stage of the product life cycle is usually a period of phaseout for the product, and little money is spent in the promotional mix. The rate of decline can be rapid when a product is replaced by an improved or lower cost product, for example, or slow if there is a loyal group of customers.

Product Characteristics

The proper blend of elements in the promotional mix also depends on the type of product. Three specific characteristics should be considered: complexity, risk, and ancillary services. *Complexity* refers to the technical sophistication of the product and hence the amount of understanding required to use it. It's hard to provide much information in a one-page magazine ad or a 30-second television ad, so the more complex the product, the greater the emphasis on personal selling. Gulfstream asks potential customers to call their senior vice president in its ads. No information is provided for simple products such as Heinz ketchup.

A second element is the degree of risk represented by the product's purchase. *Risk* for the buyer can be assessed in terms of financial risk, social risk, and physi-

How do Gulfstream aircraft and Heinz ketchup differ on complexity, risk, and ancillary services?

Gulfstream
www.gulfstreamvsp.com

Heinz
www.heinz.com

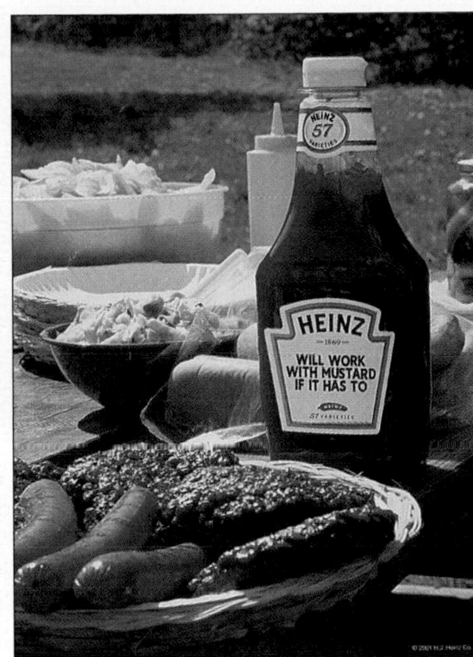

cal risk. A private jet, for example, might represent all three risks—it is expensive, employees and customers may see and evaluate the purchase, and safety and reliability are important. Although advertising helps, the greater the risk, the greater the need for personal selling. Consumers are unlikely to associate any of these risks with ketchup.

The level of ancillary services required by a product also affects the promotional strategy. *Ancillary services* pertain to the degree of service or support required after the sale. This characteristic is common to many industrial products and consumer purchases. Who will provide maintenance for the plane? Advertising's role is to establish the seller's reputation. Direct marketing can be used to describe how a product or service can be customized to individual needs. However, personal selling is essential to build buyer confidence and provide evidence of customer service.

Stages of the Buying Decision

Knowing the customer's stage of decision making can also affect the promotional mix. Figure 18–4 on the next page shows how the importance of the promotional elements varies with the three stages in the consumer purchase decision process.

Prepurchase Stage In the prepurchase stage, advertising is more helpful than personal selling because advertising informs the potential customer of the existence of the product and the seller. Sales promotion in the form of free samples also can play an important role to gain low-risk trial. When the salesperson calls on the customer after heavy advertising, there is some recognition of what the salesperson represents. This is particularly important in industrial settings in which sampling of the product is usually not possible.

Purchase Stage At the purchase stage, the importance of personal selling is highest, whereas the impact of advertising is lowest. Sales promotion in the form of coupons, deals, point-of-purchase displays, and rebates can be very helpful in encouraging demand. In this stage, although advertising is not an active influence

FIGURE 18–4
How the importance of promotional elements varies during the stages of the consumer purchase decision process

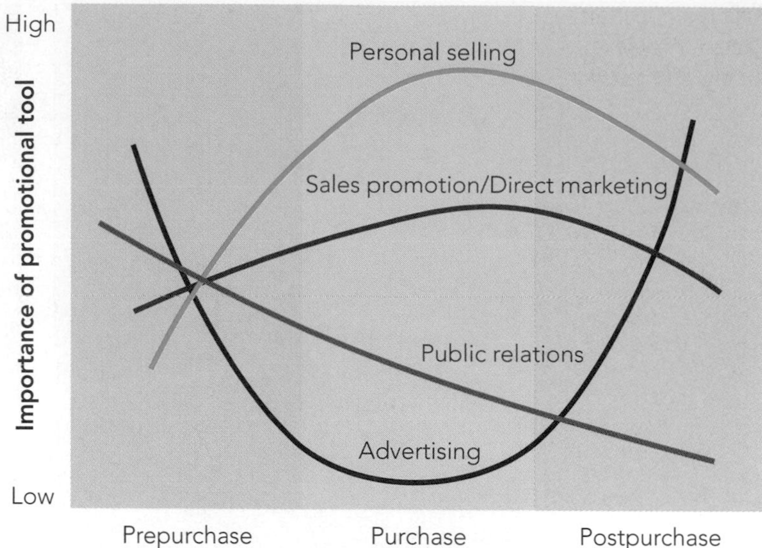

on the purchase, it is the means of delivering the coupons, deals, and rebates that are often important. Recent research indicates that direct marketing activities shorten the time consumers take to adopt a product or service.[17]

Postpurchase Stage In the postpurchase stage, the salesperson is still important. In fact, the more personal contact after the sale, the more the buyer is satisfied. Advertising is also important to assure the buyer that the right purchase was made. Advertising and personal selling help reduce the buyer's postpurchase anxiety. Sales promotion in the form of coupons and direct marketing reminders can help encourage repeat purchases from satisfied first-time triers. Public relations plays a small role in the postpurchase stage.[18]

Channel Strategies

Chapter 15 discussed the channel flow from a producer to intermediaries to consumers. Achieving control of the channel is often difficult for the manufacturer, and promotional strategies can assist in moving a product through the channel of distribution. This is where a manufacturer has to make an important decision about whether to use a push strategy, pull strategy, or both in its channel of distribution.[19]

Push Strategy Figure 18–5A shows how a manufacturer uses a **push strategy**, directing the promotional mix to channel members to gain their cooperation in ordering and stocking the product. In this approach, personal selling and sales promotions play major roles. Salespeople call on wholesalers to encourage orders and provide sales assistance. Sales promotions, such as case discount allowances (20 percent off the regular case price), are offered to stimulate demand. By pushing the product through the channel, the goal is to get channel members to push it to their customers.

Ford Motor Company, for example, provides support and incentives for its 3,700 Ford and Lincoln-Mercury dealers. Through a multi-level program, Ford provides incentives to reward dealers for meeting sales goals. Dealers receive an incentive when they are near a goal, another when they reach a goal, and a larger incentive if they exceed sales projections. Ford also offers

Why does this ad suggest readers should "Ask Your Doctor"? For the answer, see the text.

FIGURE 18–5
A comparison of push and pull promotional strategies

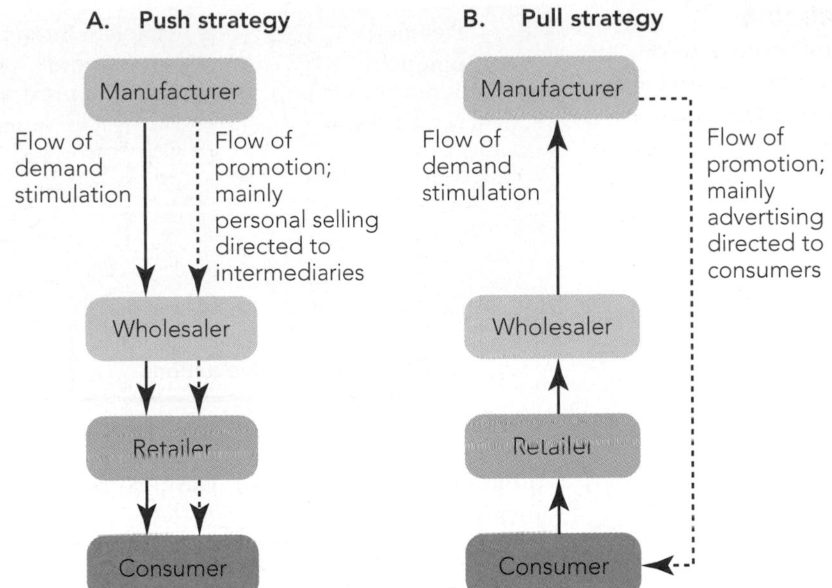

some dealers special incentives for maintaining superior facilities or improving customer service. All of these actions are intended to encourage Ford dealers to "push" the Ford products through the channel to consumers.[20]

Pull Strategy In some instances, manufacturers face resistance from channel members who do not want to order a new product or increase inventory levels of an existing brand. As shown in Figure 18–5B, a manufacturer may then elect to implement a **pull strategy** by directing its promotional mix at ultimate consumers to encourage them to ask the retailer for a product. Seeing demand from ultimate consumers, retailers order the product from wholesalers and thus the item is pulled through the intermediaries. Pharmaceutical companies, for example, now spend more than $5 billion annually on *direct-to-consumer* prescription drug advertising, to complement traditional personal selling and free samples directed only at doctors.[21] The strategy is designed to encourage consumers to ask their doctor for a specific drug by name—pulling it through the channel. Successful campaigns such as the print ad which says, "Ask your doctor if Zetia is right for you," can have dramatic effects on the sales of a product.

learning review

7. Describe the promotional objective for each stage of the product life cycle.
8. At what stage of the consumer purchase decision process is the importance of personal selling highest? Why?
9. Explain the differences between a push strategy and a pull strategy.

DEVELOPING AN IMC PROGRAM

LO4

Because media costs are high, promotion decisions must be made carefully, using a systematic approach. Paralleling the planning, implementation, and evaluation steps described in the strategic marketing process (Chapter 2), the promotion decision process is divided into (1) developing, (2) executing, and (3) assessing the promotion

FIGURE 18–6
The promotion decision process includes planning, implementation, and evaluation.

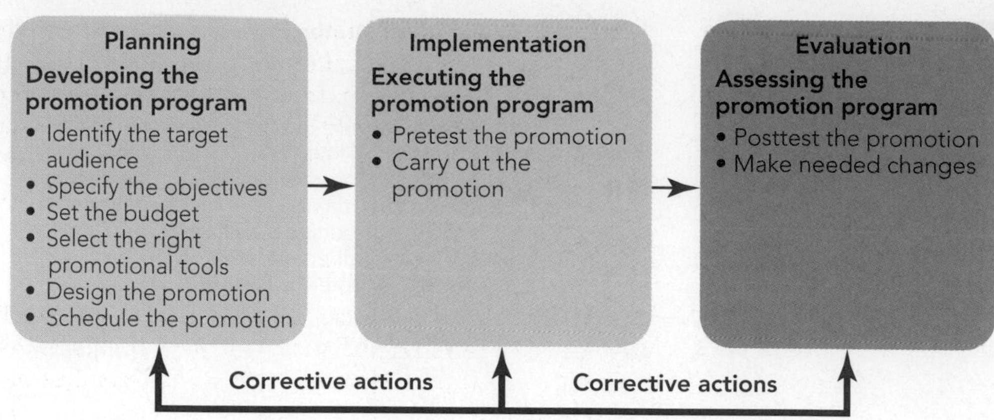

program (see Figure 18–6). Development of the promotion program focuses on the four *Ws*:

- *Who* is the target audience?
- *What* are (1) the promotion objectives, (2) the amounts of money that can be budgeted for the promotion program, and (3) the kinds of promotion to use?
- *Where* should the promotion be run?
- *When* should the promotion be run?

Identifying the Target Audience

The first decision in developing the promotion program is identifying the *target audience*, the group of prospective buyers toward which a promotion program is directed. To the extent that time and money permit, the target audience for the promotion program is the target market for the firm's product, which is identified from marketing research and market segmentation studies. The more a firm knows about its target audiences—including their lifestyle, attitudes, and values—the easier it is to develop a promotion program. If a firm wanted to reach you with television and magazine ads, for example, it would need to know what TV shows you watch and what magazines you read.

Specifying Promotion Objectives

After the target audience is identified, a decision must be reached on what the promotion should accomplish. Consumers can be said to respond in terms of a **hierarchy of effects**, which is the sequence of stages a prospective buyer goes through from initial awareness of a product to eventual action (either trial or adoption of the product).[22] The five stages are:

- *Awareness*—the consumer's ability to recognize and remember the product or brand name.
- *Interest*—an increase in the consumer's desire to learn about some of the features of the product or brand.
- *Evaluation*—the consumer's appraisal of the product or brand on important attributes.
- *Trial*—the consumer's actual first purchase and use of the product or brand.
- *Adoption*—through a favorable experience on the first trial, the consumer's repeated purchase and use of the product or brand.

For a totally new product, the sequence applies to the entire product category, but for a new brand competing in an established product category it applies to the brand itself. These steps can serve as guidelines for developing promotion objectives.

Although sometimes an objective for a promotion program involves several steps in the hierarchy of effects, it often focuses on a single stage. Regardless of what the specific objective might be, from building awareness to increasing repeat purchases, promotion objectives should possess three important qualities. They should (1) be designed for a well-defined target audience, (2) be measurable, and (3) cover a specified time period.

Setting the Promotion Budget

From Figure 18–7 it is clear that the promotion expenditures needed to reach U.S. households are enormous. Note that four companies—Procter & Gamble, AT&T, Verizon, and General Motors—each spend a total of more than $3 billion annually on promotion.[23]

After setting the promotion objectives, a company must decide how much to spend. Determining the ideal amount for the budget is difficult because there is no precise way to measure the exact results of spending promotion dollars. However, several methods can be used to set the promotion budget.[24]

Percentage of Sales In the **percentage of sales budgeting** approach, funds are allocated to promotion as a percentage of past or anticipated sales, in terms of either dollars or units sold. A common budgeting method, this approach is often stated in terms such as "Our promotion budget for this year is 3 percent of last year's gross sales."[25] The advantage of this approach is obvious: It is simple and provides a financial safeguard by tying the promotion budget to sales. However, there is a major fallacy in this approach, which implies that sales cause promotion. Using this method, a company may reduce its promotion budget because of a downturn in past sales or an anticipated downturn in future sales—situations in which it may need promotion the most. See the Using Marketing Dashboards box on the next page for an application of the promotion-to-sales ratio to the automotive industry.

Competitive Parity A second common approach, **competitive parity budgeting**, is matching the competitor's absolute level of spending or the proportion per point of market share. This approach has also been referred to as *matching competitors* or *share of market*. It is important to consider the competition in budgeting. Consumer responses to promotion are affected by competing promotional activities, so if a competitor runs 30 radio ads each week, it may be difficult for a firm to get its message across with only five messages. The competitor's budget level, however,

FIGURE 18–7
U.S. promotion expenditures of the top 10 companies

Rank	Company	Advertising (millions $)	+	All Other Promotion (millions $)	=	Total (millions $)
1	Procter & Gamble	$3,700		$1,530		$5,230
2	AT&T	$2,245		$962		$3,207
3	Verizon	$2,144		$872		$3,016
4	General Motors	$2,062		$948		$3,010
5	Time Warner	$1,738		$1,224		$2,962
6	Ford	$1,653		$872		$2,525
7	GlaxoSmithKline	$1,187		$1,270		$2,457
8	Johnson & Johnson	$1,421		$988		$2,409
9	Disney	$1,387		$906		$2,293
10	Unilever	$910		$1,336		$2,246

Using Marketing Dashboards

How Much Should You Spend on IMC?

Integrated marketing communications programs coordinate a variety of promotion alternatives to provide a consistent message across audiences. The amount spent on the various promotional elements, or on the total campaign, may vary depending on the target audience, the type of product, where the product is in the product life cycle, and the channel strategy selected. Managers often use the promotion-to-sales ratio on their marketing dashboard to assess how effective the IMC program expenditures are at generating sales.

Your Challenge As a manager at General Motors you've been asked to assess the effectiveness of all promotion expenditures during the past year. The promotion-to-sales ratio can be used by managers to make year-to-year comparisons of their programs, to compare the effectiveness of their program with competitor's programs, or to make comparisons with industry averages. You decide to calculate the promotion-to-sales ratio for General Motors. In addition, to allow a comparison, you decide to make the same calculation for one of your competitors, Ford, and for the entire automobile industry. The ratio is calculated as follows:

Promotion-to-sales ratio =
Total promotion expenditures/Total sales

Your Findings The information needed for these calculations is readily available from trade publications and annual reports. The following graph shows the promotion-to-sales ratio for General Motors and Ford (two companies featured in Figure 18–7) and the automotive industry. General Motors spent $3.01 billion on its IMC program to generate $182 billion in U.S. sales for a ratio of 1.65 (percent). Ford's ratio was 1.47, and the industry average was 1.56.

Your Action General Motors' promotion-to-sales ratio is higher than Ford's and higher than the industry average. This suggests that the current mix of promotional activities and the level of expenditures may not be creating an effective IMC program. In the future you will want to monitor the factors that may influence the ratio. The average ratio for the beverage industry has risen to 9 while the average for grocery stores is about 1.

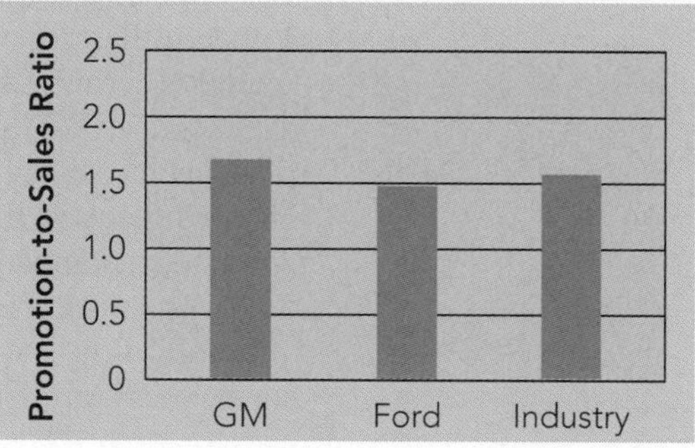

should not be the only determinant in setting a company's budget. The competition might have very different promotional objectives, which require a different level of promotion expenditures.[26]

All You Can Afford Common to many small businesses is **all-you-can-afford budgeting**, in which money is allocated to promotion only after all other budget items are covered. As one company executive said in reference to this budgeting process, "Why, it's simple. First, I go upstairs to the controller and ask how much they can afford to give us this year. She says a million and a half. Later, the boss comes to me and asks how much we should spend, and I say 'Oh, about a million and a half.' Then we have our promotion appropriation."[27]

Fiscally conservative, this approach has little else to offer. Using this budgeting philosophy, a company acts as though it doesn't know anything about a promotion-sales relationship or what its promotion objectives are.

Objective and Task The best approach to budgeting is **objective and task budgeting**, whereby the company (1) determines its promotion objectives, (2) outlines the tasks to accomplish these objectives, and (3) determines the promotion cost of performing these tasks.[28] This method takes into account what the company wants to accomplish and requires that the objectives be specified.[29] Strengths of the other budgeting methods are integrated into this approach because each previous method's strength is tied to the objectives. For example, if the costs are beyond what the company can afford, objectives are reworked and the tasks revised. The difficulty with this method is the judgment required to determine the tasks needed to accomplish objectives.

Selecting the Right Promotional Tools

Once a budget has been determined, the combination of the five basic IMC tools—advertising, personal selling, sales promotion, public relations, and direct marketing—can be specified. While many factors provide direction for selection of the appropriate mix, the large number of possible combinations of the promotional tools means that many combinations can achieve the same objective. Therefore, an analytical approach and experience are particularly important in this step of the promotion decision process. The specific mix can vary from a simple program using a single tool to a comprehensive program using all forms of promotion. The Olympics have become a very visible example of a comprehensive integrated communication program. Because the Games are repeated every two years, the promotion is continuous during "on" and "off" years. Included in the program are advertising campaigns, personal selling efforts by the Olympic committee and organizers, sales promotion activities such as product tie-ins and sponsorships, public relations programs managed by the host cities, online and digital communication, and direct marketing efforts targeted at a variety of audiences including governments, organizations, firms, athletes, and individuals.[30] At this stage, it is also important to assess the relative importance of the various tools. While it may be desirable to utilize and integrate several forms of promotion, one may deserve emphasis. The Olympics, for example, place primary importance on public relations and publicity.

The Olympics use a comprehensive IMC program.

Designing the Promotion

The central element of a promotion program is the promotion itself. Advertising consists of advertising copy and the artwork that the target audience is intended to see or hear. Personal selling efforts depend on the characteristics and skills of the salesperson. Sales promotion activities consist of the specific details of inducements such as coupons, samples, and sweepstakes. Public relations efforts are readily seen in tangible elements such as news releases, and direct marketing actions depend on written, verbal, and electronic forms of delivery. The design of the promotion will play a primary role in determining the message that is communicated to the audience. This design activity is frequently viewed as the step requiring the most creativity. In addition, successful designs are often the result of insight regarding consumer's interests and purchasing behavior. All of the promotion tools have many design alternatives. Advertising, for example, can utilize fear, humor, attractiveness, or other themes in its appeal. Similarly, direct marketing can be designed for varying levels of personal or customized appeals. One of the challenges of IMC is to design each promotional activity to communicate the same message.[31]

Scheduling the Promotion

Once the design of each of the promotional program elements is complete, it is important to determine the most effective timing of their use. The promotion schedule describes the order in which each promotional tool is introduced and the frequency of its use during the campaign.

Movie studio Columbia Pictures, for example, uses a schedule of several promotional tools for its movies. To generate interest in a movie such as *Angels and*

What promotional tools did Columbia Pictures use to support the release of this movie?

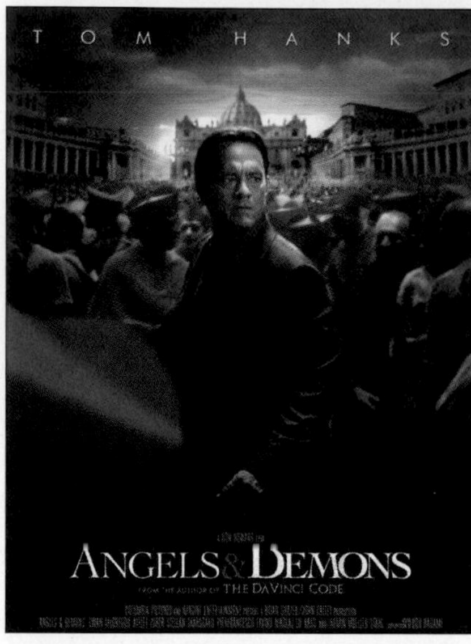

Demons, a commercial was aired during the Super Bowl. The commercial generated more than 700,000 visits to the *Angels and Demons* Web site, which provided movie previews and clips, a Facebook link, and a contest with prizes related to movie scenes. In addition, Columbia held a press conference for science, religion, and entertainment journalists to initiate a public dialog that would appear in periodicals, blogs, and social networks. It also released a movie "trailer" that was shown on television and in theaters. Then movie-related partnerships such as Mastercard's promotion offering an opportunity to win tickets to a pre-screening of the film were announced. After the movie was released another contest and VIP parties encouraged fans to consider purchasing the DVD.[32]

Overall, the scheduling of the various promotions was designed to generate interest, bring consumers into theaters, and then encourage additional purchases after seeing the movie. Several factors such as seasonality and competitive promotion activity can also influence the promotion schedule. Businesses such as ski resorts, airlines, and professional sports teams are likely to reduce their promotional activity during the "off" season. Similarly, restaurants, retail stores, and health clubs are likely to increase their promotional activity when new competitors enter the market.

EXECUTING AND ASSESSING THE PROMOTION PROGRAM

Carrying out the promotion program can be expensive and time consuming. One researcher estimates that "an organization with sales less than $10 million can successfully implement an IMC program in one year, one with sales between $200 million and $500 million will need about three years, and one with sales between $2 billion and $5 billion will need five years." In addition, firms with a market orientation are more likely to implement an IMC program.[33] To facilitate the transition, approximately 200 integrated marketing communications agencies are in operation. In addition, some of the largest agencies are adopting approaches that embrace "total communications solutions."

Media agency Initiative, which recently won *Advertising Age* magazine's Media Agency of the Year award, for example, is part of an integrated network of 2,500 marketing professionals with 91 offices in 70 countries. The agency's services include planning, media buying, digital solutions, consumer research, ROI assessment, and sports and entertainment marketing. One of its integrated campaigns for Carl's Jr. restaurants included a partnership with the cable program *Family Guy*, a rap song for radio, bus bench advertising, video gaming, sports tie-ins, and free ring tones. The campaign resulted in a 47 percent increase in sales. Initiative has used this approach with other clients including Hyundai, MillerCoors, Dr Pepper, and Bayer. CEO Tim Spengler explains that one of the keys to the agency's success is an operations committee that encourages integration by including representatives that represent all forms of promotion. While many agencies may still be specialists, the trend today is clearly toward a long-term perspective in which all forms of promotion are integrated.[34]

An important factor in developing successful IMC programs is to create a process that facilitates their design and use. A tool used to evaluate a company's current process is the IMC audit. The audit analyzes the internal communication network of the company; identifies key audiences; evaluates customer databases; assesses messages in recent advertising, public relations releases, packaging, Web sites, and e-mail communication, signage, sales promotions, and direct mail; and determines the IMC expertise of company and agency personnel.[35] This process is becoming increasingly important as consumer-generated media such as blogs, RSS, podcasts, and social networks become more popular and as the use of search engines increases. Now, in addition to ensuring that traditional forms of communication are integrated, companies must be able to monitor consumer content, respond to inconsistent messages, and even answer questions from individual customers.[36]

As shown earlier in Figure 18–6, the ideal execution of a promotion program involves pretesting each design before it is actually used to allow for changes and modifications that improve its effectiveness. Similarly, posttests are recommended to evaluate the impact of each promotion and the contribution of the promotion toward achieving the program objectives. The most sophisticated pretest and posttest procedures have been developed for advertising and are discussed in Chapter 19. Testing procedures for sales promotion and direct marketing efforts currently focus on comparisons of different designs or responses of different segments. To fully benefit from IMC programs, companies must create and maintain a test-result database that allows comparisons of the relative impact of the promotional tools and their execution options in varying situations. Information from the database will allow informed design and execution decisions and provide support for IMC activities during internal reviews by financial or administrative personnel. The San Diego Padres baseball team, for example, developed a database of information relating attendance to its integrated campaign using a new logo, special events, merchandise sales, and a loyalty program.

Currently, about one-fourth of all businesses assess program effectiveness by measuring "most of their communication tactics."[37] For most organizations, the assessment focuses on trying to determine which element of promotion works better. In an integrated program, however, media advertising might be used to build awareness, sales promotion to generate an inquiry, direct mail to provide additional information to individual prospects, and a personal sales call to complete the transaction. The tools are used for different reasons, and their combined use creates a synergy that should be the focus of the assessment.[38] Another level of assessment is necessary when firms have international promotion programs.

learning review

10. What are the characteristics of good promotion objectives?
11. What is the weakness of the percentage of sales budgeting approach?
12. How have advertising agencies changed to facilitate the use of IMC programs?

DIRECT MARKETING

LO5

Direct marketing has many forms and utilizes a variety of media. Several forms of direct marketing—direct mail and catalogs, television home shopping, telemarketing, and direct selling—were discussed as methods of nonstore retailing in Chapter 17. In addition, although advertising is discussed in Chapter 19, a form of advertising—direct response advertising—is an important form of direct marketing. Finally, interactive marketing is discussed in detail in Chapter 21. In this section, the growth of direct marketing, its value for consumers and sellers, and key global, technological, and ethical issues are discussed.

The Growth of Direct Marketing

The increasing interest in customer relationship management is reflected in the dramatic growth of direct marketing. The ability to customize communication efforts and create one-to-one interactions is appealing to most marketers, particularly those with IMC programs. While many direct marketing methods are not new, the ability

FIGURE 18–8
Business usage and response rates of popular forms of direct marketing

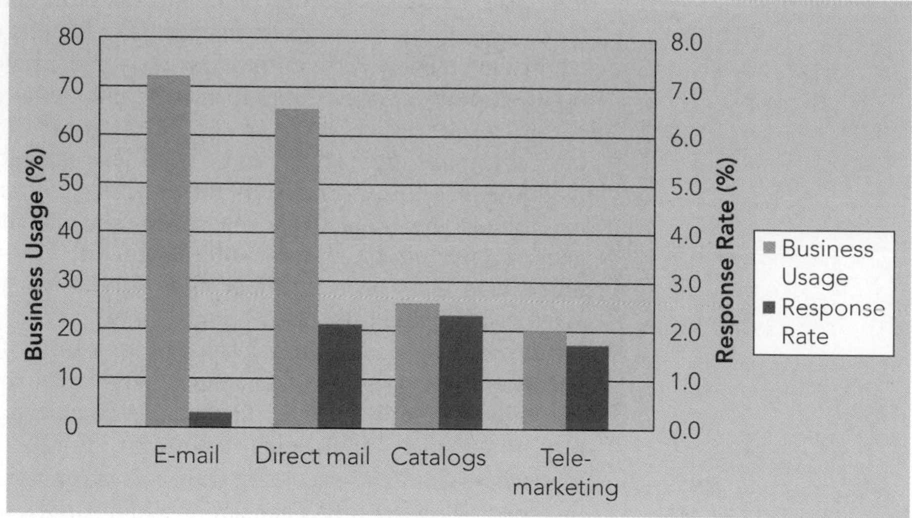

to design and use them has increased with the availability of customer information databases and new printing technologies. In recent years, direct marketing growth has outpaced total economic growth. Direct marketing expenditures of $183 billion are expected to grow at a rate of 4 percent. Similarly, 2009 revenues of $2.1 trillion are expected to grow to $2.66 trillion by 2013. Direct marketing currently accounts for 10 percent of the total U.S. gross domestic product. Figure 18–8 shows some of the most popular forms of direct marketing and their typical response rates. For example, e-mail is the most popular method. It is used by 72 percent of marketers and generates less than a 1 percent response rate.[39]

While e-mail is the most common form of direct marketing, most campaigns use several methods. JCPenney is one example of a company that has integrated its direct marketing activities. The company recently launched an interactive, virtual "runway show" by sending 15 million potential customers an e-mail inviting them to an online experience at www.jcp.com. Once consumers visit the Web site, JCPenney uses other forms of direct marketing, such as direct mail and catalogs, to follow up on the initial e-mail and online contacts. Many companies also integrate their direct marketing with other forms of promotion. Dannon, for example, uses television advertising and direct mail to promote its Activia brand yogurt products.[40]

Another component of the growth in direct marketing is the increasing popularity of the Internet. As discussed in Chapter 21, total online sales have risen from close to nothing in 1996 to projections of $903 billion in 2013. Continued growth in the number of consumers with Internet access and the number of businesses with Web sites and electronic commerce offerings is likely to contribute to the future growth of direct marketing.

The Value of Direct Marketing

One of the most visible indicators of the value of direct marketing for consumers is the level of use of various forms of direct marketing. For example, 45 percent of the U.S. population has ordered merchandise or services by mail, phone, or Internet; 68 percent of households with Internet access shop online; consumers spent more than $156 billion on products available through television offers; and more than 21 percent of all adults make three to five purchases from a catalog each year. Consumers report many benefits, including the following: They don't have to go to a store; they can usually shop 24 hours a day; buying direct saves time; they avoid hassles with salespeople; they can save money; it's fun and entertaining; and direct marketing offers more privacy than in-store shopping. Many consumers also believe that direct marketing provides excellent customer service. Toll-free telephone numbers, customer service representatives with access to information regarding purchasing preferences, overnight delivery services, and unconditional guarantees all help create value for direct marketing customers. At Landsend.com, when customers need assistance they can click the Live Help icon to receive help from a sales representative on the phone or online until the correct product is found. "It's like we were walking down the aisle in a store," says one Lands' End customer![41]

The value of direct marketing for sellers can be described in terms of the responses it generates. **Direct orders** are the result of offers that contain all the information necessary for a prospective buyer to make a decision to purchase and complete the transaction. Priceline.com, for example, will send *PriceBreaker* RSS alerts to people in its database. The messages offer discounted fares and rates to customers who can travel on very short notice. **Lead generation** is the result of an offer designed to generate interest in a product or service and a request for additional information. Four Seasons Hotels now sell private residences in several of their properties and send direct mail to prospective residents asking them to request additional information on the telephone or through a Web site. Finally, **traffic generation** is the outcome of an offer designed to motivate people to visit a business. Home Depot, for example, uses an opt-in e-mail alert to announce special sales that attract consumers to the store. Similarly, The Gap uses e-mails with coupons to increase store traffic.[42]

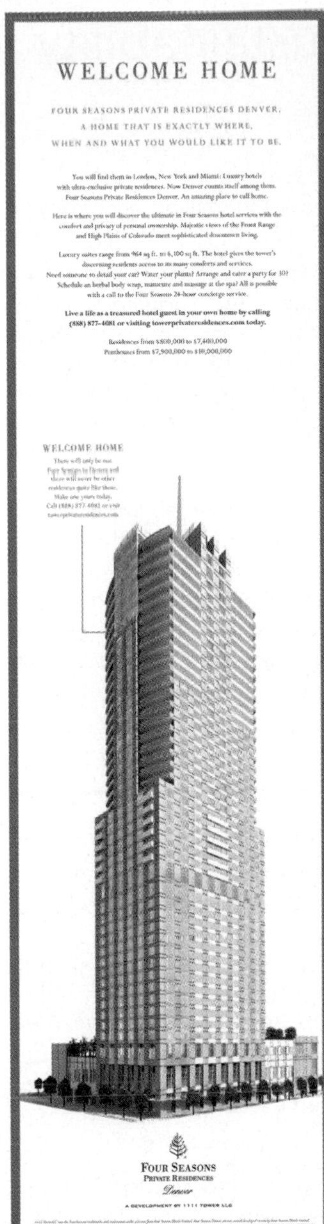

Four Seasons uses direct mail to generate leads for its private residences.

Technological, Global, and Ethical Issues in Direct Marketing

The information technology and databases described in Chapter 8 are key elements in any direct marketing program. Databases are the result of organizations' efforts to create profiles of customers so that direct marketing tools, such as e-mail and catalogs, can be directed at specific customers. While most companies try to keep records of their customer's past purchases, many other types of data are needed to use direct marketing to develop one-to-one relationships with customers. Some data, such as lifestyles, media use, and demographics, are best collected from the consumer. Other types of data, such as price, quantity, and brand, are best collected from the businesses where purchases are made. Increases in postage rates and the decline in the economy have also increased the importance of information related to the cost of direct marketing activities. Brookstone, for example, uses its database to mail more than 70 million catalogs to a specific profile of target customer each year. In addition, when the number of catalogs being sent to individual carrier routes is small, the database can add names to qualify for U.S. Postal Service discounts. This approach saves Brookstone \$5,000 to \$15,000 in postage each time it mails a catalog.[43]

Direct marketing faces several challenges and opportunities in global markets today. Several countries such as Italy and Denmark, for example, have requirements for mandatory "opt-in"—that is, potential customers must give permission to include their name on a list for direct marketing solicitations. In addition the mail, telephone, and Internet systems in many countries are not as well developed as they are in the United States. The need for improved reliability and security in these countries has slowed the growth of direct mail, while the dramatic growth of mobile phone penetration has created an opportunity for direct mobile marketing campaigns. Another issue for global direct marketers is payment. The availability of credit and credit cards varies throughout the world, creating the need for alternatives such as C.O.D. (cash on delivery), bank deposits, and online payment accounts.[44]

Global and domestic direct marketers both face challenging ethical and sustainability issues today. Concerns about privacy, for example, have led to various attempts to provide guidelines that balance consumer and business interests. The European Union passed a consumer privacy law, called the *Data Protection Directive*, after several years of discussion with the Federation of European Direct Marketing and the U.K.'s Direct Marketing Association. In the United States, the Federal Trade Commission and many state legislatures have also been concerned about privacy.

Making Responsible Decisions > > > > sustainability

Can Direct Marketing "Go Green"?

Each year consumers receive more than 100 billion pieces of direct mail. While this accounts for only 2.4 percent of the waste that ends up in landfills, it represents a huge opportunity for the direct marketing industry to adopt "green" business practices. A group of direct marketing companies and some of their corporate clients, called the Green Marketing Coalition, are developing best-practices guidelines. In addition, the United States Postal Service offers "green ideas for mailers" on its Web site. Some of the guidelines and ideas include:

- Use chlorine-free recycled paper.
- Create an "environMAIList" by removing names of people who are unlikely to respond.
- Let people easily opt out of mailings.
- Use paper from forests certified by The Sustainable Forest Initiative or the Forest Stewardship Council.
- Use printers with green certification.
- Encourage customers to recycle the mailing once they've read it.

These guidelines will have increasing importance as the direct marketing industry continues to grow. Experts have observed that there has been a 35 percent shift in spending from telemarketing to direct marketing since the Do Not Call Registry came into effect in the United States. To evaluate the environmental impact of a company, you can use the Direct Marketing Association's checklist called the Environmental Planning Tool (www.the-dma.org/envgen/envgen1.php). Can you think of other ideas that would help the direct marketing industry minimize its impact on the environment?

Several bills that call for a do-not-mail registry similar to the Do Not Call Registry are being discussed. Similarly, the proliferation of e-mail advertising, or "spam," has received increasing attention from consumers and marketers. Finally, in response to concerns raised by environmentalists, the industry is developing "green" best-practices guidelines for direct marketing companies.[45] The Making Responsible Decisions box offers examples of some of the guidelines.[46]

learning review

13. The ability to design and use direct marketing programs has increased with the availability of ________________ and ________________.
14. What are the three types of responses generated by direct marketing activities?

LEARNING OBJECTIVES REVIEW

LO1 *Discuss integrated marketing communication and the communication process.*

Integrated marketing communication is the concept of designing marketing communications programs that coordinate all promotional activities—advertising, personal selling, sales promotion, public relations, and direct marketing—to provide a consistent message across all audiences. The communication process conveys messages with six elements: a source, a message, a channel of communication, a receiver, and encoding and decoding. The communication process also includes a feedback loop and can be distorted by noise.

LO2 *Describe the promotional mix and the uniqueness of each component.*

There are five promotional alternatives. Advertising, sales promotion, and public relations are mass selling approaches, whereas personal selling and direct marketing use customized messages. Advertising can have high absolute costs but reaches large numbers of people. Personal selling has a high cost per contact but provides immediate feedback. Public relations is often difficult to obtain but is very credible. Sales promotion influences short-term consumer behavior. Direct marketing can help develop customer relationships although maintaining a database can be very expensive.

LO3 *Select the promotional approach appropriate to a product's target audience, life-cycle stage, and characteristics, as well as stages of the buying decision and channel strategies.*

The promotional mix depends on the target audience. Programs for consumers, business buyers, and intermediaries might emphasize advertising, personal selling, and sales promotion, respectively. The promotional mix also changes over the product life-cycle stages. During the introduction stage, all promotional mix elements are used. During the growth stage advertising is emphasized, while the maturity stage utilizes sales promotion and direct marketing. Little promotion is used during the decline stage. Product characteristics also help determine the promotion mix. The level of complexity, risk, and ancillary services required will determine which element is needed. Knowing the customer's stage in the buying process can help select appropriate promotions. Advertising and public relations can create awareness in the prepurchase stage, personal selling and sales promotion can facilitate the purchase, and advertising can help reduce anxiety in the postpurchase stage. Finally, the promotional mix can depend on the channel strategy. Push strategies require personal selling and sales promotions directed at channel members, while pull strategies depend on advertising and sales promotion directed at consumers.

LO4 *Describe the elements of the promotion decision process.*
The promotional decision process consists of three steps: planning, implementation, and evaluation. The planning step consists of six elements: identify the target audience, specify the objectives, set the budget, select the right promotional elements, design the promotion, and schedule the promotion. The implementation step includes pretesting. The evaluation step includes posttesting.

LO5 *Explain the value of direct marketing for consumers and sellers.*
The value of direct marketing for consumers is indicated by its level of use. For example, 68 percent of them have made a purchase by phone or mail, and 12 million people have purchased items from a television offer. The value of direct marketing for sellers can be measured in terms of three types of responses: direct orders, lead generation, and traffic generation.

FOCUSING ON KEY TERMS

advertising p. 460
all-you-can-afford budgeting p. 472
channel of communication p. 458
communication p. 458
competitive parity budgeting p. 471
decoding p. 459
direct marketing p. 463
direct orders p. 477
encoding p. 459
feedback p. 460
field of experience p. 459
hierarchy of effects p. 470
integrated marketing communications (IMC) p. 458
lead generation p. 477
message p. 458
noise p. 460
objective and task budgeting p. 472
percentage of sales budgeting p. 471
personal selling p. 461
promotional mix p. 458
public relations p. 462
publicity p. 462
pull strategy p. 469
push strategy p. 468
receivers p. 458
response p. 460
sales promotion p. 463
source p. 458
traffic generation p. 477

APPLYING MARKETING KNOWLEDGE

1 After listening to a recent sales presentation, Mary Smith signed up for membership at the local health club. On arriving at the facility, she learned there was an additional fee for racquetball court rentals. "I don't remember that in the sales talk; I thought they said all facilities were included with the membership fee," complained Mary. Describe the problem in terms of the communication process.

2 Develop a matrix to compare the five elements of the promotional mix on three criteria—to *whom* you deliver the message, *what* you say, and *when* you say it.

3 Explain how the promotional tools used by an airline would differ if the target audience were (*a*) consumers who travel for pleasure and (*b*) corporate travel departments that select the airlines to be used by company employees.

4 Suppose you introduced a new consumer food product and invested heavily both in national advertising (pull strategy) and in training and motivating your field salesforce to sell the product to food stores (push strategy). What kinds of feedback would you receive from both the advertising and your salesforce? How could you increase both the quality and quantity of each?

5 Fisher-Price Company, long known as a manufacturer of children's toys, has introduced a line of clothing for children. Outline a promotional plan to get this product introduced in the marketplace.

6 Many insurance companies sell health insurance plans to companies. In these companies the employees pick the plan, but the set of offered plans is determined by the company. Recently Blue Cross–Blue Shield, a health insurance company, ran a television ad stating, "If your employer doesn't offer you Blue Cross–Blue Shield coverage, ask why." Explain the promotional strategy behind the advertisement.

7 Identify the sales promotion tools that might be useful for (*a*) Tastee Yogurt, a new brand introduction, (*b*) 3M self-sticking Post-it® Notes, and (*c*) Wrigley's Spearmint Gum.

8 Design an integrated marketing communications program—using each of the five promotional elements—for Rhapsody, the online music service.

9 BMW recently introduced its first sport activity vehicle, the X6, to compete with other popular crossover vehicles such as the Mercedes-Benz R-class and Buick's Enclave. Design a direct marketing program to generate (*a*) leads, (*b*) traffic in dealerships, and (*c*) direct orders.

10 Develop a privacy policy for database managers that provides a balance of consumer and seller perspectives. How would you encourage voluntary compliance with your policy? What methods of enforcement would you recommend?

building your marketing plan

To develop the promotion strategy for your marketing plan, follow the steps suggested in the planning phase of the promotion decision process described in Figure 18–6.

1 You should (*a*) identify the target audience, (*b*) specify the promotion objectives, (*c*) set the promotion budget, (*d*) select the right promotion tools, (*e*) design the promotion, and (*f*) schedule the promotion.

2 Also specify the pretesting and posttesting procedures needed in the implementation and control phases.

3 Finally, describe how each of your promotion tools are integrated to provide a consistent message.

video case 18 Under Armour: Using IMC to Create a Brand for this Generation's Athletes

"Under Armour sees itself as the athletic brand of this generation. Everything that we create, every message that we put out, that's what we want to be," observes Marcus Stevens, senior creative director for Under Armour. Stevens is responsible for the complete brand aesthetic across all media, including broadcast, print, Web, and point-of-sale. His responsibility is to attract new customers and increase sales of the brand. When the company introduced its first product, a form-fitting moisture-wicking t-shirt to be worn under sportswear, the branding efforts were limited by a very small budget. Today, Under Armour is undertaking the challenge of creating an integrated marketing campaign that utilizes a much larger pool of resources and still delivers a consistent message. As a result of Under Armour's communication activities, "We are poised for growth in the future," explains Stevens.

THE COMPANY

Under Armour was founded by Kevin Plank, a University of Maryland football player who didn't like changing out of the sweat-soaked t-shirts he wore under his jersey during practice and games. In 1996 he developed a moisture-wicking fabric and modeled his first product after a typical cotton t-shirt. After several trips to the patent office, and some input from his brother, Kevin decided on the name Under Armour and set up the business in his grandmother's basement. Early sales depended entirely on word-of-mouth advertising that was generated by events such as a *USA Today* photo of an Oakland Raider football player wearing an Under Armour shirt, and Georgia Tech ordering more than 300 shirts for its entire football team. The turning point for the company came when Under Armour products were used in the movie *Any Given Sunday*. Plank decided to build on the exposure provided by the movie and purchased a full-page ad in *ESPN The Magazine*. That ad generated $750,000 in sales and began the incredible growth of the company.

As the company grew, Plank developed four "Keys of Greatness" to guide him and the Under Armour employees. The keys are:

- Build a great product
- Tell a great story about the product
- Provide great service
- Build a great team

The success of Under Armour's first product soon led to a complete line of performance sports apparel including shirts, pants, shorts, outerwear, gloves, footwear, and accessories. Telling the story was the responsibility of the marketing department and emphasized the need for integrated marketing communications. Great service required support from sales and service representatives. Finally, building a great team meant that Plank always hired the best and brightest people possible. The focus on athletes led to many applications of sports concepts to the business—meetings are called "huddles," the huddle doesn't end until a "play is called," and rapid response to changes in the environment may require "calling an audible." The approach creates a team atmosphere where everyone works together to act on the play.

Today, Under Armour's mission is to make all athletes better through passion, science, and the relentless pursuit of innovation. It offers its product assortment to men, women, and youth online and through more than 15,000 retail locations including Dick's Sporting Goods, the Sports Authority, Hibbett Sporting Goods, and Modell's Sporting Goods. International distribution includes outlets in the United Kingdom, France, Germany, Italy, New Zealand, and Japan. Headquarters has moved from Plank's grandmother's basement to Baltimore, Maryland, and the number of employees has increased to 2,200. Under Armour sales now exceed $700 million!

THE IMC PROGRAM

Stevens first met Plank at an advertising agency where Stevens worked. Plank's idea for an athletic brand for this generation's athlete was very exciting and Stevens soon left the agency to work with Plank. With a limited budget, the challenge was getting the message out to consumers. According to Stevens, "We didn't come in with a polished business plan—and a calendar to execute against; we came in with an idea and a lot of passion." To compete with much larger apparel manufacturers Stevens knew that Under Armour's marketing activities would need to provide a consistent message through advertising, public relations, personal selling and all promotional efforts. Kevin Haley, senior vice president of sports marketing, agrees, "everything has to be integrated." Integrating all promotion activities allows Under Armour to increase the effectiveness of its budget as it strives to create and maintain its brand.

Advertising

Following the release of *Any Given Sunday* and their first print ad in *ESPN the Magazine*, Under Armour began work on a new television advertising campaign. The ad, featuring Eric Ogbogu as "Big E," introduced the tagline, "We must protect this house," and was released at the same time as ESPN's new series *Playmakers*, which featured football players wearing Under Armour apparel. According to Steven Battista, senior vice president of brand, the two coinciding events "propelled the brand into the national spotlight, and then soon after that you would see fans at games holding up signs saying, 'Protect this house.'" The phrase was used by sports fans, David Letterman, Oprah Winfrey, and many others and soon became part of American lexicon. Other campaigns also helped develop the Under Armour brand and image. For example, "Click, Clack" featured the familiar sound made by cleated shoes, and appealed to athletes in many sports such as golf, lacrosse, and baseball, in addition to football.

Under Armour decided to advertise on the Super Bowl to introduce a new performance training shoe. The message in the ad focused on the athlete of tomorrow and included the tagline, "The future is ours." The athletes in the ad included Carl Weathers, a NASCAR driver; Ray Lewis, a football linebacker; Kimmie Meissner, a figure skater; and many others. The ad made a statement that Under Armour could help all athletes train like champions. "The future is ours" was a huge success ranking in the top-five ads according to *USA Today*'s Ad Meter. In addition, Web site traffic tripled following the ad and orders for the product began pouring in! The Super Bowl ad also helped make a statement about the Under Armour brand—that the company, the CEO, the product, and the consumers all represented a new prototype for the future.

Public Relations and Promotion

According to Battista, "half the benefit of a 60-second ad in the Super Bowl is the PR leading up to it and the attention you get" from producing and running the advertisement. Marketing benefits also result from promotion activities such as athlete endorsements, sponsorships, and product placements. These activities play an important role in Under Armour's integrated marketing communications

strategy. Each potential athlete endorsement, for example, is evaluated in terms of the products they will be supporting, the media that would be used, and the potential for in-store and on-field visibility. Under Armour signed Alfonso Soriano, a Chicago Cubs baseball player, to support its baseball cleats and baseball apparel, the outdoor advertising at Wrigley Field, and the retail store in the Chicago market. Under Armour looks for athletes that are "all about performance," explains Haley. They "need to be a team player, who is doing everything they can to win on every single play."

Under Armour has also developed many sponsorship relationships with teams and organizations. For example, Under Armour is the official outfitter for the football programs at Auburn University, the University of Delaware, the University of Hawaii, the University of North Texas, the University of South Carolina, and many other schools. The company recently signed a 5-year agreement with the University of Maryland to outfit all of its 27 varsity sports. Similarly, Under Armour is the supplier for all 17 varsity athletic teams at Texas Tech University. Under Armour has also sponsored high school athletes, professional soccer teams, and the NFL.

Product placements in movies, television shows, and video games have reinforced Under Armour's branding efforts and provided exposure to new audiences. In addition to *Any Given Sunday* you may remember seeing Under Armour products in the movies *Gridiron Gang* and *The Replacements*. Television programs with Under Armour product placements include *Friday Night Lights*, *The Sopranos*, and *MTV Road Rules*. Under Armour even appears in video games such as *Tiger Woods Golf* and *Fight Night 3*!

Retail and Online

When Plank first started Under Armour, its Web site (www.underarmour.com) was its only means of sales and distribution. As the company grew it gained distribution in many retailers. The point-of-sale displays in the retailers, however, offered a unique opportunity to integrate Under Armour's branding. When Under Armour moved into large retailers it noticed that the mannequins in the stores didn't look like the athletes in the advertising because the mannequins did not have muscles. To create a consistent message Under Armour made its own mannequins for the stores so that the displays would look like the athletes in the commercials. Eventually, Under Armour also began opening its own stores. The first Under Armour store opened in Annapolis, Maryland in 2008 and many others soon followed.

The Under Armour Web site remains an important part of the integrated marketing program. Approximately 15 percent of all sales come through the Web site, and many Under Armour consumers use the Web site to learn about new products, study technical details, or view print or television ads. Consumers who register on the site can receive e-mail messages about new or seasonal products and new campaigns. Currently, the Under Armour Web site attracts an average of 35,000 visitors each day. The online program also includes several social networking elements. Under Armour, for example, is building a

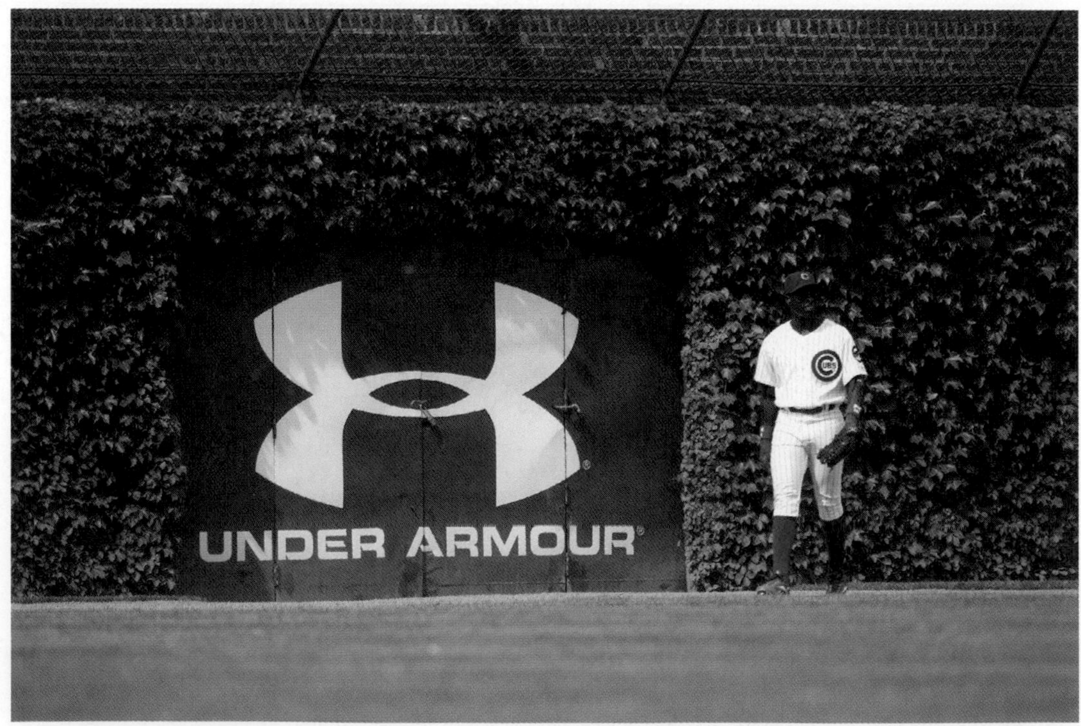

presence on Facebook and on Xbox Live marketplace. All of these activities help ensure that consumers will be exposed to a consistent message regardless of the medium they utilize.

FUTURE STRATEGY

How can Under Armour continue its incredible record of growth? Experts observe that future growth will require the company to broaden its appeal without alienating the original segment of athletes interested in performance. There are opportunities to expand exposure in many sports such as the fast-growing lacrosse segment, to attract more men, women, and youth, and to introduce new products to the current line. Under Armour, for example, recently introduced a line of running shoes—a large category with broad appeal to many consumers. Integrating the growth activities will be critical to the company's success. As Battista observes, everything has to "look right and have the same message points and the same type of branding and look and feel!"

The future is likely to be very exciting for Under Armour as it continues to introduce new products and enter new markets. For example, the company recently introduced mouth guards and a body suit that helps athletes recover from a workout faster. To expand in international markets Under Armour is creating distribution networks in Europe and Asia and signing endorsement deals with rugby players, Olympians, and other international athletes. In addition, to change perceptions that Under Armour products are used primarily by football players, the company now sponsors 27 boys' and girls' high school basketball teams. Under Armour's branding and communication strategies have been extraordinarily successful as the company now is the fastest growing performance sports brand. In fact, the company has grown so quickly that it plans to add an additional 135,000 square feet of new space across the street from its headquarters to provide showrooms and new offices. According to one newspaper headline, the company is a "runaway success"!

Questions

1 What promotional opportunities gave Under Armour its initial success?

2 Which of the promotional elements described in Figure 18-2 are used by Under Armour in its IMC campaigns?

3 What are several new strategies Under Armour might pursue as it attempts to continue its extraordinary record of growth?

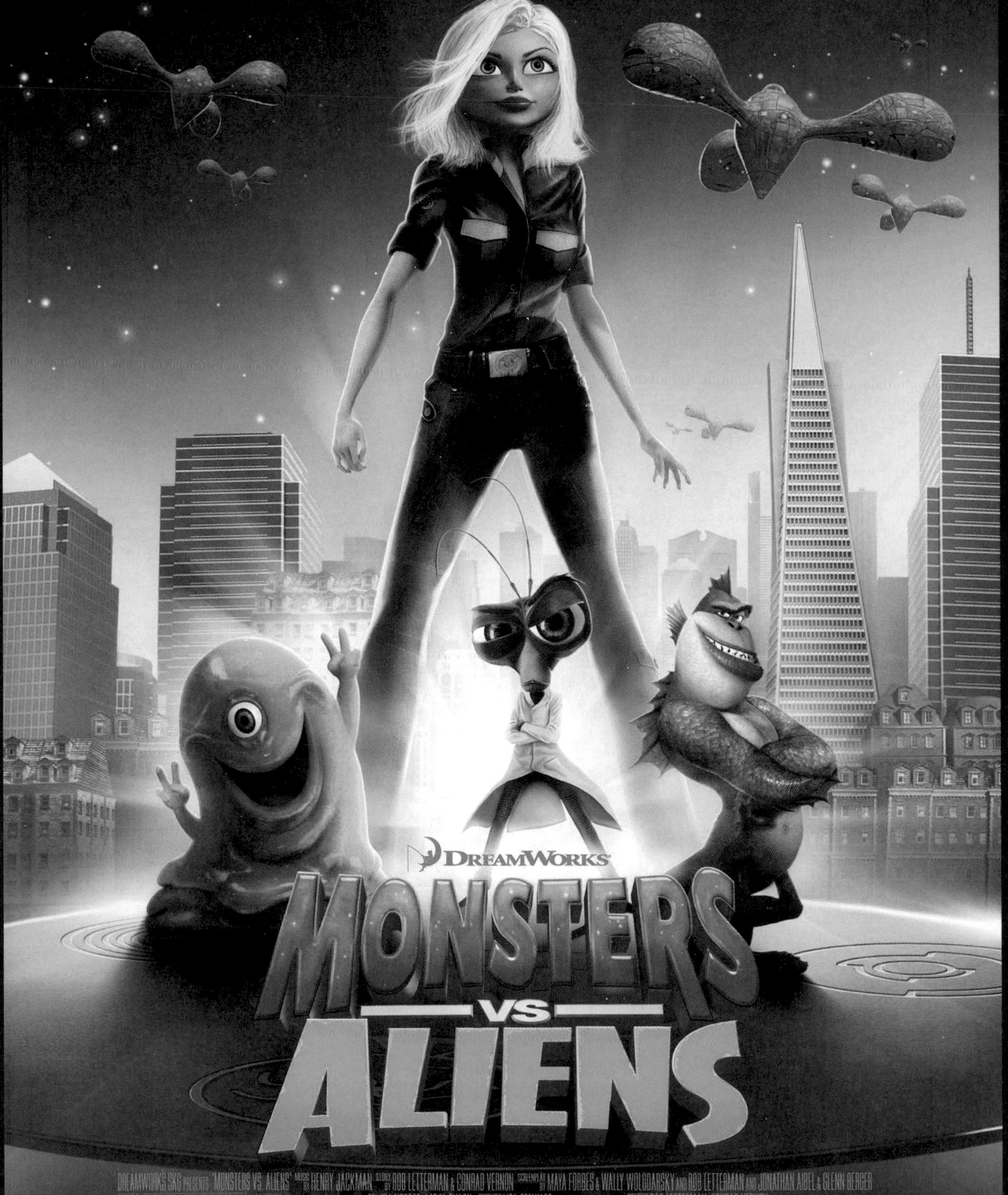
Alien Problem? Monster Solution.
DreamWorks
MONSTERS VS ALIENS
DREAMWORKS SKG PRESENTS "MONSTERS VS. ALIENS" MUSIC BY HENRY JACKMAN STORY BY ROB LETTERMAN & CONRAD VERNON SCREENPLAY BY MAYA FORBES & WALLY WOLODARSKY AND ROB LETTERMAN AND JONATHAN AIBEL & GLENN BERGER
CO PRODUCERS JILL HOPPER LATIFA OUAOU PRODUCED BY LISA STEWART DIRECTED BY ROB LETTERMAN CONRAD VERNON
PG PARENTAL GUIDANCE SUGGESTED
MonstersVsAliens.com
DreamWorks
A MONSTROUS 3D EVENT
IN TRU 3D
MARCH 2009
IN real D 3D AND IMAX 3D

19 Advertising, Sales Promotion, and Public Relations

LEARNING OBJECTIVES
After reading this chapter you should be able to:

LO1 Explain the differences between product advertising and institutional advertising and the variations within each type.

LO2 Describe the steps used to develop, execute, and evaluate an advertising program.

LO3 Explain the advantages and disadvantages of alternative advertising media.

LO4 Discuss the strengths and weaknesses of consumer-oriented and trade-oriented sales promotions.

LO5 Recognize public relations as an important form of communication.

ADVERTISING MOVES TO A NEW DIMENSION: THE THIRD DIMENSION

If Jeffery Katzenberg, James Cameron, and Steven Spielberg have their way, most visual media, including advertising, could be presented in digital 3-D in the near future. Their movie studio, DreamWorks, is developing a technology to bring a true third dimension to movie theaters and television screens!

DreamWorks' first 3-D movie, *Monsters vs. Aliens*, was a huge step for the company. "This is really a revolution," explains CEO Katzenberg. In fact, he believes the change is so important that in the future all DreamWorks' movies will be made in 3-D. The technology is not just for movies and theaters, however; it will also change broadcasting, TV displays, gaming, videos, and all forms of advertising.

The first 3-D advertisements were 30-second spots on the Super Bowl for *Monsters vs. Aliens* and Sobe Life Water energy drinks. More than 125 million pairs of free 3-D glasses, using a new technology, were distributed in the United States for use during the Super Bowl. Other forms of 3-D are being developed also. For example, a Japanese company is developing a laser system that will project 3-D outdoor advertisements. Other applications will include digital billboards and signs. The combination of the two has the potential to allow consumers to experience advertising in a virtual 3-D environment.

Unlike traditional advertising, 3-D advertising is an opportunity to immerse consumers in an experience. Today's consumers are not passive; they want to be involved and engaged. The third dimension allows viewers to participate in the ad rather than just observe it. Advertisers can use 3-D to pull the audience into an ad to feel the message being communicated. Some observers believe that 3-D viewing is so close to a real experience that it will improve retention of the message. This new generation of 3-D technology is for both animation and live action. Comcast mixed animation and live action to create its recent 3-D ad campaign called "Comcast Town." The six TV spots create an imaginary 3-D world that illustrates connectivity and entertainment for live characters. Another ad, created by NBC, encoded a clip of its TV program *Chuck* in 3-D using only the live characters and setting.

Watch for a general trend toward 3-D. Katzenberg predicts that soon everyone will own a pair of 3-D glasses![1]

The 3-D explosion is just one of the many exciting changes occurring in the field of advertising today. They illustrate the importance of advertising as one of the five promotional mix elements in marketing communications programs. This chapter describes three of the promotional mix elements—advertising, sales promotion, and public relations. Direct marketing was covered in Chapter 18, and personal selling is covered in Chapter 20.

TYPES OF ADVERTISEMENTS

Chapter 18 described **advertising** as any paid form of nonpersonal communication about an organization, a good, a service, or an idea by an identified sponsor. As you look through any magazine, watch television, listen to the radio, or browse the Internet, the variety of advertisements you see or hear may give you the impression that they have few similarities. Advertisements are prepared for different purposes, but they basically consist of two types: product advertisements and institutional advertisements.

Product Advertisements

LO1

Focused on selling a good or service, **product advertisements** take three forms: (1) pioneering (or informational), (2) competitive (or persuasive), and (3) reminder. Look at the ads for Visa, Cadillac, and M&Ms to determine the type and objective of each ad.

Used in the introductory stage of the product life cycle, *pioneering* advertisements tell people what a product is, what it can do, and where it can be found. The key objective of a pioneering advertisement (such as the ad for Visa's new Black card) is to inform the target market. Informational ads, particularly those with specific information, have been found to be interesting, convincing, and effective.[2]

Advertising that promotes a specific brand's features and benefits is *competitive*. The objective of these messages is to persuade the target market to select the firm's brand rather than that of a competitor. An increasingly common form of competitive advertising is *comparative* advertising, which shows one brand's strengths relative to those of competitors.[3] The Cadillac ad, for example, highlights the competitive advantage of the Cadillac Escalade hybrid compared to other vehicles such as the BMW X3 and the Volvo XC90. Studies indicate that comparative ads attract more attention and increase the perceived quality of the advertiser's brand although their impact may vary by product type, message content, and audience gender.[4] Firms that use comparative advertising need market research to provide legal support for their claims.[5]

Reminder advertising is used to reinforce previous knowledge of a product. The M&Ms ad shown reminds consumers about a special event, in this case, Valentine's Day. Reminder advertising is good for products that have achieved a well-recognized position and are in the mature phase of their product life cycle. Another type of

Product advertisements serve varying purposes. Which ad would be considered a (1) pioneering, (2) competitive, and (3) reminder ad?

Chevron uses an advocacy ad to communicate its position on the use of less energy. Amway uses a pioneering ad to inform readers about the company and its products.

reminder ad, *reinforcement*, is used to assure current users they made the right choice. One example is used in Dial soap advertisements: "Aren't you glad you use Dial. Don't you wish everybody did?"

Institutional Advertisements

The objective of **institutional advertisements** is to build goodwill or an image for an organization rather than promote a specific good or service. Institutional advertising has been used by companies such as Texaco, Pfizer, and IBM to build confidence in the company name.[6] Often this form of advertising is used to support the public relations plan or counter adverse publicity. Four alternative forms of institutional advertisements are often used:

1. *Advocacy* advertisements state the position of a company on an issue. Chevron places ads encouraging consumers to use less energy. Another form of advocacy advertisement is used when organizations make a request related to a particular action or behavior, such as a request by American Red Cross for blood donations.
2. *Pioneering institutional* advertisements, like the pioneering ads for products discussed earlier, are used for announcements about what a company is, what it can do, or where it is located. Recent Bayer ads stating, "We cure more headaches than you think," are intended to inform consumers that the company produces many products in addition to aspirin. Amway uses pioneering institutional ads in its "Know You Know" campaign to inform people about the company and its products.
3. *Competitive institutional* advertisements promote the advantages of one product class over another and are used in markets where different product classes compete for the same buyers. America's milk processors and dairy farmers use their "Got Milk?" campaign to increase demand for milk as it competes against other beverages.
4. *Reminder institutional* advertisements, like the product form, simply bring the company's name to the attention of the target market again. The Army branch of the U.S. military sponsors a campaign to remind potential recruits of the opportunities in the Army.

A competitive institutional ad by dairy farmers tries to increase demand for milk, and a reminder institutional ad by the U.S. Army tries to keep the attention of the target market.

learning review

1. What is the difference between pioneering and competitive ads?
2. What is the purpose of an institutional advertisement?

DEVELOPING THE ADVERTISING PROGRAM

LO2

The promotion decision process described in Chapter 18 can be applied to each of the promotional elements. Advertising, for example, can be managed by following the three steps (developing, executing, and evaluating) of the process.

Identifying the Target Audience

To develop an effective advertising program, advertisers must identify the target audience. All aspects of an advertising program are likely to be influenced by the characteristics of the prospective consumer. Understanding the lifestyles, attitudes, and demographics of the target market is essential. NBC, for example, promoted its medical/nurse drama "Mercy" to 18- to 34-year-old women, while Electronic Arts targeted 13- to 34-year-old men for The Beatles Rock Band video game. Both campaigns emphasized advertising techniques that matched the audience—program trailers for women and 30-second game demos for men.[7] Similarly, the placement of ads depends on the audience. When Porsche began its 18-month-long "Can you afford a Porsche?" campaign, it used mobile phone ads to reach its target market—young tech-savvy, connected men.[8] Even scheduling can depend on the audience. Nike schedules advertising, sponsorships, deals, and endorsements to correspond with the Olympics to appeal to "hard-core" athletes.[9] To eliminate possible bias that might result from subjective judgments about some population segments, the Federal Communications Commission suggests that advertising program decisions be based on market research about the target audience.[10]

Specifying Advertising Objectives

The guidelines for setting promotion objectives described in Chapter 18 also apply to setting advertising objectives. This step helps advertisers with other choices in the promotion decision process such as selecting media and evaluating a campaign. Advertising with an objective of creating awareness, for example, would be better matched with a magazine than a directory such as the Yellow Pages. The Magazine Publishers of America believe objectives are so important that they offer a $100,000 prize each year to the campaign that best meets its objectives. Recently, Pedigree food for dogs won with its "Adoption" campaign, which increased sales by 11 percent and raised $2.7 million for shelter dogs.[11] Similarly, the Advertising Research Foundation sponsors an Advertising Effectiveness Council to investigate new techniques for measuring the impact of all forms of advertising.[12] Experts believe that factors such as product category, brand, and consumer involvement in the purchase decision may change the importance and, possibly, the sequence of the stages of the hierarchy of effects. Snickers, for example, knew that its consumers were unlikely to engage in elaborate information processing when it designed a recent campaign. The result was ads with simple humorous messages rather than extensive factual information.[13]

Setting the Advertising Budget

During the 1990 Super Bowl, it cost companies $700,000 to place a 30-second ad. By 2009, the cost of placing a 30-second ad during Super Bowl XLIII was $3 million (see Figure 19–1). The reason for the escalating cost is the growing number of viewers: 100 million people, or about 50 percent of the viewing public, watch the game. In addition, the audience is attractive to advertisers because research indicates it is equally split between men and women and many viewers look forward to watching

FIGURE 19–1
The Super Bowl delivers a huge audience, if you can afford the cost of placing an ad.

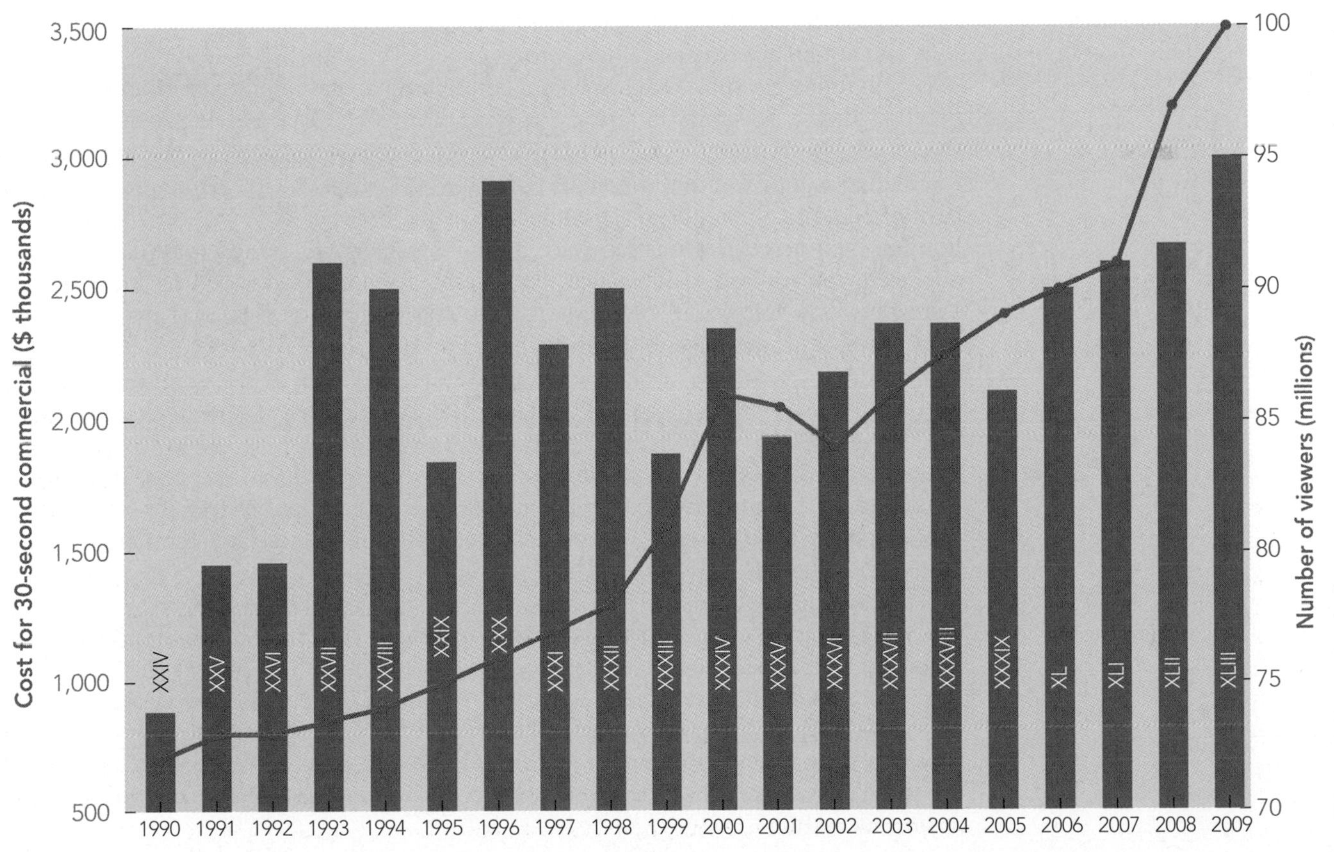

Going Online

See Your Favorite Super Bowl Ads Again, and Again!

If you missed some of the ads during the last Super Bowl, or if you liked some of them so much you want to see them again, you can review the ads at www.superbowl-ads.com. All ads for the past 12 Super Bowls and classics like the "1984" Apple Computer ad are available to view.

Which ads are your favorites? Compare the ads from different years. For example, you might compare the 2009 Coke Zero ad to the 1980 Coke ad (click All-time). Do you notice any changes?

Do you remember this Doritos ad from the Super Bowl?

the 69 "spots." The ads are effective too: Movies promoted on the Super Bowl achieve 40 percent more revenue than movies not promoted on the Super Bowl; E*TRADE increased the number of new accounts by 32 percent in the week after the game; and Go Daddy estimates that it received $11.7 million in publicity as a result of its ads. As a result, the Super Bowl attracts relatively new advertisers such as Hulu and Denny's, and regular advertisers such as Anheuser-Busch, Doritos, and Coca-Cola. Coke Zero's remake of the 1980 "Mean Joe Green" ad and Monster.com were rated the highest.[14] To learn how to see your favorite Super Bowl ad again, read the Going Online box.

While not all advertising options are as expensive as the Super Bowl, most alternatives still represent substantial financial commitments and require a formal budgeting process. In the beverage industry, for example, Coca-Cola and Pepsi have market shares of approximately 15.2 percent and 9.5 percent, and advertising and promotion budgets of $294.6 million and $162.1 million, respectively. Using a competitive parity budgeting approach, each company spends between $17 million and $19 million for each percent of market share. Using an objective and task approach, Honda allocated $50 million to introduce the Insight, its new, low-priced hybrid car. The campaign uses television, radio, magazine, newspaper, Internet, and movie theater advertising with the phrase "From Honda. For Everyone."[15]

Designing the Advertisement

An advertising message usually focuses on the key benefits of the product that are important to a prospective buyer in making trial and adoption decisions. The message depends on the general form or appeal used in the ad and the actual words included in the ad.

Message Content Most advertising messages are made up of both informational and persuasional elements. These two elements are so intertwined that it is sometimes difficult to tell them apart. For example, basic information contained in many ads such as the product name, benefits, features, and price are presented in a way that tries to attract attention and encourage purchase. On the other hand, even the most persuasive advertisements have to contain at least some basic information to be successful.

Information and persuasive content can be combined in the form of an appeal to provide a basic reason for the consumer to act. Although the marketer can use many different types of appeals, common advertising appeals include fear, sex, and humor.

Fear appeals suggest to the consumer that he or she can avoid some negative experience through the purchase and use of a product or service, a change in behavior, or a reduction in the use of a product. Examples with which you may be familiar include: automobile safety ads that depict an accident or injury; political candidate endorsements that warn against the rise of other, unpopular ideologies; or social cause ads warning of the serious consequences of drug and alcohol use. Insurance companies often try to show the negative effects on the relatives of those who die prematurely without carrying enough life or mortgage insurance. Food producers encourage the purchase of low-carb, low-fat, and high-fiber products as a means of reducing weight, cholesterol levels, and the possibility of a heart attack. The Office of National Drug Control Policy previously ran an ad with a fear appeal: The headline read "Marijuana. Harmless?" and the statement "Didn't see merging truck." When using fear appeals, the advertiser must be sure that the appeal is strong enough to get the audience's attention and concern but not so strong that it will lead them to tune out the message. In fact, research on antismoking ads indicates that stressing the severity of long-term health risks may actually enhance smoking's allure among youth.[16]

In contrast, *sex appeals* suggest to the audience that the product will increase the attractiveness of the user. Sex appeals can be found in almost any product category, from automobiles to toothpaste. The contemporary women's clothing store Bebe, for example, designs its advertising to "attract customers who are intrigued by the playfully sensual and evocative imagery of the Bebe lifestyle." Studies indicate that sex appeals increase attention by helping advertising stand out in today's cluttered media environment. Unfortunately, sexual content does not always lead to changes in recall, recognition, or purchase intent. Experts suggest that sexual content is most effective when there is a strong fit between the use of a sex appeal in the ad and the image and positioning of the brand.[17]

Humorous appeals imply either directly or subtly that the product is more fun or exciting than competitors' offerings. As with fear and sex appeals, the use of humor is widespread in advertising and can be found in many product categories. You may have smiled at the popular Geico ads that use cavemen, a gecko, and a stack of money with eyes named Kash to use humor to differentiate the company from its

These ads are examples of fear appeal, sex appeal, and humor appeal, respectively.

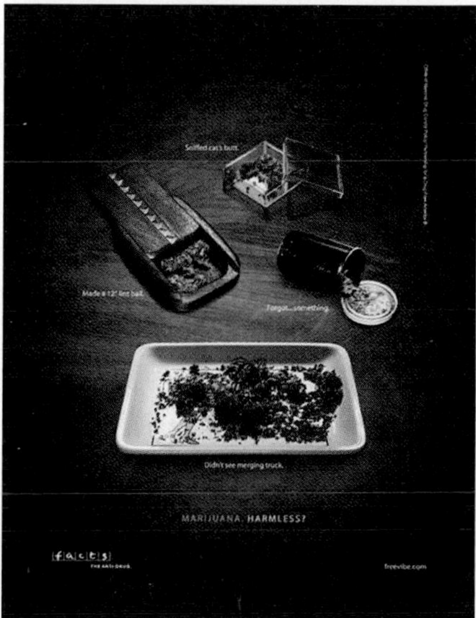

competitors. The ads have been so popular that Geico has created an interactive Web site, www.cavemanscrib.com, to allow visitors to learn more about the cavemen. In addition, Geico has created viral videos featuring the gecko and posted them on video-sharing Web sites such as YouTube, Metacafe, and Slide, where millions of viewers watch them within days.[18] You may have a favorite humorous ad character, such as the Energizer battery bunny, the AFLAC duck, or Travelocity's gnome. Advertisers believe that humor improves the effectiveness of their ads, although some studies suggest that humor wears out quickly, losing the interest of consumers. Another problem with humorous appeals is that their effectiveness may vary across cultures if used in a global campaign.[19]

Creating the Actual Message Advertising agency Crispin, Porter & Bogusky was recently designated *Advertising Age* magazine's U.S. Agency of the Year for its unique ability to take "a simple proposition" and "somehow make it entertainment." Examples of the agency's approach include the "I'm a PC" campaign for Microsoft, the "Whopper Virgin" campaign for Burger King, and the "It's What the People Want" campaign for Volkswagen. Crispin was also recognized for adding product design to the services it offers clients. Some of its design ideas include a public bike-rental program, a pen version of WD-40, and an eco-friendly sponge![20]

Crispin, Porter & Bogusky and other agencies use many forms of advertising to create their messages. A very popular form of advertising today is the use of a celebrity spokesperson. Crispin's use of well-known personalities such as Brooke Shields, David Hasselhoff, and Heidi Klum in their Volkswagen ads is an example. Many companies use athletes, movie and television stars, musicians, and other celebrities to talk to consumers through their ads. Advertisers who use a celebrity spokesperson believe that the ads are more likely to influence sales. The popular "Got Milk?" campaign reversed a steady decline in milk consumption with celebrities such as musician Taylor Swift, model Christie Brinkley, NASCAR driver Jeff Gordon, fictional characters such as Batman and Ronald McDonald, and many others. You've probably seen ads with Nicole Kidman promoting Chanel No. 5 perfume or Tiger Woods endorsing American Express. The top five corporate celebrity spokespersons today are Tom Hanks, Will Smith, Michael Jordan, Morgan Freeman, and George Clooney. The top spokespersons for causes include Lance Armstrong for LiveStrong, Angelina

The Giro campaign is one example of creative advertising that helped agency Crispin, Porter & Bogusky win *Advertising Age*'s Agency of the Year award.

Crispin, Porter & Bogusky uses a simple proposition to create a message for Microsoft.

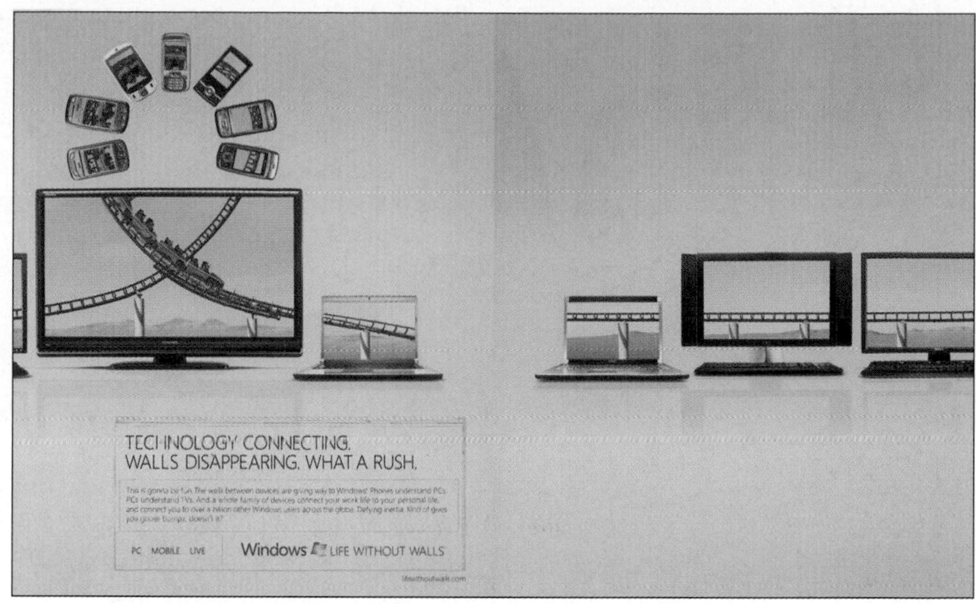

TECHNOLOGY CONNECTING.
WALLS DISAPPEARING. WHAT A RUSH.
PC MOBILE LIVE
Windows LIFE WITHOUT WALLS

Jolie for UNICEF, and Bono for his work with RED. L'Oreal Paris recently signed actress Elizabeth Banks as its exclusive worldwide spokesperson for the company and its brands. Karen Fondu, president of L'Oreal Paris, explains that Elizabeth was selected because "she has a natural charm and an incredible ability to captivate an audience."[21]

One potential shortcoming of this form of advertising is that the spokesperson's image may change to be inconsistent with the image of the company or brand. Olympic swimmer Michael Phelps lost an endorsement contract with Kellogg's after pictures of his activities at a party led to negative public attention. Many companies now probe the backgrounds of potential endorsers and consider retired athletes and legacy (deceased) athletes who are low risk and still have lasting appeal in the marketplace. Some companies are also using licensing agreements where the spokesperson's compensation is directly related to the success of the product they endorse.[22]

Another issue involved in creating the message is the complex process of translating the copywriter's ideas into an actual advertisement. Designing quality artwork, layout, and production for advertisements is costly and time consuming. The American Association of Advertising Agencies reports that high-quality TV commercials typically cost about $361,000 to produce a 30-second ad. One reason for the high costs is that as companies have developed global campaigns, the need to shoot commercials in several locations has increased. Audi recently filmed commercials in Germany, Australia, and Morocco. Actors are also expensive: Compensation for a typical TV ad is $17,000.[23]

learning review

3. What other decisions can advertising objectives influence?
4. What is a potential shortcoming of using a celebrity spokesperson?

Selecting the Right Media

Every advertiser must decide where to place its advertisements. The alternatives are the *advertising media*, the means by which the message is communicated to the

FIGURE 19–2
Television, direct mail, and newspapers account for more than 60 percent of all advertising expenditures (in millions).

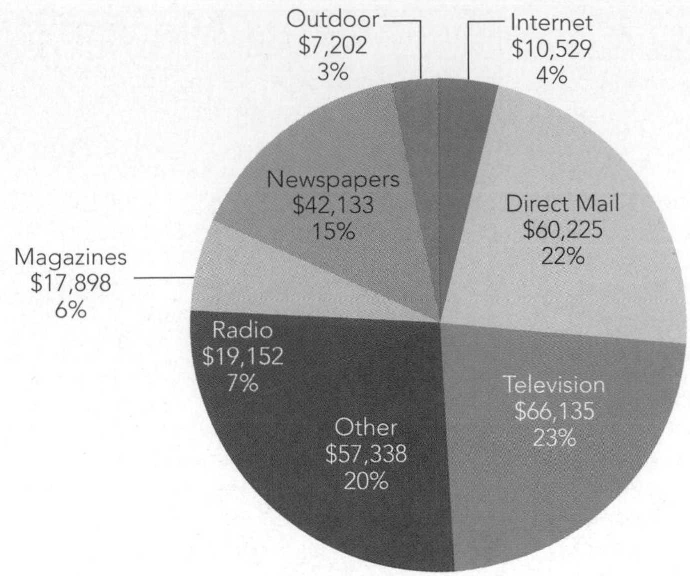

target audience. Newspapers, magazines, radio, and TV are examples of advertising media. This decision on media selection is related to the target audience, type of product, nature of the message, campaign objectives, available budget, and the costs of the alternative media. Figure 19–2 shows the distribution of the $279 billion spent on advertising among the many media alternatives.[24]

Choosing a Medium and a Vehicle Within That Medium In deciding where to place advertisements, a company has several media to choose from and a number of alternatives, or vehicles, within each medium. Often advertisers use a mix of media forms and vehicles to maximize the exposure of the message to the target audience while at the same time minimizing costs. These two conflicting goals are of central importance to media planning.

Basic Terms Media buyers speak a language of their own, so every advertiser involved in selecting the right media for their campaigns must be familiar with some common terms used in the advertising industry.

Because advertisers try to maximize the number of individuals in the target market exposed to the message, they must be concerned with reach. **Reach** is the number of different people or households exposed to an advertisement. The exact definition of reach sometimes varies among alternative media. Newspapers often use reach to describe their total circulation or the number of different households that buy the paper. Television and radio stations, in contrast, describe their reach using the term **rating**—the percentage of households in a market that are tuned to a particular TV show or radio station. In general, advertisers try to maximize reach in their target market at the lowest cost.

Although reach is important, advertisers are also interested in exposing their target audience to a message more than once. This is because consumers often do not pay close attention to advertising messages, some of which contain large amounts of relatively complex information. When advertisers want to reach the same audience more than once, they are concerned with **frequency**, the average number of times a person in the target audience is exposed to a message or advertisement. Like reach, greater frequency is generally viewed as desirable. Studies indicate that with repeated exposure to advertisements consumers respond more favorably to brand extensions.[25]

Using Marketing Dashboards
What Is the Best Way to Reach 1,000 Customers?

Marketing managers must choose from many advertising options as they design a campaign to reach potential customers. Because there are so many media alternatives (television, radio, magazines, etc.) and multiple options within each of the media, it is important to monitor the efficiency of advertising expenditures on your marketing dashboard.

Your Challenge As the marketing manager for a company about to introduce a new soft drink into the U.S. market, you are preparing a presentation in which you must make recommendations for the advertising campaign. You have observed that competitors use magazine ads, newspaper ads, and even Super Bowl ads! To compare the cost of some of the alternatives you decide to use one of the most common measures in advertising: cost per thousand impressions (CPM). The CPM is calculated as follows:

Cost per thousand impressions =
Advertising cost ($)/Impressions generated (in 1000s)

Your challenge is to determine the most efficient use of your advertising budget.

Your Findings Your research department helps you collect cost and audience size information for three options: full-page color ads in *Sports Illustrated* magazine and *USA Today* newspaper, and a 30-second television ad during the Super Bowl. With this information you are able to calculate the cost per thousand impressions for each alternative.

Media Alternative	Cost of Ad	Audience Size	Cost per Thousand Impressions
Sports Illustrated (magazine)	$336,000	3,150,000	$107
USA Today (newspaper)	$197,720	2,109,628	$94
Super Bowl (television)	$3,000,000	100,000,000	$30

Your Action Based on the calculations for these options, you see that there is a large variation in the cost of reaching 1,000 potential customers (CPM) and also in the absolute cost of the advertising. Although advertising on the Super Bowl has the lowest CPM, $30 for each 1,000 impressions, it also has the largest absolute cost! Your next step will be to consider other factors such as your total available budget, the profiles of the audiences each alternative reaches, and whether the type of message you want to deliver is better communicated in print or on television.

When reach (expressed as a percentage of the total market) is multiplied by frequency, an advertiser will obtain a commonly used reference number called **gross rating points** (GRPs). To obtain the appropriate number of GRPs to achieve an advertising campaign's objectives, the media planner must balance reach and frequency. The balance will also be influenced by cost. **Cost per thousand** (CPM) refers to the cost of reaching 1,000 individuals or households with the advertising message in a given medium (*M* is the Roman numeral for 1,000). See the Using Marketing Dashboards box for an example of the use of CPM in media selection.

Different Media Alternatives

Figure 19–3 on the next page summarizes the advantages and disadvantages of the major advertising media, which are described in more detail below. Direct mail was discussed in Chapter 18.

Television Television is a valuable medium because it communicates with sight, sound, and motion. Print advertisements alone could never give you the sense of a sports car accelerating from a stop or cornering at high speed. In addition, network television reaches 98.9 percent of all households—114.5 million—more than any other advertising option. Unfortunately, the percentage of households watching network television has declined from 56 percent in 1973 to approximately 18 percent

MEDIUM	ADVANTAGES	DISADVANTAGES
Television	Reaches extremely large audience; uses picture, print, sound, and motion for effect; can target specific audiences	High cost to prepare and run ads; short exposure time and perishable message; difficult to convey complex information
Radio	Low cost; can target specific local audiences; ads can be placed quickly; can use sound, humor, and intimacy effectively	No visual element; short exposure time and perishable message; difficult to convey complex information
Magazines	Can target specific audiences; high-quality color; long life of ad; ads can be clipped and saved; can convey complex information	Long time needed to place ad; relatively high cost; competes for attention with other magazine features
Newspapers	Excellent coverage of local markets; ads can be placed and changed quickly; ads can be saved; quick consumer response; low cost	Ads compete for attention with other newspaper features; short life span; poor color
Yellow Pages	Excellent coverage of geographic segments; long use period; available 24 hours/365 days	Proliferation of competitive directories in many markets; difficult to keep up-to-date
Internet	Video and audio capabilities; animation can capture attention; ads can be interactive and link to advertiser	Animation and interactivity require large files and more time to load; effectiveness is still uncertain
Outdoor	Low cost; local market focus; high visibility; opportunity for repeat exposures	Message must be short and simple; low selectivity of audience; criticized as a traffic hazard
Direct mail	High selectivity of audience; can contain complex information and personalized messages; high-quality graphics	High cost per contact; poor image (junk mail)

FIGURE 19–3
Advertisers must consider the advantages and disadvantages of the many media alternatives.

today. Out-of-home TV viewing, however, has been increasing as millions of viewers can now see televisions in bars, hotels, offices, airports, and college campuses.[26]

Television's major disadvantage is cost: The price of a prime-time, 30-second ad run on *Sunday Night Football* is $339,700, and the average price for all prime-time programs is $125,283. Because of these high charges, many advertisers choose less expensive "spot" ads, which run between programs in 10-, 15-, 30-, or 60-second lengths. Shorter ads reduce costs but severely restrict the amount of information and emotion that can be conveyed. Miller, however, increased sales by 8 percent in the week after it ran one-second ads on the Super Bowl. In addition, there is some indication that advertisers are shifting their interest to live events rather than programs that might be watched on a DVR days later.[27]

Another problem with television advertising is the likelihood of *wasted coverage*—having people outside the market for the product see the advertisement. The cost and wasted coverage problems of TV advertising can be reduced through the specialized cable and satellite channels. Advertising time is often less expensive on cable and satellite channels than on the broadcast networks. There are currently about 150 options, such as ESPN, MTV, Lifetime, Oxygen, the Speed Channel, the History Channel, the Science Channel, and the Food Network, that reach very nar-

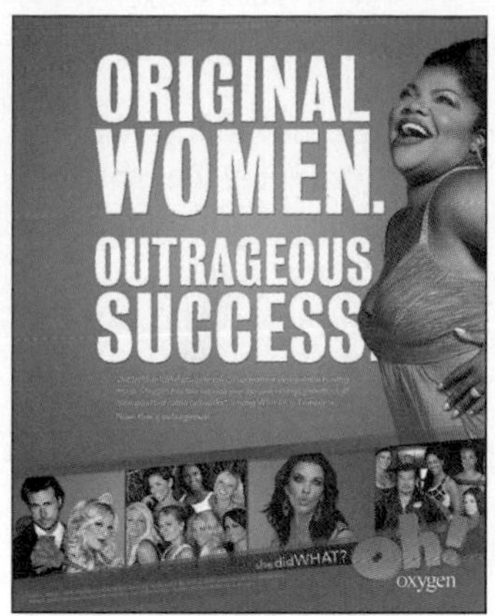

Oxygen is one of many specialized channels available to advertisers.

rowly defined audiences. Other forms of television viewing are changing advertising also. Many cable and satellite TV services offer DVRs and remotes with "skip" buttons for ad-zapping. Pay-per-view options and "download" services such as iTunes offer commercial-free viewing. In addition, Web sites such as Fancast, Hulu, Joost, and YouTube now provide access to cable and broadcast programming with limited advertising.[28]

Another popular form of television advertising is the infomercial. **Infomercials** are program-length (30-minute) advertisements that take an educational approach to communication with potential customers. Each year *Response Magazine* and Infomercial Monitoring Service Inc. report on the growth and success of infomercials as a form of television advertising. More than 470 new infomercials are produced each year. Some of the most popular included Total Gym, Nutrisystem Advanced, Bowflex, and Sleep Number. Chrysler recently produced its first infomercial for the Dodge Ram, which ran on weekend mornings on CBS, Fox, Telemundo, and Univision. What was one of the most successful infomercials? During the 2008 presidential campaign, Barack Obama ran an infomercial that attracted 33.5 million viewers—more than the final game of the World Series![29]

Radio The United States has more than 14,000 radio stations—eight times as many as there are television stations. The major advantage of radio is that it is a segmented medium. For example, there are the Farm Radio Network, the Family Life Network, Business Talk Radio, and the Performance Racing Network, all listened to by different market segments. The large number of media options today has reduced the amount of time spent listening to radio also. The average 18- to 24-year-old, however, still listens to radio an average of 2.5 hours each day, making radio an important medium for businesses with college students as a target market.[30]

A disadvantage of radio is that it has limited use for products that must be seen. Another problem is the ease with which consumers can tune out a commercial by switching stations. Satellite radio service Sirius XM offers more than 130 digital-quality, coast-to-coast channels to consumers for an annual subscription fee. Many of the channels are 100 percent commercial-free. Radio is also a medium that competes for people's attention as they do other activities such as driving, working, or relaxing. Radio listening time reaches its peak during the morning drive time (7 to 9 A.M.), remains high during the day, and then begins to decline in the afternoon (4 P.M.) as people return home and start evening activities.[31]

Magazines such as *Sports Illustrated for Kids* appeal to narrowly defined segments.

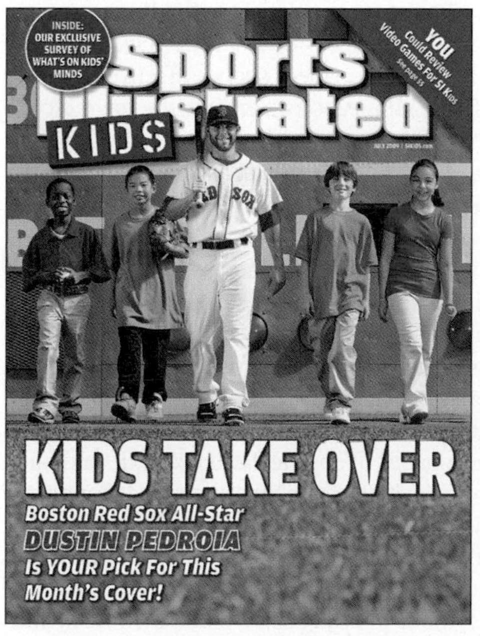

Magazines Magazines have become a very specialized medium, primarily because there are currently more than 19,532 magazines. Some 200 new magazines are introduced each year, such as *Disney Twenty-Three*, a quarterly magazine for Disney fans; *Bicycle Times*, a magazine about everyday bicycling experiences; and *Best You*, a magazine about health, diet, and exercise. A new form of existing magazines—issues containing reader-generated content—has also been introduced recently. *This Old House* and *BusinessWeek*, for example, asked readers to create substantial portions of special issues of the magazines.[32]

The marketing advantage of this medium is the great number of special-interest publications that appeal to narrowly defined segments. Runners read *Runner's World*, sailors buy *Yachting*, gardeners subscribe to *Garden Design*, and children peruse *Sports Illustrated for Kids*. More than 645 publications focus on travel, 195 are dedicated to interior design and decoration, and 139 are related to golf. Each magazine's readers often represent a unique profile. Take the *Rolling Stone* reader, who tends to listen to music more than most people; Sirius XM satellite radio knows an ad in *Rolling Stone* is reaching the desired target audience. In addition, recent studies comparing advertising in different media suggest that magazine advertising is perceived to be more "trustworthy," "inspirational," and engaging than other media.[33]

The cost of advertising in national magazines is a disadvantage, but many national publications publish regional and even metro editions, which reduces the absolute cost and wasted coverage. *Time* publishes well over 400 editions, including Latin American, Canadian, Asian, South Pacific, European, and U.S. editions. The U.S. editions include geographic and demographic options. In addition to cost, another limitation to magazines is their infrequency. At best, magazines are printed on a weekly basis, with many specialized publications appearing only monthly or less often. Although specialization can be an advantage of this medium, consumer interests can be difficult to translate into a magazine theme—a fact made clear by the hundreds of magazine failures during the past decade. *CosmoGirl*, *ElleGirl*, *Teen People*, *Virtual City*, *Business 2.0*, *PC Magazine*, *Men's Vogue*, and *Esquire Sportsman*, for example, all failed to attract and keep a substantial number of readers or advertisers.[34] Which magazine has the highest circulation? It's *AARP The Magazine* with a circulation of 24 million!

Print ads help attract readers to *USA Today*.

www.usatoday.com

Newspapers Newspapers are an important local medium with excellent reach potential. Daily publication allows advertisements to focus on specific current events, such as a 24-hour sale. Local retailers often use newspapers as their sole advertising medium. Newspapers are rarely saved by the purchaser, however, so companies are generally limited to ads that call for an immediate customer response (although customers can clip and save ads they select). Companies also cannot depend on newspapers for color reproduction as good as that in most magazines.

National advertising campaigns rarely include this medium except in conjunction with local distributors of their products. In these instances, both parties often share the advertising costs using a cooperative advertising program, which is described later in this chapter. Another exception is the use of newspapers such as *The Wall Street Journal* and *USA Today*, both of which have national distribution of more than 2 million readers.

Several important trends are influencing newspapers today. First is the dramatic decline in circulation and advertising revenue. Of the 25 largest newspapers in 1990, 21 have declined. The result has been that many papers such as Denver's *Rocky Mountain News* and the Minneapolis *StarTribune* have closed or declared bankruptcy. Other newspapers, such as the *Christian Science Monitor*, have discontinued daily editions and moved to a once-each-week model. Only the *Arizona Republic* is growing, primarily due to population growth and a focus on its Sunday edition, which accounts for most of the advertising revenue. The second trend is the growth in online newspapers. Today, hundreds of newspapers including *The Wall Street Journal*, *The New York Times*, *Chicago Tribune*, and *Washington Post* offer online versions of the print newspaper. Research by the Newspaper Association of America indicates that 71 million people visit newspaper Web sites each month and they spend an average of 5.6 minutes on the sites each time they visit. A final trend is the growth in new types of news organizations such as the *Huffington Post*, covering entertainment, media, living, business, and politics, and *Politico*, designed exclusively for the 24-hour political news consumer. Both sites have more than 5 million visitors each month![35]

Yellow pages have many advantages including a long life span.

Yellow Pages Yellow pages represent an advertising media alternative comparable to radio and magazines in terms of expenditures—about $15 billion in the United States and $25 billion globally. According to the Yellow Pages Association, consumers turn to print yellow pages more than 13 billion times annually and online yellow pages an additional 3.8 billion times per year. One reason for this high level of use is that the 6,500 yellow pages directories reach almost all households with telephones. Yellow pages are a directional medium because they help consumers know where purchases can be made after other media have created awareness and demand.

The yellow pages face several disadvantages today. First is the proliferation of directories. AT&T (Real Yellow Pages), Idearc (Verizon Superpages), and R.H. Donnelley (DEX) now produce competing directories for many cities, neighborhoods, and ethnic groups. Second, relative to other advertising options, the yellow pages have limited accountability and ROI metrics. National advertisers, which represent $2.3 billion of the $15 billion industry, believe that yellow pages need to improve audience measurement research and circulation audition practices. Finally, many yellow pages customers are migrating to the Web. For many businesses, pay-per-click search ads on Google and Yahoo! are viewed as less expensive and more effective.[36]

Internet The Internet represents a relatively new medium for advertisers although it has already attracted a wide variety of industries. Online advertising is similar to print advertising in that it offers a visual message. It has additional advantages, however, because it can also use the audio and video capabilities of the Internet. Sound and movement may simply attract more attention from viewers, or they may provide an element of entertainment to the message. Online advertising also has the unique feature of being interactive. Called *rich media*, these interactive ads have drop-down menus, built-in games, or search engines to engage viewers. Although online advertising is relatively small compared to other traditional media, it offers an opportunity to reach younger consumers who have developed a preference for online communication.

There are a variety of online advertising options. The most popular options are paid search, display (banner) ads, classified ads, and video. Paid search is one of the fastest-growing forms of Internet advertising, as approximately 80 percent of all Internet traffic begins at a search engine such as Google or Yahoo! (see Figure 19–4). *Advertising Age* magazine estimates that consumers conduct 11.8 billion

FIGURE 19–4
Google and Yahoo! have the largest shares of Internet searches and offer opportunities for online advertising.

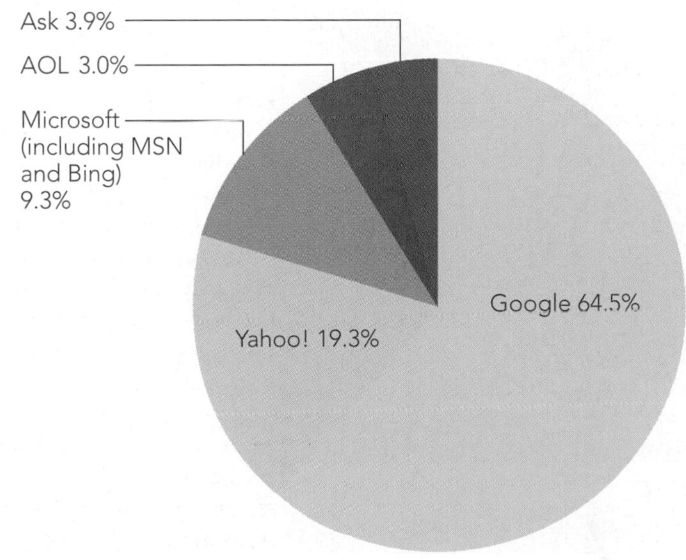

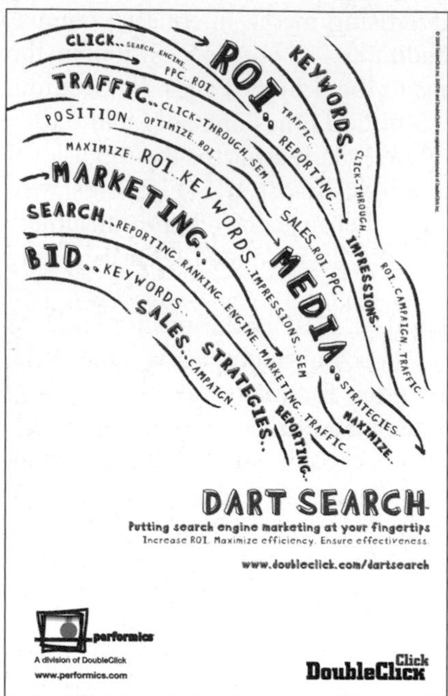

DoubleClick's Dart Search service can provide an assessment of the effectiveness of a Web site.

searches each year. Now search engine agencies help firms add tags, wikis, and RSS to the content of a site to increase search rankings. Firms such as DoubleClick provide assessment of the effectiveness of a Web site. While the use of banner ads is growing also, there is some concern that consumers are developing "banner blindness" because the click-through rate has been declining to its current level of 0.1 percent. Classified ads, such as those on CraigsList, and video ads also contribute to the growth of online advertising by providing many of the advantages and characteristics of other media such as yellow pages, magazines, newspaper, and television.[37]

One disadvantage of online advertising is that because the medium is relatively new, technical and administrative standards for the various formats are still evolving. This situation makes it difficult for advertisers to run national online campaigns across multiple sites. The Interactive Advertising Bureau provides "Standards, Guidelines & Best Practices" and creative guidelines to facilitate the use and growth of online advertising. Another disadvantage to online advertising is the difficulty of measuring impact. Several companies are testing methods of tracking where viewers go on their computer in the days and weeks after seeing an ad. Nielsen's online rating service, for example, measures actual Internet use through meters installed on the computers of 200,000 individuals in 10 countries. Measuring the relationship between online and offline behavior is also important. Recent research by ComScore, which studied 139 online ad campaigns, revealed that online ads didn't always result in a "click," but they increased the likelihood of a purchase by 17 percent and they increased visits to the advertiser's Web site by 40 percent.[38] The Making Responsible Decisions box describes how click fraud is increasing the necessity of assessing online advertising effectiveness.[39]

Outdoor A very effective medium for reminding consumers about your product is outdoor advertising, such as the scoreboard at San Diego's Qualcomm Stadium. The most common form of outdoor advertising, called *billboards*, often results in good reach and frequency and has been shown to increase purchase rates.[40] The visibility of this medium is good supplemental reinforcement for well-known products, and it is a relatively low-cost, flexible alternative. A company can buy space just in the desired geographical market. A disadvantage to billboards, however, is that no opportunity exists for lengthy advertising copy. Also, a good billboard site depends on traffic patterns and sight lines.

If you have ever lived in a metropolitan area, chances are you might have seen another form of outdoor advertising, *transit advertising.* This medium includes messages on the interior and exterior of buses, subway and light-rail cars, and taxis. As the use of mass transit grows, transit advertising may become increasingly important. Selectivity is available to advertisers, who can buy space by neighborhood or bus route. One disadvantage to this medium is that the heavy travel times, when the audiences are the largest, are not conducive to reading advertising copy. People are standing shoulder to shoulder on the subway, hoping not to miss their stop, and little attention is paid to the advertising.

Outdoor advertising can be an effective medium for reminding consumers about a product.

The outdoor advertising industry has experienced a growth surge recently. According to the Outdoor Advertising Association of America, outdoor advertising expenditures have grown to $7 billion annually. Much of the growth is the result of creative forms of outdoor

Making Responsible Decisions > > > > > > > ethics

Who Is Responsible for Click Fraud?

Spending on Internet advertising is expected to reach $36 billion in 2011 as many advertisers shift their budgets from print and TV to the Internet. For most advertisers one advantage of online advertising is that they pay only when someone clicks on their ad. Unfortunately, the growth of the medium has led to "click fraud," which is the deceptive clicking of ads solely to increase the amount advertisers must pay. There are several forms of click fraud. One method is the result of Paid-to Read (PTR) Web sites that recruit and pay members to simply click on ads. Another method is the result of "clickbots," which are software programs that produce automatic clicks on ads. While the activity is difficult to detect and stop, experts estimate that up to 17 percent of clicks may be the result of fraud, and may be costing advertisers as much as $500 million each year!

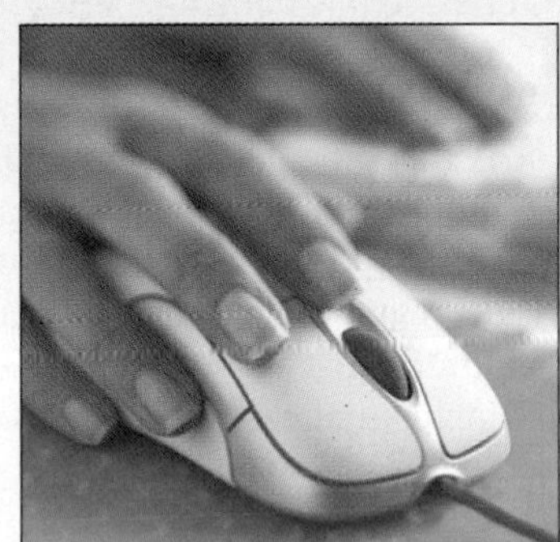

Two of the largest portals for Internet advertising are Google and Yahoo! Both firms try to filter out illegitimate clicks, although some advertisers claim that they are still being charged for PTR and clickbot traffic. Although the laws that may govern click fraud are not very clear, Google and Yahoo! have each settled class action lawsuits and agreed to provide rebates or credits to advertisers who were charged for fraudulent clicks.

Investigations of the online advertising industry have discovered a related form of click fraud that occurs when legitimate Web site visitors click on ads without any intention of looking at the site. As one consumer explains, "I always try and remember to click on the ad banners once in a while to try and keep the sites free." Stephen Dubner calls this "webtipping"!

As the Internet advertising industry grows it will become increasingly important to resolve the issue of click fraud. Consumers, advertisers, Web sites that carry paid advertising, and the large Web portals are all involved in a complicated technical, legal, and social situation. Who do you think is responsible for click fraud? Who should lead the way in the effort to find a solution?

Out-of-home advertising is also becoming interactive.

advertising and the conversion to digital billboards that allow advertisers to change their ad messages quickly and efficiently. In Toledo, Ohio, for example, the newspaper used digital billboards to display the day's headlines. Similarly, television stations now use the technology to advertise the stories that will be covered on the evening news. Digital billboards can also provide a public service by displaying Amber alerts and weather reports. A recent study found that many commuters think that digital billboards are attractive and that they make the commute more interesting. While these trends have been positive, the outdoor advertising industry also faces important environmental concerns that must be addressed through self-regulation or be restricted by legislation. For example, several states have banned billboards, and the Los Angeles City Council is considering a comprehensive billboard policy that may restrict or ban building graphics and digital billboards.[41]

Other Media As traditional media have become more expensive and cluttered, advertisers have been attracted to a variety of nontraditional advertising options called out-of-home advertising, or *place-based media*. Messages are placed in locations that attract a specific target audience such as airports, doctors' offices, health clubs, theaters (where ads are played on the screen before the movies are shown), grocery stores, even bathrooms of bars, restaurants, and nightclubs. Soon there will be advertising on video screens on gas pumps, ATMs, and in elevators, and increasingly it will be interactive. The $2.5 billion industry has attracted advertisers such as AT&T and JCPenney, which use in-store campaigns, and Geico, Sprint, and FedEx, which use out-of-home advertising to reach mobile professionals in health clubs, airports, and hotels. Research suggests that creative use of out-of-home advertising, such as preshow theater ads, enhances consumer recall of the ads.[42]

Selection Criteria Choosing between these alternative media is difficult and depends on several factors. First, knowing the media habits of the target audience is essential to deciding among the alternatives. Second, occasionally product attributes necessitate that certain media be used. For example, if color is a major aspect of product appeal, radio is excluded. Newspapers allow advertising for quick actions to confront competitors, and magazines are more appropriate for complicated messages because the reader can spend more time reading the message. The final factor in selecting a medium is cost. When possible, alternative media are compared using a common denominator that reflects both reach and cost—a measure such as CPM.

Scheduling the Advertising

There is no correct schedule to advertise a product, but three factors must be considered. First is the issue of *buyer turnover*, which is how often new buyers enter the market to buy the product. The higher the buyer turnover, the greater is the amount of advertising required. A second issue in scheduling is the *purchase frequency*; the more frequently the product is purchased, the less repetition is required. Finally, companies must consider the *forgetting rate*, the speed with which buyers forget the brand if advertising is not seen.

Setting schedules requires an understanding of how the market behaves. Most companies tend to follow one of three basic approaches:

1. *Continuous (steady) schedule.* When seasonal factors are unimportant, advertising is run at a continuous or steady schedule throughout the year.
2. *Flighting (intermittent) schedule.* Periods of advertising are scheduled between periods of no advertising to reflect seasonal demand.
3. *Pulse (burst) schedule.* A flighting schedule is combined with a continuous schedule because of increases in demand, heavy periods of promotion, or introduction of a new product.

For example, products such as breakfast cereals have a stable demand throughout the year and would typically use a continuous schedule of advertising. In contrast, products such as snow skis and suntan lotions have seasonal demands and receive flighting-schedule advertising during the seasonal demand period. Some products such as toys or automobiles require pulse-schedule advertising to facilitate sales throughout the year and during special periods of increased demand (such as holidays or new car introductions). Some evidence suggests that pulsing schedules are superior to other advertising strategies.[43] In addition, research indicates the effectiveness of a particular ad wears out quickly and, therefore, many alternative forms of a commercial may be more effective.[44]

learning review

5. You see the same ad in *Time* and *Fortune* magazines and on billboards and TV. Is this an example of reach or frequency?
6. Why has the Internet become a popular advertising medium?
7. What factors must be considered when choosing among alternative media?

EXECUTING THE ADVERTISING PROGRAM

Executing the advertising program involves pretesting the advertising copy and actually carrying out the advertising program. John Wanamaker, the founder of Wanamaker's Department Store in Philadelphia, remarked, "I know half my advertising is wasted, but I don't know what half." By evaluating advertising efforts, marketers can try to ensure that their advertising expenditures are not wasted.[45] Evaluation is done usually at two separate times: before and after the advertisements are run in the actual campaign. Several methods used in the evaluation process at the stages of idea formulation and copy development are discussed below.

Pretesting the Advertising

To determine whether the advertisement communicates the intended message or to select among alternative versions of the advertisement, **pretests** are conducted before the advertisements are placed in any medium.

Portfolio Tests Portfolio tests are used to test copy alternatives. The test ad is placed in a portfolio with several other ads and stories, and consumers are asked to read through the portfolio. Afterward, subjects are asked for their impressions of the ads on several evaluative scales, such as from "very informative" to "not very informative."

Jury Tesets Jury tests involve showing the ad copy to a panel of consumers and having them rate how they liked it, how much it drew their attention, and how attractive they thought it was. This approach is similar to the portfolio test in that consumer reactions are obtained. However, unlike the portfolio test, a test advertisement is not hidden within other ads.

Theater Tests Theater testing is the most sophisticated form of pretesting. Consumers are invited to view new television shows or movies in which test commercials are also shown. Viewers register their feelings about the advertisements either on handheld electronic recording devices used during the viewing or on questionnaires afterward.

Carrying Out the Advertising Program

The responsibility for actually carrying out the advertising program can be handled in one of three ways, as shown in Figure 19–5. The **full-service agency** provides

FIGURE 19–5
Alternative structures of advertising agencies used to carry out the advertising program

TYPE OF AGENCY	SERVICES PROVIDED
Full-service agency	Does research, selects media, develops copy, and produces artwork; also coordinates integrated campaigns with all marketing efforts
Limited-service (specialty) agency	Specializes in one aspect of creative process; usually provides creative production work; buys previously unpurchased media space
In-house agency	Provides range of services, depending on company needs

the most complete range of services, including market research, media selection, copy development, artwork, and production. In the past, agencies that assisted a client by both developing and placing advertisements often charged a commission of 15 percent of the media costs. As corporations introduced integrated marketing approaches, however, many advertisers switched from paying commissions to incentive plans based on performance. These plans typically pay for agency costs and a 5 to 10 percent profit, plus bonuses if specific performance goals are met. The Association of National Advertisers estimates that almost half of all agency clients currently use this approach. Anheuser-Busch recently introduced a new version of this approach when it announced it would begin to compensate agencies for their costs based on rigid scope-of-work agreements. Vice President of Marketing Keith Levy explains, "We want partner agencies really tied to the strategy of the brand." In the future, many clients may move to a value-based approach where compensation is dependent on sales of the advertised product or brand. This approach will add additional emphasis on agency contributions beyond advertising. In some instances, such as specialized direct-response agencies, compensation is already a percentage of revenue generated.[46]

Limited-service agencies specialize in one aspect of the advertising process such as providing creative services to develop the advertising copy, buying previously unpurchased media (media agencies), or providing Internet services (Internet agencies). Limited-service agencies that deal in creative work are compensated by a contractual agreement for the services performed. Finally, **in-house agencies** made up of the company's own advertising staff may provide full services or a limited range of services.

ASSESSING THE ADVERTISING PROGRAM

The advertising decision process does not stop with executing the advertising program. The advertisements must be evaluated to determine whether they are achieving their intended objectives, and results may indicate that changes must be made in the advertising program.

Starch scores an advertisement using aided recall.

GfK Custom Research, ® Starch Advertising Research
Cosmopolitan Magazine-November 2007
eStarch Readership Report

Garnier Fructis Advertisement

Noted	85%	Read Most	30%
Associated	84%	Brand Disposition	85% (top three score)
Read Some	69%		

Posttesting the Advertising

An advertisement may go through **posttests** after it has been shown to the target audience to determine whether it accomplished its intended purpose. Five approaches common in posttesting are discussed here.[47]

Aided Recall After being shown an ad, respondents are asked whether their previous exposure to it was through reading, viewing, or listening. The Starch test shown in the accompanying photo uses aided recall to determine the percentage of those (1) who remember seeing a specific magazine ad (*noted*), (2) who saw or read any part of the ad identifying the product or brand (*seen-associated*), (3) who read any part of the ad's copy (read some), and (4) who read at least half of the ad (*read most*). Elements of the ad are then tagged with the results, as shown in the picture.[48]

Unaided Recall A question such as "What ads do you remember seeing yesterday?" is asked of respondents without any prompting to determine whether they saw or heard advertising messages.

Attitude Tests Respondents are asked questions to measure changes in their attitudes after an advertising campaign, such as whether they have a more favorable attitude toward the product advertised.[49]

Inquiry Tests Additional product information, product samples, or premiums are offered to an ad's readers or viewers. Ads generating the most inquiries are presumed to be the most effective.

Sales Tests Sales tests involve studies such as controlled experiments (e.g., using radio ads in one market and newspaper ads in another and comparing the results) and consumer purchase tests (measuring retail sales that result from a given advertising campaign). The most sophisticated experimental methods today allow a manufacturer, a distributor, or an advertising agency to manipulate an advertising variable (such as schedule or copy) through cable systems and observe subsequent sales effects by monitoring data collected from checkout scanners in supermarkets.[50]

Making Needed Changes

Results of posttesting the advertising copy are used to reach decisions about changes in the advertising program. If the posttest results show that an advertisement is doing poorly in terms of awareness, cost efficiency, or sales it may be dropped and other ads run in its place in the future. On the other hand, sometimes an advertisement may be so successful it is run repeatedly or used as the basis of a larger advertising program.

learning review

8. Explain the difference between pretesting and posttesting advertising copy.
9. What is the difference between aided and unaided recall posttests?

SALES PROMOTION

LO4

Sales promotion has become a key element of the promotional mix, which now accounts for more than $45.8 billion in annual expenditures. In a recent survey by *Promo* magazine, marketing professionals reported that approximately 32 percent of their budgets were allocated to advertising, 37 percent to consumer promotion, 24 percent to trade promotion, and 7 percent to other marketing activities.[51] The allocation of marketing expenditures reflects the trend toward integrated promotion programs, which include a variety of promotion elements. Selection and integration of the many promotion techniques require a good understanding of the advantages and disadvantages of each kind of promotion.[52]

Consumer-Oriented Sales Promotions

Directed to ultimate consumers, **consumer-oriented sales promotions**, or simply *consumer promotions*, are sales tools used to support a company's advertising and personal selling. The alternative consumer-oriented sales promotion tools include coupons, deals, premiums, contests, sweepstakes, samples, loyalty programs, point-of-purchase displays, rebates, and product placement (see Figure 19–6).

Coupons Coupons are sales promotions that usually offer a discounted price to the consumer, which encourages trial. Approximately 302 billion coupons worth $386 billion are distributed in the United States each year. Most coupons are distributed as freestanding inserts in newspapers and reach 60 million households each week. Research indicates that 89 percent of consumers use coupons. For the first time in 16 years, coupon redemptions did not decline in 2008, as the weak economy increased the attractiveness of coupons. Consumers redeemed $2.8 billion of the coupons, which was approximately $8.57 per person. Companies that have increased their use of coupons include Procter & Gamble, Nestlé, and Kraft, while the top retailers for coupon redemption were Wal-Mart and Kroger. The number of coupons generated at Internet sites (e.g., www.valpak.com and www.coupon.com) and cell

FIGURE 19–6
Sales promotions can be used to achieve many objectives.

KIND OF SALES PROMOTION	OBJECTIVES	ADVANTAGES	DISADVANTAGES
Coupons	Stimulate demand	Encourage retailer support	Consumers delay purchases
Deals	Increase trial; retaliate against competitor's actions	Reduce consumer risk	Consumers delay purchases; reduce perceived product value
Premiums	Build goodwill	Consumers like free or reduced-price merchandise	Consumers buy for premium, not product
Contests	Increase consumer purchases; build business inventory	Encourage consumer involvement with product	Require creative or analytical thinking
Sweepstakes	Encourage present customers to buy more; minimize brand switching	Get customer to use product and store more often	Sales drop after sweepstakes
Samples	Encourage new product trial	Low risk for consumer	High cost for company
Loyalty programs	Encourage repeat purchases	Help create loyalty	High cost for company
Point-of-purchase displays	Increase product trial; provide in-store support for other promotions	Provide good product visibility	Hard to get retailer to allocate high-traffic space
Rebates	Encourage customers to purchase; stop sales decline	Effective at stimulating demand	Easily copied; steal sales from future; reduce perceived product value
Product placements	Introduce new products; demonstrate product use	Positive message in a noncommercial setting	Little control over presentation of product

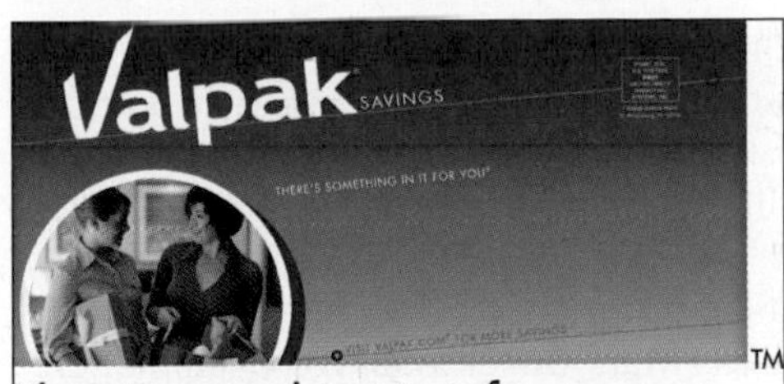

Coupons encourage trial by offering a discounted price.

phones has been increasing although they account for only 0.4 percent of all coupons. Coupons are often viewed as a key element of an integrated marketing program. Cream of Wheat recently ran banner ads on women's, parenting, food, and home and garden Web sites with the message "Free Cream of Wheat Is Just a Click Away." The link took people to a free sample order form. When the sample arrived in the mail, the package also contained a $1 coupon.[53]

Do coupons help increase sales? Studies suggest that market share does increase during the period immediately after coupons are distributed.[54] There are also indications, however, that couponing can reduce gross revenues by lowering the price paid by already-loyal consumers.[55] Therefore, the 9,000 manufacturers that currently use coupons are particularly interested in coupon programs directed at potential first-time buyers. One means of focusing on these potential buyers is through electronic in-store coupon machines that match coupons to your most recent purchases.

Coupons are often far more expensive than the face value of the coupon; a 25-cent coupon can cost three times that after paying for the advertisement to deliver it, dealer handling, clearinghouse costs, and redemption. In addition, misredemption, or attempting to redeem a counterfeit coupon or a valid coupon when the product was not purchased, should be added to the cost of the coupon. The Coupon Information Corporation estimates that companies pay out refunds of more than $300 million each year as a result of coupon fraud. Recent growth in coupon fraud has marketers considering adding holograms and visual aids to coupons to help cashiers identify valid coupons.[56]

Deals Deals are short-term price reductions, commonly used to increase trial among potential customers or to retaliate against a competitor's actions. For example, if a rival manufacturer introduces a new cake mix, the company responds with a "two packages for the price of one" deal. This short-term price reduction builds up the stock on the kitchen shelves of cake mix buyers and makes the competitor's introduction more difficult.

Premiums A promotional tool often used with consumers is the premium, which consists of merchandise offered free or at a significant savings over its retail price. This latter type of premium is called self-liquidating because the cost charged to the consumer covers the cost of the item. McDonald's, for example, used a free premium in a promotional partnership with DreamWorks during the release of the movie *Monsters vs. Aliens*. Collectible toys that portrayed movie characters were given away free with the purchase of a Happy Meal. What are the most popular premiums? According to the Promotional Products Association International, the top premiums are apparel, writing instruments, shopping bags, cups and mugs, and desk accessories. By offering a premium, companies encourage customers to return frequently or to use more of the product. Research suggests that deal-prone consumers and value seekers are attracted to premiums.[57]

Contests A fourth sales promotion in Figure 19–6, the contest, is where consumers apply their skill or analytical or creative thinking to try to win a prize. This form of promotion has been growing as requests for videos, photos, and essays are a good match with the trend toward consumer-generated content. For example, Doritos sponsored the "Crash the Super Bowl" contest, asking people to create their own 30-second ad about Doritos. A panel of judges selected five finalists from the 2,000 entries, and the public voted online for its favorite. The winner aired on the Super Bowl, and when the ad hit No. 1 on *USA Today*'s Super Bowl Ad Meter, it was awarded a $1 million bonus! If you like contests, you can enter online now at Web sites such as www.contests.about.com.[58]

Sweepstakes Sweepstakes are sales promotions that require participants to submit some kind of entry but are purely games of chance requiring no analytical or creative effort by the consumer. Popular sweepstakes include the HGTV "Dream Home Giveaway," which receives more than 40 million entries each year, and McDonald's Monopoly, which offers a grand prize of $1 million.[59]

Two variations of sweepstakes are popular now. First is the sweepstakes that offers products that consumers value as prizes. Mars Snackfood, for example, created a sweepstakes where consumers enter a UPC code from Mars products such as M&Ms, Milky Way, Snickers, Skittles, and 3 Musketeers for a chance to win a $1,000 Visa gift card. Coca-Cola has a similar sweepstakes called "My Coke Rewards" that allows consumers to use codes from bottle caps to enter to win prizes or to collect points to be redeemed for rewards. The second is the sweepstakes that offers an "experience" as the prize. For example, one of television's most popular series, *American Idol*, and AT&T sponsor a sweepstakes for a chance to win a trip for two to the season finale of *American Idol* in Los Angeles. Similarly, KFC created a sweepstakes where consumers enter for a chance to win a trip to the Super Bowl. Federal laws, the Federal Trade Commission, and state legislatures have issued rules covering sweepstakes, contests, and games to regulate fairness, ensure that the chance for winning is represented honestly, and guarantee that the prizes are actually awarded. Several well-known sweepstakes created by Publishers Clearing House and *Reader's Digest* have paid fines and agreed to new sweepstakes guidelines in response to regulatory scrutiny.[60]

Samples Another common consumer sales promotion is sampling, which is offering the product free or at a greatly reduced price. Often used for new products, sampling puts the product in the consumer's hands. A trial size is generally offered that is smaller than the regular package size. If consumers like the sample, it is hoped they will remember and buy the product. When Mars changed its Milky Way Dark to Milky Way Midnight, it gave away more than 1 million samples to college students at nightclubs, several hundred campuses, and popular spring break locations. Awareness of the candy bar rose to 60 percent, trial rose 166 percent, and sales rose 25 percent. Recent research indicates that 63 percent of college students who receive a sample will also purchase the product. Overall, companies invest more than $2.3 billion in sampling programs each year.[61]

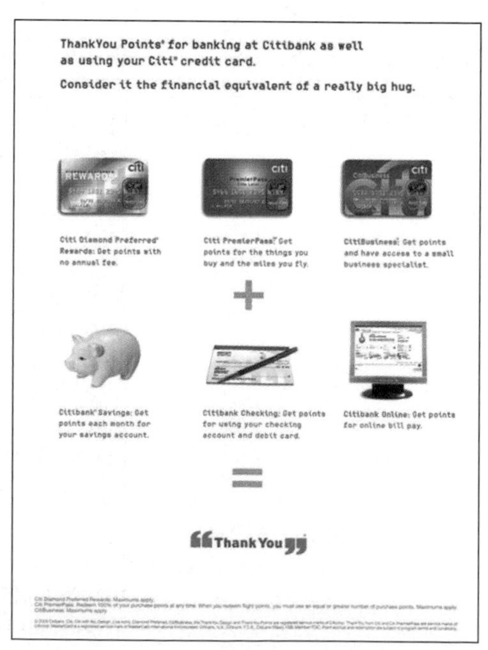

The Nestlé Crunch sweepstakes attract prospective customers while the Citi loyalty program rewards use of Citibank credit cards.

Nestlé
www.nestle.com

Citibank
www.citibank.com

Loyalty Programs Loyalty programs are a sales promotion tool used to encourage and reward repeat purchases by acknowledging each purchase made by a consumer and offering a premium as purchases accumulate. The most popular loyalty programs today are credit card reward programs. More than 75 percent of all cards offer incentives for use of their card. Citibank, for example, offers "Thank You" points for using Citi credit or debit cards. The points can be redeemed for books, music, gift cards, cash, travel, and special limited time rewards. Airlines, retailers, hotels, and grocery stores also offer popular loyalty programs. Some of the newest programs recently introduced have been by car rental and cruise line companies. There are now more than 1.8 billion loyalty program memberships, for an average of 14 for each household in the United States.[62]

The trend in loyalty programs today is to customize the rewards and benefits for different segments of program members. This approach leads to promotions targeted at new members, members with unique purchase histories, or members who have self-selected into "elite" status groups. American Airlines, for example, has offered bonus points for new members, an additional 50 percent of award points for members who fly first class, and special benefits for members who join the American Airlines Admirals Club.[63]

Point-of-Purchase Displays In a store aisle, you often encounter a sales promotion called a point-of-purchase display. These product displays take the form of advertising signs, which sometimes actually hold or display the product, and are often located in high-traffic areas near the cash register or the end of an aisle. The point-of-purchase display for Nabisco's annual back-to-school program is designed to maximize the consumer's attention to lunch box and after-school snacks, and to provide storage for the products. Annual expenditures on point-of-purchase promotions now exceed $20.3 billion and are expected to grow as point-of-purchase becomes integrated with all forms of promotion.

Point-of-purchase displays help increase consumers' attention in a store.

Some studies estimate that one-third of a consumer's buying decisions are made in the store. Grocery product manufacturers want to get their message to you at the instant you are next to their brand in your supermarket aisle, perhaps through a point-of-purchase display. At a growing number of supermarkets this may be done with digital signage. Walmart, for example, is replacing its satellite-based in-store TV network with an Internet protocol system called Walmart Smart Network, which allows eye-level screens that display short advertising clips. The advantage of these methods of promotion is that they do not rely on the consumers' ability to remember the message for long periods. Other in-store promotions such as interactive kiosks are also becoming popular.[64]

Rebates Another consumer sales promotion in Figure 19–6, the cash rebate, offers the return of money based on proof of purchase. For example, Apple recently offered a $100 rebate to consumers who purchased an Apple computer and a printer during a three-month promotion period.

When a rebate is offered on lower-priced items, the time and trouble of mailing in a proof of purchase to get the rebate check often means that many buyers never take advantage of it. However, this "slippage" is less likely to occur with frequent users of rebate promotions.[65] In addition, online consumers are more likely to take advantage of rebates.

Product Placements A final consumer promotion, **product placements**, involve the use of a brand-name product in a movie, television show, video game, or commercial for another product. It was Steven Spielberg's placement of Hershey's

Can you identify these product placements?

Reese's Pieces in *E.T.* that first brought a lot of interest to the candy. Similarly, when Tom Cruise wore Bausch and Lomb's Ray-Ban sunglasses in *Risky Business* and its Aviator glasses in *Top Gun*, sales skyrocketed from 100,000 pairs to 7,000,000 pairs in five years. After *Toy Story*, Etch-A-Sketch sales increased 4,500 percent and Mr. Potato Head sales increased 800 percent.

More recently, you might remember seeing the American Express Black Card, Ray-Ban sunglasses, and Spalding basketballs in *17 Again*, Yamaha electronic equipment in *Monsters vs. Aliens*, or Sony televisions and Pepsi in *Watchmen*. Product placement has also grown in television programs. *The Biggest Loser* ranks No. 1 in product placements with Zip-Lock baggies, Extra gum, Macy's department store, *Prevention* magazine, and many other products making appearances. Companies are usually eager to gain exposure for their products, and studios believe that product placements add authenticity to the film or program. The producers usually receive fees in exchange for the exposure. Coca-Cola, for example, reportedly pays $26 million for its placement on the television hit *American Idol*. The Federal Communications Commission is currently writing guidelines for TV product placements and how they should be disclosed.[66]

A variation of this form of promotion, called *reverse product placement*, brings fictional products to the marketplace. Bertie Bott's Every Flavor Beans, for example, began as an imaginary brand in Harry Potter books. Similarly, the movie *Forrest Gump* led to the Bubba Gump Shrimp Company restaurant chain. Finally, 7-Eleven converted 12 of its stores into Kwik-E-Marts, the imaginary convenience stores in the television cartoon series, *The Simpsons*, to coincide with the release of *The Simpsons Movie*.[67]

Trade-Oriented Sales Promotions

Trade-oriented sales promotions, or simply *trade promotions*, are sales tools used to support a company's advertising and personal selling directed to wholesalers, retailers, or distributors. Some of the sales promotions just reviewed are used for this purpose, but three other common approaches are targeted uniquely to these intermediaries: (1) allowances and discounts, (2) cooperative advertising, and (3) training of distributors' salesforces.

Allowances and Discounts Trade promotions often focus on maintaining or increasing inventory levels in the channel of distribution. An effective method for encouraging such increased purchases by intermediaries is the use of allowances and discounts. However, overuse of these price reductions can lead to retailers changing their ordering patterns in the expectation of such offerings. Although there are many variations that manufacturers can use with discounts and allowances, three common approaches are the merchandise allowance, the case allowance, and the finance allowance.[68]

Reimbursing a retailer for extra in-store support or special featuring of the brand is a *merchandise allowance*. Performance contracts between the manufacturer and trade member usually specify the activity to be performed, such as a picture of the product in a newspaper with a coupon good at only one store. The merchandise allowance then consists of a percentage deduction from the list case price ordered during the promotional period. Allowances are not paid by the manufacturer until it sees proof of performance (such as a copy of the ad placed by the retailer in the local newspaper).

A second common trade promotion, a *case allowance*, is a discount on each case ordered during a specific time period. These allowances are usually deducted from the invoice. A variation of the case allowance is the "free goods" approach, whereby retailers receive some amount of the product free based on the amount ordered, such as 1 case free for every 10 cases ordered.[69]

A final trade promotion, the *finance allowance*, involves paying retailers for financing costs or financial losses associated with consumer sales promotions. This trade promotion is regularly used and has several variations. One type is the floor stock protection program—manufacturers give retailers a case allowance price for products in their warehouse, which prevents shelf stock from running down during the promotional period. Also common are freight allowances, which compensate retailers that transport orders from the manufacturer's warehouse.

Cooperative Advertising Resellers often perform the important function of promoting the manufacturer's products at the local level. One common sales promotional activity is to encourage both better quality and greater quantity in the local advertising efforts of resellers through **cooperative advertising**. These are programs by which a manufacturer pays a percentage of the retailer's local advertising expense for advertising the manufacturer's products.

Usually, the manufacturer pays a percentage, often 50 percent, of the cost of advertising up to a certain dollar limit, which is based on the amount of the purchases the retailer makes of the manufacturer's products. In addition to paying for the advertising, the manufacturer often furnishes the retailer with a selection of different ad executions, sometimes suited for several different media. A manufacturer may provide, for example, several different print layouts as well as a few broadcast ads for the retailer to adapt and use.[70]

Training of Distributors' Salesforces One of the many functions the intermediaries perform is customer contact and selling for the producers they represent. Both retailers and wholesalers employ and manage their own sales personnel. A manufacturer's success often rests on the ability of the reseller's salesforce to represent its products.

Thus, it is in the best interest of the manufacturer to help train the reseller's salesforce. Because the reseller's salesforce is often less sophisticated and knowledgeable about the products than the manufacturer might like, training can increase their sales performance. Training activities include producing manuals and brochures to educate the reseller's salesforce. The salesforce then uses these aids in selling situations. Other activities include national sales meetings sponsored by the manufacturer and field visits to the reseller's location to inform and motivate the salesperson to sell the products. Manufacturers also develop incentive and recognition programs to motivate reseller's salespeople to sell their products.

learning review

10. What's the difference between a coupon and a deal?
11. Which sales promotional tool is most common for new products?
12. Which trade promotion is used on an ongoing basis?

PUBLIC RELATIONS

LO5

As noted in Chapter 18, public relations is a form of communication management that seeks to influence the image of an organization and its products and services. Public relations efforts may utilize a variety of tools and may be directed at many distinct audiences. While public relations personnel usually focus on communicating positive aspects of the business, they may also be called on to minimize the negative impact of a problem or crisis. Nestlé, PepsiCo, and Coca-Cola, for example, have been facing substantial negative publicity about the environmental impact of the plastic bottles used for their Nestlé Waters, Aquafina, and Dasani brands. Newspapers, blogs, the general public, and even New York and San Francisco mayors have expressed concerns that the companies' public relations departments must address.[71] The most frequently used public relations tool is publicity.

Publicity Tools

In developing a public relations campaign, several methods of obtaining nonpersonal presentation of an organization, good, or service without direct cost—**publicity tools**—are available to the public relations director. Many companies frequently use the *news release*, consisting of an announcement regarding changes in the company or the product line. The objective of a news release is to inform a newspaper, radio station, or other medium of an idea for a story.

A second common publicity tool is the *news conference*. Representatives of the media are all invited to an informational meeting, and advance materials regarding the content are sent. This tool is often used when new products are introduced or significant changes in corporate structure and leadership are being made.

Gwyneth Paltrow uses publicity to promote her movies.

Nonprofit organizations rely heavily on *public service announcements* (PSAs), which are free space or time donated by the media. For example, the charter of the American Red Cross prohibits any local chapter from advertising, so to solicit blood donations local chapters often depend on PSAs on radio or television to announce their needs.

Finally, today many high-visibility individuals are used as publicity tools to create visibility for their companies, their products, and themselves. Richard Branson uses visibility to promote the Virgin Group, Gwyneth Paltrow uses it to promote her movies, and U.S. senators use it to promote themselves as political candidates. These publicity efforts are coordinated with news releases, conferences, advertising, donations to charities, volunteer activities, endorsements, and any other activities that may have an impact on public perceptions.[72]

INCREASING THE VALUE OF PROMOTION

Today's customers seek value from companies that provide leading-edge products, hassle-free transactions at competitive prices, and customer intimacy.[73] Promotion practices have changed dramatically to improve transactions and increase customer intimacy by (1) emphasizing long-term relationships and (2) increasing self-regulation.

Building Long-Term Relationships with Promotion

Many changes in promotional techniques have been driven by marketers' interest in developing long-term relationships with their customers. Promotion can contribute to brand and store loyalty by improving its ability to target individual preferences and by engaging customers in valuable and entertaining communication. New media such as the Internet and mobile telephones have provided immediate opportunities for personalized promotion activities such as e-mail advertising. In addition, technological developments have helped traditional media such as TV and radio focus on individual preferences through services such as TiVo and Sirius XM Satellite Radio. Although the future holds extraordinary promise for the personalization of promotion, the industry will need to manage and balance consumers' concerns about privacy as it proceeds.

Changes that help engage consumers have also been numerous. Marketers have attempted to utilize interactive technologies and to integrate new media and technologies into the overall creative process. Ad agencies are increasingly integrating public relations, direct marketing, advertising, and promotion into comprehensive campaigns. In fact, some experts predict that advertising agencies will soon become "communications consulting firms." Further, increasingly diverse and global audiences necessitate multimedia approaches and sensitivity communication techniques that engage the varied groups.[74] Overall, companies hope that these changes will build customer relationships for the long term—emphasizing a lifetime of purchases rather than a single transaction.

Self-Regulation

Unfortunately, over the years many consumers have been misled, or even deceived, by some promotions. Examples include sweepstakes in which the gifts were not awarded, rebate offers that were a terrible hassle, and advertisements whose promises were great, until the buyer read the small print. In one of the worst scandals in promotion history, McDonald's assisted an FBI investigation of the firm responsible for the fast-food chain's sweepstakes, because the promotion agency security director was suspected of stealing winning game pieces.[75]

Promotions targeted at special groups such as children and the elderly also raise ethical concerns. For example, providing free samples to children in elementary schools or linking product lines to TV programs and movies have led to questions about the need for restrictions on promotions.[76] Although the Federal Trade Commission does provide some guidelines to protect consumers and special groups from misleading promotions, some observers believe more government regulation is needed.

To rely on formal regulation by federal, state, and local governments of all promotional activities would be very expensive. As a result, there are increasing efforts by advertising agencies, trade associations, and marketing organizations at *self-regulation*.[77] By imposing standards that reflect the values of society on their promotional activities, marketers can (1) facilitate the development of new promotional methods, (2) minimize regulatory constraints and restrictions, and (3) help consumers gain confidence in the communication efforts used to influence their purchases. As organizations strive for effective self-regulation, marketing executives will need to make sound ethical judgments about the use of existing and new promotional practices.

learning review

13. What is a news release?

14. What is the difference between government regulation and self-regulation?

LEARNING OBJECTIVES REVIEW

LO1 *Explain the differences between product advertising and institutional advertising and the variations within each type.*
Product advertisements focus on selling a good or service and take three forms: Pioneering advertisements tell people what a product is, what it can do, and where it can be found; competitive advertisements persuade the target market to select the firm's brand rather than a competitor's; and reminder advertisements reinforce previous knowledge of a product. Institutional advertisements are used to build goodwill or an image for an organization. They include advocacy advertisements, which state the position of a company on an issue, and pioneering, competitive, and reminder advertisements, which are similar to the product ads but focused on the institution.

LO2 *Describe the steps used to develop, execute, and evaluate an advertising program.*
The promotion decision process can be applied to each of the promotional elements. The steps to develop an advertising program include identify the target audience, specify the advertising objectives, set the advertising budget, design the advertisement, create the message, select the media, and schedule the advertising. Executing the program requires pretesting, and evaluating the program requires posttesting.

LO3 *Explain the advantages and disadvantages of alternative advertising media.*
Television advertising reaches large audiences and uses picture, print, sound, and motion; its disadvantages, however, are that it is expensive and perishable. Radio advertising is inexpensive and can be placed quickly, but it has no visual element and is perishable. Magazine advertising can target specific audiences and can convey complex information, but it takes a long time to place the ad and is relatively expensive. Newspapers provide excellent coverage of local markets and can be changed quickly, but they have a short life span and poor color. Yellow pages advertising has a long use period and is available 24 hours per day; its disadvantages, however, are that there is a proliferation of directories and they cannot be updated frequently. Internet advertising can be interactive, but its effectiveness is difficult to measure. Outdoor advertising provides repeat exposures, but its message must be very short and simple. Direct mail can be targeted at very selective audiences, but its cost per contact is high.

LO4 *Discuss the strengths and weaknesses of consumer-oriented and trade-oriented sales promotions.*
Coupons encourage retailer support but may delay consumer purchases. Deals reduce consumer risk but reduce perceived value. Premiums offer consumers additional merchandise they want, but they may be purchasing only for the premium. Contests create involvement but require creative thinking. Sweepstakes encourage repeat purchases, but sales drop after the sweepstakes. Samples encourage product trial but are expensive. Loyalty programs help create loyalty but are expensive to run. Displays provide visibility but are difficult to place in retail space. Rebates stimulate demand but are easily copied. Product placement provides a positive message in a noncommercial setting but is difficult to control. Trade-oriented sales promotions include (*a*) allowances and discounts, which increase purchases but may change retailer ordering patterns, (*b*) cooperative advertising, which encourages local advertising, and (*c*) salesforce training, which helps increase sales by providing the salespeople with product information and selling skills.

LO5 *Recognize public relations as an important form of communication.*
Public relations activities usually focus on communicating positive aspects of the business. A frequently used public relations tool is publicity. Publicity tools include new releases and news conferences. Nonprofit organization often use public service announcements.

FOCUSING ON KEY TERMS

advertising p. 486
consumer-oriented sales promotions p. 505
cooperative advertising p. 511
cost per thousand p. 495
frequency p. 494
full-service agency p. 503
gross rating points p. 495
infomercials p. 497
in-house agencies p. 504
institutional advertisements p. 487
limited-service agencies p. 504
posttests p. 504
pretests p. 503
product advertisements p. 486
product placements p. 509
publicity tools p. 512
rating p. 494
reach p. 494
trade-oriented sales promotions p. 510

APPLYING MARKETING KNOWLEDGE

1 How does competitive product advertising differ from competitive institutional advertising?

2 Suppose you are the advertising manager for a new line of children's fragrances. Which form of media would you use for this new product?

3 You have recently been promoted to be director of advertising for the Timkin Tool Company. In your first meeting with Mr. Timkin, he says, "Advertising is a waste! We've been advertising for six months now and sales haven't increased. Tell me why we should continue." Give your answer to Mr. Timkin.

4 A large life insurance company has decided to switch from using a strong fear appeal to a humorous approach. What are the strengths and weaknesses of such a change in message strategy?

5 Which medium has the lowest cost per thousand?

6 Some national advertisers have found that they can have more impact with their advertising by running a

Medium	Cost	Audience
TV show	$5,000	25,000
Magazine	2,200	6,000
Newspaper	4,800	7,200
FM radio	420	1,600

large number of ads for a period and then running no ads at all for a period. Why might such a flighting schedule be more effective than a continuous schedule?

7 Each year managers at Bausch and Lomb evaluate the many advertising media alternatives available to them as they develop their advertising program for contact lenses. What advantages and disadvantages of each alternative should they consider? Which media would you recommend to them?

8 What are two advantages and two disadvantages of the advertising posttests described in the chapter?

9 Federated Banks is interested in consumer-oriented sales promotions that would encourage senior citizens to direct deposit their Social Security checks with the bank. Evaluate the sales promotion options, and recommend two of them to the bank.

10 How can public relations be used by Firestone and Ford following investigations into complaints about tire failures?

11 Describe a self-regulation guideline you believe would improve the value of (*a*) an existing form of promotion and (*b*) a new promotional practice.

building your marketing plan

To augment your promotion strategy from Chapter 18:

1 Use Figure 19–3 to select the advertising media you will include in your plan by analyzing how combinations of media (e.g., television and Internet advertising, radio and yellow pages advertising) can complement each other.

2 Use Figure 19–6 to select your consumer-oriented sales promotion activities.

3 Specify which trade-oriented sales promotions and public relations tools you will use.

video case 19 Google, Inc.: The Right Ads at the Right Time

"So what we did, in essence, is we said advertising should be useful to a consumer just as much as the organic search results, and we don't want people just to buy advertising and be able to show an ad if it's irrelevant to the consumer's need," says Richard Holden, director of product management at Google. To accomplish this, Google developed a "Quality Score" model to predict how effective an ad will be. The model uses many factors such as click-through rates, advertiser history, and keyword performance, to develop a score for each advertisement. "Essentially, what we're trying to do is predict ahead, before we actually show an ad, how a consumer will react to that ad, and our interest is in showing fewer ads, not more ads; just the right ads at the right time," Holden continues. The Google advertising model has revolutionized the advertising industry, and it continues to improve every day!

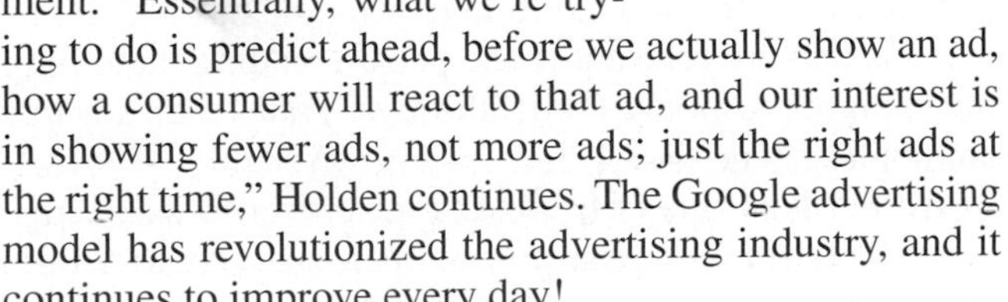

THE COMPANY

Google began in 1996 as a research project for Stanford computer science students, Larry Page and Sergey Brin. They started with a simple idea—that a search engine based on the relationships between Web sites would provide a better ranking than a search engine based only on the number of times a key term appeared on a Web site. The success of their model led to rapid growth and the founders moved the company from their dorm room, to a friend's garage, to offices in Palo Alto, California, and eventually to its current location, known as the Googleplex, in Mountain View, CA. In 2000, Google began selling advertising as a means of generating revenue. Their advertising model allowed advertisers to bid on search words and pay for each "click" by a search-engine user. The ads were required to be simple and text-based so that the search result pages remained uncluttered and the search time was as fast as possible.

Page and Brin's first search engine was called "BackRub" because their technique was based on relationships, or backlinks, between Web sites. The name quickly changed, however. The name "Google" is a misspelling of the word "googol" which is a mathematical term for a 1 followed by 100 zeros. Page and Brin used the name in the original domain, www.google.stanford.edu, to reflect their interest in organizing the immense amount of information available on the Web. The domain name, of course, became www.google.com and eventually Webster's dictionary added the verb "google" with the definition "to use the Google search engine to obtain information on the Internet." The name has become so familiar that *Advertising Age* recently reported that Google is "the world's most powerful brand"!

Today Google receives several hundred million inquiries each day as it pursues its mission: to organize the world's information and make it universally accessible and useful. The company generates more than $21 billion in annual revenue and has more than 20,000 employees. As Google has grown it has developed 10 guidelines that represent the corporate philosophy. They are:

1. Focus on the user and all else will follow.
2. It's best to do one thing really, really well.
3. Fast is better than slow.
4. Democracy on the Web works.
5. You don't need to be at your desk to need an answer.
6. You can make money without doing evil.
7. There's always more information out there.
8. The need for information crosses all borders.
9. You can be serious without a suit.
10. Great just isn't good enough.

Using these guidelines Google strives to continually improve its search engine. "The perfect search engine," explains Google co-founder Larry Page, "would understand exactly what you mean and give back exactly what you want."

ONLINE ADVERTISING

Google generates revenue by offering online advertising opportunities—next to search results or on specific Web pages. The company always distinguishes ads from the search results or the content of a Web page and it never sells placement in the search results. This approach ensures that Google Web site visitors always know when someone has paid to put a message in front of them. The advantage of online advertising is that it is measurable and allows immediate assessment of its effectiveness. As Gopi Kallayil, product marketing manager, explains: "There is a very high degree of measurability and trackability that you get through online advertising." In addition, he says, "With online advertising you can actually track the value of every single dollar that you spend, understand which particular customers the ad reached, and what they did after they received the advertising message."

The online advertising market has grown from its initial focus on simple text ads to a much larger set of options. There are five key categories of online advertising. They are:

- Search: 47%
- Display: 35%
- Classified: 10%
- Referral: 7%
- E-mail: 1%

Google is the dominant provider of online search requests and receives more than 60 percent of the search advertising revenue. The fastest-growing advertising category, however, is display advertising where Yahoo! and Microsoft are established providers. Google believes that there is an opportunity to grow its display advertising sales by making the ads useful information instead of visual clutter. According to Google co-founder Sergey Brin, "It's like search—matching people with information they want. It just happens to be promotional."

Several improvements in technology and business practice tools contributed to Google's success. First, Google developed its patented PageRank™ algorithm which evaluates the entire link structure of the Web and uses the link structure to determine which pages are most important. Then the process uses hypertext-matching analysis to determine which pages are relevant to a specific search. A combination of the importance and the relevance of Web pages provides the search results—in just a fraction of a second. Second, Google developed two business practice tools—AdWords and AdSense—to help (1) advertisers create ads, and (2) content providers generate advertising revenue. Both tools have become essential elements of Google's advertising model.

AdWords

To help advertisers place ads on their search-engine results, Google developed an online tool called AdWords. Advertisers can use AdWords to create ad text, select target keywords, and manage their account. The process allows advertisers to reach targeted audiences. Frederick Vallaeys, Adwords evangelist, explains: "One of my favorite things about AdWords is the fact that it really helps you find the right customer at the right time and show them the right message. With AdWords you can very specifically target your market because you're targeting them at a time when they do a search on Google. At that time they've told you a keyword, you know exactly what they're looking for, and here is your opportunity as a marketer to give them the exact answer to what they've just told you they wanted to find." Google has found that text ads that are relevant to the person reading them have much higher response ("clickthrough") rates than ads that are not targeted.

AdWords is also easy for any advertiser to use. Large or small businesses can simply open an account with a credit card and have ads appear within minutes. "When AdWords rolled out their self-service product, it really was one of the first times when it was very easy for a small business to put their ad up on the Internet on a search engine and compete on a level playing field along-

side Fortune 1000 companies," says Vallaeys. Google has an experienced sales and service team available to help any advertiser select appropriate keywords, generate ad copy, and monitor campaign performance. The team is dedicated to helping its advertisers improve clickthrough rates because high clickthrough rates are an indication that ads are relevant to a user's interests. Methods of improving advertising performance include changing the keywords and rewriting copy. Because there is no limit to the number of keywords that an advertiser can select and each keyword can be matched with different ad copy, the potential for many very customer-specific options is high.

Another advantage of Google's AdWords program is that it allows advertisers to easily control costs. The ads appear as a "Sponsored Link" next to search results each time the Google search engine matches the search request with the ad's keywords and Quality Score, although the advertiser is not charged unless someone "clicks" on the link. In a traditional advertising model, advertisers were charged using a CPM (cost-per-thousand) approach, which charged for the impressions made by an ad. According to Holden, the Google model "transformed that to what we call a CPC, or a cost-per-click model, and this is a model that an advertiser, instead of paying for an impression, only pays when somebody actually clicks on that ad and is delivered to their Web site. So, in effect, they may be getting the benefit from impressions being shown, but we're not actually charging them anything unless there's a definite lead being delivered to their Web site." Google also offers advertisers real-time analytical services to allow assessment of and changes to any component of an advertising campaign.

AdSense

The AdSense program was designed for Web site owners as a tool for placing ads next to their Web page content rather than next to search results. Currently, thousands of Web site managers use AdSense to place ads on their sites and generate revenue. Google applies the same general philosophy to matching ads with Web sites as it does to matching ads to search requests. By delivering ads that precisely target the content on the site's pages, Google believes the advertising enhances the experience for visitors to the Web site. In this way advertisers, Web site publishers, and information seekers all benefit.

AdSense is one of the tools Google is using to pursue its goal of increasing its display advertising business. Yahoo! and Microsoft's MSN are leaders in display advertising because they can put ads on their own Web sites such as Yahoo! Finance and MSN Money. To provide additional outlets for display ads Google recently purchased YouTube. In addition, Google purchased DoubleClick, an advertising exchange where Web sites put space up for auction and ad agencies bid to place ads for their clients. Google is also trying to make it easy for anyone to create a display ad by introducing a new tool called Display Ad Builder. Some experts observe that because Google is so dominant at search advertising, its future growth will depend on success in display advertising.

GOOGLE'S FUTURE STRATEGY

How will Google continue its success? One possibility is that it will begin to try to win advertising away from the U.S. TV industry. While this is a new type of advertising requiring creative capabilities and relationships with large advertising agencies, Google has dedicated many of its resources to becoming competitive for television advertising expenditures. For example, Google recently helped Volvo develop a campaign that included a YouTube ad and Twitter updates. Google is also likely to develop new Web sites, establish blogs, and build relationships with existing sites.

Another opportunity for Google will be mobile telephone advertising. There are currently more than 3 billion mobile phones in use, and 600 million of those are Internet-capable. Just as Google's search engine provides a means to match relevant information with consumers, phones offer a chance to provide real-time and location-specific information. Some of the challenges in mobile advertising will be that the networks are not fast and that the ad formats are not standardized. Google believes its new phone and its Android operating system will also help.

Finally, as Google pursues its mission it will continue to expand throughout the world. Search results are already available in 35 languages and volunteers are helping with many others. It is obvious that Google is determined to "organize the world's information" and make it "accessible and useful."

Questions

1 Describe several unique characteristics about Google and its business practices.

2 What is Google's philosophy about advertising? How can less advertising be preferred to more advertising?

3 Describe the types of online advertising available today. Which type of advertising does Google currently dominate? Why?

4 How can Google be successful in the display advertising business? What other areas of growth are Google likely to pursue in the future?

EROX
CHICAG
PUBLIC LIBR
C P L

20 Personal Selling and Sales Management

LEARNING OBJECTIVES

After reading this chapter you should be able to:

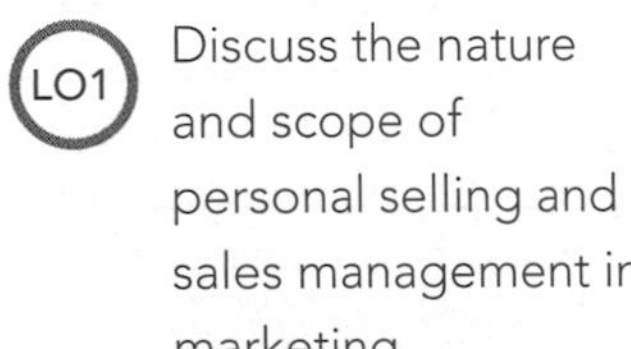

LO1 Discuss the nature and scope of personal selling and sales management in marketing.

LO2 Identify the different types of personal selling.

LO3 Explain the stages in the personal selling process.

LO4 Describe the major functions of sales management.

XEROX SUCCEEDS BY DOING WHAT'S RIGHT FOR THE CUSTOMER

Anne Mulcahy has a challenging assignment. As the chairman of the board and chief executive officer at Xerox Corporation, she is successfully managing one of the greatest feats in the annals of business history: restoring Xerox's legendary marketing and financial vitality.

Her success can be attributed to staying in sync with Xerox customers and employees. "I believe strongly that my success as a leader is driven by my commitment to understanding and meeting customers' requirements, as well as developing and nurturing a motivated and proud work force," says Mulcahy.

Mulcahy is ideally suited to the task. She began her 34-year Xerox career as a field sales representative and assumed increasingly responsible management and executive positions. These included chief staff officer, president of Xerox's General Markets Operations, and president and chief operating officer of Xerox. As chairman, Mulcahy had to muster the knowledge and experience gained from this varied background. Not surprisingly, her field sales background played a pivotal role.

"We started winning when we listened to customers," Mulcahy says. "We did that by providing greater value than our competitors—and that meant selling the way customers want to buy." She adds, "Doing what's right for the customer—that's our guiding principle." And attention to the customer buying experience has paid huge dividends. Xerox sales revenue and net income have soared during Mulcahy's tenure as chairman and CEO. Her dedicated customer focus and field sales experience bodes well for the continued success of Xerox.[1]

This chapter describes the scope and significance of personal selling and sales management in marketing and creating value for customers. It first highlights the many forms of personal selling. Next, the major steps in the selling process are outlined with an emphasis on building buyer-seller relationships. Attention is then focused on salesforce management and its critical role in achieving a company's broader marketing objectives. Three major salesforce management functions are then detailed. They are sales plan formulation, sales plan implementation, and salesforce evaluation. Finally, technology's persuasive influence on how selling is done and how salespeople are managed is described.

SCOPE AND SIGNIFICANCE OF PERSONAL SELLING AND SALES MANAGEMENT

Chapter 18 described personal selling and management of the sales effort as being part of the firm's promotional mix. Although it is important to recognize that personal selling is a useful vehicle for communicating with present and potential buyers, it is much more. Take a moment to answer the questions in the personal selling and sales management quiz in Figure 20–1. As you read on, compare your answers with those in the text.

Nature of Personal Selling and Sales Management

LO1

Personal selling involves the two-way flow of communication between a buyer and seller, often in a face-to-face encounter, designed to influence a person's or group's purchase decision. However, with advances in telecommunications, personal selling also takes place over the telephone, through video teleconferencing and Internet-enabled links between buyers and sellers.

Personal selling remains a highly human-intensive activity despite the use of technology. Accordingly, the people involved must be managed. **Sales management** involves planning the selling program and implementing and evaluating the personal selling effort of the firm. The tasks involved in managing personal selling include: setting objectives; organizing the salesforce; recruiting, selecting, training, and compensating salespeople; and evaluating the performance of individual salespeople.

Selling Happens Almost Everywhere

"Everyone lives by selling something," wrote author Robert Louis Stevenson a century ago. His observation still holds true today. The Bureau of Labor Statistics reports that about 15 million people are employed in sales positions in the United States. Included in this number are manufacturing sales personnel, real estate brokers, stockbrokers, and salesclerks who work in retail stores. In reality, however, virtually every occupation that involves customer contact has an element of personal selling. For example, attorneys, accountants, bankers, and company personnel recruiters perform sales-related activities, whether or not they acknowledge it.

About 20 percent of chief executive officers in the largest U.S. corporations have significant sales experience in their work history like Anne Mulcahy at Xerox.[2] (*What*

FIGURE 20–1
Personal selling and sales management quiz. Check your answers as you read the chapter.

1. What percentage of chief executive officers in the largest U.S. companies has significant sales experience in their work history? (check one)

   10% ________ 30% ________ 50% ________

   20% ________ 40% ________ 60% ________

2. What percentage of an average field sales representative's time each workweek is spent actually selling to customers? (check one)

   45% ________ 55% ________ 65% ________

3. "A salesperson's job is finished when a sale is made." True or false? (circle one)

   True   False

4. About what percentage of U.S. companies includes customer satisfaction as a measure of salesperson performance? (check one)

   10% ________ 30% ________ 50% ________

   20% ________ 40% ________ 60% ________

Could this be a salesperson in the operating room? Read the text to find out why Medtronic salespeople visit hospital operating rooms.

Medtronic
www.medtronic.com

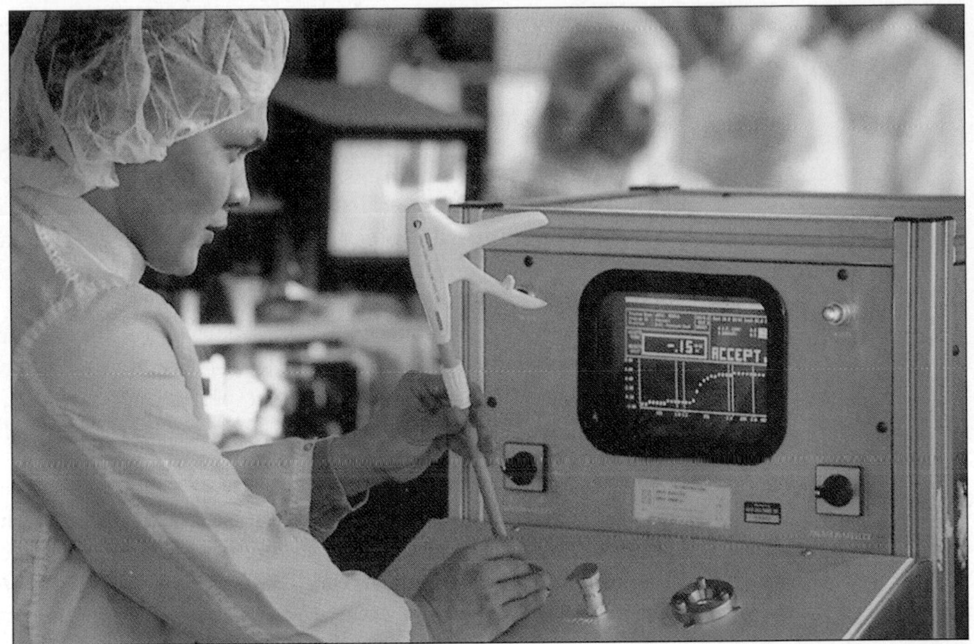

percentage did you check for question 1 in Figure 20–1?) Thus, selling often serves as a stepping-stone to top management, as well as being a career path itself.

Personal Selling in Marketing

Personal selling serves three major roles in a firm's overall marketing effort. First, salespeople are the critical link between the firm and its customers. This role requires that salespeople match company interests with customer needs to satisfy both parties in the exchange process. Second, salespeople *are* the company in a consumer's eyes. They represent what a company is or attempts to be and are often the only personal contact a customer has with the company. For example, Sam Palmisano, IBM's chief executive officer, calls the company's 40,000-strong salesforce "our face to the client."[3] Third, personal selling may play a dominant role in a firm's marketing program. This situation typically arises when a firm uses a push marketing strategy, described in Chapter 18. Avon, for example, pays almost 40 percent of its total sales dollars for selling expenses. Pharmaceutical firms and office and educational equipment manufacturers also rely heavily on personal selling in the marketing of their products.

Creating Customer Solutions and Value through Salespeople: Relationship and Partnership Selling

As the critical link between the firm and its customers, salespeople can create customer value in many ways. For instance, by being close to the customer, salespeople can identify creative solutions to customer problems. Salespeople at Medtronic, Inc., the world leader in the heart pacemaker market, are in the operating room for more than 90 percent of the procedures performed with their product and are on call, wearing pagers, 24 hours a day. "It reflects the willingness to be there in every situation, just in case a problem arises—even though nine times out of ten the procedure goes just fine," notes a satisfied customer.[4]

Salespeople can create value by easing the customer buying process. This happened at AMP, Inc., a producer of electrical products. Salespeople and customers had a difficult time getting product specifications and performance data on AMP's 70,000 products quickly and accurately. The company now records all information on CD-ROM disks that can be scanned instantly by salespeople and customers.

Customer value is also created by salespeople who follow through after the sale. At Jefferson Smurfit Corporation, a multibillion-dollar supplier of packaging products, one of its salespeople juggled production from three of the company's plants to satisfy an unexpected demand for boxes from General Electric. This person's action led to the company being given GE's Distinguished Supplier Award.

Relationship Selling Customer value creation is made possible by **relationship selling**, the practice of building ties to customers based on a salesperson's attention and commitment to customer needs over time. Relationship selling involves mutual respect and trust among buyers and sellers. It focuses on creating long-term customers, not a onetime sale. A survey of 300 senior sales executives revealed that 96 percent consider "building long-term relationships with customers" to be the most important activity affecting sales performance. Companies such as Xerox, American Express, Motorola, and Owens-Corning have made relationship building a core focus of their sales effort.[5]

Partnership Selling Some companies have taken relationship selling a step further and forged partnerships between buyer and seller organizations. With **partnership selling**, sometimes called *enterprise selling*, buyers and sellers combine their expertise and resources to create customized solutions; commit to joint planning; and share customer, competitive, and company information for their mutual benefit, and ultimately the customer.

As an approach to sales, partnership selling relies on cross-functional business specialists who apply their knowledge and expertise to achieve better customer solutions, lower cost, and greater customer value. Partnership selling complements supplier and channel partnering described in Chapters 6, 15, and 16. This practice is embraced by General Electric, Honeywell, DuPont, and IBM. For example, on any given day, IBM has 30 information technology hardware and software specialists, business consultants, and engineers working at Charles Schwab, a large brokerage firm, all under the direction of a senior IBM sales executive. Their job? Create and manage a complex state-of-the-art financial planning system that assists Schwab clients with their retirement planning.[6]

Relationship and partnership selling represent another dimension of customer relationship management. Both emphasize the importance of learning about customer needs and wants and tailoring solutions to customer problems as a means to customer value creation.

learning review

1. What is personal selling?
2. What is involved in sales management?

THE MANY FORMS OF PERSONAL SELLING

LO2

Personal selling assumes many forms based on the amount of selling done and the amount of creativity required to perform the sales task. Broadly speaking, three types of personal selling exist: order taking, order getting, and customer sales support activities. While some firms use only one of these types of personal selling, others use a combination of all three.

Order-Taking Salespeople

Typically, an **order taker** processes routine orders or reorders for products that were already sold by the company. The primary responsibility of order takers is to preserve an ongoing relationship with existing customers and maintain sales.

A Frito-Lay salesperson takes inventory of snacks for the store manager to sign. In this situation, the manager will make a straight rebuy decision.

Frito-Lay, Inc.
www.fritolay.com

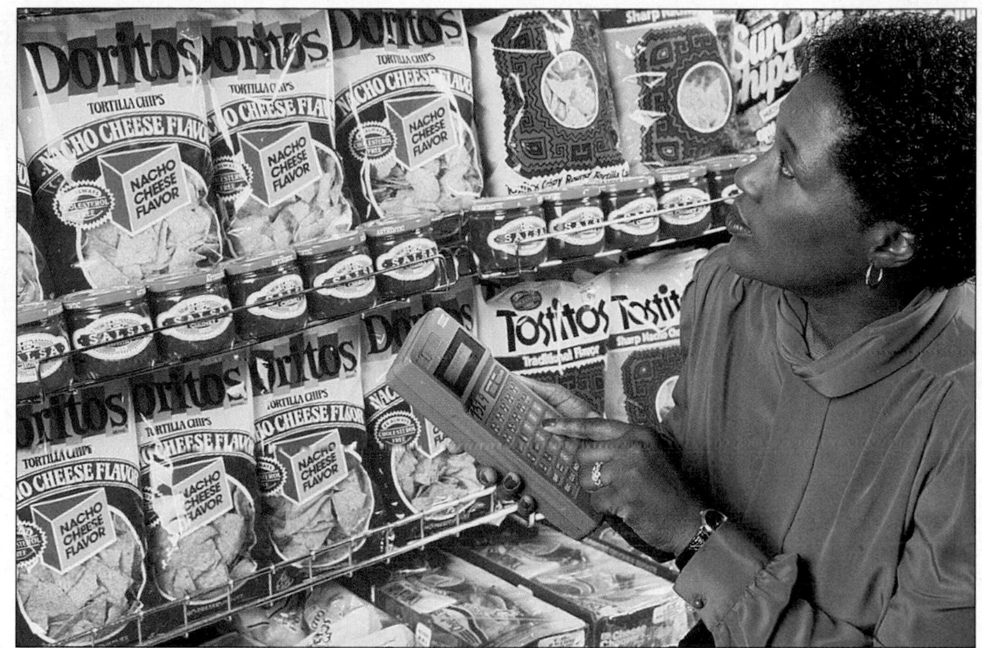

Two types of order takers exist. *Outside order takers* visit customers and replenish inventory stocks of resellers, such as retailers or wholesalers. For example, Frito-Lay salespeople call on supermarkets, convenience stores, and other establishments to ensure that the company's line of snack products (such as Doritos and Tostitos tortilla chips) is in adequate supply. In addition, outside order takers often provide assistance in arranging displays.

Inside order takers, also called *order clerks* or *salesclerks*, typically answer simple questions, take orders, and complete transactions with customers. Many retail clerks are inside order takers. Inside order takers are often employed by companies that use *inbound telemarketing*, the use of toll-free telephone numbers that customers can call to obtain information about products or services and make purchases. In business-to-business settings, order taking arises in straight rebuy situations as described in Chapter 6.

Order takers generally do little selling in a conventional sense. They engage in modest problem solving with customers. They often represent products that have few options, such as magazine subscriptions and highly standardized industrial products. Inbound telemarketing is also an essential selling activity for more "customer service" driven firms, such as Dell Inc. At these companies, order takers undergo extensive training so that they can better assist callers with their purchase decisions.

Order-Getting Salespeople

An **order getter** sells in a conventional sense and identifies prospective customers, provides customers with information, persuades customers to buy, closes sales, and follows up on customers' use of a product or service. Like order takers, order getters can be inside (an automobile salesperson) or outside (a Xerox salesperson).

Order getting involves a high degree of creativity and customer empathy and is typically required for selling complex or technical products with many options, so considerable product knowledge and sales training are necessary. In modified rebuy or new-buy purchase situations in business-to-business selling, an order getter acts as a problem solver who identifies how a particular product may satisfy a customer's need. Similarly, in the purchase of a service, such as insurance, a Metropolitan Life insurance agent can provide a mix of plans to satisfy a buyer's needs depending on income, stage of the family's life cycle, and investment objectives.

FIGURE 20–2
How do outside order-getting salespeople spend their time each week? You might be surprised after reading the text.

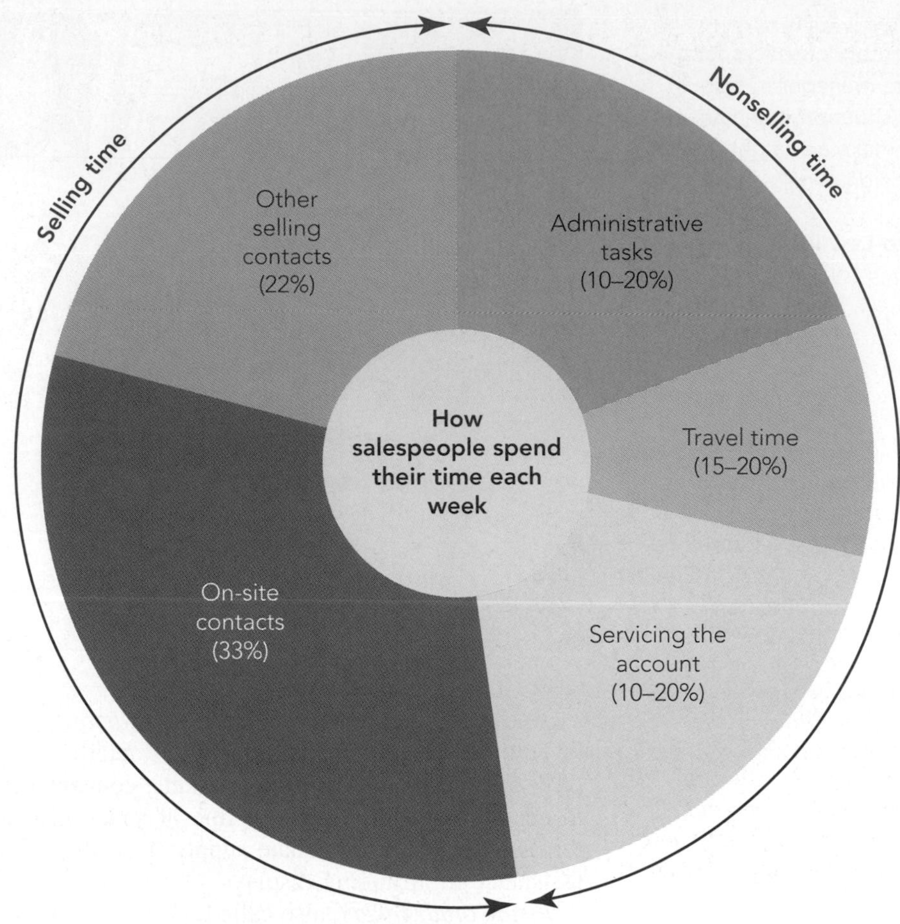

Order getting is not a 40-hour-per-week job. Industry research shows that outside order getters, or field service representatives, often work over 50 hours per week. As shown in Figure 20–2, 55 percent of their time is spent selling. (*What percent did you check for question 2 in Figure 20–1?*) Another 10 to 20 percent is devoted to customer service calls. The remainder of their workweek is occupied by getting to customers and performing administrative tasks.[7]

Order getting by outside salespeople is also expensive. It is estimated that the average cost of a single field sales call on a business customer is about $350, factoring in salespeople compensation, benefits, and travel-and-entertainment expenses. This cost illustrates why outbound telemarketing is popular. *Outbound telemarketing* is the practice of using the telephone rather than personal visits to contact current and prospective customers. A much lower cost per sales call (from $20 to $25) and little or no field expense accounts for its widespread appeal. Over 100 million outbound telemarketing calls are made to homes and businesses each year in the United States.[8]

Customer Sales Support Personnel

Customer sales support personnel augment the selling effort of order getters by performing a variety of services. For example, *missionary salespeople* do not directly solicit orders but rather concentrate on performing promotional activities and introducing new products. They are used extensively in the pharmaceutical industry, where they persuade physicians to prescribe a firm's product. Actual sales are made through wholesalers or directly to pharmacists who fill prescriptions. A *sales engi-*

Marketing Matters > > > > > > customer value

Creating and Sustaining Customer Value through Cross-Functional Team Selling

The day of the lone salesperson calling on a customer is rapidly becoming history. Today, 75 percent of companies employ cross-functional teams of professionals to work with customers to improve relationships, find better ways of doing things, and, of course, create and sustain value for their customers.

Xerox and IBM pioneered cross-functional team selling, but other firms were quick to follow as they spotted the potential to create and sustain value for their customers. Recognizing that corn growers needed a herbicide they could apply less often, a DuPont team of chemists, sales and marketing executives, and regulatory specialists created just the right product that recorded sales of $57 million in its first year. Procter & Gamble uses teams of marketing, sales, advertising, computer systems, and supply chain personnel to work with its major retailers, such as Walmart, to identify ways to develop, promote, and deliver products. Pitney Bowes, Inc., which produces sophisticated computer systems that weigh, rate, and track packages for firms such as UPS and FedEx, also uses sales teams to meet customer needs. These teams consist of sales personnel, "carrier management specialists," and engineering and administrative executives who continually find ways to improve the technology of shipping goods across town and around the world.

Efforts to create and sustain customer value through cross-functional team selling have become a necessity as customers seek greater value for their money. According to the vice president for procurement of a Fortune 500 company, "Today, it's not just getting the best price but getting the best value—and there are a lot of pieces to value."

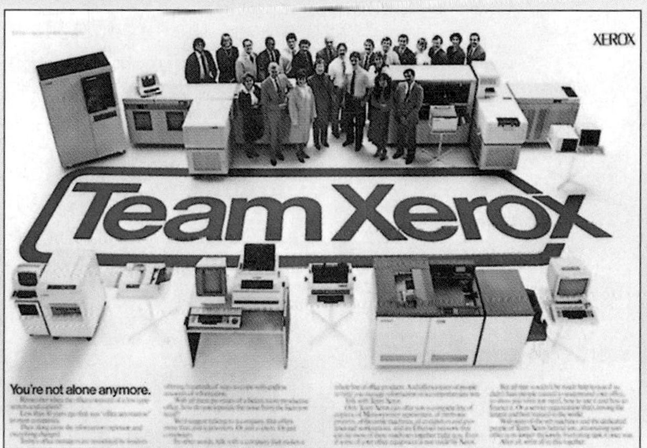

neer is a salesperson who specializes in identifying, analyzing, and solving customer problems and brings know-how and technical expertise to the selling situation but often does not actually sell products and services. Sales engineers are popular in selling business products such as chemicals and heavy equipment.

Many firms engage in cross-functional **team selling**, the practice of using an entire team of professionals in selling to and servicing major customers.[9] Team selling is used when specialized knowledge is needed to satisfy the different interests of individuals in a customer's buying center. For example, a selling team might consist of a salesperson, a sales engineer, a service representative, and a financial executive, each of whom would deal with a counterpart in the customer's firm.

Selling teams take different forms. In *conference selling*, a salesperson and other company resource people meet with buyers to discuss problems and opportunities. In *seminar selling*, a company team conducts an educational program for a customer's technical staff, describing state-of-the-art developments. IBM and Xerox pioneered cross-functional team selling in working with prospective buyers. Other firms have embraced this practice and created and sustained value for their customers, as described in the Marketing Matters box.[10]

learning review

3. What is the principal difference between an order taker and an order getter?

4. What is team selling?

THE PERSONAL SELLING PROCESS: BUILDING RELATIONSHIPS

LO3

Selling, and particularly order getting, is a complicated activity that involves building buyer–seller relationships. Although the salesperson–customer interaction is essential to personal selling, much of a salesperson's work occurs before this meeting and continues after the sale itself. The **personal selling process** consists of six stages: (1) prospecting, (2) preapproach, (3) approach, (4) presentation, (5) close, and (6) follow-up (see Figure 20–3).

Prospecting: Identifying and Qualifying Prospective Customers

Personal selling begins with the *prospecting stage*—the search for and qualification of potential customers. There are three types of prospects. A *lead* is the name of a person who may be a possible customer. A *prospect* is a customer who wants or needs the product. If an individual wants the product, can afford to buy it, and is the decision maker, this individual is a *qualified prospect*.

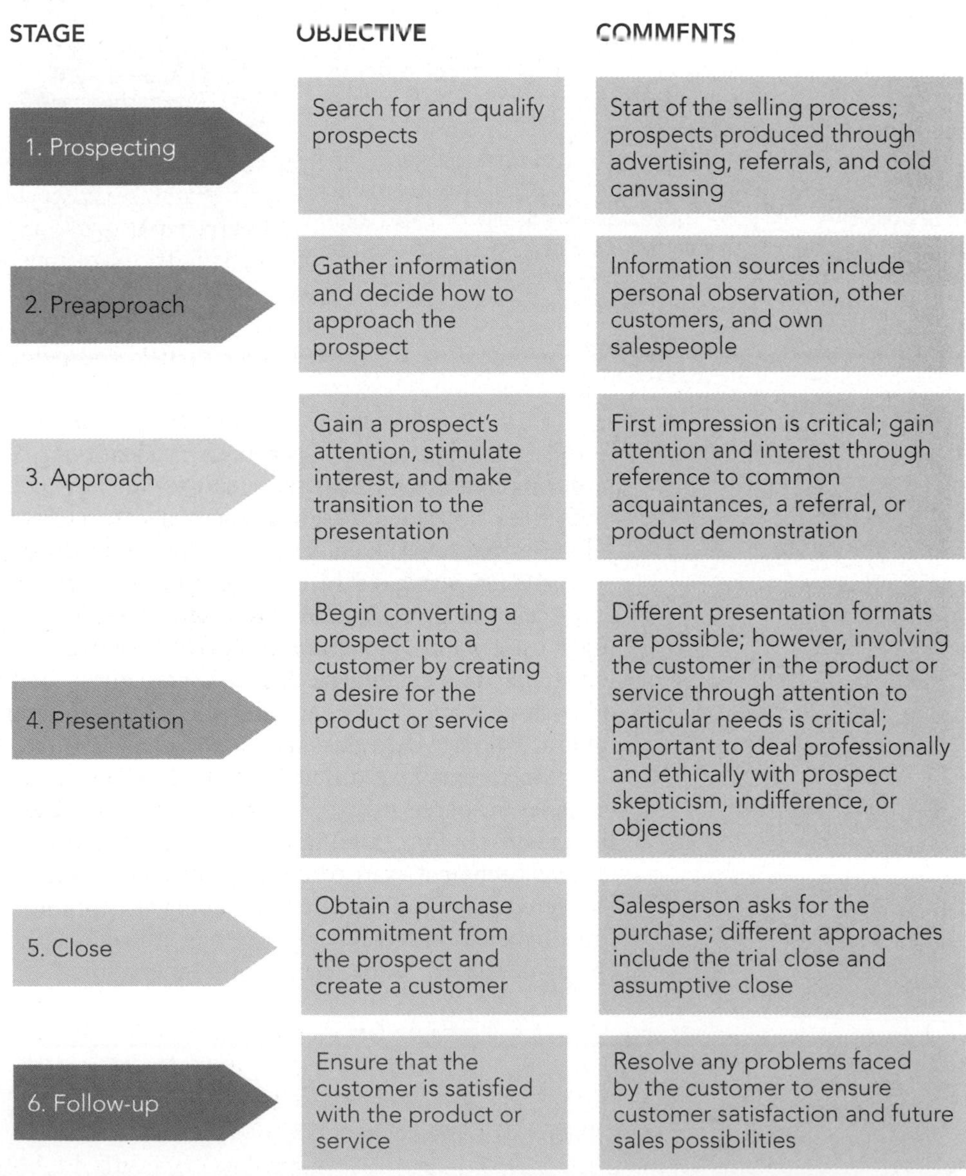

STAGE	OBJECTIVE	COMMENTS
1. Prospecting	Search for and qualify prospects	Start of the selling process; prospects produced through advertising, referrals, and cold canvassing
2. Preapproach	Gather information and decide how to approach the prospect	Information sources include personal observation, other customers, and own salespeople
3. Approach	Gain a prospect's attention, stimulate interest, and make transition to the presentation	First impression is critical; gain attention and interest through reference to common acquaintances, a referral, or product demonstration
4. Presentation	Begin converting a prospect into a customer by creating a desire for the product or service	Different presentation formats are possible; however, involving the customer in the product or service through attention to particular needs is critical; important to deal professionally and ethically with prospect skepticism, indifference, or objections
5. Close	Obtain a purchase commitment from the prospect and create a customer	Salesperson asks for the purchase; different approaches include the trial close and assumptive close
6. Follow-up	Ensure that the customer is satisfied with the product or service	Resolve any problems faced by the customer to ensure customer satisfaction and future sales possibilities

FIGURE 20–3
Stages and objectives of the personal selling process. Each stage is critical for successful selling and building a customer relationship.

Trade shows are a popular source for leads and prospects. Companies like TSCentral provide comprehensive trade show information.

TSCentral
www.tscentral.com

Leads and prospects are generated using several sources. For example, advertising may contain a coupon or a toll-free number to generate leads. Some companies use exhibits at trade shows, professional meetings, and conferences to generate leads or prospects. Staffed by salespeople, these exhibits are used to attract the attention of prospective buyers and disseminate information. Others utilize the Internet for generating leads and prospects. Today, salespeople are using Web sites, e-mail, and social networks to connect to individuals and companies that may be interested in their products or services.

Another approach for generating leads is through *cold canvassing* or *cold calling*, either in person or by telephone. This approach simply means that a salesperson may open a directory, pick a name, and contact that individual or business. Even with a high refusal rate, cold canvassing can be successful.[11] However, cold canvassing is frowned upon in most Asian and Latin American societies. Personal visits, based on referrals, are expected.

Cold canvassing is often criticized by U.S. consumers and is now regulated. A recent survey reported that 75 percent of U.S. consumers consider this practice an intrusion on their privacy, and 72 percent find it distasteful.[12] *The Telephone Consumer Protection Act* (1991) contains provisions to curb abuses such as early morning or late night calling. Additional federal regulations require more complete disclosure regarding solicitations, include provisions that allow consumers to avoid being called at any time through the Do Not Call Registry, and impose fines for violations. For example, satellite television provider DirecTV was fined $5.3 million for making thousands of calls to consumers who had put their telephone numbers on the Do Not Call Registry.[13]

Preapproach: Preparing for the Sales Call

Once a salesperson has identified a qualified prospect, preparation for the sale begins with the preapproach. The *preapproach* stage involves obtaining further information on the prospect and deciding on the best method of approach. Knowing how the prospect prefers to be approached, and what the prospect is looking for in a product or service, is essential regardless of industry or cultural setting.

For instance, a Merrill Lynch stockbroker will need information on a prospect's discretionary income, investment objectives, and preference for discussing brokerage services over the telephone or in person. For business product companies such as Texas Instruments, the preapproach involves identifying the buying role of a prospect (for example, influencer or decision maker), important buying criteria, and the prospect's receptivity to a formal or informal presentation. Identifying the best time to contact a prospect is also important. Northwestern Mutual Life Insurance Company suggests the best times to call on people in different occupations: dentists before 9:30 a.m., lawyers between 11:00 a.m. and 2:00 p.m., and college professors between 7:00 and 8:00 p.m.

This stage is very important in international selling where customs dictate appropriate protocol. In many South American countries, for example, buyers expect salespeople to be punctual for appointments. However, prospective buyers are routinely 30 minutes late. South Americans take negotiating seriously and prefer straightforward presentations, but a hard-sell approach will not work.[14]

Successful salespeople recognize that the preapproach stage should never be shortchanged. Their experience coupled with research on customer complaints indicate that failure to learn as much as possible about the prospect is unprofessional and the ruin of a sales call.

Approach: Making the First Impression

The *approach* stage involves the initial meeting between the salesperson and prospect, where the objectives are to gain the prospect's attention, stimulate interest, and build the foundation for the sales presentation itself and the basis for a working relationship. The first impression is critical at this stage, and it is common for salespeople to begin the conversation with a reference to common acquaintances, a referral, or even the product or service itself. Which tactic is taken will depend on the information obtained in the prospecting and preapproach stages.

How business cards are exchanged with Asian customers is very important. Read the text to learn the appropriate protocol in the approach stage of the personal selling process.

The approach stage is very important in international settings. In many societies outside the United States, considerable time is devoted to nonbusiness talk designed to establish a rapport between buyers and sellers. For instance, it is common for two or three meetings to occur before business matters are discussed in the Middle East and Asia. Gestures are also very important. The initial meeting between a salesperson and a prospect in the United States customarily begins with a firm handshake. Handshakes also apply in France, but they are gentle, not firm. Forget the handshake in Japan. An appropriate bow is expected. What about business cards? Business cards should be printed in English on one side and the language of the prospective customer on the other. Knowledgeable U.S. salespeople know that their business cards should be handed to Asian customers using both hands, with the name facing the receiver. In Asia, anything involving a person's name demands respect.

Presentation: Tailoring a Solution for a Customer's Needs

The *presentation* stage is at the core of the order-getting selling process, and its objective is to convert a prospect into a customer by creating a desire for the product or service. Three major presentation formats exist: (1) stimulus-response format, (2) formula selling format, and (3) need-satisfaction format.

Stimulus-Response Format The **stimulus-response presentation** format assumes that given the appropriate stimulus by a salesperson, the prospect will buy. With this format the salesperson tries one appeal after another, hoping to hit the right button. A counter clerk at McDonald's is using this approach when he or she asks whether you'd like an order of French fries or a dessert with your meal. The counter clerk is engaging in what is called *suggestive selling*. Although useful in this setting, the stimulus-response format is not always appropriate, and for many products a more formalized format is necessary.

Formula Selling Format The **formula selling presentation** format is based on the view that a presentation consists of information that must be provided in an accurate, thorough, and step-by-step manner to inform the prospect. A popular version of this format is the *canned sales presentation*, which is a memorized, standardized message conveyed to every prospect. Used frequently by firms in telephone and door-to-door selling of consumer products (for example, Kirby vacuum cleaners), this approach treats every prospect the same, regardless of differences in needs or preference for certain kinds of information.

Canned sales presentations can be advantageous when the differences between prospects are unknown or with novice salespeople who are less knowledgeable about the product and selling process than experienced salespeople. Although it guarantees a thorough presentation, it often lacks flexibility and spontaneity and, more important, does not provide for feedback from the prospective buyer—a critical component in the communication process and the start of a relationship.

Need-Satisfaction Format The stimulus-response and formula selling formats share a common characteristic: The salesperson dominates the conversation. By comparison, the **need-satisfaction presentation** format emphasizes probing and listening by the salesperson to identify needs and interests of prospective buyers. Once these are identified, the salesperson tailors the presentation to the prospect and highlights product benefits that may be valued by the prospect. The need-satisfaction format, which emphasizes problem solving and customer solutions, is the most consistent with the marketing concept and relationship building.

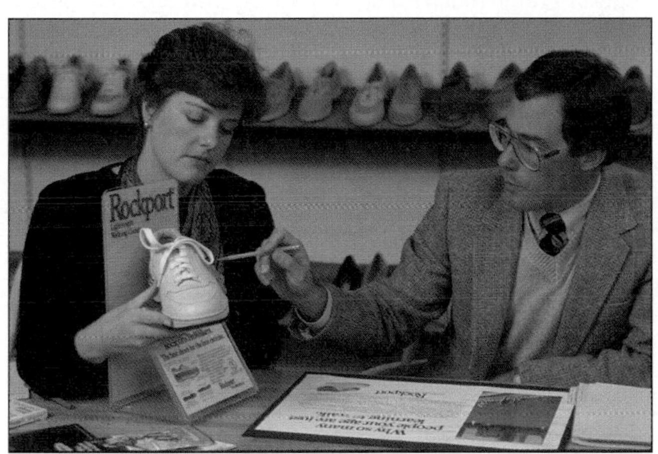

Rockport sales representatives are adept at adaptive selling to retail buyers.

The Rockport Company
www.rockport.com

Two selling styles are common with this format.[15] **Adaptive selling** involves adjusting the presentation to fit the selling situation, such as knowing when to offer solutions and when to ask for more information. Sales research and practice show that knowledge of the customer and sales situation are key ingredients for adaptive selling. Many consumer service firms such as brokerage and insurance firms and consumer product firms like Rockport, AT&T, and Gillette effectively apply this selling style.

Consultative selling focuses on problem identification, where the salesperson serves as an expert on problem recognition and resolution. With consultative selling, problem solution options are not simply a matter of choosing from an array of existing products or services. Rather, novel solutions often arise, thereby creating unique value for the customer.

Consultative selling is prominent in business-to-business marketing. Johnson Controls' Automotive Systems Group, IBM's Global Services, and DHL Worldwide Express offer customer solutions through their consultative selling style, as does Xerox. According to a senior Xerox sales executive, "Our business is no longer about selling boxes. It's about selling digital, networked-based information management

Marketing Matters > > > > > > customer value

Imagine This . . . Putting the Customer into Customer Solutions!

Solutions for problems are what companies are looking for from suppliers. At the same time, suppliers focus on customer solutions to differentiate themselves from competitors. So what is a customer solution and what does it have to do with selling?

Sellers view a solution as a customized and integrated combination of products and services for meeting a customer's business needs. But what do buyers think? From a buyer's perspective, a solution is one that (1) meets their requirements, (2) is designed to uniquely solve their problem, (3) can be implemented, and (4) ensures follow-up. This insight arose from a field study conducted by three researchers at Emory University. Their in-depth study also yielded insight into what an effective customer solution offers. According to one buyer interviewed in their study:

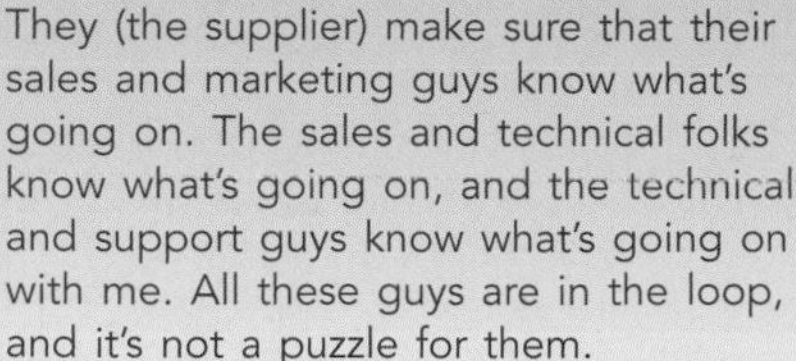

> They (the supplier) make sure that their sales and marketing guys know what's going on. The sales and technical folks know what's going on, and the technical and support guys know what's going on with me. All these guys are in the loop, and it's not a puzzle for them.

So what does putting the customer into customer solutions have to do with selling? Three things stand out. First, considerable time and effort is necessary to fully understand a specific customer's requirements. Second, effective customer solutions are based on relationships among sellers and buyers. And finally, consultative selling is central to providing novel solutions for customers, thereby creating value for them.

---

solutions, and this requires a highly customized and consultative selling process." But what does a customer solution really mean? The Marketing Matters box offers a unique answer.[16]

Handling Objections A critical concern in the presentation stage is handling objections. *Objections* are excuses for not making a purchase commitment or decision. Some objections are valid and are based on the characteristics of the product or service or price. However, many objections reflect prospect skepticism or indifference. Whether valid or not, experienced salespeople know that objections do not put an end to the presentation. Rather, techniques can be used to deal with objections in a courteous, ethical, and professional manner. The following six techniques are the most common:[17]

1. *Acknowledge and convert the objection.* This technique involves using the objection as a reason for buying. For example, a prospect might say, "The price is too high." The reply: "Yes, the price is high because we use the finest materials. Let me show you. . . ."
2. *Postpone.* The postpone technique is used when the objection will be dealt with later in the presentation: "I'm going to address that point shortly. I think my answer would make better sense then."
3. *Agree and neutralize.* Here a salesperson agrees with the objection, then shows that it is unimportant. A salesperson would say, "That's true. Others have said the same. But, they thought that issue was outweighed by other benefits."
4. *Accept the objection.* Sometimes the objection is valid. Let the prospect express such views, probe for the reason behind it, and attempt to stimulate further discussion on the objection.
5. *Denial.* When a prospect's objection is based on misinformation and clearly untrue, it is wise to meet the objection head on with a firm denial.
6. *Ignore the objection.* This technique is used when it appears that the objection is a stalling mechanism or is clearly not important to the prospect.

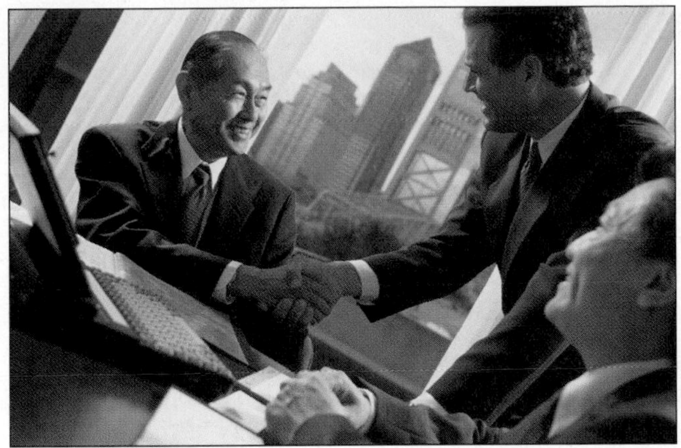

The closing stage involves obtaining a purchase commitment from the prospect. Read the text to learn how the close itself can take several forms.

Each of these techniques requires a calm, professional interaction with the prospect and is most effective when objections are anticipated in the preapproach stage. Handling objections is a skill requiring a sense of timing, appreciation for the prospect's state of mind, and adeptness in communication. Objections also should be handled ethically. Lying or misrepresenting product or service features are grossly unethical practices.

Close: Asking for the Customer's Order or Business

The *closing* stage in the selling process involves obtaining a purchase commitment from the prospect. This stage is the most important and the most difficult because the salesperson must determine when the prospect is ready to buy. Telltale signals indicating a readiness to buy include body language (prospect reexamines the product or contract closely), statements ("This equipment should reduce our maintenance costs."), and questions ("When could we expect delivery?").

The close itself can take several forms. Three closing techniques are used when a salesperson believes a buyer is about ready to make a purchase: (1) trial close, (2) assumptive close, and (3) urgency close. A *trial close* involves asking the prospect to make a decision on some aspect of the purchase: "Would you prefer the blue or gray model?" An *assumptive close* entails asking the prospect to consider choices concerning delivery, warranty, or financing terms under the assumption that a sale has been finalized. An *urgency close* is used to commit the prospect quickly by making reference to the timeliness of the purchase: "The low interest financing ends next week," or "That is the last model we have in stock." Of course, these statements should be used only if they accurately reflect the situation; otherwise, such claims would be unethical. When a prospect is clearly ready to buy, the final close is used, and a salesperson asks for the order.

Follow-Up: Solidifying the Relationship

The selling process does not end with the closing of a sale; rather, professional selling requires customer follow-up. One marketing authority equated the follow-up with courtship and marriage, by observing, "The sale merely consummates the courtship. Then the marriage begins. How good the marriage is depends on how well the relationship is managed."[18] The *follow-up* stage includes making certain the customer's purchase has been properly delivered and installed and difficulties experienced with the use of the item are addressed. Attention to this stage of the selling process solidifies the buyer–seller relationship. Research shows that the cost and effort to obtain repeat sales from a satisfied customer is roughly half of that necessary to gain a sale from a new customer.[19] In short, today's satisfied customers become tomorrow's qualified prospects or referrals. (*What was your answer to question 3 in the Figure 20-1 quiz?*)

learning review

5. What are the six stages in the personal selling process?
6. What is the distinction between a lead and a qualified prospect?
7. Which presentation format is most consistent with the marketing concept? Why?

THE SALES MANAGEMENT PROCESS

Selling must be managed if it is going to contribute to a firm's marketing objectives. Although firms differ in the specifics of how salespeople and the selling effort are managed, the sales management process is similar across firms. Sales management consists of three interrelated functions: (1) sales plan formulation, (2) sales plan implementation, and (3) salesforce evaluation (see Figure 20–4).

Sales Plan Formulation: Setting Direction

Formulating the sales plan is the most basic of the three sales management functions. According to the vice president of the Harris Corporation, a global communications company, "If a company hopes to implement its marketing strategy, it really needs a detailed sales planning process."[20] The **sales plan** is a statement describing what is to be achieved and where and how the selling effort of salespeople is to be deployed. Sales plan formulation involves three tasks: (1) setting objectives, (2) organizing the salesforce, and (3) developing account management policies.

Setting Objectives Setting objectives is central to sales management because this task specifies what is to be achieved. In practice, objectives are set for the total salesforce and for each salesperson.

Selling objectives can be output related and focus on dollar or unit sales volume, number of new customers added, and profit. Alternatively, they can be input related and emphasize the number of sales calls and selling expenses. Output- and input-related objectives are used for the salesforce as a whole and for each salesperson. A third type of objective that is behaviorally related is typically specific for each salesperson and includes his or her product knowledge, customer service satisfaction ratings, and selling and communication skills.

Increasingly, firms are also emphasizing knowledge of competition as an objective since salespeople are calling on customers and should see what competitors are doing. In fact, 89 percent of companies encourage their salespeople to gather competitive intelligence.[21] But should salespeople explicitly ask their customers for information about competitors? Read the Making Responsible Decisions box to see how salespeople view this practice.[22]

Whatever objectives are set, they should be precise and measurable and specify the time period over which they are to be achieved. Once established, these objectives serve as performance standards for the evaluation of the salesforce, the third function of sales management.

Organizing the Salesforce Organizing a selling organization is the second task in formulating the sales plan. Three questions are related to organization. First, should the company use its own salesforce, or should it use independent agents such as manufacturer's representatives? Second, if the decision is made to employ company salespeople, then should they be organized according to geography, customer type, or product or service? Third, how many company salespeople should be employed?

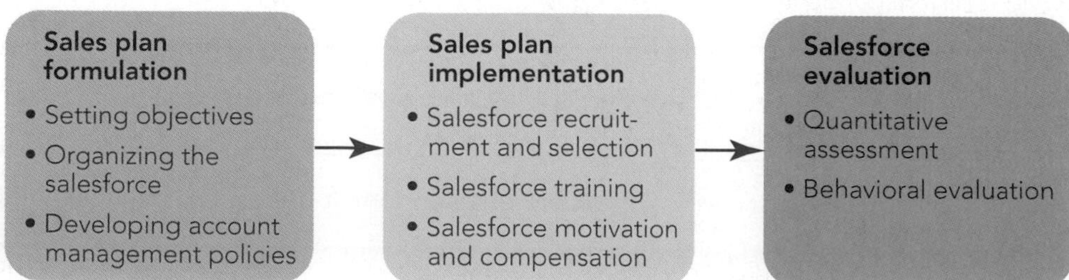

FIGURE 20–4
The sales management process involves sales plan formulation, sales plan implementation, and salesforce evaluation.

Making Responsible Decisions > > > > > > > ethics

The Ethics of Asking Customers about Competitors

Salespeople are a valuable source of information about what is happening in the marketplace. By working closely with customers and asking good questions, salespeople often have firsthand knowledge of customer problems and wants. They also are able to spot the activities of competitors. However, should salespeople explicitly ask customers about competitor strategies such as pricing practices, product development efforts, and trade and promotion programs?

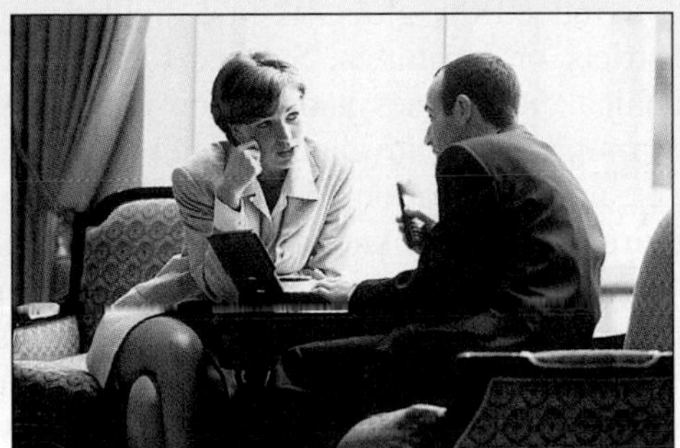

Gaining knowledge about competitors by asking customers for information is a ticklish ethical issue. Research indicates that 25 percent of U.S. salespeople engaged in business-to-business selling consider this practice unethical, and their companies have explicit guidelines for this practice. It is also noteworthy that Japanese salespeople consider this practice to be more unethical than do U.S. salespeople.

Do you believe that asking customers about competitor practices is unethical? Why or why not?

The decision to use company salespeople or independent agents is made infrequently. The decision itself is based on an analysis of economic and behavioral factors. An economic analysis examines the costs of using both types of salespeople and is a form of break-even analysis, which was discussed in Chapter 13.

Consider a situation in which independent agents would receive a 5 percent commission on sales, and company salespeople would receive a 3 percent commission, salaries, and benefits. In addition, with company salespeople, sales administration costs would be incurred for a total fixed cost of \$500,000 per year. At what sales level would independent or company salespeople be less costly? This question can be answered by setting the costs of the two options equal to each other and solving for the sales level amount, as shown in the equation:

$$\text{Total cost of company salespeople} = \text{Total cost of independent agents}$$

$$[0.03(X) + \$500{,}000] = 0.05(X)$$

where X = sales volume. Solving for X, sales volume equals \$25 million, indicating that below \$25 million in sales independent agents would be cheaper, but above \$25 million a company salesforce would be cheaper. This relationship is shown in Figure 20–5.

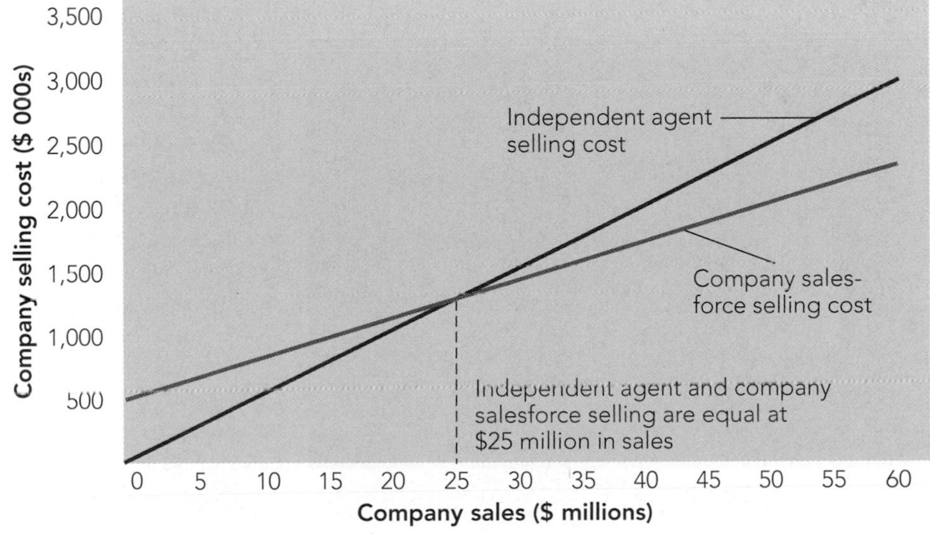

FIGURE 20–5
A break-even chart for comparing independent agents and a company salesforce includes an analysis of selling costs and sales. The break-even point occurs when company salesforce selling cost equals independent agent selling cost.

Economics alone does not answer this question. A behavioral analysis is also necessary and should focus on issues related to the control, flexibility, effort, and availability of independent and company salespeople.[23] A firm must weigh the pros and cons of the economic and behavioral factors before making this decision.

If a company elects to employ its own salespeople, then it must choose an organizational structure based on (1) geography, (2) customer, or (3) product (see Figure 20–6). A *geographical sales organization* is the simplest structure, where the United States, or indeed the globe, is first divided into regions and each region is divided into districts or territories. Salespeople are assigned to each district with defined geographical boundaries and call on all customers and represent all products sold by the company. An advantage of this structure is that it can minimize travel time, expenses, and duplication of selling effort. However, if a firm's products or customers require specialized knowledge, then a geographical structure is unsuitable.

When different types of buyers have different needs, a *customer sales organization* is used. In practice this means that a different salesforce calls on each separate type of buyer or marketing channel. For example, Kodak recently switched from a geographical to a marketing channel structure with different sales teams serving specific retail channels: mass merchandisers, photo specialty outlets, and food and drug stores. The rationale for this approach is that more effective, specialized customer support and knowledge are provided to buyers. However, this structure often leads to higher administrative costs and some duplication of selling effort, because several salesforces are used to represent the same products.

An important variation of the customer organizational structure is **key account management**—the practice of using team selling to focus on important customers so as to build mutually beneficial, long-term, cooperative relationships.[24] Key account management involves teams of sales, service, and often technical personnel who work with purchasing, manufacturing, engineering, logistics, and financial executives in customer organizations. This approach, which often assigns company personnel to a customer account, results in "customer specialists" who can provide exceptional service. Procter & Gamble uses this approach with Walmart, as does Black & Decker with Home Depot.

When specific knowledge is required to sell certain types of products, then a *product sales organization* is used. For example, Maxim Steel has a salesforce that sells drilling pipe to oil companies and another that sells specialty steel products to manufacturers. The advantage of this structure is that salespeople can develop expertise with technical characteristics, applications, and selling methods associated with a particular product or family of products. However, this structure produces high administrative costs and duplication of selling effort because two company salespeople may call on the same customer.

Steel companies such as Maxim Steel often organize their salesforces by product or product families to better serve customers.

Maxim Steel
www.maximsteel.com

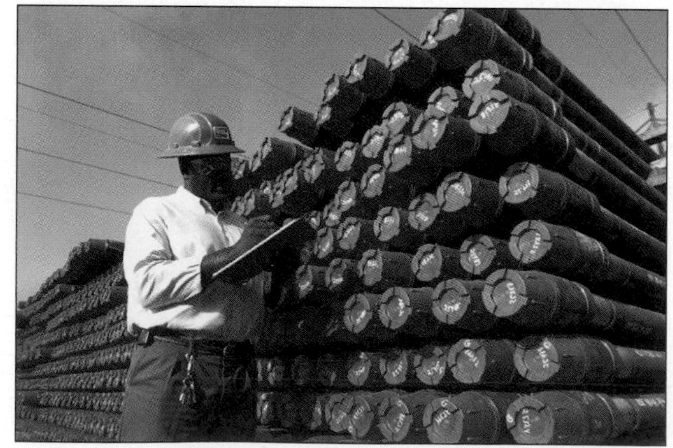

In short, there is no one best sales organization for all companies in all situations. Rather, the organization of the salesforce should reflect the marketing strategy of the firm. Each year about 10 percent of U.S. firms change their sales organizations to implement new marketing strategies.

The third question related to salesforce organization involves determining the size of the salesforce. For example, why do you think Frito-Lay has about 17,500 salespeople who call on supermarkets, convenience stores, and other establishments to sell snack foods? The answer lies in the number of accounts (customers) served, the frequency of calls on accounts, the length of an average call, and the amount of time a salesperson can devote to selling.

FIGURE 20–6
Organizing the salesforce by customer, product, and geography is common. Read the text to learn why companies use different salesforce organizations.

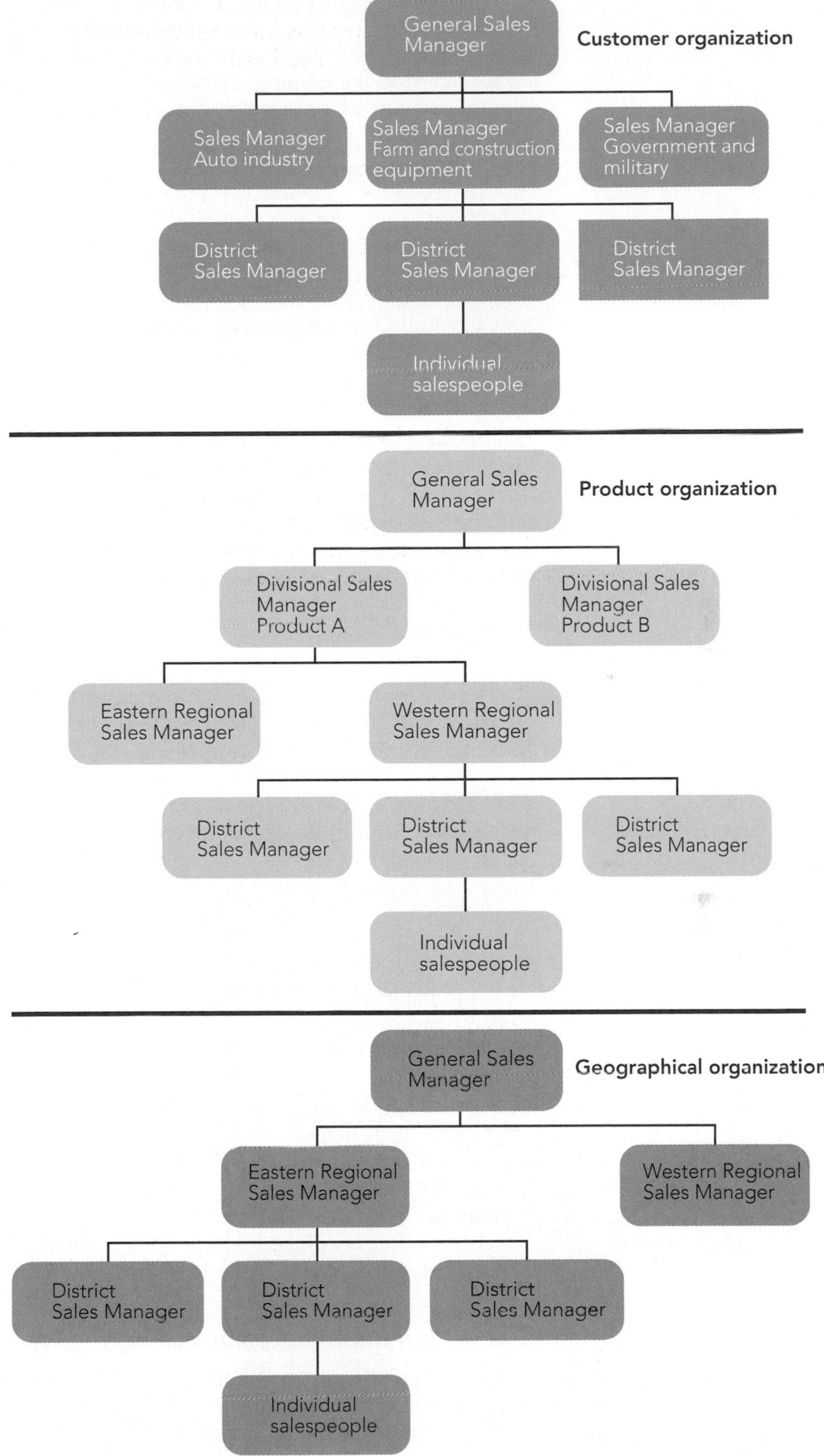

A common approach for determining the size of a salesforce is the **workload method**. This formula-based method integrates the number of customers served, call frequency, call length, and available selling time to arrive at a figure for the salesforce size. For example, Frito-Lay needs about 17,500 salespeople according to the following workload method formula:

$$NS = \frac{NC \times CF \times CL}{AST}$$

where,

NS = Number of salespeople

NC = Number of customers

CF = Call frequency necessary to service a customer each year

CL = Length of an average call

AST = Average amount of selling time available per year

Frito-Lay sells its products to 350,000 supermarkets, convenience stores, and other establishments. Salespeople should call on these accounts at least once a week, or 52 times a year. The average sales call lasts an average of 81 minutes (1.35 hour). An average salesperson works 2,000 hours a year (50 weeks × 40 hours a week), but 12 hours a week are devoted to nonselling activities such as travel and administration, leaving 1,400 hours a year. Using these guidelines, Frito-Lay would need

$$NS = \frac{350{,}000 \times 52 \times 1.35}{1{,}400} = 17{,}550 \text{ salespeople}$$

The value of this formula is apparent in its flexibility; a change in any one of the variables will affect the number of salespeople needed. Changes are determined, in part, by the firm's account management policies.

Developing Account Management Policies The third task in formulating a sales plan involves developing **account management policies** specifying whom salespeople should contact, what kinds of selling and customer service activities should be engaged in, and how these activities should be carried out. These policies might state which individuals in a buying organization should be contacted, the amount of sales and service effort that different customers should receive, and the kinds of information salespeople should collect before or during a sales call.

An example of an account management policy in Figure 20–7 shows how different accounts or customers can be grouped according to level of opportunity and the firm's competitive sales position.[25] When specific account names are placed in each cell, salespeople clearly see which accounts should be contacted, with what level of selling and service activity, and how to deal with them. Accounts in cells 1 and 2 might have high frequencies of personal sales calls and increased time spent on a call. Cell 3 accounts will have lower call frequencies, and cell 4 accounts might be contacted through telemarketing or direct mail rather than in person. For example, Union Pacific Railroad put its 20,000 smallest accounts on a telemarketing program. A subsequent survey of these accounts indicated that 84 percent rated Union Pacific's sales effort "very effective" compared with 67 percent before the switch.

Sales Plan Implementation: Putting the Plan into Action

The sales plan is put into practice through the tasks associated with sales plan implementation. Whereas sales plan formulation focuses on "doing the right things," implementation emphasizes "doing things right." The three major tasks involved in implementing a sales plan are: (1) salesforce recruitment and selection, (2) salesforce training, and (3) salesforce motivation and compensation.

Salesforce Recruitment and Selection Effective recruitment and selection of salespeople is one of the most crucial tasks of sales management. It entails finding people who match the type of sales position required by a firm. Recruitment and selection practices would differ greatly between order-taking and order-getting sales positions, given the differences in the demands of these two jobs. Therefore, recruitment and selection begin with a carefully crafted job analysis and job description followed by a statement of job qualifications.

A *job analysis* is a study of a particular sales position, including how the job is to be performed and the tasks that make up the job. Information from a job analysis is used to write a *job description*, a written document that describes job relationships and requirements that characterize each sales position. It explains: (1) to whom a salesperson reports, (2) how a salesperson interacts with other company personnel, (3) the customers to be called on, (4) the specific activities to be carried out, (5) the physical and mental demands of the job, and (6) the types of products and services to be sold.

The job description is then translated into a statement of job qualifications, including the aptitudes, knowledge, skills, and a variety of behavioral characteristics considered necessary to perform the job successfully. Qualifications for order-getting sales positions often mirror the expectations of buyers: (1) imagination and problem-solving ability, (2) strong work ethic, (3) honesty, (4) intimate product knowledge, (5) effective communication and listening skills, and (6) attentiveness reflected in responsiveness to buyer needs and customer loyalty and follow-up. Firms use a variety of methods for evaluating prospective salespeople. Personal interviews, reference checks, and background information provided on application forms are the most frequently used methods.[26]

Successful selling also requires a high degree of emotional intelligence. **Emotional intelligence** is the ability to understand one's own emotions and the emotions of people with whom one interacts on a daily basis. These qualities are important for adaptive selling and may spell the difference between effective and ineffective order-getting salespeople.[27] Are you interested in what your emotional intelligence might be? Read the Going Online box on the next page and test yourself.

The search for qualified salespeople has produced an increasingly diverse salesforce in the United States. Women now represent almost half of all professional

FIGURE 20–7
An account management policy grid grouping customers according to the level of opportunity and firm's competitive sales position

Competitive position of sales organization

Account opportunity level	High	Low
High	1 *Attractiveness:* Accounts offer a good opportunity because they have high potential and the sales organization has a strong position. *Account management policy:* Accounts should receive high level of sales calls and service to retain and possibly build accounts.	3 *Attractiveness:* Accounts may offer a good opportunity if the sales organization can overcome its weak position. *Account management policy:* Emphasize a heavy sales organization position or shift resources to other accounts if a stronger sales organization position is impossible.
Low	2 *Attractiveness:* Accounts are somewhat attractive because the sales organization has a strong position, but future opportunity is limited. *Account management policy:* Accounts should receive moderate level of sales and service to maintain current position of sales organization.	4 *Attractiveness:* Accounts offer little opportunity, and the sales organization position is weak. *Account management policy:* Consider replacing personal calls with telephone sales or direct mail to service accounts. Consider dropping account if unprofitable.

Going Online

What Is Your Emotional Intelligence or EQ?

A person's success at work depends on many talents, including intelligence and technical skills. Recent research indicates that an individual's emotional intelligence or EQ is also important, if not more important! Emotional intelligence has five dimensions: (1) self-motivation skills; (2) self-awareness, or knowing one's own emotions; (3) the ability to manage one's emotions and impulses; (4) empathy, or the ability to sense how others are feeling; and (5) social skills, or the ability to handle the emotions of other people.

What is your emotional intelligence? Visit the Web site at www.ihhp.com/quiz.php. Answer 20 questions to learn what your emotional intelligence is and obtain additional insights.

salespeople, and minority representation is growing. The fastest growth rate is among salespeople of Asian and Hispanic descent.[28]

Salesforce Training Whereas recruitment and selection of salespeople is a onetime event, salesforce training is an ongoing process that affects both new and seasoned salespeople.[29] Sales training covers much more than selling practices. For example, IBM Global Services salespeople, who sell consulting and various information technology services, take at least two weeks of in-class and Internet-based training on both consultative selling and the technical aspects of business.

Salesforce training is an ongoing process. Read the text to learn how training is conducted.

Training new salespeople is an expensive process. Salespeople in the United States receive employer-sponsored training annually at a cost of over $7 billion per year. On-the-job training is the most popular type of training, followed by individual instruction taught by experienced salespeople. Formal classes, seminars taught by sales trainers, and computer-based training are also popular.

Salesforce Motivation and Compensation A sales plan cannot be successfully implemented without motivated salespeople. Research on salesperson motivation suggests that: (1) a clear job description, (2) effective sales management practices, (3) a personal need for achievement, and (4) proper compensation, incentives, or rewards will produce a motivated salesperson.[30]

The importance of compensation as a motivating factor means that close attention must be given to how salespeople are financially rewarded for their efforts. Salespeople are paid using one of three plans: (1) straight salary, (2) straight commission, or (3) a combination of salary and commission. Under a *straight salary compensation plan*, a salesperson is paid a fixed fee per week, month, or year. With a *straight commission compensation plan*, a salesperson's earnings are directly tied to the sales or profit generated. For example, an insurance agent might receive a 2 percent commission of $2,000 for selling a $100,000 life insurance policy. A *combination compensation plan* contains a specified salary plus a commission on sales or profit generated.

Each compensation plan has its advantages and disadvantages.[31] A straight salary plan is easy to administer and gives management a large measure of control over how salespeople allocate their efforts. However, it provides little incentive to expand

Why is Jamie Cruse Vrinios, a successful Mary Kay Cosmetics Independent National Sales Director, posing with a Cadillac Escalade Hybrid? Read the text to learn how Mary Kay rewards its top sales performers.

Mary Kay Cosmetics, Inc.
www.marykay.com

sales volume. This plan is used when salespeople engage in many nonselling activities, such as account or customer servicing. A straight commission plan provides the maximum amount of selling incentive but can detract salespeople from providing customer service. This plan is common when nonselling activities are minimal. Combination plans are most preferred by salespeople and attempt to build on the advantages of salary and commission plans while reducing potential shortcomings of each. A majority of companies use combination plans today.

Nonmonetary rewards are also given to salespeople for meeting or exceeding objectives. These rewards include trips, honor societies, distinguished salesperson awards, and letters of commendation. Some unconventional rewards include the new pink Cadillacs and Buicks, and jewelry given by Mary Kay Cosmetics to outstanding salespeople. Mary Kay, with 12,000 cars, has the largest fleet of General Motors cars in the world.[32]

Effective recruitment, selection, training, motivation, and compensation programs combine to create a productive salesforce. Ineffective practices often lead to costly salesforce turnover. The expense of replacing and training a new salesperson, including the cost of lost sales, can be high. Also, new recruits are often less productive than seasoned salespeople.[33]

Salesforce Evaluation: Measuring Results

The final function in the sales management process involves evaluating the salesforce. It is at this point that salespeople are assessed as to whether sales objectives were met and account management policies were followed. Both quantitative and behavioral measures are used to tap different selling dimensions.

Quantitative Assessments Quantitative assessments are based on input- and output-related objectives set forth in the sales plan. Input-related measures focus on the actual activities performed by salespeople such as those involving sales calls, selling expenses, and account management policies. The number of sales calls made, selling expense related to sales made, and the number of reports submitted to superiors are frequently used input measures.

Output measures often appear in a sales quota. A **sales quota** contains specific goals assigned to a salesperson, sales team, branch sales office, or sales district for a stated time period. Dollar or unit sales volume, last year/current sales ratio, sales of specific products, new accounts generated, and profit achieved are typical goals. The time period can range from one month to one year.

Behavioral Evaluation Behavioral measures are also used to evaluate salespeople. These include assessments of a salesperson's attitude, attention to customers, product knowledge, selling and communication skills, appearance, and professional demeanor. Even though these assessments are sometimes subjective, they are frequently considered and, in fact, inevitable, in salesperson evaluation. Why? These factors are often important determinants of quantitative outcomes.

About 60 percent of U.S. companies now include customer satisfaction as a behavioral measure of salesperson performance. (*What percentage did you check for question 4 in Figure 20–1?*) The relentless focus on customer satisfaction by Eastman Chemical Company salespeople contributed to the company being named a recipient of the prestigious Malcolm Baldrige National Quality Award.[34] Eastman surveys its customers with multiple versions of its customer satisfaction questionnaire delivered in nine languages. Some 25 performance items are studied, including on-time and correct delivery, product quality, pricing practice, and sharing of market

Using Marketing Dashboards

Tracking Salesperson Performance at Moore Chemical & Sanitation Supply, Inc.

Moore Chemical & Sanitation Supply, Inc. (MooreChem) is a large Midwestern supplier of cleaning chemicals and sanitary products. MooreChem sells to janitorial companies that clean corporate and professional office buildings.

MooreChem recently installed a sales and account management planning software package that included a dashboard for each of its sales representatives. Salespeople had access to their dashboards as well. These dashboards included seven metrics—sales revenue, gross margin, selling expense, profit, average order size, new customers, and customer satisfaction. Each metric was gauged to show actual salesperson performance relative to target goals.

Your Challenge As a newly promoted district sales manager at MooreChem, your responsibilities include tracking each salesperson's performance in your district. You are also responsible for directing the sales activities and practices of district salespeople.

In anticipation of a performance review with one of your salespeople, Brady Boyle, you review his dashboard for the previous quarter. Provide a constructive review of his performance.

Your Findings Brady Boyle's quarterly performance is displayed below. Boyle has exceeded targeted goals for sales revenue, selling expenses, and customer satisfaction. All of these metrics show an upward trend. He has met his target for gaining new customers and average order size. But, Boyle's gross margin and profit are below targeted goals. These metrics evidence a downward trend as well. Brady Boyle's mixed performance requires a constructive and positive correction.

Your Action Brady Boyle should already know how his performance compares with targeted goals. Remember, Boyle has access to his dashboard. Recall that he has exceeded his sales target, but is considerably under his profit target. Boyle's sales trend is up, but his profit trend is down.

You will need to focus attention on Boyle's gross margin and selling expense results and trend. Boyle, it seems, is spending time and money selling lower margin products that produce a targeted average order size. It may very well be that Boyle is actually expending effort selling more products to his customers. Unfortunately, the product mix yields lower gross margins, resulting in a lower profit.

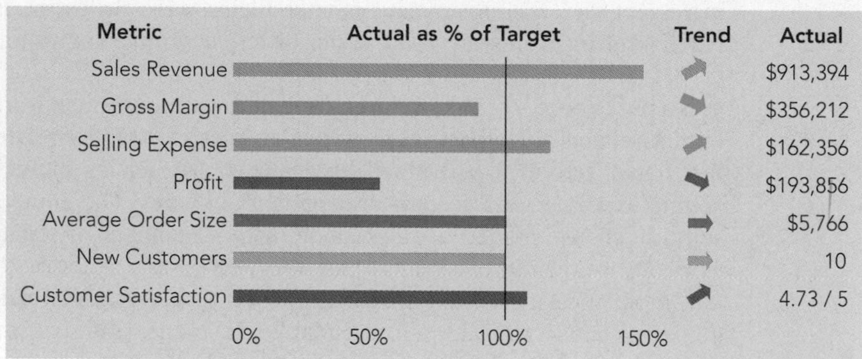

information. Salespeople review the results with customers. Eastman salespeople know that "the second most important thing they have to do is get their customer satisfaction surveys out to and back from customers," says Eastman's sales training director. "Number one, of course, is getting orders."

Increasingly, companies are using marketing dashboards to track salesperson performance for evaluation purposes. An illustration appears in the Using Marketing Dashboards box.

Salesforce Automation and Customer Relationship Management

Personal selling and sales management have undergone a technological revolution with the integration of salesforce automation into customer relationship manage-

Toshiba America Medical Systems salespeople have found computer technology to be an effective sales presentation tool and training device.

Toshiba America Medical Systems
www.toshiba.com

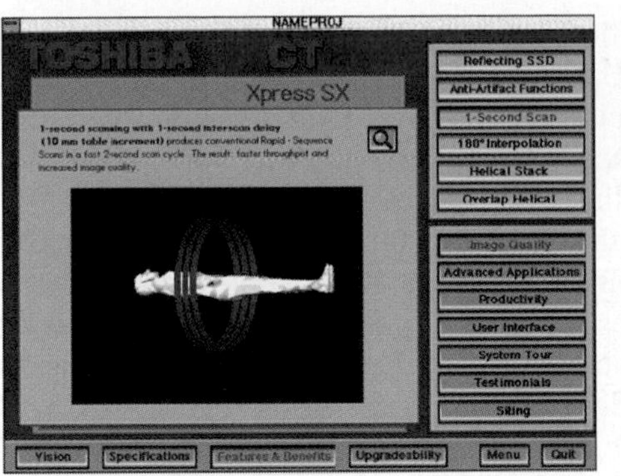

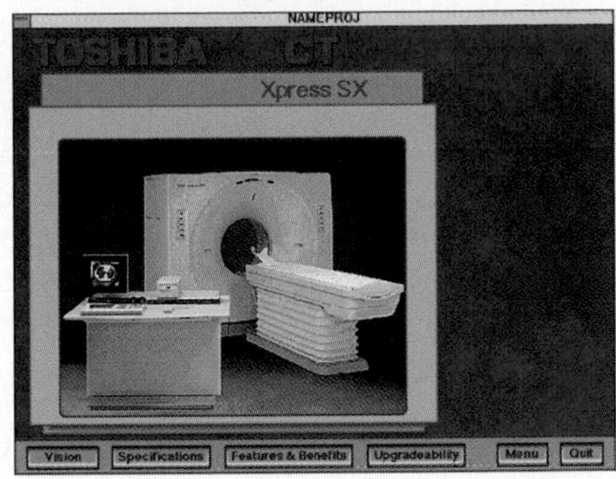

ment processes. In fact, the convergence of computer, information, communication, and Internet technologies has transformed the sales function in many companies and made the promise of customer relationship management a reality. **Salesforce automation** (SFA) is the use of these technologies to make the sales function more effective and efficient. SFA applies to a wide range of activities, including each stage in the personal selling process and management of the salesforce itself.[35]

Salesforce automation exists in many forms. Examples of SFA applications include computer hardware and software for account analysis, time management, order processing and follow-up, sales presentations, proposal generation, and product and sales training. Each application is designed to ease administrative tasks and free time for salespeople to be with customers building relationships, designing solutions, and providing service.

Salesforce Technology Technology has become an integral part of field selling.[36] Today, most companies supply their field salespeople with laptop computers. For example, salespeople for Godiva Chocolates use their laptop computers to process orders, plan time allocations, forecast sales, and communicate with Godiva personnel and customers. While in a department store candy buyer's office, such as Neiman Marcus, a salesperson can calculate the order cost (and discount), transmit the order, and obtain a delivery date within minutes from Godiva's order processing department.

Toshiba America Medical Systems salespeople use laptop computers with built-in CD-ROM capabilities to provide interactive presentations for their computerized tomography (CT) and magnetic resonance imaging (MRI) scanners. In it the customer sees elaborate three-dimensional animations, high-resolution scans, and video clips of the company's products in operation as well as narrated testimonials from satisfied customers. Toshiba has found this application to be effective both for sales presentations and for training its salespeople.

Salesforce Communication Technology has changed the way salespeople communicate with customers, other salespeople and sales support personnel, and management. Facsimile, electronic mail, and voice mail are common communication technologies used by salespeople today. Cellular (phone) technology now allows salespeople to exchange data, text, and voice transmissions. Whether traveling or in a customer's office, these technologies provide information at the salesperson's fingertips to answer customer questions and solve problems.

Advances in communication and computer technologies have made possible the mobile and home sales office. Some salespeople now equip minivans with a fully functional desk, swivel chair, light, multifunctional printer, fax machine, cellular phone, and a satellite dish. Jeff Brown, an agent manager with U.S. Cellular, uses such a mobile office. He says, "If I arrive at a prospect's office and they can't see me right away, then I can go outside to work in my office until they're ready to see me."[37]

Home offices are now common. Hewlett-Packard is a case in point. The company shifted its U.S. salesforce into home offices, closed several regional sales offices, and saved millions of dollars in staff salaries and office rent. A fully equipped home office for each salesperson includes a notebook computer, fax/copier, cellular phone, two phone lines, and office furniture.

Perhaps the greatest impact on salesforce communication is the application of Internet technology. Today, salespeople are using their company's intranet for a variety of purposes. At HP Enterprise Services, a professional services firm, salespeople access its intranet to download client material, marketing content, account information, technical papers, and competitive profiles. In addition, HP Enterprise Services offers 7,000 training classes that salespeople can take anytime and anywhere.

Salesforce automation is clearly changing how selling is done and how salespeople are managed. Its numerous applications promise to boost selling productivity, improve customer relationships, and decrease selling cost.

learning review

8. What are the three types of selling objectives?
9. What three factors are used to structure sales organizations?
10. How does emotional intelligence tie to adaptive selling?

LEARNING OBJECTIVES REVIEW

LO1 *Discuss the nature and scope of personal selling and sales management in marketing.*
Personal selling involves the two-way flow of communication between a buyer and seller, often in a face-to-face encounter, designed to influence a person's or group's purchase decision. Sales management involves planning the selling program and implementing and controlling the personal selling effort of the firm. The scope of selling and sales management is apparent in three ways. First, virtually every occupation that involves customer contact has an element of personal selling. Second, selling plays a significant role in a company's overall marketing effort. Salespeople occupy a boundary position between buyers and sellers; they *are* the company to many buyers and account for a major cost of marketing in a variety of industries; and they can create value for customers. Finally, through relationship and partnership selling, salespeople play a central role in tailoring solutions to customer problems as a means to customer value creation.

LO2 *Identify the different types of personal selling.*
Three types of personal selling exist: (*a*) order taking, (*b*) order getting, and (*c*) customer sales support activities. Each type differs from the others in terms of actual selling done and the amount of creativity required to perform the sales task. Order takers process routine orders or reorders for products that were already sold by the company. They generally do little selling in a conventional sense and engage in only modest problem solving with customers. Order getters sell in a conventional sense and identify prospective customers, provide customers with information, persuade customers to buy, close sales, and follow up on customers' use of a product or service. Order getting involves a high degree of creativity and customer empathy and is typically required for selling complex or technical products with many options. Customer sales support personnel augment the sales effort of order getters by performing a variety of services. Sales support personnel are prominent in cross-functional team selling, the practice of using an entire team of professionals in selling to and servicing major customers.

LO3 *Explain the stages in the personal selling process.*
The personal selling process consists of six stages: (*a*) prospecting, (*b*) preapproach, (*c*) approach, (*d*) presentation, (*e*) close, and (*f*) follow-up. Prospecting involves the search for and qualification of potential customers. The preapproach stage involves obtaining further information on the prospect and deciding on the best method of approach. The approach stage involves the initial meeting between the salesperson and prospect. The presentation stage involves converting a prospect into a customer by creating a desire for the product or service. The close involves obtaining a purchase commitment from the prospect. The follow-up stage involves making certain that the customer's purchase has been properly delivered and installed and difficulties experienced with the use of the item are addressed.

LO4 *Describe the major functions of sales management.*
Sales management consists of three interrelated functions: (*a*) sales plan formulation, (*b*) sales plan implementation, and (*c*) evaluation of the salesforce. Sales plan formulation involves setting objectives, organizing the salesforce, and developing account management policies. Sales plan implementation involves salesforce recruitment, selection, training, motivation, and compensation. Finally, salesforce evaluation focuses on quantitative assessments of sales performance and behavioral measures such as customer satisfaction that are linked to selling objectives and account management policies.

FOCUSING ON KEY TERMS

account management policies p. 536
adaptive selling p. 529
consultative selling p. 529
emotional intelligence p. 537
formula selling presentation p. 529
key account management p. 534
need-satisfaction presentation p. 529
order getter p. 523
order taker p. 522
partnership selling p. 522
personal selling p. 520
personal selling process p. 526
relationship selling p. 522
sales management p. 520
sales plan p. 532
sales quota p. 539
salesforce automation p. 541
stimulus-response presentation p. 529
team selling p. 525
workload method p. 536

APPLYING MARKETING KNOWLEDGE

1 Jane Dawson is a new sales representative for the Charles Schwab brokerage firm. In searching for clients, Jane purchased a mailing list of subscribers to *The Wall Street Journal* and called them all regarding their interest in discount brokerage services. She asked if they have any stocks and if they have a regular broker. Those people without a regular broker were asked their investment needs. Two days later, Jane called back with investment advice and asked if they would like to open an account. Identify each of Jane Dawson's actions in terms of the personal selling process.

2 For the first 50 years of business the Johnson Carpet Company produced carpets for residential use. The salesforce was structured geographically. In the past five years, a large percentage of carpet sales has been to industrial users, hospitals, schools, and architects. The company also has broadened its product line to include area rugs, Oriental carpets, and wall-to-wall carpeting. Is the present salesforce structure appropriate, or would you recommend an alternative?

3 Where would you place each of the following sales jobs on the order-taker/order-getter continuum shown below? (*a*) Burger King counter clerk, (*b*) automobile insurance salesperson, (*c*) Hewlett-Packard computer salesperson, (*d*) life insurance salesperson, and (*e*) shoe salesperson.

Order taker ———————————— Order getter

4 Listed here are two different firms. Which compensation plan would you recommend for each firm, and what reasons would you give for your recommendations? (*a*) A newly formed company that sells lawn care equipment on a door-to-door basis directly to consumers; and (*b*) the Nabisco Company, which sells heavily advertised products in supermarkets by having the salesforce call on these stores and arrange shelves, set up displays, and make presentations to store buying committees.

5 Tyler Automotive, Inc. supplies 1,000 independent auto parts stores throughout the United States. Each store is called on 12 times a year, and the average sales call lasts 30 minutes. Assuming a salesperson works 40 hours a week, 50 weeks a year, and devotes 75 percent of the time to actual selling, how many salespeople does Tyler Automotive need?

6 A furniture manufacturer is currently using manufacturer's representatives to sell its line of living room furniture. These representatives receive an 8 percent commission. The company is considering hiring its own salespeople and has estimated that the fixed cost of managing and paying their salaries would be $1 million annually. The salespeople would also receive a 4 percent commission on sales. The company has sales of $25 million, and sales are expected to grow by 15 percent next year. Would you recommend that the company switch to its own salesforce? Why or why not?

7 Suppose someone said to you, "The only real measure of a salesperson is the amount of sales produced." How might you respond?

building your marketing plan

Does your marketing plan involve a personal selling activity? If the answer is no, read no further and do not include a personal selling element in your plan. If the answer is yes:

1 Identify the likely prospects for your product or service.

2 Determine what information you should obtain about the prospect.

3 Describe how you would approach the prospect.

4 Outline the presentation you would make to the prospect for your product or service.

5 Develop a sales plan, focusing on the organizational structure you would use for your salesforce (geography, product, or customer).

"I'm like the quarterback of the team. I manage 250 accounts, and anything from billing issues, to service issues, to selling the products. I'm really the face to the customer," says Alison Capossela, a Washington, D.C.-based Xerox sales representative.

As the primary company contact for Xerox customers, Alison is responsible for developing and maintaining customer relationships. To accomplish this she uses a sophisticated selling process which requires many activities from making presentations, to attending training sessions, to managing a team of Xerox personnel, to monitoring competitors' activities. The face-to-face interactions with customers, however, are the most rewarding for Capossela. "It's an amazing feeling; the more they challenge me the more I fight back. It's fun!" she explains.

THE COMPANY

Xerox Corporation's mission is to "help people find better ways to do great work by constantly leading in document technologies, products, and services that improve customers' work processes and business results." To accomplish this mission Xerox employs 53,700 people in 160 countries. With annual sales of $16 billion, Xerox is the world's leading document management enterprise and a *Fortune* 500 company. Xerox offers a wide range of products and services. These include printers, copiers and fax machines, multifunction and network devices, high-speed color presses, digital imaging and archiving products and services, and supplies such as toner, paper, and ink. The entire company is guided by customer-focused and employee-centered core values (e.g., "We succeed through satisfied customers") and a passion for innovation, speed, and adaptability.

Xerox was founded in 1906 as a manufacturer of photographic paper called The Haloid Company. In 1947, the company purchased the license to basic xerographic patents. The following year it received a trademark for the word "Xerox." By 1973 Xerox had introduced the automatic, plain-paper copier, opened offices in Japan, and its Palo Alto Research Center (PARC) had invented the world's first personal computer (the Alto), the "mouse," and graphical user interface software. In 1994, Xerox adopted "The Document Company" as its signature and the partially digitized red "X" as its corporate symbol. Despite this extraordinary history of success, Xerox was $19 billion in debt by 2000 and was losing business rapidly. Many experts predicted that the company would fail.

The Xerox board of directors knew a change was needed and it asked Anne M. Mulcahy to serve as the company's CEO. Mulcahy had begun her career as a sales representative at Xerox and observed that "we had lost our way in terms of delivering value to customers." Mulcahy reduced the size of the workforce by one-third and invested in new technologies, while keeping the Xerox culture and values. The changes, coupled with Mulcahy's commitment to a sales organization that focused on customer relationships, reversed Xerox's decline. As Kevin Warren, vice president of sales, explains: "One of the reasons she has been so successful is that she absolutely resonates with all the people. I think [because of] the fact that she started out as a sales rep, people feel like she is one of them." The turnaround has been such an extraordinary success that Mulcahy was recognized by *Forbes* magazine as the 10th most powerful woman in the world!

THE SELLING PROCESS AT XEROX

When Mulcahy became CEO, Xerox began a shift to a consultative selling model that focused on helping customers solve their business problems rather than just placing more equipment in their office. The shift meant that sales reps needed to be less product-oriented and more relationship- and value-oriented. Xerox wanted to be a provider of total solutions. Today, Xerox has more than 8,000 sales professionals throughout the world who spend a large amount of their day developing customer relationships. Capossela explains: "Fifty percent of my day is spent with my customers, 25 percent is following up with phone calls or emails, and another 25 percent involves preparing proposals." The approach has helped Xerox attract new customers and keep existing customers.

The sales process at Xerox typically follows the six stages of the personal selling process identified in Figure 20–3: (1) Xerox identifies potential clients through responses to advertising, referrals, and telephone calls; (2) the salesforce prepares for a presentation by familiarizing themselves with the potential client and its document needs; (3) a Xerox sales representative approaches the prospect and suggests a meeting and presentation; (4) as the presentation begins, the salesperson summarizes relevant information about potential solutions Xerox can offer, states what he or she hopes to get out of the meeting, explains how the products and services work, and reinforces the benefits of working with Xerox; (5) the salesperson engages in an action close (gets a signed document or a firm confirmation of the sale); and then (6) continues to meet and communicate with the client to provide assistance and monitor the effectiveness of the installed solution.

Xerox sales representatives also use the selling process to maintain relationships with existing customers. In today's competitive environment it is not unusual to have customers who have been approached by competitors or who are required to obtain more than one bid before renewing a contract. Xerox has teams of people who collect and analyze information about competitors and their products. The information is sent out to sales reps or offered to them through workshops and seminars. The most difficult competitors are the ones that have also invested in customer relationships. The selling process allows Xerox to continually react and respond to new information and take advantage of opportunities in the marketplace.

THE SALES MANAGEMENT PROCESS AT XEROX

The Xerox salesforce is divided into four geographic organizations: North America, which includes the United States and Canada; Europe, which includes 17 countries; Global Accounts, which manages large accounts that operate in multiple locations; and Developing Markets, which includes all other geographic territories that may require Xerox products and services. Within each geographic area, the majority of Xerox products and services are typically sold through its direct salesforce. Xerox also utilizes a variety of other channels, including value-added resellers, independent agents, dealers, systems integrators, telephone, and Internet sales channels.

Motivation and compensation is an important aspect of any salesforce. At Xerox there is a passion for winning that provides a key incentive for sales reps. In addition, the compensation plan plays an important role. As Warren explains, "Our compensation plans are a combination of salary as well as an opportunity to leverage earnings through sales commissions and bonuses." Xerox also has a recognition program called the President's Club where the top performers are awarded a five-day trip to one of the top resorts in the world. The program has been a huge success and has now been offered for more than 30 years.

Perhaps the most well-known component of Xerox's sales management process is its sales representative training program. For example, Xerox developed the "Create and Win" program to help sales reps learn the new consultative selling approach. The components of the program consisted of interactive training sessions and distance-learning Webinars. Every new sales representative at Xerox receives eight weeks of training development in the field and at the Xerox Corporate University in Virginia. "The training program is phenomenal!" according to Capossela. The training and its focus on the customer is part of the Xerox culture outside of the sales organization also. Every senior executive at Xerox is responsible for working with at least one customer. They also spend a full day every month responding to incoming customer calls and inquiries.

WHAT IS IN THE FUTURE FOR THE XEROX SALESFORCE?

The recent growth and success at Xerox is creating many opportunities for the company and for its sales representatives. For example, Xerox is accelerating the development of its top salespeople. Mentors are used to provide advice for day-to-day issues and long-term career planning. In addition, globalization has become such an important initiative at Xerox that experienced and successful sales representatives are quickly given opportunities to manage large global accounts. Xerox is also moving toward an approach that empowers sales representatives to make decisions about how to handle accounts. The large number of Xerox customers means there are a variety of different corporate styles, and the sales reps are increasingly the best qualified to manage the relationship. This approach is just one more example of Xerox's commitment to customers and creating customer value.

Questions

1 Why was Anne Mulcahy's experience as a sales representative an important part of Xerox's growth in recent years?

2 How did the sales approach change after Mulcahy became the CEO of Xerox?

3 *(a)* How does Xerox create customer value through its personal selling process? *(b)* How does Alison Capossela provide solutions for Xerox customers?

4 Why is the Xerox training program so important to the company's success?

The Triad. Redefine Your Expectations.
• Full-Custom Carbon
• Ready in Three Weeks
• Complete Bike Prices Start at $5,195
• Beyond Your Expectations
www.sevencycles.com/gateway
One Bike. Yours.
seven cycles

21 Implementing Interactive and Multichannel Marketing

LEARNING OBJECTIVES

After reading this chapter you should be able to:

LO1 Describe what interactive marketing is and how it creates customer value, customer relationships, and customer experiences.

LO2 Identify the demographic and lifestyle profile of online consumers.

LO3 Explain why certain types of products and services are particularly suited for interactive marketing.

LO4 Describe why consumers shop and buy online and how marketers influence online purchasing behavior.

LO5 Define cross-channel shoppers and the role of transactional and promotional Web sites in reaching these shoppers.

SEVEN CYCLES. ONE BIKE. YOURS.

"One bike: Yours" is the company motto for Seven Cycles, Inc., located in Watertown, Massachusetts. And for good reason.

Seven Cycles is the largest custom bicycle frame builder. The company produces a broad range of road, mountain, cyclo-cross, tandem, touring, single-speed, and commuter bikes annually, and no two bikes are exactly alike. At Seven Cycles, attention is focused on each customer's unique cycling experience through the optimum fit, function, performance, and comfort of his or her very own bike. According to one satisfied customer, "Getting a Seven is more of a creation than a purchase."

The marketing success of Seven Cycles is due to its state-of-the-art bicycle frames. But as Rob Vandermark, company founder and president, says, "Part of our success is that we are tied to a business model that includes the Internet."

Seven Cycles uses its multi-language (English, German, Chinese, Japanese, Korean, and Flemish) Web site (www.sevencycles.com) to let customers get deeply involved in the frame building process and the selection of components to outfit their bikes. It enables customers to collaborate on the bike design using the company's Custom Kit fitting system that considers the rider's size, aspirations, and riding habits. Then customers can monitor their bike's progress through the development and production process by clicking "Where's My Frame?" on the Seven Cycles Web site.

This customization process and continuous feedback makes for a collaborative relationship between Seven Cycles, its 233 authorized dealers and distributors, and customers in 40 countries. "Each bike we build is unique, so each customer's experience deserves to be unique as well," explains Mattison Crow, marketing manager at Seven Cycles.

In addition to the order process, Web site visitors can peruse weekly news stories, learn about new-product introductions, or link to the company president's blog to get a unique perspective on the business. They can read employee biographies online to learn more about the people who build the bikes. The Web site also offers a retailer-specific section as a 24/7 repository of updated information for channel partners.

Beyond the Web site, owners of a Seven Cycles bike receive a monthly e-mail newsletter, called Communiqué, that allows them to remain in touch and be the first to learn about the company's activities, strategic partnerships, and new offerings. Seven Cycles is also experimenting with other social media tools such as Facebook and Twitter, as a means to build a stronger sense of community around the brand.[1]

This chapter describes how companies design and implement interactive marketing programs. It begins by explaining how Internet technology can create customer value, build customer relationships, and produce customer experiences in novel ways. Next, it describes how Internet technology affects and is affected by consumer behavior and marketing practice. Finally, the chapter shows how marketers integrate and leverage their communication and delivery channels using Internet technology to implement multichannel marketing programs.

CREATING CUSTOMER VALUE, RELATIONSHIPS, AND EXPERIENCES IN MARKETSPACE

LO1

Consumers and companies populate two market environments today. One is the traditional *marketplace*. Here buyers and sellers engage in face-to-face exchange relationships in a material environment characterized by physical facilities (stores and offices) and mostly tangible objects. The other is the *marketspace*, an Internet-enabled digital environment characterized by face-to-screen exchange relationships and electronic images and offerings.

The existence of two market environments has been a boon for consumers. Today, consumers can shop for and purchase a wide variety of products and services in either market environment. Actually, many consumers now browse and buy in both market environments, and more are expected to do so in the future. Figure 21–1 shows the growth in online shoppers and estimated retail sales in the United States since 2003. About 94 percent of Internet users ages 15 and older shop online in the United States. They are expected to buy $335 billion worth of products and services in 2012.[2]

Customer Value Creation in Marketspace

Why has the marketspace captured the eye and imagination of marketers worldwide? Recall from Chapter 1 that marketing creates time, place, form, and possession utilities, thereby providing value. Marketers believe that the possibilities for customer value creation are greater in the digital marketspace than in the physical marketplace.

Consider place and time utility. In marketspace, the provision of direct, on-demand information is possible from marketers *anywhere* to customers *anywhere at any time*. Why? Operating hours and geographical constraints do not exist in marketspace. For example, Recreational Equipment (www.rei.com), an outdoor gear marketer, reports

FIGURE 21–1
Trends in online shoppers and online retail sales revenue in the United States

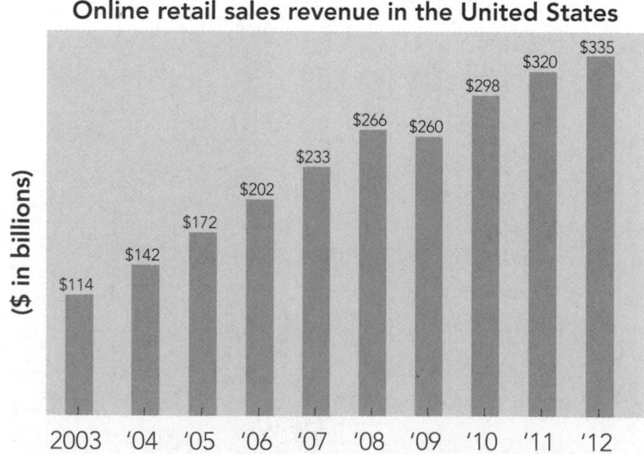

that 35 percent of its orders are placed between 10:00 P.M. and 7:00 A.M., long after and before retail stores are open for business. Similarly, a U.S. consumer from Chicago can access Marks & Spencer (www.marks-and-spencer.co.uk), the well-known British department store, to shop for clothing as easily as a person living near London's Piccadilly Square.

Possession utility—getting a product or service to consumers so they can own or use it—is accelerated. Airline, car rental, and lodging electronic reservation systems such as Orbitz (www.orbitz.com) allow comparison shopping for the lowest fares, rents, and rates and almost immediate access to and confirmation of travel arrangements and accommodations. Internet usage among people who travel on a regular basis is 20 percent higher than those who travel infrequently.[3]

The greatest marketspace opportunity for marketers, however, lies in its potential for creating form utility. Interactive two-way Internet-enabled communication capabilities in marketspace invite consumers to tell marketers specifically what their requirements are, making customization of a product or service to fit their exact needs possible.[4] For instance, Capital One lets its customers build their own mix of interest rates, fees, rewards, and cash back through its Card Lab Web site (www.capitalone.com/cardlab). Or, customers can arrange for a custom-made mountain bike from Seven Cycles as described in the chapter opening example.

Interactivity, Individuality, and Customer Relationships in Marketspace

Marketers also benefit from two unique capabilities of Internet technology that promote and sustain customer relationships. One is *interactivity*; the other is *individuality*.[5] Both capabilities are important building blocks for buyer–seller relationships. For

Seven Cycles created form utility in the creation of customized bikes for its customers in 40 countries.

Seven Cycles, Inc.
www.sevencycles.com

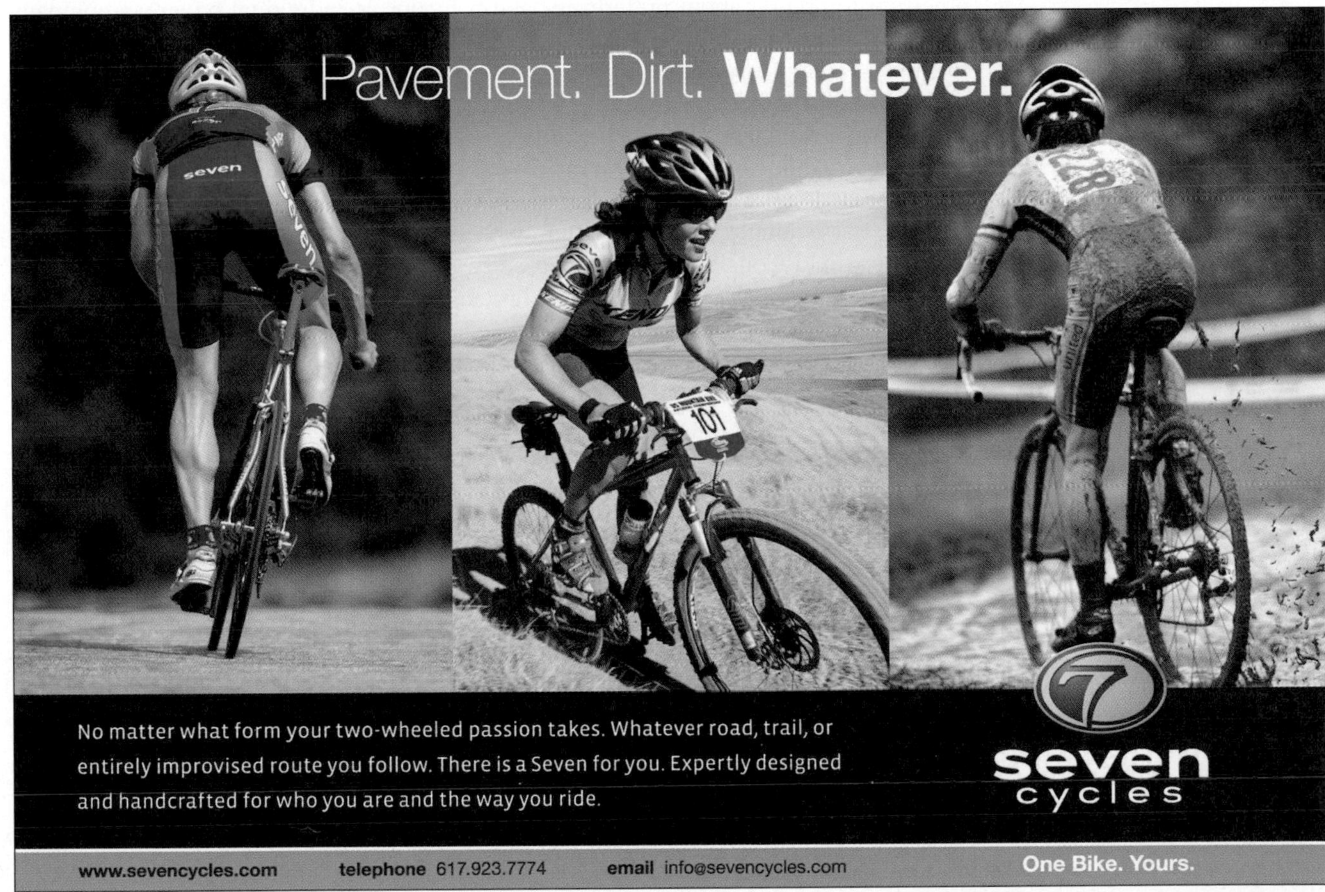

Pavement. Dirt. Whatever.
No matter what form your two-wheeled passion takes. Whatever road, trail, or entirely improvised route you follow. There is a Seven for you. Expertly designed and handcrafted for who you are and the way you ride.
seven cycles
www.sevencycles.com
telephone 617.923.7774
email info@sevencycles.com
One Bike. Yours.

Mars, Inc. uses choiceboard technology to decorate M&Ms with personal photos and messages. Other applications for choiceboards are described in the text.

Mars, Inc.
www.mymms.com

these relationships to occur, companies need to interact with their customers by listening and responding to their needs. Marketers must also treat customers as individuals and empower them to (1) influence the timing and extent of the buyer–seller interaction and (2) have a say in the kind of products and services they buy, the information they receive, and in some cases, the prices they pay.

Internet technology allows for interaction, individualization, and customer relationship building to be carried out on a scale never before available and makes interactive marketing possible. **Interactive marketing** involves two-way buyer–seller electronic communication in a computer-mediated environment in which the buyer controls the kind and amount of information received from the seller. Interactive marketing is characterized by sophisticated choiceboard and personalization systems that transform information supplied by customers into customized responses to their individual needs.

Choiceboards A **choiceboard** is an interactive, Internet-enabled system that allows individual customers to design their own products and services by answering a few questions and choosing from a menu of product or service attributes (or components), prices, and delivery options.[6] Customers today can design their own computers with Dell's online configurator, style their own athletic shoe at Reebok.com, assemble their own investment portfolios with Schwab's mutual fund evaluator, build their own bicycle at SevenCycles.com, and create a diet and fitness program at www.ediet.com that fits their lifestyle, and decorate M&Ms with photos of themselves and unique messages at www.mymms.com. Because choiceboards collect precise information about preferences and behavior of individual buyers, a company becomes more knowledgeable about a customer and better able to anticipate and fulfill that customer's needs.

Most choiceboards are essentially transaction devices. However, companies such as Dell have expanded the functionality of choiceboards using collaborative filtering technology. **Collaborative filtering** is a process that automatically groups people with similar buying intentions, preferences, and behaviors and predicts future purchases.[7] For example, say two people who have never met buy a few of the same CDs over time. Collaborative filtering software is programmed to reason that these two buyers might have similar musical tastes: If one buyer likes a particular CD, then the other will like it as well. The outcome? Collaborative filtering gives marketers the ability to make a dead-on sales recommendation to a buyer in *real time*. You see collaborative filtering applied each time you view a selection at Amazon.com and see "Customers who bought this (item) also bought. . . ."

Choiceboards and collaborative filtering represent two important capabilities of Internet technology and have changed the way companies operate today. According to an electronic commerce manager at IBM, "The business model of the past was make and sell. Now instead of make and sell, it's sense and respond."[8]

Personalization Choiceboards and collaborative filtering are marketer–initiated efforts to provide customized responses to the needs of individual buyers. Personalization systems are typically buyer-initiated efforts. **Personalization** is the consumer-initiated practice of generating content on a marketer's Web site that is custom tailored to an individual's specific needs and preferences. For example, Yahoo! (www.yahoo.com) allows users to create personalized MyYahoo! pages. Users can add or delete a variety of types of information from their personal pages, including specific stock quotes, weather conditions in any city in the world, and local television schedules. In turn, Yahoo! can use the buyer profile data entered when users register

Reebok has effectively used choiceboard technology for customizing athletic shoes.

Reebok
www.reebok.com

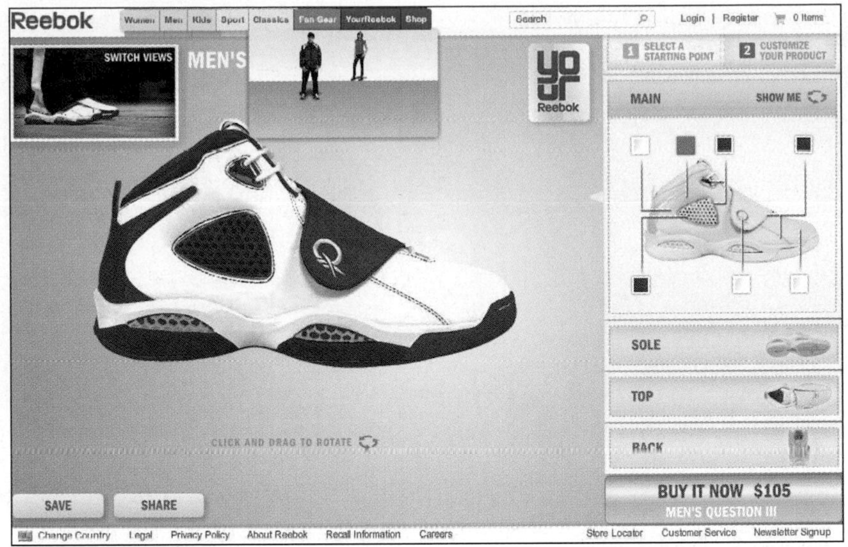

at the site to tailor e-mail messages, advertising, and content to the individual—and even post a happy birthday greeting on the user's special day.

An aspect of personalization is a buyer's willingness to have tailored communications brought to his or her attention. Obtaining this approval is called **permission marketing**—the solicitation of a consumer's consent (called *opt-in*) to receive e-mail and advertising based on personal data supplied by the consumer. Permission marketing is a proven vehicle for building and maintaining customer relationships, provided it is properly used.

Companies that successfully employ permission marketing adhere to three rules.[9] First, they make sure opt-in customers receive only information that is relevant and meaningful to them. Second, their customers are given the option to *opt-out*, or change the kind, amount, or timing of information sent to them. Finally, their customers are assured that their name or buyer profile data will not be sold or shared with others. This assurance is important because 75 percent of adult Internet users express concern about the privacy of their personal information.[10]

Creating an Online Customer Experience

A continuing challenge for companies is the design and execution of marketing programs that capitalize on the unique customer value-creation capabilities of Internet technology. Companies realize that applying Internet technology to create time, place, form, and possession utility is just a starting point for creating a meaningful marketspace presence. Today, the quality of the customer experience produced by a company is the standard by which a meaningful marketspace presence is measured.

From an interactive marketing perspective, *customer experience* is defined as the sum total of the interactions that a customer has with a company's Web site, from the initial look at a home page through the entire purchase decision process.[11] Companies produce a customer experience through seven Web site design elements. These elements are context, content, community, customization, communication, connection, and commerce. Each is summarized in Figure 21–2 on the next page. A closer look at these elements illustrates how each contributes to customer experience.

Context refers to a Web site's aesthetic appeal and functional look and feel reflected in site layout and visual design. A functionally oriented Web site focuses largely on the company's offering, be it products, services, or information. Travel Web sites, such as Travelocity.com, tend to be functionally oriented with an emphasis on destinations, scheduling, and prices. In contrast, beauty Web sites, such as Revlon.com, are more aesthetically oriented. As these examples suggest, context attempts

FIGURE 21–2
Seven Web site design elements that drive customer experience

to convey the core consumer benefit provided by the company's offerings. *Content* applies to all digital information on a Web site, including the presentation form—text, video, audio, and graphics. Content quality and presentation along with context dimensions combine to engage a Web site visitor and provide a platform for the five remaining design elements.

Web site *customization* is the ability of a site to modify itself to, or be modified by, each individual user. This design element is prominent in Web sites that offer personalized content, such as My eBay and MyYahoo! The *connection* element is the network of linkages between a company's site and other sites. These links are embedded in the Web site; appear as highlighted words, a picture, or graphic; and allow a user to effortlessly visit other sites with a mouse click. Connection is a major design element for informational Web sites such as *The New York Times*. Users of NYTimes.com can access the book review section and link to Barnes & Noble to order a book or browse related titles without ever visiting a store.

Travelocity pays close attention to creating a favorable customer experience by employing all seven Web site design elements.

Travelocity
www.travelocity.com

Communication refers to the dialogue that unfolds between the Web site and its users. Consumers—particularly those who have registered at a site—now expect that communication be interactive and individualized in real time much like a personal conversation. In fact, some Web sites now enable a user to talk directly with a customer representative while shopping the site. For example, two-thirds of the sales through Dell.com involve human sales representatives. In addition, an increasing number of company Web sites encourage user-to-user communications hosted by the company to create virtual communities, or simply, *community*. This design element is popular because it has been shown to enhance customer experience and build favorable buyer–seller relationships. Examples of communities range from the Huggies Baby Network hosted by Kimberly-Clark (www.huggies.com) to the Harley Owners Group (HOG) sponsored by Harley-Davidson (www.harley-davidson.com).

The seventh design element is *commerce*—the Web site's ability to conduct sales transactions for products and services. Online transactions are quick and simple in well-designed Web sites. Amazon.com has mastered this design element with "one-click shopping," a patented feature that allows users to order products with a single mouse click.

Most Web sites do not include every design element. Although every Web site has context and content, they differ in the use of the remaining five elements. Why? Web sites have different purposes. For example, only Web sites that emphasize the actual sale of products and services include the commerce element. Web sites that are used primarily for advertising and promotion purposes emphasize the communication element. The difference between these two types of Web sites is discussed later in the chapter in the description of multichannel marketing.

Companies use a broad array of measures to assess Web site performance. The amount of time per month visitors spend on their Web site, or "stickiness," is used to gauge customer experience.[12] Read the Using Marketing Dashboards box on the next page to learn how stickiness is measured and interpreted at Sewell Automotive Companies.

learning review

1. The consumer-initiated practice of generating content on a marketer's Web site that is custom tailored to an individual's specific needs and preferences is called ______________.
2. Companies produce a customer experience through what seven Web site design elements?

ONLINE CONSUMER BEHAVIOR AND MARKETING PRACTICE IN MARKETSPACE

Who are online consumers, and what do they buy? Why do they choose to shop and purchase products and services in the digital marketspace rather than or in addition to the traditional marketplace? Answers to these questions have a direct bearing on marketspace marketing practices.

Who Is the Online Consumer?

LO2

Many labels are given online consumers—cybershoppers, Netizens, and e-shoppers—suggesting they are a homogeneous segment of the population. They are not, but as a group, they do differ demographically from the general population.

Using Marketing Dashboards

Sizing Up Site Stickiness at Sewell Automotive Companies

Automobile dealerships have invested significant time, effort, and money in their Web sites. Why? Car browsing and shopping on the Internet is now commonplace.

Dealerships commonly measure Web site performance by tracking visit, visitor traffic, and "stickiness"—the amount of time per month visitors spend on their Web site. Web site design, easy navigation, involving content, and visual appeal combine to enhance the interactive customer experience and Web site stickiness.

To gauge stickiness, companies monitor the average time spent per unique monthly visitor (in minutes) on their Web sites. This is done by tracking and displaying the average visits per unique monthly visitor and the average time spent per visit, in minutes, in their marketing dashboards. The relationship is as follows:

Average Time Spent per Unique Monthly Visitor (minutes) =

(Average Visits per Unique Monthly Visitor) × (Average Time Spent per Visit (minutes))

Your Challenge As the manager responsible for Sewell .com, the Sewell Automotive Companies Web site, you have been asked to report on the effect recent improvements in the company's Web site have had on the amount of time per month visitors spend on the Web site. Sewell ranks among the largest U.S. automotive dealerships and is a recognized customer service leader in the automotive industry. Its Web site reflects the company's commitment to an unparalleled customer experience at its family of dealerships.

Your Findings Examples of monthly marketing dashboard traffic and time measures are displayed below for June 2006, three months before the Web site improvements (green arrow), and June 2007, three months after the improvements were made (red arrow).

The average time spent per unique monthly visitor increased from 8.5 minutes in June 2006 to 11.9 minutes in June 2007—a sizable jump. The increase is due primarily to the upturn in the average time spent per visit from 7.1 minutes to 8.5 minutes. The average number of visits also increased, but the percentage change was much less.

Your Action Improvements in the Web site have noticeably "moved the needle" on average time spent per unique monthly visitor. Still, additional action may be required to increase average visits per unique monthly visitor. These actions might include an analysis of Sewell's Web advertising program, search engine initiatives with Google, links to automobile manufacturer corporate Web sites, and broader print and electronic media advertising.

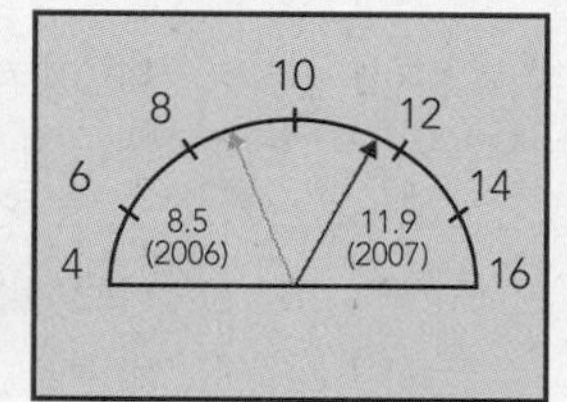

Average Time Spent per Unique Monthly Visitor (minutes)

=

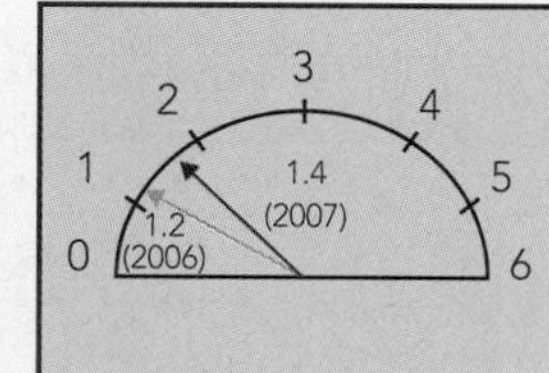

Average Visits per Unique Monthly Visitor

×

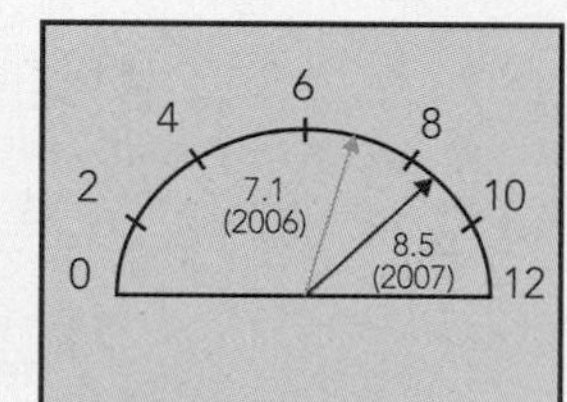

Average Time Spent per Visit (minutes)

Profiling the Online Consumer Online consumers differ from the general population in one important respect. They own or have access to a computer or an Internet-enabled device, such as a cell phone.

Online consumers are the subsegment of all Internet users who employ this technology to research products and services and make purchases. As a group, online consumers, like Internet users, are more likely to be women than men and tend to be better educated, younger, and more affluent than the general U.S. population, which makes them an attractive market.[13] Even though online shopping and buying is popular, a small percentage of online consumers still account for a disproportionate share of online retail sales in the United States. It is estimated that 20 percent of online consumers who spend $1,000-plus per year online account for 87 percent of total consumer online sales. Also, women tend to purchase more goods and services online than men.[14]

Going Online

Are You a Digital Collaborator or a Drifting Surfer?

Consumers differ in their use of information and communication technology. With that in mind, the researchers at the Pew Internet & American Life Project conducted a survey of adults ages 18 and older to classify people into different groups of information and communication technology users. Nine unique groups were identified and labeled with names such as Digital Collaborator or a Drifting Surfer.

Which group best describes you? To find out, simply go to www.pewinternet.org, click Participate, and then click "What Kind of Tech User Are You?" When finished, press the "What Kind of User Am I?" button. You will be told the group into which you fit, along with a description of the general characteristics of that group. Do you agree with the quiz results?

In general, online consumers also tend to use a range of information and communication technology as a platform to express themselves online and engage the digital marketspace. Recent research sponsored by the Pew Internet & American Life Project has categorized information and communication technology users into nine groups based on their use of devices to connect to the Internet, the activities they engage in, and their attitudes toward the marketspace.[15] To learn which group you fall into, take the quiz described in the Going Online box.

Online Consumer Lifestyle Segmentation Not all Internet users use the technology the same way, nor are they likely to be exclusive online consumers. Numerous marketing research firms have studied the lifestyles and shopping and spending habits of online consumers. A recurrent insight is that online consumers are diverse and represent different kinds of people seeking different kinds of online experiences. As an illustration, Harris Interactive, a large U.S. research firm, has identified six distinct online consumer lifestyle segments.[16]

The largest online consumer lifestyle segment, called *click-and-mortar*, consists of women who tend to browse retailer Web sites but actually buy products in traditional retail outlets. They make up 23 percent of online consumers and represent an important segment for multichannel retailers that also feature catalog and store operations, such as J. Crew and JCPenney.

Twenty percent of online consumers are *hunter-gatherers*—married couples with children at home who use the Internet like a consumer magazine to gather information and compare products and prices. They can be found visiting comparison shopping Web sites such as DealCatcher.com and mySimon.com on a regular basis. The Marketing Matters box on the next page provides an in-depth look at today's "Internet mom."[17]

Nineteen percent of online consumers are *brand loyalists* who regularly visit their favorite bookmarked Web sites and spend the most money online. They are better-educated and more affluent Internet users who effortlessly navigate familiar and trusted Web sites and enjoy the online browsing and buying experience.

Next there are *time-sensitive materialists* who regard the Internet as a convenience tool for buying music, books, computer software, and electronics. They account for 17 percent of online consumers and can be found visiting Amazon.com, Dell.com, and SonyStyle.com.

The *hooked*, *online*, and *single* segment consists of young, affluent, and single online consumers who bank, play games, and spend more time online than any other segment. They make up 16 percent of online consumers, enjoy auction Web sites such as eBay, and visit game Web sites like Slingo.com and Jigzone.com.

Five percent of online consumers are the *ebivalent newbies*—relative newcomers to the Internet who rarely spend money online but seek product information. Do any of these segments describe your online lifestyle and spending habits?

Marketing Matters > > > > > > > > > technology

Meet Today's Internet Mom—All 38 Million!

Do you have fond childhood memories of surfing the Internet with your mother? Today's children probably will.

Recent research indicates that 38 million mothers are online regularly. They're typically 38 years old and tend to be married, college educated, and working outside the home. A study conducted by C&R Research on behalf of Disney Online has identified four segments of mothers based on their Internet usage.

The *Yes Mom* segment represents 14 percent of online moms. They work outside the home, go online eight hours per week, and value the convenience of obtaining information about products and services. The *Mrs. Net Skeptic* segment accounts for 31 percent of online moms. They tend to be stay-at-home moms, are extremely family-oriented, and go online six hours per week for parenting and children's education information and food and cooking tips. The *Tech Nester* mom (32 percent of online moms) believes the Internet brings their family closer together. They average 10 hours per week online and prefer online shopping to in-store shopping. The fourth segment—*Passive Under Pressure* moms—tend to be Internet newbies and go online, but infrequently.

The first three segments, which account for 77 percent of online moms, agree that the Internet has simplified their lives. They also say that the Internet has been an invaluable information source for vacation travel, financial products, and automobiles and for useful ideas and suggestions on family-related topics. Online moms ranked weather, food and cooking, entertainment, news, health, and parenting as the most popular Web sites to visit.

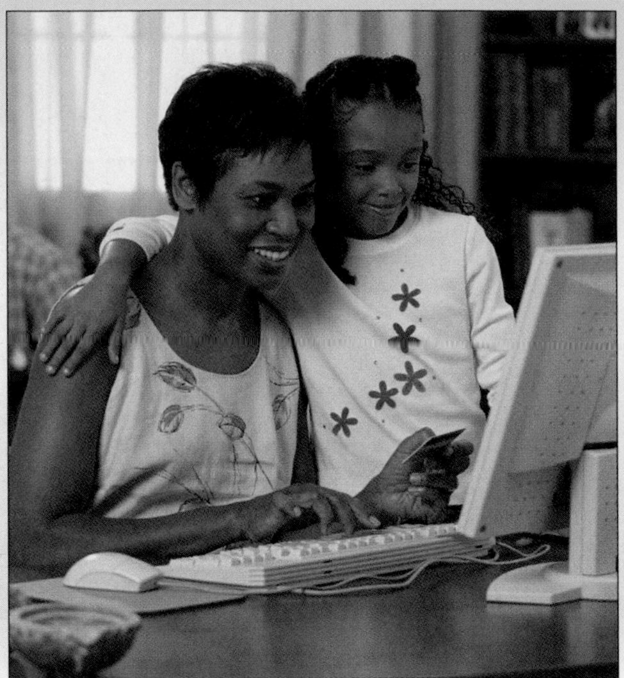

What Online Consumers Buy

LO3

Much still needs to be learned about online consumer purchase behavior. Although research has documented the most frequently purchased products and services bought online, marketers also need to know why these items are popular in the digital marketspace.

Six general product and service categories dominate online consumer buying today and for the foreseeable future as shown in Figure 21–3.[18] One category consists of items for which product information is an important part of the purchase decision, but prepurchase trial is not necessarily critical. Items such as computers, computer accessories, and consumer electronics sold by Dell.com fall into this category. So do books, which accounts for the sales growth of Amazon.com and Barnes & Noble (www.barnesandnoble.com). Both booksellers publish short reviews of new books that visitors to their Web sites can read before making a purchase decision.

A second category includes items for which audio or video demonstration is important. This category consists of CDs and DVDs sold by Columbia House.com. The third category contains items that can be delivered digitally, including computer software, travel and lodging reservations and confirmations, financial brokerage services, and electronic ticketing. Popular Web sites for these items include Travelocity.com, Ticketmaster.com, and Schwab.com.

Unique items, such as collectibles, specialty goods, and foods and gifts, represent a fourth category. Collectible auction houses (www.sothebys.com), food merchants (www.harryanddavid.com), and flower marketers (www.1800flowers.com) sell these

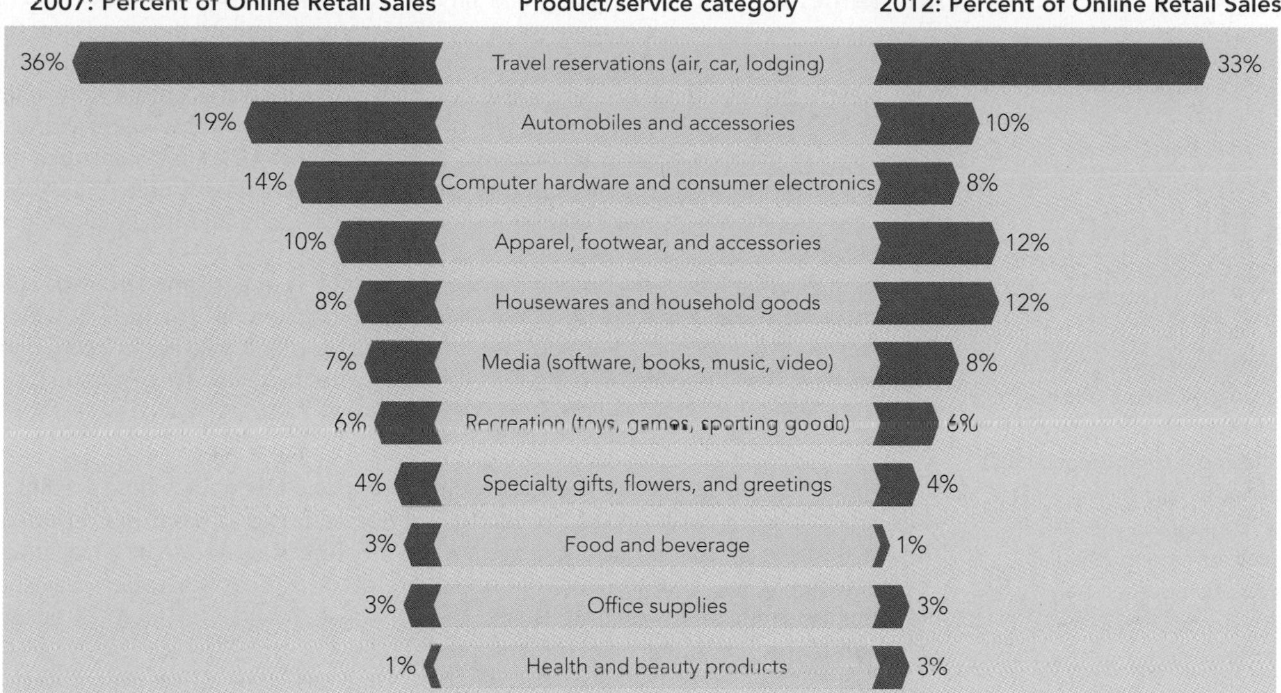

FIGURE 21–3
Estimated percentage of online retail sales by product/service category: 2007 and 2012

products. A fifth category includes items that are regularly purchased and where convenience is very important. Many consumer-packaged goods, such as grocery products, fall into this category. A final category of items consists of highly standardized products and services for which information about price is important. Certain kinds of insurance (auto and homeowners), home improvement products, casual apparel, and toys make up this category.

Why Consumers Shop and Buy Online

LO4

Marketers emphasize the customer value-creation possibilities, the importance of interactivity, individuality and relationship building, and producing customer experience in the new marketspace. However, consumers typically refer to six reasons they shop and buy online: convenience, choice, customization, communication, cost, and control (Figure 21–4).

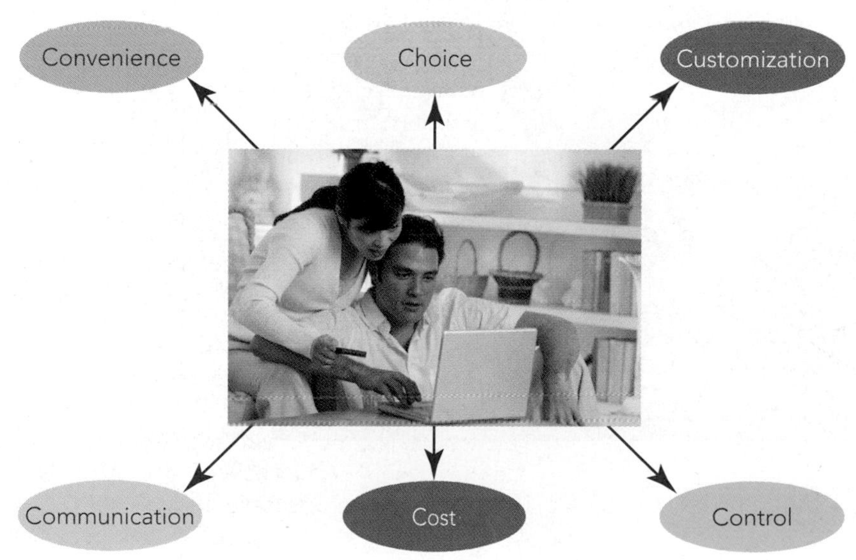

FIGURE 21–4
Why do consumers shop and buy online? Read the text to learn how convenience, choice, customization, communication, cost, and control result in a favorable customer experience.

Convenience Online shopping and buying is *convenient*. Consumers can visit Walmart at www.walmart.com to scan and order from among thousands of displayed products without fighting traffic, finding a parking space, walking through long aisles, and standing in store checkout lines. Alternatively, online consumers can use **bots**, electronic shopping agents or robots that comb Web sites to compare prices and product or service features. In either instance, an online consumer has never ventured into a store. However, for convenience to remain a source of customer value creation, Web sites must be easy to locate and navigate, and image downloads must be fast.

A commonly held view among online marketers is the **eight-second rule**: Customers will abandon their efforts to enter and navigate a Web site if download time exceeds eight seconds. Furthermore, the more clicks and pauses between clicks required to access information or make a purchase, the more likely it is a customer will exit a Web site.

Choice *Choice*, the second reason consumers shop and buy online, has two dimensions. First, choice exists in the product or service selection offered to consumers. Buyers desiring selection can avail themselves of numerous Web sites for almost anything they want. For instance, online buyers of consumer electronics can shop individual manufacturers such as Bose (www.bose.com) and QVC.com, a general merchant that offers more than 100,000 products.

Choice assistance is the second dimension. Here, the interactive capabilities of Internet-enabled technologies invite customers to engage in an electronic dialogue with marketers for the purpose of making informed choices. Choice assistance is one of the reasons for the continued success of Zappos.com. The company offers an online chat room that enables prospective buyers to ask questions and receive answers in real time. In addition, carefully designed search capabilities permit consumers to review products by brand and particular items.

Zappos.com is successful because it meets all the requirements necessary for consumers to shop and buy online. In less than 10 years, the company has posted $1 billion in annual sales of shoes, apparel, bags, accessories, housewares, and jewelry.

Zappos.com
www.zappos.com

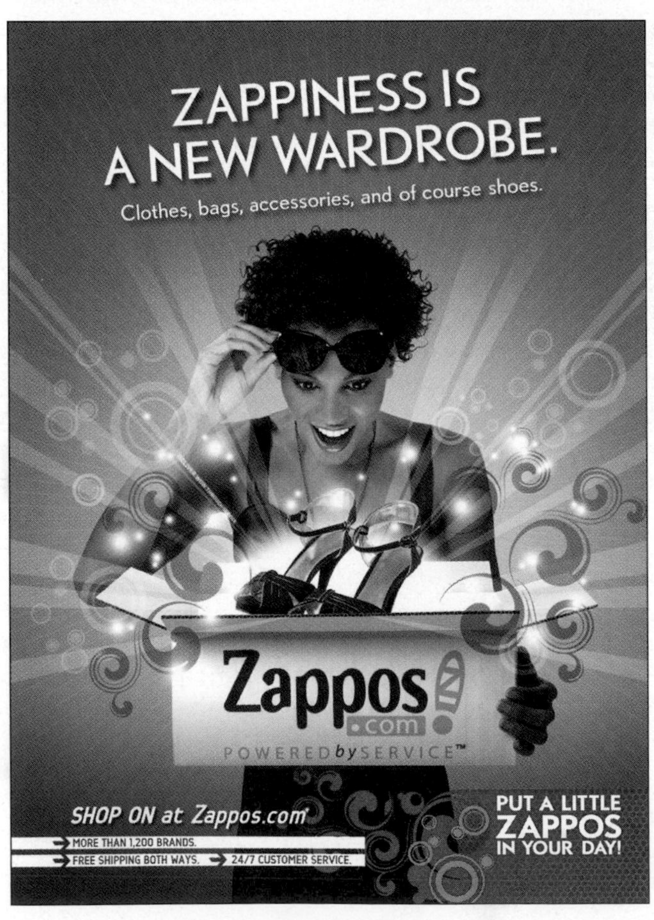

Customization Even with a broad selection and choice assistance, some customers prefer one-of-a-kind items that fit their specific needs. *Customization* arises from Internet-enabled capabilities that make possible a highly interactive and individualized information and exchange environment for shoppers and buyers. Remember the earlier Reebok, Schwab, Dell, and Seven Cycles examples? To varying degrees, online consumers also benefit from **customerization**—the growing practice of not only customizing a product or service but also personalizing the marketing and overall shopping and buying interaction for each customer.[19] Customerization seeks to do more than offer consumers the right product, at the right time, and at the right price. It combines choiceboard and personalization systems to expand the exchange environment beyond a transaction and makes shopping and buying an enjoyable, personal experience.

Communication Online consumers particularly welcome the *communication* capabilities of Internet-enabled technologies. This communication can take three forms: (1) marketer-to-consumer e-mail notification, (2) consumer-to-marketer buying and service requests, and (3) consumer-to-consumer chat rooms and instant messaging, plus social networking Web sites such as Twitter, MySpace, and Facebook.

Communication has proven to be a double-edged sword for online consumers. On the one hand, the interactive communication capabilities of Internet-enabled technologies increase consumer convenience, reduce information search costs, and make choice assistance and customization possible. Communication also promotes the development of company-hosted and independent **Web communities**—Web sites that allow people to congregate online and exchange views on topics of common interest. For instance, Coca-Cola hosts MyCoke.com, and iVillage.com is an independent Web community for women and includes topics such as career management, personal finances, parenting, relationships, beauty, and health.

Web logs, or blogs, are another form of communication. A **blog** is a Web page that serves as a publicly accessible personal journal for an individual or organization. Blogs are popular because they provide online forums on a wide variety of subjects ranging from politics to car repair. Companies such as Hewlett-Packard, Frito-Lay, and Harley-Davidson routinely monitor blogs to gather customer insights.[20]

On the other hand, communications can take the form of electronic junk mail or unsolicited e-mail, called **spam**. The prevalence of spam has prompted many online services to institute policies and procedures to prevent spammers from spamming their subscribers, and several states have antispamming laws. In 2004, the *CAN-SPAM (Controlling the Assault of Non-Solicited Pornography and Marketing) Act* became effective and restricts information collection and unsolicited e-mail promotions on the Internet.

Internet-enabled communication capabilities also make possible *buzz*, a popular term for word-of-mouth behavior in marketspace. Chapter 5 described the importance of word of mouth in consumer behavior. Internet technology has magnified its significance. According to Jeff Bezos, president of Amazon.com, "If you have an unhappy customer on the Internet, he doesn't tell his six friends, he tells his 6,000 friends![21] Buzz is particularly influential for toys, cars, sporting goods, motion pictures, apparel, consumer electronics, pharmaceuticals, health and beauty products, and health care services. Some marketers have capitalized on this phenomenon by creating buzz through viral marketing.

Viral marketing is an Internet-enabled promotional strategy that encourages individuals to forward marketer-initiated messages to others via e-mail, social networking Web sites, and blogs. There are three approaches to viral marketing. Marketers can embed a message in the product or service so that customers hardly realize they are passing it along. The classic example is Hotmail, which was one of the first companies to provide free, Internet-based e-mail. Each outgoing e-mail message has the tagline: "Get Your Private, Free Email from MSN Hotmail." Today, Windows Live Hotmail has more than 100 million users.

Marketers can also make the Web site content so compelling that viewers want to share it with others. De Beers has done this at www.adiamondisforever.com, where users can design their own rings and show them to others. One out of five Web site visitors e-mail their ring design to friends and relatives who visit the site. Similarly, eBay reports that more than half its visitors are referred by other visitors. Finally, marketers can offer incentives (discounts, sweepstakes, or free merchandise) for referrals.

About 75 percent of e-mail consists of spam. The United States is the largest source of spam, followed by China, Russia, and Brazil. These four countries produce about 40 percent of unsolicited e-mail worldwide.

De Beers effectively applies viral marketing at its custom ring Web site. How? Users of the custom ring feature can show what they have designed to friends and relatives.

De Beers
www.adiamondisforever.com

Cost Consumer *cost* is a fifth reason for online shopping and buying. Many popular items bought online can be purchased at the same price or cheaper than in retail stores.[22] Lower prices also result from Internet-enabled software that permits **dynamic pricing**, the practice of changing prices for products and services in real time in response to supply and demand conditions. As described in Chapter 14, dynamic pricing is a form of flexible pricing and can often result in lower prices. It is typically used for pricing time-sensitive items such as airline seats, scarce items found at art or collectible auctions, and out-of-date items such as last year's models of computer equipment and accessories.

A consumer's cost of external information search, including time spent and often the hassle of shopping, is also reduced. Greater shopping convenience and lower external search costs are two major reasons for the popularity of online shopping and buying among women, and particularly for those who work outside the home.

Control The sixth reason consumers prefer to buy online is the *control* it gives them over their shopping and purchase decision process. Online shoppers and buyers are empowered consumers. They deftly use Internet technology to seek information, evaluate alternatives, and make purchase decisions on their own time, terms, and conditions. For example, studies show that shoppers spend an average of five hours researching cars online before setting foot in a showroom.[23] The result of these activities is a more informed consumer and discerning shopper. In the words of one marketing consultant, "In the marketspace, the customer is in charge."[24]

Even though consumers have many reasons for shopping and buying online, a segment of Internet users refrain from making purchases for privacy and security reasons. These consumers are concerned about a rarely mentioned seventh C—cookies.

Cookies are computer files that a marketer can download onto the computer and mobile phone of an online shopper who visits the marketer's Web site. Cookies allow the marketer's Web site to record a user's visit, track visits to other Web sites, and store and retrieve this information in the future. Cookies also contain visitor information such as expressed product preferences, personal data, passwords, and financial information, including credit card numbers. Clearly, cookies make possible customized and personalized content for online shoppers. The controversy surrounding cookies is summed up by an authority on the technology: "At best a cookie makes for a user-friendly Web world: like a doorman or salesclerk who knows who you are. At worst, cookies represent a potential loss of privacy."[25] Read the Making Responsible Decisions box to learn more about privacy and security issues in the digital marketplace.[26]

Making Responsible Decisions > > > > > > > ethics

Let the E-Buyer Beware

Privacy and security are two key reasons consumers are leery of online shopping and buying. A recent Pew Internet and American Life Project poll reported that 75 percent of online consumers have privacy and security concerns about the Internet. Even more telling, many have stopped shopping a Web site or forgone an online purchase because of these concerns. Industry analysts estimate that about $24.5 million in e-commerce sales are lost annually because of privacy and security concerns among online shoppers.

Consumer concerns are not without merit. According to the Federal Trade Commission, 46 percent of fraud complaints are Internet related, costing consumers $265 million. In addition, consumers lose millions of dollars each year due to identity theft resulting from breaches in company security systems. A percolating issue is whether the U.S. government should pass more stringent Internet privacy and security laws. About 70 percent of online consumers favor such action. Companies, however, favor self-regulation. For example, TRUSTe (www.truste.com) awards its trademark to company Web sites that comply with standards of privacy protection and disclosure. Still, consumers are ultimately responsible for using care and caution when engaging in online behavior, including e-commerce. Consumers have a choice of whether or not to divulge personal information and monitor how their information is being used.

What role should the U.S. government, company self-regulation, and consumer vigilance play in dealing with privacy and security issues in the digital marketspace?

When and Where Online Consumers Shop and Buy

Shopping and buying also happen at different times in marketspace than in the traditional marketplace.[27] About 80 percent of online retail sales occur Monday through Friday. The busiest shopping day is Wednesday. By comparison, 35 percent of retail store sales are registered on the weekend. Saturday is the most popular shopping day. Monday through Friday online shopping and buying often occur during normal work hours—some 30 percent of online consumers say they visit Web sites from their place of work, which partially accounts for the sales level during the workweek. Favorite Web sites for workday shopping and buying include those featuring event tickets, auctions, online periodical subscriptions, flowers and gifts, consumer electronics, and travel. Web sites offering health and beauty items, apparel and accessories, and music and video tend to be browsed and bought from a consumer's home.

learning review

3. Which online consumer lifestyle segment spends the most money online and which spends the most time online?
4. What are the six reasons consumers prefer to shop and buy online?
5. What is the eight-second rule?

CROSS-CHANNEL SHOPPERS AND MULTICHANNEL MARKETING

LO5

Consumers are more likely to browse than buy online. Consumer marketspace browsing and buying in the traditional marketplace has given rise to the cross-channel shopper and the importance of multichannel marketing.

Who Is the Cross-Channel Shopper?

A **cross-channel shopper** is an online consumer who researches products online and then purchases them at a retail store.[28] Recent research shows that 51 percent of U.S. online consumers are cross-channel shoppers. These shoppers represent both genders equally and are only slightly younger than online consumers. They tend to have a higher education, earn significantly more money, and are more likely to embrace technology in their lives than online consumers who don't cross-channel shop.

Cross-channel shoppers want the right product at the best price, and they don't want to wait several days for delivery. The top reasons these shoppers research items online before buying in stores include: (1) the desire to compare products among different retailers; (2) the need for more information than is available in stores; and (3) the ease of comparing their options without having to trek to multiple retail locations.

Research shows that sales arising from cross-channel shoppers dwarf exclusive online retail sales. Retail sales revenue from cross-channel shoppers in 2012 is estimated to be $1.1 trillion—about five times greater than online retail sales.

Implementing Multichannel Marketing

The prominence of cross-channel shoppers has focused increased attention on multichannel marketing. Recall from Chapter 15 that *multichannel marketing* is the blending of different communication and delivery channels that are mutually reinforcing in attracting, retaining, and building relationships with consumers who shop and buy in the traditional marketplace and online—the cross-channel shopper.

The most common cross-channel shopping and buying path is to browse one or more Web sites and then purchase an item at a retail store. This shopping path might suggest that company Web sites for cross-channel shoppers should be similar. But they are not. Web sites play a multifaceted role in multichannel marketing because they can serve as either a communication or delivery channel. Two general applications of Web sites exist based on their intended purpose: (1) transactional Web sites and (2) promotional Web sites.

Multichannel Marketing with Transactional Web Sites *Transactional Web sites* are essentially electronic storefronts. They focus principally on converting an online browser into an online, catalog, or in-store buyer using the Web site design elements described earlier. Transactional Web sites are most common among store and catalog retailers and direct selling companies, such as Tupperware. Retailers and direct selling firms have found that their Web sites, while cannibalizing sales volume from stores, catalogs, and sales representatives, attract new customers and influence sales. Consider Victoria's Secret, the well-known specialty retailer of intimate apparel for women ages 18 to 45. It reports that almost 60 percent of its Web site customers are men, most of whom generate new sales volume for the company.[29]

Nestlé maintains promotional Web sites for many of its leading brands, such as its Baby Ruth snack bar. The company has found that these Web sites engage consumers. Read the text to learn the difference between transactional and promotional Web sites.

Nestlé, Inc.
www.nestleusa.com

Transactional Web sites are used less frequently by manufacturers of consumer products. A recurring issue for manufacturers is the threat of *channel conflict*, described in Chapter 15, and the potential harm to trade relationships with their retailing intermediaries. Still, manufacturers do use transactional Web sites, often cooperating with retailers. For example, Callaway Golf Company markets its golf merchandise at www.callawaygolf.com but relies on a retailer close to the buyer to fill the order. The retailer ships the order to the buyer within 24 hours and is credited with the sale. The majority of retailers that sell Callaway merchandise participate in this relationship, including retail chains Golf Galaxy and Dick's Sporting Goods. According to Callaway's chief executive officer, "This arrangement allows us to satisfy the consumer but to do so in a way that didn't violate our relationship with our loyal trade partners—those 15,000 outlets that sell Callaway products."[30]

In addition, Callaway, like other manufacturers, lists stores on the Web site where its merchandise can be shopped and bought. More often than not, however, manufacturers using multichannel marketing channels employ Web sites for advertising and promotion purposes.

Multichannel Marketing with Promotional Web Sites *Promotional Web sites* have a very different purpose than transactional sites. They advertise and promote a company's products and services and provide information on how items

FIGURE 21–5
Implementing multichannel marketing with promotional Web sites is common today. Two successes are found at Hyundai Motor America and the Clinique Division of Estée Lauder, Inc.

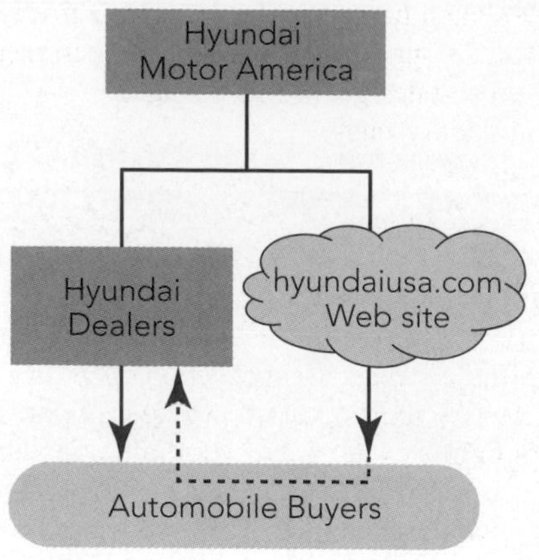

- 70% of Hyundai leads come from its Web site.
- 80% of people visiting a Hyundai dealer first visited its Web site.

- 80% of current Clinique buyers who visit its Web site later purchase a Clinique product at a store.
- 37% of non-Clinique buyers make a Clinique purchase after visiting its Web site.

can be used and where they can be purchased. They often engage the visitor in an interactive experience involving games, contests, and quizzes with electronic coupons and other gifts as prizes. Procter & Gamble maintains separate Web sites for many of its leading brands, including Pringles potato chips (www.pringles.com), Scope mouthwash (www.getclose.com), and Pampers diapers (www.pampers.com). Promotional sites are effective in generating interest in and trial of a company's products (see Figure 21–5).[31] Hyundai Motor America reports that 80 percent of the people visiting a Hyundai store first visited the brand's Web site (www.hyundaiusa.com) and 70 percent of Hyundai leads come from its Web site.

Promotional Web sites also can be used to support a company's traditional marketing channel and build customer relationships. This is the objective of the Clinique Division of Estée Lauder, Inc., which markets cosmetics through department stores. Clinique reports that 80 percent of current customers who visit its Web site (www.clinique.com) later purchase a Clinique product at a department store while 37 percent of non-Clinique buyers make a Clinique purchase after visiting the company's Web site.

The popularity of multichannel marketing is apparent in its growing impact on online retail sales.[32] Fully 70 percent of U.S. online retail sales in 2007 were made by companies that practiced multichannel marketing. Multichannel marketers are expected to register about 90 percent of U.S. online retail sales in 2012.

learning review

6. A cross-channel shopper is ________________.
7. Channel conflict between manufacturers and retailers is likely to arise when manufacturers use ______________ Web sites.

LEARNING OBJECTIVES REVIEW

LO1 *Describe what interactive marketing is and how it creates customer value, customer relationships, and customer experiences.*
Interactive marketing involves two-way buyer–seller electronic communication in a computer-mediated environment in which the buyer controls the kind and amount of information received from the seller. It creates customer value by providing time, place, form, and possession utility for consumers. Customer relationships are created and sustained through two unique capabilities of Internet technology: interactivity and individuality. From an interactive marketing perspective, customer experience represents the sum total of the interactions that a customer

has with a company's Web site, from the initial look at a home page through the entire purchase decision process. Companies produce a customer experience through seven Web site design elements. These elements are context, content, community, customization, communication, connection, and commerce.

LO2 *Identify the demographic and lifestyle profile of online consumers.*
As a group, online consumers are more likely to be women than men and tend to be better educated, younger, and more affluent than the general U.S. population. Women tend to purchase more goods and services online than men. The lifestyle profile of online consumers reflects the different kinds of online experiences they seek. Six lifestyle segments have been identified. The click-and-mortar segment consists of women who browse retailer Web sites but actually buy products at retail outlets. Hunter-gatherers use the Internet like a consumer magazine to gather information and compare products and services. Brand loyalists regularly visit their favorite bookmarked Web sites and spend the most money online. Time-sensitive materialists regard the Internet as a convenient tool for buying. The hooked, online, and single segment spends more time online than any segment. Ebivalent newbies are relative newcomers to the Internet who rarely spend money online, but seek product information.

LO3 *Explain why certain types of products and services are particularly suited for interactive marketing.*
Certain types of products and services seem to be particularly suited for interactive marketing. One category consists of items for which product information is an important part of the purchase decision, but prepurchase trial is not necessarily critical. A second category involves items for which audio or video demonstration is important. A third category contains items that can be digitally delivered. Unique items represent a fourth category. A fifth category includes items that are regularly purchased and where convenience is very important. A final category consists of highly standardized items for which information about price is important.

LO4 *Describe why consumers shop and buy online and how marketers influence online purchasing behavior.*
There are six reasons consumers shop and buy online. They are convenience, choice, customization, communication, cost, and control. Marketers have capitalized on these reasons through a variety of means. For example, they provide choice assistance using choiceboard and collaborative filtering technology, which also provides opportunities for customization. Company-hosted Web communities and viral marketing practices capitalize on the communications dimensions of Internet-enabled technologies. Dynamic pricing provides real-time responses to supply and demand conditions, often resulting in lower prices to consumers. Permission marketing is popular given consumer interest in control.

LO5 *Define cross-channel shoppers and the role of transactional and promotional Web sites in reaching these shoppers.*
A cross-channel shopper is an online consumer who researches products online and then purchases them at a retail store. These shoppers are reached through multichannel marketing. Web sites play a multifaceted role in multichannel marketing because they can serve as either a delivery or communication channel. In this regard, transactional Web sites are essentially electronic storefronts. They focus principally on converting an online browser into an online, catalog, or in-store buyer using the Web site design elements described earlier. On the other hand, promotional Web sites serve to advertise and promote a company's products and services and provide information on how items can be used and where they can be purchased.

FOCUSING ON KEY TERMS

blog p. 559
bots p. 558
choiceboard p. 550
collaborative filtering p. 550
cookies p. 560
cross-channel shopper p. 562
customerization p. 558
dynamic pricing p. 560
eight-second rule p. 558
interactive marketing p. 550
online consumers p. 554
permission marketing p. 551
personalization p. 550
spam p. 559
viral marketing p. 559
Web communities p. 559

APPLYING MARKETING KNOWLEDGE

1 Have you made an online purchase? If so, why do you think so many people who have access to the Internet are not also online buyers? If not, why are you reluctant to do so? Do you think that electronic commerce benefits consumers even if they don't make a purchase?

2 Like the traditional marketplace, marketspace offers marketers opportunities to create greater time, place, form, and possession utility. How do you think Internet-enabled technology rates in terms of creating these values? Take a shopping trip at a virtual retailer of your choice (don't buy anything unless you really want to). Then compare the time, place, form, and possession utility provided by the virtual retailer that you enjoyed during a nonelectronic experience shopping for the same product category.

3 Visit Amazon.com (www.amazon.com) or Barnes & Noble (www.barnesandnoble.com). As you tour the Web site, think about how shopping for books online compares with a trip to your university bookstore to buy books. Specifically, compare and contrast your shopping experiences with respect to convenience, choice, customization, communication, cost, and control.

4 Suppose you are planning to buy a new car so you visit www.edmunds.com. Based on your experience visiting that site, do you think you would enjoy more

or less control in negotiating with the dealer when you actually purchase your vehicle?

5 Visit the Web site for your university or college. Based on your visit, would you conclude that the site is a transactional site or a promotional site? Why? How would you rate the site in terms of the six Web site design elements that affect customer experience?

building your marketing plan

Does your marketing plan involve a marketspace presence for your product or service? If the answer is no, read no further and do not include this element in your plan. If the answer is yes, then attention must be given to developing a Web site in your marketing plan. A useful starting point is to:

1 Describe how each Web site element—context, content, community, customization, communication, connection, and commerce—will be used to create a customer experience.

2 Identify a company's Web site that best reflects your Web site conceptualization.

video case 21 Pizza Hut and imc^2: Becoming a Multichannel Marketer

It's no surprise that Pizza Hut is the world's largest pizza chain with more than 10,000 restaurants in 100 countries. But did you know that Pizza Hut is on track to becoming one of the top 35 U.S. Internet retailers in 2009?

According to Brian Niccol, Pizza Hut's chief marketing officer (CMO), "We've done what many would say is impossible. We successfully built an online business in three years that produces hundreds of millions of dollars in annual revenue. Today, Pizza Hut is a category leader in the interactive and emerging marketplace." So how did they do it? Pizza Hut simply revolutionized the quick serve restaurant (QSR) world through a multichannel marketing approach that created a customer experience and a customer engagement platform that was second to none.

THE RETAIL PIZZA BUSINESS

With three national competitors dominating the marketplace, the pizza business is very competitive. Even customers who could be considered heavy users of a particular brand regularly purchase from competitors on the basis of timing, pricing, and convenience.

In general, Pizza Hut's most frequent customers (and likely those of the other two major competitors) divide into two categories: (1) families, primarily time-starved mothers, looking for a quick and simple mealtime solution; and (2) young adult males who fuel their active lifestyle with one of the world's most versatile and convenient foods (no cooking, no utensils, no cleanup, and leftovers are perfect for breakfast). While these two groups could not be more dissimilar on the surface, value and convenience are important for both groups. Cost-conscious mothers look for a good quality product and a hassle-free eating experience. Deal-seeking young adult males seek more of the food they love with less time and cash invested in the process.

The importance of the take home and delivery segment of the U.S. pizza market is illustrated by the fact that Pizza Hut's principal national competitors focus exclusively on this aspect of the business. Most take-home and delivery sales are ordered before a customer enters the restaurant. By 2006, a growing number of retail pizza customers had become comfortable ordering pizza online. Pizza ordering, as it turned out, was an ideal product for the digital world. People understood the basic menu, generally knew that they could customize their order in a variety of ways, and were accustomed to not being in the store when ordering. Brand retail presence and established customer delivery networks also made the shift to online ordering easier for national pizza chains than other national quick serve restaurants. But as Pizza Hut understood, there is still an incredible level of complexity in making something truly sophisticated, simple, and easy for the customer.

CREATING A PLAN OF ACTION

For the most part, the intent of online ordering for the pizza business was to make transactions with the customer easier and cheaper for the brand. Pizza Hut recognized the opportunity to engage people with its brand and other people directly and do something special; namely, build sustainable relationships with their customers and enable Pizza Hut to engage people in a more meaningful and profitable way. In short, Pizza Hut set about to reinvent the retail pizza business by breaking away from a transactional platform to an efficient and powerful customer engagement platform by reaching out to customers' kitchens and couches to offer a better mealtime ordering, delivery, and dining experience.

Pizza Hut selected imc^2 (www.imc2.com) as one of its lead agencies to plan a comprehensive interactive strategy that focused first on the redesign of the Pizza Hut corporate Web site (including redefining the customer experience online and across all of the brand's touchpoints) and then on a series of progressively sophisticated and industry-leading customer engagement strategies. imc^2 brought 15 years of experience in interactive marketing and brand engagement to the assignment. Its clients included Coca-Cola, Johnson & Johnson, Pfizer, Omni Hotels, Hasbro, Procter & Gamble, and Samsung, among a host of other companies, large and small.

PIZZAHUT.COM, CUSTOMER EXPERIENCE, AND BRAND ENGAGEMENT

Pizza Hut and imc^2 executives agreed that the strategy for reinventing the retail pizza business would involve developing opportunities for customers to engage with the brand by using the right technologies to enable and encourage interaction. A new Web site was necessary to better address all major design elements. How Pizza Hut and imc^2 executed these design elements not only created value for its customers, but also served as a basis for differentiation in the retail pizza business. Let's look at these design elements and PizzaHut.com's performance.

The Pizza Hut Web site was completely redesigned to support nationwide online ordering in 2007 (including all franchise locations for the first time), and is updated frequently to keep up with the company's fast-paced marketing strategy and ambitious product innovation rollout schedule. Since promotions are an important expectation in pizza purchasing and speak to the brand's consumers in a language that clearly connects with their desire for value, the Web site *context* and *content* balances the ability to shop for a deal with quick and easy ordering access for people who arrive at PizzaHut.com ready to purchase. The site presents a number of Pizza Hut's current offers in the central viewing window as well as through the rolling navigation directly underneath the main content. Primary navigation for information, such as the menu, locations, and nutrition facts, are displayed horizontally across the top of the rotating content.

Web site *customization* is achieved in several ways, but the primary utility is to simplify ordering. For customers who have already registered, there are several personalization options, including rapid ordering called *Express Checkout*—a feature that's based on saved preferences

similar to a "playlist." For example, if you have a group of friends that likes to watch movies together, you might create an order named *Movie Night* that has your group's favorite pizzas. Using the *Express Checkout* option accessible directly on the homepage, you can select *Movie Night*, quickly review the order, click the "submit" button, and the pizzas are on their way, relying on saved delivery and payment options through a stored *cookie* (a piece of digital code that is used to identify previous visitors) to speed the transaction. With this type of functionality, you can think of convenience as an investment that creates loyalty and somewhat insulates the brand against switching down the line when customers would have to register with and learn a competitor's system, and where access to their favorite features might not be available.

Web site *content* and *communications* are integrated with the company's overall communications programs—including traditional media—with product innovations, promotions, and special events shared across platforms. True to the brand, communications are fun and energetic, matching bold images and vibrant color with a smart, clever, and light-hearted voice. One noteworthy example includes the 2008 April Fools' Day rebranding of the company as "Pasta Hut" to coincide with the launch of the brand's innovative line of Tuscani Pastas. This campaign included online support in the form of display media (banner ads) and the temporary rebranding of PizzaHut.com as PastaHut.com with special imagery and copy supporting the name change. The brand not only got plenty of coverage in the press, it deepened the connection with customers by showing their willingness to be spontaneous and fun, inviting people to play along with the joke.

Pizza Hut's integrated marketing communications approach enables the company to easily test and incorporate other items and brands under the larger corporate umbrella, such as the WingStreet operation and the pasta extension. This demonstrates the brand's ability to stretch the QSR concept way beyond its pizza roots and suggests the kind of direction the company may pursue in the future.

PizzaHut.com and the brand's other online assets are all about getting the world's favorite pizza and signature products into the hands and stomachs of customers. Since *commerce* is a huge consideration on the site, there are multiple pathways for ordering, including several onsite methods, a Facebook app (the first national pizza chain to produce an ordering application for the world's leading social networking site), a branded desktop widget, mobile ordering (aka Total Mobile Access, added in 2008, that includes both a WAP site and text ordering), and a sophisticated and simple iPhone app released in 2009 that lets customers build and submit their order visually. Additional revenue streams can also be quickly built online, as demonstrated by the eGift Card program conceived and implemented by imc^2 over a weekend during the 2008 holiday season.

Realizing that it did not make sense for the company or their customers to create a *community* on the site, Pizza Hut tapped into Facebook to achieve results in a very cost-effective manner. With approximately one million fans and the first of its kind Facebook ordering application, the brand can efficiently engage a huge group of people in a very natural way without disrupting their daily routine. Again, the brand understands that if you make something convenient, you can increase trust while securing greater transactional loyalty. Pizza Hut's 2009 program to identify a summer intern, or *Twintern*, responsible for monitoring and encouraging dialog on Twitter and other social media networks, is another example of how the brand is building on existing platforms and making effective use of the massive social marketing infrastructure.

PizzaHut.com connects mobile, desktop, social networks, and other digital gateways to complement traditional media and its retail presence. So when Pizza Hut thinks about the *connection* design element, it includes more than just linking to other Web sites online. Rather, it provides a comprehensive approach to creating a seamless customer experience wherever and whenever people want to engage the brand.

PERFORMANCE MEASUREMENT AND OUTCOMES

Pizza Hut diligently measures the performance of Pizza Hut.com. The company created a customized marketing dashboard that allows the Pizza Hut management team to monitor various aspects of the brand's marketing program and provides an almost constant stream of fresh information that it can use to optimize engagement with people or tweak various aspects of performance.

The results have been remarkable, but understand that due to the highly competitive nature of the industry, they are fluid and only represent a moment in time. Consider, for example:

1. PizzaHut.com dominates the pizza category with number one rankings in Web site traffic and search volume. According to comScore, a global leader in digital ana-

lytics and measurement, the Pizza Hut site achieves the most traffic per online dollars spent in the pizza category.

2. PizzaHut.com is on track to become one of the top 35 Internet retailers in the United States in 2009, up from 45th in 2008.
3. Pizza Hut's iPhone app had more than 100,000 downloads in the first two weeks after release (http://www.techcrunch.com/2009/08/01/pizza-huts-delicious-iphone-app-tops-100000-downloads-in-two-weeks/).

WHAT'S NEXT

So what's next for PizzaHut.com? While the brand has made huge gains in a very short time period, staying on top in the rapidly evolving digital marketplace requires constant attention. Pizza Hut envisions that its online business will surpass the one billion dollar mark within the next five years, and digital transactions leading all revenue within a decade.

While understandably protective of future strategy, Pizza Hut CMO Niccol has ambitious goals and he's not joking when he deadpans, "I want Pizza Hut to become the Amazon of foodservice and be pioneers for the digital space. I do not want us to be a brick and mortar company that just dabbles in the space." The transition to something along the lines of the Amazon model suggests that the brand might further evolve its identity as a pizza business and stretch or completely redefine the QSR model.

FIGURE 1

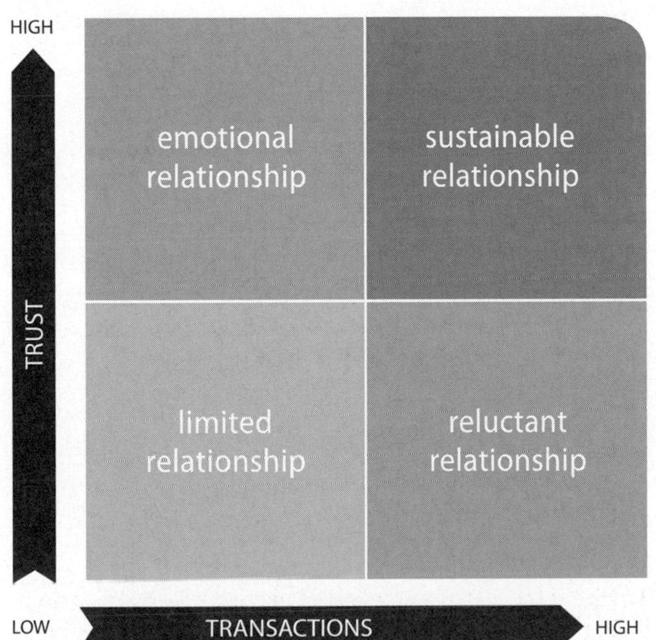

Most brands that want to grow in the evolving economy will have to think and plan long-term and be able to act swiftly as marketplace conditions change. imc² chief marketing officer Ian Wolfman, when assessing the future of the marketing, sums up the opportunity neatly. "Our agency believes that marketing's current transformation will result in a complete reorientation of how brands and companies engage with their consumers and other stakeholders. Brands that thrive will be those, like Pizza Hut, that can efficiently build sustainable relationships with people—relationships that have both high trust and high transactions" (see Figure 1). He goes on to explain that, "(B)rands taking a longer view have an unexpected advantage over traditional models that often focus too tightly on hitting near-term quarterly targets." Referring to research his agency has done on the subject, Wolfman points out that the most successful brands in the future will likely be those that resonate with people on a deeply emotional level and operate with a clearly defined sense of purpose.

Pizza Hut, with its focus on digitally enabled customer convenience and category innovation, is ideally positioned to connect with people on a level that builds trust and increases transactions. Referring to the initial time investment, however modest, that customers have to make in registering with the system and enabling various devices, Niccol sees the landscape as very promising for brands that put their customers' interests and preferences first. "If we do our job right—creating authentic engagement and making it convenient and valuable for people to interact with the brand—the numbers follow."

Questions

1 What kind of Web site is PizzaHut.com?

2 How does PizzaHut.com incorporate the seven Web site design elements?

3 How are choiceboard and personalization systems used in the PizzaHut.com Web site?

Betty Crocker
Warm Delights
Hot Fudge Brownie

22 Pulling It All Together: The Strategic Marketing Process

LEARNING OBJECTIVES
After reading this chapter you should be able to:

LO1 Explain how marketing managers allocate their limited resources.

LO2 Describe two marketing planning frameworks: Porter's generic business strategies and synergy analysis.

LO3 Explain what makes an effective marketing plan.

LO4 Use a Gantt chart to schedule a series of tasks.

LO5 Describe the alternatives for organizing a marketing department and the role of a product manager.

LO6 Explain how marketing ROI, metrics, and dashboards relate to evaluating marketing programs.

"BREAKING THE RULES" AT GENERAL MILLS TO REACH TODAY'S ON-THE-GO CONSUMER

"Sometimes you have to break the rules at every level," says Vivian Milroy Callaway about her challenges at General Mills.

Callaway is referring to the time a while back when you were growing up on Cheerios.® Then General Mills—or "Big G" from its logo—was known mainly for its breakfast cereals.

"Breaking the rules is what we did when we acquired Pillsbury in 2001," she explains. "After the acquisition, cereal went from being our No. 1 business to being one of a big three that includes meals like Hamburger Helper and Green Giant, as well as desserts like Pillsbury and Betty Crocker."[1]

As vice president of the Center for Learning and Experimentation at Big G, Callaway is responsible for helping uncover new-product ideas for the company's product portfolio. Looking over her shoulder at General Mills reveals both how competitive today's cereal business is and a few of the company's creative initiatives outside the cereal industry.

Cereal Industry Facts of Life

A quick survey of the cereal industry shows:

- Only one out of four new brands "succeeds," defined as maintaining distribution for three to four years, in the $6 billion-a-year U.S. ready-to-eat (RTE) cereal market.[2] But that RTE market has had flat or slightly declining sales in recent years.[3]
- This decline in the ready-to-eat cereals market is caused by Americans following low-carbohydrate diets, munching breakfast bars, eating breakfast at fast-food restaurants, and buying lower-priced "bagged" or generic private-label brands.[4]
- The launch of a new cereal typically costs up to $30 million and usually involves replacing one of more than 300 competing breakfast cereals already sitting somewhere on a supermarket shelf.

Callaway "broke the rules" in developing a new dessert concept: She looked at the concept *not alone* by itself—but in relation to *all* the other sweet treats people were eating. "One of my challenges," says Callaway, "is that consumers often say one thing in marketing research studies and then do something else when facing a supermarket shelf."

To overcome this problem, Callaway and her team did a lot of "iterative experimentation" in the marketplace. These marketing experiments involved putting a prototype dessert in a store, measuring

You've eaten healthy all day and want something quick for your sweet tooth? Try Warm Delights Minis microwavable desserts with only 150 calories—just add water and microwave in the container!

the results, improving the prototype, and repeating the process. The reward for Callaway and her team was a launch of its highly successful Warm Delights® microwavable desserts, followed quickly by Warm Delights Minis. Its special packaging is based on the team's research that showed extending the black microwavable bowl *outside* the edges of the Warm Delights package communicate its cooking convenience to prospective buyers.[5]

Creative Initiatives Outside Cereals

General Mills annually introduces more than 300 new food products around the world that respond to what consumers are asking for: ability to eat the product on the go, single portions, healthier eating, and greater cooking convenience.[6]

Sometimes it's possible to get all these features in the same new product and other times not. Examples of new noncereal products from General Mills include:[7]

- Eat-on-the-go products—Fiber One® Fulfill™ nutrition bars with 35 percent of the daily value of fiber needed by adults.
- Single portions—Hamburger Helper Microwave Singles meals and Green Giant Just for One microwavable vegetables.
- Healthier eating—Progresso® light soups with only 60 calories and 0 Weight Watchers Points® per serving of vegetable soup and 1 point for its soups with meat.[8]
- Greater cooking convenience—Betty Crocker® Warm Delights™ desserts (simply add water and microwave in the bowl), and Pillsbury® Ready to Bake!™ cookies (refrigerated cookie dough already formed into cookie shapes).

Introducing these new products may sound simple, but even technology can be a problem. For example, when Callaway's marketing researchers discovered that consumers actually like to *see* the chocolate chips *on top* of their chocolate chip cookies, General Mills invested in new manufacturing equipment to make this a reality. Putting the chocolate chips on top increased sales 50 percent.

This chapter discusses issues and techniques related to the planning, implementation, and evaluation phases of the strategic marketing process, which were introduced in Chapter 2. Throughout the chapter, you'll obtain insights into the marketing strategies now emerging at General Mills and other firms.

MARKETING BASICS: DOING WHAT WORKS AND ALLOCATING RESOURCES

As noted in Chapter 2, corporate and marketing executives search continuously to find a competitive advantage—a unique strength relative to what competitors are doing now and likely to do in the future.[9] Having identified this competitive advantage, they must figure out how to exploit it.[10] This involves (1) finding and using what works for their organization and industry and (2) allocating resources effectively.

These companies achieve excellence in what really matters—a clear focused strategy for Costco and a performance-oriented culture for Smucker's.

Finding and Using What Really Works

In a five-year study, researchers Nohria, Joyce, and Roberson conducted in-depth analysis of 160 companies and more than 200 management tools and techniques, such as supply chain management, customer relationship management (CRM), or use of an intranet. The result? Individual management tools and techniques had no direct relationship to superior business performance in the companies.[11]

What *does* matter? The researchers concluded that four basic business and management practices are what matter—"what really works," to use their phrase. These are: (1) strategy, (2) execution, (3) culture, and (4) structure. Firms with excellence in all four of these areas are likely to achieve superior business performance. And in terms of individual tools and techniques, the researchers concluded that which of these the firm chooses to use is less important than flawless execution of the ones it does use.

Industry leaders such as Walmart, Home Depot, and Dell do all four of the basic practices extremely well, not just two or three, and are vigilant to keep doing them well when conditions change. Coca-Cola and Kodak, superstars a decade ago, are struggling today to get these basics right and regain past success. Let's look at companies that stand out today in each of the four basics:

- *Strategy: Devise and maintain a clearly stated, focused strategy.* While Walmart may be the unstoppable force in mass-merchandise retailing, in warehouse clubs its Sam's Club is not. The winner to date: Costco Wholesale, with 60 percent as many stores as Sam's Club but almost twice the sales revenue. A key reason is its focused strategy based on the knowledge that of all U.S. retail channels, warehouse clubs attract the largest proportion of affluent shoppers. Costco's strategy: Sell a limited selection of branded high-end merchandise at low prices. In the current recession its "$1.50 hot dog and soda combo" gets customers' attention.[12]
- *Execution: Develop and maintain flawless operational execution.* Toyota is generally acknowledged as the best in the world in revolutionizing the design and manufacture of autos. Toyota managers created the doctrine of *kaizen*, or continuous improvement. For example, by speeding up decisions, Toyota reduced the time to get one model from the drawing board to the showroom to 19 months, about half the industry average.[13]
- *Culture: Develop and maintain a performance-oriented culture.* Always near the top of *Fortune*'s list of the 100 Best Companies to Work For is Smucker's—yes, the "With a name like Smucker's" company. Its straightforward culture is based on four key elements in its code of conduct: "Listen with your full attention, look for the good in others, have a sense of humor, and say thank you for a job well done." The performance result? Low employee turnover and large appreciation in the value of its stock.
- *Structure: Build and maintain a fast, flexible, flat organization.* Successful small organizations often grow into bureaucratic large ones with layers of managers and red tape that slow decision making. An exception and the unquestioned all-time leader in delivering world-class aircraft with only about 50 engineers and designers and 100 expert machinists: Lockheed's Skunk Works. Discussed later in the chapter, its first director set guidelines for organizational structure and implementation. Attempts have been made to try to apply these Skunk Works guidelines to operations as far away as France and Russia. Key guidelines are (1) give the director the authority to make quick decisions and (2) use a small number of good people who can talk to anyone in the organization to solve a problem.[14]

Of course, in practice a firm cannot allocate unlimited resources to achieving each of these business basics. It must make choices on where its resources can give the greatest return, the topic of the next section.

Allocating Marketing Resources Using Sales Response Functions

LO1

A **sales response function** relates the expense of marketing effort to the marketing results obtained.[15] For simplicity in the examples that follow, only the effects of annual marketing effort on annual sales revenue will be analyzed, but the concept applies to other measures of marketing success—such as profit, units sold, or level of awareness.

Maximizing Incremental Revenue Minus Incremental Cost Economists give managers a specific guideline for optimal resource allocation: Allocate the firm's marketing, production, and financial resources to the markets and products where the excess of incremental revenues over incremental costs is greatest. This parallels the marginal revenue–marginal cost analysis of Chapter 13.

Figure 22–1 illustrates the resource allocation principle that is inherent in the sales response function. The firm's annual marketing effort, such as sales and advertising expenses, is plotted on the horizontal axis. As the annual marketing effort increases, so does the resulting annual sales revenue, which is plotted on the vertical axis. The relationship is assumed to be S-shaped, showing that an additional $1 million of marketing effort, from $3 million to $4 million, results in far greater increases of sales revenue in the midrange ($20 million) of the curve than at either end. An increase from $2 million to $3 million in spending yields an increase of $10 million in sales; an increase from $6 million to $7 million in spending leads to an increase of $5 million in sales.

A Numerical Example of Resource Allocation Suppose Figure 22–1 shows the situation for a new General Mills product such as Banana Nut Cheerios®, which is targeted at health-conscious consumers who want a great tasting cereal. Banana Nut Cheerios is an extension of the Cheerios name, the best selling ready-to-eat cereal brand in the United States.

Also assume that the sales response function in Figure 22–1 doesn't change through time as a result of changing consumer tastes and incomes. Point A shows the position of the firm in year 1, whereas Point B shows it three years later in year 4. Suppose General Mills decides to launch new advertising and sales promotions that,

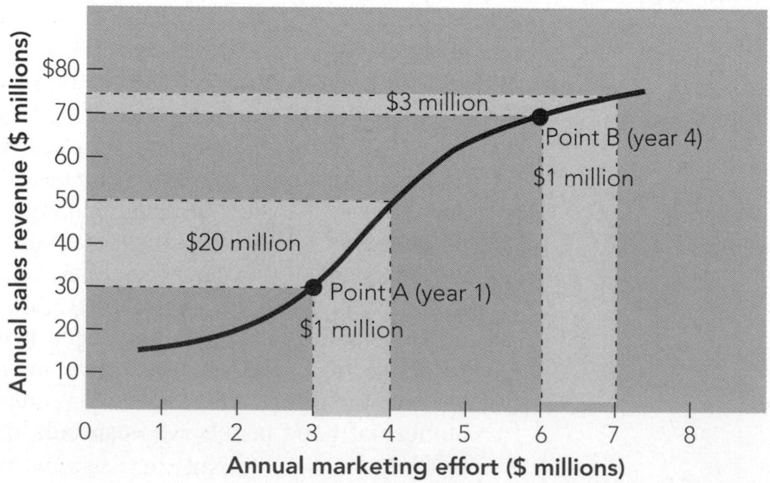

FIGURE 22–1
A sales response function shows the impact of various levels of marketing effort on annual sales revenue for two different years.

These recently introduced products reflect General Mills' increased emphasis on healthy eating.

let's say, increase its marketing effort for the brand from \$3 million to \$6 million a year. If the relationship in Figure 22–1 holds true and is a good picture of consumer purchasing behavior, the sales revenues of Banana Nut Cheerios should increase from \$30 million to \$70 million a year.

Let's look at the major resource allocation question: What are the probable increases in sales revenue for Banana Nut Cheerios in year 1 and year 4 if General Mills were to spend an additional \$1 million in marketing effort? As Figure 22–1 reveals,

Year 1

Increase in marketing effort from \$3 million to \$4 million = \$1 million.

Increase in sales revenue from \$30 million to \$50 million = \$20 million.

Ratio of incremental sales revenue to effort = \$20,000,000:\$1,000,000 20:1.

Year 4

Increase in marketing effort from \$6 million to \$7 million = \$1 million.

Increase in sales revenue from \$70 million to \$73 million = \$3 million.

Ratio of incremental sales revenue to effort = \$3,000,000:\$1,000,000 = 3:1.

Thus, in year 1 a dollar of extra marketing effort returned \$20 in sales revenue, whereas in year 4 it returned only \$3. If no other expenses are incurred, it might make sense to spend \$1 million in year 4 to gain \$3 million in incremental sales revenue. However, it may be far wiser for General Mills to invest the money in one of its other brands, such as its new line of Progresso Light soups.

The essence of resources allocation is simple: Put incremental resources where the incremental returns are greatest over the foreseeable future. For General Mills this means allocating its available resources efficiently among its broad portfolio of product lines and brands.

At General Mills extending a valuable brand name to new products provides it with important marketing synergies. For example, the Fiber One brand was used to introduce the cereal in 1985. Today the Fiber One brand name extends not only to other cereals but to snack bars, yogurt, and toaster pastries as well. Resource allocation decisions also must reflect changing consumer tastes and fluctuations in ingredient prices.[16]

How can General Mills best allocate available resources among its portfolio of brands? Several frameworks within the strategic marketing process help answer this question.

Allocating Marketing Resources in Practice General Mills, like many firms in these businesses, does extensive analysis using **share points**, or percentage points of market share, as the common basis of comparison to allocate marketing resources effectively for different product lines within the same firm. This allows it to seek answers to the question, "How much is it worth to us to try to increase our market share by another 1 (or 2, or 5, or 10) percentage point?"

This analysis enables higher-level managers to make resource allocation trade-offs among different kinds of business units owned by the company. To make these resource allocation decisions, marketing managers must estimate: (1) the market share for the product, (2) the revenues associated with each point of market share (a share point in breakfast cereals may be five times what it is in cake mixes), (3) the contribution to overhead and profit (or gross margin) of each share point, and (4) possible cannibalization effects on other products in the line (for example, new Banana Nut Cheerios might reduce sales of regular Cheerios).[17]

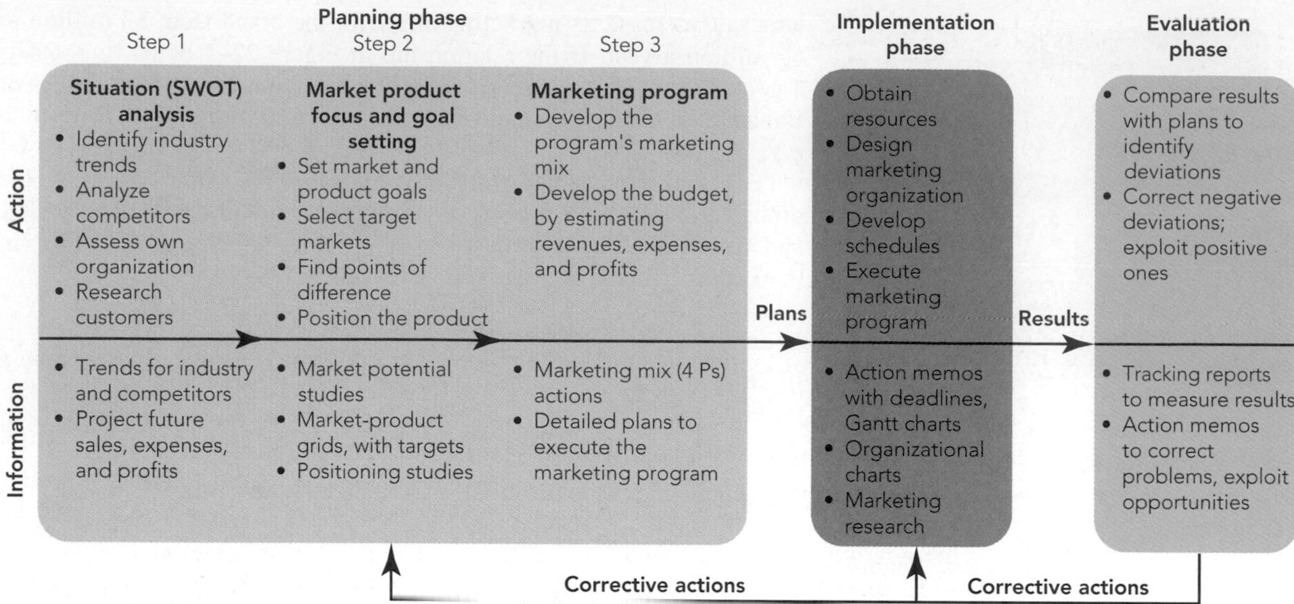

FIGURE 22–2
The actions in the strategic marketing process are supported and directed by detailed reports, studies, and memos.

Resource Allocation and the Strategic Marketing Process Company resources are allocated effectively in the strategic marketing process by converting marketing information into marketing actions. Figure 22–2 summarizes the strategic marketing process introduced in Chapter 2, along with some details of the marketing actions and information that comprise it. Figure 22–2 is really a simplification of the actual strategic marketing process: While the three phases of the strategic marketing process have distinct separations in the figure and the marketing actions are separated from the marketing information, in practice these blend and interact.

The upper half of each box in Figure 22–2 highlights the actions involved in that part of the strategic marketing process, and the lower half summarizes the information and reports used. Note that each phase has an output report:

Phase	Output Report
Planning	Marketing plans (or programs) that define goals (with pertinent marketing metrics) and the marketing mix strategies to achieve them
Implementation	Action memos that tell (1) *who* is (2) to do *what* (3) by *when*
Evaluation	Corrective action memos, triggered by comparing results with goals, often using the firm's marketing metrics and dashboards

The corrective action memos become feedback loops in Figure 22–2 that help improve decisions and actions in earlier phases of the strategic marketing process.

learning review

1. What are the four basic practices "that really work"—that are characteristics of industry-leading firms?
2. What is the significance of the S-shape of the sales response function in Figure 22–1?

THE PLANNING PHASE OF THE STRATEGIC MARKETING PROCESS

Four aspects of the strategic marketing process deserve special mention: (1) the vital importance of metrics in marketing planning, (2) the variety of marketing plans, (3) marketing planning frameworks that have proven useful, and (4) some key marketing planning and strategy lessons.

The Vital Importance of Metrics in Marketing Planning

In the past decade, measuring the effectiveness of marketing activities has become a central focus in many organizations. This boils down to defining "where the organization is going"—the goals—and "whether it is really getting there"—the marketing metrics used to measure actual performance.

Planners have a tongue-in-cheek truism: "If you don't know where you're going, any road will get you there." In making marketing plans, the "road" chosen is really the goal *plus* the metric used to measure whether the goal is achieved.

Even in today's economic turmoil, most firms stress innovation to help achieve growth. Marketing departments work closely with R&D operations departments to complete successful innovation projects.[18] So what marketing metrics might they use to measure their innovation performance?

In a recent survey, responding firms reported that on average they used eight metrics to measure their innovation. Figure 22–3 shows that among firms that use more than three different innovation metrics, they use two different kinds—output metrics and input metrics. For example, 16 percent reported using revenue growth from new products or services, which is a measure of results—an *output metric*. In contrast, Figure 22–3 also shows that 10 percent used a metric of the number of ideas in the pipeline, which clearly is an *input metric* because there is no assurance the idea will actually convert into sales revenues.[19]

FIGURE 22–3
Metric ranked No. 1 by respondents from organizations using more than three innovation metrics

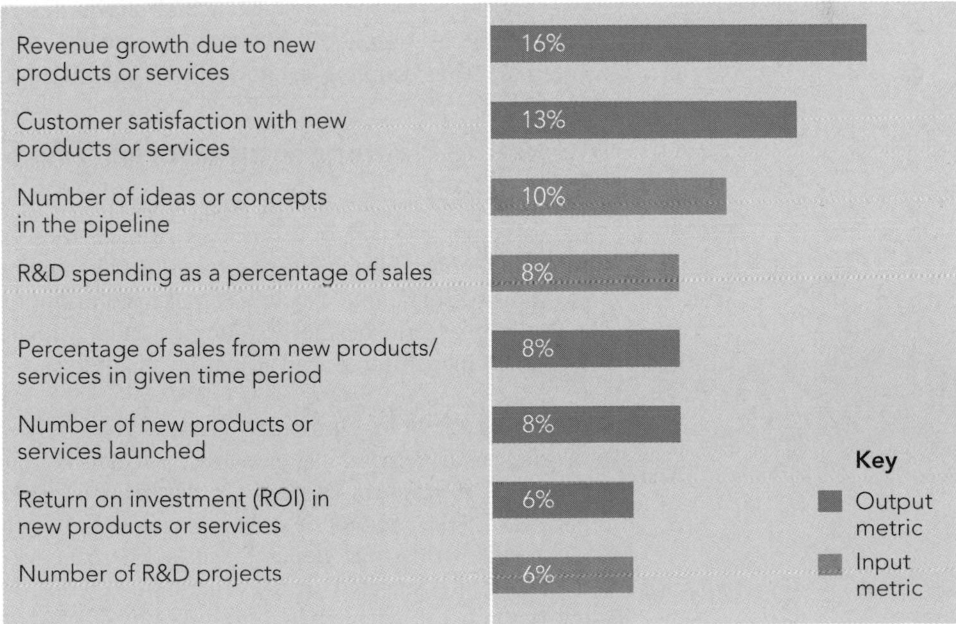

*Metrics ranked No. 1 by less than 6 percent of respondents are not shown; with these the percentages would total 100 percent.

A careful look at the innovation metrics shown in Figure 22–3 reveals that it is generally far easier to measure marketing inputs rather than marketing outputs. So measuring "the number of R&D projects" (an input) is far easier than measuring "customer satisfaction with new products or services" (an output). But as shown in Figure 22–2, the evaluation phase of the strategic marketing process involves comparing actual results—an output metric—with the goals set. So where possible, marketing managers prefer to use effective output metrics if they are available.

The Variety of Marketing Plans

The planning phase of the strategic marketing process usually results in a marketing plan that sets the direction for the marketing activities of an organization. As noted earlier in Appendix A, a marketing plan is the heart of a business plan. Like business plans, marketing plans aren't all from the same mold; they vary with the length of the planning period, the purpose, and the audience. Let's look briefly at two kinds: long-range and annual marketing plans.

Long-Range Marketing Plans Typically, long-range marketing plans cover marketing activities from two to five years into the future. Except for firms in industries such as autos, steel, or forest products, marketing plans rarely go beyond five years into the future because the tremendous number of uncertainties makes the benefits of planning less than the effort expended. Such plans are often directed at top-level executives and the board of directors.

Annual Marketing Plans Usually developed by a marketing or product manager (discussed later in the chapter) in a consumer products firm such as General Mills, annual marketing plans deal with marketing goals and strategies for a product, product line, or entire firm for a single year. This annual planning cycle typically starts with a detailed marketing research study of current users and ends after 42 weeks with the approval of the plan by the division general manager, 10 weeks before the fiscal year starts. Between these points there are continuing efforts to uncover new ideas through key-issues sessions with specialists both inside and outside the firm. The plan is fine-tuned through a series of often excruciating reviews by several levels of management, which leaves few surprises and little to chance.

It is easier to talk about planning than to do it well. The next section describes some marketing planning frameworks to aid the process.

Marketing Planning Frameworks: The Search for Growth

LO2

Marketing planning for a firm with many products competing in many markets is a complex process. Yet in a business firm all these planning efforts are directed at finding the means for increased growth in sales and profits. Two techniques that help corporate and marketing executives make important resource allocation decisions are: (1) Porter's generic business strategies and (2) synergy analysis. Both techniques relate to elements introduced in earlier chapters.

Porter's Generic Business Strategies As shown in Figure 22–4, Michael E. Porter has developed a framework in which he identifies four basic, or "generic," strategies.[20] A **generic business strategy** is one that can be adopted by any firm, regardless of the product or industry involved, to achieve a competitive advantage.

Although all the techniques discussed here involve generic strategies, the phrase is most often associated with Porter's framework. In this framework, the columns identify the two fundamental alternatives firms can use in seeking competitive advantage: becoming the low-cost producer within the markets in which it competes or differentiating itself from competitors by developing points of difference in its prod-

FIGURE 22–4
Porter's four generic business strategies involve combinations of (1) competitive scope or the breadth of the target markets and (2) a stress on costs versus product differentiation.

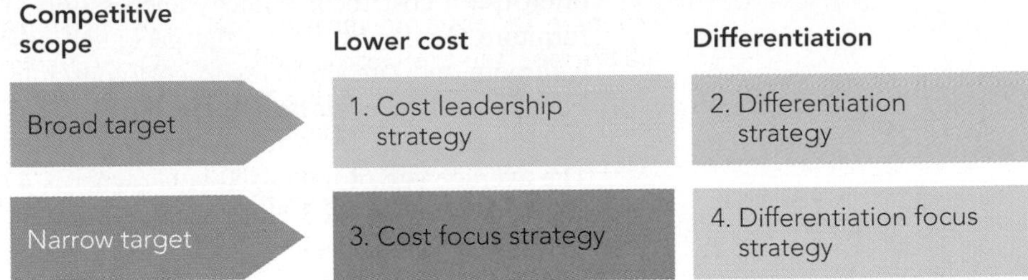

uct offerings or marketing programs. In contrast, the rows identify the competitive scope: a broad target by competing in many market segments or a narrow target by competing in only a few segments or even a single segment. The columns and rows result in four generic business strategies, any one of which can provide a competitive advantage among similar business units in the same industry:

1. A **cost leadership strategy** (cell 1) focuses on reducing expenses and, in turn, lowers product prices while targeting a broad array of market segments. One way is by securing raw materials from lower-cost suppliers. Also, significant investments in capital equipment may be necessary to improve the production or distribution process and achieve these lower unit costs. The cost leader still must have adequate quality levels. Campbell Soup's sophisticated product development and supply chain systems have led to huge cost savings. So its cost leadership strategy has resulted in lower prices for customers—causing its market share to increase in the current recession.
2. A **differentiation strategy** (cell 2) requires products to have significant points of difference in product offerings, brand image, higher quality, advanced technology, or superior service to charge a higher price while targeting a broad array of market segments. This allows the firm to charge a price premium. General Mills uses this strategy in stressing its nutritious, high-quality brands in reaching a diverse array of customer segments.
3. A **cost focus strategy** (cell 3) involves controlling expenses and, in turn, lowering product prices targeted at a narrow range of market segments. Retail

Which of Porter's generic strategies are Campbell Soup and IKEA using? For the answers and a discussion of the strategies, see the text.

chains targeting only a few market segments in a restricted group of products often use a cost focus strategy successfully. IKEA is now the world's largest furniture retailer by selling flat-pack, self-assembly furniture, accessories, and bathroom and kitchen items to cost-conscious consumers.

4. Finally, a **differentiation focus strategy** (cell 4) requires products to have significant points of difference to target one or only a few market segments. The average age of today's Toyota owner is 47. So a concerned Toyota product planning group visited cities where young people are buying and renting loft apartments. The planners discovered these young city dwellers need smaller cars they can park in cramped spaces. This suggests offering a new Toyota model with an important point of difference for a narrow segment of buyers—a differentiation focus strategy.[21]

These strategies also form the foundation for Michael Porter's theory about what makes a nation's industries successful, as discussed in Chapter 7.

Synergy Analysis **Synergy analysis** seeks opportunities by finding the optimum balance between marketing efficiencies versus R&D–manufacturing efficiencies. Using diversification analysis from Chapter 2 and the market–product grid framework from Chapter 9, we can see two kinds of synergy that are critical in developing corporate and marketing strategies: (1) marketing synergy and (2) R&D–manufacturing synergy. While the following example involves external synergies through mergers and acquisitions, the concepts apply equally well to internal synergies sought in adding new products or seeking new markets.

A critical step in the external analysis is to assess how these merger and acquisition strategies provide the organization with synergy, the increased customer value achieved through performing organizational functions more efficiently. The increased customer value can take many forms: more products, improved quality on existing products, lower prices, improved distribution, and so on. But the ultimate criterion is that customers should be better off as a result of the increased synergy. The firm, in turn, should be better off by gaining more satisfied customers resulting in increased sales and profits.

How might you segment the lawn mower market? What synergies might appear? For the answers, see the text.

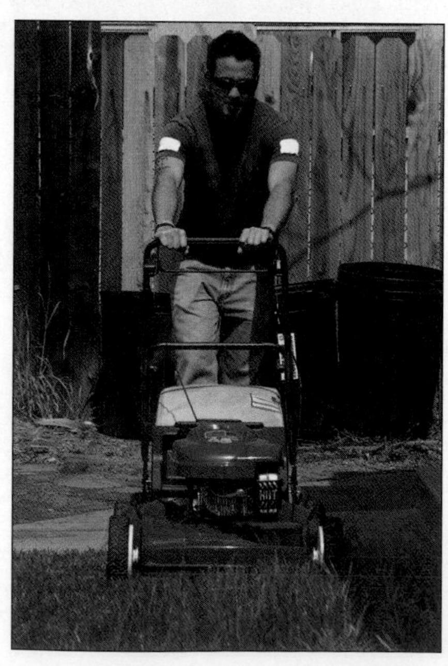

As noted in the Marketing Matters box, assume you are vice president of marketing for Great States Corp.'s line of nonpowered lawn mowers and powered walking mowers sold to the consumer market. You are looking for new product and new market opportunities to increase your revenues and profits.

You conduct a market segmentation study and develop a market–product grid to analyze future opportunities. You identify three major segments in the consumer market based on geography: (1) city, (2) suburban, and (3) rural households. These market segments relate to the size of lawn a consumer must mow. The product clusters are: (1) nonpowered, (2) powered walking, and (3) powered riding mowers. Five alternative marketing strategies are shown in the market–product grids in Figure 22–5.[22] As mentioned in Chapter 9, the important marketing synergies, or efficiencies, run horizontally across the rows in Figure 22–5. Conversely, the important R&D–manufacturing synergies, or efficiencies, run vertically down the columns. Let's look at the synergy effects for the five combinations in Figure 22–5.

A. *Market–product concentration.* The firm benefits from focus on a single product line and market segment, but it loses opportunities for significant synergies in both marketing and R&D–manufacturing.

B. *Market specialization.* The firm gains marketing synergy through providing a complete product line for the city market segment, but R&D–manufacturing has the difficulty of developing and producing three different products.

Marketing Matters > > > > > > customer value

A Test of Your Skills: Where Are the Synergies?

To try your hand in this multibillion-dollar synergy game, assume you are vice president of marketing for Great States Corp., which markets a line of nonpowered, powered walking, and powered riding lawn mowers throughout North America. A market–product grid for your business is shown. You distribute your nonpowered mowers in all three market segments shown and walking powered mowers only in suburban markets. However, you don't offer powered riding mowers for any of the three markets.

Here are your strategy dilemmas:

1. Where are the marketing synergies (efficiencies)?
2. Where are the R&D–manufacturing synergies (efficiencies)?
3. What would a market-product grid look like for an ideal company that Great States could merge with to achieve both marketing and R&D–manufacturing synergies (efficiencies)?

To consider these questions, read the text and study Figure 22–5 and the figure below.

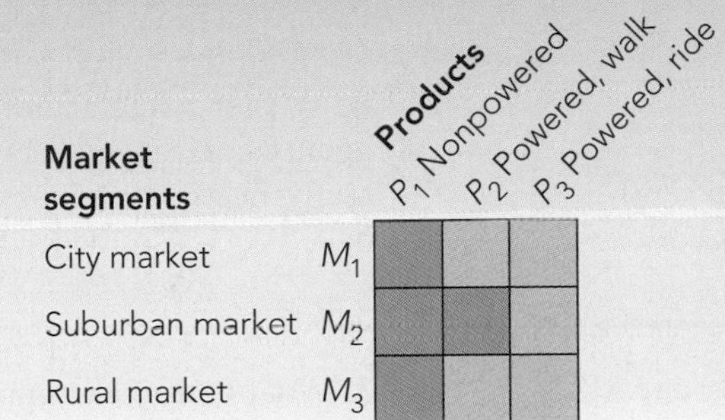

C. *Product specialization.* The firm gains R&D–manufacturing synergy through producing only a nonpowered lawn mower, but gaining market distribution in the three different geographic areas will be costly.

D. *Selective specialization.* The firm doesn't get either marketing or R&D–manufacturing synergies because of the uniqueness of the market–product combinations.

E. *Full coverage.* The firm has the maximum potential synergies in both marketing and R&D–manufacturing. The question: Is it spread too thin because of the resource requirements needed to reach all market–product combinations?

The Marketing Matters box poses the question of what the ideal partner for Great States would be if it merged with another firm, given the market–product combinations shown in the box. If, as vice president of marketing, you want to follow a full-coverage strategy, then the ideal merger partner is shown in Figure 22–6 on the next page. This would give the maximum potential synergies—if you are not spreading the resources of your merged companies too thin. Marketing gains by having a complete product line in all regions, and R&D–manufacturing gains by having access to new markets that can provide production economies of scale through producing larger volumes of its existing products.

FIGURE 22–5
Market–product grids show alternative strategies for a lawn mower manufacturer. Try to find synergies in each strategy—if any exist.

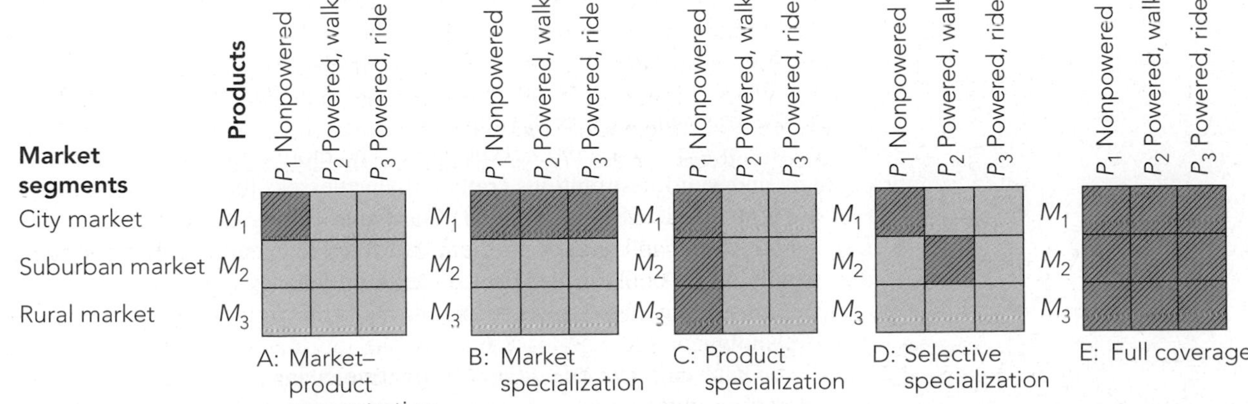

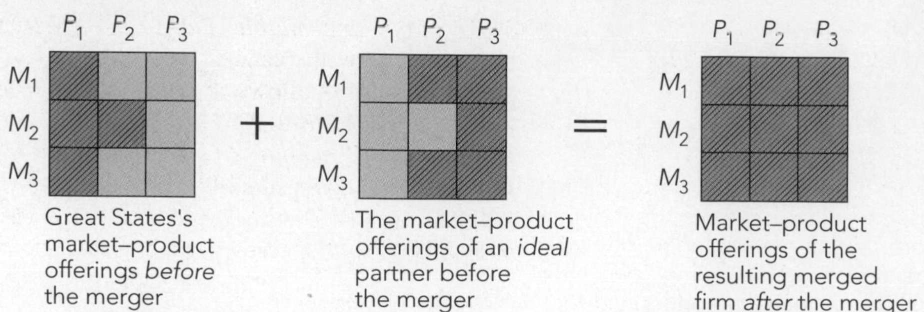

FIGURE 22–6
This is the ideal merger for Great States to obtain full market–product coverage. The ideal partner offers lawn mower products to the exact segments of customers not now served by Great States.

Often the search for synergies is within the company itself. The result often will be greater manufacturing synergies and efficiencies that in turn will lead to better quality control and happier customers. Procter & Gamble concluded the world didn't really need 31 varieties of its Head & Shoulders shampoo. Cutting the number in half, P&G also reduced its expenses and increased profits in the bargain.[23]

learning review

3. What is the difference between an input metric and an output metric?
4. Describe Porter's four generic business strategies.
5. Where do (*a*) marketing synergies and (*b*) R&D–manufacturing synergies appear when using the synergy analysis framework?

Some Marketing Planning and Strategy Lessons

LO3

Applying these frameworks is not automatic but requires a great deal of managerial judgment. Commonsense requirements of an effective marketing plan are discussed next, followed by problems that can arise.

Guidelines for an Effective Marketing Plan President Dwight D. Eisenhower, when he commanded Allied armies in World War II, made his classic observation, "Plans are nothing; planning is everything." It is the process of careful planning that focuses an organization's efforts and leads to success. The plans themselves, which change with events, are often secondary. Effective planning and plans are inevitably characterized by identifiable objectives, specific strategies or courses of action, and the means to execute them. Here are some guidelines in developing effective marketing plans:[24]

- *Set measurable, achievable goals.* Ideally, goals should be quantified and measurable in terms of what is to be accomplished and by when. So "Increase market share from 18 percent to 22 percent by December 31, 2011" is preferable to "Maximize market share given our available resources." Also, to motivate people the goals must be achievable.
- *Use a base of facts and valid assumptions.* The more a marketing plan is based on facts and valid assumptions, rather than guesses, the less uncertainty and risk are associated with executing it. Good marketing research helps.
- *Use simple, but clear and specific, plans.* Effective execution of plans requires that people at all levels in the firm understand what, when, and how they are to accomplish their tasks. Involve people with the right skills and experience in the planning.
- *Have complete and feasible plans.* Marketing plans must incorporate all the key marketing mix factors and be supported by adequate resources.

- *Make plans controllable and flexible.* Marketing plans must enable results to be compared with planned targets, often using precise marketing metrics and dashboards. This allows replanning—the flexibility to alter the original plans based on recent results.
- *Find the right person to implement the plans.* But make sure that person is heavily involved in making the plans.
- *Work toward consensus-building.* "Ownership" of the plan by team members and stakeholders increases the chances for its success.

Problems in Marketing Planning and Strategy An all-too-frequent problem in marketing planning and strategy is that bad news is filtered out as information goes up the line to give top management a very rosy picture. J.D. Power III did marketing research at Ford four decades ago. "There was no interest in finding out what customers really thought," he says. "Instead, we were constantly asked to 'torture the data until it confessed,' giving us the answers the execs wanted."[25] So he founded J.D. Power & Associates to do customer satisfaction studies. One of his first marketing research clients was Toyota, which listened and has used hundreds of J.D. Power studies over the years. Today J.D. Power & Associates is one of the world's best known marketing information companies and now serves not only the auto industry but also heath care, telecommunications, insurance, financial services, and more. Other key problems that emerge in a firm's strategic marketing process:

1. Plans may be based on very poor assumptions about environmental forces, especially changing economic conditions and competitors' actions. A Western Union plan failed because it didn't reflect the impact of deregulation and competitors' actions on business.
2. Planners and their plans may have lost sight of their customers' needs. But not at the Papa John's pizza chain. The "better ingredients, better pizza" slogan makes the hair stand up on the back of the necks of competing Pizza Hut executives. The reason is that this Papa John's slogan reflects the firm's obsessive attention to detail, which is stealing market share from much-bigger Pizza Hut. Sample detail: If the cheese on the pizza shows a single air bubble or the crust is not golden brown, the offending pizza is not served to the customer.
3. Too much time and effort may be spent on data collection and writing plans that are too complex to implement. One manufacturer cut its planning instructions "that looked like an auto repair manual" to five or six pages for operating units.
4. Line operating managers often feel no sense of ownership in implementing the plans. Andy Grove, when he was CEO of Intel, observed, "We had the very ridiculous system . . . of delegating strategic planning to strategic planners. The strategies these [planners] prepared had no bearing on anything we actually did."[26] The solution is to assign more planning activities to line operating managers, the people who actually carry them out.

General Mills' successful introduction of French-developed Yoplait yogurt to U.S. consumers . . .

Big G: Global Strategies to Find Synergies, Segments, and Partners Competing in today's global marketplace, General Mills is concerned with *both* selling its products and brands in countries around the world *and* also obtaining ideas for new products from anyone, anywhere who has a great product or technology.

Easy to understand is the benefit for General Mills of moving its existing U.S. products into foreign markets. As mentioned in Chapter 15, the company's joint venture

. . . led the way to its global search for new products today, such as Wanchai Ferry dinner kits from Hong Kong.

with Swiss-based Nestlé in Cereal Partners Worldwide provides General Mills access to European, Latin American, and Asian consumers—offering everything from cereals to ice cream bars. This joint venture has achieved great success.

Less clear is the reason for Big G's current global search for new ideas, products, and technologies. The success of Yoplait yogurt ("The Yogurt of France") has led to bringing other products developed outside the United States to our shores. Wanchai Ferry™ brand dinner kits are coming to the United States through a collaboration managed by General Mills of scientists on three continents. The dinner kits, which do not require freezing or refrigeration, are an adaptation of frozen dumplings developed by Madame Kin Wo Chong, a Hong Kong entrepreneur who started by selling her dumplings in 1977 from a cart on the city's Wanchai Ferry pier.

Have a great idea for a new technology or product General Mills might use? Under its Worldwide Innovation Network, the company wants your idea to help accelerate its innovation efforts. You can contact General Mills online through an Internet portal at www.generalmills.com/win to submit your idea. But there's a wrinkle: The new product or technology must (1) have a patent or patent pending, (2) be fully developed and be on the market somewhere in the world, and (3) fit into Big G's product lines![27]

Balancing Value and Values in Strategic Marketing Plans Two important trends are likely to influence the strategic marketing process in the future. The first, *value-based planning*, combines marketing planning ideas and financial planning techniques to assess how much a division or strategic business unit (SBU) contributes to the price of a company's stock (or shareholder wealth). Value is created when the financial return of a strategic activity exceeds the cost of the resources allocated to the activity.

The second trend is the increasing interest in *value-driven strategies*, which incorporate concerns for ethics, integrity, employee health and safety, and environmental safeguards with more common corporate values such as growth, profitability, customer service, and quality. Some experts have observed that although many corporations cite broad corporate values in advertisements, press releases, and company newsletters, they have not yet changed their strategic plans to reflect the stated values. U.S. firms, like firms and governments around the world, are increasingly called on to be good global citizens and to support sustainable development.[28]

THE IMPLEMENTATION PHASE OF THE STRATEGIC MARKETING PROCESS

The Monday morning diagnosis of a losing football coach often runs something like "We had an excellent game plan; we just didn't execute it."

Is Planning or Implementation the Problem?

The planning-versus-execution issue applies to the strategic marketing process as well: When a marketing plan fails, it's difficult to determine whether the failure is due to a poor plan or poor implementation.[29]

Effective managers tracking progress on a struggling plan first try to identify whether the problems involve: (1) the plan and strategy, (2) its implementation, or (3) both, and then they try to correct the problems. But as discussed earlier in the chapter, research on what really works shows that successful firms have excellence on both the planning and strategy side and the implementation and execution side.

Procter & Gamble's new Tide Stain Release launch shows how it has improved both planning and implementation by involving consumers earlier in its innovation activities.

For example, Procter & Gamble's consumer product success combines strong innovative products (planning and strategy) with excellent promotion and distribution (implementation and execution). Almost a decade ago P&G realized too many of its products were being pushed into the market before they were ready—really a planning glitch. P&G's mantra of "fearlessness when it comes to failure" stresses that failure isn't punished if those involved learn key lessons. So it reorganized itself around an innovation strategy to "involve some consumers in product design as soon as we have the concept," says P&G's chief executive officer, A.G. Lafley.

In the 2009 recession, consumers flocked to cheaper brands, causing Tide, P&G's biggest moneymaker, to lose market share. About half of Tide consumers already used some form of in-wash laundry additive, so P&G saw an opportunity it responded to quickly. In mid-2009 P&G launched Tide Stain Release, a new laundry additive to boost Tide's cleaning power. Its advertising tagline: "Stains Out. No Doubt."[30]

At the other extreme, most of the hundreds of dot-com firms that failed in the late 1990s had both planning *and* implementation problems. Their bad planning often resulted from their focus on getting start-up money from investors and not providing real value to customers. Bad implementation by the dot-coms frequently led to their spending huge sums on wasteful ads to try to promote their failing Web sites. While some Internet firms may have had good ideas for delivering physical products such as toys and groceries to their customers' doors, they didn't understand key implementation issues that involved inventories, warehouses, and physical distribution.

Increasing Emphasis on Marketing Implementation

Today the implementation phase of the strategic marketing process often involves moving many planning activities away from the duties of planners to those of line managers and finding effective ways to convert new marketing opportunities to completed projects.

General Electric's Jack Welch became a legend in making GE more efficient and far better at implementation. When Welch became CEO in 1981 he faced an organization mired in red tape, turf battles, and slow decision making. Further, Welch saw GE bogged down with 25,000 managers and close to a dozen layers between him and the factory floor.

In his "delayering," he sought to cut GE's levels in half and to speed up decision making and implementation by building an atmosphere of trust and autonomy among his managers and employees. Where possible, Welch made the people planning the project responsible for carrying it out. In terms of implementation and meeting key goals, Welch also insisted General Electric's departments be "winners"—or No. 1 or No. 2 in their industry in terms of revenues and profits. Although there are debates on some Welch strategies, businesses around the world are using GE's focus on implementation as a benchmark.[31]

Improving Implementation of Marketing Programs

No magic formula exists to guarantee effective implementation of marketing plans. In fact, the answer seems to be equal parts of good management skills and practices, from which have come some guidelines for improving program implementation.

Communicate Goals and the Means of Achieving Them Those called on to implement plans need to understand both the goals sought and how they are to be accomplished. Everyone in Papa John's—from founder John Schnatter to telephone order takers and make-line people—is clear on what the firm's goal

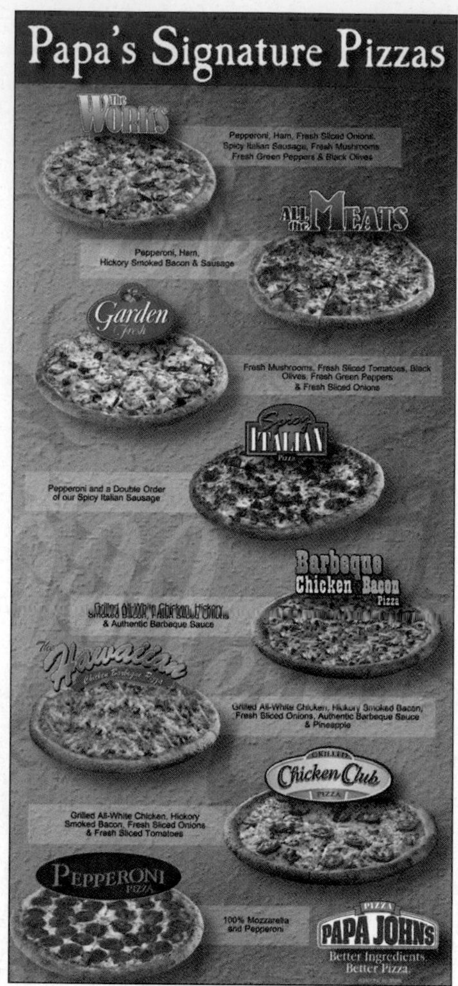

Core value #4—"PAPA"—makes very clear to all Papa John's Pizza employees what its priorities are!

is: to deliver better pizzas using better ingredients. The firm's orientation packet for employees lists its six core values that executives are expected to memorize. An example: Core value #4 is "PAPA," or "People Are Priority No. 1, Always."[32]

Have a Responsible Program Champion Willing to Act Successful programs almost always have a **product or program champion** who is able and willing to cut red tape and move the program forward. Such a person often has the uncanny ability to move back and forth between big-picture strategy questions and specific details when the situation calls for it. Program champions are notoriously brash in overcoming organizational hurdles. The U.S. Navy's Admiral Grace Murray Hopper not only gave the world an early computer language but also the word *bug*, meaning any glitch in a computer or computer program. This program champion's famous advice for moving decisions to actions by cutting through an organization's red tape: "Better to ask forgiveness than permission."

Reward Successful Program Implementation When an individual or a team is rewarded for achieving the organization's goal, they have maximum incentive to see a program implemented successfully because they have personal ownership and a stake in that success.

Take Action and Avoid Paralysis by Analysis Management experts warn against "paralysis by analysis," the tendency to excessively analyze a problem instead of taking action. To overcome this pitfall, they call for a "bias for action" and recommend a "do it, fix it, try it" approach.[33] Conclusion: Perfectionists finish last, so getting 90 percent perfection and letting the marketplace help in the fine-tuning makes good sense in implementation.

Lockheed Martin's Skunk Works got its name from the comic strip *L'il Abner* and its legendary reputation from achieving superhuman technical feats with a low budget and ridiculously short deadlines by stressing teamwork. Under the 35-year leadership of Kelly Johnson, the Skunk Works turned out a series of world-class aircraft from the world's fastest (the SR-71 Blackbird) to the nation's most untrackable aircraft (the F-117 Stealth fighter). Two of Kelly Johnson's basic tenets: (1) make decisions promptly and (2) avoid paralysis by analysis. In fact, one U.S. Air Force audit showed that Johnson's Skunk Works could carry out a program on schedule with 126 people, whereas a competitor in a comparable program was behind schedule with 3,750 people.[34]

Open communications at the Skunk Works have led to state-of-the-art aircraft like this SR-71 Blackbird.

Foster Open Communication to Surface Problems Success often lies in fostering a work environment that is open enough so employees are willing to speak out when they see problems without fear of recrimination. The focus is placed on trying to solve the problem as a group rather than finding someone to blame. Solutions are solicited from anyone who has a creative idea to suggest—from the janitor to the president—without regard to status or rank in the organization.

Two more Kelly Johnson axioms from Lockheed Martin's Skunk Works apply here: (1) When trouble develops, surface the problem immediately, and (2) get help—don't keep the problem to yourself. This may even mean getting ideas from competitors, but more often it means combing

Marketing Matters > > > > > > > > > technology

Implementation Lessons from IBM: Converting Tough Global Problems into Results

In two decades IBM has reinvented itself twice—moving (1) from computer hardware into services and software and (2) from that into today's global "data analytics."

IBM's current "Smarter Planet" ad campaign stresses its new strategy: Find tough problems and "throw in billions of dollars in R&D," as *Fortune* magazine observes, and watch what happens. The breadth of the problems IBM is tackling is mind stretching—an *E. coli* outbreak in Norway, a hurricane in Texas causing huge power outages, a fungal disease in West Africa affecting cacao trees (and your future chocolate consumption), and bogged-down rush-hour traffic in Stockholm, Sweden.

Every year people burn 2.3 billion
gallons of fuel while sitting in traffic.
A smarter planet needs
smarter traffic systems.
Let's build a smarter planet.
ibm.com/think
THINK
IBM

The Stockholm traffic problem illustrates IBM's implementation know-how: Get ideas from all over the globe to solve technical problems, thereby avoiding the "NIH syndrome"—the aversion to accept ideas "not invented here," or not originated inside one's own firm. In 2003 Stockholm put out a request for the proposal to charge drivers a fee to reduce downtown traffic by 10 to 15 percent at peak hours. The cars wouldn't be required to carry transponders, so IBM was forced to use cameras with optical character recognition to identify 500,000 cars a day traveling 60 miles an hour.

Presto! Using 18 subcontractors—and an urgent request to its R&D facility in Israel—IBM installed the system. It reduced Stockholm peak-hours traffic 22 percent and emissions 14 percent. Stockholm hired 40 lawyers to handle expected complaints and appeals. Only six were received.

your own firm and key subcontractors to find talented people with solutions. The Marketing Matters box describes how IBM today seeks tough problems and then uses its global network of subcontractors and its own labs to find and implement solutions.[35]

LO4

Schedule Precise Tasks, Responsibilities, and Deadlines Successful implementation requires that people know the tasks for which they are responsible and the deadline for completing them. To implement the thousands of tasks on a new aircraft design, Lockheed Martin typically holds weekly program meetings. The outcome of each of these meetings is an **action item list**, an aid to implementing a marketing plan consisting of four columns: (1) the task, (2) the person responsible for completing that task, (3) the date to finish the task, and (4) what is to be delivered. Within hours of completing a program meeting, the action item list is circulated to those attending. This then serves as the starting agenda for the next meeting. Meeting minutes are viewed as secondary and backward looking. Action item lists are forward looking, clarify the targets, and put strong pressure on people to achieve their designated tasks by the deadline.

Related to the action item lists are formal *program schedules*, which show the relationships through time of the various program tasks. Scheduling an action program involves: (1) identifying the main tasks, (2) determining the time required to complete each task, (3) arranging the activities to meet the deadline, and (4) assigning people the responsibilities to complete each task.

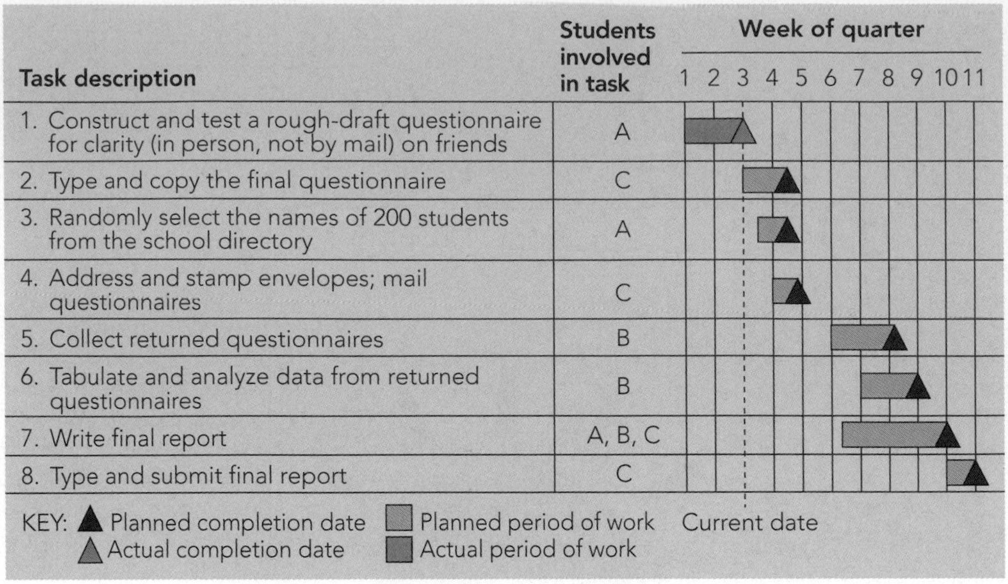

Task description	Students involved in task	Week of quarter: 1 2 3 4 5 6 7 8 9 10 11
1. Construct and test a rough-draft questionnaire for clarity (in person, not by mail) on friends	A	
2. Type and copy the final questionnaire	C	
3. Randomly select the names of 200 students from the school directory	A	
4. Address and stamp envelopes; mail questionnaires	C	
5. Collect returned questionnaires	B	
6. Tabulate and analyze data from returned questionnaires	B	
7. Write final report	A, B, C	
8. Type and submit final report	C	

KEY: ▲ Planned completion date ■ Planned period of work Current date
△ Actual completion date ■ Actual period of work

FIGURE 22–7
This Gantt chart for scheduling a student term project distinguishes the tasks that *must* be done sequentially from those that *can* be done concurrently.

Suppose, for example, that you and two friends are asked to do a term project on the problem, "How can the college increase attendance at its performing arts concerts?" And suppose further that the instructor limits the project in the following ways:

1. The project must involve a mail survey of the attitudes of a sample of students.
2. The term paper with the survey results must be submitted by the end of the 11-week quarter.

To begin the assignment, you need to identify all the project tasks and then estimate the time you can reasonably allocate to each one. To complete it in 11 weeks, your team must work on different parts at the same time, and some activities must be independent enough to overlap. This requires specialization and cooperation. Suppose that of the three of you (A, B, and C), only student C can type. Then you (student A) might assume the task of constructing the questionnaire and selecting samples, and student B might tabulate the data. You must also figure out which activities can be done concurrently to save time.

Scheduling production and marketing activities—from a term project to a new product rollout to a space shuttle launch—can be done efficiently with a *Gantt chart*, which is a graphical representation of a program schedule. Figure 22–7 shows one variation of a Gantt chart used to schedule the class project, demonstrating how the concurrent work on several tasks enables the students to finish the project on time. Developed by Henry L. Gantt, this method is the basis for the scheduling techniques used today, including elaborate computerized methods. The key to all scheduling techniques is to distinguish tasks that *must* be done sequentially from those that can be done concurrently. As in the case of the term project, scheduling tasks concurrently often reduces the total time required for a project. Software programs, such as Microsoft Project, simplify the task of developing a program schedule or Gantt chart.

learning review

6. What is the meaning and importance of a program champion?
7. What are one or two examples of lessons from Lockheed's Skunk Works that apply to implementing marketing programs?
8. Explain the difference between sequential and concurrent tasks in a Gantt chart.

Organizing for Marketing

A marketing organization is needed to implement the firm's marketing plans. Basic issues in today's marketing organizations include understanding (1) the evolving role of the chief marketing officer, (2) how line versus staff positions and divisional groupings interrelate to form a cohesive marketing organization, and (3) the role of the product manager.

The Evolving Role of the Chief Marketing Officer The senior executive responsible for a firm's marketing activities shown in Figure 22–8 is increasingly given the title of chief marketing officer (CMO), rather than vice president of marketing. This reflects the broadening of the CMO's role as the inside-the-company "voice of the consumer" in responding to dynamic marketplace changes. So today it is critical that CMOs understand (1) the changing characteristics of the global consumer segments served and (2) how to market to consumers who increasingly combine Internet online research with offline purchasing at a local store and vice versa.[36] Along with these broadened responsibilities is higher turnover among CMOs. A recent sample of 100 large firms revealed the average CMO held the job for less than two years.[37]

Line versus Staff and Divisional Groupings Although simplified, Figure 22–8 shows the organization of a typical business unit in a consumer packaged goods firm like Procter & Gamble, Kraft, or General Mills. This business unit consists of the Dinner Products, Baked Goods, and Desserts groups. It highlights the distinction between line and staff positions in marketing. Managers in **line positions**, such as the senior marketing manager for Biscuits, have the authority and responsibility to issue orders to the people who report to them, such as the two product managers shown in Figure 22–8. In this organizational chart, line positions are connected with solid lines. People in **staff positions** (connected by dotted lines) have the authority and responsibility to advise people in line positions but cannot issue direct orders to them.

FIGURE 22–8
This organization of a business unit in a typical consumer packaged goods firm shows two product or brand groups.

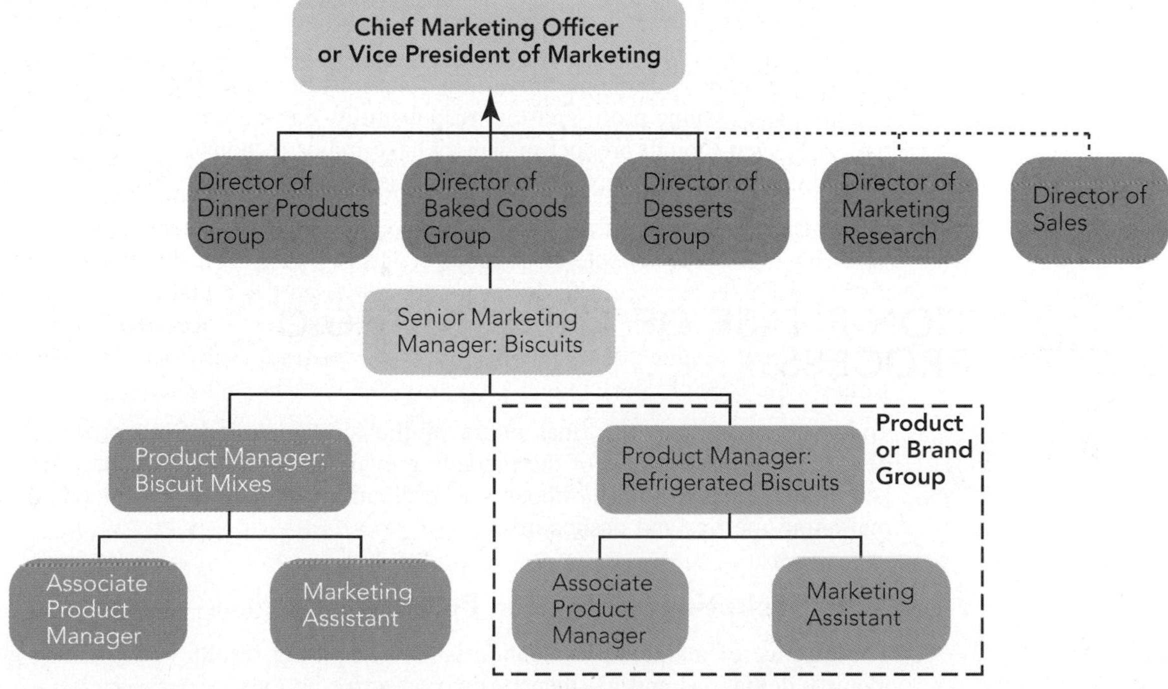

Most marketing organizations use divisional groupings—such as product line, functional, geographical, and market-based—to implement plans and achieve objectives. Only the first of these appears in the organizational chart in Figure 22–8. The top of the chart shows organization by **product line groupings** in which a unit is responsible for specific product offerings, such as Dinner Products or Baked Goods.

At higher levels than shown in Figure 22–8, grocery products firms are organized by **functional groupings**—such as manufacturing, marketing, and finance—that represent the different departments or business activities within a firm.

Most grocery products firms use **geographical groupings** in which sales territories are subdivided according to geographical location. Each director of sales has several regional sales managers reporting to him or her, such as western, southern, and so on. These, in turn, have district managers reporting to them, with the field sales representatives at the lowest level.

A fourth method of organizing a company is to use **market-based groupings**, which utilize specific customer segments, such as the banking, health care, or manufacturing segments. When this method of organizing is combined with product groupings, the result is a *matrix organization*.

A relatively new position in consumer products firms is the *category manager* (senior marketing manager in Figure 22–8). Category managers have responsibility for an entire product line—all biscuit brands, for example. They attempt to reduce the possibility of one brand's actions hurting another brand in the same category. Procter & Gamble uses category managers to organize by "global business units" such as baby care and beauty care. Cutting across country boundaries, these global business units implement standardized worldwide pricing, marketing, and distribution.

Role of the Product Manager The key person in the product or brand group is the manager who heads it. As mentioned in Chapter 10, this person is often called the *product manager* or *brand manager*. This person and his or her assistants comprise the *product group* or *brand group*, enclosed by the dashed red line in Figure 22-8. These product or brand groups are the basic building blocks in the marketing department of most consumer and business product firms. The function of a product manager is to plan, implement, and evaluate the annual and long-range plans for the products for which he or she is responsible.

There are both benefits and dangers to the product manager system. On the positive side, product managers become strong advocates for the assigned products, cut red tape to work with people in various functions both inside and outside the organization, and assume profit-and-loss responsibility for the product line. On the negative side, even though product managers have major responsibilities, they have relatively little direct authority, so they must use persuasion rather than direct orders.[38]

THE EVALUATION PHASE OF THE STRATEGIC MARKETING PROCESS

To cover evaluation, the final phase of the strategic marketing process, we can describe (1) the elements of the marketing evaluation process; (2) the roles of marketing ROI, metric, and dashboards in evaluation; and (3) how General Mills uses marketing metrics and dashboards.

The Marketing Evaluation Process

The essence of marketing evaluation is (1) comparing results with planned goals to identify deviations and (2) then taking corrective actions.

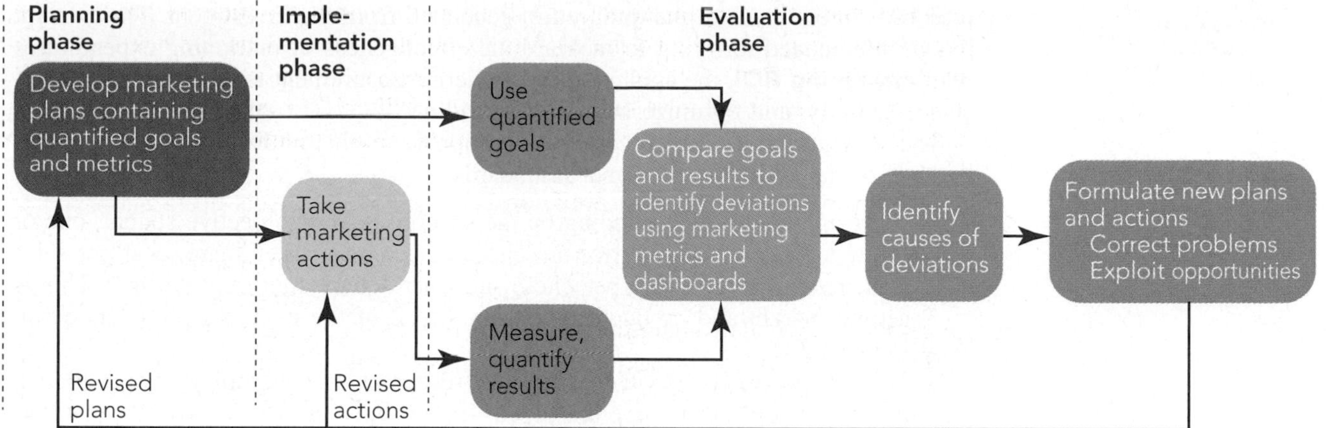

FIGURE 22–9
The evaluation phase of the strategic marketing process ties results and actions to goals, often using marketing metrics and dashboards.

Identifying Deviations from Goals Figure 22–9 shows that marketing plans made in the planning phase have both quantified goals and a specific marketing metric used to measure whether the goal is actually achieved. Marketing actions are taken in the implementation phase to attempt to achieve the goals set in the planning phase. In the evaluation phase, Figure 22–9 shows that the quantitative results are measured using the marketing metrics and compared with the actual results of the marketing actions. For speed and efficiency the results are compared with goals and often shown to marketing managers on marketing dashboards to enable them to take timely actions.

Acting on Deviations from Goals A marketing manager then interprets the marketing dashboard information using *management by exception*, which means identifying results that deviate from plans to diagnose their causes and take new actions. The marketing manager is looking for two kinds of deviations, each triggering a different kind of action:

- *Actual results fall short of goals.* This requires a corrective action. Beaten badly for years in the U.S. toothpaste market by P&G's Crest, Colgate used new technology in its labs to introduce its Total toothpaste, the first "oral pharmaceutical" ever approved by the U.S. Food and Drug Administration. Not only does Total clean teeth, but also its germ-fighting feature helps heal gingivitis, a bleeding-gum disease. Colgate marketed this feature aggressively, enabling Total to become No. 1 in the U.S. toothpaste market.[39]
- *Actual results exceed goals.* Marketing must act quickly to identify the reasons and exploit the unforeseen opportunity. In recessions, most firms tighten their belts and watch sales revenues fall. Not McDonald's! Seeing hard-pressed consumers suddenly appearing at its counters in 2009, McDonald's aggressively marketed its new "Dollar Menu" and its quirky new "McCafe" mochas, hot cocoas, and lattes and watched 58 million customers a day appear—up 2 million from a year earlier.[40]

What recession? McDonald's introduces new beverages quickly to reach hard-pressed consumers!

Evaluation Involves Marketing ROI, Metrics, and Dashboards

In the past decade, measuring the performance of marketing activities has become a central focus in many organizations. This boils down to some form of the question, "What measure can I use to determine if my company's marketing is effective?"

No single measure exists to determine if a company's marketing is effective. In finance, the return on investment (ROI) metric relates the total investment made to the total return generated from the investment. The concept has been extended to trying to measure the effectiveness of marketing expenditures with **marketing ROI**, the application of modern measurement technologies to understand, quantify, and optimize marketing spending.[41]

The strategic marketing process tries to improve marketing ROI through the effective use of marketing metrics and dashboards:

- *Marketing metrics.* Depending on the specific goal or objective sought, one or a few key marketing metrics are chosen, such as market share, cost per sales lead, retention rate, cost per click, sales per square foot, and so on.[42] This is setting market and product goals from step 2 of the planning phase shown in Figure 22–2.
- *Marketing dashboards.* If the financial resources and technology are available, the marketing metrics are displayed—often daily or weekly—on the marketing dashboard on the manager's computer. With today's syndicated scanner data, Internet clicks, and TV viewership tracking, the typical manager faces information overload. So an effective marketing dashboard displays actual results that vary significantly from plans. This alerts the manager to potential problems.[43]

These highlighted exceptions, or deviations from plans shown in the evaluation phase in Figure 22–2, are the immediate focus of the marketing manager, who then tries to improve the firm's marketing ROI.

Evaluation Using Marketing Metrics and Marketing Dashboards at General Mills

Let's assume it is mid-January and you are part of Vivian Callaway's Warm Delights team at General Mills. Your team is using the marketing data and metrics shown in the marketing dashboard in Figure 22-10. We can summarize the evaluation step of the strategic marketing process using this dashboard and the three-step challenge-findings-actions format used in the marketing dashboard boxes throughout the book.

The Distribution Challenge for Warm Delights Minis You've been asked to analyze the channel of distribution strategy of the Warm Delights Minis. This hypothetical example is based on the type of scanner data General Mills uses, but details have been modified to simplify the data and analysis.

The marketing dashboard in Figure 22-10 focuses on the distribution of the six existing Warm Delights Minis flavors and the impact of adding two new flavors introduced in the fall—Lemon Swirl cake and Cinnamon Swirl cake.[44] As with all new grocery products, the challenge is to gain distribution on retailers' shelves. So the marketing metrics in Figure 22-10 focus on the distribution of Warm Delights Minis in the five main channels of distribution used by General Mills.

The Findings for Warm Delights Minis The three "buttons" in the left-hand column titled "Select Product Option" in Figure 22-10 show that this marketing dashboard can present the situation for any one of three levels in the Warm Delights product line. The three buttons show the analysis can be done for:

- *Warm Delights Total*—the entire Warm Delights product line
- *Warm Delights (Regular)*—only for the regular size packages of Warm Delights
- *Warm Delights Minis*—only for the single-serve size packages of the brand—the Warm Delights Minis

The red "active" button in the column shows the marketing dashboard figures apply only to Warm Delights Minis. The dashboard shows five marketing metrics

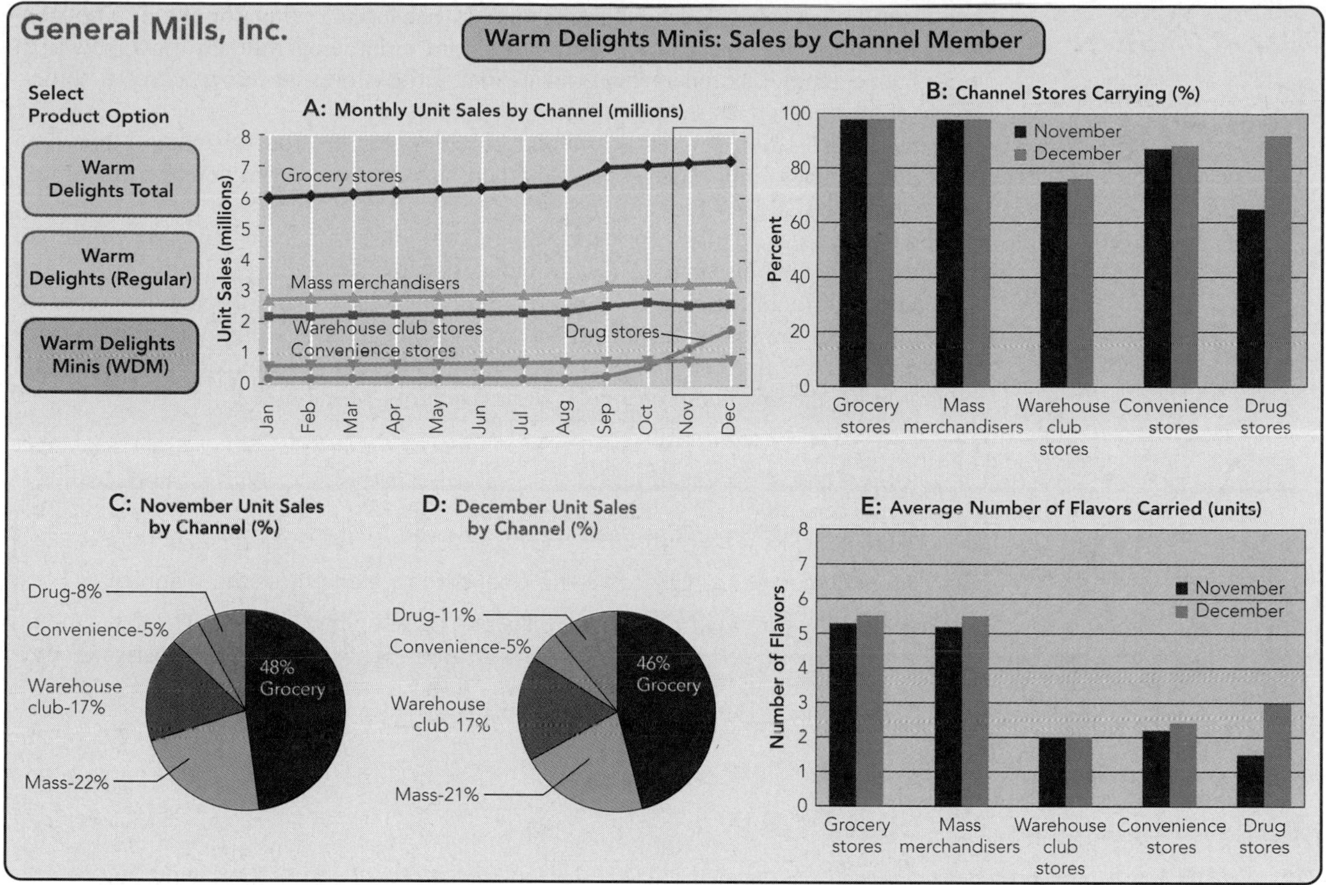

FIGURE 22–10
As a member of the Warm Delights team at General Mills, here is the marketing dashboard you can use to update the distribution channels strategy for the recently introduced line of Warm Delights Minis.

used in tracking how well Warm Delights Minis are doing in the five major channels they use:

- *Line chart A.* This shows monthly sales in millions of units for the five major channels. The grocery store channel is clearly the most important. With one exception, the sales in each channel have been increasing slightly throughout the year. The exception is the jump in sales in the drug store channel from September to December.
- *Bar chart B.* This shows the percentage of stores in each channel carrying one or more of the flavors of Warm Delights Minis in both November and December. The percentage of drug stores carrying at least one flavor jumped from 62 percent in November to 90 percent in December. Your team needs to understand better what happened.
- *Pie chart C.* This shows the percentage share of total unit sales of Warm Delights Minis going through each of the five channels in November.
- *Pie chart D.* This is similar to pie chart C, but applies to December. Comparing pie charts C and D reveals that the share of sales of Warm Delights Minis moving through the drug store channel grew from 8 percent in November to 11 percent in December—a 37.5 percent increase. Clearly your team must try to identify the reason for the increase.
- *Bar chart E.* This bar chart shows the average number of flavors of Warm Delights Minis carried by each store in the channel, the maximum possible being 8.0. But note that the Warm Delights Minis went from having only 1.4 flavors carried by the average drugstore in November to 3.0 in December, a trend worth investigating.

The Actions for Warm Delights Minis Further analysis of dashboards showing the sales by channel of individual flavors of Warm Delights Minis reveals the jump in sales in the drug store channel is because (1) a major chain (like Walgreen's) added the line and (2) drug stores are embracing the new flavors, which have made many customers more aware that drug stores are now actively selling many food lines.

Your investigation reveals a different situation for the four channels other than drug stores. The minor changes in sales there are due to the two new flavors simply replacing older, slower-moving ones.

Hot desserts normally experience an increased seasonal demand in winter. So because sales and distribution are growing, you decide to invest in the brand and schedule additional national TV advertising in late January and throughout February to exploit both the seasonal demand and recent sales trends. Seeing the jump in sales from adding a major drug store chain, you research ways to attract other potential chains in all the five main channels Warm Delights Minis uses.

learning review

9. What are four groupings used within a typical marketing organization?
10. How do marketing metrics tie the goal-setting element of the planning phase of the strategic marketing process to the evaluation phase?

LEARNING OBJECTIVES REVIEW

LO1 *Explain how marketing managers allocate their limited resources.*
Marketing managers use the strategic marketing process and marketing information, such as marketing plans, sales reports, and action memos, to effectively allocate their scarce resources to exploit the competitive advantages of their products. Marketers may use techniques like sales response functions or market share (share point) analysis to help them assess what the market's response will be to additional marketing efforts.

LO2 *Describe two marketing planning frameworks: Porter's generic business strategies and synergy analysis.*
Porter identifies four generic business strategies that firms can adopt: a cost leadership strategy, which focuses on reducing expenses to lower product prices while targeting many market segments; a differentiation strategy, which requires products to have significant points of difference to charge a premium price while targeting many market segments; a cost focus strategy, which involves controlling costs to lower prices of products targeting only a few market segments; and a differentiation focus strategy, which requires products to have significant points of difference to reach one or only a few market segments.

The synergy analysis framework focuses on two kinds of synergies: marketing synergies (efficiencies), which run horizontally across the row of the various products offered by the firm to a single market segment; and R&D–manufacturing synergies (efficiencies), which run vertically down a column of the various market segments targeted for a given product or product class. This results in five alternative combinations: market–product concentration, market specialization, product specialization, selective specialization, and full coverage.

LO3 *Explain what makes an effective marketing plan.*
An effective marketing plan has measurable, achievable goals; uses facts and valid assumptions; is simple, clear, and specific; is complete and feasible; and is controllable and flexible.

LO4 *Use a Gantt Chart to schedule a series of tasks.*
Successful implementation of a marketing plan requires that people know the tasks, responsibilities, and deadlines needed to complete it. Once the information for these three areas is generated, a program schedule can be developed. A Gantt chart is a graphical representation of this schedule. The key to this scheduling technique is to identify those tasks that must be done sequentially from those that can be done concurrently.

LO5 *Describe the alternatives for organizing a marketing department and the role of a product manager.*
First, marketing departments must distinguish between line positions, those individuals who have the authority and responsibility to issue orders to people that report to them and staff positions, those individuals who have the authority and responsibility to advise but not directly order people in line positions to do something.

Second, marketing organizations use one of four divisional groupings to implement marketing plans: product line groupings, responsible for specific product offerings; functional groupings that represent the different departments and business activities within a firm; geographical groupings, in which sales territories are subdivided on a geographical basis; and market-based groupings, which utilize specific customer segments.

Product managers interact with many people and groups both inside and outside the firm to coordinate the planning, implementation, and evaluation of the marketing plan and its budget on an annual and long-term basis for the products for which they are responsible.

LO6 *Explain how marketing ROI, metrics, and dashboards relate to evaluating marketing programs.*
The evaluation phase of the strategic marketing process involves measuring the results of the actions from the implementation phase and comparing them with goals set in the planning phase. Marketing metrics, used to help quantify the goals in the planning stage, are of two kinds: input metrics and output metrics. The marketing manager then takes action to correct negative deviations from the plan and to exploit positive ones. Today, managers want an answer to the question "Are my marketing activities effective?" One answer is in using marketing ROI, which is the application of modern measurement technologies to understand, quantify, and optimize marketing spending. Quantifying a marketing goal with a carefully defined output metric and tracking this metric on a marketing dashboard can improve marketing ROI.

FOCUSING ON KEY TERMS

action item list p. 587
cost focus strategy p. 579
cost leadership strategy p. 579
differentiation focus strategy p. 580
differentiation strategy p. 579
functional groupings p. 590
generic business strategy p. 578
geographical groupings p. 590
line positions p. 589
market-based groupings p. 590
marketing ROI p. 592
product line groupings p. 590
product or program champion p. 586
sales response function p. 574
share points p. 575
staff positions p. 589
synergy analysis p. 580

APPLYING MARKETING KNOWLEDGE

1 Assume a firm faces an S-shaped sales response function. What happens to the ratio of incremental sales revenue to incremental marketing effort at the (*a*) bottom, (*b*) middle, and (*c*) top of this curve?
2 What happens to the ratio of incremental sales revenue to incremental marketing effort when the sales response function is an upward-sloping straight line?
3 Assume General Mills has to decide how to invest millions of dollars to try to expand its dessert and yogurt businesses. To allocate this money between these two businesses, what information would General Mills like to have?
4 Suppose your Great States lawn mower company has the market–product concentration situation shown in Figure 22–5A. What are both the synergies and potential pitfalls of following expansion strategies of (*a*) market specialization and (*b*) product specialization?
5 The first Domino's Pizza restaurant was near a college campus. What implementation problems are (*a*) similar and (*b*) different for restaurants near a college campus versus a military base?
6 A common theme among managers who succeed repeatedly in program implementation is fostering open communication. Why is this so important?
7 Parts of tasks 5 and 6 in Figure 22–7 are done both concurrently and sequentially. How can this be? How does it help the students meet the term paper deadline?
8 In the organizational chart for the consumer packaged goods firm in Figure 22–8, where do product line, functional, and geographical groupings occur?
9 Why are quantified goals in the planning phase of the strategic marketing process important for the evaluation phase?

building your marketing plan

Do the following activities to complete your marketing plan:

1 Draw a simple organization chart for your organization.
2 Develop a Gantt chart to schedule the key activities to implement your marketing plan.
3 In terms of the evaluation, list (*a*) the four or five critical factors (such as revenues, number of customers, variable costs) and (*b*) how frequently (monthly, quarterly) you will monitor them to determine if special actions are needed to exploit opportunities or correct deviations.
4 Read Appendix A, "Building an Effective Marketing Plan." Then write a 600-word executive summary for your marketing plan using the numbered headings shown in Appendix A.

Vivian Milroy Callaway, vice president for the Center for Learning and Experimentation at General Mills, retells the story for the "indulgent, delicious, and gooey" Warm Delights™. She summarizes, "When you want something that is truly innovative, you have to look at the rules you have been assuming in your category and break them all!"

When a new business achieves a breakthrough, it looks easy to outsiders. The creators of Betty Crocker Warm Delights stress that if the marketing decisions had been based on the traditions and history of the cake category, a smaller, struggling business would have resulted. The team chose to challenge the assumptions and expectations of accumulated cake category business experience. The team took personal and business risks and Warm Delights is a roaring success.

PLANNING PHASE: INNOVATION, BUT A SHRINKING MARKET

"In the typical grocery store, the baking mix aisle is a quiet place," says Callaway. Shelves sigh with flavors, types, and brands. Prices are low, but there is little consumer traffic. Cake continues to be a tradition for birthdays and social occasions. But, consumer demand declines. The percentage of U.S. households that bought at least one baking mix in 2000 was 80 percent. Four years later, the percentage of households was 77 percent, a very significant decline.

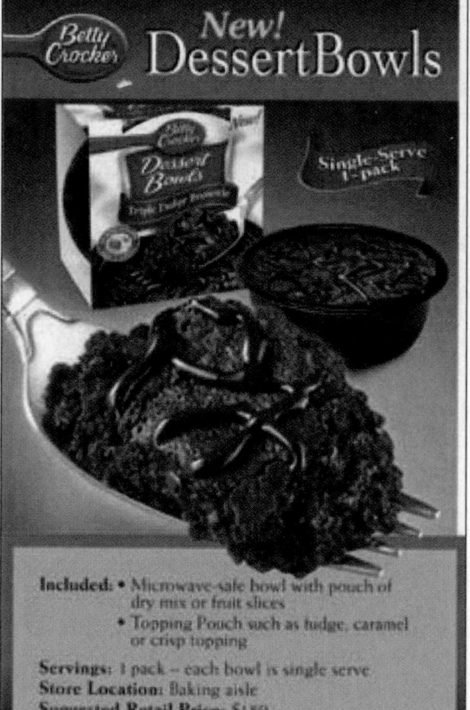

Today, a promoted price of 89 cents to make a 9×12 inch cake is common. Many choices, but little differentiation, gradually falling sales, and low uniform prices are the hallmarks of a mature category. But it's not that consumers don't buy cake-like treats. In fact, indulgent treats are growing. The premium prices for ice cream ($3.00 a pint) and chocolate ($3.00 a bar) are not slowing consumer purchases.

The Betty Crocker marketing team challenged the food scientists at General Mills to create a great tasting, easy to prepare, single-serve cake treat. The goal: Make it indulgent, delicious, and gooey. The team focused the scientists on a product that would have:

- Consistent great taste.
- Quick preparation.
- A single portion.
- No cleanup.

The food scientists delivered the prototype! Now, the marketing team began hammering out the four Ps. They started with a descriptive name "Betty Crocker Dessert Bowls" (see photo) and a plan to shelve it in the "quiet" cake aisle. This practical approach would meet the consumer need for a "small, fast, microwave cake" for dessert. Several marketing challenges emerged:

- *The comparison problem.* The easy shelf price comparison to 9×12 inch cakes selling for 89 cents would make it harder to price Dessert Bowls at $2.00.
- *The communication problem.* The product message "a small, faster-to-make cake" wasn't compelling. For example, after-school snacks should be fast and small, but "dessert" sounds too indulgent.
- *The quiet aisle problem.* The cake-aisle shopper is probably not browsing for a cake innovation.
- *The dessert problem.* Consumer's on-the-go, calorie conscious meal plans don't generally include a planned dessert.
- *The microwave problem.* Consumers might not believe it tastes good.

In sum, the small, fast-cake product didn't resonate with a compelling consumer need. But it would be a safe bet because the Dessert Bowl positioning fit nicely with the family-friendly Betty Crocker brand.

IMPLEMENTATION PHASE: LEAVING THE SECURITY OF FAMILY BEHIND

The consumer insights team really enjoyed the hot, gooey cake product. They feared that it would languish in the cake aisle under the Dessert Bowl name since this didn't capture the essence of what the food delivered. They explored who really are the indulgent treat customers. The data revealed that the heaviest buyers of premium treats are women without children. This focused the team on a target consumer: "What does she want?" They enlisted an ad agency and consultants to come up with a name that would appeal to "her." Several independently suggested the "Warm Delights" name, which became the brand name.

An interesting postscript to the team's brand name research: A competitor apparently liked not only the idea of a quick, gooey, microwavable dessert but also the "Dessert Bowls" name! You may now see its competitive product on your supermarket's shelves.

Targeting the on-the-go women who want a small, personal treat had marketing advantages:

- The $2.00 Warm Delights price compared favorably to the price of many single-serve indulgent treats.
- The product food message "warm, convenient, delightful" is compelling.
- On-the-go women's meal plans do include the occasional delicious treat.

One significant problem remained: the cake-aisle shopper is probably not browsing for an indulgent, single-serve treat.

The marketing team solved this shelving issue by using advertising and product displays outside the cake aisle. This would raise women's awareness of Warm Delights. Television advertising and in-store display programs are costly, so Warm Delights sales would have to be strong to pay back the investment.

Vivian Callaway and the team turned to market research to fine-tune the plan. The research put Warm Delights (and Dessert Bowls) on the shelf in real (different) stores. A few key findings emerged. First, the name "Warm Delights" beat "Dessert Bowls." Second, the Warm Delights with nuts simply wasn't easy to prepare, so nuts were removed. Third, the packaging with a disposable bowl beat the typical cake-mix packaging involving using your own bowl. Finally, by putting the actual product on supermarket shelves and in displays in the stores, sales volumes could be analyzed.

EVALUATION PHASE: TURNING THE PLAN INTO ACTION!

The marketing plan isn't action. Sales for "Warm Delights" required the marketing team to: (1) get the retailers to stock the product, preferably somewhere other than the cake aisle, and (2) appeal to consumers enough to have them purchase, like, and repurchase the product.

The initial acceptance of a product by retailers is important. But each store manager must experience good sales of Warm Delights to be motivated to keep its shelves restocked with the product. Also, the Warm Delights team must monitor the display activity in the store. Are the displays occurring as expected? Do the sales increase when a display is present? Watching distribution and display execution on a new product is very important so that sales shortfalls can be addressed proactively.

Did the customer buy one or two Warm Delights? Did the customer return for a second purchase a few weeks later? The syndicated services that sell household panel purchase data provide the answer. The Warm Delights team evaluates these reports to see if the number of people who tried the product matches with expectations and how the repeat purchases occur. Often, the "80/20 rule" applies. So, in the early months, is there a group of consumers that buys repeatedly and will fill this role?

For ongoing feedback, calls by Warm Delights consumers to the free consumer information line are monitored. This is a great source of real-time feedback. If a pattern emerges and these calls are mostly about the same problem, that is bad. However, when consumers call to say "thank you" or "it's great," that is good. This is an informal quick way to identify if the product is on track or further investigation is warranted.

GOOD MARKETING MAKES A DIFFERENCE

The team took personal and business risks by choosing a Warm Delights plan over the more conservative Dessert Bowl plan. Today, General Mills has loyal Warm Delights consumers who are open to trying new flavors, new sizes, and new forms. If you were a consultant to the Warm Delights team, what would you do to grow this brand?

Questions

1 What is the competitive set of desserts in which Warm Delights is located?

2 (*a*) Who is the target market? (*b*) What is the point of difference on the positioning for Warm Delights? (*c*) What are the potential opportunities and hindrances of the target market and positioning?

3 (*a*) What marketing research did Vivian Callaway execute? (*b*) What were the critical questions that she sought research and expert advice to get answers to? (*c*) How did this affect the product's marketing mix price, promotion, packaging, and distribution decisions?

4 (*a*) What initial promotional plan directed to consumers in the target market did Callaway use? (*b*) Why did this make sense to Callaway and her team when Warm Delights was launched?

5 If you were a consultant to Vivian Callaway, what product changes would you recommend to increase sales of Warm Delights?

APPENDIX C PLANNING A CAREER IN MARKETING

GETTING A JOB: THE PROCESS OF MARKETING YOURSELF

Getting a job is usually a lengthy process, and it is exactly that—a *process* that involves careful planning, implementation, and evaluation. You may have everything going for you: a respectable grade point average (GPA), relevant work experience, several extracurricular activities, superior communication skills, and demonstrated leadership qualities. Despite these, you still need to market yourself systematically and aggressively; after all, even the best products lie dormant on the retailer's shelves unless marketed effectively.

The process of getting a job involves the same activities marketing managers use to develop and introduce products and brands into the marketplace.[1] The only difference is that you are marketing yourself, not a product. You need to conduct marketing research by analyzing your personal qualities (performing a self-audit) and by identifying job opportunities. Based on your research results, select a target market—those job opportunities that are compatible with your interests, goals, skills, and abilities—and design a marketing mix around that target market. *You* are the "product";[2] you must decide how to "position" yourself in the job market. The price component of the marketing mix is the salary range and job benefits (such as health and life insurance, vacation time, and retirement benefits) that you hope to receive. Promotion involves communicating with prospective employers through written and electronic correspondence (advertising) and job interviews (personal selling). The place element focuses on how to reach prospective employers—at the career services office or job fairs, for example.

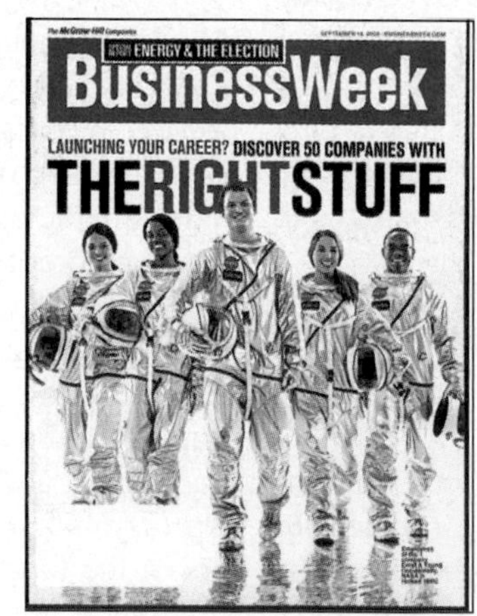

This appendix will assist you in career planning by (1) providing information about careers in marketing and (2) outlining a job search process.

CAREERS IN MARKETING

The diversity of marketing opportunities is reflected in the many types of marketing jobs, including product management, marketing research, and public relations. While many of these jobs are found at traditional employers such as manufacturers, retailers, and advertising agencies, there are also many opportunities in a variety of other types of organizations. Professional services such as law, accounting, and consulting firms, for example, have a growing need for marketing expertise. Similarly, nonprofit organizations such as universities, the performing arts, museums, and government agencies are developing marketing functions. Event organizations such as athletic teams, golf and tennis tournaments, and the Olympics are also new and visible sources of marketing jobs.

The diversity of marketing jobs is also changing because of changes in the marketing discipline. The growth of interactive marketing has created a variety of new jobs such as data miners and permission marketing managers. The growth of multichannel marketing has led to the need for communication channel managers and integration specialists. The increasing involvement and control by consumers has required public relations personnel to become social networking experts and consumer-generated content managers. Specialties in demand now include digital marketing, multicultural marketing, and viral marketing.[3]

Examples of companies that have opportunities for graduates with degrees in marketing include Altria,

Ameriprise Financial, Enterprise, Geico, Hewlett-Packard, Macy's, The Nielsen Company, Reynolds and Reynolds, Sherwin-Williams, and T-Mobile. Many of these companies have also appeared on *BusinessWeek*'s list of the "The Best Places to Start a Career."[4] Most of these career opportunities offer a chance to work with interesting people on stimulating and rewarding problems. Comments one product manager, "I love marketing as a career because there are different challenges every day."[5]

Recent studies of career paths and salaries suggest that marketing careers can also provide excellent opportunities for advancement and substantial pay. For example, one of every eight chief executive officers (CEOs) of the nation's 500 most valuable publicly held companies held positions in marketing before becoming CEO.[6] Similarly, reports of average starting salaries of college graduates indicate that salaries in marketing compare favorably with those in many other fields. The average starting salary of new marketing undergraduates in 2009 was $43,334, compared with $36,333 for journalism majors and $30,000 for advertising majors.[7] The future is likely to be even better. The U.S. Department of Labor reports that employment of advertising, marketing, promotions, public relations, and sales managers is expected to grow at a rate of 12 percent through 2016, spurred by intense domestic and global competition in products and services offered to consumers.[8]

Figure C–1 on the next page describes marketing occupations in seven major categories: product management and physical distribution, advertising and promotion, retailing, sales, marketing research, global marketing, and nonprofit marketing. One of these may be right for you. Additional sources of marketing career information are provided at the end of this appendix.

Product Management and Physical Distribution

Many organizations assign one manager the responsibility for a particular product. For example, Procter & Gamble (P&G) has separate managers for Tide, Cheer, Gain, and Bold. Product or brand managers are involved in all aspects of a product's marketing program, such as marketing research, sales, sales promotion, advertising, and pricing, as well as manufacturing. Managers of similar products typically report to a category manager, or marketing director, and may be part of a *product management team* to encourage interbrand cooperation.[9]

Product or brand managers are involved in all aspects of a product's marketing program.

College graduates with bachelor's and master's degrees—often in marketing and business—enter P&G as assistant brand managers, the only starting position in its product or brand groups. As assistant brand managers their responsibilities include developing a detailed marketing plan for a specific brand, and learning consumer, shopper, and customer insights. With good performance and demonstrated leadership, after three to six years the assistant brand manager is promoted to brand manager, then after four to eight years to associate marketing director, and after three to eight years to marketing director. These promotions often involve several brand groups. For example, a new employee might start as assistant brand manager for Folger's coffee, be promoted to brand manager for Crest toothpaste, become an associate marketing director for P&G's soap products, and finally a marketing director for a different brand group.[10]

Several other jobs related to product management (Figure C–1) deal with physical distribution issues such as storing the manufactured product (inventory), moving the product from the firm to the customers (transportation), and engaging in many other aspects of the manufacture and sale of goods. Prospects for these jobs are likely to increase as wholesalers try to differentiate themselves from competitors by increasing their involvement with selling activities and by offering more services such as installation, maintenance, assembly, and even repair.[11]

Advertising and Promotion

Although we may see hundreds of advertisements in a day, what we can't see easily is the fascinating and complex advertising profession. The entry-level advertising

Product Management and Physical Distribution

Product development manager creates a road map for new products by working with customers to determine their needs and with designers to create the product.
Product manager is responsible for integrating all aspects of a product's marketing program including research, sales, sales promotion, advertising, and pricing.
Supply chain manager oversees the part of a company that transports products to consumers and handles customer service.
Operations manager supervises warehousing and other physical distribution functions and often is directly involved in moving goods on the warehouse floor.
Inventory control manager forecasts demand for goods, coordinates production with plant managers, and tracks shipments to keep customers supplied.
Physical distribution specialist is an expert in the transportation and distribution of goods and also evaluates the costs and benefits of different types of transportation.

Sales

Direct or retail salesperson sells directly to consumers in the salesperson's office, the consumer's home, or a retailer's store.
Trade salesperson calls on retailers or wholesalers to sell products for manufacturers.
Industrial or semitechnical salesperson sells supplies and services to businesses.
Complex or professional salesperson sells complicated or custom-designed products to businesses. This requires understanding of the product technology.
Customer service manager maintains good relations with customers by coordinating the sales staff, marketing management, and physical distribution management.

Nonprofit Marketing

Marketing manager develops and directs marketing campaigns, fund-raising, and public relations.

Global Marketing

Global marketing manager is an expert in world-trade agreements, international competition, cross-cultural analysis, and global market-entry strategies.

Advertising and Promotion

Account executive maintains contact with clients while coordinating the creative work among artists and copywriters. Account executives work as partners with the client to develop marketing strategy.
Media buyer deals with media sales representatives in selecting advertising media and analyzes the value of media being purchased.
Copywriter works with art director in conceptualizing advertisements and writes the text of print or radio ads or the storyboards of television ads.
Art director handles the visual component of advertisements.
Sales promotion manager designs promotions for consumer products and works at an ad agency or a sales promotion agency.
Public relations manager develops written or video messages for the public and handles contacts with the press.
Internet marketing manager develops and executes the e-business marketing plan and manages all aspects of the advertising, promotion, and content for the online business.

Retailing

Buyer selects products a store sells, surveys consumer trends, and evaluates the past performance of products and suppliers.
Store manager oversees the staff and services at a store.

Marketing Research

Project manager for the supplier coordinates and oversees the market studies for a client.
Account executive for the supplier serves as a liaison between client and market research firm, like an advertising agency account executive.
In-house project director acts as project manager (see above) for the market studies conducted by the firm for which he or she works.
Competitive intelligence researcher uses new information technologies to monitor the competitive environment.
Data miner compiles and analyzes consumer data to identify behavior patterns, preferences, and user profiles for personalized marketing programs.

Source: Adapted from Lila B. Stair and Leslie Stair, *Careers in Marketing* (New York: McGraw-Hill, 2008); and David W. Rosenthal and Michael A. Powell, *Careers in Marketing*, ©1984, pp. 352–54.

FIGURE C–1
Seven major categories of marketing occupations

positions filled every year include jobs with a variety of firms. Advertising professionals often remark that they find their jobs appealing because the days are not routine and they involve creative activities with many interesting people.

Advertising positions are available in three kinds of organizations: advertisers, media companies, and agencies. Advertisers include manufacturers, retail stores, service firms, and many other types of companies. Often they have an advertising department responsible for preparing and placing their own ads. Advertising careers are also possible with the media: television, radio stations, magazines, and newspapers. Finally, advertising agencies offer job opportunities through their use of account management, research, media, and creative services.

Starting positions with advertisers and advertising agencies are often as assistants to employees with several years of experience. An assistant copywriter facilitates the development of the message, or copy, in an advertisement. An assistant art director participates in the design of visual components of advertisements. Entry-level media positions involve buying the media that will carry the ad or selling airtime on radio or television or page space in print media. Advancement to supervisory positions requires planning skills, a broad vision, and an affinity for spotting an effective advertising idea. Students interested in advertising should develop good communication skills and try to gain advertising experience through summer employment opportunities or internships.[12]

Growing interest in integrated marketing programs has increased opportunities for sales promotion managers, public relations managers, and Internet marketing managers. These positions require an understanding of the potential synergy of all promotional tools. Responsibilities include the design and implementation of sweepstakes, sampling programs, events and partnerships, newsletters, press releases and conferences, e-mail promotions, Web-content management, and permission marketing campaigns. In addition, as advertisers increase search marketing budgets, the number of search-marketing positions is increasing![13]

Retailing offers careers in merchandise management and store management.

Retailing

There are two separate career paths in retailing: merchandise management and store management (see Figure C–2). The key position in merchandising is that of a buyer, who is responsible for selecting merchandise, guiding the promotion of the merchandise, setting prices, bargaining with wholesalers, training the salesforce, and monitoring the competitive environment. The buyer must also be able to organize and coordinate many critical activities under severe time constraints. In contrast, store management involves the supervision of personnel in all departments and the general management of all facilities, equipment, and merchandise displays. In addition, store managers are responsible for the financial performance of each department and for the store as a whole. Typical positions beyond the store manager level include district manager, regional manager, and divisional vice president.[14]

Most starting jobs in retailing are trainee positions. A trainee is usually placed in a management training program and then given a position as an assistant buyer or assistant department manager. Advancement and responsibility can be achieved quickly because there is a shortage of qualified personnel in retailing and because superior performance of an individual is quickly reflected in sales and profits—two visible measures of success. In addition, the growth of multichannel retailing has created new

FIGURE C–2
Two common retailing career paths include merchandise management and store management.

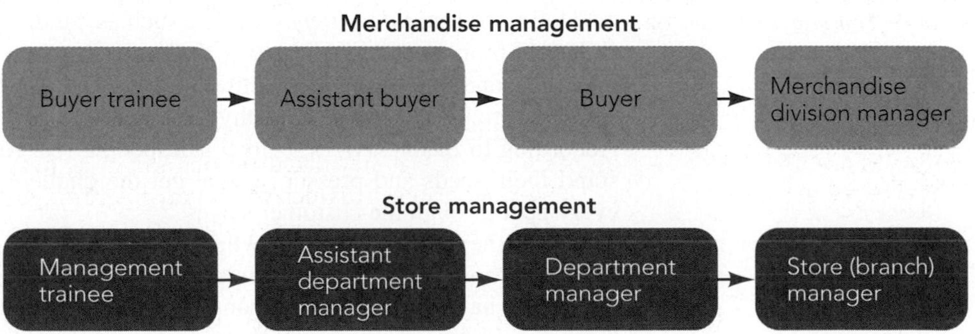

FIGURE C–3
Employment opportunities in selected sales occupations (2006 to 2016)

Occupation	2006 Employment	2016 Employment	Percentage Change 2006–2016	Average Annual Growth
Insurance sales agents	436,000	492,000	13%	5,600
Real estate brokers and sales agents	564,000	624,000	11	6,240
Retail salespersons	4,477,000	5,034,000	12	55,700
Manufacturers' and wholesalers' sales representatives	1,973,000	2,155,000	9	18,200
Securities and financial services sales agents	320,000	399,000	25	7,900

Source: "The 2006–2016 Job Outlook in Brief," *Occupational Outlook Quarterly* (Washington, DC: U.S. Department of Labor, Bureau of Labor Statistics, Spring 2008).

Xerox is well-known for its sales career opportunities.

opportunities such as Web site management and online merchandise procurement. The Bureau of Labor Statistics reports that retailing has a large number of openings and will be one of the fastest-growing employment opportunities in the future.[15]

Sales

College graduates from many disciplines are attracted to sales positions because of the increasingly professional nature of selling jobs and the many opportunities they can provide. A selling career offers benefits that are hard to match in any other field: (1) the opportunity for rapid advancement (into management or to new territories and accounts); (2) the potential for extremely attractive compensation; (3) the development of personal satisfaction, feelings of accomplishment, and increased self-confidence; and (4) independence—salespeople often have almost complete control over their time and activities.

Employment opportunities in sales occupations are found in a wide variety of organizations, including insurance agencies, retailers, and financial service firms (see Figure C–3). In addition, many salespeople work as manufacturer's representatives for organizations that have selling responsibilities for several manufacturers.[16] Activities in sales jobs include *selling duties*, such as prospecting for customers, demonstrating the product, or quoting prices; *sales-support duties*, such as handling complaints and helping solve technical problems; and *nonselling duties*, such as preparing reports, attending sales meetings, and monitoring competitive activities. Salespeople who can deal with these varying activities and have empathy for customers are critical to a company's success. According to *BusinessWeek*, "Great salespeople feel for their customers. They understand their needs and pressures; they get the challenges of their business. They see every deal through the customer's eyes."[17]

One of the fastest areas of growth in sales is in the direct marketing industry. Interest in information technology, customer relationship management (CRM), and integrated marketing has increased the demand for contact with customers. For many firms this means increasing the amount of time salespeople spend with clients; for other firms

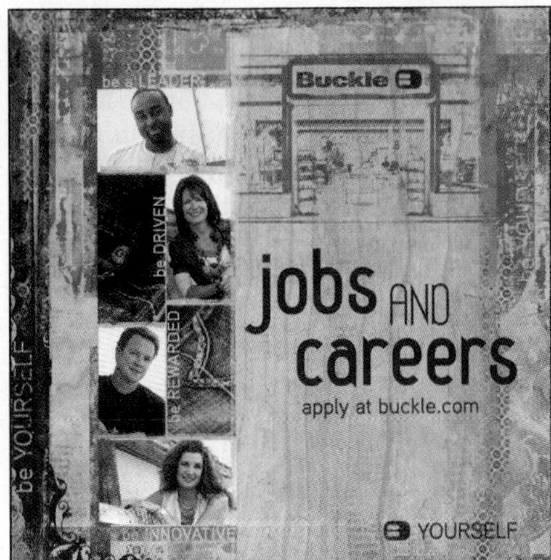

Buckle is an example of a company that encourages students to think about a job and a career.

it means increased use of Web conferencing technology; for still others it means sophisticated e-mail marketing. *Sales & Marketing Management* magazine's People's Choice Awards recently recognized companies such as GoToMeeting, Salesforce.com, and WebEx for providing innovative solutions that provide better relationships between salespeople and customers. Consultant Susan Aldrich observes that customers always say, "I want you to know about me and offer me things that are relevant to me."[18]

Marketing Research

Marketing researchers play important roles in many organizations today. They are responsible for obtaining, analyzing, and interpreting data to facilitate making marketing decisions. This means marketing researchers are basically problem solvers. Success in the area requires not only an understanding of statistical analysis, research methods, and programming, but also a broad base of marketing knowledge, writing and verbal presentation skills, and an ability to communicate with colleagues and clients.[19] Individuals who are inquisitive, methodical, analytical, and solution oriented find the field particularly rewarding.

The responsibilities of the men and women currently working in the market research industry include defining the marketing problem, designing the questions, selecting the sample, collecting and analyzing the data, and, finally, reporting the results of the research. These jobs are available in three kinds of organizations. *Marketing research consulting firms* contract with large companies to provide research about their products or services.[20] *Advertising agencies* may provide research services to help clients with questions related to advertising and promotional problems. Finally, some companies have an *in-house research staff* to design and execute their research projects. Online marketing research, which is likely to become the most common form of marketing research in the near future, requires understanding of new tools such as dynamic scripting, response validation, intercept sampling, instant messaging surveys, and online consumer panels.[21]

Although marketing researchers may start as assistants performing routine tasks, they quickly advance to broader responsibilities. Survey design, interviewing, report writing, and all aspects of the research process create a challenging career. In addition, research projects typically deal with such diverse problems as consumer motivation, pricing, forecasting, and competition. Successful candidates "like what they're doing and get excited over their work, whether it be listening to a focus group or running a complex datamining model," according to Carolyn Marconi, director of marketing research for the Vanguard Group, Inc.[22]

International Careers

Many of the careers just described can be found in international settings—in large multinational U.S. corporations, small- to medium-size firms with export business, and franchises. The international consulting firm, Accenture, for example, has thousands of consultants around the world. Similarly, many franchises such as Blockbuster Entertainment, which has 8,000 locations, are rapidly expanding outside of the United States.[23] The changes in the European Union, Brazil, Russia, India, China, and other growing markets are likely to provide many opportunities for international careers. Several methods of gaining international experience are possible. For example, some companies may alternate periods of work at domestic locations with assignments outside of the United States. In addition, working for a firm with headquarters outside of the United States at one of its local offices may be appealing. In many organizations, international experience has become a necessity for promotion and career advancement. "If you are going to succeed, an expatriate assignment is essential," says Eric Kraus of Gillette Co. in Boston.[24]

Applicants for international positions need language skills and an ability to adapt to different business models, management styles, and local practices. In addition, as multinational firms use worldwide communication technologies to build global teams of people who have never met, collaboration skills become increasingly important. Each year Accenture puts 400 of its managers into international groups who meet virtually and in many international locations to learn how to utilize the company's worldwide resources. Similarly, IBM uses Internet-based services to make it possible for its 360,000 employees to "work as one virtual team."[25]

THE JOB SEARCH PROCESS

Activities you should consider during your job search process include assessing yourself, identifying job opportunities, preparing your résumé and related correspondence, and going on job interviews.

Assessing Yourself

You must know your product—you—so that you can market yourself effectively to prospective employers. Consequently, a critical first step in your job search is conducting a self-inquiry or self-assessment. This activity involves understanding your interests, abilities, personality, preferences, and individual style. You must be confident that you know what work environment is best for you, what makes you happy, the balance you seek between personal and professional activities, and how you can be most effective at reaching your goals. This process helps ensure that you are matching your profile to the right job, or as business consultant and author Jim Collins explains, "Finding the right seat on the bus."[26]

Asking Key Questions A self-analysis, in part, entails asking yourself some very important and difficult questions (see Figure C–4). It is critical that you respond to the questions honestly, because your answers ultimately will be used as a guide in your job selection.[27] A less-than-candid appraisal of yourself might result in a job mismatch.

Identifying Strengths and Weaknesses After you have addressed the questions posed in Figure C–4, you are ready to identify your strengths and weaknesses. To do so, draw a vertical line down the middle of a sheet of paper and label one side of the paper "strengths" and the other side "weaknesses." Based on your answers to the questions, record your strong and weak points in their respective column. Ideally, this cataloging should be done over a few days to give you adequate time to reflect on your attributes. In addition, you might seek input from others who know you well (such as parents, close relatives, friends, professors, or employers) and can offer more objective views. They might even evaluate you on the questions in Figure C–4, and you can compare the results with your own evaluation. A hypothetical list of strengths and weaknesses is shown in Figure C–5 on page 606.

What skills are most important? The answer, of course, varies by occupation and employer. Recent studies, however, suggest that problem-solving skills, communication skills, interpersonal skills, analytical and computer skills, and leadership skills are all valued by employers. Personal characteristics employers seek in a job candidate include honesty, integrity, motivation, initiative, self-confidence, flexibility, and enthusiasm. Finally, most employers also look for work experience, internship experience, or co-op experience.[28]

Interests

How do I like to spend my time?
Do I enjoy working with people?
Do I like working with tangible things?
Do I enjoy working with data?
Am I a member of many organizations?
Do I enjoy physical activities?
Do I like to read?

Abilities

Am I adept at analysis?
What are my hardware, software, and operating system skills?
Do I have good verbal and written communication skills?
What special talents do I have?
At which abilities do I wish I were more adept?

Education

How have my courses and extracurricular activities prepared me for a specific job?
Which were my best subjects? My worst?
Is my GPA a good indication of my academic ability? Why?
Do I aspire to a graduate degree? Before beginning my job?
Why did I choose my major?

Personal Goals

What are my short-term and long-term goals? Why?
Am I career oriented, or do I have broader interests?
What are my career goals?
What jobs are likely to help me achieve my goals?
What do I hope to be doing in 5 years? In 10 years?
What do I want out of life?
What work–life balance do I prefer?

Personality

What are my good and bad traits?
Am I competitive?
Do I work well with others?
Am I outspoken?
Am I a leader or a follower?
Do I work well under pressure?
Do I work quickly, or am I methodical?
Do I get along well with others?
Am I ambitious?
Do I work well independently of others?

Desired Job Environment

Am I willing to relocate? Why?
Do I have a geographical preference? Why?
Would I mind traveling in my job?
Do I have to work for a large or nationally known firm to be satisfied?
Must my job offer rapid promotion opportunities?
If I could design my own job, what characteristics would it have?
How important is high initial salary to me?

Experience

What previous jobs have I held? What were my responsibilities in each job?
What internships or co-op positions have I held? What were my responsibilities?
What volunteer positions have I held? What were my responsibilities?
Were any of my jobs or positions applicable to positions I may be seeking? How?
What did I like the most about my previous jobs? Like the least?
If I had it to do over again, would I work in these jobs? Why?

FIGURE C–4
Questions to ask in your self-analysis

Taking Job-Related Tests Personality and vocational interest tests, provided by many colleges and universities, can give you other ideas about yourself. After tests have been administered and scored, test takers meet with testing service counselors to discuss the results. Test results generally suggest jobs for which students have an inclination. The most common tests at the college level are the Strong Interest Inventory and the Campbell Interest and Skill Survey. Some counseling centers and career coaches also use the Myers-Briggs® Type Indicator personality inventory and the Peoplemap™ assessments to help identify professions you may enjoy.[29] If you have not already done so, you may wish to see whether your school offers such testing services.

Identifying Your Job Opportunities

To identify and analyze the job market, you must conduct some marketing research to determine what industries *and* companies offer promising job opportunities that relate to the results of your self-analysis. Several sources that can help in your search are discussed next.

Career Services Office Your career services office is an excellent source of job information. Personnel in that office can: (1) inform you about which companies

FIGURE C–5
Hypothetical list of a job candidate's strengths and weaknesses

Strengths	Weaknesses
I enjoy being with people.	I am very demanding of team members.
I am an avid reader.	I have minimal work experience.
I have good communication skills.	I have a mediocre GPA.
I am involved in many extracurricular activities.	I am sometimes impatient.
I work well with others.	I resent close supervision.
I work well independently.	I work methodically (slowly).
I am honest and dependable.	I will not relocate.
I am willing to travel in the job.	I procrastinate unless there is a deadline.
I am a good problem solver.	I lack a customer orientation.
I have a good sense of humor.	I have poor technical skills.

Campus career centers and online databases such as Monster.com are excellent sources for job information.

will be recruiting on campus; (2) alert you to unexpected job openings; (3) advise you about short-term and long-term career prospects; (4) offer advice on résumé construction; (5) assess your interviewing strengths and weaknesses; and (6) help you evaluate a job offer. In addition, the office usually contains a variety of written materials focusing on different industries and companies and tips on job hunting. One major publication available in most career services offices is the National Association of Colleges and Employers publication *Job Choices*, which contains a list of employers, kinds of job openings for college graduates, and whom to contact about jobs in those firms. Another publication for students is *jobpostings*, which is published two times during the academic year and distributed to more than 550 colleges and universities across the United States.

Online Career and Employment Services Many companies no longer make frequent on-campus visits. Instead, they may use the many online services available to advertise an employment opportunity or to search for candidate information. The National Association of Colleges and Employers, for example, maintains a site on the Internet called JobWeb (www.jobweb.org). Similarly, Monster.com and Careerbuilder.com are online databases of employment ads, candidate résumés, and other career-related information. Some of the information resources include career guidance, a cover letter library, occupational profiles, résumé templates, and networking services.[30] Employers may contact students directly when the candidate's qualifications meet their specific job requirements. The advantage of this system for students is that regardless of the size or location of the campus they are attending, many companies have access to their résumé. Some job boards even allow applicants to post audio and video clips of themselves. One advantage for recruiters is that some of the job boards utilize software for performing background verification.[31] Your school's career center may also have a home page that offers online job search information and links to other Internet sites.

Library The public or college library can provide you with reference material that, among other things, describes successful firms and their operations, defines the content of various jobs, and forecasts job opportunities. For example, *Fortune* publishes a list of the 1,000 largest U.S. and global companies and their respective sales and profits, and Dun & Bradstreet publishes directories of more than 26 million companies in the United States. The *Occupational Outlook Handbook* is an annual publication of the U.S. Department of Labor that provides projections for specific job prospects, as well as information pertaining to those jobs. A librarian can indicate reference materials that will be most pertinent to *your* job search.

Advertisements Help-wanted advertisements provide an overview of what is happening in the job market. Local (particularly Sunday editions) and college newspapers, trade press (such as *Marketing News* or *Advertising Age*), and business magazines (such as *Sales & Marketing Management*) contain classified advertisement sections that generally have job opening announcements, often for entry-level positions. Reviewing the want ads can help you identify what kinds of positions are available and their requirements and job titles, which firms offer certain kinds of jobs, and levels of compensation.

Employment Agencies An employment agency can make you aware of several job opportunities very quickly because of its large number of job listings available through computer databases. Many agencies specialize in a particular field (such as sales and marketing). The advantages of using an agency include that it: (1) reduces the cost of a job search by bringing applicants and employers together, (2) often has exclusive job listings available only by working through the agency, (3) performs much of the job search for you, and (4) tries to find a job that is compatible with your qualifications and interests.[32] In the past, some employment agencies have engaged in questionable business practices, so check with the Better Business Bureau or your business contacts to determine the quality of the various agencies.

Personal Contacts and Networking An important source of job information that students often overlook is their personal contacts. People you know often may know of job opportunities, so you should advise them that you're looking for a job. Relatives and friends might aid your job search. Instructors you know well and business contacts can provide a wealth of information about potential jobs and even help arrange an interview with a prospective employer. They may also help arrange *informational interviews* with employers that do not have immediate openings. These interviews allow you to collect information about an industry or an employer and give you an advantage if a position does become available. It is a good idea to leave your résumé with all your personal contacts so they can pass it along to those who might be in need of your services.

Student organizations (such as the student chapter of the American Marketing Association and Pi Sigma Epsilon, the professional sales fraternity) may be sources of job opportunities, particularly if they are involved with the business community. Local chapters of professional business organizations (such as the American Marketing Association and Sales and Marketing Executives International) also can provide job information; contacting their chapter president is a first step in seeking assistance from these organizations. Creating a network of professional contacts is one of the most important career planning activities you can undertake.[33]

There are many popular social networking sites available to job seekers. LinkedIn, for example has 50 million users, including recruiters. Other sites include Plaxo, Twitter, Jobster, Facebook, Craigslist, MyWorkster, VisualCV, JobFox, and Ecademy. Some of the sites allow users to create and post a traditional résumé while others facilitate personalized Web pages with video, audio, images, and even work samples. Using all or many of these sites provides greater exposure. Remember, however, to be consistent in the image and information presented online.[34]

State Employment Office State employment offices have listings of job opportunities in their state and counselors to help arrange a job interview for you. Although state employment offices perform functions similar to employment agencies, they differ in listing only job opportunities in their state and providing their services free.

Direct Contact Another means of obtaining job information is direct contact—personally communicating to prospective employers (either by mail, e-mail, or in person) that you would be interested in pursuing job opportunities with them. Often you may not even know whether jobs are available in these firms. If you correspond with the companies in writing, a letter of introduction and an attached résumé should serve as your initial form of communication. One way to make direct contact with companies is to attend a career or job fair. These events allow many employers, recruiters, and prospective job seekers to meet in one location.[35] Your goals in direct contact are to create a positive impression and, ultimately, to arrange a job interview.

Writing Your Résumé

A résumé is a document that communicates to prospective employers who you are. An employer reading a résumé is looking for a snapshot of your qualifications to decide if you should be invited to a job interview. It is imperative that you design a résumé that presents you in a favorable light and allows you to get to that next important step.[36] Personnel in your career services office can provide assistance in designing résumés.

The Résumé Itself A well-constructed résumé generally contains up to nine major sections: (1) identification (name, address, telephone number, and e-mail address); (2) job or career objective; (3) educational background; (4) honors and awards; (5) work experience or history; (6) skills or capabilities (that pertain to a particular kind of job for which you may be interviewing); (7) extracurricular activities; (8) personal interests; and (9) personal references.[37] There is no universally accepted format for a résumé, but three are more frequently used: chronological, functional, and targeted. A *chronological* format presents your work experience and education according to the time sequence in which they occurred (i.e., in chronological order). If you have had several jobs or attended several schools, this approach is useful to highlight what you have done. With a *functional* format, you group your experience into skill categories that emphasize your strengths. This option is particularly appropriate if you have no experience or only minimal experience related to your chosen field. A *targeted* format focuses on the capabilities you have for a specific job. This alternative is desirable if you know what job you want and are qualified for it. In any of the formats, if possible, you should include quantitative information about your accomplishments and experience, such as "increased sales revenue by 20 percent" for the year you managed a retail clothing store. A résumé that illustrates the chronological format is shown in Figure C–6.[38]

Technology has created a need for a new type of résumé—the digital résumé. Although traditional versions of résumés may be visually appealing, today most career experts suggest that résumés accommodate delivery through mail, e-mail, and fax machines. In addition, résumés must accommodate employers who use scanning technology to enter résumés into their own databases or who search commercial online databases. To fully utilize online opportunities, an electronic résumé with a popular font (e.g., New Times Roman) and relatively large font size (e.g., 10–14 pt.)—and without italic text, graphics, shading, underlining, or vertical lines—must be available. In addition, because online recruiting starts with a keyword search, it is important to include keywords, focus on nouns rather than verbs, and avoid abbreviations. Related to this use of technology, don't forget that many employers may visit social networking sites such as Facebook and MySpace, or may simply "Google" your name, to see what comes up. Review your online profiles before you start your job search to provide a positive image![39]

Letter Accompanying a Résumé The letter accompanying a résumé, or cover letter, serves as the job candidate's introduction. As a result, it must gain the

FIGURE C–6
A chronological résumé presents your education and work experience in the sequence in which they occurred.

SALLY WINTER

Campus address (until 6/1/2010):	Home address:
Elm Street Apartments #2B	123 Front Street
College Town, Ohio 44042	Teaneck, NJ 07666
Phone: (555) 424-1648	Phone: (555) 836-4995
swinter@osu.stu.edu	

Education
B.S. in Business Administration, Ohio State University, 2010, cum laude—3.3 overall GPA—3.6 GPA in major

Work Experience
Paid for 70 percent of my college expenses through the following part-time and summer jobs:

Legal Secretary, Smith, Lee & Jones, Attorneys at Law, New York, NY—summer 2008
- Took dictation and transcribed tapes of legal proceedings
- Typed contracts and other legal documents
- Reorganized client files for easier access
- Answered the phone and screened calls for the partners

Salesclerk, College Varsity Shop, College Town, Ohio—2007–2009 academic years
- Helped customers with buying decisions
- Arranged stock and helped with window displays
- Assisted in year-end inventories
- Took over responsibilities of store manager when she was on vacation or ill

Assistant Manager, Treasure Place Gift Shop, Teaneck, NJ—summers and Christmas vacations—2006–2009
- Supervised two salesclerks
- Helped select merchandise at trade shows
- Handled daily accounting
- Worked comfortably under pressure during busy seasons

Campus Activities
- Elected captain of the women's varsity tennis team for two years
- Worked as a reporter and night editor on campus newspaper for two years
- Elected historian for Mortar Board chapter, a senior women's honorary society

Computer Skills
- Word, Excel, PowerPoint, Outlook

Personal Interests
- Collecting antique clocks, listening to jazz, swimming

References Available on Request

attention and interest of the reader or it will fail to give the incentive to examine the résumé carefully. In designing a letter to accompany your résumé, address the following issues:[40]

- Address the letter to a specific person.
- Identify the position for which you are applying and how you heard of it.
- Indicate why you are applying for the position.
- Summarize your most significant credentials and qualifications.
- Refer the reader to the enclosed résumé.
- Request a personal interview, and advise the reader when and where you can be reached.

A sample letter comprising these six factors is presented in Figure C–7 on the next page.

FIGURE C–7
A sample letter accompanying a résumé provides the job candidate's introduction.

Sally Winter
Elm Street Apartments, #2B
College Town, Ohio 44042
January 31, 2010

Mr. J. B. Jones
Sales Manager
Hilltop Manufacturing Company
Minneapolis, MN 55406

Dear Mr. Jones:

Dr. William Johnson, Professor of Business Administration at the Ohio State University, recently suggested that I write to you concerning your opening and my interest in a sales position. With a B.S. degree in business administration and courses in personal selling and sales management, I am confident that I could make a positive contribution to your firm.

During the past four years, I have been a salesclerk in a clothing store and an assistant manager in a gift shop. These two positions required my performing a variety of duties including selling, purchasing, stocking, and supervising. As a result, I have developed an appreciation for the viewpoints of the customer, salesperson, and management. Given my background and high energy level, I feel that I am particularly well qualified to assume a sales position in your company.

My enclosed résumé better highlights my education and experience. My extracurricular activities should strengthen and support my abilities to serve as a sales representative.

I am eager to talk with you because I feel I can demonstrate to you why I am a strong candidate for the position. I have friends in Minneapolis with whom I could stay on weekends, so Fridays or Mondays would be ideal for an appointment. I will call you in a week to see if we can arrange a mutually convenient time for a meeting. I am hopeful that your schedule will allow this.

Thank you for your kind consideration. If you would like some additional information, please feel free to contact me at (555) 424-1648. I look forward to talking with you.

Sincerely,

Sally Winter

enclosure

Interviewing for Your Job

The job interview is a conversation between a prospective employer and a job candidate that focuses on determining whether the employer's needs can be satisfied by the candidate's qualifications. The interview is a "make or break" situation: If the interview goes well, you have increased your chances of receiving a job offer; if it goes poorly, you probably will be eliminated from further consideration.

Preparing for a Job Interview To be successful in a job interview, you must prepare for it so you can exhibit professionalism and indicate to a prospective employer that you are serious about the job. When preparing for the interview, several critical activities need to be performed.

Before the interview, gather facts about the industry, the prospective employer, and the job. Relevant information might include: the general description for the occupation; the firm's products or services; the firm's size, number of employees, and financial and competitive position; the requirements of the position; and the name and personality of the interviewer. Obtaining this information will provide you with additional insight into the firm and help you formulate questions to ask the interviewer. This information might be gleaned, for example, from corporate annual reports, *The Wall Street*

Journal, Moody's manuals, Standard & Poor's *Register of Corporations, Directors, and Executives, The Directory of Corporate Affiliations*, selected issues of *Business-Week*, or trade publications. If information is not readily available, you could call the company and indicate that you wish to obtain some information about the firm before your interview.[41]

Preparation for the job interview should also involve role playing, or pretending that you are in the "hot seat" being interviewed. Before role playing, anticipate questions interviewers may pose and how you might address them (see Figure C–8). Do not memorize your answers, though, because you want to appear spontaneous, yet logical and intelligent. Nonetheless, it is helpful to practice how you might respond to the questions. In addition, develop questions you might ask the interviewer that are important and of concern to you (see Figure C–9 on the next page). "It's an opportunity to show the recruiter how smart you are," comments one recruiter.[42]

When role playing, you and someone with whom you feel comfortable should engage in a mock interview. Afterward, ask the stand-in interviewer to candidly appraise your interview content and style. You may wish to make a video of the mock interview; ask the personnel in your career services office where video equipment can be obtained for this purpose.

Before the job interview you should attend to several details. Know the exact time and place of the interview; write them down—do not rely on your memory. Get the full company name straight. Find out what the interviewer's name is and how to pronounce it. Bring a notepad and pen along to the interview, in case you need to record anything. Make certain that your appearance is clean, neat, professional, and conservative.

FIGURE C–8
Anticipate questions frequently asked by interviewers to practice how you might respond.

Interviewer Questions
1. How would you describe yourself?
2. What do you consider to be your greatest strengths and weaknesses?
3. Describe your most rewarding college experiences.
4. What do you see yourself doing in 5 years? In 10 years?
5. What are three important leadership qualities that you have demonstrated?
6. What do you really want out of life?
7. What are your long-range and short-range career goals?
8. Why did you choose your college major?
9. In which extracurricular activities did you participate? Why?
10. What jobs have you enjoyed the most? The least? Why?
11. How has your previous work experience prepared you for a marketing career?
12. Why do you want to work for our company?
13. What qualifications do you think a person needs to be successful in a company like ours?
14. Describe a creative idea you produced that led to the success of a project.
15. What criteria are you using to evaluate the company for which you hope to work?
16. Describe a project where you worked as part of a team.
17. What can I tell you about our company?
18. Are you willing to relocate?
19. Are you willing to spend at least six months as a trainee?
20. Why should we hire you?

FIGURE C–9
Interviewees should develop questions about topics that are important to them.

Interviewee Questions	
1.	Why would a job candidate want to work for your firm?
2.	What makes your firm different from its competitors?
3.	What is the company's promotion policy?
4.	Describe the typical first-year assignment for this job.
5.	How is an employee evaluated?
6.	What are the opportunities for personal growth?
7.	Do you have a training program?
8.	What are the company's plans for future growth?
9.	What is the retention rate of people in the position for which I am interviewing?
10.	How can you use my skills?
11.	Why is this position vacant?
12.	How would you describe the ideal candidate?
13.	Why do you enjoy working for your firm?
14.	How much responsibility would I have in this job?
15.	What is the corporate culture in your firm?

And be punctual; arriving tardy to a job interview gives you an appearance of being unreliable.

Succeeding in Your Job Interview You have done your homework, and at last the moment arrives and it is time for the interview. Although you may experience some apprehension, view the interview as a conversation between the prospective employer and you. Both of you are in the interview to look over the other party, to see whether there might be a good match. When you meet the interviewer, greet him or her by name, be cheerful, smile, and maintain good eye contact. Take your lead from the interviewer at the outset. Sit down after the interviewer has offered you a seat. Sit up straight in your chair, and look alert and interested at all times. Appear relaxed, not tense. Be enthusiastic.

During the interview, be yourself. If you try to behave in a manner that is different from the real you, your attempt may be transparent to the interviewer or you may ultimately get the job but discover that you aren't suited for it. In addition to assessing how well your skills match those of the job, the interviewer will probably try to assess your long-term interest in the firm.

View the interview as a conversation between the prospective employer and you.

As the interview comes to a close, leave it on a positive note. Thank the interviewer for his or her time and the opportunity to discuss employment opportunities. If you are still interested in the job, express this to the interviewer. The interviewer will normally tell you what the employer's next step is—probably a visit to the company.[43] Rarely will a job offer be made at the end of the initial interview. If it is and you want the job, accept the offer; if there is any doubt in your mind about the job, however, ask for time to consider the offer.

Following Up on Your Job Interview After your interview, send a thank-you note to the interviewer and indicate whether you are still interested in the job. If you want to continue pursuing the job, polite persistence may help you get it. The thank-you note is a gesture of appreciation and a way of maintaining visibility with the interviewer. (Remember the adage, "Out of sight, out of mind.") Even if the interview did not go well, the thank-you note may impress the interviewer so much that his or her opinion of you changes. After you have sent your thank-you note, you may wish to call the prospective employer to determine the status of the hiring decision. If the interviewer told you when you would hear from the employer, make your telephone call *after* this date (assuming, of course, that you have not yet heard from the employer); if the interviewer did not tell you when you would be contacted, make your telephone call a week or so after you have sent your thank-you note. While e-mail is a common form of communication today, it is often viewed as less personal than a letter or telephone call, so be confident that e-mail is preferred before using it to correspond with the interviewer.[44]

As you conduct your follow-up, be persistent but polite. If you are too eager, one of two things could happen to prevent you from getting the job: The employer might feel that you are a nuisance and would exhibit such behavior on the job, or the employer may perceive that you are desperate for the job and thus are not a viable candidate.

Handling Rejection You have put your best efforts into your job search. You developed a well-designed résumé and prepared carefully for the job interview. Even the interview appears to have gone well. Nevertheless, a prospective employer may send you a rejection letter. ("We are sorry that our needs and your superb qualification don't match.") Although you will probably be disappointed, not all interviews lead to a job offer because there normally are more candidates than there are positions available.

If you receive a rejection letter, you should think back through the interview. What appeared to go right? What went wrong? Perhaps personnel from your career services office can shed light on the problem, particularly if they are in the custom of having interviewers rate each interviewee. Try to learn lessons to apply in future interviews. Keep interviewing and gaining interview experience; your persistence will eventually pay off.

SELECTED SOURCES OF MARKETING CAREER INFORMATION

The following is a selected list of marketing information sources that you should find useful during your academic studies and professional career.

Business and Marketing Publications

Business Periodicals Index (BPI) (New York: H.W. Wilson Company). This is a monthly (except August) index of almost 527 periodicals from all fields of business and marketing.

Scott Dacko, *The Advanced Dictionary of Marketing: Putting Theory to Use* (Oxford: Oxford University Press, 2008). This dictionary focuses on leading-edge terminology for individuals who are serious about the theory and practice of marketing. Each term includes six elements: description, key insights, key words, implications, applications, and a bibliography.

Anne Beall, *Strategic Market Research: A Guide to Conducting Research that Drives Businesses* (Bloomington, IN: Beall Research and Training, Inc., 2008). This practical book discusses the importance of designing research around strategic questions, how to select the correct research technique, data analysis, interpreting results, and how to avoid common pitfalls.

Hoover's Handbook of World Business (Austin, TX: Hoover's Business Press, 2009). This source provides detailed information about companies outside of the United States, including firms from Canada, Europe, Japan, China, India, and Taiwan.

Rob Duncan, *Competitive Intelligence: Fast, Cheap & Ethical* (Bloomington IN: Author House, 2008). This book provides a competitive intelligence process that allows marketers to find, interpret, and respond to information about competitors. In addition, it offers many low-cost, legal, and ethical tools and techniques.

Barbara Lewis and Dale Littler, eds., *The Blackwell Encyclopedic Dictionary of Marketing* (Cambridge, MA: Blackwell Publishers, 2008). Part of the 10-volume *Blackwell Encyclopedia of Management*, this book provides clear, concise, up-to-the-minute, and highly informative definitions and explanations of the key concepts and terms in marketing management, consumer behavior, segmentation, organizational marketing, pricing, communications, retailing and distribution, product management, market research, and international marketing.

Jean L. Sears and Marilyn K. Moody, *Using Government Information Sources*, 3rd ed. (Phoenix, AZ: Oryx Press, 2001). An easy-to-use manual arranged by topics such as consumer expenditures, business and industry statistics, economic indicators,, and projections. Each chapter contains a search strategy, a checklist of courses, and a narrative description of the sources.

Cynthia L. Shamel, *Introduction to Online Market & Industry Research* (Mason, OH: Thomson Learning, 2004). This comprehensive reference provides search strategies and valuable data source information, including rankings of data sources, for industry researchers.

Linda D. Hall, *Encyclopedia of Business Information Sources*, 25th ed. (Detroit: Gale Group, 2009). A bibliographic guide to over 35,000 citations covering more than 1,100 primary subjects of interest to business personnel.

Career Planning Publications

Richard N. Bolles, *What Color Is Your Parachute? 2010: A Practical Manual for Job-Hunters and Career-Changers* (Berkeley, CA: Ten Speed Press, 2009). A companion workbook is also available. See www.jobhuntersbible.com.

Dennis V. Damp, Robert A. Juran, and Salvatori Concialdi, *The Book of U.S. Government Jobs: Where They Are, What's Available & How to Get One*, 10th ed., (McKees Rocks, PA: Bookhaven Press, 2008).

Margaret Riley Dikel and Frances E. Roehm, *Guide to Internet Job Searching* (New York : McGraw-Hill, 2008).

Diane Darling, *Networking for Career Success* (New York: McGraw-Hill, 2007).

Jay Conrad Levinson, David E. Perry, and Darren Hardy, *Guerrilla Marketing for Job Hunters 2.0: 1,001 Unconventional Tips, Tricks and Tactics for Landing Your Dream Job* (Hoboken, NJ: Wiley & Sons, 2009).

Lila B. Stair and Leslie Stair, *Careers in Marketing*, 3rd ed. (New York: McGraw-Hill, 2002).

Princeton Review: Best Entry-Level Jobs, 2009 Edition (New York: Random House Information Group, 2008).

The National Job Bank (Avon, MA: Adams Media Corporation, 2009). See www.admasmedia.com.

Martin Yate, *Cover Letters That Knock 'Em Dead; and Résumés That Knock 'Em Dead*, 8th ed. (Holbrook, MA: Adams Media Corporation, 2008). See www.adamsmedia.com.

Web sites: Resources on job searches, résumé writing, interviewing, U.S. and international job postings.

www.accessalesjobs.com
www.jobbankinfo.org
www.truecareers.com
www.careerxroads.com
www.studentjobs.gov
www.hotjobs.com
www.monster.com
www.jobbankusa.com
www.careers.org
www.careerbuilder.com
www.careers-in-marketing.com
www.studentcentral.com
www.vault.com
www.wetfeet.com

Selected Periodicals

AdWeek, Nielsen Business Media, Inc. (weekly). See www.adweek.com. Annual subscription: $299 per year.

Advertising Age, Crain Communications, Inc. (weekly). See www.adage.com. Annual subscription: $99 per year.

Barron's, Dow Jones & Co., Inc. (weekly). See www.barrons.com Annual subscription: $99 print, $79 online, $149 online and print.

BrandWeek, Nielsen Business Media, Inc. (weekly). See www.brandweek.com. Annual subscription: $299.

Business Horizons, Indiana University c/o Elsevier Science Publishing (bimonthly). See www.elsevier.com. Annual subscription: $120.

BusinessWeek, McGraw-Hill Companies (weekly). See www.businessweek.com. Annual subscription: $46.

Chain Store Age, Lebhar-Friedman, Inc. (monthly). See www.chainstoreage.com. Annual subscription: $150.

eCommerce Times, ECT News Network, Inc. (daily). See www.ecommercetimes.com.

Fortune, Time, Inc. (28 issues). See www.money.cnn.com. Annual subscription: $19.99

Forbes, Forbes Inc. (17 issues) See www.forbes.com. Annual subscription: $29.99.

Harvard Business Review, Harvard University (monthly). See www.hbsp.harvard.edu. Annual subscription: $99 online and print subscription, $129 premium subscription.

Industrial Marketing Management, Elsevier Science publishing (8 issues). See www.elsevier.com. Annual subscription: $155.

International Journal of Electronic Commerce, M. E. Sharpe publishing (quarterly). See www.mesharpe.com. Annual subscription: $92.

Journal of Advertising Research, Springer Science+Business Media (quarterly). See www.springer.com. Annual subscription: $92.

Journal of Consumer Marketing, Emerald Group Publishing, Ltd. (7 issues). See www.emeraldinsight.com. Annual subscription: $3,549.

Journal of Consumer Research, University of Chicago Press (quarterly). See www.journals.uchicago.edu. Annual subscription rates: $145 nonmembers; $55 members; $25 students.

Journal of Interactive Marketing, Direct Marketing Educational Foundation (quarterly). See www.elsevier.com. Annual subscription: $289.

Journal of Marketing, American Marketing Association (quarterly). See www.marketingpower.com. Annual subscription rates: $90 nonmembers; $53 members.

Journal of Marketing Education, Sage Publications (three times per year). See www.sagepub.com. Annual subscription: $103.

Journal of Marketing Research, American Marketing Association (bimonthly). See www.marketingpower.com. Annual subscription: $120 print, $150 print and online.

Journal of Personal Selling and Sales Marketing, American Marketing Association (quarterly). See www.jpssm.org. Annual subscription: $76.

Journal of Public Policy and Marketing, American Marketing Association (semiannually). See www.marketingpower.com. Annual subscription: $90 print; $115 online and print .

Journal of Retailing, Elsevier Science Publishing (quarterly). See www.elsevier.com. Annual subscription: $160.

Marketing Education Review, CTC Press (three times per year). See www.marketingeducationreview.com. Annual subscription: $32.

Marketing Health Services, American Marketing Association (quarterly). See www.marketingpower.com. Annual subscription: $90.

Marketing Management, American Marketing Association (six times per year). See www.marketingpower.com. Annual subscription: $95.

Marketing News, American Marketing Association (biweekly). See www.marketingpower.com. Annual subscription: $85 nonmembers; $53 members.

Marketing Research, American Marketing Association (quarterly). See www.marketingpower.com. Annual subscription: $90.

Media Week, Quantum Business Media (weekly). See www.mediaweek.co.uk. Annual subscription: $231.43

Sales and Marketing Management, VNU Business Publications. See www.salesandmarketing.com. Annual subscription: $99.

Stores, National Retail Federation (weekly). See www.nrf.com or www.stores.org. Annual subscription: $120 for nonmembers; free for members.

The Wall Street Journal Interactive, Dow Jones & Company, Inc. (weekly). See www.wsj.com. (Annual subscription: $103 online; $119 print; $140 online and print.

Professional and Trade Associations

American Association of Advertising Agencies
405 Lexington Ave.
New York, NY 10174-1801
(212) 682-2500
www.aaaa.org

American Advertising Federation
1101 Vermont Ave. N.W., Suite 500
Washington, DC 20005-6306
(202) 898-0089
www.aaf.org

American e-Commerce Association
2346 Camp St.
New Orleans, LA 70130
(504) 495-1748
www.aeaus.com

American Marketing Association
311 S. Wacker Dr., Suite 5800
Chicago, IL 60606
(800) AMA-1150
www.marketingpower.com

American Society of Transportation and Logistics
P.O. Box 3363
Warrenton, VA 20188
(202) 580-7270
www.astl.org

Business Marketing Association
1833 Centre Point Circle, Suite 123
Naperville, IL 60563
(630) 544-5054
www.marketing.org

Direct Marketing Association
1120 Avenue of the Americas
New York, NY 10036-6700
(212) 768-7277
www.the-dma.org

Direct Selling Association
1667 K Street, N.W., Suite 1100
Washington, DC 20006
(202) 452-8866
www.dsa.org

Environmental Defense: Corporate Partnerships
257 Park Avenue, S.
New York, NY 10010
(212) 505-2100
www.environmentaldefense.org

Institute for Supply Management
2055 E. Centennial Circle
Tempe, AZ 85284
(480) 752-6276
www.ism.ws

International Advertising Association
World Service Center
257 Madison Ave., Suite 2102
New York, NY 10016
(212) 557-1133
www.iaaglobal.org

International Franchise Association
1501 K Street, N.W., Suite 350
Washington, DC 20005
(202) 628-8000
www.franchise.org

Marketing Research Association
110 National Drive
Glastonbury, CT 06033-1212
(860) 682-1000
www.mra-net.org

Marketing Science Institute
1000 Massachusetts Ave.
Cambridge, MA 02138-5396
(617) 491-2060
www.msi.org

National Association of Wholesale Distributors
1325 G Street, N.W., Suite 1000
Washington, DC 20005
(202) 872-0885
www.naw.org

National Mail Order Association
2807 Polk St. NE
Minneapolis, MN 55418-2954
(612) 788-1673
www.nmoa.org

National Retail Federation
325 Seventh St., N.W., Suite 1100
Washington, DC 20004
(800) NRF-HOW2
www.nrf.com

Product Development and Management Association
15000 Commerce Parkway, Suite C
Mount Laurel, NJ 08054
(800) 232-5241
www.pdma.org

Public Relations Society of America
33 Maiden Lane
New York, NY 10038-5150
(212) 460-1400
www.prsa.org

Sales and Marketing Executive International
P.O. Box 1390
Suma, WA 98295-1390
(312) 893-0751
www.smei.org

Society for Marketing Professional Services
44 Canal Center Plaza, Suite 444
Alexandria, VA 22314
(800) 292-7667
www.smps.org

U.S. Internet Industry Association (USIIA)
1800 Diagonal Road, Suite 600
Alexandria, VA 22314
(703) 647-7440
www.usiia.org

ALTERNATE CASES

case D–1 Nike MaxSight Contact Lenses: Seeing a Need

Nike and Bausch and Lomb have teamed up to offer an exciting new addition to the eyewear market—Nike MaxSight contact lenses.

HISTORY OF CONTACT LENSES

Leonardo da Vinci first illustrated the concept of contact lenses in 1508, but it wasn't until 1887 when contact lenses were actually manufactured. These early lenses were glass and covered the entire eye. In 1948, plastic contact lenses were developed that could cover only the eye's cornea. Soft contact lenses have been around since 1971 providing greater comfort to wearers and expanding the market. Disposable contact lenses were introduced in 1987, addressing the problem of users adequately cleaning the lens to minimize irritation and even infection. What has not been available to this point is a contact lens that can provide the eye with the protection of a pair of sunglasses! Nike MaxSight contact lenses are specially tinted lenses to maximize visual acuity and are available in both prescription and nonprescription form. While designed primarily for athletes and sports participants, the market is not limited to simply those with an active lifestyle.

THE NEED

When Dr. Richard Allen, an experienced ophthamologist and faculty member at the University of Virginia Health System, revealed to his colleague Dr. Richard Edlich in 2000 that he had ocular melanoma—essentially skin cancer of the eye—the two men began researching and publishing articles on skin cancer prevention as well as prevention of ocular melanoma. Dr. Edlich contacted Dr. Reichow and Dr. Citek, two basic researchers that had conducted a comprehensive evaluation of sunglasses. The results revealed that very few brands of sunglasses offered any real protection from the sun's damaging rays and only partially protect the eyes; this despite the fact that the product may be labeled as providing 100 percent protection from the sun.

There are a number of reasons that sunglasses don't do the job. First, they have to be worn to do any good. Many sunglasses have poor quality lens material that does not adequately shield the eyes from the damaging UVA and UVB rays that also cause skin cancer. Design and fit can also minimize the effectiveness of sunglasses. Uncomfortable, unable to adequately cover the eye, and unlikely to stay in place during activity, sunglasses were not the answer.

THE SOLUTION

Doctors Reichow and Citek played a leadership role in coordinating the development of the Nike MaxSight fully tinted soft contact lens. Nike MaxSight contact lenses for athletes come in two tints: gray-green contacts for athletes who play in bright sunlight and want to be comfortable visually (golf, rugby, runners) and amber-tinted contacts for athletes in sports that require tracking of fast-moving objects (baseball, soccer, tennis, softball). The lenses come in both prescription and nonprescription form and as with most daily wear soft contacts, they must be changed monthly.

Benefits of Nike MaxSight lenses are substantial. Not only do wearers have a better field of view with no obstructions from nosepieces or frames, but there's also no fogging. You'll still sweat while exercising but that sweat isn't causing glasses to slip and slide. This lens provides distortion-free optics, whether or not you wear prescription contacts. The lenses filter out more than 90 percent of harmful blue light as well as 95 percent of UVA and UVB rays. Nike still recommends wearing sunglasses whenever possible over MaxSight lenses to protect the rest of the eye.

A box of Nike MaxSight lenses costs about $60 for a two-month supply. Conventional prescription contact lenses sell for around $25 to $70 depending on prescription.

Nike MaxSight lenses are available from selected eye care professionals. The Nike Web site (www.nikevision.com) provides information on these outlets. Consumers are unable to purchase the product unless they have an eye examination and fitting.

One primary tactic for providing information on the product for both consumers and eye care providers is the Nike Web site. A downloadable coupon is available for a free trial pair of lenses. In-store product information and displays are provided to eye care professionals to reach potential consumers. Nike also has traditional advertising on the product in selected sports magazines.[1]

Questions

1 How has Nike used an analysis of consumer needs to identify different markets and products for MaxSight? What are these different market–product combinations? Which market segments are likely to be the largest? The most likely to adopt the product?

2 Identify the elements of the marketing mix for Nike MaxSight currently. What marketing mix recommendations do you suggest beyond those Nike has already undertaken?

3 This product is positioned toward athletes who want to improve their performance and visual acuity. However, it may be difficult for anyone who does not already wear contact lenses to be motivated to adopt this product. (*a*) How likely is it that Nike will be able to capture noncontact lens-wearing athletes? (*b*) What can Nike do to encourage the noncontact lens-wearing athlete to adopt the product?

case D–2 Daktronics, Inc.: Global Displays in 68 Billion Colors

"We were looking for a way to provide jobs and keep our graduates at home," said Dr. Aelred (Al) J. Kurtenbach, board chairman of Daktronics, Inc. So in 1968, Kurtenbach, then an engineering professor at South Dakota State University (SDSU), and fellow professor Duane Sander decided to start a business. "We started a biomedical engineering company, mainly because we'd both done research in this area," continued Kurtenbach.

But even college professors make bad decisions occasionally!

THE DAKTRONICS LAUNCH: DOWNSIDE, UPSIDE

"It was a dismal failure," explains Kurtenbach, "because the electronic thermometer and automated blood-pressure gauge we'd developed worked fine but simply cost too much to produce and sell." Also, he and Sander were concerned that by the time they went through the lengthy process to receive U.S. Food and Drug Administration approval, Daktronics would run out of money.

Enter: A miracle—in the form of the South Dakota State wrestling coach who needed a portable scoreboard near the wrestling mat to tell fans the time and score without blocking their view of action on the mat. At the time, wrestling teams had to use basketball displays that couldn't show the right wrestling information and were too high and far from the mat.

In response, Daktronics designed the Matside®, a pyramid-shaped scoreboard that sits on the floor and is still in use at wrestling matches around the United States today, 35 years later. The Matside also established Daktronics' reputation as a company that could get problems solved, and quickly.

From that low-key launch, Daktronics has emerged as the world-class designer of scoreboards and electronic displays used in the United States and around the globe. The reason for Daktronics' success? "Innovation," says Kurtenbach. *Fortune Small Business* describes the company as a "geek-rich workplace," with more than 230 degreed engineers out of its 900 full-time employees in its plant in Brookings, South Dakota—population 18,504.

To start Daktronics in 1968, Kurtenbach and Sander sold shares to family and friends at $5 per share, raising a bit less than $100,000. That limited initial funding also pushed Kurtenbach and Sander into finding products that customers would buy to generate revenues for Daktronics. The company still must stay alert because it faces global competitors such as Barco from Belgium and Mitsubishi from Japan.

TODAY'S MARKET SEGMENTS

Daktronics divides its markets into three segments: sports (70 percent of Daktronics' sales), business (20 percent), and government (10 percent). The company reaches these markets today through 35 U.S. regional sales and service offices and a recently opened office in Frankfurt, Germany, to reach European and Middle Eastern customers.

In the sports segment, if you watched the Kentucky Derby at Churchill Downs or the 2004 Olympics in

Athens on television, you probably saw a sample of Daktronics electronic scoring and display systems. The same goes for 26 of 30 Major League Baseball parks, 26 of 31 National Football League stadiums, 19 of 28 National Basketball Association facilities, and 19 of 30 National Hockey League arenas, where Daktronics has created some or all of the displays. This also is true of displays at hundreds of colleges, universities, and high schools, where the prices can vary from millions of dollars to a few thousand.

A surprise to many: These displays can often pay for themselves in a year or two through the advertising shown on the units. Brad Mayne, president of the American Airlines Center in Dallas, where the NBA Mavericks and NHL Stars play, says that Daktronics' scoreboard (shown below) paid for itself in advertising by the second season.

Daktronics' largest scoreboard? It's a 36-by-149-foot giant at the Cleveland Indians' Jacobs Field. The nine full-color displays installed throughout Jacobs Field provide live videos and replays, lineups, scores, pitch information, and so on.

In the business segment, probably the biggest and best known are Daktronics' electronic displays in New York City. It recently installed a 65-foot-high display in Times Square that shows video, animation, graphics, stock quotes, and news headlines in striking shades of color.

While that may be the best-known business display, hundreds of Daktronics programmable displays dot the United States in shopping malls and outside of stores and churches. These displays show everything from current times and temperatures to financial information, gas prices, and motel room rates. James (Jim) B. Morgan, president and chief executive officer of Daktronics, now puts greater emphasis on the business accounts to make the company less dependent on the sports segment.

Less well known are Daktronics displays for the government segment. Suppose that on the way to class today, a freeway sign told you that a crash in the right lane ahead means you should move to a left lane and slow down. It was probably a Daktronics-built sign, something like that for the Cumberland Gap Tunnel that connects Virginia, Kentucky, and Tennessee, shown here. Besides highway signs, the government segment includes airport and train station displays announcing arrival and departure times.

To see what Daktronics sports, business, and government displays have been installed in your state, go to www.daktronics.com.

TECHNOLOGY

Exploiting the latest technology is critical to Daktronics' success. At the level of signage just needed to display words and numbers, a key company innovation is the Glow Cube® pixel, about the size of a Rubik's Cube. Black on one side and reflective yellow on the other, hundreds of these rotate to black or yellow to spell words or create shapes on scoreboards or highway signs. Glow Cube® pixels are the building blocks you also see on traditional signs ranging from those on professional golf tour events to portable soccer scoreboards.

For the giant programmable video displays, the basic building blocks are thousands of LEDs (light emitting diodes). LED color breakthrough in the 1990s led to today's displays capable of showing 68 billion hues of color—largely replacing tiny incandescent lamps in these displays and using only about 10 percent of the electrical power needed for those lamps. Sophisticated computer programs and video and replay systems make these screens come to life at an athletic event. Because of the low power usage and high reliability, the LED pixel has replaced the Glow Cube® pixel in most applications.

COMMUNICATIONS AND MANAGEMENT

With the engineering, manufacturing, and marketing departments housed in the same Daktronics building, many questions can be addressed with simple, direct water-cooler conversations. Kurtenbach sees this open communication as a huge competitive advantage for Daktronics.

Dr. Kurtenbach's transition from academics to business was surprisingly easy. To learn how businesses work and succeed, he checked out histories of large U.S. companies from the library. He uses what he calls his "waterboy" approach in managing—meaning that every manager is like a waterboy for the team, necessary but

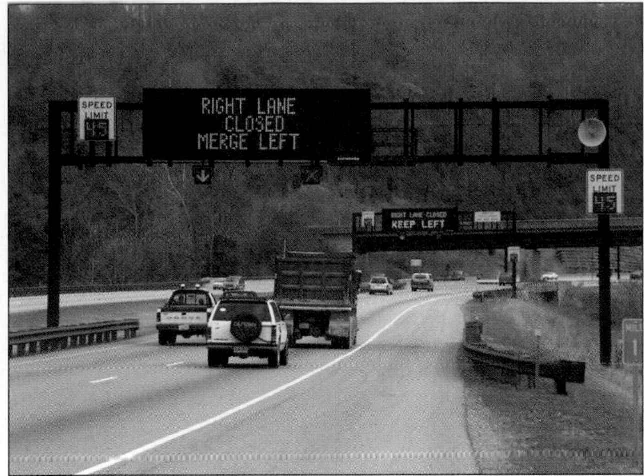

not the star. Kurtenbach developed this leadership style growing up as one of 13 children in a farm family that often involved his doing the essential tasks none of his brothers or sisters wanted to do.

STUDENT JOBS AND ECONOMIC DEVELOPMENT

How did Kurtenbach's original goal of starting a local business to help keep South Dakota State University graduates in the state turn out? Kurtenbach and Daktronics probably get a grade of A+. Not only does the company employ more than 900 full-time people in its Brookings facility, but it also provides more than 450 *paid* internships each year for students—mostly from SDSU. To help Daktronics continue to enhance its cutting-edge technology, SDSU has also responded by enhancing its graphic- and computer-design offerings.

And that $5 per share investment by family and friends in the disastrous Daktronics "biomedical device launch" in 1968? With stock splits, each share is worth about $2,700 today.[2]

Questions

1 What are the reasons or appeals that might cause potential customers in the following markets to buy a Daktronics scoreboard, electronics display, or large-screen video? (*a*) A Major League Baseball team, (*b*) a high school for its football field, (*c*) a local hardware store, and (*d*) a state highway department.

2 (*a*) Do a SWOT analysis for Daktronics. (*b*) For one entry in each of the four cells in your SWOT table (strengths, weaknesses, opportunities, and threats) suggest an action Daktronics might take to increase revenues.

3 Using Figure 2–5 in Chapter 2 as a guide, identify an action Daktronics might take to increase sales in each of the four cells: (*a*) current markets, current products; (*b*) current markets, new products; (*c*) new markets, current products; (*d*) new markets, new products.

case D–3 Jamba Juice: Scanning the Marketing Environment

What were you doing in 10th grade? Waiting to get your driver's license? Kirk Perron was thinking about his future and putting together a deal that would help launch the successful Jamba Juice chain. It sounds incredible but Kirk Perron bought the real estate for his first juice bar when he was in 10th grade. He borrowed money from a high school counselor, the librarian, and his school bus driver to put together the $12,000 down payment.

THE COMPANY

Kirk Perron opened up his first operation as The Juice Club in 1990 in San Luis Obispo, California. He hit on the idea for a convenient, delicious, healthful food store on a long weekend bike ride. An avid cyclist with a lifelong interest in health and nutrition, he wanted to offer an alternative to typical fast-food fare. The idea was a hit and quickly spread. In 1995, the company changed its name from The Juice Club to Jamba Juice. Today Jamba Juice has more than 700 stores nationwide offering a variety of healthy drinks and snacks. Jamba Juice is considered the industry leader in the smoothie market, and Perron predicts that one day Jamba Juice will be as big a brand as Coca-Cola.

THE IDEA

Jamba Juice is all about healthy food and fun. Jamba is from an African word that means "to celebrate." Walk into a Jamba Juice store and customers can choose from a wide variety of Jamba Juice specialties including smoothies, fresh-squeezed fruit and vegetable juices, breads, and pretzels. Jamba's commitment to healthy products is reflected in its mission statement, "Enriching the daily experience of our customers, our community, and ourselves through the life-nourishing qualities of fruits and vegetables."

Smoothies are the bulk of Jamba Juice's business. They are made with juice and fruit and often yogurt, sherbet, or ice milk. A typical smoothie gets most of its calories from carbohydrates and protein providing a low- or no-fat, nutritious meal. Jamba smoothies are designed to meet "heart healthy" FDA requirements. Nutritional supplements called "boosts," such as "energy juice boost," containing ginseng and gingko biloba, and "immunity juice boost," with echinacea and antioxidants, are available and can be added to smoothies. Jamba Juice also recently added a new low-calorie drink, the Enlightened Smoothie, to its menu. Learn more about Jamba at www.jambajuice.com.

As you sit at the counter in a Jamba Juice, you can watch friendly, well-trained Jamba Juice employees whip, beat, and blend your smoothie right before your eyes. Stores also feature nutrition centers where customers can get a complete nutritional breakdown for each product. Outlets also feature a merchandising area, which has Jamba Juice juicers, mugs, hats, and T-shirts.

THE COMPETITION

Juice bars have been part of a growing trend. Barriers to entry are fairly low. Single-store outlets and small chains within a city or region are common, although Jamba has several large competitors. New Orleans-based Smoothie King, for example, has 580 locations in 32 states, and Atlanta-based Planet Smoothie has more than 125 stores in 20 states. Other competitors include Juice Stop, Juice It Up!, Surf City Squeeze, and Orange Julius. Jamba Juice has positioned itself as a replacement for typical fast-food fare. This means it also considers fast-food restaurants indirect competitors.

Jamba has had to fight to maintain its trademark in a competitive market. Several years ago a San Francisco Juice bar called Jamm'n Juice was forced to change its name after Jamba complained that Jamm'n Juice and its animated fruit and vegetables were too close to the Jamba trademark and logo.

THE MARKET

Juice bars have existed for decades, often in health-food stores and gyms and were associated with what was a small group of intensely health-conscious customers. That small demographic group boomed in recent years fueling the market for fat-free foods, fitness equipment, and apparel. There has also been an increasing level of health consciousness among society generally. However, "the consumer always talks thin and eats fat," according to Allan Hickock, an industry analyst with Piper Jaffray.

However, Jamba Juice is optimistic about the opportunities for expanding the market by replacing fast food with good-for-you food. Retail sales of juice and smoothies exceeded $1.2 billion in 2006 compared with $552 million in 2000. About two-thirds of Jamba's customers are between the ages of 15 and 25—not exactly the same demographic group as the traditional health-conscious baby boomer. Age and education level are important selection criteria for opening new Jamba Juice outlets. Kirk Perron believes that the more highly educated potential customers are, the more likely they will be to stop in for a nutritious smoothie. In fact, many of current and planned Jamba outlets are in college towns, and partnerships have been formed to open outlets in universities and airports. You can find Jamba in both the Los Angeles and San Francisco airports and on campus at the University of North Carolina, George Washington University, and the University of Nevada–Las Vegas, among others. Jamba also has a licensing agreement with Whole Foods Markets, a partner that shares Jamba's values and commitment to healthy living.

THE ISSUES

Purists insist that the best drinks come from completely fresh produce. Fresh produce can be hard to work with to provide consistent-tasting drinks. Also, the price of fresh produce can change drastically throughout the year.

With fairly limited menus, juice bars are considered great as an add-on rather than a stand-alone retail establishment because they are usually not strong enough to draw customer traffic on their own. Personnel are important to the success of a juice bar—described as "bartenders" they have to be able to put on a good show for the customer.

There is a seasonality effect for smoothie and juice operators. For example, in northern climates, operators in enclosed downtown skyways or mall locations often see their business fall off in the summer when people are outdoors walking around. Business surges in the winter.[3]

Questions

1 Conduct an environmental scan for Jamba Juice as it considers a new juice bar to open near your university. Identify factors that you think have an impact on the juice bar market, and indicate whether these factors would tend to enhance opportunities or represent threats.

2 Given your environmental analysis, which environmental force do you believe is most critical for Jamba Juice and why?

3 Examine the competitive environment for juice bars. Consider the likelihood of new entrants, barriers to entry, existing competitors, and substitutes. How would you summarize the current competitive environment?

4 Do you think that the juice bar phenomenon is a fad or rooted in some fundamental environmental and market forces? Why?

case D–4 Ford and Firestone: Who's to Blame?

Ford Motor Company and Firestone Tire and Rubber enjoyed one of the longest-running relationships in American business, built upon the friendship and business relationship among the founders, Harvey Firestone and Henry Ford. From 1908 when Firestone first outfitted the Model T Ford until 2000, Firestone was the primary tire supplier to Ford. A well-publicized falling out over the blame for the deaths and accidents occurring in Ford Explorer vehicles equipped with Firestone tires buried the relationship. Firestone variously blamed Ford and consumers while Ford blamed Firestone. What went wrong?

THE FORD EXPLORER

To understand how the entire situation unfolded, it is useful to focus on the development and launch of earlier Ford automobiles. The Ford Pinto was designed in the early 1960s to compete in the lower-priced subcompact segment. Ford engineers located the Pinto's gas tank in a location vulnerable to rear-end collisions to cut costs. A Ford cost-benefit analysis estimated it would cost $11 per car to move the gas tank to a less vulnerable position. Given that it expected to produce 12.5 million Pintos over the life of the model, Ford decided not to redesign the car and spend $137 million to move the gas tank. Using insurance company claim values at the time, Ford estimated that it would "save" about $50 million in insurance claims by relocating the gas tank, netting $87 million loss. Hence, it was cheaper to leave the gas tank in its rear-end position. The decision proved fatal. Ultimately, the recall of the Pinto and related expenses cost Ford at least $1.5 billion.

The Explorer's design was based on the Ford Bronco, essentially a line of light trucks using the twin I-beam suspension to lift up the vehicle to travel over rough terrain. However, this meant that the center of gravity was higher—the vehicle became more prone to stability problems and rollovers. By the late 1980s, Ford faced more than 800 lawsuits from rollovers of the Bronco II and Ranger, forerunners of the Explorer.

Ford developed the Explorer to address a mid-1980s market looking for a rugged vehicle that was primarily image and secondarily performance. Because automobile manufacturing had a four- to five-year lead time for a new model, decisions were made about the Explorer before all the consequences of the earlier decisions on the Bronco and Ranger were in. Among the early decisions made were the use of the same twin I-beam suspension of the Bronco II and manufacturing on the same assembly line used for the Ranger. Internal company documents of tests on the Explorer prototype showed problems with rollovers and a tendency to lift its wheels and tip during turns made at speeds up to 55 mph—even worse performance than the Bronco II. In early 1987 there were calls from designers to make changes in the design of the vehicle that would improve stability and maintain passenger safety.

Consumer Reports came out with a scathing review of the Bronco II in June 1989, advising consumers to "steer clear" of the product. At this point, the Explorer's design, modeled on the Bronco II, was frozen; parts were ordered and facilities were readied for production for 1990 delivery.

Another important design decision was that of the tires for the Explorer. Both Goodyear and Firestone tires were selected for the Explorer. Examining various Firestone models, a Ford engineer reported that there was a good probability of passing the Consumer's Union testing for the Explorer with Firestone P225 tires and less confidence with the Firestone P235. Ford chose the P235. Ford's engineer, Roger Stornant, claimed, "Management is aware of the potential risk with the P235 tires and has accepted that risk. The Consumer's Union test is generally unrepresentative of the real world and I see no 'real' risk in failing except what may result in the way of spurious litigation."

Ford engineers suggested four ways to improve the stability of the Explorer: widen the chassis by two inches, lower the engine, lower the tire pressure, and stiffen the springs. Ford chose the latter two, reducing the recommended tire pressure from 30–35 psi to 26 psi. This produced more road gripping, but it also increased friction, increased the heat of the tires, and caused tread separations. The lower tire pressure also reduced fuel economy.

BRIDGESTONE/FIRESTONE

Firestone had its own history of recalls. In 1978, between 13 million and 14 million Firestone "500" tires were recalled due to faulty manufacture, costing the company more than $200 million. The National Highway Traffic Safety Administration (NHTSA) called for tougher new standards for tires and light trucks. If these standards had been in place in the late 1970s, the early and subsequent designs of SUVs would have been quite different, saving lives and money. However, the NHTSA was essentially dismantled by the Reagan administration that slashed the NHTSA's budget and revoked several new regulations, including a warning light for tire inflation problems.

In 1987, Firestone became a subsidiary of Bridgestone Tire Co. Ltd. Bridgestone, a Japanese company, was named for its founder Shojiro Ishibashi, whose name means "stone bridge." Bridgestone was proud of its technological leadership—innovations in tire performance and design—as well as its dedication to quality. The Firestone subsidiary was relabeled the Bridgestone/Firestone Company in 1990, with headquarters in Nashville, Tennessee.

The first tire separation lawsuits hit Firestone in 1992. This was followed by labor disputes and a strike at the Bridgestone/Firestone plant in Decatur, Illinois, following attempts to cut costs. Testing of both Goodyear and Firestone tire models used on the Explorer showed that the Goodyear tires significantly outperformed Firestone. In some instances, Firestone tires wore out twice as fast as Goodyears. The Firestone Wilderness tire earned the lowest-acceptable NHTSA heat resistance rating—a C. The comparable Goodyear tire received a B.

Ford began to pressure Goodyear to lower tire prices in 1995. Goodyear decided it could not manufacture tires at a price that Ford was willing to pay and actually asked for a price increase due to higher material costs. At this point, Ford discontinued using Goodyear tires on its Explorer, relying entirely upon Firestone.

LAUNCH OF THE EXPLORER AND THE LAWSUITS

The Explorer was launched in 1990 and quickly became the best-selling SUV on the market. Granted, few consumers were using it for its off-road capabilities, but they looked adventuresome whizzing down the freeway to the mall. Ford engineers were well aware of the safety risk of the Explorer. Letters to dealerships warned of the dangers of failing to follow precautions on recommended tire usage, stating that ignoring these precautions could lead to loss of control and vehicle rollover, which could result in serious injury or death.

Ford also conducted a survey in 1993 of SUV drivers, finding that these drivers drove faster, were more likely to drive in bad weather, and followed other vehicles more closely, particularly troubling since the Explorer needed 20 to 30 feet more to stop when traveling at 60 mph than a typical family car.

By 1995, a Texas jury found Ford 100 percent at fault for the death of a 20-year-old college student driving a Bronco II that rolled over due to tire separation. The $25 million verdict was the largest SUV rollover verdict at the time. In 1996, a trainee test driver lost control of an Explorer during a lane change at 52.5 mph. The driver, overcorrecting, found the car in a four-wheel slide and then a 360-degree flip.

State Farm Insurance, the largest U.S. automobile insurer, notified Firestone and NHTSA in 1998 that it was experiencing an unusual number of claims on Firestone tires. Ford quietly began replacing Firestone tires on Explorers in Venezuela and Saudi Arabia due to rollover deaths in those countries.

POINTING FINGERS

An investigative report on a Houston television station started to blow the cover off the problems at Ford and Firestone in February 2000. The vice president of public affairs at Firestone accused the television station of unfairly characterizing Firestone Radial ATX tires as dangerous. She stated that the television station would better serve viewers by telling them how to properly maintain their tires and suggested that many of the crashes were caused by external factors such as punctures.

By May 2000, NHTSA belatedly launched an investigation and sent a defect notice to Firestone. Ford accused Firestone of withholding data needed to determine which tires were defective. Ford accused NHTSA of sitting on Firestone data, and it was Ford that pinpointed where the bad tires were being produced and pressed for a recall. By late summer of 2000, the recall was announced.

Ford organized a war room of 500 people dedicated to the crisis—public affairs and media, engineering, legal, regulatory, purchasing, and finance people collecting and analyzing data, operating a 24-hour hotline for the public, and disseminating information with NHTSA and the public.

Meanwhile, Bridgestone executives in Japan had no real appreciation of what was happening with Firestone. There were few Explorers sold in Japan and very few tires subject to recall. The attitude was that the Japanese built better cars, therefore the problem must be with Ford. The first public statement by Firestone's president, Masatoshi Ono, seemed to hold the Ford Explorer responsible and advised car owners to check tire pressure every month, even better, every two weeks.

Ford's CEO, Jacques Nasser, went on the offensive claiming that there were no problems with the design of the Explorer and that there were no data pointing to faults with the Explorer; he insisted that this was a tire problem. Ford rolled out a $5 million advertising campaign to protect its reputation and brand.

In May 2001, a second recall of 13 million Firestone tires was announced by Ford in an attempt to clear the path for the 2002 Explorer. Ford claimed it did not have enough confidence in the Firestone tires, while Firestone countered that the real issue was the safety of the Explorer. Firestone-equipped Explorers accounted for most of the 174 deaths and 700 injuries sustained in accidents reported at that time. In addition, Ford faced lawsuits seeking more than $590 million in damages.

Congressional hearings were launched. Accusations and data flew back and forth. Bridgestone/Firestone announced its intention to close its Decatur, Illinois, plant in December 2001, laying off almost 1,400 people. The president of the local steelworkers union claimed that Ford blamed Firestone and then Firestone made a scapegoat of the Decatur plant.

Ford announced in July 2001 that it had taken an equity position in Top Driver, Inc., the largest chain of driving schools in the country, and would be developing a driver safety course for SUV owners. The implication was that accidents with Ford Explorers were due not only to defective Firestone tires but to driver error as well. Ford was criticized as hypocritical for presenting advertising images of invincible SUVs that can be driven with abandon, weaving in and out of traffic, giving drivers a false sense of security while at the same time claiming that SUV drivers needed safety training.[4]

Questions

1 What moral philosophy appeared to guide the decision making at Ford? At Bridgestone/Firestone? Is there any evidence that either company changed its decision-making model as lawsuits mounted?

2 Do you see Ford's handling of the situation surrounding the development, marketing, and subsequent recall as ethical but illegal, ethical and legal, unethical but legal, or unethical and illegal? Why?

3 What actions would you recommend Ford take to deal with the aftermath of this situation?

case D–5 The Jamisons Buy an Espresso Machine

At 4:52 P.M. on Friday, January 25, 2008, Brock and Alisha Jamison bought an espresso machine. There was no doubt about it. Any observer would agree that the purchase took place at precisely that time. Or did it?

When questioned after the transaction, neither Brock nor Alisha could remember which of them first suggested the idea of getting an espresso machine. They do recall that in the summer of 2006 they attended a dinner party given by a friend who specialized in French and Chinese cooking. The meal was delicious, and their friend Brad was very proud of the Krups espresso machine he had used to cap off the evening. The item was expensive, however, at about $900.

The following summer, Alisha noticed a comparison study of espresso machines in *Gourmet* magazine. The performance of four different brands was compared. At about the same time, Brock noticed that *Consumer Reports* also compared a number of brands of espresso machines. In both instances, the Krups brand come out on top.

Later that fall, new models of the Krups were introduced, and a model they liked was selling for $700 in department stores. The Jamisons searched occasionally for Krups in discount houses or in wholesale showroom catalogs, even searching the Internet, hoping to find a lower price for the product. They were simply not offered there.

For Christmas 2007, the Jamisons traveled from Los Angeles to the family home in Michigan. While there, the Jamisons received a gift of a KitchenAid mixer from Brock's grandmother. Although the mixer was beautiful, Alisha immediately thought how much more elegant and useful an espresso machine would be. One private sentence to that effect brought immediate agreement from Brock. The box was (discreetly) not opened, although many thanks were expressed. The box remained unopened the entire time the Jamisons kept the item.

Back home in Los Angeles in January, Alisha saw that the Krups was sale-priced at $600 at Sur la Table, one of the major gourmet stores in California. Brock and Alisha visited a branch location on a Saturday afternoon and saw the item. The salesperson, however, was not very knowledgeable about its features and not very helpful on explaining its attributes. The Jamisons left, very disappointed.

Two days later, Alisha called a different location for Sur la Table in a more urban location and talked to Dora Mayeur, a seemingly knowledgeable salesperson whose co-worker, Stephanie Wales, claimed to own and love exactly the model the Jamisons had in mind. Furthermore, Dora said that they did carry KitchenAid mixers and would make an exchange of the mixer, which had been received as a gift and for which no receipt was available.

On the following Friday morning, Brock put the mixer in his car trunk when he left for work. That afternoon, Alisha and six-month-old Brock, Jr., rode into town with a friend to meet Brock and make the transaction. After meeting downtown, they drove through uncharacteristic heavy rainy-day traffic to Sur la Table to meet Dora, whom they liked as much in person as they did on the telephone. Dora conducted a brief review of the types and models available.

There was the Nespresso brand, which used Nescafé coffee capsules, for about $400. There were four varieties of the FrancisFrancis brand, priced between $430 and $720. At the top of the price structure, was the multilingual, Swiss-made Jura brand, priced at $2,200. The Krups that they had coveted was also there, selling at $600, but it was much larger than they thought. In fact, the item was the shape (and seemed to be nearly the size) of the Vienna Opera House.

There was a somewhat smaller, less expensive Krups twin-tower model, and the Jamisons toyed with the idea of buying it, but Dora suggested that the more expensive version was well worth the money. The Jamisons then confirmed their initial decision to take the $600 Krups model and asked Dora about exchanging the KitchenAid mixer they had brought with them. "No problem," said Dora.

After making a quick phone call, Dora returned with bad news. Sur la Table had not carried that particular model of mixer. This model mixer was a single-color model that is usually carried at department stores and catalog sales houses. The one carried by the specialized culinary stores, such as Sur la Table, was a two-tone item. She even offered to allow the Jamisons to use her phone to verify the availability of the item. The Jamisons did exactly that.

Alisha dialed several of the suggested stores, looking for a retailer that carried both the Krups and the KitchenAid model, but she quickly learned that they were distributed through different types of retail stores. A young man who answered the phone at one store, however, seemed friendly and helpful, and Alisha was able to obtain his agreement to take the item as a return if she could get there that afternoon.

The store was about one-half mile away. Brock volunteered to brave the elements and return the mixer. He took the shopping shuttle to the store with the still-unopened mixer box under his arm. About an hour later, Brock returned cold and wet, with a refund. Together, the Jamisons bought the Krups espresso machine at 4:52 p.m. and proudly took it home.[5]

Questions

1 Which of the Jamisons decided to buy an espresso machine? The Krups brand?

2 When was the decision to buy made?

3 What were the important attributes in the evaluation of the Krups brand?

4 Would you characterize the Jamisons' purchase decision process as routine problem solving, limited problem solving, or extended problem solving? Why?

case D–6 Motetronix Technology: Marketing Smart Dust

"The next 18 months will be critical in getting the word out about our technology and products," says Ajay Gupta, president of Motetronix Technology. "The Dust Storm is on the horizon and companies that capitalize on it early have huge potential."

THE COMPANY AND TECHNOLOGY

Motetronix Technology is a developer and manufacturer of "smart dust," or tiny wireless microelectromechanical sensors that measure temperature, light, and vibration; analyze chemical compounds, including radiation and air quality; and observe surrounding movement. These sensors are powered by AA batteries and controlled by an operating system called Tiny OS. Called *motes* (short for a re*mote* wireless transceiver that both transmits and receives analog or digital signals), these sensors survey the world around them and communicate with each other wirelessly, grapevining down the line until the data get to a personal computer. The "smart dust" name comes from the ultimate goal of making each mote about one cubic millimeter small, or the size of a grain of sand.

SMART DUST APPLICATIONS

Industry analysts are predicting that smart dust will have a host of commercial, military, security, and ecological applications. Along with the Pentagon, the U.S. Department of Homeland Security has already devoted a large portion of its R&D budget to sensor technology for military and security applications. Commercial and ecological applications are still being studied. According to industry analysts, vibration sensors on a factory floor will tell when a machine is about to fail, saving millions of dollars in downtime. Air-pressure sensors on truck tires will prevent accidents and save on fuel. Sensors dropped in a forest fire's path will predict which areas will flame up next. Motes will be able to determine when a building is safe to reenter after an earthquake, monitor the vital signs (and locations) of elderly people, or monitor power consumption of household appliances. A dispersion of motes 10 to 100 feet apart could monitor traffic on a highway or measure moisture levels on farms.

Applications for motes are expected to increase with decreasing prices and smaller sizes. In 2005, a single mote was priced in the range of $50 to $100, depending on level of sophistication, and was two cubic millimeters in size (smaller than a piece of glitter). By 2012, the price of a mote is expected to fall below $1 and the size will shrink to one cubic millimeter with advances in silicon and fabrication techniques. Smart dust is projected to post industry-wide sales of $1 billion in 2012.

MARKETING SMART DUST

Motetronix Technology executives were sensitive to the fact that promising applications of smart dust had to be tempered by the reality of the marketplace and buyer behavior. Therefore, Ajay Gupta charged his marketing team with the responsibility for reviewing buying behavior associated with the adoption of a new technology. The buying process appeared to contain at least six phases: (1) need recognition, (2) identification of available products, (3) comparison with existing technology, (4) vendor or seller evaluation, (5) the decision itself, and (6) follow-up on technology performance. Moreover, there appeared to be several people within the buying organization who would play a role in the adoption of a new technology. For example, top management (such as the president and executive vice presidents) would certainly be involved. Engineering and operations management (e.g., vice presidents of engineering and manufacturing) and design engineers (e.g., persons who develop specifications for new products) would also play a major role. Purchasing personnel would have a say in such a decision and particularly in the vendor-evaluation process. The role played by each person in the buying organization was still unclear to Motetronix. It seemed that engineering management personnel could slow the adoption of smart dust if they did not feel it was appropriate for the products made by the company. Design engineers, who would actually apply fiber optics in product design, might be favorably or unfavorably disposed to the technology depending on whether they knew how to use it. Top management personnel would participate in any final decisions to use smart dust and could generate interest in the technology if stimulated to do so.

This review of buying behavior led to questions about how to influence an organization's buying process and have its technology used in a company's products or facility. Complicating the discussion was the fact that Motetronix was a comparative unknown in the industry relative to Crossbow Technology and Dust, Inc., two companies that had already commercialized the smart dust technology. In addition, issues still remained related to smart dust reliability, power consumption, and cost/price.[6]

Questions

1 What type of buying situation is involved in the purchase of smart dust, and what will be important buying criteria used by companies considering using smart dust in their products or in their facility?

2 Describe the purchase decision process for adopting smart dust, and state how members in the buying center for this technology might play a part in this process.

3 What effect will perceived risk have on a company's decision of whether to use smart dust in its products or in its facility?

case D–7 Callaway Golf: The Global Challenge

THE COMPANY HISTORY

Callaway Golf got its start in 1982 when the late Ely R. Callaway invested $400,000 for half interest in a golf club company called Hickory Stick. Callaway-Hickory, later renamed Callaway Golf, had sales of just $22 million in 1990 and was considered a small player as an OEM (original equipment manufacturer) for golf clubs. Callaway Golf made golf history and truly established itself in 1991 with the introduction of a very popular stainless-steel driver called "The Big Bertha." The Big Bertha driver was soon followed by one of the biggest selling drivers of all time, the titanium headed "Great Big Bertha."

The success of the Big Bertha products—drivers, irons, and fairway woods—made Callaway Golf a major player in the golf club business and the oversized titanium driver explosion was on. The Big Bertha name and product line continued with Steelhead, Hawkeye, ERC, C4, and ERC Fusion. Recent additions include the FT-3, FT-5, and FT-i irons and drivers, the Odyssey putter line—the most popular putter in the United States, Europe, and Japan—as well as the Callaway Golf® X Junior set for 8- to 12-year-olds with a manufacturer's suggested retail price of $275.

By 2007 Callaway revenues exceeded $1.0 billion annually, making Callaway Golf one of the major OEMs in the business of golf. Callaway sells drivers and fairway woods, irons, and putters under the Callaway, Odyssey, Ben Hogan, and Top-Flite brands and also markets balls and accessories such as golf bags, gloves, headwear, footwear, and umbrellas. The Callaway trademarks and service marks are also licensed for products such as golf apparel, watches, travel gear, and eyewear. In November 2006, Callaway launched an online store where customers can order pre-owned golf products.

BUYER BEHAVIOR

Golfers, pros and amateurs, experiment with drivers, fairway woods, and putters more than other clubs in their golf bags. Many top professionals and amateurs choose to play with their favorite irons for years before changing. Callaway Golf made a cunning decision to enter the club market the way it did in the late 1980s and early 1990s. By introducing drivers, and uniquely designed fairway woods, clubs that players often change in the constant quest for distance and accuracy, Callaway Golf quickly became a name and force in the golf club equipment business.

THE GLOBAL GOLF MARKET

The golf industry has a broad and diverse global market. The game is popular around the world. The game and the rules are essentially the same everywhere. Golfers share similar characteristics and interests—a beginning golfer or an avid golfer in the United States is not much different from a beginning golfer or an avid golfer in Australia or Germany.

The professional golf tours have done much to link golf as a global sport. Golf enthusiasts from around the world can follow their sport and stars through televised tournaments, daily newspaper coverage, weekly golf journals, monthly golf magazines, and the Internet. Golf-related Web sites are among the most popular sites on the Internet. The Golf Channel on cable television continues to be a strong venue for direct product marketing as well as international event coverage. Golf is truly a global sport. Courses and competitions exist in many countries and on every continent except Antarctica. Professional and amateur players from around the world compete and interact with a high degree of etiquette and sportsmanship. Golfers at all levels share ideas and experiences from the game.

There are notable differences among global golf markets. Japanese golfers seek out technology and products to compensate for their smaller average stature. Savvy golf equipment manufacturers have developed clubs specifically for the Japanese market with different head shapes, weight, lie angle, and shafts adjusted for the average Japanese golfer's height. And the long or distance ball is very popular. In the United States, distance balls are inexpensive and fairly low-tech. In Japan, distance balls can sell for up to 500 yen each or more than $49 per dozen. While many U.S. golfers—regardless of ability—seek out the equipment used by professional golfers, Japanese golfers often think they are "not worthy" to use top-caliber equipment.

"In the U.S. we talk about the pyramid of influence and how the best players dictate what everyone else wants to buy," says Maki Shinoda of Nike. "But in Japan, you basically need to flip the pyramid upside down." This creates an interesting challenge for golf equipment manufacturers—technology sells but how best to position the product for the market so that it does not appear to be "too professional."

COMPETITION

The golf equipment business is a highly congested and very competitive marketplace. Many merchants exist, and the field is constantly changing with new start-ups, mergers, and acquisitions. Major equipment manufacturers include Titleist, TaylorMade, Callaway, and Ping. Adams, Cleveland, Wilson, Mizuno, Nike, and others also compete for a slice of the multibillion-dollar worldwide golf equipment market. Almost all well-established club manufacturers have followed Callaway's "Bigger is Better" philosophy when it comes to the marketing and manufacturing of popular drivers. In many respects, today's design and engineering for drivers has been a contest of who can make the most forgiving, longest driving club that technology and the rules of golf allow. Premium clubs today not only offer technological innovation, forgiveness, power, distance, and accuracy, but they are also pushing the laws of physics and the rules of golf.

CALLAWAY'S INTERNATIONAL MARKETS

For Callaway Golf, the global market is a very big part of its total market with about 44 percent of all sales coming from golfers in countries outside of the United States in 2006. The global market has grown in importance since the U.S. market—estimated at 28.7 million golfers—is relatively stagnant in terms of participants and number of rounds played (around 500 million annually). In fact, for the first time since World War II, more golf courses closed in the United States in 2006 than opened.

The Japanese golf market has yet to recover from a severe economic downturn in the 1990s, and this has hurt Callaway and other golf equipment manufacturers. The typical Japanese golfer is male, spends approximately 480,000 yen ($4,500) per year on golf, and plays 6.8 times a year, practicing 9.5 times a year. Although the cost to golf in Japan has actually fallen as the economy struggled (which should have helped make golf more affordable, boosting rounds played), demographics are now a huge factor. Forecasts predicted that Japan would see negative population growth for the first time in its history in 2007. Younger golfers are working more hours to support themselves and the aging Japanese population, leaving them fewer hours on the course to enjoy themselves.

One of the hottest Asian markets is South Korea. More than 30 percent of Korea's 4 million golfers are women, compared to 10 percent of U.S. golfers. Korean women account for the lion's share of the $600 million in golf and apparel/footwear sales tallied at retail compared to hard goods sales of $275 million. The female golf market is also growing faster than the male market in Korea. Pursuing the style-conscious female golfer domestically and internationally would represent a change for most golf equipment manufacturers, including Callaway.

What appeals to style-conscious women golfers? The upscale Shisegae Department Store in Seoul provides some insight. Shisegae devotes nearly an entire floor to golf equipment and apparel and nothing is cheap. Most of the customers are women. The TaylorMade r7 driver retails for 750,000 won ($810). Nearly every shirt costs at least $300! Form-fitting, stylish apparel is the norm. No khakis found here. The sale rack has a plethora of size large items, unlike U.S. stores where small sizes dominate among unsold merchandise.

Nike has a significant head start over many of its rivals in this market. Korean consumers aspire to look and dress like celebrities, and Nike has LPGA stars Michelle Wie and Grace Park endorsing and using Nike golf products.

ISSUES

In sports, it is often said that getting to the top is easier than staying there. Callaway Golf is faced with the burdensome task of sustaining its phenomenal growth and market share against competitors in hot pursuit. Discounting and innovation by competitors are challenges that Callaway now faces. Fast followers like Adams Golf and others have developed and discounted products that cut into Callaway's mainstay, the driver, fairway wood, and specialty club market. Callaway and others were left swimming for higher ground, moving into discount stores such as Target, as discounting and dumping have changed the market share landscape. Callaway has often resisted discounting its premium product line.

Technology does drive the industry. In 2004, Adidas-Soloman A.G. (TaylorMade) released a driver with technological innovation unlike any other on the market. TaylorMade's new driver, the r7 Quad, introduced a unique interchangeable weighting system that allows golfers to customize their driver for different course conditions and desired ball flight. More than three years later, the TaylorMade r7 was still arguably the most popular driver on the market.

Other big players in the equipment business are also after Callaway's market share and may pose a greater threat to Callaway's long-term success. Titleist, TaylorMade, and Ping are large enough and strong enough to survive any market slump and also have the resources to buy smaller successful companies and the technology to provide popular products.

Steps have been taken by golf's ruling bodies—the United States Golf Association (USGA) in North America and the Royal and Ancient Golf Club of St. Andrews (R&A)—to limit driver head size (larger heads improve forgiveness on off-center hits) and coefficient of restitution (the springiness of the club face surface that creates a trampoline effect producing more distance). Many of the golf greats believe more should be done to protect the game and have bemoaned the fact that technology and equipment advances have changed the game for the worse. Jack Nicklaus says, "It used to be 80 percent shot making and about 20 percent power." Those percentages have been reversed today, according to Nicklaus. Many classic golf courses have been rendered obsolete for professional tournaments by balls and clubs that allow players to reach the greens on par four holes in one shot and par fives in two shots.

There are calls to restrict the type of equipment pros can use for tournaments. Equipment manufacturers are not eager to back away from pursuing technological advances. The vast majority of customers are amateurs looking for any edge to improve their games, and one way is through more forgiving equipment. What will happen to the "pyramid of influence" if the pros or even amateur tournaments have to be played with a "handicap" on conforming equipment rather than the latest, greatest, most forgiving equipment? Will it protect the game and put more of the emphasis back on skill?

The newest and potentially biggest golf market is now emerging in China where golf is becoming a popular choice for a growing population of young professionals. Although there are currently only about 1 million Chinese golfers, an annual growth rate of 25 percent is forecast over the next five years. The key to future global growth for the golf equipment industry may be in the budding Chinese market or the growing Indian market, also expected to grow at the same healthy rate as the Chinese market.[7]

Questions

1 What are the pros and cons of a global versus a multidomestic approach to marketing golf clubs for Callaway? Which approach do you feel would have more merit and why?

2 What are some of the significant environmental factors that could have a major impact on the marketing of golf clubs internationally? Describe each factor and what the nature of the impact would be.

3 What marketing mix recommendations would you have for Callaway as it attempts to increase international market share, especially in Asian markets?

case D–8 HOM Furniture: Where Keen Observation Pays

"Some ideas are too good *not* to steal!" The speaker isn't a CIA agent but Wayne Johansen, CEO of HOM Furniture, a group of 13 furniture stores in the upper Midwest. Johansen isn't talking about anything illegal but is describing his approach to doing very practical, commonsense marketing research: visiting dozens of first-class retailers and then weaving the best of the ideas into HOM Furniture's operations. But that gets us ahead of the story.

HOW IT ALL BEGAN

Wayne Johansen's life reads like an entrepreneurial case study. Right out of high school, Johansen started JC Imports, a wholesale import business built around jewelry and leather goods. The decision to add waterbeds to the merchandise mix proved to be a smart one, and the import business was soon closed to focus on booming waterbed sales. But all good things must come to an end; waterbeds don't wear out and the target audience of baby boomers was aging. When the market became saturated, Johansen, along with his brother, Rod, and Carl Nyberg converted their Water Bedroom stores to Total Bedroom stores. Ultimately, they wanted to expand into a full-line furniture company, but they needed larger store sizes, more warehouse capacity, and more working capital. So they took the first step in 1991 and HOM Oak and Leather stores were born. In 1997, their ultimate dream became reality as HOM Oak and Leather expanded into HOM Furniture, with sales of $30 million in 1996 growing to about $110 million in 2007.

THE CONSUMER BUYING PROCESS

Success at HOM Furniture has been built upon keen understanding of how consumers buy furniture. Furniture is a product category characterized by "complexity and significant risk," explains Johansen. A furniture purchase must fit into the consumer's overall decorating scheme, coordinating with paint, wallpaper, draperies, and floor coverings. Women are the key decision makers and they believe that their home furnishings make a statement about whether they have good taste and social status. They fear a bad decision, relying more on the expertise of the salesperson and the selection available in the store, rather than on brand names.

HOM Furniture has responded with large and inviting stores in highly visible locations, featuring great selection and knowledgeable salespeople who specialize in a given department. The smell of fresh-baked cookies greets customers as they enter the store, drawing them into a racetrack-shaped layout of the different store departments. This provides maximum exposure to merchandise and creates an airy, open feeling.

MARKETING INFORMATION AT HOM

Very quickly, Johansen and his partners recognized the value of marketing information. Before the launch of HOM Furniture in 1997, they toured 70 of the top 100 U.S. full-line furniture stores to observe the practices that contribute most to success. Some of the successful ideas gleaned from these visits include fresh-baked cookies in the stores, the use of a "house" structure in the center of the stores, and the design of two-level stores.

This benchmarking activity continues today as HOM Furniture participates in a consortium of 14 furniture retailers in the United States, Canada, and Mexico. Because the member stores do not directly compete with one another in their geographic area, they are free to share financial statements, sales data, and their best ideas. Meeting three times annually, the participants spend the first day touring the host store and reviewing store advertising. The second day is reserved for the "best idea" contest. Each participant contributes $20 and the best idea takes the pot.

Site location is widely recognized as critical to the success of any retail store. To reach a regional audience, HOM Furniture builds stores that are highly visible from the freeways leading into the city from all directions. With analytical assistance from a local newspaper, management can plot the location of all current customers on a map as well as determine the market potential within a given radius for any possible future store location. Assuming that a customer will shop at the HOM store nearest his or her home, HOM management can calculate the extent to which a future store will cannibalize business from existing stores.

This geographic analysis can be merged with MicroVision data from Claritas. MicroVision is a segmentation and consumer targeting system that classifies every U.S. household into 1 of 48 unique market segments, using demographic, lifestyle, socioeconomic, buying, media, and behavioral characteristics. For any given ZIP code, MicroVision provides a count of the number of households for each of the 48 market segments identified. This allows HOM's management to build stores in areas that are heavily populated with the types of consumers who like to shop at HOM Furniture stores.

Once the store is in operation, sales and productivity information is closely monitored. Management has easy access to a database that tracks sales by store, by department, by day of the week, and by hour of the day. In addition, the sales generated by each salesperson are recorded on a monthly basis. Productivity analysis is made possible through an electronic sensor mounted on the doorframe of the main entrance to each store to measure "door swings"—a very precise measure of customer visits. With door swing data by store, by day, and by hour, management can use sales per door swing as a measure of productivity and also relate door swings to ads, such as a Sunday insert in the local paper.

After the sale is complete, HOM Furniture wants to make sure that the customer is thoroughly satisfied. On average, a person buys $40,000 of furniture during a lifetime. A satisfied customer is more likely to be a repeat customer, worth thousands of dollars in future business. For that reason, HOM monitors the number of customer calls received and also the percentage of products sold that requires service. Expanding the system for measurement of customer satisfaction is one of Johansen's future priorities.[8]

Questions

1 (*a*) Identify the data sources HOM Furniture uses in its marketing information system. (*b*) Which would you classify as secondary data sources? (*c*) Which would be considered primary data sources?

2 When HOM Furniture advertises, it looks for a resulting spike in sales using an extensive database. (*a*) What are the advantages of this approach? (*b*) What are the possible shortcomings of this approach and how would you address them?

3 Assume that you have been hired as a marketing consultant by HOM Furniture's management. (*a*) What specific types of information should HOM collect to measure customer satisfaction with its stores and services? (*b*) For each type of information you identified in (*a*), how would HOM Furniture make use of that information to improve customer satisfaction?

case D–9 Lawn Mowers: Segmentation Challenges

BACKGROUND

The lawn mower was developed in the 1830s in England. Interest and enthusiasm for lawn care in the United States dates back to the post-World War II boom in suburban living when America's obsession with the perfect lawn began. In the 1950s, the first gas-powered, rotary-motor lawn mowers were introduced, displacing the reel (manual push) lawn mower. The surge in demand for gas-powered mowers was also accompanied by a surge in mower-related injuries, leading to improvements in the safety of these devices.

Today, the industry is challenged to come up with more environmentally sound equipment. Although today's gas mowers are 70 percent less polluting than those produced 10 years ago, using a walking gas mower for one hour produces as much hydrocarbon and nitrogen oxide emissions—greenhouse gases—as driving 11 cars for an hour. And a gas-powered riding lawn mower produces as much greenhouse gas as driving 34 cars for an hour.

PRODUCTS

A wide range of products are available for cutting lawns; they vary in terms of power source (manual, electric, gas), operator mode (walking, riding, or automatic/robotic), and additional accessories and features ranging from baggers for grass clippings, cup holders, and power steering to a cooking grill.

An estimated 6 million gas-powered, walking lawn mowers were sold in 2007, the vast majority of all mowers sold in the United States. More Craftsman (Sears) gas-powered walking mowers were sold than any other brand. Prices for gas-powered walking lawn mowers range from $200 to $700 depending on horse power, brand, and features.

Reel mowers, the manual push mowers of old, have been making a comeback. American Lawn Mower Co. of Shelbyville, Indiana, claims to be the only U.S. manufacturer of reel mowers. Estimates are that 350,000 manual mowers were sold in 2007, up almost 100,000 over the previous year. Reel mowers are priced from $100 to $400 and eliminate concerns about gas, repairs, and getting it started. However, *Consumer Reports* cautions that most reel mowers can't cut grass higher than 1½ inches or trim closer than 3 inches around obstacles.

Electric lawn mowers—major brands include Black & Decker and Craftsman—are available in both corded and cordless models. Electric mowers produce no exhaust emissions and require little maintenance besides sharpening. Less adept at tackling tall or thick grass, most electric mowers cut 18 to 19-inch swaths versus 21 inches for most gas mowers. Prices range from $125 to $250 for corded, $400 or more for cordless. Corded versions tether you to within about 100 feet of a power outlet.

Riding lawn mowers share many of the same drawbacks as gas-powered walk-behind mowers. Riding mowers can be less maneuverable and fail to cut close to obstacles. Prices range from $1,600 to $7,200. While the big advantage of riding lawn mowers is the amount of territory that can be covered, they also have a following in the little known sport of lawn mower racing. The U.S. Lawn Mower Racing Association, based in Illinois, claims more than 20 chapters in various states and a slate of regional and national races culminating in a national championship.

LAWN SIZE

According to Bruce Butterfield, research director of the National Gardening Association, it's important to pick the right type of mower for your lawn size. "I've seen people with little yards riding a big riding mower. They spend more time backing up and turning around than cutting the grass." For under a half-acre of lawn (20,000 square feet), consider an electric or battery-powered mower. For lawns up to an acre (43,560 square feet), a gas-powered walk-behind mower is recommended. And if your lawn is from 1 to 3 acres (130,680 square feet), it may be time to consider a riding mower or a lawn tractor.

BENEFITS SOUGHT

What are people looking for in a lawn mower? Is it about speed in mowing the lawn, safety, control, noise reduction, reducing their carbon footprint?

A surprising force in the demand for reel lawn mowers has been women purchasing the mowers for the exercise. Why go to the gym when you can get a workout on your lawn each week? A return to manual mowers has even been touted as a way of addressing the obesity problem in children. Get those inactive kids away from the video games this summer and out there mowing the lawn.

Mower-produced pollution and gas prices have captured the interest of the industry and consumers. Since most gasoline-powered lawn mowers do not have catalytic converters, they produce a significant amount of greenhouse gases, not to mention the fact that they are running on a nonrenewable resource—petroleum. Adding catalytic converters to gas-powered mowers is being resisted vigorously by manufacturers just as automobile manufacturers resisted the change in the 1970s. California's proposed regulation of small-engine emissions (which would necessitate the use of a catalytic converter) would cut 22 tons of smog-forming chemicals from the air *per day,* the equivalent of more than 800,000 cars per day.

While a representative for Briggs and Stratton claims that meeting new pollution standards will require a minimum of a 30 percent across-the-board price increase, the Environmental Protection Agency estimates that a catalytic converter and new hoses would cost a company about $20 to $25 per machine on average. Many consumers apparently are willing to pay more for a cleaner machine, especially when educated about the pollution problem.

Home Depot's "Mow Down Pollution" program has been a big success in Canada. Home Depot collected a record 5,000 gas-powered mowers and trimmers in a 10-day period in April, giving consumers a rebate for new manual or electric mowers. The switch was most pronounced in health-conscious urban areas such as Toronto, Montreal, and Vancouver.[9]

Questions

1 Identify at least three bases for segmenting the lawn mower market. Prepare a market–product grid illustrating at least one of these bases.

2 What criteria should a lawn equipment company use in assessing the attractiveness of market segments? What sort of information is needed to fill in the market–product grid and allow the firm to make that target market decision?

3 How might a lawn mower company use segmentation for positioning purposes? At present, the manual reel mower market is rather small but growing. What marketing mix recommendations could be used to significantly expand this market?

case D–10 Medtronic in China: Where "Simpler" Serves Patients Better

"I felt tremendous pressure to find markets and technologies to grow the business in other parts of the world," says Bobby Griffin, president of Medtronic Pacing Business. "Ninety-seven percent of Medtronic's products were being sold to 27 percent of the world. I'd read books on China and *BusinessWeek* articles about the success of

General Electric and other companies that had gone into China with scaled-down products."

THE MARKET AND THE NEED

Medtronic is the world's leading medical technology company and sells products to alleviate heart arrhythmia and neurological disorders, such as heart pacemakers, defibrillators, and angioplasty balloon catheters. But in the early 1990s, Medtronic sold only a few pacemakers in China, a country of 1.3 billion people. So Griffin interviewed a number of Chinese physicians. Their desires were very clear: They wanted a highly reliable, basic pacing device that would allow them to serve more people in need. "These doctors were motivated not by greed but by their desire to help and heal their patients," Griffin concluded. "Their relationships with their patients in the hospitals were touching. Instead of talking down to them from a standing position, they would get down on one knee and whisper in the patient's ear."

Griffin also found that only 4,000 cardiac patients a year were implanted with pacemakers in China, a small minority of the patients who needed them. "It was clear that a certain class of people in China could afford almost anything, while most could afford no treatment at all," Griffin said. "Yet more people in China could afford pacing than the populations of Germany and France combined. Of the millions of people living in the coastal cities and provinces of China, those in the middle class had $2,000 in disposable income. Ten thousand television sets were being sold every week, but health care is also vitally important."

THE NEW PACEMAKER FOR CHINA

As Griffin's plane lifted off from the Hong Kong airport, he recalled, "If we could build a pacemaker we could sell in China for $1,000 and still make our margins, we could serve many more people all over the world with a reliable product and still make a profit. I made up my mind to set an audacious goal. I'd shoot for a *radical* cost reduction in the product design."

Back at corporate headquarters, after a "You're crazy, Griffin!" reaction, Medtronic's head of development agreed to support the project. The project also received support from Medtronic's marketing organization: They liked the idea because the company could lead with an inexpensive product that could leverage sales of higher-end products later.

To meet Bobby Griffin's audacious goal, Medtronic chose its Champion pacemaker, a simplified version of the company's existing pacing systems that could meet specifications of cardiologists in China. Mechanical engineering design manager Bill Hooper had been supporting the Champion pacing system through Quest, a special program within the company that funded the work of engineers who wanted to develop projects that wouldn't otherwise receive funding. Hooper observed, "My dream was to see patients in less developed countries restored to full life in ways that had been available for years in more developed countries." His efforts exemplified Medtronic's mission: *To contribute to human welfare by application of biomedical engineering in the research, design, manufacture, and sale of instruments or appliances that alleviate pain, restore health, and extend life.*

Hooper and electrical engineer Larry Hudziak had taken the current sophisticated technology and simplified it. "We wanted to reduce the cost to make it affordable in the Chinese market. By using a proven pacing lead technology for the coil, insulator, electrode and tine, we were able to save substantially. One of the most critical parts of the Champion, the lead wire, was needed to flex whenever patients breathed, their hearts beat, or they moved. We chose a lead that had the best reliability of anything we make," Hooper explained.

The Champion design did not include more complex, state-of-the-art features like dual chamber stimulation, activity sensors, or steroid-eluding leads. The Chinese physicians Bobby Griffin had met with considered these features unnecessary, preferring high quality, low cost, longevity, and ease of use. The design team had to work hard to reduce the cost of the Champion pacemaker, which could translate into a lower selling price. Medtronic engineers also designed the Champion so that it could be programmed externally with a simple magnetic device. By February 1995, the design was complete and the product had been tested.

ON-SITE IN CHINA: A NEW PLANT AND SALESFORCE

Medtronic realized that to ensure quality control, it needed to be directly involved in the production and selling process, and available when physicians implanted the pacemaker. Bill Hooper knew how to design facilities to cut costs, but it required an almost constant presence in Shanghai, where the plant was being built. Over a three-year period, Hooper made 19 trips, and Ron Meyer, vice president of a pacing group, made 26. They reported to each other via e-mail and phone calls. "The routine was grueling," Hooper recalls. "Check into the hotel, unpack, head out to buy water and walk for exercise, then back to your room. It was such a drill."

Building a new plant was not the only challenge facing Hooper and Meyer. Medtronic also needed a salesforce, including experienced heart surgeons, to contact and train Chinese physicians. Furthermore, with the plant located in Shanghai, on the eastern coast of China, they needed a distribution system capable of serving a country roughly the size of the United States (9.6 million square kilometers).

Hooper recalled that these were tough times for both of them: "We both had families. When I was doing algebra with my daughter on the phone in the middle of the night from China, I could remind myself, 'I'm here because of Medtronic's mission and my part in fulfilling that mission.' If I hadn't had that, I would have given up."[10]

Questions

1 Assess Medtronic's decision to develop and market the new Champion heart pacemaker in terms of the following reasons for new-product success: (*a*) points of difference, (*b*) market attractiveness, (*c*) bad timing, and (*d*) economic access to doctors and patients.

2 Discuss the steps of the new-product process as they relate to the Champion pacemaker.

3 New-product development is important to a company like Medtronic, but it is hard work, and often leads to failure. How can a company encourage its employees to take initiative, make a profit, *and* be ethically and socially responsible?

4 Relate Medtronic's decision to sell pacemakers in China to its corporate mission statement. How does the decision relate to these Medtronic stakeholders: (*a*) shareholders of Medtronic stock, (*b*) Medtronic employees, and (*c*) Chinese patients?

5 Medtronic chose to design and build a new low-priced, highly reliable, reduced-feature heart pacemaker in its Shanghai plant. What are the strengths and weaknesses of this decision from (*a*) a marketing viewpoint and (*b*) an ethical viewpoint?

case D–11 Pampered Pooches Travel in Style

Can nothing be too good for man's best friend? Pampered pets can dine on Omaha Steaks' Steak Treats for Pets, 100 percent beefsteak with no additives and preservatives, and then finish off with a Frosty Paws soy-based "ice cream" treat for dessert. Fido can recline on a decadent burgundy Versailles love seat for $285 from Awesome Pet Products while wearing a faux mink coat and rhinestone tiara. If that weren't enough, burgeoning pet services include massage, chiropractic, and even liposuction.

The American Pet Products Marketing Association estimated that $40.8 billion would be spent on pets in 2007, $16.1 billion of that on food. To put this in perspective, the nearly $41 billion spent by U.S. consumers on their pets is more than the gross domestic product of all but 64 countries in the world. It's more than U.S. consumers spend annually on movies, video games, and recorded music combined. And pet spending is expected to exceed $52 billion within two years. About 63 percent of all U.S. households now own a pet, more than 71.1 million households.

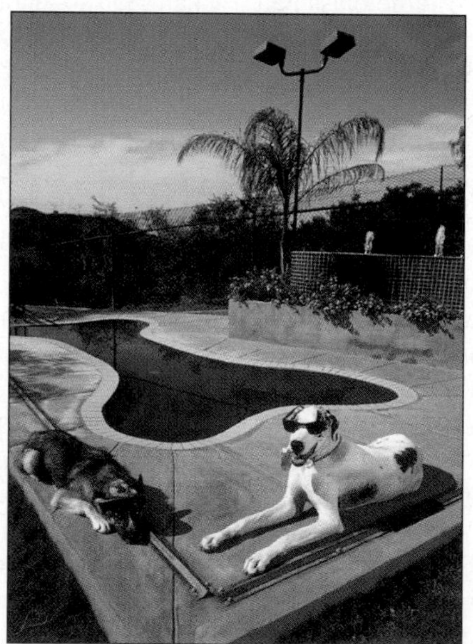

Who are these pampered pets? And perhaps more importantly, who are their owners? There are 88.3 million cats and 74.8 million dogs in the United States. Pampered pets are often surrogate children for empty nesters and childless-by-choice couples. The vast majority of pet owners consider themselves "mom" or "dad" to their pets. Pets are also considered companions and friends.

American Demographics divides pet owners into four key segments: married boomers with no kids, single/divorced boomer women, young couples with no kids, and seniors. Married boomers without kids are 27 percent more likely than the average American to have a pet and 30 percent more likely than the average American to have more than one pet. More than half (52 percent) of 35-to-45-year-old married couples without children have a pet, 31 percent have two or more. This segment also spends more money on pets than married couples with children. Among the single/divorced boomer women segment, 45 percent own a pet. This group is 18 percent more likely than the average American to own a cat.

Young couples with no kids spend more per year on their pets than any other segment. Of young couples with no kids, 52 percent own a pet and are 33 percent more likely than the average American to own more than one pet.

Among seniors, 39 percent of those 55 to 64 years of age own a pet, and 25 percent of those over 65 own a pet. Seniors are expected to be the group with the fastest rate of growth in pet ownership.

Owners of pampered pooches are likely subscribers to such lifestyle magazines as *Animal Fair, Dog Fancy, Modern Dog,* and *The Bark*—a Berkeley area newsletter started to fight for a leash-free park that has evolved into the *New Yorker* for dog enthusiasts.

One of the hottest parts of the pet market right now is pet travel. An estimated 30 million households travel with their pets, most by car. Air travel with pets is becoming more problematic. At least two North American airlines have banned pets from traveling due to complaints and concerns of passengers with allergies and asthma and because of reduced cargo space as a result of security regulations requiring passengers to check more of their baggage. The majority of those traveling pets are dogs. According to the Travel Industry Association of America, 78 percent of all traveling pets are dogs while 15 percent are cats.

The number of pet-friendly lodgings has increased 300 percent in the past three years, according to Bring YourPet.com. The American Automobile Association has added more than 1,000 pet-friendly lodgings to its 2007 pet travel guide for more than 13,000 total listings. Web sites devoted to identifying pet-friendly accommodations such as Pettravel.com and Petsonthego.com, and books such as AAA's *Traveling With Your Pet* are very popular as devoted pet owners make travel plans.

Traditional hotel and motel companies are increasingly catering to pet owners. Hotels and Resorts Worldwide (Sheraton, Westin, and W Hotels) offer oversized pet pillows; plush doggie robes; a check-in gift package that includes a pet toy, dog treat, ID tag, bone, and turn-down treat; and even have a licensed masseuse for dogs on staff. Upscale hotels are more likely to cater to pets and their owners. The Peninsula Chicago has a "pets only" room-service menu. Among other amenities, canine guests get inscribed water bowls at the Beverly Hills Hotel.

According to a survey by TripAdviser, the most pet-friendly hotel chain is Best Western followed by the Holiday Inn and then Red Roof. Among pet owners' biggest concerns when traveling are stress on the pet and care for the pet while they're touring or sightseeing. Look for pet-friendly hospitality services to address these needs.

Or how about a vacation with your best friend at a place such as Camp Unleashed in the Berkshires where you can hike, swim, and camp with your dog at your side?

Pet products companies are expanding their offerings to move into the pet hospitality area. For example, PetSmart is opening PetsHotel next to some of its stores. Starting at $21, PetsHotel provides a private kennel, two walks per day, and supervised playroom time. For a $10 "room" upgrade, you can provide your pet with a television set tuned to *Animal Planet* as well as the "Bone Booth" where pets can take phone calls from their owners.

Kennels can rival four-star hotels—pet aerobics, manicures, swim lessons—and even conventional kennels have added more upscale services. In fact, kennels have restyled themselves as pet country clubs, pet resorts, or pet care centers. Jim Krack, executive director of the American Boarding Kennel Association, put it this way: "A dog doesn't really care if he's in a place with cement walls or one with wallpaper and a brass bed, but owners today expect the same type of accommodations and services they can get for themselves."

Consider the 31-year-old woman who had her 7-year-old black lab, Daisy, as bridesmaid at her wedding. While the newlyweds were on their honeymoon in Italy, Daisy spent two weeks at the luxurious Paradise Ranch Country Club for Dogs in Sun Valley, California, at $45 per night. For this bride, nothing is too good for her best friend.[11]

Questions

1 What product attributes and benefits could an upscale hotel provide a pet owner? Are these the same product attributes and benefits provided by an upscale kennel?

2 What strategy would a company like Petco be pursuing by entering the pet hotel market? What strategy would a company like Marriott be pursuing by entering the pet hotel market?

3 What are the pros and cons of (*a*) a multiproduct branding strategy and (*b*) a multibranding strategy in the pet hospitality industry for companies such as (*a*) Petco and (*b*) Marriott?

4 What stage of the product life cycle is the pet hospitality industry in? An offering such as PetSmart's PetsHotel? Explain and support your answers.

case D–12 DigitalThink: Marketing E-Learning Services

"In 1996, two colleagues and I started discussing the possibilities that the Internet was opening up for corporate training," said Umberto Milletti, vice president of marketing and solutions management at DigitalThink. "We realized that we could harness the power of the same technologies that had revolutionized other parts of the business world to help organizations better disseminate skills and knowledge to their people."

Milletti's observation was very insightful. Over the last several decades, computer technology and, more recently, the Internet have changed the way that companies around the world do business. Increasingly powerful computers and software applications help employees work more productively; processes that once were laborious and manual are lightning fast; and geographically dispersed people can communicate and collaborate in cyberspace faster than ever before.

DigitalThink, a company that has grown from 3 employees to more than 400, and was recently ranked 22nd among the 500 fastest-growing technology companies, is at the forefront of a revolution in corporate training and education services. DigitalThink and other e-learning companies are supplementing, and occasionally replacing, traditional classroom-based training in much of the business world. The effectiveness of e-learning is causing many firms to reconsider their methods of providing training and education to employees, partners, and customers.

MARKET OPPORTUNITIES

Large companies with many locations and dispersed work forces, such as car rental agencies, hotels, airlines, retail stores, banks, and consulting firms, need to train thousands of employees frequently throughout the year. In the past, employees would gather in central locations for training courses that could last anywhere from a few days to one month. This approach to training and education was very costly and time consuming, and its effectiveness was influenced by inconsistencies in the capabilities of the trainers and the difficulty of requiring the trainers and the students to be in the same location. Using technology-based instruction saves the company time and money by increasing the reliability and effectiveness of the service and by putting the learner in control of the location and the pace of the learning experience. DigitalThink is leading the e-learning movement. Its methods have been shown to compress training time by as much as 50 percent and reduce the cost of development, maintenance, and delivery by 64 percent. A recent study reported that the global market for e-learning has grown at a 100 percent annual growth rate to $33.6 billion in 2005.

HOW DOES DIGITALTHINK ACHIEVE THESE MIRACULOUS RESULTS?

DigitalThink e-learning is tied directly to tangible outcomes. Courses are designed to develop the specific knowledge and skills that employees or salespeople need to do their jobs and to give them the opportunity to test their knowledge and apply what they've learned with a real-world situation or problem that they might encounter on the job. "Learning is most effective when students practice and demonstrate performance in a way that closely matches the performance expected of them," explains Shelly Berkowitz, manager of instructional design at DigitalThink. "We design relevant, realistic practice and assessment activities that require students to solve problems that are as complex as those they encounter in actual work situations."

Trainees can go through the courses at their own pace, allowing people to take as much or as little time as they need. Advanced students can skip over material that they already know and go directly to the exercise or assessment section to test their mastery of the material. DigitalThink e-learning can also be delivered to the learner through different media: on a CD, via a company intranet, or through a browser on the Internet. The Web-based versions of DigitalThink's training courses are the most popular—these allow companies to update and maintain the training program easily and cost effectively as well as reach all their employees smoothly and quickly.

THE MARKET

DigitalThink sees its target market as the Global 2000 companies, the largest corporations in the United States and around the world. These companies have the critical mass needed to justify large training programs, as well as continued need for training and retraining. Within these companies, key decision makers with large staffs might include the director of a call center, the vice president of sales, or the chief information officer. Hardware and software manufacturers, travel and leisure companies, major retailers, and other organizations that have typically been dependent on massive instructor-led training efforts are key markets where DigitalThink has had success selling its e-learning products and services. In fact, DigitalThink's current customers include 31 of the Fortune 100 companies and 450 organizations in 158 countries. Specific customer needs vary from ready-made courseware, to custom course development, to comprehensive learning management systems that include virtual classrooms, content management systems, and consulting services.

CUSTOMER EXAMPLES

DigitalThink developed a customized training program for an international airline's baggage and reservations departments. This airline is geographically dispersed, so it did not make sense for it to constantly transport new employees to a central location for training. Also, with the large number of people performing these jobs, training needs are almost constant. The content of the training is process oriented, which is one of the best applications for e-learning. The airline and its employees are pleased with the decision to transition the training program to a technology-based system.

Circuit City is another of DigitalThink's customers. "The e-learning program that we provide to Circuit City is centered around customer service, products that the sales counselors sell, general sales skills, and managerial skills," explains Milletti. DigitalThink has helped Circuit City create effective, interactive training for its 40,000 associates and managers, which has helped the company realize more than $100 million in cost savings. And the retailer expects to see continued improvement in customer satisfaction and sales.[12]

Questions

1 What are (*a*) the advantages and (*b*) the disadvantages of DigitalThink's technology-based instruction over conventional classroom-based educational services?

2 Given your answer to question 1 above, (*a*) what are the key criteria DigitalThink should use in identifying prospective customers for its service, (*b*) what market segments meet your criteria, and (*c*) what are possible sales objections these segments might have that you have to address?

3 Suppose a large international hotel chain asks DigitalThink to make a proposal to train its thousands of front-desk clerks and receptionists. (*a*) How would you design an e-learning program to train them how to check in a customer? (*b*) How can DigitalThink demonstrate the points of difference or benefits to the hotel chain of its technology-based instruction to obtain a contract to design an e-learning program?

case D–13 Health Cruises, Inc.: Estimating Cost, Volume, and Profit Relationships

Health Cruises, Inc., packages cruises to Caribbean islands such as Martinique and the Bahamas. Like conventional cruises, the packages are designed to be fun. But the cruise is structured to help participants become healthier by breaking old habits, such as smoking or overeating. The Miami-based firm was conceived by Susan Isom, 30, a self-styled innovator and entrepreneur. Prior to this venture, she had spent several years in North Carolina promoting a behavior-modification clinic.

Isom determined that many people were very concerned about developing good health habits, yet they seemed unable to break away from their old habits because of the pressures of day-to-day living. She reasoned that they might have a chance for much greater success in a pleasant and socially supportive environment, where good health habits were fostered. Accordingly, she established Health Cruises, Inc., hired 10 consulting psychologists and health specialists to develop a program, and chartered a ship. DeForrest Young, a Miami management consultant, became the chairperson of Health Cruises. Seven of Isom's business associates contributed an initial capital outlay totaling more than $250,000. Of this amount, $65,000 went for the initial advertising budget, $10,000 for other administrative expenses, and $220,000 for the ship rental and crew.

Mary Porter, an overweight Denver schoolteacher, has signed up to sail on a two-week cruise to Nassau, departing December 19. She and her shipmates will be paying an average of $1,500 for the voyage. The most desirable staterooms cost $2,200.

Mary learned of the cruise by reading the travel section of her Sunday newspaper on October 16. On that date, the Pittsford and LaRue Advertising Agency placed promotional notices for the cruise in several major metropolitan newspapers. Mary was fascinated by the idea of combining therapy sessions with swimming, movies, and an elegant atmosphere.

Pittsford and LaRue account executive Carolyn Sukhan originally estimated that 300 people would sign up for the cruise after reading the October 16 ads. But as of November 14, only 200 had done so. Isom and Health Cruises, Inc., faced an important decision.

"Here's the situation as I see it," explained a disturbed Isom at the Health Cruises board meeting. "We've already paid out more than a quarter of a million to get this cruise rolling. It's going to cost us roughly $200 per passenger for the two weeks, mostly for food. Pittsford and LaRue predicted that 300 people would respond to the advertising campaign, but we've only got 200.

"I see three basic options: (1) we cancel the cruise and take our losses; (2) we run the cruise with the 200 and a few more that will trickle in over the next month; or (3) we shell out some more money on advertising and hope that we can pull in more people.

"My recommendation to this board is that we try to recruit more passengers. There are simply too many empty rooms on that ship. Each one costs us a bundle."

At this point, Carolyn Sukhan addressed the board: "I've worked out two possible advertising campaigns for the November 20 papers. The first, the limited campaign, will cost $6,000. I estimate that it will bring in some 20 passengers. The more ambitious campaign, which I personally recommend, would cost $15,000. I believe this campaign will bring in a minimum of 40 passengers.

"I realize that our first attempt was somewhat disappointing. But we're dealing here with a new concept, and a follow-up ad might work with many newspaper readers who were curious and interested when they read our first notice.

"One thing is absolutely certain," Sukhan emphasized. "We must act immediately if there's any hope of getting more people on board. The deadline for the Sunday papers is in less than 48 hours. And if our ads don't appear by this weekend, you can forget it. No one signs up in early December for a December 18 sailing date."

Isom interrupted, shaking her head. "I just don't know what to say. I've looked over Carolyn's proposals, and they're excellent. Absolutely first-rate. But our problem, to be blunt, is money. Our funds are tight, and our investors are already nervous. I get more calls each day, asking me where the 300 passengers are. It won't be easy to squeeze another $6,000 out of these people. And to ask them for $15,000—well, I just don't know how we're going to be able to justify it."[13]

Questions

1 What is the minimum number of passengers that Health Cruises must sign up by November 20 to break even with the cruise? (Show your calculations.)

2 Should Health Cruises go ahead with the cruise, since 200 passengers had signed up as of November 14?

3 Would it be worthwhile for Health Cruises to spend either $6,000 or $15,000 for advertising on November 20? If so, which figure would you recommend?

4 How realistic are Carolyn Sukhan's estimates of 20 more passengers for the $6,000 advertising campaign and 40 more passengers for the $15,000 campaign?

5 Should Health Cruises consider cutting its prices for this maiden voyage health cruise?

case D–14 Bagel Bakes: Pricing a New Breakfast Product

"What a Monday morning," thought Kyoshi (Yosh) McNamara. At 8:30 A.M., Yosh expected to leisurely start the fourth and final week of the marketing analyst orientation program at Pristo-Kay, Inc., a medium-size consumer food company. By 11:30 A.M., he had sole responsibility for preparing a pricing recommendation to the vice president of breakfast products for Bagel Bakes, a new line of breakfast foods.

BACKGROUND

Yosh joined Pristo-Kay as a marketing analyst trainee in June 2007 after graduating with a BBA degree in marketing and finance. He had interned with Pristo-Kay the previous summer and worked in the department responsible for prepared breakfast foods. His first three weeks on the job were occupied by software systems training and attending a marketing research boot camp for novice marketing research professionals.

He also spent time with the marketing team for which he was assigned. This team had developed a new line of prepared breakfast foods called Bagel Bakes. These bagels have cream cheese, processed fruit, or peanut butter baked inside and are thin enough to fit in a standard one-slice toaster. Everyone agreed that the development team had done an outstanding job on this project. Consumer tests indicated that Bagel Bakes was the tastiest prepared food developed by Pristo-Kay in recent memory. Management was confident that Bagel Bakes would strengthen Pristo-Kay's breakfast product portfolio, but were aware that it was a departure from existing successful breakfast products. Management was also sensitive to the fact that hundreds of prepared breakfast products are launched annually with a very low percentage (6 percent) of these products still on the market 12 months after launch.

The Bagel Bakes marketing team consisted mainly of Tracy Jackson and Ken Byrne. Tracy was the product manager, having had a hand in developing the product (along with the food science, consumer insights, research and development, and finance teams). She had considerable experience in the food industry over the past 20 years. Ken was an associate product manager and acted as the marketing interface for sales and logistics—a key role for the upcoming product launch. His job was to prepare the sales tools that Pristo-Kay's salesforce needed to ensure that national retailers would carry Bagel Bakes. He also performed all analyses pertaining to stocking fees and point-of-sale promotion for large accounts.

On Friday of the previous week, Yosh heard a rumor that Tracy was interviewing with a competitor for a vice president position. When he arrived on Monday, he learned that Tracy had cleared out her desk over the weekend. Yosh also learned through the office grapevine that Tracy had recruited Ken to work for the competitor. As Yosh contemplated these events, Bob Smith, Pristo-Kay's vice president of breakfast products, approached his cubicle. Bob explained the situation, including the pricing recommendation request. He also said this could be an excellent opportunity for Yosh, if he made the best of it:

> "Tracy and Ken's positions will be filled quickly, but these hiring searches often take several months. Bagel Bakes needs to be launched as quickly as possible—we can't wait to fill these vacancies. The marketing plan is ready with the exception of the pricing plan, which has not yet been finalized. We are going to need you to take the lead on developing pricing recommendations for this product. Clearly, all final decisions will be made by myself and the rest of senior management, but you have a great chance to make an impression on this group. Please put together a pricing analysis and recommendation—include suggested retail prices for discount, grocery, and convenience stores. There are a number of considerations for pricing a new product like this—identify the key ones. Support your decisions well—doing this project properly would score you a lot of points right now and open up many options for your future here.
>
> One final thought for you before you get working on this: Consumer testing shows that the repurchase rate for this product should be very high, which makes me think that

promotional pricing should be used for the first few months, but this is also one of our most expensive breakfast products, in terms of production costs, making it difficult to lower prices substantially. Be sure to also include your recommendation for promotional pricing, both in terms of prices and length of promotion. I know this is a lot to ask given your short time here, but you can handle this."

BAGEL BAKES MARKETING PLAN

The targeting, positioning, promotion, and channel elements of the Bagel Bakes marketing plan had already received approval from senior management. Each element is described below.

Target Market

The primary target market for Bagel Bakes will be young adults looking for a quick, hassle-free hot breakfast. Secondary target markets include two-income families and late-night snackers of all ages.

Positioning

Bagel Bakes was to be positioned . . .

> For busy young people wanting a hot breakfast prepared in a hurry, Bagel Bites is a self-contained, quick and easy start to the day and the most delicious prepared breakfast food available.

Bagel Bakes was intended to capitalize on the growing trend toward "eating on the run" with a traditional breakfast food. In this regard, Tracy crafted a positioning map showing the competitive space for products currently available in the market. The figure below shows the proposed location for Bagel Bakes. The traditional to progressive axis denotes how similarly a product mimics a breakfast consumers could realistically prepare themselves. The sit-down to eat-on-the-run axis denotes the portability of each product. Also shown is whether a product is shelved in the frozen-food section (FRZ) or cereal section (DRY) of food stores, the number of servings per package (count), and the manufacturer's suggested retail price (MSRP). Bagel Bakes would occupy the traditional breakfast, eat-on-the-run competitive space in the frozen-food section and contain five servings (five bagels).

Retail Channels

Bagel Bakes would be sold in the freezer section of grocery, discount, and convenience chain stores currently served by Pristo-Kay. Grocery stores (e.g., Kroger) typically obtained a 23 percent margin based on the MSRP. Discount stores (e.g., Costco) obtained a 15 percent margin. Convenience stores (e.g., 7-Eleven) obtained a 50 percent margin. As a rule, discount stores priced their items 10 percent less than grocery stores.

Packaging

Bagel Bakes would be packaged in two sizes. A five-count (five bagels) package would be sold in grocery

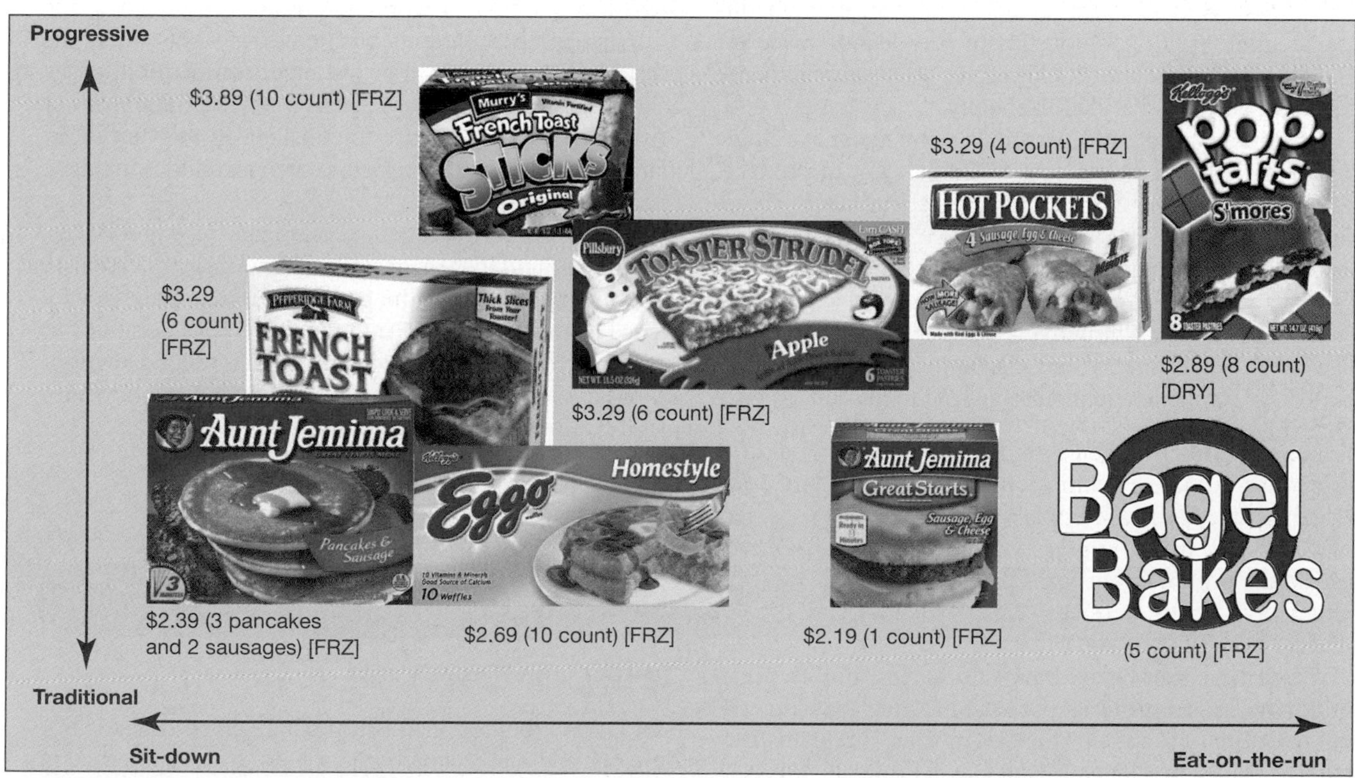

CHANNEL	BAGEL BAKES UNIT VOLUME ESTIMATES BY CHANNEL AND RETAIL PRICE		
Grocery	$3.49 1,550,000 (5-count packs)	$3.99 1,375,000 (5-count packs)	$4.49 725,000 (5-count packs)
Discount	$3.14 1,550, 000 (5-count packs)	$3.59 1,375,000 (5-count packs)	$4.04 725,000 (5-count packs)
Convenience	$0.99 380,000 (1-count packs)	$1.49 250,000 (1-count packs)	$1.99 90,000 (1-count packs)

and discount stores. A single-count (one bagel) package would be sold in convenience stores.

Advertising and Promotion

The first-year advertising and promotion plan for Bagel Bakes included $2 million for media and $750,000 for slotting fees, necessary to "buy" freezer space in stores. About 70 percent of the media expenditure would be spent in the first four months of the product's launch to create consumer awareness and trial.

Manufacturing and Delivery Costs

Bagel Bakes required specialized baking and food injection equipment. Pristo-Kay purchased this equipment for $450,000. The equipment would be depreciated over five years given frequent advances in food manufacturing technology. In addition, Pristo-Kay leased space for Bagel Bakes production and inventory. The lease expense for the space was $240,000 annually.

Pristo-Kay production personnel estimated that a single Bagel Bake bagel would cost $0.28 per unit to produce, which included the cost of ingredients and labor. Therefore, a five-count Bagel Bake package would cost $1.40 to produce. Packaging cost for a five-count package was estimated to be $0.15 per box. A one-count package would cost $0.10 per box. The delivery cost for a five-count package sold to the grocery and discount channel was $0.10 and $0.07 for a one-count package sold to the convenience channel.

PRICING CONSIDERATIONS

Pristo-Kay's consumer insights group had conducted focus groups and commissioned a simulated market test that included the marketing plan. Three grocery channel retail prices were tested for the five-count package ($3.49, $3.99, and $4.49) and three retail prices were tested for the one-count package ($0.99, $1.49, and $1.99). The test also simulated Bagel Bakes prices for the discount channel, which were 10 percent below grocery retail prices. The simulated test market yielded unit volume estimates by channel and price point. The results are shown above.

As Yosh reviewed the Bagel Bakes situation, he realized that Monday would not be the leisurely day he had expected.[14]

Questions

1 What are the different considerations when setting the price for Bagel Bakes? For instance, competition, costs, and consumer psychology. When studying the impact of Pristo-Kay's costs, be sure to consider all relevant information from the marketing plan, such as retailer margins, fixed and variable costs.

2 What MSRP would you recommend for Bagel Bakes, keeping in mind the various considerations in question 1? Recommend prices for the grocery, discount, and convenience channels, keeping in mind these considerations as well as the respective margins for each retailer category.

3 What other marketing mix tactics would you recommend for Bagel Bakes?

case D–15 Ken Davis Products, Inc.: Finding Success in Retail Channels

"We position Ken Davis Bar-B-Q Sauces, not as something you use for grilling, but as something that adds flavor to ordinary food—a 'spice kit in a jar,'" explains Barbara Jo Davis, president of Ken Davis Products, Inc.

THE COMPANY

Ken Davis Products, Inc., is a small, regional business that develops and markets barbecue sauces. It has succeeded in this fiercely competitive business against corporate giants with this spice-kit-in-a-jar positioning both for its ultimate users and also the food brokers, distributors, and retailers needed to reach them.

The company got its start when Ken Davis, Barbara's late husband, owned a restaurant where he served his grandmother's recipe for barbecue sauce. His grandmother's recipe was a little of this and a little of that—not always the same amounts or ingredients. Customers loved the sauce, but Ken finally realized he needed to standardize the recipe so that consumers would have the same great-tasting sauce every time. He called in Barbara Jo Taylor, a home economist experienced in corporate test kitchens, to help him with the recipe for the sauce. Shortly afterward, Ken married Barbara, closed the restaurant, and began marketing barbecue sauce full time. She now serves as president of Ken Davis Products.

While Ken Davis Products is a market leader regionally, it has not expanded to national distribution. Barbara Davis explains, "What I hear consumers say again and again is the reason they buy Ken Davis barbecue sauces is because it's a local company. I think the reason we're the market leaders is because it's a personal product." Obviously it's not enough just to *be* local, the product has to *appeal* to local tastes, too.

PRODUCTS AND MARKETS

Barbecue sauce is a highly regional business compared with many other condiments because of consumer taste preferences. For example, sweeter sauces are preferred in the Midwest, vinegar-based sauces in the Southeast. Ken Davis Products offers Original, 2 Carb Original, Smooth 'n Spicy, and Sweet & Smoky sauces. Barbara Davis conducts focus groups, solicits comments from shoppers in the supermarket aisles or from testers at an in-store sampling. This allows Ken Davis to continue to be the regional leader.

Barbecue sauces are categorized as base sauces, premium, or super premium brands. Super premium category sauces offer retailers margins over 20 percent; premium (Ken Davis, Bull's Eye, KC Masterpiece) typically provide a retail margin of 18 to 20 percent; and base sauces (Kraft, Heinz) offer a 12 to 15 percent retail margin.

Since consumers do most of their grilling and barbecuing in the summer, the barbecue sauce market is highly seasonal. Retailers will often cut margins on barbecue sauces seasonally and use them as loss leaders during key holidays. Margins and prices are higher "off season."

COMPETITION

The barbecue sauce market is very competitive and Ken Davis Products faces national brands offered by major consumer packaged goods companies such as Kraft and Heinz. These national companies employ their own salesforces to call on grocers and institutional accounts to purchase their products. Local or regional sauce manufacturers rely upon food brokers to represent their products. These food brokers earn a margin of 2.5 to 3.5 percent to represent the manufacturer's products. Typically food brokers demand higher margins for slower moving products and lower margins for faster turn-over items.

It's hard for national manufacturers to cater to local and regional taste preferences and still maintain a consistent brand image as well as manufacturing efficiencies. This is something that regional or local companies such as Ken Davis can do well.

LISTENING TO CONSUMERS

"You have to listen to your consumer because you're not in this business to please yourself—but to please your consumer," says Barbara Davis. Two of her "listen-to-the-consumer" insights relate to brand name and packaging.

In her test kitchen, Barbara Davis developed a sauce that's sweet (but with only 5 grams of carbohydrates per serving) and a tiny bit spicier than the original but that has a definite smoky flavor. The new smoky barbecue sauce needed a name. What to call it? Early candidates included: Original, Part II; Smoky Campfire; Test Batch #19; Sweet Roast; and Crazy Woman Creek. "Give me a break," says Barbara Davis. "Finally, we decided *not* to be cutesy, but to simply describe the flavor." So Ken Davis Sweet & Smoky Bar-B-Q Sauce was born.

Barbara Davis has talked to consumers who used Ken Davis Bar-B-Q Sauces everywhere from in the kitchen to an outdoor grill to over a campfire. This convinced her that the original cylindrical plastic bottle wasn't easy to grip in all of these places. So in 2004 the new plastic bottle with its easy-to-hold squared shape appeared.

DISTRIBUTION

Gaining access to grocers can be a significant barrier to entry for those trying to break into the market. Many grocery stores purchase from large food distributors such as Supervalu, C&S Wholesale Grocers, and C. H. Robinson. These distributors buy directly from large manufacturers such as Kraft or from food brokers utilized by smaller local and regional manufacturers. Some grocers and institutional accounts do buy directly from Kraft salespeople or from food brokers. But it's not enough to have salespeople calling on distributors and grocery accounts. Slotting allowances are less a factor for gaining access to retail shelf space these days, but are necessary for getting on the shelf at distributors. It is estimated that it may cost $40,000 per SKU (stock keeping unit) to gain entry to a distributor such as Supervalu.

Ken Davis Products pioneered the premium category and has well-established relationships in its regional market with retailers, distributors, and institutions. But as the barbecue sauce category grows more crowded with new entrants, Ken Davis will have to continue to provide not only great flavors for regional tastes but also channel relationships that maintain access to its consumers.[15]

Questions

1 Describe and compare the distribution channel for (*a*) Ken Davis Products and (*b*) Kraft, which offers products in both the base and premium categories. What distribution advantages and drawbacks does each type of channel have?

2 Under what circumstances might Ken Davis change its current distribution strategy?

3 Assume that the retail prices of Ken Davis barbecue sauces are $3.19 per 18.5-ounce bottle, Bull's Eye sauces are $2.59 per 18-ounce bottle, and Kraft Original Barbecue sauce is $1.79 for 18 ounces. (*a*) Compare how much the typical retailer will earn for each brand per bottle. (*b*) What are the implications of these retail profits for Ken Davis and its distribution strategy? (*c*) What other factors will influence retailer profits for a given barbecue sauce brand?

case D–16 Dell Inc.: A Foundation Built on Supply Chain Management

THE COMPANY

Dell is the largest direct seller of computers in the world and one of the top global PC manufacturers, though the company has struggled with disappointing performance and product-related problems. Founder Michael Dell returned as CEO in February 2007 to help put Dell back on track. Dell had revenues of $57 billion in 2007, a disappointing 2.1 percent annual increase in sales. Hewlett-Packard (HP) now claims the No. 1 market share position globally while Dell still maintains the market share lead in the United States. While Dell and HP are losing share, Apple and Lenovo are gaining ground. Dell offers PCs, notebooks, network servers, peripherals, and software. Over 90 percent of Dell's sales are to businesses and governmental customers. Recent forays into consumer electronics—digital music players, LCD television/computer monitors—have been discontinued.

SUPPLY CHAIN MANAGEMENT AT DELL

Historically, Dell's success was attributed in large part to its effective use of supply chain management. In a recent interview, Michael Dell stated, "Dell has always had a strength in its supply chain, and I think there is an opportunity to do even better there." Dell has closely aligned its suppliers with its direct channel strategy resulting in dramatic improvements in inventory management and control. Inventories are kept at ultra-low levels, one-tenth that of its competitors. A typical Dell factory runs with about five or six hours worth of inventory on hand. This is important in an industry where component costs can decline 30 to 35 percent per year and helps Dell take advantage of lower anticipated inventory costs in the future as well as minimizing the risk of holding obsolete parts in inventory. In addition, Dell has a very favorable cash conversion cycle—minus 20 days in the most recent cycle. This means that Dell gets paid faster than it pays out to vendors.

No less significant have been Dell's efforts to work with vendors to reduce vendor cycle times—the time that elapses from Dell placing an order to receiving that order in a Dell manufacturing facility. Dell communicates with its suppliers and supply chain partners through "Platinum Supplier" Web pages. These pages provide each vendor with information on Dell's forecasted demand for the vendor's products, share production schedules, and allow for e-mail communication to make adjustments and changes.

The Dell Web site (www.dell.com) allows customers to shop online. Different online "stores" are available for different types of customers such as education, government, home/home office, and businesses. Shoppers can select the items they want and place them in their shopping cart. Once the order has been submitted, the Web site has the capability to check delivery dates and monitor the status of the order with its online tracking system. More than 50,000 business customers use the Dell online purchasing and information portal. Dell has moved beyond online sales into retail sales both in the United States and globally.

Since 1996, Dell has provided its top corporate customers its "Premier Pages" program. Beyond mere customer service or e-commerce, the Dell Premier Page empowers organizations to take control. The Dell Premier Page is a Web site that is personalized specifically for your company and includes a customized online computer store where you can configure your system. The prices you see are the contract prices already negotiated with your organization. You will know instantly what the system will cost and you can place your order online.

Dell integrates all its electronic commerce and communication systems. Dell uses browser and Internet/intranet technology as the interface for all applications, so any computer in the world can interact with Dell.

Dell utilizes decision support applications for modeling and simulating materials and factory scheduling to improve supply chain efficiency. For example, Dell can look out hours or days in advance, match this with materials flow, and based on this information, optimize a manufacturing plan to execute in the factory.

And in 2006 Dell introduced its "no charge, no exceptions" free computer recycling program, offering to even pick up your old computer—any brand—while challenging its competitors to offer the same service for their computers. This adds a new dimension in closing the loop on the supply chain—"cradle to grave"—from sourcing raw materials to build and deliver finished products to reclaiming and recycling these components in an environmentally responsible manner.[16]

Questions

1 Explain how Dell's approach to supply chain management satisfies the logistical objectives of minimizing logistics costs while maximizing customer service.

2 What are the supply chain management implications for Dell now that it has followed its competitors by adopting an indirect channel strategy along with its historic direct channel strategy? What supply chain and marketing recommendations do you suggest for Dell given the competitive environment?

3 How does supply chain management relate to the marketing concept at Dell?

case D–17 Trader Joe's: Upscale Value

THE COMPANY

With a near cult following, Trader Joe's has carved out a successful position in the competitive grocery market. Started in Los Angeles in 1958 by Joe Coulombe as a convenience store, Trader Joe's was dramatically repositioned in the 1960s as a store with luxurious food at low prices. Trader Joe's has grown to 331 stores in some two dozen states. Estimated 2008 sales were $7.2 billion. The company had 10,000 employees.

THE SHOPPING EXPERIENCE

What makes Trader Joe's a unique grocery shopping experience? Trader Joe's stores are not large—about 10,000 square feet—and carry a limited number of items to keep costs down. While there are fewer items (2,500 to 3,000), the items are often unique. More than 70 percent of the merchandise is private label, including Charles Shaw wine that sells for about $3.29 per bottle! Private label has been part of Trader Joe's product strategy for more than 30 years. According to Trader Joe's president, Doug Rauch, "We went into private label because of the value opportunity, so we could put our destiny in our hands." And over the years, consumers' confidence in these offerings has grown, allowing Trader Joe's to try new things and experiment with other offerings. Private-label offerings allow Trader Joe's to knock at least 20 percent off the cost of its products. And all private-label offerings boast no artificial colors, flavors, or preservatives.

Don't let the low prices fool you—the merchandise quality is upscale. In addition to organic fruits and vegetables and other grocery staples such as milk, cheese, and meat, there are unusual items such as Trader Joe's own chocolate-covered, peanut butter-filled pretzels, and exotic cheeses such as an Indian Paneer and a white Stilton with mango and ginger chunks.

THE SEARCH FOR NEW PRODUCTS

Trader Joe's uses a group of trained employees called "the tasting panel" to evaluate, critique, and improve its varied lines of house brands. New-product ideas have been uncovered in an airport in Thailand and a small restaurant in Italy and brought back to Trader Joe's and the tasting panel. This constant influx of new, tasty, critically reviewed products replaces the bottom 10 percent of products. Rotating out the bottom 10 percent isn't easy, but it ensures a constant flow of new products for customers to try, according to Matt Sloan, vice president of merchandising.

And customers are willing to travel to take advantage of the value provided by Trader Joe's. Trader Joe's has become to Manhattan supermarkets what Walmart is to middle America grocery stores. The values offered by Trader Joe's exceed the convenience of the local market. According to Jon Hauptman of consulting firm

Willard Bishop, there are price-gap "tipping points" where consumers are willing to pay more for additional convenience. Hauptman says this price gap typically is around 10 percent. Since Trader Joe's prices are easily more than 10 percent lower for similar items (generally 20 percent lower) and offered in a more upbeat shopping environment, consumers are willing to trade convenience and tote their Trader Joe's shopping bags through the subways of Manhattan.

Sampling is a key promotional tool. For a grand opening in Newport News, Virginia, customers were able to try Atlantic smoked salmon and hot cider in the morning followed by roasted red pepper soup, sweet potato bisque, and Tuscan Italian bread in the afternoon. Employees answer customer questions and offer food suggestions. Handwritten suggestions on labels offer ideas for foods that work well together. Recipe cards are available with additional food preparation ideas.

Looking for a special dessert? How about a frozen pumpkin cheesecake or strawberries dipped in white chocolate? "People will think you've gone through so much trouble, or they'll say 'You got that at Trader Joe's,'" says Trader Joe's Danny Owens.[17]

Questions

1 How would Trader Joe's be classified as a retail outlet in terms of ownership, level of service, and merchandise line?

2 What type of retail position does Trader Joe's occupy? Who do you see as its primary competitors, given this positioning?

3 How do you reconcile Trader Joe's success with the fact that grocery stores as a category are in the maturity stage of the retail life cycle? What are the key factors behind Trader Joe's success, and what steps should it take beyond its current marketing activities to continue to prosper?

case D–18 McDonald's Restaurants: An IMC Program to Reach Different Segments

"McDonald's outstanding success in Russia is a tribute to our Russian employees, suppliers, and, of course, our customers," comments George A. Cohon, senior chairman, McDonald's in Russia. It all started in 1976 at the Olympic Games in Montreal with a chance meeting between Cohon, who was then senior chairman of McDonald's Canada, and members of the Soviet Olympic delegation.

Fourteen years and countless meetings later, the 700-seat Pushkin Square restaurant in Moscow opened on January 31, 1990. The Pushkin restaurant still is the busiest McDonald's in the world, having served more than 77 million customers during its first 11 years. But competition from Russian quick-service restaurant operators, such as Rostiks and Russian Bistro, is increasing. Therefore, the McDonald's team must continue to develop effective means of communicating with present and prospective customers.

ABOUT McDONALD'S IN RUSSIA

The amount of food McDonald's has served in Russia is staggering. Consider that in its first 11 years of operations in Russia, McDonald's has served:

- More than 300 million customers, over twice the 146 million population of Russia.
- More than 66 million Big Mac™ sandwiches, that if put side by side would be longer than the 3,476-kilometer diameter of the moon!

McDonald's currently has over 100 restaurants in Russia, from Moscow and St. Petersburg to Nizhny Novgorod and Samara. McDonald's employs more than 6,000 Russians, or about 100 for each new restaurant that opens. More than 70 managers have successfully graduated from its "Hamburger University" training course held at McDonald's head office in Chicago, part of the 2,000 hours of training they each receive. McDonald's in Russia also operates McComplex, a one-of-a-kind food-processing and distribution facility located in Moscow, which supplies products to restaurants not only in Russia but also in Germany, Ukraine, Belarus, Austria, and the Czech Republic. It features dairy, bakery, pie, liquid, and meat lines and has its own quality assurance laboratories to ensure that McDonald's strict food quality standards are met. McDonald's in Russia sources more than 75 percent of the raw ingredients it needs from over 100 independent suppliers in Russia and the Commonwealth of Independent States (CIS).

McDONALD'S COMMUNITY EFFORTS

McDonald's has a philosophy of "giving back to the communities in which we serve" in the 120 countries in which it operates. In Russia, Ronald McDonald Children's Charities (Russia) operates the Ronald McDonald Centre, a sports and play facility for physically and mentally challenged children. Located in Moscow, the Ronald McDonald Centre hosts more than 1,500 children a week, conducting music, computer, and gym classes. In addition, McDonald's in Russia contributes to various charitable children's organizations to purchase items such as medical supplies and transportation equipment. Since opening 11 years ago, McDonald's in Russia has contributed more than $5 million to benefit Russian children in need.

WHAT McDONALD'S MARKETS AND WHAT CUSTOMERS LOOK FOR

McDonald's restaurants were founded and continue to operate worldwide on the basis of the formula, Q, S, C, and V: quality, service, cleanliness, and value. The simple menu ensures convenience and quick service. McDonald's is the favorite restaurant of many Russian families because McDonald's serves a high-quality meal, in a clean environment, with a smile, at a price families can afford.

Customers all over the world count on McDonald's for consistent taste and high-quality products, no matter where the restaurant is located. The McDonald's quality assurance program ensures that only the best quality products are served to its customers. This program begins with ensuring that only top-quality ingredients are used, that each food item is prepared in a consistent manner, and that the final product meets McDonald's exacting quality standards. For example, the components of a McDonald's Big Mac sandwich in Russia will undergo more than 98 quality checks before the final sandwich is presented to the customer. This ensures that every Big Mac sandwich tastes the same whether it is ordered by a customer in London, Tokyo, or Moscow.

McDonald's offers a curious marketing dilemma. Although the same meals are served to all customers, these same customers may be looking for strikingly different eating experiences on their restaurant visits. For example, a busy manager who only has enough time to "grab a quick lunch" is seeking a different eating experience than a young couple with a six-year-old child who is celebrating a special occasion. McDonald's also practices an "act local" strategy, which allows its restaurants to cater to local tastes and laws. For example, its restaurants in Germany and France can serve beer, something prohibited in the United States.

DESIGNING AN INTEGRATED MARKETING COMMUNICATIONS (IMC) PROGRAM

These diverse customer segments, with their very different reasons for visiting a McDonald's restaurant, pose a special challenge for a McDonald's marketing manager responsible for designing and implementing an effective integrated marketing communications (IMC) program. Some of the key initial questions include:

- What are the key market segments that McDonald's might be trying to reach?
- What might each segment look for when it chooses to visit McDonald's?
- What appeals and messages might be used to attract each of these segments?
- What combination of promotional mix elements (advertising, personal selling, public relations, sales promotion, and direct marketing) could be used to reach each segment?

The decisions a McDonald's marketing manager must make become more complicated because the IMC program may vary from city to city. If McDonald's is entering a new city with its first restaurant, an IMC may be very costly. If McDonald's is adding several more restaurants in Moscow, the IMC costs can be spread across the more than 20 outlets it promotes.[18]

Questions

1 Consider these four distinct market segments for McDonald's meals in Russian cities in which it has outlets: a family with young children, busy businesspeople, an older couple, and foreign tourists who are already familiar with McDonald's. For each segment (*a*) identify the special benefit or appeal McDonald's has to offer and (*b*) compose a 10- to 12-word promotional message that might be used to reach it.

2 For the first McDonald's restaurant to open in a city, what element of an integrated marketing communications (IMC) program might be used to reach (*a*) a family with young children and (*b*) busy businesspeople?

3 For the McDonald's restaurants in Moscow, what element of an integrated marketing communications (IMC) program might be used to reach (*a*) an older couple and (*b*) foreign tourists?

case D–19 Target Corporation: Award-Winning Advertising

THE COMPANY

Recognized as one of the most respected companies in the United States, noted for its philanthropy, its commitment to health and wellness, the environment, innovation, design, and its shareholders, it is not surprising that Target Corporation is also one of the most savvy retail marketers today. Target has grown from a single Minnesota store in 1962 to more than 1,500 stores in 47 states plus the online Target.com. Estimated 2007 sales are $59.49 billion. Sales growth annually has been a healthy 13.1 percent with net income growth of 15.7 percent. Target is considered the No. 2 discount chain after Walmart.

OBJECTIVES AND STRATEGY

The company embarked on a path of differentiation more than 20 years ago that it still follows today. "We knew we would never be able to compete solely on price," says Michael Francis, senior vice president of marketing. "We knew there was a customer out there who wanted (something different)."

From a communication standpoint, the company has several important and overlapping objectives: the need to deepen the bond with the existing customer who identifies Target as a place for trendy and exclusive merchandise and to keep her coming back. The Target customer has a median age of 41, youngest among major retailers, with a median household income of $58,000; 43 percent have children at home; and 43 percent have completed college. While maintaining its base, Target is also looking to broaden its reach with younger consumers, in large part through advertising.

BREAKTHROUGH ADVERTISING

Target is second to none when it comes to award-winning advertising campaigns that reflect its affordable chic, fun, and friendly image. Its ubiquitous bull's-eye logo is recognized by 96 percent of all U.S. consumers. Not content with such high recognition, Target now wants to "own the color red."

Target has dominated the RAC (Retail Advertising Conference) awards for more than 14 years, winning awards in virtually every possible category and media as well as overall best of show.

In terms of media, Target ads are seen in newspapers, magazines, television, and outdoor billboards. Target even has its own in-store TV network (Channel Red) playing in its electronics departments that shows Target ads and promos for new CD and DVD releases. One of the biggest advertising tactics for Target is the newspaper circular listing featured items for the week.

Target also has cleverly utilized promotional events. One such event was the launch of a new apparel line by a British designer that used a London-style double-decker bus as a boutique to showcase the line around the country. Two years ago, the retailer staged a "vertical fashion show" featuring acrobats in harnesses walking down the side of Rockefeller Center while wearing items from Target's fall collection.

Sometimes the Target advertising itself becomes the story—a two-for-one advertising and public relations bonanza. Target was the sole advertiser for the August 22, 2005 issue of *The New Yorker. The New Yorker* is the paragon of style and upscale cool, perhaps the most prestigious magazine in the country, and many thought that the image of Target did not fit the media. The campaign generated controversy and buzz.

On the one hand, *The New Yorker* was roundly criticized for permitting a single advertiser, unprecedented in its history, and for not printing some statement saying the advertiser did not have any control over the issue's editorial content. On the other hand, an otherwise jaded *Adweek* columnist gushed about Target's clever illustrations, the beautifully rendered and conceptually coherent design that matched the visual design of the magazine. Describing the effort as the "smartest and most exciting example of branded entertainment I have ever seen," the columnist went on to ask, "How many contemporary American brands have a logo and a visual identity so strong and distinct that it can sustain 21 pages in a single issue without a single product mention or word of text and have it all remain immediately recognizable?"

Target has demonstrated that it is willing to take risks. Michael Francis has been known to say that if an idea sounds a bit scary, it's probably a good idea. One idea that didn't work quite as planned was painting bull's-eyes on white hermit crab shells as a means for Target to brand the Spirit Awards in Los Angeles, the week before the Academy Awards. People thought the crabs were cute until they were bit on their fingers. Well-branded hermit crabs were hanging off fingers in photographs from the event. But the stunt took on a life of its own as people from as far away as Mexico and San Diego called in over the next 18 months with reports of branded crabs on the loose. Undeterred, Target decided it was a great opportunity to send out Target gift cards and turn it into something that was completely unplanned—a find the hermit crab sweepstakes.

EFFECTIVENESS AND ASSESSMENT

What does Target spend on advertising? The Target annual report suggests that Target spent approximately $1,170 million on advertising in 2006. Newspaper circulars and media broadcast made up the bulk of the spending. How does the company evaluate the return on that expense? Winning advertising awards is fine, but what are the key measures for assessing effectiveness?

One example was the Target "Tony Bennett" campaign to leverage Bennett's 80th birthday and his new CD "Duets: An American Classic." Target negotiated an exclusive version of "Duets" featuring four exclusive tracks and a DVD of the making of the CD, sold exclusively at Target. Then the company sponsored a star-studded gala in New York City to celebrate Tony Bennett's 80th birthday and the release of his new CD/DVD complete with branded cocktail napkins and martini glasses distributed to hot New York and Los Angeles clubs. Target ads ran on A&E, TBS, TNT, as well as in *Time, People,* and *Vanity Fair* to support the CD. Target's ad agency also worked with director Rob Marshall to produce an NBC special that aired the week of Thanksgiving that was the No. 1 televised music special of the year. Tony Bennett's CD won three Grammy Awards, breaking sales records for the singer and for Target. Bennett singled out Target during his Grammy acceptance speech, thanking them for their sponsorship and support. Bottom line, it cost Target $6.2 million for the entire program. Target sold an astonishing 28 percent of all U.S. copies of the Bennett CD plus added $2.1 million in incremental nonmusic sales to its coffers.

ISSUES

It has been said that the best advertising does two things—drives sales and builds brands in the long term. It's tough to do both, and yet Target seemingly has been successful at both.

Some potential areas of concern are a substantial gap between the creativity and excitement of Target's advertising and the store shopping experience. The store shopping experience is just not as much fun as the advertising. Attempts to court the youth market have not been particularly successful. While Target advertising has a very youthful feel and energy, there hasn't been a corresponding surge in the young adult market.[19]

Questions

1 What are Target's primary promotional objectives? Have these objectives changed significantly over the years and if so, how?

2 What do you feel are the most valid measures for assessing the success of Target's advertising? Explain why you feel that these are the best means of determining effectiveness.

3 Many of Target's competitors are attempting to imitate aspects of its advertising and promotional program. (*a*) Does this present a threat to Target? (*b*) Why or why not, and how should Target respond?

case D–20 Morgantown Furniture: Making Promotion Trade-Offs

Edward Meadows, president of Morgantown Furniture, met with representatives of Kelly, Astor & Peters Advertising (KAP) and Andrew Reed, Morgantown's vice president of marketing and sales, to discuss the company's advertising program for 2008. The KAP Advertising representatives recommended that Morgantown Furniture increase its advertising in shelter magazines (such as *Good Housekeeping* and *Better Homes and Gardens,* which feature home improvement ideas and new ideas in home decorating) by $300,000 and maintain the expenditures for other promotional efforts at a constant level during 2008. The rationale given for the increase in advertising was that Morgantown Furniture had low name recognition among prospective buyers of furniture, and it intended to introduce new styles of living and dining room furniture. Reed, however, had a different opinion as to how Morgantown Furniture should spend the $300,000. He thought it was necessary to: (1) hire additional salespeople to call on the 30 new retail stores to be added by the company in 2008, (2) increase the funds devoted to cooperative advertising, and (3) improve the selling aids given to retail stores and salespeople.

THE COMPANY

Morgantown Furniture is a medium-sized manufacturer of medium- to high-priced living and dining room furniture. Sales in 2007 were $50 million. The company sells its furniture through 1,000 furniture specialty stores nationwide, but not all stores carry the company's entire line. This fact bothered Meadows because, in his words, "If they ain't got it, they can't sell it!" The company employs 10 full-time salespeople, who receive a $50,000 base salary annually and a small commission on sales. A company salesforce is atypical in the furniture industry because most furniture manufacturers use selling agents or manufacturer's representatives who carry a wide assortment of noncompeting furniture lines and receive a commission on sales. "Having our own sales group is a policy my father established 30 years ago," noted Meadows, "and we've been quite successful having people who are committed to our company. Our people don't just take furniture orders. They are expected to motivate retail salespeople to sell our line, assist in setting up displays in stores, coordinate cooperative advertising plans, and give advice on a variety of matters to our retailers and their salespeople."

In 2007, Morgantown spent $2.45 million for total promotional expenditures, excluding the salary of the vice president of marketing and sales. Promotional expenditures were categorized into four groups: (1) sales expense and administration, (2) cooperative advertising programs with retailers, (3) trade promotions, and (4) consumer advertising. Cooperative advertising allowances are usually spent on newspaper advertising in a retailer's city and are matched by the retailer's funds on a dollar-for-dollar basis. Trade promotion is directed toward retailers and takes the form of catalogs, trade magazine advertisements, booklets for consumers, and point-of-purchase materials such as displays for use in retail stores. Also included in this category is the expense of trade shows. Morgantown Furniture is represented at two trade shows a year. Consumer advertising is directed to potential consumers through shelter magazines. The typical format used in consumer advertising is to highlight new furniture and different living and dining room arrangements. Dollar allocation for each program in 2007 was as follows:

Promotional Program	Expenditure
Sales expense and administration	$ 612,500
Cooperative advertising	1,102,500
Trade advertising	306,250
Consumer advertising	428,750
Total	$2,450,000

THE INDUSTRY

The household wooden furniture industry is composed of more than 5,000 firms. Industry sales at manufacturers' prices were $10 billion. California, North Carolina, Virginia, New York, Tennessee, Pennsylvania, Illinois, and Indiana are the major U.S. furniture-producing areas. Although Ethan Allen, Bassett, Henredon, and Kroehler are well-known furniture manufacturers, no one firm captured more than 10 percent of the total household wooden furniture market.

The buying and selling of furniture to retail outlets centers around manufacturers' expositions at selected times and places around the country. At these marts, as they are called in the furniture industry, retail buyers view manufacturers' lines and often make buying commitments for their stores. However, Morgantown's experience has shown that sales efforts in the retail store by company representatives account for as much as half the company's sales in a given year. The major manufacturer expositions are held in High Point, North Carolina, in October and April. Regional expositions are also scheduled in June through August in locations such as Los Angeles, New York, and Boston.

Company research on consumer furniture-buying behavior indicated that people visit several stores when shopping for furniture, and the final decision is made jointly by a husband and wife in about 90 percent of furniture purchases. Other noteworthy findings are as follows:

- Eighty-four percent of buyers believe "the higher the price, the higher the quality" when buying home furnishings.
- Seventy-two percent of buyers browse or window shop in furniture stores even if they don't need furniture.
- Eighty-five percent read furniture ads before they actually need furniture.
- Ninety-nine percent agreed with the statement, "When shopping for furniture and home furnishings, I like the salesperson to show me what alternatives are available, answer my questions, and let me alone so I can think about it and maybe browse around."
- Ninety five percent get redecorating ideas from shelter magazines.
- Forty-one percent have written to order a manufacturer's booklet.
- Sixty-three percent feel they need decorating advice for "putting it all together."

BUDGETARY ISSUES

After the KAP Advertising representatives made their presentation, Reed again emphasized that the incremental $300,000 should not be spent for consumer advertising. He noted that Morgantown Furniture had set as an objective that each salesperson would make six calls per year at each store and spend at least four hours at each store on every call. "Given that our salespeople work a 40-hour week, 48 weeks per year, and devote only 80 percent of their time to selling due to travel time between stores, we already aren't doing the sales job," Reed added. Meadows agreed but reminded Reed that the $300,000 increment in the promotional budget was a maximum the company could spend, given other cost increases.[20]

Questions

1 How might you describe furniture buying using the purchase decision process described in Chapter 5?
2 How might each of the elements of the promotional program influence each stage in the purchase decision process?
3 What should Morgantown's promotional objectives be?
4 How many salespeople does Morgantown need to adequately service its accounts?
5 Should Morgantown Furniture emphasize a push or pull promotional strategy? Why?

case D–21 Crate and Barrel: Multichannel Marketing

THE COMPANY

Chicago-based Crate and Barrel started as a one-store operation in 1962. Gordon and Carole Segal returned from their honeymoon in Europe with a variety of unique and affordable designs for their home. Recognizing that there was no one addressing the need for those with "more taste than money," they took out a lease on an old elevator factory and Crate and Barrel was born. The entrepreneurs were so excited about the new venture that only moments before the store opened, they realized that they had forgotten to get a cash register. A simple box had to serve.

Crate and Barrel has grown to over 150 stores with 7,000 sales associates and 2006 sales of more then $2.2 billion, an 11 percent annual increase over 2005. Crate and Barrel stores, catalogs, and its Web site offer a wide variety of household items—furniture, lighting, rugs, products for bed and bath, dinnerware, flatware, cookware, kitchenware, linens, food, and gifts. In 1998, Hamburg's Otto Group, the world's largest mail-order merchant, acquired a majority stake in Euromarket Designs Inc., which does business as the Crate and Barrel brand.

Crate and Barrel competes in the retail home furnishings and housewares industry with such well-known names as Pottery Barn, Williams-Sonoma, Pier 1 Imports, and Restoration Hardware. What makes Crate and Barrel special? Crate and Barrel carves out its own unique niche with more modern styling and brighter colors than its competitors. About one-third of the merchandise is unique to Crate and Barrel. But the best news is that Crate and Barrel offers a wide selection of well-designed products that provide good customer value.

MULTICHANNELS

Crate and Barrel has successfully utilized multiple channels to make its products available to customers. The company sends out more than 15 million brightly colored catalogs annually. The catalogs are fun to look through. For the most complete selection of products, check out the Crate and Barrel Web site, www.crateandbarrel.com. Product offerings are arrayed by category so customers can browse or visit the gift ideas or bridal registry pages to select a purchase. Unlike the catalog, the Web site allows customers to zoom in on items and check out specs. Crate and Barrel customers can opt in to e-mail alerts of product offerings and sales.

Purchases can be made in one of the many retail stores, online, by mail, or by the toll-free phone line. Crate and Barrel even offers its own credit card to facilitate purchase.

The company has made significant investments in enterprise marketing systems to manage its customer database and direct-mail campaigns. The system allows Crate and Barrel to effectively design, execute, and assess the results of cross-channel marketing efforts. A Crate and Barrel customer can spot a set of Marimekko towels in the catalog, order the towels and matching bedding from the Web site, and easily stop at a Crate and Barrel store to physically test and compare wood and metal beds to complete a purchase.[21]

Questions

1 How does Crate and Barrel facilitate consumer purchases with its multichannel strategy?

2 What are the six "Cs" of e-commerce, and how does Crate and Barrel address each of these?

3 Given that all of its major competitors also attempt to utilize multiple channels, in what ways could Crate and Barrel create a competitive advantage for itself with its multichannel strategy?

case D–22 Naked® Juice: Strategy for Growth

Naked® Juice was started in 1983 in Santa Monica, California. Home-squeezed and blended juices and smoothies were peddled from towel to towel on the beaches of Southern California until they caught on with small grocery stores near the beaches, then all over Los Angeles.

Today, Naked Juice is a national brand based in Azusa, California, offering all natural, 100 percent juices and juice smoothies with no added sugar or preservatives. There's "a pound of fruit in every 15.2-ounce bottle!" More than 6 million bottles of Naked Juice are shipped every month and the brand is reportedly the fastest-growing super premium juice brand, growing at a rate of 63.9 percent annually. The top sellers are Green Machine, Protein Zone, and Mighty Mango. *Health* magazine named Mighty Mango the best smoothie, *Progressive Grocer* picked Strawberry Kiwi Kick "Best New Product" for 2006, and *Gourmet Retailer* selected Naked Juice as the "Editor's Choice" for June 2006. Naked Juice is sold through supermarkets, club stores, health food stores, and neighborhood markets across the country. Suggested retail prices for a 15.2-ounce bottle range from $2.59 for Just Juice products up to $3.19 for the smoothies with special ingredients such as acai.

PRODUCT FAMILIES

Naked Juice organizes its product offerings into "families" or categories. Currently, there are six families: Superfood Family (five different flavors of 100 percent juice smoothies), Just Juice Family (four pure juice flavors), Well Being Family (100 percent juice smoothies with immune boosters such as Vitamin C, potassium, echinacea), Protein Family (soy and whey protein-laced smoothies), Naked Energy Family (100 percent fruit juice smoothies with all-natural energy such as green tea extract, guarana, and B vitamins), and Antioxidant Family (six flavors with boosts of Vitamins A, C, E, and selium).

BEVERAGE INDUSTRY

The beverage industry is a complex and competitive environment with a wide variety of categories. In the nonalcoholic sector, the major segments are carbonated beverages (colas, lemon-lime, root beer, and other flavors), hot beverages (e.g., coffee, tea), and what are referred to as "functional" beverages—energy, sports, health, and nutritional drinks. Functional beverage sales were $7.1 billion in 2005 with a compound annual growth rate of 11.7 percent for the period 2001 to 2005.

Naked Juice competes in the energy, health, and nutritional drinks segment. Key competitors include Hansen Natural, Odwalla (owned by Coca Cola), and Pom Wonderful. Many of these beverages, as well as Naked, are located in the produce department.

SWALLOWED BY PEPSI

Pepsi "got Naked®" in early 2007 with the acquisition of the company to add to its beverage portfolio that also includes Aquafina, Gatorade, SoBe, Lipton, iced Starbucks RTDs (ready to drink), Propel, and Tropicana. PepsiCo also bought Izze Beverage Co. for $75 million, while Coca-Cola agreed to buy juice and tea maker FUZE Beverage LLC. The reasons for this buying binge of small, successful noncarbonated beverage companies is simple—the cola market is at best in the late stage of the maturity product life cycle, more likely in decline. In the first half of 2006, Pepsi-Cola's U.S. volume fell 7.2 percent while Coca-Cola Classic's fell 4.9 percent in grocery, drug, and mass merchandisers. The diet versions were also down 4.7 percent and 4.9 percent, respectively. According to Tom Pirko, president of BevMark, Coke and Pepsi executives are torn between conflicting demands of supporting declining soda brands and driving growth of noncarbonated coffee and energy drinks that younger consumers crave. The largest consumer group for cola products is not younger consumers, but 35-to-54-year-old householders. Midwesterners and those with less education index are higher on cola consumption.

Further evidence of the upheaval in the beverages market is apparent in media spending. For the first time, media spending for noncarbonated beverages and energy drinks—at $953 million in 2005, up 6.7 percent—topped the $898 million spent on traditional carbonated soft drinks.

JUICES PROSPER

"Consumption of juice may be up because of health benefits and people's interest in whole, natural, or fresh food," according to Gaff Rampersaud, a registered dietician at the University of Florida. "One hundred percent juice and other minimally processed healthy foods are gaining popularity. One benefit is the nutrient density, which means the amount of nutrients per calorie. Citrus juices and other popular juices have higher amounts of nutrients per calorie." There is also growing evidence that citrus juice consumption is beneficial in reducing the risk of oral cancer, colorectal cancer, adenomas, urinary stones, and Alzheimer's disease. Pomegranate juice is getting a lot of attention for its health benefits and has shown up in a number of new juice offerings as is acai, a rain forest berry from Brazil with a very high antioxidant content.

Consumers also continue to demand more upscale, natural and organic products. While the juice category grows, the fastest-growing part of that category is juice smoothies with a 52.4 percent one-year increase.

ISSUES

Major soft drink players have all agreed to cut back on sales of high-sugar beverages to public schools by the 2008 school year, which will further dampen carbonated sales.

The growing importance of the Hispanic market that prefers fruit-flavored beverages is part of the trend away from colas. With the explosion of variety in the beverage industry you can get your caffeine jolt with a Starbuck's latte, a Red Bull energy drink, or the green tea and guarana boosts of a Naked Juice Black & Blueberry Rush.[22]

Questions

1 What strategy(ies) has Naked Juice taken to reach its current market position?

2 Consider PepsiCo's strategy(ies) in its beverage business. What are the implications for Naked Juice in this portfolio?

3 What key marketing metrics do you think PepsiCo should use to evaluate the performance of Naked Juice? Would these measures be different for its traditional carbonated soft drinks, and if so, how?

GLOSSARY

80/20 rule A concept that suggests 80 percent of a firm's sales are obtained from 20 percent of its customers. p. 229
above-, at-, or below-market pricing Setting a market price for a product or product class based on a subjective feel for the competitors' price or market price as the benchmark. p. 354
account management policies Specifies whom salespeople should contact, what kinds of selling and customer service activities should be engaged in, and how these activities should be carried out. p. 536
action item list An aid to implementing a marketing plan consisting of four columns: (1) the task; (2) the person responsible for completing that task; (3) the date to finish the task; and (4) what is to be delivered. p. 587
adaptive selling A need-satisfaction presentation format that involves adjusting the presentation to fit the selling situation, such as knowing when to offer solutions and when to ask for more information. p. 529
advertising Any paid form of nonpersonal communication about an organization, good, service, or idea by an identified sponsor. pp. 460, 486
all-you-can-afford budgeting Allocating funds to promotion only after all other budget items are covered. p. 472
attitude A learned predisposition to respond to an object or class of objects in a consistently favorable or unfavorable way. p. 123
average revenue (AR) The average amount of money received for selling one unit of a product, or simply the price of that unit. p. 331

baby boomers The generation of children born between 1946 and 1964. p. 69
back translation The practice where a translated word or phrase is retranslated into the original language by a different interpreter to catch errors. p. 176
balance of trade The difference between the monetary value of a nation's exports and imports. p. 163
barriers to entry Business practices or conditions that make it difficult for new firms to enter the market. p. 81
barter The practice of exchanging products and services for other products and services rather than for money. p. 320
basing-point pricing Selecting one or more geographical locations (basing point) from which the list price for products plus freight expenses are charged to the buyer. p. 363
beliefs A consumer's subjective perception of how a product or brand performs on different attributes based on personal experience, advertising, and discussions with other people. p. 123
bidder's list A list of firms believed to be qualified to supply a given item. p. 152
blended family A family formed by merging two previously separated units into a single household. p. 70
blog A Web page that serves as a publicly accessible personal journal for an individual or organization. p. 559
bots Electronic shopping agents or robots that comb Web sites to compare prices and product or service features. p. 558
bottom of the pyramid The largest but poorest socioeconomic group of people in the world. p. 177
brand equity The added value a brand name gives to a product beyond the functional benefits provided. p. 283
brand licensing A contractual agreement whereby one company (licensor) allows its brand name(s) or trademark(s) to be used with products or services offered by another company (licensee) for a royalty or fee. p. 284
brand loyalty A favorable attitude toward and consistent purchase of a single brand over time. p. 122
brand name Any word, device (design, sound, shape, or color), or combination of these used to distinguish a seller's goods or services. p. 282
brand personality A set of human characteristics associated with a brand name. p. 283
branding A marketing decision in which an organization uses a name, phrase, design, symbols, or combination of these to identify its products and distinguish them from those of competitors. p. 282
breadth of product line The variety of different product items a store carries. p. 435
break-even analysis A technique that analyzes the relationship between total revenue and total cost to determine profitability at various levels of output. p. 336
break-even chart A graphic presentation of the break-even analysis that shows when total revenue and total cost intersect to identify profit or loss for a given quantity sold. p. 338
break-even point (BEP) The quantity at which total revenue and total cost are equal. p. 336
brokers Independent firms or individuals whose principal function is to bring buyers and sellers together to make sales. pp. 336, 338
bundle pricing The marketing of two or more products in a single package price. p. 349
business The clear, broad, underlying industry or market sector of an organization's offering. p. 30
business analysis The stage of the new-product process that specifies the features of the product and the marketing strategy needed to bring it to market and make financial projections. p. 260
business marketing The marketing of goods and services to companies, governments, or not-for-profit organizations for use in the creation of goods and services that they can produce and market to others. p. 140
business plan A road map for the entire organization for a specified future period of time, such as one year or five years. p. 50
business portfolio analysis A technique that managers use to quantify performance measures and growth targets to analyze its clients' strategic business units (SBUs) as though they were a collection of separate investments. p. 36
business products Products that organizations buy that assist in providing other products for resale. Also called *B2B products*, or *industrial products*. p. 246
buy classes Consists of three types of organizational buying situations: straight rebuy, new buy, and modified rebuy. p. 148
buying center The group of people in an organization who participate in the buying process and share common goals, risks, and knowledge important to a purchase decision. p. 147

capacity management Integrating the service component of the marketing mix with efforts to influence consumer demand. p. 312
category management An approach to managing the assortment of merchandise in which a manager is assigned the responsibility for selecting all products that consumers in a market segment might view as substitutes for each other, with the objective of maximizing sales and profits in the category. p. 446
cause marketing Occurs when the charitable contributions of a firm are tied directly to the customer revenues produced through the promotion of one of its products. p. 102
caveat emptor The legal concept of "let the buyer beware" that was pervasive in the American business culture prior to the 1960s. p. 95
central business district The oldest retail setting, usually located in the community's downtown area. p. 445
channel captain A channel member (producer, wholesaler, or retailer) that coordinates, directs, and supports other channel members. p. 398
channel conflict Arises when one channel member believes another channel member is engaged in behavior that prevents it from achieving its goals. p. 397
channel of communication The means (a salesperson, advertising media, or public relations tools) of conveying a message to a receiver during the communication process. p. 458
channel partnership Consists of agreements and procedures among channel members for ordering and physically distributing a producer's products through the channel to the ultimate consumer. p. 391
choiceboard An interactive, Internet-enabled system that allows individual customers to design their own products and services by answering a few questions and choosing from a menu of product or service attributes (or components), prices, and delivery options. p. 550
code of ethics A formal statement of ethical principles and rules of conduct. p. 97
cognitive dissonance The feeling of postpurchase psychological tension or anxiety consumers may experience when faced with two or more highly attractive alternatives. p. 115
collaborative filtering A process that automatically groups people with similar buying intentions, preferences, and behaviors and predicts future purchases. p. 550
commercialization The stage of the new-product process that positions and launches a new product in full-scale production and sales. p. 262
communication The process of conveying a message to others that requires six elements: a source, a message, a channel of communication, a receiver, and the processes of encoding and decoding. p. 458
community shopping center A retail location that typically has one primary store (usually a department store branch) and often 20 to 40 smaller outlets, serving a population of consumers who are within a 10- to 20-minute drive. p. 445
competition The alternative firms that could provide a product to satisfy a specific market's needs. p. 80
competitive advantage A unique strength relative to competitors that provides superior returns, often based on quality, time, cost, or innovation. p. 35
competitive parity budgeting Allocating funds to promotion by matching the competitor's absolute level of spending or the proportion per point of market share. Also called *matching competitors* or *share of market*. p. 471
consideration set The group of brands that a consumer would consider acceptable from among all the brands in the product class of which he or she is aware in the product class. p. 113
constraints In a decision, the restrictions placed on potential solutions to a problem. p. 197
consultative selling A need-satisfaction presentation format that focuses on problem identification, where the salesperson serves as an expert on problem recognition and resolution. p. 529
consumer behavior The actions a person takes in purchasing and using products and services, including the mental and social processes that come before and after these actions. p. 112
Consumer Bill of Rights (1962) A law that codified the ethics of exchange between buyers and sellers, including the rights to safety, to be informed, to choose, and to be heard. p. 95
consumer ethnocentrism The tendency to believe that it is inappropriate, indeed immoral, to purchase foreign-made products. p. 176
consumer products Products purchased by the ultimate consumer. p. 246
consumer socialization The process by which people acquire the skills, knowledge, and attitudes necessary to function as consumers. p. 128
consumerism A grassroots movement started in the 1960s to increase the influence, power, and rights of consumers in dealing with institutions. p. 83
consumer-oriented sales promotion Sales tools used to support a company's advertising and personal selling directed to ultimate consumers. Also called *consumer promotions*. p. 505
convenience products Items that the consumer purchases frequently, conveniently, and with a minimum of shopping effort. p. 247
cookies Computer files that a marketer can download onto the computer or mobile phone of an online shopper who visits the marketer's Web site. p. 560
cooperative advertising Advertising programs by which a manufacturer pays a percentage of the retailer's local advertising expense for advertising the manufacturer's products. p. 511
core values The fundamental, passionate, and enduring principles of an organization that guide its conduct over time. p. 29
corporate level The level in an organization where top management directs overall strategy for the entire organization. p. 28
cost focus strategy One of Porter's generic business strategies that involves controlling expenses and, in turn, lowering product prices targeted at a narrow range of market segments. p. 579
cost leadership strategy One of Porter's generic business strategies that focuses on reducing expenses and, in turn, lowers product prices while targeting a broad array of market segments. p. 579
cost per thousand (CPM) The cost of reaching 1,000 individuals or households with the advertising message in a given medium (M is the Roman numeral for 1,000). p. 495
cost-plus pricing Summing the total unit cost of providing a product or service and adding a specific amount to the cost to arrive at a price. p. 350
countertrade The practice of using barter rather than money for making global sales. p. 162
cross-channel shopper An online consumer who researches products online and then purchases them at a retail store. p. 562
cross-cultural analysis The study of similarities and differences among consumers in two or more nations or societies. p. 173

cross-functional teams A small number of people from different departments in an organization who are mutually accountable to accomplish a task or common set of performance goals. p. 28

cultural symbols Things that represent ideas and concepts. p. 175

culture The set of values, ideas, and attitudes that are learned and shared among the members of a group. p. 73

currency exchange rate The price of one country's currency expressed in terms of another country's currency. p. 180

customary pricing Setting a price that is dictated by tradition, a standardized channel of distribution, or other competitive factors. p. 353

customer contact audit A flowchart of the points of interaction between consumers and a service provider. p. 306

customer experience The internal response that customers have to all aspects of an organization and its offering. p. 17

customer experience management (CEM) The process of managing the entire customer experience within the firm. pp. 259, 311

customer relationship management (CRM) The process of identifying prospective buyers, understanding them intimately, and developing favorable long-term perceptions of the organization and its offerings so that buyers will choose them in the marketplace. p. 16

customer service The ability of logistics management to satisfy users in terms of time, dependability, communication, and convenience. p. 413

customer value The unique combination of benefits received by targeted buyers that includes quality, convenience, on-time delivery, and both before-sale and after-sale service at a specific price. p. 12

customerization The growing practice of not only customizing a product or service but also personalizing the marketing and overall shopping and buying interaction for each customer. p. 558

customs What is considered normal and expected about the way people do things in a specific country. p. 174

data The facts and figures related to the problem that are divided into two main parts: secondary data and primary data. p. 199

data mining The extraction of hidden predictive information from large databases to find statistical links between consumer purchasing patterns and marketing actions. p. 210

decision A conscious choice from among two or more alternatives. p. 195

decoding The process of having the receiver take a set of symbols, the message, and transform them back to an idea during the communication process. p. 459

demand curve A graph relating the quantity sold and price, which shows the maximum number of units that will be sold at a given price. p. 330

demand factors Factors that determine consumers' willingness and ability to pay for products and services. p. 330

demographics Describing a population according to selected characteristics such as age, gender, ethnicity, income, and occupation. p. 68

depth of product line The store carries a large assortment of each product item. p. 435

derived demand The demand for industrial products and services is driven by, or derived from, demand for consumer products and services. p. 143

development The stage of the new-product process that turns the idea on paper into a prototype. p. 260

differentiation focus strategy One of Porter's generic business strategies that requires products to have significant points of difference to target one or only a few market segments. p. 580

differentiation strategy One of Porter's generic business strategies that requires products to have significant points of difference to charge a higher price while targeting a broad array of market segments. p. 579

direct investment A global market-entry strategy that entails a domestic firm actually investing in and owning a foreign subsidiary or division. p. 185

direct marketing A promotion alternative that uses direct communication with consumers to generate a response in the form of an order, a request for further information, or a visit to a retail outlet. p. 463

direct marketing channels Allowing consumers to buy products by interacting with various advertising media without a face-to-face meeting with a salesperson. p. 385

direct orders The result of direct marketing offers that contain all the information necessary for a prospective buyer to make a decision to purchase and complete the transaction. p. 477

discretionary income The money that remains after paying for taxes and necessities. p. 77

disintermediation Channel conflict that arises when a channel member bypasses another member and sells or buys products direct. p. 397

disposable income The money a consumer has left after paying taxes to use for necessities such as food, housing, clothing, and transportation. p. 76

diversification analysis A tool that helps a firm search for growth opportunities from among current and new markets as well as current and new products. p. 38

dual distribution An arrangement whereby a firm reaches different buyers by employing two or more different types of channels for the same basic product. p. 386

dumping When a firm sells a product in a foreign country below its domestic price or below its actual cost. p. 188

dynamic pricing The practice of changing prices for products and services in real time in response to supply and demand conditions. p. 560

economic espionage The clandestine collection of trade secrets or proprietary information about a company's competitors. p. 95

Economic Espionage Act (1996) A law that makes the theft of trade secrets by foreign entities a federal crime in the United States. p. 165

economy Pertains to the income, expenditures, and resources that affect the cost of running a business and household. p. 75

efficient consumer response Inventory management systems that are designed to reduce a retailer's lead time for receiving merchandise, which then lowers a retailer's inventory investment, improves customer service levels, and reduces logistics expense. Also called *quick response*. p. 414

eight Ps of services marketing An expanded marketing mix for services that includes the four Ps (product, price, promotion, and place or distribution) as well as people, physical environment, process, and productivity. p. 308

eight-second rule A view that customers will abandon their efforts to enter and navigate a Web site if download time exceeds eight seconds. p. 558

electronic commerce Any activity that uses some form of electronic communication in the inventory, exchange, advertisement, distribution, and payment of goods and services. p. 80

electronic data interchange (EDI) Combining proprietary computer and telecommunication technologies to exchange electronic invoices, payments, and information among suppliers, manufacturers, and retailers. p. 412

electronic marketing channels Employing the Internet to make products and services available for consumption or use by consumers or business buyers. p. 384

e-marketplaces Online trading communities that bring together buyers and supplier organizations to make possible the real time exchange of information, money, products, and services. Also called *B2B exchanges* or *e-hubs*. p. 153

emotional intelligence The ability to understand one's own emotions and the emotions of people with whom one interacts on a daily basis. p. 537

encoding The process of having the sender transform an idea into a set of symbols during the communication process. p. 459

environmental forces The uncontrollable forces in a marketing decision involving social, economic, technological, competitive, and regulatory forces. p. 11

environmental scanning The process of continually acquiring information on events occurring outside the organization to identify and interpret potential trends. p. 66

ethics The moral principles and values that govern the actions and decisions of an individual or group. p. 92

evaluative criteria Factors that represent both the objective attributes of a brand and the subjective ones a consumer uses to compare different products and brands. p. 113

everyday low pricing (EDLP) The practice of replacing promotional allowances with lower manufacturer list prices. p. 362

exchange The trade of things of value between buyer and seller so that each is better off after the trade. p. 6

exclusive distribution A level of distribution density whereby only one retailer in a specific geographical area carries the firm's products. p. 393

experience curve pricing A method of pricing based on the learning effect, which holds that the unit cost of many products and services declines by 10 percent to 30 percent each time a firm's experience at producing and selling them doubles, resulting in possible rapid price reductions. p. 350

exporting A global market-entry strategy in which a company produces goods in one country and sells them in another country. p. 182

family life cycle The distinct phases that a family progresses through from formation to retirement, each phase bringing with it identifiable purchasing behaviors. p. 128

feedback In the feedback loop, the sender's interpretation of the response, which indicates whether the message was decoded and understood as intended during the communication process. p. 460

field of experience A mutually shared understanding and knowledge that the sender and receiver apply to the message so that it can be communicated effectively during the communication process. p. 459

fixed cost (FC) The sum of the expenses of the firm that are stable and do not change with the quantity of a product that is produced and sold. p. 335

flexible-price policy Setting different prices for products and services depending on individual buyers and purchase situations. Also called *dynamic pricing*. p. 356

FOB origin pricing The "free on board" (FOB) price the seller quotes that includes only the cost of loading the product onto the vehicle and specifies the name of the location where the loading is to occur (seller's factory or warehouse). p. 362

Foreign Corrupt Practices Act (1977) A law, amended by the *International Anti-Dumping and Fair Competition Act* (1998), that makes it a crime for U.S. corporations to bribe an official of a foreign government or political party to obtain or retain business in a foreign country. p. 174

form of ownership Distinguishes retail outlets based on whether individuals, corporate chains, or contractual systems own the outlet. p. 432

formula selling presentation A presentation format that consists of information that must be provided in an accurate, thorough, and step-by-step manner to inform the prospect. p. 529

four I's of services The four unique elements to services: intangibility, inconsistency, inseparability, and inventory. p. 299

franchising A contractual arrangement between a parent company (a franchisor) and an individual or firm (a franchisee) that allows the franchisee to operate a certain type of business under an established name and according to specific rules. p. 391

frequency The average number of times a person in the target audience is exposed to a message or an advertisement. p. 494

full-service agency An advertising agency that provides the most complete range of services, including market research, media selection, copy development, artwork, and production. p. 503

functional groupings Organizational groupings that represent the different departments or business activities within a firm. p. 590

functional level The level in an organization where groups of specialists actually create value for the organization. p. 28

gap analysis A type of analysis that compares the differences between the consumer's expectations about and experiences with a service based on dimensions of service quality. p. 306

Generation X Includes the 15 percent of the population born between 1965 and 1976. Also called *baby bust*. p. 69

Generation Y Includes the 72 million Americans born between 1977 and 1994. Also called *echo-boom* or *baby boomlet*. p. 70

generic business strategy A strategy that can be adopted by any firm, regardless of the product or industry involved, to achieve a competitive advantage. p. 578

geographical groupings Organizational groupings in which sales territories are subdivided according to geographical location. p. 590

global brand A brand marketed under the same name in multiple countries with similar and centrally coordinated marketing programs. p. 171

global competition Exists when firms originate, produce, and market their products and services worldwide. p. 169

global consumers Consumer groups living in many countries or regions of the world who have similar needs or seek similar features and benefits from products or services. p. 171

global marketing strategy Transnational firms that employ the practice of standardizing marketing activities when there are cultural similarities and adapting them when cultures differ. p. 171

goals Statements of an accomplishment of a task to be achieved, often by a specific time. Also called *objectives*. p. 31

gray market A situation where products are sold through unauthorized channels of distribution. Also called *parallel importing*. p. 188

green marketing Marketing efforts to produce, promote, and reclaim environmentally sensitive products. p. 102

gross domestic product (GDP) The monetary value of all goods and services produced in a country during one year. p. 162
gross income The total amount of money made in one year by a person, household, or family unit. Also known as *money income* at the Census Bureau. p. 76
gross rating points (GRPs) A reference number used by advertisers that is obtained by multiplying reach (expressed as a percentage of the total market) by frequency. p. 495

hierarchy of effects The sequence of stages a prospective buyer goes through from initial awareness of a product to eventual action (either trial or adoption of the product). The stages include awareness, interest, evaluation, trial, and adoption. p. 470
hypermarket A form of scrambled merchandising, which consists of a large store (more than 200,000 square feet) that offers everything in a single outlet, eliminating the need for consumers to shop at more than one location. p. 436

idea generation The stage of the new-product process that develops a pool of concepts as candidates for new products. p. 257
idle production capacity Occurs when the service provider is available but there is no demand. p. 301
industrial distributor An intermediary that performs a variety of marketing channel functions, including selling, stocking, delivering a full product assortment, and financing. p. 384
infomercials Program-length (30-minute) advertisements that take an educational approach to communication with potential customers. p. 497
information technology Involves operating computer networks that can store and process data. p. 210
in-house agencies Consist of the company's own advertising staff, who may provide full services or a limited range of services. p. 504
institutional advertisements Advertisements designed to build goodwill or an image for an organization rather than promote a specific good or service. p. 487
integrated marketing communications (IMC) The concept of designing marketing communications programs that coordinate all promotional activities—advertising, personal selling, sales promotion, public relations, and direct marketing—to provide a consistent message across all audiences. p. 458
intensive distribution A level of distribution density whereby a firm tries to place its products and services in as many outlets as possible. p. 393
interactive marketing Two–way buyer-seller electronic communication in a computer-mediated environment in which the buyer controls the kind and amount of information received from the seller. p. 550
internal marketing The notion that a service organization must focus on its employees, or internal market, before successful programs can be directed at customers. p. 311
intertype competition Competition between very dissimilar types of retail outlets that results from a scrambled merchandising policy. p. 436
involvement The personal, social, and economic significance of the purchase to the consumer. p. 115
ISO 9000 Standards for registration and certification of a manufacturer's quality management and assurance system based on an on-site audit of practices and procedures developed by the International Standards Organization (ISO). p. 145

joint venture A global market-entry strategy in which a foreign company and a local firm invest together to create a local business in order to share ownership, control, and profits of the new company. p. 184
just-in-time (JIT) concept An inventory supply system that operates with very low inventories and requires fast, on-time delivery. p. 422

key account management The practice of using team selling to focus on important customers so as to build mutually beneficial, long-term, cooperative relationships. p. 534

label An integral part of the package that typically identifies the product or brand, who made it, where and when it was made, how it is to be used, and package contents and ingredients. p. 288
laws Society's values and standards that are enforceable in the courts. p. 92
lead generation The result of a direct marketing offer designed to generate interest in a product or service and a request for additional information. p. 477
lead time The time lag from ordering an item until it is received and ready for use or sale. Also called *order cycle time* or *replenishment time*. p. 414
learning Those behaviors that result from (1) repeated experience and (2) reasoning. p. 122
level of service The degree of service provided to the customer from three types of retailers: self-, limited-, and full-service. p. 432
lifestyle A mode of living that is identified by how people spend their time and resources, what they consider important in their environment, and what they think of themselves and the world around them. p. 124
limited-service agencies Advertising agencies that specialize in one aspect of the advertising process, such as providing creative services to develop the advertising copy, buying previously unpurchased media space, or providing Internet services. p. 504
line positions Managers who have the authority and responsibility to issue orders to the people who report to them. p. 589
logistics Those activities that focus on getting the right amount of the right products to the right place at the right time at the lowest possible cost. p. 406
logistics management The practice of organizing the cost-effective flow of raw materials, in-process inventory, finished goods, and related information from point of origin to point of consumption to satisfy customer requirements. p. 406
loss-leader pricing Deliberately selling a product below its customary price, not to increase sales, but to attract customers' attention in hopes that they will buy other products as well. p. 354

make–buy decision An evaluation of whether components and assemblies will be purchased from outside suppliers or built by the company itself. p. 151
manufacturer's agents Agents who work for several producers and carry noncompetitive, complementary merchandise in an exclusive territory. Also called *manufacturer's representatives*. p. 388
marginal analysis A continuing, concise trade-off of incremental costs against incremental revenues. p. 335
marginal cost (MC) The change in total cost that results from producing and marketing one additional unit of a product. p. 335
marginal revenue (MR) The change in total revenue that results from producing and marketing one additional unit of a product. p. 331

market People with both the desire and the ability to buy a specific offering. p. 11
market modification Strategies in which a company tries to find new customers, increase a product's use among existing customers, or create new use situations. p. 278
market orientation An organization that focuses its efforts on (1) continuously collecting information about customers' needs, (2) sharing this information across departments, and (3) using it to create customer value. p. 16
market segmentation Involves aggregating prospective buyers into groups, or segments, that (1) have common needs and (2) will respond similarly to a marketing action. pp. 41, 222
market segments The relatively homogeneous groups of prospective buyers that result from the market segmentation process. p. 222
market share The ratio of sales revenue of the firm to the total sales revenue of all firms in the industry, including the firm itself. p. 31
market testing The stage of the new-product process that exposes actual products to prospective consumers under realistic purchase conditions to see if they will buy. p. 261
market-based groupings Organizational groupings that use specific customer segments. p. 590
marketing The activity for creating, communicating, delivering, and exchanging offerings that benefit the organization, its stakeholders, and society at large. p. 6
marketing channel Individuals and firms involved in the process of making a product or service available for use or consumption by consumers or industrial users. p. 380
marketing concept The idea that an organization should (1) strive to satisfy the needs of consumers (2) while also trying to achieve the organization's goals. p. 16
marketing dashboard The visual computer display of the essential information related to achieving a marketing objective. p. 32
marketing metric A measure of the quantitative value or trend of a marketing activity or result. p. 33
marketing mix The marketing manager's controllable factors—product, price, promotion, and place—that can be used to solve a marketing problem. p. 11
marketing plan A road map for the marketing activities of an organization for a specified future time period, such as one year or five years. p. 33
marketing program A plan that integrates the marketing mix to provide a good, service, or idea to prospective buyers. p. 13
marketing research The process of defining a marketing problem and opportunity, systematically collecting and analyzing information, and recommending actions. p. 195
marketing ROI The application of modern measurement technologies to understand, quantify, and optimize marketing spending. p. 592
marketing strategy The means by which a marketing goal is to be achieved, usually characterized by a specified target market and a marketing program to reach it. p. 44
marketing tactics Detailed day-to-day operational decisions essential to the overall success of marketing strategies. p. 44
market–product grid A framework to relate the market segments of potential buyers to products offered or potential marketing actions by an organization. p. 233
marketspace Information- and communication-based electronic exchange environment mostly occupied by sophisticated computer and telecommunication technologies and digitized offerings. p. 80
measures of success Criteria or standards used in evaluating proposed solutions to the problem. p. 196
merchandise line Describes how many different types of products a store carries and in what assortment. p. 432
merchant wholesalers Independently owned firms that take title to the merchandise they handle. p. 387
message The information sent by a source to a receiver during the communication process. p. 458
microfinance The practice of offering small, collateral-free loans to individuals who otherwise would not have access to the capital necessary to begin small businesses or other income-generating activities. p. 179
mission A statement of the organization's function in society, often identifying its customers, markets, products, and technologies. Often used interchangeably with *vision*. p. 29
mixed branding A branding strategy where a firm markets products under its own name(s) and that of a reseller because the segment attracted to the reseller is different from its own market. p. 288
moral idealism A personal moral philosophy that considers certain individual rights or duties as universal, regardless of the outcome. p. 99
motivation The energizing force that stimulates behavior to satisfy a need. p. 118
multibranding A branding strategy that involves giving each product a distinct name when each brand is intended for a different market segment. p. 287
multichannel marketing The blending of different communication and delivery channels that are mutually reinforcing in attracting, retaining, and building relationships with consumers who shop and buy in traditional intermediaries and online. p. 385
multichannel retailers Retailers that utilize and integrate a combination of traditional store formats and nonstore formats such as catalogs, television, and online retailing. p. 450
multicultural marketing Combinations of the marketing mix that reflect the unique attitudes, ancestry, communication preferences, and lifestyles of different races. p. 72
multidomestic marketing strategy Multinational firms that have as many different product variations, brand names, and advertising programs as countries in which they do business. p. 170
multiproduct branding A branding strategy in which a company uses one name for all its products in a product class. p. 286

need-satisfaction presentation A presentation format that emphasizes probing and listening by the salesperson to identify needs and interests of prospective buyers. p. 529
new-product process The seven stages an organization goes through to identify business opportunities and convert them to a salable good or service. p. 256
new-product strategy development The stage of the new-product process that defines the role for a new product in terms of the firm's overall objectives. p. 256
noise Extraneous factors that can work against effective communication by distorting a message or the feedback received during the communication process. p. 460

North American Industry Classification System (NAICS) Provides common industry definitions for Canada, Mexico, and the United States, which makes it easier to measure economic activity in the three member countries of the *North American Free Trade Agreement* (NAFTA). p. 141

objective and task budgeting Allocating funds to promotion whereby the company: (1) determines its promotion objectives; (2) outlines the tasks to accomplish these objectives; and (3) determines the promotion cost of performing these tasks. p. 472

objectives Statements of an accomplishment of a task to be achieved, often by a specific time. Also called *goals*. p. 31

observational data Facts and figures obtained by watching, either mechanically or in person, how people actually behave. p. 201

odd-even pricing Setting prices a few dollars or cents under an even number. p. 349

off-peak pricing Charging different prices during different times of the day or days of the week to reflect variations in demand for the service. p. 309

off-price retailing Selling brand-name merchandise at lower than regular prices. p. 444

one-price policy Setting one price for all buyers of a product or service. Also called *fixed pricing*. p. 355

online consumers The subsegment of all Internet users who employ this technology to research products and services and make purchases. p. 554

opinion leaders Individuals who exert direct or indirect social influence over others. p. 126

order getter Sells in a conventional sense and identifies prospective customers, provides customers with information, persuades customers to buy, closes sales, and follows up on customers' use of a product or service. p. 523

order taker Processes routine orders or reorders for products that were already sold by the company. p. 522

organizational buyers Those manufacturers, wholesalers, retailers, and government agencies that buy goods and services for their own use or for resale. pp. 19, 140

organizational buying behavior The decision-making process that organizations use to establish the need for products and services and identify, evaluate, and choose among alternative brands and suppliers. p. 150

organizational buying criteria The objective attributes of the supplier's products and services and the capabilities of the supplier itself. p. 145

organizational culture The set of values, ideas, attitudes, and norms of behavior that is learned and shared among the members of an organization. p. 30

packaging A component of a product that refers to any container in which it is offered for sale and on which label information is conveyed. p. 288

partnership selling The practice whereby buyers and sellers combine their expertise and resources to create customized solutions, commit to joint planning, and share customer, competitive, and company information for their mutual benefit, and ultimately the customer. Also called *enterprise selling*. p. 522

penetration pricing Setting a low initial price on a new product to appeal immediately to the mass market. p. 347

perceived risk The anxiety felt because the consumer cannot anticipate the outcomes of a purchase but believes that there may be negative consequences. p. 121

percentage of sales budgeting Allocating funds to promotion as a percentage of past or anticipated sales, in terms of either dollars or units sold. p. 471

perception The process by which an individual selects, organizes, and interprets information to create a meaningful picture of the world. p. 120

perceptual map A means of displaying or graphing in two dimensions the location of products or brands in the minds of consumers to enable a manager to see how consumers perceive competing products or brands, as well as its own product or brand to develop marketing actions to move its product or brand to an ideal position. p. 239

permission marketing The solicitation of a consumer's consent (called "*opt-in*") to receive e-mail and advertising based on personal data supplied by the consumer. p. 551

personal selling The two-way flow of communication between a buyer and seller, often in a face-to-face encounter, designed to influence a person's or group's purchase decision. pp. 461, 520

personal selling process Sales activities occurring before, during, and after the sale itself, consisting of six stages: (1) prospecting, (2) preapproach, (3) approach, (4) presentation, (5) close, and (6) follow-up. p. 526

personality A person's consistent behaviors or responses to recurring situations. p. 119

personalization The consumer-initiated practice of generating content on a marketer's Web site that is custom tailored to an individual's specific needs and preferences. p. 550

points of difference Those characteristics of a product that make it superior to competitive substitutes. p. 41

posttests Tests conducted after an advertisement has been shown to the target audience to determine whether it accomplished its intended purpose. p. 504

power center A huge shopping strip with multiple anchor (or national) stores. p. 446

predatory pricing The practice of charging a very low price for a product with the intent of driving competitors out of business. p. 365

prestige pricing Setting a high price so that quality- or status-conscious consumers will be attracted to the product and buy it. p. 347

pretests Tests conducted before an advertisement is placed in any medium to determine whether it communicates the intended message or to select among alternative versions of the advertisement. p. 503

price (P) The money or other considerations (including other products and services) exchanged for the ownership or use of a product or service. p. 320

price discrimination The practice of charging different prices to different buyers for goods of like grade and quality. p. 364

price elasticity of demand The percentage change in quantity demanded relative to a percentage change in price. p. 333

price fixing A conspiracy among firms to set prices for a product. p. 363

price lining Setting the price of a line of products at a number of different specific pricing points. p. 348
price war Successive price cutting by competitors to increase or maintain their unit sales or market share. p. 357
pricing constraints Factors that limit the range of prices a firm may set. p. 325
pricing objectives Specifying the role of price in an organization's marketing and strategic plans. p. 324
primary data Facts and figures that are newly collected for the project. p. 199
private branding A branding strategy used when a company manufactures products but sells them under the brand name of a wholesaler or retailer. Also called *private labeling* or *reseller branding*. p. 287
product A good, service, or idea consisting of a bundle of tangible and intangible attributes that satisfies consumers' needs and is received in exchange for money or something else of value. p. 246
product advertisements Advertisements that focus on selling a good or service and which take three forms: (1) pioneering (or informational), (2) competitive (or persuasive), and (3) reminder. p. 486
product class Consists of the entire product category or industry. p. 276
product differentiation A marketing strategy that involves a firm using different marketing mix activities to help consumers perceive the product as being different and better than competing products. p. 222
product form Consists of variations of a product within the product class. p. 276
product item A specific product that has a unique brand, size, or price. p. 248
product life cycle Describes the stages a new product goes through in the marketplace: introduction, growth, maturity, and decline. p. 270
product line A group of product or service items that are closely related because they satisfy a class of needs, are used together, are sold to the same customer group, are distributed through the same outlets, or fall within a given price range. p. 248
product-line pricing The setting of prices for all items in a product line to cover the total cost and produce a profit for the complete line, not necessarily for each item. p. 356
product mix Consists of all of the product lines offered by an organization. p. 249
product modification Strategies that alter a product's characteristic, such as its quality, performance, or appearance, to increase the product's value to customers and increase sales. p. 278
product or program champion A person who is able and willing to cut red tape and move the program forward. p. 586
product placements A consumer sales promotion tool that uses a brand-name product in a movie, television show, video game, or a commercial for another product. p. 509
product positioning The place a product occupies in consumers' minds on important attributes relative to competitive products. p. 238
product repositioning Changing the place a product occupies in a consumer's mind relative to competitive products. p. 238
product line groupings Organizational groupings in which a unit is responsible for specific product offerings. p. 590
profit The money left after a business firm's total expenses are subtracted from its total revenues and is the reward for the risk it undertakes in marketing its offerings. p. 26
profit equation Profit = Total revenue − Total cost; or Profit = (Unit price × Quantity sold) − (Fixed cost + Variable cost). p. 323
promotional allowances Cash payments or an extra amount of "free goods" awarded sellers in the marketing channel for undertaking certain advertising or selling activities to promote a product. p. 362
promotional mix The combination of one or more communication tools used to: (1) inform prospective buyers about the benefits of the product, (2) persuade them to try it, and (3) remind them later about the benefits they enjoyed by using the product. p. 458
protectionism The practice of shielding one or more industries within a country's economy from foreign competition through the use of tariffs or quotas. p. 166
protocol A statement that, before product development begins, identifies: (1) a well-defined target market; (2) specific customers' needs, wants, and preferences; and (3) what the product will be and do. p. 253
public relations A form of communication management that seeks to influence the feelings, opinions, or beliefs held by customers, prospective customers, stockholders, suppliers, employees, and other publics about a company and its products or services. p. 462
publicity A nonpersonal, indirectly paid presentation of an organization, good, or service. p. 462
publicity tools Methods of obtaining nonpersonal presentation of an organization, good, or service without direct cost, such as news releases, news conferences, and public service announcements. p. 512
pull strategy Directing the promotional mix at ultimate consumers to encourage them to ask the retailer for a product. p. 469
purchase decision process The five stages a buyer passes through in making choices about which products and services to buy: (1) problem recognition, (2) information search, (3) alternative evaluation, (4) purchase decision, and (5) postpurchase behavior. p. 112
push strategy Directing the promotional mix to channel members to gain their cooperation in ordering and stocking the product. p. 468

quantity discounts Reductions in unit costs for a larger order. p. 360
questionnaire data Facts and figures obtained by asking people about their attitudes, awareness, intentions, and behaviors. p. 203
quick response Inventory management systems that are designed to reduce a retailer's lead time for receiving merchandise, which then lowers a retailer's inventory investment, improves customer service levels, and reduces logistics expense. Also called *efficient consumer response*. p. 414
quota A restriction placed on the amount of a product allowed to enter or leave a country. p. 167

rating The percentage of households in a market that are tuned to a particular TV show or radio station. p. 494
reach The number of different people or households exposed to an advertisement. p. 494
receivers Consumers who read, hear, or see the message sent by a source during the communication process. p. 458

reciprocity An industrial buying practice in which two organizations agree to purchase each other's products and services. p. 146
reference groups People to whom an individual looks as a basis for self-appraisal or as a source of personal standards. p. 128
regional shopping centers Consist of 50 to 150 stores that typically attract customers who live or work within a 5- to 10-mile range, often containing two or three anchor stores. p. 445
regulation Restrictions state and federal laws place on business with regard to the conduct of its activities. p. 82
relationship marketing Links the organization to its individual customers, employees, suppliers, and other partners for their mutual long-term benefits. p. 13
relationship selling The practice of building ties to customers based on a salesperson's attention and commitment to customer needs over time. p. 522
response In the feedback loop, the impact the message had on the receiver's knowledge, attitudes, or behaviors during the communication process. p. 460
retail life cycle The process of growth and decline that retail outlets, like products, experience. Consists of the early growth, accelerated development, maturity, and decline stages. p. 449
retail positioning matrix A matrix that positions retail outlets on two dimensions: breadth of product line and value added, such as location, product reliability, or prestige. p. 442
retailing All activities involved in selling, renting, and providing products and services to ultimate consumers for personal, family, or household use. p. 430
retailing mix The activities related to managing the store and the merchandise in the store, which includes retail pricing, store location, retail communication, and merchandise. p. 443
reverse auction In an e-marketplace, it is an online auction in which a buyer communicates a need for a product or service and would-be suppliers are invited to bid in competition with each other. p. 155
reverse logistics A process of reclaiming recyclable and reusable materials, returns, and reworks from the point of consumption or use for repair, remanufacturing, redistribution, or disposal. p. 424

sales forecast The total sales of a product that a firm expects to sell during a specified time period under specified environmental conditions and its own marketing efforts. Also called a *company forecast*. p. 214
sales management Planning the selling program and implementing and evaluating the personal selling effort of the firm. p. 520
sales plan A statement describing what is to be achieved and where and how the selling effort of salespeople is to be deployed. p. 532
sales promotion A short-term inducement of value offered to arouse interest in buying a good or service. p. 463
sales quota Specific goals assigned to a salesperson, sales team, branch sales office, or sales district for a stated time period. p. 539
sales response function Relates the expense of marketing effort to the marketing results obtained. p. 574
salesforce automation (SFA) The use of computer, information, communication, and Internet technologies to make the sales function more effective and efficient. p. 541
scrambled merchandising Offering several unrelated product lines in a single store. p. 436
screening and evaluation The stage of the new-product process that internally and externally evaluates new-product ideas to eliminate those that warrant no further effort. p. 259
secondary data Facts and figures that have already been recorded before the project at hand. p. 199
selective distribution A level of distribution density whereby a firm selects a few retailers in a specific geographical area to carry its products. p. 394
self-concept The way people see themselves and the way they believe others see them. p. 119
self-regulation An alternative to government control where an industry attempts to police itself. p. 85
selling agents Agents who represent a single producer and are responsible for the entire marketing function of that producer. p. 389
semiotics A field of study that examines the correspondence between symbols and their role in the assignment of meaning for people. p. 175
service continuum The range of offerings companies bring to the market, from the tangible to the intangible or good-dominant to service-dominant. p. 301
services Intangible activities or benefits that an organization provides to satisfy consumers' needs in exchange for money or something else of value. pp. 246, 298
share points An analysis that uses percentage points of market share as the common basis of comparison to allocate marketing resources effectively for different product lines within the same firm. p. 575
shopping products Items for which the consumer compares several alternatives on criteria, such as price, quality, or style. p. 247
situation analysis Taking stock of where the firm or product has been recently, where it is now, and where it is headed in terms of the organization's marketing plans and the external forces and trends affecting it. p. 40
situational influences The five aspects of the purchase situation that impacts the consumer's purchase decision process: (1) the purchase task, (2) social surroundings, (3) physical surroundings, (4) temporal effects, and (5) antecedent states. p. 117
skimming pricing Setting the highest initial price that customers really desiring the product are willing to pay when introducing a new or innovative product. p. 346
social audit A systematic assessment of a firm's objectives, strategies, and performance in terms of social responsibility. p. 103
social class The relatively permanent, homogeneous divisions in a society into which people sharing similar values, interests, and behavior can be grouped. p. 130
social forces The demographic characteristics of the population and its values. p. 68
social responsibility The idea that organizations are part of a larger society and are accountable to that society for their actions. p. 100
societal marketing concept The view that organizations should satisfy the needs of consumers in a way that provides for society's well-being. p. 17
source A company or person who has information to convey during the communication process. p. 458
spam Communications that take the form of electronic junk mail or unsolicited e-mail. p. 559
specialty products Items that a consumer makes a special effort to search out and buy. p. 247

staff positions People who have the authority and responsibility to advise people in line positions but cannot issue direct orders to them. p. 589

standard markup pricing Adding a fixed percentage to the cost of all items in a specific product class. p. 349

stimulus-response presentation A presentation format that assumes that given the appropriate stimulus by a salesperson, the prospect will buy. p. 529

strategic alliances Agreements among two or more independent firms to cooperate for the purpose of achieving common goals. p. 170

strategic business unit (SBU) A subsidiary, division, or unit of an organization that markets a set of related offerings to a clearly defined group of customers. p. 28

strategic channel alliances A practice whereby one firm's marketing channel is used to sell another firm's products. p. 386

strategic marketing process The approach whereby an organization allocates its marketing mix resources to reach its target markets. p. 39

strategy An organization's long-term course of action designed to deliver a unique customer experience while achieving its goals. p. 27

strip mall A cluster of neighborhood stores to serve people who are within a 5- to 10-minute drive. p. 446

subcultures Subgroups within the larger, or national, culture with unique values, ideas, and attitudes. p. 131

subliminal perception Seeing or hearing messages without being aware of them. p. 121

supplier development The deliberate effort by organizational buyers to build relationships that shape suppliers' products, services, and capabilities to fit a buyer's needs and those of its customers. p. 145

supply chain A sequence of firms that perform activities required to create and deliver a product or service to ultimate consumers or industrial users. p. 406

supply chain management The integration and organization of information and logistic activities across firms in a supply chain for the purpose of creating and delivering products and services that provide value to ultimate consumers. p. 407

supply partnership A relationship that exists when a buyer and its supplier adopt mutually beneficial objectives, policies, and procedures for the purpose of lowering the cost or increasing the value of products and services delivered to the ultimate consumer. p. 146

sustainable development Conducting business in a way that protects the natural environment while making economic progress. p. 104

SWOT analysis An acronym describing an organization's appraisal of its internal **S**trengths and **W**eaknesses and its external **O**pportunities and **T**hreats. p. 40

synergy analysis Seeks opportunities by finding the optimum balance between marketing efficiencies versus R&D-manufacturing efficiencies. p. 580

target market One or more specific groups of potential consumers toward which an organization directs its marketing program. p. 11

target pricing Consists of (1) estimating the price that ultimate consumers would be willing to pay for a product, (2) working backward through markups taken by retailers and wholesalers to determine what price to charge wholesalers, and then (3) deliberately adjusting the composition and features of the product to achieve the target price to consumers. p. 349

target profit pricing Setting an annual target of a specific dollar volume of profit. p. 351

target return-on-investment pricing Setting a price to achieve an annual target return-on-investment (ROI). p. 352

target return-on-sales pricing Setting a price to achieve a profit that is a specified percentage of the sales volume. p. 352

tariffs Government taxes on goods or services entering a country that primarily serve to raise prices on imports. p. 166

team selling The practice of using an entire team of professionals in selling to and servicing major customers. p. 525

technology Inventions or innovations from applied science or engineering research. p. 78

telemarketing Using the telephone to interact with and sell directly to consumers. p. 441

third-party logistics providers Firms that perform most or all of the logistics functions that manufacturers, suppliers, and distributors would normally perform themselves. p. 417

total cost (TC) The total expense incurred by a firm in producing and marketing a product. Total cost is the sum of fixed cost and variable cost. p. 335

total logistics cost Expenses associated with transportation, materials handling and warehousing, inventory, stockouts (being out of inventory), order processing, and return goods handling. p. 412

total revenue (TR) The total money received from the sale of a product. p. 331

trade name A commercial, legal name under which a company does business. p. 282

trademark Identifies that a firm has legally registered its brand name or trade name so the firm has its exclusive use, thereby preventing others from using it. p. 282

trade-oriented sales promotions Sales tools used to support a company's advertising and personal selling directed to wholesalers, distributors, or retailers. Also called *trade promotions*. p. 510

trading down Reducing the number of features, quality, or price. p. 281

trading up Adding value to the product (or line) through additional features or higher-quality materials. p. 281

traditional auction In an e-marketplace, it is an online auction in which a seller puts an item up for sale and would-be buyers are invited to bid in competition with each other. p. 155

traffic generation The outcome of a direct marketing offer designed to motivate people to visit a business. p. 477

triple-bottom line The recognition of the need for organizations to improve the state of people, the planet, and profit simultaneously if they are to achieve sustainable, long-term growth. p. 102

ultimate consumers The people who use the goods and services purchased for a household. Also called *consumers*, *buyers*, or *customers*. p. 19

uniform delivered pricing The price the seller quotes that includes all transportation costs. p. 362

unit variable cost (UVC) Variable cost expressed on a per unit basis for a product. p. 335

unsought products Items that the consumer does not know about or knows about but does not initially want. p. 247

usage rate The quantity consumed or patronage (store visits) during a specific period. Also called *frequency marketing*. p. 228

utilitarianism A personal moral philosophy that focuses on "the greatest good for the greatest number" by assessing the costs and benefits of the consequences of ethical behavior. p. 100

utility The benefits or customer value received by users of the product. p. 19

value The ratio of perceived benefits to price; or Value = (Perceived benefits ÷ Price). p. 323

value analysis A systematic appraisal of the design, quality, and performance of a product to reduce purchasing costs. p. 151

value consciousness The concern for obtaining the best quality, features, and performance of a product or service for a given price that drives consumption behavior. p. 74

value-pricing The practice of simultaneously increasing product and service benefits while maintaining or decreasing price. p. 323

values A society's personally or socially preferable modes of conduct or states of existence that tend to persist over time. p. 173

variable cost (VC) The sum of the expenses of the firm that vary directly with the quantity of a product that is produced and sold. p. 335

vendor-managed inventory (VMI) An inventory-management system whereby the supplier determines the product amount and assortment a customer (such as a retailer) needs and automatically delivers the appropriate items. p. 423

vertical marketing systems Professionally managed and centrally coordinated marketing channels designed to achieve channel economies and maximum marketing impact. p. 390

viral marketing An Internet-enabled promotional strategy that encourages individuals to forward marketer-initiated messages to others via e-mail, social networking Web sites, and blogs. p. 559

warranty A statement indicating the liability of the manufacturer for product deficiencies. p. 292

Web communities Web sites that allow people to congregate online and exchange views on topics of common interest. p. 559

wheel of retailing A concept that describes how new forms of retail outlets enter the market. p. 448

whistle-blowers Employees who report unethical or illegal actions of their employers. p. 98

word of mouth The influencing of people during conversations. p. 127

workload method A formula-based method for determining the size of a salesforce that integrates the number of customers served, call frequency, call length, and available selling time to arrive at a figure for the salesforce size. p. 536

World Trade Organization (WTO) A permanent institution that sets rules governing trade between its members through panels of trade experts who decide on trade disputes between members and issue binding decisions. p. 167

yield management pricing The charging of different prices to maximize revenue for a set amount of capacity at any given time. p. 349

LEARNING REVIEW ANSWERS

CHAPTER 1

1. **What is marketing?**
Answer: Marketing is the activity for creating, communicating, delivering, and exchanging offerings that benefit the organization, its stakeholders, and society at large.
2. **Marketing focuses on __________ and _________ consumer needs.**
Answer: discovering; satisfying
3. **What four factors are needed for marketing to occur?**
Answer: The four factors are: (1) two or more parties (individuals or organizations) with unsatisfied needs; (2) a desire and ability to have their needs satisfied; (3) a way for the parties to communicate; and (4) something to exchange.
4. **An organization can't satisfy the needs of all consumers, so it must focus on one or more subgroups, which are its ________________.**
Answer: target market
5. **What are the four marketing mix elements that make up the organization's marketing program?**
Answer: product, price, promotion, place
6. **What are environmental forces?**
Answer: Environmental forces are those that the organization's marketing department can't control. These include social, economic, technological, competitive, and regulatory forces.
7. **What are the two key characteristics of the marketing concept?**
Answer: An organization should (1) strive to satisfy the needs of consumers (2) while also trying to achieve the organization's goals.
8. **What is the difference between ultimate consumers and organizational buyers?**
Answer: Ultimate consumers are the people who use the goods and services purchased for a household. Organizational buyers are those manufacturers, wholesalers, retailers, and government agencies that buy goods and services for their own use or for resale.

CHAPTER 2

1. **What is the difference between a business firm and a nonprofit organization?**
Answer: A business firm is a privately owned organization that serves its customers to earn a profit so that it can survive. A nonprofit organization is a nongovernmental organization that serves its customers but does not have profit as an organizational goal. Instead, its goals may be operational efficiency or client satisfaction.
2. **What are examples of a functional level in an organization?**
Answer: The functional level in an organization is where groups of specialists from the marketing, finance, manufacturing/operations, accounting, information systems, research and development, and/or human resources departments focus on a specific strategic direction to create value for the organization.
3. **What is the meaning of an organization's mission?**
Answer: A mission is a statement of the organization's function in society, often identifying its customers, markets, products, and technologies. It is often used interchangeably with *vision*.
4. **What is the difference between an organization's business and its goals?**
Answer: An organization's business describes the clear, broad, underlying industry or market sector of an organization's offering. An organization's goals (or objectives) are statements of an accomplishment of a task to be achieved, often by a specific time. Goals convert an organization's mission and business into long- and short-term performance targets to measure how well it is doing.
5. **What is the difference between a marketing dashboard and a marketing metric?**
Answer: A marketing dashboard is the visual computer display of the essential information related to achieving a marketing objective. Each variable in a marketing dashboard is a marketing metric, which is a measure of the quantitative value or trend of a marketing activity or result.
6. **What is business portfolio analysis?**
Answer: Business portfolio analysis is a technique that managers use to quantify performance measures and growth targets to analyze its clients' strategic business units (SBUs) as though they were a collection of separate investments.
7. **Explain the four market–product strategies in diversification analysis.**
Answer: The four market–product strategies in diversification analysis are: (1) Market penetration, which is a marketing strategy to increase sales of current products in current markets. There is no change in either the basic product line or the markets served. Rather, selling more of the product or selling the product at a higher price generates increased sales. (2) Market development, which is a marketing strategy to sell current products to new markets. (3) Product development, which is a marketing strategy of selling new products to current markets. (4) Diversification, which is a potentially high-risk marketing strategy of developing new products and selling them in new markets.
8. **What are the three steps of the planning phase of the strategic marketing process?**
Answer: The three steps of the planning phase of the strategic marketing process are: (1) Situation (SWOT) analysis, which involves taking stock of where the firm or product has been recently, where it is now, and where it is headed in terms of the organization's marketing plans and the external forces and trends affecting it. To do this, an organization uses a SWOT analysis, an acronym that describes an organization's appraisal of its internal Strengths and Weaknesses and its external Opportunities and Threats. (2) Market–product focus and goal setting, which determines what products an organization will offer to which customers. This is often based on market segmentation—aggregating prospective buyers into groups or segments that have common needs and will respond similarly to a marketing action. (3) Marketing program, in which an organization develops the marketing mix elements and budget for each offering.
9. **What are points of difference and why are they important?**
Answer: Points of difference are those characteristics of a product that make it superior to competitive substitutes—offerings it faces in the marketplace. They are the single most important factor in the success or failure of a new product.
10. **What is the implementation phase of the strategic marketing process?**
Answer: The implementation phase carries out the marketing plan that emerges from the planning phase and consists of: (1) obtaining resources; (2) designing the marketing organization; (3) developing schedules; and (4) executing the marketing program designed in the planning phase.
11. **How do the goals set for a marketing program in the planning phase relate to the evaluation phase of the strategic marketing process?**
Answer: The planning phase objectives are used as the benchmarks with which the actual performance results are compared in the evaluation phase to identify deviations from the written marketing plans and then correct negative ones or exploit positive ones.

CHAPTER 3

1. **Describe three generational cohorts.**
   Answer: (1) Baby boomers are those among the U.S. population born between 1946 and 1964. These Americans are growing older and are the wealthiest generation in U.S. history. (2) Generation X are those among the 15 percent of the U.S. population born between 1965 and 1976. These well-educated Americans, also known as the baby bust cohort because of declining birthrates, have a collective net worth that is less than the baby boomer generation. (3) Generation Y are the 72 million Americans among the U.S. population born between 1977 and 1994. The rising birthrate of this "baby boomlet" cohort is the result of baby boomers having children. A subset of this generational cohort are millennials, which are younger Americans born since 1994. Because each generational cohort has its distinct attitudes and behaviors, marketers have developed generational marketing programs for each of them.
2. **Why are many companies developing multicultural marketing programs?**
   Answer: Multicultural marketing programs consist of combinations of the marketing mix that reflect the unique attitudes, ancestry, communication preferences, and lifestyles of different races. The reasons for developing these programs are: (1) The racial and ethnic diversity of the United States is changing rapidly due to the increases in the African American, Asian, and Hispanic populations, which increases their economic impact. (2) An accurate understanding of the culture of each group is essential if marketing efforts are to be successful. (3) Based on an analysis of population demographic data, racial and ethnic groups tend to be concentrated in specific geographic regions.
3. **How are important values such as sustainability reflected in the marketplace today?**
   Answer: Many Americans desire and practice sustainability to preserve the environment. Specifically, these consumers buy hybrid cars and energy-efficient light bulbs. Consumers also prefer brands that have a strong link to social action (like Ben & Jerry's—see Chapter 2). Companies are responding to this consumer trend by using renewable energy in producing and reducing the packaging of their products.
4. **What is the difference between a consumer's disposable and discretionary income?**
   Answer: Disposable income is the money a consumer has left after paying taxes to use for necessities such as food, housing, clothing, and transportation. Discretionary income is the money that remains after paying for taxes and necessities and is used for luxury items.
5. **How does technology impact customer value?**
   Answers: (1) Consumers can now assess value on the basis of other dimensions, such as quality, service, and relationships, due to the decline in the cost of technology. (2) Technology provides value through the development of new products. (3) Technology has changed the way existing products are produced through recycling and precycling.
6. **In pure competition there are a __________ number of sellers.**
   Answer: large
7. **The ___________ Act was punitive toward monopolies, whereas the ____________ Act was preventive.**
   Answers: Sherman Antitrust; Clayton
8. **Describe some of the recent changes in trademark law.**
   Answer: The *Trademark Law Revision Act* (1988) allows companies to secure rights to a name before its actual use by declaring an intent to use the name. In 2003, the United States agreed to participate in the *Madrid Protocol*, which is a treaty that facilitates the protection of U.S. trademark rights. Also, the U.S. Supreme Court recently ruled that a company may obtain trademarks for colors associated with their products. Finally, the *Federal Dilution Act* of 1995 prevents someone from using a trademark on a noncompeting product (such as the "Cadillac" of brushes).
9. **How does the Better Business Bureau encourage companies to follow its standards for commerce?**
   Answer: The Better Business Bureau (BBB) uses moral suasion to get members to comply with its standards. Companies, which join the BBB voluntarily, must agree to follow these standards before they are allowed to display the BBB logo.

CHAPTER 4

1. **What are ethics?**
   Answer: Ethics are the moral principles and values that govern the actions and decisions of an individual or group. They serve as guidelines on how to act rightly and justly when faced with moral dilemmas.
2. **What are four possible reasons for the present state of ethical conduct in the United States?**
   Answer: (1) Pressure on businesspeople to make decisions in a society with diverse value systems. (2) Business decisions being judged publicly by groups with different values and interests. (3) The public's expectations of ethical business behavior have increased. (4) Ethical business conduct may have declined.
3. **What rights are included in the Consumer Bill of Rights?**
   Answer: The rights to safety, to be informed, to choose, and to be heard.
4. **Economic espionage includes what kinds of activities?**
   Answer: Economic espionage is the clandestine collection of trade secrets or proprietary information about a company's competitors. This practice includes trespassing, theft, fraud, misrepresentation, wiretapping, searching competitors' trash, and violations of written and implicit employment agreements with noncompete clauses.
5. **What is meant by moral idealism?**
   Answer: Moral idealism is a personal moral philosophy that considers certain individual rights or duties as universal, regardless of the outcome.
6. **What is meant by social responsibility?**
   Answer: Social responsibility means that organizations are part of a larger society and are accountable to that society for their actions. It comprises three concepts: (1) profit responsibility—maximizing profits for the organization's shareholders; (2) stakeholder responsibility—the obligations an organization has to those who can effect the achievement of its objectives; and (3) societal responsibility—the obligations an organization has to preserve the ecological environment and to the general public.
7. **Marketing efforts to produce, promote, and reclaim environmentally sensitive products are called __________.**
   Answer: green marketing
8. **What is a social audit?**
   Answer: A social audit is a systematic assessment of a firm's objectives, strategies, and performance in terms of social responsibility.

CHAPTER 5

1. **What is the first stage in the consumer purchase decision process?**
   Answer: problem recognition
2. **The brands a consumer considers buying out of the set of brands in a product class of which the consumer is aware is called the _________.**
   Answer: consideration set
3. **What is the term for postpurchase anxiety?**
   Answer: cognitive dissonance
4. **The problem with the Toro Snow Pup was an example of selective ___________.**
   Answer: comprehension
5. **What three attitude-change approaches are most common?**
   Answer: (1) Change beliefs about the extent to which a brand has certain attributes. (2) Change the perceived importance of the attributes. (3) Add new attributes to the product.

6. **What does *lifestyle* mean?**
Answer: Lifestyle is a mode of living that is identified by how people spend their time and resources, what they consider important in their environment, and what they think of themselves and the world around them.
7. **What are the two primary forms of personal influence?**
Answer: opinion leadership; word of mouth activity
8. **Marketers are concerned with which types of reference groups?**
Answer: membership groups; aspiration groups; dissociative groups
9. **What two challenges must marketers overcome when marketing to Hispanics?**
Answer: (1) The diversity of nationalities among this subculture. (2) The language barrier that can lead to misinterpretation or mistranslation of commercial messages.

CHAPTER 6

1. **What are the three main types of organizational buyers?**
Answer: industrial firms; resellers; government units
2. **What is the North American Industry Classification System (NAICS)?**
Answer: The NAICS provides common industry definitions for Canada, Mexico, and the United States, which makes it easier to measure economic activity in the three member countries of NAFTA.
3. **What one department is almost always represented by a person in the buying center?**
Answer: purchasing department
4. **What are the three types of buying situations or buy classes?**
Answer: new buy; straight rebuy; modified rebuy
5. **What is a make-buy decision?**
Answer: A make-buy decision is an evaluation of whether components and assemblies will be purchased from outside suppliers or built by the company itself.
6. **What is a bidder's list?**
Answer: A bidder's list is a list of firms believed to be qualified to supply a given item.
7. **What are e-marketplaces?**
Answer: E-marketplaces are online trading communities that bring together buyers and supplier organizations to make possible the real-time exchange of information, money, products, and services.
8. **In general, which type of online auction creates upward pressure on bid prices and which type creates downward pressure on bid prices?**
Answer: traditional auction; reverse auction

CHAPTER 7

1. **What is the trade feedback effect?**
Answer: The phenomenon in which one country's imports affect the exports of other countries and vice versa, thus stimulating economic activity in all the nations involved.
2. **What variables influence why some companies and industries in a country succeed globally while others lose ground or fail?**
Answers: (1) factor conditions—a nation's ability to turn its natural resources, education, and infrastructure into a competitive advantage; (2) demand conditions—includes both the number and sophistication of domestic customers for an industry's product; (3) related and supporting industries—clusters of world-class suppliers that accelerate innovation; and (4) company strategy, structure, and rivalry—the conditions governing the way a nation's businesses are organized and managed, along with the intensity of domestic competition.
3. **What is protectionism?**
Answer: Protectionism is the practice of shielding one or more industries within a country's economy from foreign competition through the use of tariffs or quotas.
4. **The North American Free Trade Agreement was designed to promote free trade among which countries?**
Answer: United States, Canada, and Mexico
5. **What is the difference between a multidomestic marketing strategy and a global marketing strategy?**
Answer: Multinational firms view the world as consisting of unique markets. As a result, they use a multidomestic marketing strategy because they have as many different product variations, brand names, and advertising programs as countries in which they do business. Transnational firms view the world as one market. As a result, they use a global marketing strategy to standardize marketing activities when there are cultural similarities and adapt it when cultures differ.
6. **Semiotics involves the study of ____________.**
Answer: the correspondence between symbols and their role in the assignment of meaning for people.
7. **When foreign currencies can buy more U.S. dollars, are U.S. products more or less expensive for a foreign consumer?**
Answer: less expensive
8. **What mode of entry could a company follow if it has no previous experience in global marketing?**
Answer: indirect exporting through intermediaries
9. **How does licensing differ from a joint venture?**
Answer: Under licensing, a company offers the right to a trademark, patent, trade secret, or other similarly valued items of intellectual property in return for a fee or royalty. In a joint venture, a foreign company and a local firm invest together to create a local business to produce some product or service. The two companies share ownership, control, and profits of the new entity.
10. **Products may be sold globally in three ways. What are they?**
Answers: Products can be sold: (1) in the same form as in their home market (product extension); (2) with some adaptations (product adaptation); and (3) as a totally new product (product invention).
11. **What is dumping?**
Answer: Dumping is when a firm sells a product in a foreign country below its domestic price or below its actual cost to produce.

CHAPTER 8

1. **What is marketing research?**
Answer: Marketing research is the process of defining a marketing problem and opportunity, systematically collecting and analyzing information, and recommending actions.
2. **What is the five-step marketing research approach?**
Answer: The five-step marketing research approach provides a systematic checklist for making marketing decisions and actions. The five steps are: (1) define the problem; (2) develop the research plan; (3) collect relevant information (data); (4) develop findings; and (5) take marketing actions.
3. **What are constraints, as they apply to developing a research plan?**
Answer: Constraints in a decision are the restrictions placed on potential solutions to a problem, such as time and money. These set the parameters for the research plan—due dates, budget, etc.
4. **What is the difference between secondary and primary data?**
Answer: Secondary data are facts and figures that have already been recorded before the project at hand, whereas primary data are facts and figures that are newly collected for the project.
5. **What are some advantages and disadvantages of secondary data?**
Answer: Advantages of secondary data are the time savings, the low cost, and the greater level of detail that may be available. Disadvantages of secondary data are that the data may be out of date, unspecific, or have definitions, categories, or age groupings that are wrong for the project at hand.
6. **What is the difference between observational and questionnaire data?**
Answer: Observational data are facts and figures obtained by watching, either mechanically or in person, how people actually behave.

Questionnaire data are facts and figures obtained by asking people about their attitudes, awareness, intentions, and behaviors.

7. **Which survey provides the greatest flexibility for asking probing questions: mail, telephone, or personal interview?**
   Answer: personal interview (or individual or depth interview, which is a special kind of individual interview)
8. **What is the difference between a panel and an experiment?**
   Answer: A panel is a sample of consumers or stores from which researchers take a series of measurements. An experiment involves obtaining data by manipulating factors under tightly controlled conditions to test cause and effect, such as changing a variable in a customer purchase decision (marketing drivers) and seeing what happens (increase/decrease in unit or dollar sales).
9. **How does data mining differ from traditional marketing research?**
   Answer: Data mining is the extraction of hidden predictive information from large databases to find statistical links between consumer purchasing patterns and marketing actions. Marketing research identifies possible drivers and then collects data.
10. **In the marketing research for Tony's Pizza, what is an example of (*a*) a finding and (*b*) a marketing action?**
   Answer: (*a*) Figure 8–8A depicts annual sales from 2006 to 2009; the finding is that annual sales are relatively flat, rising only 5 million units over the four-year period. (*b*) Figure 8–8D shows a finding (the decline in pizza consumption) that leads to a recommendation to develop an ad targeting children 6 to 12 years old.
11. **What are the three kinds of sales forecasting techniques?**
   Answer: They are: (1) judgments of the decision maker; (2) surveys of knowledgeable groups; and (3) statistical methods.
12. **How do you make a lost-horse forecast?**
   Answer: To make a lost-horse forecast, begin with the last known value of the item being forecast, list the factors that could affect the forecast, assess whether they have a positive or negative impact, and then make the final forecast.

CHAPTER 9

1. **Market segmentation involves aggregating prospective buyers into groups that have two key characteristics. What are they?**
   Answer: The groups (1) should have common needs and (2) will respond similarly to a marketing action.
2. **In terms of market segments and products, what are the three market segmentation strategies?**
   Answer: The three market segmentation strategies are: (1) one product and multiple market segments; (2) multiple products and multiple market segments; and (3) "segments of one," or mass customization.
3. **The process of segmenting and targeting markets is a bridge between which two marketing activities?**
   Answer: identifying market needs and executing the marketing program
4. **What is the difference between the demographic and behavioral bases of market segmentation?**
   Answer: Demographic segmentation is based on some objective physical (gender, race), measurable (age, income), or other classification attribute (birth era, occupation) of prospective customers. Behavioral segmentation is based on some observable actions or attitudes by prospective customers—such as where they buy, what benefits they seek, how frequently they buy, and why they buy.
5. **What are some criteria used to decide which segments to choose for targets?**
   Answer: These criteria include market size, expected growth, competitive position, cost of reaching the segment, and compatibility with the organization's objectives and resources.
6. **What factor is estimated or measured for each of the cells in a market–product grid?**
   Answer: Each cell in the grid can show the estimated market size of a given product sold to a specific market segment.
7. **How are marketing and product synergies different in a market–product grid?**
   Answer: Marketing synergies run horizontally across a market-product grid. Each row represents an opportunity for efficiency in the marketing efforts to a market segment. Product synergies run vertically down the market–product grid. Each column represents an opportunity for efficiency in research and development (R&D) and production.
8. **What is the difference between product positioning and product repositioning?**
   Answer: Product positioning refers to the place a product occupies in consumers' minds on important attributes relative to competitive products. Product repositioning involves changing the place a product occupies in a consumer's mind relative to competitive products.
9. **Why do marketers use perceptual maps in product positioning decisions?**
   Answer: Perceptual maps are a means of displaying or graphing in two dimensions the location of products or brands in the minds of consumers. Managers use perceptual maps to see how consumers perceive competing products or brands as well as their own product or brand. Then, they can develop marketing actions to move their product or brand to an ideal position.

CHAPTER 10

1. **What are the four main types of consumer products?**
   Answer: They are convenience products, shopping products, specialty products, and unsought products.
2. **What is the difference between a product line and a product mix?**
   Answer: A product line is a group of product or service items that are closely related because they satisfy a class of needs, are used together, are sold to the same customer group, are distributed through the same outlets, or fall within a given price range. The product mix consists of all the product lines offered by an organization.
3. **What marketing metric might you use in a marketing dashboard to discover which states have weak sales?**
   Answer: Annual percentage (%) sales change is a marketing metric that can measure the annual growth rate over a specified time period for each state of the United States.
4. **What kind of innovation would an improved electric toothbrush be?**
   Answer: continuous innovation—no new learning is required
5. **Why can an "insignificant point of difference" lead to new-product failure?**
   Answer: The product must have superior characteristics that deliver unique benefits to the user compared to those of competitors. Without these, the product will probably fail.
6. **How might using the Stage-Gate process reduce the chances of skipping a stage in new-product development?**
   Answer: A "gate" ensures that each step in the new-product process is completed satisfactorily before moving on to the next step. Gatekeepers make key "go/kill" decisions at each gate that determine if resources will be allocated to move the new-product process forward to the next step.
7. **What is the new-product strategy development stage in the new-product process?**
   Answer: New-product strategy development is the stage of the new-product process that defines the role for a new product in terms of the firm's overall objectives.
8. **What are the main sources of new-product ideas?**
   Answer: Customer and supplier suggestions, employee and co-worker suggestions, R&D laboratories, competitive products, and universities, inventors, and smaller firms.
9. **How do internal and external screening and evaluation approaches differ?**
   Answer: In internal screening, company employees evaluate the technical feasibility of new-product ideas to determine whether it meets the

objectives defined in the new-product strategy development step. For services, employees are assessed to determine that they have the commitment and skills to meet customer expectations and sustain customer loyalty. In external screening, evaluation consists of preliminary testing of the new-product idea (not the actual product) with consumers.

10. **How does the development stage of the new-product process involve testing the product inside and outside the firm?**
Answer: Internally, laboratory tests are done to see if the product achieves the physical, quality, and safety standards; externally, market testing is done to expose actual products to prospective consumers under realistic purchase conditions to see if they will buy.
11. **What is a test market?**
Answer: A test market is a city that is viewed as being representative of U.S. consumers in terms of demographics and brand purchase behaviors, having a cable TV system to deliver different ads to different homes, and has tracking systems to measure sales from the different advertising campaigns.
12. **What is commercialization of a new product?**
Answer: Commercialization, the last stage of the new-product process, involves positioning and launching a new product in full-scale production and sales and is the most expensive stage for most new products.

CHAPTER 11

1. **Advertising plays a major role in the __________ stage of the product life cycle, and __________ plays a major role in maturity.**
Answer: introductory; product differentiation
2. **How do high-learning and low-learning products differ?**
Answer: A high-learning product requires significant customer education and there is an extended introductory period. A low-learning product requires little customer education because the benefits of purchase are readily understood, resulting in immediate sales.
3. **What are the five categories of product adopters?**
Answer: The five categories of product adopters based on the diffusion of innovation are: (1) innovators—2.5 percent; (2) early adopters—13.5 percent; (3) early majority—34 percent; (4) late majority—34 percent; and (5) laggards—16 percent.
4. **How does a product manager help manage a product's life cycle?**
Answer: A product manager shepherds a product through its life cycle by modifying the product, modifying the market, and repositioning the product.
5. **What does "creating a new use situation" mean in managing a product's life cycle?**
Answer: Finding new uses or applications for an existing product.
6. **Explain the difference between trading up and trading down in repositioning.**
Answer: Trading up involves adding value to the product (or line) through additional features or higher-quality materials. Trading down involves reducing the number of features, quality, price, or downsizing—reducing the content of packages without changing package size and maintaining or increasing the package price.
7. **What are the five criteria mentioned most often when selecting a good brand name?**
Answer: A good brand name should: (1) suggest the product benefits; (2) be memorable, distinctive, and positive; (3) fit the company or product image; (4) have no legal or regulatory restrictions; and (5) be simple and emotional.
8. **What are the three major benefits of packaging and labeling?**
Answer: communication benefits; functional benefits; perceptual benefits
9. **What is the difference between an expressed and an implied warranty?**
Answer: Express warranties are written statements of liabilities. Implied warranties assign responsibility for product deficiencies to the manufacturer even if the retailer sells the product.

CHAPTER 12

1. **What are the four I's of services?**
Answer: intangibility, inconsistency, inseparability, and inventory
2. **To eliminate service inconsistencies, companies rely on __________ and __________.**
Answer: standardization; training
3. **Would inventory carrying costs for an accounting firm with certified public accountants be *(a)* high, *(b)* low, or *(c)* nonexistent?**
Answer: Inventory carrying costs are related to idle production capacity, which is when the service provider is available but there is no demand. A CPA typically earns a high fixed-cost salary. Therefore, if he/she is available but there is no demand for his/her service, the inventory cost of this service is *(a)* "high," because the cost of the accountant's salary must be paid regardless of whether or not the service is performed.
4. **What are the differences between search, experience, and credence properties?**
Answer: Search properties, such as color, size, and style, can be determined before purchase. Experience properties, such as with restaurants, can only be assessed during or after consumption. Credence properties, characteristics of services provided by specialized professionals such as legal advice or medical diagnostics, may be impossible to evaluate even after purchase and consumption.
5. **Hertz created its differential advantage at the points of __________ in its customer contact audit.**
Answer: interaction between consumer and service provider
6. **How does a movie theater use off-peak pricing?**
Answer: Movie theaters reduce prices for matinees and often for weekday shows due to the variation of demand for this service.
7. **Matching demand with capacity is the focus of __________ management.**
Answer: capacity
8. **What factors will influence future changes in services?**
Answer: Technology advances and the expanding global economy.

CHAPTER 13

1. **What is price?**
Answer: Price is the money or other considerations (including other products and services) exchanged for the ownership or use of a product or service.
2. **What factors impact the list price to determine the final price?**
Answer: incentives, such as cash discounts, allowances, and rebates, as well as extra fees or surcharges
3. **What is the difference between pricing objectives and pricing constraints?**
Answer: Pricing objectives involve specifying the role of price in an organization's marketing and strategic plans whereas pricing constraints are factors that limit the range of prices a firm may set.
4. **How does the type of competitive market a firm is in affect its range in setting price?**
Answer: In a market characterized by pure competition, the marketplace determines the price an individual firm can set. In a market characterized by monopolistic competition, there is some price competition among firms, which allows an individual firm to set a price within a range of prices. In an oligopoly, a firm may either be a price leader and set the market price that other firms follow or be a price follower and set a price based on the prices set by its competitors to avoid a price war. In a pure monopoly, the firm, being the only one in the market, can set any price it wants.
5. **What is the difference between a movement along and a shift of a demand curve?**
Answer: A movement along a demand curve (up or down) for a product occurs when its price is lowered/increased and the quantity demanded for it increases/decreases, assuming that other factors such as consumer

tastes, promotion (advertising and/or sales promotion), price and availability of substitute products, and/or consumer incomes, remain unchanged. However, if one or more of these factors do change, then the demand curve for a product will shift to the right or left based on whether the change(s) were favorable or not.

6. **What is total revenue and how is it calculated?**
   Answer: Total revenue (TR) is the total money received from the sale of product. Total revenue (TR) equals the product's unit price (P) times the quantity sold (Q) or $TR = P \times Q$.
7. **What does it mean if a product has a price elasticity of demand that is greater than 1?**
   Answer: Price elasticities greater than 1 indicate the product is price elastic.
8. **What is the difference between fixed costs and variable costs?**
   Answer: Fixed cost is the sum of the expenses of the firm that are stable and do not change with the quantity of a product that is produced and sold. Variable cost is the sum of the expenses of the firm that vary directly with the quantity of a product that is produced and sold.
9. **What is a break-even point?**
   Answer: A break-even point (BEP) is the quantity at which total revenue and total cost are equal.

CHAPTER 14

1. **What are the circumstances in pricing a new product that might support skimming or penetration pricing?**
   Answer: A firm introducing a new product can use skimming pricing to set the highest initial price that customers desiring the product are willing to pay because they are not very price sensitive. The firm may also want to recoup the initial R&D and promotion costs in developing and promoting the product. A firm may use penetration pricing to set a low initial price for a new product to appeal immediately to a price sensitive mass market. A firm may also use this strategy to discourage competitors from entering the market.
2. **What is odd-even pricing?**
   Answer: Odd-even pricing involves setting prices a few dollars or cents under an even number. Psychologically, a $499.99 price feels lower than $500.00, even though the difference is just 1¢.
3. **What is standard markup pricing?**
   Answer: Standard markup pricing entails adding a fixed percentage to the cost of all items in a specific product class. The price varies based on the type of product and retail store within which it is sold.
4. **What profit-based pricing approach should a manager use if he or she wants to reflect the percentage of the firm's resources used in obtaining the profit?**
   Answer: target return-on-investment pricing
5. **What is the purpose of loss-leader pricing when used by a retail firm?**
   Answer: Loss-leader pricing involves deliberately selling a product below its customary price not to increase sales but to attract customers in hopes they will buy other products as well, such as discretionary items with large markups.
6. **Why would a seller choose a flexible-price policy over a one-price policy?**
   Answer: A flexible-price policy involves setting different prices for products and services depending on individual buyers and purchasing situations instead of setting one price for all buyers. A flexible-price policy gives a firm the flexibility to change prices if consumer preferences, costs, or competitive conditions change.
7. **If a firm wished to encourage repeat purchases by a buyer throughout a year, would a cumulative or noncumulative quantity discount be a better strategy?**
   Answer: cumulative quantity discount
8. **Which pricing practices are covered by the Sherman Act?**
   Answer: horizontal price fixing and predatory pricing

CHAPTER 15

1. **What is meant by a marketing channel?**
   Answer: A marketing channel consists of individuals and firms involved in the process of making a product or service available for use or consumption by consumers or industrial users.
2. **What are the three basic functions performed by intermediaries?**
   Answer: Intermediaries perform transactional, logistical, and facilitating functions.
3. **What is the difference between a direct and an indirect channel?**
   Answer: A direct channel is one in which a producer of consumer or business products and services and ultimate consumers or industrial users deal directly with each other. An indirect channel has intermediaries that are inserted between the producer and ultimate consumers or industrial users and perform numerous channel functions.
4. **Why are channels for business products typically shorter than channels for consumer products?**
   Answer: Business channels are typically shorter than consumer channels because business users are fewer in number, tend to be more concentrated geographically, and buy in larger quantities.
5. **What is the principal distinction between a corporate vertical marketing system and an administered vertical marketing system?**
   Answer: A corporate vertical marketing system combines successive stages of production and distribution under a single ownership. An administered vertical marketing system achieves coordination by the size and influence of one channel member rather than through ownership.
6. **What are the three questions marketing executives consider when choosing a marketing channel and intermediaries?**
   Answer: The three questions to consider when choosing a marketing channel and intermediaries are: (1) Which will provide the best coverage of the target market? (2) Which will best satisfy the buying requirements of the target market? (3) Which will be the most profitable?
7. **What are the three degrees of distribution density?**
   Answer: intensive; exclusive; selective.
8. **What is meant by exclusive dealing?**
   Answer: Exclusive dealing exists when a supplier requires channel members to sell only its products or restricts distributors from selling directly competitive products. It is specifically prohibited under the *Clayton Act* when it lessens competition or creates monopolies.

CHAPTER 16

1. **What is the principal difference between a marketing channel and a supply chain?**
   Answer: A supply chain differs from a marketing channel in terms of membership. It includes suppliers who provide raw materials to a manufacturer as well as the wholesalers and retailers—the marketing channel—that deliver the finished goods to ultimate consumers.
2. **The choice of a supply chain involves what three steps?**
   Answer: (1) Understand the customer. (2) Understand the supply chain. (3) Harmonize the supply chain with the marketing strategy.
3. **The objective of information and logistics management in a supply chain is to ___________.**
   Answer: minimize logistics costs while delivering maximum customer service
4. **How does consumer demand information increase supply chain responsiveness and efficiency?**
   Answer: Demand information improves supply chain responsiveness because customers will find the products when and where they want them. Demand information improves supply chain efficiency because firms are better able to meet customer needs and to produce, transport, and store the required amount of inventory.
5. **What is the relationship between the number of warehouses a company operates, its inventory costs, and its transportation costs?**
   Answer: As the number of warehouses increases, inventory costs rise and transportation costs fall. Because more inventory is warehoused, it

can be transported in larger volumes closer to customers. The net effect is to minimize the total logistics cost.

6. **What are the basic trade-offs between the five modes of transportation?**
Answer: Each of the five modes of transportation can be evaluated against six service criteria: cost, time, capability, dependability, accessibility, and frequency.
7. **What types of inventory should use storage warehouses and which type should use distribution centers?**
Answer: Storage warehouses are best suited for products that will not be needed for substantial periods of time. Distribution centers are used if inventory needs to be in decentralized locations to facilitate sorting or consolidating products from different plants or suppliers, ingredients need to be blended, or labeling and repackaging need to be done before the products are shipped to customers.
8. **What are the strengths and weaknesses of a just-in-time system?**
Answer: A just-in-time (JIT) system saves money (production costs such as materials and labor) because lower levels of inventory for a product are required. A JIT system only works if demand forecasting is reliable. However, a JIT system is not suitable for inventories that must be stored over significant periods of time.

CHAPTER 17

1. **When Ralph Lauren makes shirts to a customer's exact preferences, what utility is provided?**
Answer: form utility
2. **Two measures of the impact of retailing in the global economy are __________ and __________.**
Answer: the total annual sales; the number of employees working at large retailers
3. **Centralized decision making and purchasing are an advantage of ______ ownership.**
Answer: corporate chain
4. **What are some examples of new forms of self-service retailers?**
Answer: Airlines (Lufthansa—self-serve check-in terminals to allow passengers to select seats, etc.); hotels (Hilton Hotels—self-serve kiosks in lobbies to allow patrons to check-in, etc.); libraries (Palm Beach County Library—self-serve machines to check out books).
5. **Would a shop for big men's clothes carrying pants in sizes 40 to 60 have a broad or deep product line?**
Answer: deep product line; the range of sizes relates to the assortment of a product item (pants) rather than the variety of product lines (pants, shirts, shoes, etc.).
6. **Successful catalog retailers often send __________ catalogs to __________ markets identified in their databases.**
Answer: specialty; niche
7. **How are retailers increasing consumer interest and involvement in online retailing?**
Answer: Retailers have improved the online retailing experience by adding experiential or interactive activities to their Web sites, allowing customers to "build" virtual products by customizing their purchases.
8. **Where are direct selling retail sales growing? Why?**
Answer: Direct-selling retailers are (1) expanding into other global markets outside the U.S. due to a specific country's lack of effective distribution channels and/or a lack of consumer knowledge about certain products and brands and (2) reaching consumers who prefer one-on-one customer service and a social shopping experience rather than shopping online or at big discount stores.
9. **What are the two dimensions of the retail positioning matrix?**
Answer: breadth of product line; value added
10. **How does original markup differ from maintained markup?**
Answer: The original markup is the difference between retailer cost and initial selling price whereas maintained markup is the difference between the final selling price and retailer cost, which is also called the gross margin.
11. **A huge shopping mall with multiple anchor stores is a __________ center.**
Answer: power
12. **According to the wheel of retailing, when a new retail form appears, how would you characterize its image?**
Answer: A low-status, low-margin, low-price outlet.
13. **Market share is usually fought out before the __________ stage of the retail life cycle.**
Answer: maturity
14. **What is an influence effect?**
Answer: An influence effect is the complementary role that different communication and delivery channels have on sales.

CHAPTER 18

1. **What are the six elements required for communication to occur?**
Answer: The six elements required for communication to occur are: a source, a message, a channel of communication, a receiver, and the processes of encoding and decoding.
2. **A difficulty for U.S. companies advertising in international markets is that the audience does not share the same __________.**
Answer: field of experience
3. **A misprint in a newspaper ad is an example of __________.**
Answer: noise
4. **Explain the difference between advertising and publicity when both appear on television.**
Answer: Since advertising space on TV is paid for, a firm can control what it wants to say and to whom and how often the message is sent over a broadcast, cable, satellite, or local TV network. Since publicity is an indirectly paid presentation of a message about a firm or its goods or services, the firm has little control over what is said to whom or when. Instead, it can only suggest to the TV medium that it run a favorable story on the firm or its offerings.
5. **Cost per contact is high with the __________ element of the promotional mix.**
Answer: personal selling
6. **Which promotional element should be offered only on a short-term basis?**
Answer: sales promotion
7. **Describe the promotional objective for each stage of the product life cycle.**
Answer: Introduction—to inform; growth—to persuade; maturity—to remind; and decline—to phase out.
8. **At what stage of the consumer purchase decision process is the importance of personal selling highest? Why?**
Answer: The purchase stage of the consumer purchase decision process because salespeople can provide sales assistance to prospective customers and negotiate terms of the sale.
9. **Explain the differences between a push strategy and a pull strategy.**
Answer: In a push strategy, a firm directs the promotional mix to channel members to gain their cooperation in ordering and stocking the product. In a pull strategy, a firm directs the promotional mix at ultimate consumers to encourage them to ask retailers for the product, who then orders it from wholesalers or the firm itself.
10. **What are the characteristics of good promotion objectives?**
Answer: Promotion objectives should possess three important qualities. They should (1) be designed for a well-defined target audience, (2) be measurable, and (3) cover a specified time period.
11. **What is the weakness of the percentage of sales budgeting approach?**
Answer: The major fallacy is that sales cause promotion. By using this method, a company may reduce its promotion budget because of downturns in past or projected future sales—situations where promotion may be needed the most.

12. **How have advertising agencies changed to facilitate the use of IMC programs?**
Answer: Some agencies have adopted: (1) a total communications solutions approach; (2) a long-term perspective in which all forms of promotion are integrated; and (3) an IMC audit to analyze the internal communication network of their clients.
13. **What are the three types of responses generated by direct marketing activities?**
Answer: They are direct orders, lead generation, and traffic generation.
14. **The ability to design and use direct marketing programs has increased with the availability of __________ and __________.**
Answer: information technology; databases

CHAPTER 19

1. **What is the difference between pioneering and competitive ads?**
Answer: Pioneering ads, used in the introductory stage of the product life cycle, tell people what a product is, what it can do, and where it can be found. Competitive ads promote a specific brand's features and benefits to persuade the target market to select the firm's brand rather than that of a competitor.
2. **What is the purpose of an institutional advertisement?**
Answer: The purpose of an institutional advertisement is to build goodwill or an image for an organization.
3. **What other decisions can advertising objectives influence?**
Answer: Advertising objectives can influence the decisions such as selecting media, evaluating an advertising campaign, and establishing the importance and sequence of the stages of the hierarchy of effects.
4. **What is a potential shortcoming of using a celebrity spokesperson?**
Answer: The spokesperson's image may change to be inconsistent with the image of the company or brand.
5. **You see the same ad in *Time* and *Fortune* magazines and on billboards and TV. Is this an example of reach or frequency?**
Answer: Reach—using more of the same media type (magazines) as well as using more of different types of media (magazines, billboards, and TV)—is an attempt to maximize the number of individuals in a target market to be exposed to the advertisement. Frequency uses the same medium/media more than once to present the advertising message.
6. **Why has the Internet become a popular advertising medium?**
Answer: The Internet offers a visual message, can use both audio and video, is interactive through rich media, and tends to reach younger consumers.
7. **What factors must be considered when choosing among alternative media?**
Answer: Knowing the media habits of the target audience; understanding the product's attributes; and calculating the reach and cost, as measured by CPM.
8. **Explain the difference between pretesting and posttesting advertising copy.**
Answer: Pretests are conducted before ads are placed in any medium to determine whether they communicate the intended message or select among alternative versions of the ad. Posttests are shown to the target audience to determine whether it accomplished its intended purpose.
9. **What is the difference between aided and unaided recall posttests?**
Answer: Aided recall involves showing an ad to respondents who then are asked if their previous exposure to it was through reading, viewing, or listening. Unaided recall involves specifically asking respondents if they remember an ad without any prompting to determine if they saw or heard its message.
10. **What's the difference between a coupon and a deal?**
Answer: A coupon provides a reduced price for an item based on redemption. A deal is a short-term price reduction.
11. **Which sales promotional tool is most common for new products?**
Answer: samples
12. **Which trade promotion is used on an ongoing basis?**
Answer: trade allowance
13. **What is a news release?**
Answer: A news release is an announcement regarding changes in the company or the product line.
14. **What is the difference between government regulation and self-regulation?**
Answer: Government regulation involves laws or other controls set by an agency of local, state, or federal government. Self-regulation involves ethical guidelines for business practices set by advertising agencies, trade associations, and marketing organizations.

CHAPTER 20

1. **What is personal selling?**
Answer: Personal selling involves the two-way flow of communication between a buyer and seller, often in a face-to-face encounter, designed to influence a person's or group's purchase decision.
2. **What is involved in sales management?**
Answer: Sales management involves planning the selling program and implementing and evaluating the personal selling effort of the firm.
3. **What is the principal difference between an order taker and an order getter?**
Answer: An order taker processes routine orders or reorders for products that were already sold by the company. An order getter sells in a conventional sense and identifies prospective customers, provides customers with information, persuades customers to buy, closes sales, and follows up on customers' use of a product or service.
4. **What is team selling?**
Answer: Team selling is the practice of using an entire team of professionals in selling to and servicing major customers.
5. **What are the six stages in the personal selling process?**
Answer: The six stages in the personal selling process are: (1) prospecting, (2) preapproach, (3) approach, (4) presentation, (5) close, and (6) follow-up.
6. **What is the distinction between a lead and a qualified prospect?**
Answer: A lead is the name of a person who may be a possible customer whereas a qualified prospect is an individual who wants the product, can afford to buy it, and is the decision maker.
7. **Which presentation format is most consistent with the marketing concept? Why?**
Answer: The need-satisfaction presentation format emphasizes probing and listening by the salesperson to identify needs and interests of prospective buyers and then tailors the presentation to the prospect and highlights product benefits, which is consistent with the marketing concept and its focus on relationship building.
8. **What are the three types of selling objectives?**
Answer: The three types of selling objectives are: (1) output-related (dollars or unit sales, new customers, profit); (2) input-related (sales calls, selling expenses); and (3) behavioral-related (product knowledge, customer service, selling and communication skills).
9. **What three factors are used to structure sales organizations?**
Answer: geography; customer; product/service
10. **How does emotional intelligence tie to adaptive selling?**
Answer: Emotional intelligence is the ability to understand one's own emotions and the emotions of people with whom one interacts on a daily basis. These qualities are important for adaptive selling.

CHAPTER 21

1. **The consumer-initiated practice of generating content on a marketer's Web site that is custom tailored to an individual's specific needs and preferences is called __________.**
Answer: personalization

2. **Companies produce a customer experience through what seven Web site design elements?**
   Answer: These design elements are: context, content, community, customization, communication, connection, and commerce.
3. **Which online consumer lifestyle segment spends the most money online and which spends the most time online?**
   Answer: The "brand loyalists" segment spends the most money online whereas the "hooked, online, and single" segment spends more time online.
4. **What are the six reasons consumers prefer to shop and buy online?**
   Answer: convenience, choice, customization, communication, cost, and control
5. **What is the eight-second rule?**
   Answer: The eight-second rule is a view that customers will abandon their efforts to enter and navigate a Web site if download time exceeds eight seconds.
6. **A cross-channel shopper is ___________.**
   Answer: an online consumer who researches products online and then purchases them at a retail store
7. **Channel conflict between manufacturers and retailers is likely to arise when manufacturers use ___________ Web sites.**
   Answer: transactional

CHAPTER 22

1. **What are the four basic practices "that really work"—that are characteristics of industry-leading firms?**
   Answer: The four basic business and management practices that matter are: (1) strategy; (2) execution; (3) culture; and (4) structure.
2. **What is the significance of the S-shape of the sales response function in Figure 22–1?**
   Answer: The sales response function relates the expense of marketing effort to the marketing results obtained. Different levels of marketing effort will cause different rates of sales revenue growth. In Figure 22–1, an additional $1 million of marketing effort results in far greater increases of sales revenue in the midrange of the curve than at either end.
3. **What is the difference between an input metric and an output metric?**
   Answer: Marketing metrics are used to measure actual organizational performance—whether its goals have been achieved. An input metric is one in which there is no assurance that it will actually convert into sales revenues, such as the number of ideas or concepts in the "pipeline," R&D spending as a percentage of sales, and the number of R&D projects. An output metric is a measure of actual results, such as sales revenues due to new offerings, customer satisfaction with new offerings, and percentage of sales from new offerings during a specified time period.
4. **Describe Porter's four generic business strategies.**
   Answer: A generic business strategy is one that can be adopted by any firm, regardless of the product or industry involved to achieve a competitive advantage. Porter's four generic business strategies are:
   - *Cost leadership strategy.* Focuses on reducing expenses and, in turn, lowers product prices while targeting a broad array of market segments.
   - *Differentiation strategy.* Requires products to have significant points of difference to charge a higher price while targeting a broad array of market segments.
   - *Cost focus strategy.* Involves controlling expenses and, in turn, lowering product prices targeted at a narrow range of market segments.
   - *Differentiation focus strategy.* Requires products to have significant points of difference to target one or only a few market segments.
5. **Where do (*a*) marketing synergies and (*b*) R&D–manufacturing synergies appear when using the synergy analysis framework?**
   Answer: Synergy analysis seeks opportunities by finding the optimum balance between marketing efficiencies versus R&D–manufacturing efficiencies using a market–product grid framework. (*a*) Marketing synergies run horizontally across the rows. As a result, a firm may experience the market specialization effect if it provides a complete product line for a given market segment. (*b*) R&D–manufacturing synergies run vertically down the columns. As a result, a firm may experience the product specialization effect if it provides a product item for all market segments. A firm can experience both marketing and R&D–manufacturing efficiencies if it offers full coverage: a complete product line targeted at all market segments.
6. **What is the meaning and importance of a program champion?**
   Answer: A program champion is able and willing to cut red tape and move the program forward to get the program implemented.
7. **What are one or two examples of lessons from Lockheed's Skunk Works that apply to implementing marketing programs?**
   Answer: Examples of lessons from Lockheed's Skunk Works are: (1) make decisions promptly; (2) avoid "paralysis by analysis," which is the tendency to excessively analyze a problem instead of taking action; (3) when trouble develops, surface the problem immediately; (4) get help—don't keep the problem to yourself; and (5) create an action item list, program schedule, and Gantt chart as aids to completing a project.
8. **Explain the difference between sequential and concurrent tasks in a Gantt chart.**
   Answer: In sequential scheduling, certain tasks must be completed before subsequent tasks can be started. In concurrent scheduling, several tasks can be worked on at the same time.
9. **What are four groupings used within a typical marketing organization?**
   Answer: product line, functional, geographical, and market-based
10. **How do marketing metrics tie the goal-setting element of the planning phase of the strategic marketing process to the evaluation phase?**
    Answer: For each marketing plan goal developed in the planning phase for an organization's offering, a marketing metric is created to measure whether the goal has actually been achieved. Marketing actions are then taken in the implementation phase. In the evaluation phase, actual results are measured using this marketing metric to compare the established goal with the results to identify any deviations that need to be either corrected or exploited.

CHAPTER NOTES

Chapter 1

1. The 3M Post-it® Flag Highlighter and Post-it® Flag Pen examples are based on a series of interviews and meetings with David Windorski, 3M, from 2004 to 2009.
2. The *Oprah Winfrey Show,* January 15, 2008.
3. John Reinan, "Millionaire Whiz Kid," *Star Tribune,* October 13, 2006, pp. A1, A18; John Cloud, "The YouTube Gurus," *Time,* December 25, 2006–January 1, 2007, pp. 66–74; Lev Grossman, "Invention of the Year 2006," *Time*, November 13, 2006, pp. 64–65; "Two Kings Get Together," *The Economist*, October 14, 2006, pp. 67–68; and Yi-Wyn Yen, "YouTube Looks for the Money Clip," CNNMoney.com, March 25, 2008.
4. Brian Stelter, "YouTube Said to Be Nearing Hollywood Deal," *The New York Times,* January 29, 2009, pp. B1, B4.
5. Thomas Lee, "YouTube Co-Founder: Be Social," *Star Tribune,* August 17, 2008, pp. D1, D2.
6. To compare the 2004 and 2007 American Marketing Association definitions of "marketing," see Lisa M. Keefe, "Marketing Defined," *Marketing News,* January 15, 2008, pp. 28–29.
7. Richard P. Bagozzi, "Marketing as Exchange," *Journal of Marketing,* October 1975, pp. 32–39; and Gregory T. Gundlach and Patrick E. Murphy, "Ethical and Legal Foundations of Relational Marketing Exchanges," *Journal of Marketing,* October 1993, pp. 35–46.
8. "The Rise of the Creative Consumer," *The Economist,* March 12, 2005, pp. 54–60.
9. Productscan® Online database of new products, from *Marketing Intelligence Service,* December 17, 2003, www.productscan.com.
10. Robert M. McMath and Thom Forbes, "What *Were* They Thinking?" (New York: Times Business, 1998), pp. 3–22.
11. From the New Product Works Web site, "Favorite Failures," www.newproductworks.com.
12. From the Hot Pockets Web site, www.chefamerica.com and www.hotpockets.com.
13. "AT&T CruiseCast℠ Will Deliver 22 Satellite TV and 20 Satellite Radio Channels into the Car for the First Time with Breakthrough Antenna and Receiver Technologies," AT&T CruiseCast press release. November 3, 2008. See www.cruisecast.com/press.html#press1. See also "Live TV in Your Car," *Fox Business News,* January 9, 2009.
14. Natalie Zmuda, "PepsiCo Still Finalizing Ad Lineup for Super Bowl," *Advertising Age*, January 27, 2009. See http://adage.com/mediaworks/article?article_id=134132 and "Pepsi Max: I'm Good (Full Version)" from Hulu.com.
15. Jonathan Clements, "Dodging the Hazards of Post-College Life: Financial Strategies for New Graduates," *The Wall Street Journal,* December 7, 2005, p. D1; Amy Hoak, "Debt 101 for College Kids," *Star Tribune,* September 17, 2006, p. D7; and John Ewoldt, "Give the Kids Credit: Teach Them About Finances Early" *Star Tribune,* August 20, 2006, pp. E1, E3.
16. E. Jerome McCarthy, *Basic Marketing: A Managerial Approach* (Homewood, IL: Richard D. Irwin, 1960); and Walter van Waterschool and Christophe Van den Bulte, "The 4P Classification of the Marketing Mix Revisited," *Journal of Marketing,* October 1992, pp. 83–93.
17. Ashish Kothari and Joseph Lackner, "A Value Based Approach to Management," *Journal of Business and Industrial Marketing,* 21, no. 4, pp. 243–49; and James C. Anderson, James A. Narius, and Wouter van Rossum, "Customer Value Propositions in Business Markets," *Harvard Business Review,* March 2006, pp. 91–99.
18. For an examination of both the drivers and outcomes of consumer satisfaction programs, see Leslie M. Fine, "Spotlight on Marketing," *Business Horizons,* 49 (2006), pp. 179–83.
19. V. Kumar, *Managing Customers for Profit,* (Upper Saddle River, NJ: Pearson Education, 2008); and "What's a Loyal Customer Worth?" *Fortune,* December 11, 1995, p. 182.
20. Michael Treacy and Fred D. Wiersema, *The Discipline of Market Leaders* (Reading, MA: Addison-Wesley, 1995); Michael Treacy and Fred Wiersema, "How Market Leaders Keep Their Edge," *Fortune* (February 6, 1995), pp. 88–89; and Michael Treacy, "You Need a Value Discipline—But Which One?" *Fortune* (April 17, 1995), p. 195.
21. Robert W. Palmatier, Rajiv P. Dant, Dhruv Grewal, and Kenneth R. Evans, "Factors Influencing the Effectiveness of Relationship Marketing: A Meta-Analysis," *Journal of Relationship Marketing,* October 2006, pp. 136–53; and William Boulding, Richard Staelin, Michael Ehret, and Wesley J. Johnson, "A Customer Relationship Management Roadmap: What Is Known, Potential Pitfalls, and Where to Go," *Journal of Marketing,* October 2005, pp. 155–66.
22. Susan Foumier, Susan Dobscha, and David Glen Mick, "Preventing the Premature Death of Relationship Marketing," *Harvard Business Review,* January–February 1998, pp. 42–51.
23. See www.oprah.com for January 15, 2008; and "Post-it® Flags Co-Sponsors Oprah's Live Web Event," *3M Stemwinder,* March 4–17, 2008, p. 3.
24. Reservations about and elaborations of these simplified stages appear in D.G. Brian Jones and Eric H. Shaw, "A History of Marketing Thought," Chapter 2 in *Handbook of Marketing,* edited by Barton Weitz and Robin Wensley (London: Sage Publications, 2006), pp. 39–65; Frederic E. Webster, Jr., "The Role of Marketing and the Firm," Chapter 3 in *Handbook of Marketing,* ed. Barton Weitz and Robin Wensley (London: Sage Publications, 2006), pp. 66–82; and Frederick E. Webster, Jr., "Back to the Future: Integrating Marketing as Tactics, Strategy and Organizational Culture," *Journal of Marketing,* October 2005, pp. 4–8.
25. Robert F. Keith, "The Marketing Revolution," *Journal of Marketing,* January 1960, pp. 35–38.
26. *Annual Report* (New York: General Electric Company, 1952), p. 21.
27. John C. Narver, Stanley F. Slater, and Brian Tietje, "Creating a Market Orientation," *Journal of Market Focused Management,* no. 2 (1998), pp. 241–55; Stanley F. Slater and John C. Narver, "Market Orientation and the Learning Organization," *Journal of Marketing,* July 1995, pp. 63–74; and George S. Day, "The Capabilities of Market-Driven Organizations," *Journal of Marketing*, October 1994, pp. 37–52.
28. The definition of customer relationship management is adapted from Rajendra K. Srivastava, Tasadduq A. Shervani, and Liam Fahey, "Marketing, Business Processes, and Shareholder Value: An Embedded View of Marketing Activities and the Discipline of Marketing," *Journal of Marketing,* special issue (1999), pp. 168–79; Gary F. Gebhardt, Gregory S. Carpenter, and John F. Sherry Jr., "Creating a Market Orientation: A Longitudinal, Multifirm, Grounded Analysis of Cultural Transformation," *Journal of Marketing,* October 2006, pp. 37–55; and Christopher Meyer and Andre Schwager, "Understanding Customer Experience," *Harvard Business Review,* February 2007, pp. 117–26.
29. Gary F. Gebhardt, Gregory S. Carpenter, and John F. Sherry Jr., "Creating a Market Orientation: A Longitudinal, Multifirm, Grounded Analysis of Cultural Transformation," *Journal of Marketing,* October 2006, pp. 37–55.

30. Christopher Meyer and Andre Schwager, "Understanding Customer Experience," *Harvard Business Review,* February 2007, pp. 117–26.
31. Michael E. Porter and Claas van der Linde, "Green and Competitive Ending the Stalemate," *Harvard Business Review,* September–October 1995, pp. 120–34; Jacquelyn Ottman, "Edison Winners Show Smart Environmental Marketing," *Marketing News*, July 17, 1995, pp. 16, 19; and Jacquelyn Ottman, "Mandate for the '90s: Green Corporate Image," *Marketing News,* September 11, 1995, p. 8.
32. Jeff Strickler, "Fran's Story," *Star Tribune,* January 17, 2009, pp. E1, E10; "What Is a Social Entrepreneur?" Schwab Foundation for Social Entrepreneurship; www.schwabfound.org/sf/SocialEntrepreneurs/index.htm; Roger L. Martin and Sally Osberg, "Social Entrepreneurship: The Case for Definition," *Stanford Social Innovation Review,* Spring 2007, pp. 34–35, www.ssireview.org/images/articles/2007SP_feature_martinosberg.pdf; Geoff Colvin, "A CEO Masters Micro-Credit," *Fortune,* January 19, 2009, p. 22; and the Hand in Hand International Web site at www.hihseed.org.
33. Shelby D. Hunt and John J. Burnett, "The Macromarketing/Micromarketing Dichotomy: A Taxonomical Model," *Journal of Marketing,* Summer 1982, pp. 9–26.
34. Philip Kotler and Sidney J. Levy, "Broadening the Concept of Marketing," *Journal of Marketing,* January 1969, pp. 10–15; and Jim Rendon, "When Nations Need a Little Marketing," *The New York Times,* November 23, 2003, p. BU6.
35. Bernard Stamler, "Temples of Culture Are Needy, Too. Tai Chi, Anyone?" *The New York Times,* April 23, 2003, p. 2.
36. Peter Gumbel, "Louvre, Inc.," *Time,* August 11, 2008, pp. 51–52.
37. William L. Wilkie and Elizabeth S. Moore, "Marketing's Relationship to Society," Chapter 1 in *Handbook of Marketing,* ed. Barton Weitz and Robin Wensley (London: Sage Publications, 2006), pp. 9–38.

3M's Post-it Flag Highlighters: This case was written by Michael J. Vessey and William Rudelius and is based on a series of personal interviews with David Windorski and 3M from 2004 to 2009.

Chapter 2

1. Information obtained from selected Web pages and press releases from the Ben & Jerry's Web site. See www.benjerry.com.
2. "Ice Cream: Global Industry Guide," *Datamonitor,* February 12, 2009, press release posted at MarketResearch.com.
3. Roger Kerin and Robert Peterson, *Strategic Marketing Problems: Cases and Comments,* 11th ed. (Upper Saddle River, NJ: Prentice Hall, 2007), p. 141.
4. Michael E. Porter, "What Is Strategy?" *Harvard Business Review* OnPoint Article, November–December 1996, p. 2.
5. Katherine Ellison, "The Bottom Line Redefined," *Nature Conservancy,* Winter 2002, pp. 45–50.
6. For a discussion on how industries are defined and offerings are classified, see the following resources: the American Marketing Association Web site, which provides one definition of an industry (www.marketingpower.com/mg-dictionary-view1509.php); and the Census Bureau's Economic Classification Policy Committee Issues Paper #1 (www.census.gov/epcd/naics/issues1), which aggregates industries in the NAICS (www.census.gov/epcd/www/naicsdev.htm) from a "production-oriented" view (see Chapter 6).
7. W. Chan Kim and Reneé Mauborgne, "Blue Ocean Strategy: From Theory to Practice," *California Management Review* 47, no. 3 (Spring 2005), p. 105; Porter, "What Is Strategy?" p. 2.
8. Costas Markides, "What Is Strategy and How Do You Know If You Have One?" *Business Strategy Review* 15, no. 2 (Summer 2004), p. 5.
9. The definition of *strategy* reflects thoughts appearing in Porter, "What Is Strategy?" pp. 4, 8; a condensed definition of strategy is found on the American Marketing Association Web site www.marketingpower.com; and Gerry Johnson, Kevan Scholes, and Richard Wittington, *Exploring Corporate Strategy* (Upper Saddle River, NJ: Prentice Hall, 2005), p. 10.
10. Roger A. Kerin, "Strategic Marketing and the CMO," *Journal of Marketing,* October 2005, pp. 12–13; and The CMO Council: Biographies of Selected Advisory Board Members. See www.cmocouncil.org/advisoryboard.html.
11. Roger A. Kerin, Vijay Mahajan, and P. Rajan Varadarajan, *Contemporary Perspectives on Strategic Marketing Planning* (Boston: Allyn & Bacon, 1990), ch. 1; and Orville C. Walker, Jr,, Harper W. Boyd, Jr., and Jean-Claude Larreche, *Marketing Strategy* (Burr Ridge, IL: Richard D. Irwin, 1992), chs. 1 and 2.
12. Taken in part from Jim Collins and Jerry I. Porras, *Built to Last: Successful Habits of Visionary Companies* (New York: HarperCollins Publishers, 2002), p. 54.
13. Ibid., p. 73; Patrick M. Lencioni "Make Your Values Mean Something," *Harvard Business Review,* July 2002, p. 6; and Aubrey Malphurs, *Values-Driven Leadership: Discovering and Developing Your Core Values for Ministry,* 2nd ed. (Grand Rapids, MI: BakerBooks, 2004), p. 31.
14. Collins and Porras, *Built to Last,* p. 73; and Lencioni, "Make Your Values Mean Something," p. 6.
15. Catherine M. Dalton, "When Organizational Values Are Mere Rhetoric," *Business Horizons* 49 (September–October 2006), p. 345.
16. Collins and Porras, *Built to Last,* pp. 94–95; and Tom Krattenmaker, "Write a Mission Statement That Your Company Is Willing to Live," *Harvard Management Communication Letter*, March 2002, pp. 3–4.
17. Nikos Mourkogiannis, "The Realist's Guide to Moral Purpose," *Strategy + Business*, no. 41 (Winter 2005), pp. 42, 45, 47.
18. Sheila M. J. Bonini, Lenny T. Mendonca, and Jeremy M. Oppenheim, "When Social Issues Become Strategic," *The McKinsey Quarterly,* 2006, no. 2, pp. 23, 25, 30–31.
19. Kenneth E. Goodpaster and Thomas E. Holloran, "Anatomy of Spiritual and Social Awareness: The Case of Medtronic, Inc.," *Third International Symposium on Catholic Social Thought and Management Education,* Goa, India, 1999, pp. 9–11.
20. Theodore Levitt, "Marketing Myopia," *Harvard Business Review,* July–August 1960, pp. 45–56.
21. David Phelps, "Debt Threat," *Star Tribune,* January 26, 2009, pp. D1, D6.
22. Brad Stone and Ashlee Vance, "A Broken Business Model?" *The New York Times,* January 26, 2009, pp .81, 84.
23. Alyssa Abkowitz, "The Movie Man," *Fortune,* February 2, 2009, p. 24; David Pogue, "Any Movie, Any Time," *Star Tribune,* February 4, 2009, p. D6; and Nick Wingfield, "Netflix Boss Plots Life After the DVD," *The Wall Street Journal*, June 23, 2009, pp. A1, A12.
24. The definition is adapted from Stephen Few, *Information Dashboard Design: The Effective Visual Communication of Data,* (Sebastopol, CA: O'Reilly Media, Inc., 2006) pp. 2–46.
25. Koen Pauwels et al., *Dashboards & Marketing: Why, What, How and What Research Is Needed?* (Hanover, NH: Tuck School, Dartmouth, May 2008).
26. Few, *Information Dashboard Design;* Bruce H. Clark, Andrew V. Abela, and Tim Ambler, "Behind the Wheel," *Marketing Management,* May–June 2006, pp. 19–23; Spencer E. Ante, "Giving the Boss the Big Picture," *BusinessWeek,* February 13, 2006, pp. 48-49; *Dashboard Tutorial,* (Cupertino, CA: Apple Computer, Inc.; 2006).
27. Few, *Information Dashboard Design,* p. 13.
28. Michael Krauss, "Balance Attention to Metrics with Intuition," *Marketing News,* June 1, 2007, pp. 6–8; John Davis, *Measuring Marketing: 103 Key Metrics Every Marketer Needs* (Singapore: John Wiley & Sons (Asia) Pte Ltd., 2007); Paul W. Farris, Neil T. Bendle, Phillip E. Pfeifer, and David J. Reibstein, *Marketing Metrics* (Upper Saddle River, NJ: Wharton School Publishing, 2006); and Marcel

Corstjens and Jeffrey Merrihue, "Optimal Marketing," *Harvard Business Review,* October 2003, pp. 114–121.

29. Jacques Bughin, Amy Guggenheim Shenkan, and Mark Singer, "How Poor Metrics Undermine Digital Marketing," *The McKinsey Quarterly,* October 2008.
30. The now-classic reference on effective graphic presentation is Edward R. Tufte. *The Visual Display of Quantitative Information,* 2nd Edition (Cheshire, CN: Graphic Press, 2001); also see Few, *Information Dashboard Design,* Chaps. 3–5.
31. George Stalk, Phillip Evans, and Lawrence E. Shulman, "Competing on Capabilities: The New Rules of Corporate Strategy," *Harvard Business Review,* March–April 1992, pp. 57–69; and Darrell K. Rigby, *Management Tools 2007: An Executive's Guide* (Boston: Bain & Company, 2007), p. 22.
32. Michael Arndt, "High-Tech and Handcrafted," *BusinessWeek,* July 5, 2004, pp. 86–87.
33. Kerin and Peterson, *Strategic Marketing Problems,* pp. 2–3; and Derek F. Abell, *Defining the Business* (Englewood Cliffs, NJ: Prentice Hall, 1980), p. 18.
34. Robert D. Hof, "How to Hit a Moving Target," *BusinessWeek,* August 21, 2006, p. 3; and Peter Kim, *Reinventing the Marketing Organization* (Cambridge, MA: Forrester, July 13, 2006), pp. 7, 9, and 17.
35. Adapted from *The Experience Curve Reviewed, IV. The Growth Share Matrix of the Product Portfolio* (Boston: The Boston Consulting Group, 1973).
36. Kerin, Mahajan, and Vardarajan, *Contemporary Perspectives,* p. 52.
37. Jim Collins, "How Great Companies Turn Crisis Into Opportunity," *Fortune,* February 2, 2009, pp. 49–52.
38. Mike Pasini, "Samsung Up, Kodak Holds on in Digicams," *Imaging Resource,* April 7, 2008; Nick Passmore, "Refocusing on Digital Cameras," *BusinessWeek,* June 4, 2008; Mike Pasini, "CIPA Releases 2009–2011 Camera Shipment Forecast," *Imaging Resource,* January 27, 2009; and "Kodak Institutional Investor Meeting," February 4, 2009, pp. 9, 15, 21–22, 64, 74.
39. "Info Trends Projects Digital Photo Frame Shipments to Achieve over 25% Annual Growth through 2012," *InfoTrends,* January 24, 2008; Karen M. Cheung, "IDC: Digital Photo Frames to Sell 42 Million Units by 2011," *DigitalCameraInfo.com,* September 13, 2007; and "New InfoTrends Report Reveals Essential Features of Digital Photo Frames," *InfoTrends,* November 14, 2008.
40. "New InfoTrends Data Indicates the Ink-Jet Photo-Centric MFPs Present Best Growth Area in Home Photo Printer Market," *InfoTrends,* August 24, 2007; Karen M. Cheung, "InfoTrends: Online Printing to Double by 2011," *DigitalCameraInfo.com,* August 13, 2007; Jefferson Graham, "Kodak Plans to Sell Inkjet Printers with Cheaper Ink," *USA Today,* February 6, 2007, p. 51; Simon Burns, "Printer Market Shows Steady Growth," VNUNET.com, September 19, 2007; Matthew Daneman, "Home Inkjet Printer Bright Spot for Kodak," *Democrat and Chronicle,* January 31, 2009; Ben Furfie, "Sector Guide: Inkjet/MFD Printers," *PC Retail,* January 8, 2009; Jennifer Nelson, "InfoTrends: Online Photo Printing Market Needs Innovation," *DigitalCameraInfo.com*, February 1, 2008; and "Kodak Institutional Investor Meeting," February 4, 2009, pp. 10, 15, 22, 38, 40–41, 64, 74.
41. Matthew Daneman, "Kodak Clings to Film," *Democrat and Chronicle,* January 4, 2009; "Kodak Institutional Investor Meeting," February 4, 2009, pp. 9, 21, 64, 74; and Robert Tomsho, "Kodak to Take Kodachrome Away," *The Wall Street Journal*, June 23, 2009, pp. B1, B6.
42. Strengths and weaknesses of the BCG technique are based on Derek F. Abell and John S. Hammond, *Strategic Market Planning: Problem and Analytic Approaches* (Englewood Cliffs, NJ: Prentice Hall, 1979); Yoram Wind, Vijay Mahajan, and Donald Swire, "An Empirical Comparison of Standardized Portfolio Models," *Journal of Marketing,* Spring 1983, pp. 89–99; and J. Scott Armstrong and Roderick J. Brodie, "Effects of Portfolio Planning Methods on Decision Making: Experimental Results," *International Journal of Research in Marketing,* Winter 1994, pp. 73–84.
43. H. Igor Ansoff, "Strategies for Diversification," *Harvard Business Review,* September–October 1957, pp. 113–24.
44. Joanna Peot, "Sweet Success," *Dairy Foods,* November 1, 2008.
45. Linda Swenson and Kenneth E. Goodpaster, *Medtronic in China (A)* (Minneapolis, MN: University of St. Thomas, 1999), pp. 4–5.
46. Ben Dobbin, "Recession-Hit Kodak Outlines New Strategy," *BusinessWeek,* February 4, 2009; Meg Tirrell, "Kodak to Cut Up to 4,500 Jobs, Restructure, Has Loss (Update 5)," *Bloomberg.com,* February 16, 2009; "Kodak Institutional Investor Meeting," February 4, 2009, pp. 6–8, 17–18, 21, 63; Josh Quittner, "Meet the Bitty Viddies," *Time,* December 15, 2008, p. 56; "Kodak Explodes onto the Pocket Video Camera Scene," Kodak press release, July 10, 2008; and "Rugged New Kodak Digital Video Camera Enables On-The-Go HD Video Capture," January 8, 2009, Kodak press release.
47. "Kodak Institutional Investor Meeting," February 4, 2009, pp. 56, 61.

BP: This case was prepared by Michael J. Vessey based on interviews with Ann Hand and Kathy Seegebrecht.

Appendix A

1. Personal interview with Arthur R. Kydd, St. Croix Management Group.
2. Examples of guides to writing marketing plans include William A. Cohen. *The Marketing Plan*, 5th ed. (New York: Wiley and Sons, 2006); and Roman G. Hiebing, Jr., and Scott W. Cooper, *The Successful Marketing Plan: A Disciplined and Comprehensive Approach* (New York: McGraw-Hill, 2008).
3. Examples of guides to writing business plans include Rhonda Abrams, *The Successful Business Plan: Secrets & Strategies*, 4th ed. (Grants Pass, OR: Oasis Press/PSI Research, 2003); Joseph A. Covello and Brian J. Hazelgren, *The Complete Book of Business Plans*, 2nd ed. (Naperville, IL: Sourcebooks, 2006); Joseph A. Covello and Brian J. Hazelgren, *Your First Business Plan*, 5th ed. (Naperville IL: Sourcebooks, 2005); and Mike McKeever, *How to Write a Business Plan*, 8th ed. (Berkeley, CA: Nolo, 2007).
4. Abrams, *The Successful Business Plan*, p. 35.
5. Some of these points are adapted from Abrams, pp. 35–43; others are adapted from William Rudelius, *Guidelines for Technical Report Writing* (Minneapolis: University of Minnesota, undated). See also William Strunk, Jr., and E. B. White, *The Elements of Style*, 4th ed. (Needham Heights, MA: Allyn & Bacon, 2000).
6. Rebecca Zimoch, "The Dawn of the Frozen Age," *Grocery Headquarters*, December 2002; see www.groceryheadquarters.com.
7. ACNielsen Strategic Planner as reported to the National Frozen & Refrigerated Foods Association for the week ending February 24, 2007; see www.nfraweb.org.
8. Chuck Van Hyning, *NPD's National Eating Trends*; see www.npdfoodworld.com
9. Jeffrey M. Humphreys, "The Multicultural Economy 2006," *Georgia Business and Economic Conditions* 66, no. 3, (Third Quarter 2006). pp. 6, 10–11; see www.selig.uga.edu/forecast.

Chapter 3

1. Erin Biba, "The GPS Revolution," *Wired*, February 2009, pp. 64–69; Mathew Honan, "I Am Here," *Wired*, February 2009, pp. 70–75; Arundhati Parmar, "On the Map," *Marketing News*, February 15, 2008, p. 12; and Graham Kelly, The GPS Revolution," ezinearticles.com, February 7, 2009.

2. "Highlights from the 2008 Report," *2008 National Coffee Drinking Trends Study* (New York: National Coffee Association of USA, Inc., February 2009); "Coffee Surpasses Soft Drinks in Daily Market Penetration," National Coffee Association of USA, Inc., April 1, 2007; and "Coffee, Tea, or Coffee?" *Marketing Management*, June 2006, p. 4.
3. "Starbucks for a Buck," *Marketing News*, March 1, 2008, p. 7; "Murky Waters," *Marketing News*, September 1, 2008, p. 6; Judith Crown, "A Wake-Up Call for Coffee," *BusinessWeek*, October 22, 2007, p. 23; and "Firms Eye Ready-to-Drink Coffee Market," *AFX International Focus*, January 3, 2007.
4. "Breakthrough Ideas for 2009," *Harvard Business Review*, February 2009, pp. 19–40; Elisabeth A. Sullivan, "We Were Right!" *Marketing News*, December 15, 2008, p. 16; Gordon A. Wyner, "Out of Control: Beware of the Forces of Economic, Technological, and Population Change," *Marketing Management*, p. 8; Elisabeth A. Sullivan, "2008 Is the Year That Social Marketing Will Reach Critical Mass," *Marketing News*, January 15, 2008, p. 12; Nikki Hopewell, "The Rules of Engagement," *Marketing News*, June 1, 2008, p. 6; "A Quarter-Century of Changes," *USA Today*, March 26, 2007, p. 8B; and "Social Networking, User-Generated Content and Green Technology Are Top Trends for 2007," *Wireless News*, January 21, 2007.
5. *2008 World Population Data Sheet* (Washington, DC: Population Reference Bureau, 2008), pp. 2, 3, 7.
6. "Gross National Income per Capita 2007," *World Development Indicators Database* (Washington, DC: World Bank, October 17, 2008); and *World Population Prospects: The 2006 Revision* (Geneva: United Nations, Department of Economic and Social Affairs, 2007), Table I.1, p. 1.
7. "Projections of the Population and Components of Change for the United States," U.S. Census Bureau, Table 1, August 14, 2008; "Projections of the Population by Selected Age Groups and Sex for the United States," U.S. Census Bureau, Table 2, August 14, 2008; Lawrence A. Crosby, Sheree L. Johnson and John Carroll III, "When We're 64," *Marketing Management*, December 2006, p. 14; and Bradley J. Fikes, "Jitterbug Phone Maker Dials into $38M," *North County Times*, June 25, 2008.
8. Emily Brandon, "10 Things You Didn't Know About Baby Boomers," USNews.com, January 15, 2009; Harry Maurer and Cristina Linblad, "Not-So-Golden Years," *BusinessWeek*, July 14, 2008, p. 8; and Christopher Musico, "The Boomer Boom," *CRM Magazine*, November 1, 2008, p. 34.
9. "New Hyatt Place Will Have No Front Desk," *Grand Rapids Press*, June 25, 2008, p. C1; Kimberly Palmer, "Gen X-ers: Stingy or Strapped?" USNews.com, February 14, 2007; Paul J. Lim, "Baby Boomers Outpace Gen X-ers," USNews.com, March 12, 2007; and Megan Rowe, "Marketing to Gen X," Financial & Insurance Meetings, July 1, 2006, p. 19.
10. Geoff Gloeckler, "Here Come the Millennials," *BusinessWeek*, November 24, 2008, p. 47; Sarah Littman, "Welcome to the New Millennials," *Response*, May 1, 2008, p. 74; "The Echo Boom Gets Louder," *Multi-Housing News*, December 4, 2008; Eileen P. Gunn, "Is Your Company Really Eco-Conscious?" USNews.com, October 9, 2008; "Welcome Generation Y," *Management Today*, July 10, 2008; Eileen P. Gunn, "10 Hot Green Careers for You," USNews.com, February 15, 2009; Sharon Jayson, "The Goal: Wealth and Fame, but 'the Good Life' Could Elude Gen Y," *USA Today*, January 10, 2007, p. 1D; Sharon Jayson, "Gen Y Makes a Mark: Their Imprint is Entrepreneurship," *USA Today*, December 7, 2006, p. 1D; "Millennial Moral," *BusinessWeek*, November 6, 2006, p. 13; and Richard H. Levey, "Gen Y Phones It In," *Direct*, September 1, 2006, p. 18.
11. Jason R. Rich, "Single Parents, Cool Vacations," *Daily News*, June 16, 2008, p. 11; and "Ocean Village Looks After Single Parents," *Travel Trade Gazette*, November 24, 2006, p. 13.
12. Alexandra Montgomery, "US Families 2025: In Search of Future Families," *Futures*, May 2008, p. 377; "Getting Hitched," *National Review*, January 24, 2007; and "Divorce Rate," www.divorcerate.org, February 10, 2009.
13. Robert Bernstein, "Utah Is Fastest-Growing State," (*U.S. Census Bureau News*, December 22, 2008); and Robert Bernstein, "Census Bureau Announces Most Populous Cities," *U.S. Census Bureau News*, June 28, 2007.
14. Thaddeus Herrick, "Aging Areas Around Cities Push Suburban Renewal," *The Wall Street Journal*, January 31, 2007, p. B1; and Stephanie McCrummen, "On the Edge of Va. Sprawl, Labels Crumble, New Lives Thrive," *The Washington Post*, March 27, 2006, p. A1.
15. "Update of Statistical Area Definitions and Guidance on their Use," Office Management and Budget, *OMB Bulletin* No. 08–01, November 20, 2007; Joshua Bolten, "Update of Statistical Area Definitions and Additional Guidance on Their Use," Office of Management and Budget, *OMB Bulletin* No. 04–03, February 18, 2004; and "About Metropolitan and Micropolitan Statistical Areas," U.S. Census Bureau, www.census.gov/population/www/estimates/aboutmetro.html.
16. Table 3: Annual estimates of the Population by Sex, Race, and Hispanic Origin, (NC-EST2007-03), Population Division, U.S. Census Bureau, May 1, 2008; and "Mapping Census 2000: The Geography of U.S. Diversity," Population Division, U.S. Census Bureau.
17. Andrew Pierce, "Multiculti Markets Demand Multilayered Marketing," *Marketing News*, May 1, 2008, p. 21; "Buying Power," *Catalyst*, May 14, 2008; and Robert Bernstein, "Census Bureau Releases Population Estimates by Race," *U.S. Census Bureau News*, August 4, 2006.
18. Laurel Wentz, "Dieste: Nissan Win, New Talent Lead to Turnaround," *Advertising Age*, January 19, 2009, p. 33; Rita Chang, "Mobile Marketers Target Receptive Hispanic Audience," *Advertising Age*, January 26, 2009, p. 18; and Marissa Miley, "Don't Bypass African-Americans," *Advertising Age*, February 2, 2009, p. 3.
19. "From 18 to 80: Women on Politics and Society," 2008 Women's Monitor Study, PR Newswire, August 20, 2008.
20. Jill Rosen, "The Gender Divide: Video-Gaming Has Been Largely a Man's—or Boy's—World, but with Games by and for Women, That's Starting to Change," *The Baltimore Sun*, September 30, 2008, p. 1C; Elisabeth A. Sullivan, "Harley-Davidson Shows Brand Strength As It Navigates Down New Roads—and Picks Up More Female Riders Along the Way," *Marketing News*, November 1, 2008, p. 8; and Stephanie Thompson, "Egg, Others Take a Shot at Gender Bending," *Advertising Age*, May 22, 2006, p. S4.
21. "Despite Economic Crisis, Consumers Value Brands' Commitment to Social Purpose," PR Newswire, November 17, 2008; John Carey and Michael Arndt, "Hugging the Tree-Huggers: Why So Many Companies Are Suddenly Linking Up With Eco Groups," *BusinessWeek*, March 12, 2007, p. 66; and David Kiley, "Toyota: How the Hybrid Race Went to the Swift," *BusinessWeek*, January 29, 2007, p. 58.
22. Sarah McBride, "How to Haggle Your Way to a Better Price," *The Seattle Times*, September 16, 2006, p. K14; and Nordstrom Rack Web site, http://about.nordstrom.com/ourstores/rackstores/about.asp, accessed February 11, 2009.
23. "College Cost in U.S. Hitting High Note," *UPI*, December 3, 2008; and "Losing Ground: A National Status Report on the Affordability of American Higher Education," The National Center for Public Policy and Higher Education, p. 2.
24. James C. Cooper, "This Recession Could Be Mild But Long," *BusinessWeek*, October 20, 2008, p. 12; and "The 2008 Economy in Recession," USNews.com, February 5, 2009.
25. Richard T. Curtin, *Surveys of Consumers* (Ann Arbor, MI: Survey Research Center, University of Michigan, October 6, 2006), p. 3.

26. Carmen Donavan-Walt, Bernadette D. Proctor, and Jessica C. Smith, "Income, Poverty and Health Insurance Coverage in the United States: 2007," *Current Population Reports* (Washington, DC: U.S. Census Bureau, August 2008), p. 29.

27. Mark Trumbull, "In Tough Times, U.S. Consumers Forging New Behaviors," *Christian Science Monitor*, February 3, 2009, p. 25.

28. "Consumer Expenditure Survey: 2007," U.S. Department of Labor, Bureau of Labor Statistics, November 28, 2008, Table 3; Kara McGuire, "Saving Back in Vogue," *Chattanooga Times Free Press*, February 4, 2009, p. C3; and Peter Coy, "Investment Outlook 2009," *BusinessWeek*, December 29, 2008, p. 34.

29. "SMEs Going Global: Eight Technology Trends," *The Edge Malaysia*, September 22, 2008; Steve Hamm, "Cheap Tech for Hard Times," *BusinessWeek*, November 24, 2008, p. 36; David Largesse, "5 Ways to Recharge Gadgets Without Plugging In," USNews.com, February 5, 2009; Stephen Doyle and Zack Zavala, "The Future of Food," *Wired*, March 2007, p. 188; "10 Emerging Technologies in 2008," *MIT Technology Review*, www.technologyreview.com/specialreports, accessed February 13, 2009; "Business Futures," Institute for Global Futures, www.globalfuturist.com/future-trends, accessed February 13, 2009; and The Project on Emerging Nanotechnologies, www.nanotechproject.org/inventories/consumer, accessed February 14, 2009.

30. Eric Griffith, "The Best Free Software of 2008," *PC Magazine*, January 13, 2009; and Koen Pauwels and Allen Weiss, "Moving from Free to Fee: How Online Firms Market to Change Their Business Model Successfully," *Journal of Marketing*, May 2008, pp. 14–31.

31. Steven Levy, "The New Reality," *Wired*, November 2008, p. 114; Bruce Nussbaum, "The Best Global Design of 2008," *BusinessWeek*, July 28, 2008, p. 44; and Urea Khan, "Kindle 2 Aims to Be iPod for Readers," *The Daily Telegraph*, February 10, 2009, p .10.

32. "2006 Rate Report Shows PET Container Recycling Rate Up for Third Year at 23.5%," National Association for PET Container Resources, Press Release, October 29, 2007; and Becky Ebenkamp, "'Precycling' Catches on with Consumers," Brandweek.com, August 12, 2008.

33. "AT&T Tries to Catch Up to Verizon," *Americas Telecommunications Insights*, December 1, 2008; Jon Fine, "Is It Better to be a Fox or a Mouse?" *BusinessWeek*, October 27, 2008, p. 85; James M. Cypher, "Economic Consequences of Armaments Production: Institutional Perspectives of J.K. Galbraith and T.B. Veblen," *Journal of Economic Issues*, March 1, 2008, p .37.

34. Tim Hughes, "Way out of this Crisis—Solution Lies in Deregulation, Not Renewed Regulation," *The Courier Mail*, February 7, 2009, p. 69; Adam Aston, "Sempra Energy: All Charged Up in California," *BusinessWeek*, June 11, 2007, p. 62; Aaron Pressman, "New Spark in Utility Stocks," *BusinessWeek*, June 4, 2007, p 102; Harry Maurer and Cristina Linblad, "Tackling Microsoft Again," *BusinessWeek*, January 28, 2008, p. 8.

35. Michael Porter, *Competitive Advantage* (New York: Free Press, 1985); and Michael Porter, *Competitive Strategy* (New York: Free Press, 1980).

36. Rebecca Sausner, "ATMs: Taking on Western Union," *Bank Technology News*, December 2008, p. 1.

37. "Frequently Asked Questions," Small Business Administration, Office of Advocacy, www.sba.gov/advo, September 2008.

38. "Legal Roundup," *Billboard*, January 31, 2009; and "A New Copyright Law?" *BusinessWeek*, August 3, 1998, p. 45.

39. "Highlights of Food Labeling," *Marketing News*, March 15, 2004, p. 14.

40. Dorothy Cohen, "Trademark Strategy Revisited," *Journal of Marketing*, July 1991, pp. 46–59.

41. Maxine L. Retsky, "Review Int'l Filing Process for Marks," *Marketing News*, September 29, 2003, p. 8.

42. Ben Walters, "The Guide: Cut, Copy and Paste," *The Guardian*, January 17, 2009, p. 4; Kevin Higgins, "Jeben Berg, YouTube's Creative Innovationist and an MPlanet Presenter, Explains How YouTube Inspires Consumers to Empower Themselves," *Marketing News*, November 15, 2008, p. 14; Michael Fielding, "Doppelgangers: Monitor Parodies to Measure Brand Value," *Marketing News*, October 15, 2006, p. 13–15; and Craig J. Thompson, Aric Rindfleisch, and Zeynep Arsel, "Emotional Branding and the Strategic Value of the Doppelganger Brand Image," *Journal of Marketing*, January 2006, pp. 50–64.

43. Paul Barrett, "High Court Sees Color as Basis for Trademarks," *The Wall Street Journal*, March 29, 1995, p. A6; Paul Barrett, "Color in the Court," *The Wall Street Journal*, January 5, 1995, p. A1; and David Kelly, "Rainbow of Ideas to Trademark Color," *Advertising Age*, April 24, 1995, pp. 20, 22.

44. Maxine L. Retsky, "Dilution of Trademarks Hard to Prove," *Marketing News*, May 12, 2003, p. 6.

45. Dick Mercer, "Tempest in a Soup Can," *Advertising Age*, October 17, 1994, pp. 25–29.

46. "FTC Refines CAN-SPAM Act," *Marketing News*, August 15, 2008, p. 4; "Time's Up," *Marketing News*, December 15, 2007, p. 14; D'Arcy Doran, "Internet Marketer Sues Over Unwanted Spam," *Marketing News*, April 1, 2007, p .20; Allison Enright, "Cingular Moves to Protect Its Turf," *Marketing News*, November 15, 2006, p. 4; Maxine L. Retsky, "Stakes Are High for Direct Mail Sweepstakes Promotions," *Marketing News*, July 3, 2000, p. 8; Catherine Arnold, "Picky, Picky, Picky," *Marketing News*, February 15, 2004, p. 17; and Catherine Arnold, "No Can Spam," *Marketing News*, January 15, 2004, p. 3.

47. BBB Online Program Standards, http://us.bbb.org, accessed February 15, 2009.

Geek Squad: This case was written by Steven Hartley. Sources: Mary Ellen Lloyd, "Camp Teaches Power of Geekdom," *The Wall Street Journal*, July 11, 2007; Dean Foust, Michael Mandel, Frederick F. Jespersen and David Henry, "The Business Week 50—The Best Performers," *BusinessWeek*, March 26, 2007, p. 58; Jessica E. Vascellaro, "What's a Cellphone For? Businesses are Finding All Sorts of New Uses for Mobile Devices," *The Wall Street Journal*, March 26, 2007, p. R5; Cade Metz, "Just How Stupid Are You? Geek Squad War Stories," *PC Magazine*, February 1, 2006; Brad Stone, "Lore of the Geek Squad," *Newsweek*, February 20, 2006, p. 44; Michelle Conlin, "Smashing the Clock," *BusinessWeek*, December 11, 2006, p. 60; "Best Buy: How to Break Out of Commodity Hell," *BusinessWeek*, March 27, 2006, p. 76; Pallavi Gogoi, "Meet Jane Geek," *BusinessWeek*, November 28, 2005, p. 94; Desiree J. Hanford, "Geek Squad Is Popular at Best Buy," *The Wall Street Journal*, December 14, 2005, p. 1; Michelle Higgins, "Getting Your Own IT Department," *The Wall Street Journal*, May 20, 2004, p. D1; and information contained on the Geek Squad Web site (www.geeksquad.com).

Chapter 4

1. www.beeresponsible.com, accessed February 2, 2009; Anheuser-Busch 2008 Corporate Social Responsibility Report; "America's Most Admired Companies," *Fortune*, March 17, 2009, p. 38.

2. For a discussion of the definition of ethics, see Patrick E. Murphy, Gene R. Laezniak, Norman E. Bowie, and Thomas A. Klein, *Ethical Marketing: Basic Ethics in Action* (Upper Saddle River, NJ: Prentice Hall, 2005).

3. Verne E. Henderson, "The Ethical Side of Enterprise," *Sloan Management Review*, Spring 1982, pp. 37–47. See also, Joseph L. Badaracco, Jr., *Defining Moments: When Managers Must Choose Between Right and Right* (Boston: Harvard Business School Press, 1997).

4. "Honorable?" *Business 2.0*, February 2000, p. 92.

5. Roger O. Crockett, "Hauling in the Hollywood Hackers," *BusinessWeek*, May 15, 2006, pp. 80–82; "Exporting Death," *Time*, April 13, 1998, p. 63; Ray O. Werner, "Marketing and the Supreme Court in Transition, 1982–1984," *Journal of Marketing*, Summer 1985, pp. 97–105; and Jane Bryant Quinn, "Computer Program Deceives Consumers," *Dallas Morning News*, March 2, 1998, p. B3.
6. *The 2007 National Business Ethics Survey* (Washington, DC: Ethics Resource Center, 2008); "Poll: Ad Execs Are Icky," *Advertising Age*, January 16, 2006, p. 26; and Ronald W. Clement, "Just How Ethical Is American Business?" *Business Horizons*, July–August 2006, pp. 313–27.
7. See, for example, Linda K. Trevino and Katherine A. Nelson, *Managing Business Ethics: Straight Talk About How to Get It Right* (New York: Wiley and Sons, 2007).
8. Thomas Donaldson, "Values in Tension: Ethics Away from Home," *Harvard Business Review*, September–October 1996, pp. 48–62.
9. Ethisphere Institute, "2008 World's Most Ethical Companies," ethisphere.com, March 2008.
10. These statistics were obtained from the Recording Industry Association of America (riaa.com), Motion Picture Association of America (mpaa.org), and the Business Software Alliance (bsa.org).
11. *Internet Piracy on Campus* (Washington, DC: IPSOS, September 16, 2003).
12. Vern Terpstra and Kenneth David, *The Cultural Environment of International Business*, 3rd ed. (Cincinnati: South-Western Publishing, 1991), p. 12.
13. Hukari Kane, "Recall Shows Battery Limits," *The Wall Street Journal*, August 18, 2006, p. A13; and "Dell Announces Recall of Notebook Computer Batteries Due to Fire Hazard," U.S. Consumer Product Safety Commission Press Release, August 15, 2006.
14. Timothy Muris, "Protecting Consumers' Privacy," FTC.gov, accessed January 3, 2005.
15. For an extensive examination on slotting fees, see Paul N. Bloom, Gregory T. Gundlach, and Joseph P. Cannon, "Slotting Allowances and Fees: Schools of Thought and Views of Practicing Managers," *Journal of Marketing*, April 2000, pp. 92–109. Also see, K. Sudhir and Vithala R. Rao, "Do Slotting Allowances Enhance Efficiency or Hinder Competition?" *Journal of Marketing Research*, May 2006, pp. 137–55.
16. Hedich Nasheri, *Economic Espionage and Industrial Spying* (Cambridge, England: Cambridge University Press, 2005).
17. "Coke Employee Faces Charges in Plot to Sell Secrets," *The Wall Street Journal*, July 6, 2006, p. B6; "Do the Right Thing? Not with a Rival's Inside Info," *Advertising Age*, July 17, 2006, p. 4; and "You Can't Beat the Real Thing," *Time*, July 17, 2006, pp. 10–11.
18. www.transparency.org, accessed January 5, 2009.
19. "U.S. Firms Raise Ethics Focus," *The Wall Street Journal*, November 28, 2005, p. B4.
20. "Coca-Cola Unit Head Resigns After Rigged Test," Forbes.com, accessed August 25, 2003.
21. *The 2007 National Business Ethics Survey*.
22. "Whistleblowers: Tales from the Back Office," *The Economist*, March 25, 2006, p. 67; and C. Fred Alford, *Whistleblowers: Broken Lives and Organizational Power* (Ithaca, NY: Cornell University Press, 2002).
23. "Scotchgard Working Out Recent Stain on its Business," Mercurynews.com, accessed June 22, 2008.
24. James O. Wilson, "Adam Smith on Business Ethics," *California Management Review*, Fall 1989, pp. 57–72.
25. Alix M. Freedman, "Bad Reaction: Nestlé's Bid to Crash Baby-Formula Market in U.S. Stirs a Row," *The Wall Street Journal*, February 16, 1989, pp. Al, A6; and Alix Freedman, "Nestlé to Drop Claim on Label of Its Formula," *The Wall Street Journal*, March 13, 1989, p. B5.
26. Harvey S. James and Farhad Rassekh, "Smith, Friedman, and Self-Interest in Ethical Society," *Business Ethics Quarterly*, July 2000, pp. 659–74.
27. "Cost of Living," *The Economist*, March 1, 2003, p. 60.
28. "Perrier—Overresponding to a Crisis," in Robert F. Hartley, *Marketing Mistakes and Successes*, 10th ed. (New York: Wiley and Sons, 2006), pp. 119–30.
29. "Ford Explorers with Firestone Tires: Ill Handling of a Killer Scenario," in Robert F. Hartley, *Marketing Mistakes and Successes*, 11th ed. (New York: Wiley and Sons, 2009) pp. 365–79.
30. Andrew W. Savitz with Karl Weber, *The Triple Bottom Line: How Today's Best Run Companies Are Achieving Economic, Social and Environmental Success* (San Francisco, CA: Jossey-Bass, 2006).
31. "Pollution Prevention Pays." 3M.com, accessed January 18, 2009; www.xerox.com/environment, accessed January 15, 2009; Elizabeth Royte, "Corn Plastic to the Rescue?" *Smithsonian*, August 2006, pp. 84–88; and "Hugging the Tree Huggers," *BusinessWeek*, March 12, 2007, pp. 66–68.
32. The ISO Survey—2007 (Geneva: International Organization for Standardization, 2008).
33. For a seminal discussion on this topic, see P. Rajan Varadarajan and Anil Menon, "Cause-Related Marketing: A Coalignment of Marketing Strategy and Corporate Philanthropy," *Journal of Marketing*, July 1988, pp. 58–74.
34. *Past.Present.Future.: The 25th Anniversary of Cause Marketing* (Boston, MA: Cone LLC, 2008); and Larry Chiagouris and Ipshita Ray, "Saving the World with Cause-Related Marketing," *Marketing Management*, July–August 2007, pp. 48–51.
35. These steps are adapted from J. J. Carson and G. A. Steiner, *Measuring Business Social Performance: The Corporate Social Audit* (New York: Committee for Economic Development, 1974). See also Risako Morinoto, John Ash, and Chris Hope, "Corporate Social Responsibility Audit: From Theory to Practice," *Journal of Business Ethics* (December 2005), pp. 315–25; and William B. Werther, Jr., and David Chandler, *Strategic Corporate Social Responsibility* (Thousand Oaks, CA: Sage Publications, Inc., 2006).
36. "Marketers Become Own Watchdogs," *Advertising Age*, June 12, 2006, p. 57; and "Sweatshops: Finally, Airing the Dirty Linen," *BusinessWeek*, June 23, 2003, pp. 100–01.
37. Unmesh Kher, "Getting Smart at Being Good . . . Are Companies Better Off for It?" *Time*, January 2006, pp. A1–A37; and Pete Engardio, "Beyond the Green Corporation," *BusinessWeek*, January 29, 2007, pp. 50–64.
38. This discussion is based on Wayne D. Hoyer and Deborah J. MacInnis, *Consumer Behavior*, 4th ed. (New York: Houghton Mifflin Company, 2007), pp. 535–37; "Factoids," *Research Alert*, December 8, 2005, p. 5; Elizabeth Woyke, "Attention Shoplifters," *BusinessWeek*, September 11, 2006, pp. 46–50; and "Putting Return Policies to the Test," *The Wall Street Journal*, February 22, 2007, p. D3.
39. "A Pirate and his Penance," *Time*, January 26, 2004, p. 60; and Crockett, "Hauling in the Hollywood Hackers."
40. Mark Dolliver, "Deflating a Myth," *Brandweek*, May 12, 2008, pp. 30–32.
41. Kenneth Hein, "'Green' Light Bulbs Symbolize a Bad Idea," *Brandweek*, January 12, 2009, p. 38.

Starbucks Corporation: This case is based on information on the company Web site (www.starbucks.com) and the following sources: "Living Our Values," *2003 Corporate Social Responsibility Annual Report*; "Starbucks Annual Shareholder meeting," Starbucks press release, March 30, 2004; Ranjay Gulati, Sarah Haffman, and Gary Neilson, "The Barista Principle: Starbucks and the Rise of Relational Capital," *Strategy and Business*, 3rd Quarter 2002, pp. 58–69; and Andy Serwer, "Hot Starbucks to Go," *Fortune*, January 12, 2004, pp. 52ff.

Chapter 5

1. Sheryll Alexander, "What Women Want . . . in a Car," CNN.com, March 14, 2008; Marti Barletta, "Who's Really Buying that Car?

Ask Her," *Brandweek*, September 4, 2006, p. 20; and Joan Voight, "The Lady Means Business," *Brandweek*, April 30, 2006, p. 28ff.

2. Roger D. Blackwell, Paul W. Miniard, and James F. Engel, *Consumer Behavior*, 10th ed. (Mason, OH: South-Western Publishing, 2006).

3. For thorough descriptions of consumer expertise, see Joseph W. Alba and J. Wesley Hutchinson, "Knowledge Calibration: What Consumers Know and What They Think They Know," *Journal of Consumer Research*, September 2000, pp. 123–57.

4. For in-depth studies on external information search patterns, see Brian T. Ratchford, Debabrata Talukdar, and Myung-Soo Lee, "The Impact of the Internet on Consumers' Use of Information Sources for Automobiles: A Re-Inquiry," *Journal of Consumer Research*, June 2007, pp. 111–19; Joel E. Urbany, Peter R. Dickson, and William L. Wilkie, "Buyer Uncertainty and Information Search," *Journal of Consumer Research*, March 1992, pp. 452–63; and Sharon E. Beatty and Scott M. Smith, "External Search Effort: An Investigation across Several Product Categories," *Journal of Consumer Research*, June 1987, pp. 83–95.

5. Smart Phone Ratings, Ratings Overview, Consumer Reports, accessed on August 6, 2009. See http://www.consumerreports.org/cro/electronics-computers/phones-mobile-devices/cell-phones-services/smart-phone-ratings/ratings-overview.htm.

6. For an extended discussion on evaluative criteria, see Del J. Hawkins and David L. Mothersbaugh, *Consumer Behavior*, 11th ed. (New York: McGraw-Hill/Irwin, 2010).

7. John A. Howard, *Buyer Behavior in Marketing Strategy*, 2nd ed. (Englewood Cliffs, NJ: Prentice Hall, 1994). For an extended discussion on consumer choice sets, see Allan D. Shocker, Moshe Ben-Akiva, Brun Boccara, and Prakesh Nedungadi, "Consideration Set Influences on Consumer Decision Making and Choice: Issues, Models, and Suggestions," *Marketing Letters*, August 1991, pp. 181–99.

8. Robert J. Donovan, John R. Rossiter, Gillian Marcoolyn, and Andrew Nesdale, "Store Atmosphere and Purchasing Behavior," Journal of Retailing, Fall 1994, pp. 283–94; and Eric A. Greenleaf and Donald R. Lehman, "Reasons for Substantial Delay in Consumer Decision Making," *Journal of Consumer Research*, September 1995, pp. 186–99.

9. Sunil Gupta and Valarie Zeithaml, "Customer Metrics and Their Impact on Financial Performance," *Marketing Science*, November–December 2006, pp. 718–39.

10. These estimates given in Jagdish N. Sheth and Banwari Mitral, *Consumer Behavior*, 2nd ed. (Mason, OH: South-Western Publishing, 2003), p. 32.

11. Frederick F. Reichheld and Thomas Teal, *The Loyalty Effect* (Boston: Harvard Business School Press, 1996); "What's a Loyal Customer Worth?" *Fortune*, December 11, 1995, p. 182; and Patricia Sellers, "Keeping the Buyers You Already Have," *Fortune*, Autumn–Winter 1993, p. 57. For an in-depth examination of this topic, see Sunil Gupta and Donald R. Lehmann, *Managing Customers as Investments* (Upper Saddle River, NJ: Pearson Education, Inc., 2005).

12. For an overview of research on involvement, see John C. Mowen and Michael Minor, *Consumer Behavior: A Framework*, 5th ed. (Upper Saddle River, NJ: Prentice Hall, 2001); and Wayne D. Hoyer and Deborah J. MacInnis, *Consumer Behavior*, 5th ed. (Florence, KY: South-Western Education Publishing, 2009).

13. Russell Belk, "Situational Variables and Consumer Behavior," *Journal of Consumer Research*, December 1975, pp. 157–63. The examples are found in Martin Lindstrom, *Buy.ology: Truth and Lies About Why We Buy* (New York: Doubleday Publishing, 2008).

14. A. H. Maslow, *Motivation and Personality* (New York: Harper & Row, 1970). Also see Richard Yalch and Frederic Brunel, "Need Hierarchies in Consumer Judgments of Product Design: Is It Time to Reconsider Maslow's Hierarchy?" in Kim Corfman and John Lynch eds., *Advances in Consumer Research* (Provo, UT: Association for Consumer Research, 1996), pp. 405–10.

15. Joel B. Cohen, "An Interpersonal Orientation to the Study of Consumer Behavior," *Journal of Marketing Research*, August 1967, pp. 270–78; and Rena Bartos, *Marketing to Women around the World* (Cambridge, MA: Harvard Business School, 1989).

16. Jane Spencer, "Lenovo Puts Style in New Laptop," *The Wall Street Journal*, January 3, 2008, p. B5.

17. This example provided in Michael R. Solomon, *Consumer Behavior*, 4th ed. (Upper Saddle River, NJ: Prentice Hall, 1999), p. 59.

18. For further reading on subliminal perception, see Lindstrom, *Buy .ology*; B. Bahrami, N. Lavie, and G. Rees, "Attentional Load Modulates Responses of Human Primary Visual Cortex to Invisible Stimuli," *Current Biology*, March 2007, pp. 39–47; J. Karremans, W. Stroebe, and J. Claus, "Beyond Vicary's Fantasies: The Impact of Subliminal Priming and Brand Choice," *Journal of Experimental Social Psychology* 42 (2006), pp. 792–98; Dennis L. Rosen and Surendra N. Singh, "An Investigation of Subliminal Embedded Effect on Multiple Measures of Advertising Effectiveness," *Psychology & Marketing*, March–April 1992, pp. 157–73; and Kathryn T. Theus, "Subliminal Advertising and the Psychology of Processing Unconscious Stimuli: A Review of the Research," *Psychology & Marketing*, May–June 1994, pp. 271–90.

19. August Bullock, *The Secret Sales Pitch* (San Jose, CA: Norwich Publishers, 2004); E. Parpis, "Sex, Crackers and Subliminal Ads," *Adweek*, March 31, 2003, p. 18; "GOP Commercial Resurrects Debate on Subliminal Ads," *The Wall Street Journal*, September 13, 2000, p. B10; and "I Will Love This Story," *U.S. News & World Report*, May 12, 1997, p. 12.

20. Sholnn Freeman, "Brand Breakdown," *The Washington Post*, March 26, 2006, p. F1ff.

21. Martin Fishbein and I. Aizen, *Belief, Attitude, Intention and Behavior: An Introduction to Theory and Research* (Reading, MA: Addison-Wesley 1975), p. 6.

22. Richard J. Lutz, "Changing Brand Attitudes through Modification of Cognitive Structure," *Journal of Consumer Research*, March 1975, pp. 49–59.

23. "The VALS™ Types," www.sric-bi.com, accessed March 10, 2009.

24. This discussion is based on Ed Keller and Jon Berry, *The Influentials* (New York: Simon and Schuster, 2003).

25. "Word of Mouth Is Where It's At," *Brandweek*, June 2, 2003, p. 26.

26. BzzAgent.com, accessed March 31, 2009; and Matthew Creamer, "BzzAgent Seeks to Turn Word of Mouth into a Saleable Medium," *Advertising Age*, February13, 2006, p. 12.

27. For an extensive review on consumer socialization of children, see Deborah Roedder John, "Consumer Socialization of Children: A Retrospective Look at Twenty-Five Years of Research," *Journal of Consumer Research*, December 1999, pp. 183–213. Also see, Gwen Bachmann Achenreinver and Deborah Roedder John, "The Meaning of Brand Names to Children: A Developmental Investigation," *Journal of Consumer Psychology* 13, no. 3 (2003), pp. 205–19; and Elizabeth S. Moore, William L. Wilkie, and Richard J. Lutz, "Passing the Torch: Intergenerational Influences as a Source of Brand Equity," *Journal of Marketing*, April 2002, pp. 17–37.

28. J. Paul Peter and Jerry C. Olson, *Consumer Behavior and Marketing Strategy*, 8th ed. (New York: McGraw-Hill/Irwin, 2008). Also see, Rex Y. Du and Wagner A. Kamakura, "Household Life Cycles and Lifestyles in the United States," *Journal of Marketing Research*, February 2006, pp. 121–32.

29. This discussion is based on Hawkins and Mothersbaugh, *Consumer Behavior: Building Marketing Strategy*; "Dad Also Is Pulling the Purse Strings," *Brandweek* September 15, 2008, p. 19; *The Kids and Tweens Market in the U.S.*, 9th ed. (Rockville, MD: Packaged Facts, August 1, 2008); and "Teens Rule," MediaBuyer.com, accessed April 7, 2007.

30. Harold R. Kerbo, *Social Stratification and Inequality* (New York: McGraw-Hill, 2000). For an extensive discussion on social class, see Eric Arnould, Linda Price, and George Zinkhan, *Consumers*, 2nd ed. (New York: McGraw Hill/Irwin, 2004).

31. Jeffrey M. Humphreys, "The Multicultural Economy in 2008," Selig Center for Economic Growth, Terry College of Business, The University of Georgia, accessed February 14, 2009.
32. The remainder of this discussion is based on Hoyer and MacInnis, *Consumer Behavior*; "Special Report: Hispanic Media," *Advertising Age*, January 30, 2008, p. S-6; and "Hispanics Wanted," *Brandweek*, April 12, 2004, p. 22.
33. The remainder of this discussion is based on Peter and Olson, *Consumer Behavior and Marketing Strategy*; and Marissa Miley, "Don't Bypass African-Americans," *Advertising Age*, February 2, 2009, pp .3, 2.
34. The remainder of this discussion is based on Hawkins and Mothersbaugh, *Consumer Behavior: Building Marketing Strategy*; and "Marketing to Asian-Americans," *Brandweek*, May 26, 2008, Special Section.

Best Buy: This case was written by David P. Brennan of the University of St. Thomas and is based on interviews with Joe Brandt, Best Buy employees and customers, and materials supplied by Best Buy.

Chapter 6

1. Interview with Kim Nagele, JCP Media, March 15, 2009.
2. John Paterson, "Evolution, Innovation are Constants," *Purchasing*, September 7, 2006, p. 55.
3. Figures reported in this discussion are found in *Statistical Abstract of the United States: 2009*, 128th ed. (Washington, DC: U.S. Census Bureau, 2009).
4. "Lockheed Wins Major Spacecraft Job," *The Wall Street Journal*, September 1, 2006, p. A3; and "Lockheed Martin Readies Historic Operations & Checkout Facility for New Orion Spacecraft Integration Work," Lockheed Martin press release, January 27, 2009.
5. Aleda V. Roth, Andy A. Tay, Madeleine E. Pullman, and John V. Gray, "Reaping What You Sow?" *International Commerce Review*, Autumn 2008, pp. 37–47.
6. *2002 NAICS United States Manual* (Washington, DC: Office of Management and Budget, 2002).
7. *North American Product Classification System* (Washington, DC: U.S. Census Bureau, 2006).
8. This listing and portions of the following discussion are based on F. Robert Dwyer and John F. Tanner, Jr., *Business Marketing*, 4th ed. (New York: McGraw-Hill/Irwin, 2009); Michael D. Hutt and Thomas W. Speh, *Business Marketing Management*, international edition (Mason, OH: South-Western, 2009); and Frank G. Bingham, Jr., Roger Gomes, and Patricia A. Knowles, *Business Marketing*, 3rd ed. (New York: McGraw-Hill/Irwin, 2006).
9. "Siemens Awarded $28 Million Contract for JetBlue Airways' Baggage Handling System with Integrated Security," Siemens USA press release, July 12, 2006.
10. Adrienne Sieko, "The Business Case for Diversity," www.industryweek.com, accessed September 1, 2008.
11. www.pg.com/supplier_diversity, accessed March 6, 2009.
12. "Boise Cascade Turns Green," *The Wall Street Journal*, September 3, 2003, p. B6. Also see Minette E. Drumwright, "Socially Responsible Organizational Buying: Environmental Concern as a Noneconomic Buying Criterion," *Journal of Marketing*, July 1994, pp. 1–18.
13. For a study of buying criteria used by industrial firms, see Daniel H. McQuiston and Rockney G. Walters, "The Evaluation Criteria of Industrial Buyers: Implications for Sales Training," *Journal of Business & Industrial Marketing*, Summer–Fall 1989, pp. 65–75.
14. For an overview on ISO 9000 certification, see Thomas H. Stevenson and Frank C. Barnes, "What Industrial Marketers Need to Know about ISO 9000 Certification: A Review, Update, and Integration with Marketing," *Industrial Marketing Management*, November 2002, pp. 695–703.
15. This example is found in Sandy D. Jap and Jakki J. Mohr, "Leveraging Internet Technologies in B2B Relationships," *California Management Review*, Summer 2002, pp. 24–38.
16. "America's Most Admired Companies," *Fortune*, March 8, 2008, pp. 80ff; Traci Parum, "Harley-Davidson: Earning Accolades, Posting Profits," www.industryweek.com, November 17, 2005; Brian Milligan, "Medal of Excellence: Harley-Davidson Wins by Getting Suppliers on Board," *Purchasing*, September 2000, pp. 52–65; and "Harley-Davidson Company," *Purchasing Magazine Online*, September 4, 2003.
17. "The Smartest Machines on Earth," *Fortune*, September 28, 2006, pp. 129–36.
18. "The Kraft/EDS Outsourcing Deal: One Year After," EDS news release, June 12, 2007; and "HP Finalizes $3 Billion Outsourcing Agreement to Manage Procter & Gamble's IT Infrastructure," Hewlett-Packard news release, May 6, 2003.
19. This discussion is based on James C. Anderson, James A. Narus, and Das Narayandas, *Business Market Management*, 3rd ed. (Upper Saddle River, NJ: Prentice Hall, 2009); and Jeffrey K. Liker and Thomas Y. Choi, "Building Deep Supplier Relationships," *Harvard Business Review*, December 2004, pp. 104–13.
20. Helen Walker and Wendy Phillips, "Sustainable Procurement: Emerging Issues," *International Journal of Procurement Management* 2, no. 1 (2009), pp. 41–61.
21. Thomas V. Bonoma, "Major Sales: Who Really Does the Buying?" *Harvard Business Review*, May–June 1982, pp. 11–19. Also see, Philip L. Dawes, Don Y. Lee, and Grahame R. Dowling, "Information Control and Influence in Emerging Buying Centers," *Journal of Marketing*, July 1998, pp. 55–68; and Thomas Tellefsen, "Antecedents and Consequences of Buying Center Leadership: An Emergent Perspective," *Journal of Business-to-Business Marketing*, 13, no. 1 (2006), pp. 53–59.
22. Allison Enright, "It Takes a Committee to Buy into B-to-B," *Marketing News*, February 15, 2006, pp. 11–13; and Bonoma, "Major Sales."
23. These definitions are adapted from Frederick E. Webster, Jr., and Yoram Wind, *Organizational Buying Behavior* (Englewood Cliffs, NJ: Prentice Hall, 1972), p. 6.
24. "Can Corning Find Its Optic Nerve?" *Fortune*, March 19, 2001, pp. 148–50.
25. Representative studies on the buy-class framework that document its usefulness include Erin Anderson, Wujin Chu and Barton Weitz, "Industrial Purchasing: An Empirical Exploration of the Buy-Class Framework," *Journal of Marketing*, July 1987, pp. 71–86; P. Matthyssens and W. Faes, "OEM Buying Process for New Components: Purchasing and Marketing Implications," *Industry Marketing Management*, August 1985, pp. 145–57; and Thomas W. Leigh and Arno J. Ethans, "A Script-Theoretic Analysis of Industrial Purchasing Behavior," *Journal of Marketing*, Fall 1984, pp. 22–32. Studies not supporting the buy-class framework include Joseph A. Bellizi and Philip McVey, "How Valid is the Buy-Grid Model?" *Industrial Marketing Management*, February 1983, pp. 57–62; Donald W. Jackson, Janet E. Keith, and Richard K. Burdick, "Purchasing Agents' Perceptions of Industrial Buying Center Influences: A Situational Approach," *Journal of Marketing*, Fall 1984, pp. 75–83; R. Vekatesh, Ajay Kohli, and Gerald Zaltman, "Influence Strategies in Buying Centers," *Journal of Marketing*, October 1995, pp. 61–72; Gary L. Lilien and Anthony Wong, "An Exploratory Investigation of the Structure of the Buying Center in the Metal Working Industry," *Journal of Marketing Research*, February 1984, pp. 1–11; and Wesley J. Johnston and Thomas V. Bonoma, "The Buying Center: Structure and Interaction Patterns," *Journal of Marketing*, Summer 1981, pp. 143–56.
26. *Machine Vision Market* (Ann Arbor, MI: Automated Imaging Association, 2009).

27. "Machine Vision Looks Well Beyond Inspection," *Packaging Digest*, August 2005, pp. 32–35.
28. This discussion is based on "B2B, Take 2," *BusinessWeek Online*, November 25, 2005; Jennifer Reinhold, "What We Learned in the New Economy," *Fast Company*, March 4, 2004, pp. 56ff; Mark Roberti, "General Electric's Spin Machine," *The Industry Standard*, January 22–29, 2001, pp .74–83; "Grainger Lightens Its Digital Load," *Industrial Distribution*, March 2001, pp .77–79; and www.boeing.com/procurement, accessed March 10, 2007.
29. "Former Ebay CEO Urges Action on Small Business," Washingtonpost.com, June 11, 2008; "New Study Reveals 724,000 Americans Rely on eBay Sales for Income," eBay press release, July 21, 2005; Robyn Greenspan, "Net Drives Profits to Small Biz," www.clickz.com, accessed March 25, 2006; Michael Krauss, "EBay 'Bids' on Small-Biz Firms to Sustain Growth," *Marketing News*, December 8, 2003, pp. 6, 7; "Ebay Realizes Success in Small-Biz Arena," *Marketing News*, May 1, 2004, p. 11; and www.ebaybusiness.com.
30. www.agentrics.com, accessed March 15, 2009.
31. www.ghx.com, accessed March 2009.
32. This discussion is based on Robert J. Dolan and Youngme Moon, "Pricing and Market Making on the Internet," *Journal of Interactive Marketing*, Spring 2000, pp. 56–73; and Ajit Kambil and Eric van Heck, *Making Markets: How Firms Can Benefit from Online Auctions and Exchanges* (Boston: Harvard Business School Press, 2002).
33. Susan Avery, "Supply Management Is Core of Success at UTF," *Purchasing*, September 7, 2006, pp. 36–39.
34. Shawn P. Daley and Prithwiraz Nath, "Reverse Auctions for Relationship Marketers," *Industrial Marketing Management*, February 2005, pp. 157–66; and Sandy Jap, "The Impact of Online Reverse Auction Design on Buyer-Seller Relationships," *Journal of Marketing*, January 2007, pp. 146–59.

Lands' End: This case is based on information available at www.landsend.com and the following sources: Robert Berner, "A Hard Bargain at Lands' End?" *BusinessWeek*, May 28, 2001, p. 14; Rebecca Quick, "Getting the Right Fit—Hips and All—Can a Machine Measure You Better than Your Tailor?" *The Wall Street Journal*, October 18, 2000, p. B1; Stephanie Miles, "Apparel E-tailers Spruce Up for Holidays," *The Wall Street Journal*, November 6, 2001, p. B6; and Dana James, "Custom Goods Nice Means for Lands' End," *Marketing News*, August 14, 2000, p. 5.

Chapter 7

1. "Dell Unveils New Computers Targeting Emerging Markets," *Marketing News*, September 15, 2008, p. 32; "Dell Wants to Sell Emerging Consumers Their First PC," Reuters.com, September 23, 2008; and "Dell Plans to Up Focus on India Biz," AdAge.com, October 24, 2008.
2. *International Trade Statistics: 2009* (Geneva: World Trade Organization, 2008). Global trade statistics in this chapter come from this source, unless otherwise indicated.
3. S. Kim and S. Kim, *Global Corporate Finance*, 6th ed. (Oxford, UK: Blackwell Publishing, 2006).
4. Michael E. Porter, *The Competitive Advantage of Nations* (New York: Free Press, 1990), pp. 577–615. For another view that emphasizes cultural differences, see David S. Landes, *The Wealth and Poverty of Nations* (New York: Norton, 1998).
5. Steven Fink, *Sticky Fingers: Managing the Global Risk of Economic Espionage* (Chicago: Dearborn Trade, 2002).
6. Dennis R. Appleyard, Alfred J. Field, Jr., and Steven Cobb, *International Economics*, 6th ed. (New York: McGraw-Hill/Irwin, 2008), chap. 15; Tansa Mesa, "Africa and Caribbean Fear EU Latam Banana Tariff Cuts," *International Herald Tribune*, August 26, 2008, p. 8; Yuri Kageyama, "Selling Rice to Japan? U.S. Plans to Try," msnbc.com, March 7, 2004; "Shot in the Foot," *The Wall Street Journal*, September 6–7, 2008, p. A10; and *Economic Report of the President* (Washington, DC: U.S. Government Printing Office, 2008).
7. This discussion is based on information provide by the World Trade Organization, www.wto.org, accessed March 25, 2009.
8. This discussion on the European Union is based on information provide at www.europa.eu, accessed, April 19, 2009.
9. This discussion is based on *Probable Effect of Certain Modifications to the North American Free Trade Agreement Rules of Origin* (Washington, DC: U.S. International Trade Commission, 2006).
10. For an overview of different types of global companies and marketing strategies, see, for example, Massaki Kotabe and Kristiaan Helsen, *Global Marketing Management*, 4th ed. (New York: Wiley and Sons, 2008), p. 221; Warren J. Keegan and Mark C. Green, *Global Marketing*, 4th ed. (Upper Saddle River, NJ: Prentice Hall, 2005); and Michael Czinkota and Ilka A. Ronkainen, *International Marketing*, 8th ed. (Mason, OH: South-Western Publishing, 2007).
11. Johnny K. Johansson and Ilkka A. Ronkainen, "The Brand Challenge," *Marketing Management*, March–April 2004, pp. 54–55.
12. Kevin Lane Keller, *Strategic Brand Management*, 3rd ed. (Upper Saddle River, NJ: Prentice Hall, 2008), p. 602; and Michael Fielding, "Global Brands Need Balance of Identity, Cultural Respect," *Marketing News*, September 1, 2006, pp. 8–10.
13. "Coca-Cola, Nike and Adidas Top Brands for Teens Globally, TRU Study Finds," www.teenresearch.com, accessed March 2, 2009; "Global Habbo Youth Survey," marketinginsight@sulake.com, accessed March 20, 2009; www.mtv.com/company, accessed January 10, 2009; Bay Fong, "Spending Spree," *U.S. News & World Report*, May 1, 2006, pp. 42–50; and "The Emerging Middle Class," *Business 2.0*, July 2006, p. 96.
14. "The World in Figures," *The Economist*, January 2, 2009.
15. For comprehensive references on cross-cultural aspects of marketing, see Paul A. Herbig, *Handbook of Cross-Cultural Marketing* (New York: Halworth Press, 1998); Jean Claude Usunier, *Marketing Across Cultures*, 4th ed. (London: Prentice Hall Europe, 2005); and John L. Graham, Mary Gilly, and Philip K. Cateora, *International Marketing*, 14th ed. (New York: McGraw-Hill/Irwin, 2009). Unless otherwise indicated, examples found in this section appear in these excellent sources.
16. Michael Esterl and David Crawford, "Siemens Pays Record Fine in Probe," *The Wall Street Journal*, December 16, 2008, p. B2.
17. R. L. Tung, *Business Negotiations with the Japanese* (Lexington, MA: Lexington Books, 1993).
18. These examples appear in Del I. Hawkins and David L. Mothersbaugh, *Consumer Behavior*, 10th ed. (New York: McGraw-Hill/Irwin, 2010), chap. 2.
19. "Greeks Protest Coke's Use of Parthenon," *Dallas Morning News*, August 17, 1992, p. D4.
20. "Some Will Not be Eager to Buy 'Made in USA,'" *AdweekMedia*, January 19, 2009, p. 14; and Graham, Gilly, and Cateora, *International Marketing*.
21. "If Only Krispy Kreme Meant 'Makes You Smarter,'" *Business 2.0*, August 2005, p. 108.
22. "Marketing by Language: Oracle Trims Teams, Sees Big Savings," *Advertising Age International*, July 2000, pp. 4, 38.
23. Terrence A. Shimp and Subhash Sharma, "Consumer Ethnocentrism, Construction and Validation of the CETSCALE," *Journal of Marketing Research*, August 1987, pp. 280–89.
24. Representative research on consumer ethnocentrism includes: Subhash Sharma, Terrence Shimp, and Jeongshin Shin, "Consumer Ethnocentrism: A Test of Antecedents and Moderators," *Journal of the Academy of Marketing Science*, Winter 1995, pp. 26–37; Joel Herche, "A Note on the Predictive Validity of the CETSCALE," *Journal of Academy of Marketing Science*, Summer 1992, pp. 261–64; Srinivas Durvasula, J. Craig Andrews, and Richard G. Netemeyer, "A Cross-Cultural Comparison of Consumer Ethnocentrism

in the United States and Russia," *Journal of International Consumer Marketing* 9, no. 4 (1997), pp. 73–93; and Hyokjin Kwak, Anupam Jaju, and Trina Larsen, "Consumer Ethnocentrism Offline and Online: The Mediating Role of Marketing Efforts and Personality Traits in the United States, South Korea, and India," *Journal of the Academy of Marketing Science* 34 (2006), pp. 367–85.

25. Vijay Mahajan and Kamini Banga, *The 86 Percent Solution: How to Succeed in the Biggest Market Opportunity of the Next 50 Years* (Upper Saddle River, NJ: Pearson Education, 2006); and C. K. Prahalad, *The Fortune at the Bottom of the Pyramid: Eradicating Poverty through Profits* (Upper Saddle River, NJ: Pearson Education, 2005).
26. "Navigating the Labyrinth: Sales and Distribution in Today's China," *Knowledge@Wharton*, October 16, 2006; and Mahajan and Banga, *The 86 Percent Soltuion.*
27. www.wto.org, accessed January 20, 2009.
28. www.hllshakti.com, accessed March 12, 2009.
29. "Burgeoning Bourgeoise," *The Economist*, February 14, 2009.
30. "Mattel Plans to Double Sales Abroad," *The Wall Street Journal*, February 11, 1998, pp. A3, A11.
31. These examples are found in Graham, Gilly, and Cateora, *International Marketing*, p. 540; "Honda Takes Currency Hit in Europe," *The Wall Street Journal*, March 28, 2001, p. A16; and "Currency Troubles Halt P&G Shipments to Turkey," *Advertising Age*, March 5, 2001, p. 32.
32. Eric Clark, *The Real Toy Story* (New York: The Free Press, 2007).
33. For an extensive and recent examination of these market-entry options, see for example, Johnny K. Johansson, *Global Marketing: Foreign Entry, Local Marketing, and Global Management*, 5th ed. (New York: McGraw-Hill/Irwin, 2008); A. Coskun Samli, *Entering & Succeeding in Emerging Countries: Marketing to the Forgotten Majority* (Mason, OH: South-Western Publishing, 2004); and Keegan, *Global Marketing*.
34. Based on an interview with Pamela Viglielmo, director of international marketing, Fran Wilson Creative Cosmetics; and "Foreign Firms Think Their Way into Japan," www.successstories.com/nikkei, accessed March 24, 2005.
35. *2008 National Export Strategy* (Washington, DC: International Trade Administration, October 2008).
36. "Made in Taiwan," *Forbes*, April 2, 2001, pp. 64–66.
37. *McDonald's 2007 Annual Report.*
38. "About Us," www.strauss-group.com, accessed March 15, 2009.
39. "FedEx Expands Reach in China with Buyout of Joint Venture," *The Wall Street Journal*, January 25, 2006; and harley-davidson.com, accessed January 10, 2007.
40. This discussion is based on Keller, *Strategic Brand Management*, pp. 709–10; Todd J. Gillman, "Chip Off the Old Block," *Dallas Morning News*, July 30, 2006, pp. 1A, 22A; "Machines for the Masses," *The Wall Street Journal*, December 9, 2003, pp. A19, A20; "The Color of Beauty," *Forbes*, November 22, 2000, pp. 170–76; "It's Goo, Goo, Goo, Goo Vibrations at the Gerber Lab," *The Wall Street Journal*, December 4, 1996, pp. A1, A6; Donald R. Graber, "How to Manage a Global Product Development Process," *Industrial Marketing Management*, November 1996, pp. 483–98; and Herbig, *Handbook of Cross-Cultural Marketing*.
41. Jagdish N. Sheth and Atul Parvatiyar, "The Antecedents and Consequences of Integrated Global Marketing," *International Marketing Review* 18, no. 1 (2001), pp. 16–29. Also see D. Szymanski, S. Bharadwaj, and R. Varadarajan, "Standardization versus Adaptation of International Marketing Strategy: An Empirical Investigation," *Journal of Marketing*, October 1993, pp. 1–17.
42. "In China, Dell Needs to Reach Consumers," *China Economic Review*, November 20, 2007.
43. "With Profits Elusive, Wal-Mart to Exit Germany," *The Wall Street Journal*, July 29, 2006, pp. A1, A6.
44. "Rotten Apples," *Dallas Morning News*, April 7, 1998, p. 14A.
45. For an in-depth discussion on gray markets, see Kersi D. Antia, Mark Bergen, and Shantanu Dutta, "Competing with Gray Markets," *Sloan Management Review*, Fall 2004, pp. 63–69.

CNS Breathe Right Strips: This case was prepared by Mary L. Brown based on interviews with Kevin McKenna, vice president, International, and Nick Naumann, senior marketing services manager of CNS, Inc., September 2004.

Chapter 8

1. See www.boxofficemojo.com for the release schedule of movies for 2009, 2010, and beyond.
2. John Horn, "Studios Play Name Games," *Star Tribune*, August 10, 1997, p. F11; and "Flunking Chemistry," *Star Tribune*, April 11, 2003, p. E13.
3. Tad Friend, "The Cobra," *The New Yorker*, January19, 2009, pp. 41–49.
4. Willow Bay, "Test Audiences Have Profound Effect on Movies," *CNN Newsstand & Entertainment Weekly*, September 28, 1998. See www.cnn.com/SHOWBIZ/Movies/9809/28/screen.test.
5. Helene Diamond, "Lights, Camera . . . Research!" *Marketing News*, September 11, 1989, pp. 10–11; and "Killer!" *Time*, November 16, 1987, pp. 72–79.
6. Carl Diorio, "Tracking Projectings: Box Office Calculations an Inexact Science," *Variety*, May 24, 2001.
7. Friend, "The Cobra," pp. 41, 48.
8. A lengthier, expanded definition from 2004 is found on the American Marketing Associations Web site at www.marketingpower.com. For a researcher's comments on this and other definitions of marketing research, see Lawrence D. Gibson, "Quo Vadis, Marketing Research?" *Marketing Research*, Spring 2000, pp. 36–41.
9. Etienne Benson, "Toy Stories," *Observer* 19, no. 12 (December 2006).
10. Lawrence D. Gibson, "Defining Marketing Problems," *Marketing Research*, Spring 1998, pp. 4–12.
11. "Inside TV Ratings" and "National Audience Sample" from the Nielsen Media Research Web site, www.nielsenmedia.com; and Richard Siklos, "Made to Measure," *Fortune*, March 3, 2008, p. 72.
12. "Top TV Ratings" from Nielsen Media Research. See www.nielsenmedia.com.
13. "U.S. Advertising Spending Totals by Medium for 2008," *Advertising Age*, June 22, 2009, p. 21.
14. David Kiley, "Counting the Eyeballs," *BusinessWeek*, January 16, 2006, pp. 84–85; and "The Ultimate Marketing Machine," *The Economist*, July 8, 2006, pp. 61–64.
15. Colleen Moore-Mezler, "Mystery Shoppers Are an Important Resource," *Alert! Magazine*, Marketing Research Association 46, no. 4 (April 2008), pp. 10,12; and Robert Frank, "How to Live Large and Largely for Free, Jennifer Voitle's Way," *The Wall Street Journal*, June 9, 2003, pp. A1, A8.
16. Sarah Ellison, "P&G Chief's Turnaround Recipe: Find Out What Women Want," *The Wall Street Journal*, June 1, 2005, p. A1; Mark Maremont, "New Toothbrush Is Big-Ticket Item," *The Wall Street Journal*, October 27, 1998, pp. B1, B6; and Emily Nelson, "P&G Checks Out Real Life," *The Wall Street Journal*, May 17, 2001, pp. B1, B4.
17. Gavin Johnson and Melinda Rea-Holloway, "Ethnography: How to Know If It's Right for Your Study," *Alert! Magazine*, Marketing Research Association 47, no. 2 (February 2009), pp. 1–4. See www.mra-net.org/alert.
18. Kenneth Chang, "Enlisting Science's Lessons to Entice More Shoppers to Spend More," *The New York Times*, September 19, 2006, p. D3; and Janet Adamy, "Cooking Up Changes at Kraft Foods," *The Wall Street Journal*, February 20, 2007, p. B1.

19. Martin Lindstrom, *Buy*ology: Truth and Lies About Why We Buy* (New York: Doubleday, 2008), pp. 8–36; C. B. Whittemore, "Martin Lindstrom's Buy*ology," *Flooring the Consumer blogspot*, March 1, 2009; Seth Brown, "Buyology Offers a Peek Inside Buyers Heads," *USA Today*, October 29, 2008; and Andrea Sachs, "Business Books," *Time*, October 23, 2008.
20. For a more complete discussion of questionnaire methods, see Joseph F. Hair, Jr., Robert P. Bush, and David J. Ortinau, *Marketing Research*, 4th ed. (New York: McGraw-Hill/Irwin, 2009), Chaps. 6 and 13.
21. Jonathan Eig, "Food Industry Battles for Moms Who Want to Cook—Just a Little," *The Wall Street Journal*, March 7, 2001, pp. A1, A10; and Susan Feyder, "It Took Tinkering by Twin Cities Firms to Saver Some Sure Bets," *Star Tribune*, June 9, 1982, p. 11A.
22. Constance Gustke, "Built to Last," *Sales & Marketing Management*, August 1997, pp. 78–83.
23. See www.trendhunter.com/about-trend-hunter.
24. "What is Online Research?" Marketing Research Association, see http://www.mra-net.org/press/online.cfm; and see also www.markettools.com/pdfs/press_releases/release_20081204.pdf.
25. Douglas D. Bates, "The Future of Qualitative Research Is Online," *Alert! Magazine*, Marketing Research Association 47, no. 2 (February 2009); Jack Neff, "The End of Consumer Surveys?" *Advertising Age*, September 15, 2008; Jack Neff, "Marketing Execs: Researchers Could Use a Softer Touch," *Advertising Age*, January 27, 2009; Bruce Mendelsohn, "Social Networking: Interactive Marketing Lets Researchers Reach Consumers Where They Are," *Alert! Magazine*, Marketing Research Association 46, no. 4 (April 2008); Toby, "Social Media Research: Interview with Joel Rubinson of ARF: Part 1," *Diva Marketing Blog*, February 16, 2009; and Toby, "Social Media Research: Interview with Joel Rubinson of ARF: Part 2," *Diva Marketing Blog*, February 23, 2009.
26. Information obtained from the Web sites of Information Resources Inc. (www.infores.com) and AC-Nielsen (www.acnielsen.com).
27. Dale Buss, "The Race to RFID," *CEO Magazine*, November 2004, pp. 32–36.
28. The step 4 discussion was written by David Ford and Don Rylander of Ford Consulting Group Inc.; the Tony's Pizza example was provided by Teré Carral of Tony's Pizza.
29. Stephanie N. Mehta, "Under Armour Reboots," *Fortune*, February 2, 2009, pp. 29–33; and Michael McCarthy, "Under Armour Is Making a Run at Nike," *USA Today*, December 9, 2008, p. 1C.

Ford Consulting Group, Inc.: This case was written by David Ford of Ford Consulting Group, Inc.

Chapter 9

1. Kimberly Weisal, "A Shine in Their Shoes," *BusinessWeek*, December 5, 2005, p. 84; and information from the "Executive Biographies" section of the Zappos.com Web site.
2. Jeffrey M. O'Brien, "Zappos Knows How to Kick It," *Fortune*, February 2, 2009, pp. 55–60.
3. Weisal, "A Shine in Their Shoes," p. 84.
4. Natalie Zmuda, "Marketer of the Year: Zappos," *Advertising Age*, October 20, 2008, p. 36.
5. Duff McDonald, "Zappos.com: Success Through Simplicity," *CIO-Insight*, November 10, 2006.
6. Jena McGregor, "Zappos' Secret: It's an Open Book," *BusinessWeek*, March 23 and 30, 2009, p. 62; Jeffrey M. O'Brien, "The 10 Commandments of Zappos," *Fortune*, January 22, 2009; http://money.cnn.com/2009/01/21/news/companies/obrien_zappos10.fortune/; and Zappos.com.
7. Zmuda, "Marketer of the Year: Zappos," p. 36.
8. Devin Leonard, "Nightmare on Madison Avenue," *Fortune*, June 28, 2004, pp. 93–108; Anthony Bianco, "The Vanishing Mass Market," *BusinessWeek*, July 12, 2004, pp. 61–65; and Geoff Colvin, "Selling P&G," *Fortune*, September 17, 2007, pp. 163–69.
9. Larry Neumeister, "Rowling to Testify Against Fan in Bid to Block Publication of 'Harry Potter' Encyclopedia," StarTribune.com from an Associated Press article, April 13, 2008; www.startribune.com/entertainment/17761909.html.
10. "Special Report on Mass Communication: A Long March," *The Economist*, July 14, 2001, pp. 63–65.
11. Amy Merrick, "Once a Bellwether, Ann Taylor Fights Its Stodgy Image," *The Wall Street Journal*, July 12, 2005, pp. A1, A8; and "Ann Taylor Launches Strategic Restructuring Program to Enhance Profitability," press release dated January 30, 2008, http://investor.anntaylor.com.
12. The relation of these criteria to implementation is discussed in Jacqueline Dawley, "Making Connections: Enhance the Implementation of Value of Attitude-Based Segmentation," *Marketing Research*, Summer 2006, pp. 16–22.
13. Ian Michiels, "Customer Analytics: Segmentation Beyond Demographics," *The Aberdeen Group*, August 2008, p. 11.
14. The discussion of fast-food trends and market share is based on Experian Simmons Spring 2009 Full-Year NCS/NHCS Choices 3 System Crosstabulation Report based on visits within the past 30 days.
15. Jennifer Ordonez, "Taco Bell Chief Has New Tactic: Be Like Wendy's," *The Wall Street Journal*, February 23, 2001, pp. B1, B4; and Jennifer Ordonez, "An Efficiency Drive: Fast-Food Lanes Are Getting Even Faster," *The Wall Street Journal*, May18, 2000, pp. A1, A10.
16. Paul Ziobro, "Arby's Brand Eats Into Wendy's Results," *The Wall Street Journal*, March 3, 2009, p. B7; and Janet Adamy, "Wendy's Comes Up with a New Strategic Recipe," *The Wall Street Journal*, September 30, 2008, p. 83.
17. Janet Adamy, "McDonald's Seeks Ways to Keep Sizzling," *The Wall Street Journal*, March 10, 2009, pp. A1, A11; and "Let Them Eat Big Macs," *BusinessWeek*, February 9, 2009, p. 8.
18. Michael Arndt, "McDonald's 24/7: By Focusing on the Hours Between Traditional Meal Times, the Fast-Food Giant is Sizzling," *BusinessWeek*, February 5, 2007, pp. 64–72.
19. The discussion of Apple's segmentation strategies through the years is based on information from its Web site, www.apple.com; and www.apple-history.com/history.html.
20. Much of the discussion about positioning and perceptual maps is based on Roger A. Kerin and Robert A. Peterson, *Strategic Marketing Problems: Cases and Comments*, 11th ed. (Upper Saddle River, NJ: Prentice Hall, 2007), pp. 147–49; John M. Mullins, Orville C. Walker Jr., Harper W. Boyd Jr., and Jean-Claude Larreche, *Marketing Management: A Strategic Decision-Marketing Approach*, 5th ed. (New York: McGraw-Hill/Irwin, 2005), p. 216.
21. Nicholas Zamiska, "How Milk Got a Major Boost by Food Panel," *The Wall Street Journal*, August 30, 2004, pp. B1, B5.
22. Rebecca Winter, "Chocolate Milk," *Time*, April 30, 2001, p. 20.

Prince Sports: This case was written by William Rudelius and is based on personal interviews with Linda Glassel, Tyler Herring, and Nick Skally in 2009.

Chapter 10

1. Geoff Colvin, "The World's Most Admired Companies: 2009," *Fortune*, March 16, 2009, pp. 76–86; and Jean McGregor, "The World's 50 Most Innovative Companies," *BusinessWeek*, April 17, 2008.
2. Apple Introduces New iPod nano With Built-in Video Camera. Apple, Inc. press release, September 9, 2009. See www.apple.com/pr/library/2009/09/09nano.html.
3. Apple Unveils iPod touch. Apple, Inc. press release, September 5, 2007. See www.apple.com/pr/library/2007/09/05touch.html.

4. Roger A. Kerin and Robert A. Peterson, *Strategic Marketing Problems: Cases and Comments*, 11th ed. (Upper Saddle River, NJ: Prentice Hall, 2007), p. 141.
5. Interview with Geek Squad founder Robert Stephens on *60 Minutes*, January 28, 2007, www.geeksquad.com; Debora Viana Thompson, Rebecca W. Hamilton, and Roland Rust, "Feature Fatigue: When Product Capabilities Become Too Much of a Good Thing," *Journal of Marketing Research*, November 2005, pp. 431–42; and Roland T. Rust, Debora Viana Thompson, and Rebecca W. Hamilton, "Defeating Feature Fatigue," *Harvard Business Review*, February 2006, pp. 98–107.
6. Youngme Moon, "Break Free from the Product Life Cycle," *Harvard Business Review*, May 2005, pp. 86–94.
7. Interview with Geek Squad founder Robert Stephens on *60 Minutes*, January 28, 2007.
8. Greg A. Stevens and James Burley, "3,000 Raw Ideas = 1 Commercial Success!" *Research-Technology Management*, May–June 1997, pp. 16–27.
9. Robert G. Cooper, "New Products: What Separates the Winners from the Losers?" in *The PDMA Handbook of New Product Development*, eds. M. D. Rosenau, A. Griffin, G. Castellion, and N. Anscheutz (New York: Wiley and Sons, 1996), pp. 3–18; Robert G. Cooper, "The Impact of Product Innovativeness on Performance," *Journal of Product Innovation Management*, April 1999, pp. 115–33; Thomas D. Kuczmarski, "Measuring Your Return on Innovation," *Marketing Management*, Spring 2000, pp. 25–32; and Merle Crawford and Anthony D. Benedetto, *New Products Management*, 9th ed. (New York: McGraw-Hill/Irwin, 2008), pp. 61–71.
10. Julie Fortser, "The Lucky Charm of Steve Sanger," *BusinessWeek*, March 26, 2001, pp. 75–76.
11. The Avert Virucidal tissues, Hey! There's A Monster In My Room spray, and Garlic Cake examples are adapted from Robert M. McMath and Thom Forbes, *What Were They Thinking?* (New York: Random House, 1998).
12. John Gilbert, "To Sell Cars in Japan, U.S. Needs to Offer More Right-Drive Models," *Star Tribune*, May 27, 1995, p. M1.
13. "Cost of Poor Quality," *SixSigma Dictionary*, www.isixsigma.com/dictionary/Cost_of_Poor_Quality_-_COPQ-63.htm; Ben Patterson, "Microsoft Fesses Up to Xbox 360 Glitches," Yahoo! Tech Blog, July 6, 2007, http://tech.yahoo.com; and Matt Richtel, "Xbox 360 Out of Order? For Loyalists, No Worries," *The New York Times*, August 13, 2007, www.nytimes.com/2007/08/13/technology/13halo.html.
14. See Productscan Online at www.productscan.com/index.cfm?nid=5.
15. Robert G. Cooper, "What Leading Companies Are Doing to Reinvent Their NPD Process," *PDMA Visions Magazine*, September 2008, pp. 6–10; Robert G. Cooper, "The Stage-Gate Idea-to-Launch Process—Update: What's New and NexGen Systems," *Journal of Product Innovation Management*, May 2008, pp. 213–32; Leland D. Shaeffer and Michael Zirkle, "Beyond 'Phase Gate'—Why Not a Tailored Solution?" *PDMA Visions Magazine*, June 2008, pp. 21–25; and Gloria Barczak, Abbie Griffin, and Kenneth B. Kahn, "Perspective: Trends and Drivers of Success in NPD Practices: Results of the 2003 PDMA Best Practices Study," *Journal of Product Innovation Management*, January 2009, pp. 3–23.
16. Dan P. Lovallo and Olivier Sibony, "Distortions and Deceptions in Strategic Decisions," *The McKinsey Quarterly*, 1 (2006), pp. 19–29; and Byron G. Augusto, Eric P. Harmon, and Vivek Pandit, "The Right Service Strategies for Product Companies, *The McKinsey Quarterly*, 1 (2006), pp. 41–51.
17. Isabelle Royer, "Why Bad Projects Are So Hard to Kill," *Harvard Business Review*, February 2003, pp. 48–56; John T. Morn, Dan P. Lovallo, and S. Patrick Viguerie, "Beating the Odds in Market Entry," *The McKinsey Quarterly* 4 (2005), pp. 35–45; Leslie Perlow and Stephanie Williams, "Is Silence Killing Your Company?" *Harvard Business Review*, May 2003, pp. 52–58; Beverly K. Brockman and Robert M. Morgan, "The Moderating Effect of Organizational Cohesiveness in Knowledge Use and New Product Development," *Journal of Marketing Science* 3 (Summer 2006), pp. 295–306; Eyal Biyalogorsky, William Boulding, and Richard Staelin, "Stuck in the Past: Why Managers Persist with New Product Failures," *Journal of Marketing*, April 2006, pp. 108–21; and Irwin L. Janis, *Groupthink* (New York: Free Press, 1988).
18. For a report on measuring and stimulating American innovation, see *Innovation Measurement: Tracking the State of Innovation in the American Economy* (Washington, DC: A Report to the Secretary of Commerce by The Advisory Committee on Measuring Innovation in the 21st Century Economy, January 2008), pp. 17–20.
19. Matt Richtel, "A Google Whiz Searches for His Place on Earth," *The New York Times*, April 12, 2009, pp. 1, 18, 19.
20. Ken Belson, "Oh, Yeah, There's a Ballgame, Too," *The New York Times*, October 22, 2006, pp. 3–1, 3–7.
21. Peter Erickson, "One Food Company's Foray into Open Innovation," *PDMA Visions Magazine*, June 2008, pp. 12–14; Benn Lawson, Kenneth J. Petersen, Paul D. Cousins, and Robert B. Handfield, "Knowledge Sharing in Interorganizational Product Development Teams: The Effect of Formal and Informal Socialization Mechanisms," *Journal of Product Innovation Management*, March 2009, pp. 156–72; and James I. Cash, Jr., Michael J. Earl, and Robert Morison, "Teaming Up to Crack Innovation and Enterprise Integration," *Harvard Business Review*, November 2008, pp. 90–100.
22. Kimberly Judson, Denise D. Schoenabachler, Geoffrey L. Gordon, Rick E. Ridnour, and Dan C. Weilbaker, "The New Product Development Process: Let the Voice of the Salesperson Be Heard," *Journal of Product & Brand Management* 15, no. 3 (2006), pp. 194–202.
23. Morgan L. Swink and Vincent A. Mabert, "Product Development Partnerships: Balancing Needs of OEMs and Suppliers," *Business Horizons*, May–June 2000, pp. 59–68.
24. C. K. Prahalad and Venkat Ramswamy, *The Future of Competition* (Boston: Harvard Business School Press, 2004); and Steve Hamm, "Adding Customers to the Design Team," *BusinessWeek*, March 1, 2004, pp. 22–23.
25. Anthony W. Ulwick, "Turn Customer Input into Innovation" *Harvard Business Review*, January 2002, pp. 91–97.
26. Sarah Ellison, "P & G Chief's Turnaround Recipe: Find Out What Women Want," *The Wall Street Journal*, June 1, 2005, pp. A1, A16.
27. Adam Aston and Gail Edmonson, "This Volvo Is Not a Guy Thing," *BusinessWeek*, March 15, 2004, pp. 84–86.
28. Daniel Turner, "The Secret of Apple Design," *MIT Technology Review*, May/June 2007; Leander Kahney, "Silicon Valley Loves Transparency and Cooperation. Not Steve Jobs. How Apple Got Everything Right By Doing Everything Wrong," *Wired Business Trends*, April 2008, pp. 137–43; and Karl T. Ulrich and Stephen D. Eppinger, *Product Design and Development* 4th ed. (New York: McGraw-Hill/Irwin, 2008), chap 10.
29. Joseph Weber, Stanley Holmes, and Christopher Palmeri, "Mosh Pits' of Creativity," *BusinessWeek*, November 7, 2005, pp. 98–100.
30. Bruce Nussbaum, "The Best Global Design of 2008," *BusinessWeek*, July 28, 2008, pp. 44–46.
31. Bruce Nussbaum, "The Power of Design," *BusinessWeek*, May 17, 2004, pp. 86–94; the article gives many techniques for idea and concept generation, as do Appendixes A, B, and C in Merle Crawford and Anthony Di Benedetto, *New Products Management*, 9th ed. (New York: McGraw-Hill/Irwin, 2008).
32. Erickson, "One Food Company's Foray into Open Innovation," p. 13.
33. Simona Covel, "My Brain, Your Brawn," *The Wall Street Journal, October 13, 2008, p. R12.*
34. Erickson, "One Food Company's Foray into Open Innovation," p. 12.
35. Steve Hoeffler, "Measuring Preferences for Really New Products," *Journal of Marketing Research*, November 2003, pp. 406–20.

36. Christopher Lovelock and Jochen Wirtz, *Services Marketing* (Englewood Cliffs, NJ: Prentice Hall, 2007), pp. 260–84.
37. Larry Huston and Nobil Sakkab, "Connect and Develop," *Harvard Business Review*, March 2006, pp. 58–66; and "Pringles Announces First-of-Its-Kind Technology that Prints Directly on Individual Crisps," www.pg.com, accessed April 6, 2004.
38. Vicki Clift, "Everyone Needs Service Flow Charting," *Marketing News*, October 23, 1995, pp. 41, 43; Mary Jo Bitner, Bernard H. Booms, and Mary Stanfield Tetreault, "The Service Encounter: Diagnosing Favorable and Unfavorable Incidents," *Journal of Marketing*, January 1990, pp. 71–84; Eberhard Scheuing, "Conducting Customer Service Audits," *Journal of Consumer Marketing*, Summer 1989, pp. 35–41; and W. Earl Susser, R. Paul Olsen, and D. Daryl Wyckoff, *Management of Service Operations* (Boston: Allyn & Bacon, 1978).
39. Laura M. Holson, "Putting a Bolder Face on Google," *The New York Times*, March 1, 2009, pp. BU1, BU8; and Julian Gutherie, "The Adventures of Marissa," *San Francisco*, March 2008.
40. Jack Neff, "White Bread, USA," *Advertising Age*, July 9, 2001, pp. 1, 12, 13.
41. Mark Leslie and Charles J. Holloway "The Sales Learning Curve," *Harvard Business Review*, July–August 2006, pp. 115–23.
42. Kim Schatzel and Roger Calantone, "Creating Market Anticipation: An Exploratory Evaluation of the Effect of Preannouncement Behavior on a New Product Launch," *Journal of the Academy of Marketing Sciences*, Summer 2006, pp. 357–66.
43. Jennifer Ordonez, "How Burger King Got Burned in Quest to Make the Perfect Fry," *The Wall Street Journal*, January 16, 2001, pp. A1, A8.
44. Kerry A. Dolan, "Speed: The New X Factor," *Forbes*, December 26, 2005, pp. 74–77.

Activeion Cleaning Solutions: This case was written by Chris Deets of Activeion Cleaning Solutions and William Rudelius.

Chapter 11

1. "G2, Zyrtec Top New Product Sales in '08," *BrandWeek*, March 23, 2009; "Gatorade Refreshes Look," *BrandWeek*, January 15, 2009, p. 4; "Gatorade Unleashes New Attitude, Enhanced Beverages," PepsiCo press release, December 28, 2008; pp. D1, 5; and Darren Rovell, *First in Thirst: How Gatorade Turned the Science of Sweat into a Cultural Phenomenon* (New York: AMACOM, 2005).
2. For an extended discussion of the generalized product life cycle, see Donald R. Lehmann and Russell S. Winer, *Product Management*, 5th ed (New York: McGraw-Hill, 2008).
3. *Gillette Fusion Case Study* (New York: Datamonitor, June 6, 2008). All subsequent references to Gillette Fusion are based on this case study.
4. John W. Mullins; Orville C. Walker, Jr.; Harper W. Boyd, Jr.; and Jean-Claude Larréché, *Marketing Management: A Strategic Decision-Making Approach*, 5th ed. (New York: McGraw-Hill/Irwin, 2005), p. 396.
5. Portions of this discussion on the fax machine product life cycle are based on Karen Prema, "Faxes are Evolving," *Purchasing Magazine Online*, March 16, 2006; and "Atlas Electronics Corporation," in Roger A. Kerin and Robert A. Peterson, *Strategic Marketing Problems: Cases and Comments*, 8th ed. (Upper Saddle River, NJ: Prentice Hall, 1998), pp. 494–506.
6. "How Many Active E-mail Mailboxes Are There in the World Today?" The Radicate Group, Inc., January 25, 2007; and "Why Are Faxes Still Around?" *Wired*, January 2009, p. 47.
7. Kate MacArthur, "Coke Energizes Tab, Neville Isdell's Fave," *Advertising Age*, August 29, 2005, pp., 3, 21.
8. "Hosiery Sales Hit Major Snag," *Dallas Morning News*, December 18, 2006 p. 50.
9. "How to Separate Trends from Fads," *BrandWeek*, October 23, 2000, pp. 30, 32.
10. *Year-End Marketing Reports on U.S. Recorded Music Shipments* (New York: Recording Industry Association of America, 2008); and "U.S. Music Forecast: 2008–2013," Forrester Research Reports, forrester.com, accessed January 17, 2009.
11. Everett M. Rogers, *Diffusion of Innovations*, 5th ed. (New York: Free Press, 2003).
12. Jagdish N. Sheth and Banwasi Mitral, *Consumer Behavior: A Managerial Perspective*, 2nd ed. (Mason, OH: South-Western College Publishing, 2003).
13. "When Free Samples Become Saviors," *The Wall Street Journal*, August 14, 2001, pp. B1, B4.
14. Amol Sharms, "Nokia Joins the Push to Do It All While on the Go," *The Wall Street Journal*, December 2, 2008, p. B5.
15. "Hop on the Back, Jack," *Marketing News*, March 15, 2009, p. 5.
16. "Dockers Adds Diversity to Message," *BrandWeek*, September 11, 2006, p. 18.
17. "New Balance Steps Up Marketing Drive," *The Wall Street Journal*, March 21, 2008, p. B3.
18. Sheth and Mitral, *Consumer Behavior*; and Marsha Cohen, *Marketing to the 50+ Population* (New York: EPM Communications, Inc., 2007).
19. Bruce Horovitz, "Shoppers Beware: Products Shrink But Prices Stay the Same," www.usatoday, June 11, 2008; John Gourville, "How to Avoid a Price Increase," *Working Knowledge for Business Leaders* (Boston: Harvard Business School, June 28, 2004); and "More for Less," *Consumer Reports*, August 2004, p. 63.
20. Judi Hasson, "Countries Mount Global Campaign to Combat Counterfeiting," www.america.gov, accessed April 24, 2009.
21. This discussion is based on Kevin Lane Keller, *Strategic Brand Management*, 3rd ed. (Upper Saddle River, NJ: Prentice Hall, 2008). Also see, Susan Fornier, "Building Brand Community on the Harley-Davidson Posse Ride," *Harvard Business School Note #5-501-502* (Boston: Harvard Business School, 2001); and Tulin Erdem, Joffre Swait, and Ana Valenzuela, "Brands as Signals: A Cross-Country Validation Study," *Journal of Marketing*, January 2006, pp. 34–49.
22. Keller, *Strategic Brand Management*.
23. This discussion is based on John Deighton, "How Snapple Got Its Juice Back," *Harvard Business Review*, January 2002, pp. 47–53; and "Breakfast King Agrees to Sell Bagel Business," *The Wall Street Journal*, September 28, 1999, pp. B1, B6. Also see, Vithala R. Rao, Manj K. Agarwal, and Denise Dahlhoff, "How Is Manifest Branding Strategy Related to the Value of a Corporation?" *Journal of Marketing*, October 2004, pp. 125–41.
24. "Judge Pooh-Poohs Lawsuit over Disney Licensing Fees," *USAToday.com*, March 30, 2004; and Keller, *Strategic Brand Management*.
25. John Brodie, "The Many Faces of Ralph Lauren," *Fortune.com*, August 29, 2007; and "Polo Ralph Lauren Enters Into Licensing Agreement with Luxottica Group, S.P.A.," www.thebusinessedition.com, February 28, 2006.
26. Beth Snyder Bulik, "What's in a (Good) Product Name? Sales," *Advertising Age*, February 2, 2009, p. 10; and Keller, *Strategic Brand Management*. Also see Chiranjeev Kohli and Douglas W. LaBahn, "Creating Effective Brand Names: A Study of the Naming Process," *Journal of Advertising Research*, January–February 1997, pp. 67–75.
27. Jack Neff, "The End of the Line for Line Extensions?" *Advertising Age*, July 7, 2008, pp. 3, 28.
28. "When Brand Extension Becomes Brand Abuse," *BrandWeek*, October 26, 1998, pp., 20, 22.
29. For an in-depth discussion on co-branding, see Akshay R. Rao and Robert W. Ruekert, "Brand Alliances as Signals of Product Quality," *Sloan Management Review*, Fall 1994, pp. 87–97.
30. David Aaker, *Brand Portfolio Strategy* (New York: Free Press, 2004).
31. "Ribbons Roll Out on Rides," *Dallas Morning News*, September 30, 2005, p. 8D.
32. Nikhil Bahadur, "How to Slim Down a Brand Portfolio," *Strategy & Business*, Winter 2006, pp. 15–16.

33. "Consumers Flock to Private Labels," *Advertising Age*, February 2, 2009, p. 27; and Lien Lamey, Barbara Deleersnyder, Marnik G. Dekimpe, and Jan-Benedict E. M. Steenkamp, "How Business Cycles Contribute to Private-Label Success: Evidence from the United States and Europe," *Journal of Marketing*, January 2007, pp. 1–15.
34. www.pez.com, accessed February `1, 2009; David Welch, *Collecting Pez* (Murphysboro, IL: Bubba Scrubba Publications, 1995); and "Elements Design Adds Dimension to Perennial Favorite Pez Brand," *Package Design Magazine*, May 2006, pp. 37–38.
35. "Market Statistics," Packaging-Gateway.com, accessed March 25, 2009.
36. "Green Bean Casserole Turns 50," *Dallas Morning News*, November 19, 2005, p. 10D.
37. "L'eggs Hatches a New Hosiery Package," *BrandWeek*, January 1, 2001, p. 6.
38. Representative scholarly research on packaging and labeling perceptions include: Priya Rgahubir and Eric A. Greenleaf, "Ratios in Proportion: What Should the Shape of the Package Be?" *Journal of Marketing*, April 2006, pp. 95–107; Peter H. Bloch, Frederic F. Brunel, and Todd Arnold, "Individual Differences in the Centrality of Visual Product Aesthetics: Concept and Measurement," *Journal of Consumer Research*, March 2003, pp. 551–65; and Pamela Anderson, Joan Giese, and Joseph A. Cote, "Impression Management Using Typeface Design," *Journal of Marketing*, October 2004, pp. 60–72.
39. Betsy McKay, "Pepsi's New Marketing Dance: Can Can," *The Wall Street Journal*, January 12, 2007, p. B3.
40. "Asian Brands Are Sprouting English Logos in Pursuit of Status, International Image," *The Wall Street Journal*, August 7, 2001, p. B7C.
41. Ellen Byron, "Consumer Products Getting a Makeover," *The Wall Street Journal*, June 2, 2008, p. B9; and Susanna Hammer, "Packaging that Pays," *Business 2.0*, July 26, 2006, pp. 68–69.
42. Betsy McKay, "Pepsi to Cut Plastic Used in Bottles," *The Wall Street Journal*, May 6, 2008, p. B2.
43. "Wal-Mart: Use Less Packaging," *Dallas Morning News*, September 23, 2006, p. 2D. For an overview of Procter & Gamble's environmental efforts, see *Sustainability Report 2007* (Cincinnati, OH: Procter & Gamble Company, 2008).
44. "Packaging," hp.com, accessed January 17, 2007.
45. Christian Twigg-Flesner, *Consumer Product Guarantees* (Aldershot, England: Ashgate Publishing, 2003).

BMW: This case was written by Giana Eckhardt and Steven Hartley based on company interviews and the following sources: April Boehm, "BMW Undergoes a Tuneup," *The Wall Street Journal,* September 28, 2007, p. A11; Gail Edmondson, "BMW's Dream Factory," *BusinessWeek,* October 16, 2006, p. 70; Claire Billings, "Continuously Building the BMW Brand for 25 Years," *Compaign,* September 24, 2004, p. 16; Larry Armstrong, BMW's Brand-new 6-series Convertible is Powerful, Elegant, and Eye-catching, *BusinessWeek,* August 9, 2004, p. 73; Gail Edmondson, "BMW: Crashing the Compact Market," *BusinessWeek,* June 18, 2004, p. 36; Troy Dreier, BMW and iPod: Two Exclusive Names That Now Go Well Together," *PC Magazine,* September 21, 2004, p. 176.

Chapter 12

1. James H. Gilmore and B. Joseph Pine II, *Authenticity* (Boston: Harvard Business School Press 2007); Scott Tillitt, "Client Meeting: L.L. Bean's Search for Authenticity," *Photo District News*, December 2008; and "PR's Goal Must Be Its Own Authenticity," *PR Week*, March 16, 2009.
2. Eugene P. Seskin and Shelly Smith, "Annual Revision of the National Income and Product Accounts," NIPA Annual Revisions, Bureau of Economic Analysis, U.S. Department of Commerce, August 2008, Table 7, p. 7; Bureau of Economic Analysis, National Accounts, Table 1.1.5 Gross Domestic Product, August 17, 2009; *World Trade Report 2008*, World Trade Organization, Table 2, p. 7; and "Employment By Major Industry Sector," U.S. Bureau of Labor Statistics, Employment Projections, Table 1, http://data.bls.gov/cgi-bin/print.pl/emp/empmajorin dustry.htm.
3. "Cruise Line Offers Tech Concierge," *Los Angeles Times*, April 5, 2009, p. 3; "Fly with the Stars and Live Like Them, Too!" *PR Newswire*, August 7, 2008; and "Who Really Loves You on Twitter? New Service Reveals All," *PC Magazine*, April 15, 2009.
4. Janet R. McColl-Kennedy and Tina White, "Service Provider Training Programs at Odds with Customer Requirements in Five Star Hotels," *Journal of Services Marketing* 11, no. 4 (1997), pp. 249–64; Ellyn A. McColgan, "How Fidelity Invests in Service Professionals," *Harvard Business Review*, January–February 1997, pp. 137–43; and Frederick F. Reichheld and W. Earl Sasser, Jr., "Zero Defections: Quality Comes to Services," *Harvard Business Review*, September–October 1990, pp. 105–11.
5. Christopher Lovelock and Event Gummesson, "Whither Services Marketing?" *Journal of Services Research* 7 (August 2004), pp. 20–41; and Christopher H. Lovelock and George S. Yip, "Developing Global Strategies for Service Businesses," *California Management Review*, Winter 1996, pp. 64–86.
6. Zhen Zhu, Cheryl Nakata, and K. Sivakumar, "Self-Service Technology Effectiveness: The Role of Design Features and Individual Traits," *Journal of the Academy of Marketing Science*, Winter 2007, pp. 492–506; and Lawrence F. Cunningham, Clifford E. Young, and James Gerlach, "A Comparison of Consumer Views of Traditional Services and Self-Service Technologies," *Journal of Services Marketing* 1 (2009), pp. 11–23.
7. "HP Positioned to Lead in New Era of Business Technology; New Solutions and Services to Help Enterprises Optimize Business Outcomes," *Business Wire,* April 24, 2007.
8. Christopher Lovelock and Jochen Wirtz, *Services Marketing* (Englewood Cliffs, NJ: Prentice Hall, 2007), p. 15.
9. Peter C. Honebein and Roy F. Cammarano, "Customers at Work: Self-Service Customers Can Reduce Costs and Become Cocreators of Value," *Marketing Management*, January/February 2006, pp. 26–31; and Matthew L. Meuter, Amy L. Ostrom, Robert I. Roundtree, and Mary Jo Bittner, "Self-Service Technologies: Understanding Customer Satisfaction with Technology-Based Service Encounters," *Journal of Marketing*, July 2000, pp. 50–64.
10. "Registered Nonprofit Organizations by Level of Total Revenue," National Center for Charitable Statistics, http://nccsdataweb.urban.org, March 2009; and "Economic Crisis: Nonprofit Statistics," National Council of Nonprofits, www.councilofnonprofits.org accessed April 7, 2009.
11. Jessi Hempl, "Selling a Cause? Better Make It Pop," *BusinessWeek*, February 13, 2006, p. 75.
12. "Red Cross Hires the Bravo Group," *PR Week*, September 1, 2008, p. 2; "NASCAR Driver Greg Biffle in Race for Blood Donations," *PR Newswire*, November 4, 2008; "American Red Cross National Celebrity Cabinet Members," American Red Cross Web site, http://www.redcross.org/portal/site/en, accessed April 8, 2009; "Nonprofit Marketer of the Year Awarded," *Marketing News*, September 1, 2008, p. 7; Aaron Baar, "Red Cross Ready to Pump Up Donations," *Brandweek.com*, February 1, 2007; and "Celebrities Commit to Supporting American Red Cross in 2007," *Lab Business Week*, March 18, 2007, p. 92.
13. Larry Chiagouris, "Nonprofits Can Take Cues from Biz World," *Marketing News*, July 15, 2006, pp. 20–22; Hempl, "Selling a Cause? Better Make It Pop"; Deborah L. Vence, "Smart Organizations Use Technology to Spark Dialogue, Cement Relationships," *Marketing News*, July 15, 2006, p. 15; and Jeffrey Gangemi, "Giving Goes Green," *BusinessWeek*, November 27, 2006, p. 84.

14. Diane C. Lade, "Postal Service Learns to Love the Internet," *South Florida Sun-Sentinel*, March 15, 2007; Stephen Barr, "Postal Service Feels Heat Over Consolidation Plans," *Washington Post*, August 3, 2006, p. D4; and Allison Enright, "Mail For Sale," *Marketing News*, June 15, 2006, p. 4.

15. Keith B. Murray, "A Test of Services Marketing Theory: Consumer Information Acquisition Activities," *Journal of Marketing*, January 1991, pp. 10–25.

16. Dawn Iacobucci, "An Empirical Examination of Some Basic Tenets in Services: Goods-Services Continua," in *Advances in Services Marketing and Management*, vol. 1 eds. Teresa Swartz, David E. Bowen, and Stephen W. Brown (Greenwich, CT: JAI Press), pp. 23–52; and Valerie A. Zeithaml, "How Consumer Evaluation Processes Differ between Goods and Services," in *Marketing of Services*, eds. James H. Donnelly and William R. George (Chicago: American Marketing Association, 1981).

17. Michael J. Dorsch, Stephen J. Grove, and William Darden, "Consumer Intentions to Use a Services Category," *Journal of Services Marketing* 2 (2000), pp. 92–117; and Murray, "A Test of Services Marketing Theory: Consumer Information Acquisition Activities," *Journal of Marketing*, January 1991, pp. 10–25.

18. Leonard L. Berry and Neeli Bendapudi, "Clueing in Customers," *Harvard Business Review*, February 2003, pp. 100–6.

19. John Ozment and Edward Morash, "The Augmented Service Offering for Perceived and Actual Service Quality," *Journal of the Academy of Marketing Science*, Fall 1994, pp. 352–63.

20. A. Parasuraman, Valerie A. Zeithaml, and Leonard L. Berry, "Reassessment of Expectations as a Comparison Standard in Measuring Service Quality: Implications for Further Research," *Journal of Marketing*, January 1994, pp. 111–24; and Leonard L. Berry, *On Great Service* (New York: Free Press, 1995).

21. Valerie A. Zeithaml, A. Parasuraman, and Leonard L. Berry, *Delivering Quality Service* (New York: Free Press, 1990); and Stephen W. Brown and Teresa Swartz, "A Gap Analysis of Professional Service Quality," *Journal of Marketing*, April 1989, pp. 92–98.

22. Amy Ostrom and Dawn Iacobucci, "Consumer Trade-Offs and the Evaluation of Services," *Journal of Marketing*, January 1995, pp. 17–28; and J. Joseph Cronin, Jr., and Steven A. Taylor, "Measuring Service Quality: A Reexamination and Extension," *Journal of Marketing*, July 1992, pp. 55–68.

23. Leslie M. Fine, "Service Marketing," *Business Horizons*, May–June 2008, pp. 163–168; and James G. Maxham III and Richard G. Netemeyer, "A Longitudinal Study of Complaining Customers' Evaluations of Multiple Service Failures and Recovery Efforts," *Journal of Marketing*, October 2002, pp. 57–71.

24. Deborah Stead, "An Unwelcome Delivery," *BusinessWeek*, May 4, 2009, p. 15; "Weblogs, Videologs," *Marketing News*, January 15, 2007, p. 21; Michelle Conlin, "Nastiness Online Can Erupt and Go Global Overnight, and 'No Comment' Doesn't Cut It Anymore," *BusinessWeek*, April 16, 2007, p. 54; and "Dell Learns Power of the Blog," *Marketing News*, December 15, 2006, p. 17.

25. Vicki Clift, "Everyone Needs Service Flow Charting," *Marketing News*, October 23, 1995, pp. 41, 43; Mary Jo Bitner, Bernard H. Booms, and Mary Stanfield Tetreault, "The Service Encounter: Diagnosing Favorable and Unfavorable Incidents," *Journal of Marketing*, January 1990, pp. 71–84; Eberhard Scheuing, "Conducting Customer Service Audits," *Journal of Consumer Marketing*, Summer 1989, pp. 35–41; and W. Earl Susser, R. Paul Olsen, and D. Daryl Wyckoff, *Management of Service Operations* (Boston: Allyn & Bacon, 1978).

26. Thorsten Hennig-Thurau, Markus Groth, Michael Paul, and Dwayne D. Gremler, "Are All Smiles Created Equal? How Emotional Contagion and Emotional Labor Affect Service Relationships," *Journal of Marketing*, July 2006, pp. 58–73.

27. Leonard L. Berry, "Relationship Marketing of Services—Growing Interest, Emerging Perspectives," *Journal of the Academy of Marketing Science*, Fall 1995, pp. 236–45; Mary Jo Bitner, "Building Service Relationships: It's All about Promises," *Journal of the Academy of Marketing Science*, Fall 1995, pp. 246–51; Kevin P. Gwinner, Dwayne D. Gremler, and Mary Jo Bitner, "Relational Benefits in Services Industries: The Customer's Perspective," *Journal of the Academy of Marketing Science*, Spring 1998, pp. 101–14; Susan Fournier, Susan Dobscha, and David Glen Mick, "Preventing the Premature Death of Relationship Marketing," *Harvard Business Review*, January–February 1998, pp. 42–51; and John V. Petrof, "Relationship Marketing: The Wheel Reinvented?" *Business Horizons*, November–December 1997, pp. 26–31.

28. Katherine N. Lemon, Tiffany Barnett White, and Russell S. Winer, "Dynamic Customer Relationship Management: Incorporating Future Considerations into the Service Retention Decision," *Journal of Marketing*, January 2002, pp. 1–14.

29. Michael Paul, Thorsten Hennig-Thurau, Dwayne D. Gremler, Kevin P. Gwinner, and Caroline Wiertz, "Toward a Theory of Repeat Purchase Drivers for Consumer Services," *Journal of the Academy of Marketing Science*, Summer 2009, pp. 215–37.

30. Thomas S. Gruca, "Defending Service Markets," *Marketing Management* 1 (1994), pp. 31–38; and Leonard L. Berry, Jeffrey S. Conant, and A. Parasuraman. "A Framework for Conducting a Services Marketing Audit," *Journal of the Academy of Marketing Science*, Summer 1991, pp. 255–68.

31. Christopher Lovelock and Jochen Wirtz, *Service Marketing: People, Technology, Strategy*, 6th ed. (Englewood Cliffs, NJ: Prentice Hall, 2007); Valerie A. Zeithaml and Mary Jo Bitner, *Services Marketing*, 3rd ed. (New York: McGraw-Hill, 2003); and Frederick G. Crane, Roger A. Kerin, Steven W. Hartley, and William Rudelius, *Marketing*, 7th Canadian ed. (New York: McGraw-Hill Ryerson, 2008).

32. Dan R. E. Thomas, "Strategy Is Different in Service Businesses," *Harvard Business Review*, July–August 1978, pp. 158–65.

33. Sundar G. Bharedwaj, P. Rajan Varadarajan, and John Fahy, "Sustainable Competitive Advantage in Service Industries: A Conceptual Model and Research Propositions," *Journal of Marketing*, October 1993, pp. 83–99.

34. Daniel B. Honigman, "Hotels at Home: In-Room Catalog and E-Commerce Service Leverages Guest Experience While Increasing Brand Awareness," *Marketing News*, March 15, 2008, p. 12.

35. Kent B. Monroe, "Buyer's Subjective Perceptions of Price," *Journal of Marketing Research*, February 1973, pp. 70–80; and Jerry Olson, "Price as an Informational Cue: Effects on Product Evaluation," in *Consumer and Industrial Buying Behavior*, eds. A. G. Woodside, J. N. Sheth, and P. D. Bennett (New York: Elsevier North-Holland, 1977), pp. 267–86.

36. Leonard L. Berry, Kathleen Seiders, and Dhruv Grewal, "Understanding Service Convenience," *Journal of Marketing* 66 (July 2002), pp. 1–17; and Charles L. Colby and A. Parasuraman, "Technology Still Matters: E-Services Are Alive and Well and Positioned for Growth," *Marketing Management* 12 (July–August 2003), pp. 28–33.

37. Robert E. Hite, Cynthia Fraser, and Joseph A. Bellizzi, "Professional Service Advertising: The Effects of Price Inclusion, Justification, and Level of Risk," *Journal of Advertising Research* 30 (August–September 1990), pp. 23–31; William R. George and Leonard L. Berry, "Guidelines for the Advertising of Services," *Business Horizons*, July–August 1981, pp. 52–56; and Eugene M. Johnson, Eberhard E. Scheuing, and Kathleen A. Gaida, *Profitable Service Marketing* (Homewood, IL: Dow Jones-Irwin, 1986).

38. Kathleen Mortimer, "Identifying the Components of Effective Service Advertisements," *Journal of Services Marketing* 22 (2008), pp. 104–13.

39. Joe Adams, "Why Public Service Advertising Doesn't Work," *Adweek*, November 17, 1980, p. 72.

40. Patriya Tansuhaj, Donna Randall, and Jim McCullough, "A Services Marketing Management Model: Integrating Internal and External

Marketing Functions," *Journal of Sciences Marketing*, Winter 1998, pp. 31–38.

41. Christian Gronroos, "Internal Marketing Theory and Practice," in *Services Marketing in a Changing Environment*, eds. Thomas Bloch, G. D. Upah, and V. A. Zeithaml, (Chicago: American Marketing Association, 1984).
42. Ibid.
43. Yong-Ki Lee, Jung-Heon Nam, Dae-Hwan Park and Kyung Ah Lee, "What Factors Influence Customer-Oriented Prosocial Behavior of Customer-Contact Employees?" *Journal o Services Marketing* 20, no. 4 (2006), pp. 251–64; Stephen W. Brown, "The Employee Experience," *Marketing Management* 12 (March–April 2003), pp. 12–13; Lawrence A. Crosby and Sheree L. Johnson, "Watch What I Do," *Marketing Management* 12 (November–December 2003), pp. 10–11; and March C. Gilly and Mary Wolfinbarger, "Advertising's Internal Audience," *Journal of Marketing*, January 1998, pp. 69–88.
44. Gabriel M. Gelb and John M. McKeever, "In Their Shoes," *Marketing Management*, July/August 2006, p. 40–45; Lynette Ryals, "Making Customer Relationship Management Work: The Measurement and Profitable Management of Customer Relationships," *Journal of Marketing*, October 2005, pp. 252–61; Bernd H. Schmitt, *Customer Experience Management* (Hoboken, NJ: Wiley and Sons, 2003); and Shaun Smith and Joe Wheeler, *Managing the Customer Experience* (Englewood Cliffs, NJ: Prentice Hall, 2002).
45. Paula Andruss, "Delivering WOW Through Service," *Marketing News*, October 15, 2008, p. 10.
46. F. G. Crane, *Professional Services Marketing: Strategy and Tactics* (London: Haworth Press, 1993); and Leonard L. Berry and Neeli Bedapudi, "Clueing in Customers," *Harvard Business Review*, February 2003, pp. 100–6.
47. Frederick H. deB. Harris and Peter Peacock, "Hold My Place, Please," *Marketing Management*, Fall 1995, pp. 34–46.
48. Christopher Lovelock and Jochen Wirtz, *Services Marketing* (Englewood Cliffs, NJ: Prentice Hall, 2007), pp. 260–84.
49. Anyuan Shen and A. Dwayne Ball, "Is Personalization of Services Always a Good Thing? Exploring the Role of Technology-Mediated Personalization (TMP) in Service Relationships," *Journal of Services Marketing* 23 (2009), pp. 80–92.
50. Regina D. Woodall, Charles L. Colby and A. Parasuraman, "E-volution to Revolution," *Marketing Management*, March/April 2007, pp. 29–34; Timothy J. Mullaney, "Online Pics: A Sure Shot," *BusinessWeek*, September 3, 2001, p. EB 12; Ramin Setoodeh, "Technology: Safer Surfing for Love," *Newsweek*, April 19, 2004, p. 66; and Ginny Parker, "Looking for Prince Charming? In Japan Check Your Cell Phone," *Time*, June 4, 2001; p. 88.
51. Stephen J. Grove, Raymond P. Fisk, and Joby John, "The Future of Services Marketing: Forecasts from Ten Services Experts," *Journal of Services Marketing* 17, no. 2 (2003), pp. 107–21; Stephen L. Vargo and Robert F. Lusch, "Evolving to a New Dominant Logic for Marketing," *Journal of Marketing* 68 (January 2004), pp.1–17; "Model of Exchange Shifts toward Services," *Marketing News*, January 15, 2004, p. 25; and G. Tomas M. Hult, "Think Global, Act Local in Global Services Marketing," *Marketing News*, March 1, 2004, p. 30.
52. Mary Jo Bitner and Stephen W. Brown, "The Service Imperative," *Business Horizons*, January–February 2008, pp. 39–46.
53. Valerie Zeithaml, Mary Jo Bitner, and Dwayne Gremler, "Services Marketing Strategy," *Marketing Strategy Encyclopedia* (Hoboken, NJ: Wiley and Sons, 2009).

Philadelphia Phillies: This case was prepared by William Rudelius based on interviews with David Montgomery, David Buck, Marisol Lezcano, and Scott Brandreth; internal company materials; http://asp.usatoday.com/sports/baseball/salaries/totalpayroll.aspx?year=2007; and the Phillies Web site (www.phillies.com).

Chapter 13

1. Steve Stecklow, "StubHub's Ticket to Ride," *The Wall Street Journal*, January 17, 2006, pp. B1, B2.
2. See "StubHub," www.wikipedia.org, February 9, 2007.
3. Sarah Lacy, "The Hot Ticket Isn't Ticketmaster," *BusinessWeek* September 4, 2006, p. 36.
4. Eric Young, "Giants Strike Online Ticket Deal," *Silicon Valley/San Jose Business Journal*, February 9, 2009.
5. Timothy Matanovich, Gary L. Lillien, and Arvind Rangaswamy, "Engineering the Price-Value Relationship," *Marketing Management*, Spring 1999, pp. 48–53.
6. Lisa Gubernick, "The Little Extras That Count (Up)," *The Wall Street Journal*, July 12, 2001, pp. B1, B4; and Donald V. Potter, "Discovering Hidden Pricing Power," *Business Horizons*, November–December 2000, pp. 41–48.
7. Scott McCartney, "Airfare Quotes That Lay Bare Hidden Fees," *The Wall Street Journal*, March 10, 2009, pp. D1, D3.
8. Aaron Robinson, "2009 Tesla Roadster Road Test," *Car and Driver*, May 2009; for a list of cost of options, see www.edmunds.com/new/2009/tesla/roadster/101147356/options.html?action-1; and the Tesla Motors Web site for press releases and other information.
9. Thomas L. Friedman, *The World Is Flat* (New York: Farrar, Straus, and Giroux, Expanded Edition, 2006), pp. 5–9; Jason Dean and Peter Wonacott, "Tech Firms Woo 'Next Billion' Users," *The Wall Street Journal*, November 3, 2006 p. A2; Dexter Roberts, "China Mobile's Hot Signal," *BusinessWeek*, February 5, 2007, pp. 42–44; Kerry Capell, "Ikea: How the Swedish Retailer Became a Global Cult Brand," *BusinessWeek*, November 5, 2005, pp. 96–106; and Mei Fong, "Ikea Hits Home in China," *The Wall Street Journal*, March 3, 2006, pp. B1, B4.
10. Adapted from Kent B. Monroe, *Pricing: Making Profitable Decisions*, 3rd ed. (New York: McGraw-Hill, 2003); and David J. Curry, "Measuring Price and Quality Competition, *Journal of Marketing*, Spring 1985, pp. 106–17.
11. Numerous studies have examined the price-quality-value relationship. See, for example, Jacob Jacoby and Jerry C. Olsen, eds., *Perceived Quality* (Lexington, MA: Lexington Books, 1985); William D. Dodds, Kent B. Monroe, and Dhruv Grewal, "Effects of Price, Brand, and Store Information on Buyers' Product Evaluations," *Journal of Marketing Research*, August 1991, pp. 307–19; and Roger A. Kerin, Ambuj Jain, and Daniel Howard, "Store Shopping Experience and Consumer Price-Quality-Value Perceptions," *Journal of Retailing*, Winter 1992, pp. 235–45. For a thorough review of the price-quality-value relationship, see Valerie A. Zeithaml, "Consumer Perceptions of Price, Quality, and Value," *Journal of Marketing*, July 1998, pp. 2–22.
12. Roger A. Kerin and Robert A. Peterson, "Crestfield Furniture Industries, Inc. (A)," *Strategic Marketing Problems: Cases and Comments*, 11th ed. (Upper Saddle River, NJ: Prentice Hall, 2007), pp. 275–86.
13. Sudeep Reddy, "Credit-Card Fees Curbed," *The Wall Street Journal*, May 20, 2009, pp. A1, A2; Kevin Diaz, "Credit Card Bill of Rights: The Fine Print," *Star Tribune*, May 22, 2009, pp. A1, A13; Jane J. Kim, "B of A to Boost Rates on Cards with Balances," *The Wall Street Journal*, April 9, 2009, pp. D1, D4; "U.S. Tightens Credit Card Issuers' Rules," *Star Tribune*, December 19, 2008, pp. D1, D6; Anna Maria Andriotis, "Avoiding College's Plastic Hangover," *The Wall Street Journal*, August 21, 2008, p. D3; Elizabeth Warren, "Making Credit Safer," *Harvard Magazine*, May–June 2008, p. 35; and Kara McGuire, "Credit Madness," *Star Tribune*, August 10, 2008, p. D3.
14. Ken Belson, "Mets Going for the Gold on Tickets for More Games," *The New York Times*, April 8, 2009, p. B13.
15. Mike Dodd, "Cards Hold 50 Years of Memories," *USA Today*, March 27, 2001, pp. 1A, 2A; J. C. Conklin, "Don't Throw Out Those Old

Sneakers, They're a Gold Mine," *The Wall Street Journal*, September 21, 1998, pp. A1, A20; and prices are quoted on eBay.com on October 25, 2007.

16. Scott McCartney, "Why Planes in the Desert May Boost Fares," *The Wall Street Journal,* April 21, 2009, pp. D1, D2.
17. Daniel Levy, Mark Bergen, Shautanu Dutta, and Robert Venable, "The Magnitude of Menu Costs: Direct Evidence from Large U.S. Supermarket Chains," *Quarterly Journal of Economics*, August 1997, pp. 791–825.
18. Gordan A. Wyner, "New Pricing Realities," *Marketing Research*, Spring 2001, pp. 34–35.
19. Akshay R. Rao, Mark E. Bergen, and Scott Davis, "How to Fight a Price War," *Harvard Business Review*, March–April 2000, pp. 107–16.
20. Arik Hesseldahl, "For Every Xbox, a Big Fat Loss," *BusinessWeek*, December 5, 2005, p. 13.
21. Ron Winslow, "How a Breakthrough Quickly Broke Down for Johnson & Johnson," *The Wall Street Journal*, September 18, 1988, pp. A1, A5.
22. Barbara Davis, "Men Who Cook!" *Ken Davis Recipe News*, Spring 2008, pp. 1, 3.
23. Frank Bruni, "Price of Newsweek: It Depends," *Dallas Times Herald*, August 14, 1986, pp. S1, S20.
24. Vanessa O'Connell, "How Campbell Saw a Breakthrough Menu Turn into Leftovers," *The Wall Street Journal*, October 6, 1998, pp. A1, A12.
25. Janice Revell, "The Price Is Not Always Right," *Fortune*, May 14, 2001, p. 240; Indrajit Sinha, "Cost Transparency: The Net's Real Threat to Prices and Brands," *Harvard Business Review*, March–April 2000, pp. 43–50; and Walter Baker, Mike Marn, and Craig Zawada, "Price Smarter on the Net," *Harvard Business Review*, February 2001, pp. 122–27.
26. Peter Coy, "Can't Stop Guzzling," *BusinessWeek*, July 31, 2006, pp. 26–29.
27. Stephanie Clifford, "A Stress Test for Magazines: Raising Prices Without Losing Readers," *The Wall Street Journal*, April 13, 2009, pp. B1, B5.
28. Ellen Byron and Anjali Cordeiro, " P&G, Others Are Confident Higher Prices Will Stick," *The Wall Street Journal*, February 20, 2009, pp. B1, B2; and Jeff D. Opdyke, "In Colgate's Profit, a Breath of Fresh Air," *The Wall Street Journal*, January 29, 2009, p. C1.
29. "Message Is Clear: Higher Prices Deter Smoking," *USA Today*, April 9, 2009, p. 10A.
30. Linda Himelstein, "Webvan Left the Basics on the Shelf," *BusinessWeek*, July 23, 2001, p. 43.

Washburn Guitar: This case was edited by Steven Hartley. Sources: Burkhard Bilger, "String Theory, Building a Better Guitar," *The New Yorker*, May 14, 2007, p. 79; and the Washburn Guitar Web site (www.washburn.com).

Chapter 14

1. "U.S. Upstart Takes on TV Giants in Price War," *The Wall Street Journal*, April 15, 2008, pp. B1, B6; Vizio press release, February 4, 2009; and "The Vizio Story," www.vizio.com, accessed March 10, 2009.
2. The conditions favoring skimming versus penetration pricing are described in Kent B. Monroe, *Pricing: Making Profitable Decisions*, 3rd ed. (New York: McGraw-Hill/Irwin, 2003).
3. Jean-Noel Kapferer, *The New Strategic Brand Management: Creating and Sustaining Brand Equity*, 4th ed. (London: Kogan Page Ltd, 2008).
4. Stacy Meichtry, "What Your Time Is Really Worth," *The Wall Street Journal*, April 7–8, 2007, pp. P1, P4.
5. "Premium AA Alkaline Batteries," *Consumer Reports*, March 21, 2002, p. 54; Kemp Powers, "Assault and Batteries," *Forbes*, September 4, 2000, pp. 54, 56; and "Razor Burn at Gillette," *BusinessWeek*, June 18, 2001, p. 37.
6. Michael Levy and Barton A. Weitz, *Retailing Management*, 7th ed. (New York: McGraw-Hill/Irwin, 2010), pp. 501–2.
7. "Bet Your Bottom Dollar on 99 Cents," NYtimes.com, February 8, 2009. For further reading on odd-even pricing, see Mark Stiving and Russell S. Winer, "An Empirical Analysis of Price Endings with Scanner Data," *Journal of Consumer Research*, June 1997, pp. 57–67; and Robert M. Schindler, "Patterns of Rightmost Digits Used in Advertised Prices: Implications for Nine-Ending Effects," *Journal of Consumer Research*, September 1997, pp. 192–201.
8. For an overview on target pricing, see Stephan A. Butscher and Michael Laker, "Market Driven Product Development," *Marketing Management*, Summer 2000, pp. 48–53.
9. Thomas T. Nagle and Reed K. Holden, *The Strategy and Tactics of Pricing*, 4th ed. (Englewood Cliffs, NJ: Prentice Hall, 2009), pp. 243–49.
10. Robert J. Dolan and Hermann Simon, *Power Pricing: How Managing Price Transforms the Bottom Line* (New York: Free Press, 1996), p. 249.
11. "What Popcorn Prices Mean for Movies," *Advertising Age*, May 19, 2008, p. 4.
12. Peter M. Noble and Thomas S. Gruca, "Industrial Pricing: Theory and Managerial Practice," *Marketing Science* 18, no. 3 (1999), pp. 435–54.
13. George E. Belch and Michael A. Belch, *Introduction to Advertising and Promotion*, 8th ed. (New York: McGraw-Hill/Irwin, 2009).
14. Andrew D. Smith, "HDTVs Are Clearly Improved," *Dallas Morning News*, September 11, 2008, pp. 1D, 6D.
15. "In Lean Times, Big Companies Make a Grab for Market Share," *The Wall Street Journal*, September 5, 2003, pp. A1, A6.
16. "Is the Music Store Over?" *Business 2.0*, March 2004, pp. 115–19.
17. "How Dell Fine-Tunes Its PC Pricing to Gain Edge in a Slow Market," *The Wall Street Journal*, June 8, 2001, pp. A1, A8.
18. Ward A. Hanson and Kirthi Kalyanam, *Internet Marketing & Electronic Commerce* (Mason, OH: Thompson Higher Education, 2007).
19. "Are Minority Shoppers Treated Unfairly? An Expensive Reason to Care," www.diversity.com, accessed May 18, 2003; Florian Zettelmeyer, Fiona Scott Morton, and Jorge Silva-Risso, "How the Internet Lowers Prices: Evidence from Matched Survey and Automobile Transaction Data," *Journal of Marketing Research*, May 2006, pp. 168–81; and Fiona Scott Morton, Florian Zettelmeyer, and Jorge Silva-Risso, "Consumer Information and Discrimination: Does the Internet Affect the Pricing of New Cars to Women and Minorities?" *Quantitative Marketing and Economics* 1 (2003), pp. 65–92.
20. For an extended discussion on product complements and substitutes, see Allan D. Shocker, Barry L. Bayus, and Namwoon Kim, "Product Complements and Substitutes in Real World: The Relevance of Other Products," *Journal of Marketing*, January 2004, pp. 28–40.
21. Monroe, *Pricing*, pp. 396–97; and "Deciding When the Price Is Right," *Dallas Morning News*, May 23, 2007, pp. 1D, 3D.
22. Jagmohan S. Raju, Raj Sethuraman, and Sanjay K. Dhar, "National Brand-Store Brand Price Differential and Store Brand Market Share," *Pricing Strategy & Practice* 3, no. 2 (1995), pp. 17–24; and Akshay R. Rao, "The Quality of Price as a Quality Cue," *Journal of Marketing Research*, November 2005, pp. 401–5.
23. "The Price Is Not Always Right," *Fortune* May 14, 2001, p. 240. Also see, Kevin P. Coyne and John Horn, "Predicting Your Competitor's Reaction," *Harvard Business Review*, April 2009, pp. 90–97.
24. For an extended discussion about price wars, see Akshay R. Rao, Mark E. Bergen, and Scott Davis, "How to Fight a Price War," *Harvard Business Review*, March–April 2000, pp. 107–16.

25. Monroe, *Pricing*, chaps. 16 and 17.
26. Kenneth C. Manning, William O,. Bearden, and Randall L. Rose, "Development of a Theory of Retailer Response to Manufacturers' Everyday Low Cost Programs," *Journal of Retailing*, Spring 1998, pp. 107–37; "Everyday Low Profits," *Harvard Business Review*, March–April 1994, p. 13; Stephen J. Hoch, Xavier Dreze, and Mary E. Purk, "EDLP, Hi-Lo, and Margin Arithmetic," *Journal of Marketing*, October 1994, pp. 16–27; and Tibbett Speer, "Do Low Prices Bore Shoppers?" *American Demographics*, January 1994, pp. 11–13. Also see Barbara E. Kahn and Leigh McAlister, *The Grocery Revolution: The New Focus on the Consumer* (Reading, MA: Addison-Wesley Educational Publishers, 1996).
27. "Six Vitamin Firms Agree to Settle Price-Fixing Suit," *The Wall Street Journal*, October 11, 2000, p. B10.
28. "Price Fixing," *USA Today*, March 7, 2000, p. C1.
29. Ronald A. Cass, "When Price 'Fixing' Makes Sense," *The Wall Street Journal*, March 24–25, 2007, p. A10; and Joseph Pereira, "Discounters, Monitors Face Battle on Minimum Pricing," *The Wall Street Journal*, December 4, 2008, pp. A1, A8.

3M Greptile Grip Golf Glove: This case was written by Michael J. Vessey based on interviews with Dr. George Dierberger, 3M personnel, and these other published sources: "3M Introduces 3M Golf Glove with Greptile Grip," 3M Press Release, May 5, 2004; National Golf Foundation Research FAQs accessed on September 14, 2009; see www.ngf.org. National Sporting Goods Association: Consumer Purchases by Sport Report accessed on September 14, 2009; see www.nsga.org/files/public/ConsumerSportsEquipmentPurchasesby Sport.A.pdf. Ruder Finn press release case study; see www.ruderfinn.com/health-wellness/fitness/case-studies/3m-golf-glove.html.

Chapter 15

1. www.callawaygolf.com, accessed April 15, 2009; Stephanie Kang, "Callaway Will Use Retailers to Sell Goods Directly to Consumers Online," *The Wall Street Journal*, November 6, 2006, p. B5; and "Justin Timberlake Putting the 'Sexy' Back in Callaway Golf," sportingoodsnewswire.com, November 19, 2008.
2. Andrew Raskin, "Who's Minding the Store?" *Business 2.0*, February 2003, pp. 70–74.
3. "Eddie Bauer's Banner Time of Year," *Advertising Age*, October 1, 2001, p. 55.
4. www.generalmills.com, accessed March 15, 2009; www.nestle.com, accessed March 15, 2009; Emily Woon, "Cereal Partners Worldwide Exploits Developing Markets," www.euromonitor.com, November 1, 2007.
5. For an extensive discussion on wholesaling, see Anne T. Coughlan, Erin Anderson, Louis W. Stern, and Adel I. El-Ansary, *Marketing Channels*, 7th ed. (Upper Saddle River, NJ: Prentice Hall, 2006), chap. 12.
6. For an overview of vertical marketing systems, see Lou Pelton, Martha Cooper, David Strutton, and James R. Lumpkin, *Marketing Channels*, 3rd ed. (New York: McGraw-Hill/Irwin, 2005).
7. For a review of channel partnering, see Jakki J. Mohr and Robert E. Spekman, "Perfecting Partnerships," *Marketing Management*, Winter–Spring 1996, pp. 35–43.
8. "Avon Regains Some Allure," *Businessweek.com*, February 6, 2007; "Avon Reports First-Quarter Results," Avon press release, May 1, 2007; and "Avon Calls, China Opens the Door," *Businessweek.com*, February 28, 2006.
9. "Kohl's Seeks Cachet in Exclusive Fila Pact," *The Wall Street Journal*, November 13, 2007, p. B4.
10. "Nike Sale of Starter Marks Shift from Low-End Market," *The Wall Street Journal*, November 16, 2007, p. B4.
11. "Dell Treads Carefully into Selling PCs in Stores," *The Wall Street Journal*, January 3, 2008, p. B1.
12. Rafi A. Mohammed, Robert J. Fisher, Bernard J. Jaworski, and Gordon J. Paddison, *Internet Marketing: Building Advantage in a Networked Economy*, 2nd ed. (New York: McGraw-Hill/Irwin, 2004).
13. "Gillette Tries to Nick Schick in Japan," *The Wall Street Journal*, February 4, 1991, pp. B3, B4.
14. Ethan Smith, "Why a Grand Plan to Cut CD Prices Went Off the Track," *The Wall Street Journal*, June 4, 2004, pp. A1, A6; and "Feud with Seller Hurts Nike Sales, Shares," *Dallas Morning News*, June 28, 2003, p. 30.
15. "Dealer Surplus," *Forbes*, October 16, 2006, pp. 50–52; and Kevin Kelleher, "Giving Dealers a Raw Deal," *Business 2.0*, December 2004, pp. 82–83.
16. Representative studies that explore the dimensions and use of power and influence in marketing channels include the following: Kenneth A. Hunt, John T. Mentzer, and Jeffrey E. Danes, "The Effect of Power Sources on Compliance in a Channel of Distribution: A Causal Model," *Journal of Business Research*, October 1987, pp. 377–98; John F. Gaski, "Interrelations among a Channel Entity's Power Sources: Impact of the Exercise of Reward and Coercion on Expert, Referent, and Legitimate Power Sources," *Journal of Marketing Research*, February 1986, pp. 62–67; Gary Frazier and John O. Summers, "Interfirm Influence Strategies and Their Application within Distribution Channels," *Journal of Marketing*, Summer 1984, pp. 43–55; George H. Lucas and Larry G. Gresham, "Power Conflict, Control, and the Application of Contingency Theory in Channels of Distribution," *Journal of the Academy of Marketing Science*, Summer 1985, pp. 27–37; F. Robert Dwyer and Julie Gassenheimer, "Relational Roles and Triangle Dramas: Effects on Power Play and Sentiments in Industrial Channels," *Marketing Letters* 3 (1992), pp. 187–200; Jean L. Johnson, Tomoaki Sakano, Joseph A. Cote, and Naoto Onzo, "The Exercise of Interfirm Power and Its Repercussions in U.S.-Japanese Channel Relationships," *Journal of Marketing*, April 1993, pp. 1–10; and Janice M. Payan and Richard G. McFarland, "Decomposing Influence Strategies: Argument Structure and Dependence as Determinants of the Effectiveness of Influence Strategies in Gaining Channel Member Compliance," *Journal of Marketing*, July 2005, pp. 66–79.
17. *Slotting Allowances in the Retail Grocery Industry* (Washington, DC: Federal Trade Commission, November 2003). Also see Paul N. Bloom, Gregory T. Gundlach, and Joseph P. Cannon, "Slotting Allowances and Fees: Schools of Thought and Views of Practicing Managers," *Journal of Marketing*, April 2000, pp. 92–109; and William L. Wilkie, Debra M. Desrochers, and Gregory T. Gundlach, "Marketing Research and Public Policy: The Case of Slotting Fees," *Journal of Public Policy & Marketing*, Fall 2002, pp. 275–89.
18. For a contemporary and comprehensive treatment of legal issues pertaining to marketing channels, see *Antitrust Law and Economics of Product Distribution* (Chicago: American Bar Association, 2006).

ACT II Microwave Popcorn: This case was prepared by Steven Hartley and Michael Vessey from company sources and State of the Industry Report: Microwave Popcorn, *Snack World*, May 2009, p. 30. Accessed September 10, 2009 at www.sfa.org.

Chapter 16

1. "Apple, Nokia, and Dell Top Supply Chain List," *Industry Week*, May 30, 2008, pp. 15–16; iPhone 3G Now Available in 22 Other Countries," *MacWorld*, August 22, 2008; and "The Apple iPhone Supply Chain, shmula.com, accessed January 5, 2009.
2. "The Physical Internet: A Survey of Logistics," *The Economist*, June 17, 2006.
3. David Simchi-Levi, Philip Kaminsky, and Edith Simchi-Levi, *Designing and Managing the Supply Chain*, 3rd ed. (New York: McGraw-Hill/Irwin, 2007), p. 6; and Tim Clark, "Driving at the Speed of Demand," *Consumer Goods Technology*, October 2005, pp. 15–18.

4. Gareth MacDonald, "FDA Launches Global Supply Chain Pilot Scheme," in-pharmatechnologist.com, accessed January 15, 2009.
5. Aleda V. Roth, Andy A. Tsay, Madeleine E. Pullman, and John V. Gray, "Reaping What You Sow?" *International Commerce Review*, Autumn 2008, pp. 37–47.
6. Jeffrey McCracken, "Ford Seeks Big Savings by Overhauling Supply System," *The Wall Street Journal*, September 29, 2005, p. A11; "Beyond Buying," *The Wall Street Journal*, March 10, 2008, p. R8; April Terreri, "Driving Efficiencies in Automotive Logistics," inbound logistics.com, January 2004; and Robyn Meredith, "Harder Than Hype," *Forbes*, April 16, 2001, pp. 188–94.
7. Major portions of this discussion are based on Sunil Chopra and Peter Meindl, *Supply Chain Management: Strategy, Planning, and Operations*, 3rd ed. (Upper Saddle River, NJ: Prentice Hall, 2007), chaps. 1–3; and Hau L. Lee, "The Triple-A Supply Chain," *Harvard Business Review*, October 2004, pp. 102–12.
8. Kevin O'Marah, "The 2008 Supply Chain Top 25: What Makes a Leader," amrresearch.com, accessed June 4, 2008; and Thomas A. Foster, "World's Best-Run Supply Chains Stay on Top Regardless of the Competition," *Global Logistics & Supply Chain Strategies*, February 2006, pp. 27–41.
9. This discussion is based on Kathryn Jones, "The Dell Way," *Business 2.0*, February 2003, pp. 61–66; Charles Fishman, "The Wal-Mart You Don't Know," *Fast Company*, December 2003, pp. 68–80; "Michael Dell: Still Betting on the Future of Online Commerce and Supply Chain Efficiencies," *Knowledge@Wharton,* September 7, 2006; and Chopra and Meindl, *Supply Chain Mangement*.
10. Portions of this discussion are based on Simchi-Levi et al., *Designing and Managing the Supply Chain*; Chopra and Meindl, *Supply Chain Management*. Also, Fan Wu, Sengun Yeniyurt, Daekwan Kim, and S. Tamer Cavusgil, "The Impact of Information Technology on Supply Chain Capabilities and Firm Performance: A Resource-Based View," *Industrial Marketing Management*, October 2006, pp. 593–604.
11. Simchi-Levi et al., *Designing and Managing the Supply Chain*, p. 6.
12. Toby G. Gooley, "How Logistics Drive Customer Service," *Traffic Management*, January 1996, p. 46.
13. Christina Passariello, "Logistics Are in Vogue with Designers," *The Wall Street Journal*, June 27, 2008, p. B1; Bill Mongelluzzo, "Logistics Makeover at Saks: Retailer Says Changes in Supply Chain Practices Have Reduced Inventory and Costs," *The Journal of Commerce*, October 24, 2005; and Michael Levy and Barton A. Weitz, *Retailing Management*, 6th ed. (New York: McGraw-Hill/Irwin, 2008).
14. "Unisys Selects DHL as Global Lead Provider for Customized Logistics Solutions," DHL press release, May 22, 2006.
15. Robert J. Bowman, "Pursuing 'On Demand,' IBM Shakes Up Its Supply Chain," www.supplychainbrain.com, accessed April 2003.
16. "Use of 3PLs by Fortune 500 Companies Remains Strong, According to Armstrong & Associates," *Global Logistics & Supply Chain Strategies*, March 27, 2009, pp. 16–17.
17. Douglas M. Lambert, *Supply Chain Management: Processes, Partnerships, and Performance*, 2nd ed. (Sarasota, FL: Supply Chain Management Institute, 2006).
18. Kris Maher, "Global Goods Jugglers," *The Wall Street Journal*, June 5, 2005, pp. A11, A12.
19. Jeffrey Davis and Martha Baer, "Some Assembly Required," *Business 2.0*, February 12, 2001, pp. 67–78.
20. Jean Murphy, "Better Forecasting, S&OP Support Transformation at Campbell's Soup Co.," *Global Logistics & Supply Chain Strategies*, June 2004, pp. 28–30.
21. Steve Miller, "Recycling Becomes Electric for CE Brands," *BrandWeek*, May 13, 2008, p. 4; "Don't Toss Out That Old Gadget," *Newsweek*, November 3, 2008, p. E8; Lorraine Woellert, "HP Wants Your Old PCs Back," *BusinessWeek*, April 10, 2006, pp. 82–83; and "Hewlett-Packard's Design for Supply Chain Program," *Global Logistics & Supply Chain Strategies*, December 2005, p. 40.
22. Brian Hindo, "Everything Old Is New Again," *BusinessWeek*, September 25, 2006, pp. 64–70.
23. Doug Bartholomew, "IT Delivers for UPS," *Industry Week*, August 2002, pp. 35–36.

Amazon.com: This case is based on material available on the company Web site and the following sources: Robert D. Hof and Heather Green, "How Amazon Cleared That Hurdle," *BusinessWeek*, February 4, 2002, p. 60; Robert D. Hof, "We've Never Said We Had to Do It All," *BusinessWeek*, October 15, 2001, p. 53; and Amazon.com 2008 Annual Report, press releases, and media image library. Accessed September 12, 2009. Mark Veverka, "The World's Best Retailer," *Barron's*, March 30, 2009. See http://online.barrons.com/article/SB123819715466061661.html.

Chapter 17

1. "Technology: Front & Forward," *The Wall Street Journal*, February 17, 2009, p. R2; Jon Fine, "Bargain-Rate Buzz," *BusinessWeek*, February 9, 2009, p. 65; Anne D'Innocenzio, "E-Retailers Push E-Mail Discounts to Lure Shoppers," *Marketing News*, November 15, 2008, p. 30; Anne D'Innocenzio, "Online Retailers See Surge on 'Cyber Monday,'" *Associated Press Financial Wire*, December 3, 2008; Pete Barlas, "Online Retailers Get Sprinkling of Yule Cheer, 'Cyber Monday' Sales Up 15%," *Investor's Business Daily*, December 4, 2008, p. A4, and "Plunkett's Retail Industry," Plunkett Research, Ltd., www.plunkettresearch.com/Industries/Retailing/Trends, accessed February 21, 2009.
2. "The Fortune 500," *Fortune*, May 5, 2008, p. F-1; *The 2008 World Factbook* (Washington, DC: Central Intelligence Agency, 2008); *Statistical Abstract of the United States: 2009*, 128th ed. (Washington, DC: U.S. Department of Commerce, Bureau of the Census, 2008), Table 19, Large Metropolitan Statistical Areas.
3. *Statistical Abstract of the United States: 2009*, Table 1009, Retail Trade and Food Services.
4. "The Global 2000," *Forbes*, April 21, 2008, p. 188.
5. "Corporate Facts: Wal-Mart By the Numbers," Wal-Mart Stores, Inc., Facts & News, www.walmartstores.com, accessed February 22, 2009.
6. "Research and Markets: Learn About Sustainability & Retailing, 2008," *Business Wire*, February 23, 2009; "Research and Markets: Going Green Isn't Just Good for the Environment—It's Good for Business Too," *Business Wire*, February 20, 2009; Jason Kirby, "Going Green for Selfish Reasons," *MacLean's*, December 8, 2008, p. 39; and Adam Aston, "Wal-Mart," *BusinessWeek*, December 22, 2008, p. 48.
7. "Retail Trade—Establishments, Employees, and Payroll," *Statistical Abstract of the United States: 2009*, 128th ed. (Washington, DC: U.S. Department of Commerce, Bureau of the Census, 2008), Table 1008; "County Business Patterns," Bureau of the Census, www.censtats.census.gov/cgi-bin/cbpnaic/cbpdetl.pl, accessed February 22, 2009.
8. "Economic Impact of Franchised Businesses," International Franchise Association, www.franchise.org, accessed February 22, 2009.
9. "Top 10 Franchises for 2009," 2009 Franchise 500, Entrepreneur.com, www.entrepreneur.com/franchise500/index.html, accessed February 22, 2009; and Scott Shane and Chester Spell, "Factors for New Franchise Success," *Sloan Management Review*, Spring 1998, pp. 43–50.
10. "Lufthansa to Replace Check-In Terminals," *Airline Industry Information*, February 13, 2009; "Hilton Hotels Corporation Place #2 In Information Week 500," *Business Wire*, September 30, 2008; "Check This Out: Palm Beach County Library System Adds Self-Service Checkouts," *South Florida Sun-Sentinel*, February 17, 2009; "Research Shows Consumers Seek More Self-Service Options Due to Pressures of Price and Time," *Business Wire*, January 12, 2009; and Peter C. Honebein and Roy F. Cammarano, "Customers at Work," *Marketing Management*, January/February 2006, pp. 26–31.

11. Michael A. Wiles, "The Effect of Customer Service on Retailers' Shareholder Wealth: The Role of Availability and Reputation Cues," *Journal of Retailing*, 2007, pp. 19–31; Cate T. Corcoran, "Nordstrom 'Simplifies' Customer Satisfaction," *Women's Wear Daily*, March 22, 2007, p. 8; and Vanessa O'Connell, "Posh Retailers Pile on Perks for Top Customers," *The Wall Street Journal*, April 26, 2007, p. D1.
12. Donna Goodison, "Circuit City Closing to Boost Big-Box Stores," *The Boston Herald*, February 1, 2009, p. 23; and "Staples Get Investment Grade Ratings on Senior Unsecured Debt From Fitch, Moody's," *Midnight Trader*, January 13, 2009.
13. "Hypermarkets Report Record Sales," *China Post*, January 20, 2009; Mark Hamstra, "Hypermarkets Capture Grocery Share in Shanghai," *Supermarket News*, June 2, 2008, p. 28; "Hypermarkets Doing Well In Some Markets," *Americas Food and Drink Insights*, November 1, 2008; and Carrefour Web site, www.carrefour.com/cdc/group/our-business/our-stores/our-stores-folder/hypermarket.html, accessed February 25, 2009.
14. "Wal-Mart to Open Few Supercenters in 2009, 2010," Associated Press Financial Wire, October 28, 2008; "About That Wal-Mart Supercenter Near You," *The San Diego Union-Tribune*, August 23, 2008, p. NC-6.
15. Andy Johns, "Healthy Vending," *Chattanooga Times Free Press*, January 12, 2009, p. B2; Alan Wolf, "Best Buy Testing Airport Vending Machines," *Video Business*, August 11, 2008, p. 6; and Gene G. Marcial, "Vending Machines Are Learning to Love Plastic," *BusinessWeek*, August 13, 2007, p. 86.
16. Leslie Berlin, "Phones As Credit Cards? Americans Must Wait," *The New York Times*, January 25, 2009, p. 4; Edward West, Dialing In Yet More Impulse Buyers," *Business Day*, January 31, 2009; Elliot Maras, "The Case for Vending," *Automatic Merchandiser*, January 2009, p. 28; and Joe Astrouski, "Eastern Illinois U. Vending Machines Go Green," *University Wire*, November 21, 2008.
17. "DMA Encourages Catalog and Direct Mail Recycling," *PR Newswire*, May 23, 2007; and Blake Gopnik, "The IKEA Idea: What to Make of these Modern Times," *The Washington Post*, August 17, 2008, p. M08.
18. Ira Teinowitz and Nat Ives, "No Day Is a Good Day for No Mail," *Advertising Age*, February 9, 2009, p. 8; "A Zip-code Screen for Catalog Customers," *The Wall Street Journal*, June 24, 2008, p. B1; and Richard H. Levey, "It's All About Me," *Direct*, November 1, 2008.
19. Paula Andruss, "Personalized URLS: Tailor-Made Web Sites Deliver the Right Content," *Marketing News*, September 1, 2008, p. 10; Crystal Uppercue, "2009: The Year of More," *Marketing News*, November 1, 2008, p. 20; and see award information at www.multichannelmerchant.com/toolbox/awards, accessed March 1, 2009.
20. "QVC Extends Global Reach to Italy," *PR Newswire*, September 26, 2008; and "Fact Sheet" from the QVC Web site, www.qvc.com/qic, accessed March 2, 2009.
21. Christine H. O'Toole, "Attention, QVC Shoppers. . ." *The Washington Post*, January 28, 2009, p. C2; "Ellen DeGeneres Says 'HALO' to QVC," *PR Newswire*, January 14, 2009; "QVC Mulls Further Channel Developments," *Retail Week*, October 17, 2008; Richard Mullins and Michael Messano, "HSN's New Deal," *Tampa Tribune*, August 20, 2008, p. 1; Laura Petrecca, "QVC Shops for Ideas for Future Sales," *USA TODAY*, May 5, 2008, p. 1B; and Jon Fine, "Lights, Camera, Shop!" *BusinessWeek*, January 12, 2009, p. 62.
22. "Walmart.com Kicks Off 'Cyber Monday' with Unbelievable Prices on Over 150 Top Online Gifts, and Extends Event for Five Straight Days," www.walmart.com; Online Specials Feature Savings of Up to 30 Percent, With Many Items Available for Free Shipping with Site to Store and 97-cent Shipping to Home," *PR Newswire*, December 1, 2008; "Over 875 Million Consumers Have Shopped Online," *The Nielsen Company News Release*, January 28, 2008; and "eMarketer Revises E-Commerce Forecast," emarketer.com, March 5, 2009.
23. "EBay Marketplaces Fact Sheet," eBay Web site, http://news.ebay.com/fastfacts.cfm, accessed March 6, 2009.
24. "HSN, Inc. to Report Fourth Quarter and Fiscal 2008 Results on March 3rd," *PR Newswire*, February 10, 2009; "Text, Shop & Ship," *Marketing News*, May 1, 2008, p. 6; and Christina Binkley, "On Style—Gucci-Stalking: New Sites Make Shopping a Game," *The Wall Street Journal*, May 1, 2008, p. D1.
25. Nicole Paitsel, "Use Web to Help Shop and Ship," *Richmond Times Dispatch*, December 7, 2008, p. J5; and Stephen Thompson, "Is Your Snazzy New Site Cloaked in Invisibility?" *Advertising Age*, October 13, 2008, p. 24.
26. "Chinese City's Internet Cafes Pushed to Open Source," *The New Zealand Herald*, December 4, 2008; "Analysis of China's $20 Billion Internet Café Industry, with an Estimated 185,000 Cafes," *Asian Business Newsweekly*, January 27, 2009, p. 15.
27. "Power of Direct Marketing Report," direct Marketing Association, 2009, p. 108.
28. "Do Not Call Registrations Permanent and Fees Telemarketers Pay To Access Registry Set," *States News Service*, April 10, 2008; and Deborah L. Vence, "Majority Rules," *Marketing News*, February 15, 2006, p. 4.
29. "Direct Selling by the Numbers," Direct Selling Association, http://www.dsa.org/pubs/numbers/, accessed March 6, 2009.
30. Betsy Verckey, "Avon Products Boosts Restructuring, Freezes Hiring," *The Associated Press*, February 19, 2009; "Avon Reports Fourth-Quarter and 2008 Results," *PR Newswire*, February 3, 2009; and "Herbalife Receives Approval for Five Provincial Direct-Selling Licenses In China," *Drug Week*, August 8, 2008.
31. Morris Kaplan, "Direct Selling Grows on the Net," *Weekend Australian*, March 7, 2009, p. 32; and "Mary Kay Inc. Offers Women Compelling Solution to Economic Downturn Through Direct Selling," *Business Wire*, March 3, 2009.
32. Dinesh Kumar Gauri, Minakshi Trivedi, and Dhruv Grewal, "Understanding the Determinants of Retail Strategy: An Empirical Analysis," *Journal of Retailing*, September 2008, p. 256.
33. The following discussion is adapted from William T. Gregor and Eileen M. Friars, *Money Merchandizing: Retail Revolution in Consumer Financial Services* (Cambridge, MA: Management Analysis Center, Inc., 1982).
34. Francis J. Mulhern and Robert P. Leon, "Implicit Price Bundling of Retail Products: A Multiproduct Approach to Maximizing Store Profitability," *Journal of Marketing*, October 1991, pp. 63–76.
35. Marc Vanhuele and Xavier Dreze, "Measuring the Price Knowledge Shoppers Bring to the Store," *Journal of Marketing*, October 2002, p. 72–85.
36. "No Frills Store Go Above and Beyond to Bring Great Savings to Customers Everyday," *Canada News Wire*, February 2, 2009; Gwen Ortmeyer, John A. Quelch, and Walter Salmon, "Restoring Credibility to Retail Pricing," *Sloan Management Review*, Fall 1991, pp. 55–66.
37. William B. Dodds, "In Search of Value: How Price and Store Name Information Influence Buyers' Product Perceptions," *Journal of Consumer Marketing*, Spring 1991, pp. 15–24.
38. "Pier 1 Imports, Inc. Reports Third Quarter Financial Results," *Business Wire*, December 18, 2008; Leonard L. Berry, "Old Pillars of New Retailing," *Harvard Business Review*, April 2001, pp. 131–37.
39. Eric Anderson and Duncan Simester, "Mind Your Pricing Cues," *Harvard Business Review*, September 2003, pp. 96–103.
40. Julie Baker, A Parasuraman, Dhruv Grewal, and Glenn B. Voss, "The Influence of Multiple Store Environment Cues on Perceived Merchandise Value and Patronage Intentions," *Journal of Marketing*, April 2002, pp. 120–41.
41. Hyeong Min Kim, "Consumer' Responses to Price Presentation Formats in Rebate Advertisements," *Journal of Retailing*, no. 4 (2006), pp. 309–17.

42. Lloyd C. Harris, "Fraudulent Return Proclivity: An Empirical Analysis," *Journal of Retailing*, December 2008, p. 461; "Survey: Returns Fraud and Abuse Costs Retailers $15.5 Billion," *Apparel*, July 1, 2008, p. 8; Kathy Grannis, "Retail Losses Hit $41.6 Billion Last Year," National Retail Security Survey, National Retail Federation, www.nrf.com, accessed March 8, 2009; and Sharna Johnson, "Businesses See Shoplifting Spike," *Clovis News Journal*, February 1, 2009.

43. Rita Koselka, "The Schottenstein Factor," *Forbes*, September 28, 1992, pp. 104, 106.

44. Kathy Lynn Gray, "Buy and Save in Bulk at Warehouse Clubs," *The Columbus Dispatch*, August 4, 2008, p. 10C; and "Industry Overview: Warehouse Clubs and Superstores," Hoovers, www.hoovers.com, accessed March 8, 2009.

45. "Merchants Go All-out to Compete with Malls; the Downtown and Outlet Stores Fight for Dwindling Shopper Dollars with Sales, Longer Hours, and Free Stuff," *Portland Press Herald*, November 28, 2008, p. A1; and "Shinsegae to Open its 20th Outlet Store in China," *Yonhap*, February 25, 2009.

46. "Fast Facts," Dollar General Web site, www.dollargeneral.com, accessed March 9, 2009.

47. "WEM Trivia," West Edmonton Mall Web site, www.westedmall.com, accessed March 9, 2009.

48. Ernesto Portillo, "Home Depot Part of Center Plan," *McClatchy-Tribune Business News*, November 20, 2008; and Lisa A. Bernard, "Anchor ID'd for 'Big Box' Power Center," *Dayton Daily News*, July 19, 2007.

49. Pierre Martineau, "The Personality of the Retail Store," *Harvard Business Review*, January–February 1958, p. 47

50. Julie Baker, Dhruv Grewal, and A. Parasuraman, "The Influence of Store Environment on Quality Inferences and Store Image," *Journal of the Academy of Marketing Science*, Fall 1994, pp. 328–39; Howard Barich and Philip Kotler, "A Framework for Marketing Image Management," *Sloan Management Review*, Winter 1991, pp. 94–104; Susan M. Keaveney and Kenneth A. Hunt, "Conceptualization and Operationalization of Retail Store Image: A Case of Rival Middle-Level Theories," *Journal of the Academy of Marketing Science*, Spring 1992, pp. 165–75; James C. Ward, Mary Jo Bitner and John Barnes, "Measuring the Prototypicality and Meaning of Retail Environments," *Journal of Retailing*, Summer 1992, p. 194; and Dhruv Grewal, R. Krishnan, Julie Baker, and Norm Burin, "The Effect of Store Name, Brand Name and Price Discounts on Consumers' Evaluations and Purchase Intentions," *Journal of Retailing*, Fall 1998, pp. 331–52. For a review of the store image literature, see Mary R. Zimmer and Linda L. Golden, "Impressions of Retail Stores: A Content Analysis of Consumer Images," *Journal of Retailing*, Fall 1988, pp. 265–93.

51. Mary Jo Bitner, "Servicescapes: The Impact of Physical Surroundings on Customers and Employees," *Journal of Marketing*, April 1992, pp. 57–71.

52. Jans-Benedict Steenkamp and Michel Wedel, "Segmenting Retail Markets on Store Image Using a Consumer-Based Methodology," *Journal of Retailing*, Fall 1991, p. 300; and Philip Kotler, "Atmospherics as a Marketing Tool," *Journal of Retailing* 49 (Winter 1973–74), p. 61.

53. Roger A. Kerin, Ambuj Jain, and Daniel L. Howard, "Store Shopping Experience and Consumer Price-Quality-Value Perceptions," *Journal of Retailing*, Winter 1992, pp. 376–97.

54. "Cannondale's 2008 PoweRanking Study," *Progressive Grocer*, November 3, 2008; "Category Management Takes a Step Forward, Becomes CMAR," *MMR*, April 16, 2007, p. 26; Kusam L. Ailwadi and Bari Harlam, "An Empirical Analysis of the Determinants of Retail Margins: The Role of Store-Brand Share," *Journal of Marketing*, January 2004, pp. 147–65; Joseph Tarnowski, "And the Awards Went to . . ." *Progressive Grocer, April 15, 2004;* Betsy Spethmann, "Shelf Sets," *Promo*, May 1, 2004, p. 6; and "Study Shows Continued Support for Category Management," *CSNews Online*, March 17, 2004.

55. John Davis, *Measuring Marketing* (Singapore: Wiley and Sons, 2007), p. 46.

56. Paul W. Farris, Neil T. Bendle, Phillip E. Pfeifer, David J. Reibstein, *Marketing Metrics* (Philadelphia: Wharton School Publishing, 2006), p. 106; Jerry Useem, "Simply Irresistible," *Fortune*, March 19, 2007, pp. 107–12; "Apple 2.0," www.blogs.business2.com; Steve Lohr, "Apple, a Success at Stores, Bets Big on Fifth Avenue," *The New York Times*, May 19, 2006; Jim Dalrymple, "Inside the Apple Stores," *MacWorld*, June 2007, pp. 16–17; and Davis, *Measuring Marketing*, pp. 280–81.

57. The wheel of retailing theory was originally proposed by Malcolm P. McNair, "Significant Trends and Development in the Postwar Period," in *Competitive Distribution in a Free, High-Level Economy and Its Implications for the University*, ed. A. B. Smith, (Pittsburgh: University of Pittsburgh Press, 1958), pp. 1–25; also see Stephen Brown, "The Wheel of Retailing—Past and Future," *Journal of Retailing*, Summer 1990, pp. 143–49; and Malcolm P. McNair and Eleanor May, "The Next Revolution of the Retailing Wheel," *Harvard Business Review*, September–October 1978, pp. 81–91.

58. Emily Bryson York and Natalie Zmuda, "McDonald's Sends McCafe onto Fashion Week Catwalks," *Advertising Age*, February 9, 2009, p. 2; Lauren Sheperd, "McDonald's Posts Profit," *The Associated Press*, January 26, 2009; Michael Arndt, "McDonald's 24/7," *BusinessWeek*, February 5, 2007, p. 64; and "Resolved: No Trans Fats in 2007," *BusinessWeek*, January 15, 2007, p. 27.

59. William R. Davidson, Albert D. Bates, and Stephen J. Bass, "Retail Life Cycle," *Harvard Business Review*, November–December 1976, pp. 89–96.

60. Anne Marie Doherty, "Who Will Weather Economic Storms on High Street?" *The Western Mail*, January 1, 2009, p. 29.

61. Umut Konus, Peter C. Verhoef, and Scott A. Neslin, "Multichannel Shopper Segments and Their Covariates," *Journal of Retailing*, December 2008, p. 398; Robert A. Peterson and Sridhar Balasubramanian, "Retailing in the 21st Century: Reflections and Prologue to Research," *Journal of Retailing*, Spring 2002, pp. 9–16.

62. Jim Carter and Norman Sheehan, "From Competition to Cooperation: E-Tailing's Integration with Retailing," *Business Horizons*, March–April 2004, pp. 71–8.

63. Ranjay Gulati and Janson Garino, "Getting the Right Mix of Bricks and Clicks," *Harvard Business Review*, May–June 2000, pp. 107–14; Marshal L. Fisher, Ananth Raman, and Anna Sheen McClelland, "Rocket Science Retailing Is Almost Here: Are You Ready?" *Harvard Business Review*, July–August 2000, pp. 115–24; Charla Mathwick, Naresh Malhotra, and Edward Rigdon, "Experiential Value: Conceptualization, Measurement and Application in the Catalog and Internet Shopping Environment," *Journal of Retailing*, Spring 2001, pp. 39–56; Lawrence M. Bellman, "Bricks and Mortar: 21st Century Survival," *Business Horizons*, May–June 2001, pp. 21–28; Zhan G. Li and Nurit Gery, "E-Tailing—for All Products?" *Business Horizons*, November–December 2000, pp. 49–54; and Bill Hanifin, "Go Forth and Multichannel: Loyalty Programs Need Knowledge Base," *Marketing News*, August 27, 2001, p. 23.

64. Robert Berner, "J.C. Penney Gets The Net," *BusinessWeek*, May7, 2007, p. 70; Multi-Channel Integration: *The New Retail Battleground* (Columbus, OH: PricewaterhouseCoopers, March 2001); and Richard Last, "JC Penney Internet Commerce," presentation at Southern Methodist University, February 12, 2001.

65. Nanette Byrnes, "Secrets of the Male Shopper," *BusinessWeek*, September 4, 2006, p. 44; Simon Brooke, "It's Different for Guys. Retailers Are Rethinking the Shop Floor with Men in Mind," *Financial Times*, April 28, 2007, p. 7; and Velitchka D. Kaltcheva and Baron A. Weitz, "When Should a Retailer Create an Exciting Store Environment?" *Journal of Marketing*, January 2006, p. 107–18.

Mall of America: This case was written by David P. Brennan and is based on an interview with Maureen Cahill and materials provided by Mall of America.

Chapter 18

1. Joseph Fullman, "Collective Communication," *Promo*, January 1, 2009, p. 18; Amy Johannes, "Sampling by Surprise," *Promo*, March 1, 2009, p. 10; Brian Quinton, "Game On!" *Promo*, February 1, 2009, p. 28; Richard Tedesco, "Big Dreams," *Promo*, November 1, 2008, p. 14; Richard Tedesco, "Alternative Viewing," *Promo*, December 1, 2008, p. 8; "Email Marketing: Time to Can Spam and Get Personal," *Precision Marketing*, December 15, 2008, p. 25; and Alyssa S. Groom, "Integrated Marketing Communication Anticipating the 'Age of Engage'" *Communication Research Trends*, December 1, 2008, p. 3.
2. Philip J. Kitchen, Ilchul Kim, and Don E. Schultz, "Integrated Marketing Communications: Practice Leads Theory," *Journal of Advertising Research*, December 2008, pp. 531–46; Bob Liodice, "Essentials for Integrated Marketing," *Advertising Age*, June 9, 2008, p. 26; Shu-pei Tsai, *Journal of Advertising* 34 (Winter 2005), pp. 11–23.
3. Wilbur Schramm, "How Communication Works," in *The Process and Effects of Mass Communication*, Wilbur Schramm, ed., (Urbana, IL: University of Illinois Press, 1955), pp. 3–26.
4. E. Cooper and M. Jahoda, "The Evasion of Propaganda," *Journal of Psychology* 22 (1947), pp. 15–25; H. Hyman and P. Sheatsley, "Some Reasons Why Information Campaigns Fail," *Public Opinion Quarterly* 11 (1947), pp. 412–23; and J. T. Klapper, *The Effects of Mass Communication* (New York: Free Press, 1960), chap. VII.
5. "Translation Bloopers," Miami News, www.miamibeach411.com, April 5, 2005; and Cynthia L. Kemper, "Biting Wax Tadpole, Other Faux Pas," *Denver Post*, August 3, 1997, p. G4.
6. Rik Pieters and Michel Wedel, "Attention Capture and Transfer in Advertising: Brand Pictorial, and Text-Size Effects," *Journal of Marketing*, April 2004, pp. 36–50.
7. Adapted from American Marketing Association, Resource Library, Dictionary, www.marketingpower.com/_layouts/Dictionary.aspx?dLetter=P, accessed March 14, 2009.
8. David Robinson, "Public Relations Comes of Age," *Business Horizons* 49 (2006), pp. 247–56; and Dick Martin, "Gilded and Gelded: Hard-Won Lessons from the PR Wars," *Harvard Business Review*, October 2003, pp. 44–54.
9. "McDonald's All-Digital Corporate Responsibility Report," *U.S. Newswire*, October 29, 2008; "RSS, Blogs, Podcast and Social Media Experts to Share Knowledge at PR Online Convergence Conference," *Business Wire*, April 11, 2007; "Business and the Media Forum Focuses on Social Media," *Business Wire*, July 9, 2007; Sarah Murray, "Public Relations: The Ease of Online Communication Is Undermining Companies' Control of Their Image and Reputation," *Financial Times*, November 8, 2006, p. 14; and Matthew Creamer, "Slowly, Marketers Learn How to Let Go and Let Blog," *Advertising Age*, October 31, 2005, p. 1.
10. Marsha d. Loda and Barbara Carrick Coleman, "Sequence Matters: A More Effective Way to Use Advertising and Publicity," *Journal of Advertising Research* 45 (December 2005), pp. 362–71.
11. Kusum L. Ailawadi, Scott A. Neslin, and Karen Gedenk, "Pursuing the Value-Conscious Consumer: Store Brands versus National Brand Promotions," *Journal of Marketing*, January 2001 , pp. 71–8.
12. Nikki Hopewell, "The Rules of Engagement: A Bevy of Rules and Best Practices Govern Promotions and Contests," *Marketing News*, June 1, 2008, p. 6; and Gerard Predergast, Yi-Zheng Shi, and Ka-Man Cheung, "Behavioural Response to Sales Promotion Tools," *International Journal of Advertising*, (2005), pp. 467–486.
13. Adapted from American Marketing Association, Resource Library, Dictionary, http://www.marketingpower.com/_layouts/Dictionary.aspx?dLetter=D, accessed March 15, 2009.
14. "New Media vs. Traditional: When Progress Meets Tradition," *Marketing Week*, January 22, 2009, p. 23; Richard H. Levey, "It's All About Me," *Direct*, November 1, 2008, p. 15; "Kraft Provides Recipe for Mobile-Marketing Success," *Advertising Age*, January 26, 2009, p. 12; Natalie Zmuda, "Marketers Push for Mobile Tuesday as the New Black Friday," *Advertising Age*, December 1, 2008, p. 21; "Multitasking Sports Viewers Engaged with Advertising," *PR Newswire US*, June 28, 2007; "How Is Multitasking Affecting TV Networks and Online Video Sites?" *Business Wire*, February 6, 2007; and Greg Lindsay, "Demanding Boomers, MultiTasking Gen Yers Decide What, How, When," *Advertising Age*, January 2, 2006, p. 22.
15. Dunn Sunnoo and Lynn Y. S. Lin, "Sales Effects of Promotion and Advertising," *Journal of Advertising Research* 18 (October 1878), pp. 37–42.
16. Andrew Scott, "The New Frontier," *Promo*, April 1, 2006, p. 16; John Palmer, "Animal Instincts," *Promo*, May 2001, pp. 25–33; and Purina Web site, http://www.purina.com/incredible-dog-challenge/2009-schedule/index.aspx, accessed March 15, 2009.
17. Remco Prins and Peter C. Verhoef, "Marketing Communication Drivers of Adoption Timing of a New E-Service Among Existing Customers," *Journal of Marketing* 71 (April 2007), pp. 169–83.
18. Anders Parment, "Distribution Strategies for Volume and Premium Brands in Highly Competitive Consumer Markets," *Journal of Retailing and Consumer Services*, July 2008, p. 250; and R. Srinivasan and Archana K. Murthy, "Integrated Brand Building Process: A Special Case," *International Journal of Business Research*, June 1, 2008, p. 174.
19. "McDonald's CMO: Erase Borders and Create Bonds," *Marketing News*, October 15, 2008, p. 20; Lauren McKay, "Holiday Humbug: Will Grinch Steal Retail's Favorite Season?" *CRM Magazine*, December 1, 2008, p. 19.
20. Terry Box, "Pressure's Rising for Ford Dealers," *Dallas Morning News*, February 10, 2007; and Richard Truett, "Ford to Dealers: We'll Support Sales," *Automotive News*, June 18, 2007, p. 3.
21. Hollie Shaw, "A Case of Much Ado?" *National Post*, October 10, 2008, p. 12; Sheng Yuan, "Public Response to Direct-to-Consumer Advertising of Prescription Drugs," *Journal of Advertising Research*, March 2008, pp. 30–41, and Fusun F. Gonul, Franklin Carter, Elina Petrova, and Kannan Srinivasan, "Promotion of Prescription Drugs and Its Impact on Physicians' Choice Behavior," *Journal of Marketing*, July 2001, pp. 79–90.
22. Robert J. Lavidge and Gary A. Steiner, "A Model for Predictive Measurement of Advertising Effectiveness," *Journal of Marketing*, October 1961, p. 61.
23. "100 Leading National Advertisers 2008," *Advertising Age*, June 23, 2008, p. S6.
24. George S. Low and Jakki J. Mohr, "Setting Advertising and Promotion Budgets in Multi-Brand Companies," *Journal of Advertising Research*, January/February 1999, pp. 67–78; Don E. Schultz and Anders Gronstedt, "Making Marcom an Investment," *Marketing Management*, Fall 1997, pp. 41–49; and J. Enrique Bigne, "Advertising Budget Practices: A Review," *Journal of Current Issues and Research in Advertising*, Fall 1995, pp. 17–31.
26. Brenda Marlin, "Adding It Up: You Can Save Time By Trying One of Three Short-Cut Approaches to an Annual Budget," *ABA Banking*, October 1, 2007, p. 36; James A. Shroer, "Ad Spending: Growing Market Share," *Harvard Business Review*, January–February 1990, pp. 44–48; and Jeffrey A. Lowenhar and John L. Stanton, "Forecasting Competitive Advertising Expenditures," *Journal of Advertising Research* 16, no .2 (April 1976), pp. 37–44.
27. Daniel Seligman, How Much for Advertising?" *Fortune,* December 1956, p. 123.

28. James E. Lynch and Graham J. Hooley, "Increasing Sophistication in Advertising Budget Setting," *Journal of Advertising Research* 30 (February–March 1990), pp. 67–75.
29. Jimmy D. Barnes, Brenda J. Muscove, and Javad Rassouli, "An Objective and Task Media Selection Decision Model and Advertising Cost Formula to Determine International Advertising Budgets," *Journal of Advertising* 11, no .4 (1982), pp. 68–75.
30. "The Olympics Come But Once Every Two Years," *Marketing News*, November 1, 2008, p. 12; "Olympics Will Bring Online Opportunities for Many Brands," *Revolution*, July 14, 2008, p. 13; and Don E. Schultz, "Olympics Get the Gold Medal in Integrating Marketing Event," *Marketing News*, April 27, 1998, pp. 5, 10.
31. "Integrated Marketing: One Message, Many Media," *Marketing Week*, September 18, 2008, p. 31; Cornelia Pechman, Guangzhi Zhao, Marvin E. Goldberg, and Ellen Thomas Reibling, "What to Convey in Antismoking Advertisements for Adolescents: The Use of Protection Motivation Theory to Identify Effective Message Themes," *Journal of Marketing*, April 2003, pp. 1–18.
32. James Quilter, "MasterCard Ties Up Sony Pictures to Promote Da Vinci Code Prequel," Brand *Republic* news release, February 6, 2009, p. 1; Steffie Nelson, "Spinners Wary of Wild Web," *Daily Variety*, February 19, 2009, p. A5–7; "Super Bowl Ads Viewed More Than 28 Million Times Online Since Sunday," *Business Wire*, February 4, 2009.
33. Mike Reid, "Performance Auditing of Integrated Marketing Communication (IMC) Actions and Outcomes," *Journal of Advertising* 34 (Winter 2005), p. 41.
34. Michael Bush, "Media Agency of the Year: Initiative," *Advertising Age*, March 2, 2009, pp. 14–15; Initiative Web site, www.initiative.com, accessed March 18, 2009; and James Quilter, "The Integrated Riddle," *Promotions and Incentive*, September 1, 2008, p. 1.
35. "Integrated Marketing: The Benefits of Integrated Marketing," *Marketing Week*, September 18, 2008, p. 33; and Tom Duncan, "Is Your Marketing Communications Integrated?" *Advertising Age*, January 24, 1994, p. 26.
36. "Integrated Marketing: Digital Fuels Integration Boom," *Marketing Week*, December 11, 2008, p. 27; Don E. Schultz, "IMC Is Do or Die in New Pull Marketplace," *Marketing News*, August 15, 2006, p. 7; and Don E. Schultz, "Integration's New Role Focuses on Customers," *Marketing News*, September 15, 2006, p. 8.
37. "Measure for Measure," *Marketing Management*, January–February 2004, p. 7.
38. Don E. Shultz, "Measure IMC's Whole—Not Just Each Part," *Marketing News*, February 15, 2006, p. 8.
39. *Statistical Factbook 2009* (New York: Direct Marketing Association), pp. 142, 143; *Direct Marketing Key Statistics at a Glance* (New York: Direct Marketing Association, 2006), pp. 1, 5.
40. "JCPenney Launches Interactive 'Runway Show,'" *Business Wire*, February 23, 2009; "JCPenney Launches Virtual Runway Show," *Promo*, February 25, 2009; and Elaine Wong, "Dannon Plans More Activity for Activia," *Brandweek*, March 2, 2009.
41. *Statistical Factbook 2009* "Six Ways Lands' End Makes Online Shopping a Joy," *PR Newswire*, November 21, 2007; and Robert Berner, "Going that Extra Inch," *BusinessWeek*, September 18, 2000, p. 84.
42. Theresa Howard, "E-mail Grows as Direct-Marketing Tool: They're Quicker To Make, Cheap to Send," *USA Today*, November 28, 2008, p. 5B.
43. Time Parry, "Fill-mail Savings," *Catalog Age*, August 1, 2008, p. 35; and Christopher Hosford, "Database Face-to-Face," *B to B*, February 9, 2009, p. 21.
44. "China: New Media Blossoming as Business Models Revamp," BBC Monitoring World Media, December 9, 2008; "The Data Dilemma," *Marketing Direct*, February 6, 2007, p. 37; and Marc Nohr, "South Africa—A Worthy Contender," *Marketing Direct*, March 5, 2007, p. 20.
45. Jeffrey Bernstein, "Ensuring Data Protection Within Singapore Non-profits," *The Business Times Singapore*, March 2, 2009; Allison Enright, "Direct Mail Challenged," *Marketing News*, April 1, 2007, p. 3; and "Spam Is Now 77% of All E-Mail," *The Calgary Herald*, February 1, 2007, p. E1.
46. Claudia H. Deutsch, "Direct Mail Tries to Go Green. No, Really," *The New York Times*, July 23, 2008, p. 7; and Jennifer Wells, "Pushing the Envelope," *The Globe and Mail*," March 22, 2008, p. B3.

Under Armour: This case was prepared by Steven Hartley. Sources: Jeremy Mullman, "Protecting This Brand While Running Ahead," *Advertising Age*, January 12, 2009, p. 16; Jeremy Mullman, "Under Armour hopes to outrun Nike," *Advertising Age*, April 28, 2008, p. 6; Jeremy Mullman, "No Sugar and Spice Here," *Advertising Age*, June 18, 2007, p. 3; Stanley Holmes, "Under Armour May Be Overstretched," *Business Week*, April 30, 2007, p. 65; interviews with Marcus Stevens, Nathan Shriver, Steven Battista, and Kevin Haley; and information contained on the Under Armour Website (www.underarmour.com).

Chapter 19

1. Mark Hachman, "What's Behind the First 3D Super Bowl Ads," *PC Magazine.com*, January 28, 2009; "Is 3D About to Boom in 2009?" *Audio Visual Magazine*, February 1, 2009, p. 6; David Hambling, "Laser Light Show Displays Adverts in Thin Air," *New Scientist*, April 25, 2009, p. 19; Burt Helm, "Blowing Up Pepsi," *Business Week*, April 27, 2009, p. 32; "Commercials: Comcast Ad Campaign," *Creative Review*, April 1, 2009, p 20; Jonathan Paul, "Commercial Convo Goes 3D," *Strategy*, May 1, 2009, p. 21; "Beam Your Ads Directly into Their Brains—Well Almost," *Revolution*, May 1, 2009, p. 42; and Josh Quittner, "The Next Dimension," *Time*, March 30, 2009, p. 54.
2. Karen V. Fernandez and Dennis L. Rosen, "The Effectiveness of Information and Color in Yellow Pages Advertising," *Journal of Advertising*, Summer 2000, p. 61; David A. Aaker and Donald Norris, "Characteristics of TV Commercials Perceived as Informative," *Journal of Advertising Research* 22, no. 2 (April–May 1982), pp. 61–70.
3. Larry D. Compeau and Dhruv Grewal, "Comparative Price Advertising: An Integrative Review," *Journal of Public Policy & Marketing*, Fall 1998, pp. 257–73; and William Wilkie and Paul W. Farris, "Comparison Advertising: Problems and Potentials," *Journal of Marketing*, October 1975, pp. 7–15.
4. Chingching Chang, "The Relative Effectiveness of Comparative and Noncomparative Advertising: Evidence for Gender Differences in Information-Processing Strategies," *Journal of Advertising*, Spring 2007, p. 21; Jerry Gotlieb and Dan Sorel, "The Influence of Type of Advertisement, Price, and Source Credibility on Perceived Quality," *Journal of the Academy of Marketing Science*, Summer 1992, pp. 253–60; and Cornelia Pechman and David Stewart, "The Effects of Comparative Advertising on Attention, Memory, and Purchase Intentions," *Journal of Consumer Research*, September 1990, pp. 180–92.
5. Kathy L. O'Malley, Jeffrey J. Bailey, Chong Leng Tan, and Carl S. Bozman, "Effects of Varying Web-based Advertising-Substantiation Information on Attribute Beliefs and Perceived Product Quality," *Academy of Marketing Studies Journal*, 2007, p. 19; Bruce Buchanan and Doron Goldman, "Us vs. Them: The Minefield of Comparative Ads," *Harvard Business Review*, May–June 1989, pp. 38–50; Dorothy Cohen, "The FTC's Advertising Substantiation Program," *Journal of Marketing*, Winter 1980, pp. 26–35; and Michael Etger and Stephen A. Goodwin, "Planning for Comparative Advertising Requires Special Attention," *Journal of Advertising* 8, no. 1 (Winter 1979), pp. 26–32.
6. David W. Schumann, Jan M. Hathcote, and Susan West, "Corporate Advertising in America: A Review of Published Studies on Use,

Measurement, and Effectiveness," *Journal of Advertising*, September 1991, p. 35; Lewis C. Winters, "Does It Pay to Advertise in Hostile Audiences with Corporate Advertising?" *Journal of Advertising Research*, June–July 1988, pp. 11–18; and Robert Selwitz, "The Selling of an Image," *Madison Avenue*, February 1985, pp. 61–69.

7. "Pandora Launches Innovative Video Platform for Entertainment Industry Advertisers," *Marketwire*, September 16, 2009.
8. Rita Chang, "Mobile Effort Gets More to Say 'I Can' Purchase a Porsche," *Advertising Age*, February 9, 2009, p. 18;
9. Jeremy Mullman, "Nike: What Slowdown?" *Advertising Age*, October 20, 2008, p. 34.
10. Ira Teinowitz, "Self-regulation Urged to Prevent Bias in Ad Buying," *Advertising Age*, January 18, 1999, p. 4
11. "$100,000 Grand Prize Will Literally Go to Dogs," *States News Service*, June 4, 2008; and Magazine Publishers of America Web site, www.magazine.org/advertising/kelly_awards, accessed April 2, 2009.
12. See the Advertising Research Foundation Web site, www.thearf.org/assets/ad-effectiveness-council accessed April 2, 2009.
13. Demetrios Vakratsas and Tim Ambler, "How Advertising Works: What Do We Really Know?" *Journal of Marketing*, January 1999, pp. 26–43.
14. Jeremy Mullman, "Yes, the Super Bowl Is Well Worth $3M a Spot," *Advertising Age*, January 26, 2009, p. 1; Bob Garfield, "Ed McMahon's Bad Ad Steals the Super Bowl," *Advertising Age*, February 2, 2009, p. 1; "NBC Sells Out Super Bowl Ads for Record $206M," *The Associated Press*, January 31, 2009; and Rama Ylkur, Chuck Tomkovick, and Patty Traczyk, "Super Bowl Effectiveness: Hollywood Finds the Games Golden," *Journal of Advertising Research*, March 2004, pp. 143–59.
15. Bradley Johnson, "U.S. Market-Share Leaders," *Advertising Age*, June 23, 2008, p. S-9; and Stuart Elliott, "A Hybrid's Niche? The Masses, It Hopes," *The New York Times*, March 13, 2009, p. 3.
16. Ioni Lewis, Barry Watson, Richard Tay, and Katherine M. White, "The Role of Fear Appeals In Improving Driver Safety," *The International Journal of Behavioral Consultation and Therapy*, June 22, 2007, p. 203; Lenore Skenazy, "Take the Fat Out of Your Food," *Advertising Age*, January 14, 2008, p. 12; and Cornelia Pechmann, Guangzhi Zhao, Marvin E. Goldberg, and Ellen Thomas Reibling, "What to Convey in Antismoking Advertisements for Adolescents: The Use of Protection Motivation Theory to Identify Effective Message Themes," *Journal of Marketing*, April 2003, pp. 1–18; Jeffrey D. Zbar, "Fear!" *Advertising Age*, November 14, 1994, pp. 18–19; John F. Tanner, Jr., James B. Hunt, and David R. Eppright, "The Protection Motivation Model: A Normative Model of Fear Appeals," *Journal of Marketing*; July 1991, pp. 36–45.
17. "About Bebe," Bebe Web site, www.bebe.com, accessed April 9, 2009; Sanjay Putrevu, "Consumer Responses Toward Sexual and Nonsexual Appeals: The Influence of Involvement, Need for Cognition (NFC), and Gender," *Journal of Advertising*, Summer 2008, p. 57.
18. Rupal Parekh, "With Strong Work for Walmart and Geico, Martin Agency Is Creating a New Specialty: Making Marketers Recession-Proof," *Advertising Age*, January 19, 2009, p. 30; and Louis Llovio, "Geico Gecko's Viral Videos," *Richmond Times Dispatch*, March 28, 2009, p. B-9.
19. Thomas W. Cline and James J. Kellaris, "The Influence of Humor Strength and Humor-Message Relatedness on Ad Memorability: A Dual Process Model," *Journal of Advertising*, Spring 2007, p. 55; Yong Zhang and George M. Zinkham, "Responses to Humorous Ads," *Journal of Advertising*, Winter 2006, p. 113; and Yih Hwai Lee and Elison Ai Ching Lim, "What's Funny and What's Not: The Moderating Role of Cultural Orientation in Ad Humor," *Journal of Advertising*, Summer 2008, p. 71.
20. "With a Growing Design Operation, Two Thriving Offices, and Successful Relationships with Massive Brands Like Coke, Crispin Is Once Again the Best Agency in the Land," *Advertising Age*, January 19, 2009, p. 22; and the Crispin Porter & Bogusky Web site, www.cpbgroup.com, accessed April 9, 2009.
21. Julie Creswell, "Nothing Sells Like Celebrity," *The New York Times*, June 22, 2008, p. 1; Barry Janoff, "Brangelina Top Cause Marketing Stars," *Brandweek.com*, September 9, 2008; and "L'Oreal Paris Signs Elizabeth Banks as New Spokesperson," *PR Newswire*, December 19, 2008.
22. Charisse Jones, "Scandals Tarnish Star Endorsements," *USA Today*, February 23, 2009, p. 5B.
23. Kipp Cheng, *2007 Television Production Cost Survey* (New York: American Association of Advertising Agencies, 2008), p. 5; and Jean Halliday, "Exotic Ads Get Noticed," *Advertising Age*, April 9, 2001, p. S4.
24. "Ad-Spending Totals By Medium," *Advertising Age*, June 23, 2008, p. S-15.
25. Vicki R. Lane, "The Impact of Ad Repetition an Ad Content on Consumer Perceptions of Incongruent Extensions," *Journal of Marketing*, April 2000, pp. 80–91.
26. David Bauder, "Prime-time Games Big in Nielsen Ratings," *The Associated Press*, March 31, 2009; James Poniewozik, "Here's to the Death of Broadcast," *Time*, April 6, 2009, p. 63; "Research and Markets: The Marketer's Guide to Digital Out-Of-Home Media," *Business Wire*, March 10, 2009; "Nielsen and Integrated Media Measurement Launch Out-of-Home Television Ratings Measurement Service," *PR Newswire*, April 12, 2007; and "Media Trends Track" based on Nielsen Media Research data, www.tvb.org/rcentral/MediaTrendsTrack, accessed April 15, 2009.
27. Brian Steinberg, "Sunday Night Football Remains Costliest TV Show," *Advertising Age*, October 26, 2009, p. 8; and Jeremy Mullman, "High Life's One-second Spots Yield 8.6% Boost After Super Bowl," *Advertising Age*, February 23, 2009, p. 3.
28. "Top 15 Cable Networks," *Advertising Age*, April 14, 2008, p. S-8; and "'TV Everywhere' May Shine Light on Cable's Week Spot," *Advertising Age*, March 9, 2009, p. 10.
29. "The IMS Top 50 Infomercials and Short-Form Spots of 2008," *Response*, December 1, 2008, p. 42; Jacqueline Renfrow, "Dodge Debuts First Infomercial for Ram Trucks," *Response*, October 1, 2008, p. 12; and Bill Carter, "Infomercial for Obama Is Big Success in Ratings," *The New York Times*, October 31, 2008, p. 19.
30. "Broadcast Station Totals As of December 31, 2008," Federal Communications Commission, February 27, 2009; "Time Spent Listening," in *Radio Today*, 2008 edition, Arbitron, www.arbitron.com, accessed April 15, 2009).
31. "Corporate Overview," Sirius Satellite Radio Web site, www.sirius.com/aboutus, accessed April 15, 2009; and "Hour-by-Hour Listening," in *Radio Today*, 2008 edition, Arbitron, www.arbitron.com, accessed April 15, 2009.
32. "A Magazine for Everyone," *The Magazine Handbook 2008–2009*, New York: Magazine Publishers of America, 2008, p. 5; "What Recession? New Magazine Launches, Up, Up, Up," MRMagazine.com, March 29, 2009, www.mrmagazine.wordpress.com; Sarah Treleaven, "The Magic Kingdom's VIP Room," *National Post*, March 14, 2009, p. WP12; and Larry Dobrow, "Idea of the Year: Reader-Generated Content," *Advertising Age*, October 6, 2008, p. S-6.
33. "Growth of Magazines by Category," *Editorial Trends and Magazine Handbook 2008–2009* (New York: Magazine Publishers of America, 2008); "Magazines Are #1 Medium of Engagement Across All Dimensions Measured," *The Magazine Handbook 2008–2009*, (New York: Magazine Publishers of America, 2008)), p. 28.
34. Marissa Miley, "Magazines We'll Miss," *Advertising Age*, December 15, 2008, p. 19; and "Average Total Paid and Verified Circulation for

Top 100 ABC Magazines," *Circulation Trends and Magazine Handbook 2008–2009* (New York: Magazine Publishers of America, 2008).

35. "Future May Be Brighter, But It's Apocalypse Now," *Advertising Age*, March 23, 2009, p. 1; Nat Ives, "Where 1990's Top Papers Are Now," *Advertising Age*, March 9, 2009, p. 4; Ken Wheaton, "The Printed Newspaper Is Not Facing Extinction (Yet)," *Advertising Age*, November 3, 2008, p. 14; Jonah Bloom, "The Newspaper Doomsayers Still Can Be Proved Wrong," *Advertising Age*, August 11, 2008, p. 13; and "Newspaper Web Sites," Newspaper Association of America, www.nna.org/trendsandnumbers, accessed April 18, 2009.

36. Carol Krol, "Yellow Pages Bleeding Red Ink," *B to B*, August 11, 2008, p. 1; and "Extinction Threatens Yellow-Pages Publishers," *The Wall Street Journal*, November 17, 2008.

37. "Search Marketing Fact Pack 2008," *Advertising Age*, November 3, 2008, p. 6; "Digital Marketing & Media Fact Pack, *Advertising Age*, April 23, 2007, p. 6; and Steve Rubel, "Banner-ad Quality Takes a Dive with the Economy," *Advertising Age*, February 16, 2009, p. 14; "comScore Releases August 2009 U.S. Search Engine Rankings," www.comscore.com, October 8, 2009.

38. See "Examine Web Audiences by Site, Size, Demographic Profile and Behavior," at Nielsen Online Web site, www.nielsen-online.com/solutions, accessed April 23, 2009; and Abbey Klaassen, "Why the Click Is the Wrong Metric for Online Ads," *Advertising Age*, February 23, 2009, p. 4.

39. Gareth Jones, "Briefing-Paid Search-Advertisers Stung By Rising Click Fraud," *Revolution*, May 1, 2009, p. 18; "30 Seconds on Click Fraud," *Marketing Direct*, December 1, 2008, p. 42; Brian Grow and Ben Elgin, "Click Fraud," *BusinessWeek*, October 2, 2006, pp. 46–57; Rob Hof, "Is Google Too Powerful?" *BusinessWeek*, April 9, 2007, p. 48; Eric J. Hansen, "Apply Online Market Data for Offline Insights," *Marketing News*, April 1, 2007, p. 30; "Out of Site at AdAge.com," *Advertising Age*, November 6, 2006, p. 12; Michael Fielding, "Click Fraud Settles Down," *Marketing News*, September 1, 2006, p. 4; and Brian Grow, "This Mouse for Hire," *BusinessWeek*, October 23, 2006, p. 104.

40. Arch G. Woodside, "Outdoor Advertising as Experiments," *Journal of the Academy of Marketing Science* 18 (Summer 1990), pp. 229–37.

41. "Digital Billboards: Outdoor Advertising's Glowing Future," Outdoor Advertising Association of America, Inc., www.oaaa.org/marketingresources, accessed April 23, 2009; Katy Bachman, "Report: Digital Billboards Not a Threat to Drivers," *Mediaweek.com*, April 13, 2009; Katy Bachman, "Billboard or Blight?" *Mediaweek.com*, February 8, 2009; and Phil Willon, "L.A. OKs 3-Month Outdoor Sign Ban," *Los Angeles Times*, December 18, 2008, p. 1.

42. "The Year Ahead for . . . Outdoor," *Campaign*, January 9, 2009, p. 28; Andrew Hampp, "Digital Out of Home. That's Those Pixilated Billboards, Right?" *Advertising Age*, March 30, 2009; Andrew Hampp, "Out of Home that Stood Out," *Advertising Age*, December 15, 2008, p. 22; and Daniel W. Baack, Rick T. Wilson, and Brian D. Till, "Creativity and Memory Effects," *Journal of Advertising*, Winter 2008, p. 85.

43. Schoon Park and Minhi Hahn, "Pulsing in a Discrete Model of Advertising Competition," *Journal of Marketing Research*, November 1991, pp. 297–405.

44. Peggy Masterson, "The Wearout Phenomenon," *Marketing Research*, Fall 1999, pp. 27–31; and Lawrence D. Gibson, "What Can One TV Exposure Do?" *Journal of Advertising Research*, March–April 1996, pp. 9–18.

45. Rob Norton, "How Uninformative Advertising Tells Consumers Quite a Bit," *Fortune*, December 26, 1994, p. 37; and "Professor Claims Corporations Waste Billions on Advertising," *Marketing News*, July 6, 1992, p. 5.

46. Stephen Fajen, "The Agency Model Is Bent but Not Broken," *Advertising Age*, July 7, 2008, p. 17; Jeremy Mullman, "Anheuser-Busch Whacks Retainers for Its Agencies," *Advertising Age*, February 16, 2009, p. 1; Jack Neff, "No One-Size-Fits-All Snuggie Model Exists for DRTV Shops," *Advertising Age*, March 23, 2009; and Ivan Pollard, "Agency Model of the Future? Keep an Eye on Media Guys," *Advertising Age*, April 2, 2007, p. 29.

47. The discussion of posttesting is based on William F. Arens, Michael F. Weigold, and Christian Arens, *Contemporary Advertising*, 12th ed. (New York: McGraw-Hill Irwin, 2009), pp. 228–30.

48. "ROI Metric Available in MRI Starch Syndicated," Mediamark Research & Intelligence, www.mediamark.com, accessed April 23, 2009.

49. David A. Aaker and Douglas M. Stayman, "Measuring Audience Perceptions of Commercials and Relating Them to Ad Impact," *Journal of Advertising Research* 30 (August–September 1990), pp. 7–17; and Ernest Dichter, "A Psychological View of Advertising Effectiveness," *Marketing Management* 1, no. 3 (1992), pp. 60–62.

50. David Krugel, "Television Advertising Effectiveness and Research Innovation," *Journal of Consumer Marketing*, Summer 1988, pp. 43–51; and Laurence N. Gold, "The Evolution of Television Advertising Sales Measurement: Past, Present, and Future, " *Journal of Advertising Research*, June–July 1988, pp. 19–24.

51. Patricia E. Odell, "Promo Lite," *Promo*, October 2008, p. 14.

52. Tom Hansen, "Media Mash," *Promo*, February 1, 2007, p. 66; Magid M. Abraham and Leonard M. Lodish, "Getting the Most Out of Advertising and Promotion," *Harvard Business Review*, May–June 1990, pp. 50–60; Steven W. Hartley and James Cross, "How Sales Promotion Can Work for and against You," *Journal of Consumer Marketing,* Summer 1988, pp. 35–42; Robert D. Buzzell, John A. Quelch, and Walter J. Salmon, "The Costly Bargain of Trade Promotion," *Harvard Business Review*, March–April 1990, pp. 141–49; and Mary L. Nicastro, "Break-Even Analysis Determines Success of Sales Promotions," *Marketing News*, March 5, 1990, p. 11.

53. Patricia Odell, "Dishing Out Discounts," *Promo*, October 2008, p. 23; "Coupon Facts," *Promo*, March 1, 2009, p. 42; and Patricia Odell, "No Lumps," *Promo*, March 1, 2009, p. 8.

54. Kapil Bawa and Robert W. Shoemaker, "Analyzing Incremental Sales from a Direct-Mail Coupon Promotion," *Journal of Marketing*, July 1998, pp. 66–78.

55. Robert A. Strang, "Sales Promotion—Fast Growth, Faulty Management," *Harvard Business Review* 54 (July–August 1976), pp. 115–24; and Ronald W. Ward and James E. Davis, "Coupon Redemption," *Journal of Advertising Research* 18 (August 1978), pp. 51–58. Similar results on favorable mail-distributed coupons were reported by Alvin Schwartz, "The Influence of Media Characteristics on Coupon Redemption," *Journal of Marketing* 30 (January 1966), pp. 41–46.

56. Amy Johannes, "Flying The Coup," *Promo*, July 1, 2008, p. 28; and "What is Coupon Misredemption?" The Coupon Information Corporation, www.cents-off.com, accessed April 23, 2009.

57. Amy Johannes, "Premium Connections," *Promo*, October 2008, p. 34; and Gerard P. Prendergast, Alex S. L. Tsang, Derek T. Y. Poon, *Journal of Advertising Research*, June 2008, p. 287.

58. "User Content Offers a New Perspective," *PR Week*, February 23, 2009, p. 21; and Randy A. Salas, "Seriously, Who Watches the Big NFL Game Just for Football? The Cool Commercials Are Really Where It's At," *StarTribune*, January 29, 2009, p. 1E.

59. "Florida Woman wins $2Million Grand Prize Package In HGTV Dream Home Giveaway 2009," *PR Newswire*, March 16, 2009; and "How I Won $1 Million By Eating Breakfast," *PR Newswire*, October 7, 2008.

60. "Mars Snackfood US Will 'Treat' Consumers to Halloween Million Dollar Contest," *Entertainment Business Newsweekly*, November 16,

2008, p. 124; "AT&T Announces Fox's 'American Idol' Seventh Season Breaks All-time Record for Text Messaging," *PR Newswire*, May 22, 2008; and Richard Tedesco, "KFC Takes Wing Title," *Promo*, December 1, 2008, p. 14.

61. Brian Quinton, "The Hands-On Experience," *Promo*, October 2008, p. 37; Larry Jaffee, "Try It," *Promo*, September 1, 2007, p. AR25; Lorin Cipolla, "Instant Gratification," *Promo*, April 1, 2004, p. 4; "Best Activity Generating Brand Awareness/Trial," *Promo*, September 2001, p. 51; and "Brand Handing," *Promo's 9th Annual Sourcebook* (2002), p. 32.
62. "Loyalty Rewards Membership on the Rise," *Brandweek.com*, April 17, 2009; "Financial Services Surpasses Airlines as Largest Single U.S. Market for Reward Programs," Colloquy Web site, www.colloquy.com, accessed April 20, 2009; and Richard Tedesco, "Winning the Customer Comeback," *Promo*, October 2008, p. 30.
63. David Rosen, "Exclusively Yours," *Promo*, February 1, 2009, p. 12.
64. Amy Johannes, "Watching the Carts," *Promo*, October 2008, p. 36.
65. Marvin A. Jolson, Joshua L. Wiener, and Richard B. Rosecky, "Correlates of Rebate Proneness," *Journal of Advertising Research*, February–March 1987, pp. 33–43.
66. Richard Tedesco, "Video Placements Proliferate," *Promo*, October 2008, p. 35; Brandchannel.com Web site, www.brandchannel.com/brandcameo-films.asp, accessed April 30, 2009; Martin Lindstrom, "Why 'Idol' Works for Coke—But Not for Ford," *Advertising Age*, November 17, 2008, p. 19; and Brian Quinton, "Fed Up," *Promo*, January 1, 2009, p. 26.
67. Amy Johannes, "Simpson Mania," *Promo*, November 1, 2008, p. 8; and Allison Enright, "Apu Buzz, Krusty—Oh My!" *Marketing News*, August 15, 2007, p. 3.
68. This discussion is drawn particularly from John A. Quelch, *Trade Promotions by Grocery Manufacturers: A Management Perspective* (Cambridge, MA: Marketing Science Institute, August 1982).
69. Michael Chevalier and Ronald C. Curhan, "Retail Promotions as a Function of Trade Promotions: A Descriptive Analysis," *Sloan Management Review* 18 (Fall 1976), pp. 19–32.
70. G. A. Marken, "Firms Can Maintain Control over Creative Co-op Programs," *Marketing News*, September 28, 1992, pp. 7, 9.
71. Emily Bryson York, "Nestlé, Pepsi, and Coke Face Their Waterloo," *Advertising Age*, October 8, 2007, p. 1.
72. Irving Rein, Philip Kotler, and Martin Stoller, *High Visibility* (New York: Dodd, Mead, 1987); and Steven Colford, "Ross Perot: A Winner after All," *Advertising Age*, December 21, 1992, pp. 4, 18.
73. Michael Treacy and Fred Wiersema, "Customer Intimacy and Other Value Disciplines," *Harvard Business Review*, January–February 1993, pp. 84–93.
74. Gerry Khermouch and Tom Lowry, "The Future of Advertising," *BusinessWeek*, March 26, 2001, p. 139; and Outlook 2001: Advertising," *Marketing News*, January 1, 2001, p. 10.
75. Betsy Spethmann, "McFallout," *Promo*, October 2001, pp. 31–38.
76. "Kid Stuff," *Promo*, January 1991, pp. 25, 42; Steven W. Colford, "Fine-Tuning Kids' TV," *Advertising Age*, February 11, 1991, p. 35; and Kate Fitzgerald, "Toys Star-Struck for Movie Tie-Ins," *Advertising Age*, February 18, 1991, pp. 3, 45.
77. Herbert J. Rotfeld, Avery M. Abernathy, and Patrick R. Parsons, "Self-Regulation and Television Advertising," *Journal of Advertising* 19, no. 4 (1990), pp. 18–26.

Google, Inc.: This case was written by Steven Hartley. Sources: Jessica E. Vascellaro, "Google Decides to Find Its Creative Side," *The Wall Street Journal*, October 7, 2009; Robert D. Hof, "Google's New Ad Weapon," *BusinessWeek*, June 22, 2009, p. 52; Maria Bartiromo, "Eric Schmidt On Where Google is Headed," *BusinessWeek*, August 17, 2009, p. 11; "Why Microsoft-Yahoo Deal Could Be Good for Google," *Advertising Age*, August 10, 2009, p. 10; Peter Burrow, "Apple and Google: Another Step Apart," *BusinessWeek*, August 17, 2009, p. 24; Jeff Jarvis, "How The Google Model Could Help," *BusinessWeek*, February 9, 2009, p. 32; Abbey Klaasen, "Google Says Print Ads Isn't the Answer for Newspapers," *Advertising Age*, January 26, 2009, p. 17; Matthew Creamer, "Recession Doesn't Dent Total Value of Top 100 Brands," *Advertising Age*, April 27, 2009; "The 500 Largest U.S. Corporations," *Fortune*, May 4, 2009, F-1; "ComScore Releases August 2009 U.S. Search Engine Rankings," www.comscore.com, October 10, 2009; interviews with Google personnel; and information contained on the Google Web site (www.google.com).

Chapter 20

1. Adam Bryant, "The Keeper of That Tapping Pen," *The New York Times*, March 22, 2009, pp .C1, 20; "Executive Biographies—Anne Mulcahy," www.xerox.com, accessed May 1, 2009; Henry Canaday, "Anne Mulcahy and the Xerox Revolution," www.sellingpower.com, accessed April 15, 2009; and "Xerox-Dedicated to Customer Success," www.sspa.com, accessed February 20, 2007.
2. "Leading CEOs: A Statistical Snapshot of S&P 500 Leaders," www.spencerstuart.com, accessed December 2008.
3. Jessi Hempel, "IBM's All-Star Salesman," www.cnnmoney.com, accessed September 26, 2008.
4. "Surgical Visits," *Business 2.0*, April 2006, p. 94.
5. Mark W. Johnson and Greg W. Marshall, *Relationship Selling*, 2nd ed. (New York: McGraw-Hill/Irwin, 2008).
6. David Kirkpatrick, "Inside Sam's $100 Billion Growth Machine," *Fortune*, June 14, 2004, pp. 80ff.
7. Barton A. Weitz, Stephen B. Castleberry, and John F. Tanner, Jr., *Selling: Building Partnerships*, 6th ed. (New York: McGraw-Hill/Irwin, 2010).
8. "Stop Calling Us," *Time*, April 29, 2003, pp. 56–58.
9. For an overview of team selling, see Eli Jones, Andrea Dickson, Lawrence B. Chonko, and Joseph P. Cannon, "Key Accounts and Team Selling: A Review, Framework, and Research Agenda," *Journal of Personal Selling & Sales Management*, Spring 2005, pp. 181–98.
10. "Group Dynamics," *Sales & Marketing Management*, January/February 2007, p. 8; and Steve Atlas and Elise Atlas, "Team Approach," *Selling Power*, May 2000, pp. 126–28.
11. Scott Sterns, "Cold Calls Have Yet to Breathe Their Last Gasp," ***The** Wall Street Journal*, December 14, 2006, p. D2.
12. Jim Edwards, "Dinner, Interrupted," *BrandWeek*, May 26, 2003, pp. 28–32.
13. Christopher Conkey, "Record Fine Levied for Telemarketing," *The Wall Street Journal*, December 14, 2005, pp. D1, D4.
14. Paul A. Herbing, *Handbook of Cross-Cultural Marketing* (New York: Halworth Press, 1998).
15. This discussion is based on Weitz, Castleberry, and Tanner, *Selling*; and Johnston and Marshall, *Relationship Selling*.
16. Kapil R. Tuli, Ajay K. Kohli, and Sundar G. Bharadwaj, "Rethinking Customer Solutions: From Product Bundles to Relational Processes," *Journal of Marketing*, July 2007, pp. 1–17.
17. For an extensive discussion of objections, see Charles M. Futrell, *Fundamentals of Selling*, 10th ed. (New York: McGraw-Hill/Irwin, 2010), chap. 12.
18. Theodore Levitt, *The Marketing Imagination* (New York: Free Press, 1983), p. 111.
19. Weitz, Castleberry, and Tanner, *Selling*.
20. *Management Briefing: Sales and Marketing* (New York: Conference Board, October 1996), pp. 3–4.

21. Ellen Neuborne, "Know They Enemy," *Sales & Marketing Management*, January 2003, pp. 29–33.
22. Alan J. Dubinsky, Marvin A. Jolson, Ronald E. Michaels, Masaaki Katobe, and Chae Un Lim, "Ethical Perceptions of Field Sales Personnel: An Empirical Assessment," *Journal of Personal Selling & Sales Management*, Fall 1992, pp. 9–21; and Alan J. Dubinsky, Marvin A. Jolson, Masaaki Katobe, and Chae Un Lim, "A Cross-National Investigation of Industrial Sales People's Ethical Perceptions," *Journal of International Business Studies*, Fourth Quarter 1991, pp. 651–70.
23. See Mark W. Johnston and Greg Marshall, *Sales Force Management*, 9th ed. (New York: McGraw-Hill/Irwin, 2009), pp. 100–4; and William T. Ross, Jr., Frederic Dalsace, and Erin Anderson, "Should You Set Up Your Own Sales Force or Should You Outsource It? Pitfalls in the Standard Analysis," *Business Horizons*, January–February 2005, pp. 23–36.
24. Eli Jones, et al., "Key Accounts and Team Selling." Also see, Arun Sharma, "Success Factors in Key Accounts," *Journal of Business & Industrial Marketing* 21, no. 3 (2006), pp. 141–50.
25. This discussion is based on William L. Cron and Thomas E. DeCarlo, *Dalrymple's Sales Management*, 10th ed. (Hoboken, NJ: Wiley and Sons, 2009).
26. René Y. Darmon, *Leading the Sales Force* (New York: Cambridge University Press, 2007).
27. Weitz, Castleberry, and Tanner, *Selling*, p. 19; Elizabeth J. Rozell, Charles E. Pettijohn, and R. Stephen Parker, "Customer-Oriented Selling: Exploring the Roles of Emotional Intelligence and Organizational Commitment," *Psychology & Marketing*, June 2004, pp. 405–24.
28. *Statistical Abstract of the United States*, 128th ed. (Washington, DC: U.S. Department of Commerce, 2009).
29. Rosann L. Spiro, Gregory A. Rich, and William J. Stanton, *Management of the Sales Force*, 12th ed. (New York: McGraw-Hill/Irwin, 2008), chap. 7.
30. Ibid., chap. 8. Also see, Julia Chang, "Wholly Motivated," *Sales & Marketing Management*, March 2007, pp. 24ff.
31. This discussion is based on Johnson and Marshall, *Sales Force Management*, chap. 11; and Andris Zoltner, Prabhakant Sinha, and Sally E. Lorimer, *The Complete Guide to Sales Force Incentive Compensation* (New York: AMACOM, 2006).
32. www.MaryKay.com, accessed April 20, 2009; Terry Box, "Mary Kay, GM in the Pink with Cadillacs," *Dallas Morning News*, August 6, 2006, p. D2.
33. René Y. Darmon, "The Concept of Salesperson Replacement Value: A Sales Force Turnover Management Tool," *Journal of Personal Selling & Sales Management*, Summer 2008, pp. 211–32.
34. Gary Hallen and Robert Latino, "Eastman Chemical's Success Story," *Quality Progress*, June 2003, pp. 50–54.
35. Mark Cotteleer, Edward Inderrieden, and Felissa Lee, "Selling the Sales Force on Automation," *Harvard Business Review*, July–August 2006, pp. 18–22.
36. "Corporate America's New Sales Force," *Fortune*, August 11, 2003, special advertising section; and www.toshiba.com/technology, accessed May 15, 2006.
37. Darmon, *Leading the Sales Force*.

Xerox: This case was written by Steven Hartley and Roger Kerin. Sources: Joseph Kornik, "Table Talk: A Sales Leaders Roundtable," *Sales & Marketing Management*, February 2007; Philip Chadwick, "Xerox Global Service," *Printweek*, October 11, 2007, p. 32; Kevin Maney, "Mulcahy Traces Steps of Xerox's Comeback," *USA Today*, September 11, 2006, p. 48; Sarah Campbell, "What It's Like Working for Xerox," *The Times*, September 14, 2006, p. 9; "Anne Mulcahy: How I Compete," *BusinessWeek* August 21, 2006, p. 55; Simon Avery, "CEO's HR Skills Turn Xerox Fortunes," *The Globe and Mail*, June 2, 2006, p. B3; Julia Chang, "Ultimate Motivation Guide: Happy Sales Force, Happy Returns," *Sales & Marketing Management*, March 2006; "The World's Most Powerful Women," www.forbes.com, August 27, 2008; and resources available on the Xerox Web site, www.xerox.com, including About Xerox, Executive Biographies, the Xerox 2007 Fact Sheet, the Online Fact Book: Historical Highlights, and the Online Fact Book: How Xerox Sells.

Chapter 21

1. Interview with Mattison Crowe, director of marketing at Seven Cycles, Inc., May 1, 2009; and www.sevencycles.com, accessed May 2, 2009.
2. "Over 875 Million Consumers Have Shopped Online," The Nielsen Company news release, January 28, 2008; and "eMarketer Revises E-Commerce Forecast," www.emarketer.com, accessed March 5, 2009.
3. "The Sky Will Now Have Some Limits," *BrandWeek*, June 18, 2007, pp. S62–63.
4. Kimberly Palmer, "The Store of You," *U.S. News & World Report*, November 10, 2008, pp. 54–56.
5. Rafi A. Mohammed, Robert J. Fisher, Bernard J. Jaworski, and Gordon J. Paddison, *Internet Marketing: Building Advantage in a Networked Economy*, 2nd ed. (New York: McGraw-Hill/Irwin, 2004).
6. Ward A. Hanson and Kirthi Kalyanam, *Internet Marketing & Electronic Commerce* (Mason, OH: Thompson Higher Education, 2007).
7. Ibid.
8. Michael Grebb, "Behavioral Science," *Business 2.0*, March 2000, p. 112.
9. Judy Strauss, Adel El-Ansary, and Raymond Frost, *E-Marketing*, 5th ed. (Upper Saddle River, NJ: Prentice Hall, 20009).
10. John B. Horrigan, "Online Shopping," www.pewinternet.org, accessed February 13, 2008.
11. This discussion is drawn form Jeffrey F. Rayport and Bernard J. Jaworski, *e-Commerce*, 2nd ed. (New York: McGraw-Hill/Irwin, 2004; and *The Essential Guide to Best Practices in eCommerce* (Portland, OR: Webtrends, Inc., 2006).
12. Mylene Mangalindan, "Web Sites Want You to Stick Around," *The Wall Street Journal*, April 15, 2008, p. B5.
13. "Demographics of Internet Users," www.pewinternet.org, accessed March 1, 2009.
14. "Statistics: U.S. Online Shoppers," accessed April 5, 2008.
15. John B. Horrigan, "A Typology of Information and Communication Technology Users," www.pewresearch.org/pubs, accessed May 7, 2007.
16. "Statistics: U.S. Online Shoppers."
17. Beth Bulik, "Technology No longer Just Kid Stuff," *Advertising Age*, February 2, 2009, p. 12; "My Mommy's Online," www.eMarketer.com, March 17, 2008; and "New Study Reveals Internet Is the Medium Moms Rely on Most," Disney Online news release, March 2004.
18. Category online retail sales estimates are based on *Statistical Abstract of the United States: 2009* (Washington, DC: Government Printing Office, 2009); Lisa Phillips, "Health and Beauty Online," www.eMarketer.com, accessed September 25, 2008; and "How Much Will Online Travel Slow?" www.eMarketer.com, accessed November 13, 2008.
19. Jerry Wind and Arvind Ranaswamy, "Customerization: The Next Wave in Mass Customization," *Journal of Interactive Marketing*, Winter 2001, pp. 13–32.
20. Tom Hayes and Michael S. Malone, "Marketing in the World of the Web," *The Wall Street Journal*, November 29–30, 2008, p. A13. Also

see, Kate Fitzgerald, "Blogs Fascinate, Frighten Marketers," *Advertising Age*, March 5, 2007, p. S-4.

21. Strauss, et al., *E-Marketing*, p. 357.
22. Hanson and Kalyanam, *Internet Marketing & Electronic Commerce*.
23. Stephen Baker, "The Online Ad Surge," *BusinessWeek*, November 22, 2004, pp. 76–81.
24. "Branding on the Net," *BusinessWeek*, November 2, 1998, pp. 78–86.
25. David Kesmodel, "Marketers Seek to Make Cookies More Palatable," *The Wall Street Journal*, June 17, 2005, pp. B1, B2.
26. Mary Lou Roberts, *Internet Marketing: Integrating Online and Offline Strategies*, 2nd ed. (Mason, OH: Thomson, 2008), chap. 12; *2008 Internet Crime Report*, www.ic3.gov; "Consumers Are Concerned About Online Privacy, But Few Understand It," www.internetretailer.com, accessed May 1, 2009.
27. "Survey: Many Admit to Online Shopping at Work," www.moneycentral.msn.com, accessed December 2, 2008; and Susan Adams, et al. "This Time It Is Personal: Employee Online Shopping at Work," *Interactive Marketing*, April 2005, pp. 326–336.
28. "This discussion is based on "Online Research Drives Offline Sales," www.eMarketer.com, accessed February 26, 2008; "Study: More Consumers Do Research Online, Shop Offline," *BrandWeek*, November 3, 2008, p. 8; "Shop Online, Spend Offline," www.eMarketer.com, accessed July 11, 2007; and Tamera Mendelsohn, "The State of Multichannel Consumers in the U.S. and Europe," www.forresterresearch.com, accessed June 25, 2007.
29. "Retailers' Panty Raid on Victoria's Secret," *The Wall Street Journal*, June 20, 2007, pp. B1, B12.
30. Stephanie Kang, "Callaway Will Use Retailers to Sell Goods Directly to Consumers Online," *The Wall Street Journal*, November 6, 2006, p. B5.
31. Erik Hauser and Max Lenderman, "Experiential Marketing," *Brandweek*, September 20, 2008, Special Section; and Timothy J. Mullaney, "E-Biz Strikes Again," *BusinessWeek*, May 10, 2004, pp. 80–90.
32. "Online Research Drives Offline Sales."

Pizza Hut: This case was prepared by Pizza Hut and imc^2 executives for exclusive use in this text.

Chapter 22

1. Personal interviews with Vivian Milroy Callaway, August 2007 and June 2009.
2. Ann Merrill, "Feeding the Beast," *StarTribune*, June 2, 2002, pp. D1, D10.
3. Matthew Boyle, "Kellogg's New Meals," *Fortune*, November 3, 2006, p. 40.
4. Matt McKinney, "General Mills Up Against Cereal Wall," *StarTribune*, June 29, 2007, pp., D1, D2.
5. Personal interview with Vivian Milroy Callaway, June 2009.
6. Kate Murphy, "Look! We Can Drive and Snack at the Same Time," *The New York Times*, November 2, 2003, p. BU4; Thomas Lee, "Big G Takes the High Road with Whole Grains," *StarTribune*, October 10, 2004, pp. D1, D4; and Thomas Lee, "More than Just Low Carbs," *StarTribune*, April 12, 2004, p. D8.
7. *2006 Annual Report* (Minneapolis, MN: General Mills, Inc., 2007, p. 8.
8. *2008 Annual Report* (Minneapolis, MN: General Mills, Inc., 2009), pp. 8, 9.
9. Hugh Courtney, John T. Horn, and Jayanti Kar, "Getting into Your Competitor's Head," *The McKinsey Quarterly*, February 2009.
10. Robert A. Kerin, P. Rajan Varadarajan, and Robert A. Peterson, "First-Mover Advantage: A Synthesis, Conceptual Framework, and Research Proposition," *Journal of Marketing*, October 1992, pp. 33–52; and Pankaj Ghemawat, "Sustainable Advantage," *Harvard Business Review*, September–October 1986, pp. 53–58.
11. Nitin Nohria, William Joyce, and Bruce Roberson, "What Really Works," *Harvard Business Review*, July 2003, pp. 42–52; and "Who Gets Eaten and Who Gets to Eat," *The Economist*, July 12, 2003, pp. 61–63.
12. Armin Harris, et al, "The Directors: Costco Wholesale," *Fortune*, May 4, 2009, pp. 100–1.
13. Kathleen Kerwin and Paul Magnusson, "Can Anything Stop Toyota?" *BusinessWeek*, November 17, 2003, pp. 114–22.
14. Ben R. Rich and Leo Janos, *Skunk Works* (Boston: Little, Brown and Company, 1994).
15. Murali K. Mantrala, Probhakant Sirha, and Andris A. Zoltners, "Impact of Resource Allocation Rules on Marketing Investment-Level Decisions and Profitability," *Journal of Marketing Research*, May 1992, pp. 162–75.
16. Anjali Cordiero and Mike Barris, "General Mills Profit Hurt by Costs," *The Wall Street Journal*, March 19, 2009, p. B11; and Stuart Elliott, "Like Comfort Food, Warm and Fuzzy Makes a Comeback," *The New York Times*, April 7, 2009, p. B3.
17. Vanitha Swaminathan, Richard J. Fox, and Srinivas K. Reddy, "The Impact of Brand Extension Introduction on Choice," *Journal of Marketing*, October 2001, pp. 1–15; Deborah Roedder-John, Barbara Loken, and Christopher Joiner, "The Negative Impact of Extensions: Can Flagship Products Be Diluted?" *Journal of Marketing*, January 1998, pp. 19–32; and Akshay R. Rao, Lu Qu, and Robert W. Ruekert, "Signaling Unobservable Product Quality through a Brand Ally," *Journal of Marketing Research*, May 1999, pp. 258–68.
18. Lisa C. Troy, Tanawat Hirunyawipada, and Audhesh K. Paswan, "Cross-Functional Integration and New Product Success: An Empirical Investigation of the Findings," *Journal of Marketing*, November 2008, pp. 132–46.
19. Vanessa Chan, Chris Musso, and Venkatesh Shankar, "Assuming Innovation Metrics," *The McKinsey Quarterly*, October 2008; and Jacques Buglin, Amy Guggenheim Shankar, and Marc Singer, "How Poor Metrics Undermine Digital Marketing," *The McKinsey Quarterly*, October 2008.
20. Adapted with permission of The Free Press, a Division of Macmillan, Inc., from *Competitive Advantage: Creating and Sustaining Superior Performance* by Michael E. Porter. Copyright 1985 by Michael E. Porter.
21. David Welch, "Staying Paranoid at Toyota," *BusinessWeek*, July 2, 2007, pp. 80–82.
22. Adapted from Philip Kotler and Kevin Lane Keller, *Marketing Management*, 12th ed. (Upper Saddle River, NJ: Prentice Hall, 2006), pp. 262–63.
23. Zachary Schiller, Greg Burns, and Karen Lowry Miller, "Make It Simple," *BusinessWeek*, September 9, 1996, pp. 96–104.
24. Several of the items in the list are adapted from Massimo Garbuio, Dan Lovallo, and Patrick Viguerie, "How Companies Make Good Decisions," *The McKinsey Quarterly*, December 2008; Renee Dye and Olivier Sibony "How to Improve Strategic Planning," *The McKinsey Quarterly*, August 2007; and Jungkiu Choi, Dan Lovallo, and Anna Tarasova, "Better Strategy for Business Units," *The McKinsey Quarterly*, June 2007.
25. University of Pennsylvania Wharton Alumni Emeritus Society, *Spring 2009 Newsletter*, p. 2.
26. Stratford Sherman, "How Intel Makes Spending Pay Off," *Fortune*, February 22, 1993, pp. 57–61.
27. Julie Jargon, "General Mills Tries to Convince Americans to Cook Chinese," *The Wall Street Journal*, May 29, 2007, pp. B1, B3; Matt McKinney, "General Public, Meet General Mills," *StarTribune*,

April 6, 2007, pp. D1, D; Julie Jargon, "General Mills Seeks Help from Iron Chief," *The Wall Street Journal*, April 4, 2007, p. B4; and "General Mills Supports Creation of New Food Science Division at Your Encore,™" General Mills press release, July 10, 2007.

28. Bjorn Lomborg, "Prioritizing the World's To-Do List," *Fortune*, May 17, 2004, p. 60; and Alfred Marcus, Donald A. Geffen, and Ken Sexton, "Business-Government Cooperation in Environmental Decision Making," *International Journal of Corporate Sustainability 9*, no. 4 (2002), pp. 345–55.
29. Charles H. Noble and Michael P. Mokwa, "Implementing Marketing Strategies: Developing and Testing a Managerial Theory," *Journal of Marketing*, October 1999, pp. 57–74.
30. J. P. Donlon, "Lafley's Law: "If You Want to Become a Game-Changer," *CEO Magazine*, July/August 2008, pp. 48–54; Steve Lohr, "How Crisis Shapes the Corporate Model," *The New York Times*, March 29, 2009, p. BU4; and Ellen Byron, "Guidance from P&G Likely to Be Cautious," *The Wall Street Journal*, May 28, 2009, p. B1.
31. Anne Fisher, "America's Most Admired Companies," *Fortune*, March 19, 2007, pp. 88–94.
32. Daniel Roth, "This Ain't No Pizza Party," *Fortune*, November 9, 1998, pp. 158–64.
33. Thomas J. Peters and Robert H. Waterman, Jr., *In Search of Excellence: Lessons from America's Best-Run Companies* (New York: Harper & Row, 1982).
34. Tom Peters, "Winners Do Hundreds of Percent over Norm," *StarTribune*, January 8, 1985, p. 5B; and Rich and Janos, *Skunk Works*, pp. 51–53.
35. Jeffrey M. O'Brien, "IBM's Grand Plan to Save the Planet," *Fortune*, May 4, 2009, pp. 85–91; and Steve Lohr, "Who Says Innovation Belongs to the Small?" *The New York Times*, May 24, 2009, p. BU4.
36. David Court, "The Downturn's New Rules for Marketers," *The McKinsey Quarterly*, December 2008; and David Court, "The Evolving Role of the CMO," *The McKinsey Quarterly, August 2007.*
37. Alexander Krasnikov and Satish Jayachandran, "The Relative Impact of Marketing, Research-and-Development, and Operations Capabilities on Firm Performance," *Journal of Marketing*, July 2008, pp. 1–11.
38. Robert W. Ruekert and Orville W. Walker, Jr., "Marketing's Interaction with Other Functional Units: A Conceptual Framework and Empirical Evidence," *Journal of Consumer Marketing*, Spring 1987, pp. 1–19; and Shikhar Sarin and Vijay Mahajan, "The Effect of Reward Structures on the Performance of Cross-Functional Product Development Teams," *Journal of Marketing*, April 2001, pp. 35–53.
39. Nelson D. Schwartz, "Colgate Cleans Up," *Fortune*, April 16, 2001, pp. 179–80.
40. Julie Jargon, "New Ads Will Stir Up Coffee Wars," *The Wall Street Journal*, May 4, 2009, p. B7; and Armin Harris, et al, "The Directors; McDonald's," *Fortune*, May 4, 2009, pp. 92–93.
41. James D. Lenskold, *Marketing ROI* (New York: McGraw-Hill, 2003).
42. Michael Krauss, "Balance Attention to Metrics with Intuition," *Marketing News*, June 1, 2007, pp. 6–8; John Davis, *Measuring Marketing: 103 Key Metrics Every Marketer Needs* (Singapore: Wiley and Sons, 2007); and Paul W. Farris, Neil T. Bendle, Phillip E. Pfeifer, and David J. Reibstein, *Marketing Metrics* (Upper Saddle River, NJ: Wharton School Publishing, 2006).
43. Malcolm Craig, *Thinking Visually: Business Applications of 14 Core Diagrams* (New York and London: Continuum, 2000).
44. The illustrative example of using a marketing dashboard at General Mills was developed by David Ford and Vivian Milroy Callaway.

Warm Delights: This case was prepared by David Ford based on interviews with Vivian Millroy Callaway.

Appendix C

1. Diane Brady, "Creating Brand You," *BusinessWeek*, August 22, 2007, pp. 72–73; and Denny E. McCorkle, Joe F. Alexander, and Memo F. Diriker, "Developing Self-Marketing Skills for Student Career Success," Journal of Marketing Education, Spring, 1992, pp. 57–67.
2. Marianne E. Green, "Marketing Yourself: From Student to Professional," *Job Choices for Business & Liberal Arts Students*, 50th ed., 2007, pp. 30–31; Joanne Cleaver, "Find a Job Through Self-Promotion," *Marketing News*, January 31, 2000, pp. 12, 16.
3. John N. Frank, "Stand Out From the Crowd, Landing a Marketing Job Today Means Touting Your Specialty and Staying Positive," *Marketing News*, January 30, 2009, p. 22.
4. "Opportunities by Occupation," *Job Choices for Business & Liberal Arts Students: 2009*, 52nd ed., National Association of Colleges and Employers, p. 101; "Opportunities by Occupation," *Job Choices: Diversity Edition 2009*, 52nd ed., National Association of Colleges and Employers, p. 154; Lindsey Gerdes, "The Best Places to Launch a Career," *BusinessWeek*, September 15, 2008, p. 36.
5. Nicholas Basta, "The Wide World of Marketing," *BW's Guide to Careers*, February–March 1984, pp. 70–72.
6. "Leading CEO's: A statistical Snapshot of S&P 500 Leaders," *Research & Insight, Spencer Stuart*, December 2008, www.spencerstuart.com/research/ceo/975/, accessed June 14, 2009.
7. "Average Yearly Salary Offers," *Salary Survey* (Bethlehem, PA: National Association of Colleges and Employers, Winter 2009), p. 4.
8 "Advertising, Marketing, Promotions, Public Relations, and Sales Managers," *Occupational Outlook Handbook*, 2008–09 Edition (Washington, DC: U.S. Department of Labor, 2008), www.bls.gov/oco/ocos020.htm, accessed June 12, 2009.
9. Matthew Creamer, "P&G Primes Its Pinpoint Marketing," *Advertising Age*, May 7, 2007.
10. "Career Functions," P&G Career Advice Center, www.pg.com/jobs/cac/functions.shtml, accessed June 14, 2009.
11. "Wholesale Trade," *Occupational Handbook*, 2008–09 Edition (Washington, DC: U.S. Department of Labor, 2008), www.bls.gov/oco/cg/cgs026.htm, accessed June 14, 2009.
12. S. William Pattis, Careers in Advertising (New York: McGraw-Hill, 2004).
13. Duane Forrester, "Search Can Offer Jobs, Decent Salaries," *Advertising Age*, May 26, 2008, p. 28; and Tanya Lewis, "Talent in Demand," *PR Week Career Guide*, 2006, pp. 4–6.
14. Roslyn Dolber, *Opportunities in Retailing Careers* (New York: McGraw-Hill, 2008).
15. Peter Coy, "Help Wanted," *BusinessWeek*, May 11, 2009, pp. 40–46; and "The Way We'll Work," *Time*, May 25, 2009, pp. 39–50.,
16. Rebecca Aronaur, "Shaping the Profession of Sales," *Sales & Marketing Management*, July 1, 2006.
17. Jack and Suzy Welch, "Dear Graduate . . . To Stand Out Among Your Peers, You Have to Overdeliver," *BusinessWeek*, June 19, 2006, p. 100.
18. "People's Choice Awards. And the Winners Are . . ." *Sales and Marketing Management*, November/December 2008, p. 20; and Elisabeth A. Sullivan, "One-to-One," *Marketing News*, June 15, 2009, pp. 10–13.
19. Edmund Hershberger and Madhav N. Segal, "Ads for MR Positions Reveal Desired Skills," *Marketing News*, February 1, 2007, p. 28.
20. "Market Research Analyst," in Les Krantz, ed., *Jobs Rated Almanac*, 6th ed. (New York: St. Martin's Press, 2002).
21. Deborah L. Vence, "In an Instant, More Researchers Use IM for Fast, Reliable Results," *Marketing News*, March 1, 2006, p. 53; and Joshua Grossnickle and Oliver Raskin, "What's Ahead on the Internet," *Marketing Research*, Summer 2001, pp. 9–13.

22. Carolyn D. Marconi, "Desperately Looking for New Talent Is a Recurring Theme," *Marketing Research*, Spring 2000, pp. 4–6.
23. International Franchise Association, http//franchise.org/Blockbuster Inc franchise.aspx.
24. Lisa Bertagnoli, "Marketing Overseas Excellent for Career," *Marketing News*, June 4, 2001, p. 4.
25. Pete Engardio, "A Guide for Multinationals: One of the Great Challenges for a Multinational Is Learning How to Build a Productive Global Team," *BusinessWeek*, August 20, 2007, p. 48; and Joann S. Lublin, "Global Experience Doesn't Have To Mean Going to Live Overseas," *The Wall Street Journal*, August 29, 2006, B1.
26. Barbara Flood, "Turbo Charge Your Job Search, Job Searching and Career Development Tips," *Information Outlook*, May 1, 2007, p. 40.
27. Robin T. Peterson and J. Stuart Devlin, "Perspectives on Entry-Level Positions by Graduating Marketing Seniors," *Marketing Education Review*, Summer 1994, pp. 2–5.
28. "Succeeding in the Job Market For the Class of 2007," *Job Choices for Business & Liberal Arts Students*, 50th ed., 2007, pp. 14–15; and Callum J. Floyd and Mary Ellen Gordon, "What Skills Are Most Important? A Comparison of Employer, Student, and Staff Perceptions," *Journal of Marketing Education*, August 1998, pp. 103–09.
29. Barbara Flood, "Turbo Charge Your Job Search, Job Searching and Career Development Tips," *Information Outlook*, May 1, 2007, p. 40.
30. Barbara Kiviat, "The New Rules of Web Hiring," *Time*, November 24, 2003, p. 57; Karen Epper Hoffman, "Recruitment Sites Changing Their Focus," *Internet World*, March 15, 1999; Pamela Mendels, "Now That's Casting A Wide Net," *BusinessWeek*, May 25, 1998: and James C. Gonyea, *The Online Job Search Companion* (New York: McGraw-Hill, 1995).
31. Peter Cappelli, "Making the Most of On-Line Recruiting," *Harvard Business Review*, March 2001, pp. 139–46.
32. Ronald B. Marks, *Personal Selling: A Relationship Approach*, 6th ed. (New York: Pearson, 1996).
33. Leonard Felson, "Undergrad Marketers Must Get Jump on Networking Skills," *Marketing News*, April 8, 2001, p. 14; Wayne E. Baker, *Networking Smart* (New York: McGraw-Hill, 1994); and Piet Levy, "AMA Chapters Across the Country Are Increasingly Using Job Boards, Networking Events and Other Techniques to Help Members in this Economy," *Marketing News*, March 15, 2009, p. 14.
34. Dan Schawbel, "Top 10 Social Sites for Finding a Job," *Mashable*, February 24, 2009.
35. "Stand Out at the Career Fair," *Job Choices for Business & Liberal Arts Students: 2009*, 52nd ed. (Bethlehem, PA: National Association of Colleges and Employers, 2008), pp. 22–23.
36. Marianne E. Green, "Marketing Yourself: From Student to Professional," *Job Choices for Business & Liberal Arts Students: 2009* (Bethlehem, PA: National Association of Colleges and Employers, 2008), pp. 28–29.
37. Marianne E. Green, "Resume Writing: Sell Your Skills to Get the Interview!" *Job Choices for Business & Liberal Arts Students*, 50th ed., 2007, pp. 39–47.
38. C. Randall Powell, "Secrets of Selling a Résumé," in Peggy Schmidt, ed., *The Honda How to Get a Job Guide* (New York: McGraw-Hill, 1984), pp. 4–9.
39. "Post With Caution: Your Online Profile and our Job Search," *Job Choices for Business & Liberal Arts Students: 20009* (Bethlehem, PA: National Association of Colleges and Employers, 2008), p. 30; "If I 'Google' You, What Will I Find?" *Job Choices for Business and Liberal Arts Students*, 50th ed., 2007, p. 16; Joyce Lain Kennedy, "Computer-Friendly Résumé Tips," Planning Job Choices: *1999*, 42nd ed. (Bethlehem, PA: National Association of Colleges and Employers, 1998), p. 49; and Joyce Lain Kennedy and Thomas J. Morrow, *Electronic Résumé Revolution* (New York: Wiley and Sons, 1994).
40. William J. Banis, "The Art of Writing Job-Search Letters," *Job Choices for Business and Liberal Arts Students*, 50th ed., 2007, pp. 32–38; and Arthur G. Sharp, "The Art of the Cover Letter," *Career Futures* 4, no. 1 (1992), pp. 50–51.
41. Alison Damast, "Recruiters' Top 10 Complaints," *BusinessWeek*, April 26, 2007; and Marilyn Moats Kennedy, "Don't List' Offers Important Tips for Job Interviews," *Marketing News*, March 15, 2007, p. 26.
42. Dana James, "A Day in the Life of a Corporate Recruiter," *Marketing News* April 10, 2000, pp. 1, 11.
43. Robert M. Greenberg, "The company Visit—Revisited," *NACE Journal*, Winter 2003, pp. 21–27.
44. Mary E. Scott, "High-Touch vs. High-Tech Recruitment," *NACE Journal*, Fall 2002, pp. 33–39.

Appendix D

1. The Nike MaxSight case was prepared by Professor Linda Rochford, University of Minnesota, Duluth, based on the following sources: Bausch and Lomb Web site, www.bausch.com/en US/consumer/visioncare/product/softcontacts/nikemaxsight.aspx; Nike Web site, www.nike.com/nikevision/main.html; "A Brief History of Contact Lenses," Contact Lens Manufacturers Association, February 2007, www.contactlenses.org/timeline.htm; Richard Edlich, "A Tribute to Dr. Robert C. Allen, an Inspirational Teacher, Humanitarian and Friend," *Journal Long Term Effects of Medical Implants*, no. 163 (2006), pp. 261–64; MayoClinic.com, "Tools for Better Health: Melanoma," www.mayoclinic.com/health/melanoma/DS00439/DSECTION-1; MayoClinic.com, "Tools for Better Health: Eye Melanoma," www.mayoclinic.com/health/eye-melanoma/DS00707; and MayoClinic.com, "Tools for Better Health: Contact Lenses: What to Know Before You Buy," www.mayoclinic.com/health/contact-lenses/WL00010.
2. The Daktronics, Inc., case was prepared by William Rudelius based on conversations with Dr. Al Kurtenbach, internal sources, and these other sources: Bill Syken, "Bright Lights, Little City," *Sports Illustrated*, May 11, 2004; Dick Youngblood, "Signs of Success" *StarTribune*, April 6, 2003, pp. D1, D2; Marilyn Alva, "Shifting Technology Helps It Score Big Wins," *Investor's Business Daily*, January 12, 2004; and Michael Hiestand, "S.D. Company Lights Up Sports World," *USA Today*, May 4, 2004, pp. C1, Cs.
3. The Jamba Juice case was prepared by Professor Linda Rochford, University of Minnesota, Duluth, and Steven Hartley from the following sources: Jamba Juice Corporation Web site and press releases: www.jambajuice.com; "Juicy Prospects," *StarTribune*, August 27, 2001, pp. D1–D2; Scott Hume, "Segment Rankings," *Restaurants and Institutions*, July 1, 2004, p. 61; Celeste Ward, "Riney Creates Good Karma for Jamba Juice," *Adweek.com*, March 18, 2004; and John Agoglia, "Squeezing Profits," *Club Industry*, December 1, 2003, p. 12.
4. The Ford and Firestone case was prepared by Professor Linda Rochford, University of Minnesota, Duluth, from the following sources: David Barboza, "Bridgestone/Firestone to Close Tire Plant at Center of Huge Recall," *The New York Times*, June 28, 2001, p. C1; Keith Bradsher, "Ford Intends to Replace 13 Million Firestone Wilderness Tires," *The New York Times*, May 23, 2001, p. C1; John Greenwald, "Tired of Each Other," *Time*, June 4, 2001, pp. 51–56; and Phil Meyerowitz, "SUV Chic: The Rugged and the Reckless," *The New York Times*, July 7, 2001, p. 12.
5. The Jamisons case was prepared by Professor Roy D. Adler, Pepperdine University, Malibu. Used with permission.
6. The Motetronix Technology case was prepared by Roger A. Kerin, based on company sources.

7. The Callaway case was prepared by Professor Linda Rochford, University of Minnesota, Duluth, from the following sources: James Achenback, "From Hickory Stick to Callaway, Ely Sought to Please Golfers," *Golfweek*, July 14, 2001, pp. 26–27; "China the Largest Growth Market for Equipment," *Golf Today*, March 2004, www.golftoday.co.uk/news/yeartodate/news04/china.html; "Opportunities in Global Golf Club Market: Market to Grow Over 25% in India and China According to E-Composites, Inc.," PR Newswire, February 18 ,2004, www.prnewswire.com; "2006 Participation by Sport," National Sporting Goods Association, www.nsga.org; "Callaway Golf Co.: Company Description, Financial Summary," Reuters, 2007; Bennet Galloway, "Adrift in a Sea of Golf Balls," *Golf In Japan*, June 10, 2006, www.golf-in-japan.com/bennetts; John Steinbreder, "Partnership Could Strengthen NGF's Research," *Golfweek Business*, June 4, 2007; Bradley Klein, "Klein: Remedies for the Malaise," *Golfweek Business*, March 5, 2007; Beth Ann Baldry, "Dispatch from South Korea," *Golfweek Business*, July 20, 2007; Paul Jones, "Japan Golf: The State of the Game," *Golf In Japan*, February 14, 2006, www.golf-in-japan.com/pauls; John Paul Newport, "Golf Journal: Spin Control; Golf's Police Are Tweaking Clubhead Rules, But a Bigger Issue Looms: The Balls," *The Wall Street Journal* (Eastern Edition), March 3, 2007, p. 7; and John Paul Newport, "Golf Journal: Crazy Driver: THE Clubs About to Shake Up Golf: Bizarre New Designs Could Improve Players' Shots—And Many in the Game Worry That's a Bad Thing," *The Wall Street Journal* (Eastern Edition), January 6, 2007, p. 1.
8. The HOM Furniture case was prepared by Kathy Chadwick based on interviews with Wayne Johansen and internal HOM Furniture materials.
9. The Lawn Mowers case was prepared by Professor Linda Rochford, University of Minnesota, Duluth, based on the following sources: Don Babwin, "Reel Mowers Cut in Quietly," *Denver Post*, May 28, 2007, www.denverpost.com; Felicity Barringer, "A Greener Way to Cut the Grass Runs Afoul of a Powerful Lobby," *The New York Times*, April 24, 2006; "It All Adds Up; Lawnmowers," *The Economist*, June 9, 2007, p. 36; "Lawn and Garden Tractors and Home Lawn and Garden Equipment," *Encyclopedia of American Industries, Online Edition*, Thomson Gale, 2007; "Canadians Switch to Push-Reel Lawn Mowers for Health and Environment," Associated Press Financial Wire, July 2, 2007; Mindy Fetterman, "Compared with Today's Mowers, Yesterday's Just Don't Cut It," *USA Today*, May 4, 2007, p. 4B; Charles J. Murray, "Mowing on Autopilot: With the Introduction of the RoboMower in the U.S., Two Israeli Inventors May Open New Door to the Fledgling Home Robotics Market," *Design News*, June 26, 2006, p. 37; Jonathan Welsh, "Splendor in the Grass; Big, Fast, 'Zero-Turn' Mowers Are Latest Status Symbol; Cruise Control and Cupholders," *The Wall Street Journal*, June 13, 2007, p. D1; Virginia Smith, "A Luscious Lawn's Lure: For Some, It's an Obsession They Never Outgrow," *Philadelphia Inquirer*, May 5, 2006; "Lawn Mowers," *Consumer Reports Buying Guide 2006*, pp. 92–95; Ray Routhier, "Mowers—They're Not Just for Grass Anymore," *Portland Press Herald*, July 15, 2007, p. A1; and Rachel Sauer, "Get Your Mower Runnin'; Speeds Reached: 30 Mph, Goal: To Mow Down the Competition," *Palm Beach Post*, June 5, 2007, p. 1E.
10. The Medtronic in China case was prepared by Mark T. Spriggs and Kenneth E. Goodpaster based on Medtronic annual reports and three Medtronic cases: *Medtronic in China (A)*, *(B)*, and *(C)* prepared by research assistant Linda Swenson under the supervision of Kenneth E. Goodpaster (Minneapolis-St. Paul, MN: University of St. Thomas).
11. The Pampered Pooches case was prepared by Professor Linda Rochford, University of Minnesota, Duluth, based on the following sources: American Pet Products Manufacturers Association, Inc., "Industry Trends, 2007–2008", Pet Owners Survey Summary, www.appma.org/press-industrytrends.asp; Diane Brady and Christopher Palmeri, "The Pet Economy," *Business Week*, August 2007; John Woestendisk, "Statistics, Trends Reflect Growing Importance of Pets in the Home," *Baltimore Sun*, July 22, 2007; Sarah Casey Newman "Traveling with Terriers and Tabbies," *St. Louis Post-Dispatch*, July 21, 2007; Leanne Ritchie, "Airline Bans Pets From Travel on Regular Flights," *Daily News*, July 20, 2007; "New Dolce Vita™ Traveler™ Pet Products Let Your Dog Travel in Warmth and Comfort; Take Your Pets Anywhere You Go," PR Newswire, February 22, 2007; and "Traveling with Pets for the Dogs, According to TripAdvisor Survey; TripAdvisor Names Top 10 Pet-Friendly Accommodations," PR Newswire, July 18, 2007.
12. The DigitalThink case was adapted by Monica Noordam and Steven Hartley from a case titled "LearningByte International" written by Giana Eckardt. Sources: Personal interviews with Umberto Milletti and Shelly Berkowitz; DigitalThink's Web site, www.digitalthink.com; Lisa Vaas, "The E-Training of America," *PC Magazine*, December 26, 2001; DigitalThink press release, "DigitalThink Ranked Number 22 Fastest Growing Technology Company in North America on 2003 Deloitte Technology Fast 500," October 14, 2003; and "Making E-Learning More than 'Pixie Dust,'" *Workforce Management*, March 1, 2003, p. 58.
13. The Health Cruises, Inc., case was prepared by Professors Maurice Mandell and Larry Rosenberg, Reprinted with permission.
14. The Bagel Bakes case was prepared by Michael A. Stanko and Matthew Fleming. Michael A. Stanko is a marketing doctoral candidate at Michigan State University. Matthew Fleming is a certified management accountant currently working in Beijing, China. Previously, Matthew was a senior financial analyst at General Mills Canada. © 2007, M. Stanko & M.SW.U., All rights reserved. Used with permission.
15. The Ken Davis Products case was prepared by Professor Linda Rochford, University of Minnesota, Duluth, based on the following sources: Ken Davis Web site: www.kendavis-bbq.com; Kelly Alexander, "'Cue It Up: Taste Testing Barbecue Sauces, From Supermarket to Specialty Brands," *Slate*, May 20, 2002; Hoovers, Food Wholesale Distributors, www.hoovers.com/industry/food-wholesale-distributors/companies; and special thanks to Patrick Miner and Tania New for their assistance with this case.
16. The Dell case was prepared by Professor Linda Rochford, University of Minnesota, Duluth, based on the following sources: Shu-ching Jean Chen, "Dell Going Small in Asia," Forbes.com, July 18, 2007; "Dell 2007 Annual Report," www.dell.com; "Dell Sets Goal of Becoming Greenest Technology Company," www.dell.com/content/topics/global.aspx; "Batteries Burn Benighted Dell," *Client Server News*, August 21, 2006; Brian Caulfield, "What Will Dell Cut Next?" Forbes.com, June 7, 2007; "HP Gains Ground As Dell's Woes Continue," *Information Week*, August 21, 2006; "PC Shipments Rose 12% in Q2, HP Had Top Share," Reuters, July 18, 2007; "Dell Computer Corporation Financial Highlights," Reuters, July 19, 2007; "High Tech Supply Chain: Michael Dell's Memo to Dell Computer Employees Leaked," *Supply Chain Digest*, February 9, 2007; and Louise Lee and Peter Burrows, "Is Dell Too Big for Michael Dell?" *Business Week*, February 12, 2007, p. 33.
17. The Trader Joe's case was prepared by Professor Linda Rochford, associate professor of marketing, University of Minnesota, Duluth, from the following sources: "Trader Joe's Company," www.hoovers.com; SN's Top 75 Retailers for 2009, supermarketnews.com, accessed October 15, 2009; David Orgel, "Trader Joe's President Shares Secrets of Success," *Supermarket News*, February 6, 2006; Joy Buchanan, "More Than Just Goat Cheese," Knight-Ridder/Tribune Business News, December 9, 2005; Mark Hamstra "Convenience Only One Small Part of Total Value Equation," *Supermarket*

News, July 17, 2006; and "Behind the Scenes at Trader Joe's" *Private Label Buyer* 20, no. 4 (April 2006).

18. The McDonald's in Restaurant case was prepared by Sarah Casanova of McDonald's Canada and Michael J. Vessey based on internal McDonald's reports and information from the McDonald's Web site, www.mcdonalds.com.

19. The Target case was prepared by Professor Linda Rochford, assistant professor of marketing, University of Minnesota, Duluth, from the following sources: Target Corporation Web site, www.target.com; "Target Makes Itself Ubiquitous," *MMR* 22, no. 16 (October 3, 2005), p. 16; "Target's Advertising Savvy," *MMR* 24, no. 1 (January 8, 2007), p. 32; Laura Heller, "Target Sweeps Awards Honoring Best Advertising; Office Max Also Wins Nod; Target Stores Inc.," *DSN Retailing Today*, February 25, 2005, p. 6; "Target Dominates RAC Awards," *Chain Store Age*, April 2004, p. 65; "Target Sees 'Red' with In-Store TV Network," *DSN Retailing Today*, March 27, 2006, p. 6; and "The New Yorker Is Scolded Over Single-Sponsor Issue," *The New York Times*, September 19, 2005, p. C7.

20. The Morgantown Furniture case was prepared by Roger A. Kerin, based on company sources.

21. The Crate and Barrel case was prepared by Professor Linda Rochford, University of Minnesota, Duluth, based on the following sources: Crate and Barrel Web site, www.crateandbarrel.com; Crate and Barrel 2007 catalogs; "Crate and Barrel Selects Unica Corporation's Affinium to Increase Effectiveness of its Multi-Channel Marketing Campaigns," *Business Wire*, April 28, 2004; "Euromarket Design, Inc.," RDS Business and Company Resource Center, 2007; and "Otto Group Takes the Lead in Online Business," Otto Group Media Centre press release, March 28, 2007, www.ottogroup.com/press.

22. The Naked Juice case was prepared by Professor Linda Rochford, University of Minnesota, Duluth, based on the following sources: Anjali Cordeiro, "Beverage Deal Gets Fuel From Desire for Less Fizz," *The Wall Street Journal*, February 14, 2007; Paul Ziobro, "Health Drinks Reward Backers," *The Wall Street Journal*, January 4, 2007, p. B10A; "Naked Juice Company," Hoovers.com; Naked Juice Web site, www.naked juice.com, and promotional materials; Hansen's Natural Web site, www.hansens.com; Kate MacArthur, "Pepsi Primes Brand Overhauls: Exclusive: $50M effort from BBDO Looks to Restore the Tone and Spirit of the 1970s Work," *AA* 77, no .42, p. 1; Bureau of Labor Statistics, *Who's Buying Alcoholic and Nonalcoholic Beverages* (Ithaca, NY: New Strategist Publications, 2005); Odwalla Products Web site, www.odwalla.com; "A Healthy Glow: Consumers Soak Up the Health Benefits of Juice and Juice Drinks," *Beverage Industry*, January 12, 2007; "Naked Juice Expands DSD, Taps Team of R&D Experts," *Beverage Industry*, August 8, 2006; "2006 State of the Industry," *Beverage Industry*, July 22, 2006; "Soda Industry to Stop Selling Non-Diet Soft Drinks in Schools," *Food Chemical News* 48, no. 13 (May 8, 2006); and "Beverages," *Media Week*, May 1, 2006, p. SR16.

CREDITS

CHAPTER 1

PP. 2–3, Courtesy 3M; Photo: Bowen Marketing. P. 4, ©M. Hruby. P. 4, ©M. Hruby. P. 4, Courtesy YouTube LLC. P. 5, ©Michael Grecco Photography. P. 5, ©Douglas Adesko. P. 7, ©M. Hruby. P. 9, Courtesy New Product Works. P. 9, This photo made available as a courtesy by Nestlé USA. P. 9, Courtesy RaySat Broadcast CorP. P. 9, Courtesy Pepsi-Cola North America Beverages. P. 12, Courtesy Southwest Airlines. P. 12, Courtesy Starbucks Corporation. P. 12, Courtesy The Home Depot, Inc. P. 14, Courtesy 3M. P. 15, Courtesy 3M. P. 16, Courtesy Toyota Motor Sales, U.S.A., Inc.; Agency: Saatchi/LA; Photo: Vic Huber Photography. P. 18, Courtesy Bridging Inc. P. 19, Réunion des Musées Nationaux/Art Resource, NY. P. 19, Annebicque Bernard/Corbis Sygma. P. 19, *No credit.* P. 22, Courtesy 3M. P. 23, Courtesy 3M.

CHAPTER 2

P. 24, *All* Courtesy Ben & Jerry's Homemade, Inc. P. 26, ©2009 Google. P. 26, Courtesy Nature Conservancy Communications. P. 29, Courtesy Medtronic. P. 30, Photography by Sean Lamb, 2004. P. 30, ©1997–2009 Netflix Inc. P. 31, ©Michael Sugrue. P. 33, Courtesy Oracle Corporation. P. 35, ©Rick Armstrong. P. 35, *All* Courtesy Eastman Kodak Company; Agency Ketchum Communications. P. 36, All Courtesy Eastman Kodak Company; Agency Ketchum Communications. P. 38, ©M. Hruby. P. 41, Courtesy Medtronic. P. 43, Courtesy Eastman Kodak Company. P. 45, Courtesy Eastman Kodak Company. P. 47, Courtesy British Petroleum. P. 48, Courtesy British Petroleum. P. 49, Courtesy British Petroleum.

APPENDIX A

P. 54, ©1996 Paradise Kitchens, Inc. All photos & ads reprinted with permission.

CHAPTER 3

P. 64, Courtesy Defense Industry Daily, LLC in association with Watershed Publishing. P. 69, ©The Procter & Gamble Company. Used by permission. P. 69, Courtesy Global Hyatt Corporation. P. 69, Courtesy Samsung. Telecommunications America, LLP. P. 71, Copyright©NetImapact. http://www.netimpact.org. P. 73, Courtesy GM Archives. P. 74, ©M. Hruby. P. 77, Courtesy ESRI. P. 77, Courtesy Regent Seven Seas Cruises. P. 78, Courtesy Sony Electronics, Inc. P. 78, Citrix, Citrix Online and GoToMeeting are registered trademarks of Citrix Systems, Inc. P. 78, Courtesy MySpace.com. P. 79, Courtesy Municipality of Central Elgin/Ontario, Canada. P. 79, Courtesy Tomra of North America. P. 83, ©M. Hruby. P. 84, Courtesy American Marketing Association/Marketing News Magazine. P. 85, Courtesy of Better Business Bureau, Inc. P. 88, Photo by Tim Boyle/Getty Images. P. 89, Photo by Tim Boyle/Getty Images.

CHAPTER 4

PP. 90–91, Courtesy Anheuser-Busch Companies. P. 95, Martin Poole/Stockbyte/Getty Images. P. 96, ©5 Creative, L.P. Illustration C. Tew & J. Robinson. P. 97, Courtesy Transparency International. P. 100, ©M. Hruby. P. 102, Courtesy Susan G. Komen Breast Cancer Foundation. P. 103, PhotoDisc Blue. P. 104, AP Photo/Elizabeth Dalziel. P. 105, AP Photo/Richard Vogel. P. 108, ©Michael Newman/PhotoEdit.

CHAPTER 5

P. 110, Courtesy TBWA Chiat Day/New York. P. 114, Karin Dreyer/Blend Images/Getty Images. P. 115, Courtesy PepsiCo, Inc./Frito-Lay, Inc. P. 117, Courtesy Campbell Soup Company. P. 120, The Secret Sales Pitch: An Overview of Subliminal Advertising. Copyright ©2004 by August Bullock. All Rights Reserved. Used with permission. SubliminalSex.com. P. 121, FRESH STEPS® is a registered trademark of The Clorox Pet Products Company. Used with permission. ©2009 The Clorox Pet Products Company. Reprinted with permission. P. 121, ©2001 Mary Kay, Inc. Photos by: Grace Huang for Sarah Laird. P. 123, Courtesy Cogate-Palmolive Company. P. 123, Courtesy Unilever U.S. Inc.; Photographer: Martin Thompson; Photography: Smoke & Mirrors. P. 124, Courtesy SRI Consulting Business Intelligence (SRIC-BI), Menlo Park, CA. VALS™ is a trademark of SRI Consulting Business Intelligence. Reprinted with permission. P. 125, Courtesy SRI Consulting Business Intelligence (SRIC-BI), Menlo Park, CA. VALS™ is a trademark of SRI Consulting Business Intelligence. Reprinted with permission. P. 126, *Both ads* Courtesy Omega SA. P. 127, Courtesy BzzAgent, LLC. P. 130, Courtesy of Haggar Clothing Co. P. 131, Courtesy ACH Food Companies, Inc. P. 132, Courtesy Bonne Bell, Inc. P. 133, Used with permission from McDonald's Corporation. P. 136, ©Gary Conner/PhotoEdit.

Figure 5-2, Copyright 2009 by Consumers Union f U.S., Inc. Yonkers, NY 10703-1057, a nonprofit organization. Reprinted with permission from the January 2009 issue of CONSUMER REPORTS® for educational purposes only. No commercial use or reproduction permitted. www.ConsumerReports.org.; Figure 5–15, Source: SRI Consulting Business Intelligence (SRIC-BI); www.sric-bi.com/VALS.

CHAPTER 6

P. 138, Courtesy J.C. Penney Company, Inc. P. 141, Courtesy Lockheed Martin Company. P. 142, Courtesy U.S. Department of Commerce/Bureau of the Census. P. 146, Lluis Gene/AFP/Getty Images. P. 147, Jewel Samad/AFP/Getty Images. P. 148, VEER Mark Adams/Photonica/Getty Images. P. 152, *No credit.* P. 154, Courtesy Slack Barshinger/Chicago. P. 155, Jim Esposito/blend Images/Getty Images. P. 155, Comstock Images/Getty Images. P. 155, Comstock Images/Getty Images. P. 155, Jim Esposito/blend Images/Getty Images. P. 159, ©M. Hruby.

CHAPTER 7

P. 160, *All* Courtesy Enfatico Agency/New York. P. 165, Courtesy Sharp Electronics Corporation. P. 165, Courtesy of Bruno Magli. P. 167, Win Initiative/The Image Bank/Getty Images. P. 170, Courtesy ALMA/BBDO São Paulo. P. 172, ©Benetton Group SPA; Photo by: Oliviero Toscani. P. 172, Courtesy Saatchi & Saatchi/Beijing. P. 173, Used with permission from McDonald's Corporation. P. 174, ©Robert Holmes. P. 174, Antonio M. Rosario/The Image Bank/Getty Images. P. 175, *Both ads:* Courtesy Microsoft Corporation. P. 176, Courtesy of Nestlé S.A. P. 178, Courtesy The Coca-Cola Company. P. 179, Courtesy Unilever U.S. P. 181, Courtesy The PRS Group, Inc./East Syracuse, NY. P. 183, Courtesy Fran Wilson Creative Cosmetics, Inc. P. 183, Courtesy McDonald's Corporation. P. 184, Courtesy Elite Industries, Ltd. P. 184, Courtesy Nestlé S.A. P. 187, *All* Courtesy The Gillette Company/Procter & Gamble. P. 190, Courtesy CNS, Inc.

Figure 7–2, Reprinted with permission from the issue of American Demographics. Copyright, Crain Communications Inc. 2004.

CHAPTER 8

P. 192, ©Shooting Star. P. 194, ©Shooting Star. P. 195, Fisher-Price, Inc. a subsidiary of Mattel, Inc. East Aurora, NY 14052 U.S.A. ©2006 Mattel, Inc. All Rights Reserved. P. 196, Fisher-Price, Inc. a subsidiary of Mattel, Inc. East Aurora, NY 14052 U.S.A. ©2006 Mattel, Inc. All Rights Reserved. P. 197, AP Photo/Morry Gash. P. 198, Photo by Business Wire via Getty Images. P. 200, Copyright © David Young-Wolff/PhotoEdit. P. 202, Courtesy The Nielsen Company. P. 203, Photo by M. Caulfield/American Idol 2008/Getty Images. P. 203, Macduff Everton/The Image Bank/Getty Images. P. 204, ©Louie Psihoyos/Science Faction/Corbis. P. 205, ©Spencer Grant/PhotoEdit. P. 205, Comstock Images/Getty Images. P. 208,

Courtesy Wendy's International, Inc. P. 209, Dan Kitwood/Getty Images. P. 209, Photo by Cancan Chu/Getty Images Asiapac. P. 211, ©Brent Jones. P. 211, Todd Warnock/Lifesize/Getty Images. P. 212, Courtesy Schwan's Consumer Brands North America, Inc. P. 214, Courtesy Schwan's Consumer Brands North America, Inc.

Figure 8–4, Nielsen data used with permission by Nielsen Business Media, Inc. 2008; emarketer.com, April 2007.

CHAPTER 9

P. 220, ©2008 Zappos.com., Inc. P. 220, ©2008 Zappos.com., Inc. P. 223, ©2008 Zappos.com., Inc. P. 223, *All* Courtesy of Sporting News Yearbooks. P. 224, ©Shooting Star. P. 224, *Both:* Jill Braaten/The McGraw-Hill Digital Library. P. 226, Microfridge® Courtesy Mac-Gray. P. 228, Courtesy Claritas. P. 230, Courtesy Xerox Corporation. P. 232, *All* ©2007 Oldemark, LLC. Reprinted with permission. The Wendy's name, design and logo, Mandarin Chicken and Frosty are trademarks of Oldemark, LLC and are licensed to Wendy's International, Inc. P. 234, Courtesy Wendy's International, Inc. P. 236, *All* Courtesy Apple Computer. P. 239, ©M. Hruby. P. 240, ©M. Hruby. P. 242, Courtesy Prince Sports. P. 243, Courtesy Prince Sports.

CHAPTER 10

P. 244, Courtesy of Apple. P. 244, AP Photo/Paul Sakuma. P. 247, QI HEN/Xinhua/Landov. P. 248, Courtesy Vetco, Inc. Consumer Health Care. P. 250, Courtesy Sony Electronics, Inc. P. 250, AP Photo/LM Otero. P, 251, Courtesy Nestle Purina Pet Care Company. P. 252, AP Photo/Dino Vournas. P. 252, ©M. Hruby. P. 253, Courtesy The New Product Works. P. 253, Courtesy of the Original Pet Drink. P.253, Courtesy The New Product Works. P. 254, Courtesy The New Product Works. P. 254, ©GfK Custom Research, LLC. P. 256, ©Erik S. Lesser/The New York Times/Redux. P. 257, Courtesy Volvo of North America. P. 258, Courtesy of IDEO. P. 259, Courtesy Gary Schwarzberg. P. 260, ©M. Hruby. P. 260, ©2009 Google. P. 261, Jim Wilson/The New York Times/Redux. P. 261, Jose Azel/Aurora. P. 262, ©M. Hruby. P. 263, Courtesy of Hewlett-Packard Company. P. 266, Courtesy Activeion Cleaning Solutions, LLC. P. 267, Courtesy Activeion Cleaning Solutions, LLC.

CHAPTER 11

PP. 268–269, Photo by Chris Weeks/WireImage/Getty Images. P. 270, ©M. Hruby. P. 272, Getty Images. P. 273, AP Photo/Mary Altaffer. P. 273, Courtesy Mullen. P. 278, ©2009 Blue Moon. P. 280, Courtesy Lowe Worldwide; Photo: Brian Kuhlman; Talent: Cameo Amato. P. 281, *No credit* P. 282, Courtesy Advanced Research Labs. P. 282, Courtesy Unilever U.S., Inc. P. 284, *No credit.* P. 287, ©M. Hruby. P. 288, Courtesy The Black & Decker Corporation. P. 288, Courtesy of De Walt Industrial Tool Company. P. 289, Courtesy of Pez Candy, Inc. P. 289, Photo by: Arthur Meyerson. "Coca-Cola, thte Contour Bottle design and the Coca-Cola Fridge Pack are trademarks of The Coca-Cola Company. Copyright 1994. All rights reserved. P. 290, ©M. Hruby. P. 290, ©M. Hruby. P. 292, Courtesy Hyundai North America. P. 295, BMW of North America, LLC.

CHAPTER 12

PP. 296–297, Photo by Angela Weis/Getty Images. P. 298, Courtesy Marriot International, Inc. P. 299, Photo courtesy of American Airlines. P. 299, Courtesy Singapore Airlines, Inc. P. 300, Courtesy Gosscreative. P. 300, Courtesy Allstate. P. 303, The American Red Cross. P. 303, Courtesy Unicef. P. 304, Courtesy Susan G. Komen For the Cure. P. 307, ©2009 Hertz System, Inc. Hertz is a registered service mark and trademark of Hertz System, Inc. P. 309, Used with permission from McDonald's Corporation. P. 309, Courtesy Sprint Nextel Corporation. P. 309, Logo used with permission of the American Red Cross. P. 309, Courtesy Laser Vision Institute. P. 310, Courtesy Accenture. P. 310, Courtesy Space Adventures, Ltd. P. 315, Photo by Rob Tringali/Sportschrome/Getty Images. P. 316, Courtesy Philadelphia Phillies.

CHAPTER 13

P. 318, *Both:* Courtesy StubHub. P. 321, ©Robert Yager. P. 322, Namas Bhojani/The New York Times/Redux Pictures. P. 322, Doug Kanter/Bloomberg News/Landov P. 323, Photo by Justin Sullivan/Getty Images. P. 325, Michael Krasowitz/Taxi/Getty Images. P. 326, ©M. Hruby. P. 327, Courtesy Coldwater Creek. P. 327, Courtesy of Ken Davis Products, Inc. P. 329, Courtesy of Ken Davis Products, Inc. P. 330, ©M. Hruby. P. 333, Alan Danaher/The Image Bank/Getty Images. P. 333, ©M. Hruby. P. 334, ©M. Hruby. P. 334, ©M. Hruby. P. 335, Chris Hondros/Getty Images. P. 335, *No credit.* P. 342, Photo by Neil Lupi/Redferns.

CHAPTER 14

P. 344, AP Photo/Chris Carlson. P. 348, ©Terry McElroy. P. 350, Courtesy of Rock & Roll Hall of Fame. P. 351, Courtesy Panasonic Consumer Electronics Company. P. 356, Courtesy Family Dollar Store. P. 358, ©M. Hruby. P. 360, Courtesy The Toro Company. P. 360, Courtesy Payless ShoeSource, Inc. P. 363, Photography by Monci Jo Williams, FORTUNE; ©1983 Time, Inc. All rights reserved. P. 368, Courtesy 3M. P. 369, Courtesy 3M.

CHAPTER 15

P. 378, Courtesy Callaway Golf; Photo by Sam Greenwood/Getty Images. P. 382, Courtesy Border's Group, Inc. P. 386, Photo by James Leynse/Corbis. P. 387, Courtesy Nestle SA. P. 389, Courtesy Century 21 Real Estate LLC. P. 389, AP Photo/Nick Ut. P. 389, ©The McGraw-Hill Companies/Photographer: Jill Braaten. P. 392, Courtesy Devries Public Relations. P. 393, An Fu/ChinaFotoPress/Redux Stock P. 394, Courtesy Jiffy Lube International, Inc. P. 394, ©Amy Etra. P. 395, Justin Sullivan/Getty Images. P. 395, *No credit.* P. 397, ©Joe & Kathy Heiner. P. 401, ©M. Hruby. P. 402, Mark Wilson/Getty Images. P. 402, Justin Sullivan/Getty Images. P. 402, Justin Sullivan/Getty Images.

CHAPTER 16

PP. 404–405, Christian Hartmann/Reuters/Landov. P. 407, ©M. Hruby. P. 408, ©M. Hruby. P. 408, ©M. Hruby. P. 408, ©M. Hruby. P. 409, Courtesy Volkswagen of America. P. 410, Courtesy IBM Corporation. P. 411, Courtesy Dell, Inc. P. 411, Courtesy Wal-Mart Stores, Inc. P. 412, Courtesy Hewlett-Packard Company. P. 415, Photo by Stefen Chow/Getty Images. P. 417, Courtesy FedEx Corporation. P. 417, Courtesy Ryder Supply Chain Solutions. P. 419, Courtesy Rapistan Demag Corporation. P. 420, Courtesy of United Airlines. P. 420, Courtesy of United Airlines. P. 422, Courtesy Microsoft Corporation. P. 423, Courtesy Porter Novelli. P. 426, ©1996–2009, Amazon.com.

APPENDIX B

P. 372, *Both* Courtesy The Caplow Company.

CHAPTER 17

P. 428, Robyn Beck/AFP/Getty Images. P. 431, ©Daniel Hambury/Corbis. P. 433, *No credit.* P. 433, Courtesy Doctor's Associates, Inc. P. 435, Courtesy Staples, Inc. P. 436, AP Photo/Christoiphe Ena. P. 436, AP Photo/Sue Ogrocki. P. 437, Courtesy Yo-Naturals Inc. P. 438, ©M. Hruby. P. 438, Courtesy Office Depot, Inc. P. 438, Courtesy L.L.Bean, Inc. P. 439, Photo by Matthew Peyton/Getty Images for QVC. P. 440, Courtesy MySimon, Inc. P. 440, Courtesy Amazon.com., Inc. P. 441, AP Photo/Jacques Brinon. P. 441, AP Photo/Greg Baker. P. 443, Photo by Justin Sullivan/Getty Images. P. 443, ©Najlah Feanny/Corbis. P. 443, AP Photo/Michael Dwyer. P. 443, ©M. Hruby. P. 444, Photo by Tim Boyle/Getty Images. P. 445, AP Photo/Paul Sakuma. P. 449, ©Brent Jones. P. 453, *Both* Courtesy Mall of America.

CHAPTER 18

P. 456, Courtesy CBS Interactive, Inc. P. 459, Courtesy Modernista! Ltd. P. 462, Courtesy

ALMAP/BBDO – São Paulo. P. 462, ©2007 Llewellyn/Frommer's Australia From $60 a Day. Reprinted with permission of John Wiley & Sons, Inc. P. 462, Courtesy International Dairy Queen, Inc. P. 464, Courtesy Nation's Restaurant News. P. 465, Courtesy Nokia North America. P. 466, Courtesy Purina Incredible Dog Challenge. P. 467, Courtesy Gulfstream Aircraft, Inc. P. 467, Courtesy H.J. Heinz Company. Used with permission. P. 469, Artwork supplied by Merck-Schering/Plough Pharmaceuticals. P. 473, Imaginechina via AP Images. P. 474, ©Shooting Star. P. 477, Courtesy 4 Seasons Hotels & Resorts. P. 478, *No credit.* P. 481, Courtesy Under Armour, Inc. P. 482, Photo by Joe Robbins/Getty Images.

CHAPTER 19

P. 484, ©Shooting Star. P. 486, BLACKCARD is a registered trademark. BLACK and BLACK CARD family of marks are trademarks of Black Card LLC. Copyright ©2007–2009. P. 486, Courtesy GM Archives. P. 486, Courtesy Mars, Inc. P. 487, Courtesy Chevron Corporation. P. 487, Courtesy Amway Global. P. 488, Courtesy National Fluid Milk Processor Promotion Board; Agency: Lowe Worldwide/New York. P. 488, Courtesy United States Army. P. 490, www.superbowl-ads.com. P. 490, Courtesy PepsiCo, Inc./Frito-Lay, Inc. P. 491, Courtesy Office of National Youth Anti Drug Media Campaign. P. 491, Courtesy BBH Tokyo. P. 491, Courtesy GEICO. P. 492, Courtesy Giro North America. P. 493, Courtesy Microsoft Corporation. P. 495, Courtesy Outdoor Channel. P. 497, Courtesy Lifetime Television. P. 497, Photo by Heinz Kluetmeier/Sports Illustrated/Getty Images. P. 498, Courtesy USA Today. P. 499, ©M. Hruby. P. 500, Courtesy Double Click, Inc. P. 500, Courtesy Nationwide Insurance. P. 501, BananaStock/PictureQuest. P. 501, Courtesy ecast. P. 504, Courtesy GfK Custom Research North America. P. 507, Courtesy of Valpak Direct Marketing Systems, Inc. P. 508, Courtesy Nestle USA/Nestle Crunch Brand. P. 508, Courtesy Mastercard Worldwide. P. 509, *No credit.* P. 510, Photo by: NBC Universal Photo Bank. P. 510, Photo by David McNew/Getty Images. P. 512, Photo by: Paul Drinkwater/BNCU Photo Bank vai AP Images. P. 515, ©2009 Google.

CHAPTER 20

P. 518, Courtesy of Xerox Corporation. P. 521, Courtesy Medtronic. P. 523, ©Mitch Kezar/ Windigo Images. P. 525, Courtesy Xerox Corporation. P. 527, ©Einzig Photography. P. 528, ©Image Source/Corbis. P. 529, ©Richard Pasley/Stock Boston, LLC. P. 530, Frank Herholdt/ Stone/Getty Images. P. 531, Purestock/ GettyImages. P. 533, Image Bank/Color Day Productions. P. 534, ©John Boykin/PhotoEdit. P. 538, Courtesy The Institute for Health & Human Potential www.ihhp.com. P. 538, Comstock Images/Getty Images. P. 539, Courtesy Mary Kay, Inc. P. 541, *Both* Courtesy of Toshiba Medical Systems & Interactive Media. P. 545, Courtesy Xerox Corporation.

CHAPTER 21

P. 546, *Both* Courtesy Seven Cycles, Inc. P. 550, ©Kainaz Amaria. P. 551, Courtesy Reebok International Ltd. P. 552, Jeffrey Coolidge/Digital Vision/Getty Images. P. 552, *No credit.* P. 552, Courtesy Travelocity. P. 556, ©Paul Barton/ Corbis. P. 557, ©Tom Grill/Corbis. P. 558, ©2008 Zappos.com., Inc. P. 559, *No credit.* P. 560, Courtesy Diamond Trading Company; Agency: J. Walter Thompson. P. 561, ©Ray Bartkus. P. 563, Courtesy Nestle USA/Nestle Confections. P. 566, Courtesy Pizza Hut, Inc. P. 567, Coutesy Pizza Hut, Inc. P.569, Courtesy Pizza Hut, Inc.

CHAPTER 22

P. 570, Courtesy General Mills; Photo: Bowen Marketing. P. 572, Courtesy General Mills; Photo: Bowen Marketing. P. 573, AP Photo/ Don Ryan. P. 573, Photo: Bowen Marketing. P. 575, Courtesy General Mills; Photo: Bowen Marketing. P. 575, Courtesy General Mills; Photo: Bowen Marketing. P. 579, Courtesy Campbell Soup Company. P. 579, Courtesy Ikea. P. 580, Fotosearch. P. 583, Courtesy General Mills; Photo: Bowen Marketing. P. 584, ©M. Hruby. P. 585, ©M. Hruby. P. 586, Courtesy Papa John's International, Inc. P. 586, Courtesy Lockheed Martin CorP. P. 587, Courtesy IBM; Agency: The Ogilvy Group/ New York. P. 591, Used with permission from McDonald's Corporation. P. 596, Courtesy General Mills.

APPENDIX C

P. 598, ©Brad Trent. P. 599, ©Paul Elledge. P. 601, Courtesy Macy's Inc. P. 602, Courtesy Xerox Corporation. P. 603, Courtesy The Buckle, Inc. P. 606, Reprinted from Job Choices 2002, with permission of the National Association of Colleges & Employers. P. 606, Courtesy Monster. P. 612, Thatch cartoon by Jeff Shesol; Reprinted with permission of Vintage Books. P. 613, White Packert/The Image Bank/Getty Images.

APPENDIX D

P. 618, Courtesy Daktronics, Inc. P. 619, Courtesy Daktronics, Inc. P. 629, Courtesy HOM Furniture. P. 632, Photo by Paul Harris/Onlien USA/Getty Images. P. 637, *All* ©M. Hruby. P. 641, AP Photo/Chris O'Connor. P. 642, Used with permission from McDonald's Corporation.

NAME INDEX

A

Aaker, David A., 681, 691, 693
Aaron, Hank, 256
Abel, Bill, 343
Abela, Andrew V., 670
Abell, Derek F., 671
Abernathy, Avery M., 694
Abkowitz, Alyssa, 670
Abraham, Maid M., 693
Abrams, Rhonda, 51, 671
Achenback, James, 699
Achenreinver, Gwen Bachman, 675
Adams, Joe, 683
Adams, Susan, 696
Adamy, Janet, 678, 679
Adler, Roy D., 699
Agarwal, Manj K., 681
Agoglia, John, 698
Ailawadi, Kusum L., 689, 690
Aizen, I., 675
Alba, Joseph W., 675
Aldrich, Susan, 603
Alexander Joe F., 697
Alexander, Kelly, 699
Alexander, Sheryll, 674
Alfond, C. Fred, 674
Allen, Richard, 616
Allen, Robert C., 698
Allman, Greg, 342
Alva, Marilyn, 698
Ambler, Tim, 670, 692
Anderson, Brad, 136
Anderson, Erin, 676, 686, 688, 695
Anderson, James C., 669, 676
Anderson, Pamela, 682
Andrews, J. Craig, 677
Andriotis, Anna Maria, 684
Andruss, Paula, 684
Anscheutz, N., 680
Ansoff, H. Igor, 671
Ante, Spencer E., 670
Antia, Kersi D., 678
Appleyard, Dennis R., 677
Arens, Christian, 693
Arens, William F., 693
Armstrong, J. Scott, 671
Armstrong, Lance, 492
Armstrong, Larry, 682
Arndt, Michael, 671, 672, 679, 689
Arnold, Catherine, 673
Arnold, Todd, 682
Arnould, Eric, 675
Arnseth, Amber, 266
Aronaur, Rebecca, 697
Arsel, Zeynep, 673
Ash, John, 674
Aston, Adam, 673, 680, 687
Astrouski, Joe, 688
Atlas, Elise, 694
Atlas, Steve, 694
Augusto, Byron G., 680
Avery, Simon, 695
Avery, Susan, 677

B

Baack, Daniel W., 693
Baar, Aaron, 682
Babwin, Don, 699
Bach, Katy, 693
Badaracco, Joseph L., 673
Baer, Martha, 687
Bagozzi, Richard P., 669
Bahadur, Nikhil, 681
Bailey, Jeffrey J., 691
Baker, Eric, 319
Baker, Julie, 688, 689
Baker, Stephen, 696
Baker, Walter, 685
Baker, Wayne E., 698
Bakken, Earl, 29
Balasubramanian, Sridhar, 689
Baldry, Beth Ann, 699
Ball, A. Dwayne, 684
Balter, David, 127
Baltrami, B., 675
Banga, Kamini, 678
Banis, William J., 698
Banks, Elizabeth, 493
Barboza, David, 698
Barczak, Gloria, 680
Barich, Howard, 689
Barlas, Pete, 687
Barnes, Jimmy D., 691
Barnes, John, 689
Barnevik, Percy, 18
Barr, Stephen, 683
Barrett, Paul, 673
Barringer, Felicity, 699
Barris, Mike, 696
Bartholomew, Doug, 687
Bartos, Rena, 675
Bass, Stephen J., 689
Basta, Nicholas, 697
Bates, Albert D., 689
Bates, Douglas D., 679
Batiromo, Maria, 694
Battista, Steven, 481, 482, 691
Bauder, David, 692
Bawa, Kapil, 693
Bay, Willow, 678
Bayus, Barry L., 685
Beall, Anne, 613
Bearden, William O., 686
Beatty, Sharon E., 675
Belch, George E., 685
Belch, Michael A., 685
Belk, Russell, 675
Bellizzi, Joseph A., 676, 683
Bellman, Lawrence M., 689
Belson, Ken, 680, 684
Ben-Akiva, Moshe, 675
Bendapudi, Neeli, 683, 684
Bendle, Neil T., 670, 689, 697
Benedetto, Antyony D., 680
Bennett, P. D., 683
Bennett, Tony, 645
Benson, Etienne, 678
Berg, Jeben, 84
Bergen, Mark E., 678, 685
Berkowitz, Shelly, 634, 699
Berlin, Leslie, 688
Bernard, Lisa A., 689
Berner, Robert, 677, 689, 691
Bernstein, Jeffrey, 691
Bernstein, Robert, 672
Berry, Jon, 675
Berry, Leonard L., 683, 684, 688
Bertagnoli, Lisa, 698
Bettencourt, Nuno, 342
Bezos, Jeff, 425, 559
Bharadwaj, Sundar G., 678, 683, 694
Bianco, Anthony, 679
Biba, Erin, 671
Bigne, J. Enrique, 690
Bilger, Burkhard, 685
Billings, Claire, 682
Bingham, Frank G., Jr., 676
Binkley, Christina, 688
Bitner, Mary Jo, 681, 682, 683, 684, 689
Biyalogorsky, Eyal, 680
Blackwell, Roger D., 675
Bloch, Peter H., 682
Bloch, Thomas, 684
Bloom, Jonah, 693
Bloom, Paul N., 674, 686
Bluestein, Jeff, 146
Boccara, Brun, 675
Boehm, April, 682
Bolles, Richard N., 614
Bolten, Joshua, 672
Bon Jovi, Jon, 342
Bonini, Shelia M., 670
Bonoma, Thomas V., 676
Booms, Bernard H., 681, 683
Boring, Christopher, 444
Boulding, William, 669, 680
Bowen, David E., 683
Bowie, Norman E., 673
Bowman, Robert J., 687
Box, Terry, 690, 695
Boyd, Harper W., Jr., 670, 679, 681
Boyle, Matthew, 696
Bozman, Carl S., 691
Bradsher, Keith, 699
Brady, Diane, 697, 699
Brandon, Emily, 672
Brandreth, Scott, 684
Brandt, Joe, 135, 136, 676
Branson, Richard, 512
Brennan, David P., 676, 690
Brin, Sergey, 515, 516
Brinkley, Christie, 492
Brockman, Beverly K., 680
Brodie, John, 681
Brodie, Roderick J., 671
Brooke, Simon, 689
Brooks, Garth, 452
Brosnan, Pierce, 304
Brown, Jeff, 541
Brown, Mary L., 678
Brown, Seth, 679
Brown, Stephen W., 683, 684, 689
Brunel, Frederic F., 675, 682
Bruni, Frank, 685
Bryant, Adam, 694
Buchanan, Bruce, 691
Buchanan, Joy, 700
Buck, David, 316, 684
Bughin, Jacques, 671, 696
Bulik, Beth Snyder, 681, 695
Bullock, August, 120, 675
Burdick, Richard K., 676
Burin, Norm, 689
Burley, James, 680
Burnett, John J., 670
Burns, Greg, 696
Burns, Simon, 671
Burrow, Peter, 694
Burrows, Carol, 295
Burrows, Peter, 699
Bush, Michael, 691
Bush, Robert P., 679
Buss, Dale, 679
Butscher, Stephen A., 685
Butterfield, Bruce, 630

Buzzell, Robert D., 693
Byrne, Ken, 626
Byrnes, Nanette, 689
Byron, Ellen, 682, 685, 697

C

Cahill, Maureen, 452, 453, 690
Calantone, Roger, 681
Callaway, Ely R., 625
Callaway, Vivian Milroy, 570, 571–572, 592, 595, 596, 597, 696, 697
Cameron, James, 485
Cammarano, Roy F., 682, 687
Campbell, Sarah, 695
Canaday, Henry, 694
Cannon, Joseph P., 674, 686, 694
Capell, Kerry, 684
Capossela, Alison, 544
Cappelli, Peter, 698
Carey, John, 672
Carpenter, Gregory S., 669
Carral, Teré, 211–214
Carroll, John, III, 672
Carry, David J., 684
Carson, J. J., 674
Carter, Bill, 692
Carter, Franklin, 690
Carter, Jim, 689
Casanova, Sarah, 700
Cash, James I., Jr., 680
Cass, Ronald A., 686
Castellion, G., 680
Castleberry, Stephen B., 694, 695
Cateora, Philip K., 677, 678
Caulfield, Brian, 699
Cavusgil, S. Tamer, 687
Chadwick, Kathy, 699
Chan, Vanessa, 696
Chandler, David, 674
Chang, Chingching, 691
Chang, Julia, 695
Chang, Kenneth, 678
Chang, Rita, 672, 692
Chen, Jean, 699
Chen, Steve, 5
Cheng, Kipp, 692
Cheung, Ka-Man, 690
Cheung, Karen M., 671
Chevalier, Michael, 694
Chiagouris, Larry, 674, 682
Choi, Jungkiu, 696
Choi, Thomas Y., 676
Chonko, Lawrence B., 694
Chopra, Sunil, 687
Chu, Wujin, 676
Cipolla, Lorin, 694
Clark, Bruce H., 670
Clark, Eric, 678
Clark, Tim, 686
Claus, J., 675
Cleaver, Joanne, 697
Clement, Ronald W., 674
Clements, Jonathan, 669
Clifford, Stephanie, 685
Clift, Vicki, 681, 683
Cline, Thomas W., 692
Clooney, George, 492
Close, Glenn, 194
Cloud, John, 669
Cobb, Steven, 677
Coccoran, Cate T., 688
Cohen, Ben, 25
Cohen, Dorothy, 673, 691
Cohen, Joel B., 675
Cohen, William A., 671
Cohon, George A., 642
Colby, Charles L., 683, 684
Coleman, Barbara Carrick, 690
Colford, Steven, 694
Collins, Jim, 670, 671
Columbus, Christopher, 322
Colvin, Geoff, 670, 679
Comer, Gary, 157
Compeau, Larry D., 691
Conant, Jeffrey S., 683
Concialdi, Salvatori, 614
Conkey, Christopher, 694
Conklin, J. C., 684
Conlin, Michelle, 673, 683
Cooper, E., 690
Cooper, James C., 672
Cooper, Martha, 686
Cooper, Robert G., 680
Cooper, Scott W., 671
Cordeiro, Anjali, 685, 696, 700
Corfman, Kim, 675
Corstjens, Marcel, 670–671
Costner, Kevin, 193
Cote, Joseph A., 682, 686
Cotteleer, Mark, 695
Coughlan, Anne T., 686
Coulombe, Joe, 641
Court, David, 697
Courtney, Hugh, 696
Cousins, Paul D., 680
Covel, Simona, 680
Covello, Joseph A., 671
Coy, Peter, 673, 685, 697
Coyne, Kevin P., 685
Craig, Malcolm, 697
Crane, Frederick G., 683, 684
Crawford, Cindy, 126, 127
Crawford, David, 677
Crawford, Merle, 680
Creamer, Matthew, 675, 690, 694, 697
Creswell, Julie, 692
Crockett, Roger O., 674
Crol, Carol, 693
Cron, William L., 695
Cronin, J. Joseph, Jr., 683
Crosby, Lawrence A., 672, 684
Cross, James, 693
Crow, Mattison, 547
Crowe, Mattison, 695
Crown, Judith, 672
Cruise, Tom, 510
Cunningham, Lawrence F., 682
Curhan, Ronald C., 694
Curtin, Richard T., 672
Cypher, James M., 673
Cyrus, Miley, 304
Czinkota, Michael, 677

D

D'Innocenzio, Anne, 687
Dacko, Scott, 613
Dae-Hwan Park, 684
Dahlhoff, Denise, 681
Dalasce, Frederic, 695
Daley, Shawn P., 677
Dalrymple, Jim, 689
Dalton, Catherine M., 670
Damast, Alison, 698
Damp, Dennis V., 614
Daneman, Matthew, 671
Danes, Jeffrey E., 686
Dant, Rajiv P., 669
Darden, William, 683
Darling, Diane, 614
Darmon, René Y., 695
David, Barbara, 329
David, John, 670
David, Kenneth, 328, 639, 674
Davidson, William R., 689
Davis, Barbara Jo, 328, 638–639, 685
Davis, James E., 693
Davis, Jeffrey, 687
Davis, John, 697
Davis, Scott, 685
Dawes, Philip L., 676
Dawley, Jacqueline, 679
Dawson, Jane, 543
Day, George S., 669
Dean, Jason, 684
DeCarlo, Thomas E., 695
Deets, Chris, 681
DeGeneres, Ellen, 266, 439
Deighton, John, 681
DeKimpe, Marnik G., 682
Deleersnyder, Barbara, 682
Dell, Michael, 161, 394, 640, 699
Desrochers, Debra M., 686
Deutsch, Claudia H., 691
Devlin, J. Stuart, 698
Dhar, Sanjay, 685
Diamond, Helene, 678
Diaz, Kevin, 684
Dichter, Ernest, 693
Dickson, Andrea, 694
Dickson, Peter R., 675
Dierberger, George, 368, 686
Dikel, Margaret Riley, 614
Diorio, Carl, 678
Diriker, M. F., 697
Dobbin, Ben, 671
Dobrow, Larry, 692
Dobscha, Susan, 13
Dodd, Mike, 684
Dodds, William D., 684, 688
Doherty, Anne Marie, 689
Dolan, Kerry A., 681
Dolan, Robert J., 677, 685
Dolber, Roslyn, 697
Dolliver, Mark, 674
Donaldson, Thomas, 674
Donavan-Walt, Carmen, 673
Donegan, Dan, 343
Donlon, J. P., 697
Donnelly, James H., 683
Donovan, Robert J., 675
Doram, D'Arcy, 673
Dorsch, Michael J., 683
Douglas, Michael, 193
Dowling, Grahame R., 676
Doyle, Stephen, 673
Dreier, Troy, 682
Dreze, Xavier, 686, 688
Drumwright, Minette E., 676
Du, Rex Y., 675
Dubinsky, Alan J., 695
Dubner, Stephen, 501
Dubscha, Susan, 669, 683
Duncan, Rob, 614
Duncan, Tom, 691
Durvasula, Srinivas, 677
Dutta, Shautanu, 678, 685
Dwyer, F. Robert, 676, 686
Dye, Renee, 696
Dylan, Bob, 342

E

Earl, Michael J., 680
Eastwood, Clint, 193
Ebenkamp, Becky, 673
Eckhardt, Giana, 682, 699
Edlich, Richard, 616, 698
Edmondson, Gail, 680, 682
Edwards, Jim, 694

Ehret, Michael, 669
Eig, Jonathan, 679
Eisenhower, Dwight D., 582
El-Ansary, Adel I., 686, 695
Elgin, Ben, 693
Elliott, Stuart, 692, 696
Ellison, Katherine, 670
Ellison, Sarah, 678, 680
Els, Ernie, 379
Engardio, Pete, 674, 698
Enright, Allison, 673, 676, 683, 691, 694
Eppinger, Stephen D., 680
Eppright, David R., 692
Erdem, Tulin, 681
Erickson, Peter, 680
Esterl, Michael, 677
Etger, Michael, 691
Ethans, Arno J., 676
Evans, Kenneth R., 669
Evans, Philip, 671
Ewoldt, John, 669

F

Faes, W., 676
Fahey, Liam, 669
Fahy, John, 683
Fajen, Stephen, 693
Farris, Paul W., 670, 689, 691, 697
Felice, Steve, 161
Fellows, George, 379
Felson, Leonard, 698
Ferguson, Sarah, 452
Fernandez, Karen V., 691
Fetterman, Mindy, 699
Few, Stephen, 670
Feyder, Susan, 679
Field, Alfred J., Jr., 677
Fielding, Michael, 673, 677, 693
Fikes, Bradley J., 672
Fine, Jon, 673, 687, 688
Fine, Leslie M., 669, 683
Fink, Steven, 677
Firestone, Harvey, 621
Fishbein, Martin, 675
Fisher, Anne, 697
Fisher, Marshal L., 689
Fisher, Robert J., 686, 695
Fishman, Charles, 687
Fisk, Raymond P., 684
Fitzgerald, Kate, 696
Fleming, Mathew, 699
Flood, Barbara, 698
Floyd, Callum J., 698
Fluhr, Jeff, 319
Fondu, Karen, 493
Fong, Bay, 677
Fong, Mei, 684
Forbes, Thom, 669, 680
Ford, David, 217–218, 679, 697
Ford, Henry, 621
Forrester, Duane, 697
Forster, Julie, 680
Foster, Thomas A., 687
Fournier, Susan, 13, 669, 681, 683
Foust, Dean, 673
Fox, Richard J., 696
Francis, Michael, 644
Frank, John N., 697
Frank, Robert, 678
Fraser, Cynthia, 683
Frazier, Gary, 686
Freedman, Alix M., 674
Freeman, Morgan, 492
Freeman, Sholnn, 675
Friars, Eileen M., 688
Friedman, Milton, 100–101, 106
Friedman, Thomas L., 322, 684
Friend, Tad, 678
Frommer, Arthur, 463
Frost, Raymond, 695
Fullman, Joseph, 690
Furfie, Ben, 671
Futrell, Charles M., 694

G

Gaida, Kathleen A., 683
Galbraith, John Kennth, 673
Galloway, Bennet, 699
Gambon, Michael, 192
Gangemi, Jeffrey, 682
Gantt, Henry L., 588
Garbuio, Massimo, 696
Garfield, Bob, 692
Garino, Janson, 689
Gaski, John F., 686
Gassenheimer, Julie, 686
Gauri, Dinesh Kumar, 688
Gebhardt, Gary F., 669
Gedenk, Karen, 690
Geffen, Donald A., 697
Gelb, Gabriel M., 684
George, William R., 683
Gerdes, Lindsey, 697
Gerlach, James, 682
Gery, Nurit, 689
Ghemawat, Pankaj, 696
Gibson, Lawrence D., 678, 693
Giese, Joan, 682
Gilbert, John, 680
Gillman, Todd J., 678
Gilly, Mary, 677, 678, 684
Gilmore, James H., 298, 682
Glassel, Linda, 241, 243, 679
Gloecker, Geoff, 672
Gogoi, Pallavi, 673
Gold, Laurence N., 693
Goldberg, Marvin E., 691, 692
Golden, Linda L., 689
Goldman, Doron, 691
Gomes, Roger, 676
Gonul, Fusum F., 690
Gonyea, James C., 698
Goodison, Donna, 688
Goodpaster, Kenneth E., 670, 671, 699
Goodwin, Stephen A., 691
Gooley, Toby G., 687
Gopnik, Blake, 688
Gordon, Geoffrey L., 680
Gordon, Jeff, 492
Gordon, Mary Ellen, 698
Gotlieb, Jerry, 691
Gourville, John, 681
Graber, Donald R., 678
Graham, Jefferson, 671
Graham, John L., 677, 678
Grannis, Kathy, 689
Gray, John V., 676, 687
Gray, Kathy Lynn, 689
Grebb, Michael, 695
Green, Heather, 687
Green, Marianne E., 697, 698
Green, Mark C., 677
Greenberg, Robert M., 698
Greenfield, Jerry, 25
Greenleaf, Eric A., 675, 682
Greenspan, Robyn, 677
Greenwald, John, 699
Gregor, William T., 688
Gremler, Dwayne D., 683, 684
Gresham, Larry G., 686
Grewal, Dhruv, 669, 683, 684, 688, 689, 691
Griffin, Abbie, 680
Griffin, Bobby, 630–631
Griffith, Eric, 673
Grint, Rupert, 192
Gronroos, Christian, 684
Gronstedt, Anders, 690
Groom, Alyssa S., 690
Grossman, Lev, 669
Grossnickle, Joshua, 698
Groth, Markus, 683
Grove, Andrew, 583
Grove, Stephen J., 683, 684
Grow, Brian, 693
Gruca, Thomas S., 683, 685
Gubernick, Lisa, 684
Gulati, Ranjay, 674, 689
Gumbel, Peter, 670
Gummesson, Event, 682
Gundlach, Gregory T., 669, 674, 686
Gunn, Eileen P., 672
Gupta, Ajay, 624
Gupta, Sunil, 675
Gustke, Constance, 679
Gutherie, Julian, 681
Gwinner, Kevin P., 683

H

Haas, Edward, III, 289
Hachman, Mark, 691
Haffman, Sarah, 674
Hahn, Minhi, 693
Hair, Joseph F., Jr., 679
Haley, Kevin, 481, 691
Hall, Linda D., 614
Hallen, Gary, 695
Hambling, David, 691
Hamilton, Rebecca W., 680
Hamm, Steve, 673, 680
Hammer, Susanna, 682
Hammond,, John S., 671
Hampp, Andrew, 693
Hamstra, Mark, 700
Hand, Amy, 671
Handfield, Robert B., 680
Hanford, Desiree J., 673
Hanifin, Bill, 689
Hanks, Tom, 492
Hansen, Eric J., 693
Hansen, Tom, 693
Hanson, Ward A., 685, 695, 696
Hardy, Darren, 614
Harmon, Eric P., 680
Harris, Armin, 696, 697
Harris, Frederick H. deB., 684
Harris, Lloyd C., 689
Harrison, George, 342
Hartley, Robert F., 674
Hartley, Steven W., 673, 682, 683, 685, 686, 691, 693, 694, 695, 698, 699
Hasselhof, David, 492
Hasson, Judi, 681
Hastings, Reed, 31
Hathcote, Jan M., 691
Hauptman, Jon, 641–642
Hauser, Erik, 696
Hawkins, Del I., 675, 676, 677
Hayes, Tom, 696
Hazelgren, Brian J., 671
Heibing, Roman G., Jr., 671
Hein, Kenneth, 674
Heitzmanm Fran, 18
Heller, Laura, 700
Helm, Burt, 691
Helsen, Kristiaan, 677
Hempel, Jessi, 682, 694
Henderson, Verne E., 673

Hennig-Thurau, Thorsten, 683
Henry, David, 673
Herbig, Paul A., 677, 678, 694
Herche, Joel, 677
Herrick, Thaddeus, 672
Herring, Tyler, 242, 679
Hershberger, Edmund, 698
Hessedahl, Arik, 685
Hickock, Allan, 620
Hiestand, Michael, 698
Higgins, Kevin, 673
Higgins, Michelle, 673
Himelstein, Linda, 685
Hindo, Brian, 687
Hite, Robert E., 683
Hoak, Amy, 669
Hoch, Stephen J., 686
Hochman, Sara, 71
Hoeffler, Steve, 680
Hof, Robert D., 671, 687, 694
Hoffman, Karen Epper, 698
Holden, Reed K., 685
Holden, Richard, 515, 517
Holloran, Thomas E., 670
Holloway, Charles J., 681
Holmes, Stanley, 680, 691
Holson, Laura M., 681
Honan, Matthew, 671
Honebein, Peter C., 682, 687
Honigman, Daniel B., 683
Hooley, Graham J., 691
Hooper, Bill, 631, 632
Hope, Chris, 674
Hopewell, Nikki, 672, 690
Hopper, Dennis, 69
Hopper, Grace Murray, 586
Horn, John, 678, 685
Horn, John T., 696
Horovitz, Bruce, 681
Horrigan, John B., 695
Hosford, Christopher, 691
Howard, Daniel L., 684, 689
Howard, John A., 675
Howard, Teresa, 691
Hoyer, Wayne D., 674, 675, 676
Hruska, Jack, 451
Hsieh, Tony, 220, 221
Hughes, Tim, 673
Hult, G. Tomas M., 684
Hume, Scott, 698
Humphreys, Jeffrey M., 671, 676
Hunt, James B., 692
Hunt, Kenneth A., 686, 689
Hunt, Shelby D., 670
Hurley, Chad, 5
Huston, Larry, 681
Hutchinson, J. Wesley, 675
Hutt, Michael D., 676
Hyman, H., 690

I

Iacobucci, Dawn, 683
Ian, Scott, 343
Inderrieden, Edward, 695
Ishibashi, Shojiro, 621–622
Isom, Susan, 635
Ives, Nat, 688, 693

J

Jackson, Donald W., 676
Jackson, Tracy, 626
Jacoby, Jacob, 684
Jaffee, Larry, 694
Jahoda, M., 690
Jain, Ambuj, 684, 689
Jaju, Anupam, 678
James, Diana, 677, 698
James, Harvey S., 674
Jamison, Alisha, 623–624
Jamison, Brock, Jr., 623–624
Janis, Irwin L., 680
Janoff, Barry, 692
Janos, Leo, 696, 697
Jap, Sandy D., 676, 677
Jargon, Julie, 697
Jarvis, Jeff, 694
Jaworski, Bernard J., 686, 695
Jayachandran, Satish, 697
Jayson, Sharon, 672
Jespersen, Frederick F., 673
Jobs, Steven, 236, 246–247, 258, 395
Johannes, Amy, 693, 694
Johansen, Ed, 628
Johansen, Wayne, 628, 629, 699
Johansson, Johnny K., 677, 678
John, Deborah Roedder, 675
John, Elton, 21, 25
John, Joby, 684
Johns, Andy, 688
Johnson, Bradley, 692
Johnson, Bruce, 190
Johnson, Eugene M., 683
Johnson, Gavin, 678
Johnson, Gerry, 670
Johnson, Jean L., 686
Johnson, Kelly, 586
Johnson, Sharma, 689
Johnson, Sheree L., 672, 684
Johnston, Mark W., 694, 695
Johnston, Wesley J., 669, 676
Joiner, Christopher, 696
Jolie, Angelina, 492–493
Jolson, Marvin A., 694, 695
Jones, Charisse, 692
Jones, D. G. Brian, 669
Jones, Eli, 694, 695
Jones, Gareth, 693
Jones, Kathryn, 687
Jones, Paul, 699
Jordan, Michael, 492
Joyce, William, 573, 696
Judson, Kimberly, 680
Jung, Andrea, 393
Jung-Heon Nam, 684
Juran, Robert A., 614

K

Kageyama, Yuri, 677
Kahn, Barbara E., 686
Kahn, Kenneth B., 680
Kahney, Leander, 680
Kallayil, Gopi, 516
Kaltcheva, Velitchka, 689
Kalyanam, Kirthi, 685, 695, 696
Kamakura, Wagner A., 675
Kambil, Ajit, 677
Kaminsky, Philip, 686
Kane, Hukari, 674
Kang, Stephanis, 696
Kapferer, Jean-Noel, 685
Kaplan, Morris, 688
Kar, Jayanti, 696
Karim, Jawed, 56
Karremans, J., 675
Katobe, Masaaki, 695
Katzenberg, Jeffrey, 485
Keaveney, Susan M., 689
Keefe, Lisa M., 669
Keegan, Warren J., 677, 678
Keith, Janet E., 676
Keith, Robert F., 669
Kellaris, James J., 692
Kelleher, Kevin, 686
Keller, Ed, 675
Keller, Kevin Lane, 677, 678, 681, 696
Kelley, David, 258, 673
Kelly, Graham, 671
Kemper, Cynthia L., 690
Kennedy, John F., 95
Kennedy, Joyce Lain, 698
Kennedy, Marilyn Moats, 698
Kennerty, Mike, 342
Kerbo, Harold R., 675
Kerin, Roger A., 670, 671, 679, 680, 681, 683, 684, 689, 695, 696, 699, 700
Kerwin, Kathleen, 696
Kesmodel, David, 696
Khan, Urea, 673
Kher, Unmesh, 674
Khermouch, Gerry, 694
Kidman, Nicole, 492
Kiley, David, 672, 678
Kim, Daekwan, 687
Kim, Hyeong Min, 688
Kim, Ilchul, 690
Kim, Jane J., 684
Kim, Namwoon, 685
Kim, Peter, 671
Kim, S., 677
Kim, W. Chan, 670
Kim, Wo Chong, 584
King, Stephanie, 686
Kirby, Jason, 687
Kirkpatrick, David, 694
Kitchen, Philip J., 690
Kiviat, Barbara, 698
Klaassen, Abbey, 693, 694
Klapper, J. T., 690
Kleese, Hilary, 159
Klein, Bradley, 699
Klein, Thomas A., 673
Klum, Heidi, 304, 439, 492
Knowles, Patricia A., 676
Kohl, Mike, 368
Kohli, Ajay K., 676, 694
Kohli, Chiranjeev, 681
Konus, Umut, 689
Kornik, Joseph, 695
Koselka, Rita, 689
Kotabe, Massaki, 677
Kothari, Ashish, 669
Kotler, Philip, 670, 689, 694, 696
Krack, Jim, 633, 634
Krantz, Lee, 698
Krasnikov, Alexander, 697
Kraus, Eric, 604
Krauss, Michael, 670, 677, 697
Krishnan, R., 689
Kroc, Ray, 448
Krugel, David, 693
Kuczmarski, Thomas D., 680
Kumar, V., 669
Kurtenbach, Alfred J., 617, 618–619, 698
Kwak, Hyokjin, 678
Kydd, Arthur R., 50, 671
Kyung Ah-Lee, 684

L

LaBahn, Douglas W., 681
LaBelle, Patti, 304
Lackner, Joseph, 669
Lacy, Sarah, 684
Laczniak, Gene R., 673

Lade, Diane C., 683
Lafley, A. G., 145, 257, 585
Laker, Michael, 685
Lambert, Douglas M., 687
Lamey, Lien, 682
Landes, David S., 677
Lane, Vicki R., 692
Largesse, David, 673
Larreché, Jean-Claude, 670, 679, 681
Larsen, Trina, 678
Latino, Robert, 695
Lauren, Ralph, 285
Lavidge, Robert J., 690
Lavie, N., 675
Lavigne, Melissa, 79
Lawson, Benn, 680
Lee, Don Y., 676
Lee, Felissa, 695
Lee, Hau L., 687
Lee, Louise, 699
Lee, Myung-Soo, 675
Lee, Thomas, 669, 696
Lee, Yin Hwai, 692
Lehmann, Donald R., 675, 681
Leigh, Thomas W., 676
Lelinwalla, Mark, 694
Lemon, Katherine N., 683
Lencioni, Patrick M., 670
Lenderman, Max, 696
Lenskold, James D., 697
Leo, Pamela, 221
Leonard, Devin, 679
Leslie, Mark, 681
Letterman, David, 481
Levey, Richard H., 672, 688, 690
Levinson, Jay Conrad, 614
Levitt, Theodore, 30, 670, 695
Levy, Daniel, 685
Levy, Keith, 504
Levy, Michael, 685, 687
Levy, Piet, 698
Levy, Sidney J., 670
Levy, Steven, 673
Lewis, Barbara, 614
Lewis, Ioni, 692
Lewis, Ray, 481
Lewis, Tanya, 697
Leyden, Peter, 71
Lezcano, Marisol, 684
Li, Zhan G., 689
Likert, Jeffrey K., 676
Lillien, Gary L., 676, 684
Lim, Chae Un, 695
Lim, Paul J., 672
Lin, Alfred, 221
Lin, Elison Ai Ching, 692
Lin, Lynn Y. S., 690
Linblad, Cristina, 672, 673
Lindsay, Greg, 690
Lindstrom, Martin, 203, 204, 675, 679, 694
Liodice, Bob, 690
Littler, Dale, 614
Littman, Sarah, 672
Llovio, Louis, 692
Lloyd, Mary Ellen, 673
Loda, Marsha D., 690
Lodish, Leonard M., 693
Lohr, Steve, 689, 697
Loiaza, Margaret, 218
Loken, Barbara, 696
Lomborg, Bjorn, 697
Lorimer, Sally E., 695
Lovallo, Dan P., 680, 696
Lovelock, Christopher H., 681, 682, 683, 684
Low, George S., 690
Lowenhar, Jeffrey A., 690
Lowry, Tom, 694
Lublin, Joann S., 698
Lucas, George H., 686
Lumpkin, James R., 686
Lusch, Robert F., 684
Lutz, Richard J., 675
Lynch, Frank, 402
Lynch, James E., 691

M

Mabert, Vincent A., 680
MacArthur, Kate, 681, 700
Maccolyn, Gillian, 675
MacDonald, Gareth, 687
MacInnis, Deborah J., 674, 675, 676
MaCrummen, Stephanie, 672
Magnusson, Paul, 696
Mahajan, Vijay, 670, 671, 678, 697
Maher, Kris, 687
Malhotra, Naresh, 689
Malone, Michael S., 696
Malphurs, Aubrey, 670
Mandel, Michael, 673
Mandell, Maurice, 699
Maney, Kevin, 695
Mangalinden, Mylene, 695
Manning, Eli, 304
Manning, Kenneth C., 686
Maras, Elliot, 688
Marcial, Gene G., 688
Marconi, Carolyn D., 603, 698
Marcus, Alfred, 697
Maremont, Mark, 678
Marken, G. A., 694
Markides, Costas, 670
Marks, Ronald B., 698
Marlin, Brenda, 690
Marn, Mike, 685
Marshall, Greg, 695
Marshall, Greg W., 694
Martin Roger L., 670
Martin, Dick, 690
Martineau, Pierre, 446, 689
Maslow, Abraham H., 675
Masterson, Peggy, 693
Matanovich, Timothy, 684
Mathwick, Charla, 689
Matthyssens, P., 676
Mauborgne, Renée, 670
Maurer, Harry, 672, 673
Maxham, James G., III, 683
May, Eleanor, 689
Mayer, Marissa, 260, 261
Mayne, Brad, 618
Mayrue, Dora, 623
McAlister, Leigh, 686
McBride, Sarah, 672
McCarthy, E. Jerome, 11, 669
McCarthy, Michael, 679
McCartney, Scott, 684, 685
McClelland, Anna Sheen, 689
McColgan, Ellyn A., 682
McColl-Kennedy, Janet R., 682
McCorkle, Denny E., 697
McCracken, Jeffrey, 687
McCullough, Jim, 683
McDonald, Duff, 679
McDonald, Hugh, 342
McDowell, Jim, 294
McFarland, Richard G., 686
McGregor, Jean, 679
McGuire, Kara, 673, 684
McKay, Betsy, 682
McKay, Lauren, 690
McKeever, John M., 684
McKeever, Mike, 671
McKenna, Kevin, 190–191, 678
McKeon, Jack, 401, 402, 403
McKinney, Matt, 696, 697
McMath, Robert M., 8, 669, 680
McNair, Malcolm P., 689
McNamara, Kyoshi, 626
McQuiston, Daniel H., 676
McVey, Philip, 676
Meadows, Edward, 645, 646
Mehta, Stephanie N., 679
Meichtry, Stacy, 685
Meindl, Peter, 687
Meissner, Kimmie, 481
Mendels, Pamela, 698
Mendelsohn, Bruce, 679
Mendelsohn, Tamera, 696
Mendonca, Lenny T., 670
Menon, Anil, 674
Mentrala, Murali K., 696
Mentzer, John T., 686
Mercer, Dick, 673
Meredity, Robun, 687
Merrick, Amy, 679
Merrill, Ann, 696
Mesa, Tansa, 677
Messano, Michael, 688
Metz, Cade, 673
Meuter, Matthew L., 682
Meyer, Christopher, 669, 670
Meyerowitz, Phil, 699
Michaels, Roland E., 695
Michiels, Ian, 679
Mick, David Glen, 13, 669, 683
Miles, Stephanie, 677
Miley, Marissa, 672, 692
Miller, Jim, 426
Miller, Karen Lowry, 696
Miller, Steve, 687
Milletti, Umberto, 633, 699
Milligan, Brian, 676
Mills, Gerard, 697
Miner, Patrick, 699
Miniard, Paul W., 675
Minor, Michael, 675
Mitral, Banwari, 675, 681
Mohammed, Rafi A., 686, 695
Mohr, Jakki J., 676, 686, 690
Monfils, Gael, 243
Mongeluzzo, Bill, 687
Monroe, Kent B., 683, 684, 685, 686
Montgomery, Alexandra, 672
Montgomery, David, 317, 684
Moody, Marilyn K., 614
Moon, Youngme, 677, 680
Moore, Elisabeth S., 670, 675
Moore-Mezler, Colleen, 678
Morash, Edward, 683
Morfitt, Marti, 190, 191
Morgan, James B., 618
Morgan, Robert M., 680
Morinoto, Risako, 674
Morison, Robert, 680
Morn, John T., 680
Morriss, John, 345
Morrow, Thomas J., 698
Mortimer, Kathleen, 683
Morton, Fiona Scott, 685
Mothersbaugh, David L., 675, 676, 677
Mourkogiannis, Nikos, 670
Mowen, John C., 675
Mudget, Joan, 158
Mukwa, Michael P., 697
Mulcahy, Anne M., 519, 520, 544, 545
Mulhern, Francis J., 688
Mullaney, Timothy J., 684, 696
Mullins, John M., 679, 681
Mullins, Richard, 688

Mullman, Jeremy, 691, 692, 693
Muris, Timothy, 674
Murphy, Jean, 687
Murphy, Kate, 696
Murphy, Patrick E., 669, 673
Murray, Charles J., 699
Murray, Keith B., 683
Murray, Sarah, 690
Murthy, Archana K., 690
Muscrove, Brenda J., 691
Musico, Christopher, 672
Musso, Chris, 696

N

N Sync, 452
Nagele, Kim, 139, 148, 676
Nagle, Thomas T., 685
Nakata, Cheryl, 682
Narayandas, Das, 676
Narus, James A., 669, 676
Narver, John C., 669
Nasheri, Hedich, 674
Nasser, Jacque, 622
Nath, Prithwiraz, 677
Naumann, Nick, 191, 678
Nedungadi, Prakesh, 675
Neff, Jack, 679, 681, 693
Neilson, Gary, 674
Nelson, Emily, 678
Nelson, Jennifer, 671
Nelson, Katherine A., 674
Nelson, Steffie, 691
Nesdale, Andrew, 675
Neslin, Scott A., 689, 690
Netemeyer, Richard G., 677, 683
Neuborne, Ellen, 695
Neumeister, Larry, 679
New, Tania, 699
Newman, Sarah Casey, 699
Newport, John Paul, 699
Newsome, Laynie, 345
Nicastro, Mary L., 693
Niccol, Brian, 566, 569
Nicklaus, Jack, 627
Nilekani, Nandan, 322
Noble, Charles H., 697
Noble, Peter M., 685
Nohr, Marc, 691
Nohria, Nitin, 573, 696
Noordan, Monica, 699
Norris, Donald, 691
Norton, Rob, 693
Nussbaum, Bruce, 673, 680
Nyberg, Carl, 628

O

Obama, Barack, 497
O'Brien, Jeffrey M., 679, 697
O'Connell, Vanessa, 685, 688
Odell, Patricia E., 693
Ogbogu, Eric, 481
O'Hagan, Sarah Rob, 270
Olsen, R. Paul, 681, 683
Olson, Jerry C., 675, 676, 683, 684
O'Malley, Kathy L., 691
O'Marah, Kevin, 687
Ono, Masatoshi, 622
Onzo, Naoto, 686
Opdyke, Jeff D., 685
Oppenheim, Jeremy M., 670
Ordonez, Jennifer, 679, 681
Orgel, David, 700
Ortinau, David J., 679
Ortmeyer, Gwen, 688
Osberg, Sally, 670
Ostrom, Amy L., 682, 683
O'Toole, Christine H., 688
Ottman, Jacquelyn, 670
Owens, Donny, 642
Ozment, John, 683

P

Paddison, Gordon J., 686, 695
Page, Larry, 515, 516
Pairsel, Nicole, 688
Palmatier, Robert W., 669
Palmer, John, 690
Palmer, Kimberly, 672, 695
Palmeri, Christopher, 680, 699
Palmisano, Samuel J., 410, 521
Paltrow, Gwyneth, 512
Pandit, Vivek, 680
Parasuraman, A., 683, 684, 688, 689
Parekh, Ripal, 692
Park, Grace, 627
Park, Schoon, 693
Parker, Ginny, 684
Parker, R. Stephen, 695
Parmar, Arundhati, 671
Parment, Anders, 690
Parpis, E., 675
Parry, Time, 691
Parsons, Petrick R., 694
Parton, Dolly, 342
Parum, Traci, 676
Parvatiyar, Atul, 678
Pasini, Mike, 671
Passariello, Christina, 687
Passmore, Nick, 671
Paterson, Ben, 680
Paterson, John, 676
Pattis, S. William, 697
Paul, Jonathan, 691
Paul, Michael, 683
Pauwels, Koen, 670, 673
Payan, Janice M., 686
Peacock Peter, 684
Pechman, Cornelia, 691, 692
Pelton, Lou, 686
Peon, Robert P., 688
Peot, Joanna, 671
Pereira, Joseph, 686
Perlow, Leslie, 680
Perron, Kirk, 619, 620
Perry, David E., 614
Peter, J. Paul, 675, 676
Peters, Leah E., 52, 53
Peters, Randall F., 52, 53
Peters, Thomas J., 697
Petersen, Kenneth J., 680
Peterson, Robert A., 670, 671, 679, 680, 681, 684, 689, 696
Peterson, Robin T., 698
Peterson, Tom, 304
Petrecca, Laura, 688
Petrof, John V., 683
Petrove, Elina, 690
Pettijohn, Charles E., 695
Pfeifer, Philip E., 670, 689, 697
Phelps, David, 670
Phelps, Michael, 126, 127, 493
Phillips, Lisa, 695
Phillips, Wendy, 676
Pierce, Andrew, 672
Pine, B. Joseph, II, 682
Pine, Joseph, 298
Pirko, Tom, 648
Plank, Kevin, 480, 481
Poeters, Rik, 690
Pogue, David, 670
Pollard, Ivan, 693
Poniewozik, James, 692
Poon, Derek T. Y., 693
Porras, Jerry I., 670
Porter, Mary, 635
Porter, Michael E., 164–165, 578–579, 580, 670, 673, 677, 696
Portillo, Ernesto, 689
Potter, Donald V., 684
Powell, C. Randall, 698
Powell, Michael A., 600
Power, J. D., III, 583
Powers, Kemp, 685
Prahalad, C. K., 678, 680
Prema, Karen, 681
Prendergast, Gerard P., 690, 693
Pressman, Aaron, 673
Price, Linda, 675
Prins, Remco, 690
Proctor, Bernadette D., 673
Pryde, Alix, 71
Pullman, Madeleine E., 676, 687
Purk, Mary E., 686
Putrevu, Sanjay, 692

Q

Qu, Lu, 696
Quelch, John A., 688, 693, 694
Quick, Rebecca, 677
Quilter, James, 691
Quinn, Jane Bryant, 674
Quinton, Brian, 690, 694
Quitner, Josh, 671, 691

R

Radcliffe, Daniel, 192
Raju, Jagmohan S., 685
Raman, Ananth, 689
Ramaswamy, Arvind, 696
Ramaswamy, Venkat, 680
Rampersaud, Gaff, 648
Randall, Donna, 683
Rao, Akshay R., 681, 685, 696
Rao, Vithala R., 674, 681
Raskin, Andrew, 686
Raskin, Oliver, 698
Rassekh, Farhad, 674
Rassouli, Javad, 691
Ratchford, Brian T., 675
Rauch, Doug, 641
Ray, Ipshita, 674
Rayport, Jeffrey F., 695
Rea-Holloway, Melinda, 678
Reddy, Srinivas K., 696
Reddy, Sudeep, 684
Reed, Andrew, 645, 646
Rees, G., 675
Rehborg, Mark, 217–218
Reibling, Ellen Thomas, 691, 692
Reibstein, David J., 670, 689, 697
Reichheld, Frederick F., 675, 682
Reid, Mike, 691
Reiman, John, 669
Rein, Irving, 694
Reinhold, Jennifer, 677
Rendon, Jim, 670
Renfrow, Jacqueline, 692
Retsky, Maxine L., 673
Revell, Janice, 685
Rgahubir, Priya, 682
Rice, Jerry, 190
Rich, Ben R., 696, 697
Rich, Gregory A., 695
Rich, Jason R., 672
Richtel, Matt, 680
Ridnour, Rick E., 680
Rigby, Darrel K., 671

Rigdon, Edward, 689
Rimes, LeAnn, 439
Rindfleisch, Aric, 673
Ritchie, Leanne, 699
Roberti, Mark, 677
Roberts, Dexter, 684
Roberts, Mary Lou, 696
Robertson, Bruce, 573, 696
Robinson, Aaron, 684
Robinson, David, 690
Rochford, Linda, 698, 699, 700
Roedder-John, Deborah, 696
Roehm, Frances E., 614
Rogers, Everett M., 681
Ronkainen, Ilka A., 677
Rose, Randall L., 686
Rosecky, Richard B., 694
Rosen, David, 694
Rosen, Dennis L., 675, 691
Rosen, Jill, 672
Rosenau, M. D., 680
Rosenberg, Larry, 699
Rosenthal, David W., 600
Ross, Ivy, 465
Ross, William T., Jr., 695
Rossiter, John R., 675
Rotfield, Herbert J., 694
Roth, Aleda V., 676, 687
Roth, Daniel, 697
Roundtree, Robert L., 682
Routhier, Ray, 699
Rovell, Darren, 681
Rowe, Megan, 672
Rowling, J. K., 224
Royer, Isabelle, 680
Royte, Elizabeth, 674
Rozell, Elisabeth J., 695
Rubel, Steve, 693
Rubinson, Joel, 679
Rudelius, William, 670, 671, 679, 681, 683, 684, 698
Ruekert, Robert W., 681, 696, 697
Rust, Roland T., 680
Ryals, Lynette, 684
Rylander, Don, 679

S

Sachs, Andrea, 679
Sakano, Tomoaki, 686
Sakkab, Nobil, 681
Salas, Randy A., 693
Salmon, Walter J., 688, 693
Samli, A Coskun, 678
Sander, Duane, 617
Sarin, Shikhar, 697
Sasser, W. Earl, Jr., 681, 682, 683
Sauer, Rachel, 699
Sausner, Rebecca, 673
Savage, Rick, 342
Savitz, Andrew W., 674
Schaecher, Phil, 157
Schatzel, Kim, 681
Scheuing, Eberhard E., 681, 683
Schiller, Zachary, 696
Schindler, Robert M., 685
Schmidt, Peggy, 698
Schmitt, Bernd H., 684
Schmitt, Genevieve, 278
Schnatter, John, 585
Schoenabachler, Denise D., 680
Scholes, Kevan, 670
Schramm, Wilbur, 690
Schultz, Don E., 690, 691
Schultz, Howard, 107, 108
Schulze, Dick, 135, 136
Schumann, David W., 691
Schwabel, Dan, 698
Schwager, Andre, 669, 670
Schwartz, Alvin, 693
Schwartz, Nelson D., 697
Schwartzberg, Gary, 259
Scott, Andrew, 690
Scott, Mary E., 698
Sears, Jean L., 614
Seegebrecht, Kathy, 49, 671
Segal, Carole, 647
Segal, Gordon, 647
Segal, Madhav N., 698
Seiders, Kathleen, 683
Seldon, Larry, 136
Seligman, Daniel, 690
Sellers, Patricia, 675
Selwitz, Robert, 692
Serwer, Andy, 674
Seskin, Eugene P., 682
Sethuraman, Raj, 685
Setoodeh, Ramin, 684
Sexton, Ken, 697
Shaeffer, Leland D., 680
Shamel, Cynthia L., 614
Shane, Scott, 687
Shankar, Amy Guggenheim, 671, 696
Shankar, Venkatesh, 696
Sharapova, Maria, 243
Sharma, Arun, 695
Sharma, Subhash, 677
Sharms, Amol, 681
Sharp, Arthur G., 698
Shaw, Eric H., 669
Shaw, Hollie, 690
Sheatsley, P., 690
Sheehan, Norman, 689
Shen, Anyuan, 684
Sheng Yuan, 690
Sheperd, Lauren, 689
Sherman, Stratford, 697
Sherry, John F., Jr., 669
Shervani, Tasadduq A., 669
Sheth, Jagdish N., 675, 678, 681, 683
Shields, Brooke, 492
Shimp, Terrence A., 677
Shin, Jeongshin, 677
Shinoda, Maki, 626
Shocker, Allan D., 675, 685
Shoemaker, Robert W., 693
Shriver, Nathan, 691
Shroer, James A., 690
Shulman, Lawrence E., 671
Sibony, Olivier, 680, 696
Sieko, Adrienne, 676
Siklos, Richard, 678
Silva-Risso, Jorge, 685
Simchi-Levi, David, 686, 687
Simchi-Levi, Edith, 686
Simester, Duncan, 688
Simon, Hermann, 685
Singer, Marc, 671, 696
Singh, Surendra N., 675
Sinha, Indrajit, 685
Sinha, Prabhakant, 695, 696
Sivakumar, K., 682
Skally, Nick, 242, 679
Skenazy, Lenore, 692
Slater, Stanley F., 669
Sloan, Matt, 641
Smidebush, Ed, 158–159
Smith, A. B., 689
Smith, Andrew D., 685
Smith, Bob, 626
Smith, Ethan, 686
Smith, Jessica C., 673
Smith, Scott M., 675
Smith, Shaun, 684
Smith, Virginia, 699
Smith, Will, 492
Solomon, Michael R., 675
Soohoo, Anthony, 457
Sorel, Dan, 691
Soriano, Alfonso, 481
Speer, Tibbett, 686
Speh, Thomas W., 676
Spekman, Robert E., 686
Spell, Chester, 687
Spencer Jane, 675
Spengler, Tim, 474
Spethman, Betsy, 689, 694
Spielberg, Steven, 485, 509–510
Spiro, Rosann L., 695
Spriggs, Mark T., 699
Srinivasan, Kannan, 690
Srinivasan, R., 690
Srinvastava, Rajendra K., 669
Staelin, Richard, 669, 680
Stair, Leslie, 600, 614
Stair, Lila B., 600, 614
Stalk, George, 671
Stamler, Bernard, 670
Stanko, Michael A., 699
Stanley, Paul, 343
Stanton, John L., 690
Stanton, William J., 695
Stayman Douglas M., 693
Stead, Deborah, 683
Stecklow, Steve, 684
Steenkamp, Jan-Benedict E. M., 682, 689
Steinberg, Brian, 692
Steinbreder, John, 699
Steiner, Gary A., 674, 690
Stelter, Brian, 669
Stephens, Robert, 87, 88, 89, 251, 252, 680
Stern, Louis W., 686
Sterns, Scott, 694
Stevens, Greg A., 680
Stevens, Marcus, 480, 481, 691
Stevenson, Robert Louis, 520
Stevenson, Thomas H., 676
Stewart, David, 691
Stiving, Mark, 685
Stoller, Martin, 694
Stone, Brad, 670, 673
Strang, Robert A., 693
Strauss, Judy, 695, 696
Strickler, Jeff, 670
Stroebe, W., 675
Strom, Travis, 368
Strunk, William, Jr., 671
Strutton, David, 686
Sudhir, K., 674
Sukhan, Carolyn, 635
Sullivan, Elizabeth A., 672, 698
Summers, John O., 686
Sunmoo, Dunn, 690
Swait, Joffre, 681
Swaminathan, Vanitha, 696
Swank, Hilary, 193
Swartz, Teresa, 683
Swenson, Linda, 671, 699
Swift, Taylor, 492
Swink, Morgan L., 680
Swinmum, Nick, 221
Swire, Donald, 671
Syken, Bill, 698
Szymanski, D., 678

T

Taludar, Debabrata, 675
Tan, Chong Leng, 691
Tanner, John F., Jr., 676, 692, 694, 695
Tansuhaj, Patriya, 683
Tarasova, Anna, 696
Tarnowski, Joseph, 689
Tay, Richard, 692
Taylor, Steven A., 683
Teal, Thomas, 675

Tedesco, Richard, 690, 694
Teinowitz, Ira, 688, 692
Teixeira, Ruy, 71
Tellefsen, Thomas, 676
Terpstra, Vern, 674
Tetreault, Mary Stanfield, 681, 683
Theus, Kathryn T., 675
Thomas, Dan R. E., 683
Thomas, Dave, 232
Thompson, Craig J., 673
Thompson, Debora Viana, 680
Thompson, Stephanie, 672
Thompson, Stephen, 688
Tietje, Brian, 669
Till, Brian D., 693
Tillitt, Scott, 682
Timberlake, Justin, 379
Tirell, Meg, 671
Toby, 679
Tomkovick, Chuck, 692
Tomsho, Robert, 671
Traczyk, Patty, 692
Treacy, Michael, 669, 694
Treleaven, Sarah, 692
Trevino, Linda K., 674
Trivedi, Minakshi, 688
Troy, Lisa C., 696
Truett, Richard, 690
Trumbull, Mark, 673
Tsai, Shu-pei, 690
Tsang, Alex S. L., 693
Tsay, Andy A., 676, 687
Tufte, Edward R., 671
Tuli, Kapil R., 694
Tung, R. L., 677
Turner, Daniel, 680
Twain, Mark, 211
Twigg-Flesner, Christian, 682

U

Ulrich, Karl T., 680
Ulwick, Anthony W., 680
Upah, G. D., 684
Urbany, Joel E., 675
Useem, Jerry, 689
Usinier, Jean Claude, 677

V

Vaas, Lisa, 699
Vakratsas, Demetrios, 692
Valenzuela, Ana, 681
Vallaeys, Frederick, 516, 517
Van den Bulte, Christophe, 669
Van der Linde, Claas, 670
Van Heck, Eric, 677
Van Hyning, Chuck, 671
Van Rossum, Wouter, 669
Van Waterschool, Walter, 669
Vance, Ashlee, 670
Vandermark, Rob, 547
Vanhuele, Marc, 688
Varadarajan, P. Rajan, 670, 671, 674, 678, 683, 696
Vargo, Stephen L., 684
Vascellaro, Jessica E., 673, 694
Veblen, Thorstein, 673
Vekatesh, R., 676
Venable, Robert, 685
Vence, Deborah L., 682, 688, 698
Verckey, Betsy, 688
Verhoef, Peter C., 689, 690
Vessey, Michael J., 670, 671, 686, 700
Veverka, Mark, 687
Viglielmo, Pamela, 678
Viguerie, S. Patrick, 680, 696
Voight, Joan, 675
Voitle, Jennifer, 202–203, 678
Voss, Glenn B., 688

W

Wales, Sterphanie, 623
Walker, Andrea K., 694
Walker, Helen, 676
Walker, Orville C., Jr., 670, 679, 681, 697
Walters, Ben, 673
Walters, Rockney G., 676
Wanamaker, John, 503
Wang, William, 345
Ward, Celeste, 698
Ward, James C., 689
Ward, Ronald A., 693
Warren, Elizabeth, 684
Warren, Kevin, 544, 545
Warterman, Robert H., Jr., 697
Watson, Barry, 692
Watson, Emma, 192
Weathers, Carl, 481
Weber, Joseph, 680
Weber, Karl, 674
Webster, Frederick E., Jr., 669, 676
Wedel, Michel, 689, 690
Weigold, Michael F., 693
Weilbaker, Dan C., 680
Weisal, Kimberly, 679
Weiss, Allen, 673
Weitz, Barton A., 669, 670, 676, 685, 687, 689, 694, 695
Welch, David, 682, 696
Welch, Jack, 697
Welch, Suzy, 697
Wells, Jennifer, 691
Welsh, Jonathan, 699
Wensley, Robin, 669, 670
Wentz, Laurel, 672
Werner, Ray O., 674
Werther, William B., Jr., 674
West, Edward, 688
West, Susan, 691
Westerlund, Jane, 370, 372, 373, 375, 376, 377
Wheaton, Ken, 693
Wheeler, Joe, 684
White, E. B., 671
White, Katherine M., 692
White, Tiffany Barnett, 683
White, Tina, 682
Whittemore, C. B., 679
Wie, Michelle, 627
Wiener, Joshua L., 694
Wiersema, Fred D., 669, 694
Wiertz, Caroline, 683
Wiles, Michael A., 688
Wilke, Jeffrey, 426
Wilkie, William L., 670, 675, 686, 691
Williams, Stephanie, 680
Willon, Phil, 693
Wilson, Alexandra, 4440
Wilson, James O., 674
Wilson, Rick T., 693
Wind, Jerry, 696
Wind, Yoram, 671, 676
Windorski, David, 3–4, 14, 15, 21–23, 670
Winer, Russell S., 681, 683, 685
Winfrey, Oprah, 3, 15, 481
Wingfield, Nick, 670
Winslow, Ron, 685
Winter, Rebecca, 679
Winters, Lewis C., 692
Wirtz, Jochen, 681, 682, 683, 684
Wittington, Richard, 670
Woellert, Lorraine, 687
Woestendisk, John, 699
Wolf, Alan, 688
Wolfinbarger, Mary, 684
Wolfman, Ian, 569
Wonacott, Peter, 684
Wong, Anthony, 676
Wong, Elaine, 691
Woodall, Regina D., 684
Woods, Tiger, 269, 368, 492
Woodside, Arch G., 683, 693
Woon, Emily, 686
Woyke, Elizabeth, 674
Wozniak, Steve, 236
Wu, Fan, 687
Wyckoff, D. Daryl, 681, 683
Wyner, Gordon A., 672, 685

Yalch, Richard, 675
Yao Ming, 133
Yate, Martin, 614
Yeniyurt, Sengun, 687
Yi Wen Yen, 669
Yi-Zheng Shi, 690
Yip, George S., 682
Ylkur, Rama, 692
Yong Ki-Lee, 684
Yong Zhang, 692
York, Emily Bryson, 689, 694
Young, Clifford E., 682
Young, DeForrest, 635
Young, Eric, 684
Youngblood, Dick, 698

Z

Zaltman, Gerald, 676
Zamiska, Nicholas, 679
Zavala, Zack, 673
Zawada, Craig, 685
Zbar, Jeffrey D., 692
Zeithaml, Valerie A., 675, 683, 684
Zettelmeyer, Florian, 685
Zhao, Guangzhi, 691, 692
Zhen Zhu, 682
Zimmer, Mary R., 689
Zimoch, Rebecca, 671
Zinkham, George M., 675, 692
Ziobro, Paul, 679, 700
Zirkle, Michael, 680
Zmuda, Natalie, 669, 679, 689, 690
Zoltner, Andris A., 695, 696

COMPANY INDEX

A

A&E, 645
AARP, 498
Abbott Laboratories, 154
ABC network, 202
Aberdeen Group, 228
Accenture, 302, 310, 603
Accutron, 285
Ace Concierge, 299
Ace Hardware, 391
ACNielsen, 154, 262
ACNielsen ScanTrack, 200, 210, 218
Activa, 476
Activeion Cleaning Solutions, case, 265–267
Activeion Friendly, 267
Activeion Pro, 266–267
Activision, 79
Act II Microwave Popcorn, case, 401–403
Adams Golf, 626, 627
Adbusters, 84
Adidas, 21, 171, 172, 280, 435
Adidas Soloman AG, 627
Advanced Bowflex, 497
Advil, 122
AEG, 453
AFLAC, 492
Agentric, 154
AIDS Foundation, 25
Airbus Industries, 169, 328
AirTran, 326
Alcoa, 328
Allbookstores.com, 440
Allstate Insurance, 300
AlphaGraphics, 360
Altria, 598
Amazon.com, 26, 79, 313, 319, 349, 380, 384, 385, 429, 440, 450, 550, 553, 555, 556, 559, 565
  case, 425–426
Amazon Conservation Association, 304
Ambassador greeting cards, 386
American Airlines, 49, 86, 304, 349, 419, 509
American Automobile Association, 633
American Boarding Kennel Association, 633
American Express Black Card, 510
American Express Company, 103, 299, 308, 522
American Express Platinum Card, 119
American Heart Association, 304
American Hospital Supply, 398
American Idol, 202, 508
American Lawn Mower Company, 629
American Marketing Association Foundation, 304
American National Can, 150
American Pet Products Marketing Association, 632
American Red Cross, 32, 140, 303, 309, 487, 512
  mission, 30
America Online, 128
Ameriprise Financial, 69, 599
Amoco, 47, 48
AMP, Inc., 521
am/pm stores, 48
Amway, 487
Anacin, 285
Angels and Demons, 473–474
Anheuser-Busch Companies, 106, 127, 132–133, 490, 504
  social responsibility, 91
Anheuser-Busch Recycling Corporation, 91
Animal Fair, 632
Animal Planet, 633
Anne Klein Couture, 165
Ann Taylor LOFT chain, 224, 225
Ann Taylor Stores Corporation, 224, 225, 450
Any Given Sunday, 480, 481
Apple II computer, 8, 236, 250
Apple Inc., 5, 8, 13, 65, 79, 130, 171, 172, 236, 252, 258, 265, 282, 284, 313, 390, 394, 447, 490, 509
  and iPhone 3G, 405
  new product innovation, 245–246
Apple Industrial Design Group, 258
Apple Stores, 297, 395, 405
  retailing mix, 447
Aquafina, 512, 648
Arby's, 127
ARCO, 47, 49
ARCO BP Express, 48
Arizona Republic, 498
Arm & Hammer, 286
Arrow shirts, 354
Arthur D. Little, 258
Associated Grocers, 390, 391, 433
AT&T, 80, 114, 175, 184, 471, 499, 502, 529
AT&T CruiseCast, 9
Atlanta Braves, 256
Aurora Foods, 284
Austad's, 368
Australia from 60 Dollars a Day, 463
Autobytel.com, 384, 385
Avert Virucidal, 253
Aviator glasses, 510
Avis Rent-A-Car, 238, 391
Avon Products, Inc., 19, 102, 170, 441, 521
  in China, 393
Awesome Pet Products, 632
Axe, 285

B

Babies "R" Us, 249
Bagel Bakes, case, 636–638
Bagel-Fuls, 259
Baked Lay's potato chips, 275
Baked Tostitos, 356
Banana Nut Cheerios, 574–575
Banana Republic, 224
Bank of America, 304
Barbie doll, 260–261
Bark, The, 632
Barnes & Noble, 102, 435, 447, 450, 552, 556, 565
Barnesandnoble.com, 440
Barney the TV dinosaur, 197
BarNone, 335
Bassett, 646
Bass Pro Store, 453
Bass Shoe Outlet, 445
Bausch and Lomb, 510, 616
BAX Global, 419
Bayer, 474, 487
Beanie Babies, 326
Beatles Rock Band video game, 488
Beatrice Foods, 415
Bebe, 491
BeBo, 241
Behold, 421
Bell bicycles, 8
Ben & Jerry's, 26, 30, 33, 35, 38, 39, 40, 47
  dashboard, 34
  founding of, 25
  mission statements, 24
  SWOT analysis, 41
Benetton, 450
Ben Franklin stores, 391
Benjamin Moore, 420
Bertie Bott's Every Flavor Beans, 510
Best Buy, 88, 89, 154, 251, 354, 394, 420, 433, 435, 436, 437, 446, 447, 452
  case, 135–137
Best Foods, 132
Best Western, 633
Best You, 497
Better Homes and Gardens, 645
Betty Crocker, 214, 572
Betty Crocker Dessert Bowls, 596, 597
Beverly Hills Hotel, 633
BevMark, 648
Bic pens, 285
Bic perfume, 281
Bicycle Times, 497
BJ's Wholesale Club, 345, 402, 445
Black & Decker, 169, 186, 265, 287, 288, 534, 630
Blackberry, 113, 115
Blockbuster Entertainment, 31, 402, 433, 603
Bloomingdale's, 298, 398, 432, 443, 445, 451, 453
Blue Cross-Blue Shield, 479
Blu-Farm Group, 191
BMW, 263, 440, 479
  case, 294–294
BMW Golf Club International tournament, 295
BMW X3, 486
Boeing Company, 80, 153, 169, 183, 215, 325, 326, 328, 350
Boise Cascade, 102
Bold, 285, 286, 599
Bon Marche, 432
Bonne Bell Cosmetics, Inc., 132
Booz, Allen & Hamilton, 302
Borders Group, Inc., 382
Bose, 283, 558
Boston Consulting Group, 36, 47
Boston Market, 449
Boucheron, 394
Boys and Girls Clubs, 102
BP, case, 47–49
BP Amoco Ultimate, 48
Brawny paper towels, 281
Breakers, 299
Breathe Right Nasal strips, 190–192
Bridgestone/Firestone, Inc., 101–102, 622
Bridgestone Tire Company, Ltd., 281, 621–622
Bridging, Inc., 18
Briggs and Stratton, 630
Brillo, 17
BringYourPet.com, 633
Brinks, 302
Brita, 74
British Airways, 114
British Broadcasting Corporation, 71
British Petroleum, 47
Bronco, 285
Brook's Brothers Clothiers, 119, 443, 453
Brookstone, 477
Brother, 274
Bruno Magli, 165
Bubba Gump Shrimp Company, 510
Budweiser Light, 122
Bufferin, 285
Buick, 115, 479, 539
Bull's Eye, 639
Bumble Bee tuna, 363
Burdines, 432
Burger Chef, 450
Burger King, 97, 207, 229, 230, 235, 236, 238, 262, 493, 543
  commercialization, 263
Burlington Coat Factory, 444

Business Talk Radio, 497
Business 2.0, 498
BusinessWeek, 35, 459, 497, 603, 630
BzzAgent Inc., marketing services, 127

C

C. H. Robinson, 639
Cadbury Schweppes, 176, 284
Cadillac, 120, 539
Cadillac Escalade, 486
Calistoga, 281
Callaway Golf Company, 369, 378, 563
  case, 625–627
  marketing channels, 379
Calloway Warbird, 369
Campbell Soup Company, 85, 131–132, 154, 279, 286, 289, 330, 422, 579
Campbell's V-8, 117
Camp Unleashed, 633
C&R Research, 556
C&S Wholesale Grocers, 639
Canon, 37, 293, 349
Cantina Corona, 453
Capital One, 549
Caplow Company
  operating ratios to analyze operations, 373–374
  operating statement, 370–373
  ratios for setting and evaluating prices, 374–377
Cap'n Crunch, 258
Careerbuilder.com, 606
Carefour, 436
CARE International, 109
Carl's Jr. restaurants, 474
CarMax, 355
Carnation Company, 100
Carnation Instant Breakfast, 21, 258
Carrefour, 431
Cartier, 347
Cartoon Network, 256
Castrol, 48
Catalyst Pepe Inc., 140
Caterpillar Inc., 145–146, 171, 384, 423
CBS network, 202, 457, 497
Celanese Chemical Company, 401
Celestial Seasonings, 290, 380
Center for Learning and Experimentation, General Mills, 572
Century 21 Real Estate, LLC, 380, 389
Cereal Partners Worldwide, 170, 387, 584
Cerezyme, 101, 106
CGCT, 184
Champion pacemakers, 41–42, 631
Chanel, 171, 188, 347
Chanel No. 5 perfume, 493
Chaps, 284
Charlesburg Furniture, 395, 396
Charles Schwab, 522, 543, 550, 558
Chatter Telephone, 196–198
Checker Drive-In Restaurants, 449
Cheer, 286, 599
Cheerios, 209, 308, 572, 574
Cheese Nips, 290
Cheetos, 184
Chef America Supreme Cuisine, 74
Chevrolet, 17
Chevrolet Cavalier, 362
Chevron, 487
Chevy Tahoe, 84
Chevy Volt, 285
Chicago Children's Museum, 304
Chicago Cubs, 481
Chicago Tribune, 498
Chicken of the Sea, 290
China Mobile Ltd., 322
Chips Ahoy, 287, 291
Chophouse bar and grill, 256
Christian Dior, 165, 354
Christian Science Monitor, 498
Christie's, 171
Chrysler Corporation, 335, 497
Church & Dwight, 286
Circle K, 402
Circuit City, 89, 135, 636
Cirque du Soleil, 297
Cirrus system, 309
Cisco Systems, 163
Claiborne for Men, 74
Clairol, 122
Cleveland Golf, 626
Cleveland Indians, 618
Cling-Free, 285
Clinique, 564
Clorox Company, 121, 285
CNBC, 9, 201
CNN, 252
CNS Breathe Right Strips, case, 190–192
Coca-Cola Company, 83, 97, 102, 114, 169, 171, 172, 175, 178, 185, 189, 275, 282, 283, 290, 291, 382, 390, 393, 434, 490, 508, 510, 512, 559, 567, 573, 619, 648
  advertising mistake, 174
  in cola wars, 96
Coccolino, 170
Coke Zero, 490
Coldwater Creek, 326
Cole Haan, 74
Colgate-Palmolive Company, 123, 124, 169, 334, 590
Colgate Total, 123, 124
Colt, 285
Columbia House, 556
Columbia Pictures, 473–474
Comcast, 485
ComScore, 500
ConAgra Foods, Inc., 401, 402
Conservation International, 108
Consumer Electronics Association, 88
Coors, 144
Corning, Inc., 140, 149
Corona Extra, 128
Cosmo Girl, 498
Costco Warehouse Club, 12, 56, 135, 154, 287, 345, 399, 402, 431, 445, 637
Costco Wholesale, 573
Cost Cutters Family Hair Salon, 309
Coupon Information Corporation, 507
Courtyard Hotels, 287
Cover Girl ColorMatch, 277
Cracker Jack, 355
Craftsman lawn mowers, 629
Craftsman power tools, 128
Craftsman radial saw, 349
Craftsman tools, 286, 292
CraigsList Inc., 31, 319, 500, 607
Crate and Barrel, 438
  case, 647
Cray, Inc., 249
Cream of Wheat, 507
Crest Neat Squeeze toothpaste, 258
Crest toothpaste, 124, 334, 398, 590, 599
Crest Whitestrips, 457
Crispin, Porter & Bogusky, 492, 493
Crossbow Technology, 625
Crunch 'n Munch, 355
CSI, 457
CSI: Miami, 202
Cub Foods, 434
Cunard, 77
CVS/Pharmacy, 402
Cybertron Transformers, 197

D

Daiei, 431
Daktronics, Inc., case, 617–619
Dallas Mavericks, 618
Dallas Museum of Art, 19
Dannon, 476
Dasani, 512
DealCatcher.com, 555
DeBeers, 171, 558, 560
Deere & Company, 145
Degree Fine Fragrance Collection, 282
Deli Creations, 203
Dell Asia Pacific and Japan, 161
Dell.com, 384, 385, 440, 555, 556
Dell Inc., 88–89, 95, 155, 184, 187, 225, 356, 385, 409, 411, 439, 523, 550, 558, 573
  case, 640–641
  in emerging markets, 160–161
  supply chain, 409–410
Del Monte, 288, 415
Delta Air Lines, 349, 419
DeWalt tools, 287, 288
DHL Worldwide, 305, 414, 417, 529
Dial soap, 288, 487
Dick's Sporting Goods, Inc., 379, 480, 563
DieHard, 285, 286
Diesel, 172
Dieste, 73
Diet Coke, 5
Diet Pepsi, 10
DigitalThink, case, 633–635
Dillard's, 436
Direct Marketing Association, 438, 441
Direct Selling Association, 442
DirecTV, 527
Disney Channel, 9
Disneyland, 297, 298, 457
Disneyland Paris, 402
Disney Online, 556
Disney Twenty-Three, 497
Dockers, 280
Dodge Ram, 497
Dog Fancy, 632
Dog World, 466
Dollar car rental, 238
Dollar General, 445
Dollar Tree, 445
Dollar Valley Stores, 356
Domino's fruit-flavored bubble gum, 284
Domino's Pizza, 307, 595
Don Miguel, 58
Donna Karan, 119, 415
Doritos, 115, 184, 281, 287, 356, 490, 507, 523
DoubleClick, 517
DoubleClick Dart Search, 500
Dr. Care Toothpaste, 8–9
DreamWorks, 484, 485
Dr Pepper, 283, 474
Drumstick Nestlé, 184
DSW Shoe Warehouse, 453
Dun & Bradstreet, 606
DuPont, 163, 522, 525
Duracell, 283, 285, 348

E

Eagle, 285
Eastman Chemical Company, 539
Eastman Kodak, 25, 27, 44, 45, 167, 381, 423, 534, 573
  product line, 35–38
Easy Off, 285

Ebags, 439
eBay, 154, 284, 319, 320, 326, 440, 559
eBayBusiness, 154
eBay Motors, 457
Ecademy, 607
Economist, The, 333–334
Eddie Bauer, 265, 385, 386, 451
Edmunds.com, 565
eHarmony, 119
Ektelon, 241
Electrolux, 441
Electronic Arts, 488
Electronic Data Systems, 146
Eli Lilly, 411
Elizabeth Arden, 288
ElleGirl, 498
Endust, 421
Energizer, 347, 492
  price perception, 348
Energizer Advanced Formula, 348
Energy Club, 71
Energy Smart light bulbs, 74
Enterprise Rent-A-Car, 599
E-Pay, 234
Epson, 286
Ericsson, 184
ESPN, 481, 496
ESPN the Magazine, 480, 481
Esquire Sportsman, 498
ESRI, 77
Estée Lauder, 127, 564
E.T., 510
Etch-A-Sketch, 510
Ethan Allen, 646
eToys, 19
E*Trade, 256, 490
Euromarket Designs Inc., 647
Eveready, 285
Excedrin, 285
Expedia, 319
EX Squirt Ketchup, 252
Exxon, 115, 186, 285

F

Facebook, 26, 208, 209, 241, 242, 297, 457, 474, 482, 547, 559, 568, 607, 608
Fairfield Inns, 258, 287
Family Dollar Stores, 356, 445
Family Fun magazine, 197
Family Guy, 474
Family Life Network, 497
Famous Barr, 432
Famous Friends Concierge, 299
Fancast, 497
Fancy Feast, 252
FAO Schwartz, 325
Farm Radio Network, 497
Fashionmall.com, 440
Fatal Attraction, 194
Federal Express, 89, 143, 185, 305, 360, 382, 502, 525
Federal Express Supply Chain Services, 417
Ferrari, 293
Fiber One, 572, 585
Fiberwise, 285
Field of Dreams, 193
Fila brand, 392
Filenes, 432
Fingos, 253
Firebird, 285
Firestone Tire and Rubber Company, 101–102
  and Ford Motor Company, 621–623
Fisher-Price, 217, 479
  marketing research, 195–198
Flickr, 65, 457
Florida Gators, 269
Florida Orange Growers Association, 280
Florsheim, 435
Focus, 287
Folgers coffee, 290, 599
Food Network, 496
FootJoy, 369
FootJoy StaSof, 369
Foot Locker, 397
Ford Bronco, 621
Ford Consulting Group, case, 217–219
Ford Motor Company, 48, 49, 102, 115, 128, 150, 169, 248, 287, 335, 383, 390, 391, 431, 434, 468, 471, 472, 583
  and Firestone problem, 621–623
Ford Pinto, 621
Forest Gump, 310
Fortune Brands, 249
Four Seasons Hotels, 477
Fox Business News, 201
Fox network, 202, 497
Fran Wilson Creative Cosmetics, 182, 183
Fresh Express, 258
Fresh Step cat litter, 121, 122
Friday Night Lights, 481
Friday Night 3, 481
Frigidaire, 435
Frito-Lay, Inc., 115, 178, 186, 275, 281, 287, 290, 356, 358, 523, 534, 536, 559
Fritos, 115
Fuji Photo, 167
Fulfill nutrition bars, 572
Fuller Brush, 441
FurReal Friends Butterscotch Pony, 197
Fusion automobile, 287
FUZE Beverage LLC, 648

G

Gain, 599
Gap, Inc., 224, 450, 465, 477
Gap.com, 440
Gap Factory Store, 445
Garden Design, 497
Garlic Cake, 254
Garmin, 65
Gatorade, 271, 282, 283, 284, 286, 648
  product and brands, 269–270
Gatorade All Stars, 269
Gatorade AM, 269, 270
Gatorade Be Tough, 270
Gatorade Bring It, 270
Gatorade Energy Bar, 269
Gatorade Energy Drink, 269
Gatorade Fierce, 270
Gatorade Frost, 269
Gatorade G2, 268, 269, 270, 286
Gatorade No Excuses, 270
Gatorade Nutritional Shake, 269
Gatorade Performance Series, 269
Gatorade Rain, 269, 270
Gatorade Shine On, 270
Gatorade Thirst Quencher, 270
Gatorade Tiger, 269, 270
Gatorade X-Factor, 269, 270
Gatorade Xtremo, 269
Gazelle.com, 429
Geant, 436
Geek Squad, 136, 251, 252
  case, 87–89
Geico, 297, 491–492, 502, 599
General Electric, 5, 16, 28, 74, 114, 153, 256, 286, 293, 326, 386, 435, 522, 585, 631
General Electric Medical Systems, 154
General Foods, 52
General Mills, 73, 90, 184, 196, 204, 209, 253, 257, 259, 278, 287, 415, 578, 579, 589, 590
  case, 595–597
  evaluation of marketing process, 592–594
  Nestlé joint venture, 170, 386, 387, 583–584
  resource allocation, 574–575
  strategic marketing at, 571–572
  Worldwide Innovation Network, 584
General Motors, 273, 335, 383, 471, 472, 539
Genzyme, 101
Georgia-Pacific, 281
Gerber, 86, 186, 286
Gigante, 169
Gillette Company, 171, 179, 185, 186, 187, 203, 283, 284, 346–347, 397, 529, 604
Gillette Fusion razor, 270, 272, 276, 347, 349
Gilt.com, 440
Gino's Hamburgers, 450
Glass Plus, 285
GlaxoSmithKline, 411, 471
Glidden, 284
Global Healthcare Exchange, 154
GNB Technologies, Inc., 423
Go Daddy, 490
Godiva Chocolates, 541
Go-Gurt Fizzix, 258–259
Golden Beauty, 186
Golden Valley Microwave Foods, 401, 402
Golf Channel, 626
Golf Galaxy, Inc., 368, 379, 563
Golfsmith, 368
Gome stores, 187
Good Housekeeping, 645
Good Start infant formula, 100
Goodyear Tire and Rubber Company, 144, 281, 390, 397, 398
Google, Inc., 5, 26, 65, 78, 117, 200, 201, 202, 260, 261, 499, 501
  case, 515–517
GoToMeeting, 78, 603
got2b.com, 282
Goya Foods, 132
Grease Monkey, 311
Great Atlantic & Pacific Tea Company, 81, 415
Great States Corporation, 580–581, 582, 595
Green Giant, 572
Green Marketing Coalition, 478
Greenpeace, 303
Grey Poupon, 203
Gridiron Game, 481
Grocery Headquarters, 56
Grumman Aircraft, 150
Gucci, 119, 171, 393–394
Gulfstream Aerospace Corporation, 144, 466, 467
Gunderson & Rosario, Inc., 254

H

H. J. Heinz Company, 18, 252, 324, 328, 415, 639
Haggar Clothing Company, 130
Hallmark Cards, Inc., 70, 386
Hamburger Helper, 195, 204, 572
Hamburger Helper Microwave Singles, 572
Hand in Hand International, 18
H&R Block, 300, 309, 389, 390, 391
Hansen Natural, 648
Hard Rock Café, 297
Harkman Electric, 384
Harley-Davidson, Inc., 74, 145, 185, 278, 279, 283, 284, 552, 553, 559
  supplier collaboration, 146
Harley Owner Group, 553
HarperCollins, 382
Harris Corporation, 532
Harris Interactive, 555

Harry and David, 439
Harryanddavid.com, 556
Harry Potter and the Half-Blood Prince, 192, 193
Harry Potter books, 224, 426, 510
Harry the K's Bar & Grill, 316
Hart Schaffner & Marx, 354
Hasbro, 197, 567
HauteLook.com, 440
Hawaiian Punch, 278, 279
Head & Shoulders, 582
Health Cruises, Inc., case, 635–636
Health magazine, 627
Heartwise cereal, 285
Heinz Ketchup, 290, 324, 466, 467
Helena Rubenstein, 186
Helios House, 48, 49
Henredon, 284, 646
Herbalife, 441
Hershey Foods, 73, 127, 131, 287, 354, 509–510
Hershey's Extra Dark Chocolate, 117
Hertz Rent-A-Car, 21, 238
  relationship marketing, 306–308
Hewlett-Packard, 39, 130, 146, 180, 263, 274, 278, 291–292, 301, 339–340, 354, 381, 412, 542, 543, 559, 599, 640–641
  Design for Supply Chain program, 423
Hewlett-Packard Enterprise Services, 542
Hey! There's A Monster In My Room spray, 254
HGTV Dream Home Giveaway, 508
Hibbett Sporting Goods, 480
Hickory Stick, 625
Hidden Valley Low-Fat Salad Dressing, 285
Hidden Valley Ranch Take Heart Salad Dressing, 285
Hi5, 241
Hilton Hotels, 434
Hindustan Lever, 179–180
History Channel, 496
Hitachi, 164
Holiday Inn, 390, 391, 443, 633
Holiday Inn Express, 74
Holiday Inn Worldwide, 74
Home Depot, 12, 102, 144, 302, 383, 429, 431, 433, 444, 446, 477, 534, 573, 630
Home Shopping Network, 385, 439
HOM Furniture, case, 628–629
HOM Oak and Leather stores, 628
Honda Civic, 321
Honda Motors, 180, 286, 490
Honey Nut Cheerios, 387
Honeywell International, 522
Hotmail, 559
Hot Pockets, 9
Howlin' Coyote chili, 33, 53–63
HTC Touch Diamond, 113
Huffington Post, 498
Huggies, 169, 281, 286
Huggies Baby Network, 553
Hulu, 497
Hummer, 459
Hyatt Corporation, 70
Hyatt Place, 70
Hyundai, 474
Hyundai Motor America, 292, 564

I

Ibane guitars, 342
IBM, 19, 97, 140, 146, 176, 384, 409, 415–416, 420, 423, 487, 521, 522, 525, 550, 604
  Global Services, 529, 538
  integrated supply chain, 410
  Smarter Planet campaign, 587
Ichiro Suzuki bobble-head doll, 326
Ideale washing machine, 186
Idearc, 499
Ideele.com, 440
IDEO, product design, 258
iFood Associates, 465
IGA Stores, 391
IKEA, 171, 172, 322, 438, 453, 579, 580
iMac, 237, 246, 265
Imagine Babyz, 74
imc^2 case, 566–569
iNap, 65
Independent Grocers Alliance, 433
Infomercial Monitoring Service Inc., 497
Information Resources, Inc., 34, 200, 210, 218
Infosys Technologies, Ltd., 322
Initiative, 474
Intel Corporation, 147, 171, 322, 583
Intelligent Quisine, 330
Interactive Advertising Bureau, 500
InterContinental Hotels, 434
International Franchise Association, 434
Iomra Systems, 79
iPhone, 79, 113, 114, 252, 313, 465
iPhone 3G, 244, 245, 246, 404, 405
iPod, 78, 172, 246, 285, 297
iTune, 497
Ivory Snow, 286
Izze Beverage Company, 648

J

J. Crew, 555
J. D. Power & Associates, 200, 583
Jack in the Box, 450
Jaguar, 440
Jamba Juice, case, 619–620
JCPenney, 131, 139–140, 144, 281, 354, 438, 446, 451, *476,* 502, 555
JCPMedia, 148
  organizational buying, 140
Jefferson Smurfit Corporation, 522
Jell-O, 269
Jelly Joes, 290
Jenn-Air, 397
JetBlue Airways, 144, 312, 326
  profitability, 313
Jewel Supermarkets, 350
Jif, 328
Jiffy Lube International, 394
Jigzone.com, 555
JobFox, 607
Jobster, 607
John Deere equipment, 145
Johnson & Johnson, 12, 28, 114, 130, 154, 255, 280, 328, 471, 567
Johnson Carpet Company, 543
Johnson Company, 86
Johnson Controls Automotive Systems Group, 529
Joosi, 497
Jose Ole, 58
JOYity, 65
Joy perfume, 285
Juice Club, 619
Juice It Up!, 620
Juice Stop, 620
Jura brand, 624
Just Born, Inc., 290
Just for One, 572
JVC, 164

K

Kanebo, 183, 397
KC Masterpiece, 639
Kellogg's, 130, 141, 144, 209, 284, 285, 407, 493
Kelly, Astor & Peters Advertising, 645–646
Ken Davis Bar-B-Q-Sauce, 329
Ken Davis Products, Inc., 328
  case, 638–640
  entrepreneurship, 329
Kenmore appliances, 286
Kentucky Fried Chicken, 460, 508
Kia Motors, 122
Kimberly-Clark Corporation, 115, 169, 253, 281, 286, 287, 553
Kindle electronic books, 79
Kirby vacuum cleaners, 529
Kirin, 397
KitchenAid, 623, 624
Kit Kat, 176
Kiwi Brands, 420–421
Kleenex, 4, 12, 115, 269, 283, 291
Kleenex diapers, 284
Kmart, 128, 397, 435, 436
Kodachrome, 39
Kodak cameras, 86
Kodak digital cameras, 36, 37
Kodak digital picture frames, 36, 37
Kodak film, 36, 39
Kodak ink jet printers, 36, 37–38
Kodak Zi6 pocket video camera, 43
Kohler, 323
Kohl's department stores, 380, 392
Komatsu, 171
Kraft American cheese, 281
Kraft Foods, Inc., 146, 203, 259, 291, 328, 386, 465, 506, 589, 639
Kraft Miracle Whip, 290
Kroehler, 646
Kroger, 287, 350, 390, 446, 506, 637
Krups, 623, 624
Kuschelweich, 170
Kwik-E-Marts, 510

L

Lalique, 347
Lands' End, 12–13, 35, 558
  case, 157–159
Landsend.com, 477
Lay's Potato Chips, 115, 178, 184, 380
Lay's snack chips, 281
Lay's Stax potato crisps, 290
Lazarus, 432
Lee jeans, 127
L'eggs, 290
Lego, 171
LEGO Land Imagination Center, 453
Lender's Bagels, 284
Lever, 179–180
Lever Europe, 170
Lever Project Shakti initiative, 174
Levi's jeans, 185, 380
Levi Strauss, 104, 171, 172
Lexmark, 274
Lexus, 398
LG, 351
LG Incite, 113
Liberty Tax Service, 434
Lifetime channel, 496
Like.com, 429
Limited, The, 450
Lincoln-Mercury dealers, 468
LinkedIn, 208, 457, 607
Lipton, 648
Liquid Paper, 274
Little Remedies, 248, 249
Liz Claiborne, 35, 74, 104
L.L. Bean, 385, 438, 439, 452
Lockheed Corporation Skunk Works, 573, 586–587
Lockheed Martin Corporation, 80, 141

Loehmann's, 434
L'Oréal, 171, 186, 284
L'Oréal Paris, 493
Louis Vuitton, 163, 283
Louvre Museum, 19
Love to Dance Bear, 197
Lowe's, 144
Lufthansa, 434
Luggage Club, 299
Luvs, 281
Luxottica Group, S. P. A., 284

M

MAB, 165
MacBook, 237, 246
MacBook Air, 237
MacBook Pro, 237
Mac-Gray Corporation, 226
MAC Group, Inc., 442
Macintosh, 246
Mac Mini, 237
Mac Pro, 236, 237
Macy's, Inc., 301, 432, 436, 510, 599, 601
Magazine Publishers of America, 489
Magnolia Home Theater, 136
Major League Baseball, 256, 315–317, 618
Mall of America, 439
 case, 453–454
M&Ms, 10, 359, 486, 508, 550
Mansar Products, Ltd., 383
MapQuest, 65
March of Dimes, 304
MarketTools, 204–205
Marks & Spencer, 549
Marlboro Light Kings, 334
Marriott Corporation, 12, 16, 18, 258
Marriott International, 287
Marriott Marquis Hotels and Vacation Clubs, 287
Mars, Inc., 383
Marshall Field's, 432
Mars Snackfood, 508
Mary Kay Cosmetics, Inc., 441, 539
Mary Kay's Velocity fragrance, 121, 122
MasterCard International, 102, 173, 474, 509
Mastro Limpio, 170
Match.com, 119
Matsushita, 164, 397
Mattel, 104, 171, 180, 181, 261
Maxim Steel, 534
Maybelline, 186
Mayo Clinic, 248, 306
Mazola Corn Oil, 132
McDonald's Corporation, 73, 103, 104, 120, 128, 133, 171, 173, 183, 184, 207, 229, 230, 234, 235, 236, 238, 262, 263, 309, 323, 391, 433, 434, 443, 448–449, 450, 461, 463, 507, 513, 529, 590
 case, 642–643
McFadden's Restaurant and Saloon, 316
McKesson Corporation, 154, 398
Medtronic, 25, 27, 30, 31, 32, 35, 47, 50, 154, 328, 521
 in Asia, 40–42
 in China, 630–632
 mission, 29
Medtronic Pacing Business, 630
Men's Vogue, 498
Mentalist, 202
Mentos, 5
Mercedes-Benz, 185, 188, 440, 479
Merck & Company, 163, 189
Merrill Lynch, 301, 528
Metacafe, 492
MetLife.com, 385
Metro Group, 431
Metropolitan Life Insurance, 132, 133, 523
Metropolitan Museum of Art, 86
Metropolitan Opera, 300
MGA Entertainment, 128
Michelin, 119, 169, 281, 284
 branding strategy, 286
MicroFridge, 226, 228
Microsoft Bing, 117
Microsoft Corporation, 31, 49, 175, 202, 283, 286, 319, 398, 422, 440, 493, 517
 antitrust problems, 80–81
Microsoft Dynamics, 422
Microsoft Excel, 338
Microsoft Project, 588
Microsoft Xbox 360, 254, 328, 457, 402
Microsoft Zune, 254
MicroVision, 628
Mike and Ike Treats, 290
Milk Processor Education Program, 280
Milky Way, 508
Milky Way Dark, 508
Milky Way Midnight, 508
Miller Brewing, 496
MillerCoors, 474
Million Dollar Baby, 193
Mimosin, 170
MINI, 294
Minneapolis Star Tribune, 498
Miramax, 287
Mission Foods, 58
Mizuno, 626
Modell's Sporting Goods, 480
Modern Dog, 632
Moen faucets, 249
Moneygram, 81
Monster.com, 127, 606
Monsters vs. Aliens, 484, 507, 510
Moodmatcher, 183
Moody's Investor Services, 611
Moore Chemical & Sanitation Supply, Inc., 540
Morgantown Furniture, case, 645–646
Motetronix Technology, case, 624–625
Motorola, Inc., 171, 177, 423, 522
Mountain Equipment Company, 433
Mpire.com, 429
MP3 players, 254
Mr. Clean, 170
Mr. Proper, 170
MSN Money, 517
MTV, 172, 496
MTV Road Rules, 481
Museum of Modern Art, 295, 304
Mustang, 285, 287
MyCoke.com, 559
MyeBay, 552
My First Craftsman, 128
MySimon.com, 440, 555
MySpace, 241, 297, 457, 559, 608
MyWorkster, 607
MyYahoo!, 550, 552

N

Nabisco Company, 130, 287, 290, 389, 509, 543
Naked Juice, case, 647–648
NASCAR, 304, 453, 493
National Association for PET Container Resources, 79
National Basketball Association, 618
National Celebrity Cabinet, 304
National Center for Public Policy and Higher Education, 75
National Football League, 618
National Gardening Association, 630
National Geographic, 21
National Golf Foundation, 368–369
National Hockey League, 618
National Retail Federation, 444
National Semiconductor, 413
National Sporting Goods Association, 369
Nationwide, 73
Nature Conservancy, 19, 26, 303
Nature Valley granola bars, 257, 265
NBC network, 485, 488
Need A Ticket.com, 319
Neighborhood Markets, 410
Neilsen Media Check, 202
Neiman Marcus, 354, 398, 432, 434, 435, 436, 447, 541
Nellie Mae, 326
Nescafé, 186–187, 624
Nespresso brand, 624
Ness Corp. Online, 202
Nestlé Food Corporation, 100, 127, 173, 176, 184, 186–187, 281, 291, 385, 415, 506, 512
 General Mills joint venture, 170, 387, 583–584
Nestlé Waters, 512
Netflix, 30
 business model, 31
Net Impact, 71
NetMarket.com, 440
New Age herbal tea, 290
New Balance, Inc., 246, 280
Newegg.com, 385
Newspaper Association of America, 498
Newsweek, demand estimation, 329–334
New Yorker, 131, 632, 644
New York Giants, 21
New York Mets, 326
New York Times, 498, 552
New York Yankees, 326
Nexcare, 368
Nickelodeon, 9
Nielsen Claritas, 227, 228
Nielsen Company, 599
Nielsen Media Research, 200, 201–202, 217
Nielsen Online Ratings, 202, 500
Nielsen Television Index Ranking Report, 202
Nike, Inc., 12, 26, 104, 105, 171, 172, 185, 248, 280, 283, 284, 297, 393, 397, 435, 488, 616, 626
NIKEID.com, 297, 298
Nike MaxSight, case, 616–617
Nike Shox NZ, 397
99 Cents Only Stores, 356
Nintendo, 254, 328, 357, 457
Nintendo GameCube, 250
Nintendo Wii, 74, 79, 250, 347, 356–357
Nissan Altima, 110
Nissan Motor Company, 73, 144, 179, 185, 397
NissanUSA.com, 110
Nokia, 65, 185, 278, 284, 423
Nordstrom, 74, 398, 435, 452, 453
Nordstrom Rack Stores, 74, 445
Norski Skog, 140
Northrup Grumman, 80
Northwest Airlines, 419
Northwestern Mutual Life Insurance Company, 528
NPD Group, 209
Nuprin, 285
NutraSweet, 84
Nutri-Grain Cereal, 141, 407
Nutrisystem, 497

O

Oakland Raiders, 480
Obsession perfume, 285
Ocean Spray Cranberries, 290
Ocean Village, 70
Odwalla, 648
ODW Logistics, Inc., 419–420
Off 5th, 445

Office Depot, 22, 89, 153, 385, 398, 426, 438, 450
Office Max, 22, 429
Olay, 69
Old Navy stores, 224
Olympus America, Inc., 273
Omaha Steaks' Steak Treats for Pets, 632
OMEGA watches, 126, 127
Omni Hotels, 567
1800flowers.com, 556
1% for the Planet, 304
Opium, 394
Oracle Corporation, 33, 176
Oral-B CrossAction toothbrush, 203
Orange Julius, 620
Orbitz.com, 335, 384, 385, 549
Oreos, 290
Orkut, 241
Orville Redenbacher popcorn, 402
Oscar Mayer, 123, 124, 130, 203
Oshman's, 435
Otto Group, 647
OUT! International, 254
Outward Bound, 303
Owens-Corning, 522
Owens-Corning Fiberglass Corporation, 84
Oxygen channel, 496, 497

P

Palm Pre, 113, 114
Palm V PDA, 258
Palo Alto Research Center, 544
Pampered Chef, 442
Pampers, 169, 281, 398, 564
Panasonic, 134, 293, 326, 351, 381, 435
Panasonic Viera television, 4
Pantene, 278
Papa John's Pizza, 583, 585–586
Paradise Kitchens, Inc., 33, 47
  marketing plan, 52–63
Paradise Ranch Country Club for Dogs, 633
Paragon Trade Brands, 287
Parker Guitar, 343
Payless Shoe Source, 360, 443, 452
PayPal, 5
PayPass, 437
PC Magazine, 498
Peapod.com, 440
Pearson, 382
Pedigree dog food, 489
Penguin Books, 127
Peninsula Chicago, 633
Pensek Logistics, 417
People, 131, 645
People en Español, 132
PepsiCo, 73, 124, 144, 169, 170, 171, 184, 269, 278, 283, 290, 291, 382, 391, 453, 490, 510, 512, 648
  in cola wars, 96
Pepsi Max, 9–10
Performance Rating Network, 497
Perrier bottled water, 101
Pert, 176
PETCO Animal Supplies, 335, 394, 395
Pets.com, 335
PetsHotel, 633
PetSmart, 335, 633
Petssonthego.com, 633
Pettravel.com, 633
Pew Internet & American Life Project, 555, 561
Pez Candy, Inc., 288
  customer value, 289
Pfizer, Inc., 487, 567
PGA America, 379
PGA Tour Superstores, 379
Phanatic Attic, 316
Philadelphia Cream Cheese, 259
Philadelphia Phillies, Inc., 300
  case, 315–317
Phoenix, 285
Photosmart, 292
Pier 1 Imports, 647
Pillsbury Company, 52, 57
Pillsbury Ready to Bake, 572
Pinto, 285
Pioneer Electronics, Inc., 164, 419–420
Piper Jaffray, 620
Pitney Bowes, Inc., 144, 525
Pittsburgh Pirates, 326
Pittsford and LaRue Advertising Agency, 635
Pivot Driver, 527
Pizza Hut, 73, 583
  case, 566–569
Planet Hollywood, 297, 298
Planet Smoothie, 620
Planter's peanuts, 389
PlasticsNet, 154
Plaxo, 607
Playboy, 284
Playmakers, 481
Playstation 3, 457
Poland Spring, 281
Politico, 498
Polo, 284
Polo/Ralph Lauren, 284, 390, 431
Pom Wonderful, 648
Popular Mechanics, 127
Porsche, 134, 488
Porsche Boxter, 286
Porsche Carrera, 286
Post-it brand products, 12
Post-it Flag, 4, 5
Post-it Flag Highlighter, 14–15
  case, 21–23
Post-It Flag Pen, 14–15
Post-it Notes, 3, 4, 14–15, 368
Pottery Barn, 647
Prevention magazine, 510
Priceline.com, 319, 477
Prince Sports, Inc., case, 241–243
Pringles, 260, 290, 564
Pristo-Kay, Inc., 636
Pristo-Kay Grocery stores, 637
Procter & Gamble, 102, 130, 144, 145, 146, 149, 169, 170, 172, 176, 180, 187, 200, 203, 209, 223, 255, 257, 260, 278, 281, 287, 290, 291, 334, 362, 390, 391, 398, 406, 457, 471, 506, 525, 534, 563, 564, 567, 582, 585, 589, 590, 599
  multibranding, 286
  and Wal-Mart, 147
Progressive Grocer, 627
Progressive Insurance, 298
Progresso, 572, 585
Progresso Light soups, 259
Promise soft spread, 122
Promo magazine, 505
Promotional Products Association International, 507
Propel, 648
Propel Fitness Water, 269
PRS Group, 180, 181
Publishers Clearing House, 508
Pure Touch Limited, 369
Purina Dog Chow, 465, 466
Purina Elegant Medleys, 252

Q

Quaker Oats Company, 258, 269, 280–281, 284
QVC, 439
QVC.com, 558

R

R. H. Donnelly, 499
Race for the Cure, 18
Radio Shack, 154, 287, 433
Rainforest Relief, 304
Ralcorp Holdings, 287
Ralph Lauren, 284, 398, 430
Ralston-Purina, 281
Random House, 382
Ray-Ban, 510
Rayovac, 287
RaySat Broadcasting, 9
Razor Gator, 319
Reader's Digest, 125, 508
Recreational Equipment, 548
Redbook, 130
Red Bull, 285
Red Cross Racing, 304
Red Lobster, 119
Red Roof, 633
Reebok International, 104, 185, 550, 551, 558
Reebok Russia, 185
Reese's Peanut Butter Puffs, 287
Reese's Pieces, 510
Regal Entertainment, 350
Regent, 77
Renaissance Hotels, 287
Replacements, The, 481
rePlanet, 79
Republic of Tea, 439
Response Magazine, 497
Restaurant News, 464
Restoration Hardware, 647
Retail Planning Associates of Ohio, 444
Revlon, 354, 551
Reynolds, 328
Reynolds and Reynolds, 599
Risky Business, 510
Rite-Aid, 402
Ritz-Carlton Hotels, 299, 300, 311
Rock and Roll Hall of Fame and Museum, 350
Rock Band 2, 74
Rockport Company, 284, 529
Rocky Mountain News, 498
Rolex, 354
Rollerblade, 282
Rolling Stone, 497
Rolls-Royce, 171, 294, 347
Ronald McDonald Children's Charities, 642
Ronald McDonald Houses, 103, 104
Rossimoda, 165
Ross Stores, 444
Rostiks, 642
Royal and Ancient Golf Club of St. Andrews, 627
RT-Mart, 436
RueLaLa.com, 440
Ruffles, 115, 184
Ruiz Foods, 58
Russian Bistro, 642

S

S. C. Johnson Company, 265
Safeguard, 287
Safeway, 147, 154, 350, 383, 415, 446
St. Croix Venture Partners, 50
St. Joseph Aspirin, 280
St. Jude Children's Research Hospital, 304
Saks Fifth Avenue, 415, 432, 435, 443, 445, 447
Salesforce.com, 603
Salvation Army, 303

Sam's Club, 135, 345, 398, 402, 410, 445, 573
Samsung Blackjack II, 113
Samsung Electronics, 69, 78, 115, 163, 274, 286, 351, 567
San Diego Padres, 475
Sanford Corporation, 274
Santitas brand tortillas, 287
Santo, 164
Saturn Corporation, 355, 430, 457
Scandinavian Airlines, 326
Schick, 395, 397
Schwab, 302
Schwab.com, 556
Schwan Food, 383
Schweppes Tonic Water, 176
Science Channel, 496
SciFlex, 369
Scope, 563, 564
Scotch-Brite floor-cleaning product, 174
Scotch-Brite Never Rust soap pads, 4, 17
Scotch-Brite Never Scratch soap pad, 204–205
Scotch Brite scouring pads, 368
Scotchgard, 99–100
Scotch tape, 368
Scripto, 291
Sears, 13, 73, 147, 287, 345, 349, 381, 383, 398, 445, 453
  and Land's End, 158
  private branding, 286
Seiko, 171, 188
Sergio Rossi, 394
Seven Cycles, Inc., 546, 549, 550, 558
  interactive marketing, 547
7-Eleven stores, 144, 147, 380, 383, 394, 402, 443, 510, 637
17 Again, 510
7Up brand, 285
Sewell Automotive Companies, 553, 554
Sharp Corporation, 164, 165, 274, 285
Sheraton catering, 302
Sheraton Hotels, 309, 633
Sherwin-Williams, 390, 420, 599
Shisegae Department Store, 627
Shiseido, 171, 183, 397
ShopCallaway.com, 379
ShopNBC, 439
Shutterfly, 426
Siemens AG, 174
  Energy & Automation's Airport Logistics Division, 144
  Industrial Automation Division, 150–151
Simpsons, 510
Simpsons Movie, 510
Singapore Airlines, 299
Sirius XM Satellite Radio, 497, 513
Skippy peanut butter, 210, 328, 354
Skippy Squeez It, 290
Skittles, 508
Sleep Number, 497
Slide, 492
Slingo.com, 555
Smithsonian, 134
Smoothie King, 620
Smucker's, 573
Snake Light flexible flashlight, 186
Snapple, 284
Snelling and Snelling, Inc., 391
Snickers, 128, 489, 508
Snuggle, 170
SoBe, 648
Sobe Life Water, 485
Sodima, 184
Sonic Dive In Restaurants, 434
Sony Corporation, 37, 78, 130, 164, 172, 179, 185, 254, 263, 286, 328, 345, 351, 381, 394, 510
Sony Energy Devices Corporation, 95
Sony PlayStation 3, 250
SonyStyle.com, 555
Sony Walkman, 326
Sopranos, The, 481
SOS, 17
Sotheby's, 171
Sothebys.com, 556
Sound of Music, 135
Source Perrier, 101
Southwest Airlines, 12, 31, 302, 311, 326
  mission, 30
Space Adventures, 310
Spalding basketballs, 510
Special K, 209
Speed Channel, 496
Sperry shoes, 435
Spic and Span, 291
Spider Man 3, 260
Sporting Goods Manufacturers, 242
Sporting News Baseball Yearbook, 223, 224
Sports Authority, 430, 431, 480
Sports Illustrated, 495
Sports Illustrated for Kids, 128, 497
Sprint, 80, 114, 309, 502
SRI Consulting Business Intelligence, 124
Stake Fastener Company, 384
Standard and Poor's *Register of Corporations,* 611
Staples, 383, 394, 435, 436
Starbucks Corporation, 12, 66–67, 84, 147, 298, 311, 386, 648
  case, 107–109
Starkist, 281
Starter athletic shoes, 393
Star Trek, 193, 194
State Farm Insurance, 622
State Hermitage Museum, Russia, 19
Steelcase Leap office chair, 258
Stewardship Council, 478
Stokely-Van Camp Inc., 269
Strauss Group, 184
ST&T, 508
StubHub.com!, 318
  pricing strategy, 319–320
Subway, 433, 434
Sunbird, 285
Sunday Night Football, 496
Sunkist, 283, 385
Superbowlads.com, 490
Supervalu, 639
Surf City Squeeze, 620
Surfrider Foundation, 304
Sur la Table, 623, 624
Susan G. Komen for the Cure organization, 304
Sustainable Forest Initiative, 478
Swatch watches, 171, 172, 252, 353
Sylvania, 144

T

Tab, 275
Taco Bell, 449
Tag Heuer, 73
Tampa Bay Rays, 315
Target Center Arena, 267
Target Corporation, 5, 18, 19, 22, 56, 147, 154, 242, 281, 325, 345, 354, 397, 402, 426, 432, 433, 435, 436, 627
  case, 644–645
Taurus, 287
TaylorMade, 369, 626, 627
TBS, 645
Teen People, 498
Telemundo, 497
Tesco, 154, 431
Tesla Roadster Sport, 321, 326
Texaco, 382, 487
Texas Instruments, 171, 528
TextBuyIt, 440
Textile Web, 154
Thirsty Cat, 253
Thirsty Dog, 253, 254
This Old House, 497
3M Corporation, 12, 17, 27, 99–100, 102, 145, 174, 204–205, 256, 259, 263, 272, 413
  case, 21–23
  innovation and marketing, 3–4
  Sports and Leisure Products Project, case, 368–369
  strategy/marketing program, 14–15
3M Greptile Grip golf glove, 368–369
3 Musketeers, 508
Ticketmaster.com, 319, 556
TicketsNow, 319
Tickle Me Elmo, 197
Tide, 223, 286, 398, 518, 585, 599
Tide StainRelease, 585
Tidy Bowl, 285
Tiffany & Company, 175, 389, 390, 443, 447
Tiger Woods Golf, 481
Time, 5, 329, 330, 472, 498, 645
Time, Inc., 128, 132
Time Warner, 80, 471
Timex, 171
Tire Rack, 426
Titleist, 249, 369, 626
TiVo, 31, 202, 513
T.J. Maxx, 444
T-Mobile, 80, 113, 114, 599
TNT, 645
Tommy Hilfiger, 172
Tom Tom, 65
Tony's Pizza
  case, 217–219
  marketing research data, 211–214
Top Driver, Inc., 623
Top Gun, 510
Toro Company, 357, 360
  multiproduct branding, 286
Toro Snow Pup, 120–121
Toshiba America Medical Systems, 541
Tostitos, 287, 356, 523
Total Bedroom stores, 628
Total Gym, 497
Total toothpaste, 334, 590
Touchstone Pictures, 287
Tower.com, 440
TownsPlace Suites, 287
Toyota Camry, 362
Toyota Motor Corporation, 16, 383, 397, 398, 573, 580, 583
Toyota Prius, 41, 74
Toy Story, 510
Trader Joe's, case, 641–642
Transformers: Revenge of the Fallen, 193
Travel Industry Association of America, 633
Travelocity.com, 335, 440, 492, 551, 556
Triarc Companies, 284
Trip Adviser, 633
Tropicana, 648
True Romance, 134
TRUSTe, 561
TSCentral, 527
Tumblr, 65
Tupperware Corporation, 392, 562
Twitter, 65, 208, 241, 242, 299, 307, 457, 517, 547, 559

Tylenol Cold & Flu, 122
Tylenol P. M., 122
Tyler Automotive, Inc., 543

U

Ugg Australia, 74
Ultra Downy, 248
Uncle Ben's Calcium Plus rice, 281
Under Armour, 214–215
  case, 480–482
UNICEF, 304
Unilever, 24, 40, 121, 170, 179–180, 209, 280, 287, 471
Union Pacific Railroad, 536
Unisys, 414
United Airlines, 419, 420–421
United Nations Children's Fund, 303
United Parcel Service, 94, 185, 305, 423, 525
United Parcel Service Supply Chain Solutions, 417
United States Golf Association, 627
U.S. Cellular, 541
U.S. Green Building Council, 49
United States Lawn Mower Racing Association, 630
U.S. News and World Report, 329
U.S. Open tennis tournament, 21
United States Postal Service, 278, 304–305, 477, 478
United States Rice Millers' Association, 166
United Technologies Corporation, 97, 155
United Way, 303
Universal Music Group, 397
Univision, 497
UPM-Kymmene Inc., 140
Urban Cofee Opportunities, 108
USA Today, 495, 498, 507

V

Vanguard Group, 603
Van Heusen Factory Store, 445
Vanity Fair, 130, 645
Verizon Communications, 80, 471, 499
Verso Paper, 140
Viacom, 80
Vicks, 176
Victoria's Secret, 435, 562
Vidal Sassoon shampoo, 354
Viking, 241
Village.com, 559
Virgin Galactic, 299
Virgin Group, 512
Virtual City, 498
Visa USA, 173, 393, 453, 486
VisualCV, 607
Vizio, Inc., 351
  pricing objectives, 345–346
Volkswagen, 127, 132, 179, 408, 493
  online retailing, 409
Volkswagen Beetle, 88
Volkswagen Golf, 294
Volvo, 257, 517
Volvo of North America, 162
Volvo XC90, 486

W

W. W. Grainger, 153
Walgreen's, 154, 402
Wall Street Journal, 201, 498, 610–611
Wal-Mart, 12, 22, 56, 74, 88, 102, 135, 147, 169, 188, 209, 242, 249, 269, 287, 288, 291, 325, 345, 354, 368, 391, 392, 393, 398, 399, 402, 409, 420, 429, 431, 433, 435, 436, 439, 443, 444, 445, 446, 452, 506, 525, 534, 573, 641, 644
  supply chain, 410–411
Wal-Mart Smart Network, 509
Wal-Mart Supercenters, 410
Walt Disney Company, 80, 283, 284, 287, 308, 311, 457, 471
Wanamaker's Department Store, 503
Wanchai Ferry, 584
Warm Delights, 572, 592, 595, 597
Warm Delights Minis, 572, 592–594
Washburn Guitars, case, 341–343
Washington Post, 498
Waterford, 163
WebEx, 603
Webvan, 335
Weight Watchers, 259, 426
Welch's grape juice, 210
Wells Fargo, 430, 431
Wendy's, 226, 238
  customer questionnaire, 206–208
  market-product grid, 233–234
  market segmentation, 229–231
  product categories, 231–233
  segmentation strategy, 235–236
West Edmonton Mall, 453
Western Auto, 390
Western Union, 81, 583
Westin Hotels, 309, 633
Weyerhaeuser, 143
Wheaties, 195, 209
Whirlpool Corporation, 144, 169, 171, 179, 186, 257, 288, 395, 412, 435
WhirlpoolWebWorld, 412
Whole Foods Markets, 620
Whopper, 83
Wild Bean Café BP Connect, 48
Wilkinson Sword, 320
Willard Bishop, 642
Williams-Sonoma, 438, 647
Wilson Sporting Goods, 626
Wilson tennis racket, 355
Wired, 7, 21
Wisk, 217
Women's Leadership Forum, 136
WorldBook, 441
Wrigley's gum, 185

Xbox, 31
Xerox Corporation, 10, 11, 83, 86, 102, 153, 215, 230, 231, 272, 423, 520–521, 522, 523, 525, 529
  case, 544–545
  Palo Alto Research Center, 544
  sales management, 519

Yahoo!, 128, 202, 499, 501, 517, 550
Yahoo! Kids/Kids Only, 128
Yamaha, 510
Yamaha guitars, 342
Yellow Pages Association, 499
YoNaturals, 437
Yoplait, 184, 304
Youniversity Ventures, 6
YouTube, 4, 43, 49, 84, 297, 307, 492, 497, 517
  founding of, 5
Yves St. Laurent, 119, 394

Z

Zappos.com, 220, 311, 558
  market segmentation, 221–222, 223
Zetia, 468
Zip-Lock, 510
Zippo, 292
Zip the Cat Beanie Baby, 326
Zoomerang, 204–205

SUBJECT INDEX

A

Above-, at-, or below-market pricing, 354
marketing dashboard, 355
Accessibility of transportation, 418
Accessory equipment, 248
Account executive, 600
Account management policies, 536
key account management, 534
Achievement-motivated groups, 125
Achievers, 125
Action item list, 587
Adaptive selling, 529
Add-on charges, 320
Administered vertical marketing systems, 391
Administrative expenses, 373
Adoption, 470
Advertising, 460–461, 486
advantages for firms, 461
by Under Armour, 481
Bagel Bakes, 638
by BP, 49
to business buyers, 464
and buyer turnover, 502
careers in, 599–601, 600
to change buying habits, 117
and change in demand, 331
comparative, 486
competitive, 486
and competitive market, 327–328
cooperative, 511
corrective, 85
and cultural symbolism, 175–176
deceptive, 85
direct-to-customer, 469
endorsements, 122
failure of sex appeals, 204
flighting schedule, 502
forgetting rate, 502
to global teenager, 172
impersonal component, 460–461
institutional, 487–488
in introduction stage, 271–272, 486
language barrier, 132
legislation on, 85
as mass selling, 460, 461
by movie industry, 485
paid aspect, 460, 461
pioneering, 486
for products, 485–487
in promotional mix, 473
pulse schedule, 502
and purchase frequency, 502
reinforcement, 487
reminder, 486
repetition in, 122
in sales promotion, 460–461
of services, 310
strengths, 461
subliminal messages, 120
by Target Corporation, 644–645
teaser campaign, 127
in 3-D, 485
weaknesses, 461
Advertising Age, 474, 492, 499–500, 607
Advertising agencies
agency costs, 504
complexity of work, 493
comprehensive campaigns, 513
cost-plus pricing, 350
Crispin, Porter & Bogusky, 492–493
full-service, 502–503
imc^{2}, 567
in-house, 503
Initiative campaign, 474
jobs in, 601
limited-service, 503
marketing research activities, 603
message content, 490–492
message creation, 492–493
Advertising and promotion-related legislation, 85
Advertising budget, 489–490
Advertising department, 458
Advertising Effectiveness Council, 489
Advertising expenditures
Coca-Cola Company and PepsiCo, 490
by media types, 494
with multiple branding, 287
with multiproduct branding, 286
outdoor advertising, 500–501
Super Bowl commercials, 489–490
by Target Corporation, 644–645
television advertising, 496
top ten companies, 471
on TV commercials, 202
Advertising media, 460–461
alternatives, 494
advantages and disadvantages, 496
Internet, 499–500
magazines, 497–498
newspapers, 498
outdoor media, 500–501
place-based media, 501–502
radio, 497
selection criteria, 502
television, 495–497
transit advertising, 500
Yellow Pages, 499
cost per thousand, 495
frequency, 494
gross rating points, 495
new forms, 465
ratings, 494
reach, 494
scheduling ads, 502
selection of, 493–495
basic terms, 494–495
vehicle within a medium, 494
Advertising message, 461
celebrity spokespersons, 492–493
components, 490
content, 490–492
costs in global campaigns, 493
creation of, 492–493
fear appeals, 491
humorous appeals, 491–492
sex appeals, 491
Advertising program
assessing
making changes, 505
posttesting, 504–505
consumer influences on, 488
development of
case, 515–517
creating message, 492–493
designing ads, 490–493
identifying target audience, 488
media alternatives, 495–502
media selection, 493–495
scheduling, 500
setting budget, 489–490
specifying objectives, 489
executing
carrying out program, 503–504
pretesting, 503
Advertising Research Foundation, 489
Advocacy advertisements, 487
Ad-zapping, 497
African Americans
buying patterns, 132
consumer potential, 72–73
and new car sales, 357
in U.S. population, 72
Age groups of world population, 68–69
Agents
for business goods, 384
functions, 380
Agricultural genome research, 78
Aided recall, 504
Aircraft manufacturers, 153
Air freight carriers, 419
Airline industry
customer service standards, 415
load factor, 312, 313
no-frills airlines, 327
off-peak pricing, 309
yield management pricing, 349
Allowances, 370
definition, 361
and everyday low prices, 363
versus everyday low pricing, 362
promotional, 362
trade-in, 362
in trade promotions, 510–511
All-you-can-afford budgeting, 472
Alternative evaluation
consumer purchases, 113–114
in organizational buying, 152
American Association of Advertising Agencies, 493
American Community Survey, 200
American Demographics, 632
American Enterprise Institute, 154
American Marketing Association, 198, 607
definition of marketing, 6
statement of ethics, 98
Anchor stores, 445
Ancillary services, 467
Annual marketing plan, 578
Antecedent states, 117
Antitrust law, 82, 84
deceptive pricing, 365
Germany, 188
and marketing channels, 398–400
per se illegal concept, 363, 364
predatory pricing, 365–366
price discrimination, 364–365
price fixing, 363–364
rule of reason, 364, 365
Sherman Act, 363, 365
Anytime Anywhere Media Measurement Initiative, 201
Approach stage, 528
Art director, 600
Art museums, 18–19
Asia
countertrade in, 162
free trade agreements, 169
Medtronic in, 40–41
U.S. export market, 163
Asian Americans
buying patterns, 132–133
consumer potential, 72–73
in U.S. population, 72
urban concentrations, 73
Aspiration group, 128
Assimilated Asian Americans, 132
Association of National Advertisers, 503
Assumptive close, 531

At-market pricing, 354
Attitude, 123
  change in, 124
  changing for men and women, 73–74
Attitude tests, 505
Auctions
  reverse, 155
  traditional, 155
Authenticity (Gilmore & Pine), 297
Automatic vending, 437–438
Automation, 339–340
  of salesforce, 540–542
Automobile industry
  BMW, 294–295
  excess inventory, 421
  Ford-Firestone problem, 621–623
  logistics aspects, 408
  marketing channels, 383
  out-of-control costs, 335
  pricing in, 321
  supply chain, 408, 409
  target markets, 224
  women new car buyers, 111
Average revenue, 331
Awareness, 470

B

Baby boomers, 69
Baby boomlet, 70
Baby bust, 69–70
Back order, 420
Back translation, 176
Backward integration, 390
Bad timing, 254
Bait-and-switch pricing, 365
Balance of trade, 163
Banner ads, 499–500
Banner blindness, 500
Bargains conditional on other purchases, 365
Barriers to entry, 81
Barter, 320
  countertrade, 162
Baseball park experience, 315–317
Basing-point pricing, 365
Basing-point pricing, 363
BBB Online, 85
Behavioral analysis
  for evaluation of salesforce, 539–540
  salesforce selection, 534
Behavioral learning process, 122
Behavioral segmentation
  consumer markets
    by product features, 227–228
    by usage rate, 228–230
    variables for, 230
  organizational markets, 231
  by usage rate, 231
Beliefs, 123
Believers, 125
Below-market pricing, 354, 356
Benchmarking, by HOM Furniture, 628
Benchmark items, 444
Better Business Bureau, 85–86
Beverage industry, 648
Bidder's list, 152
Bidding
  competitive, 144
  in reverse auctions, 155
  in traditional auctions, 155
Billboards, 500–501
  digital, 501
Biotechnology, 78
Black Friday sales, 429
Blended family, 70
Blog, 463, **559**
Borderless economic world, 166–173
Bots, 440, **558**
Bottom of the pyramid, 177
Brain scans, 204
Brainstorming, 258, 260
Brand(s)
  attitude change toward, 124
  by BMW, 294–295
  consideration set, 113–114
  criteria for evaluating, 113–114
  demand for, 326
  differentiating, 273
  establishing meaning of, 283
  fighting brands, 287
  global, 171
  hierarchy of effects, 470–471
  licensing of, 284
  limited vs. full warranty, 292
  loss in value, 284
  perceptual maps, 238–240
  positioning statement, 238
  successful, 204
  switching, 103
Brand awareness, 283
Brand development index, 278, 279
Brand equity, 283
  advantages, 283
  and brand extension, 286
  and brand licensing, 284
  creating, 283–284
  and multiproduct branding, 286
  and packaging, 290
  valuing, 284
Brand equity pyramid, 283
Brand extensions, 286
Brand identity
  BP, 48
  consumer response to, 283–284
Brand image, 290
Branding, 282
  benefits to consumers, 282–283
  legal protection, 282
  of services, 309
Branding strategies
  brand extensions, 286
  co-branding, 287
  corporate branding, 286
  family branding, 286
  at Gatorade, 269–270
  mixed branding, 288
  multibranding, 287
  multiproduct branding, 286–287
  private branding, 287
  product line extensions, 286
  in service sector, 308–309
  subbranding, 286
Brand licensing, 284
Brand logos, 204
Brand loyalists, 555
Brand loyalty, 122, 247
Brand management, Gatorade, 269–279
Brand manager, 278, 590
Brand name, 282
  and brand equity, 283–284
  economic value, 284
  and Internet domain names, 285
  language problems, 176
  in new product development, 22
  selection criteria
    company/product image, 285
    memorable and distinctive, 285
    no legal restrictions, 285
    simple and emotional, 285
    suggesting product benefits, 285
  in service sector, 309
Brand personality, 283
Breadth of product line, 425, 436, 442
Break-even analysis, 336, 336–340
  applications, 338–340
  break-even chart, 338
  calculating break-even point, 338–338
  case, 341–343
Break-even chart, 338
  salesforce analysis, 533
Break-even point, 336
  calculating, 336–338
Breakfast food, 636–638
Bribery, 174
Bribes, 96–97
Bricks and clicks retailing, 439
Brokers, 389
  functions, 380
Build-to-order, 225
Bundle pricing, 349
Bureau of Labor Statistics, 77, 520, 602
Burst schedule, 502
Business, 30
  ethical standards, 93–97
Business analysis, 260
  capacity management, 260
  off-peak pricing, 260
  prototype, 260
Business culture
  definition, 94
  ethics of competition, 95–97
  ethics of exchange, 95
Business firm, 26
Business-format franchises, 433–434
Business goods and services
  cost-plus pricing, 350
  marketing channels
    direct, 384
    electronic, 384–385
    indirect, 384
    industrial distributors, 384
Business marketing, 140
Business model
  Netflix, 31
  rethinking, 30–31
Business plan, 50–51
Business portfolio analysis, 36
  Eastman Kodak, 36–38
  growth share matrix, 36–37
  primary strengths, 38
  purpose, 36
  weaknesses, 38
Business practices, basic
  fast, flat, and flexible organization, 573
  flawless operational execution, 573
  performance-oriented culture, 573
  strategy, 573
Business products, 246
  components, 247–248
  derived demand for, 247
  life cycle of, 275
  support products
    accessory equipment, 248
    industrial services, 248
    installations, 248
    supplies, 248
Business-to-business marketing
  below-market pricing, 354
  cost-plus pricing, 350
  global marketing strategy, 171
  networked global marketplace, 171–173
Business-to-business products, 246
BusinessWeek, 245
Buy classes, 148–149
Buyer
  career as, 600
  responsibilities, 601
Buyers, 19
  in buying centers, 148
  Japanese, 148
  no economical access to, 254
  potential number of, 144
  power of, 81

satisfying requirements of
with convenience, 394–395
with information, 394
with pre- or postsale services, 395
with variety, 395
surveys of intentions of, 215
Buyer-seller relationships
in organizational buying, 146–147
reciprocity, 146
supply partnerships, 146–147
Buyer turnover, 502
Buying center, 147
buy classes
modified rebuy, 149
new buy, 148–149
straight rebuy, 148–149
buying committees, 147
buying situations, 148–149
composition of, 148
importance of, 147–148
marketing strategy, 149
questions about, 147–148
roles in
buyers, 148
deciders, 148
gatekeepers, 148
influencers, 148
users, 148
sales strategy, 149
Buying committees, 147
Buying decisions
postpurchase stage, 468
prepurchase stage, 467
purchase stage, 467–468
Buying habits, 117
Buying patterns
African Americans, 132
Asian Americans, 132–133
baby boomers, 69
and family life cycle, 128–129
Generation X, 69–70
Generation Y, 70
Hispanics, 131–132
Buying situations, 148–149
Lands' End, 158
Buy•ology (Lindstrom), 203, 204
Buzz, 127, 559

C

CAFTA-DR trade agreement, 169
Campbell Interest and Skill Survey, 605
Canada
imports from U.S., 163
and NAICS, 141–142
and North American Free Trade Agreement, 169
official languages, 176
Canned sales presentation, 529
Cannibalization, 225
minimizing, 238
CAN-SPAM Act, 85, 559
Capability of transportation, 418
Capacity management, 260, **312**
in airline industry, 312, 313
and price structure, 312
Capital costs, 421
Capital equipment, 141
Career service office, 605–606
Careers in marketing, 4–6
advertising, 599–601
diversity of, 598
getting a job, 598
identifying opportunities, 605–608
information sources, 613–615
international careers, 603–604
job search process
activities involved, 598
handling rejection, 613
job interviews, 610–613
self-assessment, 604–605
marketing research, 603
nonprofit, 598
physical distribution, 599
product management, 599
promotion, 599–601
résumés, 608–610
retailing, 601–602
sales, 602–603
starting salaries, 599
Car rental activities, 307–308
Carrying costs, 301
Case allowance, 511
Cash and carry wholesalers, 387
Cash cows
definition, 36
at Eastman Kodak, 37, 38
Cash discounts, 361
Catalog retailing, 438–439
Lands' End, 158
multichannel marketing, 385–386
transactional Web sites, 562
Category development index, 278, 279
Category killers, 436
Category management, 446
consumer marketing at retail, 446–447
Category manager, 590
Caucasians, 72
Causal research, 196
Cause marketing, 102
at American Express, 103
Caveat emptor, 95
Cease and desist orders, 85
Celebrity spokespersons, 127, 439, 492–493
potential shortcomings, 493
Cell phones, 465
Census 2000, 199–200, 202
Census 2000, 72
Central business district, 445
CEOs
careers in marketing, 599
experience in personal selling, 520–521
Channel captain, 398
Channel conflict, 397
from disintermediation, 397
horizontal, 397–398
in multichannel marketing, 563
resolving, 398
vertical, 397
Channel cost, 395
Channel influence, 398
Channel of communication, 458
Channel partnership, 391
Channels of distribution; *see* Intermediaries; Marketing channels
Channel strategies
pull strategy, 469
push strategy, 468–469
Charges, 309
Charitable contributions, 102
Charities, 26
Chief executive officers, 28
Chief marketing officer, 28, 589
Child Protection Act, 83
Children
preteen consumers, 130
socialization process, 128
teenage consumers, 130
Children's Online Privacy Protection Act, 85, 95
China
Avon Inc. in, 393
imports from U.S., 163
infrastructure, 177–178
Medtronic in, 41, 630–632
number of Internet users, 441
population, 68
tobacco production, 93
Choice
and competition, 18
in online shopping, 558
Choice assistance, 558
Choiceboard, 550
Cigarette tax, 334
Cigarette warning label, 204
Clayton Act, 82, 399
and pricing decisions, 364–365
Click-and-mortar consumers, 555
Click fraud, 501
Clickstream, 356
Closed-end questions, 206–207
Closing stage, 531
Cloud computing, 78
Co-branding, 287
Code of ethics, 97
Cognitive dissonance, 115
Cognitive learning, 122
Cohabitation, 70
Cola wars, 96
Cold calling, 527
Cold canvassing, 527
Collaborative filtering, 550
Collaborative relationships, 170
College students
credit card debt, 326
marketing to, 3–4, 14–15
tuition levels, 75
venture financing for, 6
Combination compensation plan, 538–539
Combined statistical areas, 71
Commerce, in Web site design, 553
Commercialization, 262
complexities, 263
failure fee, 263
fast prototyping, 263
regional rollout, 263
risk on grocery products, 263
slotting fee, 263
time to market, 263
Commissions, 320
Communication, 458
blogs, 463, 559
bots, 558
buzz, 559
channel of, 458
consumers, 7
in customer service, 414
in direct marketing, 463
encoding and decoding, 459–460
errors in, 459
feedback, 460
field of experience, 459–460
on first impression, 528
influence effect, 451
message, 458
new forms of, 457–458
noise, 460
in online shopping, 558–559
in packaging and labeling, 289
public relations, 512
receivers, 458
response, 460
in retailing, 446
salesforce, 541–542
social media, 463
source, 458
spam, 478, 559
tools for, 458
viral marketing, 559
in Web site design, 553
Communication infrastructure, 178
Communication technology omniverse, 555
Community, in Web site design, 553
Community shopping centers, 445–446

Companies, 26; *see also* Firms
  factor in channel choice, 392–393
  leading in promotion expenditures, 471
  overcoming consumer resistance, 277
  protection of competitive position, 82
  strategy, structure, and rivalry, 164–165
  use of social class, 131
  value of brand equity, 284
  value of satisfied customers, 115
Company analysis, Paradise Kitchens, 56
Company effects on pricing, 356–367
Company image, 285
Company salespeople, 533–534
Comparable value comparisons, 365
Comparative advertising, 486
Comparison with suggested prices, 365
Compensation plans
  combination plans, 538–539
  starting salaries in marketing, 599
  straight commission, 538–539
  straight salary, 538–539
Competencies, assessment of, 34–35
Competition, 80
  and choice, 18
  components
    barriers to entry, 81
    existing competitors, 81
    new entrants, 81
    power of buyers and suppliers, 81
    small businesses, 81
    substitutes, 81
  in distribution of services, 309–310
  fighting brands, 287
  forms of
    monopolistic competition, 80
    oligopoly, 80
    pure competition, 80
    pure monopoly, 80–81
  golf equipment industry, 625
  intertype, 436
  for Jamba Juice, 620
  for Ken Davis Products, 639
  laws protecting, 82
  price of, 328
  versus protectionism, 166–167
  and restructuring, 12
  salesforce knowledge of, 532
Competition-oriented pricing
  above-, at-, or below-market pricing, 354
  customary pricing, 353–354
  loss-leader pricing, 354
Competitive advantage, 35
  of brand equity, 283
  finding what works, 572–573
  from generic business strategies, 578–580
  Paradise Kitchens, 54
  by resource allocation, 574–576
Competitive advantage of nations, 164–165
  company strategy, structure, and rivalry, 164–165
  demand conditions, 164
  and economic espionage, 165
  factor conditions, 164
  related and supporting industries, 164
Competitive advertising
  for institutions, 487
  for products, 486
Competitive bids, 144
Competitive effects on pricing, 357–358
Competitive environment, for Jamba Juice, 620
Competitive forces
  components of competition, 81
  forms of competition, 80–81
  small businesses, 81
Competitive intelligence research, 600
Competitive markets, 327–328
Competitive parity budgeting, 490
Competitive parity budgeting, 471–472
Competitive position
  legal protection, 82
  of sales organization, 537
  of target market, 234
Competitive products, ideas from, 258
Competitors
  asking customers about, 532, 533
  distinctions among, 35
  in growth stage, 272
  for Paradise Kitchens, 56–57
  and promotion budgeting, 471–472
  repositioning as reaction to, 280
Complexity of products, 466
Components, 247–248
Concepts, 198
Concept stores, 454
Concept tests, 259
Conference Board, 75
Conference selling, 525
Connection, in Web site design, 552
Consensus-building, 583
Consideration set, 113–114
Constraints, 197
Consultative selling, 529–530
Consumer behavior, 112
  baby boomers, 69
  case, 135–137
  changes for men and women, 73–74
  and channel choice, 392
  Generation X, 69–70
  Generation Y, 70
  Internet users, 202
  mission shoppers, 451
  in online shopping
    lifestyle segmentation, 555
    profile of consumers, 554–555
    purchase decision, 556–557
    reasons for shopping, 557–560
    terms for consumers, 553
    time and place, 561
  psychological influences
    attitudes, 123–124
    beliefs, 123–124
    brand loyalty, 122–123
    learning, 122–123
    lifestyle, 124–125
    motivation, 118–119
    perceived risk, 121–122
    perception, 120–121
    personality, 119–120
    self-concept, 119–120
    values, 123–124
  purchase decision process
    achievement-motivated groups, 125
    alternative evaluation, 113–114
    case, 623–624, 624–625
    characteristics, 116
    cognitive dissonance, 115
    consideration set, 113–114
    family decision making, 129–130
    high- and low-resource groups, 125
    HOM Furniture, 628
    ideals-motivated groups, 125
    information search, 112–113
    involvement and problems solving, 115–117
    postpurchase behavior, 114–115
    problem recognition, 112
    purchase, 114
    self-expression-motivated groups, 125
    situational influences, 117
  in purchase of services
    customer contact audit, 306–308
    gap analysis, 306
    purchase process, 305–306
    quality assessment, 306
    relationship marketing, 308
  sociocultural influences
    culture, 131–133
    family, 128–130
    opinion leaders, 126–127
    personal experience, 126–129
    reference groups, 128
    social class, 130–131
    subcultures, 131–133
    word of mouth, 127–128
  women new car buyers, 111
Consumer Bill of Rights, 95, 99
Consumer-brand connection, 284
Consumer Confidence Index, 75
Consumer demand vs. industrial demand, 143
Consumer ethics, 104–105
Consumer ethnocentrism, 176–177
Consumer expectations, 114, 306, 307
Consumer Expenditure Survey, 77
Consumer goods and services
  basis of comparison, 250–251
  channel intermediaries, 382, 386–389
  classifying, 246–247
  convenience products, 247, 248
  demand estimation, 330
  marketing channels
    direct, 382–383
    electronic, 384–385
    indirect, 383
  shopping products, 247, 248
  specialty products, 247, 248
  unsought products, 247, 248
Consumer Goods Pricing Act, 364
Consumer income, 75–78
  discretionary income, 77–78
  disposable income, 76
  in global markets, 178–180
  gross income, 76
  stimulus checks of 2008, 77–78
Consumer involvement; *see* Involvement
Consumerism, 83
Consumer lifestyle, 124–125
Consumer marketing at retail, 446–447
Consumer market segmentation
  criteria for, 226
  means of, 226–230
    behavioral by product features, 227–228
    behavioral by usage rate, 228–230
    demographic, 227
    geographic, 227
    psychographic, 227
  variables to use, 230
Consumer needs
  ability to satisfy, 7
  discovering, 8
  and marketing department, 10
  new products for, 8–10
  not satisfying, 253–254
  satisfying, 11
  and type of sales organization, 534
  unsatisfied, 7
  versus wants, 10
Consumer-oriented sales promotions, 505–506, 505–510
  advantages and disadvantages, 506
  contests, 507
  coupons, 506–507
  deals, 507
  loyalty programs, 509
  point-of-purchase displays, 509
  premiums, 507
  product placements, 509–510
  rebates, 509
  reverse product placement, 510
  samples, 508
  sweepstakes, 508

Consumer products, 246
  kinds of, 247, 248
  life cycle of, 275
Consumer Product Safety Act, 83
Consumer Product Safety Commission, 83, 95
Consumer protection, 10
Consumer protection laws, 82–83
Consumer Reports, 112, 113, 621, 623, 630
Consumers; *see also* Buyers; Customers; Global consumers; Online consumers
  advantages of online retailing, 439
  baby boomers, 69
  banner blindness, 500
  baseball park experience, 315–317
  benefits from branding, 282–283
  benefits of retail chains, 433
  brain scanning, 203, 204
  brand loyalty, 122
  and brand personality, 283
  buying decision stages
    in-store decision, 509
    postpurchase, 468
    prepurchase, 467
    purchase, 467–468
  categories of product adopters, 277
  convenience of scrambled merchandising, 436
  costs of information search, 560
  coupon redemption, 506
  creating brand equity for, 283–284
  critical of cold canvassing, 527
  customized prices, 356
  in developing countries, 180
  factor in channel choice, 392
  Generation X, 69–70
  Generation Y, 70
  hierarchy of effects on, 470, 489
  influences on advertising, 488
  interaction with service provider, 300–301
  kinds of motivation, 124–125
  learning by, 122–123
  listening to, 639
  media preferences, 125
  new ways of engaging, 457–458
  not listening to, 254
  organizational, 19
  price-insensitivity, 347
  privacy rights, 95
  and product life cycle
    categories of product adopters, 276–277
    high-learning products, 275
    low-learning products, 275–276
  product success from perspective of, 251–252
  reference groups, 128
  reference value, 323
  resistance to new products, 277
  shopping experience, 641
  status-conscious, 347
  ultimate, 19
  unethical behavior by, 104–105
  use of direct marketing, 476–477
  value consciousness, 74
  videotaping, 203
Consumer socialization, 128
Consumer spending, 75
  by global teenagers, 172
  for pet products, 632
Consumers Union, 621
Consumer trends, 280–281
Consumer wants, 10
Consumption
  recent decline in, 66–67
  value in, 114–115
Consumption orientation, 74
Contact lenses, 616–617
Content, in Web site design, 552
Contests, 506, 507
Context, in Web site design, 551–552
Continuous innovation, 252
Continuous schedule, 502
Contract assembly, 183–18o4
Contract manufacturing, 183–18o4
Contractual retail systems, 433–434
Contractual vertical marketing systems, 390–391
Control, in online chopping, 560
Controllable factors, 11
Controlling the Assault of Non-Solicited Pornography and Marketing Act, 85, 559
Convenience
  as buyer requirement, 394–395
  in customer service, 415
  of online shopping, 558
Convenience products, 247, 248
Cookie cutter stores, 453
Cookies, 560
Cooperative advertising, 646
Cooperative advertising, 511
Copyright infringement, 93, 94
Copyright laws, 82
Copywriter, 600
Core competencies
  assessment of, 34–35
  Paradise Kitchens, 54
Core product, 302
Core values, 29
  at BP, 48
  at Zappos.com, 221–222
Corporate branding, 286
Corporate culture; *see* Organizational culture
Corporate level, 28
Corporate retail chains, 432–433
Corporate vertical marketing systems, 390
Corporations, 26
Corrective advertising, 85
Corruption Perception Index, 97
Cost(s)
  balanced with revenues, 358
  of distribution, 406
  of economic espionage, 165
  importance of controlling, 335
  incremental, 574
  of intellectual property theft, 94
  of magazine advertising, 498
  in online shopping, 560
  of packaging and labeling, 288–289
  of production and marketing, 327
  of protectionism, 166–167
  of reaching market segments, 234
  of Super Bowl commercials, 489–490
  of television commercials, 496
  of transportation, 418
  types of, 335–336
  of unethical consumer behavior, 104
Cost-based pricing, 351
Cost-effective flow of raw materials, 406
Cost-effectiveness of segmentation, 226
Cost elements of operating statements, 370–373
Cost focus strategy, 579–580
Cost leadership strategy, 579
Cost of goods sold
  administrative expenses, 373
  definition, 370–371
  direct labor, 372
  general expenses, 373
  gross margin, 372
  inventory, 371
  and markup, 374–375
  purchase discounts, 372
  selling expenses, 373
  stockturn rate, 376–377
Cost-oriented pricing
  cost-plus pricing, 350
  experience-curve pricing, 350–351
  standard markup pricing, 349–350
Cost per thousand, 495
Cost-plus fixed-fee pricing, 350
Cost-plus percentage-of-cost pricing, 350
Cost-plus pricing, 350
Cost reductions in packaging, 291–292
Costs of production, Bagel Bakes, 638
Cost trade-off, 339
Cost-volume-profit relationships
  break-even analysis, 336–340
  case, 635–636
  importance of cost control, 335
  marginal analysis, 335–336
  profit maximization, 335–336
Counterfeit products, 282
Countertrade, 162
Country of origin labels, 290–291
Coupons, 506–507
Co-workers
  ethical behavior, 97–98
  idea generation from, 257
Credence properties of services, 305
Credit Card Bill of Rights, 326
Cross-channel shopper, 562
Cross-cultural analysis, 173
  for services, 313–314
Cross-docking, 410
Cross-functional business specialists, 522
Cross-functional teams, 28
  for parallel development, 263
Cross-functional team selling, 525
Cruise lines, 635–636
Cues, 122
Cultural diversity
  back translation, 176
  and cross-cultural analysis, 173
  cultural ethnocentrism, 176–177
  cultural symbols, 175 176
  customs, 174–175
  language, 176
  in personal selling, 528
  values, 173–174
Cultural ethnocentrism, 176–177
Cultural symbols, 175
Cultural values, 74, 173–174
Culture, 73
  Americanization of, 172
  changing attitudes of men and women, 73–74
  changing values, 74
  consumption orientation, 74
  influence on consumers, 131–133
  as socializing force, 93–94
Cumulative quantity discounts, 360
Currency exchange rate, 180
  effect of euro, 168
Current Industrial Reports, 200
Customary pricing, 353–354
Customer analysis, Paradise Kitchens, 56–57
Customer centricity, 136
Customer contact audit, 306–307
Customer dissatisfaction, 115
Customer effects on pricing, 357
Customer experience, 17, 553
Customer experience management, 259, 311
Customer feedback, 14
Customerization, 558
Customer loyalty, 12
Customer needs, 409
Customer relationship era, 16–17
Customer relationship management, 16, 540–542, 573, 602–603
  and direct marketing, 475–476
  from personal selling, 544–545
Customer relationships, in interactive marketing, 549–551
Customer requirements, 406

Customers; *see also* Buyers; Consumers
asked about competitors, 532, 533
car rental activities, 307–308
choiceboards for, 550
dissatisfied, 306, 307
finding new, 279
idea generation by, 257
long-term relationships with, 513
need to understand, 40–41
opt-in/opt-out, 551
packaging and labeling updates for, 291
prospective, 8
repeat purchasers, 272–273
of Starbucks, 108
and strategic direction, 36
syndicated panel data, 200
understanding of, 409
women new car buyers, 111
Customer sales organization, 534, 535
Customer sales support personnel, 524–525
Customer satisfaction
as goal, 32
and salesforce evaluation, 539
and value perception, 114–115
value to companies, 115
Customer service, 413
importance in Europe, 413
Lands' End, 158
and logistics, 406, 413–415
communication, 414
convenience, 415
dependability, 414
lead time, 414
logistics costs, 413–414
at Zappos.com, 221, 223
Customer service delivery and expectations, 260
Customer service experience, 311
Customer service manager, 600
Customer service standards
differing by firms, 415
marketing dashboard for, 416
Customer value, 3–4, **12**
BzzAgent Inc., 127
Cereal Partners Worldwide, 387
in cross-functional team selling, 525
and customer satisfaction, 115
direct mail/catalog retailing, 438
fax machines, 274
global teenager, 172
Google, Inc., 261
Harley-Davidson, 146
impact of technology, 79
integrated supply chain, 410
from market orientation, 16
in marketspace, 548–549
and organizational synergy, 225
from packaging and labeling, 288–291
in personal selling, 521–522
Pez Candy, Inc., 289
from suppliers, 530
and switching brands, 103
in synergy analysis, 580, 581
Customization
by customers, 550
in online shopping, 558
services that facilitate, 297
at Seven Cycles, Inc., 547
in Web site design, 552
of Web sites, 567–568
Customized interaction, 460, 461
Customs, 174
gift-giving vs. bribery, 174
nonverbal behavior, 174–175
Cyber Monday sales, 429
Cycle time reduction, 640

D

Data, 199
from online databases, 201
primary
advantages and disadvantages, 211
data mining, 210–211
experiments, 209–210
idea evaluation, 205–208
panels, 209–210
questionnaire, 203–208
social networks, 208–209
using information technology, 210
secondary
advantages and disadvantages, 200
external, 199–200
internal, 199
syndicated panel data, 200
Data analysis, 211–212
Databases, 210
for consumer service, 114–115
for direct marketing, 463–464, 477
for integrated marketing communications, 475
Data collection
concepts, 198
methods, 198
by product managers, 278
by sampling, 198
statistical inference, 198
Data miner, 600
Data mining, 210
Data Protection Directive (EU), 477
Data warehouse, 210
Dealers, 380
Deals, 506, 507
Deceptive advertising, 85
Deceptive Mail Prevention and Enforcement Act, 85
Deceptive pricing
definition, 365
kinds of, 365
Deciders, in buying centers, 148
Decision making
by consumers, 112–117
by Generation Y, 71
involving price elasticity, 333–334
from marketing research, 195
in organizational buying, 150
on price, 320
on sustainable procurement, 147
Decisions, 195
constraints on, 197
Decision support systems, 641
Decline stage
and integrated marketing communications, 466
in product life cycle, 274–275
in retail life cycle, 450
Decoding, 459
Demand
elastic, 333
inelastic, 333
in organizational buying, 143–144
as pricing constraint, 326
primary, 271
selective, 271
for services, 312
steady vs. seasonal, 502
unitary, 333
in world trade, 163
Demand conditions, 164
Demand curve, 330
downward-sloping, 332
factors influencing, 330
movement along vs. shift of, 330–331
and prestige pricing, 347
and revenue estimation, 331–332
Demand estimation
availability of similar products, 330
consumer income, 330
consumer tastes, 330
Newsweek magazine, 329–331
for pricing, 329–331
demand curve, 330
demand factors, 330
movement along vs. shift of demand curve, 330–331
Demand factors, 330
reasons for changes, 330–331
types of, 330
Demand-oriented pricing
bundle pricing, 349
odd-even pricing, 349
penetration pricing, 347
prestige pricing, 347
price lining, 348
skimming pricing, 346–347
target pricing, 349
yield management pricing, 349
Demographics, 68
American households, 70
blended family, 70
classification system, 71
ethnic concentrations, 73
generational cohorts, 69–70
neighborhoods, 77
population of United States, 69
population shifts, 70–71
race and ethnic diversity, 72–73
of test markets, 262
world population, 68–69
Demographic segmentation
consumer markets, 226, 227
variables for, 230
organizational markets
by NAICS code, 231
by number of employees, 231
variables for, 231–232
Department of Justice, 146, 398
and Microsoft, 80–81
Department of Labor, 599, 606–607
Consumer Expenditure Survey, 77
Departments, 6–7, 28
Department stores, 433
at-market pricing, 354
full service retailing, 435
social retailing, 451
in suburban malls, 445
Dependability
in customer service, 414
of transportation, 418
Depth interviews, 204
Depth of product line, 435–436
Deregulation, 80
Derived demand, 143
Descriptive research, 196
Desk jobbers, 388
Developed countries, 177
Developing countries
defined, 177
income growth, 180
per capita income, 178
Development (new products), **260**
brainstorming, 260
customer service expectations, 260
fast prototyping, 263
parallel, 263
safety tests, 260–261
Deviations
acting on, 45
identifying, 44–45
positive or negative, 45
Diamond model of competitive advantage, 164–165
Dichotomous question, 207

Differentiation, by Target Corporation, 644
Differentiation focus strategy, 580
Differentiation positioning, 238
Differentiation strategy, 579
Diffusion of innovation, 277
Digital billboards, 501
Digital catalogs, 438–439
Digital Millennium Copyright Act, 82
Digital résumés, 608
Digital strategy, 37
Direct exporting, 182
Direct forecast, 214
Direct investment, 185
Direct labor, 372
Direct mail retailing, 438–439
  advantages and disadvantages, 496
Direct marketing, 463
  business usage, 476
  customized interaction, 460, 461, 463
  by Dell Inc., 161
  direct orders, 477
  disadvantages, 463–464
  ethical issues, 477–478
  expenditures on, 476
  first-time or repeat purchasers, 464
  forms of, 475–476
  forms of communication, 463
  global issues, 477–478
  going green, 478
  growth of, 475–476
  and information technology, 477
  on Internet, 476
  lead generation, 477
  paid aspect, 461
  regulation of, 477–478
  response rate, 476
  of services, 310–311
  strengths, 461
  technological issues, 477–478
  testing procedures, 475
  traffic generation, 477
  value of, 476–477
  weaknesses, 461
Direct Marketing Association, 478
Direct Marketing Association (UK), 477
Direct marketing channels, 385
  for business goods, 384
  for consumer goods, 382–383
Direct orders, 477
Direct selling, 441–442
  Avon in China, 393
  by Dell Inc., 640
  transactional Web sites, 562
Direct-to-consumer drug advertising, 469
Discontinuous innovation, 251, 252
Discounting, 444
Discounts
  cash, 361
  definition, 360
  purchase discounts, 372
  quantity, 360
  seasonal, 360–361
  trade, 361
  in trade promotions, 510–511
Discount stores
  versus off-price retailing, 444
  price increases, 449
Discretionary income, 77
Discrimination in new car sales, 357
Disintermediation, 397
Disposable income, 76
Dissociative groups, 128
Distribution
  costs of, 406
  electronic, 310
  Ken Davis Products, 639–640
  Medtronic, 42
  and new product development, 22
Distribution centers, 419–420
Distribution costs, Bagel Bakes, 638
Distribution-related legislation
  exclusive dealing, 84
  exclusive territorial distributorships, 85
  requirement contracts, 84
  tying contracts, 85
Distribution strategies
  Dell Inc., 161
  and dumping, 188
  in global marketing, 187
  gray market problem, 188
  in growth stage, 273
  in introduction stage, 271
  Prince Sports, Inc., 242–243
  for services, 309–310
Distributors, functions of, 380
Diversification analysis, 38
  diversification strategy, 39
  market development, 38
  market penetration, 38
  product development, 39
Diversification strategy, 39
Divisional groupings, 590
Divisions, 170
Divorce rate, 70
Dogs
  definition, 37
  at Eastman Kodak, 38
Domain names, 285
Door swing data, 629
Door-to-door selling, 441–442
Dot-com failures, 585
Downsizing of products, 281
Drivers, of marketing, 209
Drives, 122
Drop shippers, 388
Dual distribution, 386
  legality of, 399
Dues, 320
Dumping, 188
Durable goods, 246
Dynamically continuous innovation, 251, 252
Dynamic pricing, 356, **560**

E

Early adopters, 277
Early majority, 277
Ebivalent newbies, 555
Echo-boom, 70
Economic Census, 200
Economic considerations, global
  currency exchange rates, 180
  economic infrastructure, 177–178
  effect of political climate, 180–181
  financial/legal systems, 178
  income and purchasing power, 178–180
  microfinance, 179–180
  stages of development, 177
Economic development
  bottom of the pyramid, 177
  developed countries, 177
  developing countries, 177
  emerging markets, 161
Economic espionage, 95–96, 165
  activities, 96
  and Coca-Cola Company, 96
  in high-tech companies, 96
Economic Espionage Act of 1996, 165
Economic forces
  consumer income, 75–78
  macroeconomic conditions, 75
Economic influence, 398
Economic infrastructure, 177–178
Economic integration
  Asian free trade agreements, 169
  European Union, 168–169
  North American Free Trade Agreement, 169
Economies of scale, 224
Economy, 75
Education, for careers in marketing, 599
Efficient consumer response, 414, 415
Eight P's of service marketing, 308
  people, 311
  physical environment, 311
  place, 309–310
  price, 309
  process, 311–312
  product, 308–309
  productivity, 312
  promotion, 310–311
Eight-second rule, 558
80/20 rule, 229
Elastic demand, 333
Elasticity of demand, 358
E-learning services, 633–635
Electronic commerce, 80
  and euro, 168
Electronic data interchange, 412
  for inventory management, 422
  for order processing, 420–421
Electronic distribution, 310
Electronic in-store coupon machines, 506
Electronic marketing channel, 384
Electronic order processing, 420–421
Electronics industry, 351
Electronic waste, 423
E-mail
  advertising medium, 478
  for consumer surveys, 205
  for direct marketing, 476
  permission marketing, 551
  spam, 559
E-marketplaces, 153
Emerging markets, Dell sales in, 161
Emory University, 530
Emotional intelligence, 537
Employees
  idea generation from, 257
  number in service sector, 298
  in small businesses, 81
Employee welfare, as goal, 32
Employer-sponsored training, 538
Employment agencies, 607
Encoding, 459
Endorsements, 122
Enterprise resource planning, 412
Enterprise selling, 522
Entrepreneur magazine, 434
Entrepreneurship
  Avon in China, 393
  Ben & Jerry's, 25
  Crate and Barrel, 647
  Creative Cosmetics in Japan, 183
  Dell Inc., 640–641
  eBayBusiness, 154
  Jamba Juice, 619–620
  Netflix, 31
  social, 18
  Trader Joe's, 641–642
  at Vizio, Inc., 345–346
  women in India, 179
  YouTube, 5
  at Zappos.com, 221–222
Entry, 81

Environmental forces, 11
case, 87–89
competitive forces, 80–81
economic forces, 75–78
golf equipment market, 625–627
regulatory forces, 82–86
social forces, 68–74
technological forces, 78–80
trends identified, 66–67
types of, 6, 7, 66
uncontrollable, 11
Environmental issues
Anheuser-Busch, 91
at BP, 47–49
and consumer ethics, 105
and cultural values, 74
in direct marketing, 478
factor in channel choice, 392
green marketing, 102
in packaging, 291
sustainable development, 27, 104
Environmental Protection Agency, 157
Environmental scanning, 66
case, 87–89
competitive forces, 80–81
and consumer expectations, 75
economic forces, 75–78
and GPS revolution, 65
for Jamba Juice, 619–620
of neighborhoods, 77
in new-product strategy development, 256
regulatory forces, 82–86
social forces, 68–74
technological forces, 78–80
today's marketplace, 67
tracking trends, 66–67
Environmental sustainability, 71
Environmental trends, 66–67
Equipment-based services, 302, 303
Ethical behavior
of co-workers, 97–98
current perceptions, 93
personal moral philosophy, 98–100
of top management, 97–98
Ethical dilemma, whistle-blowers, 98
Ethical framework, 92–93
Ethical marketing behavior
business culture
ethics of competition, 95–97
ethics of exchange, 94–95
corporate culture and expectations
codes of ethics, 97
co-worker behavior, 97–98
top management behavior, 97–98
downsizing products, 281
industry practices, 94–97
personal moral philosophy, 97–100
moral idealism, 98–99
utilitarianism, 99
societal culture and norms, 93–94
Ethics, 17, **92;** *see also* Code of ethics
American Marketing Association statement, 98
of asking customers about competitors, 533
in cola war, 96
of consumers, 104–105
legality vs. ethicality, 92
of protectionism, 167
of slotting allowances, 399
of subliminal messages, 120
Ethics of competition
bribes and kickbacks, 96–97
Corruption Perception Index, 97
economic espionage, 95–96
Ethics of exchange, 94–95
caveat emptor, 95
right to be heard, 95
right to be informed, 95
right to choose, 95
right to safety, 95
Ethnic concentrations, 73
Ethnic diversity, 72–73
Ethnocentric consumers, 176–177
Ethnographic research, 203
Euro, 168
Europe, hypermarkets, 436
European Union
banana tariff, 166–167
Data Protection Directive, 85, 477
description, 168–169
ISO 9000 quality standards, 181
membership map, 168
and Microsoft, 80–81
number of languages, 176
packaging guidelines, 291
per capita income, 178
tariff on Japanese cars, 166
Evaluation, 470
Evaluative criteria, 113
Everyday fair pricing, 444
Everyday low pricing, 362, 444
at supermarkets, 363
Exchange, 6
in networked global marketplace, 171–173
transactions, 7–8
Exchange rate fluctuations, 180
Excise taxes, 334
Exclusive dealing, 84, 399
Exclusive distribution, 393–394
Exclusive territorial distributorships, 85
Expenses
administrative, 373
general, 373
selling, 373
Expense-to-sales ratio, 373
Experience-curve pricing, 350–351
Experience economy, 297–298
Experience properties of services, 305
Experiencers, 125
Experiments, 209–210
Expertise, channel influence, 398
Exploratory research, 196
Exporting, 182
direct, 182
indirect, 182
of services, 298–299
Exports
dollar value, 162, 163
of United States, 141, 162–163
Express companies, 419
Express warranties, 292
Extended problem solving, 116
case, 623–624
External information search, 112, 121
External screening and evaluation, 259
External secondary data, 199
Extranet, 80, 412
Extreme value stores, 445
Exurbs, 71

F

Facilitating function of intermediaries, 381–382, 384–385
Factor conditions, 164
Factory outlets, 445
Fads, 276
Failure
of dot-com companies, 585
of new products
marketing reasons, 253–254
organizational reasons, 254–255
Failure fee, 263
Fair Packaging and Labeling Act, 83
Family branding, 286
Family decision making, 129–130
Family influences
consumer socialization, 128
family decision making, 129–130
family life cycle, 128–129
Family life cycle, 128
Family Talk about Drinking, 91
Fares, 309, 320
Farm cooperatives, 26
Fashion
Americanization of, 172
products, 276
Fast food business, 642–643
Fast prototyping, 263
Fax surveys, 205
Fear appeals, 491
Feature bloat, 251, 252
Federal Bureau of Investigation, 96, 104, 513
Federal Communications Commission
on advertising, 488
on misleading promotions, 513
on product placement, 510
on subliminal messages, 120
Federal Dilution Act, 84
Federal Trade Commission
on basing-point pricing, 365
on collecting consumer data, 95
on deceptive pricing, 365
on environmental claims, 105
fraud in online shopping, 561
and marketing channels, 398–400
on newness of products, 251
powers of, 85
on privacy, 477–478
ruling on free goods/services, 366
on sweepstakes, 508
on telemarketing, 441
Federal Trade Commission Act, 85, 365–366
Federation of European Direct Marketing, 477
Feedback, 460
Feedback loop, 460
Fees, 309, 320
Feminism, 74
Field of Dreams, 453
Field of experience, 459–460
Fighting brands, 287
Finance allowance, 511
Finance department, 6
Financial data
new-product projections, 260
Paradise Kitchens, 61–62
Financial system, 178
Firms, 26; *see also* Companies
advantages of advertising, 461
backward integration, 390
business portfolio analysis, 36–38
as channel captains, 398
costs of economic espionage, 165
differing customer service standards, 415
diversification analysis, 38–39
factors in channel choice, 392–393
factors in marketing strategy change, 393
forward integration, 390
in-house research staff, 603
minority or women-owned, 144
promotional Web sites, 563–564
specializing in logistics, 414
types of goals, 31–32
using direct selling, 442
First impressions, 528
Fixed alternative questions, 206–207
Fixed costs, 335
and competitive pressures, 81
Fixed pricing, 355
Flexible-price policy, 356, **356**
and discrimination, 357

Flighting schedule, 502
Floor stock protection program, 511
FOB freight-allowed pricing, 363, 365
FOB origin pricing, 362, 365
Focus groups, 204–205
Follow-up stage, 531
Food and Drug Administration, 281, 285
Food brokers, 389
Foreign Corrupt Practices Act, 97, **174**
Forgetting rate, 502
Former price comparisons, 365
Forms of ownership, 432
contractual systems, 433–434
corporate chains, 432–433
independent retailers, 432
Formula selling presentation, 529
Form utility, 19
in interactive marketing, 549
from marketing channels, 382
in retailing, 430–431
Fortune, 91, 245, 606
Fortune 500 companies, 417
Fortune Small Business, 617
Forward integration, 390
Four I's of services, 299
inconsistency, 430
inseparability, 30–301
intangibility, 299
inventory, 301
Four P's of marketing, 11
and marketing channels, 382
marketing program, 42
at 3M Corporation, 15
Franchises fees, 434
Franchising, 391
business-format, 433–435
in international markets, 434
as market-entry strategy, 184
number of outlets, 434
product-distribution format, 433–435
top-five U.S. companies, 434
types of arrangements, 391
Fraud
in online shopping, 561
in sweepstakes, 513
Free-enterprise society, 18
Free goods/merchandise, 362
Federal Trade Commission ruling, 366
samples, 508
as trade promotion, 511
Free trade
Asian agreements, 169
benefits of, 167
Free trade agreements
and pricing strategies, 188
trade regulation in, 181
Free Trade Area of the Americas, 169
Free trials, 122
Freight absorption pricing, 363
Freight allowances, 511
Freight forwarders, 419
Frequency, 494
Frequency of transportation, 418
Full coverage, 581
Full-line forcing, 399
Full-line wholesalers, 387
Full-service agency, 503–504
Full service retailers, 435
Full warranty, 292
Functional benefits of packaging and labeling, 289–290
Functional discounts, 361
Functional groupings, 590
Functional level, 28
strategy at, 32
Functional retailing mix, 446
Furniture industry, 646
Furniture makers
Charlesburg Furniture, 396
HOM Furniture, 628–629

G

Gantt chart, 588
Gap analysis, 306
Gasoline retailing, 48–49
Gatekeepers, in buying centers, 148
Gender, and new car sales, 357
General Agreement on Tariffs and Trade, 167
General expenses, 373
Generalized life cycle, 275
General merchandise stores, 435
General merchandise wholesalers, 387
General operating ratios, 373–374
Generational cohorts
baby boomers, 69
Generation X, 69–70
Generation Y, 70, 71
Generational marketing, 70
Generation X, 69–70
Generation Y, 70
mobile marketing, 465
women of, 73–74
Generic business strategies, 578, 578–580
cost focus, 579–580
cost leadership, 579
differentiation, 579
differentiation focus, 580
Geographical groupings, 590
Geographical price adjustments
basing-point pricing, 363
FOB origin pricing, 362
FOB with freight-allowed pricing, 363
freight absorption pricing, 363
multiple-zone pricing, 362
single-zone pricing, 362
uniform delivered pricing, 362–363
Geographical sales organization, 534, 535
Geographic segmentation
consumer markets, 226, 227, 230
organizational markets, 231
GeoVALS, 125
Germany
antitrust laws, 188
packaging laws, 291
Gift-giving vs. bribery, 174
Global brand, 174
Global companies
Dell Inc., 161
effect of exchange rate fluctuations, 180
examples, 170–171
and exchange rate fluctuations, 180
Geek Squad, 88
global brands, 171
international firms, 170
marketing strategies, 171
multinational firms, 170
and societal norms, 94
Starbucks, 108
transnational firms, 170–171
Global competition, 169–170
collaborative relationships, 170
examples, 169
Global consumers, 174
companies capitalizing on, 171
and consumer ethnocentrism, 176–177
global teenagers, 172
in Japan, 164
Global economy
borderless economic world, 166–173
competitive advantage of nations, 164–165
service exporting in, 313–314
services in, 298–299
sustainable development, 27
world trade, 162–163
Global environmental scan
cultural diversity
cultural ethnocentrism, 176–177
cultural symbols, 175–176
customs, 174–175
languages, 176
values, 173–174
economic considerations
currency exchange rates, 180
economic infrastructure, 177–178
income and purchasing power, 178–180
microfinance, 179–180
stages of development, 177
and GPS revolution, 65
political-regulatory climate
political risk ratings, 181
political stability, 180
trade regulations, 181
Global marketing
by Act II Microwave Popcorn, 403
careers in, 600, 603–604
case, 190–191
consumer income/purchasing power, 178–180
cross-cultural analysis, 173–177
and currency exchange rates, 180
by Dell Inc., 161
economic considerations, 177–180
economic infrastructure, 178–179
effect on price, revenue, and costs, 322
global brands, 171
global companies, 170–171
global competition, 169–170
global consumers, 171
global teenagers, 172
golf equipment industry, 625–627
impact of retailing, 431
market-entry strategies, 181–185
marketing channels in, 395–397
McDonald's, 642–643
by Medtronics, 630–632
microfinance, 179–180
networked global marketspace, 171–172
political-regulatory climate, 180–181
prevalence of bribery in, 174
profit potential, 182
of services, 313–314
stages of economic development, 177
strategic channel alliances, 386
trends influencing
decline of protectionism, 167–168
economic integration, 169–169
World Trade Organization, 168–169
worldwide marketing program, 185–188
Global marketing entry strategies
contract assembly, 183–184
contract manufacturing, 183–184
direct investment, 185
exporting, 182
franchising, 184
general options, 181
joint ventures, 184
licensing, 182–184
profit potential, 182
Global marketing manager, 600
Global marketing program
distribution strategies, 187
pricing strategies, 188
product strategies, 185–187
promotion strategies, 186–187
Global marketing strategy, 174
to find synergies, segments, and partners, 583–584
Global organizational markets
definition, 141
and NAICS, 141–142
Global Positioning System, 65

Global suppliers, 407
Goals, 31
  acting on deviations from, 591
  communicating, 585–586
  identifying deviations from, 591
  of marketing, 6
  measurable and achievable, 582
  nonprofit organizations, 32
  Paradise Kitchens, 54
  types of, 31–32
Goal setting, in strategic marketing process, 40–42
Golf equipment industry, 379, 625–627
Golf glove development, 368–369
Good Housekeeping seal, 122
Goods, 18, 246
Government
  consumer protection, 10
  and monopoly, 80–81
  number of units in, 141
  as organizational buyer, 140
  regulatory forces, 82–85
  stimulus checks of 2008, 77–78
Government markets
  definition, 141
  and NAICS, 141–142
Government-sponsored services, 304–305
GPS revolution, 65
Gray market, 188
Green best practices guidelines, 478
Green jobs, 71
Green machines, 437–438
Green mailings, 438
Green marketing, 102, 423, 433
  by BP, 47–49
Green products, 105
Greenwashing, 105
Gross domestic product, 162
  direct marketing percentage of, 476
  per cent from small business, 81
  services component, 246, 298
Gross income, 76
Gross margin, 372
Gross profit, 372
Gross rating points, 495
Gross sales, 370
Groupthink, 255
Growth, expected in target market, 234
Growth share matrix
  market growth rate, 36
  relative market share, 36
  for strategic business units, 36–37
Growth stage; *see* Product life cycle
Growth strategies, 35–39
  business portfolio analysis, 35–38
  diversification analysis, 38–39
Guarantees, 122
Guide Against Deceptive Pricing (FTC), 365
Guide Concerning Use of the Word "Free" and Similar Representations (FTC), 366

H

Harvard Business School, 164
Harvesting strategy, 275
Head-to-head positioning, 238
Health issues in packaging, 291
Help-wanted ads, 607
Hierarchy of effects, 470
  and advertising objectives, 489
Hierarchy of needs, 118–119
High- and low-resource groups, 125
High-definition television market, 345–346
High-involvement products, 117
High-learning products, 275
Hi-Lo pricing, 363
Hispanics
  buying patterns, 131–132
  consumer potential, 72–73
  and new car sales, 357
  population concentrations, 73
  in U.S. population, 72
Holding costs, 421
Home offices, 542
Hooked, online, and single consumers, 555
Horizontal channel conflict, 397–398
Horizontal price fixing, 363–364
Households
  American, 70
  American Community Survey, 200
  family life cycle, 128–129
  income, 75–78
  nontraditional, 129
  purchasing power level, 179
  with television, 201–202
  traditional family, 128–129
Human resources department, 6
Humorous appeals, 491
Hunter-gatherers, 555
Hypermarket, 436

I

Ice cream industry, 24
Idea evaluation methods
  closed-end questions, 206–207
  dichotomous questions, 207
  with electronic technology, 208
  fax surveys, 205
  fixed alternative questions, 206–207
  Likert scale, 207
  mail surveys, 205
  mall intercept interviews, 205–206
  online surveys, 205
  open-ended questions, 206
  problems to guard against, 208
  semantic differential scale, 207
  telephone surveys, 205
Idea generation, 257
  brainstorming sessions, 258
  from competitive products, 258
  customer suggestions, 257
  employee/co-worker suggestions, 257
  from inventors, 259
  open innovation, 257
  research and development labs, 257–258
  from small technology firms, 259
  supplier suggestions, 257
  from universities, 258–259
Idea generation methods, 203–205
  depth interviews, 204
  focus groups, 204–205
  individual interviews, 203–204
  trend hunting, 205
Ideals-motivated groups, 125
Ideas, 18, 246
  marketing of, 19
Idle production capacity, 301
Image, of retail outlets, 446
Implementation plan, Paradise Kitchens, 63
Implied warranties, 292
Importers of U.S. goods, 163
Importing, parallel, 188
Imports
  dollar value, 162–163
  quotas on, 167
  tariffs on, 166–167
  of United States, 163
Inbound telemarketing, 523
Income
  of consumers, 75–78
  global, 68
  worldwide disparities, 178–179
Income statement, 370
Inconsistency of services, 300
Incremental costs and revenues, 358–359, 574
Independent agents, 533–534
Independent e-marketplace, 153–154
Independent retailers, 432
Index of Consumer Sentiment, 75, 76
India
  Medtronic in, 41
  population, 68
  women entrepreneurs, 179
Indifferents, 555
Indirect exporting, 182
Indirect marketing channels
  for business goods, 384
  for consumer goods, 383
  industrial distributors, 384
Individual interviews, 203–204
Individuality, in interactive marketing, 549–550
Industrial design, 258
Industrial distributor, 384
Industrial firms, 140
Industrial markets
  definition, 140
  and NAICS, 141–142
Industrial products, 246
Industrial salesperson, 600
Industrial services, 248
Industrial supplies, 141
Industries, 26
  marketing plan, 50
  related and supporting, 164
Industry analysis, Paradise Kitchens, 56
Industry practices, and ethics, 94–97
Industry structure, 80–81
Inelastic demand, 333
Infant Formula Act, 82
Inflationary economy, 75
Influence effect, 451
Influencers, in buying centers, 148
Infomercial, 497
Information
  as buyer requirement, 394
  inadequate, 113
  right to, 95
Information search
  by consumers, 112–113
  in organizational buying, 151–152
  and perceived risk, 121–122
  and selective retention, 121
Information systems department, 6
Information technology, 210
  for direct marketing, 477
  electronic data interchange, 412
  enterprise resource planning, 412
  extranet, 412
  and flexible pricing, 356
  for logistics management, 407, 411–412
  for marketing research, 210–211
  for supply chain management, 407, 411–412
  at Wal-Mart, 411
Infrastructure, 177–178
In-house agencies, 504
In-house project director, 600
In-house research staff, 603
Innovation
  continuous, 251
  diffusion of, 277
  discontinuous, 151, 252
  dynamically continuous, 251, 252
  open, 257
  at 3M Corporation, 3–4, 14–15
Innovation metrics, 577–578
Innovators, 125, 277

Input metric, 577–578
Input-related sales plan objectives, 532, 539
Inquiry tests, 505
Inseparability of services, 300–301
Inside order takers, 523
Installations, 248
Institutional advertisements, 487–488
advocacy, 487
competitive, 487
pioneering, 487
reminder, 487
Intangibility of services, 299
Integrated marketing communications, 458
basic tools of, 473
case, 480–481
costs of, 474
to develop promotional mix
buying decision stages, 467–468
channel strategies, 468–469
product characteristics, 466–467
product life cycle, 465–466
target audience, 464–465
to engage consumers, 457–458
marketing dashboard for, 472
McDonald's, 642–643
types of promotion, 457–458
value of publicity, 463
Integrated marketing communications program, 469–475
designing promotion, 472
execution and assessment, 474–475
identifying target audience, 470
scheduling promotion, 472–473
selecting promotional tools, 472
setting budget, 471–473
specifying objectives, 470–471
Integrated supply chain, 410
Intellectual property, lost sales from theft of, 94
Intelligent failures, 255
Intelligent mail, 438
Intensive distribution, 393
Interactive marketing, 550
case, 566–569
characteristics, 548
choiceboards, 550
collaborative filtering, 550
consumer lifestyle segmentation, 555–556
consumer profile, 554–555
and cookies, 560
cross-channel shoppers, 562
customer experience, 551–553
customer relationships, 549–550
customer value creation, 548–549
customization, 558
dynamic pricing, 560
eight-second rule, 558
fraud complaints, 561
Internet moms, 556
marketing dashboard for, 554
multichannel marketing, 562–564
number of consumers, 548
permission marketing, 551
personalization, 550–551
privacy and security concerns, 561
projected sales, 548
purchase behavior, 556–557
reasons for shopping, 557–561
self-regulation, 561
at Seven Cycles, Inc., 547
times and marketspaces, 561
utilities provided by, 548–549
and viral marketing, 559
Web communities, 559
Web site design, 551–553
Web site elements, 551–553
Interactive marketing source of new jobs, 598
Interactivity, 549–550
Interest, 320, 470
Intermediaries
activities, 386–387
agents, 388–389
brokers, 389
cash and carry wholesalers, 387
and channel conflict, 397–398
choice considerations, 393
consumer benefits from, 382
desk jobbers, 388
and disintermediation, 387
drop shippers, 388
electronic marketing channels, 384–385
facilitating function, 381–382, 384–385
food brokers, 389
and four utilities, 382
functions and types, 380
general merchandise wholesalers, 387
in Japan, 396–397
logistical function, 381–382
longer lead times, 414
manufacturer's agents, 388–389
manufacturer's branches/offices, 389
merchant wholesalers, 387–388
minimizing transactions, 381
object of promotion, 464
overseas, 395–397
rack jobbers, 387
satisfying buyer requirements, 394–395
selling agents, 389
specialty merchandise wholesalers, 387
transactional function, 384–385
transactional functions, 381–382
truck jobbers, 388
value created by, 380–381
Intermittent schedule, 502
Intermodal transportation, 418–419
Internal information search, 112, 121
Internal marketing, 311
Internal screening and evaluation, 259
Internal secondary data, 199
International Anti-Dumping and Fair Competition Act, 174
International firms, 170
International marketing careers, 603–604
International Standard Industrial Classification of All Economic Activities (UN), 142
International Standards Organization, 102, 145
International trade; *see* World trade
Internet, 80
for direct marketing, 476
domain names, 285
effect on baseball, 317
for electronic marketing channels, 384–385
for interactive marketing
choiceboards, 550
collaborative filtering, 550
for networked global marketplace, 171–173
new market opportunities on, 392
number of users in China, 441
online databases, 201
for organizational buying, 153–154
product management on, 295
for salesforce communication, 542
worldwide access to, 171–173
Internet access, 441
Internet advertising
advantages and disadvantages, 496
banner ads, 499–500
click fraud, 501
comparative statistics, 499
Google, Inc., 516–517
key categories, 516
options, 499–500
rating service, 500
as rich media, 499
search engines, 499–500
Internet cafes, 441
Internet-enabled marketspace, 548
Internet-enabled technologies, 558–559
Internet kiosks, 441
Internet marketing manager, 600
Internet moms, 556
Internet shopping, 13
Internet Tax Freedom Act, 85
Internet users behavior, 202
Intertype competition, 436
Interviews
depth, 204
individual, 203–204
for jobs, 610–613
kinds of questions, 206–207
mall intercept, 205–206
by telephone, 205
using electronic technology, 208
Intranet, 80
Introduction stage; *see* Product life cycle
Inventors, new product ideas from, 259
Inventory
definition, 371
reasons for carrying, 421
and seasonal discounts, 360–361
in service sector, 301
stockouts, 412–414
stockturn rate, 376–377
total logistics costs, 412–413
Inventory control managers, 600
Inventory costs
capital costs, 421
carrying costs, 301
holding costs, 421
risk costs, 421
service costs, 421
storage costs, 421
Inventory management
cross-docking, 410
efficient customer response, 414
electronic data interchange for, 422
inventory costs, 421
just-in-time systems, 421–422
order cycle time, 414
quick response, 414
quick response delivery, 414
reasons for inventory, 421
replenishment time, 414
supply chain strategies, 421–422
vendor-managed inventory, 422
at Wal-Mart, 433
Inventory service costs, 421
Investment, direct, 185
Involvement, 115–116
high-involvement purchases, 115–116
low-involvement purchases, 116
and marketing strategy, 116–117
problem-solving levels, 116
ISO 14000 initiative, 102
ISO 9000 standards, **145,** 181

J

Japan
buyers in, 148
consumers in, 164
Creative Cosmetics in, 183
imports from U.S., 163
keiretsu, 397
marketing channels, 395–397
negotiating in, 174–175
rice exports to, 166
trade barriers, 181

Job analysis, 537
Job applicants
  personality tests, 605
  vocational interest tests, 605
Job Choices, 606
Job description, 537
Job interviews
  follow-up, 613
  frequently asked questions, 611, 612
  handling rejection, 613
  preparing for, 610–612
  succeeding in., 612–613
Job opportunities, identifying
  career service office, 605–606
  direct contact, 608
  employment agencies, 607
  help-wanted ads, 607
  libraries, 606–607
  networking, 607
  online employment services, 606
  personal contact, 607
  state employment office, 607
Job postings, 606
Job qualifications, 537
Jobs, in direct mail retailing, 438
Job search process
  activities involved in, 598
  handling rejection, 613
  identifying opportunities, 605–608
  job interviews, 610–613
  résumés, 608–610
  self-assessment, 604–605
Joint ventures, 184
Journal of Marketing Research, 198
Judgment, 92–93
Judgments of decision makers, 214–215
Junk mail, 559
Jury tests, 502
Just-in-time concept, 145–146, **421–422**

K

Keiretsu, 397
Kelley Blue Book, 321
Key account management, 534
Key personality traits, 119
Kickbacks, 96–97, 174
Kiosks, 434, 441

L

Label, 288
Labeling
  and brand image, 290
  challenges
    connecting with customers, 291
    cost reductions, 291–292
    environmental concerns, 291
    health, safety, and security, 291
  communication benefits, 289
  country of origin, 290–291
  creating customer value, 288–291
  functional benefits, 289–290
  perceptual benefits, 290–291
Laboratory test markets, 262
Laggards, 277
Language(s)
  back translation, 176
  in global marketing, 176
  number of, 176
  and semiotics, 175
Language barrier, 132
Lanham Act, 83, 282
Late majority, 277
Lawn mower makers, 629–630
Lawrence Livermore National Laboratory, 146
Laws, 92; *see also* Regulation
  advertising and promotion-related, 84–85
  antitrust, 82, 84
  and brand names, 285
  CAN-SPAM Act, 85, 559
  cease and desist orders, 85
  Child Protection Act, 83
  Children's Online Privacy Protection Act, 85, 95
  Clayton Act, 82, 364, 399
  Consumer Bill of Rights, 99
  Consumer Goods Pricing Act, 364
  Consumer Product Safety Act, 83
  corrective advertising, 85
  Deceptive Mail Prevention and Enforcement act, 85
  Digital Millennium Copyright Act, 82
  distribution-related, 84–85
  Economic Espionage Act, 97
  European Union Data Protection Act, 85
  Fair Packaging and Labeling act, 83
  Federal Dilution Act, 84
  Federal Trade Commission Act, 85, 365
  Foreign Corrupt Practices Act, 97
  Infant formula Act, 82
  Internet Tax Freedom Act, 83
  Lanham Act, 83
  Madrid Protocol, 83
  on marketing channels
    dual distribution, 399
    exclusive dealing, 399
    Federal Trade Commission monitoring, 398–399
    full-line forcing, 399
    refusal to deal, 399–400
    resale restrictions, 400
    tying arrangements, 399
    vertical integration, 399
  and moral standards, 94
  Nutritional Labeling and Education Act, 82
  on parallel importing, 188
  per se illegal concept, 84
  on pricing
    deceptive pricing, 365
    geographical pricing, 365
    predatory pricing, 365–366
    price discrimination, 364–365
    price-fixing, 363–364
  pricing-related, 84
  product-related, 82–84
  protecting competition, 82
  Robinson-Patman Act, 82, 85, 364–365
  Sherman Antitrust Act, 82, 84, 363, 365, 399, 400
  Telephone Consumer Protection Act, 85, 527
  Trademark Law Revision Act, 83
Lawyers, cost-plus pricing, 350
Lead, 526–527
Leadership in Energy and Environmental Design, 68
Lead generation, 477
Lead time, 414
Learning, 122
  behavioral, 122
  and brand loyalty, 122–123
  cognitive, 122
Learning effect, 350–351
Legal framework, 92–93
Legal system, 178
Less-than-truckload shipments, 419
Level of service, 432
  full service, 435
  limited service, 435
  self-service, 434–435
Library services, 606–607
Licensing
  by Act II Microwave Popcorn, 402
  of brands and trademarks, 284
  contract assembly, 183–184
  contract manufacturing, 183–184
  franchising, 184
  as market-entry strategy, 182–183
Life cycle, family, 128–129
Lifestyle, 124
  segmentation of online consumers, 555
  VALS profiles, 124–125
Likert scale, 207
Limited-coverage warranty, 292
Limited-line stores, 435
Limited-line wholesalers, 387
Limited problem solving, 116
Limited-service agencies, 504
Limited service retailers, 435
Linear trend extrapolation, 215–216
Line positions, 589
List price
  adjustments to, 359–363
    allowances, 362–362
    discounts, 360–361
    geographical adjustments, 362–363
  setting
    balancing incremental costs and revenues, 358–359
    choosing a policy, 355–356
    company effects on, 356
    competitive effects on, 357–358
    customer effects on, 357
Litigation, Ford-Firestone problem, 622
Little Dragons of Asia, 169
Living standards, global, 68
Load factor, 312, 313
Lobbying, 82
Location-awareness services, 65
Location-based marketing, 65
Logistical function of intermediaries, 381–382
Logistics, 406
  decisions involved in, 406
  key supply chain functions
    inventory management, 421–422
    order processing, 420–421
    third-party providers, 417
    transportation, 418–419
    warehousing/materials handling, 419–420
  related to marketing channels, 406
  related to supply chain management, 406
  reverse, 422–423
  supplier networks, 407
Logistics management, 406
  auto industry, 408, 409
  case, 425–426
  cost-effective, 406
  customer-driven, 406
  customer-driven supply chain
    customer service concept, 413–415
    customer service standards, 415–416
    information technology, 411–412
    marketing dashboard for, 416
    total logistics cost concept, 412–413
  customer requirements, 406
  firms specializing in, 414
  at Procter & Gamble, 406
Logotype/Logo, 282
Long-range marketing plan, 578
Long-run profit, 325
Los Angeles City Council, 501
Loss-leader pricing, 354
Lost-horse forecast, 214–215
Lower class, 130–131
Low-involvement products, 116–117
Low-learning products, 275–276
Loyalty programs, 506, 509
Luxury goods, 347

M

Machine vision systems, 150–153
Macroeconomic conditions, 75
Macromarketing, 17–18
Madrid Protocol, 83
Magazine advertising
  advantages and disadvantages, 496

costs of, 498
number of magazines, 497
special interest types, 497–498
Magnusson-Moss Warranty/FTC Improvement Act, 292
Mail surveys, 205
Maintained markup, 444
Make-buy decision, 151
Makers, 125
Malcolm Baldrige National Quality Award, 539
Mall intercept interviews, 205–206
Mall of America, 439
case, 453–454
Management by exception, 591
Managing for long run profit, 325
Manufacturers
above-market pricing, 354
allowances to supermarkets, 398
and chain stores, 433
contract assembly, 183–184
contract manufacturing, 183–184
cooperative advertising, 511
cost-plus pricing, 350
customer service standards, 415
as direct marketing channels, 382–383, 384
dual distribution, 386
evolution of market orientation, 16–17
joint ventures, 184
for Lands' End, 158
of original equipment, 150
performance contracts, 510–511
pull strategy, 469
push strategy, 468–469
and relationship marketing, 13
and reseller profits, 357
salesforce training, 511
and slotting allowances, 399
target pricing, 349
trade discounts, 361
transactional Web sites, 563
Manufacturer's agents, 388–389
Manufacturer's branch offices, 389
Manufacturer-sponsored retail franchise system, 391
Manufacturer-sponsored wholesale systems, 391
Manufacturer's representative, 388
Manufacturer's sales offices, 389
Manufacturer's suggested retail price, 364, 409, 638
Manufacturing
build-to-order, 225
capacity management, 260
lawn mower makers, 629–630
mass customization, 224–225
in new product development, 22
organizational chart, 43
precycling, 79
recycling products, 79
in synergy analysis, 580
Manufacturing department, 6
Marginal analysis, 335–336
advantage and difficulty of, 359
definition, 358
power and limitations of, 358
and profit calculation, 336–337
Marginal cost, 335, 336–337, 358
Marginal revenue, 331, 337, 358
calculating, 332
Marginal revenue = marginal cost, 337
Maricopa County Medical Society, Arizona, 93
Markdown, 375–376
timing of, 444
Market, 11
global teenager, 172
for golf products, 368–369
for Ken Davis Products, 639
reaching new, 280
Market attractiveness, too little, 254
Market-based groupings, 590
Market development strategy, 38
Marketer-dominated information sources, 112
Market growth rate, 36
Marketing, 6
breadth and depth of
benefits to consumers, 19
organizational buyers, 19
ultimate consumers, 19
what is marketed, 18–19
who benefits, 19
who markets, 18
business marketing, 140
and career planning, 4–6
changes in discipline of, 598
to consumer needs vs. wants, 10
costs of, 327
discovering consumer needs, 8
and entrepreneurship, –56
ethical/legal framework, 92–93
ethics in, 17
evolution of
customer relationship era, 16–17
marketing concept era, 16
market orientation, 16
production era, 16
sales era, 16
factors required for
ability to satisfy needs, 7
communication, 7
transactions, 7–8
unsatisfied needs, 7
financial aspects
operating ratios, 373–374
operating statement, 370–373
ratios for setting prices, 374–377
four Ps of, 11
goals of, 6
impact of technology, 79
implication of population trends, 68–69
implication of reference groups, 128
internal, 311
location-based, 65
macroeconomic conditions, 75
macromarketing, 17–18
micromarketing, 18
mobile, 465
new products, 8–10
opportunities in European Union, 168–169
organizing for
brand manager, 590
category manager, 590
chief marketing officer, 589
divisional groupings, 590
line vs. staff positions, 589
product manager, 590
personal selling in, 521
of services
capacity management, 312
customer experience management, 311
distribution, 309–310
internal marketing, 311
marketing mix, 308–309
off-peak pricing, 309
physical environment, 311
price, 309
process, 311–312
promotion, 310–311
social responsibility, 17–18
societal marketing concept, 17–18
at 3M Corporation, 3–4, 14–15
utility created by, 19
Marketing actions/activities, 212
and behavioral learning theory, 122
at BP, 48
case, 217–219
from data presentation, 212–213
evaluation of results, 214
factors influencing, 6–7
identifying, 196–197
identifying data for, 197–198
implementation, 214
information technology for, 211–212
linking needs to, 222
measures of success, 196–197
to reach segments, 226
to reach target markets, 234–236
Apple Inc., 236
Wendy's, 235–236
recommendations, 213
scheduling, 588
from SWOT analysis, 40
United States Postal Service, 304–305
Marketing channels, 380
auto industry, 408
for business goods, 383–386
direct channel, 384
indirect channel, 384
industrial distributors, 384
Callaway Golf, 379
case, 401–403
channel partnerships, 391
channel relationships
channel captains, 398
channel influences, 398
securing cooperation, 398
sources of conflict, 397–398
consumer benefits, 382
for consumer goods
direct channel, 382–383
indirect channel, 383
direct channels, 385
direct selling and lack of, 441–442
discounts for, 360
and disintermediation, 397
dual distribution, 386
electronic, 384–385
factors affecting choice/management
company factors, 392–393
consumers, 392
environment, 392
products, 392
profitability, 395
satisfying buyer requirements, 394–395
target market coverage, 393–394
functions performed by, 381–382
global dimensions
channel relationships, 397
intermediaries, 395–396
need for understanding, 397
in global marketing, 187
gray market, 188
intermediaries, 386–389
legal considerations, 398–400
monitoring performance of, 395, 396
multichannel marketing, 385–386
promotional allowances, 362
related to logistics, 406
related to supply chain management, 406
strategic channel alliances, 386
versus supply chain, 406–407
value created by, 380–381
vertical marketing systems
administered, 391
contractual, 390–391
corporate, 390
Marketing communications program, 458
Marketing concept, 16
Marketing concept era, 16
Marketing dashboards, 32
for above-, at-, or below-market pricing, 355
advertising media selection, 495
Ben & Jerry's, 34
for brand development index, 279
case, 218
for category development index, 279
customer service standards, 415
for data presentation, 212–213

Marketing dashboards—*Cont.*
to evaluate strategic marketing process, 592–594
for evaluating marketing channels, 396
Integrated marketing communications expenditures, 472
JetBlue profitability, 313
marketing matrix, 33
marketing plan, 33
for retailing strategy, 447
salesforce evaluation, 540
sales problems, 249–250
Marketing department, 6
and consumer needs, 10
key role, 28
responsibilities, 7
Marketing drivers, 209
Marketing evaluation process, 590–591
Marketing goals, 41
Marketing implementation, 585
Marketing information research, case, 628–629
Marketing manager, 600
Marketing managers
advertising media options, 494
and price elasticities, 333
Marketing metrics, 33
to evaluate strategic marketing process, 592–594
innovation metrics, 577–578
in marketing planning, 577–578
Marketing mix, 11
controllable factors, 11
in introduction stage, 270–272
Nike MaxSight, 616–617
poor execution, 254
price component, 598
price in, 323–324
promotion element, 458
for services
branding, 308–309
capacity management, 312
distribution, 309–310
internal marketing, 311
physical environment, 311
price, 309
process, 311–312
productivity, 312
promotion, 310–311
at 3M Corporation, 15
Marketing mix activities, 42
"Marketing Myopia" (Levitt), 30
Marketing News, 607
Marketing objectives
goal setting, 41
Paradise Kitchens, 58–59
Marketing organization design, 43
Marketing plan, 33
annual, 578
Bagel Bakes, 637–638
compared to business plan, 50–51
elements of, 50, 51
guidelines, 582–583
industry plan, 50
kind and complexity of organization, 50
long-range, 578
metrics, 577–578
most-asked questions, 51
Paradise Kitchens, Inc., 52–63
planning gap, 44–45
problems in., 583–584
target audience and purpose, 50
writing style and suggestions, 51–52
Marketing planning framework
diversification analysis, 580–581
generic business strategies, 578–580
market segmentation study, 580–581
synergy analysis, 580–582
Marketing program, 13; *see also* Global marketing program
action item list, 587
avoiding paralysis by analysis, 586
cohesive, 42
communicating goals, 585–586
and components of competition, 81
customer relationships, 12–13
customer value, 12–13
execution of, 44
four Ps of marketing, 11
Gantt chart, 588
generational, 70
marketing mix activities, 42
and marketing organization, 43
multicultural, 73
open communication, 586–587
Paradise Kitchens, 60–61
planning gap, 44–45
product or program champion, 586
program schedules, 587–588
relationship marketing, 13
rewarding success, 586
scheduling, 587–588
in strategic marketing process, 576, 585–588
from SWOT analysis, 39–40
at 3M Corporation, 14–15, 22–23
at Wendy's, 236
Marketing research, 195
careers in, 603
case, 217–219
causal, 196
challenges of, 195
on college students, 3–4
consumer marketing at retail, 446–447
for decision making, 195
descriptive, 196
expenditures on, 204
exploratory, 196
feedback for future research, 196
by Fisher-Price, 195–198
measures of success, 196–197
Morgantown Furniture, 646
by movie industry, 193–194
objectives, 196–197
and sales forecasting, 214–216
at 3M Corporation, 21–23
Marketing research consulting firms, 603
Marketing research process
collect relevant data
marketing dashboards, 212–213
syndicated panel data, 200
collect relevant information
data types, 199
information technology for, 210–211
primary data, 201–210
secondary data, 199–200
develop findings
data analysis, 211–212
present findings, 212–213
five-step approach, 195
marketing actions
evaluation of results, 214
implementation, 213
recommendations, 213
by neuromarketing, 193, 194
plan development
identify needed data, 197–198
means of data collection, 198
specify constraints, 197
problem definition, 195–197
develop measures of success, 196–197
identify possible actions, 196–197
setting objectives, 196
Marketing ROI, 592
Marketing strategies, 44
aligned with supply chain
Apple Inc., 405
Dell Inc., 409–410
IBM, 410
steps, 409
Wal-Mart, 410–411
at BP, 47–49
in buying centers, 149
company factors in changes, 393
to counter perceived risk, 122
diversification analysis
diversification strategy, 39
market development, 38
market penetration, 38
product development, 39
global, 171
by international firms, 170
and involvement, 116–117
for Jamba Juice, 620
multidomestic, 170
Naked Juice, 647–648
and organization of salesforce, 534
pan-European, 168–169
for pet products, 632–633
problems in, 583–584
during product life cycle, 270–275
by transnational firms, 171
two-tier, 224
word of mouth, 127
Marketing synergy, 237–238, 580
Marketing tactics, 44
Market modification, 278
creating new use, 280
finding new customers, 278–279
increasing product use, 279–280
Market niche, product positioning for, 238
Market orientation, 16
Market penetration strategy, 38
Marketplace
changing attitudes and roles in, 73–74
compared to marketspace, 548
trends identified in, 67
Market-product concentration, 580
Market-product focus
Paradise Kitchens, 58–59
in strategic marketing process, 40–42, 576
Market-product grid, 233
Apple Inc., 237
forming, 233
market size estimation, 233
in strategic marketing process, 580–582
Wendy's, 233
Market-product synergies, 236–238
Market segmentation, 40, 222
at Apple Inc., 237
case, 241–243
consumer markets, 226–230
key factors in, 222
for lawn mowers, 629–630
linking needs to actions, 222
meaning of, 222–223
in multichannel retailing, 450–451
organizational markets, 230–231
product differentiation strategy, 222
reasons for, 224
strategies for
build-to-order, 225
mass customization, 224–225
multiple products in multiple segments, 224
one product in multiple segments, 223–224
synergies vs. cannibalization, 225
two-tier strategy, 224
at Zappos.com, 220–222, 223
Market segmentation steps
actions to reach target markets
Apple Inc., 236
Wendy's, 235–236
grouping potential buyers
bases of segmentation, 226–230
criteria for forming segments, 226
variables for, 230–231
at HOM Furniture, 628–629

marketing actions
at Apple Inc., 236
recognizing key synergies, 236–238
at Wendy's, 235–236
market-product grid, 233
product groupings, 231–233
target market selection, 233–234
Market segmentation study, 580–581
Market segments, 222
in Asia, 41–42
at Best Buy, 136
criteria for forming, 226
Daktronics, Inc., 617–618
and generic business strategies, 579–580
for mass customization, 224–225
McDonald's, 642–643
multiple
with multiple products, 224
with one product, 223–224
Nike MaxSight, 616–617
online consumers, 555
pet owners, 632
Prince Sports, Inc., 243
synergies vs. cannibalization, 225
variables in forming, 230
Washburn Guitar, 342
Market share, 31
Coca-Cola Company and PepsiCo, 490
competitive parity budgeting, 471
Eastman Kodak, 35, 37
as goal, 31
in maturity stage, 273–274
penetration pricing for, 347
as pricing objective, 325
relative, 36
in retail life cycle, 450
in test market, 262
Market size
estimation for market-product grid, 233
estimation for target market, 234
Marketspace, 80; *see also* Interactive marketing
customer experience, 551–553
customer relationships, 549–551
customer value creation, 548–549
online consumer behavior, 553–561
Market specialization, 580
Market structure, 327–328
Market testing, 261
major U.S. test markets, 262
problems with, 262
simulated test markets, 262
test markets, 261–262
Markup
definitions of, 374–375
maintained, 444
original, 444
in pricelining, 348
standard markup pricing, 349–350
and target pricing, 349
Massachusetts Institute of Technology, 78
Mass customization, 224–225
Mass markets, 223
Mass production industries, 339
Mass selling, 460, 461
Materials handling, 420
Materials handling costs, 406
Matrix organization, 590
Maturity stage
and integrated marketing communications, 466
in product life cycle, 273–274
in retail life cycle, 450
Maximizing current profit, 325
Measures of success, 196–197
Mechanical data collection, 201–202
Media buyer, 600
Media preferences of consumers, 125
Medical technology, 630–632
Membership group, 128
Men
changing attitudes and roles, 73–74
as mission shoppers, 451
Merchandise allowances, 510–511
Merchandise line, 432
breadth of, 435, 436
breadth of product line, 442
category management, 446–447
consumer marketing at retail, 446–447
depth of, 435–436
intertype competition, 436
scrambled merchandising, 436
Merchandise management, 601
Merchant wholesalers, 387
Mergers and acquisitions
PepsiCo and Naked Juice, 648
PepsiCo and Quaker Oats, 269
Quaker Oats and Stokely-Van Kamp, 269
in synergy analysis, 580
Message, 458; *see also* Advertising message; Communication
Methods, 198
Metropolitan divisions, 71
Metropolitan statistical area, 71
Mexico
imports from U.S., 163
and NAICS, 141–142
and North American Free Trade Agreement, 169
Microfinance, 179–180
Micromarketing, 18
Micropolitan statistical areas, 71
Micro trends, 205
Microwave popcorn business, 401–403
Middle-aged couples, 129
Middle class, 130–131
Middleman, 380
Millennials, 70, 71
Minority, 69
Minority-owned firms, 144
Mission, 29
Paradise Kitchens, 53
Missionary salespeople, 524
Mission shoppers, 451
Mission statement
Ben & Jerry's, 24
BP, 47
definition, 30
examples, 29–30
of Starbucks, 107
Mixed branding, 288
Mobile marketing, 465
Modified rebuy, 149, 158
Monopolistic competition, 80, 327–328
Monopoly, 80–81, 327–328
Moral idealism, 99–100
Moral philosophy
based on moral idealism, 99–100
based on utilitarianism, 100
Motivation, 118
in consumer lifestyle, 124–125
by consumer needs, 118–119
of salesforce, 538–539
Motor carriers, 419
Movement along a demand curve, 330–331
Movie industry
advertising by, 485
ending switches, 194
film title problem, 193
marketing research, 193–194
product placements, 509–510
risks faced by, 193
sneak previews, 193
Super Bowl commercials, 490
test screenings, 193–194
3-D films, 485
tracking studies, 194
Multibranding, 287
Multichannel marketing, 385, 598
Crate and Barrel, 647
cross-channel shoppers, 562
implementing
promotional Web sites, 563–564
transactional Web sites, 562–563
at Pizza Hut, 566–569
Multichannel marketing multiplier, 41
Multichannel Merchant, 439
Multichannel retailers, 450
Multicultural Agency of the Year, 73
Multicultural marketing, 72
Multidomestic marketing strategy, 170
case, 625–627
Multinational firms, 170
Multiple-zone pricing, 362
Multiproduct branding, 286
Multiracials, 72
Myers-Briggs Type Indicator, 605
Mystery shopper, 202–203

N

NAICS; *see* North American Industry Classification System
Nanotechnology, 78
National Aeronautics and Space Administration, 141, 350
National Association of Colleges and Employers, 606
National Bureau of Economic Research, 357
National Do Not Call Registry, 85, 441, 478, 527
National Highway Traffic Safety Administration, 621–622
Necessities, price inelastic, 333–334
Needs; *see also* Consumer needs
of buyers in a segment, 226
consumer perception of, 112
definition, 10
hierarchy of, 118–119
personal, 119
physiological, 118–119
safety, 119
self-actualization, 119
social, 119
Need-satisfaction presentation, 529
Negative deviation, 45
Neighborhoods, 77
Net sales, 370
Networked global marketplace, 171–173
Networking, 607
Network technologies, 80
Neuromarketing, *203,* 204
Neuroscience, 203, 204
New buy, 148–149, 158
New car sales
race or gender discrimination, 357
trade-in allowances, 362
to women, 111
New entrants, 81
New-product concept, 198
New product development
incomplete protocol, 253
product invention, 186
from technology, 79
at 3M Corporation, 14–15
New product launch, 22
New-product process, 256
business analysis, 260
capacity management, 260
case, 265–267
commercialization, 262–263
complexities, 263
failure fee, 263
fast prototyping, 263
parallel development, 263
regional rollouts, 263
risks in grocery products, 263
slotting fee, 263
time to market, 263

- **New-product process**—*Cont.*
  - design rules at Google, 261
  - development stage
    - brainstorming, 260
    - customer service expectations, 260
    - safety tests, 260–261
  - idea generation
    - case, 619–620
    - competitive products, 258
    - consumer suggestions, 257
    - employee/co-worker suggestions, 257
    - by inventors, 259
    - open innovation, 257
    - research and development labs, 257–258
    - by small tech firms, 259
    - supplier suggestions, 257
    - by universities, 258–259
  - market testing
    - major U.S. test markets, 262
    - problems with, 262
    - simulated test markets, 262
    - test markets, 261–262
  - at Medtronic, 631
  - prototypes, 260
  - screening and evaluation
    - external approach, 259
    - internal approach, 259
  - skipping stages in, 253–255
  - strategy development, 256
  - at 3M Corporation, 21–23, 368
- New products
  - from Apple Inc., 245–246
  - compared to existing products, 250–251
  - from consumer perspective, 251–252
  - continuous innovation, 251
  - discontinuous innovation, 251, 252
  - dynamically continuous innovation, 251, 252
  - feature bloat, 251, 252
  - Federal Trade Commission on, 251
  - hierarchy of effects, 470–471
  - ideas needed for success of, 253
  - introduction stage
    - advertising and promotion, 270–271
    - consumer resistance, 277
    - gaining distribution, 271
    - microwave popcorn, 402
    - penetration pricing, 272
    - primary demand, 271
    - selective demand, 271
    - skimming pricing, 271–272, 346–347
    - stimulating trial, 270
  - in legal terms, 251
  - marketing reasons for failure
    - bad timing, 254
    - incomplete protocol, 253
    - insignificant differences, 253
    - no economical access to buyers, 254
    - not satisfying customer needs, 253–254
    - poor execution of marketing mix, 254
    - poor quality, 254
    - too little attractiveness, 254
  - to meet consumer needs, 8–10
  - from organizational perspective, 251
  - organizational reasons for failure
    - desire for quick revenues, 255
    - not learning from past failures, 255
    - not listening to customers, 254
    - skipping process stages, 254–255
    - task force groupthink, 255
  - prelaunch issues, 22
  - preventing failure, 8
  - protocol statement, 252–253
  - regular distribution, 251
  - search for, 641–642
- **New-product strategy development, 256**
  - at 3M Corporation, 14–15, 21–23
- News conferences, 512
- Newspapers
  - advantages and disadvantages, 496
  - declining circulation, 498
  - online versions, 498
- News releases, 512
- *New York Times,* 225, 261, 322
- No-frills airlines, 327
- **Noise, 460**
- Nonassimilated Asian Americans, 132
- Noncumulative quantity discounts, 360
- Nondurable goods, 246
- Nonmonetary rewards, 539
- Nonprofit organizations, 26, 140
  - goals, 32
  - marketing careers in, 598
  - public service announcements, 512
  - services provided by, 302–304
- Nonselling duties, 602
- Nonstore retailing
  - automatic vending, 437–438
  - catalog sales, 438–439
  - direct mail, 438–439
  - direct selling, 441–442
  - online retailing, 439–441
  - telemarketing, 441
  - TV home shopping, 439
- Nonverbal behavior, 174–175
- Norms, 93–94
- North American Free Trade Agreement, 142, 167
  - description, 169
- **North American Industry Classification System, 141–142**
- North American Product Classification System, 142
- Nutritional Labeling and Education Act, 82

O

- Objections, handling, 530–531
- **Objective and task budgeting, 472–473,** 490
- **Objectives, 31**
  - of advertising, 489
  - of integrated marketing communications, 470–471
  - of marketing research, 196–197
  - new-product strategy development, 257
  - organizational, 234
  - organizational buying, 144–145
  - in personal selling, 529
  - of pricing, 324–325
  - of sales plan, 532
  - and target market compatibility, 234
- **Observational data, 201**
  - mechanical collection, 201–202
  - neuromarketing methods, 203, 204
  - personal methods, 202–203
- *Occupational Outlook Handbook,* 606–607
- **Odd-even pricing, 349**
- Offering, 26
  - strategy varying by, 32
- Office of National Drug Control Policy, 491
- **Off-peak pricing,** 260, **309**
- Off-price retailing, 449
  - extreme value retailers, 445
  - outlet stores, 445
  - warehouse clubs, 445
- **Off-price selling, 444**
- Oligopoly, 80, 327–328
- Olympic Games, 473
- **One-price policy, 355–354**
- Online advertising, 516–517
- Online auctions, 440
  - reverse, 155
  - traditional, 155
- Online consumer experience, 551–553
- **Online consumers,** 548, **554**
  - clickstream, 356
  - costs of fraud, 561
  - cross-channel shoppers, 562
  - Dell Inc., 640
  - eight-second rule, 558
  - lifestyle segmentation
    - brand loyalists, 555
    - click-and-mortar segment, 554
    - ebivalent newbies, 555
    - hooked, online, and single, 555
    - hunter-gatherers, 555
    - time-sensitive materialists, 555
  - main product/service categories, 556–557
  - multichannel marketing, 562–564
  - privacy and security issues, 561
  - profile of, 554–555
  - reasons for shopping
    - choice, 558
    - communication, 558–559
    - control, 560
    - convenience, 558
    - cost, 560
    - customization, 558
    - dynamic pricing, 560
  - terms for, 553
  - users of information, 555
- Online databases, 201
- Online employment services, 606
- Online malls, 440
- Online organizational buying
  - auctions
    - reverse, 155
    - traditional, 155
  - eBayBusiness, 154
  - e-marketplaces, 153–154
  - forms of, 153
  - prominence of, 153
  - reasons for, 153
- Online panels, 205
- Online retailing, 429–430, 450–451
  - advantages for consumers, 439–440
  - Under Armour, 481–482
  - checkout problem, 440
  - improvement in, 440–441
  - Pizza Hut, 566
  - varying approaches, 440
  - at Zappos.com, 221–222, 223
- Online sales, multichannel marketing, 564
- Online shopping, sales projections, 476
- Online surveys, 205
- Open-ended questions, 206
- Open innovation, 257
- Operating ratios, 373–374
- Operating statement
  - cost elements, 370–373
  - definition, 370
  - profit element, 373
  - projecting, 353
  - sales element, 370
- Operational execution, flawless, 573
- **Opinion leaders, 126**
- Opt-in customers, 551
- Opt-out, 551
- Order clerks, 523
- Order cycle time, 414
- **Order getters, 523**
- Order processing, 420–421
- Order size, in organizational buying, 144
- **Order takers, 522**
  - inside, 523
  - outside, 523
- **Organizational buyers, 19, 140**
  - from Dell Inc., 640
  - environmental concerns, 147
  - global organizational markets, 141
  - government markets, 141
  - Harley-Davidson, 146
  - industrial markets, 140

  - JCPMedia, 139
  - and NAICS, 141–142
  - reseller markets, 140
- Organizational buying
  - advertising in, 464
  - bidder's list, 152
  - buying centers, 147–149
  - buying criteria, 145–146
  - buy-seller relationships, 146–147
  - case, 157–159
  - competitive bids, 144
  - demand characteristics, 143–144
  - as derived demand, 143–144
  - from minority or women-owned firms, 144
  - number of potential buyers, 144
  - objectives, 144–145
  - online, 153–155
  - reciprocity, 146
  - size of purchase or order, 144
  - supply partnerships, 146–147
  - sustainable procurement, 147
- **Organizational buying behavior, 150**
  - key characteristics, 143
- **Organizational buying criteria, 145**
  - commonly used, 145
  - just-in-time systems, 145–146
  - for machine vision system, 150–152
  - standards certification, 145
  - supplier development, 145
- Organizational buying process
  - alternative evaluation, 152
  - information search, 151–152
  - make-buy decision, 151
  - postpurchase behavior, 152–153
  - problem recognition, 150–151
  - purchase decision, 152
  - stages, 150, 151
  - value analysis, 151–152
- Organizational chart, 27, 43
  - Paradise Kitchens, 62
- Organizational culture
  - code of ethics, 97
  - co-worker behavior, 97–98
  - definition, 97
  - top management behavior, 97–98
  - whistle-blowers, 98
- **Organizational culture, 30**
  - performance-oriented, 573
- Organizational direction
  - Ben & Jerry's, 24–25
  - business model, 30–31
  - goals and objectives, 31–32
- Organizational foundation
  - core values, 29
  - definition, 29
  - key elements, 29
  - mission, 29–30
  - organizational culture, 30
- Organizational goals, profit vs. nonprofit, 26
- Organizational markets
  - e-marketplaces, 153–154
  - global, 141
  - government, 141
  - industrial, 140
  - measurement of, 141–142
  - online auctions, 155
  - organizational buyers, 140
  - prominence of online buying, 153
  - reseller, 140–141
  - virtual, 153–154
  - ways of segmenting, 230–231
- Organizational objectives, 234
- Organizational strategies, 32
- Organizational structure, 27–28
  - corporate level, 28
  - cross-functional teams, 28
  - delayering, 585
  - Paradise Kitchens, 62–63
  - strategic business unit level, 28
- Organizational synergy, 225
- Organizations
  - customer experience management, 259
  - definition, 25
  - departments within, 6–7
  - functional groupings, 590
  - geographical groupings, 590
  - kinds of, 25
  - market-based groupings, 590
  - marketing plan complexity, 50
  - with market orientation, 16
  - matrix, 590
  - product line groupings, 590
  - product success from perspective of, 231
  - profit vs. nonprofit, 302–304
  - reasons for existence, 29–32
  - reasons for new product failure, 254–255
  - relationship marketing, 12
  - restructuring, 12
  - stakeholders, 30
  - strategic directions
    - current status, 34–35
    - growth strategies, 35–39
  - strategy, 27
  - terminology for, 26
  - visionary, 28–32
- Original equipment manufacturers, 150
- Original markup, 444
- Orion lunar spacecraft, 141
- Outbound telemarketing, 524
- Outdoor advertising
  - advantages and disadvantages, 496
  - billboards, 500–501
  - case, 617–619
  - digital billboards, 501
  - expenditures, 500–501
  - growth of, 500–501
  - transit advertising, 500
- Outdoor Advertising Association of America, 500
- Outlet stores, 445
- Output metric, 577–578
- Output-related sales plan objectives, 532, 539
- Outside order takers, 523

P

- Pacemaker market, 41–42
- **Packaging, 288**
  - annual company costs, 288–289
  - Bagel Bakes, 637–638
  - brand image, 290
  - challenges
    - connecting with customers, 291
    - cost reductions, 291–292
    - environmental concerns, 291
    - health, safety, and security, 291
  - communication benefits, 289
  - consumer protection, 290
  - convenience dimension, 290
  - creating customer value, 288–291
  - European guidelines, 291
  - functional benefits, 289–290
  - Gatorade, 270
  - perceptual benefits, 290–291
  - and product quality, 290
  - and product shelf life, 291
- Palm Beach County library, 434–435
- Panels, 209
- Paper manufacturers, 139
- Parallel development, 263
- Parallel importing, 188
- Paralysis by analysis, 587
- **Partnership selling,** 521–522, **522**
- Patents, and licensing, 182–183
- Pay-per-view TV, 497
- *PC Magazine,* 79
- **Penetration pricing,** 272, **347**
  - conditions favoring, 347
  - in electronics industry, 351
- People-base services, 302, 303
- People meter, 201
- Per capita income, 178–179
- **Perceived risk, 121**
- **Percentage of sales budgeting, 471**
- **Perception, 120**
  - or risk, 121–122
  - selective, 120–121
  - subliminal, 121
- **Perceptual maps, 239**
  - for product positioning, 238–240
- Performance contracts, 510–511
- Performance measures
  - business portfolio analysis, 36–38
  - marketing dashboards, 32–34
- Performance-oriented culture, 573
- **Permission marketing, 551**
- Per se illegal concept, 84, 363, 364
- Personal computer industry
  - feature bloat, 252
  - supply chain management, 409–410
- Personal influence
  - buzz, 127
  - family, 128–130
  - opinion leaders, 126–127
  - reference groups, 128
  - and rumors, 128
  - social class, 130–131
  - word of mouth, 127–218
- Personal interview surveys, 205
- **Personality, 119**
- Personality tests, 605
- Personality traits, 119
- **Personalization, 550**–551
- Personalization of services, 313
- Personalized URLs, 439
- Personal job contact, 607
- Personal moral philosophy, 98–100
- Personal needs, 119
- Personal observation methods
  - ethnographic research, 203
  - mystery shoppers, 22–203
  - videotaping consumers, 203
- **Personal selling, 461–462,** 519–531, **520**
  - advantages and disadvantages, 462
  - case, 544–545
  - CEO experience in, 520 521
  - conference selling, 525
  - creating customer value, 521–522
  - cross-functional business specialists, 522
  - cross-functional team selling, 525
  - customer sales support, 524–525
  - customized interaction, 461
  - as customized interaction, 460, 461
  - marketing role, 521
  - missionary salespeople, 524
  - number of employees, 520
  - order getters, 523–524
  - order takers, 522–523
  - paid aspect, 461
  - partnership selling, 521–522
  - in promotional mix, 473
  - relationship selling, 521–522
  - sales engineer, 524–525
  - seminar selling, 525
  - of services, 310–311
  - strengths, 461
  - team selling, 525
  - technological changes, 540–542
  - wasted coverage reduced by, 462
  - weaknesses, 461

Personal selling process, 526
approach, 528
closing stage, 531
cold canvassing, 527
follow-up, 531
preapproach, 527–528
presentation stage
adaptive selling, 529
consultative selling, 529–530
formula selling format, 529
handling objections, 530–531
need-satisfaction format, 529–530
stimulus-response format, 529
prospecting, 526–527
stages of, 526
at Xerox, 519
Personal sources of information, 112
Personal values, 123
Pet products, 632–633
Petroleum business, 47–49
Pet travel, 632–633
Pew Internet and American Life Project, 555
Philanthropy, McDonald's, 643
Physical distribution, careers in, 599
Physical environment of services, 311
Physical surroundings, 117
Physiological needs, 118–119
Piggyback, 419
Pioneering advertisements
for institutions, 487
for products, 486
Pi Sigma Epsilon, 607
Place, 11; *see also* Distribution
Place-based media, 501–502
Place strategy
Medtronic, 631–632
at 3M Corporation, 15
Place utility, 19
in interactive marketing, 548–549
from marketing channels, 382
in retailing, 430–431
Planning
acting on deviations, 491
versus execution, 584–585
identifying deviations, 491
strategic marketing process, 39–45
in strategic marketing process, 577–584
value-based, 584
Planning gap, 44–45
Planning schedules, 43–44
Point-of-purchase displays, 506, 509
Points of difference, 41
insignificant differences, 253
Paradise Kitchens, 59
Political-regulatory climate
political risk ratings, 181
political stability, 180
trade regulations, 181
Political risk ratings, 181
Political stability, 180
Pollution Prevention Pays program, 27
Population
percent in developing countries, 177
racial and ethnic diversity, 72–73
statistical areas, 71
of United States, 69
world, 68–69
Population explosion, 68
Population shift, 70–71
Portfolio tests, 502
Positioning, 41–42
Bagel Bakes, 637
Nike MaxSight, 616–617
Paradise Kitchens, 59
Positioning statement, 238
Positive deviation, 45
Possession utility, 19
in interactive marketing, 549
from marketing channels, 382
in retailing, 430–431
Postpurchase behavior
of consumers, 114–115
in organizational buying, 152–153
Postsale services, 395
Posttests, 504
aided recall, 504
attitude tests, 505
inquiry tests, 505
of promotion program, 475
sales tests, 505
Starch test, 504
unaided recall, 505
Power centers, 446
Preapproach stage, 527–528
Precycling, 79
Predatory pricing, 365–366
Premium, from brand equity, 283
Premium price, 320
Premiums, 506, 507
Pre- or postsale services, 395
Presentation stage
formula selling format, 529
handling objections, 530–531
need-satisfaction format, 529–530
objective, 528
stimulus-response format, 529
Prestige pricing, 347
Preteen consumers, 130
Pretests, 460, **503**
jury tests, 502
portfolio tests, 502
of promotion program, 475
theater tests, 502
Price(s), 11, **320**
add-on charges, 320
and barter, 320
and business decisions, 320
characteristics of, 320–321
of competition, 328
customizing, 356
factors increasing or decreasing, 321
final, 321
and global marketplace, 322
indicator of value, 322–323
with inflation, 75
in marketing mix, 323–324
and new product development, 22
in online shopping, 560
during recessions, 75
in service sector, 309
for setting/evaluating, 374–377
suggested retail, 349, 354
terms for, 309, 320
Price bargaining, 357
Price change
cost of, 327
on deals, 507
duration of, 327
effect on sales, 320
Price competition, 327–328
Price cutting, 357–358
Price differences, 365
Price differentials, 357
Price discounting, 84
Price discrimination, 364
Price elasticity of demand, 333
decisions involving, 333–334
determining factors, 333
elastic demand, 333
inelastic demand, 333, 334
and marketing managers, 333
unitary demand, 333
Washburn Guitar, 342–343
Price equation
calculating, 321
illustration, 321
Price fixing, 84, **363–364**
horizontal, 363–364
and manufacturer's suggested retail price, 364
resale price maintenance, 364
vertical, 364
Price-insensitivity, 347
Price lining, 348
Price points, 348
Price policy
balancing costs and revenues, 358–359
basing-points pricing, 363
company effects, 356–357
competition-oriented, 353–354
competitive effects, 357–358
cost-oriented, 349–351
customer effects, 357
demand-oriented, 346–349
flexible price policy, 356
Hi-Lo pricing, 363
legal and regulatory aspects
deceptive pricing, 365
free merchandise offers, 366
geographic pricing, 365
predatory pricing, 365–366
price discrimination, 364–365
one-price policy, 355–356
and price wars, 357–358
product-line pricing, 356–357
profit-oriented, 351–353
at 3M Corporation, 369
Price premium, 354
Price sensitivity, 33
Price-setting steps, 323–324
Price-value position, 345–346
Price war, 357–358
Pricing
court ruling, 93
laws on, 84
Pricing constraints, 325
competitors' prices, 328
cost of price changes, 327–328
costs of marketing, 327
costs of production, 327
demand, 326
identifying, 325–328
newness of product, 326
single product vs. product line, 326
Pricing decisions, 320
case, 341–343
Clayton Act, 364–365
cost-volume-profit relationships, 334–340
demand estimation, 329–331
identify constraints, 325–328
identify objectives, 324–325
Medtronic, 42
revenue estimation, 331–334
Pricing objectives, 324
identifying, 324–325
market share, 325
profit, 324–325
sales, 325
social responsibility, 325
Stubhub.com, 319–320
survival, 325
unit volume, 325
at Vizio, Inc., 345–346
Pricing strategies
above-, at-, or below-market pricing, 354
adjustments to list price, 359–363
Bagel Bakes, 638
bundle pricing, 349
case, 368–369
cost-plus pricing, 350
customary pricing, 353–354

and dumping, 188
dynamic pricing, 560
Energizer, 348
experience-curve pricing, 350–351
flexible pricing, 356
in global marketing, 187
gray market problem, 188
loss-leader pricing, 354
odd-even pricing, 349
off-peak pricing, 260
one-price policy, 355–356
Paradise Kitchens, 60
penetration pricing, 272, 347
prestige pricing, 347
price lining, 348
promotional allowances, 84
quantity discounts, 84
select approximate level, 346–354
in services sector, 309
setting list price, 354–359
skimming pricing, 346–347
skimming strategy, 271–272
in small business, 329
standard markup, 349–350
steps, 346
at StubHub.com, 319–320
target pricing, 349
target profit pricing, 351–352
target return-on-investment pricing, 352–353
target return-on-sales pricing, 352
value pricing, 33
at Vizio, Inc., 345–346
yield management pricing, 349

Primary data, 199
advantages and disadvantages, 211
data mining, 210–211
experiments, 209–210
neuromarketing methods, 203, 204
panels, 209–210
personal methods, 202–203
questionnaire
idea evaluation methods, 205–208
idea generation methods, 203–205
social networks, 208–209
using information technology, 210–211

Primary demand, 271
Privacy
in direct marketing, 477–478
in online shopping, 561
Privacy rights, 95
Private branding, 287
Private labeling, 287, 641
Private online exchange, 154
Problem definition, in marketing research, 195–197
identify possible actions, 196–197
set objectives, 196
Problem recognition
by consumers, 112
in organizational buying, 150–151
Problem solving, 116–117
Process, in service marketing, 311–312
Procurement, sustainable, 147
Product(s), 11, 246; *see also* New product *entries*
attitude change toward, 124
availability of substitutes, 330
benchmark items, 444
brand loyalty, 123
classifying
business products, 247–249
consumer products, 246–247
creating new use situation, 280
demand for, 326
downsizing, 281
factor in channel choice, 392
free trials, 122
global brands, 171
green, 105
grouped into categories, 231–233
hierarchy of effects, 470–471, 489
high-involvement, 117
high-learning, 275
increasing the use of, 279–280
from Ken Davis Products, 639
low-involvement, 116–117
low-learning, 275–276
luxury goods, 347
multiple segments with multiple, 224
multiple segments with one, 223–224
North American classification system, 142
point-of-purchase displays, 509
points of difference, 41
in pricing, 326
versus product line in pricing, 326
recycled by technology, 79
safety standards, 95
shelf life, 291
sold in vending machines, 437

Product adaptation, 186
Product advertisements, 486
comparative, 486
competitive, 486
pioneering, 486
reinforcement, 487
reminder, 486
Product benefits, 285
Product bundling, 278–279
Product characteristics
ancillary services, 467
complexity, 466
risk, 466–467
Product class, 276
demand for, 326
standard markup pricing, 349–350
Product counterfeiting, 282
Product deletion, 274
Product development strategy, 39
Product differentiation, 222
and competitive market, 327–328
in maturity stage, 273–274
and organizational synergy, 225
Product-distribution format franchises, 433–434
Product extension, 185
Product form, 276
Product goals, 41
Product image, 285
Product invention, 186
Production costs, 327
Production era, 16
Production scheduling, 588
Product item, 248
Productivity, in service sector, 312
Product liability claims, 292
Product life cycle, 270
advertising in, 486
case, 284–285
and consumers, 276–277
consumer vs. business products, 275
decline stage, 466
drop in sales, 274
harvesting strategy, 275
product deletion, 274
diffusion of innovation, 277
factor in channel choice, 392
for fax machines, 272–274
generalized, 275
growth stage, 466
changes during, 273
gaining distribution, 273
repeat purchasers, 273–274
sales increase, 272
and integrated marketing communications, 465–466
introduction stage, 465–466
advertising and promotion, 270–271
gaining distribution, 271
pricing strategies, 271–272
primary demand, 271
reasons for consumer resistance, 277
selective demand, 271
stimulating trial, 270
length of, 275
managing
market modification, 278–280
product modification, 278
product repositioning, 280–281
role of product manager, 278
marketing objectives, 271
maturity stage, 466
holding market share, 273–274
slowing sales, 273
as pricing constraint, 326
product class, 276
product form, 276
shape of
fads, 276
fashion products, 276
high-learning products, 275
low-learning products, 275–276
stages, 271

Product line, 248
Eastman Kodak, 36, 37–38
Naked Juice, 648
and price lining, 348
versus single product, 326
trade discounts, 361
Product line extensions, 286
Product line groupings, 590
Product-line pricing, 356–357
Product management
careers in, 599
on Internet, 295
Product management team, 599
Product managers, 278, 590, 600
Product mix, 249
Product objectives, Paradise Kitchens, 58–59
Product or program champion, 586
Product placement, 506
Product placements, 509–510
Product positioning, 41–42, **238**
differentiation, 238
head-to-head, 238
perceptual maps, 238–240
positioning statement, 238
and repositioning, 238
Product-related legislation
company protection, 82
consumer protection, 82–83
trademark protection, 83–84
Product repositioning, 238
catch rising trend, 280–281
changing value offered, 281
reaching new markets, 280
reaction to competitors, 280
Product sales organization, 534, 535
Product specialization, 581
Product strategies
Medtronic, 42
Paradise Kitchens, 60
product adaptation, 186
product extension, 185
product invention, 186
at 3M Corporation, 15
Product synergy, 237–238
Product warranties, 292
Profit, 26
effect of price on, 323–324
as goal, 31
measures of, 324–325
pricing objective, 324–325

Profitability
 and channel choice, 395
 of JetBlue Airways, 313
 and price, 320
 of Starbucks, 109
Profit-and-loss statement, 370
Profit before taxes, 373
Profit element of operating statements, 373
Profit equation, 323, 336–338
Profit margins, disagreements over, 397
Profit maximization, 335–336
Profit organizations, 302–304
Profit-oriented pricing
 target profit pricing, 351–352
 target return-on-investment pricing, 352–353
 target return-on-sales pricing, 352
Profit potential
 in global marketing, 182
 in segments, 226
Profit responsibility, 100–101
Program schedules, 587–588
Project manager, 600
Project Shakti initiative, 179
Promotion, 11
 by Under Armour, 481
 Bagel Bakes, 638
 by BP, 49
 building long-term relationships, 513
 careers in, 599–601
 costs with multiple branding, 287
 costs with multiproduct branding, 286
 designing, 473
 directed at intermediaries, 464
 executing and assessing, 474–475
 expenditures by top ten firms, 471
 in introduction stage, 271–272
 legislation on, 85
 loss-leader pricing, 354
 by Morganwtown Furniture, 645–646
 multimedia approaches, 513
 and new product development, 22
 scheduling, 473–474
 selecting tools for, 473
 self-regulation, 513
 of services, 310–311
Promotional allowances, 84, **362**
 Robinson-Patman Act, 365
Promotional mix, 458
 advertising, 460–461, 486–505
 ancillary services, 467
 Bagel Bakes, 637–638
 buying decision stages, 467–468
 case, 480–481
 channel strategies, 468–469
 direct marketing, 463–464
 increasing value of, 512–513
 in integrated marketing communications, 464–469
 Major League Baseball, 316–317
 mass selling, 460, 461
 new forms of communication, 457–458
 personal selling, 460, 461–462, 520–531
 product characteristics, 466–467
 and product life cycle, 465–466
 publicity, 462–463, 512
 public relations, 462, 512
 right combination of, 473
 sales promotion, 463, 505–511
 strengths and weaknesses, 461
 target audience, 464–465
 Target Corporation, 644
 uses of, 468
Promotional Web sites, 563–564
Promotion budget
 allocated to sales promotion, 505
 all-you-can-afford budgeting, 472
 case, 645–646
 competitive parity budgeting, 471–472, 490
 objective and task budgeting, 472–473, 490
 percentage of sales budgeting, 471
Promotion-related legislation, 85
Promotion strategies
 dual adaptation, 186–187
 Medtronic, 42
 Paradise Kitchens, 60–61
 Prince Sports, Inc., 242–243
 product adaptation, 186
 product extension, 185
 product invention, 186
 at 3M Corporation, 15
 viral marketing, 559
Prospect, 526
Prospecting stage
 cold canvassing, 527
 leads, 526–527
Protectionism, 166
 arguments for, 166
 benefits to producers, 167
 case for, 167
 cost to consumers, 166–167
 decline of, 167–168
 effects on trade, 166
 and General Agreement on Tariffs and Trade, 167
 by quotas, 167
 by tariffs, 166–167
 and World Trade Organization, 167–168
Protocol, 253, 256
 incomplete, 253
Prototypes, 260
Psychographics, 124–125
Psychographic segmentation
 of consumer lifestyle, 125
 of consumer markets, 226, 227
 variables for, 230
Psychological influences; *see* Consumer behavior
Publicity, 462
 versus advertising and personal selling, 462
 credibility advantage, 462–463
 disadvantages, 463
 in promotional campaigns, 463
 for services, 310
Publicity tools, 512
Public relations, 462
 by Under Armour, 481
 as communication management, 512
 mass selling, 460, 461
 news conferences, 512
 news releases, 512
 paid aspect, 461
 in promotional mix, 473
 public service announcements, 512
 strengths, 461
 tools of, 462
 weaknesses, 461
Public relations manager, 600
Public service announcements, 310, 512
Public sources of information, 112
Pull strategy, 469
Pulse schedule, 502
Purchase decision
 of buying committees, 147
 by consumers, 114
 determining factors, 114
 high-involvement, 115–116
 Internet use, 114
 low-involvement, 116
 online shoppers, 556–557
 in organizational buying, 152
 for services, 305–306
Purchase decision process, 112
 achievement-motivated groups, 125
 characteristics, 116
 cognitive dissonance, 115
 consideration set, 113–114
 evaluation of alternatives, 113–114
 high- and low-resource groups, 125
 ideals-motivated groups, 125
 information search, 112–113
 involvement and problem solving, 115–117
 at JCPMedia, 139
 perception of need, 112
 postpurchase behavior, 114–115
 problem recognition, 112
 purchase, 114
 self-expression-motivated groups, 125
 situational influences, 117
 value of customer satisfaction, 115
Purchase discounts, 372
Purchase frequency, 502
Purchases, syndicated panel data, 200
Purchase size, in organizational buying, 144
Purchasing power
 and global consumer income, 178–180
 in poorest nations, 177
 regional comparisons, 179
Pure competition, 80, 327–328
Pure monopoly, 80–81, 327–328
Push strategy, 468

Q

Qualified prospect, 526–527
Quality
 Ford-Firestone problem, 621–623
 as goal, 31
 ISO standards, 181
 poor, 254
 price as indicator of, 33, 309
Quality assessment of services, 306
Quality management and assurance, 145
Quantitative assessment of salesforce, 539
Quantity discounts, 84, **360**
Question marks
 definition, 37
 at Eastman Kodak, 37, 38
Questionnaire data, 203
 closed-end questions, 206–207
 depth interviews, 204
 dichotomous question, 207
 fax surveys, 205
 fixed alternative questions, 206–207
 focus groups, 204–205
 fuzzy front-end methods, 205
 idea evaluation methods, 205–208
 idea generation methods, 203–205
 individual interviews, 203–204
 Likert scale, 207
 mail surveys, 205
 mall intercept interviews, 205–206
 online surveys, 205
 open-ended questions, 206
 personal interview surveys, 205
 problems to guard against, 208
 semantic differential scale, 207
 telephone surveys, 205
 trend hunting, 205
Quick response, 159, **414**
Quick response delivery time, 415
Quota, 167
Quoted price; *see* List price

R

Race, and new car sales, 357
Racial diversity, 72–73
Rack jobbers, 387

Radio advertising
  advantages and disadvantages, 496
  compared to television, 498
Radio frequency identification tags, 434, 445
Radio frequency identification technology, 210–211
Railroads
  advantages and disadvantages, 418
  decline of, 30
  intermodal transportation, 418–419
  lobbying against, 82
  unit trains, 418
Rates, 309
Rating, 494
Ratios
  to analyze operations, 373–374
  expense-to-sales ratio, 373
  operating ratios, 373–374
  for setting/evaluating prices
    markdown, 375–376
    markup, 374–375
    return on investment, 377
    stockturn rate, 376–377
Raw materials, cost-effective flow of, 406
Reach, 494
  of television advertising, 495–496
Reagan administration, 621
Real time, 550
Rebates, 506, 509
Receivers, 458
Recession, 75
Reciprocity, 146
Recruitment/selection of salesforce
  emotional intelligence, 537, 538
  job analysis, 537
  job description, 537
  women and minorities, 537–538
Recycling, 91, 291
  of electronic waste, 423
  of products, 79
Recycling program, 641
Reference groups, 128
Reference value, 323
Refusal to deal, 399–400
Regional rollouts, 263
Regional shopping centers, 445
Regional trade agreements, 167
Regular distribution, 251
Regulation, 82
Regulatory forces; *see also* Laws
  advertising and promotion-related laws, 85
  on cold canvassing, 527
  in direct marketing, 477–478
  distribution-related laws, 84–85
  on pricing, 363–366
  pricing-related laws, 84
  product relate laws, 82–84
  protecting competition, 82
  and self-regulation, 85–86
  self-regulation of promotion, 513
Reinforcement, 122
Reinforcement advertisements, 487
Related and supporting industries, 164
Relationship marketing, 13, 308
Relationship selling, 521–**522**
Relative market share, 36
Reminder advertising
  for institutions, 487
  for products, 486
Rent, 320
Repeat purchasers, 272–273
Replenishment time, 414
Requirement contracts, 84
Resale price maintenance, 364
Resale restrictions, 400
Research and development
  in synergy analysis, 580
  at 3M Corporation, 14–15
Research and development department, 6
Research and development labs, idea generation from, 257–258
Research objectives, 196–197
Reseller branding, 287
Reseller markets
  definition, 140
  and NAICS, 141–142
  prices in, 357
Resource allocation
  numerical example, 574–575
  optimal, 574
  in strategic marketing process, 576
  using sales response function, 574
  using share points, 575
Resources, obtaining, 43
Response, 122, **460**
Restaurants, customer service standards, 415
Restructuring, 12
Résumés
  accompanying letter, 608–610
  chronological format, 608
  digital, 608
  functional format, 608
  target format, 608
Retail communication, 446
Retailers
  cash discounts for, 361
  and channel conflict, 397–398
  cooperative advertising, 511
  customer service standards, 415
  finance allowances, 511
  functions, 380
  of golf equipment, 379
  Lands' End, 157–159
  marketing channels, 383
  multichannel marketing, 385–386
  number of, 140
  number of companies online, 429
  as organizational buyers, 140
  situational influences on, 117
  size of different types, 431
  supplier partnerships, 147
  trade discounts for, 361
  transactional Web sites, 562
Retailer-sponsored cooperatives, 391, 433
Retailing, 430
  Under Armour, 481–482
  by Best Buy, 135–137
  Black Friday sales, 429
  career paths, 601–602
  case, 453–454
  changing nature of
    retail life cycle, 449–450
    wheel of retailing, 448–449
  Cyber Monday sales, 429
  efficient consumer response, 414
  electronic data interchange for, 412
  environmentally friendly, 433
  form of ownership
    contractual systems, 433–434
    corporate chains, 432–433
    independent retailers, 432
  future changes
    managing customer experience, 451
    multichannel retailing, 40–451
  global economic impact, 431
  level of service
    full service, 435
    limited service, 435
    self-service, 434–435
  merchandise line
    breadth of line, 436
    depth of line, 435–436
  nonstore
    automatic vending, 437–438
    direct mail and catalogs, 438–439
    direct selling, 441–442
    online, 439–441
    telemarketing, 441
    TV home shopping, 439
  online shopping, 429–430
  supply chain management, 410–411
  Target Corporation, 644–645
  types of careers in, 600
  utilities offered by, 430–431
Retailing mix, 443
  functional, 446
  at Mall of America, 453–454
Retailing strategy
  HOM Furniture, 628–629
  Ken Davis Products, 639
  marketing dashboard for, 447
  measures
    sales per square foot, 447
    same store growth rate, 447
  retailing mix
    communication, 446
    merchandise, 446–447
    pricing, 444–445
    store location, 445–446
  retail positioning matrix, 442–443
Retail life cycle, 449–450
Retail outlets
  anchor stores, 445
  Bagel Bakes, 637
  category killers, 436
  concept stores, 454
  contractual systems, 433–434
  cookie cutter stores, 453
  corporate chains, 432–433
  cost of acquiring customers, 438
  department stores, 433, 445
  extreme value stores, 445
  factory outlets, 445
  franchise operations, 434
  full service, 435
  functional, 446
  general merchandise stores, 435, 436
  hypermarkets, 436
  image, 446
  independent retailers, 432
  intertype competition, 436
  limited-line stores, 435
  limited service, 435
  at Mall of America, 453–454
  number in franchising, 434
  in retail life cycle, 449–450
  sales per square foot, 447
  same store growth, 447
  self-service, 434–435
  single-line stores, 435
  single-price retailers, 445
  specialty outlets, 435–436
  supercenters, 436
  Trader Joe's, 641–642
  warehouse clubs, 445
  in wheel of retailing, 48–449
Retail positioning matrix, 442–443
Retail pricing; *see also* Pricing *entries*
  benchmark/signpost items, 444
  everyday fair pricing, 444
  everyday low prices, 363, 444
  gross margin, 444
  maintained markup, 444
  manufacturer's suggested retail price, 364
  markdown, 375–376, 444

Retail pricing—*Cont.*
markup, 374–375
off-price retailing, 444–445
original markup, 444
shrinkage, breakage, and theft, 444
standard markup pricing, 349–350
store vs. manufacturer brands, 357
Retail salesperson, 600
Return on assets, 324–325
Return on investment, 31, 324–325, 352–353, 377, 591–592
Returns, 370
Revenue
balanced with costs, 358
and break-even analysis, 336–338
incremental, 574
from Major League Baseball, 317
and poorly conceived products, 255
types of, 331, 332
Revenue estimation
and demand curve, 331–332
Newsweek magazine, 331–334
and price elasticity of demand, 333–334
for pricing, 331–333
revenue concepts, 331
Reverse auction, 155
Reverse logistics, 422–423
Reverse product placement, 510
RFID; *see* Radio frequency identification technology
Rice import tariffs, 167
Rich media, 499
Risk
costs of, 421
perceived, 121–122
in product purchase, 466–467
Robinson-Patman Act, 82, 85
and basing-point pricing, 365
and flexible pricing, 356
and price discrimination, 364
and promotional allowances, 365
Roles, changing for men and women, 73–74
Routine problem solving, 116
Rule of reason, 364, 365
Rumors, 128
Rural-to-urban shift, 71
Russia
legal red tape, 178
McDonald's in, 642–643

S

Safety
automobile, 111
Ford-Firestone problem, 621–623
in packaging, 291
right to, 95
Safety need, 119
Safety standards, 95
Safety tests, 260–261
Salary, 320, 599
Sales
Apple iPhone, 246
on Black Friday, 429
careers in, 600
and coupons, 506
customer relationship management, 602–603
on Cyber Monday, 429
in decline stage, 274
by Dell in emerging markets, 161
from direct mail retailing, 438
from direct selling, 441
effect of price changes, 320
in global marketing, 431
as goal, 31
gross and net, 370
in growth stage, 272–273
marketing dashboard, 249–250
in maturity stage, 273
nonselling duties, 602
in online retailing, 557
as pricing objective, 325
rebates on, 509
sales-support duties, 602
selling duties, 602
and theft of intellectual property, 94
from TV home shopping, 439
types of careers in, 602–603
by types of retailers, 431
from vending machines, 437
Sales and Marketing Management, 603, 607
Salesclerks, 523
Sales elements of operating statements, 370
Sales engineer, 524–525
Sales era, 16
Salesforce
as company representative, 521
compensation of
advantages and disadvantages, 538–539
combination plan, 538–539
straight commission, 538
straight salary, 538
and differing buyer needs, 534
evaluation of
behavioral, 530–540
with marketing dashboard, 540
quantitative, 539
in home offices, 542
knowledge of competitors, 532
and marketing strategy, 534
of Medtronic in China, 631–632
motivation of, 538–539
nonmonetary rewards, 539
organizing
customer organization, 534, 535
geographical organization, 534, 535
independent agents or company hires, 533–534
key account management, 534
product organization, 534, 535
size of, 534–536
workload method, 532–533
recruitment and selection
emotional intelligence, 537
job analysis, 537
job description, 537
training of, 511, 538
women and minorities in, 537–538
at Xerox, 544–545
Salesforce automation, 540–542, **541**
Salesforce communication, 541–542
Salesforce survey forecast, 215
Salesforce technology, 541
Sales forecast, 214
on toy sales, 197
Sales forecasting techniques
judgments of decision makers
direct forecast, 214
lost-horse forecast, 214–215
statistical methods
linear trend extrapolation, 215–216
trend extrapolation, 215–216
surveys of knowledgeable groups
buyers' intentions, 215
salesforce, 215
Sales management, 520
salesforce communication, 541–542
salesforce technology, 541
at Xerox, 519, 544–545
Sales management process
account management policies, 536
customer relationship management, 540–542
recruitment and selection, 537–538
salesforce automation, 540–542
salesforce evaluation, 539–540
salesforce training, 538
sales plan formulation, 532–536
sales plan implementation, 536–539
Sales occupation opportunities, 602
Sales organization, competitive position of, 537
Salespeople
in direct selling, 441
missionary, 524
order getters, 523–524
order takers, 522–523
relationship and partnership selling, 521–522
role in personal selling, 521
selling and nonselling time, 524
Sales per square foot, 447
Sales plan, 532
formulation
account management policies, 536
organizing salesforce, 532–536
setting objectives, 532
implementation, 534–539
motivation and compensation, 538–539
recruitment and selection, 537–358
training, 538
Sales promotion, 463
advertising support, 463
annual expenditures, 404
components, 463
consumer-oriented, 505–510
mass selling, 461
paid aspect, 461
in promotional mix, 473
push strategy, 468
for services, 310
short-term advantage, 463
strengths, 461
testing procedures, 475
trade-oriented, 510–511
weaknesses, 461
Sales promotion manager, 600
Sales quota, 537
Sales response function, 574
Sales strategy, in buying centers, 149
Sales-support duties, 602
Sales tests, 505
Sales volume, potential, 262
Same store growth rate, 447
Samples, 506, 508
Sampling, 198
Satellite radio, 497
Savings rate, 77–78
Scale, 207
Scheduling
action item lists, 587
of advertising, 502
Gantt chart, 588
program schedules, 587–588
of tasks, responsibilities, and deadlines, 587–588
Scrambled merchandising, 436
Screening and evaluation, 259
concept tests, 259
customer experience management, 259
external approach, 259
internal approach, 259
Seals of approval, 122
Search engines, 499–500
Google, 515–517
Search properties of services, 305
Seasonal discounts, 360–361
Secondary data, 199
advantages and disadvantages, 200

    external, 199–200
    internal, 199
    online databases, 201
Secret Sales Pitch (Bullock), 120
Security
    in online shopping, 561
    in packaging, 291
Selective comprehension, 120–121
Selective demand, 271
Selective distribution, 394
Selective exposure, 120
Selective perception, 120–121
Selective retention, 121
Selective specialization, 581
Self-actualization need, 119
Self-assessment
    job-related tests, 605
    key questions, 604
    strengths and weaknesses, 604, 606
Self-concept, 119
Self-expression-motivated groups, 125
Self liquidating premium, 507
Self-regulation, 85
    by Better Business Bureau, 85–86
    of online shopping, 561
    of promotion, 513
Self-service retailers, 434–435
Self-service technologies, 300–301
Selling agents, 389
Selling duties, 602
Selling expenses, 373
Semantic differential scale, 207
Seminar selling, 525
Semiotics, 175
Semitechnical salesperson, 600
Sensitivity analysis, 210
Service continuum, 301
Service failure, 306, 307
Services, 18, **246, 298**
    brand names, 309
    carrying costs, 301
    classifying
        delivery by people or equipment, 302
        government-sponsored, 304–305
        profit or nonprofit organizations, 302–304
    component of Gross domestic product, 246
    consumer purchase
        assessing quality, 306
        customer contact audit, 306–308
        purchase process, 305–306
        relationship marketing, 308
    continuum of, 301–302
    core product, 302
    cost-plus pricing, 350
    credence properties, 305
    dimensions of quality, 306
    as experience economy, 297–298
    experience properties, 305
    four I's of
        inconsistency, 300
        inseparability, 300–301
        intangibility, 299
        inventory, 301
    gap analysis, 306
    in global economy, 298–299, 313–314
    and idle production capacity, 301
    marketing of
        capacity management, 312
        customer experience management, 311
        distribution, 309–310
        internal marketing, 311
        off-peak pricing, 309
        physical environment, 311
        price, 309
        process, 311–312
        productivity, 312
        product/service, 308–309
        promotion, 310–311
    monitoring failure of, 307
    new product development in, 256
    new types, 299
    number of employees, 298–299
    percent of Gross domestic product, 298–299
    personalization of, 313
    search properties, 305
    Space Adventures, 310
    sports marketing, 315–317
    supplementary, 302
    technological advances, 312–313
    that facilitate customization, 297
    uniqueness, 298–299
Services market, 140
Service-sponsored franchise systems, 391
Service-sponsored retail franchise systems, 391
Sex appeals, 491
    failure of, 204
Share points, 575
Shelf life, 291
Sherman Antitrust Act, 82, 84, 363, 365, 399, 400
Shift of a demand curve, 330–331
Shoe sales, 221–222, 223
Shopping bots, 440
Shopping experience, 111
Shopping products, 247, 248
Signpost items, 444
Simulated test markets, 262
Single-line stores, 435
Single parents, 129
Single-price retailers, 445
Single product vs. product line, 326
Single-zone pricing, 362
Situational influences, 117
Situation analysis, 39
    Paradise Kitchens, 55–58
Skimming pricing, 271–272, **346**
    as effective strategy, 346–347
    in electronics industry, 351
    followed by penetration pricing, 347
Slotting allowances, 95, 263, 399, 639
Small businesses
    as competitors, 81
    exporting by, 182
    marketing careers, 5
    number of, 81
    pricing in, 329
    and Robinson-Patman Act, 82
Small technology firms, new product ideas from, 259
Smart phones, 113
Smoking-related illnesses, 93
Social audit, 103
Social class, 130
Social entrepreneurship, 18
Social forces, 68
    culture, 73–74
    demographics, 68–73
    generational cohorts, 69–70
    households, 70
    population shifts, 70–71
Socialization process, 128
Social media, 463
Social needs, 119
Social networks, 208–209
Social responsibility, 17–18, **100**
    at Anheuser-Busch, 91
    case, 107–109
    cause marketing, 102
    concepts of
        profit responsibility, 100–101
        societal responsibility, 102
        stakeholder responsibility, 101–102
    and consumer ethics, 104–105
    Generation Y, 68
    as goal, 32
    green marketing, 102
    pricing objective
    social audit, 103
    social entrepreneurship, 18
    and student credit cards, 326
    sustainable development, 103–104
Social retailing, 451
Social shopping experience, 442
Social surroundings, 117
Societal culture, 93–94
Societal marketing concept, 17, 100
Societal responsibility
    cause marketing, 102
    green marketing, 102
    triple-bottom line, 102
Sociocultural influences; *see* Consumer behavior
Source, 458
Spam, 478, **559**
Spam-blocker, 205
Special fees, 320
Specialty merchandise wholesalers, 387
Specialty outlets, 435–436
Specialty products, 247, 248
Specialty stores, full service retailing, 435
Speed, 111
Sports marketing, 315–317
Spouse dominant decisions, 130
Spreadsheet simulation, 353
Staff positions, 589
Stakeholder responsibility, 101–102
Stakeholders, 30
    definition, 29
Standard Industrial Classification system, 142
Standard markup pricing, 349–350
Standards certification, 145
Starch test, 504
Stars
    definition, 36
    at Eastman Kodak, 37, 38
Start-up firms, 50
State employment office, 607
Statistical area, 71
Statistical forecasting methods, 215–216
Statistical inference, 198
Status-conscious consumers, 347
Steady schedule, 502
Stereotyping, eliminating, 74
Stimulus discrimination, 122
Stimulus generalization, 122
Stimulus-response presentation, 529
Stockholm traffic problem, 587
Stock keeping units, 248
    number of, 254
Stockouts, 412–414
Stockturn rate, 376–377
Stop Counterfeiting in Manufactured Goods Act, 282
Storage costs, 421
Storage warehouses, 419
Store locations
    case, 453–454
    central business district, 445
    community shopping centers, 445–446
    HOM Furniture, 628
    power centers, 446
    regional shopping centers, 445
    strip location, 446
    value added aspect, 442–443
Store management, 601
Store manager, 600
Straight-commission compensation plan, 538–539
Straight rebuy, 148–149, 158
Straight-salary compensation plan, 538–539

Strategic alliances, 170
Strategic business units, 28
business portfolio analysis, 36–38
cash cows, 36
dogs, 37
at Eastman Kodak, 36–38
question marks, 37
stars, 36
strategy at level of, 32
Strategic channel alliances, 386
Strategic directions
current status
competitive advantage, 35
competitors, 35
core competencies, 34–35
customers, 35
growth strategies, 35–39
business portfolio analysis, 36–38
diversification analysis, 38–39
Strategic marketing process, 39
basics
fast, flexible, and flat organization, 573
operational execution, 573
performance-oriented culture, 573
strategy, 573
BP case, 47–49
case, 595–597
evaluation phase, 576
acting on deviations, 45, 591
at General Mills, 592–594
identifying deviations, 44–45, 591
management by exception, 591
marketing dashboards, 591–592
marketing metrics, 591–592
marketing ROI, 591–592
taking marketing actions, 591
finding what works, 573–574
at General Mills, 571–572, 583–584, 592–594
goal setting, 576
implementation phase, 576
action item list, 587
avoiding paralysis by analysis, 586
brand manager, 590
category manager, 590
chief marketing officer, 589
communicate goals, 585–586
delayering organization, 585
designing marketing organization, 43
developing schedules, 43–44
divisional groupings, 590
executing program, 44
Gantt chart, 588
line and staff positions, 589
marketing strategy, 44
marketing tactics, 44
obtaining resources, 43
open communication, 586–587
planning vs. execution issue, 584–585
product manager, 590
product or program champion, 586
program schedules, 587–588
rewarding success, 586
scheduling precision, 587–588
marketing program, 576
market-product focus, 576
planning phase, 577–582
annual marketing plan, 578
diversification analysis, 580
generic business strategies, 578–580
global strategies, 583–584
goal setting, 40–42
long-range plans, 578
marketing metrics, 577–578
marketing planning framework, 578–582
marketing planning guidelines, 582–583
marketing program, 42
market-product focus, 40–42
market segmentation, 40
problems in planning, 583–584
sources of competitive advantage, 579
SWOT analysis, 39–40
synergy analysis, 580–582
value-based planning, 584
value-driven strategy, 584
variety of marketing plans, 578
questions for, 39
resource allocation
reports, studies, and memos, 576
using sales response function, 574–575
using share points, 575
seeking competitive advantage, 572–576
SWOT analysis, 576
Strategic performance units, 47
Strategy, 27
clearly stated and focused, 573
organizational, 32
Paradise Kitchens, 53–54
value-driven, 584
in visionary organizations, 29
Strict liability rulings, 292
Strip location, 446
Strivers, 125
Strong Interest Inventory, 605
Student credit cards, 325
Styling, in car purchase, 111
Subbranding, 286
Subcultures, 131
African Americans, 132
Asian Americans, 132–133
Hispanics, 131–132
Subliminal messages, 120
Subliminal perception, 121
Subsidiaries, 170
Substitutes
as competition, 81
price and availability of, 330
reference value, 323
Sugar import quotas, 167
Suggested retail price, 349, 354
Suggestive selling, 529
Super Bowl
commercials, 127, 297
cost of commercials, 489–490
size of audience, 489
Supercenters, 436
Supermarkets
allowances from manufacturers, 398
cost of price changes, 327
everyday low pricing, 363
slotting allowances, 95, 263, 399, 639
standard markup pricing, 349–350
target return-on-sales pricing, 352
Trader Joe's, 641–642
Supplementary services, 302
Supplier development, 145
Supplier diversity, 108, 145
Supplier networks, 407
Suppliers, 248
bidder's list, 152
collaboration with, 146
competitive bids from, 144
cost-plus fixed-fee pricing, 350
focus on customer relations, 530
global, 407
idea generation by, 257
to Lands' End, 158
in online buying, 153
performance monitoring, 152
power of, 81
in reverse auctions, 155
vendor-managed inventory, 422
Supply, in world trade, 163
Supply chain, 406
customer-driven
customer service concept, 413–415
customer service standards, 415–416
information technology, 411–412
marketing dashboard for, 415
total logistics costs, 412–413
global suppliers, 407
integrated, 410
key logistics functions
inventory management, 421–422
order processing, 420–421
third-party providers, 417
transportation, 418–419
warehousing/materials handling, 419–420
versus marketing channels, 406–407
output, 413
understanding of, 409
Supply chain management, 407
aligned with marketing strategy
at Apple Inc., 405
at Dell Inc., 409–410
steps, 409
at Wal-Mart, 410–411
auto industry, 408, 409
in auto industry, 408
balancing logistics costs and customer service, 413–414
case, 425–426
Dell Inc., 640–641
elements of, 406
inventory management, 421–422
inventory strategies, 421–422
order cycle time, 414
reducing lead time, 414
related to logistics, 406
related to marketing channels, 406
replenishment time, 414
reverse logistics, 422–423
supplier networks, 407
Supply chain managers, 409, 600
Supply partnership, 146–147
Support products, 248
Surcharges, 320
Survey Research Center, 75
Surveys of buyer's intentions, 215
Surveys of knowledgeable groups, 215
Survival, as pricing objective, 325
Survivors, 125
Sustainable development, 27, **104**
global dilemma, 27
in retailing, 433
Sustainable growth, 147
Sustainable procurement, 147
Sweepstakes, 506, 508
fraud in, 513
Switching costs, 81
SWOT analysis, 39
actions called for, 40
basis of, 39
identifying critical factors, 40
in new-product strategy development, 256
Paradise Kitchens, 55
in strategic marketing process, 576
Symbolism, 175–176
Syndicated panel data, 200
Synergy
versus cannibalization, 225
market-product, 236–238
Synergy analysis, 580
customer value in, 580, 581
full coverage, 581
market product concentration, 580
market segmentation study, 580–581
market specialization, 580
mergers and acquisitions strategy, 580

Now with *Marketing*, 10e by Kerin/Hartley/Rudelius!

Less Managing. More Teaching. Greater Learning.

McGraw-Hill *Connect*tm *Marketing* is an online assignment and assessment solution that connects students with the tools and resources they'll need to achieve success. It meets you where you are!

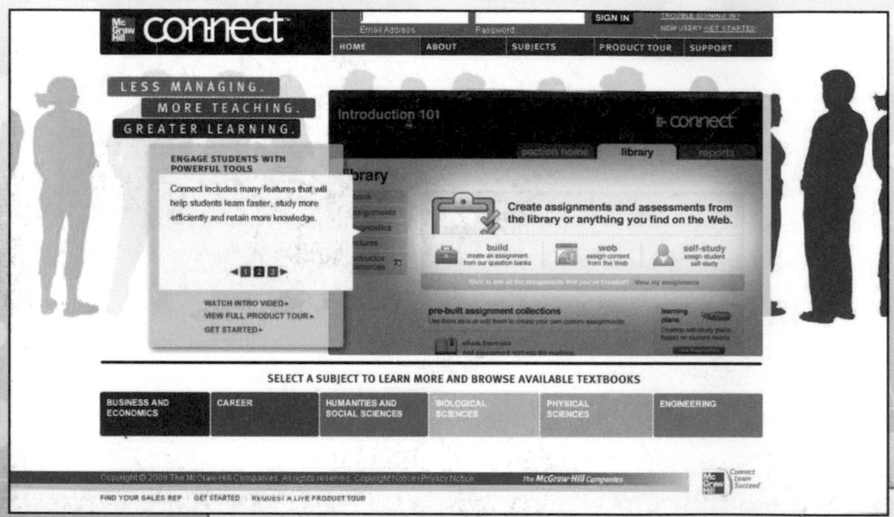

McGraw-Hill *Connect Marketing* features

Connect Marketing offers a number of powerful tools and features to make managing assignments easier, so faculty can spend more time teaching. With *Connect Marketing*, students can engage with their coursework anytime and anywhere, making the learning process more accessible and efficient.

95% of faculty who have seen *Connect Marketing* say that it is good or excellent!*

91% of faculty say that the interactive content is good or excellent!*

*Survey results from over 400 professors who have seen *Connect Marketing*.

Discover for yourself how *Connect Marketing* ensures students will **connect** with the content, **learn** more effectively, and **succeed** in your course.